CRIMINAL LITIGATION AND SENTENCING

Sixth Edition

Cavendish
Publishing
Limited

London • Sydney • Portland, Oregon

This book is supported by a Companion Website, created to keep *Criminal Litigation and Sentencing* up to date and to provide enhanced resources for both students and lecturers.

Key features include:

- termly updates
- links to useful websites
- links to 'ebooks' for introductory and further reading
- 'ask the author' – your questions answered

www.cavendishpublishing.com/criminallit

CRIMINAL LITIGATION
AND SENTENCING

THE OLDHAM C

Return o

by th Welch, LLB, PGC(TLHE), Barrister

Dean and Director of Teaching Staff Resources
Inns of Court School of Law
City University, London

Cavendish
Publishing
Limited

London • Sydney • Portland, Oregon

Sixth edition first published in Great Britain 2004 by
Cavendish Publishing Limited, The Glass House,
Wharton Street, London WC1X 9PX, United Kingdom
Telephone: + 44 (0)20 7278 8000   Facsimile: + 44 (0)20 7278 8080
Email: info@cavendishpublishing.com
Website: www.cavendishpublishing.com

Published in the United States by Cavendish Publishing
c/o International Specialized Book Services,
5804 NE Hassalo Street, Portland,
Oregon 97213-3644, USA

Published in Australia by Cavendish Publishing (Australia) Pty Ltd
3/303 Barrenjoey Road, Newport, NSW 2106, Australia

© Hungerford-Welch, P	2004
First edition	1994
Second edition	1995
Third edition	1996
Fourth edition	1998
Fifth edition	2000
Sixth edition	2004

British Library Cataloguing in Publication Data
Hungerford-Welch, Peter
Criminal litigation and sentencing – 6th ed
1 Criminal justice, administration of – England
2 Criminal justice, administration of – Wales
3 Sentences (criminal procedure) – England
4 Sentences (criminal procedure) – Wales I Title
345.4'2'05

Library of Congress Cataloguing in Publication Data
Data available

ISBN 1-85941-849-X
ISBN 978-185941-849-9

3 5 7 9 10 8 6 4 2

Printed and bound in Great Britain by Antony Rowe Ltd.,Chippenham, Wiltshire

Dedicated to Jane Hungerford-Welch

PREFACE

This book started life as *Lecture Notes on Criminal Litigation and Sentencing*, a comparatively slim volume based on lectures given to students on the Bar Vocational Course at the Inns of Court School of Law. After three editions under the *Lecture Notes* banner, it was felt that the book should be expanded to make it more useful for practitioners (barristers, solicitors and legal executives) as well as for students, pupil barristers and trainee solicitors.

This edition, the 6th, has been revised completely in order to take account of the extensive changes to the criminal justice system brought about by the Criminal Justice Act 2003 (and, to a lesser extent, by the Courts Act 2003).

This version is different from previous versions in that, as well as setting out the rules governing procedure and sentencing (based on statute law and on case law), there are also contextual materials to help the reader understand how the rules have come into existence and to evaluate those rules. This will be of assistance to law students, both at the LLB and the LLM stage.

Indeed, I hope that this book will be of interest to anyone who is interested in how our system of criminal justice operates.

My thanks go to Cavendish Publishing for their hard work in putting this book together (and their patience with last-minute amendments). I owe a special debt of gratitude to my wife Jane, without whose help, encouragement and support this book would never have seen the light of day.

I have endeavoured to state the law as at July 2004.

Criminal justice is a fast-moving area, with a seemingly endless flow of statutes and case law. To keep this book up-to-date, Cavendish have created a companion website where updated material will be placed regularly (for the address, see p ii).

Peter Hungerford-Welch
Inns of Court School of Law
City University, London
August 2004

CONTENTS

TABLE OF CASES

TABLE OF STATUTES

TABLE OF STATUTORY INSTRUMENTS

TABLE OF EUROPEAN LEGISLATION

CHAPTER 1

PRELIMINARIES

1.1   INTRODUCTION

In this chapter, we examine how a defendant is brought before the criminal courts; we consider what happens when a suspect is taken to a police station for questioning; we see how the decision to prosecute a suspect is taken; and we look at the structure and personnel of the criminal courts, and at the advocates who appear before them.

1.1.1   Some basic terminology

A defendant in a criminal case always makes his first appearance in a magistrates' court. Some cases are tried in the magistrates' court (comprising a bench of lay justices or a District judge); others are tried by a judge (a Circuit judge, a recorder, or a High Court judge) and jury in the Crown Court. An offence is a 'summary offence' if it must be tried in a magistrates' court. An offence is an 'indictable offence' if it may or must be tried in the Crown Court; where an indictable offence may be tried by a magistrates' court instead of the Crown Court, it is known as an 'either way' offence.

Section 66 of the Courts Act 2003 (in force since January 2004) provides that High Court judges, Circuit judges and recorders may exercise the jurisdiction of magistrates when exercising their criminal (and family) jurisdiction, thus enabling a Crown Court judge to make orders and to sentence in relation to cases normally reserved to magistrates' courts when disposing of related cases in the Crown Court.

1.2   COMMENCING PROCEEDINGS

There are currently three ways of bringing someone before the criminal courts:

- summons;
- arrest without warrant, followed by charge;
- arrest with warrant, followed by charge.

When Pt 4 of the Criminal Justice Act 2003 comes into force, the first of these three methods will be replaced with a new method for instituting proceedings, namely a 'written charge' and a 'requisition' requiring the person so charged to attend court.

1.3   SUMMONS

This is a two-stage process: the laying of an information, followed by the issue and service of a summons.

1.3.1 Laying an information

Before a summons can be issued, an 'information' has to be laid at a magistrates' court. Where proceedings are commenced by the police, this will be done by a police officer. The information must state:

- the name and address of the person laying the information, who is known as the 'informant' (in the case of a police prosecution this will be the police officer who reported the offence or a senior officer, depending on the policy of that police force);
- the name and address of the accused;
- the brief facts of the case as alleged by the informant;
- the statutory provision (if any) allegedly contravened by the accused.

In *Rubin v Director of Public Prosecutions* [1990] 2 QB 80, it was held that an information must be laid in the name of an individual, not a body. Thus, an information laid by the police must state the name of an individual officer and not, for example, 'Thames Valley Police'. However, this point is of limited practical significance; a police prosecution can continue even if the officer who signs the information dies before the case has been disposed of (*Hawkins v Bepey* [1980] 1 WLR 419; [1980] 1 All ER 797).

The information may be laid before a magistrate or a magistrates' clerk, and this may be done orally (in which case, the informant attends the magistrates' court) or in writing. Usually, an information is laid in writing; the information is simply sent to the nearest magistrates' court. The volume of prosecutions means that a bundle of informations in respect of all the cases where a decision to prosecute has been taken will be prepared by the police process department and sent to the magistrates' court.

A written information is laid as soon as it is received in the clerk's office, even if it is not considered by a clerk or a magistrate until later (*R v Manchester Justices ex p Hill* [1983] 1 AC 328; [1982] 2 All ER 963). No standard form has to be used; all that matters is that the document sent to the magistrates' court contains the essential elements of an information (*R v Kennet Justices ex p Humphrey and Wyatt* [1993] Crim LR 787).

Many courts now have computer links with local police stations. In those cases, the information is laid when it is fed by the police into the computer link, even if a print-out is not produced at the court until later (*R v Pontypridd Juvenile Court ex p B* (1989) 153 JP 213).

As we shall see in Chapter 4, an information may allege only one offence (r 12 of the Magistrates' Courts Rules 1981). This means that if a suspect is alleged to have committed more than one offence, a separate information has to be laid in respect of each offence. We shall also see in Chapter 4 that an information alleging a summary offence must be laid within six months of the alleged commission of the offence (s 127 of the Magistrates' Courts Act 1980). Thus, the date when the information is laid can be important.

1.3.2 Issuing a summons

Once an information has been laid, a summons may then be issued by a magistrate or clerk (usually the latter). The original version of ss 1 and 2 of the Magistrates' Courts Act 1980 contained detailed provisions regarding the territorial jurisdiction of magistrates' courts to issue a summons. Those complexities were swept away by the Courts Act 2003, which gives magistrates national jurisdiction (see Chapter 4).

In deciding whether or not to issue a summons, the magistrate or clerk should ensure that the facts stated in the information disclose an offence known to law, and that any time limits relating to the commencement of the prosecution have been complied with (*R v Gateshead Justices ex p Tesco Stores Ltd* [1981] QB 470; [1981] 1 All ER 1027). In *R v Liverpool Justices ex p Knibb* [1991] COD 53, it was held that, before issuing a summons, a clerk or magistrate must ascertain that the essential ingredients of the offence are *prima facie* present (that is, that the facts alleged in the information contain all the ingredients of the offence); that the offence alleged is not out of time; that the court has jurisdiction; that the informant has the necessary authority to prosecute and that the application for the summons is not vexatious. In *R v Bradford Justice ex p Sykes* (1999) 163 JP 224, it was argued that a clerk or magistrate, before issuing a summons, must make inquiries into the background of the information which has been laid. The Divisional Court held that, where an information has been laid, a clerk or a magistrate is entitled to make inquiries beyond the material before him before issuing a summons, but there is no duty to do so. It is submitted that it would, in most cases, be impracticable to expect the court to investigate the background to the case before issuing the summons. It is perhaps not surprising that the new method of instituting proceedings established by the Criminal Justice Act 2003 (see below) enables proceedings to be commenced without reference to the court.

1.3.3 Contents of the summons

Rule 98 of the Magistrates Courts Rules 1981 provides that:

(2) A summons requiring a person to appear before a magistrates' court to answer to an information or complaint shall state shortly the matter of the information or complaint and shall state the time and place at which the defendant is required by the summons to appear.

(3) A single summons may be issued against a person in respect of several informations or complaints; but the summons shall state the matter of each information or complaint separately and shall have effect as several summonses, each issued in respect of one information or complaint.

Rule 100 of the Magistrates Courts Rules 1981 provides that:

(1) Every information, summons, warrant or other document laid, issued or made for the purposes of, or in connection with, any proceedings before a magistrates' court for an offence shall be sufficient if it describes the specific offence with which the accused is charged, or of which he is convicted, in ordinary language avoiding as far as possible the use of technical terms and without necessarily stating all the elements of the offence, and gives such particulars as may be necessary for giving reasonable information of the nature of the charge.

(2) If the offence charged is one created by or under any Act, the description of the offence shall contain a reference to the section of the Act, or, as the case may be, the rule, order, regulation, byelaw or other instrument creating the offence.

Thus, the summons must give the substance of the allegation against the accused. It will set out the statutory provision contravened (if appropriate, as it usually will be since most offences are statutory), together with a short summary of the facts of the case.

In the case of an allegation of careless driving, for example, the particulars would be set out as follows:

> On 26 August 2004, driving a mechanically propelled vehicle, namely, a Ford Cortina motor car registration number Y123 ABC, on a road, namely, Warmington High Street, without due care and attention, contrary to s 3 of the Road Traffic Act 1988.

Although an information may allege only one offence, there is no objection to a summons referring to more than one information. So, if the accused is alleged to have committed a number of offences, the allegations will be detailed in a schedule on the summons.

The summons will also show the address of the court which the defendant is to attend, and the date and time of the first court appearance which the accused has to make in respect of this offence.

1.3.4 Serving the summons

Rule 99(1) of the Magistrates' Court Rules 1981 provides that:

> Service of a summons issued by a justice of the peace on a person other than a corporation may be effected:
>
> (a)   by delivering it to the person to whom it is directed; or
>
> (b)   by leaving it for him with some person at his last known or usual place of abode; or
>
> (c)   by sending it by post in a letter addressed to him at his last known or usual place of abode.

The summons is usually served by the court posting it to the defendant's last known address (that is, the address he gave to the police). If this is ineffective (for example, it is returned undelivered by the Post Office), the summons may be served by personal delivery (a police officer will hand the summons to the defendant) or even by leaving it with someone at the defendant's last known address.

1.3.5 A new method of instituting proceedings

In his *Review of the Criminal Courts of England and Wales*, Lord Justice Auld recommended the abolition of the laying of informations, mainly on the basis that the magistrates' courts are providing very little scrutiny of informations before issuing summonses. In para 55 of Chapter 10, Lord Justice Auld describes it an 'anomaly' that, in the most serious cases, the police charge a suspect without the intervention of the court and notes that the role of the court in the summons procedure is exercised in so 'notional' a manner as to make it unnecessary. His recommendations were as follows:

> 162   All public prosecutions should take the form of a charge, issued without reference to the courts, which should remain the basis of the accusation against the defendant throughout all stages of the case, irrespective of the level of court in which it is tried.
>
> 163   The charge may be oral or in writing, a written copy or original, as the case may be, being served manually or by postal service.
>
> 164   In either case, under arrangements with the court's administration, the charge should specify the date of first attendance at court on pain of arrest on warrant.

165 The present procedure for application for a warrant, by swearing an oath as to service of process, in summary offences should be abolished and replaced by paper application considered and determined in open court.

166 The same regime for commencing proceedings should apply to private prosecutions, save that: 1) the charge should only be administered in writing; 2) it should be subject to the prior permission of the court; 3) the permission should be endorsed on the charge sheet by an officer of the court; and 4) the court, before listing the matter, should notify the Director of Public Prosecutions.

...

168 The form of charge should be common to summary and indictable offences.

169 The prosecution should be entitled to amend the charge up to the pre-trial assessment date (or in a summary trial without such an assessment, up to a date to be specified), but thereafter only with the permission of the trial court.

170 The procedure for issue of warrants should be simplified.

Section 29 of the Criminal Justice Act 2003 gives effect to these proposals by creating a new method of commencing criminal proceedings to replace the laying of informations and issue of summonses. Section 29 provides as follows:

(1) A public prosecutor may institute criminal proceedings against a person by issuing a document (a 'written charge') which charges the person with an offence.

(2) Where a public prosecutor issues a written charge, it must at the same time issue a document (a 'requisition') which requires the person to appear before a magistrates' court to answer the written charge.

(3) The written charge and requisition must be served on the person concerned and a copy of both must be served on the court named in the requisition.

(4) In consequence of sub-sections (1) to (3), a public prosecutor is not to have the power to lay an information for the purpose of obtaining the issue of a summons under section 1 of the Magistrates' Courts Act 1980.

For these purposes, a public prosecutor is defined (in s 29(5)) as meaning:

(a) a police force or a person authorised by a police force to institute criminal proceedings,

(b) the Director of the Serious Fraud Office or a person authorised by him to institute criminal proceedings,

(c) the Director of Public Prosecutions or a person authorised by him to institute criminal proceedings,

(d) the Attorney General or a person authorised by him to institute criminal proceedings,

(e) a Secretary of State or a person authorised by a Secretary of State to institute criminal proceedings,

(f) the Commissioners of Inland Revenue or a person authorised by them to institute criminal proceedings,

(g) the Commissioners of Customs & Excise or a person authorised by them to institute criminal proceedings, or

(h) a person specified in an order made by the Secretary of State for the purposes of this section or a person authorised by such a person to institute criminal proceedings.

The effect of this is that notification of the requirement to attend court will be communicated to the accused by the prosecutor, not by the magistrates' court. Indeed, the magistrates' court will have no involvement whatsoever until the accused makes his first appearance before the court.

Section 29(4) makes it clear that the new procedure is intended to replace the existing procedure of laying an information (by removing the power of a public prosecutor to commence a case by laying an information). Section 30(4) further clarifies the ambit of the new procedure. It provides that:

Nothing in section 29 affects—

(a)   the power of a public prosecutor to lay an information for the purpose of obtaining the issue of a warrant under section 1 of the Magistrates' Courts Act 1980,

(b)   the power of a person who is not a public prosecutor to lay an information for the purpose of obtaining the issue of a summons or warrant under section 1 of that Act, or

(c)   any power to charge a person with an offence whilst he is in custody.

Thus, an information will still need to be laid in order to secure the grant of an arrest warrant; where a person is arrested, the case against them will continue to be commenced by way of a charge; and the new procedure is not available in the case of private prosecutions (which will have to be commenced by laying an information).

1.4   ARREST WITHOUT WARRANT

Section 24 of the Police and Criminal Evidence Act 1984 (PACE) provides that:

(4)   Any person may arrest without a warrant—

(a)   anyone who is in the act of committing an arrestable offence;

(b)   anyone whom he has reasonable grounds for suspecting to be committing such an offence.

(5)   Where an arrestable offence has been committed, any person may arrest without a warrant—

(a)   anyone who is guilty of the offence;

(b)   anyone whom he has reasonable grounds for suspecting to be guilty of it.

(6)   Where a constable has reasonable grounds for suspecting that an arrestable offence has been committed, he may arrest without a warrant anyone whom he has reasonable grounds for suspecting to be guilty of the offence.

(7)   A constable may arrest without a warrant—

(a)   anyone who is about to commit an arrestable offence;

(b)   anyone whom he has reasonable grounds for suspecting to be about to commit an arrestable offence.

In summary, a police officer may arrest someone without a warrant if:

• the person is committing (or the officer has reasonable grounds to believe that he is committing) an arrestable offence; or

• the officer has reasonable grounds to believe that an arrestable offence has been committed and also has reasonable grounds to believe that the person arrested has committed that offence; or

- the person is about to commit (or the officer has reasonable grounds to believe that the person is about to commit) an arrestable offence.

1.4.1 Meaning of 'arrestable offence'

An arrestable offence is defined by s 24 of PACE as one which is:

- punishable by a fixed term of imprisonment (for example, murder); or
- punishable by a maximum sentence of imprisonment of five years or more; or
- in the list contained in Sched 1A to PACE.

Schedule 2 to PACE preserves other statutory powers of arrest, such as arrest for breach of a condition of bail (s 7 of the Bail Act 1976) and arrest for failure to provide a road-side breath specimen (s 6(5) of the Road Traffic Act 1988).

1.4.2 Meaning of 'reasonable grounds'

In *O'Hara v Chief Constable of the RUC* [1997] AC 286, the House of Lords considered the meaning of 'reasonable grounds' in the context of anti-terrorism legislation, which applied the same test as s 24 of PACE. It was held that, for a police officer to have reasonable grounds to effect an arrest, the question is whether a reasonable person would be of that opinion, having regard to the information which was in the mind of the arresting officer. In other words, the test is partly subjective (the officer must have formed a genuine suspicion in his own mind that the suspect has committed the offence in question) and partly objective (there must be reasonable grounds for that suspicion). The House of Lords went on to hold that the information acted on by the officer need not be based on his own observations: he is entitled to form a suspicion on the basis of what he has been told. It is not necessary to prove what was known to the person who gave the information to the police officer or to prove that any facts on which the officer based his suspicion were actually true.

This test is compatible with the requirements of Art 5 of the European Convention on Human Rights (the right to liberty). On appeal to the European Court of Human Rights (*O'Hara v UK* (2002) 34 EHRR 32), it was held that, for an arrest to be lawful, it is necessary to provide some information capable of assuring the court that the arrest was based on reasonable suspicion. However, that information does not have to be as compelling as that required to justify a conviction or the bringing of a charge. In the earlier case of *Fox, Campbell and Hartley v UK* (1990) 13 EHRR 157, the test was expressed as requiring an arrest to be based on reasonable suspicion, in the sense of the existence of facts or information which would satisfy an objective observer that the suspect may have committed the offence.

The application of this test is illustrated by a civil case, *Hough v Chief Constable of Staffordshire* [2001] EWCA Civ 39; (2001) *The Times*, 14 February. The claimant was a passenger in a vehicle stopped by police. A routine check on the police computer said that the owner of the vehicle might be armed. The claimant was arrested but no weapon was found in his possession. He brought an action for damages. The Court of Appeal held that, where the arresting officer's suspicion is formed on the basis of a national police computer entry, the entry itself is capable of providing the necessary objective justification to afford the arresting officer the required reasonable suspicion under s 24(6) of PACE. The court said that an arresting officer could never be the 'mere conduit' for another, and so the crucial question remained as to what was in the mind of the arresting officer. Whether the computer entry in question sufficed to provide the necessary objective justification depended on the circumstances of the individual case. If the situation lacked urgency, and some further inquiry was clearly called for before the suspicion could properly be said to crystallise, then the computer entry alone would not suffice. In the present case, however, the entry itself provided ample justification for an arrest and the claim for wrongful arrest was defeated.

1.4.3   Information to be given on arrest

Section 28 of PACE set out what the accused must be told when is he arrested:

(1)   Subject to sub-section (5) below, where a person is arrested, otherwise than by being informed that he is under arrest, the arrest is not lawful unless the person arrested is informed that he is under arrest as soon as is practicable after his arrest.

(2)   Where a person is arrested by a constable, sub-section (1) above applies regardless of whether the fact of the arrest is obvious.

(3)   Subject to sub-section (5) below, no arrest is lawful unless the person arrested is informed of the ground for the arrest at the time of, or as soon as is practicable after, the arrest.

(4)   Where a person is arrested by a constable, sub-section (3) above applies regardless of whether the ground for the arrest is obvious.

(5)   Nothing in this section is to be taken to require a person to be informed—

(a) that he is under arrest; or

(b) of the ground for the arrest,

if it was not reasonably practicable for him to be so informed by reason of his having escaped from arrest before the information could be given.

Article 5(2) of the European Convention on Human Rights requires that everyone who is arrested shall be informed promptly, in a language which he understands, of the reasons for his arrest and of any charge against him. This means that the suspect must be told 'in simple, non-technical language that he can understand, the essential legal and factual grounds for his arrest so as to be able, if he sees fit, to apply to a court to challenge its lawfulness' (*Fox, Campbell and Hartley v UK* (1990) 13 EHRR 157 and *Taylor v Chief Constable of Thames Valley Police* [2004] EWCA Civ 858).

Thus, when someone is arrested, they should, at the time of the arrest, be informed in non-technical language of the reason for the arrest. This is so even if the reason is obvious (*Abbassy v Metropolitan Police Commissioner* [1990] 1 WLR 385; [1990] 1 All ER 193).

The information is normally given by the officer making the arrest, but s 28 of PACE is satisfied if an officer other than the arresting officer informs the person arrested of the reason for the arrest (*Dhesi v Chief Constable of West Midlands Police* (2000) *The Times*, 9 May).

Code C of the PACE Codes of Practice provides that:

10.3 A person who is arrested, or further arrested, must be informed at the time, or as soon as practicable thereafter, that they are under arrest and the grounds for their arrest.

10.4 A person who is arrested, or further arrested, must also be cautioned unless:

(a) it is impracticable to do so by reason of their condition or behaviour at the time;

(b) they have already been cautioned immediately prior to arrest as in paragraph 10.1.

Note 10B supplements Code 10.3 and provides that:

An arrested person must be given sufficient information to enable them to understand they have been deprived of their liberty and the reason they have been arrested, eg when a person is arrested on suspicion of committing an offence they must be informed of the suspected offence's nature, when and where it was committed. If the arrest is made under the general arrest conditions in PACE, section 25, the grounds for arrest must include an explanation of the conditions which make the arrest necessary. Vague or technical language should be avoided.

The terms of the caution under para 10.5 inform the suspect that if he does not mention, when questioned, something he later relies on in court, it may harm his defence, and that anything he does say may be given in evidence.

1.4.4 'Citizen's arrest'

Under s 24 of PACE, a member of the public may arrest someone who is in the act of committing (or whom he has reasonable grounds to suspect is committing) an arrestable offence.

Where an arrestable offence has already been committed, a member of the public can arrest someone who is (or whom he has reasonable grounds for suspecting is) guilty of that offence.

The police powers of arrest are wider, in that a police officer only has to have reasonable grounds for suspecting that an arrestable offence has been committed before he can arrest anyone whom he reasonably suspects of committing it.

Thus, if a member of the public (for example, a store detective) arrests someone who he reasonably suspects of committing an arrestable offence, the arrest will not be valid if an arrestable offence has not in fact been committed (*R v Self* [1992] 1 WLR 657; [1992] 3 All ER 476). In *Self*, the defendant was arrested by a store detective, with the help of a member of the public, on suspicion of shoplifting. There was a struggle in which the member of the public was kicked and punched by the defendant. The defendant was charged with theft and assault. He was acquitted of the theft but convicted of assault. The Court of Appeal held that the conviction for the assault could not be sustained. The store detective and the person assisting him had no right to detain the defendant: no arrestable offence had in fact been committed by the defendant and therefore there was no right to effect a 'citizen's arrest'.

Furthermore, a member of the public cannot arrest someone who is apparently about to commit an arrestable offence, whereas a police officer can.

A citizen who makes an arrest should deliver the person arrested into the hands of the police as soon as practicable: s 30(1)(b) of PACE. The police will then be responsible for charging the suspect if they decide to proceed with the case.

1.4.5   Non-arrestable offences

It is possible (perhaps surprisingly) to be arrested for a non-arrestable offence. In the case of non-arrestable offences (that is, those not within s 24), the police may only arrest a suspect if one or more of the so-called 'general arrest conditions' set out in s 25 of PACE is satisfied. These conditions are set out in s 25(3), and are as follows:

(3)   The general arrest conditions are—
    (a) that the name of the relevant person is unknown to, and cannot be readily ascertained by, the constable;
    (b) that the constable has reasonable grounds for doubting whether a name furnished by the relevant person as his name is his real name;
    (c) that—
        (i)   the relevant person has failed to furnish a satisfactory address for service; or
        (ii) the constable has reasonable grounds for doubting whether an address furnished by the relevant person is a satisfactory address for service;
    (d) that the constable has reasonable grounds for believing that arrest is necessary to prevent the relevant person—
        (i)   causing physical injury to himself or any other person;
        (ii) suffering physical injury;
        (iii) causing loss of or damage to property;
        (iv) committing an offence against public decency; or
        (v) causing an unlawful obstruction of the highway;
    (e) that the constable has reasonable grounds for believing that arrest is necessary to protect a child or other vulnerable person from the relevant person.

Section 25(3) will be satisfied where:

- the suspect refuses to give his name, and his identity cannot readily be ascertained (for example, from a document such as a driving licence in his possession); or
- the police officer has reasonable grounds for doubting whether the name given by the suspect is his real name; or
- the suspect has failed to supply his address; or
- the police officer has reasonable grounds for doubting whether the address given by the suspect is one at which it will be possible to effect service of a summons on the suspect; or
- the police officer has reasonable grounds for believing that it is necessary to arrest the suspect in order to prevent him from causing physical injury to another person or to himself; or
- the police officer has reasonable grounds for believing that it is necessary to arrest the suspect in order to prevent him from causing damage to property; or
- the police officer reasonably thinks that it is necessary to arrest the suspect in order to prevent him from committing an offence against public decency or from obstructing the highway; or

- the police officer reasonably thinks that it is necessary to arrest the suspect in order to protect a child or other vulnerable (for example, mentally ill) person.

The first four of these situations are cases where arrest is appropriate because it is doubtful that a summons could be served and therefore arrest is the only way of commencing proceedings. The remaining grounds enable the police to deal with emergency situations.

In *Edwards v DPP* (1993) 97 Cr App R 301, it was held that, for an arrest under s 25 of PACE to be valid, the relevant ground should be in the mind of the police officer at the time the arrest is made. Furthermore, there must be evidence (especially what is said by the police officer to the suspect when the arrest is made) that this is the case.

Only a police officer may make an arrest for a non-arrestable offence.

Thus, unless the general arrest conditions set out above apply, a suspect can only be arrested if it is alleged that he has committed an arrestable offence. On the other hand, an information may be laid and a summons issued in respect of any offence.

1.5   VOLUNTARY ATTENDANCE AT A POLICE STATION

Sometimes, a person will agree to go to a police station to be interviewed by the police without first being arrested. Someone who has not been arrested but who is 'helping the police with their inquiries' is free to leave at any time unless and until he is arrested – see s 29 of PACE, which provides that:

Where for the purpose of assisting with an investigation a person attends voluntarily at a police station or at any other place where a constable is present or accompanies a constable to a police station or any such other place without having been arrested—

(a)   he shall be entitled to leave at will unless he is placed under arrest;

(b)   he shall be informed at once that he is under arrest if a decision is taken by a constable to prevent him from leaving at will.

Code C 3.21 provides that:

Anybody attending a police station voluntarily to assist with an investigation may leave at will unless arrested. If it is decided they shall not be allowed to leave, they must be informed at once that they are under arrest and brought before the custody officer, who is responsible for making sure they are notified of their rights in the same way as other detainees ...

1.6   PROCEDURE AFTER ARREST

After the suspect has been arrested, he will (unless granted 'street bail' – see below) be taken to a 'designated police station' (that is, under s 35, one with facilities for the detention of suspects) as soon as practicable after arrest: s 30(1) of PACE. The suspect will not be taken immediately to the police station if the case is one where the presence of the suspect elsewhere 'is necessary in order to carry out such investigations as it is reasonable to carry out immediately' (s 30(10)); it may be necessary, for example, to search the suspect's home.

The time of the suspect's arrival at the police station is called the 'relevant time'. This is the moment from which the length of the suspect's detention starts to be measured.

On arrival at the police station, the suspect is taken to the custody officer, defined by s 36 as an officer of the rank of a Sergeant or above (s 36(3) who is unconnected with the investigation of the case (s 36(5)).

1.6.1 'Street bail'

Section 30 of PACE is amended by s 4 of the Criminal Justice Act 2003, which came into force in January 2004. The requirement that 'the person must be taken by a constable to a police station as soon as practicable after the arrest' is set out in s 30(1A) and is (under s 30(1)(B)) made subject to s 30A. Sections 30A–30D provide for what may be termed 'street bail'. This provision empowers police officers to grant bail to persons following their arrest without the need to take them to a police station first. Section 30A provides that a constable may release on bail a person who has been arrested 'at any time before he arrives at a police station' (s 30A(2)). It requires that the person released on bail 'must be required to attend a police station' (s 30A(3)) and that any police station may be specified for that purpose (s 30A(5)). No other requirement may be imposed on the person as a condition of bail (s 30A(4)). Under s 30B, the police officer must give the person bailed, before he is released, a written notice setting out (a) the offence for which he was arrested, and (b) the ground on which he was arrested (s 30B(2)), and informing him that he is required to attend a police station (s 30B(3)); the notice may also specify the police station and the time at which he is required to attend (s 30B(5)). If these details are not included in the notice, they must be supplied in a further written notice provided to the person later. The police can specify a different police station or a different time by giving the person written notice to that effect (s 30B(6), (7)). Under s 30C(1), the police can give the person a written notice that his attendance at the police station is no longer required.

Section 30C(2) provides that, if the person is required to attend a police station which is not a designated police station (that is, one without facilities for detention of suspects), he must be released, or taken to a designated police station, within six hours of his arrival at the non-designated station. Section 30C(4) provides that a person who has been released on bail under s 30A can be re-arrested if new evidence justifying a further arrest has come to light since his release (s 30C(4)).

Section 30D deals with failure to answer to bail granted under s 30A. Where the person fails to attend the police station at the specific time, he may be arrested without warrant (s 30D(1)).

Home Office Circular 61/2003 gives guidance on the implementation of s 4 of the 2003 Act. The Circular sets out the key aims of 'street bail', which are:

- to enable officers to remain on patrol for longer periods and raise visibility;
- to give officers greater flexibility to decide how best to use their time and organise their casework; and
- to remove the need for suspects to be taken to a police station only to be bailed on arrival.

The Circular goes on to identify the benefits of this new power:

Who does it benefit?

• The police:

– reduce the amount of time travelling to and from the station

– better plan the investigation and work caseload

– spend less time waiting at the police station to progress the investigation

– ensure appropriate representation on answering bail

- The suspect:

– reduce the need to travel to a police station

– avoid spending time in detention whilst awaiting representation etc

– ensure that time spent in detention is focused on the investigation and not awaiting representation

- Legal representatives, parents, appropriate adults

– ability to plan and prepare for attendance

- The community

– increased police presence on the street

– more officer time spent patrolling than dealing with 'bureaucratic' delays.

Part A (para 3) of the Circular goes on to identify the key matters to be taken into account by the police:

Street bail enables front-line officers to apply their discretion at the point of arrest. There are four key considerations:

- the nature of the offence

- the ability to progress the investigation at the station

- confidence in the suspect answering bail

- the level of awareness and understanding of the procedure by the suspect.

It may be a source of some confusion that Pt F of the Circular (namely 'pocket-sized guide') provides guidance in slightly different terms. It states that:

It is a matter for the discretion of the constable when street bail should be given. The primary considerations are:

- the nature and seriousness of the offence

- fitness, vulnerability and awareness of the detainee

- potential for further offences to be committed

- preservation of evidence.

The date for attendance should be no more than six weeks from the date of arrest.

Part A of the Circular adds (paras 5 and 6) that:

Officers must ensure that street bail is used fairly, objectively and without any bias against ethnic or other groups within the community. Supervising officers must monitor the use of street bail and consider whether officers under their supervision are making appropriate use of the power.

Supervising officers should satisfy themselves that the decision to use or decline use of street bail is not on the basis of stereotyped image or inappropriate generalisations. Appropriate action should be taken by supervising officers if examination of the records reveals any trends or patterns which give cause for concern.

Part C contains more detailed guidance on the considerations to be applied when deciding whether or not to grant street bail:

What type of offence has been committed? There is no definitive list of offences to which street bail can be granted. It is a matter for the officer's discretion. However, it is unlikely that street bail would be granted in relation to a serious arrestable offence.

What impact has the offence had? How has the offence impacted on the victim and any bystanders – what impact has it had on the offender – how serious is the offence?

Would a delay in dealing with the offender result in loss of vital evidence? It might be necessary to take an arrested person to a police station to preserve and examine forensic evidence, which could be lost if the suspect is released.

Is the arrested person fit to be released back on to the streets? A drunken driver, or those with mental health problems, for example, may not be in a fit state to be returned to the streets. In the case of a juvenile, consideration must be given to the welfare of the child. Detailed factors are given below.

Does the arrested person understand what is happening? This particularly applies to vulnerable people who would normally require the assistance of an appropriate adult (ie mentally disordered or mentally vulnerable people and juveniles) but may also include those suspected to be under the influence of drink and/or drugs.

If released on bail is the arrested person likely to commit a further offence? The arresting officer must/should not grant street bail if there are reasonable grounds to believe that the arrested person might continue to commit that or another offence if released eg where fighting is involved.

Am I satisfied that the arrested person has provided a correct name and address? The bailing officer must not grant bail if he is not satisfied that the identification and address details provided are correct.

What about juveniles and other vulnerable people? You should assess the level of risk to the safety and welfare of a juvenile or vulnerable person.

1.6.2 Arrival at the police station: duties of the custody officer

The duties of the custody officer are:

- to decide whether there is sufficient evidence for the suspect to be charged or whether to authorise detention without charge (see s 37 of PACE);
- to inform the suspect of his rights (for example, the right under s 56 to have someone informed of his arrest and the right under s 58 to consult in private with a solicitor);
- to keep a custody record documenting all that occurs during the suspect's detention, for example, meal breaks and interviews;
- to seize and retain anything in the possession of the prisoner, except for clothes and personal effects (which may only be seized if the custody officer thinks the prisoner will use them to cause injury to himself or others, or damage to property, or to escape).

1.6.2.1 The right to have someone informed of the arrest

Under s 56 of PACE, the suspect has the right to have someone informed of their arrest. However, the exercise of this right can be delayed for up to 36 hours on the authority of an officer of the rank of Inspector or above (the rank was reduced from Superintendent to Inspector by s 74 of the Criminal Justice and Police Act 2001). Section 56 provides as follows:

(1) Where a person has been arrested and is being held in custody in a police station or other premises, he shall be entitled, if he so requests, to have one friend or relative or other person who is known to him or who is likely to take an interest in his welfare told, as soon as is practicable except to the extent that delay is permitted by this section, that he has been arrested and is being detained there.

(2) Delay is only permitted—

    (a) in the case of a person who is in police detention for a serious arrestable offence; and

    (b) if an officer of at least the rank of Inspector authorises it.

(3) In any case the person in custody must be permitted to exercise the right conferred by sub-section (1) above within 36 hours from the relevant time, as defined in section 41(2) above.

(4) An officer may give an authorisation under sub-section (2) above orally or in writing but, if he gives it orally, he shall confirm it in writing as soon as is practicable.

(5) Subject to sub-section (5A) below an officer may only authorise delay where he has reasonable grounds for believing that telling the named person of the arrest—

    (a) will lead to interference with or harm to evidence connected with a serious arrestable offence or interference with or physical injury to other persons; or

    (b) will lead to the alerting of other persons suspected of having committed such an offence but not yet arrested for it; or

    (c) will hinder the recovery of any property obtained as a result of such an offence.

(5A) An officer may also authorise delay where he has reasonable grounds for believing that—

    (a) the person detained for the serious arrestable offence has benefited from his criminal conduct, and

    (b) the recovery of the value of the property constituting the benefit will be hindered by telling the named person of the arrest.

(5B) For the purposes of sub-section (5A) above the question whether a person has benefited from his criminal conduct is to be decided in accordance with Part 2 of the Proceeds of Crime Act 2002.

(6) If a delay is authorised—

    (a) the detained person shall be told the reason for it; and

    (b) the reason shall be noted on his custody record.

(7) The duties imposed by sub-section (6) above shall be performed as soon as is practicable.

(8) The rights conferred by this section on a person detained at a police station or other premises are exercisable whenever he is transferred from one place to another; and this section applies to each subsequent occasion on which they are exercisable as it applies to the first such occasion.

(9) There may be no further delay in permitting the exercise of the right conferred by sub-section (1) above once the reason for authorising delay ceases to subsist.

1.6.3 Charging the suspect

To charge a suspect, the custody officer tells the suspect what offence(s) he is accused of. The suspect is cautioned that he does not have to say anything, that it may harm his defence if he does not mention something he later relies on in court, and that anything he does say will be written down and may be given in evidence. The suspect is then asked if he has anything to say. Any reply must be noted down.

Section 37(7) originally provided that:

... if the custody officer determines that he has before him sufficient evidence to charge the person arrested with the offence for which he was arrested, the person arrested—

(a)   shall be charged; or

(b)   shall be released without charge, either on bail or without bail.

However, s 37(7) is amended by the Criminal Justice Act 2003 to enable the Crown Prosecution Service (CPS) to have more direct involvement in the charging process. The prospect of the defendant pleading guilty, or being found guilty, depends in large measure on the defendant being charged with the right offence(s). The Auld Review recommended that all public prosecutions should take the form of a charge, issued without reference to the courts and for which the prosecutor (in all but minor, routine or urgent cases) would have initial responsibility. In particular, the Review recommended early involvement of CPS in charging decisions. The relevant Recommendations are as follows:

152   The Crown Prosecution Service should be given greater legal powers, in particular the power to determine the initial charge, and sufficient resources to enable it to take full and effective control of cases from the charge or pre-charge stage, as appropriate.

...

154   The Crown Prosecution Service should determine the charge in all but minor, routine offences or where, because of the circumstances, there is a need for a holding charge before seeking the advice of the Service.

155   In minor, routine cases in which the police charge without first having sought the advice of the Service, they should apply the same evidential test as that governing the Service in the Code for Crown Prosecutors.

156   Where the police have preferred a holding charge, and in other than minor, routine offences, a prosecutor should review and, if necessary, reformulate the charge at the earliest possible opportunity.

These reforms are aimed at ensuring two key objectives:

(a) that the defendant is charged with the appropriate offence (rather than one which is too serious); and

(b) that the defendant is only charged if there is sufficient evidence, so that there is a realistic prospect of conviction.

As regards private prosecutions, Lord Justice Auld recommends that:

158   The right of private prosecution should continue, subject to the power of the Director of Public Prosecutions, on learning of a private prosecution, to take it over and discontinue it.

159   Any court before which a private prosecution is initiated should be under a duty forthwith to notify the Director of it in writing.

160   The Director, in deciding whether to discontinue a private prosecution that he has taken over, should apply the public interest test as well as the evidential test set out in the Code for Crown Prosecutors.

Paragraph 2 of Sched 2 to the Criminal Justice Act 2003 amends s 37(7) of PACE and adds two new sub-sections, (7A) and (7B), as follows:

(a) shall be released without charge and on bail for the purpose of enabling the Director of Public Prosecutions to make a decision under section 37B below,

(b) shall be released without charge and on bail but not for that purpose,

(c) shall be released without charge and without bail, or

(d) shall be charged.

(7A) The decision as to how a person is to be dealt with under sub-section (7) above shall be that of the custody officer.

(7B) Where a person is released under sub-section (7)(a) above, it shall be the duty of the custody officer to inform him that he is being released to enable the Director of Public Prosecutions to make a decision under section 37B below.

Section 37A(1) of PACE empowers the Director of Public Prosecutions (DPP) to issue general guidance to enable custody officers to deal with people under s 37(7) and set out what information should be sent to the DPP under s 37B(1). Such guidance, and any revisions thereto, must be published (s 37A(5)).

According to the Explanatory Notes which accompany the Criminal Justice Act 2003, it is envisaged that the DPP's guidance will set out the circumstances in which it will be appropriate for the police to charge or otherwise deal with a suspect without reference to the CPS. This is likely to include minor cases (such as the majority of road traffic offences); cases where there is an admission by the suspect and which could be disposed of by the magistrates' court; and cases where there is a need to bring the suspect before a court with a view to seeking a remand in custody. In other cases it will be appropriate for the police to release the suspect without charge but on bail while (as required by s 37B) the case is referred to the CPS.

Section 37B provides as follows:

(1)   Where a person is released on bail under section 37(7)(a) above, an officer involved in the investigation of the offence shall, as soon as is practicable, send to the Director of Public Prosecutions such information as may be specified in guidance under section 37A above.

(2)   The Director of Public Prosecutions shall decide whether there is sufficient evidence to charge the person with an offence.

(3)   If he decides that there is sufficient evidence to charge the person with an offence, he shall decide—

(a) whether or not the person should be charged and, if so, the offence with which he should be charged, and

(b) whether or not the person should be given a caution and, if so, the offence in respect of which he should be given a caution.

(4)   The Director of Public Prosecutions shall give written notice of his decision to an officer involved in the investigation of the offence.

(5)   If his decision is—

(a) that there is not sufficient evidence to charge the person with an offence, or

(b) that there is sufficient evidence to charge the person with an offence but that the person should not be charged with an offence or given a caution in respect of an offence, a custody officer shall give the person notice in writing that he is not to be prosecuted.

(6)   If the decision of the Director of Public Prosecutions is that the person should be charged with an offence, or given a caution in respect of an offence, the person shall be charged or cautioned accordingly.

(7)   But if his decision is that the person should be given a caution in respect of the offence and it proves not to be possible to give the person such a caution, he shall instead be charged with the offence.

Thus, if a suspect is released without charge but on bail, it is then for the CPS to determine whether there is sufficient evidence to charge the suspect with the offence and, if so, whether the suspect should be charged (and, if so, with what offence) or whether he should be given a caution (and, if so, in respect of what offence). The suspect is then to be charged, cautioned or informed in writing that he is not to be prosecuted.

One possible disadvantage of this new system is that there might be a risk that, if Crown Prosecutors have more direct involvement at the charging stage (especially if they are based in police stations), some of the independence from the police which is supposed to be a hallmark of the CPS may be lost (reverting to the days before the institution of the CPS, when police forces instructed firms of solicitors to act for them and to prosecute cases on their behalf in court).

The use of Crown Prosecutors to decide whether the suspect should be charged and, if so, with what offence(s) was piloted during 2004 in Kent, West Yorkshire, South Yorkshire, Cleveland, Lancashire and Northumbria. The scheme was judged a success by the CPS and the Home Office. The benefits identified in the pilot areas included:

- increases in early guilty pleas and conviction rates (up to 40%);
- decreases in discontinued cases, ineffective trials and changed charges (as much as 90% was achieved in one area);
- improvements in file quality; and
- improved understanding and co-operation between the CPS and police.

The Auld Review also recommended that the charge should remain the basis of the case against a defendant regardless of the court which ultimately deals with his case, thus replacing the present mix of charges, summonses and indictments. These proposals were accepted for the most part, in that Pt 4 of the Criminal Justice Act 2003 makes provision for instituting proceedings by way of a written charge (instead of by the laying of an information and issue of a summons). However, the indictment will remain the basis of Crown Court trials.

1.6.4   Police bail

After a suspect has been charged, he must be released on police bail (with the condition that he attend a specified magistrates' court on a specified date and at a specified time) unless any of the exceptions contained in s 38 of PACE apply.

Section 38(1) provides as follows:

(1) Where a person arrested for an offence otherwise than under a warrant endorsed for bail is charged with an offence, the custody officer shall ... order his release from police detention, either on bail or without bail, unless—

    (a) if the person arrested is not an arrested juvenile—

        (i) his name or address cannot be ascertained or the custody officer has reasonable grounds for doubting whether a name or address furnished by him as his name or address is his real name or address;

        (ii) the custody officer has reasonable grounds for believing that the person arrested will fail to appear in court to answer to bail;

        (iii) in the case of a person arrested for an imprisonable offence, the custody officer has reasonable grounds for believing that the detention of the person arrested is necessary to prevent him from committing an offence;

        (iiia) in the case of a person who has attained the age of 18, the custody officer has reasonable grounds for believing that the detention of the person is necessary to enable a sample to be taken from him under section 63B below;

        (iv) in the case of a person arrested for an offence which is not an imprisonable offence, the custody officer has reasonable grounds for believing that the detention of the person arrested is necessary to prevent him from causing physical injury to any other person or from causing loss of or damage to property;

        (v) the custody officer has reasonable grounds for believing that the detention of the person arrested is necessary to prevent him from interfering with the administration of justice or with the investigation of offences or of a particular offence; or

        (vi) the custody officer has reasonable grounds for believing that the detention of the person arrested is necessary for his own protection;

    (b) if he is an arrested juvenile—

        (i) any of the requirements of paragraph (a) above is satisfied; or

        (ii) the custody officer has reasonable grounds for believing that he ought to be detained in his own interests.

Under s 38, therefore, bail may only be withheld from a person who has been charged if:

- the suspect refuses to give his name or address (or there are doubts as to the correctness of the name or address given); or
- if the custody officer has reasonable grounds to believe that:

(i) the suspect will fail to appear in court; or

(ii) continued detention of the suspect is necessary to prevent the suspect from committing an offence (provided that the person has been arrested for an imprisonable offence); or

(iii) continued detention of the suspect is necessary to prevent him from causing physical injury to any other person or from causing damage to property (this ground applies only where the person has been arrested for a non-imprisonable offence; there is no need for this specific ground where the suspect has been arrested for an imprisonable offence because such conduct would be covered by the other ground – risk of a subsequent offence – for withholding bail in the case of imprisonable offences); or

(iv) continued detention of the suspect is necessary to prevent the suspect from interfering with the administration of justice or with police investigations; or

(v) continued detention of the suspect is necessary for his own protection.

In deciding whether there is a risk that the defendant will abscond, or commit a further offence, or interfere with witnesses, the custody officer will have to apply the same criteria as a magistrates' court (s 38(2A) of PACE). These criteria are considered in 2.4.1 below.

By virtue of an amendment to s 38 of PACE made by s 57 of the Criminal Justice and Court Services Act 2000, the custody officer is empowered, after charge, to detain the person charged in order to enable a sample to be taken to test for the presence of a specified Class A drug; this is subject to the conditions set out in s 63B of PACE. This provision is extended by s 5 of the Criminal Justice Act 2003 to cover anyone who has attained the age of 14.

1.6.5 Imposition of conditions on police bail

Where a person is released on police bail (under s 38 of PACE) having been charged with an offence, the custody officer has power (under s 3A of the Bail Act 1976) to impose any condition on the grant of bail which a court could impose (with certain exceptions, such as a requirement of residence in a bail hostel).

Section 3A(5) of the Bail Act 1976 says that:

Where a constable grants bail to a person no conditions shall be imposed ... unless it appears to the constable that it is necessary to do so for the purpose of preventing that person from—

(a) failing to surrender to custody, or

(b) committing an offence while on bail, or

(c) interfering with witnesses or otherwise obstructing the course of justice, whether in relation to himself or any other person.

Section 3A(4) of the Bail Act 1976 allows a custody officer, at the request of the accused, to vary the conditions of bail which were imposed when the defendant was charged, and adds that 'in doing so he may impose conditions or more onerous conditions'.

Where conditions are attached to police bail, reasons have to be given and recorded (s 5A of the Bail Act 1976). Furthermore, where conditions have been attached to police bail, the defendant may apply to a magistrates' court to vary those conditions, although it should be borne in mind that the court also has the power to withhold bail altogether or to 'impose more onerous conditions' (s 43B(2) of the Magistrates' Courts Act 1980).

Section 47(3A) of PACE (inserted by s 46 of the Crime and Disorder Act 1998) provides that, where a custody officer grants bail to someone who has been charged with an offence, he must specify the date of the person's appearance in the magistrates' court; that date should normally 'be not later than the first sitting of the court after the person is charged with the offence'. This has the effect that the first court appearance of the accused should take place at the next available sitting of the magistrates whether the suspect is released on police bail or not.

1.6.6 Release without charge on police bail

Sometimes police release a suspect without charge but require him to return to the police station at a later date (for example, for further questioning or to give the police or CPS further time in which to decide whether or not to charge him). In such a case, the suspect is released on police bail.

Paragraph 6(3) of Sched 2 to the Criminal Justice Act 2003 amends s 47(1A) of PACE to enable conditions to be imposed where a person is released on bail pending consultation with the CPS.

Where a suspect has been released on police bail with the condition that he should return to the police station on a specified date, he may be arrested without a warrant if he fails to attend the police station at the appointed time: s 46A of PACE. He may also (by virtue of the amended version of s 46A set out in para 5 of Sched 2 to the Criminal Justice Act 2003) be arrested if the police have reasonable grounds for suspecting that he has broken any conditions of bail.

If a person is arrested under s 46A and, by that stage, the investigating officer has not received notice (under s 37B(4)) from the DPP as to whether the suspect should be charged or cautioned, he '(a) shall be charged, or (b) shall be released without charge, either on bail or without bail' (s 37C(2)); the decision as to how he is to be dealt with is taken by the custody officer (s 37C(3)).

Section 34(7) of PACE provides that, where a person returns to the police station to answer police bail, including 'street bail' (see above), or is arrested for failing to do so, he is to be regarded as having been arrested for the original offence at that moment. It follows that the suspect is in the same position as a person who is being detained without charge and so the custody timetable (set out below) applies.

1.6.7 Detention without charge

Section 37 of PACE covers the situation where the custody officer decides that there is insufficient evidence to charge the suspect:

(2) If the custody officer determines that he does not have such evidence before him, the person arrested shall be released either on bail or without bail, unless the custody officer has reasonable grounds for believing that his detention without being charged is necessary to secure or preserve evidence relating to an offence for which he is under arrest or to obtain such evidence by questioning him.

(3) If the custody officer has reasonable grounds for so believing, he may authorise the person arrested to be kept in police detention.

If there is insufficient evidence for the suspect to be charged, he must be released (either unconditionally or with the proviso that he return to the police station on a specified date) unless it is necessary for the police to detain him without charge in order to:

- secure or preserve evidence relating to the offence for which the suspect has been arrested (for example, the police fear that the suspect would hide relevant evidence or warn accomplices); or
- obtain such evidence by questioning the suspect.

Ed Cape, in 'Detention without charge: what does "sufficient evidence to charge" mean?' [1999] Crim LR 874, points out (drawing on research including Brown, D: *PACE Ten Years On: A Review of the Research* (Home Office Research Study 155, 1997) that the examination by the custody officer of the need for the suspect's detention rarely amounts to a searching scrutiny, with the effect that almost all of those who are arrested are detained. Custody officers who were observed during the research did not ask arresting officers for much information at all about the evidence against the suspect before authorising the detention of the suspect. Cape's main concern in this article is to address the question whether the 'sufficient evidence to charge' test in s 37 'leaves unanswered the question of whether the police must decide upon charge once satisfied there is a *prima facie* case against the suspect, or whether they can delay charge until some higher threshold is met, such as whether there is sufficient evidence to give a realistic prospect of conviction'. Cape takes the view that the test applied by the police ('sufficient evidence to charge') and that applied by the CPS ('realistic prospect of conviction') are necessarily different. However, it seems logical that – in practice, if not in theory – the two tests should amount to the same thing, since the police are sending to the CPS a case with sufficient evidence, they hope, for that case to be taken forward by the CPS. Perhaps the key difference between the two tests is their mode of application – the decision of the custody officer is taken by a non-lawyer (in the potentially chaotic atmosphere of the police station custody area), whereas when the case is reviewed by the CPS, the review is carried out by a qualified lawyer. Given that, as a result of the reforms brought about by the Criminal Justice Act 2003, charging is to be taken over in most cases by Crown Prosecutors, it seems inexorable that the two tests will be interpreted to mean the same thing.

1.6.8　Detention without charge: reviews

If the suspect is detained without charge, the detention is subject to periodic reviews according to the timetable set out in ss 40–44 of PACE.

Under s 40(3), reviews take place as follows:

(a)　the first review shall be not later than six hours after the detention was first authorised;

(b)　the second review shall be not later than nine hours after the first;

(c)　subsequent reviews shall be at intervals of not more than nine hours.

Thus, the first review takes place six hours after detention was first authorised; the second review at 15 hours after detention was first authorised; and the third review at 24 hours after detention was first authorised.

At each of these reviews, the review officer has to be satisfied that the conditions of continued detention set out at 1.6.7 above continue to be satisfied.

Before deciding whether to authorise the continued detention of the suspect, the review officer must give the suspect (unless he is asleep or otherwise unfit by reason of his condition or behaviour), or any solicitor who is representing him and who is available at the time of the review, the opportunity to make representations about the continued detention (s 40(12)–(14)).

A review may be postponed if, having regard to the circumstances prevailing at the latest time when that review should take place, it is not practicable to carry out the review then (for example, because the suspect is then being interviewed and it would wreck the interview if it were to be suspended for a review to take place, or because no review officer is readily available at that time). Where a review is postponed, it must take place as soon as practicable after the time it should have taken place, and a reason for the delay must be noted on the custody record (s 40(4), (5), (7)). Importantly, a postponement of one review does not affect the time when subsequent reviews have to take place (s 40(6)).

Section 40A of PACE (as amended by s 6 of the Criminal Justice Act 2003) enables reviews of detention to be conducted by telephone rather than in person at the police station. The reviewing officer will usually speak to the custody officer, and to the detained person (or their legal representative) if he wishes to exercise the right to make representations about the continuing need for detention. Prior to this amendment, telephone reviews were only permissible where it was not reasonably practicable for the reviewing officer to be present at the police station; that restriction is removed by the 2003 Act. However, under s 40(A)(2) of the 1984 Act, telephone reviews must not be conducted where it is reasonably practicable to carry out the review using video-conferencing facilities in accordance with regulations under s 45A of PACE.

The Home Office Circular (60/2003) on the implementation of the amended version of s 40A (which came into force in January 2004) contains the following guidance:

3.2 The review officer has the straightforward alternative of reviewing in person or by telephone.

3.3 The review officer must consider each case individually and decide whether a telephone review is sufficient, or whether a review in person is most appropriate in the circumstances.

3.4 It will enable operational flexibility and provide scope to save the review officer's time by minimising effort that would otherwise be used up in travelling to conduct reviews.

3.5 But, importantly, the decision on the type of review must always take full account of the needs of the person in custody. The benefits of carrying out a review in person should always be considered, based on the individual circumstances of each case with specific additional consideration if the person is:

– a juvenile (and the age of the juvenile); or

– mentally vulnerable; or

– has been subject to medical attention for other than routine minor ailments; or

– there are presentational or community issues around the person's detention.

3.6 Should a telephone review be undertaken, the officer responsible for authorising continued detention shall ensure that the opportunity to make representations is given to the detainee (unless asleep), the detainee's solicitor if available at the time; and the appropriate adult if available at the time.

3.7 The review officer can decide at any stage that a telephone review should be terminated and that the review will be conducted in person. The reasons for doing so should be noted in the custody record.

3.8 Telephone reviews will not be permitted where facilities for review by video conferencing exist and it is practicable to use them.

1.6.9   Detention beyond 24 hours

After 24 hours from the time when detention was first authorised have elapsed, the suspect can only be detained without charge if the provisions of s 42ff apply (s 41). Otherwise he must be released (with or without bail): s 41(7).

If the suspect is released because 24 hours have elapsed, he cannot be re-arrested without a warrant for the offence for which he was previously arrested 'unless new evidence justifying a further arrest has come to light after his release' (s 41(9)). This does not, however, prevent the arrest of the suspect under s 46A of PACE (arrest for failure to answer police bail).

Section 42(1) of PACE provides that:

Where a police officer of the rank of superintendent or above who is responsible for the police station at which a person is detained has reasonable grounds for believing that—

(a)   the detention of that person without charge is necessary to secure or preserve evidence relating to an offence for which he is under arrest or to obtain such evidence by questioning him;

(b)   an offence for which he is under arrest is an arrestable offence; and

(c)   the investigation is being conducted diligently and expeditiously,

he may authorise the keeping of that person in police detention for a period expiring at or before 36 hours after the relevant time.

Section 42(1)(b) was amended by s 7 of the Criminal Justice Act 2003. Prior to this amendment, s 42 applied only to serious arrestable offences (as defined by s 116 of the 1984 Act). This meant that the maximum period of detention in a case which did not involve a serious arrestable offence was 24 hours, and it was only where the offence was a 'serious arrestable offence' that the police could authorise detention for up to a further 12 hours. The amendment of s 42 (which took effect in January 2004) means that the police have the power to detain a suspect without charge for up to 36 hours in the case of all arrestable offences, not just serious arrestable offences. Home Office Circular 60/2003 makes the point that:

4.3   The extension of the detention period for the broader category of arrestable offences represents a significant additional power for the police.

4.4   It should be used sparingly and only where there is full justification.

The Circular also makes the point that:

... detaining a juvenile or a mentally vulnerable person for longer than 24 hours without charge will only normally be justifiable where the offence is a serious arrestable offence (para 4.8).

To authorise detention beyond 24 hours, the officer giving permission for continued detention must be satisfied that:

- the investigation is being carried out diligently and expeditiously; and
- the suspect's continued detention is necessary to secure or preserve evidence relating to the offence for which the suspect has been arrested or to obtain such evidence by questioning the suspect (in other words, the same requirement that applies to earlier reviews, pursuant to s 37(2)).

1.6.10 Detention beyond 36 hours

After 36 hours have elapsed since the 'relevant time', the suspect can only be detained further without being charged if this is permitted by a magistrates' court (s 43).

The application for a warrant for continued detention is made *in camera* (that is, with the public excluded) before two or more lay justices (s 45). The application has to be made on oath. The suspect has a right to be present and, if he so wishes, to be legally represented at this hearing (s 43(3)).

Section 43(4) provides that:

A person's further detention is only justified for the purposes of this section or section 44 below if—

(a) his detention without charge is necessary to secure or preserve evidence relating to an offence for which he is under arrest or to obtain such evidence by questioning him;

(b) an offence for which he is under arrest is a serious arrestable offence; and

(c) the investigation is being conducted diligently and expeditiously.

Section 43(14) stipulates that any information submitted in support of an application for a warrant of continued detention must state:

(a) the nature of the offence for which the suspect has been arrested;

(b) the general nature of the evidence on which he was arrested;

(c) what inquiries have been made by the police and what inquiries they propose to make; and

(d) the reasons for believing that the continued detention of the suspect is necessary for the purpose of making such further inquiries.

The police should apply for permission to detain the suspect before the initial 36 hour period has expired; if this is not practicable, then the application must be made to the magistrates not later than 42 hours after the initial detention (s 43(5)). In other words, there is a six hour period of grace; thereafter, the suspect's continued detention can no longer be authorised and his continued detention is unlawful.

The magistrates can issue a warrant allowing a maximum period of no more than a further 36 hours' detention: s 43(12). If the police need even more time, they can make a further application to the magistrates, under s 44, for continued permission to detain the suspect without charge. However, the magistrates cannot authorise a period of detention which would mean that the suspect has been in custody for a total of more than 96 hours from the relevant time (s 44(3)).

Once 96 hours have elapsed from the relevant time, the suspect must be released, either unconditionally or on bail to return to the police station. Following his release, the suspect cannot be re-arrested without a warrant for the same offence unless new evidence has come to light (s 43(19)).

It should be noted that this timetable does not apply to suspects detained under the Prevention of Terrorism legislation (which permits a longer period of detention without charge).

1.6.11 Non-compliance with review timetable

Where the suspect's detention is not reviewed in accordance with PACE (and none of the circumstances in s 40 which allow for postponement of the review are applicable), the detention is unlawful from the time when the review should have taken place, giving rise to a civil claim for damages for false imprisonment. It is immaterial in such a case that there were grounds to justify the continued detention, and so the suspect's continued detention would have been authorised had a review taken place: see *Roberts v Chief Constable of the Cheshire Constabulary* [1999] 2 All ER 326. In *Roberts,* it was said to be arguable that a late review may render lawful a person's detention from the time it takes place (leaving only the period immediately preceding the review as unlawful detention).

1.7   INTERVIEWING SUSPECTS

Code of Practice C, issued to the police under PACE, sets out detailed rules for the detention and interviewing of suspects. It requires, for example, that suspects be given two light meals and a main meal each day and that they are given at least eight hours' rest per day: Code C 8 and Code C 12.2. In *R v Weerdesteyn* [1995] 1 Cr App R 405, the Court of Appeal confirmed that, where customs officers interview a suspect, the provisions of PACE and the Codes of Practice apply just as they do in the case of a police interview.

1.7.1   The caution

Code C 10.1 says that:

10.1 A person whom there are grounds to suspect of an offence must be cautioned before any questions about an offence, or further questions if the answers provide the grounds for suspicion, are put to them if either the suspect's answers or silence, (ie failure or refusal to answer or answer satisfactorily) may be given in evidence to a court in a prosecution. A person need not be cautioned if questions are for other necessary purposes, eg:

(a) solely to establish their identity or ownership of any vehicle;

(b) to obtain information in accordance with any relevant statutory requirement (see paragraph 10.9);

(c) in furtherance of the proper and effective conduct of a search, e.g. to determine the need to search in the exercise of powers of stop and search or to seek co-operation while carrying out a search ...

Note 10A provides that for there to be grounds to suspect someone of an offence:

... there must be some reasonable, objective grounds for the suspicion, based on known facts or information which are relevant to the likelihood the offence has been committed and the person to be questioned committed it.

Thus, a person whom there are grounds to suspect of an offence must be cautioned before any questions about it are put to him regarding his involvement or suspected involvement in that offence. This definition of when a caution must be administered excludes preliminary questions, for example, to establish the suspect's identity.

Code C 10.5 sets out the terms of the caution as follows:

10.5 The caution which must be given on:

(a) arrest;

(b) all other occasions before a person is charged or informed they may be prosecuted, (see section 16),

should, unless the restriction on drawing adverse inferences from silence applies (see Annex C), be in the following terms:

'You do not have to say anything. But it may harm your defence if you do not mention when questioned something which you later rely on in Court. Anything you do say may be given in evidence.'

10.6 Annex C, paragraph 2 sets out the alternative terms of the caution to be used when the restriction on drawing adverse inferences from silence applies.

10.7 Minor deviations from the words of any caution given in accordance with this Code do not constitute a breach of this Code, provided the sense of the relevant caution is preserved.

10.8 After any break in questioning under caution, the person being questioned must be made aware they remain under caution. If there is any doubt the relevant caution should be given again in full when the interview resumes.

It must be emphasised that the caution must be given both upon arrest and before the suspect is questioned. When there is a break in questioning, the interviewing officer must ensure that the suspect is aware that he remains under caution. When the suspect is charged, the caution is repeated in the same terms except that the word 'now' replaces the words 'when questioned' (Code C 16.2).

1.7.2   The interview

Code C 11.1A provides that:

... an interview is the questioning of a person regarding their involvement or suspected involvement in a criminal offence or offences which, under paragraph 10.1, must be carried out under caution.

One approach is to say that if a person is being questioned only as a potential witness, there is no need to caution that person; however, if a person is about to be questioned as a potential suspect, a caution must be administered before that stage of the questioning process begins.

Code C 11.1 provides that, except in emergencies, an interview may only take place at a police station.

If the interview is not tape-recorded, a record must be made showing what is said; this should be done during or as soon as practicable after the interview. The record should be signed by the maker and the person interviewed should be given the opportunity to read and correct the record: Code C 11.7–14.

Under Code C 11.6, the interview must cease once the police have enough evidence to provide a 'realistic prospect of conviction' (the same test that is applied by the CPS when deciding whether or not to continue a prosecution):

The interview or further interview of a person about an offence with which that person has not been charged or for which they have not been informed they may be prosecuted, must cease when:

(a) the officer in charge of the investigation is satisfied all the questions they consider relevant to obtaining accurate and reliable information about the offence have been put to the suspect, this includes allowing the suspect an opportunity to give an innocent explanation and asking questions to test if the explanation is accurate and reliable, eg to clear up ambiguities or clarify what the suspect said;

(b) the officer in charge of the investigation has taken account of any other available evidence; and

(c) the officer in charge of the investigation, or in the case of a detained suspect, the custody officer, (see paragraph 16.1), reasonably believes there is sufficient evidence to provide a realistic prospect of conviction for that offence.

1.7.3 Role of the solicitor during police interviews

Since April 2001, publicly-funded advice at police stations is given (irrespective of the client's means) by solicitors or accredited representatives, acting under a contract with the Legal Services Commission known as the Criminal Defence Service General Criminal Contract.

Code C provides as follows:

6   *Right to legal advice*

6.1   Unless Annex B applies [delaying access to a solicitor], all detainees must be informed that they may at any time consult and communicate privately with a solicitor, whether in person, in writing or by telephone, and that free independent legal advice is available from the duty solicitor.

...

6.4   No police officer should, at any time, do or say anything with the intention of dissuading a detainee from obtaining legal advice.

6.5   The exercise of the right of access to legal advice may be delayed only as in Annex B. Whenever legal advice is requested, and unless Annex B applies, the custody officer must act without delay to secure the provision of such advice. If, on being informed or reminded of this right, the detainee declines to speak to a solicitor in person, the officer should point out that the right includes the right to speak with a solicitor on the telephone. If the detainee continues to waive this right the officer should ask them why and any reasons should be recorded on the custody record or the interview record as appropriate. Reminders of the right to legal advice must be given as in paragraphs 3.5, 11.2, 15.4, 16.4 and 16.5 and Code D, paragraphs 3.17(ii) and 6.3. Once it is clear a detainee does not want to speak to a solicitor in person or by telephone they should cease to be asked their reasons.

6.5A In the case of a juvenile, an appropriate adult should consider whether legal advice from a solicitor is required. If the juvenile indicates that they do not want legal advice, the appropriate adult has the right to ask for a solicitor to attend if this would be in the best interests of the person. However, the detained person cannot be forced to see the solicitor if he is adamant that he does not wish to do so.

6.6   A detainee who wants legal advice may not be interviewed or continue to be interviewed until they have received such advice unless:

(a) Annex B applies, when the restriction on drawing adverse inferences from silence in Annex C will apply because the detainee is not allowed an opportunity to consult a solicitor; or

(b) an officer of superintendent rank or above has reasonable grounds for believing that:

   (i) the consequent delay might:

   - lead to interference with, or harm to, evidence connected with an offence;
   - lead to interference with, or physical harm to, other people;
   - lead to serious loss of, or damage to, property;
   - lead to alerting other people suspected of having committed an offence but not yet arrested for it;
   - hinder the recovery of property obtained in consequence of the commission of an offence.

   (ii) when a solicitor, including a duty solicitor, has been contacted and has agreed to attend, awaiting their arrival would cause unreasonable delay to the process of investigation.

   Note: In these cases the restriction on drawing adverse inferences from silence in Annex C will apply because the detainee is not allowed an opportunity to consult a solicitor;

(c) the solicitor the detainee has nominated or selected from a list:

   (i) cannot be contacted;

   (ii) has previously indicated they do not wish to be contacted; or

   (iii) having been contacted, has declined to attend; and

   the detainee has been advised of the Duty Solicitor Scheme but has declined to ask for the duty solicitor.

   In these circumstances the interview may be started or continued without further delay provided an officer of Inspector rank or above has agreed to the interview proceeding.

   Note: The restriction on drawing adverse inferences from silence in Annex C will not apply because the detainee is allowed an opportunity to consult the duty solicitor;

(d) the detainee changes their mind, about wanting legal advice.

In these circumstances the interview may be started or continued without delay provided that:

   (i) the detainee agrees to do so, in writing or on tape; and

   (ii) an officer of Inspector rank or above has enquired about the detainee's reasons for their change of mind and gives authority for the interview to proceed.

...

6.8 A detainee who has been permitted to consult a solicitor shall be entitled on request to have the solicitor present when they are interviewed unless one of the exceptions in paragraph 6.6 applies.

6.9 The solicitor may only be required to leave the interview if their conduct is such that the interviewer is unable properly to put questions to the suspect.

6.10 If the interviewer considers a solicitor is acting in such a way, they will stop the interview and consult an officer not below Superintendent rank, if one is readily available, and otherwise an officer not below Inspector rank not connected with the investigation. After speaking to the solicitor, the officer consulted will decide if the interview should continue in the presence of that solicitor. If they decide it should not, the suspect will be given the opportunity to consult another solicitor before the interview continues and that solicitor given an opportunity to be present at the interview.

6.11 The removal of a solicitor from an interview is a serious step and, if it occurs, the officer of superintendent rank or above who took the decision will consider if the incident should be reported to the Law Society. If the decision to remove the solicitor has been taken by an officer below superintendent rank, the facts must be reported to an officer of superintendent rank or above who will similarly consider whether a report to the Law Society would be appropriate. When the solicitor concerned is a duty solicitor, the report should be both to the Law Society and to the Legal Services Commission.

6.12 'Solicitor' in this Code means:
- a solicitor who holds a current practising certificate;
- an accredited or probationary representative included on the register of representatives maintained by the Legal Services Commission.

The Guidance Notes for this Part of the Code state:

6D   A detainee has a right to free legal advice and to be represented by a solicitor. The solicitor's only role in the police station is to protect and advance the legal rights of their client. On occasions this may require the solicitor to give advice which has the effect of the client avoiding giving evidence which strengthens a prosecution case. The solicitor may intervene in order to seek clarification, challenge an improper question to their client or the manner in which it is put, advise their client not to reply to particular questions, or if they wish to give their client further legal advice. Paragraph 6.9 only applies if the solicitor's approach or conduct prevents or unreasonably obstructs proper questions being put to the suspect or the suspect's response being recorded. Examples of unacceptable conduct include answering questions on a suspect's behalf or providing written replies for the suspect to quote.

6E   An officer who takes the decision to exclude a solicitor must be in a position to satisfy the court the decision was properly made. In order to do this they may need to witness what is happening.

Thus, a solicitor (or other accredited representative) who is present when a suspect is being interviewed by the police should intervene if the police officers:
- ask unfair questions;
- ask questions which do not relate to the alleged offence(s);
- misrepresent the law;
- claim to know things but without having any factual basis for that knowledge;
- produce or refer to evidence which has not been shown to the suspect or the solicitor;
- misrepresent information;
- put pressure on the suspect by questioning him in a burdensome manner, by behaving abusively, or by attempting to influence the suspect's decision making.

In 'Incompetent police station advice and the exclusion of evidence' [2002] Crim LR 471, Ed Cape notes that there is a continuing cause for concern about the quality of advice given to suspects at police stations (despite the accreditation scheme for police station representatives, training materials produced by the Law Society, the quality targets incorporated into the General Criminal Contract, and a description of the role of the lawyer contained in the Code of Practice). He argues that the European Court of Human Rights has recognised that the fairness of a trial depends not only on what is done after charge, but may also be affected by what occurs at the police station stage. Accordingly, he concludes that the courts should exclude evidence which was obtained as a result of incompetence of the lawyer advising at the police station.

1.7.4 Special rules for juveniles and persons at risk

Special rules apply to protect juveniles and other vulnerable groups. For example:

- a juvenile should not be placed in a cell unless no other secure accommodation is available and the custody officer takes the view that secure accommodation is necessary;

- a juvenile, or someone who is mentally disordered or mentally handicapped, must not be interviewed regarding their involvement or suspected involvement in a criminal offence or offences or asked to provide or sign a written statement under caution unless an 'appropriate adult' (that is, a parent, guardian, or social worker) is present (see Code C 11.15).

Code 11.17 provides that:

If an appropriate adult is present at an interview, they shall be informed:

- they are not expected to act simply as an observer; and
- the purpose of their presence is to:
  — advise the person being interviewed;
  — observe whether the interview is being conducted properly and fairly;
  — facilitate communication with the person being interviewed.

See also *DPP v Blake* [1989] 1 WLR 432; (1989) 88 Cr App R 179, where it was held that a parent is not an appropriate adult if the juvenile and parent are estranged; a social worker should be the appropriate adult in such a case.

In *DPP v Cornish* (1997) *The Times*, 27 January, the Divisional Court held that where a juvenile is interviewed by the police in the absence of an appropriate adult and there is an application for the interview to be excluded under s 76 of PACE, the court should hear evidence as to who was at the interview and how the interview went in order to determine the effect of the absence of an appropriate adult. In other words, evidence from the interview should not be excluded automatically.

In *R v Aspinall* [1999] 2 Cr App R 115, the defendant suffered from schizophrenia, and so was a 'person at risk'; however, he was interviewed by the police in the absence of an appropriate adult. The Court of Appeal held that even though the defendant appeared able to understand procedures and answer questions, this did not obviate the need for the presence of an appropriate adult. The interview should therefore have been ruled inadmissible under s 78 of PACE.

1.8 DETENTION AFTER CHARGE

As soon as the investigating officer thinks there is sufficient evidence to prosecute the suspect, the suspect must be taken to the custody officer. If the custody officer agrees that there is sufficient evidence against the suspect, the suspect will be charged. The custody officer tells the suspect what offence(s) he is accused of and, after cautioning the suspect, asks if he has anything to say. Anything said by the suspect in answer to the charge must be noted down.

If the suspect is not granted bail under s 38 of PACE, he must be taken before the magistrates' court not later than the day after the day he is charged (ignoring Sundays, Christmas Day and Good Friday (s 46)). The magistrates will then decide whether or not to grant bail, using the criteria laid down in the Bail Act 1976 (set out in Chapter 2).

1.8.1 Further questioning

Code C 16.5 provides that, once the suspect has been charged, he cannot be asked further questions about the offence(s) with which he has been charged unless further questions are necessary:

- to prevent or minimise harm or loss to some other person or to the public; or
- for clearing up an ambiguity in a previous answer or statement; or
- in the interests of justice to enable the suspect to have put to him, and to have an opportunity to comment on, information concerning the offence which has come to light since he was charged.

1.9   ACCESS TO LEGAL ADVICE: s 58 OF PACE

Under s 58 of PACE, the suspect has a right, upon request, to consult with a solicitor in private at any time. The solicitor can be the defendant's own solicitor or a duty solicitor.

1.9.1 Denial of access to legal advice

The power to delay access to a solicitor for up to 36 hours is contained in s 58 of PACE. This provides as follows:

> 58   *Access to legal advice*
>
> (1) A person arrested and held in custody in a police station or other premises shall be entitled, if he so requests, to consult a solicitor privately at any time.
>
> (2) Subject to sub-section (3) below, a request under sub-section (1) above and the time at which it was made shall be recorded in the custody record.
>
> (3) Such a request need not be recorded in the custody record of a person who makes it at a time while he is at a court after being charged with an offence.
>
> (4) If a person makes such a request, he must be permitted to consult a solicitor as soon as is practicable except to the extent that delay is permitted by this section.
>
> (5) In any case he must be permitted to consult a solicitor within 36 hours from the relevant time, as defined in section 41(2) above.
>
> (6) Delay in compliance with a request is only permitted—
>
> (a) in the case of a person who is in police detention for a serious arrestable offence; and
>
> (b) if an officer of at least the rank of superintendent authorises it.

(7) An officer may give an authorisation under sub-section (6) above orally or in writing but, if he gives it orally, he shall confirm it in writing as soon as is practicable.

(8) Subject to sub-section (8A) below an officer may only authorise delay where he has reasonable grounds for believing that the exercise of the right conferred by sub-section (1) above at the time when the person detained desires to exercise it—

    (a) will lead to interference with or harm to evidence connected with a serious arrestable offence or interference with or physical injury to other persons; or

    (b) will lead to the alerting of other persons suspected of having committed such an offence but not yet arrested for it; or

    (c) will hinder the recovery of any property obtained as a result of such an offence.

(8A) An officer may also authorise delay where he has reasonable grounds for believing that—

    (a) the person detained for the serious arrestable offence has benefited from his criminal conduct; and

    (b) the recovery of the value of the property constituting the benefit will be hindered by the exercise of the right conferred by sub-section (1) above.

(8B) For the purposes of sub-section (8A) above the question whether a person has benefited from his criminal conduct is to be decided in accordance with Part 2 of the Proceeds of Crime Act 2002.

(9) If delay is authorised—

    (a) the detained person shall be told the reason for it; and

    (b) the reason shall be noted on his custody record.

(10) The duties imposed by sub-section (9) above shall be performed as soon as is practicable.

(11) There may be no further delay in permitting the exercise of the right conferred by sub-section (1) above once the reason for authorising delay ceases to subsist.

(12) Nothing in this section applies to a person arrested or detained under the terrorism provisions.

In summary, the right of access to a solicitor can be denied by the police for up to 36 hours from the relevant time, but only if the following conditions are satisfied:

- denial is on the authority of a superintendent or more senior officer; and
- the offence is a 'serious arrestable offence' (see below); and
- there are reasonable grounds for believing that allowing immediate access to a solicitor would lead to:

    (a) interference with evidence connected with a serious arrestable offence; or

    (b) interference with or injury to other persons; or

    (c) alerting of other persons suspected of committing a serious arrestable offence (that is, other miscreants would be tipped off); or

    (d) hindrance to the recovery of the proceeds of a serious arrestable offence.

In *R v Samuel* [1988] QB 615; [1988] 2 All ER 135, it was held that the suspicion must relate to the particular solicitor whom the suspect wishes to see. The police must therefore have grounds to suspect the honesty of that solicitor or else think him particularly naive. In *R (Thompson) v Chief Constable of Northumbria* [2001] EWCA Civ

321; [2001] 1 WLR 1342, a chief constable had made a blanket order banning a probationary solicitor's representative from attending police stations in the force's area to advise persons in custody. The Court of Appeal held, following *R v Chief Constable of Avon & Somerset ex p Robinson* [1989] 1 WLR 793, that such a blanket ban was unlawful. However, a senior police officer could issue advice to his officers that a particular representative was likely to hinder an investigation (the basis for exclusion under s 58). It would then be for the appropriate officer in the specific case to decide whether or not that particular person should in fact be excluded.

Given the importance of the right to legal advice while being detailed (and questioned) by the police, and the risk that evidence will be excluded by the court if obtained where this right has been withheld, it is very rare for the police to invoke the power to delay access to a solicitor.

1.9.2 Serious arrestable offence

The term 'serious arrestable offence' is defined in s 116 of PACE as:

- an offence from the list in Sched 5 to the Act,
- under s 116(3):

    any other arrestable offence is serious only if its commission—

    (a) has led to any of the consequences specified in sub-section (6) below; or

    (b) is intended or is likely to lead to any of those consequences.

The consequences listed in sub-s (6) are:

    (a) serious harm to the security of the State or to public order;

    (b) serious interference with the administration of justice or with the investigation of offences or of a particular offence;

    (c) the death of any person;

    (d) serious injury to any person;

    (e) substantial financial gain to any person; and

    (f) serious financial loss to any person.

(7) Loss is serious for the purposes of this section if, having regard to all the circumstances, it is serious for the person who suffers it.

(8) In this section 'injury' includes any disease and any impairment of a person's physical or mental condition.

The latter two provisions generally mean that a substantial amount of money is involved. However, as regards the last item on this list, serious financial loss, s 116(7) provides that the test is a subjective one: loss is serious for these purposes if it is serious for the person who suffers it. In *R v McIvor* [1987] Crim LR 409, for example, it was held that the loss of £800 was not a 'serious financial loss' to a relatively prosperous loser.

1.9.3 Wrongful denial of access to legal advice

Should there be wrongful exclusion of a solicitor, any confession obtained by the police may well be held inadmissible at trial under s 78 of PACE, which allows the court to exclude any prosecution evidence which would have an adverse effect on the fairness of the proceedings. See, for example, *R v Mason* [1988] 1 WLR 139; [1987] 3 All ER 481, where the police deceived a solicitor into thinking that the case against his client was stronger than it was and, because the legal advice was based on this fact, the police had effectively denied legal advice to the defendant. The Court of Appeal said that his subsequent confession should have been excluded.

In *Cullen v Chief Constable of the RUC* [2003] UKHL 39; [2004] 2 All ER 237, it was held (by a majority of 3:2) that the denial of a statutory right of access to a solicitor is incapable of causing loss or injury of a kind for which damages may be awarded. The appropriate remedy is the public law remedy of judicial review. This case was decided under Northern Ireland legislation but would be equally applicable to the right of access to a solicitor conferred by s 58 of PACE. With respect to the majority of their Lordships, it is difficult to see how judicial review would provide an adequate remedy, since the court would effectively be limited to granting a declaration that the police had acted unlawfully. It remains the case, therefore, that the main sanction where incriminating evidence is obtained in an interview following an improper denial of access to a solicitor is that the evidence is liable to be ruled inadmissible under s 78 of PACE. This would not have assisted Cullen, as he pleaded guilty to the charge and so the question of exclusion of evidence did not arise.

1.9.4 European Convention on Human Rights

Article 6 of the European Convention on Human Rights guarantees the right to legal representation. Denial of access to a solicitor during a police interview may violate this provision, especially if adverse inferences can be drawn from the defendant's failure to answer questions (*Murray v UK* (1996) 22 EHRR 29). It is for this reason that s 58 of the Youth Justice and Criminal Evidence Act 1999 prevents adverse inferences being drawn (under s 34 of the Criminal Justice and Public Order Act 1994) from a suspect's silence where the suspect was not allowed the opportunity to consult a solicitor. To give effect to s 58 of the 1999 Act, a new Annex (Annex C) was added to Code C. It provides as follows:

RESTRICTION ON DRAWING ADVERSE INFERENCES FROM SILENCE AND TERMS OF THE CAUTION WHEN THE RESTRICTION APPLIES

(a) *The restriction on drawing adverse inferences from silence*

1   The Criminal Justice and Public Order Act 1994, sections 34, 36 and 37 as amended by the Youth Justice and Criminal Evidence Act 1999, section 58 describe the conditions under which adverse inferences may be drawn from a person's failure or refusal to say anything about their involvement in the offence when interviewed, after being charged or informed they may be prosecuted. These provisions are subject to an overriding restriction on the ability of a court or jury to draw adverse inferences from a person's silence. This restriction applies:

(a) to any detainee at a police station, [see Note 10C] who, before being interviewed, see section 11 or being charged or informed they may be prosecuted, (see section 16), has:

(i)   asked for legal advice, (see section 6, paragraph 6.1);

(ii) not been allowed an opportunity to consult a solicitor, including the duty solicitor, as in this Code: and

(iii) not changed their mind about wanting legal advice, (see section 6, paragraph 6.6(d)).

...

(b) to any person charged with, or informed they may be prosecuted for, an offence who:

    (i) has had brought to their notice a written statement made by another person or the content of an interview with another person which relates to that offence, (see section 16, paragraph 16.4);

    (ii) is interviewed about that offence, or

    (iii) makes a written statement about that offence.

(b) *Terms of the caution when the restriction applies*

2   When a requirement to caution arises at a time when the restriction on drawing adverse inferences from silence applies, the caution shall be:

'You do not have to say anything, but anything you do say may be given in evidence.'

3   Whenever the restriction either begins to apply or ceases to apply after a caution has already been given, the person shall be re-cautioned in the appropriate terms. The changed position on drawing inferences and that the previous caution no longer applies shall also be explained to the detainee in ordinary language.

When the suspect was first arrested, he would have been given the normal caution. Where the suspect then asks to speak to a solicitor but has not been allowed an opportunity to do so, he has to be told of the consequence. The suggested form of words is:

This means that from now on, adverse inferences cannot be drawn at court and your defence will not be harmed just because you choose to say nothing. Please listen carefully to the caution I am about to give you because it will apply from now on. You will see that it does not say anything about your defence being harmed.

If the suspect is then allowed to speak with a solicitor, he becomes once again at risk of adverse inference being drawn and so should be told:

The caution you were previously given no longer applies. This is because after that caution you have been allowed an opportunity to speak to a solicitor. Please listen carefully to the caution I am about to give you because it will apply from now on. It explains how your defence at court may be affected if you choose to say nothing.

In *Averill v UK* (2000) 31 EHRR 839, the defendant was denied access to a solicitor for the first 24 hours of his detention for questioning. He failed to mention when questioned matters he later relied on at his trial, and adverse inferences were drawn at trial from his silence. The European Court of Human Rights held that the defendant had been fully apprised of the implications of remaining silent. It was clear from the reasoning of the judge (this was a Northern Ireland trial by judge alone) that there was substantial evidence against the defendant irrespective of the adverse inferences, and so the defendant had not been convicted on the basis of adverse inferences alone. There was therefore no violation of Art 6(1) (the right to a fair hearing) in the drawing of the adverse inferences. However, there was a violation of Art 6(3)(c) (right to access to legal assistance): as a matter of fairness, access to a lawyer should have been guaranteed to the applicant before his interrogation began; the denial of access to a solicitor during the first 24 hours of detention failed to comply with the requirements of Art 6(3)(c). This seems to go further than *Murray*.

In *Magee v UK* (2001) 31 EHRR 35, the defendant had been held by the police for over 48 hours without access to legal advice under Prevention of Terrorism legislation. The European Court of Human Rights held that to deny access to a lawyer for such a long period was incompatible with the rights of the accused under Art 6 of the Convention. However, the Court took particular account of the austerity of the conditions of the Holding Centre where the defendant had been detained and the fact that he had been held incommunicado during the breaks between bouts of questioning by teams of police officers. The intimidating atmosphere was specifically devised to sap his will; as a matter of procedural fairness, said the Court, this should have been counterbalanced by access to a solicitor.

In *Brennan v UK* (2002) 34 EHRR 18, the European Court held that Art 6(3) of the European Convention on Human Rights normally requires that an accused be allowed to benefit from the assistance of a lawyer in the initial phases of an interrogation. An accused's right to communicate with his advocate out of hearing of a third person is part of the basic requirements of a fair trial (Art 6(3)(c)). If a lawyer is unable to confer with his client and receive confidential instructions from him without surveillance, his assistance would lose much of its usefulness. However, the right of access to a solicitor can be subject to restrictions for good cause. The question in each case is whether the restriction, in the light of the entirety of the proceedings, deprived the accused of a fair hearing. While it is not necessary for the applicant to prove that the restriction had a prejudicial effect on the course of the trial, he has to have been directly affected by the restriction in the exercise of the rights of the defence. In the instant case, the presence of the police officer within hearing during the applicant's first consultation with his solicitor would have inevitably prevented the applicant from speaking frankly to his solicitor and would have given him reason to hesitate before broaching questions of potential significance to the case against him. The Court therefore held that the presence of the police officer was a violation of Art 6(3)(c).

1.10   ARREST WITH A WARRANT

Under s 1 of the Magistrates' Courts Act 1980, a warrant for the suspect's arrest may only be issued if:

(a) the information is in writing; and

(b) either:

  (i)   the offence to which the warrant relates is an indictable offence or is punishable with imprisonment; or

  (ii) the person's address is not sufficiently established for a summons to be served on him.

Section 1 used to require that the information be 'substantiated on oath'; however, s 31(1) of the Criminal Justice Act 2003 removed that requirement (in effect since January 2004).

Whereas a magistrate or a justices' clerk may issue a summons, only a magistrate is empowered to issue an arrest warrant.

The warrant requires the police to arrest the suspect and take him before the magistrates' court named on the warrant (usually the issuing court).

Where the offence charged is an indictable offence, a warrant may be issued even if a summons has previously been issued; this would be appropriate if, for example, the summons was returned by the Post Office undelivered.

In practice, it is quite rare for an arrest warrant to be sought. The more serious offences carry a power of arrest without warrant (so a warrant is unnecessary) and in other cases it is preferable to issue a summons (or adopt the new written charge procedure established by the Criminal Justice Act 2003). If the summons cannot be served, however, the police can go back to the magistrate to apply for an arrest warrant.

An arrest warrant issued to commence criminal proceedings can be endorsed with a requirement that the accused be released on bail after his arrest. It is unlikely that such a warrant would be so endorsed, however, as a warrant will normally be sought only where the defendant is clearly evading service of the summons.

In *R v Enfield Magistrates' Court ex p Caldwell* (1997) 161 JP 336, the Divisional Court held that an information laid to secure an arrest warrant has the effect of commencing a prosecution in that case (and so has the same effect as laying an information without also asking for an arrest warrant). This will presumably cease to be the case when the power to commence public prosecutions by information is abolished.

1.11   THE CODES OF PRACTICE

The five Codes of Practice issued under PACE are known as Codes A, B, C, D and E. These Codes are subject to periodic revision (s 67 of PACE). The last revision of the Codes took place in August 2004. For a brief discussion of some of the earlier changes, from the perspective of a defence solicitor, see Ed Cape's article, 'The revised PACE Codes of Practice: a further step towards inquisitorialism' [2003] Crim LR 355.

Section 11 of the Criminal Justice Act 2003 (in force since January 2004) amends s 67 of PACE. Before a Code can be revised, or a new Code issued, the Secretary of State must consult:

(a)   persons whom he considers to represent the interests of police authorities,

(b)   persons whom he considers to represent the interests of chief officers of police,

(c)   the General Council of the Bar,

(d)   the Law Society of England and Wales,

(e)   the Institute of Legal Executives, and

(f)   such other persons as he thinks fit (s 67(4), as amended).

The requirements for parliamentary approval are set out in the amended s 67(7)–(7C):

(7)   An order bringing a code into operation may not be made unless a draft of the order has been laid before Parliament and approved by a resolution of each House.

(7A) An order bringing a revision of a code into operation must be laid before Parliament if the order has been made without a draft having been so laid and approved by a resolution of each House.

(7B) When an order or draft of an order is laid, the code or revision of a code to which it relates must also be laid.

(7C) No order or draft of an order may be laid until the consultation required by sub-s (4) has taken place.

This simplifies the process for revising the Codes of Practice. Paragraph 6.3 of the Home Office Circular 60/2003 says that: 'The intention is to enable more frequent updating of the Codes to ensure their relevance to statutory requirements and to any changes impacting on the powers of the police and the investigation of crime.'

1.11.1 Code A

This is the Code of Practice for the exercise by police officers of their statutory powers of stop and search (and so this Code deals with the exercise of the power vested in the police to stop people and search them for stolen or prohibited articles under s 1 of PACE) (see below).

1.11.2 Code B

This Code of Practice governs the searching of premises by police officers and the seizure of property found by police officers on persons or premises (and so this Code deals with the exercise of the powers of search conferred on the police by ss 8, 15 and 17 of PACE).

1.11.3 Code C

This is the Code of Practice for the detention, treatment and questioning of persons by police officers (see above).

1.11.4 Code D

This is the Code of Practice for the 'identification of persons by police officers'. This Code governs matters such as the conduct of video identifications, identification parades and the taking of fingerprints or DNA.

Key provisions from Code D include the following:

(a) *Cases when the suspect's identity is not known*

3.2 In cases when the suspect's identity is not known, a witness may be taken to a particular neighbourhood or place to see whether they can identify the person they saw. Although the number, age, sex, race, general description and style of clothing of other people present at the location and the way in which any identification is made cannot be controlled, the principles applicable to the formal procedures under paragraphs 3.5 to 3.10 shall be followed as far as practicable. For example:

(a) where it is practicable to do so, a record should be made of the witness' description of the suspect, as in paragraph 3.1 (a), before asking the witness to make an identification;

(b) care must be taken not to direct the witness's attention to any individual unless, taking into account all the circumstances, this cannot be avoided. However, this does not prevent a witness being asked to look carefully at the people around at the time or to look towards a group or in a particular direction, if this appears necessary to make sure that the witness does not overlook a possible suspect simply because the witness is looking in the opposite direction and also to enable the witness to make comparisons between any suspect and others who are in the area;

(c) where there is more than one witness, every effort should be made to keep them separate and witnesses should be taken to see whether they can identify a person independently;

(d) once there is sufficient information to justify the arrest of a particular individual for suspected involvement in the offence, eg, after a witness makes a positive identification, the provisions set out from paragraph 3.4 onwards shall apply for any other witnesses in relation to that individual. Subject to paragraphs 3.12 and 3.13, it is not necessary for the witness who makes such a positive identification to take part in a further procedure;

(e) the officer or police staff accompanying the witness must record, in their pocket book, the action taken as soon as, and in as much detail, as possible. The record should include: the date, time and place of the relevant occasion the witness claims to have previously seen the suspect; where any identification was made; how it was made and the conditions at the time (eg, the distance the witness was from the suspect, the weather and light); if the witness's attention was drawn to the suspect; the reason for this; and anything said by the witness or the suspect about the identification or the conduct of the procedure.

3.3 A witness must not be shown photographs, computerised or artist's composite likenesses or similar likenesses or pictures (including 'E-fit' images) if the identity of the suspect is known to the police and the suspect is available to take part in a video identification, an identification parade or a group identification. If the suspect's identity is not known, the showing of such images to a witness to obtain identification evidence must be done in accordance with Annex E.

(b)   Cases when the suspect is known and available

3.4 If the suspect's identity is known to the police and they are available, the identification procedures set out in paragraphs 3.5 to 3.10 may be used. References in this section to a suspect being 'known' mean there is sufficient information known to the police to justify the arrest of a particular person for suspected involvement in the offence. A suspect being 'available' means they are immediately available or will be within a reasonably short time and willing to take an effective part in at least one of the following which it is practicable to arrange:

- video identification;
- identification parade; or
- group identification.

Video identification

3.5 A 'video identification' is when the witness is shown moving images of a known suspect, together with similar images of others who resemble the suspect. (See paragraph 3.21 for circumstances in which still images may be used.)

3.6 Video identifications must be carried out in accordance with Annex A.

Identification parade

3.7 An 'identification parade' is when the witness sees the suspect in a line of others who resemble the suspect.

3.8 Identification parades must be carried out in accordance with Annex B.

Group identification

3.9 A 'group identification' is when the witness sees the suspect in an informal group of people.

3.10 Group identifications must be carried out in accordance with Annex C.

...

Circumstances in which an identification procedure must be held

3.12 Whenever:

(i) a witness has identified a suspect or purported to have identified them prior to any identification procedure set out in paragraphs 3.5 to 3.10 having been held; or

(ii) there is a witness available, who expresses an ability to identify the suspect, or where there is a reasonable chance of the witness being able to do so, and they have not been given an opportunity to identify the suspect in any of the procedures set out in paragraphs 3.5 to 3.10,

and the suspect disputes being the person the witness claims to have seen, an identification procedure shall be held unless it is not practicable or it would serve no useful purpose in proving or disproving whether the suspect was involved in committing the offence. For example, when it is not disputed that the suspect is already well known to the witness who claims to have seen them commit the crime.

3.13 Such a procedure may also be held if the officer in charge of the investigation considers it would be useful.

Selecting an identification procedure

3.14 If, because of paragraph 3.12, an identification procedure is to be held, the suspect shall initially be offered a video identification unless:

(a) a video identification is not practicable; or

(b) an identification parade is both practicable and more suitable than a video identification; or

(c) paragraph 3.16 applies.

The identification officer and the officer in charge of the investigation shall consult each other to determine which option is to be offered. An identification parade may not be practicable because of factors relating to the witnesses, such as their number, state of health, availability and travelling requirements. A video identification would normally be more suitable if it could be arranged and completed sooner than an identification parade.

3.15 A suspect who refuses the identification procedure first offered shall be asked to state their reason for refusing and may get advice from their solicitor and/or, if present, their appropriate adult. The suspect, solicitor and/or appropriate adult shall be allowed to make representations about why another procedure should be used. A record should be made of the reasons for refusal and any representations made. After considering any reasons given, and representations made, the identification officer shall, if appropriate, arrange for the suspect to be offered an alternative that the officer considers suitable and practicable. If the officer decides it is not suitable and practicable to offer an alternative identification procedure, the reasons for that decision shall be recorded.

3.16 A group identification may initially be offered if the officer in charge of the investigation considers it is more suitable than a video identification or an identification parade and the identification officer considers it practicable to arrange.

It is clear from the Code that 'video identification' (rather than the traditional identity parade) is now the preferred option. The set of images used must include the suspect and at least eight other persons who, so far as possible, resemble the suspect in age, height, general appearance and position in life.

Where an identification parade takes place, it should consist of at least eight people (in addition to the suspect) who so far as possible resemble the suspect in age, height, general appearance and position in life. The participants stand in line and each one must be clearly numbered. Witnesses are brought in one at a time; they are told that the person they saw may or may not be on the parade and that, if they can make a positive identification, they should do so by indicating the number of the person concerned. In *R v Quinn* [1995] 1 Cr App R 480, the Court of Appeal said that if the Code of Practice on identification parades is not complied with, a conviction based on evidence of identification from the parade will be quashed.

1.11.5 Code E

This Code of Practice deals with the procedure to be adopted in tape-recorded interviews; all interviews in respect of indictable (including triable either way) offences must be tape-recorded unless it is not reasonably practicable to do so as a result of equipment failure and the custody officer considers that the interview should not be delayed.

1.11.6 Code F

This Code deals with video recording of police interviews with suspects. It is in very similar terms to Code E.

1.11.7 Breaches of the Codes

Breaches of the provisions of the Codes do not mean that any evidence obtained in breach of the Code in question (for example, a confession) is automatically inadmissible, but if there have been breaches of the Code, any evidence so obtained may well be ruled inadmissible as a result. See, for example, *R v Delaney* (1988) 88 Cr App R 338, *R v Bryce* [1992] 4 All ER 567 and *R v Joseph* [1993] Crim LR 206. It should be borne in mind that evidence will not be excluded automatically because there has been a breach of a Code. For example, in *R v Senior* [2004] EWCA Crim 454; [2004] 3 All ER 9, where questions had been asked by customs officers to establish the ownership of suspicious baggage prior to administering a caution (even though the passengers were effectively suspects at that stage), the questioning amounted to a breach of para 10.1 of Code C, but the court held that that did not require the evidence to be excluded at the trial.

1.12   POLICE POWERS OF SEARCH

PACE also contains powers regarding police searches of people, vehicles and premises. Section 117 of PACE confers upon the police the power to use reasonable force when exercising these powers. It provides that:

> Where any provision of this Act (a) confers a power on a constable; and (b) does not provide that the power may only be exercised with the consent of some person, other than a police officer, the officer may use reasonable force, if necessary, in the exercise of the power.

It is reasonable, for the purpose of s 117, that police officers executing a search warrant should seek, by no more force than necessary, to restrict the movement of those in occupation of premises while those premises are being searched (*DPP v Meaden* [2003] EWHC 3005; [2004] 1 WLR 945).

1.12.1 Power to stop and search

The power to stop and search is contained in s 1 of PACE:

(1) A constable may exercise any power conferred by this section—

   (a) in any place to which at the time when he proposes to exercise the power the public or any section of the public has access, on payment or otherwise, as of right or by virtue of express or implied permission; or

   (b) in any other place to which people have ready access at the time when he proposes to exercise the power but which is not a dwelling.

(2) Subject to sub-section (3) to (5) below, a constable—

   (a) may search—

      (i) any person or vehicle;

      (ii) anything which is in or on a vehicle,

   for stolen or prohibited articles or any article to which sub-section (8A) below applies; and

   (b) may detain a person or vehicle for the purpose of such a search.

(3) This section does not give a constable power to search a person or vehicle or anything in or on a vehicle unless he has reasonable grounds for suspecting that he will find stolen or prohibited articles or any article to which sub-section (8A) below applies.

(4) If a person is in a garden or yard occupied with and used for the purposes of a dwelling or on other land so occupied and used, a constable may not search him in the exercise of the power conferred by this section unless the constable has reasonable grounds for believing—

   (a) that he does not reside in the dwelling; and

   (b) that he is not in the place in question with the express or implied permission of a person who resides in the dwelling.

(5) If a vehicle is in a garden or yard occupied with and used for the purposes of a dwelling or on other land so occupied and used, a constable may not search the vehicle or anything in or on it in the exercise of the power conferred by this section unless he has reasonable grounds for believing—

   (a) that the person in charge of the vehicle does not reside in the dwelling; and

   (b) that the vehicle is not in the place in question with the express or implied permission of a person who resides in the dwelling.

(6) If in the course of such a search a constable discovers an article which he has reasonable grounds for suspecting to be a stolen or prohibited article [or an article to which sub-section (8A) below applies], he may seize it.

(7) An article is prohibited for the purposes of this Part of this Act if it is—

   (a) an offensive weapon; or

   (b) an article—

      (i) made or adapted for use in the course of or in connection with an offence to which this sub-paragraph applies; or

(ii) intended by the person having it with him for such use by him or by some other person.

(8) The offences to which sub-section (7)(b)(i) above applies are—

(a) burglary;

(b) theft;

(c) offences under section 12 of the Theft Act 1968 (taking motor vehicle or other conveyance without authority); and

(d) offences under section 15 of that Act (obtaining property by deception)

(e) offences under section 1 of the Criminal Damage Act 1971 (destroying or damaging property) [this sub-section added by s 1 of the Criminal Justice Act 2003, in force January 2004].

(8A) This sub-section applies to any article in relation to which a person has committed, or is committing or is going to commit an offence under section 139 of the Criminal Justice Act 1988.

(9) In this Part of this Act 'offensive weapon' means any article—

(a) made or adapted for use for causing injury to persons; or

(b) intended by the person having it with him for such use by him or by some other person

In summary, s 1 of PACE empowers a police officer to search any person or vehicle for stolen or prohibited articles provided that the officer has reasonable grounds for suspecting that such articles will be found. The term 'stolen' article is self-explanatory.

The term 'prohibited' article means:

• an offensive weapon (that is, made or adapted for use for causing injury to person or intended by the person having it for such use); or

• an article made or adapted for use in burglary, theft, taking a conveyance without authority, or obtaining property by deception; or

• an article made or adapted to cause criminal damage.

Sections 2 and 3 of PACE set out detailed rules regarding the procedure to be followed by a police office when exercising the powers conferred by s 1 and the details that have to be recorded. Failure to comply with these provisions may make an otherwise lawful search unlawful, and thereby deprive police officers who face resistance of the protection afforded by the offence of assaulting a constable acting in the execution of his duty. Section 2(3), for example, requires a constable conducting a search to inform the person to be searched, before the search commences, of his name and police station; failure to do so renders the search unlawful, and the illegality is not cured either by the fact that the search was reasonable or that the person concerned consented to it (*Osman v DPP* (1999) 163 JP 725).

Home Office Circular 60/2003 emphasises that the stop and search powers must be used 'fairly, objectively, and without any bias against ethnic or other groups within the community'.

Key provisions from Code A include the following:

1.1 Powers to stop and search must be used fairly, responsibly, with respect for people being searched and without unlawful discrimination. The Race Relations (Amendment) Act 2000 makes it unlawful for police officers to discriminate on the grounds of race, colour, ethnic origin, nationality or national origins when using their powers.

...

1.4   The primary purpose of stop and search powers is to enable officers to allay or confirm suspicions about individuals without exercising their power of arrest. Officers may be required to justify the use or authorisation of such powers, in relation both to individual searches and the overall pattern of their activity in this regard, to their supervisory officers or in court. Any misuse of the powers is likely to be harmful to policing and lead to mistrust of the police. Officers must also be able to explain their actions to the member of the public searched. The misuse of these powers can lead to disciplinary action.

1.5   An officer must not search a person, even with his or her consent, where no power to search is applicable. Even where a person is prepared to submit to a search voluntarily, the person must not be searched unless the necessary legal power exists, and the search must be in accordance with the relevant power and the provisions of this Code. The only exception, where an officer does not require a specific power, applies to searches of persons entering sports grounds or other premises carried out with their consent given as a condition of entry.

...

2.2   Reasonable grounds for suspicion depend on the circumstances in each case. There must be an objective basis for that suspicion based on facts, information, and/or intelligence which are relevant to the likelihood of finding an article of a certain kind or, in the case of searches under section 43 of the Terrorism Act 2000, to the likelihood that the person is a terrorist. Reasonable suspicion can never be supported on the basis of personal factors alone without reliable supporting intelligence or information or some specific behaviour by the person concerned. For example, a person's race, age, appearance, or the fact that the person is known to have a previous conviction, cannot be used alone or in combination with each other as the reason for searching that person. Reasonable suspicion cannot be based on generalisations or stereotypical images of certain groups or categories of people as more likely to be involved in criminal activity.

2.3   Reasonable suspicion can sometimes exist without specific information or intelligence and on the basis of some level of generalisation stemming from the behaviour of a person. For example, if an officer encounters someone on the street at night who is obviously trying to hide something, the officer may (depending on the other surrounding circumstances) base such suspicion on the fact that this kind of behaviour is often linked to stolen or prohibited articles being carried. Similarly, for the purposes of section 43 of the Terrorism Act 2000, suspicion that a person is a terrorist may arise from the person's behaviour at or near a location which has been identified as a potential target for terrorists.

2.4   However, reasonable suspicion should normally be linked to accurate and current intelligence or information, such as information describing an article being carried, a suspected offender, or a person who has been seen carrying a type of article known to have been stolen recently from premises in the area. Searches based on accurate and current intelligence or information are more likely to be effective. Targeting searches in a particular area at specified crime problems increases their effectiveness and minimises inconvenience to law-abiding members of the public. It also helps in justifying the use of searches both to those who are searched and to the general public. This does not however prevent stop and search powers being exercised in other locations where such powers may be exercised and reasonable suspicion exists.

...

2.6   Where there is reliable information or intelligence that members of a group or gang habitually carry knives unlawfully or weapons or controlled drugs, and wear a distinctive item of clothing or other means of identification to indicate their membership of the group or gang, that distinctive item of clothing or other means of identification may provide reasonable grounds to stop and search a person.

...

2.10   If, as a result of questioning before a search, or other circumstances which come to the attention of the officer, there cease to be reasonable grounds for suspecting that an article is being carried of a kind for which there is a power to stop and search, no search may take place. In the absence of any other lawful power to detain, the person is free to leave at will and must be so informed.

2.11   There is no power to stop or detain a person in order to find grounds for a search. Police officers have many encounters with members of the public which do not involve detaining people against their will. If reasonable grounds for suspicion emerge during such an encounter, the officer may search the person, even though no grounds existed when the encounter began. If an officer is detaining someone for the purpose of a search, he or she should inform the person as soon as detention begins.

...

4.1   An officer who has carried out a search in the exercise of any power to which this Code applies, must make a record of it at the time, unless there are exceptional circumstances which would make this wholly impracticable (eg in situations involving public disorder or when the officer's presence is urgently required elsewhere). If a record is not made at the time, the officer must do so as soon as practicable afterwards. There may be situations in which it is not practicable to obtain the information necessary to complete a record, but the officer should make every reasonable effort to do so.

4.2   A copy of a record made at the time must be given immediately to the person who has been searched. The officer must ask for the name, address and date of birth of the person searched, but there is no obligation on a person to provide these details and no power of detention if the person is unwilling to do so.

...

4.6   The record of the grounds for making a search must, briefly but informatively, explain the reason for suspecting the person concerned, by reference to the person's behaviour and/or other circumstances.

4.7   Where officers detain an individual with a view to performing a search, but the search is not carried out due to the grounds for suspicion being eliminated as a result of questioning the person detained, a record must still be made in accordance with the procedure outlined above.

...

5.1   Supervising officers must monitor the use of stop and search powers and should consider in particular whether there is any evidence that they are being exercised on the basis of stereotyped images or inappropriate generalisations. Supervising officers should satisfy themselves that the practice of officers under their supervision in stopping, searching and recording is fully in accordance with this Code. Supervisors must also examine whether the records reveal any trends or patterns which give cause for concern, and if so take appropriate action to address this.

...

5.3   Supervision and monitoring must be supported by the compilation of comprehensive statistical records of stops and searches at force, area and local level. Any apparently disproportionate use of the powers by particular officers or groups of officers or in relation to specific sections of the community should be identified and investigated.

5.4 In order to promote public confidence in the use of the powers, forces in consultation with police authorities must make arrangements for the records to be scrutinised by representatives of the community, and to explain the use of the powers at a local level.

Ed Cape, in 'The revised PACE Codes of Practice: a further step towards inquisitorialism' [2003] Crim LR 355, notes that much of the research on the PACE powers of stop and search (including Brown, D, *PACE Ten Years On: A Review of the Research*, Home Office Research Study 155, 1997, Chapter 2) has questioned the efficacy of the provisions, and points out that the Macpherson Report concluded that the 'perception and experience of the minority communities that discrimination is a major element in the stop and search problem is correct' (*Report of the Stephen Lawrence Inquiry*, Cm 4262, para 45.8). Macpherson recommended that all 'stops', as well as 'stops and searches', should be recorded; that the recording requirements be extended to 'voluntary' stops and searches; and that the records should be monitored and scrutinised and the results published (Recommendations 61–63).

These recommendations were accepted by the Home Office. A new section has been added to Code A (A4.11–4.20) to set out the procedures to be followed for recording encounters where a police officer requests a person in a public place to account for themselves (actions, behaviour, presence in the area, possession of anything). Recorded details must include the reason why the officer questioned the person, the person's ethnicity and the outcome of the encounter.

1.12.2 Searching premises

It may also be necessary for the police to enter and search premises. Usually a search warrant is required, but there are circumstances where the police can proceed without a warrant:

- *Entry with a warrant*

    Section 8 of PACE provides as follows:

    (1) If on an application made by a constable a justice of the peace is satisfied that there are reasonable grounds for believing—

    (a) that a serious arrestable offence has been committed; and

    (b) that there is material on premises specified in the application which is likely to be of substantial value (whether by itself or together with other material) to the investigation of the offence; and

    (c) that the material is likely to be relevant evidence; and

    (d) that it does not consist of or include items subject to legal privilege, excluded material or special procedure material; and

    (e) that any of the conditions specified in sub-section (3) below applies,

    he may issue a warrant authorising a constable to enter and search the premises.

    (2) A constable may seize and retain anything for which a search has been authorised under sub-section (1) above.

    (3) The conditions mentioned in sub-section (1)(e) above are—

    (a) that it is not practicable to communicate with any person entitled to grant entry to the premises;

(b) that it is practicable to communicate with a person entitled to grant entry to the premises but it is not practicable to communicate with any person entitled to grant access to the evidence;

(c) that entry to the premises will not be granted unless a warrant is produced;

(d) that the purpose of a search may be frustrated or seriously prejudiced unless a constable arriving at the premises can secure immediate entry to them.

(4) In this Act 'relevant evidence', in relation to an offence, means anything that would be admissible in evidence at a trial for the offence.

Important points to note are that s 8 applies only to cases where the police suspect that a 'serious arrestable offence' has been committed; the police must have reasonable grounds to believe that there is relevant evidence on the premises; and there must be a good reason for requiring a warrant (usually that entry would not be permitted without a warrant being produced or that the purpose of the search would be frustrated if the police were unable to effect immediate entry onto the premises).

Under s 15 of PACE, certain safeguards are set out:

(2) Where a constable applies for any such warrant, it shall be his duty—

(a) to state—

(i) the ground on which he makes the application; and

(ii) the enactment under which the warrant would be issued;

(b) to specify the premises which it is desired to enter and search; and

(c) to identify, so far as is practicable, the articles or persons to be sought.

(3) An application for such a warrant shall be made *ex parte* and supported by an information in writing.

(4) The constable shall answer on oath any question that the justice of the peace or judge hearing the application asks him.

(5) A warrant shall authorise an entry on one occasion only.

(6) A warrant—

(a) shall specify—

(i) the name of the person who applies for it;

(ii) the date on which it is issued;

(iii) the enactment under which it is issued; and

(iv) the premises to be searched; and

(b) shall identify, so far as is practicable, the articles or persons to be sought.

Thus, an application for a search warrant must specify the premises which the police wish to enter and search and must identify the material to be sought. Where a constable knows that premises include or consist of a number of dwellings in separate occupation, the application must specify the particular dwelling(s) which the police wish to enter and search: *R v South Western Magistrates' Court ex p Cofie* [1997] 1 WLR 885.

In *R v Chesterfield Justices ex p Bramley* [2000] 1 All ER 411, the Divisional Court held as follows:

(a) when executing a search warrant under s 8(1) of the 1984 Act, a police officer is not entitled to remove items from the premises in order to sift through them for the purpose of deciding whether or not they fall within the scope of the warrant;

(b) there is no absolute prohibition on seizing an item which is in fact subject to legal professional privilege, provided that the police officer who seizes it does not have reasonable grounds for believing that it is privileged; and

(c) if there is no lawful authority for seizing some of the items that are seized during a search, those items must be returned, but the search remains valid for the items that were properly seized.

The restrictive aspect of this case was reversed by Pt 2 of the Criminal Justice and Police Act 2001. Section 50 of that Act covers the situation where it cannot be conveniently determined *in situ* whether an article or its contents are subject to seizure, or where there are complex issues relating to the status of material as special procedure or excluded material or legally privileged material. In essence, s 50 empowers a person who is lawfully on premises, and who is authorised to search for something, to seize anything which he has reasonable grounds for believing to be something for which he may search and which he is empowered to seize. These powers enable the person to seize the article and to remove it from the premises for the purpose of determining whether it falls within the power. It is a condition of exercise of the power that the determination cannot be reasonably practicably made on the premises (s 50(1)). Where the seizable property cannot reasonably practicably be separated from something else in which it is comprised, both the article and the container may be seized (s 50(2)). The factors to be considered in determining reasonable practicability include length of time, numbers of persons needed, damage to property from separation, the apparatus necessary and prejudice to the use of separated property (s 50(3)).

In *R (Cronin) v Sheffield Magistrates' Court* [2002] EWHC 2568 (Admin); [2003] 1 WLR 752, an application for a search warrant of the claimant's premises was made by the police (under the Misuse of Drugs Act 1971). The application was supported by an information and by oral evidence from a police officer. The claimant argued that, following the coming into force of the Human Rights Act 1998, it was necessary for a written record to be kept of the reasons for the grant of a warrant, including a record of the questions and answers which were asked of the police officer who was seeking the warrant; he contended that his rights under Art 8 of the European Convention on Human Rights had been breached by the failure to do so. It was held that when justices accept an information as containing all the material required to satisfy them that a search warrant should be issued, it is unreasonable to require them to make a note unless a particular matter was elicited during the course of questioning the police officer seeking the warrant (in which case it is highly desirable that a note should be made of that matter). It is only in exceptional circumstances that any further record will be required. The court went on to hold that if a person whose premises have been searched following the issue of a warrant asks for a copy of the information, it should be provided unless it contains details of an informer or other statements to which public interest immunity would apply, in which case disclosure would be contrary to the public interest.

Rules regarding the execution of the search warrant are set out in s 16 of PACE (which is amended by s 2 of the Criminal Justice Act 2003, in force since January 2004, to enable any person authorised to accompany the police when executing the warrant to search for and seize property, thus enabling civilians to take an active role in search and seizure operations).

- *Entry without warrant*

  Two statutory provisions enable the police to enter and search premises without a warrant.

(a) Section 17 of PACE empowers the police to enter and search premises to execute an arrest warrant, to arrest someone for an arrestable offence, or to save life or limb or prevent serious damage to property.

(b) Section 18(1) of PACE allows a police officer to enter and search any premises occupied or controlled by a person who is under arrest for an arrestable offence, if the officer has reasonable grounds to suspect that there is on the premises evidence relating to the offence for which the suspect has been arrested or to some other arrestable offence which is connected with, or similar to, that offence.

The text of those two provisions is as follows:

17   *Entry for purpose of arrest etc*

(1)   Subject to the following provisions of this section, and without prejudice to any other enactment, a constable may enter and search any premises for the purpose—

    (a) of executing—

        (i) a warrant of arrest issued in connection with or arising out of criminal proceedings; or

        ...

    (b) of arresting a person for an arrestable offence;

    (c) of arresting a person for an offence under [various statutory provisions]

    (ca) of arresting, in pursuance of section 32(1A) of the Children and Young Persons Act 1969, any child or young person who has been remanded or committed to local authority accommodation under section 23(1) of that Act;

    (cb) of recapturing any person who is, or is deemed for any purpose to be, unlawfully at large ...

    (d) of recapturing any person whatever who is unlawfully at large and whom he is pursuing; or

    (e) of saving life or limb or preventing serious damage to property.

(2)   Except for the purpose specified in paragraph (e) of sub-section (1) above, the powers of entry and search conferred by this section—

    (a) are only exercisable if the constable has reasonable grounds for believing that the person whom he is seeking is on the premises; and

    (b) are limited, in relation to premises consisting of two or more separate dwellings, to powers to enter and search—

        (i) any parts of the premises which the occupiers of any dwelling comprised in the premises use in common with the occupiers of any other such dwelling; and

        (ii) any such dwelling in which the constable has reasonable grounds for believing that the person whom he is seeking may be.

(3)   The powers of entry and search conferred by this section are only exercisable for the purposes specified in sub-section (1)(c)(ii) or (iv) above by a constable in uniform.

(4)   The power of search conferred by this section is only a power to search to the extent that is reasonably required for the purpose for which the power of entry is exercised.

(5)   Subject to sub-section (6) below, all the rules of common law under which a constable has power to enter premises without a warrant are hereby abolished.

(6)   Nothing in sub-section (5) above affects any power of entry to deal with or prevent a breach of the peace.

18   *Entry and search after arrest*

(1)   Subject to the following provisions of this section, a constable may enter and search any premises occupied or controlled by a person who is under arrest for an arrestable offence, if he has reasonable grounds for suspecting that there is on the premises evidence, other than items subject to legal privilege, that relates—

   (a) to that offence; or

   (b) to some other arrestable offence which is connected with or similar to that offence.

(2)   A constable may seize and retain anything for which he may search under sub-section (1) above.

(3)   The power to search conferred by sub-section (1) above is only a power to search to the extent that is reasonably required for the purpose of discovering such evidence.

(4)   Subject to sub-section (5) below, the powers conferred by this section may not be exercised unless an officer of the rank of Inspector or above has authorised them in writing.

(5)   A constable may conduct a search under sub-section (1) above—

   (a) before the person is taken to a police station; and

   (b) without obtaining an authorisation under sub-section (4) above,

   if the presence of that person at a place other than a police station is necessary for the effective investigation of the offence.

(6)   If a constable conducts a search by virtue of sub-section (5) above, he shall inform an officer of the rank of Inspector or above that he has made the search as soon as practicable after he has made it.

(7)   An officer who—

   (a) authorises a search; or

   (b) is informed of a search under sub-section (6) above, shall make a record in writing—

      (i) of the grounds for the search; and

      (ii) of the nature of the evidence that was sought.

(8)   If the person who was in occupation or control of the premises at the time of the search is in police detention at the time the record is to be made, the officer shall make the record as part of his custody record.

In summary, the officer may seize and retain anything for which he may search, but the scope of the search must be restricted to whatever is reasonably required to search for the evidence referred to in s 18(1) (s 18(2), (3)).

Normally, such a search should be authorised in writing by an officer of at least the rank of Inspector (s 18(4)). A search may take place without such authorisation and without taking the suspect to the police station first if his presence is necessary at some other place for the effective investigation of the offence (s 18(5)).

A police officer who is exercising a statutory power to enter someone's home by the use of the reasonable force should explain the reason for exercising that power of entry to any occupant unless it is impracticable to do so (*O'Loughlin v Chief Constable of Essex* [1998] 1 WLR 374).

Key parts of Code B of the PACE Codes of Practice include the following:

1.3   The right to privacy and respect for personal property are key principles of the Human Rights Act 1998. Powers of entry, search and seizure should be fully and clearly justified before use because they may significantly interfere with the occupier's privacy. Officers should consider if the necessary objectives can be met by less intrusive means.

1.4   In all cases, police should:

- exercise their powers courteously and with respect for persons and property
- only use reasonable force when this is considered necessary and proportionate to the circumstances.

...

7.7   The Criminal Justice and Police Act 2001, Part 2 gives officers limited powers to seize property from premises or persons so they can sift or examine it elsewhere. Officers must be careful they only exercise these powers when it is essential and they do not remove any more material than necessary. The removal of large volumes of material, much of which may not ultimately be retainable, may have serious implications for the owners, particularly when they are involved in business or activities such as journalism or the provision of medical services. Officers must carefully consider if removing copies or images of relevant material or data would be a satisfactory alternative to removing originals. When originals are taken, officers must be prepared to facilitate the provision of copies or images for the owners when reasonably practicable.

7.8   Property seized under the Criminal Justice and Police Act 2001, sections 50 or 51 must be kept securely and separately from any material seized under other powers. An examination under section 53 to determine which elements may be retained must be carried out at the earliest practicable time, having due regard to the desirability of allowing the person from whom the property was seized, or a person with an interest in the property, an opportunity of being present or represented at the examination.

7.8A   All reasonable steps should be taken to accommodate an interested person's request to be present, provided the request is reasonable and subject to the need to prevent harm to, interference with, or unreasonable delay to the investigatory process. If an examination proceeds in the absence of an interested person who asked to attend or their representative, the officer who exercised the relevant seizure power must give that person a written notice of why the examination was carried out in those circumstances. If it is necessary for security reasons or to maintain confidentiality officers may exclude interested persons from decryption or other processes which facilitate the examination but do not form part of it.

7.9   It is the responsibility of the officer in charge of the investigation to make sure property is returned in accordance with sections 53 to 55. Material which there is no power to retain must be:

- separated from the rest of the seized property;
- returned as soon as reasonably practicable after examination of all the seized property.

7.9A   Delay is only warranted if very clear and compelling reasons exist, eg the:

- unavailability of the person to whom the material is to be returned;
- need to agree a convenient time to return a large volume of material.

7.9B   Legally privileged, excluded or special procedure material which cannot be retained must be returned:

- as soon as reasonably practicable;
- without waiting for the whole examination.

1.12.3 Legal privilege

The police cannot gain access to material which is subject to legal privilege. This material is defined by s 10(1) of PACE:

Subject to sub-section (2) below, in this Act 'items subject to legal privilege' means—

(a) communications between a professional legal adviser and his client or any person representing his client made in connection with the giving of legal advice to the client;

(b) communications between a professional legal adviser and his client or any person representing his client or between such an adviser or his client or any such representative and any other person made in connection with or in contemplation of legal proceedings and for the purposes of such proceedings; and

(c) items enclosed with or referred to in such communications and made—

(i) in connection with the giving of legal advice; or

(ii) in connection with or in contemplation of legal proceedings and for the purposes of such proceedings,

when they are in the possession of a person who is entitled to possession of them.

(2) Items held with the intention of furthering a criminal purpose are not items subject to legal privilege.

In summary, therefore, this definition covers communications between a lawyer and his client (or any person representing his client) made in connection with the giving of legal advice to the client; and communications between a lawyer and his client (or any person representing his client) or between such an adviser or his client or any such representative and any other person made in connection with or in contemplation of legal proceedings and for the purpose of such proceedings.

1.12.4 Excluded and special procedure material

The police can only gain access to 'excluded material' or 'special procedure material' by obtaining a warrant from a Circuit judge under s 9 of PACE.

Excluded material is defined by s 11(1) of PACE:

(a) personal records which a person has acquired or created in the course of any trade, business, profession or other occupation or for the purposes of any paid or unpaid office and which he holds in confidence;

(b) human tissue or tissue fluid which has been taken for the purposes of diagnosis or medical treatment and which a person holds in confidence;

(c) journalistic material which a person holds in confidence and which consists:

(i) of documents; or

(ii) of records other than documents.

Special procedure material is defined by s 14:

(a) material other than items subject to legal privilege and excluded material, in the possession of a person who:

(i) acquired or created it in the course of any trade, business, profession or other occupation or for the purpose of any paid or unpaid office (s 14(1), (2)); and

    (ii) holds it in confidence;

(b)   journalistic material, other than excluded material.

The procedure for applying to a Circuit judge for access to excluded material or special procedure material under s 9 is set out in Sched 1.

The judge may only make an access order if satisfied on the balance of probabilities that one of the sets of access conditions is fulfilled.

The first set of access conditions (Sched 1, para 2) requires that:

(a)   there are reasonable grounds for believing—

    (i)   that a serious arrestable offence has been committed;

    (ii) that there is material which consists of special procedure material or also includes special procedure material and does not also include excluded material on premises specified in the application;

    (iii) that the material is likely to be of substantial value (whether by itself or together with other material) to the investigation in connection with which the application is made; and

    (iv) that the material is likely to be relevant evidence;

(b)   other methods of obtaining the material—

    (i)   have been tried without success; or

    (ii) have not been tried because it appeared that they were bound to fail; and

(c)   it is in the public interest, having regard—

    (i)   to the benefit likely to accrue to the investigation if the material is obtained; and

    (ii) to the circumstances under which the person in possession of the material holds it,

    that the material should be produced or that access to it should be given.

The second set of access conditions (Sched 1, para 3) requires that there be reasonable grounds for believing that there is excluded material on the premises, in respect of which a magistrate would have had power to grant a search warrant but for the removal of that power by s 9(2).

A judge also has the power to issue a warrant authorising a constable to enter and search premises (Sched 1, para 12). Where the material is excluded material, the judge must be satisfied that the second set of access conditions (see previous paragraph) is fulfilled and that there has been a failure to comply with an access order.

A judge may also issue a warrant to enter and search premises if satisfied that either set of access conditions is fulfilled and that any of the following conditions are also fulfilled:

(a)   that it is not practicable to communicate with any person entitled to grant entry to the premises to which the application relates;

(b)   that it is practicable to communicate with a person entitled to grant entry to the premises but it is not practicable to communicate with any person entitled to grant access to the material;

(c)   that the material contains information which—

    (i)   is subject to a restriction or obligation such as is mentioned in section 11(2)(b) above; and

    (ii) is likely to be disclosed in breach of it if a warrant is not issued;

(d)   that service of notice of an application for an order under paragraph 4 above may seriously prejudice the investigation.

1.13 ALTERNATIVES TO PROSECUTION

1.13.1 Adults

Not every arrest results in the person arrested being charged and having to go to court. The police have the alternative of administering a 'caution' instead. This is not to be confused with the warning given before questioning; rather it is a warning that committing a further offence will result in court action.

The present arrangements for cautions of adults are set out in Home Office Circular 18/1994.

The purpose of a formal caution is:

- to deal quickly and simply with less serious offenders;
- to divert them from unnecessary appearance in the criminal courts;
- to reduce the chances of their re-offending.

A caution does not count as a previous conviction but, if the person re-offends, the caution will be cited in court. Records of a caution are usually kept for three years or until the offender attains the age of 18, whichever is the longer.

Before administering a caution, the police should consider two questions:

- are the circumstances such that a caution is likely to be effective in preventing the offender from re-offending?;
- is a caution appropriate to the offence?

As regards the latter question, the guidelines make it clear that a caution is never appropriate for really serious indictable-only offences, such as rape. A caution may, in exceptional circumstances, be appropriate for an indictable-only offence (for example, a very minor robbery where there is only a mild threat of violence and very little is stolen).

Offences that are triable either way may not be appropriate for cautioning if they are serious in the present case (for example, an offence which is racially motivated; theft in breach of trust; an offence carried out in a systematic and organised way).

The following conditions must be met before a caution can be administered:

- there must be evidence of the offender's guilt sufficient to give a realistic prospect of conviction;
- the offender must admit the offence; and
- the offender (or, in the case of a juvenile, his parents or guardian) must understand the significance of a caution and give informed consent to being cautioned.

There is a presumption against prosecuting certain categories of offender (for example, the elderly, those who suffer from mental illness or impairment and those who are severely disabled). The guidance from the Home Office makes it clear, however, that members of these groups should be prosecuted if the seriousness of the offence so requires. That guidance also says that the presumption in favour of diverting juveniles from the courts does not mean that they should automatically be cautioned merely because they are juveniles (such cautioning would now take place under the system of reprimands and warnings established by the Crime and Disorder Act 1998).

The guidelines go on to say that a practical demonstration of regret (for example, apologising to the victim or offering to put matters right) may support the use of a caution.

The police are encouraged to seek the views of the victim as to the seriousness of the offence, the extent of any harm or loss, and whether the offender has made any form of reparation or paid compensation.

A caution should normally be administered at a police station by a uniformed officer of the rank of Inspector or above. A juvenile should only be cautioned in the presence of a parent or guardian.

If the offender is elderly, infirm or otherwise vulnerable, a caution may be administered at the offender's home in the presence of a friend or relative.

It is the intention of the Home Office that offenders should not usually receive more than one caution; subsequent offences should lead to prosecution. Cautioning for a subsequent offence should only take place if:

• the later offence is trivial; or
• there has been a sufficient lapse of time since the first caution to suggest that the caution had some effect in preventing re-offending.

The Home Office Circular adds that there is no intention to inhibit the practice of taking action short of a formal caution by giving an oral warning. Such a warning, or informal caution, is not recorded and cannot be cited in subsequent court proceedings.

If a formal caution is administered in breach of the Home Office guidelines, then judicial review may be sought to quash the caution and have it deleted from police records. See *R v Metropolitan Police Commissioner ex p P* (1996) 8 Admin LR 6, where a caution was quashed because the recipient of the caution had not admitted the offence and also because the police had made no attempt to establish whether the person, a child under 14, knew that his behaviour had been seriously wrong. A caution is a criminal matter within s 18(1) of the Supreme Court Act 1981 (which provides that no appeal lies to the Court of Appeal from any judgment of the High Court in any criminal cause or matter), and so the Court of Appeal has no jurisdiction to entertain an appeal from the decision of the High Court in judicial review proceedings challenging the lawfulness of the caution; the only appeal is to the House of Lords (provided that there is a question of law raising a point of public importance): *R (Aru) v Chief Constable of Merseyside* [2004] EWCA Civ 199; [2004] 1 WLR 1697.

Where the suspect makes a clear and unequivocal admission, it is acceptable to administer a formal caution (as an alternative to commencing a prosecution) even if the admission was not obtained in an interview complying with Code C of the Codes of Practice; however, as a matter of good practice, the police should ensure that a formal interview (complying with Code C) takes place (*R v Chief Constable of Lancashire Constabulary ex p Atkinson* (1998) 192 JP 275).

Normally, where someone has been cautioned for an offence, they will not subsequently be prosecuted for that same offence. However, in *Hayter v L* [1998] 1 WLR 854, the prosecutor's son was assaulted by the respondents. The respondents admitted the offence and were cautioned by the police. The prosecutor then commenced a private prosecution. The magistrates stayed the prosecution as an abuse of process. The Divisional Court held that the administration of a caution did not mean that a subsequent private prosecution would be an abuse of process and so the justices were wrong to stay the prosecution. It should be borne in mind, however, that the DPP has power under the Prosecution of Offences Act 1985 to take over and terminate a private prosecution if it is in the public interest to do so.

Part 3 of the Criminal Justice Act 2003 introduces 'conditional cautions' (in force from July 2004). Section 22 of the Act defines conditional cautions and says who can administer them. It states:

(1) An authorised person may give a conditional caution to a person aged 18 or over ('the offender') if each of the five requirements in section 23 is satisfied.

(2) In this Part 'conditional caution' means a caution which is given in respect of an offence committed by the offender and which has conditions attached to it with which the offender must comply.

(3) The conditions which may be attached to such a caution are those which have either or both of the following objects—
    (a) facilitating the rehabilitation of the offender,
    (b) ensuring that he makes reparation for the offence.

(4) In this Part 'authorised person' means—
    (a) a constable,
    (b) an investigating officer, or
    (c) a person authorised by a relevant prosecutor for the purposes of this section [defined in s 27 as meaning the Attorney General, the Director of the Serious Fraud Office, the DPP, a Secretary of State, the Commissioners of Inland Revenue, the Commissioners of Customs & Excise, or a person who is specified in an order made by the Secretary of State as being a relevant prosecutor].

Before a conditional caution can be administered, there are five requirements. These are set out in s 23 of the Act, as follows:

(1) The first requirement is that the authorised person has evidence that the offender has committed an offence.

(2) The second requirement is that a relevant prosecutor decides—
    (a) that there is sufficient evidence to charge the offender with the offence, and
    (b) that a conditional caution should be given to the offender in respect of the offence.

(3) The third requirement is that the offender admits to the authorised person that he committed the offence.

(4) The fourth requirement is that the authorised person explains the effect of the conditional caution to the offender and warns him that failure to comply with any of the conditions attached to the caution may result in his being prosecuted for the offence.

(5) The fifth requirement is that the offender signs a document which contains—
    (a) details of the offence,
    (b) an admission by him that he committed the offence,
    (c) his consent to being given the conditional caution, and
    (d) the conditions attached to the caution.

The sanction for non-compliance with the conditions is set out in s 24(1):

If the offender fails, without reasonable excuse, to comply with any of the conditions attached to the conditional caution, criminal proceedings may be instituted against the person for the offence in question.

In 2004, a Code of Practice on Conditional Cautions was issued. The Code:

- sets out as the basic criteria for a conditional caution that the suspect is 18 or over, that he admits the offence, and that there is enough evidence to charge;
- explains that it is the 'relevant prosecutor' (usually the CPS) who determines whether a conditional caution is appropriate;
- advises that a conditional caution will usually be appropriate where conditions that facilitate the rehabilitation of the offender or ensure that the offender makes reparation for the offence, or both, will provide a proportionate response to the offence, bearing in mind the public interest;
- makes clear that only exceptionally should a person who has recently been cautioned for a similar offence be given a conditional caution;
- requires that a suspect should have made a clear and reliable admission under a cautioned interview before the prospect of a conditional caution is mentioned;
- explains that conditions must be proportionate, achievable and appropriate, and have reparation or rehabilitation as their objectives, and that a deadline should be set for their completion;
- requires that it should be a standard condition not to re-offend within the period of the conditional caution;
- emphasises the importance of robust monitoring of an offender's compliance with conditions, requiring as a standard condition that they co-operate with monitoring arrangements, and report any failure to complete conditions and the reasons for this;
- sets out the action to be taken in the event of non-compliance; the decision will rest with the prosecutor, but the usual outcome will be prosecution for the original offence;
- encourages contact with victims to ascertain their views; and
- includes guidance about the use of restorative justice processes, for those areas which choose to deliver conditional cautions in a restorative manner.

1.13.2 Juveniles

A slightly different system applies to young offenders. Section 65 of the Crime and Disorder Act 1998 applies (by virtue of s 65(1)) to cases where:

(a) the police have evidence that a child or young person has committed an offence;

(b) there is sufficient evidence against the youngster that, if he were prosecuted, there would be a realistic prospect that he would be convicted of the offence;

(c) the youngster admits to the police that he committed the offence;

(d) the youngster has not previously been convicted of any offence; and

(e) the police are satisfied that it would not be in the public interest for the youngster to be prosecuted.

In such a case, s 65(2) provides that the police may *reprimand* the youngster if he has not previously been reprimanded or warned.

Under s 65(3), the police may *warn* a youngster who comes within s 65(1) if:

(a) he has not previously been warned; or

(b) where he has previously been warned, the present offence was committed more than two years after the date of the previous warning and the police consider that the present offence is not sufficiently serious to require a charge to be brought.

Section 65(3) goes on to state that no person may be warned more than twice.

Under s 65, the usual sequence of events would be:

- first offence: reprimand;
- second offence: warning;
- third offence: prosecution (or a second warning if the present offence is more than two years after the first warning and the present offence is not so serious as to require prosecution).

However, s 65(4) states that where the youngster has not previously been reprimanded, a warning may be administered, rather than a reprimand, if the police consider that the offence is so serious as to require a warning.

Similarly, there is nothing to stop the police from prosecuting a youngster for a first or second offence where the seriousness of the offence makes that an appropriate course of action.

Under s 65(5), reprimands and warnings must be administered in the presence of an appropriate adult. The effect of re-offending must be explained to the youngster and to the adult.

Under s 66(2), where a warning has been administered, a youth offending team must, unless they consider it inappropriate to do so, arrange for the youngster to participate in a rehabilitation programme, with the aim of preventing him from re-offending.

Where a person has been warned under s 65 and is subsequently convicted of an offence committed within two years of the warning, the court dealing with him for the later offence cannot impose a conditional discharge unless it takes the view that there are exceptional circumstances relating to the offence or to the offender which justify its doing so (s 66(4)).

Reprimands, warnings and failure to participate in a rehabilitation programme may be cited in criminal proceedings in the same way as previous convictions may be cited (s 66(5)).

It used to be the case that reprimands and warnings had to be given in a police station; however, that requirement was removed by s 56 of the Criminal Justice and Court Services Act 2000. This gives the police flexibility to arrange for 'restorative conferences' in more suitable locations, such as the offices of the youth offending team responsible for assessing the young offender and providing the intervention programme.

In *R (on the Application of U) v Commissioner of Police of the Metropolis* [2002] EWHC 2486; [2003] 1 WLR 897; [2003] 1 Cr App R 29, the claimants, who were both aged 15 at the relevant time, were suspected of having committed indecent assaults on young girls. The police administered final warnings pursuant to ss 65 and 66 of the Crime and Disorder Act 1998. The claimants were not informed that, since the offences fell within the ambit of the Sex Offenders Act 1997, they would be put on the Sex Offenders Register. They sought judicial review, arguing that, in the absence of express informed consent, a final warning should not have been given. It was held that informed consent is required before the procedure for administering final warnings can comply with Art 6 of the European Convention on Human Rights. Although the decision was taken not to prosecute, the claimants were nonetheless required to subject themselves to a procedure that had the effect of publicly pronouncing their guilt of the offence of indecent assault. Therefore, they had been denied a right to a trial of the charges against them, and were declared guilty by an administrative process. The court ruled that the system of cautions will only be compliant with the Convention if the procedures can properly be said to amount to a waiver of the right to have one's case dealt with by a court of law. That would require the informed consent by the offender to the procedure being adopted. The proper practice has to be to ensure that, before a reprimand or final warning is administered, the offender and his parent, carer or other appropriate adult should be told of the consequences and asked whether or not they consent to that course being taken.

In November 2002, the Secretary of State published revised guidance pursuant to s 65(6) of the 1998 Act. Paragraph 1.3 reads:

> The final warning scheme aims to divert children and young people from their offending behaviour before they enter the court system.

Paragraph 1.4 provides:

> The scheme was designed to do this by:
> - ending repeat cautioning and providing a progressive and effective response to offending behaviour;
> - providing appropriate and effective interventions to prevent re-offending; and
> - ensuring that young people who do re-offend after being warned are dealt with quickly and effectively by the courts.

Paragraph 1.9 says that:

> The scheme has now been in operation for over two years and is proving its worth ... in 2001, 28,339 young people received final warnings and 70% were accompanied by an intervention programme. Research shows that effective intervention at the final warning stage significantly reduces the rate of re-offending. The Youth Justice Board has set a target that 80 per cent of all final warnings should have an intervention programme by 2004.

Several paragraphs refer to the need for speed in the operation of the scheme. If a young offender is to be dealt with by means of a reprimand or a final warning, it is important (in the public interest, and for the effective operation of the scheme) that that reprimand or final warning should be administered swiftly, in order to maximise the impact of such reprimand or final warning upon the young offender. One consequence of this is that if the police decide against this course of action (for example, because – at that stage – the juvenile denies the offence), the court will not usually require the police or the CPS to reconsider offering a reprimand or warning after the juvenile has been charged (see *R (F) v CPS* [2003] EWHC 3266; (2004) 168 JP 93).

1.14 THE DECISION TO PROSECUTE

Assuming the case is not one where the police consider that a caution is appropriate, or one where the suspect is bailed and the CPS decides whether or not to charge or caution him, the decision to charge someone following their arrest, or to lay an information, is taken by the police, often with guidance from the CPS. The CPS then takes over the conduct of the prosecution (s 3(2)(a) of the Prosecution of Offences Act 1985). The case will be reviewed by a Crown Prosecutor, who may decide to continue with the original charge(s), substitute different ones, or even discontinue proceedings altogether.

Under s 3(2) of the Prosecution of Offences Act 1985, it is the duty of the DPP (as head of the CPS) to take over the conduct of all criminal proceedings instituted on behalf of a police force. Proceedings are only instituted on behalf of a police force where the police force has investigated and arrested the suspect and brought him before the custody officer: *R v Criminal Cases Review Commission ex p Hunt* [2001] QB 1108 (QBD) (*R v Stafford Justices ex p Commissioners of Customs & Excise* [1991] 2 QB 339 followed; *R v Ealing Justices ex p Dixon* [1990] 2 QB 91 not followed).

1.14.1 Discontinuing proceedings

The DPP can, at any 'preliminary stage' of the proceedings, discontinue any criminal proceedings by serving a notice of discontinuance under s 23 of the Prosecution of Offences Act 1985.

This will be done where it becomes apparent that the case against the defendant is not as strong as it first seemed (for example, new evidence comes to light or a prosecution witness changes his story). According to figures released by the CPS, in the period 2001–04, an average of 15% of cases in the magistrates' court were discontinued each year.

Section 23(2) of the 1985 Act defines the term 'preliminary stage'. In the case of a summary offence, it is too late to serve a notice under s 23 once the trial has begun. In the case of an indictable offence, it is too late to serve a notice if committal proceedings have taken place, or the case has been transferred to the Crown Court under s 51 of the Crime and Disorder Act 1998, or summary trial has begun. The exclusion (by s 23(2)) of cases that have been sent for trial to the Crown Court is mitigated to a large extent by s 23A of the Act. This specifically provides for notice of discontinuance to be served where a case has been sent to the Crown Court under s 51 of the Crime and Disorder Act 1998. The notice may be served, 'at any time before the indictment is preferred', on the Crown Court sitting at the place specified in the notice transferring the case to that court. This provision will be of even greater importance when the relevant provisions of Sched 3 to the Criminal Justice Act 2003 come into force, extending the scope of s 51 of the 1998 Act so that it encompasses either way offences as well as those triable only on indictment.

To discontinue proceedings under s 23, the DPP simply serves a notice on the clerk to the justices. The DPP must inform the defendant and must give reasons for the decision to discontinue the proceedings. As discontinuance does not prevent the institution of further proceedings in respect of the offence (s 23(9)), the defendant may serve a counter-notice requiring that the proceedings continue; this would be appropriate in a case where the defendant wishes to have his name cleared by an acquittal.

If the decision to discontinue the prosecution is taken after the preliminary stages have been completed, the prosecution can only discontinue proceedings at trial by offering no evidence at trial. According to CPS figures, in the period 2000–03, an average of 13.5% of cases were not proceeded with in the Crown Court.

In *Cooke v DPP* (1992) 95 Cr App R 233, it was held that s 23 only provides an additional method of discontinuing proceedings. The other ways of discontinuing proceedings (such as withdrawing a summons or charge or offering no evidence) remain available.

In *R v Grafton* [1992] QB 101; [1992] 4 All ER 609, it was held that the decision to discontinue proceedings is entirely a matter for the prosecution; the agreement of the court is not required. This applies both in the magistrates' court and the Crown Court.

The powers of the DPP to discontinue a prosecution under s 23 of the Prosecution of Offences Act may be contrasted with the power of the Attorney General (who is a member of the government but who is also responsible to Parliament) to enter a *nolle prosequi*. This power enables the Attorney General to terminate a prosecution at any time after the bill of indictment has been signed. This power is exercised only rarely but its exercise cannot be challenged in the courts (*Gouriet v Union of Post Office Workers* [1978] AC 435).

There has been some criticism of the fact that the CPS can only discontinue Crown Court proceedings prior to the stage when the case is sent to the Crown Court; if they wish to drop the case after that stage, they have to offer no evidence at the plea and directions hearing or at the start of the trial. The ongoing review of the evidence in a case may well mean that the CPS wish to discontinue the case after the 'preliminary' stages are over, especially with the abolition of committal proceedings resulting in cases reaching the Crown Court much sooner. The Auld Review discusses this (at paras 64–68 of Chapter 10) and recommends that:

171 The law should be amended to provide a form of procedure common to all courts to enable a prosecutor, without the consent of the defendant or the approval of the court, to discontinue proceedings at any stage before close of the prosecution case on trial.

172 In the event of the prosecution discontinuing at any time before pre-trial assessment or, where there is no pre-trial assessment, before a stage to be specified, the prosecution should be entitled to reinstate the prosecution, subject to the court's power to stay it as an abuse of process.

173 In the event of the prosecution discontinuing after that stage, the defendant should be entitled to an acquittal, save where the court for good reason permits the prosecution to 'lie on the file'.

174 There should be common provision for all courts, subject to their approval and the agreement of the parties, to give formal effect to such discontinuance and, where appropriate, acquittal in the absence of the parties.

1.14.2 Deciding to prosecute

The Code of Conduct for Crown Prosecutors (set out in full at the end of this chapter) states that a prosecution should only be started or continued if there is a 'realistic prospect of conviction'. This means that a court is 'more likely than not' to convict the defendant of the charge alleged. In deciding whether or not this 51% test is satisfied, the Crown Prosecutor should consider both the admissibility and the likely reliability of the evidence against the defendant. Thus, the Crown Prosecutor must take account of any challenges which the defence may make to the admissibility of evidence and must also see if there are discrepancies between what the various prosecutions witnesses have said to the police and whether a prosecution witness might have a motive for lying.

The CPS should also consider whether a prosecution is in the public interest. For example, if the offence is a trivial one, and so in the event of conviction the court would be likely to impose only a very small or nominal penalty, the CPS might take the view that it is not in the public interest to continue proceedings. Similarly, a prosecution may not be in the public interest if it is likely to have an adverse effect on the physical or mental health of the victim or the offender. However, the Code makes it clear that 'the more serious the offence, the more likely it is that a prosecution will be needed in the public interest'.

In *R v DPP ex p C* [1995] 1 Cr App R 136, it was held that the decision by the CPS not to prosecute a person is susceptible to judicial review if the Crown Prosecutor who took the decision failed to act in accordance with the policy set out in the Code of Conduct for Crown Prosecutors. In that case, which involved an allegation that a man had committed buggery on his wife, a Crown Prosecutor decided that there was sufficient evidence against the man but that it was not in the public interest to prosecute him. The Code of Conduct states that, in the case of a serious sexual assault, where the evidential sufficiency criterion is satisfied (so that there is a realistic prospect of conviction), it will normally be in the public interest to prosecute the alleged offender. The Divisional Court emphasised that the power to review the decisions of the CPS will be exercised sparingly: it would only be used if the decision not to prosecute was arrived at because of an unlawful policy, or because of a failure to act in accordance with the Code of Practice or where a decision was perverse.

In *R v DPP ex p Manning* [2001] QB 330, the Divisional Court repeated that, although a decision by the DPP not to prosecute is susceptible to judicial review, the review power is to be exercised sparingly. The court went on to hold that there is no general obligation on the CPS to give reasons for a decision not to prosecute. However, in a case where one might reasonably expect there to be a prosecution (in this case, there had been a death in custody and a properly directed coroner's jury had returned a verdict of unlawful killing implicating a person who, although not named, was clearly identified and whose whereabouts were known), reasons for a decision not to prosecute should be given.

In *R v DPP ex p Treadaway* (1997) *The Times*, 31 October, the Divisional Court held that, when deciding whether or not to prosecute a person for conduct which a civil court has found proven, the prosecutor must analyse the civil court's findings very carefully.

In the absence of dishonesty or bad faith or other exceptional circumstances, the decision to prosecute is not amenable to judicial review; challenges to such proceedings should be made in the context of the criminal trial or by way of appeal against conviction following such trial (*R v DPP ex p Kebilene* [2000] 2 AC 326; [1999] 4 All ER 801). *Kebilene* was followed in *R (Pepushi) v CPS* [2004] EWHC 798 (Admin); (2004) *The Times*, 21 May, where the court reiterated that a decision to prosecute is not ordinarily amenable to judicial review. Thomas LJ said (at paras 49–50):

> In view of the frequency of applications seeking to challenge decisions to prosecute, we wish to make it clear and, in particular, clear to the Legal Services Commission (which funds applications of this kind which seek to challenge the bringing of criminal proceedings) that, save in wholly exceptional circumstances, applications in respect of pending prosecutions that seek to challenge the decision to prosecute should not be made to this court. The proper course to follow, as should have been followed in this case, is to take the point in accordance with the procedures of the criminal courts ...

The circumstances in which a challenge is made to the bringing of a prosecution should be very rare indeed ... We stress that the Legal Services Commission and those advising prospective applicants for judicial review should always realise that judicial review is very rarely appropriate where an alternative remedy is available. If such a remedy is available, a judicial review application should not be pursued.

1.14.3 Private prosecutions

Where a member of the public commences a 'private prosecution', they do so by laying an information. A member of the public can bring a private prosecution for any offence unless the offence is one for which the consent of the Attorney General or the DPP is required before a prosecution can take place. This is because s 6(1) of the Prosecution of Offences Act 1985 preserves the right of any person to institute criminal proceedings in any case unless the consent of the DPP or the Attorney General is necessary in order to commence a prosecution. Such consent is only needed for a very small number of offences.

A member of the public can only commence criminal proceedings by laying an information as he will not be granted an arrest warrant by a magistrate; someone who effects a 'citizen's arrest' (an arrest without a warrant) has to hand the suspect over to the police (who will then decide whether or not to charge the suspect).

Section 6(2) of the Prosecution of Offences Act 1985 enables the DPP to take over the conduct of any criminal proceedings. Once the DPP has taken over the conduct of the proceedings, he is free to discontinue them if he thinks it appropriate to do so.

Where the CPS have already commenced proceedings against a defendant and a member of the public seeks to lay an information against that defendant alleging another offence arising out of the same incident, the court should be reluctant to issue a summons. In *R v Tower Bridge Magistrates ex p Chaudhry* [1993] 3 WLR 1154; [1994] 1 All ER 44, for example, the applicant's son was killed in a road accident. The CPS brought proceedings against the other driver alleging driving without due care and attention. The applicant laid an information which alleged causing death by reckless driving (it would now be causing death by dangerous driving). The magistrate refused to issue a summons and that refusal was upheld by the Divisional Court.

1.14.4 Prosecutions by public bodies other than the police

Where a public body, such as the Inland Revenue, HM Customs & Excise or a local authority, commences a prosecution, this is currently done by an employee of the public body laying an information at a magistrates' court. Indeed, this is the only way for the proceedings to be commenced if the offence is not an arrestable offence. Even in the case of arrestable offences, the usual method for a public body to commence a prosecution is by laying down an information. It should be noted, however, that the new written charge and requisition procedure established by the Criminal Justice Act 2003 (replacing the laying of informations) applies to all public prosecutions, including those brought by government departments.

Provided that the offence is an arrestable offence, as defined in s 24 of PACE, the suspect may be arrested by a representative of the public body. Representatives of such bodies are not police officers and so are, in effect, making a 'citizen's arrest'. The person arrested will be taken to a police station to be charged by the custody officer.

In *R v Stafford Justices ex p Customs & Excise Commissioners* [1990] 3 WLR 656, followed in *R v Croydon Justices ex p Holmberg* [1992] Crim LR 892, it was held that proceedings commenced in this way are not taken over by the police (and thence by the CPS) but are conducted by the relevant public body.

1.14.5 What happens next?

As we shall see in Chapter 3, some offences have to be tried in the magistrates' court ('summary trial', dealt with in Chapter 4) while others *may* be tried in that court if the defendant and the magistrates agree; the remaining offences have to be tried before a judge and jury in the Crown Court ('trial on indictment', dealt with in Chapter 10).

Even if a case is ultimately tried in the Crown Court, the case will nevertheless start in the magistrates' court:

- In the case of proceedings which are commenced by the laying of an information and the issue of a summons, it is the magistrates' court which issues the summons and the summons will require the defendant to attend the magistrates' court which issued it. When this procedure is replaced by the written charge and requisition procedure established by the Criminal Justice Act 2003, the requisition will require the accused to attend a magistrates' court.
- If the suspect is arrested and charged by the police, he may be granted police bail under s 38 of PACE. In that case, he will be handed a charge sheet which tells him the date, time and place of his first court appearance, which will be in the magistrates' court.
- If, after charge, the suspect is not granted police bail, then he will be held in custody by the police until the next sitting of the magistrates' court. At that hearing, the magistrates will decide whether to grant him bail or not (see Chapter 2).

1.15   THE MAGISTRATES' COURT

The magistrates' court usually comprises three lay justices and a legally qualified clerk.

The lay justices are ordinary members of the public who have put themselves forward to sit as justices of the peace (JPs). They are appointed by the Lord Chancellor. They are unpaid, although they can claim reimbursement for travel expenses and loss of earnings. Each magistrate has to sit at least 26 times a year (although many sit more often than this). They receive basic training in the law, the evidence and the procedure which they are likely to encounter.

Because they have only very elementary training, the lay justices need the help of their clerk. Section 27 of the Courts Act 2003 re-enacts s 43 of the Justices of the Peace Act 1997; under s 27(2) a person may be designated as a justices' clerk only if he:

(a)   has a 5 year magistrates' court qualification,

(b)   is a barrister or solicitor who has served for not less than 5 years as an assistant to a justices' clerk, or

(c)   has previously been a justices' clerk.

Section 27(6) of the 2003 Act empowers the Lord Chancellor to make regulations setting out the requirements that a person must fulfil in order to be designated as an assistant to a justices' clerk. Assistant clerks will continue to be limited to advising lay justices (and so are not able to exercise those powers of a single justice that may be exercised by a justices' clerk).

In the larger cities, there may well be a District judge (formerly known as a 'stipendiary magistrate'). District judges are appointed by the Queen, on the recommendation of the Lord Chancellor, from amongst barristers and solicitors of at least seven years' standing. A District judge can try a case sitting alone whereas at least two lay justices must be sitting for a summary trial to take place. Section 26(1) of the Courts Act 2003 is in similar terms to s 10E of the Justices of the Peace Act 1997, empowering District judges (magistrates' courts) to sit alone. It provides that:

> Nothing in the 1980 Act (a) requiring a magistrates' court to be composed of two or more justices, or (b) limiting the powers of a magistrates' court when composed of a single justice, applies to a District Judge (Magistrates' Courts).

Because a District judge is legally qualified and sits alone, cases in front of such magistrates tend to be disposed of more quickly than those that are heard by lay justices.

The Courts Act 2003 expands the role of the District judges by empowering them to exercise some of the powers of Crown Court judges. This is achieved by s 65 of the Act, which has the effect of making District judges judges of the Crown Court; this section amends s 8(1)(b) of the Supreme Court Act 1981 Act (persons who are judges of the Crown Court), to include District judges (magistrates' courts) as well as recorders. Schedule 4 to the 2003 Act sets out a number of specific interlocutory proceedings and rulings that fall within the jurisdiction of a District judge before a case is ready to go before a Crown Court judge.

Both solicitors and barristers have complete rights of audience in the magistrates' court.

1.16   THE CROWN COURT

The Crown Court is always presided over by a judge. Where the Crown Court is trying a case, the judge always sits with a jury. Very serious offences are usually tried by a High Court judge; most cases, however, will be tried by a Circuit judge or a part-time judge called a recorder. Thus, murder must be tried by a High Court judge; manslaughter and rape will usually be tried by a High Court judge but may be tried by a Circuit judge; other offences can be tried by a High Court judge, a Circuit judge or a recorder. See ss 8 and 75 of the Supreme Court Act 1981 and s 24 of the Courts Act 1971.

A Circuit judge or recorder is addressed as 'your Honour'; a High Court judge (or any judge sitting at the Central Criminal Court) is addressed as 'my Lord'.

High Court judges are appointed by the Queen, on the recommendation of the Lord Chancellor, from amongst the ranks of barristers of at least 10 years' standing. Most will have acted as deputy (that is, part-time) High Court judges beforehand. A Circuit judge may also be made a High Court judge.

Circuit judges and recorders are appointed by the Queen on the recommendation of the Lord Chancellor. Barristers and solicitors of at least 10 years' standing may be appointed recorders. Only barristers of 10 years' standing or solicitors or barristers who have been recorders for at least three years are eligible for appointment as Circuit judges.

The allocation of work in the Crown Court is governed by the *Practice Direction (Criminal Proceedings: Consolidation)* [2002] 1 WLR 2870 (para III.21.1). Offences triable in the Crown Court are classified as follows:

Class 1: (a) misprision of treason and treason felony; (b) murder; (c) genocide; (d) torture, hostage-taking and offences under the War Crimes Act 1991; (e) an offence under the Official Secrets Acts; (f) soliciting, incitement, attempt or conspiracy to commit any of the above offences.

Class 2: (a) manslaughter; (b) infanticide; (c) child destruction; (d) abortion (s 58 of the Offences against the Person Act 1861); (e) rape; (f) sexual intercourse with a girl under 13; (g) incest with girl under 13; (h) sedition; (i) an offence under s 1 of the Geneva Conventions Act 1957; (j) mutiny; (k) piracy; (l) soliciting, incitement, attempt or conspiracy to commit any of the above offences.

Class 3: (a) all offences triable only on indictment other than those in classes 1, 2 and 4; (b) soliciting, incitement, attempt or conspiracy to commit any of the above offences.

Class 4: (a) wounding or causing grievous bodily harm with intent (s 18 of the Offences against the Person Act 1861); (b) robbery or assault with intent to rob (s 8 of the Theft Act 1968); (c) soliciting, incitement or attempt to commit any of the above offences; (d) conspiracy at common law, or conspiracy to commit any offence other than those included in classes 1, 2 and 3; (e) all offences which are triable either way.

Crown Courts are classified as first, second or third tier. The first tier courts can try all indictable offences; the third tier can try only less serious indictable offences. This is because third tier Crown Courts do not have the services of a High Court judge; first tier courts always do and second tier courts sometimes do.

Recommendation 68.1 of the Auld Review is that 'all work within the jurisdiction of the Crown Court should be triable by a Circuit Judge unless, on referral to a Presiding Judge, he specially reserves it for trial by a High Court Judge' and Recommendation 69 is that 'the formal "tiering" of court centres for the trial of certain classes of cases should be abolished and replaced by a more flexible system, overseen by the Presiding Judges, for the assignment of cases, adapted to the needs of each circuit and the work, and having regard to the physical constraints and convenience of location of different courts'. These recommendations have not so far been taken up.

When the Crown Court is sitting as an appellate court from the magistrates' court, it comprises a Circuit judge or recorder and two lay justices (though up to four lay justices may sit).

Barristers and solicitors with rights of audience in the higher courts have rights of audience for trials on indictment. However, where the Crown Court is hearing an appeal from the magistrates' court, or a committal for sentence from the magistrates' court (see Chapter 4), all barristers and solicitors have rights of audience.

1.17 CROWN PROSECUTORS

Crown Prosecutors have to be either barristers or solicitors (s 1(3) of the Prosecution of Offences Act 1985).

Crown Prosecutors have 'all the powers of the Director [of Public Prosecutions] as to the institution and conduct of proceedings' (s 1(6)). Thus, a Crown Prosecutor can authorise the commencement of proceedings where the consent of the DPP is required (s 1(7)). Similarly, a Crown Prosecutor can discontinue proceedings under s 23 of the Prosecution of Offences Act 1985.

Crown Prosecutors, whether barrister or solicitors, may conduct trials in the magistrates' court and in the Crown Court but, in most cases, the CPS will brief counsel to prosecute in trials on indictment.

Crown Prosecutors obviously play a key role in ensuring that criminal cases are dealt with fairly and efficiently. In his *Review of the Criminal Courts*, Lord Justice Auld notes (in para 13 of Chapter 2) that the key to better preparation for, and efficient and effective disposal of, criminal cases is early identification of the issues. He identified four 'essential' components in this process:

- strong and independent prosecutors;
- efficient and properly paid defence lawyers;
- ready access by defence lawyers to their clients in custody; and
- a modern communications system.

1.18 OPEN COURT

Both the magistrates' court and the Crown Court normally sit in open court and there is a strong presumption that they should do. However, any court does have a discretion to sit *in camera* (that is, to exclude the public) if this is necessary for the administration of justice. Decisions to sit *in camera* are therefore very rare (see, generally, *Attorney General v Leveller Magazine Ltd* [1979] AC 440; [1979] 1 All ER 745).

1.19 ETHICAL ISSUES

For a discussion of ethical issues that arise in criminal cases, see:

- Boon, A and Levin, J, *The Ethics and Conduct of Lawyers in the UK*, 1999, Oxford: Hart Publishing.
- Blake, M and Ashworth, A, 'Some ethical issues in prosecuting and defending' [1998] Crim LR 16–34.

It is also instructive to look at Annex N of the Bar's Code of Conduct, part of which deals with Criminal Cases. It provides as follows:

STANDARDS APPLICABLE TO CRIMINAL CASES

10 *Introduction*

10.1 These standards are to be read together with the General Standards and the Code of Conduct. They are intended as a guide to those matters which specifically relate to practice in the criminal courts. They are not an alternative to the General Standards, which apply to all work carried out by a barrister. Particular reference is made to those paragraphs in the General Standards relating to the general conduct of a case (5.8), conduct in Court (5.10), discussion with witnesses (6.1, 6.2) and the use of documents belonging to other parties (7.1, 7.2, 7.3), which are not repeated in these standards.

11 *Responsibilities of Prosecuting Counsel*

11A The Standards and principles contained in this paragraph apply as appropriate to all practising barristers, whether in independent practice or employed and whether appearing as counsel in any given case or exercising any other professional capacity in connection with it.

11.1 Prosecuting counsel should not attempt to obtain a conviction by all means at his command. He should not regard himself as appearing for a party. He should lay before the Court fairly and impartially the whole of the facts which comprise the case for the prosecution and should assist the Court on all matters of law applicable to the case.

11.2 Prosecuting counsel should bear in mind at all times whilst he is instructed:

(i) that he is responsible for the presentation and general conduct of the case;

(ii) that he should use his best endeavours to ensure that all evidence or material that ought properly to be made available is either presented by the prosecution or disclosed to the defence.

11.3 Prosecuting counsel should, when instructions are delivered to him, read them expeditiously and, where instructed to do so, advise or confer on all aspects of the case well before its commencement.

11.4 In relation to cases tried in the Crown Court, prosecuting counsel:

(a) should ensure, if he is instructed to settle an indictment, that he does so promptly and within due time, and should bear in mind the desirability of not overloading an indictment with either too many defendants or too many counts, in order to present the prosecution case as simply and as concisely as possible;

(b) should ask, if the indictment is being settled by some other person, to see a copy of the indictment and should then check it;

(c) should decide whether any additional evidence is required and, if it is, should advise in writing and set out precisely what additional evidence is required with a view to serving it on the defence as soon as possible;

(d) should consider whether all witness statements in the possession of the prosecution have been properly served on the defendant in accordance with the Attorney General's Guidelines;

(e) should eliminate all unnecessary material in the case so as to ensure an efficient and fair trial, and in particular should consider the need for particular witnesses and exhibits and draft appropriate admissions for service on the defence;

(f) should in all Class 1 and Class 2 cases and in other cases of complexity draft a case summary for transmission to the Court.

11.5 Paragraphs 6 to 6.3.4 of the Written Standards for the Conduct of Professional Work refer.

11.6 Prosecuting counsel should at all times have regard to the report of Mr Justice Farquharson's Committee on the role of Prosecuting Counsel which is set out in Archbold. In particular, he should have regard to the following recommendations of the Farquharson Committee:

(a) Where counsel has taken a decision on a matter of policy with which his professional client has not agreed, it would be appropriate for him to submit to the Attorney General a written report of all the circumstances, including his reasons for disagreeing with those who instructed him;

(b) When counsel has had an opportunity to prepare his brief and to confer with those instructing him, but at the last moment before trial unexpectedly advises that the case should not proceed or that pleas to lesser offences should be accepted, and his professional client does not accept such advice, counsel should apply for an adjournment if instructed to do so;

(c) Subject to the above, it is for prosecuting counsel to decide whether to offer no evidence on a particular count or on the indictment as a whole and whether to accept pleas to a lesser count or counts.

11.7 It is the duty of prosecuting counsel to assist the Court at the conclusion of the summing-up by drawing attention to any apparent errors or omissions of fact or law.

11.8 In relation to sentence, prosecuting counsel:

(a) should not attempt by advocacy to influence the Court with regard to sentence: if, however, a defendant is unrepresented it is proper to inform the Court of any mitigating circumstances about which counsel is instructed;

(b) should be in a position to assist the Court if requested as to any statutory provisions relevant to the offence or the offender and as to any relevant guidelines as to sentence laid down by the Court of Appeal;

(c) should bring any such matters as are referred to in (b) above to the attention of the Court if in the opinion of prosecuting counsel the Court has erred;

(d) should bring to the attention of the Court any appropriate compensation, forfeiture and restitution matters which may arise on conviction, for example pursuant to sections 35–42 of the Powers of Criminal Courts Act 1973 and the Drug Trafficking Offences Act 1986;

(e) should draw the attention of the defence to any assertion of material fact made in mitigation which the prosecution believes to be untrue: if the defence persist in that assertion, prosecuting counsel should invite the Court to consider requiring the issue to be determined by the calling of evidence in accordance with the decision of the Court of Appeal in *R v Newton* (1983) 77 Cr App R 13.

12 *Responsibilities of Defence Counsel*

12.1 When defending a client on a criminal charge, a barrister must endeavour to protect his client from conviction except by a competent tribunal and upon legally admissible evidence sufficient to support a conviction for the offence charged.

12.2 A barrister acting for the defence:

(a) should satisfy himself, if he is briefed to represent more than one defendant, that no conflict of interest is likely to arise;

(b) should arrange a conference and if necessary a series of conferences with his professional and lay clients;

(c) should consider whether any enquiries or further enquiries are necessary and, if so, should advise in writing as soon as possible;

(d) should consider whether any witnesses for the defence are required and, if so, which;

(e) should consider whether a Notice of Alibi is required and, if so, should draft an appropriate notice;

(f) should consider whether it would be appropriate to call expert evidence for the defence and, if so, have regard to the rules of the Crown Court in relation to notifying the prosecution of the contents of the evidence to be given;

(g) should ensure that he has sufficient instructions for the purpose of deciding which prosecution witnesses should be cross-examined, and should then ensure that no other witnesses remain fully bound at the request of the defendant and request his professional client to inform the Crown Prosecution Service of those who can be conditionally bound;

(h) should consider whether any admissions can be made with a view to saving time and expense at trial, with the aim of admitting as much evidence as can properly be admitted in accordance with the barrister's duty to his client;

(i) should consider what admissions can properly be requested from the prosecution;

(j) should decide what exhibits, if any, which have not been or cannot be copied he wishes to examine, and should ensure that appropriate arrangements are made to examine them as promptly as possible so that there is no undue delay in the trial.

(k) should as to anything which he is instructed to submit in mitigation which casts aspersions on the conduct or character of a victim or witness in the case, notify the prosecution in advance so as to give prosecuting Counsel sufficient opportunity to consider his position under paragraph 11.8(e).

12.3 A barrister acting for a defendant should advise his lay client generally about his plea. In doing so he may, if necessary, express his advice in strong terms. He must, however, make it clear that the client has complete freedom of choice and that the responsibility for the plea is the client's.

12.4 A barrister acting for a defendant should advise his client as to whether or not to give evidence in his own defence but the decision must be taken by the client himself.

12.5.1 Where a defendant tells his counsel that he did not commit the offence with which he is charged but nevertheless insists on pleading guilty to it for reasons of his own, counsel should:

(a) advise the defendant that, if he is not guilty, he should plead not guilty but that the decision is one for the defendant; counsel must continue to represent him but only after he has advised what the consequences will be and that what can be submitted in mitigation can only be on the basis that the client is guilty.

(b) explore with the defendant why he wishes to plead guilty to a charge which he says he did not commit and whether any steps could be taken which would enable him to enter a plea of not guilty in accordance with his profession of innocence.

12.5.2 If the client maintains his wish to plead guilty, he should be further advised:

(a) what the consequences will be, in particular in gaining or adding to a criminal record and that it is unlikely that a conviction based on such a plea would be overturned on appeal;

(b) that what can be submitted on his behalf in mitigation can only be on the basis that he is guilty and will otherwise be strictly limited so that, for instance, counsel will not be able to assert that the defendant has shown remorse through his guilty plea.

12.5.3 If, following all of the above advice, the defendant persists in his decision to plead guilty:

(a) counsel may continue to represent him if he is satisfied that it is proper to do so;

(b) before a plea of guilty is entered counsel or a representative of his professional client who is present should record in writing the reasons for the plea;

(c) the defendant should be invited to endorse a declaration that he has given unequivocal instructions of his own free will that he intends to plead guilty even though he maintains that he did not commit the offence(s) and that he understands the advice given by counsel and in particular the restrictions placed on counsel in mitigating and the consequences to himself; the defendant should also be advised that he is under no obligation to sign; and

(d) if no such declaration is signed, counsel should make a contemporaneous note of his advice.

13   *Confessions of Guilt*

13.1   In considering the duty of counsel retained to defend a person charged with an offence who confesses to his counsel that he did commit the offence charged, it is essential to bear the following points clearly in mind:

(a) that every punishable crime is a breach of common or statute law committed by a person of sound mind and understanding;

(b) that the issue in a criminal trial is always whether the defendant is guilty of the offence charged, never whether he is innocent;

(c) that the burden of proof rests on the prosecution.

13.2   It follows that the mere fact that a person charged with a crime has confessed to his counsel that he did commit the offence charged is no bar to that barrister appearing or continuing to appear in his defence, nor indeed does such a confession release the barrister from his imperative duty to do all that he honourably can for his client.

13.3   Such a confession, however, imposes very strict limitations on the conduct of the defence. a barrister must not assert as true that which he knows to be false. He must not connive at, much less attempt to substantiate, a fraud.

13.4   While, therefore, it would be right to take any objections to the competency of the Court, to the form of the indictment, to the admissibility of any evidence or to the evidence admitted, it would be wrong to suggest that some other person had committed the offence charged, or to call any evidence which the barrister must know to be false having regard to the confession, such, for instance, as evidence in support of an alibi. In other words, a barrister must not (whether by calling the defendant or otherwise) set up an affirmative case inconsistent with the confession made to him.

13.5   A more difficult question is within what limits may counsel attack the evidence for the prosecution either by cross-examination or in his speech to the tribunal charged with the decision of the facts. No clearer rule can be laid down than this, that he is entitled to test the evidence given by each individual witness and to argue that the evidence taken as a whole is insufficient to amount to proof that the defendant is guilty of the offence charged. Further than this he ought not to go.

13.6   The foregoing is based on the assumption that the defendant has made a clear confession that he did commit the offence charged, and does not profess to deal with the very difficult questions which may present themselves to a barrister when a series of inconsistent statements are made to him by the defendant before or during the proceedings; nor does it deal with the questions which may arise where statements are made by the defendant which point almost irresistibly to the conclusion that the defendant is guilty but do not amount to a clear confession. Statements of this kind may inhibit the defence, but questions arising on them can only be answered after careful consideration of the actual circumstances of the particular case.

14 *General*

14.1 Both prosecuting and defence counsel:

(a) should ensure that the listing officer receives in good time their best estimate of the likely length of the trial (including whether or not there is to be a plea of guilty) and should ensure that the listing officer is given early notice of any change of such estimate or possible adjournment;

(b) should take all reasonable and practicable steps to ensure that the case is properly prepared and ready for trial by the time that it is first listed;

(c) should ensure that arrangements have been made in adequate time for witnesses to attend Court as and when required and should plan, so far as possible, for sufficient witnesses to be available to occupy the full Court day;

(d) should, if a witness (for example a doctor) can only attend Court at a certain time during the trial without great inconvenience to himself, try to arrange for that witness to be accommodated by raising the matter with the trial Judge and with his opponent;

(e) should take all necessary steps to comply with the *Practice Direction (Crime: Tape Recording of Police Interviews)* [1989] 1 WLR 631.

14.2 If properly remunerated (paragraph 502 of the Code), the barrister originally briefed in a case should attend all plea and directions hearings. If this is not possible, he must take all reasonable steps to ensure that the barrister who does appear is conversant with the case and is prepared to make informed decisions affecting the trial.

15 *Video Recordings*

15.1 When a barrister instructed and acting for the prosecution or the defence of an accused has in his possession a copy of a video recording of a child witness which has been identified as having been prepared to be admitted in evidence at a criminal trial in accordance with Section 54 of the Criminal Justice Act 1991, he must have regard to the following duties and obligations:

(a) Upon receipt of the recording, a written record of the date and time and from whom the recording was received must be made and a receipt must be given.

(b) The recording and its contents must be used only for the proper preparation of the prosecution or defence case or of an appeal against conviction and/or sentence, as the case may be, and the barrister must not make or permit any disclosure of the recording or its contents to any person except when, in his opinion, it is in the interests of his proper preparation of that case.

(c) The barrister must not make or permit any other person to make a copy of the recording, nor release the recording to the accused, and must ensure that:

(i) when not in transit or in use, the recording is always kept in a locked or secure place, and:

(ii) when in transit, the recording is kept safe and secure at all times and is not left unattended, especially in vehicles or otherwise.

(d) Proper preparation of the case may involve viewing the recording in the presence of the accused. If this is the case, viewing should be done:

(i) if the accused is in custody, only in the prison or other custodial institution where he is being held, in the presence of the barrister and/or his instructing solicitor.

      (ii) if the accused is on bail, at the solicitor's office or in counsel's chambers or elsewhere in the presence of the barrister and/or his instructing solicitor.

    (e) The recording must be returned to the solicitor as soon as practicable after the conclusion of the barrister's role in the case. A written record of the date and time despatched and to whom the recording was delivered for despatch must be made.

16   *Attendance of Counsel at Court*

16.1 Prosecuting counsel should be present throughout the trial, including the summing-up and the return of the jury. He may not absent himself without leave of the Court; but, if two or more barristers appear for the prosecution, the attendance of one is sufficient.

16.2.1 Defence counsel should ensure that the defendant is never left unrepresented at any stage of his trial.

16.2.2 Where a defendant is represented by one barrister, that barrister should normally be present throughout the trial and should only absent himself in exceptional circumstances which he could not reasonably be expected to foresee and provided that:

    (a) he has obtained the consent of the professional client (or his representative) and the lay client; and

    (b) a competent deputy takes his place.

16.2.3 Where a defendant is represented by two barristers, neither may absent himself except for good reason and then only when the consent of the professional client (or his representative) and of the lay client has been obtained, or when the case is legally aided and the barrister thinks it necessary to do so in order to avoid unnecessary public expense.

16.2.4 These rules are subject to modification in respect of lengthy trials involving numerous defendants. In such trials, where after the conclusion of the opening speech by the prosecution defending counsel is satisfied that during a specific part of the trial there is no serious possibility that events will occur which will relate to his client, he may with the consent of the professional client (or his representative) and of the lay client absent himself for that part of the trial. He should also inform the judge. In this event it is his duty:

    (a) to arrange for other defending counsel to guard the interests of his client;

    (b) to keep himself informed throughout of the progress of the trial and in particular of any development which could affect his client; and

    (c) not to accept any other commitment which would render it impracticable for him to make himself available at reasonable notice if the interests of his client so require.

16.3.1 If during the course of a criminal trial and prior to final sentence the defendant voluntarily absconds and the barrister's professional client, in accordance with the ruling of the Law Society, withdraws from the case, then the barrister too should withdraw. If the trial judge requests the barrister to remain to assist the Court, the barrister has an absolute discretion whether to do so or not. If he does remain, he should act on the basis that his instructions are withdrawn and he will not be entitled to use any material contained in his brief save for such part as has already been established in evidence before the Court. He should request the trial judge to instruct the jury that this is the basis on which he is prepared to assist the Court.

16.3.2 If for any reason the barrister's professional client does not withdraw from the case, the barrister retains an absolute discretion whether to continue to act. If he does continue, he should conduct the case as if his client were still present in Court but had decided not to give evidence and on the basis of any instruction he has received. He will be free to use any material contained in his brief and may cross-examine witnesses called for the prosecution and call witnesses for the defence.

17   *Appeals*

17.1.1 Attention is drawn to the Guide to Proceedings in the Court of Appeal Criminal Division ('the Guide') which is set out in full its original form at (1983) 77 Crim App R 138 and is summarised in a version amended in April 1990 Volume 1 of Archbold at 7–173 to 7–184.

17.1.2 In particular when advising after a client pleads guilty or is convicted, defence counsel is encouraged to follow the procedures set out at paragraphs 1.2 and 1.4 of the Guide.

17.2 If his client pleads guilty or is convicted, defence counsel should see his client after he has been sentenced in the presence of his professional client or his representative. He should then proceed as follows:

(a) if he is satisfied that there are no reasonable grounds of appeal he should so advise orally and certify in writing. Counsel is encouraged to certify using the form set out in Appendix 1 to the Guide. No further advice is necessary unless it is reasonable for a written advice to be given because the client reasonably requires it or because it is necessary eg in the light of the circumstances of the conviction, any particular difficulties at trial, the length and nature of the sentence passed, the effect thereof on the defendant or the lack of impact which oral advice given immediately after the trial may have on the particular defendant's mind.

(b) if he is satisfied that there are more reasonable grounds of appeal or if his view is a provisional one or if he requires more time to consider the prospects of a successful appeal he should so advise orally and certify in writing. Counsel is encouraged to certify using the form set out in Appendix 1 to the Guide. Counsel should then furnish written advice to the professional client as soon as he can and in any event within 14 days.

17.3 Counsel should not settle grounds of appeal unless he considers that such grounds are properly arguable, and in that event he should provide a reasoned written opinion in support of such grounds.

17.4 In certain cases counsel may not be able to perfect grounds of appeal without a transcript or other further information. In this event the grounds of appeal should be accompanied by a note to the Registrar setting out the matters on which assistance is required. Once such transcript or other information is available, counsel should ensure that the grounds of appeal are perfected by the inclusion of all necessary references.

17.5 Grounds of Appeal must be settled with sufficient particularity to enable the Registrar and subsequently the Court to identify clearly the matters relied upon.

17.6 If at any stage counsel is of the view that the appeal should be abandoned, he should at once set out his reasons in writing and send them to his professional client.

Code for Crown Prosecutors

1   **Introduction**

1.1   The decision to prosecute an individual is a serious step. Fair and effective prosecution is essential to the maintenance of law and order. Even in a small case a prosecution has serious implications for all involved — victims, witnesses and defendants. The Crown Prosecution Service applies the Code for Crown Prosecutors so that it can make fair and consistent decisions about prosecutions.

1.2 The Code helps the Crown Prosecution Service to play its part in making sure that justice is done. It contains information that is important to police officers and others who work in the criminal justice system and to the general public. Police officers should take account of the Code when they are deciding whether to charge a person with an offence.

1.3 The Code is also designed to make sure that everyone knows the principles that the Crown Prosecution Service applies when carrying out its work. By applying the same principles, everyone involved in the system is helping to treat victims fairly and to prosecute fairly but effectively.

2 General Principles

2.1 Each case is unique and must be considered on its own facts and merits. However, there are general principles that apply to the way in which Crown Prosecutors must approach every case.

2.2 Crown Prosecutors must be fair, independent and objective. They must not let any personal views about ethnic or national origin, sex, religious beliefs, political views or the sexual orientation of the suspect, victim or witness influence their decisions. They must not be affected by improper or undue pressure from any source.

2.3 It is the duty of Crown Prosecutors to make sure that the right person is prosecuted for the right offence. In doing so, Crown Prosecutors must always act in the interests of justice and not solely for the purpose of obtaining a conviction.

2.4 It is the duty of Crown Prosecutors to review, advise on and prosecute cases, ensuring that the law is properly applied, that all relevant evidence is put before the court and that obligations of disclosure are complied with, in accordance with the principles set out in this Code.

2.5 The CPS is a public authority for the purposes of the Human Rights Act 1998. Crown Prosecutors must apply the principles of the European Convention on Human Rights in accordance with the Act.

3 Review

3.1 Proceedings are usually started by the police. Sometimes they may consult the Crown Prosecution Service before starting a prosecution. Each case that the Crown Prosecution Service receives from the police is reviewed to make sure it meets the evidential and public interest tests set out in this Code. Crown Prosecutors may decide to continue with the original charges, to change the charges, or sometimes to stop the case.

3.2 Review is a continuing process and Crown Prosecutors must take account of any change in circumstances. Wherever possible, they talk to the police first if they are thinking about changing the charges or stopping the case. This gives the police the chance to provide more information that may affect the decision. The Crown Prosecution Service and the police work closely together to reach the right decision, but the final responsibility for the decision rests with the Crown Prosecution Service.

4 Code Tests

4.1 There are two stages in the decision to prosecute. The first stage is the evidential test. If the case does not pass the evidential test, it must not go ahead, no matter how important or serious it may be. If the case does meet the evidential test, Crown Prosecutors must decide if a prosecution is needed in the public interest.

4.2 This second stage is the public interest test. The Crown Prosecution Service will only start or continue with a prosecution when the case has passed both tests. The evidential test is explained in section 5 and the public interest test is explained in section 6.

5 The Evidential Test

5.1 Crown Prosecutors must be satisfied that there is enough evidence to provide a 'realistic prospect of conviction' against each defendant on each charge. They must consider what the defence case may be, and how that is likely to affect the prosecution case.

5.2 A realistic prospect of conviction is an objective test. It means that a jury or bench of magistrates, properly directed in accordance with the law, is more likely than not to convict the defendant of the charge alleged. This is a separate test from the one that the criminal courts themselves must apply. A jury or magistrates' court should only convict if satisfied so that it is sure of a defendant's guilt.

5.3 When deciding whether there is enough evidence to prosecute, Crown Prosecutors must consider whether the evidence can be used and is reliable. There will be many cases in which the evidence does not give any cause for concern. But there will also be cases in which the evidence may not be as strong as it first appears. Crown Prosecutors must ask themselves the following questions:

Can the evidence be used in court?

(a) Is it likely that the evidence will be excluded by the court? There are certain legal rules which might mean that evidence which seems relevant cannot be given at a trial. For example, is it likely that the evidence will be excluded because of the way in which it was gathered or because of the rule against using hearsay as evidence? If so, is there enough other evidence for a realistic prospect of conviction?

Is the evidence reliable?

(b) Is there evidence which might support or detract from the reliability of a confession? Is the reliability affected by factors such as the defendant's age, intelligence or level of understanding?

(c) What explanation has the defendant given? Is a court likely to find it credible in the light of the evidence as a whole? Does it support an innocent explanation?

(d) If the identity of the defendant is likely to be questioned, is the evidence about this strong enough?

(e) Is the witness's background likely to weaken the prosecution case? For example, does the witness have any motive that may affect his or her attitude to the case, or a relevant previous conviction?

(f) Are there concerns over the accuracy or credibility of a witness? Are these concerns based on evidence or simply information with nothing to support it? Is there further evidence which the police should be asked to seek out which may support or detract from the account of the witness?

5.4 Crown Prosecutors should not ignore evidence because they are not sure that it can be used or is reliable. But they should look closely at it when deciding if there is a realistic prospect of conviction.

6 The Public Interest Test

6.1 In 1951, Lord Shawcross, who was Attorney General, made the classic statement on public interest, which has been supported by Attorneys General ever since: 'It has never been the rule in this country — I hope it never will be — that suspected criminal offences must automatically be the subject of prosecution'. (House of Commons Debates, volume 483, column 681, 29 January 1951.)

6.2 The public interest must be considered in each case where there is enough evidence to provide a realistic prospect of conviction. A prosecution will usually take place unless there are public interest factors tending against prosecution which clearly outweigh those tending in favour. Although there may be public interest factors against prosecution in a particular case, often the prosecution should go ahead and those factors should be put to the court for consideration when sentence is being passed.

6.3 Crown Prosecutors must balance factors for and against prosecution carefully and fairly. Public interest factors that can affect the decision to prosecute usually depend on the seriousness of the offence or the circumstances of the suspect. Some factors may increase the need to prosecute but others may suggest that another course of action would be better.

The following lists of some common public interest factors, both for and against prosecution, are not exhaustive. The factors that apply will depend on the facts in each case.

Some common public interest factors in favour of prosecution

6.4 The more serious the offence, the more likely it is that a prosecution will be needed in the public interest. A prosecution is likely to be needed if:

(a) a conviction is likely to result in a significant sentence;

(b) a weapon was used or violence was threatened during the commission of the offence;

(c) the offence was committed against a person serving the public (for example, a police or prison officer, or a nurse);

(d) if the identity of the defendant is likely to be questioned, is the evidence about this strong enough?

(e) the defendant was in a position of authority or trust;

(f) there is evidence that the offence was premeditated;

(g) there is evidence that the offence was carried out by a group;

(h) the victim of the offence was vulnerable, has been put in considerable fear, or suffered personal attack, damage or disturbance;

(i) the offence was motivated by any form of discrimination against the victim's ethnic or national origin, sex, religious beliefs, political views or sexual orientation, or the suspect demonstrated hostility towards the victim based on any of those characteristics;

(j) there is a marked difference between the actual or mental ages of the defendant and the victim, or if there is any element of corruption;

(k) the defendant's previous convictions or cautions are relevant to the present offence;

(l) the defendant is alleged to have committed the offence whilst under an order of the court;

(m) there are grounds for believing that the offence is likely to be continued or repeated, for example, by a history of recurring conduct;

(n) the offence, although not serious in itself, is widespread in the area where it was committed.

Some common public interest factors against prosecution

6.5 A prosecution is less likely to be needed if:

(a) the court is likely to impose a nominal penalty;

(b) the defendant has already been made the subject of a sentence and any further conviction would be unlikely to result in the imposition of an additional sentence or order, unless the nature of the particular offence requires a prosecution;

(c) the offence was committed as a result of a genuine mistake or misunderstanding (these factors must be balanced against the seriousness of the offence);

(d) the loss or harm can be described as minor and was the result of a single incident, particularly if it was caused by a misjudgement;

(e) there has been a long delay between the offence taking place and the date of the trial, unless:

- the offence is serious;
- the delay has been caused in part by the defendant;
- the offence has only recently come to light; or
- the complexity of the offence has meant that there has been a long investigation;

(f) a prosecution is likely to have a bad effect on the victim's physical or mental health, always bearing in mind the seriousness of the offence;

(g) the defendant is elderly or is, or was at the time of the offence, suffering from significant mental or physical ill health, unless the offence is serious or there is a real possibility that it may be repeated. The Crown Prosecution Service, where necessary, applies Home Office guidelines about how to deal with mentally disordered offenders. Crown Prosecutors must balance the desirability of diverting a defendant who is suffering from significant mental or physical ill health with the need to safeguard the general public;

(h) the defendant has put right the loss or harm that was caused (but defendants must not avoid prosecution solely because they pay compensation); or

(i) details may be made public that could harm sources of information, international relations or national security.

6.6 Deciding on the public interest is not simply a matter of adding up the number of factors on each side. Crown Prosecutors must decide how important each factor is in the circumstances of each case and go on to make an overall assessment.

The relationship between the victim and the public interest

6.7 The Crown Prosecution Service prosecutes cases on behalf of the public at large and not just in the interests of any particular individual. However, when considering the public interest test Crown Prosecutors should always take into account the consequences for the victim of the decision whether or not to prosecute, and any views expressed by the victim or the victim's family.

6.8 It is important that a victim is told about a decision which makes a significant difference to the case in which he or she is involved. Crown Prosecutors should ensure that they follow any agreed procedures.

Youths

6.9 Crown Prosecutors must consider the interests of a youth when deciding whether it is in the public interest to prosecute. However Crown Prosecutors should not avoid prosecuting simply because of the defendant's age. The seriousness of the offence or the youth's past behaviour is very important.

6.10   Cases involving youths are usually only referred to the Crown Prosecution Service for prosecution if the youth has already received a reprimand and final warning, unless the offence is so serious that neither of these were appropriate. Reprimands and final warnings are intended to prevent re-offending and the fact that a further offence has occurred indicates that attempts to divert the youth from the court system have not been effective. So the public interest will usually require a prosecution in such cases, unless there are clear public interest factors against prosecution.

Police Cautions

6.11   These are only for adults. The police make the decision to caution an offender in accordance with Home Office guidelines.

6.12   When deciding whether a case should be prosecuted in the courts, Crown Prosecutors should consider the alternatives to prosecution. This will include a police caution. Again the Home Office guidelines should be applied. Where it is felt that a caution is appropriate, Crown Prosecutors must inform the police so that they can caution the suspect. If the caution is not administered because the suspect refuses to accept it or the police do not wish to offer it, then the Crown Prosecutor may review the case again.

7   Charges

7.1   Crown Prosecutors should select charges which:

(a) reflect the seriousness of the offending;

(b) give the court adequate sentencing powers; and

(c) enable the case to be presented in a clear and simple way.

This means that Crown Prosecutors may not always continue with the most serious charge where there is a choice. Further, Crown Prosecutors should not continue with more charges than are necessary.

7.2   Crown Prosecutors should never go ahead with more charges than are necessary just to encourage a defendant to plead guilty to a few. In the same way, they should never go ahead with a more serious charge just to encourage a defendant to plead guilty to a less serious one.

7.3   Crown Prosecutors should not change the charge simply because of the decision made by the court or the defendant about where the case will be heard.

8   Mode Of Trial

8.1   The Crown Prosecution Service applies the current guidelines for magistrates who have to decide whether cases should be tried in the Crown Court when the offence gives the option and the defendant does not indicate a guilty plea. (See the 'National Mode of Trial Guidelines' issued by the Lord Chief Justice.) Crown Prosecutors should recommend Crown Court trial when they are satisfied that the guidelines require them to do so.

8.2   Speed must never be the only reason for asking for a case to stay in the magistrates' courts. But Crown Prosecutors should consider the effect of any likely delay if they send a case to the Crown Court, and any possible stress on victims and witnesses if the case is delayed.

9   Accepting Guilty Pleas

9.1   Defendants may want to plead guilty to some, but not all, of the charges. Alternatively, they may want to plead guilty to a different, possibly less serious, charge because they are admitting only part of the crime. Crown Prosecutors should only accept the defendant's plea if they think the court is able to pass a sentence that matches the seriousness of the offending, particularly where there are aggravating features. Crown Prosecutors must never accept a guilty plea just because it is convenient.

9.2 Particular care must be taken when considering pleas which would enable the defendant to avoid the imposition of a mandatory minimum sentence. When pleas are offered, Crown Prosecutors must bear in mind the fact that ancillary orders can be made with some offences but not with others.

9.3 In cases where a defendant pleads guilty to the charges but on the basis of facts that are different from the prosecution case, and where this may significantly affect sentence, the court should be invited to hear evidence to determine what happened, and then sentence on that basis.

10 Re-starting a Prosecution

10.1 People should be able to rely on decisions taken by the Crown Prosecution Service. Normally, if the Crown Prosecution Service tells a suspect or defendant that there will not be a prosecution, or that the prosecution has been stopped, that is the end of the matter and the case will not start again. But occasionally there are special reasons why the Crown Prosecution Service will re-start the prosecution, particularly if the case is serious.

10.2 These reasons include:

(a) rare cases where a new look at the original decision shows that it was clearly wrong and should not be allowed to stand;

(b) cases which are stopped so that more evidence which is likely to become available in the fairly near future can be collected and prepared. In these cases, the Crown Prosecutor will tell the defendant that the prosecution may well start again; and

(c) cases which are stopped because of a lack of evidence but where more significant evidence is discovered later.

HUMAN RIGHTS ACT 1998

The provisions of the European Convention on Human Rights that have effect under the Act are set out in Sched 1. Those that are relevant to criminal litigation and sentencing are set out below.

Schedule 1

THE ARTICLES

Article 2: Right to life

1 Everyone's right to life shall be protected by law. No one shall be deprived of his life intentionally save in the execution of a sentence of a court following his conviction of a crime for which this penalty is provided by law.

2 Deprivation of life shall not be regarded as inflicted in contravention of this Article when it results from the use of force which is no more than absolutely necessary:

(a) in defence of any person from unlawful violence;

(b) in order to effect a lawful arrest or to prevent the escape of a person lawfully detained;

(c) in action lawfully taken for the purpose of quelling a riot or insurrection.

Article 3: Prohibition of torture

No one shall be subjected to torture or to inhuman or degrading treatment or punishment.

Article 4: Prohibition of slavery and forced labour

1 No one shall be held in slavery or servitude.

2 No one shall be required to perform forced or compulsory labour.

3 For the purpose of this Article the term 'forced or compulsory labour' shall not include:

(a) any work required to be done in the ordinary course of detention imposed according to the provisions of Article 5 of this Convention or during conditional release from such detention;

(b) any service of a military character or, in case of conscientious objectors in countries where they are recognised, service exacted instead of compulsory military service;

(c) any service exacted in case of an emergency or calamity threatening the life or well-being of the community;

(d) any work or service which forms part of normal civic obligations.

Article 5: Right to liberty and security

1 Everyone has the right to liberty and security of person. No one shall be deprived of his liberty save in the following cases and in accordance with a procedure prescribed by law:

(a) the lawful detention of a person after conviction by a competent court;

(b) the lawful arrest or detention of a person for non-compliance with the lawful order of a court or in order to secure the fulfilment of any obligation prescribed by law;

(c) the lawful arrest or detention of a person effected for the purpose of bringing him before the competent legal authority on reasonable suspicion of having committed an offence or when it is reasonably considered necessary to prevent his committing an offence or fleeing after having done so;

(d) the detention of a minor by lawful order for the purpose of educational supervision or his lawful detention for the purpose of bringing him before the competent legal authority;

(e) the lawful detention of persons for the prevention of the spreading of infectious diseases, of persons of unsound mind, alcoholics or drug addicts or vagrants;

(f) the lawful arrest or detention of a person to prevent his effecting an unauthorised entry into the country or of a person against whom action is being taken with a view to deportation or extradition.

2 Everyone who is arrested shall be informed promptly, in a language which he understands, of the reasons for his arrest and of any charge against him.

3 Everyone arrested or detained in accordance with the provisions of paragraph 1(c) of this Article shall be brought promptly before a judge or other officer authorised by law to exercise judicial power and shall be entitled to trial within a reasonable time or to release pending trial. Release may be conditioned by guarantees to appear for trial.

4 Everyone who is deprived of his liberty by arrest or detention shall be entitled to take proceedings by which the lawfulness of his detention shall be decided speedily by a court and his release ordered if the detention is not lawful.

5 Everyone who has been the victim of arrest or detention in contravention of the provisions of this Article shall have an enforceable right to compensation.

Article 6: Right to a fair trial

1 In the determination of his civil rights and obligations or of any criminal charge against him, everyone is entitled to a fair and public hearing within a reasonable time by an independent and impartial tribunal established by law. Judgment shall be pronounced publicly but the press and public may be excluded from all or part of the trial in the interest of morals, public order or national security in a democratic society, where the interests of juveniles or the protection of the private life of the parties so require, or to the extent strictly necessary in the opinion of the court in special circumstances where publicity would prejudice the interests of justice.

2 Everyone charged with a criminal offence shall be presumed innocent until proved guilty according to law.

3 Everyone charged with a criminal offence has the following minimum rights:
   (a) to be informed promptly, in a language which he understands and in detail, of the nature and cause of the accusation against him;
   (b) to have adequate time and facilities for the preparation of his defence;
   (c) to defend himself in person or through legal assistance of his own choosing or, if he has not sufficient means to pay for legal assistance, to be given it free when the interests of justice so require;
   (d) to examine or have examined witnesses against him and to obtain the attendance and examination of witnesses on his behalf under the same conditions as witnesses against him;
   (e) to have the free assistance of an interpreter if he cannot understand or speak the language used in court.

Article 7: No punishment without law

1 No one shall be held guilty of any criminal offence on account of any act or omission which did not constitute a criminal offence under national or international law at the time when it was committed. Nor shall a heavier penalty be imposed than the one that was applicable at the time the criminal offence was committed.

2 This Article shall not prejudice the trial and punishment of any person for any act or omission which, at the time when it was committed, was criminal according to the general principles of law recognised by civilised nations.

Article 8: Right to respect for private and family life

1   Everyone has the right to respect for his private and family life, his home and his correspondence.

2   There shall be no interference by a public authority with the exercise of this right except such as is in accordance with the law and is necessary in a democratic society in the interests of national security, public safety or the economic well being of the country, for the prevention of disorder or crime, for the protection of health or morals, or for the protection of the rights and freedoms of others.

Article 9: Freedom of thought, conscience and religion

1   Everyone has the right to freedom of thought, conscience and religion; this right includes freedom to change his religion or belief and freedom, either alone or in community with others and in public or private, to manifest his religion or belief, in worship, teaching, practice and observance.

2   Freedom to manifest one's religion or beliefs shall be subject only to such limitations as are prescribed by law and are necessary in a democratic society in the interests of public safety, for the protection of public order, health or morals, or for the protection of the rights and freedoms of others.

Article 10: Freedom of expression

1   Everyone has the right to freedom of expression. This right shall include freedom to hold opinions and to receive and impart information and ideas without interference by public authority and regardless of frontiers. This Article shall not prevent States from requiring the licensing of broadcasting, television or cinema enterprises.

2   The exercise of these freedoms, since it carries with it duties and responsibilities, may be subject to such formalities, conditions, restrictions or penalties as are prescribed by law and are necessary in a democratic society, in the interests of national security, territorial integrity or public safety, for the prevention of disorder or crime, for the protection of health or morals, for the protection of the reputation or rights of others, for preventing the disclosure of information received in confidence, or for maintaining the authority and impartiality of the judiciary.

Article 11: Freedom of assembly and association

1   Everyone has the right to freedom of peaceful assembly and to freedom of association with others, including the right to form and to join trade unions for the protection of his interests.

2   No restrictions shall be placed on the exercise of these rights other than such as are prescribed by law and are necessary in a democratic society in the interests of national security or public safety, for the prevention of disorder or crime, for the protection of health or morals or for the protection of the rights and freedoms of others. This Article shall not prevent the imposition of lawful restrictions on the exercise of these rights by members of the armed forces, of the police or of the administration of the State.

Article 14: Prohibition of discrimination

The enjoyment of the rights and freedoms set forth in this Convention shall be secured without discrimination on any ground such as sex, race, colour, language, religion, political or other opinion, national or social origin, association with a national minority, property, birth or other status.

Article 18: Limitation on use of restrictions on rights

The restrictions permitted under this Convention to the said rights and freedoms shall not be applied for any purpose other than those for which they have been prescribed.

CHAPTER 2

BAIL

2.1 INTRODUCTION

In this chapter, we see what happens at the defendant's first court appearance and the subsequent adjournments before the case is ready to proceed to its next stage. In particular, we examine the principles which govern whether the defendant should be held in custody or granted bail prior to the trial.

2.2 ADJOURNMENTS

Adjournments are often necessary to enable the defendant to instruct solicitors or to give the prosecution a chance to prepare advance information or committal statements. At each adjournment, the defendant is told the next date upon which he must attend court.

The granting of an adjournment is a matter for the court's discretion, but the rules of natural justice require that both sides should be allowed to prepare and present their cases properly (*R v Thames Magistrates' Court ex p Polemis* [1974] 1 WLR 1371; [1974] 2 All ER 1219).

In *R v Kingston-upon-Thames Justices ex p Martin* [1994] Imm AR 172, it was said that the following factors should be taken into account in deciding whether or not to grant an adjournment:

- the importance of the proceedings;
- the likely adverse consequences for the person seeking the adjournment;
- the risk of prejudice if the application is not granted;
- the convenience of the court;
- the interests of justice in ensuring that cases are dealt with efficiently; and
- the extent to which the applicant has been responsible for the circumstances which have led to the application for an adjournment.

At the heart of the law relating to adjournments is the principle that the parties should be given every reasonable opportunity to prepare their cases. For example, in *R v Sunderland Justices ex p Dryden* (1994) *The Times*, 18 May, it was held that, where a defendant applied for an adjournment in order to obtain expert evidence, the magistrates could not refuse that application on the ground that the expert called by the prosecution was independent.

Usually, the fact that there have been previous adjournments in a case will militate against further adjournments. However, in *R v Highbury Juvenile Court ex p DPP* [1993] COD 390, the case had been adjourned three times. On the next occasion the case was listed, a prosecution witness failed to attend. The defendant argued that his recollection of the events leading up to the charge was becoming dim and that the case should be dismissed. The magistrates refused a prosecution application for an adjournment and, as the prosecution was unable to call any evidence, dismissed the case. It was held by the Divisional Court (rather surprisingly) that the magistrates had acted perversely in refusing a fourth adjournment. However, in view of the delay, the Divisional Court took no action and so the acquittal stood.

In practice, an adjournment is only refused if the court takes the view that the party requesting the adjournment *should* be in a position to proceed now.

2.3   REMANDS: PROCEDURE IN COURT

Where a defendant is before the court because he has been arrested and charged, an adjournment is called a 'remand'. The remand may be in custody or on bail. This is governed by the Bail Act 1976.

It is usually the Crown Prosecution Service (CPS) who makes the formal application for the adjournment (although there is no reason why it could not be the defence, if the prosecution are ready to proceed but the defence are not).

The CPS representative is asked by the court if there are any objections to bail and, if so, to summarise them. The objections are based on a form in the CPS file which has been filled in by the police. A list of the defendant's previous convictions (if any) will also be handed to the court.

There is no requirement for formal evidence of the matters which give rise to the objections to bail to be given (*R v Mansfield Justices ex p Sharkey* [1985] QB 613). The objections to bail are simply given by the CPS representative in court; a police officer will not be called to give evidence.

The defendant may then make an application for bail. The defence will try to show that the prosecution objections are ill-founded or that the objections can be met by the imposition of conditions.

In *R v Isleworth Crown Court ex p Commissioner of Customs & Excise* [1990] Crim LR 859, it was said that the prosecution have a right to reply to the defence submissions if this is necessary to correct alleged mis-statements of fact in what the defence have said.

The court then comes to a decision. If bail is refused, the court must say why. The reason(s) must be based on the grounds for withholding bail set out in the Bail Act 1976 and must be recorded in a certificate which is handed to the defendant.

The Schedule to the Justices' Clerks Rules 1999 (SI 1999/2784) empowers a justices' clerk (or a person appointed to assist a justices' clerk) to perform the following functions connected with bail:

- para 8: to extend bail on the same conditions as those (if any) previously imposed, or, with the consent of the prosecutor and the accused, impose or vary conditions of bail.
- para 9: to further adjourn criminal proceedings with the consent of the prosecutor and the accused, but only if '(a) the accused, not having been remanded on the previous adjournment, is not remanded on the further adjournment; or (b) the accused, having been remanded on bail on the previous adjournment, is remanded on bail on the like terms and conditions, or, with the consent of the prosecutor and the accused, on other terms and conditions'.
- para 10: (1) to further adjourn criminal proceedings, where there has been no objection by the prosecutor, where the accused, having been remanded on bail on the previous adjournment, is remanded on bail on the like terms and conditions in

his absence; (2) to remand the accused on bail in his absence at the time of further adjourning the proceedings in pursuance of para 10(1).

2.4   THE BAIL ACT 1976

Section 4(1) of the Bail Act 1976 provides that, 'A person to whom this section applies shall be granted bail except as provided in Schedule 1 to this Act'. This is sometimes said to create a 'right to bail'. This description is rather inaccurate. It would be better to say that s 4 creates a (rebuttable) presumption in favour of bail.

Section 4(2) sets out the scope of s 4. It applies to:

... a person who is accused of an offence when—

(a)   he appears or is brought before a magistrates' court or the Crown Court in the course of or in connection with proceedings for the offence, or

(b)   he applies to a court for bail [or for a variation of the conditions of bail] in connection with the proceedings.

Section 4(4) provides that s 4 also applies:

... to a person who has been convicted of an offence and whose case is adjourned by the court for the purpose of enabling inquiries or a report to be made to assist the court in dealing with him for the offence.

In summary, therefore, the presumption in favour of bail applies at all stages prior to conviction, and also after conviction, but only where the case is adjourned for a pre-sentence report.

Where s 4 does not apply (for example, when the defendant appeals against conviction or sentence or where the defendant is committed for sentence following summary conviction of an either way offence), the court nevertheless has a discretion to grant bail.

2.4.1   Imprisonable offences

If the defendant is charged with (or has been convicted of) an offence which is punishable with imprisonment, the presumption in favour of bail may be rebutted if the court finds that one or more of the grounds for withholding bail set out in Pt 1 of Sched 1 to the Bail Act applies.

2.4.1.1 Grounds for withholding bail

Those grounds are as follows:

• Under para 2:

the defendant need not be granted bail if the court is satisfied that there are substantial grounds for believing that the defendant, if released on bail (whether subject to conditions or not) would:

(a)   fail to surrender to custody; or

(b)   commit an offence while on bail; or

(c)   interfere with witnesses or otherwise obstruct the course of justice, whether in relation to himself or any other person.

These are grounds that are most commonly invoked in practice.

- Under para 2A:

The defendant need not be granted bail if (a) the offence with which he is charged is an indictable offence or an offence triable either way; and (b) it appears to the court that he was on bail in criminal proceedings on the date of the offence.

This exception to the presumption in favour of bail (that, at the time of the present offence, the defendant was already on bail in respect of earlier alleged offences) is amended by s 14(1) of the Criminal Justice Act 2003 to read as follows:

2A(1)If the defendant falls within this paragraph he may not be granted bail unless the court is satisfied that there is no significant risk of his committing an offence while on bail (whether subject to conditions or not).

(2)   The defendant falls within this paragraph if—
     (a) he is aged 18 or over, and
     (b) it appears to the court that he was on bail in criminal proceedings on the date of the offence.

This amendment was made to ensure conformity with the Human Rights Act 1998. The Law Commission (Law Com No 269) had recommended that the Bail Act 1976 be amended to make it plain that the fact that the defendant was on bail at the time of the alleged offence is not an independent ground for the refusal of bail, as para 2A (as originally drafted) appeared to suggest, but is one of the considerations that the court should take into account when considering withholding bail on the ground that there is a real risk that the defendant will commit an offence while on bail. It is, of course, important in this context to remember the presumption of innocence: the accused is *alleged* to have committed an offence while on bail as a result of *allegations* of an earlier offence; at this stage, it cannot be assumed that he is guilty of either offence, since neither offence has been proved.

- Under para 3:

... the defendant need not be granted bail if the court is satisfied that the defendant should be kept in custody for his own protection or, if he is a child or young person, for his own welfare.

- Under para 4:

... the defendant need not be granted bail if he is in custody in pursuance of the sentence of a court.

In other words, the accused is already serving a custodial sentence imposed for an earlier offence.

- Under para 5:

... the defendant need not be granted bail where the court is satisfied that it has not been practicable to obtain sufficient information for the purpose of taking the decisions required by this Part of this Schedule for want of time since the institution of the proceedings against him.

In other words, the court is satisfied that lack of time since the commencement of proceedings means that it has been impracticable to obtain the information needed to decide the question of bail properly.

- Under para 6:

  ... the defendant need not be granted bail if, having been released on bail in or in connection with the proceedings for the offence ... he has been arrested in pursuance of section 7 of this Act.

  In other words, the accused has been arrested for absconding under s 7 of the Bail Act.

  This paragraph is amended by s 15(1) of the Criminal Justice Act 2003 to read as follows:

  (1) If the defendant falls within this paragraph, he may not be granted bail unless the court is satisfied that there is no significant risk that, if released on bail (whether subject to conditions or not), he would fail to surrender to custody.

  (2) Subject to sub-paragraph (3) below, the defendant falls within this paragraph if—

     (a) he is aged 18 or over, and

     (b) it appears to the court that, having been released on bail in or in connection with the proceedings for the offence, he failed to surrender to custody.

  (3) Where it appears to the court that the defendant had reasonable cause for his failure to surrender to custody, he does not fall within this paragraph unless it also appears to the court that he failed to surrender to custody at the appointed place as soon as reasonably practicable after the appointed time.

  (4) For the purposes of sub-paragraph (3) above, a failure to give to the defendant a copy of the record of the decision to grant him bail shall not constitute a reasonable cause for his failure to surrender to custody.

  The Law Commission (Law Com No 269) had recommended that para 6 be repealed, on the basis that it is superfluous (in that the circumstances leading to the defendant being arrested under s 7 may properly be taken into account, under para 9(c) of Pt I of Sched 1 to the Bail Act 1976, as a possible reason for concluding that one of the Convention-compatible grounds for withholding bail is satisfied).

  Under the revised version of para 6, the court is required to refuse bail to an adult defendant who has failed without reasonable cause to surrender to custody in answer to bail in the same proceedings, unless the court is satisfied that there is no significant risk that he would fail again to surrender if released.

- Section 19(4) of the Criminal Justice Act 2003 (in force since April 2004) adds paras 6A–6C to Schedule 1. These provide that a defendant aged 18 or over who has been charged with an imprisonable offence will not be granted bail (unless the court is satisfied that there is no significant risk of his committing an offence while on bail), where the three conditions set out in para 6B apply, namely:

  (a) there is drug test evidence that the person has a specified Class A drug in his body (by way of a lawful test obtained under s 63B of the Police and Criminal Evidence Act 1984 or s 161 of the Criminal Justice Act 2003);

  (b) either he is charged with an offence under s 5(2) or (3) of the Misuse of Drugs Act 1971 and the offence relates to a specified Class A drug; or the court is satisfied that there are substantial grounds for believing that the misuse of a specified Class A drug caused or contributed to the offence with which he is charged or that offence was motivated wholly or partly by his intended misuse of a specified Class A drug; and

(c)   the person does not agree to undergo an assessment (carried out by a suitably qualified person) of whether he is dependent upon or has a propensity to misuse any specified Class A drugs, or he has undergone such an assessment but does not agree to participate in any relevant follow-up which has been offered.

If an assessment or follow-up is proposed and agreed to, it will be a condition of bail that they be undertaken (s 3(6E) of the Bail Act 1976).

• Where the defendant has been convicted and the case is adjourned for a pre-sentence report to be prepared, there is an additional ground, under para 7, for withholding bail, namely:

... where his case is adjourned for inquiries or a report, the defendant need not be granted bail if it appears to the court that it would be impracticable to complete the inquiries or make the report without keeping the defendant in custody.

In other words, it would be impracticable to produce the pre-sentence report without keeping the defendant in custody.

2.4.1.2 Factors to be taken into account

The factors which have to be taken into account in deciding whether or not the grounds set out in Sched 1 have been established are listed in para 9 of that Schedule. They are as follows:

(a)   'The nature and seriousness of the offence or default (and the probable method of dealing with the defendant for it)': in other words, the gravity of the offence. The point is that if a custodial sentence is likely, that is an incentive to abscond.

(b)   'The character, antecedents, associations and community ties of the defendant.' The phrase 'character and antecedents' refers to any previous convictions. These may make a custodial sentence more likely (especially if the defendant, if convicted of the present offence, will be in breach of a suspended sentence of imprisonment).

Note that, currently, if a magistrate hears about a defendant's previous convictions in the course of a bail application, that magistrate is disqualified from trying the defendant if a summary trial takes place subsequently (s 42 of the Magistrates' Courts Act 1980). However, this provision will be repealed when the repeals in Pt 4 of Sched 37 to the Criminal Justice Act 2003 come into effect.

The word 'associations' is generally taken to refer to undesirable friends with criminal records. Examining the defendant's 'community ties' involves looking at how easy it would be for the defendant to abscond and how much he has to lose by absconding. How long has the defendant lived at his present address? Is he single or married? Does he have dependant children? Is he in employment? How long has he had his present job? Does he have a mortgage or a protected tenancy?

(c)   'The defendant's record as respects the fulfilment of his obligations under previous grants of bail in criminal proceedings.' In other words, the defendant's bail record: has he absconded or committed offences while on bail in the past? Absconding in earlier proceedings is regarded as evidence of a risk that he may do so again.

(d) 'Except in the case of a defendant whose case is adjourned for inquiries or a report, the strength of the evidence of his having committed the offence ...' The strength of the prosecution case is relevant in that, if the defendant has a good chance of acquittal (for example, the prosecution case rests on uncorroborated identification evidence), it can be argued that there is no point in the defendant absconding. Conversely, if the prosecution case is strong, so that conviction is likely, the defendant may abscond rather than 'face the music' (especially if a custodial sentence is likely).

Paragraph 9 concludes with the words, 'as well as to any others [ie considerations] which appear to be relevant', thus making it clear that the list of factors set out above is not exhaustive.

In particular, it should also be noted that s 4(9) of the Bail Act (added by s 58 of the Criminal Justice and Court Services Act 2000) stipulates that, 'in taking any decisions required by Part I or II of Schedule 1 to this Act, the considerations to which the court is to have regard include, so far as relevant, any misuse of controlled drugs by the defendant'.

Also, s 14(2) of the Criminal Justice Act 2003 inserts a para 9AA (applicable to juvenile defendants), which reads as follows:

(1)   This paragraph applies if—
   (a) the defendant is under the age of 18, and
   (b) it appears to the court that he was on bail in criminal proceedings on the date of the offence.

(2)   In deciding for the purposes of paragraph 2(1) of this Part of this Schedule whether it is satisfied that there are substantial grounds for believing that the defendant, if released on bail (whether subject to conditions or not), would commit an offence while on bail, the court shall give particular weight to the fact that the defendant was on bail in criminal proceedings on the date of the offence.

Section 15(2) of the Criminal Justice Act 2003 also inserts a para 9AB (applicable to juvenile defendants), which provides as follows:

(1)   Subject to sub-paragraph (2) below, this paragraph applies if—
   (a) the defendant is under the age of 18, and
   (b) it appears to the court that, having been released on bail in or in connection with the proceedings for the offence, he failed to surrender to custody.

(2)   Where it appears to the court that the defendant had reasonable cause for his failure to surrender to custody, this paragraph does not apply unless it also appears to the court that he failed to surrender to custody at the appointed place as soon as reasonably practicable after the appointed time.

(3)   In deciding for the purposes of paragraph 2(1) of this Part of this Schedule whether it is satisfied that there are substantial grounds for believing that the defendant, if released on bail (whether subject to conditions or not), would fail to surrender to custody, the court shall give particular weight to—
   (a) where the defendant did not have reasonable cause for his failure to surrender to custody, the fact that he failed to surrender to custody, or
   (b) where he did have reasonable cause for his failure to surrender to custody, the fact that he failed to surrender to custody at the appointed place as soon as reasonably practicable after the appointed time.

Thus, the court is required, in assessing the risk of future absconding in the case of defendants under the age of 18, to give particular weight to the fact that they have failed to surrender to custody.

2.4.2 Murder, manslaughter and rape

Section 25 of the Criminal Justice and Public Order Act 1994 (as amended by s 56 of the Crime and Disorder Act 1998) applies where the defendant is charged with murder, attempted murder, manslaughter, rape or attempted rape and has previously been convicted of one of these offences in the past. In a case to which s 25 applies, bail may only be granted if there are 'exceptional circumstances' which justify the grant of bail. In *R (O) v Harrow Crown Court* [2003] EWHC 868; [2003] 1 WLR 2756, the Divisional Court held that s 25 of the Criminal Justice and Public Order Act 1994 is compatible with the right to liberty guaranteed by Art 5 of the European Convention on Human Rights. However, the judges differed as to how s 25 actually operates, Kennedy LJ holding that s 25 effectively imposes a neutral burden (the court having to be 'satisfied' that there are exceptional circumstances), but Hooper J holding that s 25 should be regarded as placing an evidential burden on the defendant to produce or point to material which supports the existence of exceptional circumstances, so that it is then for the prosecution to satisfy the court that bail should not be granted.

2.4.3 Non-imprisonable offences

The grounds for withholding bail where the offence, or every offence, of which the defendant is accused or convicted is one which is not punishable with imprisonment are contained in Pt 2 of Sched 1 to the Bail Act 1976. This provides that a defendant who is charged with (or convicted of) a non-imprisonable offence need not be granted bail if:

- Under para 2:

  (a)   it appears to the court that, having been previously granted bail in criminal proceedings, he has failed to surrender to custody in accordance with his obligations under the grant of bail; and (b) the court believes, in view of that failure, that the defendant, if released on bail (whether subject to conditions or not) would fail to surrender to custody.

- Under para 3:

  ... the court is satisfied that the defendant should be kept in custody for his own protection or, if he is a child or young person, for his own welfare.

- Under para 4:

  ... he is in custody in pursuance of the sentence of a court.

  (that is, he is already serving a custodial sentence).

- Under para 5:

  (a)   having been released on bail in or in connection with the proceedings for the offence, he has been arrested in pursuance of section 7 of this Act; and (b) the court is satisfied that there are substantial grounds for believing that the defendant, if released on bail (whether subject to conditions or not) would fail to surrender to custody, commit an offence on bail or interfere with witnesses or otherwise obstruct the course of justice (whether in relation to himself or any other person).

This version of para 5 was substituted by s 13(4) of the Criminal Justice Act 2003 (in force since April 2004) to ensure conformity with the Human Rights Act 1998. The Law Commission (Law Com No 269) recommended that the paragraph be amended by adding a requirement that the court must be satisfied that there are substantial grounds for believing that the defendant, if released on bail (whether subject to conditions or not), would fail to surrender to custody; commit an offence while on bail; or interfere with witnesses or otherwise obstruct the course of justice.

It is very rare for bail to be refused in the case of non-imprisonable offences. Note that bail cannot be refused on the grounds that the defendant is likely to abscond or to commit offences while on bail.

2.5   CONDITIONS

If the magistrates grant unconditional bail, the defendant's only duty is to attend court on the date of the next hearing (s 3(1) of the Bail Act).

It is, however, open to the court to attach conditions to the grant of bail. Section 3 of the Act provides as follows:

(4)   He may be required, before release on bail, to provide a surety or sureties to secure his surrender to custody.

(5)   He may be required, before release on bail, to give security for his surrender to custody.
      The security may be given by him or on his behalf.

(6)   He may be required to comply, before release on bail or later, with such requirements as appear to the court to be necessary—

      (a) to secure that he surrenders to custody,

      (b) to secure that he does not commit an offence while on bail,

      (c) to secure that he does not interfere with witnesses or otherwise obstruct the course of justice whether in relation to himself or any other person,

      (ca) for his own protection or, if he is a child or young person, for his own welfare or in his own interests,

      (d) to secure that he makes himself available for the purpose of enabling inquiries or a report to be made to assist the court in dealing with him for the offence

      (e) to secure that before the time appointed for him to surrender to custody, he attends an interview with an authorised advocate or authorised litigator, as defined by section 119(1) of the Courts and Legal Services Act 1990;

   ...

(6ZAA) Subject to section 3AA below, if he is a child or young person he may be required to comply with requirements imposed for the purpose of securing the electronic monitoring of his compliance with any other requirement imposed on him as a condition of bail.

(6ZA) Where he is required under sub-section (6) above to reside in a bail hostel or probation hostel, he may also be required to comply with the rules of the hostel.

Paragraph 3(6)(ca) was added by s 13 of the Criminal Justice Act 2003 (in force since April 2004) in response to concern by the Law Commission that there was no power to impose a bail condition for the protection of the defendant even though one of the exceptions to the right to bail, in the Bail Act 1976, is based on the need for protection of the defendant, and Convention case law recognises that, in certain circumstances, the protection of the defendant is capable of being a relevant and sufficient reason for detention.

Section 3 does not provide a comprehensive list of conditions that may be attached to the grant of bail, but it does set out, in sub-s (6), the basis on which conditions may be attached.

It should be noted that s 3(2) provides that 'No recognizance for his surrender to custody shall be taken from him'. In other words, an accused cannot act as surety for himself.

Section 19(2) of the Criminal Justice Act 2003 (in force since April 2004) adds sub-ss 6C–6E to s 3 of the Bail Act 1976. These provide that, where (a) the conditions set out in para 6B of Part 1 of Sched 1 are satisfied (namely, there is drug test evidence that the person has a specified Class A drug in his body, and either the offence is a drugs offence associated with a specified Class A drug or the court is satisfied that there are substantial grounds for believing that the misuse of a specified Class A drug caused or contributed to that offence or provided its motivation), and (b) the person has been offered an assessment of whether he is dependent upon or has a propensity to misuse any specified Class A drugs (or such an assessment has been carried out and he has been offered follow-up), and (c) he has agreed to undergo that assessment and participate in any follow-up, then the court, if it grants bail, shall impose as a condition of bail that the defendant both undergoes the relevant assessment and participates in any relevant follow-up proposed to him or, if a relevant assessment has been carried out, that the defendant participates in the relevant follow-up (s 3(6D)).

2.5.1   Examples of commonly imposed conditions

Sureties and security are the only conditions specifically mentioned in the Bail Act 1976. However, the court can impose any condition it thinks appropriate, provided that the condition is necessary on the grounds set out in the previous paragraph.

Commonly imposed conditions include the following:

- surety (where one or more persons, other than the defendant, promise to pay a specified sum to the court if the defendant absconds: see 2.6 below for further details);
- security (where the defendant deposits money or one or more valuable items with the court). If the defendant absconds the court can order the forfeiture of some or all of the security;
- residence (that is, living and sleeping at a specified address);
- residence in a bail hostel (in which case, it is also a condition that the defendant must comply with the hostel rules (s 3(6ZA));
- reporting to a specified police station (on specified days and at specified times);
- curfew (requiring the defendant to stay indoors during specified hours at night);
- not to enter a particular building or to go to a specified place or to go within a specified distance of a certain address;
- not to contact, directly or indirectly, the victim or any named prosecution witnesses;

- surrender of defendant's passport to the police;
- the court can require the defendant, before the time appointed for him to surrender to custody, to attend an interview with his solicitor (s 3(6)(e)).

In *McDonald v Procurator Fiscal, Elgin* (2003) *The Times*, 17 April (a case which came before the High Court of Justiciary in Scotland), the defendant had been granted bail subject to a condition that he remain in his dwelling at all times except between 10 am and 12 noon. The court held that this (rather onerous) requirement did not amount to detention or deprivation of his freedom and did not constitute an infringement of Art 5 of the European Convention on Human Rights.

In *R (CPS) v Chorley Justices* [2002] EWHC 2162; (2002) 166 JP 764, the question at issue was whether justices are empowered to attach a condition to the grant of bail, that the defendant will present himself at the door of his residence when required to do so by a police officer during the hours of curfew. It was held that there is power, under s 3(6) of the Bail Act 1976, to impose such 'door-step' conditions, but it is a question of fact in each case whether such a condition would be necessary.

In *R (Stevens) v Truro Magistrates' Court* [2001] EWHC 558 (Admin); [2002] 1 WLR 144, it was held that it is permissible for a third party to make available an asset to a defendant in order to enable him to give it as security for his release on bail and the court can accept such an asset. However, as it is the defendant himself who gives the security, the arrangements the defendant might make with those who helped him put up the requisite security are not to be a matter for the court. There is no obligation for the third party to be notified before the security is forfeited on the defendant's non-attendance.

Under ss 131 and 132 of the Criminal Justice and Police Act 2001, where a juvenile is granted bail, compliance with any bail conditions can be enforced through electronic monitoring, provided that (a) he has attained the age of 12; (b) either (i) he is charged with a violent or sexual offence, or an offence carrying at least 14 years' imprisonment, or (ii) he is charged with an imprisonable offence and he has a recent history of repeatedly committing imprisonable offences while on bail or to local authority accommodation; and (c) a youth offending team has informed the court of its opinion that the imposition of the requirement is suitable for the juvenile.

2.5.2 When may conditions be imposed?

Paragraph 8(1) of Sched 1, Pt 1 (as amended by the Criminal Justice Act 2003) makes it clear that no conditions shall be imposed:

> ... unless it appears to the court that it is necessary to do so for the purpose of preventing the occurrence of any of the events mentioned in paragraph 2 of this Part of this Schedule [namely, the court is satisfied that there are substantial grounds for believing that the defendant, if released on bail, will fail to surrender to custody, or commit an offence while on bail, or interfere with witnesses or otherwise obstruct the course of justice, whether in relation to himself or any other person] or for the defendant's own protection or, if he is a child or young person, for his own welfare or in his own interests.

In *R v Mansfield Justices ex p Sharkey* [1985] QB 613; [1985] 1 All ER 193, Lord Lane CJ said that whereas there have to be substantial grounds for believing that the defendant will abscond, commit further offences, etc, for bail to be withheld altogether, the test for the imposition of conditions is a lower one. To impose conditions on the grant of bail, it is enough if the justices 'perceive a real and not a fanciful risk' of the defendant absconding, committing further offences, etc. In *R (CPS) v Chorley Justices* [2002] EWHC 2162; (2002) 166 JP 764, the court noted that the only prerequisite for imposing conditions on bail under s 3(6) is that, in the circumstances of the particular case, imposition of the condition is necessary to achieve the aims specified in the section.

2.5.3   Non-imprisonable offence

In *R v Bournemouth Magistrates ex p Cross* (1989) 89 Cr App R 90, it was held that conditions may be imposed when bail is granted to someone who is charged with a non-imprisonable offence.

2.5.4   Breaking conditions of bail

If the defendant is granted conditional bail but then breaches a condition of that bail, he is liable to be arrested under s 7(3) of the Bail Act 1976, which provides that:

> A person who has been released on bail in criminal proceedings and is under a duty to surrender into the custody of a court may be arrested without warrant by a constable—
>
> ...
>
> (b)   if the constable has reasonable grounds for believing that that person is likely to break any of the conditions of his bail or has reasonable grounds for suspecting that that person has broken any of those conditions; or
>
> (c)   in a case where that person was released on bail with one or more surety or sureties, if a surety notifies a constable in writing that that person is unlikely to surrender to custody and that for that reason the surety wishes to be relieved of his obligations as a surety.

When the defendant has been arrested under s 7(3), he should be taken before the court as soon as practicable and in any event within 24 hours after his arrest (excluding Christmas Day, Good Friday and any Sunday): s 7(4). In *R v Governor of Glen Parva Young Offender Institution ex p G* [1998] 2 All ER 295, the defendant was arrested for breach of bail conditions; he was taken to the cells of a magistrates' court within 24 hours of arrest but was not brought before a magistrate until two hours after the expiry of the 24 hour time limit. The Divisional Court held that the detention after 24 hours was unlawful: s 7(4) of the Bail Act 1976 requires the defendant to be brought before a justice of the peace (not merely brought within the court precincts) within 24 hours of arrest. In *R v Liverpool Justices ex p DPP* [1993] QB 233; [1992] 3 All ER 249, it was held that where the police arrest someone who is in breach of a bail condition or whom the police believe to be about to abscond (powers conferred by s 7 of the Bail Act 1976), a single lay justice has the power to remand the defendant in custody or to grant bail subject to further conditions.

Section 7(5) of the Bail Act provides that:

> A justice of the peace before whom a person is brought under sub-section (4) ... may ... if of the opinion that that person—
>
> (a)   is not likely to surrender to custody, or
>
> (b)   has broken or is likely to break any condition of his bail,

remand him in custody or commit him to custody, as the case may require or, alternatively, grant him bail subject to the same or to different conditions, but if not of that opinion shall grant him bail subject to the same conditions (if any) as were originally imposed.

In other words, the court has to decide whether the accused is indeed likely to fail to surrender to custody or has broken (or is likely to breach) any condition of his bail. It is likely that the defendant's bail will be withdrawn, so that he will be held in custody pending trial, or else bail will be granted again but subject to more stringent conditions.

The effect of the Human Rights Act 1998 on the procedure to be followed in such cases has been considered in several cases by the Divisional Court. In *R (Hussain) v Derby Magistrates' Court* [2002] 1 Cr App R 4, the defendant was arrested for breach of bail conditions. The magistrates made a preliminary ruling and adjourned the case to the afternoon of the same day. The Divisional Court held that, under s 7(4) and (5) of the Bail Act 1976, justices have power to stand an application out of their list after the case has been called on and make a preliminary ruling, with the effect that a different bench should embark on the hearing afresh and determine it on the same day. What has to be ensured is that the question of the defendant's continuing detention is placed before a justice or justices within the 24 hour period. The court went on to confirm that the investigation into alleged breach of a bail condition is not concerned with the trial of a criminal charge; there is nothing in the language of s 7(5) which demands that the court should adopt the procedural rigidities appropriate for a more formal hearing such as a summary trial. It follows that there is no need for the court to hear evidence; instead it can base its decision on representations from the prosecution and the defence.

In *R (on the Application of the DPP) v Havering Magistrates' Court; R (McKeown) v Wirral Borough Magistrates' Court* [2001] 1 WLR 805, the Divisional Court again considered s 7 in the context of Arts 5 and 6 of the Convention. The court confirmed that Art 6 has no direct relevance where justices are exercising their judgment whether or not to commit a person to custody following breach of bail conditions, since s 7 does not create any criminal offence. However, the court went on to hold that Art 5 is directly relevant, but said that the procedures applicable under domestic law are entirely compatible with the requirements of Art 5. The court went on to give detailed guidance on proceedings under s 7. These proceedings are, by their nature, emergency proceedings to determine whether or not a person who was not considered to present risks, which would have justified a remand in custody in the first instance, did subsequently present such risks. When exercising the power to detain, the magistrate is not entitled to order detention (or impose additional conditions) by reason simply of the finding of a breach. The fact of a breach is evidence of a relevant risk arising, but it is no more than one of the factors which the magistrate has to consider when exercising his discretion. The magistrate is required, on the material before him, to come to a fair and rational opinion. That material is not restricted to admissible evidence in the strict sense. In doing so, the magistrate has to bear in mind the consequences to the defendant (namely the fact that he is at risk of losing his liberty) in the context of the presumption of innocence. Article 5 does not require any different approach. The procedural task of the magistrate is to ensure that the defendant has a full and fair opportunity to comment on, and answer, the material before the court. If that material includes evidence from a witness who gives oral testimony, the accused has to be given an opportunity to cross-examine. Likewise, if he wishes to give oral evidence, he is entitled to do so. The court went on to hold that the fact that, under domestic law, there is no power in a justice to adjourn the hearing once a defendant has been brought before him under s 7(4) of the 1976 Act does not result in a breach of Art 5. Parliament has to be taken to have determined that there should be a swift and relatively informal resolution of the issues raised, and so the court has to do its best to come to a fair conclusion on the relevant day; if it cannot do so, it will not be of the opinion that the relevant matters have been made out which could justify detention.

R (DPP) v Havering Magistrates' Court was followed in R (Vickers) v West London Magistrates' Court [2003] EWHC 1809; (2003) 167 JP 473. The defendant was arrested and brought before the justices for failing to comply with the bail conditions. Before the justices, he sought to raise a defence of reasonable excuse; however, the justices held that no such defence exists under s 7 of the Bail Act 1976. The defendant sought judicial review of that decision, contending that, when considering the matter under s 7(5), the justices were obliged to first decide whether a breach had occurred and, in reaching that decision, must have regard to any reasonable excuse which the accused put forward. The Divisional Court held that s 7(5) of the 1976 Act requires a two-stage approach. First, the justices have to determine whether there has been a breach of a bail condition; secondly, if there has been a breach, the justices are obliged to consider whether or not the bailed person should be granted bail again. In carrying out the first stage, the justices must act fairly and give the accused a chance to answer the accusations against him. That does not, however, include an inquiry as to whether the accused had any reasonable excuse for breaching bail. At the second stage, assuming that the justices are satisfied that there has been a breach, the reasons for the breach of bail become relevant, and the justices would be obliged to consider all the evidence (including the reason for the breach). If that procedure is followed, there will be no breach of Art 5 of the European Convention.

Where a defendant is granted conditional bail by the Crown Court following an appeal to that court against the refusal of bail by a magistrates' court, if the defendant is arrested under s 7 of the Bail Act 1976 for breach of a condition of his bail, he must be taken before a magistrate, not a judge of the Crown Court (Re Marshall (1994) 159 JP 688). In R (Ellison) v Teeside Magistrates' Court [2001] EWHC 12 (Admin); (2001) 165 JP 355, the defendant was arrested for breaking bail conditions imposed by the Crown Court. He was taken before a magistrates' court (under s 7 of the Bail Act 1976). The magistrates remanded him in custody to appear at Crown Court to deal with the question of bail. It was held by the Divisional Court that, where a defendant is brought before a magistrates' court for breaching a condition of his bail, the magistrates must deal with the matter. They have no power to commit the defendant to the Crown Court to be dealt with for the breach.

Failure to comply with conditions of bail can amount to contempt of court. However, that fact is of limited practical relevance. In R v Ashley [2003] EWCA Crim 2571; (2003) 167 JP 548, the defendant was convicted of contempt of court, arising out of breaches of bail conditions. He had been released on bail subject to conditions that required him to surrender his passport and not to leave the country. He broke both conditions but returned to face trial on the appointed day. The Divisional Court held that the purpose of placing restrictions on an individual's movements under the Bail Act 1976 is to ensure that he attends the trial. If the conduct breaching bail is known about at the time, that bail could be revoked. Furthermore, there may be cases where breach of a bail condition gives rise to a further offence (for example, where witnesses are intimidated). However, s 7 of the Bail Act 1976 does not create any offence. Although the defendant had breached bail conditions by leaving the country, he did return for his trial. It followed that the judge did not have power to deal with him by way of contempt of court.

Home Office Circular 34/1998 (para 11) discusses breach of the condition under s 3(6)(e) of the Bail Act 1976, namely that the defendant must attend an interview with his lawyer. The Circular emphasises that this condition carries the same sanctions as apply to breach of any other bail condition. Thus, the defendant is liable to arrest without a warrant and the court may vary his remand status. The Circular says that, as with any other condition, the consequences of failing to comply should be explained to the defendant at the time the requirement is imposed. However, the Circular does make the point that the defendant's solicitor should not be expected to report a breach if the defendant fails to attend an interview.

2.5.5   Application for variation of conditions

Section 3(8) of the Bail Act 1976 provides that:

Where a court has granted bail in criminal proceedings that court or, where that court has committed [or sent] a person on bail to the Crown Court for trial or to be sentenced or otherwise dealt with, that court or the Crown Court may on application—

(a)   by or on behalf of the person to whom bail was granted, or

(b)   by the prosecutor or a constable,

vary the conditions of bail or impose conditions in respect of bail which [has been] granted unconditionally.

In other words, where bail is granted subject to conditions, the defendant or the prosecution may apply to vary those conditions. Similarly, if unconditional bail was granted, the prosecution may apply to the court for conditions to be added.

The power to vary conditions of bail under s 3(8) of the Bail Act 1976 is conferred on the court which imposed those conditions and, where that court has committed a defendant on bail to the Crown Court for trial or to be sentenced, on the Crown Court. During the period between committal to the Crown Court by the magistrates and the defendant's surrender to custody at the Crown Court, the magistrates' court and the Crown Court have concurrent jurisdiction (so either could vary the conditions). Once the arraignment has taken place (and so the defendant has surrendered to the custody of the Crown Court) the magistrates no longer have any jurisdiction in relation to the grant of bail. So, in *R v Lincoln Justices ex p Mawer* (1995) 160 JP 21, the defendant was granted conditional bail by the Crown Court following her arraignment, the conditions being the same as those which the magistrates had originally imposed; the Divisional Court held that the magistrates' court could not entertain an application to vary the conditions imposed by the Crown Court.

2.6   SURETIES

In this section, we examine in greater detail one of the commonly imposed conditions of bail, namely sureties. A surety makes a formal promise to pay a fixed sum of money if the defendant fails to surrender to custody.

Section 3(4) of the Bail Act 1976 provides that the accused 'may be required, before release on bail, to provide a surety or sureties to secure his surrender to custody'. Section 8 of the Act sets out the procedure to be followed where the court grants bail on condition that the defendant provides one or more surety for the purpose of ensuring that he surrenders to custody.

2.6.1   Granting of bail subject to surety

In deciding whether to grant bail subject to a surety, the court has to consider the suitability of the proposed surety. Section 8(2) provides that:

> In considering the suitability for that purpose of a proposed surety, regard may be had (amongst other things) to—
>
> (a)   the surety's financial resources;
>
> (b)   his character and any previous convictions of his; and
>
> (c)   his proximity (whether in point of kinship, place of residence or otherwise) to the person for whom he is to be surety.

Thus, regard must be had to:

- the 'financial resources' of the proposed surety: could the surety pay the sum which he is promising to pay?;
- the 'character' of the proposed surety and whether he has 'any previous convictions': is the surety a trustworthy person?;
- the 'proximity (whether in point of kinship, place of residence or otherwise)' of the proposed surety to the person for whom he is to be surety: is the proposed surety a friend, relative or employer? How far away does he live from the defendant? The most important consideration under this heading is the relationship of proposed surety to the defendant: will the surety have the ability to control the defendant so as to ensure that he attends court when he should? Put another way, would the fact the surety stands to lose money if the defendant absconds operate on the mind of the defendant so as to deter him from absconding?

In fixing the amount of the surety, the court has regard to the seriousness of the offence, the degree of risk that the defendant will abscond, and to the means of the proposed surety.

It is quite common to have two or more sureties. If the court will only grant bail subject to a recognisance of a certain amount and that amount is beyond the means of the proposed surety, then another person will have to be found. It should be noted that the defendant cannot stand as a surety for himself (s 3(2) of the Bail Act 1976).

The financial circumstances of the proposed surety are crucial. In *R v Birmingham Crown Court ex p Ali* (1999) 163 JP 145, the Divisional Court said that 'it is irresponsible (and possibly a matter for consideration by a professional disciplinary body) for a qualified lawyer or legal executive to tender anyone as a surety unless he or she has reasonable grounds for believing that the surety will, if necessary, be able to meet his or her financial undertaking' (at p 147, *per* Kennedy LJ). The same goes for a court official; unless the surety has the benefit of separate legal advice, the court official should make some inquiries to satisfy himself that the surety will, if necessary, be able to pay.

If the proposed surety is in court, he gives evidence of these matters and confirms that he understands the obligations he will be undertaking.

If the defence are aware that someone has offered to act as a surety but that person is not in court, and the magistrates are satisfied that the person is a satisfactory surety, the court may grant bail subject to that named surety entering into the recognisance (that is, signing the formal document which sets out the agreement to act as surety) in front of a justice of the peace or a justices' clerk, or at a police station in front of an officer of the rank of inspector or above (s 8(4)), or the governor of the prison where the accused is detailed (r 86 of the Magistrates' Courts Rules 1981). The defendant remains in custody until this has been done.

If there is no one whom the defence can offer as a surety at the time of the hearing, the magistrates may grant bail subject to a surety who is acceptable to the police entering into a recognisance (for the amount fixed by the court) at a magistrates' court or a police station (s 8(3)). Again, the defendant stays in custody until a satisfactory surety has entered into a recognisance. If the potential surety is rejected by the magistrates, court clerk or police inspector (as the case may be) because that person is not satisfied of the surety's suitability, the potential surety may apply to the magistrates' court to take his recognisance (s 8(5)). Under s 8(7), where a recognisance is entered into otherwise than before the court that fixed the amount of the recognisance, 'the same consequences shall follow as if it had been entered into before that court'.

2.6.2 Forfeiture of recognisance

If the defendant fails to surrender to custody when he should, there is a presumption that the full sum promised by the surety will be forfeited, unless it appears fair and just that a lesser sum should be forfeited or none at all. The burden of showing that the amount promised by the surety should not be forfeited (or that only part of that sum should be forfeited) lies on the surety (*R v Uxbridge Justices ex p Heward-Mills* [1983] 1 WLR 56).

The relevant factors were considered in *R v Southampton Justices ex p Green* [1976] QB 11, *R v Horseferry Road Justices ex p Pearson* [1976] 1 WLR 511, *R v Reading Crown Court ex p Bello* [1992] 3 All ER 353 and *R v Wood Green Crown Court ex p Howe* [1992] 1 WLR 702:

- *The surety's means*

  Has there been a change in financial circumstances since he agreed to act as surety which would make it unfair to order him to forfeit the sum promised?

- *Culpability*

  Did the surety take all reasonable steps to secure the defendant's attendance at court, again making it unfair to penalise the surety?

If a surety has a change of mind (for example, he decides that the defendant is unlikely to attend court after all) and wishes to withdraw from the surety, he should give written notice to this effect to the police (see *Bello* above). The police can then arrest the defendant without a warrant, under s 7(3)(c) of the Bail Act 1976, which provides that there is a power of arrest:

> ... in a case where that person was released on bail with one or more surety or sureties, if a surety notifies a constable in writing that that person is unlikely to surrender to custody and that for that reason the surety wishes to be relieved of his obligations as a surety.

Even though the surety can only formally withdraw from the recognisance with the agreement of the court, a surety who has given written notice to the police may seek to argue that they should not forfeit the money promised if the defendant does indeed abscond (see *Howe* above). However, in *R v Maidstone Crown Court ex p Lever and Connell* [1995] 1 WLR 928, the Court of Appeal took a rather tougher line. In that case, one of two sureties discovered that the defendant had not been home for two nights. That surety telephoned the other surety and the police. Attempts by the police to apprehend the defendant were unsuccessful. The judge ordered the first surety to forfeit £35,000 (out of a recognisance of £40,000) and the other £16,000 (out of a recognisance of £19,000). The two sureties sought judicial review of this decision. The Court of Appeal upheld the judge's decision. It was said that a lack of culpability on the part of the surety (or even commendable diligence by the surety), although a relevant factor, was not in itself a reason for reducing or setting aside the obligation into which the surety had freely entered. It was added that the court had a broad discretion as to whether and to what extent it would be fair and just to remit some or all of a recognisance and that the exercise of that discretion will only be set aside if it is perverse. In the instant case, a remission of about 15% could not be said to be perverse.

In *Lever and Connell*, the court endeavoured to give general guidance. Butler-Sloss LJ said (at p 930) that 'the presence or absence of culpability is a factor but the absence of culpability ... is not in itself a reason to reduce or set aside the obligation entered into by the surety to pay in the event of a failure to bring the defendant to court'. However, there may be circumstances where the amount forfeited might be reduced because the surety had made considerable efforts to carry out his undertakings.

The reason for the adoption of a fairly strict approach to the forfeiture of recognisances was set out by Butler-Sloss LJ at p 931, where her Ladyship quotes from Lord Widgery CJ in *R v Southampton Justices ex p Corker* (1976) 120 SJ 214 (also quoted by McCullough J in *R v Uxbridge Justices ex p Heward-Mills* [1983] 1 WLR 56, p 59) where Lord Widgery refers to 'the real pull of bail':

> The real pull of bail, the real effective force that it exerts, is that it may cause the offender to attend his trial rather than subject his nearest and dearest who has gone surety for him to undue paid and discomfort.

It should be noted that s 120 of the Magistrates' Courts Act 1980 (as amended by s 55 of the Crime and Disorder Act 1998) provides that, where a person stands as a surety but the accused fails to attend court, the magistrates' court must:

(a) declare the recognisance to be forfeited; and

(b) issue a summons to the surety requiring him to appear before the court to show cause why he should not be ordered to pay the sum promised.

If the surety fails to attend that hearing, the court may proceed in his absence if satisfied that he was served with the summons.

Section 120(3) states that 'the court which declares the recognizance to be forfeited may, instead of adjudging any person to pay the whole sum in which he is bound, adjudge him to pay part only of the sum or remit the sum'. In *Kaur v DPP* (2000) 164 JP 127, the Divisional Court held that the justices can only have regard to the assets of the surety; assets of third parties are irrelevant. Regard must be had to the surety's share in the equity of the matrimonial home; however, the impact on the surety and others, if the matrimonial home has to be sold to satisfy the recognisance, is a relevant factor in deciding whether to remit all or part of the recognisance. The court went on to confirm that lack of culpability on the part of the surety is not in itself a reason for not remitting the recognisance.

In *R v Birmingham Crown Court ex p Ali* (1999) 163 JP 145, it was held that where there has been no proper means inquiry and the surety then applies for a reduction in the amount of the recognisance to be forfeited (under s 120 of the Magistrates' Courts Act 1980), the sum should be reduced (if necessary) to a sum that the surety could be expected to pay in full within two, or at the most three, years.

The obligation entered into by the surety is a personal obligation. Under s 9 of the Bail Act 1976, if a person agrees with another to indemnify a surety against any liability under the recognisance, that person is guilty of an offence. This is so whether the agreement is made before or after the person to be indemnified becomes a surety, whether or not he in fact becomes a surety, and whether the agreement contemplates compensation in money or in money's worth (s 9(2)). The penalty is up to three months' imprisonment and/or a fine of up to £5,000 (or the offender can be committed to the Crown Court for sentence, where the maximum penalty is 12 months' imprisonment and/or a fine). Proceedings for an offence under s 9 can only be brought by (or with the consent of) the Director of Public Prosecutions (s 9(5)).

2.7 REPEATED BAIL APPLICATIONS

Schedule 1, Pt IIA of the Bail Act 1976 (inserted by s 154 of the Criminal Justice Act 1988) provides as follows:

(1) If the court decides not to grant the defendant bail, it is the court's duty to consider, at each subsequent hearing while the defendant is a person to whom section 4 above applies and remains in custody, whether he ought to be granted bail.

(2) At the first hearing after that at which the court decided not to grant the defendant bail he may support an application for bail with any argument as to fact or law that he desires (whether or not he has advanced that argument previously).

(3) At subsequent hearings the court need not hear arguments as to fact or law which it has heard previously.

Thus, at the first hearing after that at which bail was refused, the defendant can make a bail application whether or not it is based on arguments which were advanced on the first occasion. This means that the defendant may make bail applications on his first and second appearances before the court and may advance precisely the same arguments in each application if he so wishes. Or, if no application is made on the first appearance, the defendant may make an application on his second appearance.

Thereafter, a material change of circumstances (that is, something relevant to bail) is required if a further bail application is to be made. So, in subsequent remands, the court should only consider whether the circumstances have changed since the last fully argued bail application was heard (for example, a possible surety comes forward or the defendant is offered employment).

This provision is based on *R v Nottingham Justices ex p Davies* [1981] 1 QB 38, in which the Divisional Court said the defendant should be allowed two fully argued applications. This was because the first application is often under-prepared due to lack of time, and so fairness demands that a second application be heard. Thereafter, however, the court would simply be hearing arguments that had been heard before; hence, the requirement of a change in circumstances so that a third application for bail can only be made if there is some fresh material for the court to consider.

In *R v Dover and East Kent Justices ex p Dean* [1992] Crim LR 33, the defendant did not make a bail application on his first appearance at court and he consented to being remanded in his absence (under s 128 of the Magistrates' Courts Act 1980) for the next three weeks. On the occasion of his next appearance before the court (a month after his first appearance), the defendant sought to make a bail application. The magistrates would not let him do so, but the Divisional Court held that remands in the defendant's absence do not count as hearings for the purpose of determining whether a bail application can be made. The defendant's second appearance was to be regarded as the second hearing (even though the case had been listed in the intervening weeks) and so he had a right to make a bail application.

In *R v Calder Justices ex p Kennedy* (1992) 156 JP 716, it was similarly held that if the magistrates remand the defendant in custody on the basis that there is insufficient information before the court to make a decision on bail (a permitted ground for refusing bail under Sched 1, Pt I, para 5 of the Bail Act 1976), this hearing does not count for the purposes of s 154. So, a full bail application may be made on the occasion of the defendant's next appearance and, if that application is unsuccessful, a second fully argued bail application can be made on his subsequent appearance before the court.

2.8   BAIL AND THE EUROPEAN CONVENTION ON HUMAN RIGHTS

Under Art 5 of the European Convention, which safeguards the right to liberty, a person charged with an offence must be released pending trial unless there are 'relevant and sufficient' reasons to justify continued detention (*Wemhoff v Germany* (1968) 1 EHRR 55). The case law of the European Court shows that this is interpreted in a way that is very similar to the UK's Bail Act 1976. The grounds accepted by the European Court of Human Rights for withholding bail include:

- the risk that the defendant will fail to appear at the trial. This has been defined as requiring 'a whole set of circumstances which give reason to suppose that the consequences and hazards of flight will seem to him to be a lesser evil than continued imprisonment' (*Stogmuller v Austria* (1969) 1 EHRR 155). The court can take account of 'the character of the person involved, his morals, his home, his occupation, his assets, his family ties, and all kinds of links with the country in which he is being prosecuted' (*Neumeister v Austria* (1979) 1 EHRR 91). The likely sentence is relevant but cannot of itself justify the refusal of bail (*Letellier v France* (1991) 14 EHRR 83);

- the risk that the defendant will interfere with the course of justice (for example, interfering with witnesses, warning other suspects, destroying relevant evidence). There must be an identifiable risk and there must be evidence in support (*Clooth v Belgium* (1992) 14 EHRR 717);

- preventing the commission of further offences; there must be good reason to believe that the defendant will commit offences while on bail (*Toth v Austria* (1991) 14 EHRR 551);

- the preservation of public order: bail may be withheld where the nature of the alleged crime and the likely public reaction to it are such that the release of the accused may give rise to public disorder (*Letellier v France* (1991) 14 EHRR 83).

Article 5 of the Convention also allows the imposition of conditions on the grant of bail.

It should be noted that the 'equality of arms' principle applies to bail applications (*Woukam Moudefo v France* (1991) 13 EHRR 549). This includes:

- the right to disclosure of prosecution evidence for purposes of making a bail application: *Lamy v Belgium* (1989) 11 EHRR 529 (the decision of the Divisional Court in *R v DPP ex p Lee* [1999] 2 Cr App R 304 largely accords with this);

- the requirement that the court should give reasons for the refusal of bail (*Tomasi v France* (1992) 15 EHRR 1) and should permit renewed applications for bail at reasonable intervals (*Bezicheri v Italy* (1990) 12 EHRR 210). Both these requirements are satisfied by the Bail Act 1976.

The Law Commission (Law Com No 269, www.lawcom.gov.uk/files/lc269.pdf) considered the impact of the Human Rights Act 1998 on the law governing decisions taken by the police and the courts to grant or refuse bail in criminal proceedings.

The Commission noted that Art 5 of the Convention states that, although reasonable suspicion that the detained person has committed an offence can be sufficient to justify pre-trial detention for a short time, the national authorities must thereafter show additional grounds for detention. They summarised the five additional grounds recognised under the Convention as follows, namely where the purpose of detention is to avoid a real risk that, were the defendant to be released:

(1) he or she would:

    (a)   fail to attend trial; or

    (b)   interfere with evidence or witnesses, or otherwise obstruct the course of justice; or

    (c)   commit an offence while on bail; or

    (d)   be at risk of harm against which he or she would be inadequately protected; or

(2) a disturbance to public order would result.

The Law Commission concluded that there are no provisions in the Bail Act which are incompatible with Convention rights. However, the Commission did identify some areas of the law which they believed would benefit from legislative reform. They also produced a Guide to assist decision-makers to apply the Bail Act 1976 in a way that is compatible with the Convention (a copy of the Guide can be accessed at www.lawcom.gov.uk/files/guide.pdf).

The Guide emphasises that a defendant should only be refused bail where detention is necessary for a purpose which Strasbourg jurisprudence has recognised as legitimate, in the sense that detention may be compatible with the defendant's right to release under Art 5(3). Thus, a domestic court exercising its powers in a way which is compatible with the Convention rights should refuse bail only where it can be justified both under the Convention, as interpreted in Strasbourg jurisprudence, and domestic legislation.

The Guide also points out that detention will only be necessary if the risk relied upon as the ground for withholding bail could not be adequately addressed by the imposition of appropriate bail conditions. Thus, the Commission concluded that conditional bail should be used in preference to detention where a bail condition could adequately address the risk that would otherwise justify detention.

Furthermore, the court refusing bail should give reasons for finding that detention is necessary. Those reasons should be closely related to the individual circumstances pertaining to the defendant, and be capable of supporting the conclusion of the court.

The Law Commission's *Guidance for Bail Decision-Takers and their Advisers* makes a number of important points:

General principles applicable to the refusal of bail

Detention will only be necessary if the risk could not be adequately addressed by the imposition of appropriate bail conditions that would make detention unnecessary. Any court refusing bail should give reasons that explain why detention is necessary. Those reasons should be closely related to the individual circumstances of the defendant.

...

The risk of offending on bail

The decision-taker must consider whether it may properly be inferred from any previous convictions and other circumstances relating to the defendant that there is a real risk that the defendant will commit an offence if granted bail, and that the defendant therefore falls within paragraph 2(b) of Part I of Schedule 1 to the Act. Provided that a decision to withhold bail is a necessary and proportionate response to a real risk that, if released, the defendant would commit an offence while on bail, such a decision will comply with the Convention.

Defendant on bail at the time of the alleged offence

The factor in paragraph 2A of Part I of Schedule 1 to the Act (a defendant who commits an indictable offence whilst on bail) does not, in itself, establish any Article 5(3) purpose. Consequently, a court should not base a decision to withhold bail solely on paragraph 2A. To do so would infringe Article 5 and would be unlawful under sections 3 and 6 of the Human Rights Act 1998 (HRA). That factor may, however, be relevant to a decision whether to withhold bail on the basis of another relevant exception, for example the risk that the defendant will commit an offence while on bail.

Detention for the defendant's own protection

A decision to refuse bail to a defendant under the exception in paragraph 3 of Part I of Schedule 1 to the Act, that is for the defendant's own protection (from self-harm or harm from others) would comply with the Convention, where:

(1)   detention is necessary to address a real risk that, if granted bail, the defendant would suffer harm, against which detention could provide protection; and

(2)   there are exceptional circumstances in the nature of the alleged offence and/or the conditions or context in which it is alleged to have been committed.

A decision of a court to order detention because of a risk of self-harm may be compatible with the ECHR even where the circumstances giving rise to the risk are unconnected with the alleged offence, provided that the court is satisfied that there is a real risk of self-harm, and that a proper medical examination will take place rapidly so that the court may then consider exercising its powers of detention under the Mental Health Act 1983.

Detention because of a lack of information

The refusal of bail under paragraph 5 of Part I of Schedule 1 to the Act, where it has not been practicable to obtain sufficient information for the taking of a full bail decision for want of time since the institution of proceedings against the defendant, would be compatible with Article 5 provided that:

(1)   detention is for a short period, which is no longer than necessary to enable the required information to be obtained, and

(2)   the lack of information is not due to a failure of the prosecution, the police, the court, or another state body to act with 'special diligence'.

There is no need in such a case for the court to be satisfied of any of the recognised purposes set out in paragraph 2 above.

After the initial short period of time has passed, a lack of information that is not due to a failure of a state body to act with 'special diligence' may be taken into account as a factor militating in favour of detention on another Convention compliant ground for detention.

Detention following arrest under section 7

Paragraph 6 of Part I and paragraph 5 of Part II of Schedule 1 The broad provisions in paragraph 6 of Part I and paragraph 5 of Part II of Schedule 1 to the Act, that a defendant arrested pursuant to section 7 need not be granted bail, should be read subject to the narrower provisions governing bail following a section 7(3) arrest, set out in section 7(5) of the Act. That provision requires that bail should again be granted unless the justice is of the opinion that the defendant is not likely to surrender to custody, or has broken or is likely to break any condition of bail. Detention on one of these grounds will comply with the Convention only where this is necessary for one or more of the recognised purposes set out above in paragraph 2.

Section 7(5) hearings

At the hearing of section 7(5) proceedings there is no requirement that oral evidence should be heard in every case, but account should be taken of the quality of material presented. This may range from mere assertion to documentary proof. If the material includes oral evidence, the defendant must be given an opportunity to cross-examine. Likewise, a defendant should be permitted to give relevant oral evidence if he or she wishes to do so.

Section 25 of the Criminal Justice and Public Order Act 1994

The expression 'exceptional circumstances' in section 25 of the Criminal Justice and Public Order Act 1994 should be construed so that it encompasses a defendant who, if released on bail, would not pose a real risk of committing a serious offence. This construction achieves the purpose of Parliament to ensure that, when making bail decisions about defendants to whom section 25 applies, decision-takers focus on the risk the defendant may pose to the public by reoffending. It is possible that some other circumstance might constitute 'exceptional circumstances'. Even if 'exceptional circumstances' do exist, bail may, nonetheless, be withheld on a Convention-compatible ground if this is deemed to be necessary in the individual case.

Conditional bail

Conditional bail as an alternative to custody

A defendant must be released, if need be subject to conditions, unless:

(1)   that would create a risk of the kind which can, in principle, justify pre-trial detention (set out above in paragraph 2), and

(2)   that risk cannot, by imposing suitable bail conditions, be averted, or reduced to a level at which it would not justify detention.

Conditional bail as an alternative to unconditional bail

A court should only impose bail conditions for one of the purposes which Strasbourg jurisprudence recognises as capable of justifying detention (set out above in paragraph 2). A bail condition should only be imposed where, if the defendant were to break that condition or be reasonably thought likely to do so, it may be necessary to arrest the defendant in order to pursue the purpose for which the condition was imposed.

Reasons for imposing conditions

Decision-takers should state their reasons for imposing bail conditions and specify the purposes for which any conditions are imposed. Decision-takers should also be alert to ensure that any bail conditions they impose do not violate the defendant's other Convention rights, such as those protected by Articles 8–11 of the Convention (the right to respect for family life, freedom of thought, conscience and religion, freedom of expression and freedom of assembly and association).

Giving reasons for bail decisions

It is of particular importance that decision-takers or their clerks make, and retain for the file, a note of the gist of the arguments for and against the grant of bail, and the oral reasons given by the tribunal for their decision.

Form of evidence

It is not necessary to hear sworn evidence in the great majority of cases. Courts should, in particular cases, consider whether fairness requires the calling of evidence on oath for the determination of the application, as a failure to call such evidence may cause a particular decision to fall foul of Article 5(4).

A court hearing bail proceedings should take account of the quality of the material presented. It may range from mere assertion to documentary proof. If the material includes sworn oral evidence, the defendant must be given an opportunity to cross-examine. Likewise, the defendant should be permitted to give relevant oral evidence if he or she wishes to do so.

Disclosure

Ex parte Lee [1999] Cr App R 304 recognises an ongoing duty of disclosure from the time of arrest. The Court of Appeal emphasised that at the stage before committal, there are continuing obligations on the prosecutor to make such disclosure as justice and fairness may require in the particular circumstances of the case, that is, where it could reasonably be expected to assist the defence when applying for bail. This will ensure that the defendant enjoys 'equality of arms' with the prosecution. Compliance with this requirement, together with those imposed by the Attorney-General's guidelines to prosecutors, should ensure compliance with the Convention. This will apply equally to hearings pursuant to s 7(5). The duty of disclosure does not require that the whole of the prosecution file be disclosed to the defence prior to the hearing. It is sufficient if disclosure is provided of the material the defendant needs in order to enjoy 'equality of arms' with the prosecution in relation to the matter to be decided by the court.

Public hearing

Where normally the hearing would be in chambers, if the defendant requests that the bail hearing be held in public, it should be held in public unless there is a good reason not to do so.

The right to challenge pre-trial detention

The Convention gives a detained person the right to make further court challenges to the legality of his or her detention despite having already made one or more such challenges, where for example, with the passage of time, the circumstances which once were considered by a court to justify detention may have changed.

To ensure compliance with the Convention, Part IIA of Schedule I to the Act should be applied on the basis that courts should be willing, at intervals of 28 days, to consider arguments that the passage of time constitutes, in the particular case, a change in circumstances relevant to the need to detain the defendant, so as to require the hearing of all the arguments on the question of bail. It may be, for example, that the time served on remand may have reduced the risk of the defendant absconding.

If the court finds that the passage of time does amount to a relevant change of circumstances then a full bail application should follow in which all the arguments, old and new, could be put forward and taken into account.

Lord Justice Auld, in his *Review of the Criminal Courts of England and Wales*, notes the view of the Law Commission that the provisions of the Bail Act 1976 are compatible with the European Convention on Human Rights. However, he does note some shortcomings in the procedure (see paras 69–82 of Chapter 10) and recommends as follows:

175 Magistrates and judges in all courts should take more time to consider matters of bail.

176 Listing practices should reflect the necessity to devote due time to bail applications and allow the flexibility required for all parties to gather sufficient information for the court to make an appropriate decision.

177 Courts, the police, prosecutors and defence representatives should be provided with better information for the task than they are at present, in particular, complete and up to date information of the defendant's record held on the Police National Computer, relevant probation or other social service records, if any, verified information about home living conditions and employment, if any, and

sufficient information about the alleged offence and its relationship, if any, to his record so as to indicate whether there is a pattern of offending.

178   Courts and all relevant agencies should be equipped with a common system of information technology ... to facilitate the ready availability to all who need it of the above information.

179   There should be appropriate training for magistrates and judges in the making of bail decisions, with Article 5 ECHR and risk assessment particularly in mind, as the Law Commission has proposed.

...

181   Bail notices should be couched in plain English, printed and given to the defendant as a formal court order when the bail decision is made, so that he understands exactly what is required of him and appreciates the seriousness of the grant of bail and of any attached conditions.

182   All courts should be diligent in adopting the Law Commission's proposals for the recording of bail decisions in such a way as to indicate clearly how they have been reached.

2.9   CHALLENGING THE REFUSAL OF BAIL

In this section, we consider the various ways of challenging a refusal of bail. The starting point is the right of the defendant to know why bail was refused in the first place.

2.9.1   Record of reasons

Sub-sections 5(3) and 5(4) of the Bail Act 1976 provide as follows:

(3)   Where a magistrates' court or the Crown Court—

    (a)   withholds bail in criminal proceedings, or

    (b)   imposes conditions in granting bail in criminal proceedings, or

    (c)   varies any conditions of bail or imposes conditions in respect of bail in criminal proceedings,

and does so in relation to a person to whom section 4 of this Act applies, then the court shall, with a view to enabling him to consider making an application in the matter to another court, give reasons for withholding bail or for imposing or varying the conditions.

(4)   A court which is by virtue of sub-section (3) above required to give reasons for its decision shall include a note of those reasons in the record of its decision and shall (except in a case where, by virtue of sub-section (5) below, this need not be done) give a copy of that note to the person in relation to whom the decision was taken.

Thus, the defendant receives a document setting out which ground or grounds for withholding bail (from those specified in Sched 1 to the Act) were held to be applicable, and what factors were taken into account (that is, from the list in Sched 1, para 9) in deciding that the grounds were made out.

For example, the record of the decision might say that bail is being withheld because the court is satisfied that there are substantial grounds for believing that the accused will:

- *Fail to surrender to custody*
  Reasons: accused has two previous convictions for absconding;

  accused lacks community ties, being unemployed and of no fixed abode.
- *Commit an offence while on bail*
  Reasons: accused has three previous convictions for offences similar to that presently charged;

  accused has no apparent income;

  two of accused's previous convictions are for offences committed while on bail.

2.9.2   Certificate that full argument has been heard

Furthermore, s 5(6A) says that if a magistrates' court refuses bail after hearing a fully argued bail application, it must provide the defendant with a certificate that this is the case. If the magistrates allow a defendant to make a third application because there has been a material change of circumstances but do not grant bail, they must state in the certificate what change of circumstances persuaded them to hear the application.

Once the defendant has a certificate that full argument has been heard, he may apply for bail to the Crown Court if the magistrates refuse bail.

2.10   OPTIONS OPEN TO THE DEFENDANT WHEN BAIL HAS BEEN REFUSED OR CONDITIONS IMPOSED

In order to challenge the refusal of bail:

- The defendant may make a further application in the magistrates' court if this is permissible under Sched 1, Pt IIA of the Bail Act 1976 (see above) – namely if this is only the defendant's second bail application or the defendant can show that there has been a material change of circumstances.
- The defendant may apply for bail to the Crown Court under s 81(1) of the Supreme Court Act 1981.

Furthermore, s 22 of the Criminal Justice Act 1967 formerly empowered the High Court to grant bail in cases where bail has been refused by magistrates. However, under s 17 of the Criminal Justice Act 2003, s 22(1) of the 1967 Act is amended (in effect since April 2004) so that it applies only in cases 'where an application to the court to state a case for the opinion of the High Court is made'. Thus, it is only in the context of appeals by way of case stated (following the final disposal of the case by the magistrates) that the High Court will continue to have the jurisdiction to grant bail in criminal cases. This provision is based on Recommendation 183 of the Auld Review, that the right of application to a High Court judge for bail after determination by any criminal court exercising its original or appellate jurisdiction should be removed. This recommendation was made by Lord Justice Auld because the possibility of an application for bail to the High Court is unnecessary given the jurisdiction of the Crown Court (see paras 84–86 of Chapter 10 of the Review). For the sake of completeness, it should be noted that, under s 37 of the Criminal Justice Act 1948, the

High Court may also grant bail where a person is appealing to the High Court by way of case stated from a decision of the Crown Court (in practice, this will be where a defendant appeals from the magistrates' court to the Crown Court and then seeks to appeal to the High Court from the decision of the Crown Court), where he is appealing from the Crown Court to the High Court by way of judicial review, seeking an order quashing the decision of the Crown Court (again this will be the case where the defendant is challenging a decision of the Crown Court in its appellate capacity), and where he has been convicted or sentenced by a magistrates' court and is appealing to the High Court by way of judicial review, seeking an order quashing the decision of the magistrates. In summary, then, the High Court can no longer hear appeals against refusal of bail, but it can grant bail to those who are appealing to it against conviction or sentence.

Section 16(1) of the Criminal Justice Act 2003 (in force since April 2004) also enables the defendant to appeal to the Crown Court against the imposition of certain bail conditions (based on Recommendation 184 of the Auld Review, that defendants should have a right of appeal to the Crown Court in respect of conditions imposed by magistrates as to residence away from home and/or to the provision of a surety or sureties or the giving of security). This right of appeal may only be exercised in respect of certain conditions, set out in s 16(3):

(a)   that the person concerned resides away from a particular place or area,

(b)   that the person concerned resides at a particular place other than a bail hostel,

(c)   for the provision of a surety or sureties or the giving of a security,

(d)   that the person concerned remains indoors between certain hours,

(e)   [a condition] imposed under section 3(6ZAA) of the 1976 Act (requirements with respect to electronic monitoring), or

(f)   that the person concerned makes no contact with another person.

Furthermore, the right of appeal under s 16 can only be exercised if the defendant has previously made an application to the magistrates (under s 3(8)(a) of the Bail Act) for the conditions to be varied (s 16(4), (5) and (6)). Once the Crown Court has disposed of the appeal, no further appeal can be brought unless a further application has been made to the magistrates under s 3(8)(a) (see s 16(8)).

2.10.1   Crown Court bail application: procedure

An application may be made to the Crown Court if the defendant has a certificate (under s 5(6A) of the Bail Act 1976) from the magistrates' court that a fully argued bail application was made there.

The defendant must give at least 24 hours' notice to the CPS. The defendant has no right to be present at the Crown Court hearing (and usually is not present) (r 19(5) of the Crown Court Rules 1982). The hearing is usually (though not invariably) in chambers (that is, the public are excluded and robes are not worn): r 27(2)(a). Otherwise, the procedure is the same as the magistrates' court, with the prosecution summarising the objections to bail and the defence replying. It is perhaps questionable whether the practice of hearing bail appeals in private and in the absence of the accused fully accords with the European Convention.

2.11   PROSECUTION CHALLENGES TO THE GRANT OF BAIL

2.11.1   Records of reasons for decision to grant bail

Section 5(2A) of the Bail Act provides that:

> Where a magistrates' court or the Crown Court grants bail in criminal proceedings to a person to whom section 4 of this Act applies after hearing representations from the prosecutor in favour of withholding bail, then the court shall give reasons for granting bail.

In a case where s 5(2A) applies, the court is required (by s 5(2B)) to: 'include a note of those reasons in the record of its decision and, if requested to do so by the prosecutor, shall cause the prosecutor to be given a copy of the record of the decision ...'

Two mechanisms exist to enable the prosecution to challenge the grant of bail to a defendant.

2.11.2   Prosecution appeals against grant of bail

The Bail (Amendment) Act 1993 allows the prosecution to appeal, in certain circumstances, against decisions by magistrates to grant bail.

> Section 1 of the Bail (Amendment) Act 1993 provides that:
>
> Where a magistrates' court grants bail to a person who is charged with or convicted of—
>
> (a)   an offence punishable by a term of imprisonment of 5 years or more, or
>
> (b)   an offence under section 12 (taking a conveyance without authority) or 12A (aggravated vehicle taking) of the Theft Act 1968,
>
> the prosecution may appeal to a judge of the Crown Court against the granting of bail.

When s 18 of the Criminal Justice Act 2003 comes into force, the scope of the Bail (Amendment) Act will be extended to cover all offences punishable by imprisonment (not just those punishable by five years' or more), following Recommendation 185 of the Auld Review. Section 1 of the 1993 Act will then read as follows:

> Where a magistrates' court grants bail to a person who is charged with, or convicted of, an offence punishable by imprisonment, the prosecution may appeal to a judge of the Crown Court against the granting of bail.

Under s 1(2) of the 1993 Act, this power only applies where the prosecution is conducted (a) by or on behalf of the DPP, or (b) 'by a person who falls within such class or description of person as may be prescribed for the purposes of this section by order made by the Secretary of State'. It follows that private prosecutions (that is, prosecutions other than those brought by the CPS or other public bodies) are excluded from the scope of the Bail (Amendment) Act 1993.

Furthermore, for the Act to apply, the prosecution must have opposed the grant of bail in the magistrates' court (s 1(3)).

If the prosecution wish to exercise the right of appeal, oral notice of appeal is given to the magistrates 'at the conclusion of the proceedings at which such bail has been granted and before the release from custody of the person concerned' (s 1(4) of the

1993 Act) and written notice of appeal must be served on the magistrates' court and on the defendant within two hours of the conclusion of the bail hearing (s 1(5)).

Where oral notice of appeal has been given, the court must remand the accused in custody (s 1(6) of the 1993 Act and r 93A(4) of the Magistrates' Courts Rules 1981). If the prosecution serves written notice of appeal within the prescribed time, the accused is again formally remanded in custody (r 93A(5)). The defendant is then held in custody pending the Crown Court hearing, which must take place within 48 hours from the date on which oral notice of appeal is given (excluding weekends and public holidays): s 1(8) of the 1993 Act.

If, having given oral notice of appeal, the prosecution fails to serve a written notice of appeal within the two hour period specified in s 1(5) of the 1993 Act, 'the appeal shall be deemed to have been disposed of' (s 1(7) of the Act) and the clerk must direct the release of the accused (r 93A(7) of the 1981 Rules).

The courts have accorded some latitude to prosecutors when interpreting the apparently strict time limitations in the Act. For example, in *R v Isleworth Crown Court ex p Clarke* [1998] 1 Cr App R 257, the Divisional Court held that the requirement that the prosecutor must give oral notice of appeal against the decision to grant bail 'at the conclusion of the proceedings' was satisfied in a case where such notice was given to the magistrates' court clerk about five minutes after the court rose.

Similarly, in *R (Jeffrey) v Warwick Crown Court* [2002] EWHC 2469; [2003] Crim LR 190, the prosecutor wished to appeal against the grant of bail to the accused but the notice of appeal was served on the accused three minutes late. The Divisional Court held that Parliament did not intend that the time limit for serving notice of appeal should defeat an appeal if the prosecution had given itself ample time to serve the notice on the defendant within the two hour period, had used due diligence to serve the notice within that period, and the failure to do so was not the fault of the prosecution, but was due to circumstances outside its control. Furthermore, the delay of three minutes had not caused the accused any prejudice (since he knew at the conclusion of the proceedings before the magistrates that the prosecution was exercising its right of appeal and he knew that he was being detained in custody as a result of the oral application for him to be remanded in custody until the appeal was disposed of).

In *R v Middlesex Guildhall Crown Court ex p Okoli* [2001] 1 Cr App R 1, the Divisional Court had to consider the effect of the 48 hour time limit (contained in s 1(8)). On 7 June 2000, the defendant was granted bail by a magistrates' court. The prosecution sought to appeal under the Bail (Amendment) Act 1993. The appeal was listed for 3 pm on 9 June. The defendant argued that this was more than 48 hours after the notice of appeal had been given, and so the Crown Court had no jurisdiction to hear the appeal. It was held that where an oral notice of appeal against a decision to grant bail has been given, the appeal hearing must commence within 48 hours (counting only working days) of the date – not the time – on which notice of appeal was given. The Crown Court therefore had jurisdiction in the present case.

The need to have a written notice following the oral notice of appeal is to enable the question of whether or not to appeal to be considered by a Senior Crown Prosecutor. Guidance issued to Crown Prosecutors by the CPS (www.cps.gov.uk/Home/legalguidance/14/bail.htm#2.12) says that this right of appeal should only be used in:

... cases of grave concern where there are substantial grounds under Bail Act 1976 which would allow the Court to refuse bail. The Prosecutor considering whether an appeal is appropriate should apply an overarching test of whether there is a serious risk of harm to any member of the public or any other significant risk of harm to any member of the public or any other significant public interest ground.

...

The seriousness of the offence is a factor to be considered. The public interest ground should not be used to justify appeals in less serious cases. The nature of the offence which the defendant faces is relevant if it illustrates the risk created by granting bail. Examples might be extreme cases of personal violence such as murder, rape, robbery or aggravated burglary, particularly if it is alleged that weapons have been used in offences of violence or during the commission of sexual offences.

...

A serious risk of harm to public safety and property may give grounds to justify an appeal. Examples might be arson with intent to endanger life or being reckless as to whether life is endangered, terrorist offences or riot.

The risk to the individual victim or victims will be a factor. The following situations may justify the exercise of the right of appeal:

- A record which discloses previous convictions, particularly of a similar kind against the same victim or victims with similar characteristics;
- Evidence of violence or threats of violence to the victim or his or her family; or
- Evidence of undue influence over the victim, for example where there are alleged sexual offences against young people or children.

A strong indication that the defendant may abscond may be relevant, particularly if he or she has no right to remain in Britain or has substantial assets or interests abroad. On the other hand the right of appeal should not be used simply because the defendant has no fixed address or settled way of life, particularly where this may be coupled with mental health problems (unless of course there are genuine indications of danger to the public).

This guidance is not intended to be exhaustive and each case will need to be decided on its merits after consideration of any representations made to the Court and any other information which may become available.

The appeal takes the form of a re-hearing. The judge hearing the appeal may remand the defendant in custody or may grant bail subject to such conditions (if any) as he thinks fit (s 1(9) of the 1993 Act). Where a Crown Court judge allows a prosecution appeal against the grant of bail by a magistrates' court under the 1993 Act, the judge must state the period for which the defendant is to be remanded in custody (in other words, the judge must specify the date on which the defendant is to appear in the magistrates' court), and that period must be in accordance with the periods specified in s 128 or 128A of the Magistrates' Courts Act 1980 (see below). This is because the defendant is still under the jurisdiction of the magistrates' court: *R v Szakal* [2000] 1 Cr App R 248.

2.11.3 Prosecution application for reconsideration of grant of bail

Section 5B of the Bail Act 1976 provides that where a magistrates' court has granted bail or the defendant has been granted police bail, the prosecution may apply to the magistrates' court for that decision to be reconsidered, asking the court to:

- vary the conditions of bail;
- impose conditions in respect of bail which has been granted unconditionally; or
- withhold bail.

Rule 93B of the Magistrates' Courts Rules 1981 requires that:

An application under section 5B(1) of the Bail Act 1976 shall—

(a) be made in writing;

(b) contain a statement of the grounds on which it is made;

(c) specify the offence which the proceedings in which bail was granted were connected with, or for;

(d) specify the decision to be reconsidered (including any conditions of bail which have been imposed and why they have been imposed); and

(e) specify the name and address of any surety provided by the person to whom the application relates to secure his surrender to custody.

Under r 93B(4), the time fixed for the hearing must be not later than 72 hours after receipt of the application (ignoring Sundays and public holidays).

The court has power to impose conditions if the original grant of bail was without condition, to vary any conditions that were imposed originally, or to withhold bail. This provision only applies where the defendant is accused of an indictable (including triable either way) offence (s 5B(2)). Section 5B (together with r 93B(6) and (7) of the 1981 Rules) clearly envisages the possibility of such an application being made in the absence of the defendant; however, s 5B(9) requires notice of the application to be given to the defendant and for the defendant to be given an opportunity to make written or oral representations to the court.

Section 5B(3) provides that 'no application for the reconsideration of a decision under this section shall be made unless it is based on information which was not available to the court or constable when the decision was taken'. Thus, an application is only possible under s 5B if it is based on new information (in the sense of information which was not available when the original decision regarding bail was taken). The basis of the application is therefore not to impugn the original decision to grant bail but to draw to the court's attention a relevant change in circumstances.

2.11.4 The two procedures compared

It follows that the two main differences between the prosecution appeal against the grant of bail and the prosecution application for re-consideration of the grant of bail are:

- an application for re-consideration depends on new information coming to light (and so is not impugning the original decision);
- an appeal is made to the Crown Court whereas an application for re-consideration is made to the magistrates' court.

2.12 WHAT HAPPENS IF THE DEFENDANT FAILS TO ATTEND COURT?

Section 2 of the Bail Act 1976 defines 'surrender to custody' to mean the accused 'surrendering himself into the custody of the court ... at the time and place for the time being appointed for him to do so'. In other words, the defendant 'surrenders' to custody by attending the correct court on the correct date and at the correct time and by complying with that court's procedure for surrender, for example, reporting to a particular office or a particular person (*DPP v Richards* [1988] QB 701; [1988] 3 All ER 406). As it was put in *R v Central Criminal Court ex p Guney* [1996] AC 616; [1996] 2 All ER 705, a defendant surrenders to custody when he puts himself at the direction of the court or an officer of the court. Having surrendered, the defendant must remain within the precincts of the court.

2.12.1 The offence of absconding

Section 6(1) of the Bail Act 1976 states that: 'If a person who has been released on bail in criminal proceedings fails without reasonable cause to surrender to custody he shall be guilty of an offence.' Under s 6(2), if the defendant had a reasonable excuse for non-attendance but thereafter 'fails to surrender to custody at the appointed place as soon after the appointed time as is reasonably practicable he shall be guilty of an offence' (in other words, if it is not reasonably practicable for the defendant to surrender at the appointed time, he must do so as soon as it is reasonably practicable).

The burden of proof rests on the accused to prove (on the balance of probabilities) that he had reasonable cause for his failure to surrender to custody: s 6(3).

The procedure to be followed is set out in the *Practice Direction (Criminal Proceedings: Consolidation)* [2002] 1 WLR 2870, as amended. When handing down the amendment, Lord Woolf CJ said that the failure of defendants to surrender to custody in accordance with the terms of their bail could undermine the administration of justice. Accordingly, it is most important that defendants appreciate the significance of their obligation to do so and, where they fail, that courts take appropriate action. An additional section was added to Pt I of the Practice Direction, replacing Pt V, para 56. The amendment also takes explicit account of the judgment of the Court of Appeal in *R v White; R v McKinnon* [2003] 2 Cr App R(S) 133 and the judgment of the House of Lords in *R v Jones (Anthony)* [2003] AC 1. The revised direction applies to persons released on bail in all criminal proceedings, including appeals to the Court of Appeal (Criminal Division):

Part I

13   *Failure to surrender*

13.1   The following directions take effect immediately.

13.2   The failure of defendants to comply with the terms of their bail by not surrendering can undermine the administration of justice. It can disrupt proceedings. The resulting delays impact on victims, witnesses and other court users and also waste costs. A defendant's failure to surrender affects not only the case with which he is concerned, but also the courts' ability to administer justice more generally by damaging the confidence of victims, witnesses and the public in the effectiveness of the court system and the judiciary. It is, therefore, most important that defendants who are granted bail appreciate the significance of the obligation to surrender to custody in accordance with the terms of their bail and that courts take appropriate action if they fail to do so.

13.3 There are at least three courses of action for the courts to consider taking: (a) imposing penalties for the failure to surrender; (b) revoking bail or imposing more stringent bail conditions; and (c) conducting trials in the absence of the defendant.

Penalties for failure to surrender

13.4 A defendant who commits a s 6(1) or s 6(2) Bail Act 1976 offence commits an offence that stands apart from the proceedings in respect of which bail was granted. The seriousness of the offence can be reflected by an appropriate penalty being imposed for the Bail Act offence.

13.5 The common practice at present of courts automatically deferring disposal of a s 6(1) or s 6(2) Bail Act 1976 offence (failure to surrender) until the conclusion of the proceedings in respect of which bail was granted should no longer be followed. Instead, courts should now deal with defendants as soon as is practicable. In deciding what is practicable, the court must take into account when the proceedings in respect of which bail was granted are expected to conclude, the seriousness of the offence for which the defendant is already being prosecuted, the type of penalty that might be imposed for the breach of bail and the original offence as well as any other relevant circumstances. If there is no good reason for postponing dealing with the breach until after the trial, the breach should be dealt with as soon as practicable. If the disposal of the breach of bail is deferred, then it is still necessary to consider imposing a separate penalty at the trial and the sentence for the breach of the bail should usually be custodial and consecutive to any other custodial sentence (as to which see paragraph 13.13). In addition, bail should usually be revoked in the meantime (see paragraph 13.14 to 13.16). In the case of offences which cannot, or are unlikely to, result in a custodial sentence, trial in the absence of the defendant may be a pragmatic sensible response to the situation (see paragraph 13.17 to 13.19). This was not a penalty for the Bail Act offence and a penalty might also be imposed for the Bail Act offence.

Initiating proceedings – bail granted by a police officer

13.6 When a person has been granted bail by a police officer to attend court and subsequently fails to surrender to custody, the decision whether to initiate proceedings for a s 6(1) or s 6(2) offence will be for the police/prosecutor.

13.7 The offence in this form is a summary offence and should be initiated as soon as practicable after the offence arises in view of the six months time limit running from the failure to surrender. It should be dealt with on the first appearance after arrest, unless an adjournment is necessary, as it will be relevant in considering whether to grant bail again.

Initiating proceedings – bail granted by a court

13.8 When a person has been granted bail by a court and subsequently fails to surrender to custody, on arrest that person should normally be brought as soon as appropriate before the court at which the proceedings in respect of which bail was granted are to be heard. (The six months time limit does not apply where bail was granted by the court.) Should the defendant commit another offence outside the jurisdiction of the bail court, the Bail Act offence should, where practicable, be dealt with by the new court at the same time as the new offence. If impracticable, the defendant may, if this is appropriate, be released formally on bail by the new court so that the warrant may be executed for his attendance before the first court in respect of the substantive and Bail Act offences.

13.9   Given that bail was granted by a court, it is more appropriate that the court itself should initiate the proceedings by its own motion. The court will be invited to take proceedings by the prosecutor, if the prosecutor considers proceedings are appropriate.

Conduct of proceedings

13.10 Proceedings under s 6 of the Bail Act 1976 may be conducted either as a summary offence or as a criminal contempt of court. Where the court is invited to take proceedings by the prosecutor, the prosecutor will conduct the proceedings and, if the matter is contested, call the evidence. Where the court initiates proceedings without such an invitation the same role can be played by the prosecutor at the request of the court, where this is practicable.

13.11 The burden of proof is on the defendant to prove that he had reasonable cause for his failure to surrender to custody (s 6(3) of the Bail Act 1976).

Proceedings to be progressed to disposal as soon as is practicable

13.12 If the court decides to proceed, the s 6 Bail Act offence should be concluded as soon as practicable.

Sentencing for a Bail Act offence

13.13 In principle, a custodial sentence for the offence of failing to surrender should be ordered to be served consecutively to any other sentence imposed at the same time for another offence unless there are circumstances that makes this inappropriate (see *R v White; R v McKinnon*).

Relationship between the Bail Act offence and further remands on bail or in custody

13.14 When a defendant has been convicted of a Bail Act offence, the court should review the remand status of the defendant, including the conditions of that bail, in respect of the main proceedings for which bail had been granted.

13.15 Failure by the defendant to surrender or a conviction for failing to surrender to bail in connection with the main proceedings will be a significant factor weighing against the re-granting of bail or, in the case of offences which do not normally give rise to a custodial sentence, in favour of trial in the absence of the offender.

13.16 Whether or not an immediate custodial sentence has been imposed for the Bail Act offence, the court may, having reviewed the defendant's remand status, also remand the defendant in custody in the main proceedings.

Trials in absence

13.17 A defendant has a right, in general, to be present and to be represented at his trial. However, a defendant may choose not to exercise those rights by voluntarily absenting himself and failing to instruct his lawyers adequately so that they can represent him and, in the case of proceedings before the magistrates' court, there is an express statutory power to hear trials in the defendant's absence (s 11 of the Magistrates' Courts Act 1980). In such circumstances, the court has a discretion whether the trial should take place in his/her absence.

13.18 The court must exercise its discretion to proceed in the absence of the defendant with the utmost care and caution. The overriding concern must be to ensure that such a trial is as fair as circumstances permit and leads to a just outcome.

13.19 Due regard should be had to the judgment of Lord Bingham of Cornhill in *R v Jones* [2003] AC 1 in which Lord Bingham identified circumstances to be taken into account before proceeding, which include: the conduct of the defendant, the disadvantage to the defendant, the public interest, the effect of any delay and whether the attendance of the defendant could be secured at a later hearing. Other relevant considerations are the seriousness of the offence and likely outcome if the defendant is found guilty. If the defendant is only likely to be fined for a summary offence this can be relevant since the costs that a defendant might otherwise be ordered to pay as a result of an adjournment could be disproportionate. In the case of summary proceedings the fact that there can be an appeal that is a complete rehearing is also relevant, as is the power to re-open the case under s 142 of the Magistrates' Court Act 1980.

In summary, if the defendant was granted bail by the court and then absconded, but is now before the court, it should be left to the prosecution to invite the court to take action if the prosecutor thinks it appropriate to do so. There is then a hearing to determine whether or not the defendant is guilty of absconding.

The prosecution are generally quite keen for action to be taken where a defendant has absconded. This is because if the defendant is convicted of failing to answer his bail, this conviction can be used in any later proceedings against the defendant to show a risk that he will abscond again (Sched 1, Pt I, para 9(c) to the Bail Act 1976).

Failure to answer bail which was granted by a court (that is, rather than the police) will be dealt with by the court at which the proceedings in respect of which bail was granted are to be heard. In other words, if the defendant is to be tried for the substantive offence in the magistrates' court, the Bail Act 1976 offence will be dealt with in that court. If the defendant is to be tried in the Crown Court, the Bail Act 1976 offence will be dealt with in that court (by a judge sitting alone, not by a jury). Paragraph 13.5 of the Practice Direction makes it clear that it is no longer appropriate to postpone consideration of the Bail Act 1976 offence until the conclusion of the substantive proceedings (as was formerly the practice).

Under s 6(5), an offence under s 6 is punishable 'either on summary conviction or as if it were a criminal contempt of court'. In *R v Lubega* (1999) 163 JP 221, the appellant arrived at the Crown Court 20 minutes late. The judge dealt with the matter as a contempt of court. The question for the Court of Appeal was whether the judge was entitled to treat the late arrival as a contempt of court. The court held that if the appellant had committed any offence, it was contrary to s 6(1) of the Bail Act 1976. The effect of s 6(5) is not to convert an offence under the Act into a contempt of court, but rather to provide a speedy method of disposing of the matter. The judge was therefore not entitled to deal with the matter as a contempt of court.

Section 6(7) of the Bail Act 1976 provides that a person convicted of absconding is liable to up to three months' imprisonment and/or a fine of up to £5,000 in the magistrates' court or to 12 months' imprisonment and an unlimited fine in the Crown Court; the latter applies whether the defendant has been committed to the Crown Court for sentence (under s 6(6) of the Bail Act 1976) or if the offence is being dealt with by the Crown Court because the defendant had been sent for trial in the Crown Court before he absconded (see *Schiavo v Anderton* [1987] QB 20; [1986] 3 All ER 10).

In *R v White; R v McKinnon* [2002] EWCA Crim 2952; [2003] 2 Cr App R(S) 29, the Court of Appeal said that a custodial sentence imposed for failure to surrender to custody (s 6 of the Bail Act 1976) should normally be ordered to be served consecutively to any sentence of imprisonment imposed for the substantive offence for which the defendant was before the court. The court also made it clear that there is no principle of law that the sentence for failing to surrender to custody should be proportionate to the sentence for the substantive offence of which the defendant stands convicted. Indeed, the court pointed out that in *R v Neve* (1986) 8 Cr App R(S) 270, the Court of Appeal had upheld the imposition of a sentence of six months' imprisonment for failing to surrender to custody even though the defendant had been acquitted of the substantive offence.

Failure to answer police bail is dealt with by the police laying an information; the allegation is then tried at the magistrates' court. When this form of commencement of criminal proceedings is abolished (under the Criminal Justice Act 2003), the new written charge and requisition procedure will be used for this purpose. Also, s 15(3) of the Criminal Justice Act 2003 (in force since April 2004) disapplies s 127 of the Magistrates' Court Act 1980 (which prevents summary proceedings from being instituted more than six months after the commission of an offence) in respect of offences under s 6 of the Bail Act 1976, and instead provides that such an offence may not be tried unless an information is laid either within six months of the commission of the offence, or within three months of the date when the defendant surrenders to custody, is arrested in connection with the offence for which bail was granted, or appears in court in respect of that offence. This will ensure that a defendant cannot escape prosecution under s 6 of the Bail Act 1976 merely by succeeding in absconding for more than six months.

2.12.2 Reasonable cause

An offence is only committed under s 6 if the defendant has no reasonable cause for the failure to surrender.

Section 6(3) states that it is for the accused to prove that he had reasonable cause for his failure to surrender to custody. As is always the case when a defendant bears a burden of proof, it is the civil standard that is the balance of probabilities.

In *R v How* [1993] Crim LR 201, following the earlier decision in *R v Watson* (1990) 12 Cr App R(S) 227, the Court of Appeal emphasised that, when the court is dealing with an allegation of absconding, the defendant must be given an opportunity to explain the failure to surrender to custody, or (if the defendant admits the offence) to put forward any mitigation. Furthermore, where the defendant denies the offence, he should be given the chance to adduce evidence that he had good cause for the failure to surrender (*R v Boyle* [1993] Crim LR 40). Likewise, in *R v Hourigan* [2003] EWCA Crim 2306; [2003] All ER (D) 229 (Jul), where the defendant arrived late at the Crown Court (in breach of his bail), the Court of Appeal noted that, because the failure to surrender has to have been without reasonable cause, it is incumbent on the court, before deciding whether to impose a penalty, to decide whether the s 6(1) offence has been made out. The allegation that he has committed an offence under s 6(1) should be put to the defendant (either directly or through counsel). If the defendant admits the breach, the court can go on to consider the question of penalty. Where the defendant does not admit the breach, the court should make the necessary enquiries (for example, through questioning the defendant) and then make a formal announcement of whether the allegation is found to be proven or not, with reasons for that finding.

In *R v Liverpool City Justices ex p Santos* (1997) *The Times*, 23 January, QBD, it was held that a mistake by a solicitor may, depending on the circumstances, be a reasonable excuse for a defendant's failure to surrender to bail.

If reasonable cause exists at the time the defendant should have surrendered, then he should surrender as soon as reasonably practicable thereafter.

2.12.3 Bench warrant

If the defendant was originally arrested and charged, failing to attend court is not only an offence itself (s 6 of the Bail Act 1976) but also enables the court to grant a warrant for the defendant's arrest – s 7(1) of the Bail Act 1976 provides that:

> If a person who has been released on bail in criminal proceedings and is under a duty to surrender into the custody of a court fails to surrender to custody at the time appointed for him to do so the court may issue a warrant for his arrest.

Such a warrant is known as a 'bench warrant'.

If a defendant fails to attend court but there is a suggestion that he has a good reason for not doing so (but there is insufficient information to be sure of this), the court may issue a bench warrant but 'back it for bail'. In other words, the warrant is endorsed with a direction to the police to release the defendant once he has been arrested and informed of the next date he must attend court. This serves to warn the defendant that failure to attend court may lead to his arrest.

If the defendant clearly has a good reason for not attending court, the court should simply adjourn the case in the absence of the defendant, with the defendant being remanded on bail as before (s 129(3) of the Magistrates' Courts Act 1980). This is sometimes known as 'enlarging bail'.

If no good reason is apparent, an arrest warrant (not backed for bail) will be issued.

Under the Magistrates' Courts (Miscellaneous Amendments) Rules 1993, a clerk is empowered to issue an arrest warrant (whether or not endorsed for bail) if there is no objection on behalf of the accused.

Under s 7(2), if the defendant surrenders to custody by attending court on the appropriate day, but then absents himself from the court at any time after he has surrendered to the custody of the court and before the court is ready to begin or to resume the hearing of the proceedings, this is a breach of bail and a bench warrant may be issued.

2.12.4 Failure to attend to answer summons

If the defendant was supposed to attend court to answer a summons (that is, he was not originally arrested and charged), a bench warrant can only be granted if the information upon which the summons was based is substantiated on oath and the offence alleged is one which is imprisonable (s 1 of the Magistrates' Courts Act 1980).

2.12.5 After arrest under a bench warrant

After arrest pursuant to a bench warrant not backed for bail, the defendant will be taken before the court which granted bail and the question of whether or not he should be released on bail (perhaps with more stringent conditions) or kept in custody will be decided by the court. The defendant should be taken before the court within 24 hours of arrest (excluding Sundays).

As a result of absconding, the defendant's chance of being granted bail in the same proceedings are reduced because the court is entitled (under Sched 1, Pt I, para 6 to the Bail Act 1976) to give particular weight to the fact that the defendant has already absconded in connection with those proceedings.

2.12.6 Police powers

The police have the power to arrest without warrant a person who is on bail if there are reasonable grounds to believe that he will abscond. Section 7(3) of the Bail Act 1976 provides that:

A person who has been released on bail in criminal proceedings and is under a duty to surrender into the custody of a court may be arrested without warrant by a constable—

(a)   if the constable has reasonable grounds for believing that that person is not likely to surrender to custody; …

After arrest, the defendant will be brought before the court.

2.12.7 Proceeding with the case in the defendant's absence

In some instances, it may be possible to continue with the case even though the defendant is not present in the courtroom. This is dealt with in the chapters which follow as we examine the various hearings that may take place in a criminal case.

2.13 PERIOD OF REMAND IN CUSTODY PRIOR TO CONVICTION

The maximum period of a remand in custody prior to conviction is 'eight clear days' unless s 128A of the Magistrates' Courts Act 1980 applies (s 128(6) of the Magistrates' Courts Act 1980).

The term 'eight *clear* days' means that if a hearing takes place on Monday, the next hearing must take place no later than the following Wednesday.

Section 128A provides as follows:

A magistrates' court may remand the accused in custody for a period exceeding 8 clear days if—

(a)   it has previously remanded him in custody for the same offence; and

(b)   he is before the court,

but only if, after affording the parties an opportunity to make representations, it has set a date on which it expects that it will be possible for the next stage in the proceedings, other than a hearing relating to a further remand in custody or on bail, to take place, and only—

(i)   for a period ending not later than that date; or

(ii)   for a period of 28 clear days,

whichever is the less.

Thus, s 128A allows a remand in custody for up to 28 days but does not apply to the first remand hearing, as the defendant must have previously been remanded in custody for the same offence. Furthermore, for s 128A to apply, the next hearing must be 'effective', in the sense that the mode of trial hearing or committal proceedings or summary trial will take place. Both the prosecution and the defendant must be allowed to make representations before a remand in excess of eight days is ordered, but the defendant's consent is not required. It should be noted that s 128A(3) provides that 'nothing in this section affects the right of the accused to apply for bail during the period of the remand'.

2.13.1   Remands in absence of the defendant

The provisions of s 128A should be contrasted with remands in the absence of the defendant which are possible, under s 128(3A)–(3E), provided that (a) the defendant 'has the assistance of a legal representative to represent him in the proceedings in that court' (s 128(1B)), and (b) the defendant consents to not being present at future remand hearings (s 128(1C)). The defendant must be brought before the court on at least every fourth application for his remand (s 128(1A)(ii)). Thus, there can be a maximum of three remands *in absentia*, and so the defendant has to appear in court at least once a month.

It is open to the defendant to withdraw his consent to be remanded in his absence (s 128(3A)(d)). It follows that the defendant can still apply for bail during the 28 day period by giving notice to the court that he wishes to do so.

2.13.2   Remand after conviction

Following summary conviction, there may be a remand in custody of up to three weeks to enable the preparation of a pre-sentence report (dealing with the most suitable method of dealing with the defendant). Section 10(3) of the Magistrates' Courts Act 1980 provides that:

> A magistrates' court may, for the purpose of enabling inquiries to be made or of determining the most suitable method of dealing with the case, exercise its power to adjourn after convicting the accused and before sentencing him or otherwise dealing with him; but, if it does so, the adjournment shall not be for more than 4 weeks at a time unless the court remands the accused in custody and, where it so remands him, the adjournment shall not be for more than 3 weeks at a time.

2.13.3   Place of remand

Remand in custody means that the defendant is held in prison or (if aged 18–20) in a remand centre. However, s 128(7) of the Magistrates' Courts Act 1980 allows a remand to police custody for a maximum of three clear days; s 128(8) states that this is only possible if it is necessary for the purpose of making inquiries into offences other than those presently before court). The defendant must be brought back to the magistrates' court as soon as the need to question him ceases.

Where a defendant has been remanded in custody, he will have to be brought to the court from the place he is detained on the next date when he is due to appear in court (this is sometimes known as being 'produced'). The defendant will be kept in cells adjacent to the court until his case is called on. At that point he will be escorted into the dock.

Section 57 of the Crime and Disorder Act 1998 allows preliminary hearings (that is, hearings before the start of the trial) to take place even though the defendant is not present in court provided that he is in custody in prison and, by means of a live television link or otherwise, he is able to see and hear the court and to be seen and heard by it.

It should be noted that a person who is in remand in the cells of the court (for example, waiting to be taken up to the courtroom) has a common law right to consult a solicitor as soon as reasonably practicable if he so wishes (*R v Chief Constable of South Wales ex p Merrick* [1994] 1 WLR 663; [1994] 2 All ER 560).

2.14   EARLY ADMINISTRATIVE HEARINGS

Section 50 of the Crime and Disorder Act 1998 provides for 'early administrative hearings' in the magistrates' court. It provides that where the accused has been charged with an offence at a police station, the magistrates' court before whom he appears for the first time may (unless the offence or one of them is triable only on indictment) consist of a single magistrate (s 50(1)). At this hearing, the accused must be asked 'whether he wishes to be granted a right to representation funded by the Legal Services Commission as part of the Criminal Defence Service and, if he does, the justice shall decide whether or not to grant him such a right' (s 50(2)). The single justice may then remand the accused in custody or on bail (s 50(3)). Such a hearing may also be conducted by a justices' clerk, with the important proviso that the clerk is not empowered to remand the accused in custody and may only vary conditions of bail imposed by the police if the prosecution and accused both consent to the clerk doing so (s 50(4)).

2.15   CUSTODY TIME LIMITS

Section 22 of the Prosecution of Offences Act 1985 provides for 'custody time limits'. The custody time limits are set out in the Prosecution of Offences (Custody Time Limits) Regulations 1987 (SI 1987/299). For indictable offences, the custody time limit from first appearance to committal proceedings is 70 days; for offences which are triable either way and the case is to be tried summarily, the custody time limit from first appearance to the start of the trial is 70 days unless the mode of trial hearing takes place within 56 days in which case the time limit is 56 days (reg 4). Following committal proceedings, the time limit from committal to arraignment at the Crown Court is 112 days (reg 5).

These provisions apply to proceedings in the youth court even though the usual distinction between summary and indictable offences does not apply there (*R v Stratford Youth Court ex p S* [1998] 1 WLR 1758).

For the purposes of s 22, proceedings for an offence are taken to have begun when the accused is charged with the offence or an information is laid charging him with the offence (s 22(11ZA)).

The start of a trial on indictment is taken to occur when 'a jury is sworn to consider the issue of guilt or fitness to plead or, if the court accepts a plea of guilty before a jury is sworn, when that plea is accepted' (s 22(11A)). The start of a summary trial is taken to occur '(a) when the court begins to hear evidence for the prosecution at the trial or to consider whether to exercise its power under section 37(3) of the Mental Health Act 1983 (power to make hospital order without convicting the accused), or (b) if the court accepts a plea of guilty without proceeding as mentioned above, when that plea is accepted' (s 22(11B)).

In *R v Leeds Crown Court ex p Whitehead* (2000) 164 JP 102, the custody time limit applicable to the defendant was due to expire on 15 October 1998. The trial commenced on 14 October 1998. On 26 January 1999, the trial was stopped and the jury were discharged. A fresh trial date was set for 13 September 1999; the defendant was remanded in custody. The defendant argued that the custody time limit provisions were applicable to the period after the abandonment of the first trial. The Divisional Court held that, since the custody time limit provisions cease to apply at the start of the trial (that is, when a jury is sworn in), the time limit provisions did not apply to the period between when a trial is aborted in the Crown Court and the re-trial. However, the court went on to say that if a trial is aborted and a re-trial ordered, the judge should be vigilant to protect the interests of the accused by taking steps to fix a speedy re-trial, or by considering the grant of bail, or even staying the proceedings as an abuse of process.

2.15.1 Expiry of the time limit

Under reg 8 of the Prosecution of Offences (Custody Time Limits) Regulations 1987 (SI 1987/299), where a custody time limit has expired:

- the defendant has an absolute right to bail;
- the court cannot require sureties, or the giving of security as a condition of granting bail (but it can impose other conditions, such as conditions of residence, reporting to a police station, etc); and
- following the grant of bail, the defendant may not be arrested without warrant merely on the ground that a police officer believes he is unlikely to surrender to custody.

If the defendant is granted bail because the custody time limit has expired, his right to bail continues only until he is arraigned (that is, when he pleads guilty or not guilty). Thereafter, the court can withhold bail if any of the reasons for doing so under the Bail Act 1976 apply (*R v Croydon Crown Court ex p Lewis* (1994) 158 JP 886).

Also, under s 22(4) of the Prosecution of Offences Act 1985, where the overall time limit expires, the court must stay the proceedings against the accused. Section 22B enables the proceedings to be re-instituted in certain limited circumstances.

2.15.2 Extending the time limit

Section 22(3) of the 1985 Act empowers the appropriate court, at any time before the expiry of a time limit imposed by the regulations, to extend (or further extend) that limit. The appropriate court to do so is the Crown Court if the defendant has been committed or sent for trial to the Crown Court; otherwise the application should be made to the magistrates' court.

The court can only extend the custody time limit under s 22(3) if it is satisfied:

(a)   that the need for the extension is due to:

    (i)   the illness or absence of the accused, a necessary witness, a judge or a magistrate;

    (ii) a postponement which is occasioned by the ordering by the court of separate trials in the case of two or more accused or two or more offences; or

    (iii) some other good and sufficient cause,

and

(b)   that the prosecution has acted with all due diligence and expedition.

In *R v Leeds Crown Court ex p Bagoutie* (1999) *The Times*, 31 May, the Divisional Court held that, where there is an application for an extension of the custody time limits and the court is satisfied that there is good and sufficient cause for the extension but is not satisfied that the prosecution have acted with all due expedition, the court is not obliged to refuse the application for an extension if it concludes that the failure to exercise due expedition has not caused or contributed to the need for the extension. It follows that the court is not obliged to refuse an extension in a case where there has been avoidable delay by the prosecution but that delay has had no effect on the ability of the prosecution and the defence to be ready for trial on a predetermined trial date.

Further guidance was given by the Court of Appeal in *R v Manchester Crown Court ex p McDonald* [1999] 1 All ER 805. The court held that to grant an extension of the custody time limit, the court must first be satisfied on the balance of probabilities that both statutory conditions in s 22(3) are met. First, the prosecutor must show that there is a sufficient basis for the court to be satisfied that there is good reason to grant an extension (sub-s (3)(a)). The court still has to make this decision even if the parties agree to the extension or if there is no objection to it from the defence. This requirement will not be satisfied merely because of the seriousness of the offence or by the fact that only a short extension is required. To satisfy the second requirement (under sub-s 3(b)), it must be shown that the prosecutor has acted with the diligence and expedition to be shown by a competent prosecutor conscious of his duty to bring the case to trial as quickly as reasonably and fairly possible. This involves having regard to the nature and complexity of the case, the extent of preparation necessary, the conduct of the defence, and the extent to which the prosecutor depends on the co-operation of people outside his control. Staff shortages are not relevant. Difficulty in finding an appropriate judge will only be relevant if the case needs to be tried by a judge of particular seniority. Further, the Divisional Court will only interfere if the court below reaches a decision that no reasonable court could reach.

Similarly, it was held in *R (Bannister) v Guildford Crown Court* [2004] EWHC 221 that a routine case with no particular facts capable of constituting a good and sufficient cause will not qualify for an extension of custody time limits merely because of listing difficulties. The court pointed out that if the difficulty of providing judicial resources is too readily accepted as a good and sufficient reason for extending custody time limits, there is a danger that the purpose of the statutory provisions will be undermined. The court accepted, however, that there may be exceptional situations where the particular case can only be tried by a particular class of judge, where such a judge is only going to be available at a particular trial centre for a particular time, where other similar cases are already awaiting trial, and where there is no reasonable alternative but to make the defendant wait because the case cannot readily be transferred to another court centre.

However, in *R (Gibson) v Crown Court at Winchester* [2004] EWHC 361; [2004] 1 WLR 1623, Lord Woolf CJ considered *Bannister* and held that the availability of resources (whether of courtrooms or of judges) is not an irrelevant consideration. Courts cannot ignore the fact that resources are limited and that at certain times the pressures on those resources would be greater than at other times. It is important that courts strive to overcome any difficulties that occurred; if they do not, that might debar them from extending the custody time limits. However, it is certainly not correct that judges should ignore questions of the non-availability of resources. Thus, unavailability of a suitable judge and courtroom for the trial of a defendant are relevant considerations when deciding whether to extend a custody time limit. In that case, the court also confirmed that (as had been held in *Bagoutie*) the extension does not have to be refused if the prosecution's failure had not caused the need for the extension. Thus, a judge may extend the custody time limit of a defendant who is awaiting trial, despite the fact that the prosecution have not acted with all due diligence and expedition, if the prosecution's failure has not caused the need for the extension.

Delays caused by police under-staffing will not amount to a good reason for extending time (*R v Southampton Crown Court ex p Roddie* [1991] 1 WLR 303).

In *R v Leeds Crown Court ex p Briggs (No 1)* [1998] 2 Cr App R 413, the Divisional Court noted that the seriousness of the offence is not, of itself, enough to justify an extension of time but the complexity of the case might be. The Divisional Court in that case also held that the court should give reasons explaining its decision that there is good and sufficient cause to extend time and that the prosecution has acted with all due expedition.

It must be borne in mind that matters relevant to granting or refusing bail under the Bail Act 1976, such as the seriousness of the offence, the need to protect the public and the shortness of the extension required, cannot of themselves provide a good and sufficient cause for extending a custody time limit under the Prosecution of Offences Act 1985 (*R v Sheffield Crown Court ex p Headley* [2000] 2 Cr App R 1; *R (Eliot) v Reading Crown Court* [2001] EWHC 464 (Admin); [2001] 4 All ER 625).

The application to extend the time limit must be made prior to the expiry of the limit: once the limit has expired, there is no power to extend it (*R v Sheffield Justices ex p Turner* [1991] 2 QB 472).

What happens if the defendant is charged with another offence? In *R v Great Yarmouth Magistrates ex p Thomas* [1992] Crim LR 116, the defendant was charged with importing cannabis. The prosecution applied for an extension of the custody time limit, but the court refused to extend time. The defendant was released on bail but was immediately arrested by police for possessing cannabis with intent to supply. The Divisional Court held that there was nothing to stop the prosecution from bringing several charges against a defendant based on the same or similar facts, even if this results in there being several custody time limits in operation. However, the magistrates should ensure that the prosecution are not abusing the process of the court by doing so. Likewise, in *R v Stafford Crown Court ex p Uppall* (1995) 159 JP 86, where the defendant was charged with rape, at the expiry of the custody time limit (an application for an extension of time having been refused), the prosecution preferred an additional charge of false imprisonment arising out of the same facts as the rape. It was held that, where an additional charge is brought against a defendant who is already charged with an offence, the second offence has its own custody time limit and this is the case whether or not the second charge is based on additional evidence. It was also said that when the CPS are considering bringing further charges against a defendant, they should review the evidence at the earliest opportunity and, wherever possible, comply with the initial custody time limit. However, the CPS would not be guilty of abuse of process unless it was established that they brought further charges simply for the purpose of extending the time limit.

In a case being tried in the Crown Court, the arraignment has to take place before the expiry of the custody time limit if the accused is to remain in custody, otherwise the prosecution have to apply for an extension of the time limit. In *R v Maidstone Crown Court ex p Hollstein* [1995] 3 All ER 503, the defendant had been arrested for arson on 19 January 1994. The custody time limit following committal for trial was extended to 22 July, the date the trial was expected to start. The trial did not start on 22 July, but no application to extend the custody time limit was made. On 27 July, the defendant was arraigned (although the trial did not in fact start on that date) and was remanded in custody. It was said by the Queen's Bench Division that it was not permissible to arraign a defendant simply to deprive the accused of the right to bail he would otherwise have enjoyed upon the expiry of the custody time limit. See also *R v Maidstone Crown Court ex p Clark* [1995] 1 WLR 831, where the defendant was served with a large amount of evidential material on the date he was supposed to be entering a plea. As the custody time limit was about to expire, the prosecution wanted the defendant to be arraigned, even though he needed more time to consider the evidence just served on him. Again, the Divisional Court said that it was improper to arraign a defendant simply to defeat the custody time limit provisions.

A similar situation arose in *R (Wardle) v Leeds Crown Court* [2001] UKHL 12; [2002] 1 AC 754, where the appellant was charged with murder. On the day that the custody time limit expired, the prosecution offered no evidence on the murder charge but charged the appellant with manslaughter arising out of the same facts. The question to be decided was whether the later charge caused a fresh custody time limit to start running. The House of Lords held that, on a proper construction of reg 4(4) of the Prosecution of Offences (Custody Time Limits) Regulations 1987, each separate offence attracts its own custody time limit; however, there would be no fresh custody time limit if the new charge is simply a restatement of the other offence with different particulars. Thus, the new offence has to be a different offence in law if it is to attract a fresh custody time limit. The House of Lords went on to hold that the bringing of a new charge would be an abuse of process if the prosecution could not demonstrate, on the facts of the case, that the bringing of the new charge was justified, so that the court was satisfied that it had not been brought solely with a view to obtaining the substitution of a fresh custody time limit. On this basis, it was held that there is no incompatibility with the European Convention on Human Rights.

Where the defendant wishes to argue that the arraignment in the Crown Court was improper, judicial review is not available to challenge the arraignment. This is because judicial review cannot be sought in respect of matters relating to Crown Court trials (s 29(3) of the Supreme Court Act 1981). Therefore, the only remedy available to a defendant in such a case is to seek a writ of habeas corpus (*R v Leeds Crown Court ex p Hussain* [1995] 1 WLR 1329).

Under s 22(7) of the Prosecution of Offences Act 1985, where a magistrates' court decides to extend, or further extend, a time limit, the accused may appeal against the decision to the Crown Court. Under sub-s (8), where a magistrates' court refuses to extend, or further extend, a time limit, the prosecution may similarly appeal against the refusal to the Crown Court. Sub-section (9) provides that an appeal under sub-s (8) may not be commenced after the expiry of the limit in question and also provides that where such an appeal is commenced before the expiry of the limit, the limit shall be deemed not to have expired before the determination or abandonment of the appeal.

The court can decide whether or not to extend time on the basis of submissions from counsel; in other words, there is no need for evidence to be called if the court thinks that this would be unnecessary (*R v Norwich Crown Court ex p Parker and Ward* (1992) 96 Cr App R 68).

In *Wildman v DPP* [2001] EWHC 14 (Admin); (2001) 165 JP 543, the Divisional Court considered the procedure for seeking an extension of a custody time limit in light of the coming into force of the Human Rights Act 1998. It was held that this procedure could be more informal than a normal trial process, and so it is unnecessary to comply with the formal rules of evidence. The burden is on the prosecution to obtain an extension of time: it has to satisfy the justices that it is a proper application and it also has to enable the defendant to test the appropriateness of the application. In the majority of cases, it should be possible for the prosecution to make information available to the defendant, prior to the application, which will enable him to be satisfied as to the propriety of the application. In so far as it is necessary for a defendant to test any aspect of the application, the means must be provided to enable him to do that. However, the court said that formal disclosure of the sort which is appropriate prior to trial is not normally necessary for an application for bail or for an extension of custody time limits.

In *R (Siraju) v Crown Court at Snaresbrook* [2001] EWHC 638 (Admin); [2001] All ER (D) 55, the Divisional Court pointed out that it is settled law that a court can only be satisfied that the conditions for extending custody time limits under the Prosecution of Offences Act 1985 are fulfilled if it has conducted an inquiry into the matter. The court has to satisfy itself of the matters set out in the Act, and cannot abdicate its responsibility by assuming that the matter has been adequately dealt with by a different judge on a previous occasion. The court therefore cannot assume fulfilment of the conditions from the fact that another court had seen fit to fix a trial date outside the limit, or that counsel have accepted that date for their convenience. In the present case, the judge was unaware of the history of the case and, even though he had no material evidence before him upon which to make any findings as to due expedition, he had simply inferred due expedition from the order of the previous judge fixing the trial date. It followed that there had been procedural impropriety and the decision would accordingly be quashed.

The Auld Review considers the custody time limits contained in the Prosecution of Offences Act 1985 (see paras 262–70 of Chapter 10). Recommendation 226 says that:

> Section 22 of the Prosecution of Offences Act 1985 should be amended to enable a court to consider and grant an extension of the custody time limit after its expiry, but only if such power is closely circumscribed, including a provision that the court should only grant an extension where it is satisfied that there is a compelling public interest in doing so.

2.16   DELAY BEFORE OR DURING PROCEEDINGS

We have already seen that if a defendant is remanded in custody prior to trial, the custody time limits restrict the length of time that the defendant can be kept in custody unless the prosecution are able to justify extending the custody time limit. Once the custody limit has expired, then, unless the prosecution obtain an extension, the defendant has to be released on bail. However, the prosecution continues against him.

Nevertheless, there are instances when a case can be terminated as a result of delay.

In *R v Willesden Justices ex p Clemmings* (1987) 87 Cr App R 280, and in *R v Derby Crown Court ex p Brooks* (1984) 80 Cr App R 164, it was said that there are two types of delay which empower the court to stop the proceedings against the accused:

- where the prosecution have deliberately manipulated or misused the process of the court so as to take unfair advantage of the accused (for example, deliberately delaying proceedings in the hope that a defence witness will no longer be available to give evidence); or
- where the accused is able to show that he has been, or will be, prejudiced in the preparation or conduct of his defence by delay on the part of the prosecution which, although not deliberate, was nonetheless unjustifiable.

Delay may arise before or after proceedings are commenced. The two types of delay which have been identified – abuse of process and prejudice to the defendant – have been considered in a number of cases.

2.16.1   Deliberate delay: abuse of process

In *R v Brentford Justices ex p Wong* [1981] QB 445, the prosecution laid an information alleging careless driving. The information was laid just before the expiry of the six month time limit which applies to summary offences. The prosecution asked for the summons not to be served straight away, however, as they had not yet decided whether or not to proceed with the case. The summons was served five months later. The Divisional Court said that the magistrates had a discretion to dismiss the case because of the delay, which had been a deliberate attempt to gain further time in which to reach a decision.

2.16.2   Inadvertent delay: prejudice to defendant

In *Dyer v Watson* [2002] UKPC D1; [2004] 1 AC 379, the Privy Council had to consider the effect of delay in criminal proceedings. It was held that the threshold of proving that a trial has not taken place within a reasonable time is a high one, not easily crossed. If the period which has elapsed is one which, on its face, gives ground for real concern, then (a) it is necessary to look into the detailed circumstances of the particular case, and (b) it must be possible to justify any lapse of time which appears to be excessive. Regard must be had to (a) the complexity of the case; (b) the conduct of the defendant (since a defendant cannot properly complain of delay of which he is the author); and (c) the manner in which the case has been dealt with by the prosecution and the courts (there is no general obligation on a prosecutor to act with all due expedition and diligence; however, a marked lack of expedition, if unjustified, would point towards a breach of the reasonable time requirement).

To succeed in having a case dismissed on the basis of delay which is not deliberate, the defence must show both inordinate delay as a result of inefficiency on the part of the prosecution and that the defendant has been, or will be, prejudiced by that delay (*per* Lloyd LJ in *R v Gateshead Justices ex p Smith* (1985) 149 JP 681). In that case, there was a delay of more than two years between the issue and the service of the summons and the trial was eventually fixed for a date over three years after the alleged offences. This was said to be inordinate and prejudicial delay and it was therefore held that the case should therefore proceed no further. Similarly, in *R v Oxford City Justices ex p Smith* (1982) 75 Cr App R 200, the summons was inadvertently sent to the wrong address; the summons was eventually served nearly two years later. The prosecution had the correct address and the delay was a result of their inefficiency; further, it was found that the defence would be handicapped as a result of the delay and its effect on the memories of any relevant witnesses. It was held that the case should be dismissed.

On the other hand, in *R v Grays Justices ex p Graham* [1982] QB 1239; [1982] 3 All ER 653, committal proceedings held more than two years after the alleged offences were held not to cause undue prejudice to the accused. The Court of Appeal held that the delay was not sufficiently prolonged to amount to an abuse of process and apparently accepted the prosecution contention that the offences involved (cheque fraud) take a long time to investigate. Likewise, in *R v Central Criminal Court ex p Randle* [1991] 1 WLR 1087, the defendants were charged with offences arising out of the escape from prison of the spy George Blake. The offences had occurred some 23 years ago but the defendants had published a book about what they had done in 1989. The prosecution case was based on the book and so the Divisional Court held that the defendants could not claim that they were prejudiced by the failing memory of witnesses.

In *R v Canterbury and St Augustine's Justices ex p Barrington* (1994) 158 JP 325, an information was laid against the defendant alleging a drink-driving offence. The defendant had left the address he had given the police before the summons was served. The police had no other address for him. The summons was not served until nearly four years after the alleged offence. The court reiterated the familiar principle that a stay would only be ordered if the defendant could show, on the balance of probabilities, that no fair trial could take place because of the degree of prejudice caused by the delay. That involved looking at the case as a whole. Here, the defendant conceded that it was unlikely that he would have any defence to the summons; in the circumstances, the court concluded that the justices had not erred in deciding that a fair trial was possible despite the delay.

In *R v Telford Justices ex p Badhan* [1991] 2 QB 78; [1991] 2 All ER 854, the defendant was charged with a rape which was alleged to have occurred over 14 years ago. The Divisional Court reiterated that the test to be applied was not whether the prosecution could be blamed for the delay but whether the accused could show, on the balance of probabilities, that a fair trial was no longer possible. In that case, it was not and so the case stopped there. In *R v Dutton* [1994] Crim LR 910, it was re-emphasised that it is for the defendant to show, on the balance of probabilities, that the delay is such that a fair trial is not possible.

These decisions followed the Court of Appeal decision on the *Attorney General's Reference (No 1 of 1990)* [1992] 1 QB 630, in which it was said that a stay of proceedings on the ground of delay should rarely be ordered in the absence of fault on the part of the prosecution and should never be ordered where the delay was due merely to the complexity of the case or contributed to by the actions of the defendant himself.

Where the events giving rise to the charges took place a long time ago, it is important that full account is taken (by the magistrates or jury, as the case may be) of the difficulties this fact presents to the defence. In *R v Birchall* (1995) *The Times*, 23 March, the defendant faced charges of rape and indecent assault arising out of incidents which allegedly took place 15–20 years ago. The judge refused to stay the proceedings for abuse of process. The Court of Appeal (perhaps surprisingly) upheld this decision but allowed the defendant's appeal against conviction because the judge had failed to warn the jury about the difficulties which the defendant would have in defending himself against such old charges. Similarly, in *R v B* [1996] Crim LR 406, the appellant was charged with rape and indecent assault, the offences allegedly having been committed 19 years earlier. The Court of Appeal, upholding the decision of the trial judge to allow the trial to take place, said that, provided that there could still be a fair trial, a lapse of time was not a sufficient reason for granting a stay of the case. However, the judge in this case had failed to direct the jury on the difficulties which the defendant faced in defending the case in the light of the lapse of time; it was on that basis that the appeal was allowed. Likewise, in *R v Wilkinson* [1996] 1 Cr App R 81, convictions for indecent assault, gross indecency and incest were upheld even though the acts were committed some 15–28 years ago. The judge had held that a fair trial was possible and the Court of Appeal would not impugn that decision. Also, the judge had given a warning to the jury that the defence had difficulties in adducing precise evidence because of the lapse of time.

A note of caution on the use of authorities in applications to stay proceedings on the ground of delay was sounded by the Divisional Court in *R v Newham Justices ex p C* [1993] Crim LR 130. The court said that comparing the facts of the instant case with the facts of earlier reported cases will rarely be of assistance: it is a question of fact whether the particular defendant is able to show that a fair trial is no longer possible.

The right to a fair trial under Art 6 of the European Convention on Human Rights includes the right to have a trial within a reasonable time. However, it appears that this right adds little or nothing to the rights founded upon the common law. In *Attorney General's Reference (No 2 of 2001)* [2003] UKHL 68; [2004] 2 WLR 1, the House of Lords considered the effect of delay. In that case, the charges arose from incidents which took place in April 1998; proceedings were started in February 2000 and the trial was scheduled to start in January 2001. The defendants submitted that the proceedings should be stayed because the delay meant that a fair trial was no longer possible. The judge agreed, and ordered that the proceedings should be stayed. The stay was later lifted, but the prosecution offered no evidence, and the defendants were therefore acquitted. The Attorney General referred two points of law for the opinion of the Court of Appeal: (i) whether criminal proceedings could be stayed on the ground that there had been a violation of the reasonable time requirement in Art 6(1) of the European Convention on Human Rights in circumstances where the accused could not demonstrate any prejudice arising from the delay; and (ii) when the relevant time period commences in the determination of whether, for the purposes of Art 6(1), a criminal charge had been heard within a reasonable time. The House of Lords held that criminal proceedings could be stayed on the ground that there had been a violation of the reasonable time requirement in Art 6(1) of the Convention only if a fair hearing is no longer possible, or it is for any compelling reason unfair to try the defendant. It was said that it would be anomalous if breach of the reasonable time requirement were to have an effect that is more far-reaching than breach of the defendant's other rights under Art 6(1). It was held that if, through the action or inaction of a public authority, a criminal charge is not determined at a hearing within a reasonable time, there is necessarily a breach of the defendant's Convention right, and such remedy has to be afforded as is just and appropriate. If the breach is established before the hearing, the appropriate remedy might be a public acknowledgment of the breach, action to expedite the hearing to the greatest extent practicable and perhaps, if the defendant were in custody, his release on bail. If the breach is established after the hearing, the appropriate remedy might be a public acknowledgment of the breach, a reduction in the penalty imposed on a convicted defendant or the payment of compensation to an acquitted defendant. Unless the hearing was unfair, or it was unfair to try the defendant at all, it would not be appropriate to quash any conviction. Cases where the delay is of such an order, or the prosecutor's breach of professional duty is such as to make it unfair that proceedings against the defendant should continue would be recognisable, although very exceptional. A stay would never be an appropriate remedy if any lesser remedy would adequately vindicate the defendant's Convention right. On the second question, the House of Lords held that, for the purposes of the requirement under Art 6(1) of the Convention that a criminal charge must be heard within a reasonable time, the relevant time period commences at the earliest time at which the defendant was officially alerted to the likelihood of criminal proceedings against him. This will normally be when he was charged or served with a summons to attend court.

It follows that if there has been prejudice caused to a defendant which interferes with his right to a fair trial in a way which could not otherwise be remedied, a stay of the proceedings is the appropriate remedy. However, in the absence of prejudice of that sort, there is normally no justification for granting a stay. The proceedings should be stayed only if it would amount to an abuse of the process of the court to proceed with the prosecution.

When should a point about delay amounting to abuse of process be taken? In *R v Smolinski* [2004] EWCA Crim 1270; (2004) *The Times*, 28 May, the Court of Appeal said that where there was delay in bringing a criminal case to trial, the developing practice of making an application for a stay of proceedings on the ground of abuse of process would not always be appropriate and is to be discouraged. If such an application is to be made, the court said that it is preferable to do so after the evidence has been called, so that the court has had the opportunity to see the witnesses.

2.16.3 Code of Conduct for Crown Prosecutors

According to the Code of Conduct for Crown Prosecutors, it may not be in the public interest to prosecute where there has been a long delay between the offence taking place and the date of the trial. However, this will not be so if the offence is serious, or the delay has been caused in part by the defendant, or the offence has only recently come to light, or the complexity of the offence has meant that there has been a long investigation.

CHAPTER 3

CLASSIFICATION AND ALLOCATION OF OFFENCES

3.1 INTRODUCTION

In this chapter, we examine how the decision is made as to which court (magistrates' court or Crown Court) the offence should be tried in, if that offence is one which can be tried in either court.

Mode of trial can be determined in any magistrates' court; it does not matter where in England and Wales the offence was allegedly committed (s 2 of the Magistrates' Courts Act 1980).

3.2 CLASSIFICATION OF OFFENCES

According to Sched 1 to the Interpretation Act 1978, there are three types of criminal offence:

- summary offences (offences which are triable only in the magistrates' court);
- indictable offences, which are either:
  (a) triable only on indictment (triable only in the Crown Court); or
  (b) triable either way (triable either in the magistrates' court or the Crown Court).

To determine which category a particular offence falls into one should look at:

- Sched 1 to the Magistrates' Courts Act 1980, which lists a number of offences that are triable either way; or
- the statute which creates the offence: if the penalty refers both to summary conviction and to conviction on indictment, the offence is triable either way; if it refers only to conviction on indictment, the offence can be tried only in the Crown Court; if it refers only to summary conviction, the offence can be tried only in the magistrates' court.

Thus, if an offence is in the list in Sched 1 to the 1980 Act or its penalty is expressed in a way which refers to both summary trial and trial on indictment, it is triable either way.

The rest of this chapter examines how it is decided where an offence which is triable either way should be tried.

3.3 INDICATION AS TO A DEFENDANT'S INTENDED PLEA: THE 'PLEA BEFORE VENUE' HEARING

The 'mode of trial' procedure begins with the court seeking to find out the defendant's intended plea, a practice known to practitioners as 'plea before venue'. This process is set out in ss 17A and 17B of the Magistrates' Courts Act 1980 (inserted by s 49 of the Criminal Procedure and Investigations Act 1996).

Section 17A applies where a defendant who has attained the age of 18 is charged with an offence that is triable either way (s 17A(1)). The s 17A procedure has to be carried out in the presence of the defendant (s 17A(2)). It begins with the charge being written down (if this has not already been done) and being read to the defendant (s 17A(3)). The court then explains to the defendant that he may indicate whether he intends to plead guilty or not guilty; the defendant must also be warned that if he indicates an intention to plead guilty, he will be regarded as having actually pleaded guilty and that the magistrates then have the power to commit him for sentence to the Crown Court (under s 3 of the Powers of Criminal Courts (Sentencing) Act 2000) if they take the view that their sentencing powers are inadequate (s 17A(4)).

The defendant is then asked whether he intends to plead guilty or not guilty (s 17A(5)). If the defendant indicates that he intends to plead guilty, the magistrates must proceed as if the case were a summary trial and the defendant had pleaded guilty (s 17(6)). In other words, the indication of an intention to plead guilty is to be regarded as an actual plea of guilty.

If the defendant indicates that he intends to plead not guilty, the court goes through the mode of trial procedure set out in ss 18–21 of the Magistrates' Courts Act 1980 (described below): s 17A(7). Where the defendant declines to indicate how he intends to plead, the court must assume that he intends to plead not guilty and so must go through the mode of trial procedure (s 17A(8)).

The effect of these provisions is that where a defendant is charged with an either way offence and indicates to the magistrates that he intends to plead guilty, he will be regarded as having agreed to summary trial and as having pleaded guilty. If the case is a serious one, in the sense that it calls for a sentence beyond the powers of the magistrates, the defendant will be committed for sentence to the Crown Court. The object of this reform was to ensure that defendants who intend to plead guilty do not end up in the Crown Court unless the case is a serious one.

Where the defendant indicates an intention to plead guilty to one or more either way offences but is also committed to the Crown Court for trial in respect of an either way offence to which he intends to plead not guilty, or in respect of an offence which is triable only on indictment, the magistrates may commit him to the Crown Court for sentence (under s 4 of the Powers of Criminal Courts (Sentencing) Act 2000) in respect of the offence(s) to which he had indicated a guilty plea (even if their sentencing powers would be adequate to deal with the offence(s)).

A Home Office Circular (45/1997) makes the point that some defendants, especially unrepresented defendants, may find the 'plea before venue' hearing difficult to understand. The Circular says (at para 15):

The court may wish to take account of the following points in framing its invitation:

- the defendant will want to know whether his case will be dealt with that day in court. The court may wish to make this clear when explaining what will happen if the defendant indicates a plea of guilty or not guilty;

- the defendant must understand that an indication of a guilty plea will lead to conviction and sentence. But some defendants may be confused if the court tries to distinguish between plea indication and plea taking. It may be clearer to inform the defendant that if he tells the court that he intends to plead guilty, the outcome will be that he will be convicted of the offence, that the prosecutor will tell the court about the facts of the case, that the defence will have the opportunity to respond, and that the court will then proceed to consider sentence either on the same day or at a later date if the court requires more information about the case before deciding on the appropriate sentence;

- the defendant must also understand that the court has the discretion to commit him to Crown Court for sentence [under s 3 of the Powers of Criminal Courts (Sentencing) Act 2000] if it considers the offence to be so serious that its own sentencing powers are not sufficient to impose a great enough punishment;

- the defendant should be given every opportunity to say that he understands what is likely to happen if he takes a particular course. It may be preferable, during the explanation of the procedure, to pause at the end of each stage and ask the defendant whether he understands what has just been said;

- the defendant should be asked at the end of the explanation whether he understands and whether there is anything on which he would like further explanation.

The Home Office Circular contains an Annex with a suggested form of wording for the use of the magistrates' court when inviting the defendant to indicate his plea. It is as follows:

This/these offence(s) may be tried either by this court or by the Crown Court before a Judge and jury.

Whether or not this court can deal with your case today will depend upon your answers to the questions which I am going to put to you. Do you understand?

You will shortly be asked to tell the court whether you intend to plead guilty or not guilty to (certain of) the offence(s) [that is, only the offences which are triable either way] with which you are charged. Do you understand?

If you tell us that you intend to plead guilty, you will be convicted of the offence(s). We may then be able to deal with (part of) your case at this hearing. The prosecutor will tell us about the facts of the case, you (your representative) will have the opportunity to respond (on your behalf), and we shall then go on to consider how to sentence you. Do you understand?

We may be able to sentence you today, or we may need to adjourn the proceedings until a later date for the preparation of a pre-sentence report by the Probation Service. If we believe that you deserve a greater sentence than we have the power to give you in this court, we may decide to send you to the Crown Court, either on bail or in custody, and you will be sentenced by that court, which has greater sentencing powers. Do you understand?

[In cases where s 4 of the Powers of Criminal Courts (Sentencing) Act 2000 applies:]

If you indicate a guilty plea for this/these offence(s), even if we believe that our own sentencing powers are great enough to deal with you here, we may still send you to the Crown Court to be sentenced for this/these offence(s) because you have also been charged with [a] related offence(s) [for which you have already been committed for trial in that court [for which you will be committed for trial in that court]. Do you understand?

If, on the other hand, you tell us that you intend to plead not guilty, or if you do not tell us what you intend to do, we shall go on to consider whether you should be tried by this court or by the Crown Court on some future date. If we decide that it would be appropriate to deal with your case in this court, we shall ask you if you are content for us to do so or whether you wish to have your case tried in the Crown Court.

Before I ask you how you intend to plead, do you understand everything I have said
or is there any part of what I have said which you would like me to repeat or explain?

Section 17B of the Magistrates' Courts Act 1980 deals with the situation where (a) a
person who has attained the age of 18 years appears or is brought before a
magistrates' court on an information charging him with an offence triable either way;
(b) the accused is represented by a legal representative; (c) the court considers that by
reason of the accused's disorderly conduct before the court it is not practicable for
proceedings under s 17A to be conducted in his presence; and (d) the court considers
that it should proceed in the absence of the accused (s 17B(1)). In such a case, the
charge is written down (if not already done) and read to the lawyer; the lawyer is then
asked whether the defendant intends to plead guilty or not guilty; if the lawyer
indicates that the defendant intends to plead guilty, the case is regarded as a summary
trial in which the defendant has pleaded guilty; if the lawyer indicates that the client
intends to plead not guilty, or if the lawyer declines to indicate the defendant's
intention regarding the plea, the court proceeds to the mode of trial hearing (s 17B(2),
(3)).

Guidance on the impact of the 'plea before venue' procedure was given by the
Court of Appeal in *R v Rafferty* [1999] 1 Cr App R 235. The court held that: (i) where the
defendant is charged with an either way offence and indicates a guilty plea at the 'plea
before venue' hearing and is then committed for sentence to the Crown Court, he is
entitled to a greater discount for his guilty plea than the defendant who delays
pleading guilty until he appears in the Crown Court; (ii) when a person who is on bail
enters a guilty plea at the 'plea before venue' hearing, the usual practice should be to
continue his bail, even if it is anticipated that a custodial sentence will be imposed by
the Crown Court, unless there is good reason for remanding him in custody. In *R v
Barber* [2001] EWCA Crim 2267; [2002] 1 Cr App R(S) 130, the Court of Appeal said that
it is of the greatest importance that those who enter pleas of guilty before venue is
decided receive the maximum possible discount for so doing. Pleas entered before
venue has been decided therefore attract a greater discount than pleas which are
delayed and entered to an indictment in the Crown Court. The appropriate discount
for a prompt guilty plea entered at the Crown Court to an offence triable only on
indictment is one-third. The Court said that a greater discount than one-third is often
appropriate for a plea entered before venue is decided in relation to an offence triable
either way. Unfortunately, the court did not indicate how much more than a one-third
discount would be appropriate.

Where the court does not pass sentence immediately, the magistrates must be
careful not to create an expectation that the defendant will ultimately be sentenced in
that court if they wish the option of committal for sentence to the Crown Court to
remain open. In *R v Horseferry Road Magistrates' Court ex p Rugless* (2000) 164 JP 311, the
defendant indicated a guilty plea at the 'plea before venue' hearing; the court accepted
jurisdiction and ordered a pre-sentence report, stating that all sentencing options were
to remain open with the exception of committal to the Crown Court for sentence. At
the next hearing, the magistrates committed the defendant to the Crown Court for
sentence (under s 3 of the Powers of Criminal Courts (Sentencing) Act 2000). The
Divisional Court held that the defendant had a legitimate expectation that he would be
sentenced in the magistrates' court. The subsequent decision to commit him for
sentence was in breach of this legitimate expectation; accordingly it was appropriate to
quash the decision to commit for sentence. In *R (White) v Barking Magistrates' Court*
[2004] EWHC 417, the defendant was charged with production of cannabis contrary to

s 4(2) of the Misuse of Drugs Act 1971. The charges related to a large-scale production operation. When he appeared before the justices, they adjourned the matter. At the next hearing they committed him to the Crown Court for sentence. He applied for judicial review of the decision to commit, contending that, at the first hearing, the justices had created a legitimate expectation that they would deal with sentence themselves. It was held that although an expectation had been created by the justices at the earlier hearing that they would not commit the defendant to the Crown Court, that expectation would not be fulfilled, since it would have been an unreasonable decision by the justices. Given the severity of the offending, it would have been unreasonable, and therefore unlawful, for the justices not to have committed the defendant for sentencing in the Crown Court.

3.4   MODE OF TRIAL HEARING: PROCEDURE

The procedure to be followed for the part of the mode of trial hearing after 'plea before venue' where the defendant indicates an intention to plead not guilty (or gives no indication of his intended plea) in respect of one or more offences is set out in ss 18–21 of the Magistrates' Courts Act 1980.

It applies where the defendant has attained the age of 18 and is charged with an either way offence (s 18(1)):

- The court asks if the accused is aware of his right to receive advance information of the prosecution case (see below); if a request for disclosure has been made, the court will ask if the request has been complied with.

- The prosecution make representations as to the appropriate mode of trial. This involves a brief summary of the facts of the alleged offence so that the magistrates can assess the seriousness of the offence. The prosecution will base their submissions on the criteria contained in s 19(3) of the 1980 Act and in the Mode of Trial Guidelines.

- The defence then have the chance of making representations as to the appropriate mode of trial. If the defendant wishes to be tried at the Crown Court, no representations will be made since, even if the magistrates decide that the case is suitable for summary trial, the defendant can nevertheless choose trial on indictment. If, on the other hand, the prosecution ask for trial on indictment but the defendant wishes to be tried summarily, the defendant will first have to persuade the magistrates to accept jurisdiction (that is, to rule that the case is suitable for summary trial).

- Having heard the representations, the magistrates come to their decision whether or not to offer the defendant the option of summary trial (that decision being based on the criteria set out in s 19(3) of the 1980 Act and the Mode of Trial Guidelines).

- If the magistrates decide that the case is not suitable for summary trial, committal proceedings will take place either immediately or else on a later occasion. Paragraph 7 of Sched 3 to the 2003 Act replaces s 21 of the Magistrates' Courts Act 1980 with a new version which provides that where the magistrates decline jurisdiction (deciding that the case is not suitable for summary trial), they should then send the case to the Crown Court for trial in accordance with the procedure contained in s 51 of the Crime and Disorder Act 1998 (which previously applied solely to offences triable only on indictment).

- If the magistrates decide that the case is suitable for summary trial, the defendant will be asked whether he wishes to be tried in the magistrates' court or by a judge and jury in the Crown Court. Before the defendant announces his choice, the court must first warn him that if he consents to a summary trial and is convicted, he may be sent to the Crown Court to be sentenced (under s 3 of the Powers of Criminal Courts (Sentencing) Act 2000). The defendant then announces his choice. In *R v Southampton Magistrates Court ex p Sansome* [1999] 1 Cr App R(S) 112, the court approved the form of wording in Stone's *Justices' Manual* (para 1-438) to be used where the magistrates decide that the case is suitable for summary trial:

> It appears to this court more suitable for you to be tried here. You may now consent to be tried by this court, but if you wish, you may choose to be tried by a jury instead. If you are tried by this court and are found guilty, this court may still send you to the Crown Court for sentence if it is of the opinion that greater punishment should be inflicted for the offence than it has power to impose. Do you wish to be tried by this court or do you wish to be tried by a jury?

Thus, summary trial of an either way offence is only possible if both the magistrates and the defendant agree to it.

3.5   MODE OF TRIAL: RELEVANT FACTORS

Section 19(3) of the Magistrates' Courts Act 1980 states that in deciding whether or not a case is suitable for summary trial, the magistrates should have regard to:

> ... the nature of the case; whether the circumstances make the offence one of serious character; whether the punishment which a magistrates' court would have power to inflict for it would be adequate; and any other circumstances which appear to the court to make it more suitable for the offence to be tried in one way rather than the other.

Section 19(1) also requires the court to take account of any representations made by the prosecution and the defence.

The key question which the magistrates must ask themselves is whether six months' imprisonment (12 months if the accused is charged with two or more offences which are triable either way) would be adequate punishment.

3.5.1   Guidelines

To help the magistrates decide which is the appropriate mode of trial in any case, para V.51 of the *Practice Direction (Criminal Proceedings: Consolidation)* [2002] 1 WLR 2870 contains Mode of Trial Guidelines:

51   *Mode of trial*

51.1   The purpose of these guidelines is to help magistrates decide whether or not to commit defendants charged with 'either way' offences for trial in the Crown Court. Their object is to provide guidance not direction. They are not intended to impinge on a magistrate's duty to consider each case individually and on its own particular facts. These guidelines apply to all defendants aged 18 and above.

General mode of trial considerations

51.2 Section 19 of the Magistrates' Courts Act 1980 requires magistrates to have regard to the following matters in deciding whether an offence is more suitable for summary trial or trial on indictment: (a) the nature of the case; (b) whether the circumstances make the offence one of a serious character; (c) whether the punishment which a magistrates' court would have power to inflict for it would be adequate; (d) any other circumstances which appear to the court to make it more suitable for the offence to be tried in one way rather than the other; (e) any representations made by the prosecution or the defence.

51.3 Certain general observations can be made: (a) the court should never make its decision on the grounds of convenience or expedition; (b) the court should assume for the purpose of deciding mode of trial that the prosecution version of the facts is correct; (c) the fact that the offences are alleged to be specimens is a relevant consideration (although it has to be borne in mind that difficulties can arise in sentencing in relation to specimen counts (see *R v Clark* [1996] 2 Cr App R(S) 351 and *R v Kidd* [1998] 1 WLR 604)); the fact that the defendant will be asking for other offences to be taken into consideration, if convicted, is not; (d) where cases involve complex questions of fact or difficult questions of law, including difficult issues of disclosure of sensitive material, the court should consider committal for trial; (e) where two or more defendants are jointly charged with an offence each has an individual right to elect his mode of trial; (f) in general, except where otherwise stated, either way offences should be tried summarily unless the court considers that the particular case has one or more of the features set out in paragraphs 51.4–51.18 and that its sentencing powers are insufficient; (g) the court should also consider its power to commit an offender for sentence under sections 3 and 4 of the Powers of Criminal Courts (Sentencing) Act 2000 if information emerges during the course of the hearing which leads it to conclude that the offence is so serious, or the offender such a risk to the public, that its powers to sentence him are inadequate. This means that committal for sentence is no longer determined by reference to the character and antecedents of the offender.

Features relevant to individual offences

51.4 Where reference is made in these guidelines to property or damage of 'high value' it means a figure equal to at least twice the amount of the limit (currently £5,000) imposed by statute on a magistrates' court when making a compensation order.

The Guidelines then give guidance in respect of some of the offences most commonly encountered in the magistrates' court.

To summarise the key principles set out in the Guidelines:

- the court should never make its decision on the ground of convenience;
- the court should assume for the purpose of deciding mode of trial that the prosecution version of the facts is correct (and so there is little point in the defence making representations that the offence is not as serious as the prosecution allege);
- the fact that the defendant will, in the event of conviction, be asking for other offences to be taken into consideration (TICs) is *not* a relevant consideration (this is slightly surprising, as the presence of 'TICs' could affect the sentence that is passed);
- if the case involves complex questions of fact or difficult questions of law, the court should consider committing the defendant to the Crown Court for trial;

- where two or more defendants are jointly charged, the magistrates must consider each defendant separately; thus, it would be wrong to refuse to try a defendant summarily in a case which is suitable for summary trial merely because another defendant is to be tried in the Crown Court. This provision is based on the decision of the House of Lords in *R v Brentwood Justices ex p Nicholls* [1992] 1 AC 1; [1991] 3 All ER 359, followed in *R v Ipswich Justices ex p Callaghan* (1995) 159 JP 748 and *R v Wigan Justices ex p Layland* (1995) 160 JP 223: s 19 of the Magistrates' Courts Act 1980 requires the justices to make a decision about mode of trial before the defendant or defendants are put to their election. Once a decision has been made, it should not be changed on the basis that one or more of the defendants elects Crown Court trial;

- the original version of the Guidelines (issued in 1990) said that the magistrates, in determining mode of trial, should assume that the defendant has no previous convictions (indeed it was held in *R v Colchester Justices ex p NE Essex Building Co* [1977] 1 WLR 1109 that any previous convictions must not be revealed to the magistrates at this stage) and should not take account of any personal mitigating circumstances. However, the revised version of the Mode of Trial Guidelines omits the principle that the defendant's antecedents are irrelevant. Similarly, the revised Guidelines omit the principle stated in the original version that the magistrates should ignore any personal mitigating circumstances. The present position thus appears to be that in determining mode of trial the magistrates may take account of all the factors (except 'TICs') to which they would have regard if they were passing. When the amended version of s 19 of the Magistrates' Courts Act 1980 (see para 5 of Sched 3 to the Criminal Justice Act 2003) comes into effect, this question will be put beyond doubt, since s 19(2) will specifically provide that the court 'shall give the prosecution an opportunity to inform the court of the accused's previous convictions (if any)';

- there is a presumption in favour of summary trial unless the case has aggravating features which render the magistrates' sentencing powers inadequate. The Guidelines go on to give examples of aggravating features for particular offences. For example:
  (a) burglary of a dwelling house is more serious if committed when the building is likely to be occupied, or if there is also vandalism;
  (b) theft is more serious if committed in breach of trust or over a prolonged period;
  (c) offences of violence are more serious if a weapon is used or if the victim is vulnerable (for example, elderly or infirm) or if the victim is someone whose job brings him into contact with the public (for example, a bus driver, a publican or a police officer);
  (d) dangerous driving is more serious if there is grossly excessive speed or a prolonged course of dangerous driving or other related offences are committed as well;

- amount involved: where property has been stolen and not recovered, regard should be had to its value. The guidelines say that the magistrates should decline jurisdiction if the value involved exceeds twice the amount they can order to be paid by way of compensation. Since the magistrates can order compensation of £5,000 per offence, this means that they should decline jurisdiction if the value of unrecovered property exceeds £10,000.

3.5.2   Summary

The question which the magistrates should ask themselves at a mode of trial hearing is: 'Assuming that what the prosecution say about the offence is correct and assuming the defendant has no previous convictions, is six months' imprisonment (or 12 months for two or more offences) likely to be sufficient punishment?'

3.6   PRESENCE OF THE DEFENDANT

The defendant must be present at the mode of trial hearing unless either:

- under s 18(3) of the Magistrates' Courts Act, 'the court considers that by reason of his disorderly conduct before the court it is not practicable for the proceedings to be conducted in his presence'; or
- under s 23(1) of the Magistrates' Courts Act, '(a) the accused is represented by a legal representative who in his absence signifies to the court the accused's consent to the proceedings for determining how he is to be tried for the offence being conducted in his absence; and (b) the court is satisfied that there is good reason for proceeding in the absence of the accused'.

3.7   WHERE SHOULD THE DEFENDANT CHOOSE TO BE TRIED?

If the magistrates do not offer the defendant the chance of summary trial, the defendant has no choice in the matter: the trial can only take place in the Crown Court. If the magistrates do accept jurisdiction, should the defendant agree to summary trial?

3.7.1   The advantages of summary trial

The advantages of summary trial are as follows:

- The main advantage of summary trial is that the trial procedure is less formal. This means that the trial is less daunting, a fact which may be particularly relevant if the defendant is going to be unrepresented at trial, as will be the case if the defendant is not granted public funded representation and yet cannot afford legal representation.
- Summary trial takes a shorter time than does a trial in the Crown Court. A case which would take half a day in the magistrates' court would take probably a whole day in the Crown Court. This means that summary trial is cheaper. This too is relevant if the defendant is not publicly funded but has chosen to pay for representation.
- It is sometimes said that an advantage of summary trial is that there is a limit on the sentence which the magistrates' court can pass (six months' imprisonment for one either way offence, 12 months for two or more). However, this advantage is largely nullified by the power of the magistrates to commit the defendant to be sentenced in the Crown Court under s 3 of the Powers of Criminal Courts

(Sentencing) Act 2000. It should be borne in mind that when the relevant provisions of the Criminal Justice Act 2003 come into force, magistrates will be empowered to pass a sentence of 12 months' custody for a single either way offence, but the power to commit for sentence following summary trial of a either way offence will be abolished.

3.7.2 The advantages of trial on indictment

The advantages of trial on indictment are as follows:

- Jurors tend to be less 'case hardened' than magistrates. Magistrates, who sit regularly, may well have heard the same story before and therefore find it less convincing. Also, magistrates tend to be more trusting of police evidence than do jurors.
- In the magistrates' court, the justices are triers of law and fact whereas in the Crown Court, the judge is the trier of law and the jurors are the triers of fact. Two advantages of Crown Court trial flow from this fact:

   (a) Where the admissibility of a piece of evidence is challenged in the Crown Court, the challenge is made in the absence of the jury and, if the judge rules the evidence inadmissible, the jury hear nothing of this evidence. In the magistrates' court, however, the justices themselves have to rule on any question concerning the admissibility of evidence. If they decide that a particular piece of evidence is inadmissible, they must then put it from their minds. It is difficult to be sure that the justices are able to ignore, for example, evidence that the defendant made a confession even where they have ruled that the confession is inadmissible. In *R v Ormskirk Justices ex p Davies* (1994) 158 JP 1145, it was held that one bench cannot delegate to another bench the duty of hearing and determining questions of admissibility; such decisions must be taken by the bench actually trying the case. It should be borne in mind, however, that when Sched 3 to the Courts Act 2003 comes into effect, a bench will be able to give a pre-trial ruling on the admissibility of evidence and that ruling will bind the bench that eventually tries the case. This will effectively negate the advantage of Crown Court trial where there is an issue over the admissibility of evidence.

   (b) (i) If there is a point of law to be decided, it is easier to deal with that point in the Crown Court, presided over by a professional judge, than in the magistrates' court, where the justices (who have only elementary legal training) depend on their clerk for advice on questions of law (unless the trial takes place before a legally qualified District judge).

   (ii) Legal errors are also easier to detect in the Crown Court, as the judge has to set out the relevant law in the summing up to the jury.

- Another advantage of trial on indictment is said to be that the prosecution have to disclose copies of the statements made by the witnesses they will be calling at the Crown Court. This is because committal proceedings cannot take place unless the prosecution have served their witness statements on the defence. This advantage is less marked as a result of the advance information rules which have to be complied with before mode of trial is decided. This is especially so in light of para 43 of the Attorney General's Guidelines on disclosure, which provides that in the case of summary trial:

The prosecutor should, in addition to complying with the obligations under the CPIA, provide to the defence all evidence upon which the Crown proposes to rely in a summary trial. Such provision should allow the accused or their legal advisers sufficient time properly to consider the evidence before it is called. Exceptionally, statements may be withheld for the protection of witnesses or to avoid interference with the course of justice.

The effect of this is to place a defendant who is being tried in the magistrates' court in the same position as a defendant who is being tried in the Crown Court as regards obtaining copies of the statements of the people to be called as prosecution witnesses.

Another factor which might be relevant is the length of time the defendant will have to wait for a summary trial or a trial on indictment to take place. This depends very much on local conditions, as waiting lists vary considerably.

It is a widely held belief that trial on indictment offers a more thorough examination of the issues in a case and a trial procedure that is fairer to the accused than summary trial. It may well be the case that this is more a matter of perception than reality. Nonetheless, in his *Review of the Criminal Courts of England and Wales*, Lord Justice Auld did recommend (Recommendation 8) that:

Steps should be taken to provide benches of magistrates that reflect more broadly than at present the communities they serve by:

...

8.5   equipping local Advisory Committees with the information to enable them to submit for consideration for appointment, candidates that will produce and maintain benches broadly reflective of the communities they serve, including the establishment and maintenance of national and local data-bases of information on the make-up of the local community and on the composition of the local magistracy;

8.6   instituting a review of the ways in which the role and terms of service of a magistrate might be made more attractive and manageable to a wider range of the community than is presently the case; and

8.7   persisting with the current search for occupational and/or social groupings as a substitute for political affiliations as a measure of local balance.

He also recommended that in order to strengthen the training of magistrates, the Judicial Studies Board should be made responsible for the content and manner of the training of magistrates. The Courts Act 2003 achieves this objective to a large extent by revising arrangements for training of justices (see s 19).

3.8   FAILURE TO FOLLOW THE CORRECT PROCEDURE IN DETERMINING MODE OF TRIAL

If the magistrates fail to follow the correct procedure in the mode of trial hearing (for example, the defendant is not warned of the possibility of being committed for sentence to the Crown Court) and a summary trial then takes place, the summary trial will be invalid and the Divisional Court will order the magistrates to go through the mode of trial procedure again. See *R v Kent Justices ex p Machin* [1952] 2 QB 355, where a conviction by the magistrates was quashed by the Divisional Court because the magistrates' court failed to warn the defendant of the possibility of being committed for sentence following summary conviction; and *R v Cardiff Justices ex p Cardiff City Council* (1987) *The Times*, 24 February, where an acquittal following summary trial which took place after a defective mode of trial hearing was quashed by the Divisional Court.

In *R v Northampton Justices ex p Commissioners of Customs & Excise* [1994] Crim LR 598, the defendant was charged with fraudulent evasion of VAT (triable either way) involving £193,000. The magistrates, having heard representations, held that the case was suitable for summary trial. The prosecution appealed against this decision. The Divisional Court held that, in view of the seriousness of the alleged offence, the decision reached by the magistrates was so unreasonable that it should be quashed.

3.9   CHANGING THE DECISION AS TO MODE OF TRIAL

Once the decision as to mode of trial has been taken, it is nonetheless possible for that decision to be altered.

3.9.1   From summary trial to trial on indictment

Section 25(2) of the Magistrates' Courts Act 1980 says that, during a summary trial, the magistrates may terminate the trial at any time before the close of the prosecution case and hold committal proceedings instead (so that, if there is a case to answer, the defendant will be committed for trial to the Crown Court). This may happen if either the defendant or the magistrates have a change of mind or if the defendant is allowed to change his plea from guilty to not guilty. In *R v Horseferry Road Magistrates' Court ex p K* [1996] 3 All ER 719, the Divisional Court held that the power to change from summary trial applies only once the trial has begun. The fact that the defendant has entered a plea of not guilty does not mean that the trial has begun. That only happens once the court has started to hear evidence or, for example, submissions on a preliminary point of law which has a direct bearing on the guilt or innocence of the accused.

3.9.2   The magistrates have a change of mind

The magistrates may have a change of mind regarding mode of trial if, during a summary trial, they decide as they hear the prosecution evidence that the case is in fact more serious than they thought when they agreed to summary trial. However, in such a case, it should be noted that they could simply continue with the summary trial and, if they convict the defendant, commit him to the Crown Court to be sentenced.

If the defendant consents to summary trial and pleads guilty, it is then too late to change to committal proceedings unless the defendant asks to change his plea first (*R v Dudley Justices ex p Gillard* [1986] AC 442; [1985] 3 All ER 634). In the case of a plea of guilty, the only course of action if the magistrates, on hearing the facts of the case set out more fully by the prosecution, decide that the case is too serious for them to deal with is to commit the defendant to the Crown Court for sentence under s 3 of the Powers of Criminal Courts (Sentencing) Act 2000.

In *R (on the Application of K) v Leeds Youth Court* [2001] EWHC 177 (Admin); (2001) 165 JP 694, it was held that the exercise of the discretion under s 25(6) has to be based on good, proper and relevant reasons, relating to the seriousness of the offence. The magistrates are entitled to keep the trial under review and to change their decision, if it becomes apparent that the original decision is no longer appropriate. Circumstances justifying such a decision are likely to vary from case to case, but include a change in circumstances and instances where new material is adduced; also cases where, as the evidence unfolds, the manner in which it is presented would justify such a decision. In the present case, once it became clear to the justices that the oral testimony had put a different perspective on the bare statement of the offences, they were entitled to exercise their powers under s 25(6).

3.9.3   The defendant has a change of mind

The magistrates have a discretion to allow the defendant to withdraw his consent to summary trial.

The test to be applied in deciding whether to exercise this discretion in the defendant's favour was set out in *R v Birmingham Justices ex p Hodgson* [1985] 1 QB 1131, where the defendant did not realise that he had a defence to the charge, and *R v Highbury Corner Magistrates ex p Weekes* [1985] 1 QB 1147, where a 17 year old defendant did not understand what a Crown Court was. The test to be applied in deciding whether to allow a defendant to withdraw his consent to summary trial is: did the defendant understand the 'nature and significance' of the choice which was put before him at the mode of trial hearing? In deciding this question, the magistrates should have regard to factors such as:

- whether the defendant knew that he had a possible defence to the charge;
- whether the defendant had access to legal advice before making his decision as to mode of trial;
- the defendant's age and apparent intelligence;
- possibly, whether the defendant has previous convictions (and so is likely to know something about criminal procedure); it should be remembered, however, that if the magistrates are made aware of the defendant's previous convictions, those magistrates will not be able to continue with the trial anyway, and so if the defendant's application is not allowed, the trial will have to begin again in front of a bench which is unaware of the defendant's criminal record.

It should be noted that the burden of proof lies on the defendant to show that he did not understand the nature and significance of the choice (*R v Forest Magistrates ex p Spicer* (1989) 153 JP 81).

3.9.4   The defendant successfully applies to change his plea

In *R v Bow Street Magistrates ex p Welcombe* (1992) 156 JP 609, it was held that if, during a summary trial, the defendant is allowed to change his plea from guilty to not guilty, the defendant must also be given the opportunity to elect trial on indictment if he so wishes.

3.9.5   From trial on indictment to summary trial

Section 25(3) of the Magistrates' Courts Act 1980 provides that, at any time during committal proceedings, the justices may offer the defendant the chance of summary trial. This is the case whether it is the defendant or the justices who have a change of mind. It must be emphasised, however, that summary trial can only take place if both the defendant and the magistrates agree to it. It follows that if the magistrates decide that the case is not as serious as they thought when they declined jurisdiction, a summary trial cannot take place without the defendant's consent. The defendant should be warned (or reminded if he was informed earlier) that he may be committed for sentence to the Crown Court if he is convicted by the magistrates.

Where the magistrates decide that the case is, in fact, suitable for summary trial, there will have to be an adjournment before the summary trial can start. This is because all the evidence at committal proceedings is in the form of written statements. Witnesses will have to attend court to give oral evidence at the summary trial.

3.10   CRIMINAL DAMAGE: THE SPECIAL PROVISIONS

Section 22 of the Magistrates' Courts Act 1980 sets out a special procedure to be applied in cases of criminal damage (excluding arson) where the value involved is less than £5,000. Under s 22(2), if the amount involved does not exceed the 'relevant sum' (£5,000), the court must 'proceed as if the offence were triable only summarily' (and so there is no mode of trial hearing). So, where the value involved is £5,000 or less, the case *must* be tried summarily. Under s 33 of the Magistrates' Courts Act 1980, the maximum sentence in such a case is three months' imprisonment or a fine of up to £2,500 (that is, half the usual penalty); furthermore, there can be no committal for sentence to the Crown Court under s 3 of the Powers of Criminal Courts (Sentencing) Act 2000. However, when para 27 of Sched 32 to the Criminal Justice Act 2003 comes into force, the maximum sentence of imprisonment under s 33 will be increased to 51 weeks.

If 'it appears to the court clear that, for the offence charged, the value involved exceeds the relevant sum', the court will proceed to determine mode of trial in the usual way (sub-s (3)). Thus, where the value is more than £5,000, the usual mode of trial procedure applies. If the defendant consents to summary trial and is convicted, the usual penalties apply and a s 3 committal is possible.

Under s 22(4), if 'it appears to the court for any reason not clear whether, for the offence charged, the value involved does or does not exceed the relevant sum', the court proceeds in the manner set out in sub-s (5):

(5)   The court shall ... explain to him in ordinary language—

   (a) that he can, if he wishes, consent to be tried summarily for the offence and that if he consents to be so tried, he will definitely be tried in that way; and

   (b) that if he is tried summarily and is convicted by the court, his liability to imprisonment or a fine will be limited as provided in section 33 below [s 33(1) provides that '(a) ... the court shall not have power to impose on him in respect of that offence imprisonment for more than 3 months [under the Criminal Justice Act 2003, 51 weeks] or a fine greater than level 4 on the standard scale; and (b) section 3 of the Powers of Criminal Courts

(Sentencing) Act 2000 (committal to Crown Court for sentence) shall not apply as regards that offence.

If there is doubt as to whether the value involved is more or less than £5,000, the magistrates must offer the defendant the chance of summary trial. If the defendant accepts summary trial, the lower penalties (three months' imprisonment (51 weeks under the Criminal Justice Act 2003) or a fine of up to £2,500 and no s 3 committal) apply; if he does not consent to summary trial, he will be sent to the Crown Court for trial (s 22(6)).

It follows that the first step in a case involving criminal damage is to ascertain the 'value involved'. This is defined as the cost of repair or, if the article is damaged beyond repair, replacement. The value may be ascertained on the basis of representations by the prosecution and defence. There is no obligation on the magistrates to hear evidence as to the value (though they have a discretion to do so) (*R v Canterbury Justices ex p Klisiak* [1982] QB 398; [1981] 2 All ER 129). Section 22(11) provides that where the accused is charged with two or more offences to which the section applies and which 'constitute or form part of a series of two or more offences of the same or a similar character', the court should take the value involved as being the aggregate of the values involved in each offence for the purpose of determining whether the special procedure applies.

There is no appeal against the decision of the magistrates as to the value involved.

It must be emphasised that these special provisions apply only to criminal damage (and to offences under s 12A of the Theft Act 1968 – aggravated vehicle taking – but only where the only aggravating feature alleged is criminal damage). In the case of theft, for example, the defendant has an unfettered right to Crown Court trial no matter how small the value of the property stolen.

In *R (Abbott) v Colchester Justices* [2001] EWHC 136 (Admin); (2001) 165 JP 386, the defendant was charged with criminal damage to crops on a farm. The value of the damage itself was £750. However, there was also consequential loss of £5,000. The Divisional Court held that the correct measure of the value of damage caused is the value of the property in the open market at the material time. This does not include consequential loss. The value involved in the present case therefore did not exceed the relevant sum and so the case had to be tried summarily. In *R (DPP) v Prestatyn Magistrates' Court* [2002] EWHC 1177; (2002) *The Times*, 17 October, the defendants were charged with causing criminal damage to genetically-modified crops. The District judge was uncertain as to the value of the crops and so treated the offence as triable either way (under s 22(4)). It was held that, where there is no open market value, the magistrates have to find a market value of something in order to determine the value of the property damaged. In the instant case, the crop was being grown for research and not for sale. That gave it a real value but it was a different and probably greater value than maize grown for food. The District judge was entitled to reach the conclusion that the crop was neither worthless nor limited in value to the price of ordinary maize but he could not say whether or not the value was greater or less than £5,000, so that the case fell within s 22(4).

In *R v Ward and Others* (1997) 161 JP 297, the Court of Appeal held that where a defendant is convicted of conspiracy to cause criminal damage, and the value of the damage is less than £5,000, the Crown Court can impose a sentence in excess of the maximum for the substantive offence (since conspiracy is an entirely separate offence).

The 'plea before venue' procedure established by s 17A of the Magistrates' Courts Act 1980 applies to all offences which are triable either way, including cases of criminal damage where the value involved is less than £5,000. The defendant should therefore be given an opportunity to indicate his plea at a 'plea before venue' hearing. On a guilty indication, the court will deal with the case summarily and proceed to consider sentence. Home Office Circular 45/1997 says that the limitation on the court's sentencing powers under s 33 of the Act (three months' imprisonment and/or a £2,500 fine in cases where the value involved in the criminal damage is less than £5,000) does not apply in such cases, since the procedure set out in s 17A is not subject to s 22. This means, says the Circular, that the court has the power to impose the maximum penalties or to commit the defendant for sentence to the Crown Court under s 3 or 4 of the Powers of Criminal Courts (Sentencing) Act 2000. If the defendant indicates that he will plead not guilty (or gives no indication), the court should then go through the s 22 procedure, hearing representations as to the value involved and trying the case summarily if the value is £5,000 or less, or going through the standard mode of trial procedure if the value is more than £5,000. It is questionable whether this interpretation is correct, since it would appear to exclude the operation of s 22 from cases where the defendant pleads guilty.

3.11   MODE OF TRIAL: SOME STATISTICS

Figures from the 2004 Annual Report of the CPS show the following case results:

Magistrates' courts

Case results for the year 2003–04:

- Excluding cases proved in the absence of the defendant, 8% of cases were contested (the defendant pleading guilty in 92% of cases).
- Of those pleading not guilty, 73% were convicted (27% were acquitted).

Figures for previous years were:

- 1998–99: 26% of those pleading not guilty were acquitted.
- 1999–00: 28% of those pleading not guilty were acquitted.
- 2000–01: 29% of those pleading not guilty were acquitted.
- 2001–02: 30% of those pleading not guilty were acquitted.
- 2002–03: 29% of those pleading not guilty were acquitted.

Crown Court

(a)   Either way offences in the Crown Court 2003–04:

- 24% of cases went to the Crown Court because the defendant elected Crown Court trial (76% because the magistrates declined jurisdiction).

Previous years:

- 1998–99: 29% because of defendants' election.
- 1999–00: 32% because of defendants' election.
- 2000–01: 30% because of defendants' election.
- 2001–02: 29% because of defendants' election.
- 2002–03: 27% because of defendants' election.

(b)   Case results 2003–04:

- 26% of cases were contested (the defendant pleading guilty in 74% of cases).

Of those pleading not guilty, 62% were convicted (38% were acquitted).

Previous years:

- 1998–99: 43% of those pleading not guilty were acquitted.
- 1999–00: 43% of those pleading not guilty were acquitted.
- 2000–01: 44% of those pleading not guilty were acquitted.
- 2001–02: 42% of those pleading not guilty were acquitted.
- 2002–03: 38% of those pleading not guilty were acquitted.

These figures can be compared with the official Judicial Statistics, which cover all prosecutions, not just those conducted by the CPS (and so they include, for example, prosecutions brought by HM Excise and Customs and the Inland Revenue).

The Judicial Statistics for 2003 show a noticeable drop in the number of cases committed for trial between 1997 and 1998 (91,110 and 75,815 cases respectively). Indeed, the average number of cases committed for trial each year between 1989 and 1997 was 93,244; the average for the period 1998–2003 was 78,246.

The number of cases committed for sentence shows more clearly the effect of the 'plea before venue' procedure. In 1997, a total of 14,871 cases were committed for sentence to the Crown Court. In 1998, that figure rose steeply to 29,774 cases. The average number of cases committed for sentence each year was 13,251 in the period 1989–97; in the period 1998–2003, the average figure rose to 28,643 committals for sentence per year.

In 2003, the percentage of cracked trials as a proportion of all cases disposed of in the Crown Court was 24%. Of these cracked trials, 62% occurred where the defendant pleaded guilty on the day of the trial; in 17% of cases the prosecution accepted a plea of guilty to an alternative charge; in 19% of cases the prosecution offered no evidence; and in 2% of cases the defendant was bound over to keep the peace.

In 2003, the defendant pleaded guilty to all counts (or pleaded guilty to some counts but the prosecution did not proceed with the others, or else pleaded not guilty to the counts on the indictment but guilty pleas to alternative offences were accepted by the prosecution) in 58% of cases.

During 2003, 67% of defendants who pleaded not guilty were acquitted.

From these figures we can see that the proportion of acquittals in the Crown Court is indeed higher than the acquittal rate in the magistrates' court (suggesting that defendants really are more likely to be acquitted in the Crown Court). However, a number of points can be made about this conclusion:

- the gap between the acquittal rates of the two courts is not perhaps as high as some people might expect;
- national figures may well mask significant local variations (tough juries/lenient magistrates);
- it may well be that a number of cases which resulted in acquittal in the Crown Court would also have resulted in acquittal had they been tried in the magistrates' court; and

- considerably more either way cases are tried in the Crown Court because the magistrates declined jurisdiction than are sent there because the defendant elected trial on indictment.

3.12   THE ADVANCE INFORMATION RULES

The Magistrates' Courts (Advance Information) Rules 1985 provide that in the case of offences which are triable either way, the prosecution must, if the defence so request, supply the defence with either (a) a summary of the prosecution case, or (b) copies of the statements of the prosecution witnesses. The purpose of the Advance Information Rules is to make it unnecessary for the defendant to elect Crown Court trial simply so that committal proceedings (in which the prosecution case has to be revealed) then have to take place. The choice of whether to supply a summary or the witness statements lies with the prosecution (r 4(1)).

The prosecution may only refuse to comply with a request under the Rules if they think that compliance would lead to the intimidation of witnesses or other interference with the course of justice (r 5).

At the mode of trial hearing, the court must ensure that the defendant is aware of the right to advance information and that, if advance information has been requested, the prosecution have complied with that request (r 6(1)).

If the prosecution fail to comply with the request for advance disclosure, the magistrates' court has no power to order the prosecution to comply (*R v Dunmow Justices ex p Nash* (1993) 157 JP 1153). All the court can do is adjourn the mode of trial hearing (if necessary more than once) or, if satisfied that the defence have not been prejudiced by the prosecution's failure to comply with the Rules, proceed to determine mode of trial anyway (r 7(1)).

Furthermore, the court cannot dismiss the charges brought by the prosecution because of non-compliance with the Rules (*King v Kucharz* (1989) 153 JP 336). In *R (on the Application of AP, MD and JS) v Leeds Youth Court* [2001] EWHC 215 (Admin); (2001) 165 JP 684, the case against the defendants was adjourned for the prosecution to serve papers on the defence by a specified date; the youth court stated that failure to serve the papers would lead to dismissal of the case. On the adjourned hearing, the second bench refused to dismiss the charge even though the order for service of the papers had not been complied with. The Divisional Court held (following *King v Kucharz*) that, even taking account of Art 6 of the European Convention on Human Rights, the court does not have jurisdiction to dismiss proceedings for abuse of process simply on the basis of non-compliance with the Magistrates' Courts (Advance Information) Rules 1985.

A similar point arose in *R v Calderdale Magistrates Court ex p Donahue* [2001] Crim LR 141. The defendant sought judicial review of a decision by the magistrates refusing to direct the prosecution to disclose videotape evidence or accede to a request for an adjournment before proceeding to a 'plea before venue' hearing. Once the defence lawyers saw the videotape, the defendant entered a guilty plea. He argued that, as a result of the magistrates' refusal to order disclosure of the tape, he had been unable to make an informed decision on plea and so he had elected for Crown Court trial; it followed that there was a risk that he would not receive the appropriate credit for his guilty plea (given that it was not entered at the 'plea before venue' hearing). The

Divisional Court held that the defendant was entitled to view the videotape evidence by way of advance disclosure under the Magistrates' Court (Advance Information) Rules 1985 and so the magistrates had erred in refusing the request for an adjournment. The purpose of disclosure under the 1985 Rules is to enable the defendant to make an informed choice as to his plea and mode of trial. In the present case, the only evidence against the defendant was the video and he ought to be given the opportunity to withdraw his election for committal and be given credit for entering a guilty plea at the earliest opportunity.

If the prosecution offer only a summary of their case, they can sometimes be encouraged to supply copies of the witness statements if the defence indicate that they may well consent to summary trial if they do not have to elect Crown Court trial merely in order to obtain witness statements.

In the case of summary offences, the Advance Information Rules do not apply. However, the prosecution may make voluntary disclosure and so it is worthwhile for the defence to ask.

Home Office Circular 45/1997 points out that early service of advance information will help the defendant and his legal representatives to prepare for the 'plea before venue' hearing. The Circular notes that the CPS aims to serve advance information on the first of the following occasions:

- a request by the defendant or his representative;
- notification by the court that publicly-funded representation has been granted;
- the defendant's first appearance in court (where he is remanded on bail).

In *R v Stratford Justices ex p Imbert* [1999] 2 Cr App R 276, the Divisional Court held that Art 6 of the European Convention on Human Rights (which guarantees the right to a fair trial) does not require that prosecution witness statements should be disclosed to the defence before summary trial in the magistrates' court. The court held that disclosure of the witness statements is not necessary to achieve the 'equality of arms' required by the European Court of Human Rights in cases such as *Foucher v France* (1997) 25 EHRR 234. The decision in *Imbert* seems to accord with the view taken by the European Court of Human Rights that the accused must be informed of the nature of the charge against him and the material facts on which it is based, but not necessarily the evidence in support (*Brozicek v Italy* (1999) 12 EHRR 371).

However, para 43 of the *Attorney General's Guidelines: Disclosure of Information in Criminal Proceedings* provides as follows:

Summary trial

43 The prosecutor should, in addition to complying with the obligations under the Criminal Procedure and Investigations Act 1996, provide to the defence all evidence upon which the Crown proposes to rely in a summary trial. Such provision should allow the accused or their legal advisers sufficient time properly to consider the evidence before it is called. Exceptionally, statements may be withheld for the protection of witnesses or to avoid interference with the course of justice.

The effect of these guidelines seems to be to supersede the Advance Information Rules, by providing that there should be full disclosure, automatically, before all summary trials.

3.13   SECTION 40 OF THE CRIMINAL JUSTICE ACT 1988

Section 40 of the Criminal Justice Act 1988 provides as follows:

40   *Power to join in indictment count for common assault etc*

(1)   A count charging a person with a summary offence to which this section applies may be included in an indictment if the charge—

(a) is founded on the same facts or evidence as a count charging an indictable offence; or

(b) is part of a series of offences of the same or similar character as an indictable offence which is also charged,

but only if (in either case) the facts or evidence relating to the offence were disclosed to a magistrates' court inquiring into the offence as examining justices or are disclosed by material which, in pursuance of regulations made under paragraph 1 of Schedule 3 to the Crime and Disorder Act 1998 (procedure where person sent for trial under section 51), has been served on the person charged.

(2)   Where a count charging an offence to which this section applies is included in an indictment, the offence shall be tried in the same manner as if it were an indictable offence; but the Crown Court may only deal with the offender in respect of it in a manner in which a magistrates' court could have dealt with him.

(3)   The offences to which this section applies are—

(a) common assault;

(aa) an offence under section 90(1) of the Criminal Justice Act 1991 (assaulting a prisoner custody officer);

(ab) an offence under section 13(1) of the Criminal Justice and Public Order Act 1994 (assaulting a secure training centre custody officer);

(b) an offence under section 12(1) of the Theft Act 1968 (taking motor vehicle or other conveyance without authority etc);

(c) an offence under section 103(1)(b) of the Road Traffic Act 1988 (driving a motor vehicle while disqualified);

(d) an offence mentioned in the first column of Schedule 2 to the Magistrates' Courts Act 1980 (criminal damage etc) which would otherwise be triable only summarily by virtue of section 22(2) of that Act; and

(e) any summary offence specified under sub-section (4) below.

(4)   The Secretary of State may by order made by statutory instrument specify for the purposes of this section any summary offence which is punishable with imprisonment or involves obligatory or discretionary disqualification from driving.

To summarise, s 40 of the Criminal Justice Act 1988 applies if the defendant is sent for trial in respect of an indictable (that is, indictable-only or triable either way) offence and the witness statements also disclose any one or more of the following summary offences:

• common assault;

• taking a conveyance without the owner's consent (s 12 of the Theft Act 1968);

• driving a motor vehicle while disqualified;

• criminal damage where the value involved is £5,000 or less;

• assaulting a prison officer or a secure training centre officer.

The summary offence(s) may then be included on the indictment if they are founded on the same facts as the indictable offence, or if they form part of a series of offences (along with the indictable offence) of the same or a similar character as that offence. This is the same test as that which applies to the joinder of counts on an indictment under r 9 of the Indictment Rules 1971.

The effect of this provision is that the getaway driver at a robbery who has taken the car without the owner's consent can be indicted for robbery and for taking the conveyance (even though the latter is a summary offence) and the burglar who commits criminal damage in order to effect entry to the premises can be charged with burglary and criminal damage (even if the value of the criminal damage is less than £5,000).

It is the prosecution who decide whether or not the linked summary offence(s) should appear on the indictment so that the Crown Court can try the summary offence(s) as well as the indictable offence.

Where s 40 applies, the summary offence(s) appear on the indictment and are tried as if indictable. Note, however, that if the defendant is convicted of a s 40 summary offence, the Crown Court cannot impose more than six months' imprisonment and/or a £5,000 fine (that is, the maximum which the magistrates' court could have imposed) for that offence.

3.14   SECTION 41 OF THE CRIMINAL JUSTICE ACT 1988

Section 41 of the Criminal Justice Act 1988 provides as follows:

41   *Power of Crown Court to deal with summary offence where person committed for either way offence*

(1)   Where a magistrates' court commits a person to the Crown Court for trial on indictment for an offence triable either way or a number of such offences, it may also commit him for trial for any summary offence with which he is charged and which—

(a)   is punishable with imprisonment or involves obligatory or discretionary disqualification from driving; and

(b)   arises out of circumstances which appear to the court to be the same as or connected with those giving rise to the offence, or one of the offences, triable either way,

whether or not evidence relating to that summary offence appears on the depositions or written statements in the case; and the trial of the information charging the summary offence shall then be treated as if the magistrates' court had adjourned it under section 10 of the Magistrates' Courts Act 1980 and had not fixed the time and place for its resumption.

...

(4)   The committal of a person under this section in respect of an offence to which section 40 above applies shall not preclude the exercise in relation to the offence of the power conferred by that section; but where he is tried on indictment for such an offence, the functions of the Crown Court under this section in relation to the offence shall cease.

(5)   If he is convicted on the indictment, the Crown Court shall consider whether the conditions specified in sub-section (1) above were satisfied.

(6)   If it considers that they were satisfied, it shall state to him the substance of the summary offence and ask him whether he pleads guilty or not guilty.

(7)   If he pleads guilty, the Crown Court shall convict him, but may deal with him in respect of that offence only in a manner in which a magistrates' court could have dealt with him.

(8)   If he does not plead guilty, the powers of the Crown Court shall cease in respect of the offence except as provided by sub-section (9) below.

(9)   If the prosecution inform the Court that they would not desire to submit evidence on the charge relating to the summary offence, the Court shall dismiss it.

In summary, s 41 of the Criminal Justice Act 1988 provides that if the magistrates commit the defendant for trial on indictment in respect of one or more offences which are triable either way, they may also commit the defendant for a plea to be taken in respect of any summary offence, provided that the summary offence:

- is punishable with imprisonment or with disqualification from driving; and
- arises out of circumstances which are the same as or connected with the either way offence(s).

If, and only if, the defendant is convicted of the either way offence (either pleading guilty or being found guilty by the jury), the summary offence(s) will be put to the defendant for plea. The summary offence(s) will thus not appear on the indictment and will not be tried by the jury. Thereafter:

- if, having been convicted of the either way offence(s), the defendant pleads guilty to the summary offence(s), the Crown Court can pass any sentence which the magistrates could have imposed in respect of the summary offence(s) to which the defendant has pleaded guilty;
- if the defendant is acquitted of the either way offence(s) or, having been convicted of the either way offence(s), pleads not guilty to the summary offence(s), the prosecution can either indicate that it does not wish to proceed with the summary offence(s) or proceedings in respect of the summary offence(s) must be continued in the magistrates' court.

It is the magistrates, rather than the prosecution, who decide whether or not to commit a summary offence to the Crown Court for the plea to be taken.

In *R v Miall* [1992] QB 836, the defendant was committed for trial for perverting the course of justice. The magistrates tried to commit him, under s 41, for the plea to be taken in respect of a summary offence, driving with excess alcohol. It was held that s 41 could not be invoked as the offence on the indictment (perverting the course of justice, a common law offence) was triable only on indictment, not triable either way.

In *R v Foote* (1992) 94 Cr App R 82, the defendant was committed for trial to the Crown Court in respect of a charge of reckless (now called dangerous) driving. The magistrates also tried to commit him under s 41 of the Criminal Justice Act 1988 for a plea to be taken in respect of a charge of careless driving arising out of the same incident. The defendant pleaded not guilty to the reckless driving and the prosecution decided to accept that plea; the court then tried to invoke s 41 to take a plea in respect of the charge of careless driving. This was held to be wrong, because s 41 could not apply where the defendant had not been convicted of the either way offence.

In *R v Bird* [1995] Crim LR 745, the defendant was sent for trial in the Crown Court on charges of possession of an offensive weapon (an either way offence) and driving while disqualified (a summary offence to which s 40 applies). By virtue of s 41, he was committed for plea in respect of a charge of driving without insurance. He was acquitted of the charge of possession of an offensive weapon but was convicted of driving while disqualified. The Court of Appeal held that, since the defendant had been convicted on indictment of driving while disqualified, that offence was to be treated as an indictable offence. It followed that the Crown Court was entitled to deal with the summary offence of no insurance under s 41.

Section 41 is amended by para 303 of Sched 8 to the Courts Act 2003. Under that Act, s 41(8) will read, 'If he does not plead guilty, the Crown Court may try him for the offence, but may deal with him only in a manner in which a magistrates' court could have dealt with him', and s 41(9) is repealed. This amendment is the corollary of the enactment of s 66 of the Courts Act 2003, which empowers Crown Court judges to exercise the powers of magistrates. This means that if the defendant is convicted of the either way offence and then pleads not guilty to the linked summary offence, the Crown Court judge (sitting without a jury) will be able to try the summary offence (following the procedure which would have been adopted had that offence been tried in the magistrates' court). If the judge decides not to try the summary offence, the case can be remitted to the magistrates for them to try it.

It should be noted that s 41 will be repealed when the repeals contained in Sched 3 (Pt 2) to the Criminal Justice Act 2003 come into effect. This is because s 51(3) of the Crime and Disorder Act 1998, as amended by Sched 3 to the Criminal Justice Act 2003, provides that where a defendant is sent to the Crown Court for trial in respect of an indictable-only or either way offence, the justices may also send him for trial in respect of any related offence (provided that if the related offence is a summary one, it is punishable with imprisonment or disqualification from driving).

Although the government chose not to implement Lord Justice Auld's proposals (in his *Review of the Criminal Courts of England and Wales*) for a completely unified criminal court, it is significant that High Court judges (and deputies), Circuit judges (and deputies) and recorders will, under s 66 of the Courts Act 2003, have the same powers as magistrates in criminal cases. The Explanatory Notes that accompany the Act say that it is not expected that extensive use will be made of the provision, but it would (for example) be possible for a Circuit judge in the Crown Court to deal with a summary offence without the case having to go back to a magistrates' court. Thus, if the court is dealing with a summary offence which has been committed under s 41 of the Criminal Justice Act 1988 and the summary offence would otherwise have to be remitted to the magistrates' court (because the accused is acquitted of the either way offence to which the summary offence was linked, or the accused pleads not guilty to the summary offence), s 66 will enable the Crown Court judge to deal with the summary offence acting as a magistrate (and following the appropriate magistrates' courts' procedure).

3.15 ADJUSTING THE CHARGES TO DICTATE MODE OF TRIAL

It is possible for the prosecution to drop an existing charge and replace it with a new charge. This will usually be done in open court. The prosecution will indicate that they do not wish to proceed on the existing charge (by offering no evidence if the defendant has already pleaded not guilty, by giving notice of discontinuance or by withdrawing the summons if he has not entered a plea). The new charge is brought either by the police further charging the defendant outside court or by the prosecution laying an information orally in open court. Under r 4(1) of the Magistrates' Courts Rules 1981, an information may be laid by the prosecutor or by counsel or solicitor (or someone else) authorised on behalf of the prosecutor.

Sometimes the effect of replacing one charge with another will be to replace an offence which is triable either way with one which is triable only summarily, thus depriving the accused of the possibility of Crown Court trial. In *R v Canterbury Justices ex p Klisiak* [1982] QB 398, it was held that the prosecution could only be prevented from doing this in 'the most obvious circumstances which disclose blatant injustice' (*per* Lord Lane CJ).

In *R v Sheffield Justices ex p DPP* [1993] Crim LR 136, the magistrates stayed proceedings against a defendant where the prosecution declined to proceed with a charge of assault occasioning actual bodily harm (triable either way) and substituted a charge of common assault (a summary offence). The Divisional Court granted a prosecution application for judicial review, holding that it is a matter for the prosecution to decide which charge to proceed with. The court would only intervene where there was evidence of bad faith (that is, manipulating the system). In the present case, the charge of common assault was appropriate on the facts and there was no prejudice to the defendant.

It is also possible for a charge which is triable either way to be replaced by an offence which is triable only on indictment. However, in *R v Brooks* [1985] Crim LR 385, the Court of Appeal warned that it would be unjust and wrong for the prosecution to do this if the magistrates have already accepted jurisdiction in respect of the either way offence; the prosecution would be frustrating that decision by changing the charge.

The Code of Conduct for Crown Prosecutors says that charges should be chosen which reflect the seriousness of the offending, give the court adequate sentencing powers, and enable the case to be presented in a clear and simple way. The Code goes on to say that Crown Prosecutors should not continue with more charges than necessary and should never go ahead with a more serious charge just to encourage a defendant to plead guilty to a less serious one. Finally, the Code states that the charge should not be changed simply because of the decision made by the court or the defendant about where the case will be heard.

3.16   ALLOCATION OF CASES UNDER THE CRIMINAL JUSTICE ACT 2003

In this section, we look at various proposals for reform of the mode of trial procedure and then examine in details the reforms brought about by the Criminal Justice Act 2003.

3.16.1 Proposals for reform

In Chapter 6 of his 'Review of delay in the criminal justice system' ('Managing the distribution of cases between the courts') (www.homeoffice.gov.uk/docs/crimrev6.html), published in 1997, Martin Narey recommended that defendants should no longer be able to veto the decision of magistrates to retain jurisdiction of cases.

The Narey Review noted that:

> It is frequently claimed that the right of a defendant to elect trial by jury is an ancient one, enshrined in Magna Carta. In fact, there was no right to claim trial by jury until 1855. Up to that time, there were only two categories of offence: those triable only on indictment and those triable only summarily. Felonies (as opposed to misdemeanours) were always tried on indictment. But there was no element of defendant election.

> From the middle of the nineteenth century the simple distinction between cases triable on indictment and those triable summarily began to be eroded ...

> The underlying principle that the defendant should consent to summary trial was preserved in these changes. But in the 1870s statutes began to introduce hybrid offences which could be tried either summarily or on indictment. The crucial point here was that some hybrid offences could be retained by magistrates without the defendant's consent.

The Review then considered the recommendations made in 1975 by the James Committee:

> By the time the James Committee reported ('The Distribution of Criminal Business between the Crown Court and Magistrates' Courts: Report of the Interdepartmental Committee 1975') the distinction between cases triable only on indictment, summary only cases and those indictable cases triable summarily with the defendant's consent was confused by three other types of case: hybrid cases carrying a right to elect trial by jury, hybrid cases without that right and summary cases which under certain circumstances could be tried on indictment. The James Committee concluded that this proliferation of categories had evolved as a result of largely unrelated developments in the summary jurisdiction of magistrates' courts which had not been considered as a whole. The Committee's recommendations led to the present threefold classification of offences as summary, either way and indictable-only.

> The James Committee was clearly alive to the resource implications of jury trial. And they were conscious of the circumstances which made it important for some defendants more than others to be able to protect their reputation:

>> A professional person of good character, if convicted of a minor offence of dishonesty for example, will suffer in reputation and may lose his livelihood, whereas for a person with a long record of similar offences the only penalty will probably be the sentence actually imposed.

> The committee also noted that few jurisdictions had found it necessary, or even regarded it as desirable, to build into their systems of criminal justice an element of personal choice by the defendant of the court in which he should be tried. But they concluded that, however anomalous the English system, account had to be taken of:

>> the regard in which the present right of election is held ... There is a substantial body of opinion in favour of removing the defendant's right of election [but] this is almost entirely confined to those directly responsible for the administration of justice, whether as judges, court staff or prosecutors. Virtually all the organisations representing practitioners and almost every individual solicitor and barrister who wrote to us, together with most of the organisations representing a wider interest, took the contrary view.

The Narey Review noted that those who argue in favour of preserving the defendant's right to elect trial rely on the seriousness of either way offences: 'It is pointed out that, for example, the right to elect trial for theft is vital because of the effect of a conviction for dishonesty on a person's character.' However, Narey countered this by pointing out that 'there are a number of offences involving dishonesty including false representation for obtaining a benefit and fraudulent use of a telecommunications system, as well as offences such as soliciting, keeping a brothel, impersonation of a police officer, common assault and assault on a constable which have equally serious implications for a person's reputation and which are triable summarily only'.

The Review then examined the reasons defendants have for electing trial on indictment:

> There appear to be three objectives for defendants who elect trial. The first is to delay proceedings and therefore to put off conviction and sentence. (Some defence lawyers will admit that they will advise clients to do this in the hope of persuading the CPS to accept a plea to a less serious charge, or simply to make it more likely that prosecution witnesses will not attend the trial or will be vague in their recollections.) The second is to retain location in a local prison, close to family and friends (including friends in the prison) and with the additional visits available to unconvicted prisoners.

> The third objective is acquittal, the chances of which are higher at the Crown Court than at magistrates' courts (this does not imply that the Crown Court is fairer). Whatever the chances of acquittal at the Crown Court, a very large majority of defendants electing trial subsequently plead guilty. It is difficult to be precise, but it appears that about two thirds of defendants electing trial subsequently plead guilty and about three quarters of all defendants electing are subsequently convicted.

The Review noted the suggestion of reclassifying some either way offences as summary-only and pointed out that it is 'frequently' suggested (for example, by the James Committee in 1975) that theft of a small monetary value should also be reclassified. However, Narey said that:

> I believe that reducing the number of cases going to the Crown Court through reclassifying minor theft would be an unsatisfactory solution, although I acknowledge that it might divert a significant number of cases from the Crown Court, perhaps in the region of two thousand (including cases committed by magistrates). Reclassification would mean that there would be no circumstances in which a theft of small monetary value could go to the Crown Court even where, because of the nature of the offence, magistrates considered that Crown Court trial was appropriate. (A minor theft from an elderly or other vulnerable person or a minor theft by a person in a position of trust are two examples.)

> There would also be circumstances, because of matters of reputation, or because a conviction for theft might lead to defendants losing their job, where it might be considered proper for a case to be heard in front of a jury. For those reasons, I recommend that the possibility of a defendant being tried at the Crown Court for any current either way offence should not be removed. But the final decision on venue should be one for the magistrates to make rather than the defendant.

Narey went on to discuss in more detail his recommendation that magistrates should decide venue in all either way cases:

> Defendants should no longer be able to veto the decision of magistrates to retain jurisdiction of cases: instead, the decision should rest with magistrates, with the prosecutor making recommendations as to venue and the defence having the opportunity to make representations as well. Where the defence were able to produce convincing reasons for Crown Court trial, magistrates would be free to accept them and commit the case for trial.

The 1993 Royal Commission made a similar recommendation and considered that in making their decision magistrates should consider a number of factors including the defendant's reputation and past record, the gravity of the offence, the complexity of the case and its likely effect on the defendant. (An alternative option would be to remove the right of election from defendants where they were being prosecuted for an offence similar in nature to an earlier conviction, since in those circumstances matters of reputation are not paramount. But this option, whilst initially attractive, would expose the Government to criticisms that it was offering a lower standard of justice to those with criminal convictions who, it might be argued, are most vulnerable to wrongful arrest and charge.)

The Runciman Commission further suggested that in circumstances where prosecutor and defence agreed on venue, magistrates should not be involved in the decision. Presentationally this might be difficult. It is important that magistrates should take, and be seen to take, this decision. (It is true that in Scotland there is no role for the court in deciding venue – the decision being one for the prosecution alone, and with no right of appeal – and this appears to cause no controversy whatsoever; but any attempt to confer similar rights on the prosecution in England and Wales would be greeted with alarm.)

Narey went on to note that the government's final response to the Royal Commission, published in June 1996, was that the removal of the right to elect trial on indictment 'should not be undertaken unless it is clear that it would be the only possible way of achieving the objective' and that the question should be reconsidered in the light of the effect of the 'plea before venue' procedure implemented by the Criminal Procedure and Investigations Act 1996.

Narey commented that:

This rather suggests that plea before venue provides an alternative to removing the defendant's veto on the mode of trial decision. In fact the two initiatives would be complementary: plea before venue is likely to reduce unnecessary committals by magistrates, whereas removing the right of election would remove unnecessary committals prompted by defendants. However successful the plea before venue initiative, it will not reduce defendant elections.

Narey was very conscious of the controversial nature of the proposal to remove the right to choose Crown Court trial. He tried to counter the arguments he expected to be raised against the proposal.

The first argument he anticipated is that the proposal amounts to erosion of a fundamental privilege. He answered this argument by saying:

The belief that the removal of the defendant's veto on the magistrates' decision on mode of trial would erode fundamental individual liberties established in the Middle Ages is widely shared but is not undisputed. At least one eminent historian regards the later interpretation of Magna Carta's 'lawful judgement of peers' to mean trial by jury as going far beyond the detailed intention and sense of the original charter; and the jury was not an independent tribunal but a group of local people selected because of their familiarity with the district and the accused, and certainly much less likely to be independent than a modern bench of magistrates.

The decision in the middle and late nineteenth century to allow cases to be tried summarily only with the consent of the accused has to be set in the context of a criminal justice process which extended very few of the protections currently afforded to defendants.

Narey concluded that:

> If accepted, these recommendations would not rule out Crown Court trial for any defendant charged with an either way offence, but it would stop an improper manipulation of the justice system. Magistrates would be well able to distinguish those defendants who, because of potential loss of reputation, or for other reasons, were justified in seeking a Crown Court hearing. Those cases would be a minority. The majority of cases in which the defendant elects trial result, eventually, in guilty pleas, but only after significantly increased inconvenience to victims and witnesses and at considerable extra cost.

In 1998, the government published a Consultation Paper, *Determining Mode of Trial in Either Way Cases* (www.homeoffice.gov.uk/docs/contrial.html), with the following purpose:

> ... to consider whether a defendant in an either way case which the magistrates are willing to hear should continue to be able to decide where he should be tried; to consider whether some possible options for reform would be more consistent with the interests of justice and efficiency; and to invite comments on the alternatives. The paper is concerned not with the merits of jury trial, but only with the defendant's ability to choose it.

Given the fact that many defendants choose Crown Court trial because they perceive it as fairer and more thorough than summary trial, the exclusion of consideration of the merits of jury trial may perhaps be considered a little disingenuous.

The Consultation Paper started by putting the question of the defendant's right to elect Crown Court trial in its historical context, much as Narey had done.

In para 6, the Paper noted that the proportion of cases where the magistrates decline jurisdiction exceeds, by a significant margin, those cases where the defendant elects Crown Court trial. The Paper suggested that a 'possible explanation is that some defendants have concluded that (as Home Office research has demonstrated) those who plead guilty having elected Crown Court trial are likely to receive a substantially heavier sentence than if they had pleaded guilty in the magistrates' court'.

The Paper went on to note (para 8) that:

> ... defendants in the Crown Court are more likely to plead not guilty than those who are tried in magistrates' courts: around one-third of defendants who go to the Crown Court plead not guilty to some or all charges, compared with fewer than one in ten in magistrates' courts. The percentage of defendants pleading not guilty in the Crown Court appears to be much the same whether they have elected to be tried there or have been directed there by the magistrates. At first sight this seems surprising since it might have been expected that defendants who elect would have a greater propensity to plead not guilty; but on the other hand, directed cases are likely to be relatively serious and possibly more likely to be contested for that reason.

In para 9, the Paper noted the disparity in acquittal rates between the Crown Court and the magistrates' court and said that:

> It is unclear ... whether this is because juries are more inclined to acquit – rightly or wrongly – than magistrates, or because defendants with a good defence are more likely to be tried in the Crown Court, either as a result of having elected or (conceivably) by direction of the magistrates.

The Paper went on to summarise the arguments for and against (a) maintaining the status quo, (b) reclassifying some offences as summary offences, or (c) abolishing the right of the defendant to elect Crown Court trial.

Dealing first with maintaining the status quo, the Paper first summarised the arguments in favour of preserving the status quo:

11   The fundamental argument in favour of the present arrangement is that allowing defendants charged with any non-summary offence to have access to trial by jury (which is the mode of trial which is considered appropriate for all serious cases) helps to promote confidence in the criminal justice system.

12   The considerations to which magistrates must have regard in deciding whether a case is suitable to be tried by them or should be tried by a jury, which are set out in the National Mode of Trial Guidelines, are broadly concerned with the seriousness of the case. The effect that conviction would have on the defendant's reputation is not one of these considerations. But reputation is widely perceived, at least in certain sorts of case, as a justification for continuing to allow the defendant to elect Crown Court trial. As the James Committee put it,

> A professional person of good character, if convicted of a minor offence of dishonesty for example, will suffer in reputation and may lose his livelihood, whereas for a person with a long record of similar offences the only penalty will probably be the sentence actually imposed.

13   When people who have never been accused of a criminal offence argue the case for the right to elect jury trial, it is usually on the basis that this is what they would want were they unfortunate enough to be charged with an offence which they had not committed.

14   Underlying the argument for allowing defendants to defend their reputation before a jury is the assumption that a jury is 'fairer' than a bench of magistrates. Home Office research has shown that defendants who elect Crown Court trial tend to do so mainly because they believe that their chances of acquittal are higher at the Crown Court than at magistrates' courts. Indeed that belief is borne out by the statistics, although the case in favour of election depends more on the existence of these perceptions that jury trial is advantageous than on whether they are well founded.

15   Some other arguments which are adduced in favour of election for trial – for example, the fact that a jury can acquit in the face of evidence which legally establishes the offence ('nullification') – go to the merits of trial by jury rather than to whether a defendant should be able to choose to be tried in this way.

Turning to the arguments that the present systems requires reform, the Paper said:

16   The fundamental argument against the present system is that it means that the additional delay and cost inseparable from Crown Court proceedings are incurred in cases which do not need to be tried there but which defendants have themselves chosen to take to the Crown Court because, rightly or wrongly, they see some advantage in doing so. Elected cases, by definition, are cases which the magistrates considered were suitable for them to deal with and which, but for the defendant's veto, they would have tried. The Royal Commission on Criminal Justice and the 'Review of Delay in the Criminal Justice System' (the Narey report) both considered that the court, and not the defendant, is best qualified to make the final decision where a case should be heard. That decision should be based on an objective assessment by the court of the gravity of the case, and not on defendants' own perception of what is advantageous for them (eg that there would be a better prospect of acquittal in the higher court).

17   It is open to question how many accused persons elect Crown Court trial out of a desire to defend their reputation. The Narey report quoted a senior and distinguished magistrate:

> In considering elections for trial I cannot remember the last time someone elected for reasons of reputation. Inevitably, the ones who elect are experienced defendants, the ones who know how to play the system.

18   This assessment is borne out by Home Office research suggesting that only one in ten of the defendants who elect Crown Court trial are without previous convictions. Defendants who have a criminal record are less likely than those with none to be motivated primarily by a wish to clear their name. They may be attracted (especially where their previous record is such as to put them at risk, if convicted, of losing their liberty) by the better prospects for acquittal afforded by the Crown Court. But these prospects are insufficient to prevent two-thirds of defendants from eventually pleading guilty before the start of trial, and are irrelevant to the significant proportion of defendants who (according to the same research) intended to plead guilty from the outset.

19   For the great majority of defendants, the decision to elect Crown Court trial may be founded on a wish to delay the proceedings, for any of the following reasons:
    (a) to apply pressure on the Crown to accept a plea to a less serious charge;
    (b) to make it more likely that prosecution witnesses will fail to attend the trial or, if they do attend, will be vague in their recollections;
    (c) to put off the evil day. If it achieves nothing else, electing Crown Court trial will at least postpone conviction and sentence and the consequent removal from a local prison, where defendants are close to family and friends and enjoy the additional visits and other privileges available to unconvicted prisoners.

20   The majority of cases in which the defendant elects trial result, eventually, in guilty pleas, but only after significantly greater inconvenience and worry to victims and witnesses, and at considerable extra cost. This cost arises not only in court time and legal aid funds, but also in prison places, because defendants who are sentenced to imprisonment by the Crown Court having elected to be tried there tend to receive substantially longer terms than would have been imposed by the magistrates.

Turning to possible reforms of the system of allocating either way offences, the Paper considered first reclassification of particular either way offences as summary-only (as was done by the Criminal Justice Act 1988, when criminal damage (up to £5,000 in value), common assault, driving while disqualified, and taking a conveyance without authority became summary offences).

The Paper cited simplicity as the main argument in favour of this approach:

Reclassification would be straightforward, and would have the potential to divert some of the more obviously minor cases from the Crown Court. The James Committee recommended in 1975 that theft involving a small monetary value should be reclassified. They suggested a cut-off point of £20, which would be rather more than £90 now; if this were adopted, it is estimated that reclassification of minor theft would enable the magistrates to deal with some 2,000 cases in which defendants now elect Crown Court trial (para 22).

However, the Paper went on to suggest that this sort of reclassification could well cause injustice:

The problem with reclassification is that it is a blunt instrument: it would deprive magistrates of the power to send cases in the reclassified categories to the Crown Court even where they considered the particular offence to be such that Crown Court trial was appropriate. For example, theft of even a small sum may be a serious matter where the victim is an elderly or other vulnerable person, or where the culprit is in a position of trust, or where a conviction for dishonesty might lead to the defendant losing his job (para 23).

The other disadvantage noted in the Paper is that the reclassification option would not affect the offences which are not reclassified and so defendants could still elect Crown Court trial of offences that the magistrates could deal with.

The Paper therefore moved to what was plainly the government's preferred option, namely the abolition of the right to elect Crown Court trial. Paragraph 25 introduced this section of the Paper by saying:

> It is less obvious why the defendant should be allowed to insist on taking a case to the Crown Court which the magistrates have decided would be suitable for them to try. It is sometimes argued that no-one should be tried for a serious offence in a magistrates' court unless he is content to be tried there, but (as the James Committee noted in 1975) few other jurisdictions allow the defendant such an element of personal choice.

Paragraph 26 recalls that the 'Royal Commission on Criminal Justice recommended that venue in either way cases should be decided by the parties where they were in agreement on the issue. Where they did not agree, it would be for the magistrates to decide where the case should be tried; they would have regard not only to any defence representations (as legislation already requires), but also to such factors as the gravity of the offence, the complexity of the case, the defendant's past record if any (which would be an innovation), and the effect of conviction (and the likely sentence) on the defendant's livelihood and reputation ...'; para 27 recalls that the 'Review of Delay in the Criminal Justice System recommended simply that the decision as to where either way cases are heard should rest with the magistrates, having regard to recommendations as to venue from the prosecutor and from the defence, and that defendants should no longer be able to veto their decision'. On either basis, the defendant would no longer be able to veto summary trial.

Turning to the arguments for this approach, the Paper said:

28   The main argument for removing defendants' ability to choose jury trial is that it is not they, but the court, which is best qualified to determine where a case should be tried. Abolition would not automatically rule out Crown Court trial for any defendant charged with particular either way offences (as reclassification would). It would prevent what some regard as manipulation of the justice system by defendants demanding Crown Court trial for no good reason.

29   The proposal that magistrates should be required to take account of those factors (such as harm to a hitherto unblemished reputation) which might justify a defendant in seeking a Crown Court hearing would go some way towards meeting the concerns of those who see election for trial primarily as a safeguard for defendants with a reputation to lose. It would mean that some of the cases in which the defendant now elects jury trial would go to the Crown Court by direction of the magistrates. But even on the assumption that this might happen in as many as a quarter of elected cases, there would still be a fall of some 15,000 in the number of committals for trial. By way of comparison, the implementation of the 'plea before venue' provision in s 49 of the Criminal Procedure and Investigations Act 1996 has led to a similar reduction in the number of cases committed to the Crown Court for trial.

Next, the arguments against the removal of the right to elect were set out:

30   The objection to the removal of election is essentially that it would result in
      defendants being tried summarily for indictable offences without their consent,
      and that the benefits of the present arrangement which are listed in paragraphs
      11–14 above would be lost.

31   The system proposed by the Royal Commission is open to a particular objection
      in that it would admit of the possibility (albeit an unlikely one) that by agreeing
      on summary trial the Crown and the defence could together require magistrates
      to hear a case which they considered unsuitable for their jurisdiction.

Given the obviously controversial nature of the suggestion that the right to elect trial
on indictment should be abolished, it is perhaps surprising that the arguments against
were not set out in greater detail.

The Paper then considered a more limited proposal to limit the right to elect trial
on indictment, namely that the right should be lost only where a defendant was
prosecuted for an offence similar in nature to an earlier conviction. The basis for
drawing a distinction between such offences and other accusations was that matters of
reputation would not be paramount where the accused had previous convictions for
similar offences.

Paragraph 33 set out the arguments in favour of this approach:

A defendant who has already been convicted of the same sort of offence can hardly be
said to have as strong a reason for defending his reputation as a defendant with an
unblemished record, and is arguably less likely to have a genuine intention of doing so
when electing Crown Court trial. The clearest examples of manipulation are where
defendants with long criminal records elect Crown Court trial and then plead guilty at
the last moment or are convicted after a trial. This option would enable the magistrates
to deal with such cases.

The arguments against the proposal were set out in para 34:

Not everyone would accept that those with criminal convictions should, for that
reason alone, be denied a privilege accorded to other defendants. That a defendant has
a criminal record does not imply that he or she is necessarily guilty of the offence
charged; indeed it is arguable that it might be the existence of previous convictions
which brought the defendant under suspicion. A defendant whose previous
convictions were such as to put him at risk of a custodial sentence if convicted might
even be regarded as having greater justification for seeking jury trial than those who
were at no such risk.

3.16.2   Mode of Trial Bills

Two Criminal Justice (Mode of Trial) Bills were placed before Parliament in the late
1990s. The government's intention was to remove the defendant's right to elect trial for
either way offences. Under both Bills, the choice of mode of trial would have been a
matter for the magistrates. They would have heard representations from the
prosecution and from the defence, and would then have decided whether the case was
to be tried in the magistrates' court or the Crown Court.

The main impetus for reform was the fact that too much of the Crown Court's
workload was felt to comprise cases that could have been dealt with in the
magistrates' court, in the sense that they were not serious enough to justify the much
more expensive form of trial. This proposal was intensely controversial, and many

people argued that it was wrong to take away a person's right to choose trial by jury for any either way offence.

The first version of the Bill required the magistrates to have regard to the likely effect of conviction on the defendant's reputation. However, this was felt to discriminate unfairly against those with previous convictions. The second Bill went to the other extreme, and excluded all consideration of the circumstances of the offender. The accused would have had a right of appeal to the Crown Court (to a judge sitting alone, without lay justices) against a decision that he ought to be tried summarily. Both Bills failed to complete their passage through Parliament.

3.16.3   The Auld Review

In Sir Robin Auld's *Review of the Criminal Courts of England and Wales*, he argued that there should be a unified Criminal Court, with the Crown Court and magistrates' courts being replaced by a unified Criminal Court consisting of three Divisions: the 'Crown Division' (constituted as the Crown Court now is and exercising jurisdiction over all indictable-only matters and the more serious either way offences allocated to it); the 'District Division' (consisting of a judge, normally a District judge or recorder, and at least two lay magistrates, and exercising jurisdiction over a range of either way offences of sufficient seriousness to merit up to two years' custody); and the 'Magistrates' Division' (constituted as magistrates' courts now are, with either lay justices or a District judge, and dealing with all summary matters and the less serious either way cases allocated to them). Auld's plan was that the Magistrates' Division would allocate all either way cases, according to the seriousness of the alleged offence and the circumstances of the defendant. In the event of a dispute as to venue, a District judge would determine the matter after hearing representations from the prosecution and the defendant. The defendant would no longer have the right to choose trial by jury for an either way offence. The main rationale for mixed tribunals was that they would 'combine the advantages of the legal knowledge and experience of the professional judge with community representation in the form of lay magistrates' (para 276). For a discussion of these proposals, see John Jackson's article 'Modes of trial: shifting the balance towards the professional judge' [2002] Crim LR 249.

The government rejected the proposal to restructure the criminal courts in this way. However, the Courts Act 2003 does make provision for a much closer working relationship between the Crown Court and the magistrates' court, as well as a single committee to devise rules for both courts (making it likely that, eventually, there will be a set of rules common to both courts, along the lines of the Civil Procedure Rules that are applicable in both the county court and the High Court).

The Auld Review also tackled the highly controversial question of determining mode of trial for either way offences. This topic is considered at length in paras 119–72 of Chapter 5. The question was perhaps made all the more difficult by the failure of the two Mode of Trial Bills. Having reviewed all the arguments, Lord Justice Auld concludes that there is no good reason why a defendant should be able to choose the court in which he is tried (and he notes that this right is, in international terms, a rarity).

Accordingly, the relevant recommendations are as follows:

32 In all 'either way' cases, magistrates' courts, not defendants, should determine venue after representation from the parties.

33 In the event of a dispute on the issue, a District Judge should decide.

34 The defence and the prosecution should have a right of appeal on paper from any mode of trial decision on which they were at issue to a Circuit Judge nominated for the purpose, and provision should be made for the speedy hearing of such appeals.

...

36 The procedure of committal for sentence should be abolished.

In the Criminal Justice Act 2003, the government approached the concerns about the workload of the Crown Court from a different angle. Rather than seeking to restrict the defendant's right to elect Crown Court trial, the Act increases the sentencing powers of the magistrates. The effect of this is intended to be that the magistrates will find more cases suitable for summary trial; if more defendants are offered summary trial, the likelihood is that there will be an increase in the number of summary trials and a corresponding decrease in the number of Crown Court trials. This may seem to be a sensible approach given the fact that approximately two-thirds of either way cases tried in the Crown Court are in that court because the magistrates declined jurisdiction (only one-third are there because the defendant, having been offered the option of summary trial, elected Crown Court trial). However, some commentators argue that it is inappropriate to increase the sentencing powers of the magistrates in this way, since (a) the magistrates' courts could not cope with a significant increase in workload, and (b) many magistrates would regard themselves as ill-equipped to try more serious cases. See, for example, Andrew Herbert, 'Mode of trial and magistrates' sentencing powers: will increased powers inevitably lead to a reduction in the committal rate?' [2003] Crim LR 313 (an article based on a study which involved interviewing magistrates, clerks and defence solicitors). Herbert notes that the 'plea before venue' procedure met with only limited success in encouraging the entry of early guilty pleas. He says that the proportion of defendants who admit guilt at the 'plea before venue' hearing would appear to be lower than had been anticipated, and comments that:

... [M]agistrates appear to view the decision to order reports as equating to an acceptance of jurisdiction and being virtually conclusive that they will finalise a case. The consequence of this practice is that they seem unwilling, or at the very least reluctant, to order reports in cases which might be outside their sentencing powers, opting instead to commit these defendants to the Crown Court at the PBV hearing.

On the increase in the sentencing powers of magistrates by the Criminal Justice Bill (or Act, as it now is), he says that these enhanced powers 'might result in magistrates imposing longer prison sentences on offenders who currently receive six months or less rather than lead to them accepting jurisdiction in a wider and more serious compass of cases'.

He concludes as follows:

... There can be little doubt that increased powers would have some effect on the committal rate. It is virtually inconceivable that magistrates would not retain any additional cases or that these cases would be completely offset by greater exercise of the right of election. It has been argued in this article, however, that the anticipated effect of increased powers on committal rates may well not be as significant as expected. The underlying reasons for this present as being the culture of the lay magistracy and the lack of impetus coming from within magistrates' courts to finalise more serious cases.

The findings of this study suggest that attempts to change procedure cannot afford to underestimate the strength of the culture of the lay magistracy ... Magistrates have traditionally viewed the purpose of a mode of trial hearing as being to provide a clearly defined path for a case. They have a belief that a decision to accept jurisdiction is essentially final. They adopt a cautious approach towards retaining cases in order to minimise the possibility of colleagues having to make an implicitly conflicting decision at the sentencing hearing. This conservative attitude provides one reason for the limited impact of plea before venue on committal rates. Magistrates view the decision to order reports as equating to an acceptance of jurisdiction and, therefore, tend to commit cases which might prove to be outside their sentencing powers.

The effect of a cautious approach towards accepting jurisdiction is heightened by an apparent lack of impetus coming from within magistrates' courts to hear more serious cases. The objective of a reduced committal rate is, quite simply, seen by many court participants as being flawed. Almost all of the magistrates interviewed for this study believed that current mode of trial procedure was satisfactory and produced a fair and realistic division of business between the higher and lower courts in the interests of justice. Lawyers expressed the opinion that lay magistrates were already being asked to handle cases at the extreme of their ability. This view is crucial as magistrates are nearly always faced with an agreed or unchallenged application of the Crown and almost invariably endorse that recommendation. Increased sentencing powers may have the effect of net widening and lead to the imposition of longer custodial sentences. It may even be that a reduction in the committal rate would have the paradoxical consequence of the increased use of imprisonment as many defence solicitors believe that judges tend to be more lenient, and show greater faith in the efficacy of community orders, in some borderline categories of offence.

... It is, however, possible to reach one positive and constructive conclusion. The prime implication of this study is that reform is more likely to be effected from within than imposed from without. Magistrates need to be made aware of the reasons why judges more often than not sentence either way defendants *within* lower court powers. Their current knowledge of Crown Court sentences would appear to be largely confined to that gleaned from reading the local press ... A significant reduction in the committal rate will only materialise when all magistrates' court participants believe that the objective of a lower rate equates with the interests of justice.

3.16.4   The Criminal Justice Act 2003

Section 41 of the Criminal Justice Act 2003 gives effect to Sched 3 to the Act, which contains detailed rules setting out the procedure to be followed by magistrates' courts when determining mode of trial for either way offences and for sending cases to the Crown Court for trial.

The Explanatory Notes that accompany the Act state that these new procedures are designed to enable cases to be dealt with in the level of court which is appropriate to their seriousness, and to ensure that they reach that court as quickly as possible. It should be noted that the government abandoned its plans to remove the right of the defendant to elect Crown Court trial even though Lord Justice Auld recommended that this be done; the decision to drop this proposal was probably not unconnected with the fierce opposition that met the two Mode of Trial Bills introduced (unsuccessfully) by the government.

Important changes include:

- making magistrates aware, when they determine mode of trial, of any previous convictions recorded against the defendant;

- removing the option of committal for sentence in cases where the magistrates accept jurisdiction;

- allowing defendants, in cases where the magistrates offer the option of summary trial, to seek a broad indication of the sentence they would face if they were to plead guilty at that stage;

- abolishing committal proceedings and transfers in serious fraud and child witness cases, and replacing them with a common system for sending cases to the Crown Court, based on the present arrangements for indictable-only cases (under s 51 of the Crime and Disorder Act 1998).

The procedure for giving an indication of plea is extended to defendants under the age of 18 who are charged with offences which may be committed for trial to the Crown Court (under s 24 of the Magistrates' Courts Act 1980, which applies to those cases where a sentence of detention under s 91 of the Powers of Criminal Courts (Sentencing) Act 2000 may be imposed following conviction in the Crown Court, or where the juvenile defendant is charged alongside an adult co-accused). This brings the procedure applicable to those defendants into line with the procedure which applies to adult defendants. The Explanatory Notes make the point that the intention of this is to avoid cases involving young defendants being sent to the Crown Court unnecessarily.

Paragraphs 3 and 4 of Sched 3 make it clear that the 'plea before venue' and mode of trial ('allocation') hearing may take place before a single lay justice. However, if the accused is given the option of summary trial and accepts that option, a single justice cannot try the case (and so, where the preliminary hearing takes place before a single justice and the accused pleads not guilty, the case will have to be adjourned for hearing before a full bench (or a District judge)). Similarly, although a single lay justice may take a guilty plea, sentence must be imposed by a full bench (or a District judge).

Paragraph 5 of Sched 3 substitutes an amended version of s 19 of the Magistrates' Courts Act 1980, which sets out the procedure to be followed when the magistrates' court decides whether a case involving an either way offence to which the defendant has not indicated a guilty plea should be tried summarily or in the Crown Court. This new procedure for 'allocation' differs from the present one in that the court is to be informed about any previous convictions recorded against the defendant when deciding whether its sentencing powers are adequate. This settles once and for all the controversy over whether the magistrates should have regard to previous convictions when considering whether a case is suitable for summary trial. Bearing in mind that the magistrates are trying to predict whether the ultimate sentence will be one that is within their powers, it seems to make sense that they should be made aware of factors that would be relevant to that sentence.

As well as taking account of the Mode of Trial Guidelines set out in the 2002 *Consolidated Practice Direction* (and to any representations made by the prosecution or defence), the magistrates will be required to have regard to any allocation guidelines issued by the newly-created Sentencing Guidelines Council under s 170 of the 2003 Act.

The amended version of s 19 of the 1980 Act, inserted by para 5, is as follows:

Decision as to allocation

(1)   The court shall decide whether the offence appears to it more suitable for summary trial or for trial on indictment.

(2)   Before making a decision under this section, the court—

(a)   shall give the prosecution an opportunity to inform the court of the accused's previous convictions (if any); and

(b)   shall give the prosecution and the accused an opportunity to make representations as to whether summary trial or trial on indictment would be more suitable.

(3)   In making a decision under this section, the court shall consider—

(a)   whether the sentence which a magistrates' court would have power to impose for the offence would be adequate; and

(b)   any representations made by the prosecution or the accused under sub-section (2)(b) above,

and shall have regard to any allocation guidelines (or revised allocation guidelines) issued as definitive guidelines under section 170 of the Criminal Justice Act 2003.

(4)   Where—

(a)   the accused is charged with two or more offences; and

(b)   it appears to the court that the charges for the offences could be joined in the same indictment or that the offences arise out of the same or connected circumstances,

sub-section (3)(a) above shall have effect as if references to the sentence which a magistrates' court would have power to impose for the offence were a reference to the maximum aggregate sentence which a magistrates' court would have power to impose for all of the offences taken together.

…

(6)   If, in respect of the offence, the court receives a notice under section 51B or 51C of the Crime and Disorder Act 1998 (which relate to serious or complex fraud cases and to certain cases involving children respectively), the preceding provisions of this section and sections 20, 20A and 21 below shall not apply, and the court shall proceed in relation to the offence in accordance with section 51(1) of that Act.

Paragraph 6 of Sched 3 replaces s 20 of the Magistrates' Courts Act 1980, and adds a new section, s 20A. These amendments have the effect of revising the procedure to be followed by the magistrates' court where it decides that a case is suitable for summary trial. As now, defendants will be told that they can either consent to be tried summarily or, if they wish, be tried in the Crown Court. A major change made by the 2003 Act is to remove the possibility that the defendant may be committed for sentence to the Crown Court after the magistrates have accepted jurisdiction. Thus, a defendant who accepts summary trial will have a finite limit placed on the sentence that can be imposed for that offence.

Where the defendant indicates a guilty plea under s 17A or 17B of the 1980 Act, the option of committal to the Crown Court for sentence under s 3 of the Powers of Criminal Courts (Sentencing) Act 2000 will continue to be available (as is inevitable given the fact that defendants may plead guilty to very serious either way offences at the 'plea before venue' hearing).

The new procedure also gives defendants the opportunity of requesting an indication from the magistrates whether, if they plead guilty at that stage, the sentence would be custodial or not. The magistrates are given a broad discretion whether or not to give such an indication. Where an indication is given, the defendant will be given the opportunity to reconsider his original indication as to plea. If he then decides to plead guilty, the magistrates' court will proceed to sentence (if necessary adjourning for a pre-sentence report); in such a case, a custodial sentence will be available only if such a sentence was indicated by the court.

If the defendant declines to reconsider his plea indication, or if no sentence indication is given by the magistrates, the defendant will be given the choice of accepting summary trial or electing Crown Court trial. Where an indication of sentence is given and the defendant does not choose to plead guilty on the basis of it, the sentence indication is not binding on the magistrates who later try the case summarily, or on the Crown Court if the defendant elects trial on indictment.

The amended s 20 of the 1980 Act, substituted by para 6, and the new s 20A inserted by that paragraph provide as follows:

20   *Procedure where summary trial appears more suitable*

(1)   If the court decides under section 19 above that the offence appears to it more suitable for summary trial, the following provisions of this section shall apply (unless they are excluded by section 23 below).

(2)   The court shall explain to the accused in ordinary language—

    (a) that it appears to the court more suitable for him to be tried summarily for the offence;

    (b) that he can either consent to be so tried or, if he wishes, be tried on indictment;

    ...

(3)   The accused may then request an indication ('an indication of sentence') of whether a custodial sentence or non-custodial sentence would be more likely to be imposed if he were to be tried summarily for the offence and to plead guilty.

(4)   If the accused requests an indication of sentence, the court may, but need not, give such an indication.

(5)   If the accused requests and the court gives an indication of sentence, the court shall ask the accused whether he wishes, on the basis of the indication, to reconsider the indication of plea which was given, or is taken to have been given, under section 17A or 17B above.

(6)   If the accused indicates that he wishes to reconsider the indication under section 17A or 17B above, the court shall ask the accused whether (if the offence were to proceed to trial) he would plead guilty or not guilty.

(7)   If the accused indicates that he would plead guilty the court shall proceed as if—

    (a) the proceedings constituted from that time the summary trial of the information; and

    (b) section 9(1) above were complied with and he pleaded guilty under it.

(8)   Sub-section (9) below applies where—

    (a) the court does not give an indication of sentence (whether because the accused does not request one or because the court does not agree to give one);

(b) the accused either—

   (i) does not indicate, in accordance with sub-section (5) above, that he wishes; or

   (ii) indicates, in accordance with sub-section (5) above, that he does not wish,

   to reconsider the indication of plea under section 17A or 17B above; or

(c) the accused does not indicate, in accordance with sub-section (6) above, that he would plead guilty.

(9) The court shall ask the accused whether he consents to be tried summarily or wishes to be tried on indictment and—

(a) if he consents to be tried summarily, shall proceed to the summary trial of the information; and

(b) if he does not so consent, shall proceed in relation to the offence in accordance with section 51(1) of the Crime and Disorder Act 1998.

20A *Procedure where summary trial appears more suitable: supplementary*

(1) Where the case is dealt with in accordance with section 20(7) above, no court (whether a magistrates' court or not) may impose a custodial sentence for the offence unless such a sentence was indicated in the indication of sentence referred to in section 20 above.

(2) Sub-section (1) above is subject to sections 3A(4), 4(8) and 5(3) of the Powers of Criminal Courts (Sentencing) Act 2000.

(3) Except as provided in sub-section (1) above—

(a) an indication of sentence shall not be binding on any court (whether a magistrates' court or not); and

(b) no sentence may be challenged or be the subject of appeal in any court on the ground that it is not consistent with an indication of sentence.

Where the magistrates decline jurisdiction, the case is sent to the Crown Court under s 51 of the Crime and Disorder Act 1998: see s 21 of the Magistrates' Courts Act 1980 (as substituted by para 7 of Sched 3 to the Criminal Justice Act 2003), which provides that:

If the court decides under section 19 above that the offence appears to it more suitable for trial on indictment, the court shall tell the accused that the court has decided that it is more suitable for him to be tried on indictment, and shall proceed in relation to the offence in accordance with section 51(1) of the Crime and Disorder Act 1998.

Where the defendant is charged with several related either way offences, pleads guilty to one or some, but not all, of them at the 'plea before venue' hearing and is sent to the Crown Court to be tried for the rest, s 4 of the Powers of Criminal Courts (Sentencing) Act 2000 continues to empower the magistrates to commit the defendant to the Crown Court to be sentenced for the offence to which he has pleaded guilty.

Paragraph 11 of Sched 3 amends s 25 of the Magistrates' Courts Act 1980. The existing power to switch from summary trial to committal proceedings, or vice versa, is abolished. Instead, there is a new power for the prosecution to apply for an either way case which has been allocated for summary trial to be tried on indictment instead. This application must be made before the summary trial begins and must be dealt with by the court before any other application or issue in relation to the summary trial is dealt with (s 25(2A)). Under s 25(2B), the court may only accede to the application 'if it is satisfied that the sentence which a magistrates' court would have power to impose for the offence [or offences that constitute or form part of a series of two or more offences of the same or a similar character] would be inadequate'. If the court agrees to the prosecution application, the case is transferred to the Crown Court under s 51 of the Crime and Disorder Act 1998. The amended s 25 of the Magistrates' Courts Act 1980 will read as follows:

(1)   Sub-sections (2) to (2D) below shall have effect where a person who has attained the age of 18 appears or is brought before a magistrates' court on an information charging him with an offence triable either way.

(2)   Where the court is required under section 20(9) above to proceed to the summary trial of the information, the prosecution may apply to the court for the offence to be tried on indictment instead.

(2A) An application under sub-section (2) above—

(a) must be made before the summary trial begins; and

(b) must be dealt with by the court before any other application or issue in relation to the summary trial is dealt with.

(2B) The court may grant an application under sub-section (2) above but only if it is satisfied that the sentence which a magistrates' court would have power to impose for the offence would be inadequate.

(2C) Where—

(a) the accused is charged on the same occasion with two or more offences; and

(b) it appears to the court that they constitute or form part of a series of two or more offences of the same or a similar character,

sub-section (2B) above shall have effect as if references to the sentence which a magistrates' court would have power to impose for the offence were a reference to the maximum aggregate sentence which a magistrates' court would have power to impose for all of the offences taken together.

(2D) Where the court grants an application under sub-section (2) above, it shall proceed in relation to the offence in accordance with section 51(1) of the Crime and Disorder Act 1998.

Paragraphs 21–28 of Sched 3 amend the Powers of Criminal Courts (Sentencing) Act 2000. Most importantly, the power to commit a defendant to the Crown Court for sentence in the case of an either way offence will cease to be available where the magistrates' court has accepted jurisdiction at the 'plea before venue'/allocation hearing.

Paragraph 22 substitutes a new version of s 3 of the Powers of Criminal Courts (Sentencing) Act 2000. It reads as follows:

Committal for sentence on indication of guilty plea to serious offence triable either way

(1)   Subject to sub-section (4) below, this section applies where—

(a) a person aged 18 or over appears or is brought before a magistrates' court ('the court') on an information charging him with an offence triable either way ('the offence');

(b) he or his representative indicates under section 17A or (as the case may be) 17B of the Magistrates' Courts Act 1980 (initial procedure: accused to indicate intention as to plea), but not section 20(7) of that Act, that he would plead guilty if the offence were to proceed to trial; and

(c) proceeding as if section 9(1) of that Act were complied with and he pleaded guilty under it, the court convicts him of the offence.

(2)   If the court is of the opinion that—

    (a) the offence; or

    (b) the combination of the offence and one or more offences associated with it,

    was so serious that the Crown Court should, in the court's opinion, have the power to deal with the offender in any way it could deal with him if he had been convicted on indictment, the court may commit him in custody or on bail to the Crown Court for sentence in accordance with section 5(1) below.

(3)   Where the court commits a person under sub-section (2) above, section 6 below (which enables a magistrates' court, where it commits a person under this section in respect of an offence, also to commit him to the Crown Court to be dealt with in respect of certain other offences) shall apply accordingly.

(4)   This section does not apply in relation to an offence as regards which this section is excluded by section 17D of the Magistrates' Courts Act 1980 (certain offences where value involved is small).

To understand the operation of these various provisions, it is necessary to distinguish between two different situations:

• where the accused is asked (at the 'plea before venue hearing') whether he wishes to indicate a plea, and indicates a guilty plea (thereby in fact pleading guilty), this is done before the magistrates hear representations as to venue. Thus, the defendant may well be pleading guilty to an offence which is beyond the sentencing powers of the magistrates. In such a case, the magistrates retain their power to commit the defendant to the Crown Court for sentence (under s 3 of the Powers of Criminal Courts (Sentencing) Act 2000);

• where the accused is asked (at the 'plea before venue' hearing) whether he wishes to indicate a plea, and he either indicates an intention to plead not guilty (or declines to state his intention), the magistrates will proceed to consider mode of trial (or allocation as it is termed in the Criminal Justice Act 2003). If the magistrates decide that the case is beyond their sentencing powers, they will simply transfer the defendant to the Crown Court for trial (under the new transfer provisions that apply s 51 of the Crime and Disorder Act 1998 to either way offences). If the magistrates decide that the case is suitable for summary trial (in particular, that their sentencing powers would be adequate), the defendant is then put to his election. If he chooses Crown Court trial, the magistrates will transfer the case to the Crown Court for trial. If he opts for summary trial, the case will remain in the magistrates' court. If the defendant then enters a guilty plea, or is convicted by the magistrates, there is no power to commit him to the Crown Court for sentence for that offence. Thus, a defendant who consents to summary trial cannot receive a sentence in excess of the sentence available to the magistrates for that offence.

It should also be noted that para 23 of Pt 1 of Sched 3 to the Criminal Justice Act 2003 inserts a s 3A into the Powers of Criminal Courts (Sentencing) Act 2000. This applies where an offender is convicted of a specified either way offence (as defined in s 224 of the 2003 Act) and it appears to the court that the criteria for the imposition of a sentence under s 225(3) or 227(2) of the Criminal Justice Act 2003 (dangerous offenders) are satisfied. In such a case, the court must commit the offender (in custody or on bail) to the Crown Court for sentence. Under s 6 of the 2000 Act, the offender can also be committed for sentence for other offences to be dealt with by the Crown Court.

Section 3A(5) clarifies that nothing in s 3A prevents the court from committing the offender for sentence under s 3 if the provisions of that section are satisfied.

Under s 5 of the Powers of Criminal Courts (Sentencing) Act 2000 (amended by para 26 of Sched 3 to the 2003 Act), where an offender has been committed for sentence under s 3, 3A or 4, the Crown Court may deal with the offender in any way in which it could deal with him if he had just been convicted of the offence on indictment before the court.

CHAPTER 4

SUMMARY TRIAL

In this chapter, we look at the procedure for trying cases in the magistrates' court.

It should be borne in mind that, under s 29(5) of the Criminal Justice Act 2003, references to the 'information' will be taken to refer to the 'written charge', and references to the 'summons' will be taken to refer to the 'requisition', when the new method of instituting proceedings established by s 29 come into force.

4.1   TERRITORIAL JURISDICTION

It should be considered that all criminal cases start life in the magistrates' court, in the sense that (however serious the alleged offence may be) the accused makes his first appearance in a magistrates' court. The basic jurisdictional rules for criminal cases are set out in ss 1 and 2 of the Magistrates' Courts Act 1980. Under the original version of these provisions, a magistrates' court could try a summary offence which was alleged to have been committed in the county served by that court. The court could try a summary offence not committed in its county if the defendant was already appearing before that court in respect of another offence or the accused was to be tried jointly with someone who is already appearing before that court. It could try an offence which was triable either way, no matter where in England or Wales the offence was allegedly committed.

In *R v Croydon Magistrates' Court ex p Morgan* (1998) 162 JP 521, the defendant was charged with 10 either way offences and two summary offences. The summary offences were committed outside the commission area for that magistrates' court. The defendant was committed for trial in respect of the either way offences. The Divisional Court held that, since the Croydon magistrates had committed the defendant for trial of the either way offences rather than trying those offences themselves, that magistrates' court did not have jurisdiction to try the two summary offences committed outside its area.

The Auld Review recommended (Recommendation 3) that, 'Whilst magistrates should continue to be appointed to one commission area, there should be a ready mechanism for enabling them, when required, to sit in adjoining areas'.

Under Pt 2 of the Courts Act 2003, however, magistrates are given national jurisdiction. The Act abolishes commission areas and petty session areas and replaces them with 'local justice areas'. Lay justices will be appointed for the whole of England and Wales; however, each lay magistrate will be assigned to a local justice area. It is planned that lay magistrates will continue to be assigned to the local justice area where they live or (if more convenient) where they work.

These reforms make it necessary to amend ss 1 and 2 of the Magistrates' Courts Act 1980. These sections are amended by ss 43 and 44 of the Courts Act 2003 so as to give magistrates the power to deal with cases no matter where the offence was committed. Consequently, any magistrate will have jurisdiction to issue a summons or warrant (although it should be borne in mind that, under the Criminal Justice Act 2003, the issue of a summons following the laying of an information as a way of commencing criminal proceedings will no longer be available to public prosecutors), and any magistrates' court will have jurisdiction to try an offence, irrespective of where that offence was committed.

Section 43 of the Courts Act 2003 replaces s 1(1) of the 1980 Act (issue of summons to accused or warrant for his arrest) with the following:

(1)   On an information being laid before a justice of the peace that a person has, or is suspected of having, committed an offence, the justice may issue—

   (a) a summons directed to that person requiring him to appear before a magistrates' court to answer the information, or

   (b) a warrant to arrest that person and bring him before a magistrates' court.

Section 44 of the Courts Act 2003 replaces s 2 of the 1980 Act (trial of summary offences) with the following:

(1)   A magistrates' court has jurisdiction to try any summary offence.

(2)   A magistrates' court has jurisdiction as examining justices over any offence committed by a person who appears or is brought before the court.

(3)   Subject to—

   (a) sections 18 to 22, and

   (b) any other enactment (wherever contained) relating to the mode of trial of offences triable either way,

   a magistrates' court has jurisdiction to try summarily any offence which is triable either way.

(4)   A magistrates' court has jurisdiction, in the exercise of its powers under section 24, to try summarily an indictable offence.

The proviso that the new s 2(3) is subject to ss 18–22 of the 1980 Act makes it clear that the jurisdiction of the magistrates to conduct a summary trial of an either way offence is dependent both upon the magistrates accepting jurisdiction and the accused consenting to summary trial.

Even though ss 43 and 44 give all magistrates national jurisdiction, it is anticipated that, in practice, a local link (often seen as one of the strengths of the magistracy) will be retained at least to some extent; after all, most cases will continue to be tried in the court that serves the area where the offence was committed, and most magistrates will be (fairly) local to that area. It should be borne in mind, however, that the closure in recent years of some smaller courts, and the centralisation of the magistrates' courts so they sit mainly in the larger centres of population, has tended to undermine the local nature of magisterial justice.

4.2   TIME LIMITS

There are no time limits applicable to indictable (including either way) offences. However, an information alleging a summary offence must be laid within six months of the commission of the offence unless the statute creating the offence provides otherwise (s 127 of the Magistrates' Courts Act 1980). Where a statute creates a continuing summary offence, a prosecution can be brought at any time until six months have elapsed from the date when the offence ceased to be committed: *British Telecommunications plc v Nottinghamshire CC* [1999] Crim LR 217 (here, the offence was that of failing to reinstate the highway after street works had been carried out; the last date when the offence ceased to be committed was when the reinstatement of the road was completed satisfactorily).

In *Atkinson v DPP* [2004] EWHC 1457; [2004] 3 All ER 971, it was held that where there is uncertainty as to whether an information has been laid in time, the question should be determined according to the criminal burden and standard of proof and the magistrates should decline to hear the matter unless satisfied so that they are sure that the information was laid in time (see also *Lloyd v Young* [1963] Crim LR 703).

There is no specific time limit within which the summons must be served once the information has been laid, although excessive delay in serving the summons could amount to an abuse of process, giving the court the power to dismiss the case. This would only arise where the prosecution ask the court not to post the summons to the defendant or where the police were dilatory in serving a summons on a defendant personally where postal service had proved ineffective.

4.3   A CHARGE EQUIVALENT TO AN INFORMATION

The rules of procedure which apply to summary trial refer to the trial of an information. The same rules apply where proceedings are commenced by arrest and charge, as a charge is regarded as an information for these purposes.

4.4   THE DUPLICITOUS INFORMATION

Rule 12 of the Magistrates' Courts Rules 1981 (as amended by r 3 of the Magistrates' Courts (Miscellaneous Amendments) Rules 1993) provides as follows:

(1)   … a magistrates' court shall not proceed to the trial of an information that charges more than one offence.

(2)   Nothing in this rule shall prohibit two or more informations being set out in one document.

(3)   If, notwithstanding paragraph (1) above, it appears to the court at any stage in the trial of an information that the information charges more than one offence, the court shall call upon the prosecutor to elect on which offence he desires the court to proceed, whereupon the offence or offences on which the prosecutor does not wish to proceed shall be struck out of the information; and the court shall then proceed to try that information afresh.

(4)   If a prosecutor who is called upon to make an election under paragraph (3) above fails to do so, the court shall dismiss the information.

(5)   Where, after an offence has or offences have been struck out of the information under paragraph (3) above, the accused requests an adjournment and it appears to the court that he has been unfairly prejudiced, it shall adjourn the trial.

Thus, an information should allege only one offence. If an information alleges more than one offence, the court must call upon the prosecution to decide which offence to proceed with. The other offence will then be struck out. If the prosecution fail to choose between the offences, the court must strike out the entire information.

In *Carrington Carr v Leicestershire County Council* (1994) 158 JP 570, it was held that there are five situations where informations may be duplicitous:

- where two or more discrete offences are charged conjunctively in one information, for example, a single information alleges both dangerous driving and careless driving;
- where two offences are charged disjunctively or in the alternative in one information, for example, a single information alleges dangerous driving or careless driving;
- where an offence was capable of being committed in more ways than one, for example, driving under the influence of drink or drugs, and both ways are referred to in one information;
- where a single offence was charged in respect of an activity but the activity involved more than one act; and
- where a single activity was charged but a number of particulars are relied on by the prosecution to prove the offence, for example, a single act of obtaining by deception where the deception involved several misrepresentations.

In the latter two instances, a single information may well be appropriate. However, if the defendant wishes to admit some but not other allegations, or wishes to raise different defences to different allegations, separate informations would be necessary. An information would be duplicitous if, for example, the defendant were charged with receiving stolen goods and another form of handling stolen goods in the same information. Note, however, that a series of acts may amount to a single offence if those acts constitute a course of conduct (for example, stealing a number of items from a supermarket would be charged in one information under a single allegation of theft) (*Heaton v Costello* (1984) 148 JP 688).

It was also held in *Ministry of Agriculture, Fisheries and Food v Nunn* [1990] Crim LR 268 that an information will be duplicitous if it alleges more than one victim of the alleged offence. Whilst this will usually be the case (separate victims should be dealt with in separate informations as separate offences have been committed), there may be circumstances where a single offence can be committed against more than one victim.

4.5   TRYING MORE THAN ONE OFFENCE OR MORE THAN ONE DEFENDANT

Where several defendants are charged with the same offence, they will be tried together.

Where an accused faces more than one information or there are several defendants charged in separate informations, a joint trial is possible.

More than one information may be tried at the same time if the magistrates feel that there is a sufficient link between the offences charged. This is a matter for the discretion of the justices, who should ask themselves whether the interests of justice are best served by a joint trial or separate trials, balancing convenience for the prosecution against the risk of any prejudice to the defendant. *Per* Lord Roskill in *Chief Constable of Norfolk v Clayton* [1983] 2 AC 473:

> The justices should always ask themselves whether it would be fair and just to the defendant or defendants to allow a joint trial.

If the magistrates decide against a single trial where the defendant is accused of more than one offence, those justices should not hear any of the cases, as a magistrate trying a case should be unaware that the defendant faces other charges (*R v Liverpool Justices ex p Topping* [1983] 1 WLR 119; [1983] 1 All ER 490). Each case would thus have to be heard by a different bench.

4.6   DISMISSING A CASE WITHOUT HEARING THE EVIDENCE

Section 15 of the Magistrates' Courts Act 1980 provides as follows:

(1)   Where at the time and place appointed for the trial or adjourned trial of an information the accused appears or is brought before the court and the prosecutor does not appear, the court may dismiss the information or, if evidence has been received on a previous occasion, proceed in the absence of the prosecutor.

(2)   Where, instead of dismissing the information or proceeding in the absence of the prosecutor, the court adjourns the trial, it shall not remand the accused in custody unless he has been brought from custody or cannot be remanded on bail by reason of his failure to find sureties.

Thus, s 15 empowers the court to adjourn the case or dismiss the information if the prosecution fail to appear at the time and place fixed for the summary trial. Where a magistrates' court dismisses an information under s 15 without consideration of the merits of the case because of the non-attendance of the prosecutor, there is no rule of law which prevents the court from dealing with an identical information subsequently laid against the same defendant; the question to be decided is whether the new information amounts to an abuse of process, and so the court must consider what prejudice would be caused to the defendant by the preferment of the new information (*Holmes v Campbell* (1998) 162 JP 655).

A case can also be dismissed without a hearing if there has been delay. The circumstances where a case may be dismissed because of delay are considered in Chapter 2.

However, in *R v Watford Justices ex p DPP* [1990] RTR 374; [1990] Crim LR 422, it was held that the justices cannot dismiss an information on the ground that the case is too trivial to justify the continuance of the proceedings. If the prosecution wish to adduce evidence, the magistrates must hear that evidence unless the prosecution are guilty of abuse of process.

In *DPP v Shuttleworth* [2002] EWHC 621 (Admin); (2002) 166 JP 417, a magistrates' court dismissed an information for want of prosecution. The prosecution were represented at the hearing but the prosecutor did not have the relevant file; the justices dismissed the information without taking plea. They relied on s 15(1) of the Magistrates' Courts Act 1980. It was held that, in the circumstances, the justices were not entitled to dismiss the information when they did. Section 15 of the Act has to be read with the procedure on trial prescribed by s 9 of the Act. The first stage of that procedure is that an information should be put to a defendant and a plea taken. In the instant case, there was enough information before the justices, notwithstanding the absence of the prosecution's file, to enable that to happen. The court said that, although the frustration of justices when faced with the absence of a prosecution file was understandable, s 15(1) of the Act is not a provision that should be used in a punitive or disciplinary fashion against the Crown Prosecution Service (CPS). Instead, where an additional hearing is required through the fault of one of the parties, the justices should consider making a costs order against the defaulting party.

4.7   PLEADING GUILTY BY POST

Section 12 of the Magistrates' Courts Act 1980, which provides that the defendant may be offered the opportunity of pleading guilty by post, applies only to summary offences which have a maximum sentence of no more than three months' imprisonment (although s 308 of the Criminal Justice Act 2003, when it comes into force, will repeal s 12(1)(a)(i) of the Magistrates' Courts Act 1980 so as extend the range of cases in which a defendant in the magistrates' court can plead guilty and be dealt with in his absence by removing the limitation which excludes offences punishable with more than three months' imprisonment).

The defendant is sent a special form along with the summons. On the form, the defendant can indicate a plea of guilty and can also draw to the court's attention any mitigating circumstances which may persuade the court to impose a more lenient sentence.

At court, neither the prosecution nor the defence are represented. In open court, the clerk will read out the statement of facts which is sent out to the defendant along with the summons and whatever the defendant has written on the form or in an accompanying letter. The court then proceeds to pass sentence.

Note, however, that a sentence of imprisonment or disqualification from driving cannot be imposed in the absence of the defendant. If the court is minded to impose such a sentence, the defendant will be summoned to attend on a later occasion (see sub-ss 11(3) and (4) of the Magistrates' Courts Act 1980).

Section 12A of the Magistrates' Courts Act 1980 makes provision for the application of s 12 of the Magistrates' Courts Act 1980 where the defendant appears in court. If the accused has indicated that he wishes to plead guilty by post but nevertheless appears before the court, the court may (if the accused consents) proceed as if the defendant were absent. Similarly, if the accused has not indicated that he wishes to plead guilty by post but, when he attends court, indicates that he wishes to plead guilty, the court may (if the accused consents) proceed as if he were absent and he had indicated an intention to plead guilty by post. Where the court proceeds as if the defendant were absent, the prosecution summary of the facts of the case must not go beyond the statement served on the defendant when he was given the option of pleading guilty by post. However, if the accused is in fact present in court, he must be given the opportunity to make an oral submission with a view to mitigation of sentence.

A large number of defendants do not respond to the summons in which they are given the opportunity to plead guilty by post. The Magistrates' Courts (Procedure) Act 1998 allows for the police to prepare witness statements (rather than just a statement of facts) and to serve them along with the summons. The witness statements will be admissible as evidence unless the defendant objects. If the defendant fails to plead guilty by post or to attend court to plead not guilty, and so fails to object to the use of the witness statements as evidence, the court can proceed to try the defendant in his absence, the prosecution case being based upon the witness statements already served on the defendant.

The pleading guilty by post system is used most commonly for driving offences, and so the 1998 Act also makes provision for a print-out from the Driver and Vehicle Licensing Agency to be admissible as evidence of previous convictions for traffic offences without the need to give the defendant advance notice of intention to refer to these previous convictions.

4.8   PRESENCE OF THE DEFENDANT

Section 122 of the Magistrates' Courts Act 1980 provides that:

(1)   A party to any proceedings before a magistrates' court may be represented by a legal representative.

(2)   Subject to sub-section (3) below, an absent party so represented shall be deemed not to be absent.

(3)   Appearance of a party by a legal representative shall not satisfy any provision of any enactment or any condition of a recognizance expressly requiring his presence.

Where proceedings were commenced by summons (rather than by arrest and charge), the defendant is deemed to be present if his legal representative is in court. The legal representative may enter a plea on behalf of the defendant if the latter is not in court.

Where proceedings were begun by summons, but s 122 is inapplicable, s 13 of the Magistrates' Courts Act 1980 says that a warrant for the defendant's arrest may be issued. Section 13 provides that:

(1)   Subject to the provisions of this section, where the court, instead of proceeding in the absence of the accused, adjourns or further adjourns the trial, the court may ... issue a warrant for his arrest.

(2)   Where a summons has been issued, the court shall not issue a warrant under this section unless the condition in sub-section (2A) below or that in sub-section (2B) below is fulfilled.

(2A)   The condition in this sub-section is that it is proved to the satisfaction of the court, on oath or in such other manner as may be prescribed, that the summons was served on the accused within what appears to the court to be a reasonable time before the trial or adjourned trial.

(2B)   The condition in this sub-section is that—

(a)   the adjournment now being made is a second or subsequent adjournment of the trial,

(b)   the accused was present on the last (or only) occasion when the trial was adjourned, and

(c)   on that occasion the court determined the time for the hearing at which the adjournment is now being made.

(3)   A warrant for the arrest of any person who has attained the age of 18 shall not be issued under this section unless—

(a)   the offence to which the warrant relates is punishable with imprisonment, or

(b)   the court, having convicted the accused, proposes to impose a disqualification on him.

(3A)   A warrant for the arrest of any person who has not attained the age of 18 shall not be issued under this section unless—

    (a) the offence to which the warrant relates is punishable, in the case of a person who has attained the age of 18, with imprisonment, or

    (b) the court, having convicted the accused, proposes to impose a disqualification on him.

(4)   This section shall not apply to an adjournment on the occasion of the accused's conviction in his absence under sub-section (5) of section 12 above or to an adjournment required by sub-section (9) of that section.

(5)   Where the court adjourns the trial—

    (a) after having, either on that or on a previous occasion, received any evidence or convicted the accused without hearing evidence on his pleading guilty under section 9(3) above; or

    (b) after having on a previous occasion convicted the accused without hearing evidence on his pleading guilty under section 12(5) above,

the court shall not issue a warrant under this section unless it thinks it undesirable, by reason of the gravity of the offence, to continue the trial in the absence of the accused.

Thus, the preconditions to the issue of an arrest warrant under s 13 are:

(a) if the present hearing is the first hearing, it is proved that the summons was served on the defendant;

(b) if the present hearing is a second or subsequent hearing, the defendant was present on the last occasion and the date for the present hearing was fixed at that hearing.

In other words, it has to be proved that the defendant knew of the date of today's hearing.

However, where the defendant was originally arrested and charged, he must attend court personally or else is in breach of his bail, entitling the court to grant a bench warrant for his arrest under s 7 of the Bail Act 1976.

4.8.1   Trial in absence of the defendant

Under s 11(1) of the Magistrates' Courts Act 1980, a defendant may be tried in his absence in the magistrates' court. However, if the offence charged is triable either way, the defendant can only be tried *in absentia* in the magistrates' court if, on an earlier occasion, he consented to summary trial.

According to CPS figures, in the period 2000–04, the prosecution secured a conviction in the absence of the defendant in an average of approximately 13% of the cases brought by the CPS.

Where an application for an adjournment is made on behalf of the defence on the ground that the defendant cannot attend court by reason of illness, and there is a medical certificate or doctor's letter to support this claim, but the magistrates think that the excuse is spurious, they should nevertheless give the defendant the chance to answer their doubts and not simply proceed with the trial (*R v Bolton Justices ex p Merna* [1991] Crim LR 848).

In *R (on the Application of R) v Thames Youth Court* [2002] EWHC 1670 (Admin); (2002) 166 JP 613, the defendant was a juvenile. On the day his trial was listed for hearing before the youth court, he was arrested in connection with an unrelated offence and so was unable to attend the youth court. The District judge decided to try the defence in his absence. It was held that in cases where a defendant has plainly not absented himself from his trial voluntarily, the threshold of prejudice and fairness that the defendant has to demonstrate in order to establish that a guilty verdict might be unsafe is a comparatively low one, particularly where the defendant is a youth and where there is material about which counsel for the defendant would have wished to have taken instructions. It is an important consideration, said the court, that a juvenile might not have the same level of understanding as an adult. Even though the case concerned a juvenile, it is submitted that it would be wrong in principle for a defendant to be tried in his absence in any case where the court is aware that the absence is unavoidable and out of the defendant's control. Some support for this view may be derived from the decision in *R v Jones* [2002] UKHL 5; [2003] 1 AC 1, where the House of Lords held (in the context of trial on indictment) that a judge has a discretion to commence a trial in the absence of the defendant, but this discretion should be exercised with great caution, and if the absence is attributable to involuntary illness or incapacity it would be very rarely, if ever, right to do so, at any rate unless the defendant was represented and asked that the trial should begin.

4.8.2   Setting aside conviction where the defendant did not know of proceedings (s 14 of the Magistrates' Courts Act 1980)

We saw in Chapter 1 that a summons could be served by posting it to the defendant's last known address or even by leaving it with someone at that address. There is therefore a risk that the summons will not in fact come to the attention of the defendant, and that the defendant will be tried and convicted in his absence under s 11 of the Magistrates' Courts Act 1980.

Section 14 of the Magistrates' Courts Act 1980 provides that in these circumstances the conviction may be set aside. It provides as follows:

(1)   Where a summons has been issued under section 1 above and a magistrates' court has begun to try the information to which the summons relates, then, if—

    (a) the accused, at any time during or after the trial, makes a statutory declaration that he did not know of the summons or the proceedings until a date specified in the declaration, being a date after the court has begun to try the information; and

    (b) within 21 days of that date the declaration is served on the justices' chief executive for the court,

without prejudice to the validity of the information, the summons and all subsequent proceedings shall be void.

...

(3)   If on the application of the accused it appears to a magistrates' court (which for this purpose may be composed of a single justice) that it was not reasonable to expect the accused to serve such a statutory declaration as is mentioned in sub-section (1) above within the period allowed by that sub-section, the court may accept service of such a declaration by the accused after that period has expired; and a statutory declaration accepted under this sub-section shall be deemed to have been served as required by that sub-section.

(4)   Where any proceedings have become void by virtue of sub-section (1) above, the information shall not be tried again by any of the same justices.

Thus, the procedure to achieve the setting aside of the conviction is as follows:

- The defendant must make a statutory declaration (a written statement under oath rather like an affidavit) averring that he did not know of the summons or the subsequent proceedings until after the court had begun to try the information. The declaration must also state the date on which the defendant first became aware of the proceedings.
- This statement must be served on the clerk to the justices who convicted the defendant within 21 days of the date when the defendant first knew of the proceedings.
- The effect of the declaration is to render void the summons and all subsequent proceedings. However, the information itself remains unaffected and so a fresh summons can be served on the basis of the original information.
- The defendant may attend the court in person to make the statutory declaration (in which case, it is sworn before a magistrate) or else he may swear the declaration before a solicitor or commissioner for oaths and then send it by post to the court.
- A magistrate or a clerk may allow a declaration to take effect even if it is served after the 21 day time limit if, in the circumstances of the case, it was not reasonable to expect the defendant to effect service of the declaration within that time.

The problem of a defendant not knowing about proceedings never arises where proceedings are commenced by arrest and charge: the charge sheet tells the defendant the date of his first court appearance.

4.9   SUMMARY TRIAL PROCEDURE

The court will consist either of three lay justices or a District judge; there will also be a clerk/legal adviser to assist the court. It is very rare for a District judge to sit with lay justices. The Auld *Review of the Criminal Courts of England and Wales* recommended that:

> District Judges and magistrates should not routinely sit as mixed tribunals to deal with the general range or any particular type of case or form of proceeding, though there may be training and local 'cultural' advantages in their doing so from time to time depending on their respective availability and case loads (Recommendation 5.1).

And that:

> District Judges should concentrate on case allocation and management, cases of legal or factual complexity, cases of priority, such as those involving young offenders or offences of a sexual nature, and long cases (Recommendation 5.3).

The latter recommendation was perhaps largely unnecessary, as District judges tend to be deployed in that way already.

Given the fact that District judges are legally qualified, the Auld Review also recommends that they should normally sit without a legal adviser (Recommendation 6).

The first stage in a summary trial is for the plea to be taken. The clerk puts the allegation(s) to the defendant who has to plead guilty or not guilty. A separate plea should be entered in respect of each charge faced by the defendant.

4.9.1   Procedure where the defendant pleads guilty

The procedure where the defendant pleads guilty is as follows:

- The prosecution summarise the facts of the offence.

  It should be noted that if there is a significant difference between the prosecution version of the facts and the version to be put forward by the defence (for example, in the case of an offence of dishonesty, there is a dispute over the value involved in the offence), the court must either accept the defence version or else hear evidence on the question and then come to a decision on which version to believe (*R v Newton* (1983) 77 Cr App R 13).

- The prosecutor hands the magistrates details of the defendant's previous convictions, if any. The prosecutor will have asked the defence to confirm that these details are correct. The magistrates will indicate which of the previous convictions they wish the prosecutor to read out loud on the basis that they are relevant to the sentence for the present offence; usually, it is only the most recent convictions that are read out. The prosecutor will also tell the court what is known about the personal circumstances of the defendant (employment, housing, etc); this is based on what the defendant has told the police and will be very brief.

- Once the prosecution have summarised the facts, the magistrates may decide to adjourn for a pre-sentence report. If not, the defence will make a plea in mitigation in order to try to persuade the court to impose a lenient sentence. Having heard the plea in mitigation, the magistrates may then decide to adjourn for a pre-sentence report. The adjournment cannot be for more than four weeks if the defendant is on bail, and three weeks if he is in custody (s 10(3) of the Magistrates' Courts Act 1980).

- If there has been an adjournment for a pre-sentence report, it is unlikely that the same magistrates will be sitting on the next occasion, so the prosecution will have to summarise the facts of the offence and the defence will have to do a full plea in mitigation.

- Sentence is then passed.

4.9.2   Procedure where the defendant pleads not guilty

The procedure where the defendant pleads not guilty is as follows:

- The prosecution may make an opening speech, briefly setting out what they hope to prove.

- The prosecution witnesses give evidence (each one being examined-in-chief by the prosecution, cross-examined by the defence and, if necessary, re-examined by the prosecution).

- The written statements of any prosecution witnesses may be read to the court if the defence consent to this being done, as will be the case where the defence accept that the contents of the statement are true and so this evidence is not disputed (s 9 of the Criminal Justice Act 1967).

- After the close of the prosecution case, the defendant may make a submission that there is no case to answer. This submission is considered more closely below.

- If the defence do not make a submission of no case to answer, or make a submission which is rejected by the magistrates, the defence may then call evidence.

- If there are defence witnesses in addition to the defendant, the defendant should give evidence first. Each defence witness is examined-in-chief by the defence, cross-examined by the prosecution and, if necessary, re-examined by the defence.
- After the defence witnesses have given evidence, the defence may make a closing speech.
- The magistrates consider their verdict. A bench of lay magistrates usually retires to consider its decision, whereas a District judge usually announces his decision immediately. Brief reasons for the verdict should be given (as this is regarded as an important aspect of the right to a fair trial under Art 6 of the European Convention on Human Rights).
- If the defendant is convicted, the prosecution supply the court with details of any previous convictions recorded against the defendant, together with brief details of the defendant's personal circumstances. The court will either adjourn the case for a pre-sentence report to be obtained or hear a plea in mitigation on behalf of the defendant and then pass sentence. Again, the maximum period of the adjournment for reports to be prepared is four weeks if the defendant is on bail, three weeks if he is custody (s 10(3) of the Magistrates' Courts Act 1980).

4.9.3 Sentencing powers

The sentencing powers of the magistrates are dealt with in later chapters. In summary, a magistrates' court cannot impose a custodial sentence of more than six months unless the offender has been convicted of two or more offences which are triable either way, in which case, the maximum is 12 months. These powers will be increased when the relevant provisions of the Criminal Justice Act 2003 come into force: the magistrates will then be empowered to impose up to a year's custody for a single offence.

4.10 PRE-TRIAL HEARINGS

Paragraphs 204–35 of Chapter 10 of the Auld Review consider the practice and procedure relating to pre-trial hearings and pre-trial assessments. Recommendation 210 is that:

> In the preparation for trial in all criminal courts, there should be a move away from plea and direction hearings and other forms of pre-trial hearings to co-operation between the parties according to standard or adapted time-tables, wherever necessary seeking written directions from the court.

The Review goes on to recommend:

- that there should be national standard timetables and lists of key actions for preparation for trial (Recommendation 211); that the parties should be at liberty to seek leave from the trial court to vary the standard timetable (Recommendation 213);
- that the parties should endeavour to prepare for trial in accordance with the timetable and list of key actions to resolve between themselves any issues of law, procedure or evidence that may shape and/or affect the length of the trial and when it can start (Recommendation 214);

- that the timetable in each case should set a date for the 'pre-trial assessment' – ie, an assessment by the parties and the court as to the state of readiness for trial (Recommendation 215);
- that, by the pre-trial assessment date, the parties should complete and send to the trial court a checklist showing progress in preparation and as to readiness for trial, and seeking, if appropriate, written directions (Recommendation 216);
- that there should only be a pre-trial hearing if the court or the parties consider it is necessary for the timely and otherwise efficient preparation for, and conduct of, the trial – for example, where one or other of the parties cannot comply with the timetable, or where there are unresolved issues affecting the efficient preparation for or conduct of the trial, or when the case is sufficiently serious or complex to require the guidance of the court (Recommendation 217);
- that the judge or magistrates conducting an oral pre-trial hearing should be empowered to give binding directions or rulings subject to subsequent variation or discharge if justice requires it (Recommendation 219);
- that where a pre-trial hearing is necessitated by one or other or both parties' failure without good cause to comply with the timetable or other directions of the court, or to resolve issues of procedure, law or fact between them, the court should have power:

  (1) to make such order as to payment of a publicly funded defence advocate for his attendance at the hearing as may be appropriate in the circumstances; and/or publicly to reprimand either party's advocate or those instructing them as appropriate; any such public reprimand to be communicated to and taken into account by the professional body of the person reprimanded and, where the person is franchised for publicly funded defence work, by the Legal Services Commission; and/or

  (2) to make such order of costs against one or other or both sides as may be appropriate (Recommendation 220).

It should be noted that magistrates' courts already have pre-trial hearings: where a guilty plea is anticipated, an 'Early First Hearing' is scheduled; where a not guilty plea is expected, there will be an 'Early Administrative Hearing'. Where the defendant is charged with an either way offence and indicates a not guilty plea and consents to summary trial, a date for a pre-trial review is set, if this is felt to be necessary. Pre-trial reviews are intended to assist the court in assessing the readiness of the parties for trial. However, practices do differ across the country. Moreover, magistrates sitting at pre-trial hearings may make directions or recommendations as to appropriate preparation or conduct of the case, but (whilst such directions may be noted in the court's records) they do not bind the magistrates who eventually hear the case (although the trial bench may well take the earlier direction into account when making any decision).

The Courts Act 2003 builds on this existing practice and empowers magistrates to make binding rulings and directions at pre-trial hearings in criminal cases that are to be tried in the magistrates' courts, where it is in the interests of justice to do so. It will only be possible to make such rulings once a not guilty plea has been entered. The power will be exercisable at any stage up to the commencement of the trial once the accused has entered a not guilty plea. The magistrates will be able to give binding rulings on questions of law and admissibility of evidence.

Before making a binding ruling, the magistrates must give the parties an opportunity to be heard and, when the accused is unrepresented but wishes to be represented, must consider whether to grant legal representation at public expense.

A pre-trial ruling made by a magistrates' court will remain binding until the case is disposed of or is sent to the Crown Court. The magistrates' court may discharge or vary a pre-trial ruling on application by a party to the case (where there has been a material change of circumstances) or, where it is in the interests of justice, of its own motion. However, there is no separate right of appeal against a pre-trial ruling (if the accused is ultimately convicted, he can appeal to the Crown Court in the usual way; in the case of an acquittal, the prosecution could ask the magistrates to state a case to the Divisional Court).

The power to make rulings at pre-trial hearings is contained in s 45 of the Courts Act 2003, which gives effect to the detailed provisions in Sched 3 (and states that these provisions 'apply in relation to pre-trial hearings beginning on or after the day on which [Sched 3] comes into force').

Schedule 3 inserts new sections into the 1980 Act. First of all, there is a new s 8A. This provides as follows:

8A *Power to make rulings at pre-trial hearing*

(1) For the purposes of this section a hearing is a pre-trial hearing if—

(a) it relates to an information—

(i)   which is to be tried summarily, and

(ii) to which the accused has pleaded not guilty, and

(b) it takes place before the start of the trial.

(2) For the purposes of sub-section (1)(b), the start of a summary trial occurs when the court begins—

(a) to hear evidence from the prosecution at the trial, or

(b) to consider whether to exercise its power under section 37(3) of the Mental Health Act 1983 (power to make hospital order without convicting the accused).

(3) At a pre-trial hearing, a magistrates' court may make a ruling as to any matter mentioned in sub-section (4) if—

(a) the condition in sub-section (5) is met,

(b) the court has given the parties an opportunity to be heard, and

(c) it appears to the court that it is in the interests of justice to make the ruling.

(4) The matters are—

(a) any question as to the admissibility of evidence;

(b) any other question of law relating to the case.

(5) The condition is that, if the accused is not legally represented, the court must—

(a) ask whether he wishes to be granted a right to representation funded by the Legal Services Commission as part of the Criminal Defence Service, and

(b) if he does, decide whether or not to grant him that right.

(6) A ruling may be made under this section—

(a) on an application by a party to the case, or

(b) of the court's own motion.

The binding effect of rulings under s 8A is set out in s 8B, which provides that:

Effect of rulings at pre-trial hearing

(1) Subject to sub-sections (3) and (6), a ruling under section 8A has binding effect from the time it is made until the case against the accused or, if there is more than one, against each of them, is disposed of.

(2) The case against an accused is disposed of if—

    (a) he is acquitted or convicted,

    (b) the prosecutor decides not to proceed with the case against him, or

    (c) the information is dismissed.

(3) A magistrates' court may discharge or vary (or further vary) a ruling under section 8A if—

    (a) the condition in section 8A(5) is met,

    (b) the court has given the parties an opportunity to be heard, and

    (c) it appears to the court that it is in the interests of justice to do so.

(4) The court may act under sub-section (3)—

    (a) on an application by a party to the case, or

    (b) of its own motion.

(5) No application may be made under sub-section (4)(a) unless there has been a material change of circumstances since the ruling was made or, if a previous application has been made, since the application (or last application) was made.

(6) A ruling under section 8A is discharged in relation to an accused if—

    (a) the magistrates' court commits or sends him to the Crown Court for trial for the offence charged in the information, or

    (b) a count charging him with the offence is included in an indictment by virtue of section 40 of the Criminal Justice Act 1988.

Pre-trial reporting restrictions apply already under the 1980 Act, but s 8C extends the ambit of these restrictions to pre-trial rulings. Section 8C imposes restrictions on reporting of pre-trial hearings in order to avoid prejudicing the right to a fair trial (particularly important if the case is ultimately tried in the Crown Court). The publishing of anything other than basic factual information (defined in sub-s (7) as including the identity of the court and the names of the justices; the names, ages, home addresses and occupations of the accused and witnesses; the offence(s) with which the accused is accused; the names of counsel and solicitors in the proceedings; where the proceedings are adjourned; the date and place to which they are adjourned; any arrangements as to bail; whether a right to representation by the Criminal Defence Service was granted to the accused) is prohibited – unless the court orders that reporting restrictions should not apply – until such time as the case against the accused is disposed of.

The power to lift the reporting restrictions is conferred by sub-s (3). Where the court is minded to order that the reporting restrictions do not apply and there is only one accused, and he objects to the making of an order removing the restrictions, the court may make the order if (and only if) satisfied after hearing the representations of the accused that it is in the interests of justice to do so (sub-s (4)(a)); where there are two or more accused and one or more of them objects to the lifting of the restrictions, the court may make the order if (and only if) satisfied after hearing the representations of each of the accused that it is in the interests of justice to do so (sub-s (5)(b)).

Breach of these reporting restrictions is a summary offence punishable (under s 8D of the 1980 Act) with a level 5 fine (currently £5,000). Under s 8D(6), proceedings for this offence may not be instituted otherwise than by or with the consent of the Attorney General.

The implementation of the power to make binding pre-trial rulings will bring the powers of magistrates in pre-trial hearings heard in the magistrates' courts into line with those of the judges in the Crown Court (where the Criminal Procedure and Investigations Act 1996 empowers a judge to give binding rulings on matters of law and admissibility of evidence). Indeed, the new sections inserted into the 1980 Act broadly follow ss 40 and 41 of the Criminal Procedure and Investigations Act 1996, which set out the Crown Court's power to make binding rulings in pre-trial hearings.

This is meant not only to assist in ensuring more efficient preparation of cases for trial in the magistrates' courts but also to bring the procedures adopted in magistrates' courts into line with Crown Court procedures (a necessary consequence of the desire for closer integration between the magistrates' courts and the Crown Court, which was strongly advocated by Lord Justice Auld).

4.11 SUMMARY TRIAL IN MORE DETAIL

Several matters need to be considered in more detail.

4.11.1 Securing the attendance of witnesses

Section 97 of the Magistrates' Courts Act 1980 provides as follows:

(1) Where a justice of the peace ... is satisfied that any person in England or Wales is likely to be able to give material evidence, or produce any document or thing likely to be material evidence, at the summary trial of an information ... by a magistrates' court ... and that that person will not voluntarily attend as a witness or will not voluntarily produce the document or thing, the justice shall issue a summons directed to that person requiring him to attend before the court at the time and place appointed in the summons to give evidence or to produce the document or thing.

(2) If a justice of the peace is satisfied by evidence on oath of the matters mentioned in sub-section (1) above, and also that it is probable that a summons under that sub-section would not procure the attendance of the person in question, the justice may instead of issuing a summons issue a warrant to arrest that person and bring him before such a court or justice, as the case may be, as aforesaid at a time and place specified in the warrant; but a warrant shall not be issued under this sub-section where the attendance is required for the hearing of a complaint.

(2A) A summons may also be issued under sub-section (1) above if the justice is satisfied that the person in question is outside the British Islands but no warrant shall be issued under sub-section (2) above unless the justice is satisfied by evidence on oath that the person in question is in England or Wales.

(2B) A justice may refuse to issue a summons under sub-section (1) above in relation to the summary trial of an information if he is not satisfied that an application for the summons was made by a party to the case as soon as reasonably practicable after the accused pleaded not guilty.

...

(3) On the failure of any person to attend before a magistrates' court in answer to a summons under this section, if—

    (a) the court is satisfied by evidence on oath that he is likely to be able to give material evidence or produce any document or thing likely to be material evidence in the proceedings; and

    (b) it is proved on oath, or in such other manner as may be prescribed, that he has been duly served with the summons, and that a reasonable sum has been paid or tendered to him for costs and expenses; and

    (c) it appears to the court that there is no just excuse for the failure,

the court may issue a warrant to arrest him and bring him before the court at a time and place specified in the warrant.

(4) If any person attending or brought before a magistrates' court refuses without just excuse to be sworn or give evidence, or to produce any document or thing, the court may commit him to custody until the expiration of such period not exceeding one month as may be specified in the warrant or until he sooner gives evidence or produces the document or thing or impose on him a fine not exceeding £2,500, or both.

Thus, under s 97 of the Magistrates' Courts Act 1980, a magistrate (or a clerk) may issue a summons requiring a person to attend court to give evidence or to produce a document or other item of evidence. This applies whether the summons is sought by the prosecution or the defence.

Before ordering a person to attend as a witness, the magistrate (or clerk) must be satisfied that the person will be able to give 'material evidence' and that the person will not attend voluntarily. Material evidence is evidence of some value to the party seeking the order. In *R v Marylebone Magistrates ex p Gatting and Emburey* (1990) 154 JP 549, the applicant was refused a witness order against two England cricketers, as the motive for seeking the order was political rather than evidential.

Similarly, before the magistrate (or clerk) can issue a summons requiring the production of documents under s 97 of the Magistrates' Courts Act 1980, he must be satisfied that the respondent is likely to be able to produce the requested documents, and that the documents contain material evidence (that is, evidence which is both relevant and admissible). It is for the party who seeks the production of the documents to adduce evidence which satisfies the justices that there is a real possibility that the documents are material. Documents which are requested merely for the purpose of possible cross-examination are not material (see *R v Reading Justices ex p Berkshire County Council* [1996] 1 Cr App R 239).

If the witness fails to comply with the summons, a warrant for his arrest may be granted by a magistrate (s 97(3)). A magistrate (but not a clerk) may issue a warrant rather than a summons if satisfied by evidence (on oath) that a summons would be ineffective (s 97(2)).

Under s 97(2B) of the Magistrates' Courts Act 1980, a witness summons may be refused if the application is not made as soon as reasonably practicable after the defendant has pleaded not guilty.

4.11.2   Defects in the information: amendment

Section 123 of the Magistrates' Courts Act 1980 provides that:

(1)   No objection shall be allowed to any information or complaint, or to any summons or warrant to procure the presence of the defendant, for any defect in it in substance or in form, or for any variance between it and the evidence adduced on behalf of the prosecutor or complainant at the hearing of the information or complaint.

(2)   If it appears to a magistrates' court that any variance between a summons or warrant and the evidence adduced on behalf of the prosecutor or complainant is such that the defendant has been misled by the variance, the court shall, on the application of the defendant, adjourn the hearing.

The effect of s 123 is that no objection shall be allowed in respect of an information or summons where that objection is based on a defect in substance or form, or on any variance between it and the evidence adduced by the prosecution. The practical result of this provision is that all but the gravest of errors can be ignored or cured by amendment.

It appears from the case law that there are three categories of defect in the information.

(a)   Minor defects

First, there are minor defects which do not require amendment. This would include a minor mis-spelling or other inconsequential error that has misled no one. In *R v Sandwell Justices ex p West Midlands Passenger Transport Executive* [1979] RTR 17; [1979] Crim LR 56, for example, the information alleged a defective rear nearside tyre, when in fact it was a near offside tyre which was defective; a conviction based on this unamended information was upheld.

(b)   Defects requiring amendment

Secondly, there are defects which require amendment (which is possible under s 123 of the Magistrates' Courts Act 1980) but which are not so grave as to be incurable. If the defendant has been misled by the error, the court should remedy this by granting an adjournment to enable the defence to prepare their case in the light of the amendment.

An example of this sort of defect is where the information alleges an offence under a section of an Act which has been repealed and re-enacted in identical terms in a later statute (*Meek v Powell* [1952] 1 KB 164; [1952] 1 All ER 347).

Similarly, in *Wright v Nicholson* [1970] 1 WLR 142; [1970] 1 All ER 12, it was held that an information can be amended to show a different date for the alleged commission of the offence, provided that an adjournment is granted if the defence need more time to prepare their case in the light of the amendment. This was so even though the defendant had an alibi for the date originally alleged.

Indeed, in *R v Norwich Crown Court ex p Russell* [1993] Crim LR 518, the Divisional Court went even further. The information in that case alleged that the offence (criminal damage) had been committed on 19 February 1991. In fact, it was the prosecution's case that the offence was committed on 18 February. The discrepancy was not noticed until after the defendant had been convicted. The Divisional Court said that the justices had clearly ignored the confusion as to dates and there was no reason why the conviction could not stand, even though the information had not been amended.

In *R v Scunthorpe Justices ex p McPhee and Gallagher* (1998) 162 JP 635, the defendant was charged with robbery; the prosecution sought to amend the information to allege theft and common assault (a summary offence) instead. An information alleging a summary offence must be laid within six months of the commission of the alleged offence (s 127(1) of the Magistrates' Courts Act 1980). The Divisional Court held that an information laid within that time limit can be amended under s 123 even if the amendment is more than six months after the commission of the alleged offence. This is so even if the amendment involves alleging a different offence, provided that (a) the new offence alleges the 'same misdoing' as the original offence (in other words, 'the new offence should arise out of the same (or substantially the same) facts as gave rise to the original offence'); and (b) the amendment can be made in the interests of justice. In considering whether it is in the interests of justice for the amendment to be made, the court should pay particular regard to the interests of the accused. If the amendment would result in the defendant facing a 'significantly more serious charge', it is likely to be against the interests of justice to allow such an amendment; similarly, the need for an adjournment would militate against the court granting leave for the amendment of the information.

The same approach had been taken in *R v Newcastle-upon-Tyne Justices ex p John Bryce (Contractors) Ltd* [1976] 1 WLR 517, where the prosecution were allowed to amend an information to allege 'use' rather than 'permitting use' of a vehicle, even though the effect was to charge a different summary offence and even though a new information could not have been laid because more than six months had elapsed from the date of the alleged offence. It was said that the defence were not prejudiced by this amendment as the true nature of the offence was clear from the statement of facts on the summons. Similarly, in *R v Thames Magistrates' Court ex p Stevens* (2000) 164 JP 164, the defendant was charged with assault occasioning actual bodily harm (s 47 of the Offences Against the Persons Act 1861). The prosecution subsequently indicated that they wished to withdraw the s 47 charge and lay a charge alleging the summary offence of common assault (s 39 of the Criminal Justice Act 1988) instead. However, it was more than six months since the commission of the offence. The Divisional Court held that the magistrate had correctly concluded that what was being sought by the prosecution was an amendment of the original charge, rather than a substitution or withdrawal of that charge. Section 127 of the Magistrates' Courts Act 1980 therefore did not apply to prevent the court from dealing with the charge of common assault. The magistrate, in considering whether the amendment was in the interests of justice, had taken proper account of the fact that:

(a) the offences had arisen out of the same facts;

(b) the applicant had not been misled or prejudiced by the amendment;

(c) she was not deprived by the amendment of any substantive defence that she had;

(d) the evidence to be adduced by the prosecution was not different after the amendment; and

(e) the effect of the amendment was in fact to reduce the gravity of the original charge.

In *DPP v Short* [2001] EWHC 885 (Admin); (2002) 166 JP 474, the information alleged that the defendant 'used' a vehicle with excess alcohol (rather than 'drove') under s 5 of the Road Traffic Act 1988. At the end of the evidence, the prosecution invited the justices to exercise their power under s 123 of the Magistrates' Courts Act 1980 to amend the information to substitute 'drove' for 'used', thus bringing the information within the wording of s 5. The magistrates refused to allow the information to be amended. It was held by the Divisional Court that the correct approach to determine whether an information discloses an offence not known to law is to look at the information as a whole. Any reference to a statute cannot be ignored. Section 123 of the Magistrates' Courts Act 1980 confers a wide discretion on justices to amend an information, and that discretion should ordinarily be exercised in favour of amendment unless so amending would result in injustice to a defendant. In the present case, taking account of the reference to s 5 of the 1988 Act, it could not be said that the information disclosed an offence not known to law. Moreover, no injustice would have been caused to the defendant by the proposed amendment, since he was aware of the case against him. Accordingly, the justices had erred in refusing the prosecution amendment.

(c)   Irremediable defects

Thirdly, there are fundamental errors which cannot be corrected by amendment (despite the wide wording of s 123 of the Magistrates' Courts Act 1980). This would include an information which names the wrong person (for example, *Marco (Croydon) Ltd v Metropolitan Police* [1984] RTR 24 and *City of Oxford Tramway v Sankey* (1890) 54 JP 564). The only remedy for the prosecution in such a case is to lay a new information (which, in the case of a summary offence, is only possible if less than six months have elapsed since the commission of the offence). There must then be an adjournment so that a fresh summons can be served on the new defendant (*R v Greater Manchester Justices ex p Aldi GmbH & Co KG* (1995) 159 JP 717).

4.11.3   Withdrawal of summons/offering no evidence

If the defendant has not entered a plea, the prosecution can (with the agreement of the justices) withdraw the summons (*R v Redbridge Justices ex p Sainty* [1981] RTR 13). The prosecution may make such an application if one of their witnesses is not available but the court will not grant an adjournment because it takes the view that the prosecution should be in a position to proceed.

Withdrawal of a summons does not constitute an acquittal, so a fresh summons can be issued (*R v Grays Justices ex p Low* [1990] 1 QB 54). Presumably, the same applies to charges, if proceedings were commenced by arrest and charge rather than by laying an information.

If the defendant has entered a plea of not guilty it is too late to withdraw the summons and so the prosecution must:

• proceed with the trial; or

• seek an adjournment; or

• offer no evidence.

The usual situations where the prosecution offer no evidence are where:

- the defendant has pleaded guilty to one offence and the prosecution do not wish to proceed with another (closely related) charge; or

- where new evidence exonerating the defendant has come to light; or

- where the CPS reviews the evidence and decides that there is insufficient prospect of securing a conviction to merit continuing the proceedings.

If the prosecution offer no evidence, and an acquittal is recorded, fresh proceedings may be brought if (but only if) the defendant was never in jeopardy of conviction (*R v Dabhade* [1993] QB 329; [1992] 4 All ER 796).

In *Holmes v Campbell* (1998) 162 JP 655, a magistrates' court dismissed the information against the defendants when the prosecutor failed to appear at the hearing. The prosecutor subsequently laid a fresh information (containing the same allegations) but the magistrates' court declined to try that information on the ground that it would be an abuse of process. The Divisional Court held that by virtue of s 15 of the Magistrates' Courts Act 1980 the accused could not have been convicted at a hearing where the prosecutor was absent. They had therefore not been in jeopardy of conviction at that hearing and so, following *R v Dabhade*, the doctrine of *autrefois acquit* did not prevent the hearing of the fresh information. Furthermore, the magistrates were wrong to hold that the fresh information was an abuse of process, since before the hearing of the first information the defendants had indicated to the prosecution that they would be pleading guilty.

4.11.4 Making speeches in a summary trial

The making of speeches in a summary trial is governed by r 13 of the Magistrates' Courts Rules 1981:

(1) On the summary trial of an information, where the accused does not plead guilty, the prosecutor shall call the evidence for the prosecution, and before doing so may address the court.

(2) At the conclusion of the evidence for the prosecution, the accused may address the court, whether or not he afterwards calls evidence.

(3) At the conclusion of the evidence, if any, for the defence, the prosecutor may call evidence to rebut that evidence.

(4) At the conclusion of the evidence for the defence and the evidence, if any, in rebuttal, the accused may address the court if he has not already done so.

(5) Either party may, with the leave of the court, address the court a second time, but where the court grants leave to one party it shall not refuse leave to the other.

(6) Where both parties address the court twice the prosecutor shall address the court for the second time before the accused does so.

The trial will therefore usually begin with an opening speech by the prosecutor (unless the prosecutor waives his right to make an opening speech). Such speeches are generally very brief. Unlike a trial in the Crown Court, however, the prosecutor has no entitlement to make a closing speech.

The defence are entitled to make only one speech, and so they may make *either* an opening speech or a closing speech. Most defence advocates would invariably choose to make a closing speech, since that is the last chance to address the magistrates before they consider their verdict and it is useful to be able to draw together the threads of the defence case and to highlight any reasonable doubt in the prosecution case.

Rule 13(5) says that either party may, with the leave of the court, make a second speech. Thus, if the prosecutor wishes to make a closing speech or the defence wish to make a closing speech as well as an opening speech, an application must be made to the magistrates.

Where one party is allowed to make a second speech, the other party must also be allowed to make a second speech. Where the case is a complex one, the justices may well allow both parties to make two speeches. Rule 13(6) stipulates that, where both parties address the court twice, the closing speech for the accused takes place after the closing speech for the prosecution. Thus, the defence always have the last word.

4.11.5   Pre-trial disclosure

Under the Criminal Procedure and Investigations Act 1996, the prosecution have to disclose to the defence any material not previously disclosed which might undermine the prosecution case against the accused. The defendant then has the chance to make voluntary disclosure of the nature of the defence case (setting out the matters where the defence take issue with the prosecution and giving particulars of any alibi the defence will rely on at trial). If the defence provide voluntary disclosure of their case, the prosecution then has to reveal any previously undisclosed material which might reasonably be expected to assist the defence case.

4.11.6   Witnesses the prosecution must call

Where the prosecutor serves a bundle of witness statements on the defence prior to summary trial, the prosecution must call as witnesses all the people whose statements have been served (unless any of the exceptions which relate to Crown Court trials are applicable (*R v Haringey Justices ex p DPP* [1996] 1 All ER 828)).

4.11.7   Reading witness statements

Under s 9 of the Criminal Justice Act 1967, a written statement may be read aloud to the court as evidence (instead of the maker of the statement giving oral evidence) if:

* the statement is signed by its maker;
* the statement contains a declaration by the maker that it is true to the best of his knowledge and belief and that he makes it knowing that he is liable to prosecution if he has wilfully stated in it anything which he knows to be false or does not believe to be true;
* a copy of the statement has been served on all the other parties to the proceedings; and
* none of the parties on whom the statement is served objects within seven days of service to the statement being used as evidence.

The last two requirements do not apply if the parties agree immediately before or during the hearing that the statement may be used as evidence rather than the witness giving 'live' testimony.

Where the statement refers to a document or other object as an exhibit, a copy of that document must accompany the statement when it is served on the other parties or the other parties must be told how they can inspect a copy of that document. When the statement is read out at the trial, any document or exhibit referred to in it becomes an exhibit just as if it has been produced by a witness giving oral evidence.

It is usually the statements of prosecution witnesses which are read out in this way, with the consent of the defence, on the basis that the defence concedes that the evidence of that witness is uncontroversial and so the defence do not wish to cross-examine that witness. However, there is no reason why the evidence of a defence witness cannot be given in this way (if the prosecution agree).

4.11.8   Objecting to prosecution evidence in a summary trial

Objections to prosecution evidence are made under s 76 or 78 of the Police and Criminal Evidence Act 1984 (PACE).

If the defence invoke s 76 and allege that a confession has been obtained by oppression or in circumstances where anything said by the defendant is likely to be unreliable, the magistrates have to hold a *voir dire* or 'trial within a trial' (*R v Liverpool Juvenile Court ex p R* [1988] QB 1; [1987] 2 All ER 668). This simply means that evidence has to be heard on the admissibility of the confession. The prosecution will have to call the police officers who were present when the defendant confessed and they can be cross-examined by the defence; the defendant may then give evidence (and be cross-examined by the prosecution). At this stage, it is only the admissibility of the confession, not its truth, which is in issue.

If the magistrates decide that the confession is inadmissible, the trial will continue (assuming there is other evidence against the accused), but no further mention may be made of the confession. If the confession is ruled admissible, the trial will resume with the police officer giving evidence of what the defendant said (unless this has already been done in the *voir dire*, in which case the evidence does not have to be repeated as the magistrates have already heard it).

Where the defendant asks for evidence to be excluded under s 78 of PACE (that is, on the ground that its admission would be unfairly prejudicial to the defendant) the justices may either consider the admissibility of the evidence when that issue arises or postpone consideration of admissibility until the end of the hearing. Whereas the magistrates must allow evidence to be given on a *voir dire* if there is an application to exclude evidence under s 76, there is no such obligation where the application is under s 78 (*Vel v Owen; Vel v Chief Constable of North Wales* (1987) 151 JP 510; *Halawa v Federation Against Copyright Theft* [1995] 1 Cr App R 21). In *Halawa,* the Divisional Court said that, in most cases, it is generally better for the magistrates to hear all the prosecution evidence (including the disputed evidence) before considering an application to exclude evidence under s 78. This does of course leave the justices with the very difficult (some might say impossible) task of putting from their minds prejudicial evidence that they have heard but then decide is inadmissible.

In *Johnson v Leicestershire Constabulary* (1998) *The Times,* 7 October, it was held by the Divisional Court that where magistrates wrongly become aware that a defendant has previous convictions, or has been before the court before, the test to be applied is whether there is any real danger of bias arising from the magistrates finding out something they should not have discovered. The court said that it has to be borne in mind that lay justices are capable of putting out of their minds matters which are irrelevant.

In *R v Bow Street Magistrates' Court ex p Proulx* [2001] 1 All ER 57, it was held that the approach to be adopted by the Divisional Court when exercising its supervisory jurisdiction over a decision of a magistrate who had rejected an application to exclude evidence of a confession under ss 76 and 78 of PACE is as follows: provided the magistrate has correctly directed himself on the law, the Divisional Court will only interfere with his findings of fact, and his assessment of their significance when ruling on the admissibility of evidence, if they are outside the range of conclusions open to a reasonable magistrate (that is, the Divisional Court will determine whether they could be interfered with on grounds of *Wednesbury* unreasonableness). The court went on to say that the test is not whether the actual confession was untruthful or inaccurate. The test is whether whatever was said or done was, in the circumstances existing as at the time of the confession, likely to have rendered such a confession unreliable, whether or not it might be seen subsequently, with hindsight and in the light of all the material available at trial, that it did or did not actually do so.

4.11.9 Dock identifications

Where the identity of the defendant as the person who committed the offence is in issue, the court will generally not allow a witness who has not previously identified the defendant at an identification parade to be asked 'do you see the person who committed the offence in court today?' (a so-called 'dock identification'). The reason for not allowing this to be done is that the defendant is at a great disadvantage – the eyes of the witness are bound to go to the person sitting in the dock.

However, in *Barnes v DPP* [1997] 2 Cr App R 505, the defendant was charged with failing to provide a breath specimen. There had been no identity parade and the only evidence that the defendant was the person who refused to provide a specimen was a 'dock identification' by a police officer. The Divisional Court held that the justices had a discretion to allow a defendant to be identified in court even if there had not been a previous identification parade. In *Karia v DPP* [2002] EWHC 2175; (2002) 166 JP 753, the defendant appealed against conviction for a number of motoring offences on the ground that the magistrates should not have allowed the police officer who had stopped the vehicle to make a 'dock identification' of him, and that an identification parade should have been held. He argued that the decision in *Barnes v DPP* permitting dock identifications in such cases was incompatible with the Human Rights Act 1998. It was held that the aim of a dock identification in a case such as the present one is usually to avoid an unmeritorious dismissal of a prosecution case resulting from a failure to make a purely formal identification of the defendant. In the present case, the defendant had not notified the prosecution that identity was in issue, and so the dock identification was not unfair. Since there had been no prior notification that identity was in issue, there was no basis on which the police could have considered that it would be useful to hold an identification parade. As far as the Human Rights Act point was concerned, a requirement that the issues should be made known to the court before or during the proceedings cannot infringe Art 6; a requirement that a defendant should indicate before or at his trial what are the issues in the trial does not infringe his right to silence. On this basis, it would appear that dock identifications are only to be ruled out where the defendant has already indicated that identity is in issue in the case. Both *Barnes* and *Karia* appear to conflict with *North Yorkshire Trading Standards Department v Williams* (1994) 159 JP 383, where the court rejected the notion that less strict identification rules should apply in respect of summary offences. See further Watkin, T, 'In the dock – an overview of decisions of the High Court on dock identifications in the magistrates' court' [2003] Crim LR 463.

4.11.10 The submission of no case to answer

We have already seen that the defence may make a submission that there is no case to answer once the prosecution have called all their evidence. The principles to be applied to a submission of no case to answer in a magistrates' court were originally set out in *Practice Direction (Submission of No Case to Answer)* [1962] 1 WLR 227. This provided as follows:

> A submission that there is no case to answer may properly be made and upheld: (a) when there has been no evidence to prove an essential element in the alleged offence; (b) when the evidence adduced by the prosecution has been so discredited as a result of cross-examination or is so manifestly unreliable that no reasonable tribunal could safely convict upon it.

> Apart from these two situations a tribunal should not in general be called upon to reach a decision as to conviction or acquittal until the whole of the evidence which either side wishes to tender has been placed before it. If however a submission is made that there is no case to answer, the decision should depend not so much on whether the adjudicating tribunal (if compelled to do so) would at that stage convict or acquit but on whether the evidence is such that a reasonable tribunal might convict. If a reasonable tribunal might convict on the evidence so far laid before it, there is a case to answer.

However, this Practice Direction was revoked by *Practice Direction (Criminal Proceedings: Consolidation)* [2002] 1 WLR 2870; [2002] 3 All ER 904 and nothing was put in its place. This leaves justices without clear guidance on the test to be applied when considering a submission of no case.

It seems likely that justices will continue to take the view that, if a submission of no case to answer is made, the decision should depend not so much on whether they would, at that stage, convict or acquit but on whether the evidence is such that a reasonable tribunal might convict. If a reasonable tribunal might convict on the evidence so far laid before it, there is a case to answer.

Thus, the basic question to be answered is whether or not there is sufficient evidence on which a reasonable bench of magistrates could convict. In other words, the submission should succeed if a conviction would be perverse, in the sense that no reasonable bench could convict.

Where the justices are minded to dismiss a case prior to the start of the defence case (whether following a submission of no case to answer by the defence or of their own motion), the prosecution should be given the opportunity to address the court to show why the case should not be dismissed (*R v Barking and Dagenham Justices ex p DPP* (1995) 159 JP 373). This means that the prosecution have the right to reply to the defence submission that there is no case to answer unless, having heard the defence submission, the magistrates decide to rule against the defence and indicate this fact to the prosecutor.

If the submission is successful, the defendant is acquitted. If it is unsuccessful, the trial continues.

An important question that arises in the context of submissions of no case to answer in the magistrates' court is the extent to which the justices may have regard to the credibility of prosecution witnesses when considering such a submission. In the Crown Court, the judge has to be careful not to trespass on the territory of the jury. The test to be applied by the judge when ruling on a submission of no case to answer is set out in *R v Galbraith* [1981] 1 WLR 1039: is the prosecution evidence so tenuous that, even taken at its highest, a jury properly directed could not properly convict on it? The requirement that the Crown Court judge should 'take the prosecution evidence at its highest' is intended to leave questions of credibility to the jury. Submissions of no case to answer based on the credibility of the prosecution evidence should only succeed in the Crown Court where the prosecution evidence is clearly incredible. In *R v Barking and Dagenham Justices ex p DPP*, the Divisional Court said that questions of credibility should, except in the clearest of cases, not normally be taken into account by justices considering a submission of no case to answer in the magistrates' court.

Nonetheless, some justices may well take the pragmatic view that it would be inappropriate for them to go through the motions of hearing defence evidence if they have already formed the view that the prosecution evidence is so unconvincing that they will not convict on it in any event. The general principle remains that, so long as the necessary minimum amount of prosecution evidence has been adduced so as to raise a case on which a reasonable tribunal could convict, the justices should allow the trial to run its course rather than acquitting on a submission of no case to answer.

In some cases, the deficiency in the prosecution case can be cured by allowing the prosecution to re-open their case, rather than upholding the submission of no case to answer and acquitting the accused. In *Hughes v DPP* [2003] EWHC 2470; (2003) 167 JP 589, it was said that when, on a submission of no case to answer, a point is raised which has no bearing on the merits of the prosecution, and the defect in the prosecution case is one of omission (and probably oversight), the advocate acting for the prosecution should request leave to recall the relevant witness to supplement the prosecution evidence. The court added that, in such a case, the magistrates should normally exercise their discretion to permit the prosecution to re-open their case so that such evidence can be given, particularly where the fact in question is likely to be uncontroversial. Indeed, if necessary, the magistrates should consider inviting the prosecution to recall the relevant witness. It is submitted that it may well be appropriate for the justices to allow the prosecution to re-open their case, and thus adduce evidence that was inadvertently omitted, even if the missing evidence does have a more direct bearing on the merits of the prosecution case. If the defect in the prosecution case is one that could be cured simply and speedily by allowing them to re-open their case and recall a witness, it may well be that the interests of justice require that the prosecution be given the chance to remedy the defect. It is difficult to see how the defendant would be prejudiced by this decision. However, if the re-opening of the prosecution case would require an adjournment, and thus cause delay in the disposal of the case, the balance of the interests of justice might require that the submission is upheld and the defendant acquitted. From the perspective of professional conduct and ethics, it is also noteworthy that in his judgment in *Hughes*, Stanley Burnton J went on to say that 'Ambushes of the kind attempted in this case are to be discouraged and discountenanced. Criminal proceedings are not a game: their object is to achieve a fair determination of the innocence or guilt of the defendant'.

There is no legal obligation on magistrates to give reasons for rejecting a submission of no case to answer (*Moran v DPP* [2002] EWHC 89; (2002) 166 JP 467).

If a submission of no case to answer is made by the defence, it should be made clear to the magistrates that evidence will be called if the submission is unsuccessful. This avoids confusion, since the magistrates might otherwise think that the defence have simply chosen to make a closing speech without calling any evidence.

In certain very limited circumstances, the case can be re-opened even after the magistrates have held that there is no case to answer. In *Steward v DPP* [2003] EWHC 2251; [2003] 4 All ER 1105, the justices acceded to a submission of no case to answer, and gave reasons why they had done so. The prosecutor then pointed out that the reasons given by the magistrates contained an error of fact. The justices reviewed their decision and concluded that there was a case to answer. The defendant, who was subsequently convicted, appealed by way of case stated on the basis that the justices had been acting *functus officio* by proceeding to hear the case after reaching a finding of no case to answer. The Divisional Court said that the justices were entitled to re-open a case despite having acceded to a submission of no case to answer where an error had been identified by the prosecution and it had been agreed by the defendant that there was an error in the reasons given by the justices. In those circumstances, the process of adjudication had not been completed and the justices were not *functus officio*. The present case was said to be distinguishable from *R v Essex Justices ex p Final* [1963] 2 QB 816 (where it was held that justices should not re-open a case once they have reached their decision), as that case had been re-opened in order to hear further submissions on the evidence whereas, in the present case, the justices had identified their error straight away, admitted it and rectified it; also, the earlier case was decided at a time when it was less common for justices to give reasons for accepting a submission of no case to answer (and so errors in their reasoning were less likely to be immediately apparent).

4.11.11 The defendant's evidence

If a submission of no case to answer is not made (or is unsuccessful), the defence then have the opportunity to present evidence to the court. If the defendant is going to call other witnesses as well as giving evidence himself, the defendant should give evidence first unless the court otherwise directs (see s 79 of PACE).

If the defendant decides not to give evidence, he runs the risk that the magistrates will be entitled to draw adverse inferences from his silence under s 35 of the Criminal Justice and Public Order Act 1994.

The magistrates should warn the defendant of the possible consequences of not testifying (this warning is required by s 35(2) of the Criminal Justice and Public Order Act 1994). However, in *Radford v Kent County Council* (1998) 162 JP 697, the magistrates failed to warn the defendant that adverse inferences could be drawn if he failed to testify. However, in their stated case, the justices said that 'we drew no inferences whatsoever from the failure of the appellant to give evidence, but simply were aware that the evidence for the prosecution was not rebutted by evidence from or on behalf of the appellant'. The Divisional Court held that, although the warning of the consequences of not testifying is very important, the failure to give the warning in the present case did not render the appellant's conviction unsafe.

4.11.12 Re-opening the prosecution case

Rule 13(3) of the Magistrates' Courts Rules 1981 provides that, after any evidence called by the defence, 'the prosecutor may call evidence to rebut that evidence'. In practice, this provision is used quite sparingly (see *Price v Humphries* [1958] 2 QB 353; *Hammond v Wilkinson* (2001) 165 JP 786). It can be used, for example, to deal with something that has arisen *ex improviso* – something that could not reasonably have been foreseen – during the course of the defence case. It can also be used where the prosecution seek to adduce evidence that is intended to remedy a technical deficiency in their case. However, the power to allow the prosecution to re-open their case can go beyond such technical difficulties. For example, in *James v South Glamorgan County Council* [1993] RTR 312, the main prosecution witness had not arrived but the trial proceeded nonetheless; after the prosecution case had been closed and while the defendant was giving evidence, the witness arrived. It was accepted by the magistrates that the witness had a good reason for being late and the prosecution were allowed to call him as a witness. It was held by the Divisional Court that, since the evidence had not been available at the proper time and there was no unfairness to the defendant, the decision of the magistrates was correct. Similarly, in *Khatibi v DPP* [2004] EWHC 83; (2004) 168 JP 361, the court said that the discretion to admit evidence after the close of the prosecution case is not confined to the well-established exceptions of rebuttal and mere formality. The discretion must, however, be exercised with great caution. The magistrates should bear in mind the strictly adversarial nature of the English criminal process, whereby the cases for the prosecution and the defence are presented consecutively in their entirety. The normal order of events should not be departed from substantially unless justice really demands such a course of action. In deciding whether to exercise their discretion to permit the calling of evidence after the close of the prosecution case, the magistrates must look carefully at the interests of justice overall, and in particular at the risk of any prejudice to the defendant. The court also pointed out that it has generally been accepted that an application to call further evidence cannot succeed after the bench has retired to consider its verdict.

4.11.13 Change of plea

The magistrates have a discretion to allow a defendant to change his plea from guilty to not guilty at any stage before sentence is passed (*S (An Infant) v Recorder of Manchester* [1971] AC 481). The question for the magistrates is whether the original plea was unequivocal and entered with a proper understanding of what the charge entailed.

If the defendant is allowed to change his plea to one of not guilty, he should also be allowed to re-consider his consent to summary trial (*R v Bow Street Magistrates ex p Welcombe* (1992) 156 JP 609).

Similarly, the magistrates can allow a defendant to change his plea from not guilty to guilty at any time before a verdict is returned.

4.11.14 Seeing the magistrates in private

It is open to the justices to hear representations from the parties in private, but they should do so only in exceptional cases. Steps must be taken to ensure that all parties are aware of the private hearing and are represented at it. The clerk must take a contemporaneous note of the hearing (see *R v Nottingham Justices ex p Furnell* (1995) 160 JP 201).

In *R v Faversham and Sittingbourne Justices ex p Stickings* (1996) 160 JP 801, the magistrates, during the course of a trial and acting on the advice of their clerk, ruled that certain prosecution evidence was inadmissible. During an adjournment, the prosecutor telephoned the clerk to say that the ruling was wrong in law. The clerk agreed that the ruling was wrong. The defence were not given notice of this until the court reconvened, whereupon the magistrates reversed their earlier ruling and ordered that the case be retried by another bench. The Divisional Court said that it was procedurally unfair for a matter to be drawn to the clerk's attention by telephone. The proper method was to do so in writing, sending a copy to all other parties to the case. Furthermore, the general principle was that decisions reached by justices should not be reversed. Accordingly, a re-trial should not have been ordered.

4.11.15 The risk of bias

Unless there are special circumstances, interlocutory ruling on the admissibility of evidence does not deprive District judges and lay justices of the ability to continue the hearing of the trial (*R v Stipendiary Magistrate for Norfolk ex p Taylor* (1997) 161 JP 773). Therefore, District judges and lay justices should not normally disqualify themselves from hearing a trial merely because they have ruled in favour of an application by the prosecution for non-disclosure of material on the ground of public interest immunity (*R (DPP) v Acton Youth Court* [2001] EWHC 402 (Admin); [2001] 1 WLR 1828, expressly approved in *R v H* [2004] UKHL 3; [2004] 2 WLR 335).

In *KL and LK v DPP* [2001] EWHC 1112 (Admin); (2002) 166 JP 1112, the prosecution made an application for the use of screens in relation to a prosecution witness, on the grounds that she would feel intimidated having to give evidence in the defendant's presence. The question to be decided was whether the justices should withdraw from the case after hearing the application. It was held that there is no objection in principle to justices hearing a case after having heard an application for the use of screens.

4.11.16 Special Measures Directions

An application can be made under s 19 of the Youth Justice and Criminal Evidence Act 1999 for special measures:

• screening the witness from the accused (s 23);

• giving evidence by live link (s 24) (this provision will become less relevant, as s 51 of the Criminal Justice Act 2003 enables a court to authorise witnesses, other than the defendant, to give evidence through a live link in criminal proceedings);

• giving evidence in private, in a sexual case, or where there is a fear that the witness may be intimidated (s 26);

• video recording of evidence-in-chief (s 27) (again, this provision is made less relevant, as s 137 of the Criminal Justice Act 2003 extends the circumstances in which evidence-in-chief can take the form of a video recorded statement);

• video recording of cross-examination and re-examination where the evidence-in-chief of the witness has been video recorded (s 28);

- examination through an intermediary in the case of a young or incapacitated witness (s 29); provision of aids to communication for a young or incapacitated witness (s 30).

These measures are also applicable in the Crown Court, and are dealt with fully in Chapter 10. The procedure for making (and opposing) applications for special measures directions is set out in the Magistrates Courts (Special Measures Directions) Rules 2002 (SI 2002/1687) and (for the use of intermediaries) the Magistrates' Courts (Special Measures Directions) (Amendment) Rules 2004 (SI 2004/184).

In *R (on the Application of D) v Camberwell Green Youth Court* [2003] EWHC 227 (Admin); (2003) 167 JP 210, the Divisional Court considered six cases concerning special measures directions. Section 21(5) of the 1999 Act establishes a presumption that the court will give a special measures direction to admit a video recording of the evidence-in-chief and/or the giving of evidence over a live link unless special measures are not available or, in the case of a video recording, the interests of justice dictate otherwise. The issue for determination was whether s 21(5) is compatible with the right to a fair trial guaranteed by Art 6 of the European Convention on Human Rights. It was held that s 21(5) does not breach Art 6. The court reasoned that eligible witnesses are assured from an early stage that they will receive the protection of a special measures direction, and that assurance benefits witnesses and increases the quality of their evidence. If it subsequently appears that the direction had caused unfairness, 'safety valves' are provided by ss 20(2) and 24(3) of the Act, and by the common law power of the court to prevent unfairness. The court observed that there is nothing in the Convention which prohibits vulnerable witnesses from being allowed to give evidence in a different room from the accused, and that witnesses have rights and are entitled to protection. This decision is a useful reminder that even though Art 6 of the Convention is concerned with the rights of the accused, the court has also to consider the fairness of the trial from the perspective of the prosecution, the complainant and the witnesses.

4.1117 Fitness to plead

In *R (P) v Barking Youth Court* [2002] EWHC 734; [2002] 2 Cr App R 19, the defendant was 16 years old and was to be tried in a youth court. His solicitor raised the issue of fitness to plead. The question at issue was the approach to be taken in such a case. It was held that, in the case of offences to be tried summarily, s 37(3) of the Mental Health Act 1983 and s 11 of the Powers of Criminal Courts (Sentencing) Act 2000 together provide a statutory framework for all the issues that arise in cases of defendants who are (or might be) mentally ill or suffering from severe mental impairment. Fitness to plead is dealt with more fully in the context of Crown Court trial.

4.12   THE ROLE OF THE CLERK

Whereas a lay justice receives only a very small amount of legal training, their clerk is a qualified lawyer. The functions of the clerk are set out in s 28 of the Courts Act 2003 and in para V.55.7 of the *Practice Direction (Criminal Proceedings: Consolidation)* [2002] 1

WLR 2870; [2002] 3 All ER 904. Section 28 of the Courts Act 2003 (which is based on s 45 of the Justices of the Peace Act 1997) says that:

(4) The functions of a justices' clerk include giving advice to any or all of the justices of the peace to whom he is clerk about matters of law (including procedure and practice) on questions arising in connection with the discharge of their functions, including questions arising when the clerk is not personally attending on them.

(5) The powers of a justices' clerk include, at any time when he thinks he should do so, bringing to the attention of any or all of the justices of the peace to whom he is clerk any point of law (including procedure and practice) that is or may be involved in any question so arising.

Paragraph V.55 of the Practice Direction states as follows:

55 *Clerk retiring with justices*

55.1 A justices' clerk is responsible for:

(a) the legal advice tendered to the justices within the area;

(b) the performance of any of the functions set out below by any member of his staff acting as legal adviser;

(c) ensuring that competent advice is available to justices when the justices' clerk is not personally present in court; and

(d) the effective delivery of case management and the reduction of unnecessary delay.

55.2 Where a person other than the justices' clerk (a 'legal adviser'), who is authorised to do so, performs any of the functions referred to in this direction he will have the same responsibilities as the justices' clerk. The legal adviser may consult the justices' clerk or other person authorised by the justices' clerk for that purpose before tendering advice to the bench. If the justices' clerk or that person gives any advice directly to the bench, he should give the parties or their advocates an opportunity of repeating any relevant submissions prior to the advice being given.

55.3 It shall be the responsibility of the legal adviser to provide the justices with any advice they require properly to perform their functions, whether or not the justices have requested that advice, on:

(a) questions of law (including European Court of Human Rights jurisprudence and those matters set out in section 2(1) of the Human Rights Act 1998);

(b) questions of mixed law and fact;

(c) matters of practice and procedure;

(d) the range of penalties available;

(e) any relevant decisions of the superior courts or other guidelines;

(f) other issues relevant to the matter before the court; and

(g) the appropriate decision-making structure to be applied in any given case.

In addition to advising the justices it shall be the legal adviser's responsibility to assist the court, where appropriate, as to the formulation of reasons and the recording of those reasons.

55.4 A justices' clerk or legal adviser must not play any part in making findings of fact, but may assist the bench by reminding them of the evidence, using any notes of the proceedings for this purpose.

55.5 A justices' clerk or legal adviser may ask questions of witnesses and the parties in order to clarify the evidence and any issues in the case. A legal adviser has a duty to ensure that every case is conducted fairly.

55.6   When advising the justices the justices' clerk or legal adviser, whether or not previously in court, should:

   (a) ensure that he is aware of the relevant facts; and

   (b) provide the parties with the information necessary to enable the parties to make any representations they wish as to the advice before it is given.

55.7   At any time justices are entitled to receive advice to assist them in discharging their responsibilities. If they are in any doubt as to the evidence which has been given, they should seek the aid of their legal adviser, referring to his notes as appropriate. This should ordinarily be done in open court. Where the justices request their adviser to join them in the retiring room, this request should be made in the presence of the parties in court. Any legal advice given to the justices other than in open court should be clearly stated to be provisional and the adviser should subsequently repeat the substance of the advice in open court and give the parties an opportunity to make any representations they wish on that provisional advice. The legal adviser should then state in open court whether the provisional advice is confirmed or, if it is varied, the nature of the variation.

55.8   The performance of a legal adviser may be appraised by a person authorised by the magistrates' courts committee to do so. For that purpose the appraiser may be present in the justices' retiring room. The content of the appraisal is confidential, but the fact that an appraisal has taken place, and the presence of the appraiser in the retiring room, should be briefly explained in open court.

55.9   The legal adviser is under a duty to assist unrepresented parties to present their case, but must do so without appearing to become an advocate for the party concerned.

55.10 The role of legal advisers in fine default proceedings or any other proceedings for the enforcement of financial orders, obligations or penalties is to assist the court. They must not act in an adversarial or partisan manner. With the agreement of the justices a legal adviser may ask questions of the defaulter to elicit information which the justices will require to make an adjudication, for example to facilitate his explanation for the default. A legal adviser may also advise the justices in the normal way as to the options open to them in dealing with the case. It would be inappropriate for the legal adviser to set out to establish wilful refusal or neglect or any other type of culpable behaviour, to offer an opinion on the facts, or to urge a particular course of action upon the justices. The duty of impartiality is the paramount consideration for the legal adviser at all times, and this takes precedence over any role he may have as a collecting officer. The appointment of other staff to 'prosecute' the case for the collecting officer is not essential to ensure compliance with the law, including the Human Rights Act 1998. Whether to make such appointments is a matter for the justices' chief executive.

Clark v Kelly [2003] UKPC D1; [2003] 2 WLR 1586 was a case which concerned the role of the clerk to the justices in the District Court, the Scottish equivalent of the magistrates' court. The Privy Council held that the role of the clerk as legal assessor is not incompatible with the defendant's right to a fair trial under Art 6 of the European Convention on Human Rights. Complaint was made of the fact that the clerk gives advice to the justices in private. The Privy Council ruled that any advice which the clerk gives to the justices in private (whether on matters of law, practice or procedure) should be regarded by the justices as provisional advice until the substance of that advice has been repeated in open court and the parties have had an opportunity to comment on it. The clerk should then state in open court whether that advice is confirmed or varied (and if it is varied, in what way) before the justices act upon it. The approach taken by the Privy Council closely mirrors the requirements set out in para V.55.7 of the Practice Direction.

When the clerk gives advice to the justices in the course of the hearing, this should be done in open court, so that the prosecution and defence can make submissions to the bench on that advice.

If the clerk advises the justices after they have retired to consider their decision and the clerk cites authority which was not cited in open court, he should inform the advocates in the case and give them the opportunity to make further submissions to the magistrates (*W v W* (1993) *The Times*, 4 June).

In *R v Chichester Justices ex p DPP* [1994] RTR 175, it was held (*obiter*) that if the clerk who advises the justices is not the clerk who was present in court when the parties made their submissions on the point of law at issue, it is essential that the clerk should hear informal submissions on the relevant law from the parties before advising the justices.

What the clerk must not do is to express a view on questions of fact; these questions are solely for the magistrates. So, for example, the clerk should not say whether or not he believes a particular witness. See, for example, *R v Stafford Justices ex p Ross* [1962] 1 WLR 456, where a conviction was quashed because the clerk had passed a note to the bench suggesting that the defence case was implausible. Nor should the clerk recommend a particular type of sentence in the event of the defendant being convicted (although he can advise the justices on what sentences are available).

The clerk should not leave the courtroom with the justices when they retire to consider their verdict. If the magistrates require assistance from the clerk, he should only join them when asked to do so and should return to the courtroom once the advice has been given (see *R v Eccles Justices ex p Farrelly* (1993) 157 JP 77 and *R v Birmingham Justices ex p Ahmed* [1995] Crim LR 503).

Where the accused is unrepresented, the clerk may assist the defendant by asking any necessary questions of prosecution witnesses (although the clerk should not assume the role of defence counsel and cross-examine the prosecution witnesses).

4.13 THE DECISION OF THE JUSTICES

Usually, there are three lay magistrates. Their decision (whether to acquit or to convict) is by simple majority.

The chairman does not have a second or casting vote. If only two lay justices hear a case but cannot agree on a verdict, they have no option but to adjourn the case for re-trial in front of a bench with three justices (*R v Redbridge Justices ex p Ram* [1992] 1 QB 384).

In reaching their decision on a question of fact, it is open to magistrates to use their personal local knowledge, but they should inform the prosecution and the defence that they are doing so, so that those representing the parties have the opportunity of commenting upon the knowledge which the justices claim to have: *Bowman v DPP* [1991] RTR 263; *Norbrook Laboratories (GB) Ltd v Health and Safety Executive* [1998] EHLR 207.

In *Gibbons v DPP* [2000] All ER (D) 2250, the appellants were charged with assault. They said they had been acting in self-defence. An eye-witness gave evidence that she was 25 yards from the fight and that the appellants were responsible. After the closing speeches had been made, the District judge had cause to visit the place where the alleged offence had occurred. While there, he checked the site of the assault, the distance the witness was located from the attack and whether her view would have been obstructed. The Divisional Court held that those were all critical issues at the trial. At the very least, the magistrate should have informed the parties of his intention of taking a view, so that they could have had the opportunity to make submissions as to where the witness had actually been located. It followed that, in the circumstances, there had been a defect in the trial process; the convictions were quashed and a re-trial ordered.

The magistrates' decision is announced in open court by the chairman. Where the defendant is convicted the magistrates have to give brief reasons for their decision. In *R (McGowan) v Brent Justices* [2001] EWHC Admin 814; (2002) 166 JP 29, the Divisional Court held that, in a summary trial, it is enough for justices to indicate the basis of their decision without stating their reasons in the form of a judgment or giving reasons in any elaborate form (see *McKerry v Teesdale & Wear Valley Justices* (2000) 164 JP 355), and that this is still the case following the implementation of the Human Rights Act 1998. What is necessary is for the justices to show that they have put their mind to the ingredients of the offence. The essence of the exercise, said the court, is to inform the defendant why he has been found guilty: that could be done in a few sentences.

4.13.1 Alternative verdicts

Whereas a jury can sometimes convict the defendant of a lesser offence even though that offence is not on the indictment (for example, theft instead of robbery) under s 3 of the Criminal Law Act 1967, the magistrates have no such power (*Lawrence v Same* [1968] 2 QB 93). In that case, a conviction for common assault on an information alleging unlawful wounding was set aside by the Divisional Court because it was in excess of jurisdiction.

However, there are certain statutory exceptions to this rule, such as the power to convict of careless driving instead of dangerous driving (see s 24 of the Road Traffic Offenders Act 1988). In *R (on the Application of H) v Liverpool City Youth Court* [2001] Crim LR 487 the defendant was charged with aggravated vehicle taking (s 12A of the Theft Act 1968) but the magistrates convicted him of the lesser offence of taking a vehicle without the owner's consent. The Divisional Court rejected the argument that the power to convict of the lesser offence under s 12(5) of the 1968 Act was confined to the Crown Court.

If the prosecution wish the justices to consider alternative offences, those offences must be charged (in separate informations). The informations can then be tried together. If the defendant only faces one charge to begin with, but the prosecution want the court to have the power to convict the defendant of a different offence, an information alleging the new offence may be laid in open court or the defendant may be 'further charged' by the police outside court. This course of action will be appropriate if the defendant is willing to plead guilty to an offence which is less serious than that originally charged and the prosecution are willing to accept that plea and drop the more serious charge. If the defendant is charged with alternative offences at the outset and pleads not guilty to both, and the magistrates convict the defendant of the more serious of the two offences, the magistrates should either adjourn the other information *sine die* (that is, with no date being set, the understanding being that the defendant will hear no more of that information) or else convict the defendant of the lesser offence too and impose only a nominal penalty in respect of it (*DPP v Gane* (1991) 155 JP 846).

4.13.2   Setting aside conviction or sentence

Section 142 of the Magistrates' Courts Act 1980 provides as follows:

(1)   A magistrates' court may vary or rescind a sentence or other order imposed or made by it when dealing with an offender if it appears to the court to be in the interests of justice to do so; and it is hereby declared that this power extends to replacing a sentence or order which for any reason appears to be invalid by another which the court has power to impose or make.

...

(2)   Where a person is convicted by a magistrates' court and it subsequently appears to the court that it would be in the interests of justice that the case should be heard again by different justices, the court may so direct.

...

(3)   Where a court gives a direction under sub-section (2) above—

(a) the conviction and any sentence or other order imposed or made in consequence thereof shall be of no effect;

...

(5)   Where a sentence or order is varied under sub-section (1) above, the sentence or other order, as so varied, shall take effect from the beginning of the day on which it was originally imposed or made, unless the court otherwise directs.

Section 142(2) of the Magistrates' Courts Act 1980 thus enables a defendant who was convicted in the magistrates' court (whether he pleaded guilty or was found guilty) to ask the magistrates to set the conviction aside. This application can be considered by the same magistrates who convicted the defendant or by a different bench. If the conviction is set aside, the case is re-heard by different magistrates from those who convicted the defendant. An application under s 142(2) may be appropriate if, for example, the magistrates made an error of law or there was some defect in the procedure which led to the conviction.

The magistrates can re-open the case under s 142 regardless of whether the defendant pleaded guilty or was found guilty. However, s 142 cannot operate where the defendant was acquitted (see *Coles v East Penwith Justices* (1998) 162 JP 687, where the Divisional Court held that there was no power under s 142(1) to revoke a defendant's costs order where the prosecution had withdrawn the charges).

In *R v Dewsbury Magistrates ex p K* (1994) *The Times*, 16 March, the defendant (who was aware that the case was due to be heard) was convicted in his absence, but his failure to attend court was not intentional. He sought a re-hearing but the justices refused. This refusal was quashed by the Divisional Court, which said that any inconvenience to the court or to the prosecution should not outweigh the right of the defendant to have an opportunity of defending himself. However, in *R v Gwent Magistrates' Court ex p Carey* (1996) 160 JP 613, the Divisional Court held that magistrates have a broad discretion in deciding whether or not to re-open a case under s 142. They are entitled to have regard to the fact that the defendant failed to attend the original hearing through his own fault and that witnesses would be inconvenienced if a re-trial were to be ordered. Henry LJ also said that the magistrates were entitled to take account of the apparent strength of the prosecution case, although little weight should be given to it, since an apparently strong case can collapse during the course of a trial. His Lordship also pointed out that the magistrates, by refusing to re-open the case, were not 'finally shutting out the defendant from the judgment seat' because he still had his unfettered right of appeal to the Crown Court.

Section 142(1) of the Magistrates' Courts Act 1980 empowers a magistrates' court to vary or rescind a sentence if it is in the interests of justice to do so. Again, this power may be exercised by a different bench from that which passed the original sentence. The main use of this power is to remedy the situation where an illegal sentence is inadvertently passed on an offender.

There is no time limit within which applications for the setting aside of a conviction or sentence under s 142 must be made. However, where a defendant applies under s 142(2) for the trial to be re-heard, delay in making the application is a relevant consideration for the magistrates in deciding whether or not to grant that application (*R v Ealing Magistrates' Court ex p Sahota* (1998) 162 JP 73).

4.14   COMMITTAL FOR SENTENCE

Even if a defendant is tried and convicted by a magistrates' court, he may still in certain circumstances be sentenced by the Crown Court.

4.14.1   Section 3 of the Powers of Criminal Courts (Sentencing) Act 2000

The first type of committal for sentence is under s 3 of the Powers of Criminal Courts (Sentencing) Act 2000, which applies where a defendant is convicted in a magistrates' court of an offence which is triable either way. The effect of a committal under s 3 is that the defendant will be sentenced by the Crown Court, whose sentencing powers are greater than those of the magistrates' court.

Section 3 provides as follows:

(1)   Subject to sub-section (4) below, this section applies where on the summary trial of an offence triable either way a person aged 18 or over is convicted of the offence.

(2)   If the court is of the opinion—

   (a) that the offence or the combination of the offence and one or more offences associated with it was so serious that greater punishment should be inflicted for the offence than the court has power to impose, or

   (b) in the case of a violent or sexual offence, that a custodial sentence for a term longer than the court has power to impose is necessary to protect the public from serious harm from him,

   the court may commit the offender in custody or on bail to the Crown Court for sentence in accordance with section 5(1) below.

(3)   Where the court commits a person under sub-section (2) above, section 6 below (which enables a magistrates' court, where it commits a person under this section in respect of an offence, also to commit him to the Crown Court to be dealt with in respect of certain other offences) shall apply accordingly.

(4)   This section does not apply in relation to an offence as regards which this section is excluded by section 33 of the Magistrates' Courts Act 1980 (certain offences where value involved is small).

Section 3(2)(a) of the Powers of Criminal Courts (Sentencing) Act 2000 thus provides that where the magistrates take the view that the offence (or, where there is more than one offence, the combination of offences before the court) is so serious that greater punishment should be inflicted than the magistrates' court has power to impose, the magistrates' court can commit the defendant to the Crown Court to be sentenced. Usually, this test is taken to mean that committal for sentence is appropriate where the justices think that more than six months' custody is appropriate. However, in *R v Chelmsford Justices ex p Lloyd* [2001] 2 Cr App R(S) 15, the defendant pleaded guilty to an either way offence. The justices decided that a custodial sentence was wholly inappropriate. The justices wished to impose a fine, but felt that a fine in excess of their powers (limited to £5,000 per offence in the case of either way offences) was appropriate. Accordingly, they committed the defendant to the Crown Court to be sentenced (under s 3 of the Powers of Criminal Courts (Sentencing) Act 2000). The Divisional Court held that there is no reason why justices cannot commit for sentence under s 3 if they are of the opinion that, while imprisonment would not be appropriate, the offence merits a larger fine than they have the power to impose.

Section 3(2)(b) allows committal for sentence for a violent or sexual offence (as defined in s 161 of the 2000 Act) where a longer sentence is necessary to protect the public from serious harm from the offender.

Where the defendant is committed for sentence, there is no presumption in favour of bail, as s 4 of the Bail Act 1976 does not apply. The committal may be on bail or in custody (s 3(1)); it is usually in custody, since the defendant faces a relatively long custodial sentence (*R v Coe* [1968] 1 WLR 1950; [1969] 1 All ER 65).

In *R v Manchester Justices ex p Kaymanesh* (1994) 15 Cr App R(S) 838, the Divisional Court held that magistrates should normally exercise the power to commit the defendant for sentence under s 3 only if new information came to light which was not available to the magistrates when the decision to try the case summarily was reached. However, it was held in *R v Dover Justices ex p Pamment* (1994) 15 Cr App R(S) 778, dismissing an application for judicial review of the decision of the magistrates to commit the defendant for sentence under s 3, that if the justices do exercise their power to commit a defendant for sentence under s 3 having earlier accepted jurisdiction to try the case, the exercise of that power was unfettered.

Similarly, in *R v Sheffield Crown Court ex p DPP* (1994) 15 Cr App R(S) 768, it was held that where the magistrates commit a defendant for sentence under s 3, the Crown Court usually has no power to remit the case to the magistrates' court. If the order is plainly bad on its face (for example, s 3 is invoked by the magistrates in respect of an offence which is triable only summarily), the Crown Court could remit the case to the magistrates' court, but the proper course of action is usually for the defendant to apply to the Divisional Court for judicial review.

R v Sheffield Crown Court ex p DPP and *R v Dover Justices ex p Pamment* were followed and approved in *R v North Sefton Justices ex p Marsh* (1995) 16 Cr App R(S)

401. In that case, the Divisional Court held that the discretion to commit for sentence under s 3 is unfettered. It was said that *Kaymanesh* was wrongly decided and should not be followed. It was said by the Divisional Court that the decision to commit for sentence under s 3 did not have to be based on information received by the court after the decision to try the defendant summarily. However, the court went on to say that magistrates should think carefully when deciding the appropriate mode of trial, since a defendant should be able to conclude that, once summary jurisdiction has been accepted, he will not be committed to the Crown Court on the same facts. Indeed, in the instant case, some of the information which caused the magistrates to commit for sentence had come to light after the mode of trial hearing. In *R v Southampton Magistrates' Court ex p Sansome* [1999] 1 Cr App R(S) 112, the Divisional Court confirmed that the correct approach was that set out in *ex p Marsh* (above).

The mode of trial guidelines in the *Consolidated Practice Direction* (see para V.51.3(l)) say that the magistrates should consider exercising their power to commit the defendant to the Crown Court under s 3 if information emerges during the course of the summary trial which leads them to conclude that their sentencing powers are inadequate.

In *R v Flax Burton Justices ex p Commissioners of Customs & Excise* (1996) 160 JP 481, the Divisional Court stressed the need for the justices to consider carefully whether their powers of sentencing are adequate to deal with an offence before accepting jurisdiction to try that offence.

Thus, in summary, magistrates should not normally commit a defendant for sentence under s 3 unless new information has come to light since the mode of trial decision was taken. However, if magistrates do commit a defendant for sentence on the basis of information which was already known to the court when the decision to try the case was reached, judicial review will not be granted since the magistrates have not acted beyond their powers.

The question of whether a s 3 committal can only be triggered by new information, or whether the magistrates can in effect simply change their minds about the adequacy of their sentencing powers, is now only relevant in those cases where the defendant indicates an intention to plead not guilty (or gives no indication as to plea) at the 'plea before venue' hearing. Where the defendant indicates an intention to plead guilty, he will do so in the magistrates' court, and so will be convicted by the magistrates, however serious the offence is and before the magistrates are given any information about the seriousness of the offence.

Home Office Circular 45/1997 deals with the situation where the defendant indicates a guilty plea and the magistrates, having heard the prosecution outline the brief facts of the case, immediately come to the view that their sentencing powers are insufficient to deal with the defendant. In such a case, the magistrates should allow the defence to make representations on the question of committal for sentence, or to put forward a plea in mitigation, but should not hesitate to make it clear that it is their firm intention to commit the defendant to the Crown Court for sentence. The Circular also makes the point that where the offence is obviously a serious one, a pre-sentence report will not be prepared before committal for sentence.

Guidance on several issues that may arise in this context was given by the Divisional Court in *R v Warley Magistrates' Court ex p DPP* [1999] 1 All ER 251. The court held as follows:

(a) Where a defendant indicates a guilty plea under the 'plea before venue' procedure in s 17A of the Magistrates' Courts Act 1980, the magistrates must take account of the discount to be granted for that guilty plea when deciding whether or not their sentencing powers are adequate to deal with the defendant.

(b) Where it is clear that the case is beyond the sentencing powers of the magistrates, they should be prepared to commit the defendant to the Crown Court for sentence without first seeking a pre-sentence report or hearing a plea in mitigation (although they should warn the defence that they have this in mind so that the defence can make brief representations to oppose that course of action; if the magistrates are persuaded to change their minds, the prosecutor should be given a chance to reply).

(c) In other cases, the hearing should proceed as usual; if the question of whether or not to commit for sentence remains a live issue at the end of the hearing, the court should seek representations on this issue from the prosecution and the defence.

(d) Where there is a difference between the prosecution and defence versions of the facts of the offence (a *Newton* dispute):

   (i) if the magistrates think that their sentencing powers will be adequate however the dispute is resolved, they should adopt the procedure laid down in *R v Newton* (1983) 77 Cr App R 13 (either accepting the defence version or hearing evidence and making findings of fact);

   (ii) if they think that their sentencing powers will not be adequate however the dispute is resolved, they should simply commit for sentence, leaving the Crown Court to follow the *Newton* procedure;

   (iii) if the decision whether or not to commit turns or may turn on which version is found to be correct, the magistrates should follow the *Newton* procedure; if the offender is then committed for sentence, the Crown Court should adopt the findings of fact made by the magistrates at the *Newton* hearing unless the defendant can point to some significant development, such as the discovery of important new evidence in his favour.

Where the defendant indicates a not guilty plea (or gives no indication) at the 'plea before venue' hearing, and the court decides to accept jurisdiction at the mode of trial hearing, it may be that information emerges during the summary trial which makes the offence appear more serious than it did when the magistrates accepted jurisdiction. In such a case, it is open to magistrates to continue with the trial and, if they convict the defendant, to commit him for sentence under s 3; alternatively, they can terminate the summary trial and hold committal proceedings instead, so that the trial will start again in the Crown Court (s 25(2) of the Magistrates' Courts Act 1980).

If a defendant is aggrieved at a decision to commit him for sentence to the Crown Court, there is little that can be done about it. The decision to commit for sentence could be challenged by means of judicial review, but such a challenge would only succeed if the committal were perverse (in the sense that no reasonable bench of magistrates could have decided to commit the defendant for sentence). However, the defendant may derive some comfort from two points: firstly, it is by no means inevitable that the Crown Court will in fact impose a sentence which is more severe than the sentence which the magistrates' court could have imposed; secondly, if the Crown Court does impose a sentence which is greater than the sentence the magistrates' court could have imposed, the Court of Appeal has jurisdiction to entertain an appeal against that sentence if it is in fact excessive.

One basis which has, however, been accepted for challenging the decision to commit for sentence under s 3 of the 2000 Act is where the defendant had a legitimate expectation that he would be sentenced in the magistrates' court. To succeed, the defendant has to show that there was conduct amounting to a clear and unequivocal representation that sentence would be determined by the magistrates (*R v Sheffield Magistrates' Court ex p Ojo* (2000) 164 JP 659). In *R (Rees) v Feltham Justices* [2001] 2 Cr App R(S) 1, the magistrates invited the defendant's solicitor to mitigate before them and then adjourned the matter for the preparation of a pre-sentence report without stating that committal to the Crown Court was an option still open to them; this was held to be sufficient to give rise to a legitimate expectation that the justices themselves would pass sentence.

It should be borne in mind that the power to commit for sentence, where the defendant has been convicted in the magistrates' court following a not guilty plea, will be abolished when the relevant provisions of the Criminal Justice Act 2003 come into force. There will, however, still be a power to commit for sentence where the defendant indicates a guilty plea at the 'plea before venue' hearing (see Chapter 3).

4.14.2 Procedure in the Crown Court

The Crown Court when hearing a s 3 committal comprises a Circuit judge or recorder (s 74 of the Supreme Court Act 1981).

The hearing takes the same form as the sentencing procedure in the magistrates' court, that is, the prosecution summarise the facts of the case and give details of the defendant's previous convictions (if any), followed by a defence plea in mitigation.

We have already seen that if there is a significant divergence between prosecution and defence versions, then there has to be a *Newton* hearing. In the context of a s 3 committal, if a *Newton* hearing took place at the magistrates' court, the Crown Court should adopt the outcome. If the divergence between prosecution and defence versions becomes apparent for the first time at the Crown Court (or no *Newton* hearing was held at the magistrates' court), the Crown Court should hold a *Newton* hearing to determine the issue (see *Munroe v Crown Prosecution Service* [1988] Crim LR 823).

Where the defendant is sentenced by the Crown Court following a s 3 committal, the maximum sentence which the Crown Court can impose is the same as if the defendant had just been convicted on indictment (so, the limit of six months' imprisonment for one offence, 12 months' for two or more offences, no longer applies) (s 5 of the Powers of Criminal Courts (Sentencing) Act 2000).

Some sentences depend on the age of the offender (for example, imprisonment is only possible if the defendant has attained the age of 21). If the defendant's age has changed between the date he was committed for sentence under s 3 and the date the Crown Court passes sentence, he will be dealt with according to his age at the date of his Crown Court appearance (*Robinson* [1962] Crim LR 47).

4.14.3 Committal for breach of Crown Court order

The second form of committal for sentence is where a magistrates' court has convicted a defendant of any offence committed during the currency of a suspended sentence or a community order or conditional discharge imposed by the Crown Court. In such a case, the magistrates' court can commit the defendant to be dealt with by the Crown Court for the breach of the Crown Court order (which may mean the Crown Court re-sentencing the defendant for the offence originally dealt with by the Crown Court). The relevant provisions in the Powers of Criminal Courts (Sentencing) Act 2000 are: s 13(5) (breach of Crown Court conditional discharge); s 116(3)(b) (offence during period of early release from prison sentence imposed by Crown Court); s 120(2) (breach of Crown Court suspended sentence); para 4(4) of Sched 3 (breach of Crown Court community orders).

Where the offender is committed for sentence because he is in breach of a Crown Court order, the Crown Court comprises a judge sitting alone.

4.14.4 Section 4 of the Powers of Criminal Courts (Sentencing) Act 2000

Section 4 of the Powers of Criminal Courts (Sentencing) Act 2000 provides as follows:

(1) This section applies where—

    (a) a person aged 18 or over appears or is brought before a magistrates' court ('the court') on an information charging him with an offence triable either way ('the offence');

    (b) he or his representative indicates that he would plead guilty if the offence were to proceed to trial; and

    (c) … the court convicts him of the offence.

(2) If the court has committed the offender to the Crown Court for trial for one or more related offences, that is to say, one or more offences which, in its opinion, are related to the offence, it may commit him in custody or on bail to the Crown Court to be dealt with in respect of the offence in accordance with section 5(1) below.

…

(4) Where the court—

    (a) under sub-section (2) above commits the offender to the Crown Court to be dealt with in respect of the offence, and

    (b) does not state that, in its opinion, it also has power so to commit him under section 3(2) above,

    section 5(1) below shall not apply unless he is convicted before the Crown Court of one or more of the related offences.

(5) Where section 5(1) below does not apply, the Crown Court may deal with the offender in respect of the offence in any way in which the magistrates' court could deal with him if it had just convicted him of the offence.

(6) Where the court commits a person under sub-section (2) above, section 6 below (which enables a magistrates' court, where it commits a person under this section in respect of an offence, also to commit him to the Crown Court to be dealt with in respect of certain other offences) shall apply accordingly.

(7)   For the purposes of this section one offence is related to another if, were they both to be prosecuted on indictment, the charges for them could be joined in the same indictment.

The effect of s 4(1) and (2) is that, where the defendant has indicated that he will plead guilty to an either way offence (and so is deemed to have pleaded guilty to it) and he is also committed for trial for one or more related offences, the magistrates may commit him to the Crown Court for sentence in respect of the either way offence to which he has pleaded guilty. For the purposes of these provisions, one offence is related to another if the charges for them could be joined (under r 9 of the Indictment Rules 1971) in the same indictment if both were to be tried in the Crown Court (s 4(7)). So, the two charges must be founded on the same facts or must be a series (or part of a series) of offences of the same or similar character.

Section 4(4) provides that, where the justices have committed a defendant for sentence pursuant to s 4(2), the Crown Court can only exceed the sentencing powers of the magistrates' court in respect of the either way offence to which the defendant indicated a plea of guilty if either:

(a) the magistrates stated that they considered their sentencing powers were inadequate to deal with the defendant for that offence (and so they also had power to commit him for sentence under s 3); or

(b) he is also convicted by the Crown Court of one or more of the related offences.

The relationship between ss 3 and 4 of the Powers of Criminal Courts (Sentencing) Act 2000 may seem rather confusing. The purpose of s 4 is to ensure that if the defendant is to be tried in the Crown Court for an offence which is related to an offence to which the defendant has indicated a guilty plea at the 'plea before venue' hearing, then the magistrates can commit him to the Crown Court for sentence for that latter offence even if their sentencing powers are adequate to deal with that offence (and so a committal under s 3 would be inappropriate).

If the magistrates take the view that their sentencing powers are adequate to deal with the offence in respect of which the defendant has indicated a guilty plea, then only s 4 allows the justices to commit the defendant to the Crown Court for sentence for that offence. On the other hand, if the magistrates take the view that their sentencing powers are not adequate to deal with that offence, they have two options: they can either commit him for sentence for that offence under s 3, or they can commit him for sentence under s 4 but indicate that they took the view that their sentencing powers were inadequate and so could have invoked s 3.

Obviously, the best practice will be to use s 3 where the magistrates' sentencing powers are not adequate and to use s 4 where their powers are adequate. In any event, Home Office Circular 45/1997 says that, when committing a defendant for sentence, the court should state whether it is doing so under s 3 or s 4. If the magistrates use s 4 but do not consider that their sentencing powers are adequate to deal with the offence, they should state (under s 4(4)) that they also had the power to commit the defendant for sentence under s 3, so as to avoid inadvertently fettering the powers of the Crown Court when dealing with the offence.

4.14.5 Section 6 of the Powers of Criminal Courts (Sentencing) Act 2000

Section 6 of the Powers of Criminal Courts (Sentencing) Act 2000 provides as follows:

(1)   This section applies where a magistrates' court ('the committing court') commits a person in custody or on bail to the Crown Court under any enactment mentioned in sub-section (4) below to be sentenced or otherwise dealt with in respect of an offence ('the relevant offence').

(2)   Where this section applies and the relevant offence is an indictable offence, the committing court may also commit the offender, in custody or on bail as the case may require, to the Crown Court to be dealt with in respect of any other offence whatsoever in respect of which the committing court has power to deal with him (being an offence of which he has been convicted by that or any other court).

(3)   Where this section applies and the relevant offence is a summary offence, the committing court may commit the offender, in custody or on bail as the case may require, to the Crown Court to be dealt with in respect of—

(a)   any other offence of which the committing court has convicted him, being either—

(i)   an offence punishable with imprisonment; or

(ii) an offence in respect of which the committing court has a power or duty to order him to be disqualified under section 34, 35 or 36 of the Road Traffic Offenders Act 1988 (disqualification for certain motoring offences); or

(b)   any suspended sentence in respect of which the committing court has under section 120(1) below power to deal with him.

(4)   The enactments referred to in sub-section (1) above are—

...

(b)   sections 3 and 4 above (committal for sentence for offences triable either way);

(c)   section 13(5) below (conditionally discharged person convicted of further offence);

(d)   section 116(3)(b) below (offender convicted of offence committed during currency of original sentence); and

(e)   section 120(2) below (offender convicted during operational period of suspended sentence).

In summary, s 6 provides that where the magistrates have exercised any of the following powers of committal:

• under s 3 of the 2000 Act; or

• under s 4 of the 2000 Act; or

• under s 13(5) of the 2000 Act (breach of Crown Court conditional discharge); or

• under s 116(3)(b) of the 2000 Act (offence during early release period of Crown Court prison sentence); or

• under s 120(2) of the 2000 Act (offence during operational period of Crown Court suspended sentence),

then they may also commit the defendant to the Crown Court to be sentenced for any other offence that the magistrates' court could sentence him for.

Therefore, if the defendant is committed to the Crown Court under s 3 of the 2000 Act for a triable either way offence, he can also be committed under s 6 of the Act in respect of any summary offence of which he has been convicted on the same occasion.

Similarly, if the defendant is committed to the Crown Court to be dealt with for the breach of a particular Crown Court order (see above), he can also be committed to be dealt with for the offence which gave rise to the breach.

Two examples may assist in illustrating the scope of s 6 of the 2000 Act:

(a) The defendant is charged with theft (triable either way) and common assault (a summary offence) and the magistrates convict him of both charges. The magistrates decide that their sentencing powers are inadequate to deal with the theft and so they commit the defendant to the Crown Court in respect of that offence under s 3 of the 2000 Act. This section does not apply to summary offences and so cannot be used to enable the magistrates to commit the defendant to the Crown Court for the common assault. However, s 6 of the 2000 Act enables the magistrates to commit the defendant to the Crown Court for the common assault, and so the Crown Court can sentence him for both offences.

(b) The defendant is charged with theft. The theft is a very minor offence and so the magistrates cannot invoke s 3 of the 2000 Act (since their sentencing powers are plainly adequate to deal with the theft). However, the defendant committed the theft while he was subject to a suspended sentence of imprisonment imposed by the Crown Court. If the magistrates want the Crown Court to deal with the defendant for the theft as well as dealing with him for the breach of the suspended sentence, they can commit him to the Crown Court under s 120(2) of the Act in respect of the suspended sentence and under s 6 of the Act in respect of the theft.

The sentencing powers of the Crown Court in respect of offences committed under s 6 are the same as those of the magistrates' court (s 7(1)). This is because the purpose of s 6 is for the defendant to be sentenced by one court in respect of all outstanding matters, not to increase the sentence which may be imposed.

4.15 TRANSFER OF CASES BETWEEN MAGISTRATES' COURTS

The Courts Act 2003 makes it easier to transfer criminal proceedings between magistrates' courts. Section 3B of the Magistrates' Courts Act 1980 (inserted by the Access to Justice Act 1999) enabled either the prosecution or the defence to apply to have a summary case transferred to a magistrates' court in another commission area. This provision has not been brought into force, and s 46(2) of the Courts Act 2003 repeals it and provides instead that the court, either on the application of one of the parties or at its own motion, may transfer a criminal case at any stage in the proceedings. Section 46(1) achieves this by inserting a new section, s 27A, into the 1980 Act. This new section provides as follows:

Power to transfer criminal proceedings

(1) Where a person appears or is brought before a magistrates' court—

(a) to be tried by the court for an offence, or

(b) for the court to inquire into the offence as examining justices,

the court may transfer the matter to another magistrates' court.

(2) The court may transfer the matter before or after beginning the trial or inquiry.

(3) But if the court transfers the matter after it has begun to hear the evidence and the parties, the court to which the matter is transferred must begin hearing the evidence and the parties again.

(4) The power of the court under this section to transfer any matter must be exercised in accordance with any directions given under section 30(3) of the Courts Act 2003.

Thus, s 46 enables magistrates' courts to transfer criminal cases to other magistrates' courts at any stage in the proceedings. It is submitted that this power may be exercised either on the application of the prosecution or the defence, or of the court's own motion (in the latter case the court should listen to representations from the parties before transferring the case to another court).

Furthermore, s 10 of the Powers of Criminal Courts (Sentencing) Act 2000 provides that, if one magistrates' court convicts a defendant and then discovers that he has been convicted of another offence at another magistrates' court but has not yet been sentenced, he may be remitted to that other court to be sentenced for both offences so long as:

- the offence being remitted is imprisonable or carries disqualification from driving; and

- the other court consents.

Section 27A(4) of the Magistrates' Courts Act 1980 requires the court to have regard to any directions given under s 30(3) of the Courts Act 2003, which empowers the Lord Chancellor (with the concurrence of the Lord Chief Justice) to give directions as to the distribution and transfer of magistrates' courts business. Where a person is charged with an offence, the prosecution decide which court that person should appear before and this decision will have to take account of any directions issued under s 30(3). It is likely that the directions will stipulate that the defendant should be taken to a court in a local justice area either where the offence is alleged to have been committed, where the accused resides or where any witnesses reside.

CHAPTER 5

JUVENILE OFFENDERS – THE YOUTH COURT

5.1 INTRODUCTION

In this chapter, we look at the way in which young offenders are dealt with by the courts. We examine the jurisdiction of the youth court and also what happens if the juvenile has committed a very serious offence or is jointly charged with an adult offender.

The powers of the courts to deal with young offenders are a matter of considerable political importance. In the Home Office Consultation Paper, *Preventing Children Offending*, Chapter 1 (www.homeoffice.gov.uk/docs/prev1.html), the government worked on the assumption that 20% of all offences are committed by juveniles (para 10). Added to this, 'Some of the worries that people have about crime are underpinned by the threat of juvenile crime, and by unruly juvenile behaviour' (para 9). In the Home Office Consultation Paper *Tackling Youth Crime* (www.homeoffice.gov.uk/docs/tyc.html), it was pointed out that:

> Youth crime is one of the most serious problems facing England and Wales today. Young offenders can wreck their chances of leading worthwhile and fulfilled adult lives and they can wreck the lives of those whom they victimise.

> Involvement in offending and drug use amongst young people is widespread – one in two males and one in three females admitted to committing offences and the same number admitted using drugs at some time, though most offending is infrequent and minor. We know that a disproportionate amount of crime is committed by a hard core of persistent young offenders, with about 3% of offenders responsible for 25% of offences.

A detailed Consultation Paper was issued by the Home Office in November 1997. It was entitled *No More Excuses – A New Approach to Tackling Youth Crime in England and Wales* (Cmnd 3809). It begins by setting out the importance of youth crime, referring to Home Office research that showed that, among 14–25 year olds, one in two males and one in three females admitted to having committed an offence and to statistics from 1996 showing that, for offenders convicted or cautioned for an indictable offence, 10–15 year olds accounted for around 14% of known offenders, and 10–17 year olds account for around 25% (para 1.1). In other words, young people commit a disproportionate amount of crime. The Paper went on to note that it is a 'small hard core of persistent offenders' who are responsible for that disproportionate amount of crime. Paragraph 1.2 refers to Home Office research showing that about 3% of young offenders commit 26% of youth crime.

Paragraph 1.5 of the Consultation Paper sets out what are perceived to be the key factors related to youth criminality, namely:

- being male;
- being brought up by a criminal parent or parents;
- living in a family with multiple problems;
- experiencing poor parenting and lack of supervision;
- poor discipline in the family and at school;

- playing truant or being excluded from school;
- associating with delinquent friends; and
- having siblings who offend.

Paragraph 1.6 highlights 'two important influences', namely 'persistent school truancy and associating with offenders', but concludes that 'the single most important factor in explaining criminality is the quality of a young person's home life, including parental supervision'.

The Paper goes on to consider whether there is a need for active intervention, or whether juveniles will simply grow out of their offending behaviour. It says that:

> 1.9 A prevailing assumption behind youth justice policy has been the idea that youngsters will grow out of their offending behaviour. For many young offenders it is true that their first caution – or court appearance is enough to divert them from crime. But this assumption is wide of the mark when it comes to the hard core of persistent offenders who cause so much crime.
>
> 1.10 While many young offenders do grow out of their delinquent behaviour, research shows that this happens less markedly and far more slowly for young men than young women. For young men, the positive effects of personal and social development completing education, getting a job, leaving home, settling down with a partner – tend to be outweighed by the more powerful influences of the peer group and siblings. Desistance from offending is even less likely for young male offenders involved in regular drug or alcohol misuse.
>
> ...
>
> 1.13 We know that those who start committing offences at an early age are more likely to become serious and persistent offenders. So the Government's youth justice reforms will focus efforts on preventing offending, on early and effective intervention to stop children and young people being drawn into crime and, if they are, to halt their offending before it escalates.

It is doubtless because of concern over the level of youth crime that s 37(1) of the Crime and Disorder Act provides that 'It shall be the principal aim of the youth justice system to prevent offending by children and young persons'.

Section 37(2) goes on to require that: 'In addition to any other duty to which they are subject, it shall be the duty of all persons and bodies carrying out functions in relation to the youth justice system to have regard to that aim.'

However, s 44(1) of the Children and Young Persons Act 1933 provides that:

> Every court in dealing with a child or young person who is brought before it, either as an offender or otherwise, shall have regard to the welfare of the child or young person and shall in a proper case take steps for removing him from undesirable surroundings, and for securing that proper provision is made for his education and training.

5.2   TERMINOLOGY

The youth court has jurisdiction to deal with juvenile offenders, that is, offenders aged 10–17 years (inclusive). 10–13 year olds are called 'children' and 14–17 year olds are called 'young persons'. This distinction is relevant as sentencing powers differ to some extent according to whether the juvenile is a child or a young person.

The youth court has jurisdiction where the offender is under 18. The choice of the age of 17 as the cut-off point is in some senses arbitrary. In the *Review of Delay in the Criminal Justice System*, Martin Narey (in Chapter 8, 'Managing the Youth Court') (www.homeoffice.gov.uk/docs/crimrev8.html) suggests that 17 year olds should be dealt with by the adult court (a recommendation that was not accepted by the government). He points out that:

> ... when the youth court replaced juvenile courts in October 1992, the age limit was raised from 17 to 18 on the basis that 16 and 17 year olds ought to be treated in the same way as 'near adults'. Almost everyone I have spoken to has agreed that defendants of 17, who were previously dealt with by magistrates' courts, are unsuitable for the jurisdiction of the youth court, where they now account for a third of all cases. They tend to be experienced as offenders (about 60 per cent of 17 year olds before the youth court have previous convictions, compared with about 50 per cent of 16 year olds and 45 per cent of 15 year olds) and, I am told, they are often disruptive and unco-operative. There certainly are 17 year olds whose immaturity makes them suitable for the youth court, just as there are defendants of 16 for whom the adult court would be the proper forum. But a line has to be drawn, and in my view it should be the 17th rather than the 18th birthday. 17 year olds already count as adults at the police station, where they can be questioned without the presence of an adult; and they remain the responsibility of the Probation Service, who otherwise deal only with adult offenders. I therefore recommend that 17 year olds should be returned to the jurisdiction of the adult court ... The removal of this large group of relatively serious and troublesome offenders would enable the youth court to concentrate on dealing more promptly and effectively with children up to school leaving age.

5.3   THE AGE OF CRIMINAL RESPONSIBILITY

There is an irrebuttable presumption that a person who is under the age of 10 cannot be guilty of a criminal offence. There used to be a rebuttable presumption that a child aged between 10 and 14 was incapable of committing an offence. This presumption was, however, abolished by s 34 of the Crime and Disorder Act 1998.

In Part 1 of the Home Office Consultation Paper *Tackling Youth Crime* (www.homeoffice.gov.uk/docs/tyc.html), the government dealt with this presumption, often called *doli incapax*, that children under 14 did not know the difference between right and wrong (and therefore were incapable of committing a crime) unless the prosecution were able to prove that they did have this understanding. Hence, a child aged under 14 could only be convicted of a criminal offence if the presumption of *doli incapax* was first rebutted. To rebut the presumption, the prosecution had to adduce evidence to prove that the child knew that what he was doing was seriously wrong, rather than simply naughty.

In *C v DPP* [1996] AC 1, the House of Lords had ruled that the doctrine of *doli incapax* remained part of English law (allowing an appeal from the Divisional Court, which held that it no longer formed part of the law). However, the House of Lords recommended that Parliament should review this presumption. Three main arguments were put forward (in the Consultation Paper) by the government in favour of reform, namely that the presumption was:

• archaic;

• illogical; and

• unfair in practice.

It was believed to be *archaic* on the grounds that the notion that the average 10-13 year old did not know right from wrong seemed contrary to common sense in an age of compulsory education from the age of five and that the doctrine developed at a time when punishments were much harsher (whereas now the emphasis is as much on preventing re-offending as on punishment for the crime).

The presumption was thought to be *illogical* since, in practice, the presumption could be rebutted if the prosecution produced evidence that the child was of normal mental development for his age. However, the doctrine itself presumed that children of that age normally did not know right from wrong, so to rebut the presumption by proving the child's normality was logically inconsistent.

The presumption was said to be *unfair in practice*, in that it placed a very heavy burden on the prosecution to provide the evidence necessary to show that a child knew his act was seriously wrong. To rebut the presumption, the prosecution had to produce evidence separate from the facts of the offence (for example, evidence of the child's response to police questioning, or reports from his teachers or from an educational psychologist). There was authority that previous findings of guilt could be used as evidence that the child knew right from wrong, but if this evidence were adduced, different magistrates would have to try the case.

The government noted that discontinuance of a case because of insufficient evidence to rebut the presumption was not in the young offender's best interests, since it could mean that an opportunity to take appropriate action to prevent re-offending was missed.

The government considered two options for reform: outright abolition of the presumption (so that young defendants aged 10–17 would all be treated in the same way) or reversal of the presumption (so that the court would start with the presumption that a child aged 10–13 was capable of forming criminal intent but that child would be acquitted if the defence adduced evidence that the child did not know that what they did was seriously wrong and the prosecution were unable to show beyond reasonable doubt that the child did indeed know that the action was seriously wrong). The option taken by the government in the Crime and Disorder Act 1998 was outright abolition of the presumption.

However, it remains the case that there is a conclusive presumption that a child under 10 cannot commit an offence and so is outside the jurisdiction of the criminal courts. Note, however, that if a child is beyond the control of her parents and is therefore at risk of harm, a family proceedings court can make a care or supervision order under s 31 of the Children Act 1989.

5.4   JUVENILES AND BAIL

The Bail Act 1976 (with the presumption in favour of bail) applies to juveniles.

The criteria for granting bail are virtually the same as for adults. Two differences are that a juvenile can be refused bail where this is necessary for his own welfare (not just if necessary for her own protection, as is the case with adults) and that a parent or guardian may be asked to act as a surety not only for the juvenile's attendance at court (the function of the surety in the case of adult defendants) but also for compliance with any other conditions of bail which the court may impose (s 3(7) of the Bail Act 1976).

The most significant difference between adults and juveniles is in what happens to a juvenile under the age of 17 if bail is withheld, whether before or after conviction.

Where a juvenile is refused bail, they are remanded to local authority accommodation unless the criteria laid down in s 23(5) of the Children and Young Persons Act 1969 (set out below) are satisfied.

Section 23(7) provides that where a juvenile is remanded to local authority accommodation, the court can impose such conditions as it would be able to impose on an adult offender under s 3(6) of the Bail Act 1976. These conditions can include electronic monitoring under s 23AA of the Act. Section 23A of the Children and Young Persons Act 1969 provides that where a juvenile has been remanded to local authority accommodation and conditions have been imposed under s 23(7), the juvenile may be arrested without a warrant if the police have reasonable grounds for suspecting that the youngster has broken any of the conditions.

Under s 23(5), all remands of juveniles who are not granted bail are to local authority accommodation. However, the court is empowered (after consultation with the local authority) to require the local authority to place and keep the juvenile in 'secure accommodation' (run by the local authority). The power to impose such a security requirement is confined to cases where the juvenile has attained the age of 15, and:

(a) either:

    (i)   he is charged with or has been convicted of a violent or sexual offence or an offence punishable in the case of an adult offender with at least 14 years' imprisonment; or

    (ii)   he has a recent history of absconding while remanded to local authority accommodation, and is charged with or has been convicted of an imprisonable offence alleged or found to have been committed while he was so remanded; and

(b) the court is of the opinion that imposing a security requirement is the only way to protect the public from serious harm from the juvenile.

In deciding whether the public needs to be protected from the juvenile, it is necessary for the court to assess the risk of serious harm to the public by reference to the nature of the offences in respect of which the young person has been charged or convicted, and the manner in which these offences have been carried out (or are alleged to have been carried out if the defendant has not yet been convicted); it is not enough to consider only the risk that such offences might be repeated (*R v Croydon Youth Court ex p G (A Minor)* (1995) *The Times*, 3 May).

5.5   YOUTH COURTS

A youth court must consist of justices from the youth court panel, which comprises a number of magistrates who have received extra training to equip them to deal with juveniles (r 11 of the Youth Court (Constitution) Rules 1954; Sched 2 to the Children and Young Persons Act 1933).

Rule 12(1) of the 1954 Rules provides that 'each youth court shall consist of either: (a) a District Judge (Magistrates' Courts) sitting alone; or (b) not more than three justices who shall include a man and a woman'. Rule 12(2) says that:

If at any sitting of a youth court other than one constituted in accordance with paragraph (1)(a) of this rule [ie, a District judge sitting alone] no man or no woman is available owing to circumstances unforeseen when the justices to sit were chosen under rule 11 of these Rules, or if the only man or woman present cannot properly sit as a member of the court, and in any such case the other members of the panel present think it inexpedient in the interests of justice for there to be an adjournment, the court may be constituted without a man or, as the case may be, without a woman.

Thus, where the youth court comprises a bench of lay magistrates, there should be no more than three justices and there should (unless a properly constituted court is not available and it is inexpedient to adjourn) be at least one male and one female. In *R v Birmingham Justices ex p F* (2000) 164 JP 523, only two male magistrates were available to sit in the youth court. Both parties were legally represented and no issue was taken by the parties as to the constitution of the court. The Divisional Court held that the proceedings were a nullity; the justices should have invited representations from the parties; the defendant's conviction was quashed and a re-trial ordered.

The distinction between indictable, triable either way and summary offences does not apply to juvenile defendants. Thus, a bench of justices in the youth court may try an offence which, in the case of an adult defendant, would be triable only in the Crown Court. Furthermore, a juvenile has no right to elect Crown Court trial in any case where an adult defendant would have such a right. The justices in the youth court may, however, decline jurisdiction in respect of certain indictable offences.

Section 50 of the Courts Act 2003 sets out a new framework under which lay magistrates and District judges are to be authorised to hear youth court cases. The Act also enables the higher judiciary (including circuit judges and recorders) to hear these cases, without particular authorisation; this occurs as a result of the extension of their jurisdiction, by s 66 of the Act, to include that of a District judge (magistrates' courts).

Currently, lay magistrates who sit in youth courts do so because they are members of the specialist youth court 'panel'. Under s 50, the 'panel' system is to be abolished. Instead, the Lord Chancellor will have to authorise a lay justice or District judge before he can sit in the youth court. These personal authorisations will be valid throughout England and Wales, reflecting the new national jurisdiction conferred on magistrates. Regulations will be published dealing with the allocation and removal of authorisations for justices and District judges to sit as members of youth courts, the appointment of chairmen of youth courts, and the composition of youth courts.

District judges will continue to be empowered to sit in youth courts. However, to quote from the Explanatory Notes that accompany the Act, 'because of the often sensitive nature of youth cases, and the specific knowledge and understanding that is required, these rules [will] help to ensure that only trained and suitable magistrates (or District Judges (Magistrates' Courts)) sit on youth courts'.

Section 50(1) of the Courts Act 2003 substitutes a new version of s 45 of the Children and Young Persons Act 1933, dealing with the constitution of youth courts. The new s 45 provides as follows:

Youth courts

(1) Magistrates' courts—

    (a) constituted in accordance with this section or section 66 of the Courts Act 2003 (judges having powers of District Judges (Magistrates' Courts)), and

(b) sitting for the purpose of—

    (i)   hearing any charge against a child or young person, or

    (ii) exercising any other jurisdiction conferred on youth courts by or under this or any other Act,

    are to be known as youth courts.

(2)   A justice of the peace is not qualified to sit as a member of a youth court for the purpose of dealing with any proceedings unless he has an authorisation extending to the proceedings.

(3)   He has an authorisation extending to the proceedings only if he has been authorised by the Lord Chancellor or a person acting on his behalf to sit as a member of a youth court to deal with—

    (a) proceedings of that description, or

    (b) all proceedings dealt with by youth courts.

(4)   The Lord Chancellor may by rules make provision about—

    (a) the grant and revocation of authorisations,

    (b) the appointment of chairmen of youth courts, and

    (c) the composition of youth courts.

Section 50(2) of the 2003 Act repeals Sched 2 to the 1933 Act (constitution of youth courts) and sub-s (3) repeals s 146 of the Magistrates' Courts Act 1980 (rules relating to youth court panels and the composition of youth courts).

Under s 66 of the Courts Act 2003, a Crown Court judge will be able to make orders, and to pass sentence, in relation to cases normally reserved to magistrates' courts when disposing of related cases in the Crown Court. This would appear to mean (although this possibility is not mentioned in the Explanatory Notes that accompany the Act) that, in particularly difficult or sensitive cases, a senior judge could sit (as a magistrate) in the youth court. The fact that long-term detention (s 91 of the Powers of Criminal Courts (Sentencing) Act 2000) of offenders under the age of 18 is confined to cases where the offender was convicted on indictment means that serious cases involving juveniles will, in any event, continue to be tried in the Crown Court.

5.6   DIFFERENCES BETWEEN THE YOUTH COURT AND ADULT MAGISTRATES' COURT

There is less formality in the youth court than in an adult magistrates' court. For example:

- the juvenile sits on a chair, not in a dock, and usually has a parent or guardian sitting nearby;
- the juvenile and any juvenile witnesses are addressed by their first names;
- the oath taken by witnesses is to promise (not swear) to tell the truth;
- the terminology differs slightly, for example, a 'finding of guilt' (not a 'conviction') and an 'order made upon a finding of guilt' (not a 'sentence'). Note, however, that the juvenile pleads 'guilty' or 'not guilty'.

5.6.1   Exclusion of the public

The public are excluded from the courtroom under s 47(2) of the Children and Young Persons Act 1933, which provides that:

> No person shall be present at any sitting of a [youth court] except—
>
> (a)   members and officers of the court;
>
> (b)   parties to the case before the court, their solicitors and counsel, and witnesses and other persons directly concerned in that case;
>
> (c)   *bona fide* representatives of newspapers or news agencies [news gathering or reporting organisations];
>
> (d)   such other persons as the court may specially authorise to be present.

Thus, the only people entitled to be present in the youth court apart from the accused, the parents and the justices and their clerk are:

- the lawyers representing the juvenile or the prosecution in the present case; the lawyers cannot enter the courtroom if a case they are appearing in is not yet being dealt with;
- court officials (for example, the usher);
- reporters (but note the reporting restrictions set out below);
- probation officers and social workers;
- witnesses giving evidence (and they are allowed to remain in court once they have given evidence);
- anyone else directly concerned in the case;
- anyone whom the magistrates allow to be present (for example, law students).

Note that if a juvenile is appearing as an accused, or as a witness, in the adult magistrates' court or the Crown Court, the public have the right to be present unless the court takes the exceptional step of sitting *in camera*.

5.7   REPORTING RESTRICTIONS

Section 49 of the Children and Young Persons Act 1933 imposes automatic reporting restrictions. This section applies to newspaper reports and to broadcast programmes (s 49(3)). Section 49(1)(a) prevents the publication of material that 'reveals the name, address or school of any child or young person concerned in the proceedings or includes any particulars likely to lead to the identification of any child or young person concerned in the proceedings'. Thus, the essence of the restrictions is that details should not be published or broadcast which would enable the accused, or any juvenile witness in the case, to be identified. Section 49(1)(b) provides that no picture of the accused, or of any juvenile witness, shall be published or broadcast.

Breach of these reporting restrictions is punishable, on summary conviction, by a fine not exceeding level 5 (£5,000): s 49(9).

In *DPP v Todd* [2003] EWHC 2408; (2004) 168 JP 194, the defendant was convicted and sentenced in the youth court. During the course of those proceedings, he attained the age of 18. The justices ruled that s 49 no longer applied, since the defendant was no longer aged under 18. It was held by the Divisional Court that a defendant in proceedings before the youth court ceases to benefit from the reporting restrictions contained in s 49 as soon as he attains the age of 18. The specific purpose of s 49, said the court, is to protect children and young persons from adverse publicity. Such restrictions are an exception to the general right to report proceedings, and so should be interpreted narrowly. The fact that a person had been a young person at the commencement of proceedings could not, said the court, justify such a person continuing to benefit from s 49 once he has ceased to be a young person.

5.7.1 Lifting the restrictions

The court has a discretion to lift the restrictions if it is appropriate to do so in order to avoid injustice (for instance, where the defence wish to make an appeal for potential witnesses to come forward). Under s 49(5)(a), the court may dispense to any specified extent with the requirements of s 49 in relation to the accused or a juvenile witness, if it is satisfied that it is 'appropriate to do so for the purpose of avoiding injustice to the child or young person'.

Furthermore, s 49(5)(b) provides that the court may dispense to any specified extent with the requirements of s 49 in respect of a child or young person who is 'unlawfully at large' (for example, the juvenile was granted bail but has absconded), and the court is satisfied that it is 'necessary to dispense with those requirements for the purpose of apprehending him and bringing him before a court or returning him to the place in which he was in custody'. This provision only applies to a child or young person who is charged with, or has been convicted of, a violent or sexual offence, or an offence punishable (in the case of an adult) with imprisonment for 14 years or more. This power can only be exercised following an application by or on behalf of the Director of Public Prosecutions (DPP) (which includes applications by the Crown Prosecution Service (CPS)); the juvenile's legal representative must be given notice of the application (s 49(7)).

The power to lift the reporting restrictions may be exercised by a single justice (s 49(8)).

Under s 49(4A) of the Children and Young Persons Act 1933, the court, if it is satisfied that it would be in the public interest to do so, may order that restrictions on the publication of reports of proceedings in a youth court be lifted in relation to a child or young person who has been convicted of an offence. The parties to the proceedings must be given an opportunity to make representations before such an order is made (s 49(4B)).

In *McKerry v Teesdale Justices* (2000) 164 JP 355, the Divisional Court noted that there was a tension between the juvenile's right to privacy and the 'hallowed principle that justice is administered in public, open to full and fair reporting of the proceedings in court'. Lord Bingham CJ stressed that the power to dispense with anonymity must be exercised with very great care, caution and circumspection. The statutory provisions on the welfare of juveniles involved in criminal proceedings, and on the imposition and removal of reporting restrictions in such cases, have to be read against the background of international law and practice on the topic. It would be wholly wrong, for example, for a court to dispense with a young person's *prima facie* right to anonymity as an additional punishment. The court added that it was very difficult to see any place for 'naming and shaming'. The court has to be satisfied that the statutory criterion, that it is in the public interest to dispense with the reporting restrictions, is satisfied. That will very rarely be the case, and the court making such an order must set out clearly why it is in the public interest to dispense with the restrictions. The Divisional Court also held that, in weighing up the public interest, it is open to the court to hear representations from a representative of the press (even from a reporter present in court, who will of course have no formal right of audience).

5.7.2   Juveniles appearing in adult courts

If a juvenile appears in the adult magistrates' court (or the Crown Court), there are no reporting restrictions to prevent the reporting of the identity of the juvenile unless such restrictions are ordered by the court under s 39 of the Children and Young Persons Act 1933. Again, breach of an order under s 39 is punishable with a fine not exceeding level 5 (£5,000).

In *R v Central Criminal Court ex p S* (1999) 163 JP 776, the Divisional Court held that there has to be a good reason for making an order under s 39 preventing identification of a juvenile who appears before an adult court. The court said that in deciding whether or not to make such an order, the weight which the court should attach to the various factors relevant to the decision might be different at differing stages of the proceedings. For example, after the juvenile has been convicted, it might be appropriate to place greater weight on the interest of the public in knowing the identity of those who have committed serious crimes.

In *Briffet & Bradshaw v DPP* (2002) 166 JP 841, a newspaper editor appealed against his conviction for an offence under s 39 after publishing information about a juvenile in breach of an order imposing reporting restrictions. It was held that a person would only be guilty of an offence under s 39 if the terms of the order imposing reporting restrictions are clear and unambiguous: the order must leave no doubt in the mind of a reasonable reader as to precisely what it is that is prohibited. The court added that the making of a s 39 order is only justified if Art 10 of the European Convention on Human Rights is complied with, in the sense that the restriction of free expression is required to meet a pressing social need.

In *R v Tyne Tees TV Ltd* (1997) *The Times*, 20 October, the defendant published material in breach of an order under s 39 of the Children and Young Persons Act 1933. The judge dealt with this as a contempt of court. The Court of Appeal said that the proper course would have been for the judge to report the matter so that proceedings for the summary offence created by s 39 could be taken, not to treat it as a contempt of court.

The court has the power to lift the restrictions imposed under s 39 of the 1933 Act. So, after a s 39 order has been made, it is open to the court to discharge the order. In *R v Central Criminal Court ex p S*, the Divisional Court declined to follow *R v Leicester Crown Court ex p S* (1992) 94 Cr App R 153 and held that it is not the case that a s 39 order should only be discharged in rare and exceptional circumstances.

5.8   ATTENDANCE OF PARENT OR GUARDIAN

Section 34A(1) of the Children and Young Persons Act 1933 provides that if the juvenile is under 16, the court *must* (or if the juvenile is 16 or 17 the court *may*) require a parent or guardian 'to attend at the court during all the stages of the proceedings, unless and to the extent that the court is satisfied that it would be unreasonable to require such attendance, having regard to the circumstances of the case'. This was intended by the government, at least in part, to underline parental responsibility for the wrong-doings of their children. Where the child is in local authority care, he will be accompanied by a local authority social worker or foster parent (see s 34A(2)).

If the juvenile is not legally represented, the parent or guardian may assist in the conduct of the defence, for example, in cross-examination of prosecution witnesses (see r 5 of the Magistrates' Courts (Children and Young Persons) Rules 1992).

5.9   YOUTH COURT TRIAL PROCEDURE

Apart from the attempt to make the atmosphere less forbidding, the procedure for a trial in the youth court is the same as the procedure for summary trial in the adult magistrates' court.

5.10   PROCEDURE FOR SENTENCING JUVENILES

Under r 10(2)(a) of the Magistrates' Courts (Children and Young Persons) Rules 1992, before passing sentence on a juvenile (whether the juvenile was found guilty or pleaded guilty), the court must give a parent or guardian the chance to address the court; under r 10(2)(b), the court must consider all available information as to the juvenile's general conduct, home surroundings, school record and medical history. If such information is not available, the court should consider adjourning the case to enable such information to be produced.

There will usually be a pre-sentence report (written by a social worker, rather than a probation officer, as would be the case for an adult offender) and also a school report.

The contents of the reports do not have to be read out in court (and usually will not be read out). If they are read out, r 10(2)(e) provides that if the court considers it necessary in the interests of the juvenile, it may require him or his parent or guardian, if present, to withdraw from the court. However, under r 10(3), the court is required to arrange for copies of any written report before the court to be made available to the juvenile's legal representative, to a parent or guardian if present at the hearing, and to the juvenile (unless the court decides that it would be impracticable to disclose the report to the juvenile, having regard to his age and understanding or that it would be undesirable to do so having regard to potential serious harm which might thereby be suffered by him). Under r 10(4), if the juvenile is not legally represented and a particular report is not made available to him and has been considered by the court without being read aloud, or the juvenile or the parent/guardian have been required to withdraw from the court, then the juvenile must be told 'the substance of any part of the information given to the court bearing on his character or conduct which the court considers to be material to the manner in which the case should be dealt with unless it appears to it impracticable so to do having regard to his age and understanding' (para (a)), and the parent/guardian (if present) must be told the following:

> ... the substance of any part of such information which the court considers to be material as aforesaid and which has reference to his character or conduct or to the character, conduct, home surroundings or health of the relevant minors, and if such a

person, having been told the substance of any part of such information, desires to produce further evidence with reference thereto, the court, if it thinks the further evidence would be material, shall adjourn the proceedings for the production thereof and shall, if necessary in the case of a report, require the attendance at the adjourned hearing of the person who made the report (para (b)).

Where a juvenile has been tried in the youth court, he or she will be sentenced by that court. The youth court has no power to commit the juvenile to the Crown Court for sentence (indeed, the Crown Court has no greater powers of sentence in respect of a juvenile convicted by the youth court).

5.11   PLACE OF FIRST APPEARANCE

The juvenile's first court appearance in respect of an offence will be in the youth court unless the case is one of the exceptional ones where the first appearance is in the adult magistrates' court. Those exceptional cases are:

- the juvenile is jointly charged with an adult; or
- the juvenile is charged with aiding and abetting an adult to commit an offence (or vice versa); or
- the juvenile is charged with an offence which arises out of circumstances which are the same as (or connected with) those which resulted in the charge faced by an adult accused.

These exceptions exist because no one who is 18 or older at the time of their first court appearance should ever appear in the youth court, yet defendants who are jointly charged (or charged with closely connected offences) should appear together in court. The result is that a juvenile in such a case appears alongside the adult in the adult magistrates' court.

5.12   PLACE OF TRIAL

We have already seen that a juvenile may be tried in the youth court for an offence which is triable only on indictment in the case of an adult offender and that a juvenile never has a right to elect trial on indictment.

In this section, we consider the circumstances in which a juvenile may be tried in the Crown Court or in an adult magistrates' court.

The law in this area seems to be rather complicated, as it is to be found in a combination of statutory sources:

- s 46 of the Children and Young Persons Act 1933;
- s 18 of the Children and Young Persons Act 1963;
- s 24 of the Magistrates' Courts Act 1980;
- s 29 of the Magistrates' Courts Act 1980.

However, the key points may be summarised briefly:

(a) There are three circumstances in which the trial of a juvenile may take place in the Crown Court:

(i)   where the juvenile is accused of murder or manslaughter;

(ii)   where the juvenile is accused of a very serious offence; or

(iii) where the juvenile is charged alongside an adult.

(b) There is only one situation where the trial of a juvenile may take place in an adult magistrates' court, namely where the juvenile is charged alongside an adult.

5.12.1   Crown Court trial of juveniles

We look first at the three situations in which a juvenile may or must be tried by a judge and jury in the Crown Court.

5.12.1.1 *Murder and manslaughter; certain firearms offences*

Where a juvenile is charged with homicide (that is, murder or manslaughter), or with offences covered by s 51A of the Firearms Act 1968 (mandatory minimum sentence for certain firearms offences), the trial must take place in the Crown Court (s 24(1) of the Magistrates' Courts Act 1980).

5.12.1.2 *Section 91 of the Powers of Criminal Courts (Sentencing) Act 2000*

The second situation where a juvenile may be tried in the Crown Court is where the provisions of s 91 of the Powers of Criminal Courts (Sentencing) Act 2000 apply to the offence. Section 91, which empowers the Crown Court to order that a juvenile be detained for a period not exceeding the maximum sentence of imprisonment which may be imposed on an adult offender for the offence in question, applies only in the following cases:

* where a juvenile who has attained the age of 10 is charged with an offence which carries at least 14 years' imprisonment in the case of an adult offender;
* where a juvenile who has attained the age of 10 is charged with certain offences under the Sexual Offences Act 2003:

    (i)   s 3 (sexual assault);

    (ii)   s 13 (child sex offences committed by juveniles);

    (iii) s 25 (sexual activity with a child family member);

    (iv)   s 26 (inciting a child family member to engage in sexual activity).

The offences of causing death by dangerous driving, and causing death by careless driving while under the influence of drink or drugs, were specifically mentioned in the original version of s 91; however, this was made unnecessary when the maximum penalty for these offences was increased (by the Criminal Justice Act 2003) to 14 years' imprisonment (and so both offences come within s 91 automatically).

The power to commit a juvenile for trial in the Crown Court if the juvenile is charged with one or more of these offences is contained in s 24(1)(a) of the Magistrates' Courts Act 1980. This gives the magistrates power to commit the juvenile to the Crown Court for trial:

* if s 91 of the 2000 Act applies to the offence; and
* the court 'considers that if he is found guilty of the offence it ought to be possible to sentence him' to long-term detention under s 91.

These provisions are necessary because of the relatively limited ambit of the custodial sentence that would normally be applicable in the case of an offender under the age of 18, namely a detention and training order: this order is limited to a total of 24 months (12 months' custody followed by 12 months' supervision); where the offender has not attained the age of 15, a detention and training order can only be made if he is a 'persistent offender'; and the detention and training order is not available at all where the offender is under 12. Section 91 of the 2000 Act enables the Crown Court to pass a longer term of detention than would otherwise be possible (given the 24 month limit on the duration of the detention and training order), and it enables the Crown Court to impose a term of detention where otherwise no detention would be possible (in the case of an offender under the age of 12, or an offender under the age of 15 who is not a persistent offender).

Paragraph 27 of Sched 3 to the Criminal Justice Act 2003 inserts a new section, s 5A, into the Powers of Criminal Courts (Sentencing) Act 2000. This provides that where an offender is committed for sentence under s 3B, 3C or 4A, the Crown Court may deal with the offender in any way in which it could deal with him if he had just been convicted of the offence on indictment before the court.

Even if a juvenile is tried and convicted in the Crown Court, the Crown Court is not obliged to pass a sentence of detention under s 91 of the 2000 Act. The court retains the power to deal with the offender in any way that the youth court could have done. It would generally be undesirable for the Crown Court to remit the case to the youth court for sentence under s 8 of the 2000 Act, since the youth court will already have expressed the view that the case is too serious for its powers (see *R v Allen and Lambert* (1999) 163 JP 841).

5.12.1.3 *The decision to commit in a s 91 case*

If the allegations against a juvenile are of such a nature that (in the event of his being convicted) there ought to be the option of sentencing him to a term of detention under s 91, s 24(1)(a) of the Magistrates' Courts Act 1980 enables the magistrates in the youth court to decline jurisdiction and to commit the case to the Crown Court for trial. Magistrates in the youth court should only commit a juvenile for trial in the Crown Court if, on its facts, the case is sufficiently serious to justify a sentence of detention under s 91 of the 2000 Act.

In *R v Inner London Youth Court ex p DPP* (1996) 161 JP 178, the Divisional Court said that the proper question for magistrates to ask themselves when deciding whether or not to commit a juvenile to the Crown Court for trial under s 24 of the Magistrates' Courts Act 1980 is this: 'If this defendant were convicted of the offence with which he stands charged, would it be proper for a Crown Court when sentencing to exercise its powers under [s 91]?' If the answer is 'yes', the juvenile should be committed to the Crown Court for trial. The same approach was taken in *R v AM* [1998] 1 WLR 63, where the Court of Appeal said that magistrates should commit a juvenile for Crown Court trial in any case where a sentence under s 91 might be merited.

This question was re-visited in *R (D) v Manchester City Youth Court* [2001] EWHC 860 (Admin); [2002] 1 Cr App R(S) 135. Gage J said that the effect of s 24 is that a magistrates' court should not decline jurisdiction unless the offence and the circumstances surrounding it and the offender are such as to make it 'more than a vague or theoretical possibility that a sentence of detention for a long period may be passed'.

Of course, this means that the justices must take into account the sentencing practice of the Crown Court and the Court of Appeal (Criminal Division) in relation to s 91 (see, for example, *R v AM* [1998] 1 WLR 63), since the youth court could not reasonably consider that 'it ought to be possible to sentence' a defendant under that provision if there were in fact no possibility that the Crown Court would so sentence him. As Stanley Burnton J observed in *R (C and D) v Sheffield Youth Court; R (N) v Sheffield Youth Court* [2003] EWHC 35 (Admin); (2003) 167 JP 159, 'in deciding whether it considers that it ought to be possible to sentence a defendant pursuant to s 91, the youth court must consider the sentencing powers of the Crown Court and the guidance that has been given as to their exercise. If, on the basis of that guidance, there is no real possibility of such a sentence, committal is inappropriate'. His Lordship added that, in making its decision, the youth court should take into account any undisputed facts put forward as mitigation (such as the good character of the accused). However, contentious mitigation should be ignored: if the case is committed to the Crown Court and the defendant is convicted, mitigation will be a matter for that court.

In *R (D) v Manchester City Youth Court*, Gage J noted that there is nothing in the statute to prevent the Crown Court using its powers under s 91 to impose a sentence of less than two years' detention (indeed, Lord Lane CJ in *R v Fairhurst* (1986) 8 Cr App R(S) 346 (at p 349) had said that a sentence of less than two years may well be appropriate in some cases). However, his Lordship said that: 'it will only be in very exceptional and restricted circumstances that it will be appropriate to do so, rather than make a detention and training order. The fact that an offender ... does not qualify for a detention and training order because he is not a persistent offender does not seem to me such an exceptional circumstance as to justify the passing of a period of detention of less than two years under s 91.'

Gage J modified his view slightly in *R (W) v Thetford Youth Court* [2002] EWHC 1252; [2003] 1 Cr App R(S) 67, where he said that he remained of the opinion that where an offence or offences are likely to attract a sentence of less than two years' custody, the appropriate sentence will be a detention and training order. In the case of an offender under 15 who is not a persistent offender, or a child under 12, the most likely sentence will be a non-custodial sentence. It follows that in most cases the appropriate place of trial will be the youth court. However, he went on to say that he accepted that there may be cases where, despite the fact that the offender is under 15 and no detention and training order can be made, the only appropriate sentence is a custodial sentence pursuant to s 91 and possibly for a period of less than two years. He said that he remained of the opinion that the circumstances of the offence and the offender will only rarely call for a sentence pursuant to s 91, particularly if the court is dealing with an offender under the age of 12. However, he added that his use, in the earlier case, of the expression 'very exceptional' may have been unduly restrictive. Nonetheless, he remained of the view that the mere fact that a youth court, unable to make a short detention and training order, considers that the option to pass a short custodial sentence should be available does not mean that it should decline jurisdiction. He said: '[i]t seems to me that in such circumstances the fact that a detention and training order is not available indicates that Parliament intended that generally a non-custodial sentence should be passed. Perhaps it would be better to say that cases involving offenders under 15 for whom a detention and training order is not available will only rarely attract a period of detention, under s 91; the more rarely if the offender is under 12.'

A key element of uncertainty is whether the magistrates are entitled to have regard to the fact that Crown Court is inherently a less suitable forum for the trial of younger defendants. In *R v Devizes Youth Court ex p A* (2000) 164 JP 330, it was held that where a youth court decides that a custodial sentence (where that is only available in the Crown Court) or a longer period of custody than would be available (under a detention and training order) needed to be an option available to the sentencing court, the youth court has no option but to commit the youth for trial. The court specifically ruled out the argument that the Crown Court is not a suitable place to deal with a case against a youth, holding that the relevant provisions of international conventions (the United Nations' Standard Minimum Rules for the Administration of Juvenile Justice, the United Nations' Convention on the Rights of the Child and the European Convention on Human Rights) affect the way in which the trial is conducted and not the decision as to whether the case is dealt with in the Crown Court or the youth court. As Brooke LJ put it, at p 334: 'if the justices do form the judgement that if the defendant is found guilty of the offence it ought to be possible to sentence him to detention under [s 91] under s 24(1), they are bound to proceed with a view to transferring the proceedings against the accused for trial.'

It follows from *Devizes* that if the defendant before the youth court is charged with an offence to which s 24(1)(a) applies, the only question for a youth court is whether it considers that if he is found guilty of the offence, it ought to be possible to sentence him pursuant to s 91. Once it so considers, the youth court has no discretion in the matter. Questions of the suitability of the Crown Court for the trial of the offender are irrelevant to the decision to be made by the youth court.

However, in *R (W) v Southampton Youth Court* [2002] EWHC 1640 (Admin); [2003] 1 Cr App R(S) 87, Lord Woolf (sitting with Kay LJ) said that: '[w]hile the need to impose the appropriate sentence is important, so is the need to ensure that wherever possible the trial should take place in the appropriate setting. That is more satisfactorily achieved in a youth court than in a Crown Court ... Justices should start off with a strong presumption against sending young offenders to the Crown Court unless they are satisfied that that is clearly required, notwithstanding the fact that the forum for trial will not be so appropriate as the youth court.' In *R (C and D) v Sheffield Youth Court; R (N) v Sheffield Youth Court* [2003] EWHC 35 (Admin); (2003) 167 JP 159, Stanley Burnton J said that he did not think that Lord Woolf intended to suggest that a youth court which considers that it ought to be possible to sentence the defendant pursuant to s 91 nonetheless has a discretion whether or not to commit him to the Crown Court. His Lordship said that: '[i]f he did, his observation was inconsistent with the decision in *Devizes*, where the point was the basis of its decision, and I should follow *Devizes*. In any event, in my judgment, *Devizes* was correctly decided. Section 24(1) unambiguously requires the youth court to commit to the Crown Court if the conditions for the exercise of the power to commit are satisfied: the words are "the Court shall commit the accused for trial". Parliament has decided that the Crown Court is the suitable venue for the trial of persons under the age of 18 if the conditions expressly laid down by s 24(1) are satisfied.'

In *R v AM* [1998] 1 WLR 63, the Court of Appeal confirmed that where a juvenile is charged with more than one offence, and s 91 of the 2000 Act applies to one or some, but not all, of those offences, the court may, when considering the seriousness of the offence(s) to which s 91 applies, consider the seriousness of the combination of all offences, since they are 'associated offences' within the meaning of s 161(1) of the Powers of Criminal Courts (Sentencing) Act 2000.

The decision to commit a juvenile for trial under s 24(1)(a) of the Magistrates' Courts Act 1980 is based on representations made by the prosecution and the defence. No evidence is called (*R v South Hackney Juvenile Court ex p RB and CB* (1983) 77 Cr App R 294).

It used to be the case that the youth court should not be told of any previous findings of guilt recorded against the juvenile (*R v Hammersmith Juvenile Court ex p O* (1987) 86 Cr App R 843). However, that rule is no longer applicable. When a youth court is deciding whether or not to commit a juvenile to stand trial in the Crown Court in a case where there is a possibility of a sentence of detention under s 91 of the Powers of Criminal Courts (Sentencing) Act 2000, the court is entitled to know about any previous findings of guilt recorded against the juvenile: *R (Tullet) v Medway Magistrates' Court* [2003] EWHC 2279 (Admin); (2003) 167 JP 541.

5.12.1.4 *Juveniles charged with several offences in s 91 cases*

Where a juvenile appears before a youth court charged with a number of offences and is sent to the Crown Court in respect of some (but not all) of them, the youth court is not required to adjourn proceedings in respect of the other offences (s 10(3A) of the Magistrates' Courts Act 1980, inserted by s 47(5) of the Crime and Disorder Act 1998).

Section 24(1A) of the Magistrates' Courts Act 1980 (inserted by s 47(6) of the Crime and Disorder Act 1998 and confirming the effect of *R v Stephenson* [1999] 1 Cr App R 1) provides that where a magistrates' court commits a juvenile to the Crown Court in a case to which s 91 of the Powers of Criminal Courts (Sentencing) Act 2000 applies, the court may also commit him for trial for any other indictable offence with which he is charged at the same time, even if the other indictable offence is not within the ambit of s 91, provided that the charges for both offences can properly be joined in the same indictment. This will be the case where the offences are founded on the same facts or form (part of) a series of offences of the same (or a similar) character. So, to use the facts of *Stephenson* as an example: the juvenile was charged with five offences; three (indecent assault) fell within the scope s 91 but the other two (assault causing actual bodily harm) did not. Under s 24(1A), all five indictable offences can appear on the same indictment (so long as there is a sufficient link between the offences). Obviously, in the event of conviction, the Crown Court could only order long-term detention in respect of those offences to which s 91 applied.

5.12.1.5 *Revisiting the decision to try the case summarily where s 91 applies*

In *R (H) v Balham Youth Court* [2003] EWHC 3267; (2004) 168 JP 177, the Divisional Court confirmed that a youth court has the power under s 25(2) of the Magistrates' Courts Act 1980 to re-open its decision as to mode of trial in cases where there is a power to commit for trial with a view to the imposition of a sentence under s 91. Thus, if the youth court decides to try the case, it has power under s 25(2) to terminate the trial and send the case to the Crown Court for trial instead.

In *R v Herefordshire Youth Court ex p J* (1998) 95(20) LSG 34, the juvenile was charged with indecent assault (an offence for which he could have been committed for trial to the Crown Court with a view to a sentence of detention being imposed in the event of conviction under s 91 of the Powers of Criminal Courts (Sentencing) Act 2000). The charge was put and he pleaded guilty. At the next hearing, the justices purported to commit the juvenile for Crown Court trial. The Divisional Court held that the justices had the power to discontinue summary trial in favour of Crown Court trial only where a summary trial, in the sense of determining the defendant's guilt or innocence, had actually started. In the instant case, as a plea of guilty had been entered by a defendant who had been properly represented, no trial could be said to be in progress. It is open to them to re-visit the question of jurisdiction.

In *R v Fareham Youth Court and Morey ex p CPS* (1999) 163 JP 812, the defendant was charged with indecent assault and attempted rape. The magistrates decided that, although the offences fell within s 91 of the Powers of Criminal Courts (Sentencing) Act 2000, it would not be necessary to sentence the defendant under that section in the event of conviction and that he should therefore be tried summarily. The applicant then pleaded guilty to the indecent assault but not guilty to the attempted rape. At a later hearing, the CPS asked a differently constituted bench to reconsider the question of the appropriate penalty in the event of conviction. The court concluded that all the offences should be dealt with by the Crown Court and transferred the case to the Crown Court. The defendant challenged the validity of that transfer. The Divisional Court held that once the justices had concluded that there should be a summary trial, the matter cannot be re-opened before the court has begun to try the case summarily (whether as a result of new circumstances or because existing circumstances were not brought to the justices' attention at the earlier hearing). Where the magistrates in the youth court accept jurisdiction in a case that the prosecution think ought to be tried in the Crown Court, the appropriate remedy is for the prosecution to seek judicial review of the magistrates' decision to try the case. The court added (unsurprisingly) that attempted rape ought to be tried in the Crown Court, not the youth court.

5.12.1.6 Challenging refusal to commit for trial in a s 91 case

If the magistrates decide to proceed by way of summary trial in a case where committal for trial under s 24 of the Magistrates' Courts Act 1980 is possible (that is, it is a case where detention under s 91 of the Powers of Criminal Courts (Sentencing) Act 2000 is possible following conviction in the Crown Court), the prosecution may seek judicial review to quash that decision if it is unreasonable (*R v Inner London Youth Court ex p DPP* (1996) 161 JP 178).

5.12.1.7 Challenging the decision to commit for trial in a s 91 case

The appropriate forum for challenging a decision to commit to the Crown Court is in the High Court by way of judicial review. In *R v AH* [2002] EWCA Crim 2938; (2003) 167 JP 30, the defendant (who was 14 years old) was charged with robbery. The youth court declined jurisdiction on the ground of insufficient sentencing powers and committed the defendant for trial in the Crown Court under s 24(1)(a) of the 1980 Act. At the start of the trial in the Crown Court, an application to stay the proceedings as an abuse of process was made on the ground that the case should not have been committed for trial. It was held that the appropriate forum for challenging the decision to commit for trial is the Divisional Court (by way of an application for judicial review) rather than by making an abuse of process application in the Crown Court.

It used to be thought that the Divisional Court would apply the well known *Wednesbury* 'perversity' test to any challenge to a decision to commit for trial. However, it is clear from *R (W) v Thetford Youth Court* [2002] EWHC 1252; [2003] 1 Cr App R(S) 67, *R (W) v Southampton Youth Court* [2002] EWHC 1640 (Admin); [2003] 1 Cr App R(S) 87 and *R (C and D) v Sheffield Youth Court* [2003] EWHC 35 (Admin); (2003) 167 JP 159 that the test is less restrictive than that. As Stanley Burnton J put it in the latter case:

> [t]he test to be applied by the High Court on judicial review of a decision of a youth court under s 24(1) is: in the judgment of the High Court, was the decision of the youth court wrong? It is not sufficient for the High Court to consider that it would have made a different decision under s 24(1) to that of the youth court. Only if the High Court is satisfied that the original decision was wrong may it interfere.

Where a youth court intends to decline jurisdiction to hear a case and commits a young defendant for trial at the Crown Court with a view to the imposition of a sentence of detention under s 91 of the Powers of Criminal Courts (Sentencing) Act 2000, it is a useful discipline for that court to give reasons for its decision, to make certain that there are better prospects of ensuring that it applies the appropriate legal test, namely that there is a real possibility of the Crown Court passing a sentence of detention under s 91 in the event of conviction: *R (C) v Balham Youth Court* [2003] EWHC 1332 (Admin); (2003) 167 JP 525.

5.12.1.8 Joint charge with adult to be tried in the Crown Court

The third situation where a juvenile may be tried in the Crown Court is where the juvenile is jointly charged with an adult. Where a juvenile and an adult are jointly charged, their first court appearance will be in an adult magistrates' court (not a youth court, which would be an inappropriate forum for a case involving an adult defendant).

Section 24(1)(b) of the Magistrates' Courts Act 1980 provides that a juvenile may be sent to the Crown Court to be tried jointly with an adult if:

• the juvenile is jointly charged with the adult (in practice, this will include cases where one is alleged to have aided and abetted the other, since both will usually be charged as principal offenders); and

• the adult is going to be tried in the Crown Court (either because the offence is triable only on indictment in the case of an adult, or else the mode of trial hearing resulted in a decision in favour of trial on indictment rather than summary trial); and

• the justices decide that it is 'necessary in the interests of justice' that the juvenile and the adult should both be sent to the Crown Court for trial.

In deciding whether or not it is necessary in the interests of justice to send the juvenile to the Crown Court under s 24(1)(b), the court has to balance what may well be conflicting interests. On one hand, it is desirable that there should be a joint trial, to avoid prosecution witnesses having to give their evidence twice, to avoid the risk of inconsistent verdicts, and to avoid the risk of disparity in the sentences which are passed in the event of conviction. On the other hand, a juvenile may well find appearing in the Crown Court an unduly traumatic experience.

Generally speaking, the younger the juvenile and the less serious the charge, the more reluctant the justices should be to send the juvenile to the Crown Court.

Also relevant are the likely plea of the juvenile and the degree of his involvement in the offence. If the juvenile is likely to plead guilty and it is accepted by the prosecution that he played only a minor role in the offence, it is likely to be more appropriate to deal with him separately.

It should also be noted that if a juvenile is sent for trial in the Crown Court because he is jointly charged with an adult, he may also be tried in the Crown Court for any other indictable offence which is charged at the same time, provided that it arises out of circumstances which are the same as or connected with those giving rise to the joint charge (s 24(2) of the Magistrates' Courts Act 1980).

Normally, s 24(1)(b) of the Magistrates' Courts Acts 1980 will be relevant where a juvenile and an adult appear together in an adult magistrates' court. However, in *R v Coventry City Magistrates ex p M* [1992] Crim LR 810, it was held that the power to send a juvenile for trial in the Crown Court under s 24(1)(b) is not confined to an adult magistrates' court in which the adult and the juvenile appear together. A youth court can also exercise this power in a case where a juvenile before it is to be jointly indicted with an adult who has already been sent for trial by an adult magistrates' court.

In *R v Tottenham Youth Court ex p Fawzy* [1998] 1 All ER 365, the Divisional Court held that, where an adult and juvenile are jointly charged (and so make their first appearance in an adult magistrates' court) with an offence that falls within the ambit of s 91 of the 2000 Act, and the justices, following an application under s 6(1) of the Magistrates' Courts Act 1980, hold that there is no case to answer against the adult, the adult magistrates' court must consider whether the case is one in which a sentence under s 91 might be justified. If so, they should commit the juvenile to the Crown Court for trial; if not, they should take a plea from the juvenile. If the juvenile pleads guilty, he should normally be remitted to the youth court for sentence (unless the very limited powers of the adult magistrates' court when dealing with a juvenile are appropriate). If he pleads not guilty, the adult court has the option whether to send him to the youth court for trial. However, the adult court has no power to send the case to the youth court for that court to decide mode of trial. The mode of trial question, in these circumstances, is one which must be decided by the adult court. This will cease to be of relevance when the abolition (by the Criminal Justice Act 2003) of committal proceedings for either way offences comes into effect.

5.12.1.9 Special arrangements where a juvenile is tried in the Crown Court

Special arrangements have to be made for the Crown Court trial of young defendants in order to take account of the judgment of the European Court of Human Rights in *V v UK; T v UK* (2000) 30 EHRR 121. These arrangements are set out in detail in para IV.39 of *Practice Direction (Criminal Proceedings: Consolidation)* [2002] 1 WLR 2870; [2002] 3 All ER 904, which provides as follows:

39 *Trial of children and young persons*

39.1 This direction applies to trials of children and young persons in the Crown Court. In it children and young persons are together called 'young defendants'.

39.2 The steps which should be taken to comply with paragraphs 39.3–39.17 should be judged, in any given case, taking account of the age, maturity and development (intellectual and emotional) of the young defendant on trial and all other circumstances of the case.

The overriding principle

39.3 Some young defendants accused of committing serious crimes may be very young and very immature when standing trial in the Crown Court. The purpose of such trial is to determine guilt (if that is in issue) and decide the appropriate sentence if the young defendant pleads guilty or is convicted. The trial process should not itself expose the young defendant to avoidable intimidation, humiliation or distress. All possible steps should be taken to assist the young defendant to understand and participate in the proceedings. The ordinary trial process should, so far as necessary, be adapted to meet those ends. Regard should be had to the welfare of the young defendant as required by section 44 of the Children and Young Persons Act 1933.

Before trial

39.4 If a young defendant is indicted jointly with an adult defendant, the court should consider at the plea and directions hearing whether the young defendant should be tried on his own and should ordinarily so order unless of opinion that a joint trial would be in the interests of justice and would not be unduly prejudicial to the welfare of the young defendant. If a young defendant is tried jointly with an adult the ordinary procedures will apply subject to such modifications (if any) as the court may see fit to order.

39.5 At the plea and directions hearing before trial of a young defendant, the court should consider and so far as practicable give directions on the matters covered in paragraphs 39.9–39.15.

39.6 It may be appropriate to arrange that a young defendant should visit, out of court hours and before the trial, the courtroom in which the trial is to be held so that he can familiarise himself with it.

39.7 If any case against a young defendant has attracted or may attract widespread public or media interest, the assistance of the police should be enlisted to try to ensure that a young defendant is not, when attending for the trial, exposed to intimidation, vilification or abuse.

39.8 The court should be ready at this stage (if it has not already done so) to give a direction under section 39 of the 1933 Act or, as the case may be, section 45 of the Youth Justice and Criminal Evidence Act 1999. Any such order, once made, should be reduced to writing and copies should on request be made available to anyone affected or potentially affected by it.

The trial

39.9 The trial should, if practicable, be held in a courtroom in which all the participants are on the same or almost the same level.

39.10 A young defendant should normally, if he wishes, be free to sit with members of his family or others in a like relationship and in a place which permits easy, informal communication with his legal representatives and others with whom he wants or needs to communicate.

39.11 The court should explain the course of proceedings to a young defendant in terms he can understand, should remind those representing a young defendant of their continuing duty to explain each step of the trial to him and should ensure, so far as practicable, that the trial is conducted in language which the young defendant can understand.

39.12 The trial should be conducted according to a timetable which takes full account of a young defendant's inability to concentrate for long periods. Frequent and regular breaks will often be appropriate.

39.13 Robes and wigs should not be worn unless the young defendant asks that they should or the court for good reason orders that they should. Any person responsible for the security of a young defendant who is in custody should not be in uniform. There should be no recognisable police presence in the courtroom save for good reason.

39.14 The court should be prepared to restrict attendance at the trial to a small number, perhaps limited to some of those with an immediate and direct interest in the outcome of the trial. The court should rule on any challenged claim to attend.

39.15 Facilities for reporting the trial (subject to any direction given under section 39 of the 1933 Act or section 45 of the 1999 Act) must be provided. But the court may restrict the number of those attending in the courtroom to report the trial to such number as is judged practicable and desirable. In ruling on any challenged claim to attend the courtroom for the purpose of reporting the trial the court should be mindful of the public's general right to be informed about the administration of justice in the Crown Court. Where access to the courtroom by reporters is restricted, arrangements should be made for the proceedings to be relayed, audibly and if possible visually, to another room in the same court complex to which the media have free access if it appears that there will be a need for such additional facilities.

39.16 Where the court is called upon to exercise its discretion in relation to any procedural matter falling within the scope of this practice direction but not the subject of specific reference, such discretion should be exercised having regard to the principles in paragraph 39.3.

Appeal and committals for sentence

39.17 This practice direction does not in terms apply to appeals and committals for sentence, but regard should be paid to the effect of it if the arrangements for hearing any appeal or committal might otherwise be prejudicial to the welfare of a young defendant.

Lord Justice Auld, in his *Review of the Criminal Courts of England and Wales,* considers (in paras 207–11) the trial of young defendants. He makes the point that youth court justices are specially trained to deal with juveniles, whereas a randomly selected jury has no such training; also, he notes that the period of delay between arrest and disposal is much greater in the Crown Court than in the youth court (he quotes figures from 2001, where the period between arrest and sentence for young offenders was 197 days in the Crown Court as against 66 days in the youth court).

In any event, despite the changes made to the trial process where the accused is young, there remains the question of whether Crown Court trial is really appropriate for young defendants, even if the trial process is modified. The Review recommends that:

48   All cases involving young defendants who are presently committed to the Crown Court for trial or for sentence should in future be put before the youth court consisting, as appropriate, of a High Court Judge, Circuit Judge or Recorder sitting with at least two experienced magistrates and exercising the full jurisdiction of the present Crown Court for this purpose.

49   The only possible exception should be those cases in which the young defendant is charged jointly with an adult and it is considered necessary in the interests of justice for them to be tried together.

50 The youth court so constituted should be entitled, save where it considers that public interest demands otherwise, to hear such cases in private, as in the youth court exercising its present jurisdiction.

This proposal was only accepted to a limited extent in that, under the Courts Act 2003, all High Court and Crown Court judges are given the power to act as justices of the peace (and so are entitled to exercise the jurisdiction of justices); using this power, a senior judge could theoretically sit as a justice in a magistrates' court or youth court. Thus, the Courts Act 2003 in effect lays the foundation for the reform suggested by Lord Justice Auld.

The danger of Crown Court trial being inappropriate for some young defendants is highlighted by the decision of the European Court of Human Rights in *SC v UK* (2004) *The Times*, 29 June (ECtHR, App No 60958/00). The applicant, who was aged 11 years at the time, challenged the fairness of his Crown Court trial. The European Court held that there had been a breach of the applicant's right to a fair trial. The Court said that the right of an accused to effective participation in his criminal trial generally includes not only the right to be present, but also to hear and follow the proceedings. In the case of a child, it is essential that he be dealt with in a manner which takes full account of his age, level of maturity and intellectual and emotional capacities, and that steps are taken to promote his ability to understand and participate in the proceedings, including conducting the hearing in such a way as to reduce as far as possible his feelings of intimidation and inhibition. In the present case, two experts had assessed the juvenile as having a very low intellectual level for his age. The Court said that it could not conclude that the juvenile was capable of participating effectively in his trial. The Court considered that when the decision is taken to deal with a child who risks not being able to participate effectively because of his young age and limited intellectual capacity, by way of criminal proceedings rather than some other form of disposal directed primarily at determining the child's best interests and those of the community, it is essential that he be tried in a specialist tribunal which is able to give full consideration to and make proper allowance for the handicaps under which he labours, and adapt its procedure accordingly. The trial in this case took place before the Practice Direction came into effect, but it is unlikely that the measures in that Practice Direction would have brought about a different result. However, the effect of the decision of the European Court would seem to be confined to children whose intellectual level is unusually low.

5.12.1.10 Sentencing juveniles after Crown Court trial alongside adult

If a juvenile is convicted at the Crown Court following joint trial with an adult, the Crown Court should remit the juvenile to the youth court for sentence unless it is undesirable to do so (s 8 of the Powers of Criminal Courts (Sentencing) Act 2000).

In *R v Lewis* (1984) 79 Cr App R 94, it was held that remission to the youth court would generally be undesirable because:

- the Crown Court judge is better informed on the facts of the case (having presided over the trial);
- there would otherwise be a risk of disparity in the sentences passed on the adult and the juvenile;
- there would be unnecessary duplication of proceedings (causing unnecessary delay and public expense).

5.12.1.11 The Criminal Justice Act 2003

The procedure for sending juveniles to the Crown Court for trial will change when the relevant provisions of the Criminal Justice Act 2003 come into force. Sub-sections 51A(2) and (3) of the Crime and Disorder Act 1998 (added by para 18 of Sched 3 to the Criminal Justice Act 2003) enable the court to send the juvenile forthwith to the Crown Court for trial where the juvenile is charged with:

- homicide; or
- · a firearms offence where there is a mandatory minimum sentence (under s 51A of the Firearms Act 1968); or
- an offence to which the provisions of s 91 of the Powers of Criminal Courts (Sentencing) Act 2000 apply and the court considers that it ought to be possible to sentence the juvenile to detention under that section in the event of his being convicted of the offence; or
- · notice has been given to the court under s 51B (serious or complex fraud cases) or s 51C (certain cases involving children) of the Crime and Disorder Act 1998.

Section 51A(4) of the 1998 Act will enable linked offences to be transferred to the Crown Court at the same time (if the linked offence is a summary one, it can only be sent to the Crown Court if it is punishable with imprisonment or disqualification from driving). The function of the court under s 51A can be exercised by a single justice.

Section 51A provides that:

(1)   This section is subject to sections 24A and 24B of the Magistrates' Courts Act 1980 (which provide for certain offences involving children or young persons to be tried summarily).

(2)   Where a child or young person appears or is brought before a magistrates' court ('the court') charged with an offence and any of the conditions mentioned in sub-section (3) below is satisfied, the court shall send him forthwith to the Crown Court for trial for the offence.

(3)   Those conditions are—
   (a)   that the offence falls within sub-section (12) below;
   (b)   that the offence is such as is mentioned in sub-section (1) of section 91 of the Powers of Criminal Courts (Sentencing) Act 2000 (other than one mentioned in paragraph (d) below in relation to which it appears to the court as mentioned there) and the court considers that if he is found guilty of the offence it ought to be possible to sentence him in pursuance of sub-section (3) of that section;
   (c)   that notice is given to the court under section 51B or 51C below in respect of the offence;
   (d)   that the offence is a specified offence (within the meaning of section 224 of the Criminal Justice Act 2003) and it appears to the court that if he is found guilty of the offence the criteria for the imposition of a sentence under section 226(3) or 228(2) of that Act would be met.

(4)   Where the court sends a child or young person for trial under sub-section (2) above, it may at the same time send him to the Crown Court for trial for any indictable or summary offence with which he is charged and which—
   (a)   (if it is an indictable offence) appears to the court to be related to the offence mentioned in sub-section (2) above; or

(b) (if it is a summary offence) appears to the court to be related to the offence mentioned in sub-section (2) above or to the indictable offence, and which fulfils the requisite condition (as defined in sub-section (9) below).

(5) Where a child or young person who has been sent for trial under sub-section (2) above subsequently appears or is brought before a magistrates' court charged with an indictable or summary offence which—

(a) appears to the court to be related to the offence mentioned in sub-section (2) above; and

(b) (in the case of a summary offence) fulfils the requisite condition,

the court may send him forthwith to the Crown Court for trial for the indictable or summary offence.

(6) Where—

(a) the court sends a child or young person ('C') for trial under sub-section (2) or (4) above; and

(b) an adult appears or is brought before the court on the same or a subsequent occasion charged jointly with C with an either way offence for which C is sent for trial under sub-section (2) or (4) above, or an either way offence which appears to the court to be related to that offence,

the court shall where it is the same occasion, and may where it is a subsequent occasion, send the adult forthwith to the Crown Court for trial for the either way offence.

(7) Where the court sends an adult for trial under sub-section (6) above, it shall at the same time send him to the Crown Court for trial for any either way or summary offence with which he is charged and which—

(a) (if it is an either way offence) appears to the court to be related to the offence for which he was sent for trial; and

(b) (if it is a summary offence) appears to the court to be related to the offence for which he was sent for trial or to the either way offence, and which fulfils the requisite condition.

(8) The trial of the information charging any summary offence for which a person is sent for trial under this section shall be treated as if the court had adjourned it under section 10 of the 1980 Act and had not fixed the time and place for its resumption.

(9) A summary offence fulfils the requisite condition if it is punishable with imprisonment or involves obligatory or discretionary disqualification from driving.

(10) In the case of a child or young person charged with an offence—

(a) if the offence satisfies any of the conditions in sub-section (3) above, the offence shall be dealt with under sub-section (2) above and not under any other provision of this section or section 51 above;

(b) subject to paragraph (a) above, if the offence is one in respect of which the requirements of sub-section (7) of section 51 above for sending the child or young person to the Crown Court are satisfied, the offence shall be dealt with under that sub-section and not under any other provision of this section or section 51 above.

(11) The functions of a magistrates' court under this section, and its related functions under section 51D below, may be discharged by a single justice.

(12) An offence falls within this sub-section if—

(a) it is an offence of homicide; or

(b) each of the requirements of section 51A(1) of the Firearms Act 1968 would be satisfied with respect to—

(i) the offence; and

(ii) the person charged with it,

if he were convicted of the offence.

Paragraph 10 of Sched 3 to the Criminal Justice Act 2003 inserts a number of new sections into the Magistrates' Courts Act 1980 (ss 24A–24D). The effect of these new sections is to apply a procedure similar to that contained in ss 17A–17C (the 'plea before venue' hearing) to cases involving a defendant who is under the age of 18 where the court has to decide whether to send him to the Crown Court for trial (because he is charged alongside an adult co-accused or because he is charged with an offence to which s 91 of the Powers of Criminal Courts (Sentencing) Act 2000 applies). These new sections provide as follows:

24A(1) This section applies where—

(a) a person under the age of 18 years appears or is brought before a magistrates' court on an information charging him with an offence other than one falling within section 51A(12) of the Crime and Disorder Act 1998 ('the 1998 Act'); and

(b) but for the application of the following provisions of this section, the court would be required at that stage, by virtue of section 51(7) or (8) or 51A(3)(b), (4) or (5) of the 1998 Act to determine, in relation to the offence, whether to send the person to the Crown Court for trial (or to determine any matter, the effect of which would be to determine whether he is sent to the Crown Court for trial).

(2) Where this section applies, the court shall, before proceeding to make any such determination as is referred to in sub-section (1)(b) above (the 'relevant determination'), follow the procedure set out in this section.

(3) Everything that the court is required to do under the following provisions of this section must be done with the accused person in court.

(4) The court shall cause the charge to be written down, if this has not already been done, and to be read to the accused.

(5) The court shall then explain to the accused in ordinary language that he may indicate whether (if the offence were to proceed to trial) he would plead guilty or not guilty, and that if he indicates that he would plead guilty—

(a) the court must proceed as mentioned in sub-section (7) below; and

(b) in cases where the offence is one mentioned in section 91(1) of the Powers of Criminal Courts (Sentencing) Act 2000) he may be sent to the Crown Court for sentencing under section 3B or (if applicable) 3C of that Act if the court is of such opinion as is mentioned in sub-section (2) of the applicable section.

(6) The court shall then ask the accused whether (if the offence were to proceed to trial) he would plead guilty or not guilty.

(7) If the accused indicates that he would plead guilty, the court shall proceed as if—

(a) the proceedings constituted from the beginning the summary trial of the information; and

(b) section 9(1) above was complied with and he pleaded guilty under it,

and, accordingly, the court shall not (and shall not be required to) proceed to make the relevant determination or to proceed further under section 51 or (as the case may be) section 51A of the 1998 Act in relation to the offence.

(8)   If the accused indicates that he would plead not guilty, the court shall proceed to make the relevant determination and this section shall cease to apply.

(9)   If the accused in fact fails to indicate how he would plead, for the purposes of this section he shall be taken to indicate that he would plead not guilty.

(10)   Subject to sub-section (7) above, the following shall not for any purpose be taken to constitute the taking of a plea—

(a) asking the accused under this section whether (if the offence were to proceed to trial) he would plead guilty or not guilty;

(b) an indication by the accused under this section of how he would plead.

24B(1) This section shall have effect where—

(a) a person under the age of 18 years appears or is brought before a magistrates' court on an information charging him with an offence other than one falling within section 51A(12) of the Crime and Disorder Act 1998;

(b) but for the application of the following provisions of this section, the court would be required at that stage to make one of the determinations referred to in paragraph (b) of section 24A(1) above ('the relevant determination');

(c) the accused is represented by a legal representative;

(d) the court considers that by reason of the accused's disorderly conduct before the court it is not practicable for proceedings under section 24A above to be conducted in his presence; and

(e) the court considers that it should proceed in the absence of the accused.

(2)   In such a case—

(a) the court shall cause the charge to be written down, if this has not already been done, and to be read to the representative;

(b) the court shall ask the representative whether (if the offence were to proceed to trial) the accused would plead guilty or not guilty;

(c) if the representative indicates that the accused would plead guilty the court shall proceed as if the proceedings constituted from the beginning the summary trial of the information, and as if section 9(1) above was complied with and the accused pleaded guilty under it;

(d) if the representative indicates that the accused would plead not guilty the court shall proceed to make the relevant determination and this section shall cease to apply.

(3)   If the representative in fact fails to indicate how the accused would plead, for the purposes of this section he shall be taken to indicate that the accused would plead not guilty.

(4)   Subject to sub-section (2)(c) above, the following shall not for any purpose be taken to constitute the taking of a plea—

(a) asking the representative under this section whether (if the offence were to proceed to trial) the accused would plead guilty or not guilty;

(b) an indication by the representative under this section of how the accused would plead.

24C(1) A magistrates' court proceeding under section 24A or 24B above may adjourn the proceedings at any time, and on doing so on any occasion when the accused is present may remand the accused.

(2)   Where the court remands the accused, the time fixed for the resumption of proceedings shall be that at which he is required to appear or be brought before the court in pursuance of the remand or would be required to be brought before the court but for section 128(3A) below.

24D(1) The functions of a magistrates' court under sections 24A to 24C above may be discharged by a single justice.

(2)   Sub-section (1) above shall not be taken as authorising—

(a) the summary trial of an information (other than a summary trial by virtue of section 24A(7) or 24B(2)(c) above); or

(b) the imposition of a sentence, by a magistrates' court composed of fewer than two justices.

It should also be noted that para 11(4) of Sched 3 to the Criminal Justice Act 2003 repeals s 25(3)–(8) of the Magistrates' Courts Act 1980 (the power to switch from summary trial to committal proceedings or vice versa) to reflect the abolition of committal proceedings.

At the moment, the power to pass a sentence of detention under s 91 of the Powers of Criminal Courts (Sentencing) Act 2000 can only be exercised by the Crown Court where the juvenile was convicted on indictment (ie, where the juvenile either pleaded guilty in the Crown Court or was convicted in that court). However, under s 24A or 24B of the Magistrates' Court Act 1980, where the juvenile is charged with an offence to which s 91 of the 2000 Act applies or is charged alongside an adult who is to be tried in the Crown Court, and he (the juvenile) indicates a guilty plea, he will be deemed to have pleaded guilty before the justices. If the offence is one to which the provisions of s 91 of the 2000 Act apply, the magistrates will then be empowered by s 3B of the 2000 Act (added by para 23 of Sched 3 to the Criminal Justice Act 2003) to commit the juvenile to the Crown Court for sentence. In other words, s 3B of the 2000 Act will enable committal for sentence where the juvenile indicates a guilty plea under the 'plea before venue' procedure applicable to juveniles. This power to commit is available where the court is of the opinion that the offence (or the combination of the offence and one or more offences associated with it) is such that the Crown Court should, in the court's opinion, have power to deal with the offender under s 91. In such a case, the court may commit the juvenile (in custody or on bail) to the Crown Court for sentence. Section 3B(3) provides that where a juvenile is committed for sentence under s 3B, s 6 of the 2000 Act (which enables a magistrates' court to commit the offender to the Crown Court to be dealt with in respect of certain other offences) is applicable.

Section 3B reads as follows:

(1)   This section applies where—

(a) a person aged under 18 appears or is brought before a magistrates' court ('the court') on an information charging him with an offence mentioned in sub-section (1) of section 91 below ('the offence');

(b) he or his representative indicates under section 24A or (as the case may be) 24B of the Magistrates' Courts Act 1980 (child or young person to indicate intention as to plea in certain cases) that he would plead guilty if the offence were to proceed to trial; and

(c) proceeding as if section 9(1) of that Act were complied with and he pleaded guilty under it, the court convicts him of the offence.

(2)   If the court is of the opinion that—

(a) the offence; or

(b) the combination of the offence and one or more offences associated with it,

was such that the Crown Court should, in the court's opinion, have power to deal with the offender as if the provisions of section 91(3) below applied, the court may commit him in custody or on bail to the Crown Court for sentence in accordance with section 5A(1) below.

(3)   Where the court commits a person under sub-section (2) above, section 6 below (which enables a magistrates' court, where it commits a person under this section in respect of an offence, also to commit him to the Crown Court to be dealt with in respect of certain other offences) shall apply accordingly.

Paragraph 25 of Sched 3 to the Criminal Justice Act 2003 inserts a new section, s 4A, into the Powers of Criminal Courts (Sentencing) Act 2000. This section applies where a juvenile is charged with an offence to which s 91 of the 2000 Act applies and, at the plea before venue hearing, the juvenile indicates an intention to plead guilty to that offence. Under s 4A(2), if the court has sent the offender to the Crown Court for trial for one or more offences that are related to the s 91 offence, it may commit him (in custody or on bail) to the Crown Court to be dealt with in respect of the s 91 offence. Under s 4A(4), if the magistrates commit the s 91 offence to the Crown Court for sentence but do not state that, in their opinion, the case is one where it ought to be possible to impose detention under s 91, the Crown Court cannot impose detention under s 91 for that offence (and so is limited to the sentences that could be imposed by the youth court). This provision thus mirrors s 4 of the 2000 Act which is applicable to adult offenders.

Section 3C of the Powers of Criminal Courts (Sentencing) Act 2000 (added by para 23 of Sched 3 to the Criminal Justice Act 2003) enables committal for sentence of dangerous young offenders. Where a juvenile is convicted of an offence specified in s 224 of the 2003 Act, and it appears to the court that the criteria for the imposition of a sentence under s 226(3) or 228(2) of the 2003 Act (dangerous offenders) would be met, the court must commit the offender (in custody or on bail) to the Crown Court for sentence. The offender can also be committed (s 6 of the 2000 Act) to be sentenced for other offences that the magistrates would otherwise be dealing with.

Under s 5A of the Powers of Criminal Courts (Sentencing) Act 2000 (added by para 27 of Sched 3 to the Criminal Justice Act 2003), where an offender is committed for sentence under s 3B, 3C or 4A of the 2000 Act, the Crown Court may deal with the offender in any way in which it could deal with him if he had just been convicted of the offence on indictment before the court.

5.12.2 Summary trial of juveniles

5.12.2.1 Procedure where juvenile is not to be tried in the Crown Court

If the justices decide that it is not necessary in the interests of justice to send the juvenile to the Crown Court, even though the adult co-accused is to be tried by the Crown Court, the charge will be put to the juvenile in the adult magistrates' court and a plea taken from him.

If the juvenile pleads guilty, the magistrates will consider whether their sentencing powers in respect of the juvenile are adequate. Those powers are to make any one or more of the following orders:

- absolute discharge (that is, no action is taken against the juvenile);
- conditional discharge (that is, no action is taken against the juvenile unless he re-offends during the period specified by the court);

- a fine (up to £1,000 for a juvenile who has attained the age of 14; up to £250 for one who has not (s 135 of the Powers of Criminal Courts (Sentencing) Act 2000));
- requiring the juvenile's parents to enter into a recognisance to keep proper control of him.

If these powers, which are contained in s 8(8) of the 2000 Act, are not sufficient, the justices will remit the juvenile to the youth court to be sentenced (under s 8(6) of the 2000 Act).

If the juvenile pleads not guilty, the adult magistrates' court may try him (under s 29(2) of the Magistrates' Courts Act 1980); however, in the absence of a good reason to the contrary (for example, the prosecution wish to offer no evidence), he should normally be remitted to the youth court for trial.

5.12.2.2 Trial of juvenile in adult magistrates' court – joint charge

Where the juvenile is jointly charged with an adult who is to be tried summarily (that is, it is a summary offence or else an either way offence where the adult defendant and the justices agree to summary trial), the place of trial for the juvenile may differ depending on the plea entered by the adult and on whether the charge is a joint charge or merely a related charge:

- *If the adult pleads not guilty to the joint charge*

  The adult magistrates' court will ask the juvenile to plead (guilty or not guilty). If the juvenile pleads not guilty, the adult court *must* try him (s 46(1)(a) of the Children and Young Persons Act 1933). If he pleads or is found guilty, the magistrates will remit him to the youth court for sentence if the sentences which the adult court can impose (see above) are inappropriate.

- *If the adult pleads guilty to the joint charge*

  If the juvenile pleads not guilty, the adult magistrates' court *may* try him under s 29(2) of the Magistrates' Courts Act 1980 or remit him to the youth court for trial. Although the magistrates could theoretically try the juvenile (even though the adult has pleaded guilty, so that there will be no trial of the adult), it is much more likely that they will remit him to the youth court for trial. There is little justification for trying a juvenile on his own in the magistrates' court. If the juvenile pleads guilty (or the adult court does try him and he is found guilty), the adult court will remit him to the youth court if none of the sentences which the adult court can impose are appropriate.

- *Aiding and abetting, etc*

  If the juvenile is charged with aiding and abetting the adult or the adult is charged with aiding and abetting the juvenile, the adult magistrates' court has a *discretion* to try them both if they both plead not guilty (s 46(1)(b) of the Children and Young Persons Act 1933; s 18(a) of the Children and Young Persons Act 1963). If the adult and juvenile are charged with offences which arise out of the same circumstances and both plead not guilty, the adult magistrates' court may either try the juvenile or remit him to the youth court for trial (s 18(b) of the Children and Young Persons Act 1963). If the adult pleads guilty and the juvenile not guilty, the magistrates are likely to remit the juvenile to the youth court for trial; if the adult magistrates' court tries the juvenile and convicts him, he will be remitted to the youth court for sentence if the magistrates' sentencing powers (see above) are inappropriate.

Where one offender is charged with taking a conveyance without the owner's consent and another is charged with allowing himself to be carried in a conveyance which has been taken without the owner's consent, although these are in reality separate offences, they are to be regarded as jointly charged for the purposes of s 24 of the Magistrates' Courts Act 1980 (see *R v Peterborough Justices ex p Allgood* (1995) 159 JP 627).

5.12.2.3 *Mistake in age*

If an adult magistrates' court starts to deal with a defendant believing him to be 18 or over and it then transpires that he is a juvenile, the court can either continue to hear the case or remit it to the youth court, whichever seems most appropriate in the circumstances (s 46(1)(c) of the Children and Young Persons Act 1933).

5.13   RELEVANT DATE – AGE

Section 29(1) of the Children and Young Persons Act 1963 provides that:

> Where proceedings in respect of a young person are begun for an offence and he attains the age of eighteen before the conclusion of the proceedings, the court may continue to deal with the case and make any order which it could have made if he had not attained that age.

Thus, the youth court has jurisdiction if the accused is under 18 when the proceedings are begun. In *R v Uxbridge Youth Court ex p H* (1998) 162 JP 327, the defendant was 17 when arrested and charged but, by the time he made his first appearance at the youth court, he had turned 18. The Divisional Court held (construing s 29) that proceedings are begun when the defendant first appears before the justices; it followed that the youth court did not have jurisdiction to deal with this defendant.

What happens if a 17 year old has his 18th birthday during the course of proceedings in the youth court?

The House of Lords held in *R v Islington North Juvenile Court ex p Daley* [1983] 1 AC 347, which was followed in *R v Nottingham Justices ex p Taylor* [1992] QB 557, that:

> ... the only appropriate date at which to determine whether an accused person has attained an age which entitles him to elect to be tried by jury is the date of his appearance before the court on the occasion when the court makes its decision as to mode of trial.

In other words (as there is no mode of trial hearing as such in the youth court), the date when the juvenile pleads guilty or not guilty is the relevant date.

Cases where the defendant attains the age of 18 between conviction and sentence are dealt with by s 9 of the Powers of Criminal Courts (Sentencing) Act 2000. Under s 9(1), the youth court is empowered, in such a case, to remit the defendant to the adult magistrates' court to be sentenced. The adult magistrates' court may then 'deal with the case in any way in which it would have power to deal with it if all proceedings relating to the offence which took place before the youth court had taken place before [the adult court]' (s 9(2)(b)). There is no right of appeal against the order of remission (s 9(4)).

In *R (Denny) v Acton Youth Court* [2004] EWHC 948 (Admin); [2004] 2 All ER 961, a 17 year old was charged with attempted robbery. He entered a plea of not guilty at the youth court. By the time the matter came on for trial and he was found guilty, he was 18. The justices in the youth court adjourned sentence and remitted him to the adult court pursuant to s 9. The adult court remitted the case to the youth court for that court to reconsider (under s 142 of the Magistrates' Courts Act 1980) the decision to remit. The Divisional Court held that the order remitting the case to the adult magistrates' court under s 9 was defective by reason of illegality: youth courts should never remit a defendant to a magistrates' court for sentence in relation to an offence which, in the case of an adult, is triable only on indictment. The court went on to say that, provided the adult court has not reached the stage of considering sentence, it is possible for the youth court to rescind a remittal to an adult magistrates' court under s 142 of the 1980 Act, since a remittal under s 9 is an 'order made when dealing with an offender'.

It should be noted that the *type* of sentence is generally fixed by the offender's age at the date of conviction (*Danga* [1992] QB 476). Nevertheless, the court should have regard to the offender's age at the date when the offence was committed when considering the severity of the penalty to impose. In *R v Jones* [2003] EWCA Crim 1609; (2003) 167 JP 536, the defendant was aged 17 at the time of the offence; however, by the sentencing hearing, he had attained the age of 18. He was sentenced to 15 months' detention in a young offender institution. It was held (following *R v Ghafoor* [2002] EWCA Crim 1857; [2003] 1 Cr App R(S) 84) that where a defendant crosses an age threshold between the date of the offence and the date of conviction, it is appropriate to consider the sentence which could have been passed had the defendant been sentenced at the time he committed the offence. It is then appropriate to consider other factors, and if there are good reasons to depart from that starting point, then that can be done.

5.14   APPEALS FROM THE YOUTH COURT

For discussion on appeals from the youth court, see Chapter 6, which deals with appeals from magistrates' courts.

5.15   ASSESSING THE EFFECTIVENESS OF THE YOUTH COURT

In the Home Office Consultation Paper *Tackling Youth Crime* (www.homeoffice.gov.uk/docs/tyc.html), the perceived failings of the youth justice system were summarised as follows:

- it lacks public credibility and clear aims;
- the system of repeat cautioning was not working;
- re-offending continues on bail;
- the youth court system is too cumbersome and slow, taking on average 4½ months to deal with young offenders. 4 out of 5 cases observed by an audit commission in their study were adjourned;
- there is a lack of supervised community based intervention programmes aimed at changing the behaviour of young offenders early in their careers;

- the current system of custodial orders and facilities is disjointed and variable and needs radical overhaul. Too little emphasis is given to changing offending behaviour.

In the 1997 Consultation Paper issued by the Home Office, *No More Excuses – A New Approach to Tackling Youth Crime in England and Wales* (Cmnd 3809), Chapter 2 considers the aims of the youth justice system and refers to the Crime and Disorder Bill (now Act) which sets out in statutory form the aim of the youth justice system, namely to prevent offending by young people.

Paragraph 2.9 refers to proposals made by the Home Secretary's Youth Justice Task Force (an advisory group comprising a range of people with varied experience of the youth justice system, including victim issues, plus representatives of relevant government departments), which suggested that the aim of preventing offending by young people should be achieved through the following objectives:

- the swift administration of justice so that every young person accused of breaking the law has the matter resolved without delay;
- confronting young offenders with the consequences of their offending, for themselves and their family, their victims and their community;
- punishment proportionate to the seriousness and persistence of offending;
- encouraging reparation to victims by young offenders;
- reinforcing the responsibilities of parents; and
- helping young offenders to tackle problems associated with their offending and to develop a sense of personal responsibility.

Chapter 9 of the Paper sets out the government's vision for a youth court for the 21st century. Paragraph 9.2 notes that:

> ... a frank assessment of the current approach of the youth court must conclude that, all too often, inadequate attention is given to changing offending behaviour. This is not the fault of individuals working within the system. It is encouraged by the court's very structures and procedures ... The purpose of the youth court must change from simply deciding guilt or innocence and then issuing a sentence. In most cases, an offence should trigger a wider enquiry into the circumstances and nature of the offending behaviour, leading to action to change that behaviour. This requires in turn a fundamental change of approach within the youth court system.

Paragraph 9.3 lists some of the reforms needed to enable this to happen:

- speedier decisions on guilt or innocence, much closer to the date of the offence and with less tolerance of adjournments;
- a system which is more open, and which commands the confidence of victims and the public;
- processes which engage young offenders and their parents and focus on the nature of their offending behaviour and how to change it;
- a stronger emphasis on using sentencing to prevent future offending; and
- more efficient arrangements for the scheduling and management of cases.

An important aspect of the approach commended by the government is engaging with the offender. Paragraph 9.6 notes that this requires:

- training magistrates so that they understand the value of talking directly to both the young defendant and his or her parents during court proceedings, even where the young person has legal representation;

- encouraging magistrates to question young defendants about the reasons for their behaviour, before reaching a final decision on sentencing; and
- encouraging youth courts to ensure that the physical environment of the court room promotes proceedings which involve the young person directly and which are less adversarial.

Paragraph 9.7 encourages 'opening up the youth court'. It says:

There must also be more openness in youth court proceedings. In law, youth courts have some discretion over who can attend proceedings and over the lifting of reporting restrictions. But present practice places too much emphasis on protecting the identity of young offenders at the expense of the interests of victims and the community. Justice is best served in an open court where the criminal process can be scrutinised and the offender cannot hide behind a cloak of anonymity.

To achieve this, para 9.8 says that:

The Government believes that the youth court should make full use of its discretion to lift reporting restrictions in the public interest following conviction. This is particularly important where the offence is a serious one; where the offending is persistent or where it has affected a number of people or the local community; and at the upper age range of the youth court. Occasions when it would not be in the best interests of the public, and others concerned with the case, to lift reporting restrictions might include cases where an early guilty plea was entered or where naming the young offender would result in revealing the identity of a vulnerable victim.

This part of the Paper concludes:

9.9 Though the Government does not want to make youth courts entirely open in the same way as adult courts, it believes that magistrates should make use of their existing discretion to admit victims and members of the public to youth courts. Victims, in particular, have a strong claim to be present during the trial to see justice being done, unless in the circumstances of the particular case this would be contrary to the interests of justice.

Of course, in the case of adult defendants, a trial in open court is fundamental to the fairness guaranteed by Art 6 of the European Convention on Human Rights. However, this approach has to be modified in the case of young defendants, where trial in open court may be regarded as inimical to fairness (see *T and V v UK* (2000) 30 EHRR 121 and the provisions of the *Consolidated Practice Direction* on dealing with young defendants in the Crown Court).

Turning to the sentencing process, the government indicates in para 9.21 that it wants youth court sentencing to be built on the concept of restorative justice:

restoration: young offenders apologising to their victims and making amends for the harm they have done;

reintegration: young offenders paying their debt to society, putting their crime behind them and rejoining the law abiding community; and

responsibility: young offenders – and their parents – facing the consequences of their offending behaviour and taking responsibility for preventing further offending.

In para 9.22, it is said that this approach is intended to:

- ensure that the most serious offenders continue to be dealt with in a criminal court to provide punishment, protect the public and prevent re-offending;

- provide an opportunity for less serious offending to be dealt with in a new non-criminal panel, enforced by a criminal court;
- involve young people more effectively in decisions about them – encouraging them to admit their guilt and face up to the consequences of their behaviour;
- involve the victim in proceedings, but only with their active consent; and
- focus on preventing offending.

5.16   YOUTH JUSTICE: WHAT HAPPENS NEXT?

In March 2004, the Home Office published *Youth Justice – the Next Steps: Summary of Responses and the Government's Proposals*. In its Consultation Paper, *Every Child Matters – Next Steps*, the government said (at para 4.20):

> ... Where [young people] do commit crimes the focus for the people who work with them will continue to be preventing offending and tackling the factors that underlie it. We intend to clarify the law so that preventing offending is also the main purpose of sentencing, but we shall require courts also to have regard to public protection, welfare, punishment and reparation when deciding an appropriate sentence for a young offender. We shall make fuller use of parenting programmes, both with young offenders' families and with young offenders who are themselves parents. We propose also to take steps to help as much as possible young defendants and their carers understand and prepare for their experience in court. We shall make sentencing simpler and more flexible, drawing on a broad menu of interventions that may be chosen from to meet individual need. The new Intensive Supervision and Surveillance Order will provide a robust alternative to custody, which will be a last resort for only the most serious or persistent young offenders. With the help of other children's services, the youth justice system will focus in particular on helping young offenders re-engage with education, training and employment in the community.

The Paper goes on to set out the government's conclusions and intentions, making the point that some of the action to put its decisions into effect will depend on resources or parliamentary time. It says that: 'Our youth justice approach ... focuses on preventing offending but also on tackling the factors which underlie it.' The conclusions are set out under a series of headings:

Pre-court interventions

We have decided not to change the existing statutory framework on Reprimands and Final Warnings because it provides speed, simplicity and effective sanctions for failure to comply. We do propose to take administrative action to ensure that the scheme is used to its full capacity and we shall issue guidance so that reasons are stated in open court whenever the scheme is bypassed. We also intend to put forward legislation at a suitable opportunity to amend the Rehabilitation of Offenders Act to ensure that Reprimands and Final Warnings are not citable to prospective employers.

General sentencing principles and structure

We unreservedly accept that welfare is an important consideration when a court has to make a decision on the appropriate sentence for a young offender. But we believe that the main purpose of a sentence imposed by a court on conviction of a criminal offence by a juvenile should be to prevent their further offending and we shall legislate to clarify this in law. Courts will also be required to have regard to other factors including public protection, welfare, punishment and reparation. The interventions which are used to help the young person deal with their offending behaviour would include activities and support which have been assessed as appropriate for the individual. The Sentencing Guidelines Council will also provide guidance to courts on juveniles. In addition, we will include preventing anti-social behaviour in the duties of the Youth Justice Board and youth offending teams.

Families and communities

We shall promote the fuller use of parenting measures, including Family Group Conferencing and family therapy, by youth justice agencies and shall issue guidance. We shall also provide parenting programmes for young offenders who are themselves parents. We recognise that some of these offenders are 'hard to reach' and their needs are not being met by current programmes. We plan to establish family group conferencing in 15 youth offending team areas to promote this technique as a form of restorative justice.

Policing, public order and courts

We propose to develop a Young Defendant's Pack to help young people and their parents or carers understand and prepare for their court experience – to promote understanding and acceptance of responsibility. We shall also examine the scope for involving voluntary agencies in supporting them at and before court, and further promote simpler language in court. We propose to discuss with the Judicial Studies Board ways in which the particular needs of young defendants can be met through training for crown court judges and with the relevant professional bodies in respect of training for lawyers.

Remands

We shall issue guidance to ensure pre-sentence reports are consistently well targeted and provide the information courts need. We propose to provide a wider range of supported accommodation for young people on bail or community sentence. We also propose to encourage the use of remand fostering and consider how to increase the provision of places.

We also propose to legislate to treat 17 year olds as juveniles for the purposes of remand and bail. There will be separate consultation on the question of the status of 17 year olds being interviewed by the police under PACE legislation.

Sentencing in the community

We believe that it is important for the sentencing options to be simpler and more flexible. The Reparation Order and Referral Order will maintain their distinct roles but otherwise we shall legislate to introduce a new generic juvenile community sentence with a wide menu of interventions. This new Juvenile Rehabilitation Order will replace the eight current community sentences.

… Youth Justice Centres [will] provide a wider range of activities in support of the sentence – including counselling, sport, education (basic and life skills), training, employment and community service.

… [W]e shall build on the success of Acceptable Behaviour Contracts and encourage their use with positive requirements as part of the early intervention work by Youth Inclusion and Support Panels.

We propose to improve the leverage of Youth Offending Teams in accessing local accommodation for young defendants on bail and for convicted young offenders through buying retainers on emergency beds, bonds and specialist advice or placement services. They need to be able to make full use of existing accommodation in the community – whether provided by local authorities, housing associations or private landlords. We also propose to pilot intensive fostering as an alternative to custody for convicted young offenders.

We shall establish outreach services for young offenders serving sentences in the community, including those leaving custody. These services will provide practical advice and help to the young person to re-engage with the statutory and other services in the community. We shall also negotiate with local authorities to identify more reparation projects suitable for juvenile offenders which help local communities.

We propose a limited extension to Referral Orders to allow them on a later court appearance, for example where the young person has not previously received one or did so at least two years ago.

More intensive sentences, including custody

... [W]e shall legislate to establish a new Intensive Supervision and Surveillance Order as a robust alternative to custody for the more serious or persistent offenders. We shall retain the Detention and Training Order (DTO) and also provide that 12–14 year olds would no longer need to be both serious and persistent to receive a DTO, but that the maximum term for them would drop from 24 to 12 months.

During the community part of a DTO we shall bring a particular focus on activities to help young offenders re-engage with education, training and employment. In addition supervising officers will be able to choose from the same range of interventions as are available to offenders serving a community sentence. We shall explore further how to improve the continuity between education in custody and in the community.

For a critique of these proposals in the context of the history of juvenile justice, see 'Youth justice? Half a century of responses to youth offending' [2004] Crim LR 167, by Caroline Ball.

CHAPTER 6

APPEALS FROM MAGISTRATES' COURTS AND YOUTH COURTS

6.1   INTRODUCTION

In this chapter, we look at the mechanisms which exist for appealing against the decisions of a magistrates' court or a youth court. We examine the appellate jurisdiction of the Crown Court (completely different to its jurisdiction as a court of first instance when defendants are tried on indictment) and we also consider the supervisory jurisdiction which the High Court exercises over magistrates' courts and youth courts by means of appeal by way of case stated and by means of judicial review.

Thus, there are three forms to appeal against the decisions of a magistrates' court or a youth court:

- appeal to the Crown Court;
- appeal to the High Court by way of case stated; and
- judicial review.

6.2   APPEAL TO THE CROWN COURT

The most common form of appeal from the magistrates' court and youth court is to the Crown Court. This is governed by s 108 of the Magistrates' Courts Act 1980. If the defendant pleaded guilty, he can appeal against sentence only (unless the plea was equivocal, considered later in this chapter). If he pleaded not guilty but was convicted by the magistrates, he can appeal against conviction and/or sentence.

Section 108 provides as follows:

(1)   A person convicted by a magistrates' court may appeal to the Crown Court—

    (a) if he pleaded guilty, against his sentence;

    (b) if he did not, against the conviction or sentence.

(1A) Section 14 of the Powers of Criminal Courts (Sentencing) Act 2000 (under which a conviction of an offence for which … an order for conditional or absolute discharge is made is deemed not to be a conviction except for certain purposes) shall not prevent an appeal under this section, whether against conviction or otherwise.

(2)   A person sentenced by a magistrates' court for an offence in respect of which an order for conditional discharge has been previously made may appeal to the Crown Court against the sentence.

(3)   In this section 'sentence' includes any order made on conviction by a magistrates' court, not being—

    …

    (b) an order for the payment of costs; …

6.2.1   Procedure for appeal to the Crown Court

The procedure for appeal is as follows:

- notice of appeal is given to the clerk of the magistrates' court and to the prosecutor within 21 days of the passing of the sentence (r 7 of the Crown Court Rules 1982);
- leave to appeal is not required;
- grounds of appeal need not be given;
- the Crown Court can extend the 21 day period but will take account of the merits of the case as well as the reason for the delay if asked to extend the time limit (r 7(5), (6)).

The 21 day period for giving notice of appeal runs from the date when sentence is passed even if the appeal is against conviction only.

6.2.2   Bail pending appeal

Where the defendant is given a custodial sentence, bail pending appeal may be granted by the magistrates who passed sentence (s 113 of the Magistrates' Courts Act 1980), although there is no presumption in favour of bail as s 4 of the Bail Act 1976 does not apply. If the magistrates do not grant bail, the Crown Court may do so (under s 81(1) of the Supreme Court Act 1981). The strongest argument that can be advanced in support of bail pending the hearing of the appeal is that a short sentence may have been served before the appeal is heard.

The right to apply for bail to a High Court judge in chambers under s 22(1) of the Criminal Justice Act 1967 is removed by the Criminal Justice Act 2003.

6.2.3   The hearing of the appeal in the Crown Court

The appeal is heard by a Circuit judge or recorder and at least two lay justices.

An appeal against conviction takes the form of a complete re-hearing (so the procedure is the same as the trial in the magistrates' court or youth court) (s 79(3) of the Supreme Court Act 1981).

Because an appeal against conviction is a re-hearing, the parties are not limited to evidence which was called at the original trial. This has the important consequence that either party can call witnesses who were not called in the magistrates' court trial, or refrain from calling witnesses who did give evidence in the magistrates' court. Note, however, that the Crown Court cannot amend the information on which the appellant was convicted (*Garfield v Maddocks* [1974] QB 7; *R v Swansea Crown Court ex p Stacey* [1990] RTR 183).

An appeal against sentence similarly mirrors the sentencing procedure in the magistrates' court or youth court, with the prosecution summarising the facts and the defence making a plea in mitigation. In *R v Swindon Crown Court ex p Murray* (1998) 162 JP 36, the Divisional Court held that, when dealing with an appeal against sentence, the Crown Court should not ask itself whether the sentence was within the discretion of the magistrates (the test which would be appropriate in judicial review) but should consider whether, in the light of all the matters which the Crown Court had heard, the sentence passed by the magistrates was the correct one. If it was not the correct sentence, the Crown Court should replace it with the sentence that that court holds to be the right one.

In *Bussey v DPP* [1999] 1 Cr App R(S) 125, the defendant pleaded guilty to the offence of driving whilst disqualified. He maintained that he only drove because his wife had been taken ill and he had to take her to hospital. The Crown disputed this version of events, but the magistrates decided (without hearing evidence) to accept the defendant's version. The defendant felt that the sentence imposed was nonetheless excessive and he appealed to the Crown Court. It was held that, since the Crown Court is not bound by findings of fact made by a magistrates' court in a way that could limit the Crown Court's sentencing powers, where a defendant appeals against sentence to the Crown Court, the court is entitled to decide the appeal on a different factual basis from that accepted by the magistrates' court. However, where the Crown Court rejects the view taken by the magistrates' court, the court should make the position plain to the appellant and give him an opportunity, under the *Newton* principle (see *R v Newton* (1983) 77 Cr App R 13), to challenge the factual basis adopted by the court.

6.2.4   Decision

The decision of the Crown Court is a majority decision. This means that the lay justices can out-vote the judge. The lay justices must, however, accept any decisions on questions of law made by the judge.

Where the Crown Court dismisses an appeal against conviction, the judge must give reasons; judicial review can be sought to compel the judge to do so if necessary (*R v Warwick Crown Court ex p Patel* [1992] COD 143; *R v Harrow Crown Court ex p Dave* [1994] 1 WLR 98; *R (Taylor) v Maidstone Crown Court* [2003] EWHC 2555). In *R v Snaresbrook Crown Court ex p Input Management Ltd* (1999) 163 JP 533, the Divisional Court defined the obligation to give reasons: the reasons given by the Crown Court should enable the defendant: (i) to see the nature of the criminality found to exist by the Court; and (ii) to consider properly whether there are grounds for a further appeal to the Divisional Court by way of case stated. In *R v Kingston Crown Court ex p Bell* (2000) 164 JP 633, the Divisional Court said that failure by the Crown Court to give reasons for its decision will usually vitiate the decision. However, the court said that this is not a universal rule; if, for example, the reasons are obvious, then the failure to give reasons will not necessarily be fatal.

According to the official Judicial Statistics for 2003, nearly 42% of defendants appealing to the Crown Court had their appeals against conviction allowed or their sentence varied; of the remainder, 31% of appeals were dismissed and 26% were abandoned.

6.2.5   Equivocal pleas

The usual rule is that a defendant who pleads guilty in the magistrates' court cannot challenge that conviction by appealing to the Crown Court. However, if the plea of guilty was 'equivocal', the defendant can appeal against conviction despite having pleaded guilty. There are two main types of equivocal plea:

- The plea which is equivocal in court (that is, becomes equivocal because of something said prior to the passing of sentence).

This will be the case if either:

(i) when the charge is put, the defendant says 'Guilty but ...', that is, some form of words raising a defence (for example, 'guilty of theft but I thought the property was mine'); or

(ii) when the charge is put, the defendant says only 'Guilty', but this straightforward plea is followed by a plea in mitigation which raises a defence and so is inconsistent with the guilty plea (for example, *R v Durham Quarter Sessions ex p Virgo* [1952] 2 QB 1).

- The plea which is made equivocal not because of anything the defendant says in court but because the defendant pleaded guilty as a direct result of threats from a third party. Then, at some time after the passing of sentence, the defendant alleges that he only pleaded guilty as a result of duress and now maintains that he is innocent (for example, *R v Huntingdon Crown Court ex p Jordan* [1981] QB 857).

In the case of the first type of equivocal plea, the problem should be dealt with at the original hearing. The charge should be put again by the magistrates' court once the relevant law has been explained to the defendant. If the plea remains equivocal, a not guilty plea should be entered by the court on the defendant's behalf.

If this does not occur, or if the plea is equivocal because of duress, the defendant should apply to the Crown Court to declare the plea equivocal. In this type of appeal, the only enquiry undertaken by the Crown Court is whether the plea was equivocal or not. If the Crown Court decides that the plea was indeed equivocal, it will remit the case to the magistrates' court for trial.

Provided the Crown Court conducts a proper inquiry into what happened in the magistrates' court (the clerk or the chairman of the bench which convicted the defendant may have to supply a statement to assist the Crown Court in that inquiry), a direction from the Crown Court regarding remission for trial is binding on the magistrates' court (*R v Plymouth Justices ex p Hart* [1986] 1 QB 950; [1986] 2 All ER 452).

There are no other grounds for going behind a plea of guilty and so no other cases where a defendant can appeal to the Crown Court after pleading guilty (*R v Marylebone Justices ex p Westminster London Borough Council* [1971] 1 WLR 567). It is therefore not sufficient for the defendant merely to show that he regrets pleading guilty and that he has an arguable defence.

6.2.6　Powers of the Crown Court

Section 48(2) of the Supreme Court Act 1981 provides that, following an appeal from the magistrates' court, the Crown Court:

(a) may confirm, reverse or vary any part of the decision appealed against, including a determination not to impose a separate penalty in respect of an offence; or

(b) may remit the matter with its opinion thereon to the authority whose decision is appealed against; or

(c) may make such other order in the matter as the court thinks just, and by such order exercise any power which the said authority might have exercised.

Section 48(4) and (5) goes on to provide that:

(4)　... if the appeal is against a conviction or a sentence, the preceding provisions of this section shall be construed as including power to award any punishment, whether more or less severe than that awarded by the magistrates' court whose decision is appealed against, if that is a punishment which that magistrates' court might have awarded.

(5) This section applies whether or not the appeal is against the whole of the decision.

Thus, s 48 allows the Crown Court to:

- quash the conviction;
- remit the case to the magistrates' court (for example, in the case of an equivocal plea);
- vary the sentence imposed by the magistrates (this includes the power to increase the sentence, but not beyond the maximum sentence which the magistrates' court could have passed).

The wording of s 48(2) has the effect that, if the defendant appeals against only part of the decision of the magistrates' court, every aspect of the magistrates' decision can be reconsidered by the Crown Court. For example:

- even if the defendant appeals only against conviction, the Crown Court can still vary the sentence;
- if the defendant was convicted of two offences and appeals against only one conviction, the Crown Court could allow the appeal but vary the sentence for the other offence;
- if the defendant was convicted by the magistrates of one offence but acquitted of another and he now appeals against the conviction, the Crown Court could convict the defendant of the offence of which the magistrates' court acquitted him.

It should be noted that, if the Crown Court does vary the sentence, it cannot impose a sentence greater than the sentence that the magistrates could have imposed.

6.2.7 Abandonment of appeal

Under r 11 of the Crown Court Rules 1982, the appellant may abandon his appeal by giving written notice to the magistrates' court, the Crown Court and the prosecution. Notice should be given at least three days before the appeal is due to be heard. It is open to the Crown Court to allow an appeal to be abandoned even if these requirements are not satisfied. In *R v Gloucester Crown Court ex p Betteridge* (1997) 161 JP 721, the Divisional Court held that, once the Crown Court gives leave to an appellant to abandon his appeal from the decision of the magistrates' court, the Crown Court no longer has the power to increase the sentence imposed by the magistrates.

In *Hayes v DPP* (2003) *The Times*, 30 January, the defendant was sentenced to six months' imprisonment by a magistrates' court. He was released on bail pending appeal. The terms of his bail required him to be present at the appeal. The defendant failed to attend court on the date fixed for the hearing of the appeal. He also failed to appear on subsequent dates, although he was represented by counsel. The judge dismissed the appeal, holding that the defendant had effectively abandoned his appeal. The Divisional Court said that in any case where it appears to the Crown Court, sitting in an appellate capacity, that an appellant is not attending in spite of being obliged to do so, but is represented by counsel, the proper course is for the court to hear the appeal in the absence of the appellant. It is not open to the Crown Court to treat the absence of the appellant as *de facto* abandonment of the appeal.

6.2.8   Further appeal from the Crown Court

The decision of the Crown Court on an appeal from a magistrates' court or youth court can only be challenged by means of an appeal to the Divisional Court by way of case stated or judicial review. There is no appeal to the Court of Appeal.

Recommendation 306.3 of the Auld Review was that there should no longer be an appeal to the High Court (either by way of case stated or judicial review) from the Crown Court sitting in its appellate capacity, but that there should be an appeal to the Court of Appeal; however, this appeal should be subject to the permission of the Court of Appeal, which it should only give in a case involving an important point of principle or practice or where there is some other compelling reason for the court to hear it. This suggestion was not taken up by the government.

6.3   APPEAL TO THE DIVISIONAL COURT BY WAY OF CASE STATED

This is possible under s 111 of the Magistrates' Courts Act 1980, which provides as follows:

(1) Any person who was a party to any proceeding before a magistrates' court or is aggrieved by the conviction, order, determination or other proceeding of the court may question the proceeding on the ground that it is wrong in law or is in excess of jurisdiction by applying to the justices composing the court to state a case for the opinion of the High Court on the question of law or jurisdiction involved ...

(2) An application under sub-section (1) above shall be made within 21 days after the day on which the decision of the magistrates' court was given.

(3) For the purpose of sub-section (2) above, the day on which the decision of the magistrates' court is given shall, where the court has adjourned the trial of an information after conviction, be the day on which the court sentences or otherwise deals with the offender.

(4) On the making of an application under this section in respect of a decision any right of the applicant to appeal against the decision to the Crown Court shall cease.

(5) If the justices are of opinion that an application under this section is frivolous, they may refuse to state a case, and, if the applicant so requires, shall give him a certificate stating that the application has been refused ...

(6) Where justices refuse to state a case, the High Court may, on the application of the person who applied for the case to be stated, make an order of *mandamus* requiring the justices to state a case.

Unlike the appeal to the Crown Court, it is available to the prosecution as well as the defence. However, it only applies where the decision of the magistrates' court or youth court is:

• wrong in law; or
• in excess of jurisdiction.

The right to appeal by way of case stated is only available where there has been a final determination of the case in the magistrates' court; this form of appeal is not available, for example, to challenge the decision of the magistrates to send the accused for trial or sentence in the Crown Court (see *Streames v Copping* [1985] 1 QB 920 and *Loade v DPP* [1990] 1 QB 1052).

In *McKnight v Sheppard* [1999] 1 WLR 1333, it was held that on an appeal by way of case stated a party is not entitled to take a new point, the decision of which might be affected by evidence which could have been, but was not, adduced before the tribunal of fact. Similarly, where a defendant has been convicted by the magistrates and appeals to the Divisional Court, it is not possible to raise the issue that certain prosecution evidence should have been excluded under s 78 of the Police and Criminal Evidence Act 1984 if the defence had not asked the magistrates to exclude the evidence under s 78. In other words, such matters cannot be raised for the first time in the Divisional Court (see *Braham v DPP* (1995) 159 JP 527).

The appellant makes an application to the magistrates to state a case. This application must be made within 21 days of conviction (or sentence, if later) identifying the question of law or jurisdiction at issue. This 21 day period cannot be extended (*Michael v Gowland* [1977] 1 WLR 296; *R v Clerkenwell Magistrates' Court ex p DPP* [1984] QB 821). It should be noted, however, that where the final termination of proceedings is a decision on an application for costs, the 21 day time limit for asking the magistrates to state a case under s 111 of the Magistrates' Courts Act 1980 begins to run from the date of the decision on costs (*Liverpool City Council v Worthington* [1999] EHLR 225).

6.3.1 Refusal to state a case

The justices may refuse to state a case if they regard the application as frivolous and issue a certificate to that effect (s 111(5) of the Magistrates' Courts Act 1980). If they do refuse to state a case, the appellant can apply for judicial review of this refusal (s 111(6)).

The test of whether a request to state a case is frivolous is whether the application raises an arguable point of law (*R v City of London Justices ex p Ocansey* (1995) unreported, and *R v East Cambridgeshire Justices ex p Stephenson* (1995) unreported). In *R v Mildenhall Magistrates' Court ex p Forest Heath District Council* (1997) 161 JP 401, it was held that the word 'frivolous' in this context means that the justices consider the application to be 'futile, misconceived, hopeless, or academic'. The court went on to say that such a conclusion will be reached only rarely: it is not enough that the justices consider that their original decision was correct. Furthermore, where justices do refuse to state a case, they should give brief reasons explaining why they have done so. The court went on to say that a finding of fact may be challenged if it is perverse (see *Bracegirdle v Oxley* [1947] 1 KB 349, p 353, *per* Lord Goddard CJ); this would be the case if, for example, the finding had no evidential foundation whatsoever. However, a decision (even if mistaken) is not perverse if the justices prefer A's evidence to that of B and resolve the question of fact on the basis of A's evidence.

Where the magistrates refuse to state a case and the appellant seeks judicial review of that refusal, the usual remedy (if the Divisional Court holds that the refusal to state a case was wrong) is for the Divisional Court to quash the refusal to state a case, so the magistrates have to state a case. However, it is open to the Divisional Court, when considering the application for judicial review of the refusal to state a case, to regard the written evidence used in the judicial review proceedings as the case stated (see *R v Reigate Justices ex p Counsell* (1983) 148 JP 193) and to treat the application for judicial review as if it were an appeal by way of case stated. In this way, the Divisional Court can, for example, quash a conviction without waiting for the case to go back to the magistrates to state a case (see, for example, *R v Ealing Justices ex p Woodman* (1994) 158 JP 997).

This approach was followed in *R v Crown Court at Blackfriars ex p Sunworld Ltd* [2000] 1 WLR 2102, where the Divisional Court gave guidance on the approach to be adopted by that court in a case where the magistrates' court (or indeed the Crown Court, on appeal from the magistrates' court) has refused to state a case. Where a magistrates' court or Crown Court refuses to state a case, the aggrieved party should, without delay, apply for permission to bring judicial review (either seeking a mandatory order to require the court to state a case or a quashing order to quash the order sought to be appealed). If the court below has already given a reasoned judgment containing all the necessary findings of fact and/or has explained its refusal to state a case in terms which clearly raise the true point of law in issue, the single judge should, if he thinks the point properly arguable, grant permission for judicial review which directly challenges the order complained of, thereby avoiding the need for a case to be stated at all. If the court below has stated a case but in respect of some questions only, the better course may be to apply for the case stated to be amended, unless there already exists sufficient material to enable the Divisional Court to deal with all the properly arguable issues in the case. The Divisional Court will adopt whatever course involves the fewest additional steps and the least expense, delay and duplication of proceedings. Whether (as in *R v Thames Magistrates Court ex p Levy* (1997) *The Times*, 17 July) it will be possible to proceed at once to a substantive determination of the issues must inevitably depend in part upon whether all interested parties are represented and prepared, and on the availability of court time.

Another reason for refusing to state a case is contained in s 114 of the Magistrates' Courts Act 1980, which provides that:

> Justices to whom application has been made to state a case for the opinion of the High Court on any proceeding of a magistrates' court shall not be required to state the case until the applicant has entered into a recognisance, with or without sureties, before the magistrates' court, conditioned to prosecute the appeal without delay and to submit to the judgment of the High Court and pay such costs as that Court may award ...

This empowers the magistrates to require the appellant to enter into a recognisance (that is, promise to pay a specified sum of money if the condition is not complied with) to pursue the appeal without delay. If this power is invoked, a case will not be stated until the appellant has entered into a recognisance.

The fact that the applicant's defence is publicly funded does not, of itself, mean that the justices cannot require him to enter into a recognisance; the defendant must satisfy the court that he has no means of raising sufficient capital to comply with the condition (*R v Croydon Magistrates' Court ex p Morgan* (1997) 161 JP 169).

6.3.2   Statement of case

Rule 76 of the Magistrates Courts Rules 1981 provides as follows:

(1)   An application under section 111(1) of the Act of 1980 shall be made in writing and signed by or on behalf of the applicant and shall identify the question or questions of law or jurisdiction on which the opinion of the High Court is sought.

(2) Where one of the questions on which the opinion of the High Court is sought is whether there was evidence on which the magistrates' court could come to its decision, the particular finding of fact made by the magistrates' court which it is claimed cannot be supported by the evidence before the magistrates' court shall be specified in such application.

(3) Any such application shall be sent to the justices' chief executive for the magistrates' court whose decision is questioned.

Rule 81 governs the contents of the statement of case. It provides that:

(1) A case stated by the magistrates' court shall state the facts found by the court and the question or questions of law or jurisdiction on which the opinion of the High Court is sought.

(2) Where one of the questions on which the opinion of the High Court is sought is whether there was evidence on which the magistrates' court could come to its decision, the particular finding of fact which it is claimed cannot be supported by the evidence before the magistrates' court shall be specified in the case.

(3) Unless one of the questions on which the opinion of the High Court is sought is whether there was evidence on which the magistrates' court could come to its decision, the case shall not contain a statement of evidence.

Thus, the statement of the case should set out:

- the charge(s) being tried by the magistrates;
- the facts as found by the magistrates (but not the evidence upon which those findings of fact were based, unless the basis of the appeal is that the decision of the justices was entirely unsupported by the evidence which they had heard);
- any submissions (including names of any authorities cited in argument) made to the magistrates by the prosecution and defence (see *DPP v Kirk* [1993] COD 99), and the magistrates' decision on those submissions;
- the question(s) for determination by the High Court.

In *Vehicle Inspectorate v George Jenkins Transport Ltd* [2003] EWHC 2879 (Admin); (2003) *The Times*, 5 December, it was said that a stated case should set out the facts as found or accepted for the purposes of the magistrates' ruling (with reference to any relevant documents); it should set out in summary form the submissions made on each side; it should set out the conclusions of the magistrates' court on the matters in issue and the question(s) for the consideration of the Divisional Court. Kennedy LJ added (at para 39), 'Where advocates appear in the magistrates' court, there is no reason why the court, if minded to state a case, should not invite the advocates for the parties to submit a first draft, indicating any areas of disagreement'.

The magistrates' clerk prepares a draft case and sends it to the prosecution and defence for comment. A properly drafted question should not be altered without the party who framed the original question being given the opportunity to commit on the changes (*R v Waldie* (1995) 159 JP 514). The final version (amended in the light of any comments made by prosecution or defence and signed by the clerk or by two of the magistrates whose decision is under appeal) is sent to the appellant.

The appellant should lodge the stated case at the Administrative Court Office (in the Royal Courts of Justice) within 10 days of receiving it from the clerk (CPR Practice Direction 52, para 18.4) and must serve the appellant's notice and accompanying documents on all respondents within four days after they are filed or lodged at the appeal court (para 18.6).

It should be borne in mind that when magistrates are asked to state a case, it is not open to them to put forward reasons why the respondent should not be able to challenge their decision where those reasons were not part of their original decision (*Kent County Council v Curtis* (1998) EGCS 100). Furthermore, the justices should not change, or put a gloss on, the reasons which they gave in court for convicting or acquitting the defendant (*Evans v DPP* [2001] EWHC 369 (Admin); (2001) *The Times,* 9 July).

6.3.3   Bail pending appeal

If the defendant was given a custodial sentence, the magistrates may grant bail pending appeal under s 113 of the Magistrates' Courts Act 1980. If the magistrates refuse, the defendant can apply to a High Court judge in chambers under s 37(1)(b) of the Criminal Justice Act 1948. This jurisdiction to grant bail is preserved by the Criminal Justice Act 2003 (which otherwise removed the bail jurisdiction of the High Court).

6.3.4   The hearing

The appeal is heard by a Divisional Court (that is, two or more High Court judges in open court). If a two judge court hears the appeal but cannot agree on the outcome, the appeal fails (*Flannagan v Shaw* [1920] 3 KB 96).

No evidence is heard. The appeal takes the form of legal argument based on the facts stated in the case; no evidence is called, and so there are no witnesses.

6.3.5   Powers of the Divisional Court

The powers of the Divisional Court on an appeal by way of case stated are contained in s 112 of the Magistrates' Courts Act 1980, which provides that:

> Any conviction, order, determination or other proceeding of a magistrates' court varied by the High Court on an appeal by case stated, and any judgment or order of the High Court on such an appeal, may be enforced as if it were a decision of the magistrates' court from which the appeal was brought.

Section 28A of the Supreme Court Act 1981 provides as follows:

> (3)   The High Court shall hear and determine the question arising on the case (or the case as amended) and shall—
>
>   (a) reverse, affirm or amend the determination in respect of which the case has been stated; or
>
>   (b) remit the matter to the magistrates' court, or the Crown Court, with the opinion of the High Court,
>
>   and may make such other order in relation to the matter (including as to costs) as it thinks fit.
>
> (4)   Except as provided by the Administration of Justice Act 1960 (right of appeal to House of Lords in criminal cases), a decision of the High Court under this section is final.

It follows that:

- where the defendant was convicted by the magistrates, the Divisional Court may replace the conviction with an acquittal;
- where the defendant was acquitted after a full trial (that is, not after a successful submission of no case to answer at the close of the prosecution case), the Divisional Court may remit the case back to the magistrates' court with a direction to convict and proceed to sentence (or if it is plain what sentence should be passed, the Divisional Court may itself convict and proceed to sentence the appellant);
- where the defendant was acquitted otherwise that after a full trial (for example, following a successful submission of no case to answer), the Divisional Court may remit the case to the magistrates' court with a direction to continue with the trial or to start the trial afresh in front of a fresh bench.

The Divisional Court cannot quash only part of an order and leave the rest intact. So, in *R v Old Street Magistrates ex p Spencer* (1994) *The Times*, 8 November, a costs order for £930 had been made. The Divisional Court felt that £150–250 was the appropriate bracket. However, the Divisional Court lacked the power to substitute a different amount. All it could do was to quash the original order and remit the case to the magistrates.

In *Griffith v Jenkins* [1992] 2 AC 76, the House of Lords confirmed that the Divisional Court has the power to remit a case for a re-hearing before the same or a different bench of magistrates. Thus, it does not matter if the original court cannot be reconstituted for some reason (for example, one of the justices has retired or died). A re-hearing of the case will only be ordered if a fair trial is still possible given the lapse of time since the alleged offence.

6.3.6   Abandonment of appeal

An appellant who has made an appeal by way of case stated is entitled to withdraw that appeal without the leave of the High Court (*Collett v Bromsgrove District Council* (1996) 160 JP 593).

6.3.7   Effect on the right of appeal to the Crown Court

The making of an application to the magistrates to state a case removes the defendant's right to appeal to the Crown Court (s 111(4) of the Magistrates' Courts Act 1980). It is therefore tactically wise to appeal to the Crown Court first and, if that appeal is unsuccessful, to appeal against the decision of the Crown Court to the Divisional Court.

6.4   JUDICIAL REVIEW

Like appeal by way of case stated, judicial review is available to the prosecution as well as the defence. However, an acquittal will not be quashed unless the trial was a nullity and so the defendant was not in danger of a valid conviction (for example, the purported summary trial of an indictable-only offence, or where the magistrates acquit without hearing any prosecution evidence (*R v Dorking Justices ex p Harrington* [1984] AC 743)).

For judicial review to be available, there does not have to have been a final determination of the case.

Where the defendant pleaded guilty, the court will only entertain an application for judicial review of the conviction where the prosecution has acted in a way which has misled the defendant (*R v Burton-on-Trent Justices ex p Woolley* (1995) 159 JP 165, following *R v Home Secretary ex p Al Mehdawi* [1990] 1 AC 876).

6.4.1 Grounds

The grounds for seeking judicial review are:

- error of law on the face of record (that is, an error disclosed in the court records). This would include passing a sentence in excess of the relevant statutory maximum for that offence;
- excess of jurisdiction (that is, the decision was *ultra vires*). In *R v Kent Justices ex p Machin* [1952] 2 QB 355, for example, the defendant was asked to agree to summary trial without first being warned that if he did so he could be committed for sentence to the Crown Court; the summary trial was therefore void;
- breach of the rules of natural justice (for example, bias or failing to allow both sides to put their case).

In *R v Gough* [1993] AC 646, the House of Lords held that the court should ask itself whether there was a 'real danger' of bias. In *Porter v Magill* [2002] 2 AC 357, the House of Lords considered the question of bias in relation to the courts generally, and approved the test derived from *Re Medicaments and Related Classes of Goods (No 2)* [2000] 1 WLR 700: would a fair-minded and informed observer conclude that there was a real possibility, or real danger (the two being the same) that the tribunal was biased? This test is in accordance with that adopted by the European Court of Human Rights in *Sander v UK* (2001) 31 EHRR 44. This is effectively the same as the test propounded in *R v Liverpool Justices ex p Topping* [1983] 1 WLR 119: would a reasonable and fair minded person sitting in court and hearing all the relevant facts have a reasonable suspicion that a fair trial of the appellant was not possible?

Breach of natural justice has been widely construed. It includes, for example:

(a) failing to give the accused adequate time to prepare a defence (*R v Thames Magistrates' Court ex p Polemis* [1974] 1 WLR 1371);

(b) failing to allow an adjournment where a witness could not attend on the day of the trial (*R v Bracknell Justices ex p Hughes* (1990) 154 JP 98):

(c) failure by the prosecution to notify the defence of the existence of a witness who could support the defence case (*R v Leyland Justices ex p Hawthorn* [1979] QB 283);

(d) failure by the prosecution to inform the defence in a shoplifting case that the key prosecution witness had a previous conviction for wasting police time, arising out of a false allegation of theft (*R v Knightsbridge Crown Court ex p Goonatilleke* [1986] QB 1);

(e) ordering a defendant to pay costs without considering his means to pay them (*R v Newham Justices ex p Samuels* [1991] COD 412).

However, there are some restrictions on the use of judicial review to challenge decisions of magistrates. For example, in *R v Greater Manchester Justices ex p Aldi GmbH & Co KG* (1995) 159 JP 717, it was held that it is inappropriate to challenge interlocutory decisions of magistrates by way of judicial review. The exception to this is where the magistrates allow the information to be amended to show a different defendant and adjourn in order for the summons to be served on the new defendant. Furthermore, in *R v Dolgellau Justices ex p Cartledge; R v Penrith Justices ex p Marks* [1996] RTR 207, the Divisional Court held that it has no jurisdiction to quash a summary conviction following an unequivocal plea of guilty where no complaint is made of the conduct of the tribunal and the conduct of the prosecution cannot fairly be categorised as analogous to fraud.

In *R v Peterborough Justices ex p Dowler* [1996] 2 Cr App R 561, where the appellant claimed that his conviction for careless driving should be set aside because the prosecution had failed to disclose a witness statement which might have helped his case, it was held that it is unnecessary to grant judicial review of a conviction by magistrates where the procedural unfairness complained of could be rectified by a fair hearing (by way of appeal) before the Crown Court. However, in *R v Hereford Magistrates' Court ex p Rowlands* [1998] QB 110, the Divisional Court held that the decision of the QBD in *Dowler*, although correct on its facts, should not be treated as authority that a party complaining of procedural unfairness in a magistrates' court should invariably exercise his right of appeal to the Crown Court rather than seek judicial review. The existence of a right of appeal to the Crown Court, particularly if it has not been exercised, should not ordinarily weigh against the grant of permission to seek judicial review or the granting of substantive relief once leave has been granted. However, permission to seek judicial review should only be granted if the applicant can show an apparently plausible complaint which, if upheld, might vitiate the proceedings in the magistrates' court. The Divisional Court should be slow to intervene, and should only do so when good (or arguably good) grounds are shown. It follows that the Divisional Court will not intervene if there have been only minor deviations from best practice.

6.4.2   Procedure

Judicial review is governed by Pt 54 of the Civil Procedure Rules (CPR). There is a strict time limit of three months from the date of the decision complained of (and the applicant must act promptly even within the three months):

(a) The first step in a claim for judicial review is to file a claim form. As well as the matters that normally have to appear in a claim form (see CPR 8.2), CPR Pt 54.6 provides that the claimant has to identify interested parties and must state the remedy sought. The claim form has to be accompanied by the documents required by the Practice Direction which supplements CPR Pt 54. Paragraph 5.6 of the Practice Direction says that the claim form must include or be accompanied by a detailed statement of the claimant's grounds for bringing the claim for judicial review, a statement of the facts relied upon, and a time estimate for the hearing. Paragraph 5.7 of the Practice Direction says that the claim form must also be accompanied by any written evidence in support of the claim (or in support of any application to extend time), a copy of any order that the claimant seeks to have quashed, an approved copy of the lower court's reasons for reaching the decision under challenge, copies of any documents on which the claimant proposes to rely, copies of any relevant statutory material, and a list of essential documents for reading in advance by the court (with page references to the passages relied on).

Where the claim is for judicial review of a decision of a magistrates' court or the Crown Court, the prosecution must always be named as an interested party (para 5.2 of the Practice Direction). The defendant must file an acknowledgment of service not more than 21 days after the service of the claim form. The acknowledgment of service must be served on the claimant, and on any other person named in the claim form, not later than seven days after it is filed. The acknowledgment of service must (if the person filing it intends to contest the claim) set out a summary of the grounds for contesting the claim (and must state the name and address of anyone whom the person filing it considers to be an interested party).

(b) Paragraph 8.4 of the Practice Direction that supplements CPR Pt 54 says that the court will generally consider the question of permission without a hearing. Where there is a hearing, neither the defendant nor any other interested party need attend the hearing unless the court directs otherwise (para 8.5 of the Practice Direction). Where the defendant or any interested party does attend a hearing, the court will not generally make an order for costs against the claimant (para 8.6 of the Practice Direction). If there has not been undue delay, the judge will go on to consider the merits of the application. The test applied by the single judge is whether the claimant's application for judicial review discloses an arguable case. CPR Pt 54.12 provides that if the court, without a hearing, refuses permission to proceed or gives permission that is subject to conditions or on certain grounds only, the court will serve its reasons for making the order along with the order itself. Under CPR Pt 54.12, 'the claimant may not appeal but may request the decision to be reconsidered at a hearing' (and must file a request for such a hearing within seven days of the service of the court's reasons for the decision). Neither the defendant nor anyone else serviced with the claim form may apply to set aside an order giving the claimant permission to proceed (CPR Pt 54.13).

(c) Under CPR Pt 54.14, once the claimant has been given permission to proceed, the defendant (and anyone else served with the claim form who wishes to contest the claim or support it on additional grounds) must, within 35 days after service of the order giving permission, serve detailed grounds for contesting the claim (or supporting it on additional grounds), and any written evidence.

(d) Where all the parties agree, the court may decide the claim for judicial review without a hearing (CPR Pt 54.18). Otherwise, the claimant must file and serve a skeleton argument not less than 21 working days before the date of the hearing of the judicial review claim (para 15.1 of the Practice Direction). The defendant (and any other party wishing to make representations at the hearing) must file and serve a skeleton argument not less than 14 working days before the date of the hearing (para 15.2 of the Practice Direction). The skeleton arguments must contain a list of issues, a list of the legal points to be taken (together with any relevant authorities), a chronology of events, a list of essential documents for advance reading by the court, and a list of persons referred to.

(e) Where the claimant seeks to rely on grounds other than those for which the court gave permission to proceed, he must first obtain the court's permission (CPR Pt 54.15). Where the claimant intends to rely on additional grounds at the hearing of the claim for judicial review, he must give notice to the court and to any person served with the claim form no later than seven clear days before the hearing.

(f) The hearing takes place before a Divisional Court (that is, two or more High Court judges sitting in an open court). It usually takes the form of legal argument based on the written evidence, though it is possible for oral evidence to be called if necessary. The court then reaches its decision and, if it decides in favour of the claimant, can make any of the orders set out below.

Usually any application for judicial review will be made at the conclusion of the proceedings in the magistrates' court. However, there will be some cases where an application may be made before that point. In *R (Hoar-Stevens) v Richmond-upon-Thames Magistrates* [2003] EWHC 2660, the Divisional Court held that it has jurisdiction to hear applications for judicial review in respect of questions as to whether proceedings should go ahead at all. However, there is a distinction between that type of case and the type of case where the Divisional Court is being asked to examine, during the course of a trial, the way in which a magistrates' court has in fact proceeded. In the latter case there is no jurisdiction for the court to entertain an application for judicial review until the proceedings before the magistrates have been concluded (see *R v Rochford Justices ex p Buck* (1978) 68 Cr App R 114).

6.4.3   Bail

Where the defendant was given a custodial sentence by the magistrates and is applying to the Divisional Court for a quashing order to quash the conviction, the magistrates do not have the power to grant bail pending the hearing of the application for judicial review. An application for bail may be made to a single High Court judge in chambers under s 37(1)(d) of the Criminal Justice Act 1948.

6.4.4   Remedies

The main judicial review remedies are:

* *Quashing order (formerly called certiorari)*

  This has the effect of quashing the original decision; where a conviction is quashed, the defendant stands acquitted of the offence.

* *Mandatory order (formerly called mandamus)*

  This requires the lower court to do something, for example, to go through the mode of trial procedure again or to re-hear an application for public funding of the case.

* *Prohibiting order (formerly called prohibition)*

  This prevents the lower court from doing something that it should not do, for example, committal proceedings where there have been several previous attempts to have the defendant committed for trial and so further attempts amount to an abuse of process.

Sometimes more than one order is made: for example, there might be a quashing order to quash the decision of the court below, and a mandatory order compelling the lower court to reconsider the matter.

It should be noted that granting of a judicial review remedy is always discretionary. Even if the applicant is able to succeed on the merits, the High Court may decide that it is inappropriate to grant a remedy (see, for example, *R v Oxford City Justices ex p Berry* [1988] QB 507).

Delay is a fairly common ground for withholding relief. In *R v Neath and Port Talbot Justices ex p DPP* [2000] 1 WLR 1376, the Divisional Court said that the circumstances to be taken into account when the court is exercising its discretion in criminal proceedings whether to grant relief in a judicial review application (or indeed an appeal by way of case stated) where there has been delay include:

- the seriousness of the offence;
- the nature of the evidence in the case (particularly the extent to which its quality would be affected by the delay);
- the extent, if any, to which the defendant had contributed to the magistrates' error;
- the extent, if any, to which the defendant had contributed to the delay in hearing the challenge;
- how far the complainant would be justifiably aggrieved by the proceedings being abandoned;
- how far the defendant would be justifiably aggrieved by the proceedings being continued.

6.5   APPEAL AGAINST SENTENCE

Although it would theoretically be possible to appeal by way of case stated (or to seek judicial review), if the magistrates impose a sentence which is beyond their powers, it is quicker and easier simply to appeal to the Crown Court against sentence.

Where the appeal is on the basis that the sentence is wrong in law (or outside jurisdiction) because it is so severe that no reasonable bench could impose such a sentence, the proper appeal is to the Crown Court rather than to the Divisional Court (*Tucker v DPP* [1992] 4 All ER 901; *R v Battle Justices ex p Shepherd* (1983) 5 Cr App R(S) 124).

In *Allen v West Yorkshire Probation Service* [2001] EWHC 2 (Admin); (2001) 165 JP 313, the Divisional Court repeated that appeals by way of case stated or applications for judicial review are not usually appropriate procedures for appeals against sentence. If a sentence imposed by magistrates is wrong, the defendant should appeal to the Crown Court unless there are clear and substantial reasons for believing that an appeal by way of case stated or judicial review would be appropriate.

6.6   CASE STATED OR JUDICIAL REVIEW?

The grounds on which judicial review can be sought and an appeal by way of case stated made are virtually the same: an error of law or jurisdiction.

In *R v Oldbury Justices ex p Smith* (1994) 159 JP 316, it was said that where appeal by way of case stated is available, it is preferable to challenge a decision of a magistrates' court by means of appeal by way of case stated rather than judicial review. This is because judicial review is to be regarded as a remedy of last resort and because on an appeal by way of case stated the Divisional Court is presented with all the findings of fact made by the magistrates. In other words, judicial review applications should be confined to cases where there has not been a final determination of the case, such as committal for sentence (*R v Ipswich Crown Court ex p Baldwin* [1981] 1 All ER 596).

It should also be added that judicial review is particularly appropriate where the procedure adopted by the lower court is being questioned. In *R v North Essex Justices ex p Lloyd* (2001) 165 JP 117, the Divisional Court said that the most appropriate procedure for challenging a decision of a magistrates' court where the issue is the extent of their jurisdiction, and the procedure which should ordinarily be used, is judicial review.

On the other hand (provided that there has been a final determination), if the magistrates have misconstrued a statutory provision, appeal by way of case stated is preferable as it enables the question at issue to be set out more clearly.

6.7   APPEALS FROM THE YOUTH COURT

Appeal from the youth court against conviction and/or sentence lies to the Crown Court. The only difference from appeals from magistrates' courts is that, in the case of an appeal from the youth court, the Crown Court comprises a Circuit judge or recorder and lay justices drawn from the youth court panel.

Appeals by way of case stated and judicial review are also available.

If a juvenile is convicted in the Crown Court (having been committed for the trial there because he was jointly charged with an adult or with a view to a sentence of long-term detention under s 91 of the Powers of Criminal Courts (Sentencing) Act 2000 being imposed in the event of conviction), appeal lies to the Court of Appeal (Criminal Division), as is always the case with conviction on indictment.

6.8   FURTHER APPEALS

If the initial appeal is unsuccessful, a further appeal may be possible.

6.8.1   From the Crown Court

Where the Crown Court is sitting in an appellate capacity from the magistrates' court, the appellant may appeal against the decision of the Crown Court to the Divisional Court by way of case stated, or seek judicial review, but only where the Crown Court has made an error of law or jurisdiction (ss 28(1) and 29(1) of the Supreme Court Act 1981).

In *R v Gloucester Crown Court ex p Chester* [1998] COD 365, it was held by the Divisional Court that, where a person is convicted by a magistrates' court and appeals to the Crown Court, further appeal against conviction to the High Court on a point of law should be by way of case stated, not judicial review.

An application to the Crown Court to state a case for the opinion of the Divisional Court (following the Crown Court's determination of an appeal from a magistrates' court) must be made within 21 days of the decision complained of (r 26(1) of the Crown Court Rules 1982). Unlike the time limit applicable to challenging the decision of a magistrates' court, r 26(14) allows any time limit (including the initial 21 day period) under r 26 to be extended by the Crown Court. The decision to extend time can be taken by a judge alone (that is, without lay justices); the respondent must be given the chance to make representations. Extensions of time should only be granted for cogent reasons (*DPP v Coleman* [1998] 1 WLR 1708).

6.8.2   From the Divisional Court

Appeal from the Divisional Court lies direct to the House of Lords, by-passing the Court of Appeal (s 1(1)(a) of the Administration of Justice Act 1960). The Divisional Court must certify that there is a point of law of general public importance involved and either the Divisional Court or the House of Lords must give leave to appeal.

6.9   THE AULD REVIEW

Lord Justice Auld, in his *Review of the Criminal Courts in England and Wales*, argued that it was anomalous that a defendant should be able to appeal from the magistrates' court to the Crown Court without leave (whereas a defendant convicted on indictment can only appeal with leave) and that the appeal should take the form of a re-hearing (rather than legal argument based on specific grounds of appeal, as in an appeal to the Court of Appeal following conviction on indictment). He therefore recommended that the same tests for appeal against conviction and sentence should apply throughout the appellate system (Recommendation 300). This would involve the abolition of the defendant's right of appeal against conviction and/or sentence in the magistrates' court to the Crown Court by way of re-hearing (Recommendation 302). The current entitlement to appeal without leave and to have the case re-heard should be replaced by a requirement for leave to appeal to the Crown Court, on the same grounds as are applicable in the Court of Appeal (Recommendation 303), with the appeal being heard in the Crown Court by a judge sitting alone, not sitting with justices (Recommendation 304), and hearing submissions about the safety of the conviction or the severity of the sentence in the same way that the Court of Appeal hears appeals.

The Auld Review also considered the fact that there are currently three separate forms of appeal from the magistrates' court. Lord Justice Auld took the view that it was unnecessary to have three different avenues of appeal, and accordingly recommended that there should be no right of appeal from the magistrates' courts to the High Court by an appeal by way of case stated or by a claim for judicial review (Recommendation 305).

These proposals, which were not enacted in either the Criminal Justice Act or Courts Act 2003, are discussed by Kate Malleson in 'Streamlining and clarifying the appellate process' [2002] Crim LR 272. She points out that the Auld Review itself comments that the current appeal rate from magistrates' courts is very low: 1% (see para 16 of Chapter 12). She points out that this figure includes both conviction and sentence appeals; for conviction appeals alone, the rate was a mere 0.4% in 2000 (compared with 4% of defendants convicted in the Crown Court appealing against conviction during the same period). The fact that so few defendants appeal against the decisions of magistrates (even though there is no requirement to obtain leave to appeal) might appear to suggest an extremely high satisfaction rating for summary trial. However, it should be borne in mind that the power of the Crown Court to review sentence (with the risk that the sentence might be increased) may be a significant deterrent to would-be appellants.

CHAPTER 7

DISCLOSURE: THE CRIMINAL PROCEDURE AND INVESTIGATIONS ACT 1996

7.1 DISCLOSURE OF UNUSED MATERIAL UNDER THE CRIMINAL PROCEDURE AND INVESTIGATIONS ACT 1996

We have already seen that the prosecution have to disclose the evidence that they will be adducing against the defendant (under the Advance Information Rules in cases tried in the magistrates' court or through the process of committal or transfer in the Crown Court cases). It is noteworthy that, in his *Review of the Criminal Courts of England and Wales*, Lord Justice Auld notes (paras 117–20 of Chapter 10) that the rules on disclosure of evidence that the prosecution intend to adduce are rather piecemeal. He recommends that:

> There should be a single set of statutory rules imposing on the prosecution in all cases a duty to provide its proposed evidence in sufficient time to enable the defence adequately to prepare for trial, the precise timescale to be prescribed by rules (Recommendation 194).

The government chose not to take up this recommendation. However, the Criminal Justice Act 2003 does amend the Criminal Procedure and Investigations Act (CPIA) 1996. This Act created additional duties of pre-trial disclosure, both by the prosecution to the defence and by the defence to the prosecution. The duty of disclosure placed on the prosecution by the CPIA 1996 is to disclose certain material that they do not intend to use at the trial (commonly referred to as 'unused material'). The CPIA 1996 is supplemented by a Code of Practice issued under s 23 of the CPIA 1996 and by *Attorney General's Guidelines on Disclosure of Information in Criminal Proceedings* (November 2000). Detailed guidance to the police and to the Crown Prosecution Service (CPS) on the operation of the CPIA 1996 can be found in the Joint Operational Instructions (JOPI): www.cps.gov.uk/publications/docs/jopimay2004.pdf.

Under s 1 of the CPIA 1996, the statutory disclosure provisions apply to all trials in the magistrates' court or youth court where the defendant pleads not guilty and to all cases being tried in the Crown Court.

7.1.1 The duty of the investigator

A system of disclosure of unused material held by the prosecution will only be as good as the investigation which was conducted by the police, since the prosecution cannot disclose material that has not been found during the investigation. Furthermore, the system depends on relevant information that is discovered during the investigation being retained and its existence accurately recorded. For this reason, the investigating officer is under a duty to retain material obtained in a criminal investigation which may be relevant to that investigation. Paragraph 5.4 of the Code of Practice issued under s 23 of the CPIA 1996 provides a non-exhaustive list of the material that should be retained, which includes:

- crime reports (including crime report forms, relevant parts of incident report books or police officers' notebooks);
- custody records;

- records derived from tapes of telephone messages (for example, 999 calls) containing descriptions of the alleged offence or offender;
- final versions of witness statements (and draft versions where their content differs from the final version);
- interview records;
- communications between police and experts (for example, forensic scientists) and reports of work carried out by experts;
- any material casting doubt of the reliability of a confession;
- any material casting doubt on the reliability of a witness;
- any other material that would fall within the test for primary prosecution disclosure (see below).

Because of concerns about this important stage of the process, the Auld Review recommends that:

> 199   The police should retain responsibility for retaining, collating and recording any material gathered or inspected in the course of the investigation; police officers should be better trained for what, in many cases, may be an extensive and difficult exercise regardless of issues of disclosability, and subject, in their exercise of it to statutory guidelines and a rigorous system of 'spot' audits by HM Inspectorates of Constabulary and/or of the Crown Prosecution Service.
>
> 200   Such responsibility as the police have for identifying and considering all potentially disclosable material should be removed to the prosecutor.
>
> 201   The prosecutor should retain ultimate responsibility for the completeness of the material recorded by the police and assume sole responsibility for primary and all subsequent disclosure.

The suggestion that the responsibility that the police currently have for identifying all potentially disclosable material should be transferred to the prosecutor might raise some practical difficulties, not least because of the massive increase in workload for prosecutors that this would entail. The Criminal Justice Act 2003 did not enact this suggestion.

7.1.2   Disclosure of unused material by the prosecution

Section 3(1) of the CPIA 1996 currently requires the prosecutor to:

> (a)   disclose to the accused any prosecution material which has not previously been disclosed to the accused and which in the prosecutor's opinion might undermine the case for the prosecution against the accused; or
>
> (b)   give to the accused a written statement that there is no material of a description mentioned in para (a).

'Prosecution material' is defined by s 3(2) as material 'which is in the prosecutor's possession, and came into his possession in connection with the case for the prosecution against the accused' or which 'he has inspected in connection with the case for the prosecution against the accused'. This would seem to represent a narrowing of the common law duty of disclosure, which extended to material of which the prosecuting lawyers were unaware (for example, forensic evidence which had not been passed on to the lawyers).

The test in the current version of the CPIA 1996 is a subjective one (based on the opinion of the prosecutor). When the amendments contained in the Criminal Justice Act 2003 come into force, the test will become an objective one (see below).

Section 3 covers a wide range of material – anything which has an adverse effect on the strength of the prosecution case. There is detailed guidance in paras 36–38 of the *Attorney General's Guidelines: Disclosure of Information in Criminal Proceedings*. For example, s 3 covers any material which:

- casts doubts on the accuracy on any prosecution evidence;
- may point to another person having involvement in the commission of the offence;
- may cast doubt on the reliability of a confession;
- might affect the credibility of a prosecution witness;
- might support a defence that has already been raised by the defence or which is apparent from the prosecution papers;
- may have a bearing on the admissibility of any prosecution evidence.

A useful rule-of-thumb test is that material ought to be disclosed if it would give the defence a useful basis for cross-examination or if it would support defence arguments that prosecution evidence is inadmissible or that the proceedings should be stayed.

Plainly, this includes information which casts doubt on the reliability of a prosecution witness by undermining their credibility. So, for example, the prosecution should disclose any previous convictions of their witnesses (see *R v Vasiliou* [2000] Crim LR 845), or the fact that a prosecution witness has sought a reward payable on the defendant's conviction (as in *R v Rasheed* (1994) 158 JP 914). Likewise, in *R v Guney* [1998] 2 Cr App R 242, the Court of Appeal held that the defence are entitled to be informed of any convictions or disciplinary findings recorded against a police officer involved in the present case, and of any decisions by trial judges where a trial was stopped, or Court of Appeal judgments where a conviction was quashed, because of misconduct or lack of veracity of identified police officers who are also involved in the present case.

Section 3(6) enables the prosecutor to withhold material if 'the court, on an application by the prosecutor, concludes it is not in the public interest to disclose it and orders accordingly'. The question of 'public interest immunity' is considered in detail later in this chapter.

7.1.3 Disclosure by the defence

Where the case is to be tried in the Crown Court, the defence are required, by s 5 of the CPIA 1996, to serve a 'defence statement'. Where the case is to be tried in a magistrates' court or youth court, service of a defence statement is voluntary (see s 6 of the Act).

The requirement in s 5 of the CPIA 1996 for compulsory disclosure by the defendant where the case is to be tried in the Crown Court applies once the prosecution have made disclosure of their material under s 3. The defence statement must be served within 14 days of the date on which the prosecution comply (or purport to comply) with the duty of primary disclosure under s 3 of the CPIA 1996 (see para 2 of the Criminal Procedure and Investigations Act 1996 (Defence Disclosure Time Limits) Regulations 1997 (SI 1997/684)).

Section 5(5) requires the defendant to give a 'defence statement to the court and the prosecutor'. This 'defence statement' is defined by s 5(6) as 'a written statement':

(a)   setting out in general terms the nature of the accused's defence;

(b)   indicating the matters on which he takes issue with the prosecution; and

(c)   setting out, in the case of each such matter, the reason why he takes issue with the prosecution.

Defence statements are normally drafted by the accused's solicitor, since counsel may not be involved during the early stages of the life of the case. However, counsel will sometimes be instructed to draft a defence statement. The General Council of the Bar has given guidance on the involvement of counsel in the drafting of defence statements (see *Guidance on Preparation of Defence Case Statements*). Counsel must ensure that the defendant:

(a) understands the importance of the accuracy and adequacy of the defence statement; and

(b) has had the opportunity of carefully considering the statement drafted by counsel and has approved it.

What can go wrong is illustrated by *R v Wheeler* (2000) 164 JP 565. The defendant was convicted of an offence contrary to s 170(2) of the Customs & Excise Management Act 1979 following his arrest at Gatwick airport, when he was found to be concealing drugs internally. At trial, an inconsistency had become apparent between the defence statement which had been served by his solicitors (in which he said that he knew he was carrying the drugs when he arrived in the UK) and his evidence during cross-examination (in which he maintained that he believed he had vomited up all of the packets before travelling to the UK). The defence statement had not been signed by the defendant, who alleged that his solicitor had made a mistake in serving an incorrect statement of his case. Whilst referring to the alleged mistake in his summing up, the trial judge had provided the jury with no specific guidance. The Court of Appeal held that the judge had erred in failing to give specific directions as to the inconsistency, given that the jury would be affected by it. The court added that it is advisable that defence statements be signed by a defendant in preference to them being permitted to be served by solicitors on a defendant's behalf without procedures being followed to verify accuracy.

Even though it is desirable that the defendant should sign the defence statement, it should be noted that the Crown Court has no power to impose a requirement that a defence statement be signed personally by the defendant (*R (Sullivan) v Maidstone Crown Court* [2002] EWHC 967; [2002] 1 WLR 2747).

The defence also have a duty to disclose expert evidence to the prosecution (see the Crown Court (Advance Notice of Expert Evidence) Rules 1987 and the Magistrates' Courts (Advance Notice of Expert Evidence) Rules 1997). In *R v Davies* [2002] EWCA Crim 85; (2002) 166 JP 243, the defendant was charged with murder. The main defence to the murder charge was diminished responsibility. Prior to the trial, a consultant psychiatrist had been instructed by the defendant's solicitors to examine him and to write a report on him. After she had provided her report, the defence decided that she would not be called to give evidence and that the report would not be disclosed. The prosecution applied for an order that the report be disclosed. The judge ordered disclosure. It was held by the Court of Appeal (applying the case of *R v R (Blood Sample: Privilege)* [1994] 1 WLR 758) that the judge had erred in ordering disclosure of the report. Where, in criminal proceedings, the opinion of an expert has been obtained at the request of the solicitors to a party to the proceedings in circumstances where s 10(1)(b) of the Police and Criminal Evidence Act 1984 applies, and that opinion is derived from privileged information from which it cannot be separated, it is itself privileged. The predominant purpose of the psychiatrist's examination had been to report on the defendant's mental state to his solicitors; she had not examined him for the purposes of treating him. The judge was therefore wrong to conclude that the psychiatrist's opinion resulted from a doctor/patient relationship.

7.1.3.1 Alibi evidence

Special provisions apply where the defendant relies on an alibi. Evidence in support of an alibi is defined by s 5(8) as:

> ... evidence tending to show that by reason of the presence of the accused at a particular place or in a particular area at a particular time he was not, or was unlikely to have been, at the place where the offence is alleged to have been committed at the time of its alleged commission.

The defence of alibi applies only to offences which are linked to a particular time and place. If, for example, the defendant is charged with living off immoral earnings and claims in his defence that he was out of the country at the time he is alleged to have been so doing, this defence does not amount to an alibi because the allegation is not specific to a particular place (*R v Hassan* [1970] 1 QB 423).

An alibi is concerned with the defendant's whereabouts at the time of the offence itself, not at times which are related to circumstantial evidence relied on by the prosecution. In *R v Lewis* [1969] 2 QB 1, the defendant was charged with dishonestly receiving two stolen postal orders on 14 February. The prosecution adduced evidence that he cashed the two postal orders on 16 February, as part of the evidence showing that he had dishonestly received them on 14 February. It was held that his whereabouts on 16 February were so removed from the offence itself as not to amount to an alibi. This case should be contrasted with *R v Fields* [1991] Crim LR 38. The defendant was allegedly seen twice by a prosecution witness, once during the robbery with which he was charged and once three hours before the robbery. The defendant had no alibi for the time of the robbery itself but said that three hours before the robbery he was 25 miles away and so could not have been the person seen by the witness. This was held to amount to an alibi even though it did not relate to the time of the offence itself. This decision of the Court of Appeal is a rather surprising one; however, it may be justified on the basis that the two sightings were very close together in time and that they were inextricably linked given the evidence of the witness; also, that the person seen three hours before the robbery was at the scene in order to prepare for the robbery and so his presence there could (loosely) be said to be part of the robbery itself. Nonetheless, this decision should probably be confined to its facts.

In *R v Johnson* (1994) 15 Cr App R(S) 827, it was held that evidence only amounts to alibi evidence if it is evidence that the defendant was somewhere other than the place where the offence was committed at the relevant time; evidence which simply shows that the defendant was not present at the commission of the offence is not alibi evidence.

Where the defence statement discloses an alibi, s 5(7) requires the defence statement to give particulars of the alibi. Those particulars must include:

(a)   the name and address of any witness the accused believes is able to give evidence in support of the alibi, if the name and address are known to the accused when the statement is given;

(b)   any information in the accused's possession which might be of material assistance in finding any such witness, if his name or address is not known to the accused when the statement is given.

Presumably the particulars of alibi should set out where the defendant claims to have been at the relevant time even if the only evidence in support of that alibi is to come from the defendant himself (cf *R v Jackson* [1973] Crim LR 356, a case decided under the legislation which dealt with alibis prior to the enactment of the CPIA 1996).

7.1.3.2 *Voluntary disclosure by defence*

Where the defendant is to be tried in the magistrates' court (or, if a juvenile, the youth court), s 6 of the CPIA 1996 makes provision for voluntary disclosure by the defence. Section 6(2) provides that in those cases the defendant *may* give a defence statement to the prosecutor and, if he does so, must also give such a statement to the court.

The incentive for the defence to make disclosure even though it is not compulsory is that, if they do so, a further duty of disclosure is then imposed upon the prosecution.

7.1.3.3 *Amendments to law relating to defence statements (Criminal Justice Act 2003)*

Defence statements have tended to be fairly brief, somewhat anodyne, documents. Lord Justice Auld, in his *Review of the Criminal Courts of England and Wales*, says:

202   The requirements of a defence statement should remain as at present, as should the requirements for particulars where the defence is alibi and/or the defence propose to adduce expert evidence.

203   More effective use of defence statements should be facilitated by the general improvements to the system for preparation for trial that I have recommended, and encouraged through professional conduct rules, training and, in the rare cases where it might be appropriate, discipline, to inculcate in criminal defence practitioners the propriety of and need for compliance with the requirements.

Thus, the Review recommends no more than greater encouragement, through professional conduct rules and otherwise, for the provision of adequate defence statements. The Criminal Justice Act 2003 goes further by making the statutory duty of the defence more onerous.

Section 33(2) of the Criminal Justice Act 2003 inserts a new section, s 6A, into the 1996 Act. The effect of the amended section is to require the accused to provide a more detailed defence statement, setting out the nature of his defence, including any particular defences on which he intends to rely, and indicate any points of law he wishes to take. Section 6A provides:

6A *Contents of defence statement*

(1) For the purposes of this Part a defence statement is a written statement—

    (a) setting out the nature of the accused's defence, including any particular defences on which he intends to rely,

    (b) indicating the matters of fact on which he takes issue with the prosecution,

    (c) setting out, in the case of each such matter, why he takes issue with the prosecution, and

    (d) indicating any point of law (including any point as to the admissibility of evidence or an abuse of process) which he wishes to take, and any authority on which he intends to rely for that purpose.

(2) A defence statement that discloses an alibi must give particulars of it, including—

    (a) the name, address and date of birth of any witness the accused believes is able to give evidence in support of the alibi, or as many of those details as are known to the accused when the statement is given;

    (b) any information in the accused's possession which might be of material assistance in identifying or finding any such witness in whose case any of the details mentioned in paragraph (a) are not known to the accused when the statement is given.

(3) For the purposes of this section evidence in support of an alibi is evidence tending to show that by reason of the presence of the accused at a particular place or in a particular area at a particular time he was not, or was unlikely to have been, at the place where the offence is alleged to have been committed at the time of its alleged commission.

(4) The Secretary of State may by regulations make provision as to the details of the matters that, by virtue of sub-section (1), are to be included in defence statements.

Section 5 as originally enacted envisaged a single defence statement. Section 33(3) of the Criminal Justice Act 2003, which inserts a further new section, s 6B, into the 1996 Act, requiring defence statements to be updated. It provides that where the accused has already served a defence statement under s 5 or 6, he must (before the trial) serve an updated defence statement or else give a written statement stating that he has no changes to make to the defence statement that was served under s 5 or 6 as the case may be.

Section 34 of the Criminal Justice Act imposes a new obligation on the defendant, to identify witnesses he proposes to call. It adds s 6C to the CPIA 1996:

6C *Notification of intention to call defence witnesses*

(1) The accused must give to the court and the prosecutor a notice indicating whether he intends to call any persons (other than himself) as witnesses at his trial and, if so—

    (a) giving the name, address and date of birth of each such proposed witness, or as many of those details as are known to the accused when the notice is given;

    (b) providing any information in the accused's possession which might be of material assistance in identifying or finding any such proposed witness in whose case any of the details mentioned in paragraph (a) are not known to the accused when the notice is given.

(2) Details do not have to be given under this section to the extent that they have already been given under section 6A(2).

...

(4) If, following the giving of a notice under this section, the accused—
  (a) decides to call a person (other than himself) who is not included in the notice as a proposed witness, or decides not to call a person who is so included, or
  (b) discovers any information which, under sub-section (1), he would have had to include in the notice if he had been aware of it when giving the notice,

  he must give an appropriately amended notice to the court and the prosecutor.

The proposal that the defence should have to reveal details of their witnesses to the prosecution was a cause of some concern. It is highly likely that the police will want to interview some or all of the witnesses who are named, and there is a risk that the witnesses may be put off from testifying. In an attempt to allay these fears, s 21A(1) of the 1996 Act (inserted by s 40 of the Criminal Justice Act 2003) requires the Secretary of State to:

... prepare a code of practice which gives guidance to police officers, and other persons charged with the duty of investigating offences, in relation to the arranging and conducting of interviews of persons—

(a) particulars of whom are given in a defence statement in accordance with section 6A(2), or

(b) who are included as proposed witnesses in a notice given under section 6C.

Section 21A(2) requires that:

The code must include (in particular) guidance in relation to—

(a) information that should be provided to the interviewee and the accused in relation to such an interview;

(b) the notification of the accused's solicitor of such an interview;

(c) the attendance of the interviewee's solicitor at such an interview;

(d) the attendance of the accused's solicitor at such an interview;

(e) the attendance of any other appropriate person at such an interview taking into account the interviewee's age or any disability of the interviewee.

The sanction against the defendant for failure to comply with these new disclosure requirements is the drawing of adverse inferences by the court. Section 6E(2), inserted by s 36 of the Criminal Justice Act 2003, provides that, if the judge thinks that the accused has failed to supply a defence statement under s 5 or has failed to supply an updated defence statement under s 6B or a witness notice under s 6C, 'so that there is a possibility of comment being made or inferences drawn under section 11(5), he shall warn the accused accordingly'.

The obligations of the defence extend beyond witnesses they propose to call in the case of experts, where there is a new obligation to reveal the identity of experts who have been instructed on behalf of the defence, whether or not they are called as defence witnesses. This obligation is contained in s 6D of the 1996 Act (inserted by s 35 of the Criminal Justice Act 2003). It provides:

6D   *Notification of names of experts instructed by accused*

(1)   If the accused instructs a person with a view to his providing any expert opinion for possible use as evidence at the trial of the accused, he must give to the court and the prosecutor a notice specifying the person's name and address.

(2)   A notice does not have to be given under this section specifying the name and address of a person whose name and address have already been given under section 6C.

(3)   A notice under this section must be given during the period which, by virtue of section 12, is the relevant period for this section.

Section 33(1) of the Criminal Justice Act 2003 added some new sub-sections to s 5; these provide for service of defence statements on co-defendants, if the court so orders. It provides:

(5A)   Where there are other accused in the proceedings and the court so orders, the accused must also give a defence statement to each other accused specified by the court.

(5B)   The court may make an order under sub-section (5A) either of its own motion or on the application of any party.

The new s 5(5A) essentially gives statutory effect to the decision of the Court of Appeal in *R v Cairns* [2002] EWCA Crim 2838; [2003] 1 WLR 796, where the Court of Appeal held that, in cases in which there are a number of co-defendants, the prosecution are not automatically required to disclose to any defendant the defence statement of another. However, if the prosecution, having received the defence statements of the co-defendants, form the view that the statement of one might reasonably be expected to assist the defence of another, that statement should be disclosed under s 7 of the CPIA 1996 (see below). Disclosure in these circumstances is necessary in order to give effect to the defendant's right to a fair trial under Art 6 of the Convention.

Section 36 of the Criminal Justice Act 2003 further increases the importance of the defence statement by making provision for it to be shown to the jury. Section 6E(4)–(6) provides as follows:

(4)   The judge in a trial before a judge and jury—

(a)   may direct that the jury be given a copy of any defence statement, and

(b)   if he does so, may direct that it be edited so as not to include references to matters evidence of which would be inadmissible.

(5)   A direction under sub-section (4)—

(a)   may be made either of the judge's own motion or on the application of any party;

(b)   may be made only if the judge is of the opinion that seeing a copy of the defence statement would help the jury to understand the case or to resolve any issue in the case.

(6)   The reference in sub-section (4) to a defence statement is a reference—

(a)   where the accused has given only an initial defence statement (that is, a defence statement given under section 5 or 6), to that statement;

(b)   where he has given both an initial defence statement and an updated defence statement (that is, a defence statement given under section 6B), to the updated defence statement;

(c)   where he has given both an initial defence statement and a statement of the kind mentioned in section 6B(4), to the initial defence statement.

To remove doubt as to whether a defence statement served by the defendant's solicitor is to be regarded as being given on behalf of the defendant, s 6E(1) of the 1996 Act (inserted by s 36 of the Criminal Justice Act 2003) provides that:

Where an accused's solicitor purports to give on behalf of the accused—

(a)   a defence statement under section 5, 6 or 6B, or

(b)   a statement of the kind mentioned in section 6B(4),

the statement shall, unless the contrary is proved, be deemed to be given with the authority of the accused.

7.1.4 Secondary disclosure by the prosecution

Section 7 of the CPIA 1996 imposes a further duty of disclosure on the prosecution whenever the defence have made compulsory disclosure (under s 5, in the case of Crown Court trials) or voluntary disclosure (under s 6, in the case of magistrates' court or youth court trials). Section 7(2) requires the prosecutor, once a defence statement has been given, to:

(a)   disclose to the accused any prosecution material which has not previously been disclosed to the accused and which might be reasonably expected to assist the accused's defence as disclosed by the defence statement given under s 5 or 6; or

(b)   give to the accused a written statement that there is no material of a description mentioned in para (a).

'Prosecution material' has the same definition as under s 3. The test under s 7 is an objective one but is confined to material that is relevant to the defence case in so far as that case has been disclosed in the statutory defence statement.

Paragraph 40 of the *Attorney General's Guidelines* suggests certain types of material may be particularly relevant at the stage of secondary disclosure. The list includes the following:

- recorded scientific or scenes of crime findings relevant to an issue raised in the defence statement;
- where identification is or may be in issue, all previous descriptions of suspects, together with all records of identification procedures in respect of the offence(s) and photographs of the accused taken by the investigator around the time of the suspect's arrest;
- information that any prosecution witness has received, has been promised, or has requested any payment or reward in connection with the case;
- names of people whom the investigator thinks may have relevant information but whom the investigator does not intend to interview.

As with the initial duty of disclosure, it is open to the prosecution to seek an order from the court that material should be withheld on the ground that it is not in the public interest to disclose it (s 7(5)). Again, the relevant court is the one in which the trial is to take place.

7.1.5   Revised test for prosecution disclosure under the Criminal Justice Act 2003

There was some criticism of the subjective nature of the test contained in s 3, depending as it does on the prosecutor's opinion, and of the potential difficulty of deciding whether a particular item of unused material undermines the prosecution case or supports the defence case. The Auld Review concludes that:

195   The Criminal Procedure and Investigations Act 1996 scheme of material disclosure should be retained, in particular, two stages of prosecution disclosure under which the second stage is informed by and conditional on a defence statement indicating the issues that the defendant proposes to take at trial.

196   The present mix of primary and subsidiary legislation, Code, Guidelines and Instructions should be replaced by a single and simply expressed instrument setting out clearly the duties and rights of all parties involved.

197   There should be the same test of disclosability for both stages of prosecution disclosure providing in substance and, for example, for the disclosure of 'material which, in the prosecutor's opinion, might reasonably affect the determination of any issue in the case of which he knows or should reasonably expect' or, more simply but tautologically, 'material which in the prosecutor's opinion might weaken the prosecution case or assist that of the defence'.

Following these recommendations, s 32 of the Criminal Justice Act 2003 amends s 3 of the 1996 Act so that it requires the prosecutor to:

... disclose to the accused any prosecution material which might reasonably be considered capable of undermining the case for the prosecution against the accused or of assisting the case for the accused.

This amendment makes the test an objective one, and effectively combines primary and secondary disclosure.

In many ways, the amended version of s 3 reflects current practice as regards disclosure. In *R v Makin* [2004] EWCA Crim 1607, for example, the Court of Appeal summarised the existing disclosure obligations as including a duty to disclose material that assists the defence by allowing a defendant to put forward a tenable case in the best possible light or material that assists the defence to make further enquiries which might assist in showing the defendant's innocence or in avoiding a miscarriage of justice. The court also pointed out that this duty of disclosure continues as long as proceedings remain, whether at first instance or on appeal.

In 'Criminal Justice Act 2003: disclosure and its discontents' [2004] Crim LR 441, Mike Redmayne comments that:

These changes ... make the prosecution's obligations clearer and simpler. But their significance should not be overstated. The problems that afflict prosecution disclosure are too deep-rooted to be cured by legislative tweaking. They stem from the fact that the police are naturally reluctant to reveal information which may damage the prosecution case, and that they know that undisclosed material will often not be discovered. Because the police are the ones with the key obligations here – to draw up accurate schedules which contain sufficient detail for judgments to be made by prosecutors, and for challenges to be made by the defence – failings on their part are difficult to remedy later in the process. The Criminal Justice Act does nothing to address these problems.

7.1.6 Continuing disclosure duty of the prosecution

Section 9(2) of the CPIA 1996 applies to all times between disclosure by the prosecution under s 3 and the end of the case (that is, the acquittal or conviction of the defendant or the prosecution deciding not to proceed with the case). This continuing duty of the prosecutor is defined by s 9(2) as a duty to:

> ... keep under review the question whether at any given time there is prosecution material which:
>
> (a) in his opinion might undermine the case for the prosecution against the accused; and
>
> (b) has not been disclosed to the accused.

Section 9(2) then provides that 'if there is such material at any time the prosecutor must disclose it to the accused as soon as is reasonably practicable'.

Section 9(5) places a slightly different duty on the prosecutor once secondary disclosure has been made by the prosecution under s 7. This duty is to:

> ... keep under review the question whether at any given time there is prosecution material which:
>
> (a) might reasonably be expected to assist the accused's defence as disclosed by the defence statement given under s 5 or 6; and
>
> (b) has not been disclosed to the accused.

Again, any such material must be disclosed as soon as is reasonably practicable.

'Prosecution material' has the same definition as under s 3.

Section 9(8) enables the prosecution to apply for an order that it is not in the public interest to disclose material which would otherwise have to be disclosed under s 9.

7.1.7 The continuing duty under the Criminal Justice Act 2003

Section 37 of the Criminal Justice Act 2003 inserts a new s 7A in the 1996 Act. The new s 7A replaces the existing ss 7 and 9 of the 1996 Act (which are both repealed: Sched 37, Pt 3). The new s 7A imposes a continuing duty on prosecutors to disclose unused material. It provides as follows:

> 7A Continuing duty of prosecutor to disclose
>
> (1) This section applies at all times—
>
> (a) after the prosecutor has complied with section 3 or purported to comply with it, and
>
> (b) before the accused is acquitted or convicted or the prosecutor decides not to proceed with the case concerned.
>
> (2) The prosecutor must keep under review the question whether at any given time (and, in particular, following the giving of a defence statement) there is prosecution material which—
>
> (a) might reasonably be considered capable of undermining the case for the prosecution against the accused or of assisting the case for the accused, and
>
> (b) has not been disclosed to the accused.
>
> (3) If at any time there is any such material as is mentioned in sub-section (2) the prosecutor must disclose it to the accused as soon as is reasonably practicable (or within the period mentioned in sub-section (5)(a), where that applies).

(4)   In applying sub-section (2) by reference to any given time the state of affairs at that time (including the case for the prosecution as it stands at that time) must be taken into account.

(5)   Where the accused gives a defence statement under section 5, 6 or 6B—

(a) if as a result of that statement the prosecutor is required by this section to make any disclosure, or further disclosure, he must do so during the period which, by virtue of section 12, is the relevant period for this section;

(b) if the prosecutor considers that he is not so required, he must during that period give to the accused a written statement to that effect.

(6)   For the purposes of this section prosecution material is material—

(a) which is in the prosecutor's possession and came into his possession in connection with the case for the prosecution against the accused, or

(b) which, in pursuance of a code operative under Part 2, he has inspected in connection with the case for the prosecution against the accused.

...

(8)   Material must not be disclosed under this section to the extent that the court, on an application by the prosecutor, concludes it is not in the public interest to disclose it and orders accordingly.

(9)   Material must not be disclosed under this section to the extent that it is material the disclosure of which is prohibited by section 17 of the Regulation of Investigatory Powers Act 2000.

7.1.8   Faults in disclosure by the defence

If the defendant:

(a) fails to give a defence statement under s 5 (compulsory disclosure prior to Crown Court trial) or does so but fails to comply with the time limit; or

(b) gives voluntary disclosure under s 6 (prior to summary trial) but does so after the expiry of the time limit; or

(c) sets out inconsistent defences in the defence statement; or

(d) at his trial puts forward a defence which is different from any defence set out in the defence statement; or

(e) at his trial adduces evidence in support of an alibi without having given particulars of the alibi in the defence statement (this applies to all Crown Court trials but it only applies to summary trials if the defendant has made voluntary disclosure under s 6); or

(f) at his trial calls a witness to give evidence in support of an alibi without having given particulars of that witness in the alibi notice (again, this applies to all Crown Court trials but it only applies to summary trials if the defendant has made voluntary disclosure under s 6),

then s 11(3) of the CPIA 1996 enables the court or, with the leave of the court, the prosecution (or a co-defendant where two defendants are running different defences) to 'make such comment as appears appropriate' (s 11(3)(a)). Section 11(3) also enables the magistrates or the jury, as the case may be, to 'draw such inferences as appear proper in deciding whether the accused is guilty of the offence concerned' (s 11(3)(b)).

Section 11(4) provides that where the accused puts forward at trial a defence which is different from any defence set out in a defence statement given under s 5 (trial on indictment) or s 6 (summary trial), the court, in deciding whether comments should be made or adverse inferences drawn, should have regard:

(a) to the extent of the difference in the defences; and

(b) to whether there is any justification for it.

The risk of adverse inferences being drawn is, of course, a very significant sanction. It should be noted, however, that s 11(5) provides that 'a person shall not be convicted of an offence solely on an inference drawn under sub-section (3)'. This mirrors the other 'adverse inference' cases (under the Criminal Justice and Public Order Act 1994).

Although permission from the judge is required before comment can be made under s 11, there is no requirement for the prosecution (or a co-accused) to seek leave before cross-examining the accused on discrepancies between the defence statement and the defence case at trial (*R v Tibbs* [2001] 2 Cr App R 309).

In *R v Terry* [2003] EWCA Crim 1800, the defendant served a defence statement in which he alleged that police officers had entrapped him to commit the offence. At trial, however, he ran a defence of duress. The prosecution were granted leave to cross-examine the defendant on his apparent change of defence from entrapment to duress. The judge subsequently directed the jury that it was a matter for them if they chose to draw an inference from the defendant's change of defence. The defendant appealed against conviction on the ground that the judge had erred in his ruling because entrapment was not capable of constituting a defence but would only have been potential grounds for an abuse of process argument. The Court of Appeal held that the defence statement contained material which the defendant sought to put forward to prevent his conviction. It might or might not amount to a defence in law or on the facts; nevertheless, it was within s 5 of the Act and therefore was capable of being used to fulfil the requirements of s 11 of the Act. Accordingly, the judge had been entitled to rule that the prosecution could cross-examine the defendant and to allow the jury to draw appropriate inferences.

7.1.9 Sanctions against the defendant under the Criminal Justice Act 2003

Section 39 of the Criminal Justice Act 2003 substitutes a new version of s 11. This new version extends the existing list of defence disclosure failures and removes the requirement to obtain leave before making comments on some of them. Section 11 (as amended) applies in three cases:

(1) Where the accused is to be tried in the Crown Court (and so is required by s 5 to provide a defence statement) and the accused:

    (a)   fails to give an initial defence statement under s 5; or

    (b)   provides an initial defence statement but does so late; or

    (c)   fails to provide an updated defence statement (or a statement that there are no changes); or

    (d)   provides an updated statement (or a statement that there are no changes) but does so late; or

    (e)   sets out inconsistent defences in the defence statement; or

    (f)   at the trial, puts forward a defence which was not mentioned in his defence statement or is different from any defence set out in that statement; or

(g)   at the trial, relies on a matter which was not mentioned in his defence statement but which should have been so mentioned; or

(h)   at the trial, adduces evidence in support of an alibi without having given particulars of the alibi in the defence statement; or

(i)   at the trial, calls an alibi witness without have given appropriate notice of the alibi, or details of that particular witness, in the defence statement.

(2) Where the accused is to be tried in a magistrates' court and gives an initial defence statement voluntarily but does so late or does any of the things set out in paragraphs (c) to (i) in the preceding paragraph.

(3) Where the accused gives a witness notice (under s 6C) but does so late or, at the trial, calls a witness who was not included, or not adequately identified, in a witness notice.

Under s 11(5), where s 11 applies:

(a) the court or any other party may make such comment as appears appropriate;

(b) the court or jury may draw such inferences as appear proper in deciding whether the accused is guilty of the offence concerned.

Section 11(6) provides that where adverse inferences could be drawn as a result of failure to mention a point of law (including any point as to the admissibility of evidence or an abuse of process) or an authority, comment by another party may be made only with the leave of the court. Sub-section (7) provides that where the failure in question is a failure to comply with the witness notice requirements, comment by another party may be made only with the leave of the court. Section 11(9) stipulates that where the accused calls a witness whom he has failed to include, or to identify adequately, in a witness notice, the court must have regard to whether there is any justification for the failure.

Under s 11(8), where the accused puts forward a defence which is different from any defence set out in his defence statement, the court must have regard (a) to the extent of the differences in the defences, and (b) to whether there is any justification for it.

Section 11(10) importantly confirms that 'a person shall not be convicted of an offence solely on an inference drawn under sub-section (5)'.

7.1.10 Defence application for disclosure

Section 8(2) of the CPIA 1996 provides that, where the accused has given a defence statement under s 5, 6 or 6B and has, at any time, reasonable cause to believe that there is prosecution material which should have been disclosed to him but which has not been disclosed, he may apply to the court for an order requiring the prosecution to disclose it to him. Again, it is open to the prosecutor to argue that disclosure is not in the public interest (s 8(4)).

7.1.11 Time limits

Regulation 2 of the CPIA 1996 (Defence Disclosure Time Limits) Regulations 1997 (SI 1997/684) defines the 'relevant period' for ss 5 and 6 as beginning with the day when the prosecutor complies (or purports to comply) with s 3 of the CPIA 1996 and expiring 14 days later.

Regulation 3 provides for the extension of that period by the court, on application by the accused, if the court is satisfied that the accused could not reasonably have acted within that period. No limit is prescribed for the length of such extension. Regulation 4 enables the accused to apply for further extensions of time.

Regulation 5 provides that where the 14 day period would otherwise expire on a Saturday or Sunday, or on Christmas Day or Good Friday or any other bank holiday, it will be deemed to expire on the next working day.

For s 3, the prosecutor must act 'as soon as is reasonably practicable' after the accused has pleaded not guilty (in the case of summary trials) or has been committed or transferred for trial, etc (in the case of Crown Court trials). For s 7, the prosecutor must act 'as soon as is reasonably practicable after the accused gives a defence statement under s 5 or 6'.

Rule 8(4) of the Crown Court (Criminal Procedure and Investigations Act 1996) (Disclosure) Rules 1997 (SI 1997/698) and r 8(4) of the Magistrates' Courts (Criminal Procedure and Investigations Act 1996) (Disclosure) Rules 1997 (SI 1997/703) provide that where the accused applies for an extension of time, the prosecutor may make written representations to the court within 14 days of being given notice of the application by the accused. On receipt of these representations (or at the expiry of the 14 day period, where no representations have been made), the court considers the application and may, if it wishes, do so at a hearing (r 8(5)). If there is a hearing, it is *inter partes* and the prosecutor and applicant are entitled to make representations to the court (r 8(6)). The hearing is held in open court (r 9(2)).

Section 10 of the CPIA 1996 provides that a failure by the prosecution to observe those time limits does not constitute grounds for staying the proceedings for abuse of process (s 10(2)) unless the delay is such that the accused is denied a fair trial (s 10(3)).

7.1.12 Third party disclosure

Sometimes material that may support the defence case is in the hands of a third party. For example, the accused might be charged with a sexual offence involving a child, and the child's school, or the relevant social services department, might have records of false allegations made by the child who is the alleged victim of the offence (as in *R v Brushett* [2001] Crim LR 471). If the material comes into the hands of the police, it should be retained and would fall within the ordinary disclosure regime under the CPIA 1996.

The *Attorney General's Guidelines on Disclosure* distinguish between two situations. First, there is material held by government departments or other Crown bodies. Paragraph 29 says that:

> Where it appears to an investigator, disclosure officer or prosecutor that a Government department or other Crown body has material that may be relevant to an issue in the case, reasonable steps should be taken to identify and consider such material. Although what is reasonable will vary from case to case, prosecutors should inform the department or other body of the nature of its case and of relevant issues in the case in respect of which the department or body might possess material, and ask whether it has any such material ...

Secondly, there is material held by other agencies. Paragraphs 30–33 state that:

30   There may be cases where the investigator, disclosure officer or prosecutor suspects that a non-government agency or other third party (for example, a local authority, a social services department, a hospital, a doctor, a school, providers of forensic services) has material or information which might be disclosable if it were in the possession of the prosecution. In such cases consideration should be given as to whether it is appropriate to seek access to the material or information and if so, steps should be taken by the prosecution to obtain such material or information. It will be important to do so if the material or information is likely to undermine the prosecution case, or assist a known defence.

31   If the investigator, disclosure officer or prosecutor seeks access to the material or information but the third party declines or refuses to allow access to it, the matter should not be left. If despite any reasons offered by the third party it is still believed that it is reasonable to seek production of the material or information, and the requirements of section 2 of the Criminal Procedure (Attendance of Witnesses) Act 1965 or as appropriate section 97 of the Magistrates Courts Act 1980 are satisfied, then the prosecutor or investigator should apply for a witness summons causing a representative of the third party to produce the material to the Court.

32   Information which might be disclosable if it were in the possession of the prosecution which comes to the knowledge of investigators or prosecutors as a result of liaison with third parties should be recorded by the investigator or prosecutor in a durable or retrievable form (for example potentially relevant information revealed in discussions at a child protection conference attended by police officers).

33   Where information comes into the possession of the prosecution in the circumstances set out in paragraphs 30–32 above, consultation with the other agency should take place before disclosure is made: there may be public interest reasons which justify withholding disclosure and which would require the issue of disclosure of the information to be placed before the court.

If material remains in the hands of the third party, then the accused is obviously entitled to request it. If the third party is not prepared to hand it over, then the accused can seek a witness summons (using the procedure laid down by s 2 of the Criminal Procedure (Attendance of Witnesses) Act 1965 in Crown Court cases, or s 97 of the Magistrates' Courts Act 1980 in magistrates' court cases). The accused would have to be able to show that the third party is likely to be able to give or produce material evidence in the case, and will not voluntarily attend or produce the evidence.

At the hearing of the application, the third party is able to argue, for example, that there is no evidence held, or that it is not material, or that it should not be disclosed on grounds of public interest immunity (see below).

The Auld Review also considers the question of third party disclosure, and recommends that:

206   There should be consideration of a new statutory scheme for third party disclosure, including its cost implications to all concerned, to operate alongside and more consistently with the general provisions for disclosure of unused material.

So far, this suggestion has not been taken up by the government.

7.2   PUBLIC INTEREST IMMUNITY

Section 3(6) enables the prosecutor to withhold material that would normally have to be disclosed under s 3 (primary disclosure) if the court, on an application by the prosecutor, concludes that it is not in the public interest to disclose it and orders accordingly. Section 7(5) similarly enables the prosecutor to seek an order permitting non-disclosure of material that would otherwise have to be disclosed under s 7 (secondary disclosure). The relevant court is the court in which the defendant is to be tried (so the magistrates' court has no jurisdiction in respect of disclosure once the defendant has been sent to the Crown Court for trial: *R v CPS ex p Warby* (1994) 158 JP 190).

A common example of a case where public interest immunity (PII) is raised is where the prosecution wish to protect the identity of an informant whom the prosecutor does not intend to call as a witness at the trial (as in *R v Turner* [1995] 1 WLR 264) or where the police wish to keep secret the location of an observation post from which they were watching the movements of the accused (as in *R v Johnson* [1988] 1 WLR 1377).

The essence of the PII provisions in the CPIA 1996 is that if material should otherwise be disclosed because it undermines the prosecution case or assists the defence case, that material must be disclosed to the defence unless the court gives permission for it to be withheld from the defence.

The *Attorney General's Guidelines on Disclosure*, dealing with applications for non-disclosure in the public interest, state that:

41   Before making an application to the court to withhold material which would otherwise fail to be disclosed, on the basis that to disclose would not be in the public interest, a prosecutor should aim to disclose as much of the material as he properly can (by giving the defence redacted or edited copies of summaries).

42   Prior to or at the hearing, the court must be provided with full and accurate information. The prosecution advocate must examine all material which is the subject matter of the application and make any necessary enquiries of the prosecutor and/or investigator. The prosecutor (or representative) and/or investigator should attend such applications.

Where a magistrates' court has ruled that it is not in the public interest to disclose prosecution material, the defendant may apply to the magistrates for a review of the question whether it is still not in the public interest to disclose that material (s 14(2)).

Where a Crown Court has ruled that it is not in the public interest to disclose prosecution material, the court itself must keep under review the question whether it is still not in the public interest to disclose that material (s 15(3)). Although the Crown Court has to keep the matter under review without the need for any application by the defence, it is open to the defendant to apply to the court for a review of the question (s 15(4)).

Where magistrates rule on disclosure, it may be that they hear matters which are prejudicial to the defendant. In these circumstances, it is a matter for their discretion whether they disqualify themselves from conducting the trial itself (*R v South Worcestershire Justices ex p Lilley* [1995] 1 WLR 1595).

In *R v Botmeh and Alami* [2001] EWCA Crim 2226; [2002] 1 WLR 531, the defendants appealed against conviction on the basis of evidence which became available to the

Crown after the trial. The Crown made an application to withhold this information from the defence on the basis of public interest immunity. It was held that the Court of Appeal is empowered to consider an *ex parte* application to withhold relevant evidence on the ground of public interest immunity even where that evidence has not been the subject of a public interest immunity application to the trial judge.

7.2.1 Public interest immunity and the European Court of Human Rights

In *Jasper v UK* (2000) 30 EHRR 441, where the European Court held that (by a bare majority of nine votes to eight) there was no violation of Art 6, the defence had been informed that a PII application was to be made by the prosecution (although they were not told into which category the material being withheld was said to fall); the defence had thus had the opportunity to make submissions and to participate (albeit to a comparatively limited extent) in the decision-making process. The Court said (at para 51):

> It is a fundamental aspect of the right to a fair trial that criminal proceedings ...should be adversarial and that there should be equality of arms between the prosecution and defence. The right to an adversarial trial means, in a criminal case, that both prosecution and defence must be given the opportunity to have knowledge of and comment on the observations filed and the evidence adduced by the other party. In addition Article 6(1) requires ... that the prosecution authorities should disclose to the defence all material evidence in their possession for or against the accused.

In para 52, however, the Court noted that it is not only the interests of the accused that have to be taken into account. It follows that:

> ... the entitlement to disclosure of relevant evidence is not an absolute right. In any criminal proceedings there may be competing interests, such as national security or the need to protect witnesses at risk of reprisals or keep secret police methods of investigation of crime, which must be weighed against the rights of the accused. In some cases it may be necessary to withhold certain evidence from the defence so as to preserve the fundamental rights of another individual or to safeguard an important public interest. However, only such measures restricting the rights of the defence which are strictly necessary are permissible under Article 6(1). Moreover, in order to ensure that the accused receives a fair trial, any difficulties caused to the defence by a limitation on its rights must be sufficiently counterbalanced by the procedures followed by the judicial authorities.

The Court emphasised that its role was to 'scrutinise the decision-making procedure to ensure that, as far as possible, it complied with the requirements to provide adversarial proceedings and equality of arms and incorporated adequate safeguards to protect the interests of the accused' (para 53).

In this case, the defence had been notified that an application to withhold material was to be made, but were not told of the category of material which the prosecution sought to withhold. The defence was given the opportunity to outline the defence case to the trial judge and to ask the judge to order disclosure of any evidence relevant to that case. On this basis, the Court (at para 55) said that it was:

> ... satisfied that the defence were kept informed and permitted to make submissions and participate in the above decision-making process as far as was possible without

revealing to them the material which the prosecution sought to keep secret on public interest grounds.

Jasper was decided in favour of the UK government by the slenderest of majorities. It is worthwhile examining briefly the views of some of the judges who were in the minority:

> We note that, although the defence in this case were notified that an ex parte application was to be made by the prosecution for material to be withheld on grounds of public interest immunity, they were not informed of the category of material which the prosecution sought to withhold, they were not – by definition – involved in the *ex parte* proceedings, and they were not informed of the reasons for the judge's subsequent decision that the material should not be disclosed. This procedure cannot, in our view, be said to respect the principles of adversarial proceedings and equality of arms, given that the prosecuting authorities were provided with access to the judge and were able to participate in the decision-making process in the absence of any representative of the defence. We do not accept that the opportunity given to the defence to outline their case before the trial judge took his decision on disclosure can affect the position, as the defence were unaware of the nature of the matters they needed to address. It was purely a matter of chance whether they made any relevant points.
>
> The fact that the judge monitored the need for disclosure throughout the trial cannot remedy the unfairness created by the defence's absence from the *ex parte* proceedings. In our view, the requirements ... that any difficulties caused to the defence by a limitation on defence rights must be sufficiently counterbalanced by the procedures followed by the judicial authorities, are not met by the mere fact that it was a judge who decided that the evidence be withheld ... Our concern is that, in order to be able to fulfil his functions as the judge in a fair trial, the judge should be informed by the opinions of both parties, not solely the prosecution.

The minority went on to suggest that the use of special counsel (see below) might go some way to redress the balance.

The European Court also considered the question of disclosure in *Rowe and Davis v UK* (2000) 30 EHRR 1, where the European Court found that there had been a breach of Art 6. The Court repeated the point made in *Jasper* (quoted above).

In *R v Davis, Rowe and Johnson* (2000) *The Times*, 24 April, the Court of Appeal noted that the judgment of the European Court of Human Rights in the case of *Rowe and Davis v UK* had been highly critical of the procedure adopted prior to the coming into force of the CPIA 1996 but did not criticise the procedure used under that Act to deal with public interest immunity applications.

In *Edwards and Lewis v UK* (2003) 15 BHRC 189, again the European Court of Human Rights quoted extensively from its judgment in *Jasper*. However, the Court distinguished *Jasper* on the basis that, in the present case, it appeared that 'the undisclosed evidence related, or may have related, to an issue of fact decided by the trial judge' (namely whether or not there had been entrapment). At para 57, the Court noted that:

> Had the defence been able to persuade the judge that the police had acted improperly, the prosecution would, in effect, have had to be discontinued. The applications in question were, therefore, of determinative importance to the applicants' trials, and the public interest immunity evidence may have related to facts connected with those applications.

The Court (para 58) said that:

> Despite this, the applicants were denied access to the evidence. It was not, therefore, possible for the defence representatives to argue the case on entrapment in full before the judge.

The Court went on to hold that it did:

> ... not consider that the procedure employed to determine the issues of disclosure of evidence and entrapment complied with the requirements to provide adversarial proceedings and equality of arms and incorporated adequate safeguards to protect the interests of the accused. It follows that there has been a violation of Article 6 § 1 in this case.

It has to be noted that this decision has a fairly limited application. It appears to be relevant only where the defendant's ability to make an application to the judge for the case to be dismissed or stayed is diminished through the withholding of potentially relevant evidence. It does not apply where the guilt or innocence of the accused is a matter for the jury.

7.2.2 Domestic case law on public interest immunity

Prior to the enactment of the CPIA 1996, disclosure was governed almost exclusively by case law. Section 21 of the CPIA 1996 provides that the Act replaces the common law regarding the circumstances in which disclosure has to be made (s 21(1)). However, the Act does not 'affect the rules of common law as to whether disclosure is in the public interest' (s 21(2)).

Many of the public interest cases are ones where the prosecution did not want to reveal to the defence the identity of a person because the prosecution feared that the person would be intimidated or otherwise put at risk (for example, a regular police informant). However, as was said in *R v Keane* [1994] 1 WLR 746, if the evidence proves the defendant's innocence, or would assist in avoiding a miscarriage of justice, the balance must come down resoundingly in favour of disclosing that evidence.

In *R v Reilly* [1994] Crim LR 279, the prosecution refused to disclose the identity of an informant who was not going to be called as a prosecution witness. It was held by the Court of Appeal that the need to protect an informant had to give way to the need to allow the defence to present a tenable case in its best light (which may involve impugning the informant). The Crown had to choose between disclosing the identity of the informant or discontinuing the case against the defendant (and in fact chose the latter course). This invidious choice meant that a large number of prosecutions had to be dropped rather than placing informants at risk. In *R v Turner* [1995] 1 WLR 264, the Court of Appeal took a slightly tougher line and said that the court should only accede to an application by the defence for disclosure of the identity of an informant if it was satisfied that the information was essential to the running of the defence. In the instant case, it appeared that the informant had participated in the events surrounding the crime and the defence case was that the defendant had been set up. Accordingly, the judge should have decided that the balance came down firmly in favour of disclosure.

The prosecution generally cannot claim immunity from disclosure in respect of documents which the trial judge has not viewed personally (*R v K* (1993) 97 Cr App R 342). However, in *R v W* (1996) *The Times*, 12 July, it was said to be sufficient for the judge to rely on the judgment of an independent barrister appointed to read the documents where the volume of papers is such that the judge does not have time to read them personally.

In *R v Brown* [1997] 3 WLR 447, the Crown had failed to disclose to the defence information which reflected on the credibility of two defence witnesses. It was held by the House of Lords that the Crown is not under a duty to disclose to the defence material which is relevant only to the credibility of defence witnesses. Although this case was not one to which the CPIA 1996 applied (since the relevant provisions of the Act were not in force at the relevant time), the House of Lords held that such material is not material which might assist the defence case. It follows that it would not be disclosable under the CPIA 1996.

In *R v Mills* [1998] AC 382, the House of Lords held that the prosecution should provide the defence with a copy of the statement containing relevant material made by a witness whom the prosecution does not propose to call at the trial (not just supply the defence with the name and address of that witness) even if the prosecution take the view that the witness is not a credible witness. Failure to do so may render a conviction unsafe. Such statements would now have to be disclosed under the CPIA 1996 if they might assist the defence case.

In *R v DPP ex p Lee* [1999] 1 WLR 1950, the Divisional Court noted that the CPIA 1996 does not specifically address disclosure during the period between arrest and the case being sent to the Crown Court. The court said that, in most cases, prosecution disclosure can wait until after the case has been sent to the Crown Court without jeopardising the defendant's right to a fair trial. However, the court said that the prosecutor must always be alive to the need to make advance disclosure of material that should be disclosed at an earlier stage. Examples given by the court include:

(a) previous convictions of the alleged victim if that information could reasonably be expected to assist the defence when applying for bail;

(b) material which might enable a defendant to make an application to stay the proceedings as an abuse of process;

(c) material which might enable a defendant to submit that he should only be sent for trial on a lesser charge, or even that he should not be sent for trial at all;

(d) depending on what the defendant chooses to reveal about his case at this early stage, material which would enable the defendant and his legal advisers to make preparations for trial which would be significantly less effective if disclosure were delayed, for example, names of any witnesses whom the prosecution do not intend to use.

Any disclosure by the prosecution prior to committal would not normally exceed the primary disclosure which, after committal, would be required by s 3 of the 1996 Act (that is, material which in the prosecutor's opinion might undermine the case for the prosecution). Indeed, in *DPP v Ara* [2001] 4 All ER 559, it was held that, where the police are willing to caution a suspect in relation to an offence, rather than prosecute him, the suspect is entitled to disclosure of such material as is necessary to enable his legal adviser to assess the prosecution case and to give informed advice as to whether or not the suspect should consent to the caution. The court added that this does not mean that there is a general obligation on the police to disclose material prior to charge on any wide-ranging basis.

In *R v Feltham Magistrates' Court ex p Ebrahim* [2001] EWHC 130 (Admin); [2001] 1 WLR 1293, the claimant sought to have criminal proceedings against him stayed as an abuse of process, on the basis that potentially relevant video footage had not been preserved by the prosecution. The Divisional Court held that there is jurisdiction to stay proceedings for abuse of process: (i) where the defendant could not receive a fair trial; or (ii) where it would be unfair for the defendant to be tried (for example, where the prosecution had conducted itself badly). Where an abuse of process application is made on the ground that relevant material is no longer available, the court should ascertain whether the prosecution was under a duty to obtain or retain that evidence (under the Code of Practice issued under the CPIA 1996 or the *Attorney General's Guidelines on Disclosure*). If there was no such duty, the prosecution could not have abused the process of the court simply because the material is no longer available. However, if the prosecution was in breach of its duty, the court would have to consider whether to take the exceptional course of staying the proceedings for abuse of process on that ground. In such a case, the court should bear in mind: (i) the ultimate objective of the discretion to stay is to ensure a fair trial according to the law; and (ii) the trial process itself is equipped to deal with most of the complaints on which applications for a stay are founded. No stay should be imposed unless the defendant shows, on the balance of probabilities, that because of the lack of evidence he would suffer serious prejudice to the extent that no fair trial could be held (see *Attorney General's Reference (No 1 of 1990)* [1992] 1 QB 630).

Before the enactment of the CPIA 1996, there was concern that the common law duty of disclosure on the prosecution had become too onerous. In particular, there was concern that in many cases the defence were simply engaging in a 'fishing expedition'. For example, in *R v Turner* [1995] 1 WLR 264, the Court of Appeal expressed concern at the number of cases where the defence were seeking undisclosed information from the prosecution. The court said:

> We wish to alert judges to the need to scrutinise applications for disclosure of details about informants with very great care. They will need to be astute to see that assertions of a need to know such details, because they are essential to the running of the defence, are justified. If they are not so justified, then the judge will need to adopt a robust approach in declining to order disclosure. Clearly, there is a distinction between cases in which the circumstances raise no reasonable possibility that information about the informant will bear upon the issues and cases where it will. Again, there will be cases where the informant is an informant and no more; other cases where he may have participated in the events constituting, surrounding, or following the crime. Even when the informant has participated, the judge will need to consider whether his role so impinges on an issue of interest to the defence, present or potential, as to make disclosure necessary ....

In *R v Templar* [2003] EWCA Crim 3186, the Court of Appeal accepted the assertion by prosecuting counsel that if the material in respect of which immunity is sought 'was properly the subject of public interest immunity, the judge was entitled to order that it be withheld from the [defendant] unless it provided any support for the [defendant]'s case or could be said to harm or undermine that of the prosecution'. This raises a key problem in the law of disclosure: if the material is not relevant (in the sense that it undermines the prosecution case or supports the defence case) it does not have to be disclosed in the first place. On the other hand, if it does in fact undermine the prosecution case or support the defence case to any significant extent, it seems inconsistent with the defendant's right to a fair trial for that material to be withheld, however sensitive it might be. In 'Fairness and public interest immunity: inconsistent concepts?' (2004) 154 NLJ 46, Stephen Parkinson suggests that where the public interest in withholding the material is weak and it has a central relevance to the defence case, the judge must clearly order disclosure; equally, where the public interest against disclosure is strong and the material is of peripheral relevance to the defence case (though falling within the CPIA 1996 tests), the judge will rule against disclosure; if both competing interests are equally strong (or equally weak), the judge should apply the test that would be used by the Court of Appeal on an appeal against conviction, namely whether the conviction would be unsafe if disclosure were to be withheld (and so disclosure should only be withheld if doing so would not render the conviction unsafe).

The fact that some applications for permission to withhold material held by the prosecution take place without the defence even knowing that such an application is being made (see below), has raised a number of concerns about the fairness of the procedure that is adopted for the determination of PII applications.

In *R v H; R v C* [2004] UKHL 3; [2004] 2 WLR 335, the House of Lords considered the question of public interest immunity. The Court of Appeal had certified that two points of law of general public importance were involved in its decision:

(1) Are the procedures for dealing with claims for public interest immunity made on behalf of the prosecution in criminal proceedings compliant with Article 6 of the European Convention for the Protection of Human Rights and Fundamental Freedoms?

(2) If not, in what way are the procedures deficient and how might the deficiency be remedied?

The opinion of the House of Lords was delivered by Lord Bingham on behalf of all the Law Lords who heard this appeal. Lord Bingham took as his starting point the principle established in *R v Horseferry Road Magistrates' Court ex p Bennett* [1994] 1 AC 42 at 68, and *Attorney General's Reference (No 2 of 2001)* [2003] UKHL 68; [2004] 2 WLR 1, para 13, that it is 'axiomatic' that a person charged with a criminal offence should receive a fair trial and that, if he cannot be tried fairly for that offence, he should not be tried for it at all.

Lord Bingham noted that Art 6 of the European Convention requires that the trial process, viewed as a whole, must be fair; it followed that the answers to the questions posed by the Court of Appeal (and the other issues considered by the House of Lords) had to be governed by that 'cardinal and overriding requirement' (para 10).

At para 12, Lord Bingham quotes from Lord Steyn in *Attorney General's Reference (No 3 of 1999)* [2001] 2 AC 91, 118:

The purpose of the criminal law is to permit everyone to go about their daily lives without fear of harm to person or property. And it is in the interests of everyone that serious crime should be effectively investigated and prosecuted. There must be fairness to all sides. In a criminal case this requires the court to consider a triangulation of interests. It involves taking into account the position of the accused, the victim and his or her family, and the public.

Lord Bingham makes the point that, while the focus of Art 6 is on the right of a criminal defendant to a fair trial, it is a right that has to be exercised within the framework of the administration of the criminal law. It follows from this that rights of people other than the defendant have to be taken into account. His Lordship also repeats (in para 13) that the duty of prosecuting counsel is not to obtain a conviction at all costs but to act as a minister of justice (*Randall v The Queen* [2002] UKPC 19; [2002] 1 WLR 2237, para 10).

In para 14, Lord Bingham refers to what he calls 'the golden rule': that fairness ordinarily requires disclosure to the defence of any material held by the prosecution which weakens its case or strengthens that of the defendant (assuming this material is not part of the formal prosecution case against the defendant, in which it will have been disclosed anyway). This duty has been enshrined in statute, in the CPIA 1996. His Lordship noted that s 3 of the 1996 Act does not require disclosure of material which is either neutral in its effect or which is adverse to the defendant (in that it strengthens the prosecution or weakens the defence).

Turning to public interest immunity justifying the withholding of material that tends to undermine prosecution or assist the defence, Lord Bingham notes that the public interest most regularly engaged in this context is the need for the effective investigation and prosecution of serious crime; this may involve the following:

> ... resort to informers and under-cover agents, or the use of scientific or operational techniques (such as surveillance) which cannot be disclosed without exposing individuals to the risk of personal injury or jeopardising the success of future operations. In such circumstances some derogation from the golden rule of full disclosure may be justified but such derogation must always be the minimum derogation necessary to protect the public interest in question and must never imperil the overall fairness of the trial (para 18).

Although perhaps not strictly necessary to its decision, the House of Lords (at the invitation of the parties) also considered the correctness of the decision of the Court of Appeal in *R v Smith (Joe)* [2001] 1 WLR 1031. In that case, the defendant was charged with burglary. At the outset of his trial, the prosecution made an *ex parte* public interest immunity application, following which the judge ordered that disclosure need not be made to the defence. Defence counsel, having been notified of that application and ruling, submitted that there was no evidence that the officers in the case had had reasonable grounds to arrest the defendant or to suspect his involvement in the offence for which he had been arrested. The judge ruled that he was satisfied that the police had had reasonable grounds for suspicion based on information that had been the subject of the PII application. The defendant was convicted. The Court of Appeal held that there was no principle in English law that information received by a judge in the course of a PII application could not be used in order to determine whether the police had reasonable grounds for suspecting that the defendant had committed an offence or had reasonable cause to arrest the defendant. The court said that, while 'equality of arms' between the prosecution and the defence is a fundamental aspect of the right to a fair trial (and both sides have to be afforded the opportunity to have knowledge of the case), that right is not absolute because competing interests, such as national security and protection of police investigative methods, also have to be taken into account. The Court of Appeal held that the trial judge had properly addressed those competing interests in making his decision. This decision was overruled in *R v H* [2004] UKHL 3; [2004] 2 WLR 335, where Lord Bingham says (at para 42):

> By analogy with the course adopted in *PG and JH v United Kingdom*, the judge could have ascertained the questions the defence wished to put to the witness, and himself put the questions to the witness in chambers. That would have enabled him to reach a conclusion whether the police had had reasonable grounds for suspicion or not. It may be that the judge could, by inviting submissions from prosecution and defence, have

devised a better procedure. In any event, it was incumbent upon him to involve and inform the defence to the maximum extent possible and to ensure that disclosure was made to the extent that it could be made without unjustified damage to the public interest. As it was, the main plank of the defence was destroyed by evidence given to the judge privately which the defence never had the opportunity to meet in any way. Such a procedure does not meet the minimum standards required by the Convention, and the Court of Appeal erred in holding otherwise ... *R v Smith* should no longer be treated as good law.

7.2.3 Procedure for determining public interest immunity claims

The procedure for determining claims of public interest immunity was originally set out in *R v Ward* [1993] 1 WLR 619 and *R v Davis* [1993] 1 WLR 613 at 617–18. The Court of Appeal identified three classes of case, which Lord Bingham, in *R v H*, summarised in the following terms:

In the first, comprising most of the cases in which a PII issue arises, the prosecution must give notice to the defence that they are applying for a ruling of the court, and must indicate to the defence at least the category of the material they hold (that is, the broad ground upon which PII is claimed), and the defence must have the opportunity to make representations to the court. There is thus an *inter partes* hearing conducted in open court with reference to at least the category of the material in question. The second class comprises cases in which the prosecution contend that the public interest would be injured if disclosure were made even of the category of the material. In such cases the prosecution must still notify the defence that an application to the court is to be made, but the category of the material need not be specified: the defence will still have an opportunity to address the court on the procedure to be adopted but the application will be made to the court in the absence of the defendant or anyone representing him. If the court considers that the application falls within the first class, it will order that procedure to be followed. Otherwise it will rule. The third class, described as 'highly exceptional', comprises cases where the public interest would be injured even by disclosure that an *ex parte* application is to be made. In such cases application to the court would be made without notice to the defence. But if the court considers that the case should be treated as falling within the second or the first class, it will so order (see para 20).

Thus, the prosecution should, whenever possible, notify the defence that it is applying for a ruling by the court, and indicate to the defence at least the category of the material to which the application relates. The defence should then be given the opportunity of making representations to the court.

Where disclosure even of the category of material would be tantamount to revealing whatever it is that the prosecution are seeking not to disclose, the prosecution should still notify the defence of the application, but need not specify the category of material; in such a case, the application will be *ex parte*. If the court, on hearing the application, considers that the normal procedure should have been followed, it will order that the application should be renewed *inter partes*, otherwise it will rule on the *ex parte* application.

If the prosecution believe that to reveal even the fact that an *ex parte* application is to be made could 'let the cat out of the bag' (thereby defeating the purpose of the application), they may apply to the court *ex parte* without notice. If the court, on hearing the application considers that notice should have been given to the defence, or even that the normal *inter partes* procedure should have been adopted, it will so order.

The Court of Appeal also made the point that, even if the judge rules in favour of non-disclosure, the position may change during the course of the trial, and so the court will have to monitor the question of disclosure. If the public interest in non-disclosure is then outweighed by the need to order disclosure in the interests of securing fairness to the defendant, the prosecution will have to decide whether to disclose the material in question or to offer no further evidence in the case.

The procedural regime established by *R v Davis* and *R v Ward* was given statutory effect in the Crown Court (Criminal Procedure and Investigations Act 1996) (Disclosure) Rules 1997 (SI 1997/698) and by the Magistrates' Courts (Criminal Procedure and Investigations Act 1996) (Disclosure) Rules 1997 (SI 1997/703). Where the prosecutor wishes to make an application to withhold material, a notice of application must be served on:

(a) the appropriate officer of the Crown Court or the clerk to the justices, as the case may be; and

(b) (unless the defence is being given no notice of the application) on the accused.

This notice must (unless the defence are not being told the basis of the application) 'specify the nature of the material to which the application relates' (r 2(2) of both sets of Rules).

Where the prosecutor 'has reason to believe that to reveal to the accused the nature of the material to which the application relates would have the effect of disclosing that which the prosecutor contends should not in the public interest be disclosed', the prosecutor does not have to specify the nature of the material to which the application refers (r 2(3) of the Crown Court Rules and r 2(4) of the Magistrates' Courts Rules). This would be the case, for example, where the material in question is from an informant whom the prosecutor does not intend to call as a witness at the trial and the prosecutor believes that, once the accused finds out that there was an informant, he would be able to work out who that informant was.

Where the prosecutor 'has reason to believe that to reveal to the accused the fact that an application is being made would have the effect of disclosing that which the prosecutor contends should not in the public interest be disclosed', the prosecutor does not have to inform the accused that an application is being made (r 2(4) of the Crown Court Rules and r 2(5) of the Magistrates' Courts Rules).

In a case where the prosecutor serves notice on the accused that an application is being made, the hearing is *inter partes* and both the prosecutor and the accused are entitled to make representations to the court (r 3(3) of the Crown Court Rules and r 3(2) of the Magistrates' Courts Rules).

Rule 3(4) of the Crown Court Rules (r 3(3) of the Magistrates' Courts Rules) provides that where the prosecutor applies to the court for leave to make representations in the absence of the accused, the court may for that purpose sit in the absence of the accused and any legal representative of his. Thus, the accused (and his legal representatives) can be excluded from part of the hearing.

In a case where the prosecutor did not serve notice of the application on the accused, the hearing is *ex parte* and only the prosecutor is entitled to make representations to the court (r 3(5) of the Crown Court Rules and r 3(4) of the Magistrates' Courts Rules).

A hearing under r 3 may be held in private (r 9(2) of both sets of Rules).

Where the court rules that it is in the public interest that material should not be disclosed, the court must state, and record, its reasons for doing so (r 4(2) of both sets of Rules).

The accused must be notified of the making of the order unless the case was one where the accused was not informed that an application was being made (r 4(3) of both sets of Rules).

In *R v H*, the House of Lords (after considering the background of both English law and the jurisprudence of the Strasbourg Court) concluded that:

> If material does not weaken the prosecution case or strengthen that of the defendant, there is no requirement to disclose it ... Neutral material or material damaging to the defendant need not be disclosed and should not be brought to the attention of the court. Only in truly borderline cases should the prosecution seek a judicial ruling on the disclosability of material in its hands ... (para 35).

In other words, in most cases the prosecution will not need to make an application: if it is clear that a judge would order disclosure, then the prosecution should either disclose the material to the defence or drop the case.

The House of Lords went on to give detailed guidance on how the courts should approach public interest immunity hearings:

36   When any issue of derogation from the golden rule of full disclosure comes before it, the court must address a series of questions:

(1)   What is the material which the prosecution seek to withhold? This must be considered by the court in detail.

(2)   Is the material such as may weaken the prosecution case or strengthen that of the defence? If No, disclosure should not be ordered. If Yes, full disclosure should (subject to (3), (4) and (5) below) be ordered.

(3)   Is there a real risk of serious prejudice to an important public interest (and, if so, what) if full disclosure of the material is ordered? If No, full disclosure should be ordered.

(4)   If the answer to (2) and (3) is Yes, can the defendant's interest be protected without disclosure or disclosure be ordered to an extent or in a way which will give adequate protection to the public interest in question and also afford adequate protection to the interests of the defence?

This question requires the court to consider, with specific reference to the material which the prosecution seek to withhold and the facts of the case and the defence as disclosed, whether the prosecution should formally admit what the defence seek to establish or whether disclosure short of full disclosure may be ordered. This may be done in appropriate cases by the preparation of summaries or extracts of evidence, or the provision of documents in an edited or anonymised form, provided the documents supplied are in each instance approved by the judge. In appropriate cases the appointment of special counsel may be a necessary step to ensure that the contentions of the prosecution are tested and the interests of the defendant protected (see paragraph 22 above). In cases of exceptional difficulty the court may require the appointment of special counsel to ensure a correct answer to questions (2) and (3) as well as (4).

(5)   Do the measures proposed in answer to (4) represent the minimum derogation necessary to protect the public interest in question? If No, the court should order such greater disclosure as will represent the minimum derogation from the golden rule of full disclosure.

(6) If limited disclosure is ordered pursuant to (4) or (5), may the effect be to render the trial process, viewed as a whole, unfair to the defendant? If Yes, then fuller disclosure should be ordered even if this leads or may lead the prosecution to discontinue the proceedings so as to avoid having to make disclosure.

(7) If the answer to (6) when first given is No, does that remain the correct answer as the trial unfolds, evidence is adduced and the defence advanced?

It is important that the answer to (6) should not be treated as a final, once-and-for-all, answer but as a provisional answer which the court must keep under review.

37 Throughout his or her consideration of any disclosure issue the trial judge must bear constantly in mind the overriding principles referred to in this opinion. In applying them, the judge should involve the defence to the maximum extent possible without disclosing that which the general interest requires to be protected but taking full account of the specific defence which is relied on. There will be very few cases indeed in which some measure of disclosure to the defence will not be possible, even if this is confined to the fact that an ex parte application is to be made. If even that information is withheld and if the material to be withheld is of significant help to the defendant, there must be a very serious question whether the prosecution should proceed, since special counsel, even if appointed, cannot then receive any instructions from the defence at all.

Importantly, Lord Bingham concludes that:

Provided the existing procedures for dealing with claims for public interest immunity made on behalf of the prosecution in criminal proceedings are operated with scrupulous attention to the governing principles referred to and continuing regard to the proper interests of the defendant, there should be no violation of Article 6 of the Convention.

The House of Lords also gave general guidance on PII hearings in magistrates' courts. Lord Bingham affirmed the approach taken in R (DPP) v Acton Youth Court [2001] EWHC 402 (Admin); [2001] 1 WLR 1828:

If PII applications are confined, as they should be, to material which undermines the prosecution case or strengthens that of the defence, the bench will not be alerted to material damaging to the defendant. If it is, the principles which should govern the court's decision whether to recuse itself are the same as in the case of any other tribunal of fact, but the court's duty of continuing review ordinarily militates in favour of continuing the proceedings before the court which determines the PII application. If a case raises complex and contentious PII issues, and the court has discretion to send the case to the crown court for trial, the magistrates' court should carefully consider whether those issues are best resolved in the crown court. The occasions on which it will be appropriate to appoint special counsel in the magistrates' court will be even rarer than in the Crown Court (para 44).

In R v G [2004] EWCA Crim 1368; (2004) The Times, 8 June, the Court of Appeal had to consider a case where sensitive information had been disclosed inadvertently. In a PII hearing, held ex parte, the judge had ordered non-disclosure of certain material to the defence. Subsequently, the prosecution had inadvertently disclosed some highly confidential and sensitive material in a document sent to the defendants' counsel. The judge ordered a ban on dissemination by the lawyers 'in the know' to anyone, including their clients. The judge made an express finding that the legal representatives could continue to represent their clients properly and effectively. The

Court of Appeal said that it is not appropriate for a judge in a criminal trial to make an order prohibiting defence counsel and solicitors from divulging to their clients evidence which has been inadvertently and wrongly disclosed to them by the prosecution. Furthermore, the court said that it is not for the judge to determine whether counsel or solicitors are capable of continuing to represent their client: the question of whether a lawyer can properly continue to represent his client is one for the lawyer, not the court.

7.2.4   Use of 'special counsel' in public interest immunity applications

The role of the judge in PII hearings is clearly a crucial one so far as the European Court is concerned. Indeed, in *PG and JH v UK* (2001) *The Times*, 19 October, the Court said that:

> ... The fact that the need for disclosure was at all times under assessment by the trial judge provided a further, important safeguard in that it was his duty to monitor throughout the trial the fairness or otherwise of the evidence being withheld. It has not been suggested that the judge was not independent and impartial within the meaning of Article 6(1). He was fully versed in all the evidence and issues in the case and in a position to monitor the relevance to the defence of the withheld information both before and during the trial.

Two points arise from this. First, in a case such as *Jasper* (where the defendant knew that an application to withhold material was being made and had a chance to make representations to the judge), the judge can only safeguard the interests of the accused if he or she has received sufficient information from the defence as to its case. Inevitably, the judge will not be as well-briefed on the details of the defence case as defence counsel would be. Nonetheless, it is probably true that (in most cases at least) knowledge of the broad thrust of the defence case will be sufficient to evaluate the potential relevance of the material that the prosecution are seeking to withhold. However, the second point is that, in a case where the defence do not know that an application to withhold material is being made, the only information that the judge is likely to have about the defence case will be based on (a) what the accused said when interviewed by the police, and (b) the content of the 'defence statement' served under the CPIA 1996. This information may be inadequate to brief the judge sufficiently to appreciate the relevance of the withheld material. Also, if the defendant remains silent in interview and/or serves a defence statement that lacks detail, he not only faces the possibility of adverse inferences being drawn by the jury but also is depriving the judge of information that might help in assessing the relevance of withheld material. This in turns makes it more difficult, if not impossible, for the judge to ensure that the accused has a fair trial.

The Auld Review (2001) recommended the use of 'special counsel' in cases where the prosecution wished to seek non-disclosure on grounds of public interest immunity on an *ex parte* basis. Paragraph 194 of the Review refers to a paper prepared for the Review by Tim Owen QC, who argued that the use of special counsel would:

> ... restore some adversarial testing of the issues presently absent in the determination of these often critical and finely balanced applications. It should not be generally necessary for special counsel to be present throughout the trial. Mostly the matter should be capable of resolution by the court before trial and, if any question about it arises during trial, he could be asked to return ...

However, at para 197 of the Review, Lord Justice Auld notes that the efficacy of the disclosure regime does not depend wholly on court procedures. He says that:

> ... even the introduction of special counsel ... would not solve the root problem ... of police failure, whether out of incompetence or dishonesty, to indicate to the prosecutor the existence of critical information. Unless ... the police significantly improve their performance in that basic exercise, there will be no solid foundation for whatever following safeguards are introduced into the system.

Recommendation 206 of the Auld Review is as follows:

> A scheme should be introduced for instruction by the court of special independent counsel to represent the interests of the defendant in those cases at first instance and on appeal where the court now considers prosecution applications in the absence of the defence in respect of the non-disclosure of sensitive material.

This recommendation was apparently not accepted by the government. The Criminal Justice Act 2003 makes a number of changes to the law relating to the disclosure of unused material, but does not make provision for use of special counsel.

It therefore fell to the courts to decide whether to sanction the use of special counsel. In *R v H; R v C* [2004] UKHL 3; [2004] 2 WLR 335, the House of Lords considered the potential role for 'special independent counsel' in PII hearings. It is interesting that the role of special independent counsel was not mentioned specifically in the questions certified by the Court of Appeal, even though the role of such counsel was central to the appeal. It seems likely that the Court of Appeal did not want to limit the scope of the enquiry by the House of Lords into general issues surrounding the fairness or otherwise of PII hearings.

At para 21, Lord Bingham turns to what he describes as the 'novel procedure' of appointing special independent counsel or a 'special advocate' to protect the interests of the defendant but who may not disclose to the defendant the secret material that is disclosed to him in order to make representations on behalf of the defendant and who is not, in the ordinary sense, professionally responsible to the defendant. Despite describing the procedure as 'novel', his Lordship goes on to identify a number of cases where the use of special advocates has been sanctioned by statute or by the courts. It is interesting to note in this context that the government did not include any reference to the use of special counsel when it amended the CPIA 1996 in the Criminal Justice Act 2003.

Turning to the jurisprudence of the European Court of Human Rights, Lord Bingham referred to *Chahal v UK* (1996) 23 EHRR 413 (an immigration case which raised issues of national security and where security-cleared counsel, instructed by the court, was appointed to cross-examine the witnesses and generally assist the court to test the strength of the State's case). The European Court accepted (at para 131) 'that there are techniques which can be employed which both accommodate legitimate security concerns about the nature and sources of intelligence information and yet accord the individual a substantial measure of procedural justice'. A similar point was made in *Tinnelly & Sons Ltd and McElduff v UK* (1998) 27 EHRR 249, where special counsel was appointed in a discrimination case that raised national security issues.

Of relevance to the appeal in *R v H*, the European Court in *Jasper* had held that the use of special counsel was not necessary in that case. At para 56, the Court said that:

The fact that the need for disclosure was at all times under assessment by the trial judge provided a further, important, safeguard in that it was his duty to monitor throughout the trial the fairness or otherwise of the evidence being withheld ... He was fully versed in all the evidence and issues in the case and in a position to monitor the relevance to the defence of the withheld information both before and during the trial.

Lord Bingham, in *R v H*, expresses concern (at para 22) that the appointment of special counsel raises:

... ethical problems, since a lawyer who cannot take full instructions from his client, nor report to his client, who is not responsible to his client and whose relationship with the client lacks the quality of confidence inherent in any ordinary lawyer-client relationship, is acting in a way hitherto unknown to the legal profession. While not insuperable, these problems should not be ignored, since neither the defendant nor the public will be fully aware of what is being done. The appointment is also likely to cause practical problems: of delay, while the special counsel familiarises himself with the detail of what is likely to be a complex case; of expense, since the introduction of an additional, high-quality advocate must add significantly to the cost of the case; and of continuing review, since it will not be easy for a special counsel to assist the court in its continuing duty to review disclosure, unless the special counsel is present throughout or is instructed from time to time when need arises.

However, his Lordship concludes that:

None of these problems should deter the court from appointing special counsel where the interests of justice are shown to require it. But the need must be shown. Such an appointment will always be exceptional, never automatic; a course of last and never first resort. It should not be ordered unless and until the trial judge is satisfied that no other course will adequately meet the overriding requirement of fairness to the defendant.

Finally, the House of Lords considered whether it was right to question the suitability of the Attorney General (who effectively oversees the work of the Director of Public Prosecutions) to be the officer responsible for the appointment of special counsel in cases where the necessity for such appointment arises.

Lord Bingham says (at para 46):

In our opinion such doubt is misplaced. It is very well-established that when exercising a range of functions the Attorney-General acts not as a minister of the Crown ... and not as the public officer with overall responsibility for the conduct of prosecutions, but as an independent, unpartisan guardian of the public interest in the administration of justice ... It is in that capacity alone that he approves the list of counsel judged suitable to act as ... special counsel ... It would perhaps allay any conceivable ground of doubt, however ill-founded, if the Attorney-General were to seek external approval of his list of eligible advocates by an appropriate professional body or bodies, but such approval is not in current circumstances essential to the acceptability of the procedure.

7.3 CONFIDENTIALITY

Where prosecution material has been disclosed to the defendant, the defendant may only use that material in connection with the forthcoming trial or an appeal following that trial unless the material is in the public domain because it has been displayed or communicated to the public in open court (s 17).

Contravention of s 17 is a contempt of court (s 18(1)). Where the prosecution disclosure was in the context of a summary trial, the contempt will be dealt with by the magistrates' court and the penalty is a custodial sentence of up to six months and/or a fine of up to £5,000; where the prosecution disclosure was in the context of trial on indictment, the contempt will be dealt with by the Crown Court and the penalty is up to two years' custody and/or a fine.

7.4   APPLICATIONS BY THE ACCUSED UNDER THE CPIA 1996

Such applications are governed by the Crown Court (Criminal Procedure and Investigations Act 1996) (Disclosure) Rules 1997 (SI 1997/698) and by the Magistrates' Courts (Criminal Procedure and Investigations Act 1996) (Disclosure) Rules 1997 (SI 1997/703).

Where the accused wishes to make an application for review of an order for non-disclosure under s 15(4) of the CPIA 1996, the application must be in writing and must 'specify the reason why the accused believes the court should review the question' whether it is still in the public interest for the material to be withheld (r 5(2) of both sets of Rules).

The court is empowered to determine the application without a hearing (r 5(5) of the Crown Court Rules and r 5(6) of the Magistrates' Courts Rules). However, under r 5(6) of both sets of Rules, an application may only be determined without a hearing if the court is satisfied that there are no grounds on which the court might conclude that it is in the public interest to disclose material to any extent. Thus, it is only hopeless applications that can be determined without a hearing.

The hearing is *inter partes*, and the accused and the prosecutor are entitled to make representations to the court (r 5(7) of the Crown Court Rules and r 5(5) of the Magistrates' Courts Rules). However, after hearing the accused's representations, the prosecutor can apply to the court for leave to make representations in the absence of the accused (r 5(8) of the Crown Court Rules and r 5(7) of the Magistrates' Courts Rules). Furthermore, where the order to which the application relates was one made after an application where the accused was not informed that the application was being made, the review hearing is *ex parte* and only the prosecutor is entitled to make representations to the court (r 5(9) of the Crown Court Rules and r 5(8) of the Magistrates' Courts Rules).

A hearing under r 5 may be held in private (r 9(2) of both sets of Rules).

Where the accused believes that the prosecution are withholding information that should have been disclosed and wishes to make an application under s 8(2) of the CPIA 1996, the application must be made in writing and must specify the material to which the application relates, that the material has not been disclosed to the accused, and the reason why the material might be expected to assist the applicant's defence as disclosed by the defence statement (r 7(2) of both sets of Rules).

The prosecutor has to give written notice to the court within 14 days of being informed of the accused's application that either he wishes to make representations to the court concerning the material to which the application relates or, if he does not wish to make representations, that he is willing to disclose that material (r 7(6) of the Crown Court Rules and r 7(4) of the Magistrates' Courts Rules).

Rule 7(5) of the Crown Court Rules (r 7(6) of the Magistrates' Courts Rules) enables the court to determine the application without a hearing, but r 7(7) of the Crown Court Rules (r 7(6) of the Magistrates' Courts Rules) stipulates that the application must not be determined without a hearing if:

- the prosecutor has given notice that he wishes to make representations and the court considers that those representations should be made at a hearing; or
- the court considers a hearing to be necessary in the interests of justice.

The hearing is *inter partes* and the prosecutor and the applicant are entitled to make representations to the court (r 7(8) of the Crown Court Rules and r 7(5) of the Magistrates' Courts Rules). Rule 7(9) of the Crown Court Rules (r 7(7) of the Magistrates' Courts Rules) enables the prosecutor to apply for leave to make representations in the absence of the accused and any legal representative of the accused.

A hearing under r 7 may be held in private (r 9(2) of both sets of Rules).

CHAPTER 8

TRANSFERRING CASES TO THE CROWN COURT FOR TRIAL

8.1   INTRODUCTION

We have already seen that all criminal cases begin in the magistrates' court (either an information is laid and a summons is issued requiring the defendant to attend the magistrates' court, or else the defendant is arrested, charged and required to appear at the magistrates' court). If the offence is triable only in the Crown Court, it must be transferred to that court. If it is triable either way, it will be transferred to the Crown Court for trial only if the accused indicates a not guilty plea at the 'plea before venue' hearing (or gives no indication of plea and so is deemed to be indicating a not guilty plea) and the mode of trial hearing that follows results in a decision in favour of Crown Court trial (either because the magistrates decline jurisdiction or because the accused elects Crown Court trial).

8.1.1   Background

When magistrates are conducting committal proceedings, they are known as 'examining justices'. They have jurisdiction to hold committal proceedings no matter where in England and Wales the offence was allegedly committed.

The original version of the Magistrates' Courts Act 1980 provided two alternative methods for transferring a case from the magistrates' court so that it could be tried in the Crown Court. The first, committal 'without consideration of the evidence' under s 6(2) of the Magistrates' Courts Act 1980, remains in force for either way offences (but not indictable-only offences) and is described below.

The second was a version of committal 'with consideration of the evidence', which was significantly different from the version of committal under s 6(1) of the 1980 Act which is described below. Under the original version of s 6(1), the procedure for a committal with consideration of the evidence was very similar to that of an ordinary trial, with witnesses being subject to examination-in-chief, cross-examination and re-examination. A contemporaneous note of the evidence was taken down and when a witness had finished testifying, the notes were read back to the witness, who was then given an opportunity to make any amendments. The witness then signed the notes (which became a 'deposition'). After the prosecution witnesses had given evidence, the defence had a chance to make a submission that there was no case to answer. If that submission was unsuccessful, the defence had the opportunity to call evidence and make a second submission of no case to answer (though it was very rare for the defence to call any evidence at this stage). If a submission of no case to answer was successful, the defendant was 'discharged'.

Under the Criminal Justice and Public Order Act 1994, a new system called transfer for trial was set up to replace both forms of committal. The essence of the system was that the prosecution would serve a notice on the defendant and on the magistrates' court and that, following receipt of the notice, the magistrates would transfer the case to the Crown Court for trial. This procedure did not involve a hearing in court. It was, however, open to a defendant to make representations to the effect that the prosecution witness statements did not disclose a case to answer and in that case there could be a hearing. These provisions never came into force and were, by s 47 of the Criminal Procedure and Investigations Act (CPIA) 1996, replaced by a new system of committal proceedings set out in Sched 1 to the CPIA 1996.

Under this new system, committal without consideration of the evidence remained in its original version, but committal with consideration of the evidence was amended so that witness statements are read out but witnesses do not attend the hearing.

A further change was made by the enactment of s 51 of the Crime and Disorder Act 1998, which effectively abolished committal proceedings in the case of indictable-only offences, replacing them with a system under which the case was transferred to the Crown Court at a very early stage (often after only one appearance in the magistrates' court).

Finally, the Criminal Justice Act 2003 abolishes committal proceedings for either way offences, and applies the system of transfer in s 51 of the Crime and Disorder Act 1998 to either way offences as well as indictable-only offences. It is anticipated that these provisions of the 2003 Act will come into force in 2005/06.

8.2 THE TWO FORMS OF COMMITTAL

Section 6 of the Magistrates' Courts Act 1980 (as amended by Sched 1, para 4 to the CPIA 1996) provides for two methods of committing a defendant from the magistrates' court to the Crown Court. One method (under s 6(1) of the Magistrates' Courts Act 1980) involves a consideration of the evidence by the magistrates; the other (under s 6(2) of the 1980 Act) does not. Each of these is examined in more detail later in this chapter. First, however, some preliminary matters have to be considered.

If there is more than one defendant, and the defendants are jointly charged, there will be joint committal proceedings. If the defendants are not jointly charged, joint committal proceedings only take place if the charges against the defendants are sufficiently linked that it is likely that they will be tried together in the Crown Court (*R v Camberwell Green Magistrates ex p Christie* [1978] QB 602).

Section 4(3) of the Magistrates' Courts Act 1980 provides that the defendant must be present at committal proceedings unless (under s 4(4)):

(a) his disorderly conduct makes it impracticable for him to remain in court; or

(b) he is unwell but is legally represented and consents to the proceedings taking place in his absence.

In *R v Liverpool City Magistrates' Court ex p Quantrell* [1999] 2 Cr App R 24, the defendant was unwell and wanted committal proceedings under s 6(2) of the Magistrates' Courts Act 1980 (that is, committal without consideration of the evidence) to take place in his absence. Because s 4(4) of the 1980 Act refers to examining justices hearing evidence in the absence of the defendant where he is ill but is legally represented and consents to the evidence being given in his absence, the magistrates held that they had no power to conduct a hearing without consideration of evidence in the absence of the defendant. The Divisional Court held that the magistrates were wrong and that it was open to a magistrates' court to commit a defendant under s 6(2) in his absence, although they were not obliged to do so.

If the defendant fails without good cause to attend the committal proceedings, he will be in breach of his bail and a warrant for his arrest will be issued.

8.3   COMMITTAL WITHOUT CONSIDERATION OF THE EVIDENCE

The vast majority of committals are without consideration of the evidence, under s 6(2), and so we will consider them first. This form of committal is only possible if all of the following requirements are satisfied.

8.3.1   Pre-conditions for a s 6(2) committal

First, under s 5A of the Magistrates' Courts Act 1980, the prosecution evidence must comprise:

(a) written statements which comply with s 5B of the Magistrates' Courts Act 1980. In order for a statement to comply with s 5B:

  (i)   the statement must be signed by its maker;

  (ii)   the statement must contain a declaration by the maker that 'it is true to the best of my knowledge and belief and I make it knowing that, if it is tendered in evidence, I shall be liable to prosecution if I have wilfully stated in it anything which I know to be false or do not believe to be true'.

  (iii) a copy of the statement must be served on the defendant (or, if there is more than one defendant, on all the defendants);

  and/or

(b) depositions (under s 5C of the Magistrates' Courts Act), that is, sworn statements taken before a magistrate under s 97A of the Magistrates' Courts Act;

  and/or

(c) statements made admissible by virtue of s 23 or 24 of the Criminal Justice Act 1988: s 5D of the Magistrates' Courts Act 1980.

Secondly, under s 6(2)(a), the defendant (or, if more than one defendant, each of them) must have a legal representative acting for him in the case.

Thirdly, under s 6(2)(b), the defendant must not have requested the magistrates' court to consider a submission that there is insufficient evidence to put the defendant on trial by jury for the offence. If there is more than one defendant, committal under s 6(2) is not possible if any of them wishes to submit that there is no case to answer.

8.3.2   Procedure

Prior to the hearing, the prosecution will have served on the defendant(s) the bundle of prosecution witness statements (assuming these statements have not already been served on the defence pursuant to the advance information rules).

At the hearing, the bundle of witness statements will be handed to the magistrates. The magistrates will not read the witness statements but will check that there is no submission on behalf of the defendant(s) that there is no case to answer. Assuming there is no such submission, the defendant will be committed to stand trial at the

Crown Court and will be told the date of his first appearance at the Crown Court (for the Plea and Directions Hearing).

The magistrates will also consider ancillary matters such as bail, publicly funded representation and publicity.

Under the Schedule to the Justices' Clerks Rules 1999, a clerk may commit a defendant for trial provided that he is already on bail and is committed to the Crown Court on bail with the same conditions (if any) as before.

The presumption in favour of bail continues to apply where the defendant has been committed for trial to the Crown Court. Where the defendant was on bail prior to committal, bail will be continued unless the prosecution can satisfy the magistrates that any of the statutory reasons for withholding bail now apply. Where the defendant is in custody at the time of the committal proceedings, the committal hearing may present an opportunity to make a bail application, not least because the strength of the prosecution case (something which the magistrates have to consider under the Bail Act 1976) may well be much clearer.

8.4   PUBLICITY: REPORTING RESTRICTIONS

Section 8(1) of the Magistrates' Courts Act 1980 makes it unlawful to publish a report (written or broadcast) of any information other than that specified by s 8(4) of the Magistrates' Courts Act 1980. This allows the publication of only basic details about the case such as:

(a) the identity of the court;

(b) names of examining justices, counsel and solicitors;

(c) names, addresses, ages and occupations of parties and witnesses;

(d) charges against the accused and those on which he was committed for trial;

(e) decisions on the granting of bail and of publicly funded representation through the Criminal Defence Service.

These restrictions mean that any evidence read out, and any arguments put forward, at committal proceedings cannot be reported by the media. This is so that the people who eventually sit on the jury that tries the defendant will not be biased against the defendant because of unfavourable pre-trial publicity.

Breach of the restrictions is a summary offence carrying a maximum fine of £5,000.

Under s 8(3) of the Magistrates' Courts Act 1980, these restrictions apply to all stages of the case against the defendant prior to and including the committal and, unless lifted, also apply until the Crown Court trial is over. The restrictions automatically lapse if the committal proceedings result in the discharge of the defendant.

8.4.1   Lifting the restrictions

These statutory reporting restrictions can be lifted by the magistrates. An application for the restrictions to be lifted may be made at the committal proceedings or at any remand hearing before those proceedings take place.

If there is only one defendant and he asks for the reporting restrictions to be lifted, the magistrates must comply with this request and lift the restrictions (s 8(2)).

If there is more than one defendant and one defendant asks for the reporting restrictions to be lifted, but another defendant opposes this application, the defendant who wants the restrictions lifted must show that it is in the interests of justice for this to be done (s 8(2A); *R v Leeds Justices ex p Sykes* [1983] 1 WLR 132; [1983] 1 All ER 460).

To ensure that the application is dealt with fairly, all the defendants must be given a chance to make representations on the lifting of the restrictions (s 8(2A); *R v Wirral Justices ex p Meikle* (1990) 154 JP 1035).

A strong argument in favour of lifting the restrictions is that publicity is necessary in order to encourage potential witnesses to come forward.

8.4.2   Defining what can be reported

If the restrictions are lifted, then all of the restrictions have to be lifted: the justices cannot pick and choose which of the restrictions are lifted and which remain. Furthermore, once the restrictions are lifted, they cannot be reimposed (*R v Bow Street Magistrates ex p Kray* [1969] 1 QB 473).

However, if the justices wish to lift the reporting restrictions which apply under s 8 of the Magistrates' Courts Act 1980 but nonetheless wish to prevent the full reporting of all the details of the case, they can lift the s 8 restrictions but then make an order under s 4 of the Contempt of Court Act 1981. This allows the court to order postponement of the contemporaneous reporting of some or all of any legal proceedings where such action is necessary to prevent a 'substantial risk of prejudice to the administration of justice'. Thus, if the s 8 restrictions have been lifted, the court can effectively define what may be reported by making an order under the Contempt of Court Act 1981.

In *R v Sherwood ex p Telegraph Group plc* [2001] EWCA Crim 1075; [2001] 1 WLR 1983, the Court of Appeal issued guidance on applications to postpone media coverage of court proceedings under s 4(2) of the Contempt of Court Act 1981: they should be approached by way of a three-stage test:

(1) The first question is whether reporting would give rise to a not insubstantial risk of prejudice to the administration of justice in the relevant proceedings. If not, that is the end of the matter.

(2) If such a risk is perceived to exist, then the second question arises: would an order under s 4(2) eliminate that risk? If not, there could clearly be no necessity to impose such a ban and that would be the end of the matter. On the other hand, even if the judge is satisfied that an order would achieve the objective, he would still have to consider whether the risk could satisfactorily be overcome by some less restrictive means. If so, it could not be said to be necessary to take the more drastic approach.

(3) If the judge concludes that there is no other way of eliminating the perceived risk of prejudice, it still does not follow necessarily that an order has to be made. The judge might still have to ask whether the degree of risk contemplated should be regarded as tolerable in the sense of being the lesser of two evils. It is at that stage that value judgments might have to be made as to the priority between competing public interests. Where there is an appeal, it is the duty of the Court of Appeal not merely to review the decision of the trial judge but to come to its own independent conclusions on the materials placed before it.

These guidelines are equally applicable to magistrates' courts.

Where the court is minded to make an order under the Contempt of Court Act 1981, it should listen to any representations made on behalf of the press (*R v Clerkenwell Magistrates ex p The Telegraph plc* [1993] 2 All ER 183 and para I.3.2 of the *Consolidated Practice Direction*).

8.5 COMMITTAL WITH CONSIDERATION OF THE EVIDENCE

As we have seen, committal without consideration of the evidence under s 6(2) is only possible if the defendant concedes that the prosecution witness statements disclose a case to answer against him. In those comparatively rare cases where the defendant does not concede that this is so, the magistrates have to consider the evidence against the defendant under s 6(1). Section 6(1) of the Magistrates' Courts Act 1980 provides that a:

> ... magistrates' court inquiring into an offence as examining justices shall on consideration of the evidence:
>
> (a) commit the accused for trial if it is of opinion that there is sufficient evidence to put him on trial by jury for any indictable offence;
>
> (b) discharge him if it is not of that opinion and he is in custody for no other cause than the offence under inquiry.

Sections 5B(4), 5C(4) and 5D(4) of the Magistrates' Courts Act 1980 each provide that, unless the committal is without consideration of the evidence under s 6(2), each statement or deposition must:

> ... be read aloud at the hearing; and where the court so directs, an account shall be given orally of so much of any [statement or deposition, as the case may be] as is not read aloud.

The hearing at which the magistrates consider whether the witness statements disclose a case to answer against the defendant will begin with a short opening speech by the prosecutor. The prosecutor will then read out the written statements made by the witnesses upon whose evidence the prosecution case is based (or, with the permission of the court, the prosecutor will summarise the effect of any part of a statement which is not read out loud). No witnesses will be called to give oral evidence.

When the prosecution statements have been read to the court, the defence will have the opportunity to submit that there is no case to answer on the basis of those witness statements; the prosecutor will be entitled to reply to that submission in order to try to persuade the magistrates that there is a case to answer.

Having heard the submission of no case to answer from the defence and a reply from the prosecution, the examining justices consider whether there is sufficient evidence to justify committing the defendant to stand trial at the Crown Court. The test they have to apply is whether there is a *prima facie* case against the accused. In other words, they have to ask themselves whether there is sufficient evidence on which a reasonable jury *could* convict him (not whether they *would* convict the defendant). Thus, the only evidence tendered at a s 6(1) committal is prosecution evidence, and all that evidence must be in writing. There is no defence evidence at all.

This procedure for committal with consideration of the evidence is of comparatively little use to defendants. It will not often be the case that the witness statements do not disclose a case to answer. Because the new procedure does not allow oral evidence to be heard, there is no possibility of cross-examining a prosecution witness to probe potential weaknesses in their evidence. Furthermore (under Sched 1, paras 25 and 26 to the CPIA 1996), ss 76 and 78 of PACE (which enable a court to exclude prosecution evidence as being inadmissible) do not apply to committal proceedings.

In *Wilkinson v CPS* (1998) 162 JP 591, the Crown Prosecution Service (CPS) served a bundle of witness statements on the defendant. The defendant opted for committal proceedings with consideration of the evidence under s 6(1) of the Magistrates' Courts Act 1980. At the committal proceedings, the CPS relied solely on the statement of the alleged victim of the offence. The defendant argued that part of that statement was inadmissible and that the decision not to read any of the other witness statements created a false picture. The Divisional Court held that there was plainly sufficient admissible evidence in the complainant's statement and so it did not matter that other parts of the statement might be inadmissible at trial and, more generally, the prosecution may choose which witnesses to rely on for the purposes of committal proceedings.

Under s 6(1), it is open to the magistrates to decide that there is insufficient evidence to justify the defendant being committed for trial in respect of the offence for which the prosecution seek committal but that there is sufficient evidence to justify committal for trial for another offence. Provided that the offence in respect of which the magistrates find a case to answer is an indictable offence (whether triable only in the Crown Court or triable either way), they may commit him for trial for that offence. An example would be where the prosecution seek committal for murder but the magistrates decide that there is only sufficient evidence to support a charge of manslaughter. Where the justices are minded to hold that there is a case to answer on a charge other than the original one, the parties should be given the opportunity to address the bench before the magistrates have made up their minds (*R v Gloucester Magistrates Court ex p Chung* (1989) 153 JP 75).

Where the magistrates decide that there is insufficient evidence to justify a Crown Court trial in respect of any indictable offence, they must discharge the defendant. A 'discharge' at committal proceedings does not have the same effect as an acquittal, since the prosecution can re-prosecute the defendant for the same offence (something that cannot be done where the defendant has been acquitted following a trial).

If the prosecution wish to challenge a discharge, there are two ways of doing so:

(1) The prosecution can bring fresh committal proceedings alleging the same offence (*R v Manchester Justices ex p Snelson* [1977] 1 WLR 911; [1978] 2 All ER 62). Normally, the prosecution will only bring fresh proceedings if, for example, the decision to discharge the defendant was clearly unreasonable, or new evidence against the accused comes to light. If the prosecution behave oppressively by bringing fresh committal proceedings where the defendant has already been discharged, the Divisional Court may (on an application for judicial review) grant an order of prohibition to prevent further committal proceedings which amount to an abuse of process (*R v Horsham Justices ex p Reeves* (1980) 75 Cr App R 236).

(2) Instead of bringing fresh committal proceedings the prosecution may decide instead to seek a 'voluntary bill of indictment' (see below).

8.6   CHALLENGING THE DECISION TO COMMIT FOR TRIAL

In most cases, there will be no remedy for a defendant who thinks that he should not have been committed for trial; all he can do is wait for the Crown Court trial and make a submission that there is no case to answer at the close of the prosecution case.

If the defendant is committed for trial, there is no possibility of an appeal to the Divisional Court by way of case stated as there has been no final determination of the case (*Cragg v Lewes District Council* [1986] Crim LR 800).

In *R v Bedwellty Justices ex p Williams* [1997] AC 225, the House of Lords, following their earlier decision in *Neill v North Antrim Magistrates' Court* [1992] 1 WLR 1221, held that the decision of a magistrates' court to commit a defendant for trial is susceptible to judicial review. In *Williams*, the only evidence relied on by the prosecution was the fact that the defendant was implicated in statements made to the police by other people who were charged in the same proceedings: these statements (being out of court statements by co-defendants) were inadmissible against Williams. There was, therefore, no admissible evidence against her. The House of Lords held that, because examining justices are required by s 6(1) of the Magistrates' Courts Act 1980 to consider the evidence adduced by the prosecution, a committal should be quashed if there was no admissible evidence of the defendant's guilt. The House of Lords went on to hold that where there was *some* admissible evidence against the accused, but it was insufficient to amount to a *prima facie* case against him, the remedy of judicial review is available, but the Divisional Court should be slow to interfere with the decision of the justices. Presumably, a decision based on admissible evidence that there is a *prima facie* case against the accused would only be quashed if no reasonable bench of magistrates could have come to the view that there was sufficient evidence (that is, the decision to commit the accused for trial was perverse).

8.7   OTHER METHODS OF SECURING TRIAL ON INDICTMENT

Committal proceedings are the usual way of making a defendant stand trial in the Crown Court for an either way offence. There are, however, two other ways: the voluntary bill of indictment and the notice of transfer procedure.

8.7.1   A voluntary bill of indictment

A 'voluntary bill of indictment' is an order made by a High Court judge that the defendant should stand trial in the Crown Court for the offence(s) specified in the order. The obtaining of a voluntary bill of indictment is governed by s 2(2)(b) of the Administration of Justice (Miscellaneous Provisions) Act 1933.

To obtain a voluntary bill of indictment, the prosecution have to make a written application to a High Court judge. Paragraph IV.35 of the *Practice Direction (Criminal Proceedings: Consolidation)* [2002] 1 WLR 2870; [2002] 3 All ER 904 provides as follows:

35   *Voluntary bills of indictment*

35.1 Section 2(2)(b) of the Administration of Justice (Miscellaneous Provisions) Act 1933 allows the preferment of a bill of indictment by the direction or with the consent of a judge of the High Court. Bills so preferred are known as voluntary bills.

35.2 Applications for such consent must not only comply with each paragraph of the Indictment (Procedure) Rules 1971 (SI 1971/2084), but must also be accompanied by: (a) a copy of any charges on which the defendant has been committed for trial; (b) a copy of any charges on which his committal for trial was refused by the magistrates' court; (c) a copy of any existing indictment which has been preferred in consequence of his committal; (d) a summary of the evidence or other document which:

(i)   identifies the counts in the proposed indictment on which he has been committed for trial (or which are substantially the same as charges on which he has been so committed) and

(ii) in relation to each other count in the proposed indictment, identifies the pages in the accompanying statements and exhibits where the essential evidence said to support that count is to be found;

(e) marginal markings of the relevant passages on the pages of the statements and exhibits identified under (d)(ii). These requirements should be complied with in relation to each defendant named in the indictment for which consent is sought, whether or not it is proposed to prefer any new count against him.

35.3 The preferment of a voluntary bill is an exceptional procedure. Consent should only be granted where good reason to depart from the normal procedure is clearly shown and only where the interests of justice, rather than considerations of administrative convenience, require it.

35.4 Neither the 1933 Act nor the 1971 Rules expressly require a prosecuting authority applying for consent to the preferment of a voluntary bill to give notice of the application to the prospective defendant or to serve on him a copy of documents delivered to the judge; nor is it expressly required that the prospective defendant have any opportunity to make any submissions to the judge, whether in writing or orally.

35.5 The prosecuting authorities for England and Wales have issued revised guidance to prosecutors on the procedures to be adopted in seeking judicial consent to the preferment of voluntary bills. These procedures direct prosecutors:

(a) on the making of application for consent to preferment of a voluntary bill, forthwith to give notice to the prospective defendant that such application has been made;

(b) at about the same time, to serve on the prospective defendant a copy of all the documents delivered to the judge (save to the extent that these have already been served on him);

(c) to inform the prospective defendant that he may make submissions in writing to the judge, provided that he does so within nine working days of the giving of notice under (a) above.

Prosecutors will be directed that these procedures should be followed unless there are good grounds for not doing so, in which case prosecutors will inform the judge that the procedures have not been followed and seek his leave to dispense with all or any of them. Judges should not give leave to dispense unless good grounds are shown.

35.6   A judge to whom application for consent to the preferment of a voluntary bill is made will, of course, wish to consider carefully the documents submitted by the prosecutor and any written submissions timeously made by the prospective defendant, and may properly seek any necessary amplification. The judge may invite oral submissions from either party, or accede to a request for an opportunity to make such oral submissions, if the judge considers it necessary or desirable to receive such oral submissions in order to make a sound and fair decision on the application. Any such oral submissions should be made on notice to the other party, who should be allowed to attend.

The Practice Direction makes it clear that the voluntary bill procedure should not be used unless there is very good reason to depart from normal procedure. The main uses of this procedure are as follows:

(a) Where committal proceedings have taken place and the defendant has been discharged, the voluntary bill procedure is an alternative to bringing fresh committal proceedings. However, in *Brooks v DPP of Jamaica* [1994] 1 AC 568, the Privy Council said that a judge should only direct the preferment of a voluntary bill of indictment in a case where magistrates have discharged a defendant in exceptional circumstances.

(b) Where the defendant disrupts the committal proceedings but for some reason the justices decide not to use their power (under s 4 of the Magistrates' Courts Act 1980) to proceed in his absence, the voluntary bill procedure can be used.

(c) Where one defendant has already been committed for trial and another suspect is arrested shortly before the trial of the first defendant, it is desirable that there be a joint trial. If there is insufficient time for committal proceedings to take place and it is undesirable to seek an adjournment of the first defendant's trial, the voluntary bill procedure is a speedy way of getting the second suspect to the Crown Court so that there can be a joint trial.

If the judge directs that a voluntary bill of indictment be preferred (that is, orders the defendant to stand trial in the Crown Court), that decision cannot be challenged by judicial review (*R v Manchester Crown Court ex p Williams* (1990) 154 JP 589). Similarly, the judge who presides over the trial in the Crown Court cannot quash the indictment if he disagrees with the decision of the High Court judge (*R v Rothfield* (1937) 26 Cr App R 103).

Even though the decision of a High Court judge to issue a voluntary bill of indictment is not subject to judicial review, the decision of a prosecutor to seek a voluntary bill is susceptible to review, but only on very limited grounds (such as alleged malice on the part of the prosecutor (*R v Inland Revenue Commissioners ex p Dhesi* (1995) *The Independent*, 14 August)).

Simon Farrell and Daniel Friedman, in 'Voluntary bills of indictment: the administration of justice or a rubber stamp' [1998] Crim LR 616, are highly critical of this procedure, contending that the defendant loses the right to make representations that (for example) he has been the victim of administrative inefficiency or that criminal proceedings have been initiated by way of misleading information, and they argue that in such cases the defendant should have the right to object to the initiation of criminal proceedings from the outset. They contend that the system of voluntary bills is defective because it does not readily allow for such objections. Recommendation 167 of the Auld Review is that the voluntary bill of indictment should be abolished, on the basis that it no longer serves a useful purpose (especially bearing in mind that its main use is to by-pass committal proceedings, which have been abolished in the case of indictable-only offences and will be abolished in the case of either way offences when the relevant provisions of Sched 3 to the Criminal Justice Act 2003 come into force).

8.7.2 Notices of transfer

In certain cases, the prosecution can by-pass the need for committal proceedings merely by serving a notice on the defendant transferring the case to the Crown Court.

This procedure applies in two cases:

(1) *Section 4 of the Criminal Justice Act 1987*

Cases involving serious or complex fraud where the prosecution is brought by the Director of Public Prosecutions (DPP) (this includes Crown Prosecution Service (CPS) cases as the DPP is head of the CPS), the Serious Fraud Office, the Inland Revenue and Her Majesty's Customs & Excise.

(2) *Section 53 of the Criminal Justice Act 1991*

Specified offences of a violent or sexual nature where there is a child witness (either the victim of the offence or a witness to its commission) who will be called at the trial. In such a case, the DPP (who can delegate this function to Crown Prosecutors) may use the transfer procedure if he is of the opinion that it is necessary to transfer the case direct to the Crown Court in order to avoid prejudice to the welfare of the child.

In *R v T (Jean Pierre)* [2001] 1 Cr App R 32, the Court of Appeal said that proceedings against a child should not be transferred to the Crown Court unless the offences were so serious as to come within s 91 of the Powers of Criminal Courts (Sentencing) Act 2000.

To by-pass committal proceedings under either of these statutes, a notice of transfer is served on the magistrates' court and on the defendant. The notice must be accompanied by the written witness statements which show there is sufficient evidence for the accused to be committed for trial.

In *R v Wrench* [1996] 1 Cr App R 340, it was held that, if one of the offences of which the defendant is accused is one to which the transfer provisions apply, then the procedure can also be used in respect of any other offences which can validly be joined on the same indictment.

When a notice of transfer has been served, the defendant may apply to a Crown Court judge to dismiss the charge(s) on the ground that there is no case to answer (s 6 of the Criminal Justice Act 1987 and Sched 6, para 5 to the Criminal Justice Act 1991).

Section 6 of the Criminal Justice Act 1987 provides that, in fraud case transfers, oral evidence may only be given at the hearing of the application to dismiss the case with leave of the judge, which is very rarely given.

Schedule 6 of the Criminal Justice Act 1991 provides that, in child witness case transfers, the judge may give leave for oral evidence to be called at the hearing of the application to dismiss the case, but he must not hear oral evidence from the child in whose interests the notice of transfer was given in deciding whether there is a case to answer.

In either case, the judge must dismiss the case if it appears to him that the evidence against the defendant would not be sufficient for a jury properly to convict him.

Further proceedings in respect of the dismissed charge may only be brought by way of an application for a voluntary bill of indictment.

In *R (on the Application of IRC) v Kingston Crown Court* [2001] EWHC 581 (Admin); [2001] 4 All ER 721, it was held that the test to be applied by the judge on the application to dismiss under s 6 of the Criminal Justice Act 1987 is whether the evidence would be sufficient for a jury properly to convict. That requires the judge to take into account the whole of the evidence against the defendant. On an application under s 6, it is not appropriate for the judge to view any evidence in isolation from its context and other evidence. The judge is not bound to assume that a jury would make every possible inference capable of being drawn against the defendant. The judge has to decide not only whether there is any evidence to go to a jury, but also whether that evidence is sufficient for a jury properly to convict. That exercise requires the judge to assess the weight of the evidence. This is not to say that the judge is entitled to substitute himself for the jury. The question for him is not whether the defendant should be convicted on the evidence put forward by the prosecution, but the sufficiency of that evidence. Where the evidence is largely documentary, and the case depends on the inferences or conclusions to be drawn from it, the judge must assess the inferences or conclusions that the prosecution propose to ask the jury to draw from the documents, and decide whether it appears to him that the jury could properly draw those inferences and come to those conclusions. The judge's conclusion as to the weight to be given to any evidence, and his conclusion that the evidence against the defendant is or is not sufficient for a jury properly to convict him, can only be impugned if they can be shown to be conclusions that no reasonable judge could have come to, and so the Divisional Court will not interfere if the decision of the judge was within the range of decisions open to a reasonable judge properly directing himself as to the law. The court observed that Parliament clearly intended the judge to have a wide margin of appreciation in this respect.

8.8 INDICTABLE-ONLY OFFENCES: TRANSFER TO THE CROWN COURT

Section 51 of the Crime and Disorder Act 1998 abolishes the requirement of committal proceedings in the case of offences which are triable only on indictment. The detailed provisions for the transfer of indictable-only offences to the Crown Court are set out in Sched 3 to the 1998 Act.

Section 51(1) provides that, where an adult appears before a magistrates' court charged with an offence which is triable only on indictment, the magistrates' court must immediately send him to the Crown Court for trial for that offence and for any either way or summary offence which appears to the court to be related to the indictable-only offence (under sub-s (11), this only applies to summary offences which are punishable with imprisonment or disqualification from driving).

Under s 51(7), the magistrates' court must provide a notice, which is served on the defendant and on the relevant Crown Court, specifying the offence(s) for which the defendant has been sent for trial. Section 51(8) requires that, where there is more than one indictable-only offence, and the defendant is also sent for trial in respect of an either way or summary offence, the notice must specify which indictable-only offence the either way or summary offence is linked to.

In selecting which location of the Crown Court to send the defendant to for trial, the magistrates' court must have regard to the convenience of the defence, the prosecution and the witnesses, the desirability of expediting the trial, and directions given by the Lord Chief Justice on the allocation of Crown Court business (s 51(10)).

In *R (Salubi) v Bow Street Magistrates' Court* [2002] EWHC 919 (Admin); [2002] 1 WLR 3073, it was held that (a) where a charge alleges an indictable-only offence arising out of the same facts as an earlier indictable-only charge or either way offence, it is caught by the s 51 procedure and has to be sent to the Crown Court. If the earlier charge is of a related either way offence and has not yet been committed for trial, the magistrates' court should send both to the Crown Court; and (b) the fact that a magistrates' court has a duty under s 51(1) to send an indictable-only case to the Crown Court 'forthwith' does not necessarily preclude it from exercising its jurisdiction to stay the proceedings as an abuse of process in an appropriate case, but such cases will be very rare (not least because an abuse of application can be made immediately after the case arrives at the Crown Court). Even in such rare cases where it might be appropriate to make an abuse of process application in the magistrates' court at the sending stage, it should be remembered that the onus is on the defence to establish bad faith or serious misconduct and that innocent mistakes based on lack of judgment do not suffice.

Within 42 days of the transfer, the prosecution must serve on the defence copies of the documents containing the evidence on which the charge is based: reg 2 of the Crime and Disorder Act (Service of Prosecution Evidence) Regulations 2000. In *Fehily v Governor of Wandsworth Prison* [2002] EWHC 1295; [2003] 1 Cr App R 10, it was held that failure by the prosecution to comply with the 42 day time limit does not render the prosecution a nullity: the Crown Court has jurisdiction to extend time on an application by the prosecution even if the application is made after the expiry of the time limit.

8.8.1   Submission of no case to answer

Paragraph 1 of Sched 3 requires the defendant to be served with copies of the documents containing the evidence on which the charge(s) are based.

Paragraph 2(1) says that at any time after the service of these documents but before he has been arraigned, the defendant may apply, orally or in writing, to the Crown Court to which he has been sent for trial for the charge(s) to be dismissed. The application is heard by a judge, who is required (under para 2(2)) to dismiss a charge (and where the indictment has been preferred, to quash any count on the indictment relating to that charge) if it appears to him 'that the evidence against the applicant would not be sufficient for a jury properly to convict him'.

Paragraph 2(3) says that an oral application can only be made if the applicant has given written notice of his intention to make the application. Paragraph 2(4) says that oral evidence may only be given on such an application with the leave of the judge, and leave is only to be given where it is in the interests of justice to do so. Paragraph 2(4) also envisages the possibility of the judge making an order that oral evidence should be heard (again, only if in the interests of justice to do so). Under para 2(5), if the judge gives leave or makes an order for someone to give evidence, but that person fails to give evidence, the judge may disregard any document indicating the evidence which that witness might have given at the hearing of the application.

Paragraph 2(6) provides that where a charge has been dismissed under para 2(2), further proceedings on that charge can only be brought by means of an application to a High Court judge for a voluntary bill of indictment.

8.8.2 Reporting restrictions

Paragraph 3 of Sched 3 imposes reporting restriction: they are the same as those applicable to committal proceedings under s 6 of the Magistrates' Courts Act 1980 (see above).

8.8.3 Linked offences

Paragraph 6 of Sched 3 deals with the power of the Crown Court to deal with cases where summary offences are sent to the Crown Court under s 51. Indictable-only and either way offences can actually appear on the indictment. If the defendant is convicted on that indictment, the Crown Court must first consider whether the summary offence is related to the indictable-only offence(s). Paragraph 6(12) provides that an offence is related to another offence for these purposes 'if it arises out of circumstances which are the same as or connected with those giving rise to the other offence'. If the summary offence is related to the indictable offence of which the defendant has been convicted, the court asks the defendant whether he pleads guilty or not guilty to the summary offence. If he pleads guilty, the Crown Court will proceed to sentence him for that offence (but may not impose a greater sentence than a magistrates' court could have imposed). If he pleads not guilty, the Crown Court has no further part to play in respect of that offence (unless the prosecution indicate that they do not wish to proceed with the offence, in which case the Crown Court can formally dismiss it, with the effect that the defendant is acquitted of it). Paragraph 6(8) makes it clear that the provisions of para 6 do not apply where the summary offence is tried on indictment under s 40 of the Criminal Justice Act 1988.

This procedure is of course very similar to that set out in s 41 of the Criminal Justice Act 1988 and achieves the same objectives. It is for this reason that s 41 of the 1988 Act will be repealed when the relevant provisions of the 2003 Act come into force, making s 51 applicable to either way as well as indictable-only offences.

Paragraph 6(9) provides that where the Court of Appeal quashes a conviction for an indictable-only offence, it must also set aside any conviction for a summary offence where the accused was dealt with for that offence by the Crown Court following conviction for the indictable-only offence.

Section 51(2) provides that, where an adult has already been sent for trial under s 51(1) and then appears before a magistrates' court charged with a related either way offence (or a related summary offence, provided that it carries imprisonment or disqualification from driving), the magistrates may send him to the Crown Court for trial for that either way or summary offence.

Paragraph 7 of Sched 3 deals with the situation where the defendant is sent for trial for an indictable-only offence but is not arraigned for such an offence. If the indictment still contains any either way offences, the Crown Court must go through the indication as to plea ('plea before venue') procedure and, where the defendant indicates a not guilty plea or gives no indication, the mode of trial procedure which would have been followed in the magistrates' court.

In *R v Nembhard* [2002] EWCA Crim 134; (2002) 166 JP 363, the defendant was charged with attempted robbery (an indictable-only offence) and was transferred to the Crown Court under s 51 of the 1998 Act; he was also sent to the Crown Court under s 51(1)(b) for the summary offence of assaulting a police officer. The attempted robbery charge was subsequently replaced with a charge of attempted theft (an either way offence). The defendant indicated a guilty plea to that charge, and so was deemed to have pleaded guilty to it (para 7(6) of Sched 3). The defendant also pleaded guilty to the summary offence (para 6(2) of Sched 3). The question to be resolved was whether the Crown Court had jurisdiction to sentence the defendant for the summary offence, given the fact that the indictable-only offence was no longer before the court. It was held that the court had jurisdiction to deal with the summary offence in these circumstances (its sentencing powers being limited to those of the magistrates' court).

In *R v Haye* [2002] EWCA Crim 2476; [2003] Crim LR 287, the defendant was charged with robbery. He was sent for trial at the Crown Court under s 51 of the Crime and Disorder Act 1998. At the plea and directions hearing, the prosecution dropped the charge of robbery and replaced it with a charge of theft. The defendant pleaded not guilty to theft. When the matter came on for trial, the defendant was re-arraigned on the theft charge and entered a guilty plea. He appealed against conviction on the ground that the procedure set out in para 7 of Sched 3 to the 1998 Act had not been followed prior to the arraignment on the theft charge; in particular, he complained that proper consideration had not been given to the question of whether he should be tried summarily or whether the Crown Court should continue to deal with the case. He argued that the proceedings which followed the plea of guilty were, therefore, a nullity. It was held that any failure to comply with the statutory procedure in relation to the right of a defendant to make representations and/or to exercise choice as to mode of trial would have the consequence that, if the matter proceeded to trial, the hearing would be regarded as *ultra vires* and liable to be quashed. In the present case, there had been not merely a departure from the prescribed procedure for determining mode of trial but an absence of any determination, in the sense of a conscious decision, as to the appropriate mode of trial. The defendant had therefore been deprived of an opportunity of seeking to persuade the judge that summary trial would be more suitable. It followed that the proceedings in relation to the indictment alleging theft were a nullity.

When the amendments made by Sched 3 to the Criminal Justice Act 2003 come into force, where the Crown Court has to decide mode of trial under para 7, it must follow the procedure set out in amended versions of paras 9(2), (3) and (4), which (as amended by para 20 of Sched 3 to the 2003 Act) provide as follows:

(2)   Before deciding the question, the court—

    (a)   shall give the prosecution an opportunity to inform the court of the accused's previous convictions (if any); and

    (b)   shall give the prosecution and the accused an opportunity to make representations as to whether summary trial or trial on indictment would be more suitable.

(3)   In deciding the question, the court shall consider—

    (a)   whether the sentence which a magistrates' court would have power to impose for the offence would be adequate; and

>   (b) any representations made by the prosecution or the accused under sub-paragraph (2)(b) above,
>
> and shall have regard to any allocation guidelines (or revised allocation guidelines) issued as definitive guidelines under section 170 of the Criminal Justice Act 2003.

(4)   Where—

>   (a) the accused is charged on the same occasion with two or more offences; and
>
>   (b) it appears to the court that they constitute or form part of a series of two or more offences of the same or a similar character;
>
> sub-paragraph (3)(a) above shall have effect as if references to the sentence which a magistrates' court would have power to impose for the offence were a reference to the maximum aggregate sentence which a magistrates' court would have power to impose for all of the offences taken together.

Where the Crown Court decides that the offence is suitable for summary trial, under para 10(2) (as amended):

(2)   The court shall explain to the accused in ordinary language—

>   (a) that it appears to the court more suitable for him to be tried summarily for the offence;
>
>   (b) that he can either consent to be so tried or, if he wishes, be tried on indictment; and
>
>   (c) in the case of a specified offence (within the meaning of section 224 of the Criminal Justice Act 2003), that if he is tried summarily and is convicted by the court, he may be committed for sentence to the Crown Court under section 3A of the Powers of Criminal Courts (Sentencing) Act 2000 if the committing court is of such opinion as is mentioned in sub-section (2) of that section.

These amendments are to ensure that the Crown Court follows the same mode of trial procedure to that adopted by the magistrates' court when that court is determining mode of trial.

8.8.4   Other defendants

Section 51(3) provides that where an adult is sent to the Crown Court for trial under s 51(1), and another adult, either then or on a subsequent occasion, appears at the magistrates' court charged jointly with him with an either way offence which is related to the indictable only offence, the court must (if it is the same occasion) or may (if it is a subsequent occasion) send the other adult to the Crown Court for trial for the either way offence. Under s 51(4), the magistrates must also send him to the Crown Court for trial for any either way or summary offence (in the case of the latter, provided that it is imprisonable or carries disqualification from driving) which is related to the indictable offence.

Under s 51(5), where an adult is sent for trial under s 51(1) or (3) and a juvenile is charged jointly with the adult with the indictable offence for which the adult has been sent for trial, the magistrates' court should only send the juvenile to the Crown Court for trial for the indictable offence 'if it considers it necessary in the interests of justice'. Where a juvenile is sent for trial for an indictable offence under s 51(5), the court may also send him for trial for a related either way or summary offence (in the case of the latter, provided that it is imprisonable or carries disqualification from driving).

8.9   MOVING THE TRIAL

The justices will usually send the defendant to the nearest location of the Crown Court which is competent to deal with the case.

It may be, however, that there are reasons why this may not be appropriate. For example, the offence with which the defendant is charged may have aroused such ill feeling locally that a fair trial at the nearest location of the Crown Court may not be possible. In such a case, the magistrates may be asked to send the defendant to a different Crown Court.

If the magistrates do not accede to this application, or if no such application is made, there are two other ways of moving the trial:

- paragraph 76(2) of the Supreme Court Act 1981 empowers an officer of the Crown Court to alter the place of trial;
- if the transfer is not effected administratively, either party may make an application to the Crown Court, under s 76(3) of the Supreme Court Act 1981, for the venue of the trial to be altered. Such applications formerly had to be heard by a High Court judge sitting in open court; however, s 86 of the Courts Act 2003 amends s 76 so that it is no longer necessary to apply to a High Court judge. Such applications are now heard by a Crown Court judge, sitting in chambers.

In *R v Croydon Crown Court ex p Britton* (2000) 164 JP 729, it was held that the scope of s 76 extends to altering the place of trial for an indictable-only offence transferred to the Crown Court without committal proceedings under s 51 of the Crime and Disorder Act 1998 (and so would also apply to either way offences even after committal proceedings for such offences are abolished by the Criminal Justice Act 2003).

8.10   SUMMONS TO A POTENTIAL PROSECUTION WITNESS TO MAKE A DEPOSITION

The CPIA 1996 added s 97A to the Magistrates' Courts Act 1980. The section enables a magistrate, prior to sending a case to the Crown Court, to issue a summons to a *potential* prosecution witness. The summons requires the potential witness to attend before a magistrate so that the magistrate can take a deposition from the witness. The requirements which have to be met are:

(a) the person is likely to be able to make, on behalf of the prosecution, a written statement containing material evidence (or to produce a document or other exhibit likely to be material evidence), for the purposes of committal proceedings which have not yet taken place; and

(b) the person would not make the statement (or produce the document or exhibit) voluntarily.

Where the magistrate is satisfied that the person will not attend even if a summons is issued, then an arrest warrant can be issued instead.

The deposition is taken before a single magistrate. A court does not have to be convened for this to be done; indeed, the deposition does not have to be taken in a court building. The defendant and his legal representative have no right to attend the taking of the deposition, and if they do attend have no right to cross-examine the witness. Indeed, the magistrate does not even have to notify the accused that a deposition is being taken (and would not notify the accused if the prosecution feared that the witness might be the subject of intimidation if the defence knew that a statement was being taken). The prosecutor questions the witness and a note is taken of the answers given by the witness. The witness is then asked to confirm the accuracy of the note. The magistrate must ensure that the questions asked by the prosecutor are relevant to the charge faced by the accused.

This procedure is not available to the defence, since its object is to facilitate the gathering of evidence for committal proceedings. It represents the first time that magistrates have become part of the criminal investigation process (along the lines of the examining magistrate on the Continent).

The Divisional Court considered this power in *R (CPS) v Bolton Magistrates' Court* [2003] EWHC 2697 (Admin); (2004) 168 JP 10. The court held as follows:

- The procedure for taking a deposition from a witness who will not voluntarily make a statement is a proceeding in open court. However, in the circumstances of a particular case, the justices might, exceptionally, exclude persons from the taking of the deposition or otherwise modify the procedure where that would assist in the reception of the evidence or is in the interests of justice.

- A deposition does not have to be taken at a court house but can be taken elsewhere. However, that flexibility can only properly be exercised in very unusual circumstances. Any prejudice to the administration of justice caused by members of the public being present can be dealt with by orders under s 4(2) of the Contempt of Court Act 1981 or by the general power to restrict access.

- Normally those representing the defendant will not be allowed to cross-examine the witness, but there might be cases where the reluctant witness is unlikely to be available at the Crown Court, or could perhaps be spared attendance there if one or two questions were asked; in such a situation, it would be open to the justices to permit cross-examination.

- Where a witness who has been summoned to give a deposition refuses to answer questions on the ground of privilege against self-incrimination, that claim should be the subject of proper investigation by the justices in respect of each and every question for which it is claimed. Before acceding to a claim to privilege, the court should satisfy itself, from the circumstances of the case and the nature of the evidence which the witness is called to give, that there is a reasonable ground to apprehend real and appreciable danger to the witness with reference to the ordinary operation of the law in the ordinary course of things, and not a danger of an imaginary or insubstantial character.

8.11   EXTENDING s 51 TO EITHER WAY OFFENCES (THE CRIMINAL JUSTICE ACT 2003)

Lord Justice Auld, in his *Review of the Criminal Courts of England and Wales*, concluded that committal proceedings should be abolished for either way offences in the same way that they were abolished for indictable-only offences. Committal proceedings seem to serve little useful purpose, and it was perhaps inevitable that they should be abolished altogether. Accordingly, Recommendation 35 was that:

> The procedure of committal of 'either way' cases to the Crown Court for trial should be abolished and ... such cases should be 'sent' to the Crown Court in the same way as indictable-only cases.

This proposal was accepted and the new procedure is contained in Sched 3 to the Criminal Justice Act 2003.

Paragraphs 15–20 of Sched 3 to the 2003 Act amend the procedure contained in the Crime and Disorder Act 1998 for transferring cases to the Crown Court.

Paragraph 17 inserts a new section, s 50A, into the Magistrates' Courts Act 1980, setting out the order in which a magistrates' court is to apply various procedures in respect of either way offences.

Paragraph 18 of Sched 3 replaces s 51 of the 1998 Act with an amended version that applies to both indictable-only offences (and charges that are related to such offences), but also to either way offences (where the mode of trial process results in a decision that the defendant should be tried on indictment).

Paragraph 18 also inserts three new sections, ss 51A–C, into the Crime and Disorder Act 1998. Section 51A makes provision for cases where the defendant is under 18. Sections 51B and 51C effectively subsume the transfer provisions originally contained in s 4 of the Criminal Justice Act 1987 (serious fraud cases) and s 53 of the Criminal Justice Act 1991 (child witness cases) respectively.

Section 50A(3) of the Crime and Disorder Act 1998 sets out the order in which the magistrates must take the various steps. It provides that, where an adult defendant is charged with an either way offence, the magistrates should take the following steps:

- 'plea before venue';
- in the event of an indication of a not guilty plea, mode of trial procedure;
- if the magistrates decline jurisdiction or the defendant elects trial on indictment, transfer the case to the Crown Court under s 51.

If the defendant is also charged with an indictable-only offence or an offence in respect of which there is a notice under s 51B (serious or complex fraud cases) or 51C (child witnesses) and is sent to the Crown Court for trial for that offence, the magistrates must decide whether the either way offence is related to the other offence and so should be sent to the Crown Court alongside that other offence; if the either way offence is not related to the other offence, the magistrates should go through the 'plea before venue' and mode of trial procedure for that either way offence.

The amended version of s 51(1) of the Crime and Disorder Act 1998 provides that where an adult defendant appears before a magistrates' court charged with:

- an indictable-only offence;
- an either way offence; or
- an offence in respect of which the prosecutor has served a notice under s 51B (serious or complex fraud) or 51C (child witnesses),

then the magistrates 'shall send him forthwith to the Crown Court for trial for the offence'.

Under s 51(3), where the magistrates send an adult for trial under s 51(1), they *must* also send him for trial in respect of any either way offence, or a summary offence which is punishable with imprisonment or disqualification from driving, which appears to the court to be related to the offence that they have sent for trial. Under s 51(4), the magistrates *may* send a defendant for trial in the Crown Court in respect of such a related either way or summary offence if he subsequently appears in the magistrates' court charged with that offence after he has been sent for trial for the 'main' offence. Where an either way offence is sent to the Crown Court under sub-s (3) or (4), this is done without first going through 'plea before venue' or mode of trial procedure.

Under s 51(5), where the magistrates send an adult defendant for trial under s 51 and another adult appears before the court on the same or a subsequent occasion charged jointly with the first adult with an either way offence that appears to the court to be related to an offence for which the first adult was sent for trial, the court must (where it is the same occasion) and may (where it is a subsequent occasion) send the second adult forthwith to the Crown Court for trial for the either way offence. Under s 51(6), where the court sends an adult for trial under sub-s (5), it must at the same time send him to the Crown Court for trial for any either way offence, or a summary offence punishable with imprisonment or disqualification from driving, with which he is charged if that offence is related to the offence for which he is sent for trial.

Under s 51(7), if an adult is sent for trial under s 51, and a child or young person appears before the court on the same or a subsequent occasion charged jointly with the adult with an indictable offence for which the adult is sent for trial or with an indictable offence which appears to the court to be related to that offence, the court 'shall, if it considers it necessary in the interests of justice to do so, send the child or young person forthwith to the Crown Court for trial for the indictable offence'. Under sub-s (8), if a juvenile has been sent for trial under sub-s (7), it may at the same time send him to the Crown Court for trial for any indictable offence (or summary offence punishable with imprisonment or disqualification from driving) with which he is charged and which is related to the offence for which he is sent for trial.

Section 51E provides that:

(c) an either way offence is related to an indictable offence if the charge for the either way offence could be joined in the same indictment as the charge for the indictable offence;

(d) a summary offence is related to an indictable offence if it arises out of circumstances which are the same as or connected with those giving rise to the indictable offence.

Section 51(13) makes it clear that the functions of a magistrates' court under s 51 may be discharged by a single justice.

Section 51D sets out the contents of the notice provided by the magistrates' court under s 51 or (for young defendants, s 51A). The notice must specify:

(a) the offence or offences for which a person is sent for trial; and

(b) the place at which he is to be tried.

A copy of the notice is served on the accused and given to the Crown Court sitting at the place specified in the notice.

In selecting the place of trial, the court is required (by s 51D(4)) to have regard to:

(a) the convenience of the defence, the prosecution and the witnesses;

(b) the desirability of expediting the trial; and

(c) any direction given under s 75(1) of the Supreme Court Act 1981.

The amended text of s 51 of the Crime and Disorder Act 1998 will read as follows:

(1)   Where an adult appears or is brought before a magistrates' court ('the court') charged with an offence and any of the conditions mentioned in sub-section (2) below is satisfied, the court shall send him forthwith to the Crown Court for trial for the offence.

(2)   Those conditions are—

(a) that the offence is an offence triable only on indictment other than one in respect of which notice has been given under section 51B or 51C below;

(b) that the offence is an either way offence and the court is required under section 20(9)(b), 21, 23(4)(b) or (5) or 25(2D) of the Magistrates' Courts Act 1980 to proceed in relation to the offence in accordance with sub-section (1) above;

(c) that notice is given to the court under section 51B or 51C below in respect of the offence.

(3)   Where the court sends an adult for trial under sub-section (1) above, it shall at the same time send him to the Crown Court for trial for any either way or summary offence with which he is charged and which—

(a) (if it is an either way offence) appears to the court to be related to the offence mentioned in sub-section (1) above; or

(b) (if it is a summary offence) appears to the court to be related to the offence mentioned in sub-section (1) above or to the either way offence, and which fulfils the requisite condition (as defined in sub-section (11) below).

(4)   Where an adult who has been sent for trial under sub-section (1) above subsequently appears or is brought before a magistrates' court charged with an either way or summary offence which—

(a) appears to the court to be related to the offence mentioned in sub-section (1) above; and

(b) (in the case of a summary offence) fulfils the requisite condition,

the court may send him forthwith to the Crown Court for trial for the either way or summary offence.

(5)   Where—

(a) the court sends an adult ('A') for trial under sub-section (1) or (3) above;

(b) another adult appears or is brought before the court on the same or a subsequent occasion charged jointly with A with an either way offence; and

(c) that offence appears to the court to be related to an offence for which A was sent for trial under sub-section (1) or (3) above,

the court shall where it is the same occasion, and may where it is a subsequent occasion, send the other adult forthwith to the Crown Court for trial for the either way offence.

(6)   Where the court sends an adult for trial under sub-section (5) above, it shall at the same time send him to the Crown Court for trial for any either way or summary offence with which he is charged and which—

(a) (if it is an either way offence) appears to the court to be related to the offence for which he is sent for trial; and

(b) (if it is a summary offence) appears to the court to be related to the offence for which he is sent for trial or to the either way offence, and which fulfils the requisite condition.

(7) Where—

    (a) the court sends an adult ('A') for trial under sub-section (1), (3) or (5) above; and

    (b) a child or young person appears or is brought before the court on the same or a subsequent occasion charged jointly with A with an indictable offence for which A is sent for trial under sub-section (1), (3) or (5) above, or an indictable offence which appears to the court to be related to that offence, the court shall, if it considers it necessary in the interests of justice to do so, send the child or young person forthwith to the Crown Court for trial for the indictable offence.

(8) Where the court sends a child or young person for trial under sub-section (7) above, it may at the same time send him to the Crown Court for trial for any indictable or summary offence with which he is charged and which—

    (a) (if it is an indictable offence) appears to the court to be related to the offence for which he is sent for trial; and

    (b) (if it is a summary offence) appears to the court to be related to the offence for which he is sent for trial or to the indictable offence, and which fulfils the requisite condition.

(9) Sub-sections (7) and (8) above are subject to sections 24A and 24B of the Magistrates' Courts Act 1980 (which provide for certain cases involving children and young persons to be tried summarily).

(10) The trial of the information charging any summary offence for which a person is sent for trial under this section shall be treated as if the court had adjourned it under section 10 of the 1980 Act and had not fixed the time and place for its resumption.

(11) A summary offence fulfils the requisite condition if it is punishable with imprisonment or involves obligatory or discretionary disqualification from driving.

(12) In the case of an adult charged with an offence—

    (a) if the offence satisfies paragraph (c) of sub-section (2) above, the offence shall be dealt with under sub-section (1) above and not under any other provision of this section or section 51A below;

    (b) subject to paragraph (a) above, if the offence is one in respect of which the court is required to, or would decide to, send the adult to the Crown Court under—

        (i) sub-section (5) above; or

        (ii) sub-section (6) of section 51A below,

    the offence shall be dealt with under that sub-section and not under any other provision of this section or section 51A below.

(13) The functions of a magistrates' court under this section, and its related functions under section 51D below, may be discharged by a single justice.

8.11.1 Serious or complex fraud cases and cases involving child witnesses

Section 51B sets out the procedure for transferring serious or complex fraud cases to the Crown Court. It applies where the prosecution is brought by the DPP, the Director of the Serious Fraud Office, the Commissioners of the Inland Revenue, the Commissioners of Customs & Excise, or the Secretary of State and the evidence 'reveals a case of fraud of such seriousness or complexity that it is appropriate that the management of the case should without delay be taken over by the Crown Court'. The prosecuting authority serves a notice on the magistrates' court.

Section 51C enables the DPP to serve a notice on the magistrates' court where he is of the opinion that a child would be called as a witness at the trial and that, for the purpose of avoiding any prejudice to the welfare of the child, the case should be taken over and proceeded with by the Crown Court without delay. This provision applies only to certain offences: any offence that involves an assault on, or injury or a threat of injury to, a person; offences under the Protection of Children Act 1978 or the Sexual Offences Act 2003; kidnapping, false imprisonment, or child abduction under the Child Abduction Act 1984.

8.11.2   Reporting restrictions

Section 52A sets out reporting restrictions to prevent prejudicial pre-trial reportage of cases. Section 52A(1) provides as follows:

(1)   Except as provided by this section, it shall not be lawful—

   (a)   to publish in the United Kingdom a written report of any allocation or sending proceedings in England and Wales; or

   (b)   to include in a relevant programme for reception in the United Kingdom a report of any such proceedings,

   if (in either case) the report contains any matter other than that permitted by this section.

Section 52A(6) provides that it is unlawful to publish, or include in a broadcast programme, any matters except those specified in sub-s (7). In other words, s 52A(7) sets out the matters that can be reported, namely:

(a)   the identity of the court and the name of the justice or justices;

(b)   the name, age, home address and occupation of the accused;

(c)   in the case of an accused charged with an offence in respect of which notice has been given to the court under section 51B [serious or complex fraud cases] above, any relevant business information [defined by sub-s (9) to mean any address used by the accused for carrying on a business on his own account; the name of any business which he was carrying on on his own account at any relevant time; the name of any firm in which he was a partner at any relevant time or by which he was engaged at any such time; the address of any such firm; the name of any company of which he was a director at any relevant time or by which he was otherwise engaged at any such time; the address of the registered or principal office of any such company; any working address of the accused in his capacity as a person engaged by any such company];

(d)   the offence or offences, or a summary of them, with which the accused is or are charged;

(e)   the names of counsel and solicitors engaged in the proceedings;

(f)   where the proceedings are adjourned, the date and place to which they are adjourned;

(g)   the arrangements as to bail;

(h)   whether a right to representation funded by the Legal Services Commission as part of the Criminal Defence Service was granted to the accused or any of the accused.

Under s 52A(2), the magistrates have the power to lift these reporting restrictions. This power is governed by sub-ss (3) and (4), which provide as follows:

(3)   Where there is only one accused and he objects to the making of an order under sub-section (2) above, the court shall make the order if, and only if, it is satisfied, after hearing the representations of the accused, that it is in the interests of justice to do so.

(4)   Where in the case of two or more accused one of them objects to the making of an order under sub-section (2) above, the court shall make the order if, and only if, it is satisfied, after hearing the representations of the accused, that it is in the interests of justice to do so.

It would appear that if there is only one defendant and he asks for the restrictions to be lifted, the court should make an order lifting the restrictions.

Under s 52B, breach of the reporting restrictions set out in s 52A is a summary offence, punishable (under s 52A(2)) with a level 5 fine (currently up to £5,000). Proceedings under s 52B can only be brought by, or with the consent of, the DPP (s 52B(3)).

CHAPTER 9

INDICTMENTS

9.1   INTRODUCTION

In this chapter, we examine the rules which govern the form and content of the indictment upon which a Crown Court trial is based. The key legislative provisions governing the form and content of indictments are to be found in ss 3 and 5 of the Indictments Act 1915, s 2 of the Administration of Justice (Miscellaneous Provisions) Act 1933, and in rr 4–9 of the Indictment Rules 1971 (SI 1971/1253).

9.2   TERMINOLOGY

The indictment is the formal document setting out the charges which the defendant faces at the Crown Court. Each offence is known as a 'count'. An indictment is only valid when it is signed by an appropriate officer of the Crown Court. A draft indictment which has not yet been signed by an officer of the Crown Court is known as a 'bill of indictment'.

No 04/01321

INDICTMENT

THE CROWN COURT AT CROYDON

THE QUEEN v VICTOR JAMES WARD

VICTOR JAMES WARD is charged as follows:

COUNT 1

Statement of Offence

Burglary, contrary to s 9(1)(b) of the Theft Act 1968.

Particulars of Offence

VICTOR JAMES WARD, on 2 September 2004, having entered as a trespasser a building known as 17 Maidwell Avenue, Croydon, stole therein a television set and a video recorder, the property of John Green.

COUNT 2

Statement of Offence

Unlawful wounding, contrary to section 20 of the Offences Against the Person Act 1861.

Particulars of Offence

VICTOR JAMES WARD, on 2 September 2004, unlawfully and maliciously wounded John Green.

BR SMITH
Officer of the Crown Court
Date: 1 December 2004

9.3 DRAFTING THE INDICTMENT

It used to be the case that an officer of the Crown Court would look through the witness statements used by the prosecution at committal proceedings to establish a *prima facie* case, and would decide what offences should appear on the indictment on the basis of those statements.

Nowadays, however, the Crown Prosecution Service will usually send a 'bill of indictment' (that is, a draft indictment) to the Crown Court and a proper officer of the court simply signs it.

In most cases, the drafting is done by a Crown Prosecutor, although in difficult cases the Crown Prosecution Service will instruct counsel to do the drafting.

Although the drafting of the indictment is the responsibility of the prosecution, under s 2(1) of the Administration of Justice (Miscellaneous Provisions) Act 1933, a proper officer of the Crown Court must sign a bill of indictment before it can become an indictment. In *R v Morais* [1988] 3 All ER 161, it was held by the Court of Appeal that this requirement is a mandatory requirement. It followed that a bill of indictment which had been initialled by a High Court judge after giving leave to the prosecution to prefer a voluntary bill of indictment, but which had not been signed by the proper office of the court, was not a valid indictment.

9.4 TIME LIMIT

The bill of indictment should be 'preferred' (that is, delivered to the Crown Court) within 28 days of the committal proceedings or (in the case of transfers under s 51 of the Crime and Disorder Act 1998, within 28 days of the service of the documents on the defendant).

This period may be extended by up to 28 days by an officer of the Crown Court and may be extended for any period by a Crown Court judge.

The application for an extension of time may be made after the time limit has expired: r 5 of the Indictment Rules 1971.

In any event, preferment out of time is not a ground of appeal against conviction as it does not constitute a material irregularity (*R v Sheerin* (1976) 64 Cr App R 68 and *R v Soffe* (1982) 75 Cr App R 133).

9.5   FORM OF INDICTMENT

Section 3 of the Indictments Act 1915 provides that:

(1)   Every indictment shall contain, and shall be sufficient if it contains, a statement of the specific offence or offences with which the accused person is charged, together with such particulars as may be necessary for giving reasonable information as to the nature of the charge.

(2)   Notwithstanding any rule or law or practice, an indictment shall, subject to the provisions of this Act, not be open to objection in respect of its form or contents if it is framed in accordance with the rules under this Act.

The rules which govern the form and content of an indictment are to be found in the Indictment Rules. Rule 5 provides that:

... every indictment shall contain, and shall be sufficient if it contains, a statement of the specific offence with which the accused person is charged describing the offence shortly, together with such particulars as may be necessary for giving reasonable information as to the nature of the charge.

Rule 6 of the Indictment Rules goes on to set out the components of a count. Each count comprises:

*   *Statement of offence*

    This is a brief description of the offence; if the offence is a statutory one, the relevant section will be given: r 6(a).

*   *Particulars of offence*

    This must 'disclose the essential elements of the offence' (r 6(b)). Rule 6 goes on to provide that 'an essential element need not be disclosed if the accused person is not prejudiced or embarrassed in his defence by the failure to disclose it'; and r 6(c) says that 'it shall not be necessary to specify or negative an exception, proviso excuse or qualification'. To comply with r 6(b), the particulars will set out who is charged, the date of the alleged offence, the act allegedly done, an allegation of *mens rea* (that is, the mental element of the crime), and the identity of the alleged victim.

Rule 4 of the Indictment Rules applies where more than one offence is alleged. It provides that:

Where more than one offence is charged in an indictment, the statement and particulars of each offence shall be set out in a separate paragraph called a count, and rules 5 and 6 of these rules shall apply to each count in the indictment as they apply to an indictment where one offence is charged.

Precedents to assist in the drafting of indictments can be found in *Blackstone's Criminal Practice* and in *Archbold*.

Where the date of the commission of the offence is not known for certain, it is usual to say either 'on or about [date]' or 'on a date unknown between [day before the earliest date when the offence could have been committed] and [day after the latest date when the offence could have been committed]'. If the date is incorrectly stated, that is not fatal to the prosecution case since the indictment can be amended, though the defendant may well be entitled to an adjournment if necessary to prepare his defence on the basis of the new date (cf *Wright v Nicholson* [1970] 1 WLR 142).

In *R v Ike* [1996] STC 391, the defendant was charged with tax offences relating to VAT. On appeal against conviction, she argued that the indictment was defective because it failed to spell out the *mens rea* which the prosecution had to prove in relation to acts which she was alleged to have done (in this case, fraudulent intent or intent to deceive). The Court of Appeal held that the indictment should indeed have spelled out the necessary *mens rea* and that those words should have appeared before any reference to the conduct which was alleged (so each count should have alleged that, with the necessary *mens rea*, the defendant carried out the *actus reus*). However, the jury had been correctly directed on the mental element of the offences and so the conviction was not unsafe; the appeal was therefore dismissed.

Where there is more than one defendant, the order in which the names of defendants are placed on an indictment is the responsibility of the prosecutor, who has a discretion as to that order. The mere fact that a co-defendant named later on the indictment might give evidence adverse to a defendant after that defendant has given evidence provides no basis for regarding the prosecution's exercise of its discretion in drafting the indictment as improper. Nor does it provide grounds for severing the indictment and ordering a separate trial since, in principle, defendants jointly charged should be tried in a single trial: *R v Cairns* [2002] EWCA Crim 2838; [2003] 1 WLR 796.

Each count in an indictment is a separate entity. In *R v O'Neill* [2003] EWCA Crim 411, the defendant was charged in an indictment which included a count that was defective, in that it was based on a statutory provision which had not been in force at the relevant time. The Court of Appeal confirmed that even if one count charges an offence not known to the law, any other counts in the same indictment can stand and need not be quashed.

9.6   RULE 4: THE RULE AGAINST DUPLICITY

Rule 4 of the Indictment Rules requires that each count on an indictment should allege only one offence. Rule 4(2) provides:

> Where more than one offence is charged in an indictment, the statement and particulars of each offence shall be set out in a separate paragraph called a count, and rules 5 and 6 of these rules shall apply to each count in the indictment as they apply to an indictment where one offence is charged.

The specimen indictment shown above has as its first count an allegation of burglary involving the theft of two items. This does not contravene r 4 as the activity of burglary can and usually will involve more than one act. Where the acts form part of 'the same transaction', they may properly be said to amount to a single offence (*DPP v Merriman* [1973] AC 584).

This means that if a defendant steals a number of items from the same person at more or less the same time, it will be regarded as a single act of theft (*R v Wilson* (1979) 69 Cr App R 83). In that case, the defendant was charged with stealing three jumpers, a pair of shorts, two pairs of trousers, four dimmer switches and a cassette tape from

Debenhams (count 1) and stealing eight records and a bottle of aftershave from Boots (count 2). It was argued on behalf of the defendant that both counts were bad for duplicity as the stolen items came from different departments of the stores in question. The argument was rejected on the basis that each count alleged acts forming a single activity. Neither count was duplicitous, therefore. Thus, where a series of acts in effect amounts to a single course of conduct, those acts can validly be regarded as amounting to a single offence. For example, in *DPP v McCabe* (1993) 157 JP 443, it was held by the Divisional Court that an allegation that the defendant stole 76 library books between two specified dates was a single offence and so a count alleging this theft was not bad for duplicity.

Where there are several victims, it is usual to have a separate count for each victim, as in *R v Mansfield* [1977] 1 WLR 1102, where the defendant was charged with seven different counts of murder arising from a single act of arson. This is so even though a single count would have been valid in that particular, since only one act was involved.

However, a count which alleged that the defendant stole £200 from A one day and £200 from B the next would be duplicitous because there are two separate acts of theft.

9.6.1 Rule 7

Rule 7 of the Indictment Rules provides that:

> Where an offence created by or under an enactment states the offence to be the doing or the omission to do any one of any different acts in the alternative, or the doing or the omission to do any act in any one of any different capacities, or with any one of any different intentions, or states any part of the offence in the alternative, the acts, omissions, capacities or intentions, or other matters stated in the alternative in the enactment or subordinate instrument may be stated in the alternative in an indictment charging the offence.

The effect of r 7 is that if a section of a statute creates one offence which may be committed in a number of ways, the alternatives may be charged in a single count. If, however, the section creates more than one offence, each offence the prosecution wish the jury to consider must be put in a separate count.

A good example of the operation of r 7 (in practice, if not in strict legal theory) is to be found in respect of handling stolen goods contrary to s 22 of the Theft Act 1968. Handling effectively comprises two offences. The first is that of dishonestly receiving stolen goods; the second comprises all the other ways of handling and these ways are all different ways of committing a single offence. The various ways of committing the second form of handling can, and usually will, be charged in a single count. However, a count which charged receiving and the other forms of handling together would be regarded as defective.

Thus, there are two basic handling counts; either:

- AB on [date] dishonestly received stolen goods, namely [description of goods], knowing or believing the same to be stolen goods; or

- AB on [date] dishonestly undertook or assisted in the retention, removal, disposal or realisation of stolen goods, namely [description of goods], by or for the benefit of another, or dishonestly arranged to do so, knowing or believing the same to be stolen goods.

9.6.2   Breach of r 4 or r 7

The defence may make an application to quash the indictment if a count is bad for duplicity, but the prosecution may defeat this application by asking for leave to amend the indictment under s 5(1) of the Indictments Act 1915 to split the duplicitous count into two separate counts.

In *R v Levantiz* [1999] 1 Cr App R 465, several discrete acts of supplying a controlled drug were alleged in a single count in the indictment. The Court of Appeal held (following *R v Thompson* [1914] 2 KB 99) that where a count in an indictment is duplicitous (that is, charges more than one offence), that count is not void and the conviction is not necessarily unsafe. It follows that an appeal against conviction on that count can be dismissed if the Court of Appeal decides that the conviction is safe despite the irregularity in the indictment. In deciding whether a conviction based on a duplicitous count is safe, it is submitted that the court should ask itself whether the accused was prejudiced by the duplicitous nature of the count. If it is the case that the defendant must have been guilty of everything alleged in the count – or nothing alleged in the count – it is unlikely that he would have been prejudiced by the duplicity.

9.7   CO-DEFENDANTS

Rules 4 and 7 apply whether the count in question alleges that one defendant or more than one defendant committed the offence. Thus, where there is alleged to have been more than one participant in the offence, all the parties to an offence may be joined in a single count (*Director of Public Prosecutions v Merriman* [1973] AC 584). The jury will be directed that they must consider each defendant separately, so where there are two defendants, they may acquit both defendants, convict both defendants or convict one and acquit the other.

9.7.1   Secondary parties

Secondary parties (that is, those who aid, abet, counsel or procure the commission of the offence) are usually charged as principal offenders (s 8 of the Accessories and Abettors Act 1861).

Thus, in a burglary case where one person enters the premises and another person stays outside as a look-out, both will usually be charged with burglary contrary to s 9(1)(b) of the Theft Act 1968 and the particulars will allege that both entered the premises and stole. Similarly, the getaway driver in a robbery will usually be charged in the same count as the defendants who actually carry out the robbery.

The fact that a defendant is really alleged to have been a secondary party is thus not apparent from the indictment itself, but is made clear to the jury in the course of the prosecution opening speech.

Nonetheless, there will be cases where the prosecution choose to draft a count which specifically alleges aiding and abetting.

9.8 RULE 9: JOINDER OF COUNTS

We now consider the indictment which contains more than one count. Each indictment containing two or more counts must comply with r 9, which states:

> Charges for any offences may be joined in the same indictment if those charges are founded on the same facts, or form or are a part of a series of offences of the same or a similar character.

The effect of r 9 is to require that all the counts on the indictment must be either:

- founded on the same facts; or
- form, or be part of, a series of offences of the same or a similar character.

Thus, joinder is permissible if either or these two 'limbs' of r 9 is satisfied.

9.8.1 Same facts

Two offences may be said to be founded on the same facts if either:

- they arise from a single incident or are part of the same 'transaction'. For example, in the specimen indictment shown above, the defendant wounds the householder in the course of committing the burglary. The same principles would apply where someone steals a car in order to use it as a getaway vehicle in a robbery: the theft of the car and the robbery would be charged in a single indictment. Similarly, someone who causes criminal damage in order to commit a burglary may be charged with both offences in a single indictment (the criminal damage being charged pursuant to s 40 of the Criminal Justice Act 1988 if the value of the damage is less than £5,000); or
- a later offence would not have been committed but for the commission of an earlier offence. For example, see *R v Barrell and Wilson* (1979) 69 Cr App R 250, where a defendant was charged with affray and assault (both arising out of a single incident) and with attempting to pervert the course of justice, as the defendant had tried to bribe witnesses to the affray and assault not to give evidence against him. The defence objected to the joinder of the latter charge. However, the Court of Appeal held that, because the attempt at bribery would not have taken place but for the charges arising out of the affray, the charges all had a 'common factual origin' (*per* Shaw LJ). It was held, therefore, that all these charges could appear in a single indictment.

9.8.1.1 Contradictory counts

In *R v Bellman* [1989] AC 836, the House of Lords held that counts can be joined in an indictment even if they are mutually contradictory. The defendant in that case was charged with conspiracy to evade the prohibition on the importation of controlled drugs and with obtaining property by deception. If the defendant had intended to import the drugs, he was guilty of the first offence; if he took the money from the buyers but did not intend to import the drugs to give to them, he was guilty of the second offence. The House of Lords ruled that these inconsistent allegations could properly appear in a single indictment.

Another example is *R v Shelton* (1986) 83 Cr App R 379, where the defendant was charged with two counts, one alleging theft and the other alleging the second form of handling. The Court of Appeal said that it did not matter that these allegations were contradictory.

It will generally be unusual for the prosecution to include inconsistent counts on an indictment. The jury will be directed to consider each count separately. A conviction in respect of a given count is only possible if the jury are satisfied beyond reasonable doubt that the defendant is guilty under that particular count. If the prosecution are making contradictory allegations, the jury may well think that the defendant is guilty of something but may not be satisfied so that they are sure that he is guilty of a particular offence.

9.8.2 Same or similar character

In *Ludlow v Metropolitan Police Commissioner* [1971] AC 29, the House of Lords had to construe the second limb of r 9. The defendant faced two allegations, one of attempted theft on 20 August 1968 (the theft allegedly taking place at a public house in Acton) and one of robbery on 5 September 1968 (the allegation arising out of an altercation with a barman in a public house in Acton). The House of Lords held that these two allegations could be made in the same indictment. In coming to this conclusion, the following points were made:

- two offences are capable of amounting to a 'series';
- for counts to be joined in an indictment, there must be a 'nexus' between them both in law and in fact. In other words, the offences must be both legally and factually similar;
- the evidence in respect of one count need not be admissible by way of similar fact evidence in respect of the other count(s).

In *R v Harward* (1981) 73 Cr App R 168, the defendant was charged with conspiracy to defraud and with handling stolen goods. Despite the legal similarity (dishonesty), there was no factual link between the offences (apart from the fact that the stolen goods were found when his home was being searched during the fraud investigation). Two offences do not form (part of) a series of offences merely because evidence relating to one offence is uncovered during the investigation into the other. The indictment was therefore defective.

In *R v Marsh* (1985) 83 Cr App R 165, the defendant was charged with criminal damage and reckless driving (the same victim) and assault (a different victim). It was held that criminal damage and reckless driving were validly joined as they arose out of a single act (causing damage by using the car). However, there was an insufficient legal link between either of these offences and the assault, and the only factual link between those offences was the use of violence. The addition of the assault charge thus rendered the indictment defective.

In *R v McGlinchey* (1983) 78 Cr App R 282, it was held that two counts alleging handling stolen goods were correctly joined. The first alleged receiving photographic equipment on 19 July 1982 and the second receiving a stolen credit card on 2 September 1982. There was clearly a legal nexus, in that the same offence was alleged in both counts. The only factual nexus was that they were committed two months apart, but that was held to be sufficient.

In *R v Mariou* [1992] Crim LR 511, the defendant was charged with burglary, robbery, aggravated burglary and possession of a firearm with intent to endanger life.

The Court of Appeal upheld the joinder of these counts as the burglary and robbery charges were legally similar and were all linked by violent entry into a dwelling-house and the subsequent use or threat of violence. The firearms offence was validly joined as it arose on the same facts as the others – the gun was carried when the offences were being committed.

In *R v Baird* (1993) 97 Cr App R 308, the defendant was charged with indecent assault on two different boys. The alleged offences were separated by a period of nine years. The Court of Appeal held that the offences nevertheless formed a series and so could validly be joined in a single indictment.

In *R v Williams* [1993] Crim LR 533, the defendant was charged with indecently assaulting a 13 year old girl on 8 June 1991 and with false imprisonment of the same girl on 13 June 1991. It was held that, had these two offences been committed on the same occasion, they could have been joined in a single indictment; however, they were different incidents (it was the same victim but different offences, thus lacking a legal nexus) and so they could not be validly joined on the same indictment.

9.8.3 Joinder of defendants under r 9

The provisions of r 9 apply whether the counts are against the same defendant or different defendants; all that matters is that the offences themselves are sufficiently linked to satisfy the provisions of r 9. Thus, a number of defendants may be joined in the same indictment even if no count applies to all of them, provided that the counts are sufficiently linked for r 9 to be satisfied. For example, the person who is alleged to have handled the proceeds of a burglary could be charged in the same indictment as the alleged burglar.

For example, in *R v Assim* [1966] 2 QB 249, there were two defendants, a receptionist and a doorman at a night club. The receptionist was charged with wounding one person (s 20 of the Offences Against the Person Act 1861) and the doorman with assault occasioning actual bodily harm (s 47 of the same Act) against a different person. Even though there was no joint count in the indictment, the indictment was held to be valid as there was sufficient link in time and place: both victims had tried to leave without paying; D1 allegedly attacked one victim with a knife; the other victim intervened and was attacked by D2. Thus, there was sufficient legal and factual nexus for the two counts to be joined in the same indictment.

9.8.4 Joinder of summary offences under s 40 of the Criminal Justice Act 1988

The requirement of s 40 of the Criminal Justice Act 1988, that a summary offence to which that section applies can only be added to an indictment alongside an indictable offence if it is founded on the same facts as the indictable offence or forms or is part of a series of offences of the same or a similar character to the indictable offence, mirrors the requirement of r 9 of the Indictment Rules 1971.

In *R v Callaghan* (1992) 94 Cr App R 226, the appellant was charged with six offences: one count of arson (an indictable offence), two counts of theft (an indictable offence), two counts of taking a conveyance without the consent of the owner (a summary offence to which s 40 of the Criminal Justice Act 1988 applies) and one count of driving while disqualified (a summary offence to which s 40 applies). The two counts of taking a conveyance without the owner's consent were held to be properly joined since they were of the same or a similar character to the two theft charges (which both involved motor vehicles). However, the charge of driving while disqualified related to his driving of a vehicle which he had taken without consent (the subject of one of the other counts on the indictment). The Court of Appeal held that the charge of driving while disqualified should not have been included in the indictment, since that charge was not linked with an *indictable* offence. The only link was with a summary offence validly added under s 40, and that was held not to be enough.

9.9   DISCRETION TO ORDER SEPARATE TRIALS

Where an indictment validly alleges that a defendant committed more than one offence or alleges that more than one defendant was involved in the offence(s), the judge may nevertheless order that separate trials take place.

9.9.1   Separate counts

Section 5(3) of the Indictments Act 1915 provides:

> Where, before trial, or at any stage of a trial, the court is of opinion that a person accused may be prejudiced or embarrassed in his defence by reason of being charged with more than one offence in the same indictment, or that for any other reason it is desirable to direct that the person should be tried separately for any one or more offences charged in an indictment, the court may order a separate trial of any count or counts of such indictment.

This provision thus empowers a Crown Court judge to order separate trials of offences on an indictment. This power is sometimes known as 'severing the indictment'. It applies both to a defendant who seeks separate trials for a number of offences and to co-defendants who seek separate trials.

This power applies only to a valid indictment (that is, one which satisfies r 9), and so this power to 'sever' cannot be used to cure misjoinder of counts (*Newland* [1988] QB 402).

The power to 'sever' applies if the defendant can show that he would be 'prejudiced or embarrassed in his defence' or there is some other good reason. In other words, the defendant has to show that he will not receive a fair trial if all the counts are dealt with together.

In *Ludlow v Metropolitan Police Commissioner* [1971] AC 29, the House of Lords said that if the counts are validly joined under r 9, those counts should usually be tried together and the defendant must show a 'special feature' (*per* Lord Pearson) in the case if there are to be separate trials. In other words, the burden rests on the defendant to show that exceptional circumstances merit separate trials.

In *R v Christou* [1996] 2 WLR 620, the House of Lords held that where the defendant is charged with sexual offences against more than one person, and the evidence of one complainant is not so related to that of the others as to render that evidence admissible on the other charges (under the similar fact evidence rule), the judge has a discretion to sever the indictment. The essential criterion for the exercise of this discretion is the achievement of a fair resolution of the issues in the case. Factors which might have to be considered include: how closely related are the facts upon which the various charges are based; the effect of having two or more trials on the defendant and his family and on the victims and their families; the effect of press publicity; whether the judge can give directions to the jury which will enable there to be a fair trial if the counts are tried together.

In *R v Trew* [1996] 2 Cr App R 138, the defendant was charged with attacks on four different women. Only one of the women (B) picked him out at an identification parade. The trial judge refused to sever the counts relating to the attack on B from the counts relating to the other attacks. The Court of Appeal said that the judge should have taken account of the fact that evidence relating to the attack on B was inadmissible as regards the other alleged attacks. It followed that the presence of all the counts in the same indictment would have the sole effect of making it more likely that the appellant would be convicted. Accordingly, the appeal was allowed and a re-trial ordered.

Another example may be found in *R v D* [2003] EWCA Crim 2424; [2004] 1 Cr App R 19, where the defendant was charged with serious sexual offences against his two young step-daughters. He appealed against conviction on the grounds that the judge had failed in the summing up to deal adequately with how the jury should approach the fact that they were considering cases against two complainants on the same indictment. The Court of Appeal held that the two sets of charges had been properly joined, since they constituted a series of offences of the same or a similar character. However, once the prosecution had decided that the case was not one of similar fact, the first complainant's evidence about the allegations in relation to her was not admissible as proof of the allegations in relation to the other complainant (and vice versa), and in such circumstances the issue of severance arose. Dealing with the question of severance, the court said that there will be cases where, without legitimate mutual evidential support between the charges, the offences should not be tried together, but there will also be cases where joint trials of all counts might well be appropriate whether or not the principles as to cross-admissibility apply. In cases where the prosecution do not rely on similar fact and the charges are not severed, it is essential for the jury to be directed in clear terms that the evidence on each set of allegations is to be treated separately and that the evidence in relation to an allegation in respect of one complainant cannot be treated as proof of an allegation relating to the other complainant.

Arguments in favour of severance which may succeed in appropriate cases include the following:

- the jury may find it difficult to disentangle the evidence, with the risk that they will rely on evidence which does not relate to a particular count when considering that count;
- one count is of a nature likely to arouse hostility in the minds of the jurors, and so they may not approach the other counts with open minds;
- the evidence on one count is strong but on the other is weak, and there is a risk that the jury will assume the defendant is guilty of the second count merely because they find him guilty of the first;
- the evidence in respect of each count is weak, but the jury may convict on the basis that there is no smoke without fire, taking an overview of the allegations rather than considering each count individually;

- the number of counts and/or defendants is such that the jury will be overwhelmed by the sheer weight of evidence, and the interests of justice are therefore better served by having a number of shorter trials (see, for example, *R v Novac* (1976) 65 Cr App R 107).

It has to be borne in mind that the effect of these risks can be minimised, if not removed altogether, by appropriately worded directions from the judge on how the jury should approach the task of analysing the evidence. A defendant seeking separate trials would therefore have to show why such a direction would not provide sufficient protection in his case.

An example of where severance would have been appropriate is *R v Laycock* [2003] EWCA Crim 1477; [2003] Crim LR 803, where the defendant was charged with a number of offences, including possession of a firearm when a prohibited person, namely having been sentenced to imprisonment for more than three years (an offence under s 21 of the Firearms Act 1968). The very nature of this offence revealed the fact that he had previously been convicted of a serious offence. The court criticised the number of counts, saying that in formulating an indictment an excessive number of counts should not be included, since this overloads the indictment. Furthermore, the court went on to say that prosecutors should be careful not to charge counts that would prejudice a defendant unless there is a real purpose to be served. In the present case, the s 21 offence should not have been joined in the indictment since it did not give the judge any additional sentencing powers. If the prosecution were determined to seek a conviction for the offence in question, a separate trial of that count would have been fairer.

If the trial judge refuses to order separate trials, the exercise of his discretion will not be interfered with by the Court of Appeal unless it is manifestly wrong (*R v Tickner* [1992] Crim LR 44 and *R v Mariou* [1992] Crim LR 511).

9.9.2   Co-defendants

Where two or more defendants are charged in a single count, the judge has a discretion to order separate trials. Again, it has to be shown that a fair trial cannot be achieved without severance. Judges are reluctant to order separate trials of defendants charged with the same offence: if there are two separate trials, the cost of the proceedings will be doubled, the witnesses will have to testify twice, and there is a risk of inconsistent verdicts. It is for this reason that separate trials will only be ordered if there are exceptional circumstances which require this course of action.

In *R v Lake* (1976) 64 Cr App R 172, the trial judge's refusal to order separate trials was upheld by the Court of Appeal even though there was some evidence in the case which was admissible against one defendant but inadmissible against (and highly prejudicial to) the other. This will be the case if D1 confesses to the police and in that confession implicates D2 (the out-of-court statement by D1 is inadmissible against D2, but the jury will hear about that statement as they hear about the case against D1). The Court of Appeal agreed with the trial judge that the danger of prejudice could be removed by an appropriate direction to the jury.

Similarly, in *R v Crawford* [1998] 1 Cr App R 338, the Court of Appeal upheld the decision of the trial judge not to order separate trials in a case where D1 was going to give evidence (in the course of her defence) against D2 and so D2 would be able to cross-examine D1 on her previous convictions (and it should be borne in mind that if D1 gives evidence in the witness box that implicates D2, that is admissible evidence against D2). In some cases, it may be possible to remove the problem caused by an out-of-court statement (such as a police interview) which implicates a co-accused simply by editing the statement to remove the name of the co-accused. However, this will be ineffective if either the defendant who made the statement intends to rely on the full version (as he is entitled to do when he goes into the witness box to testify on his behalf) or the out-of-court statement would not make sense if it were to be edited in this way.

In *R v Grondkowski and Malinowski* [1946] KB 369, separate trials were not ordered even though the defendants were blaming each other (the so called 'cut throat defence'), a defence which often results in both defendants being convicted. Similarly, in *R v Kennedy* [1992] Crim LR 37, two defendants were charged with affray. One defendant indicated that he would be referring to the previous convictions of the other (one for an offence of violence and others for offences of dishonesty) in the hope of persuading the jury that he had been acting in self-defence (a permissible course of action according to the House of Lords in *R v Randall* [2003] UKHL 69; [2004] 1 WLR 56). Even though this was evidence which the prosecution would not have been able to adduce, and was clearly prejudicial to the other defendant, the judge's decision not to order separate trials was upheld. Similarly, in *R v Eriemo* [1995] 2 Cr App R 206, it was held that a judge was justified in refusing an application to sever an indictment where one defendant intends to argue that he was acting under the duress of another defendant.

In *R v Johnson* (1994) 15 Cr App R(S) 827, it was held that although there is no firm rule that where an indictment contains an allegation that A assaulted B, and a second count alleging that C assaulted A, it would often be appropriate to order separate trials. However, the Court of Appeal went on to say that if that had been the only ground of appeal, it would not have been a sufficient basis for allowing the appeal.

The usual response to the assertion that the jury will hear evidence that is inadmissible against one defendant, or that they might give undue weight to the evidence of one defendant if he gives evidence that implicates his co-accused, is that the jury will be directed by the judge to consider the case of each defendant separately and to ignore any evidence that has been ruled inadmissible against a particular defendant when they consider the case against that defendant (and that they should bear in mind that one defendant might be serving his own interests by giving evidence against a co-accused). Critics of the efficacy of such directions suggest that jurors are being asked to perform 'mental gymnastics'. In 'The prejudiced defendant: unfairness suffered by a defendant in a joint trial' [2003] Crim LR 432, Peter Thornton QC suggests that:

> There is certainly an argument that severance should take place more frequently than at present, with the object of achieving fairness for all defendants. The decision whether to order severance is now made much easier for judges in the light of modern rules of disclosure, both by prosecution and defence. It is not right that a defendant should be put at risk of a conviction based partly on inadmissible evidence. There is no way of knowing, in the absence of jury research, how juries cope with this problem and what notice they take of the judge's warnings. After all, the necessity for consistency, the principle that drives the concept of the joint trial, is frequently not achieved in a joint trial. The evidence against one defendant may be weaker than against another, producing different verdicts, even where it is alleged that both

defendants were present and jointly participating in the crime. That applies whether they are tried together or separately. Similarly unequal 'treatment' can easily be avoided by one judge trying both cases and passing sentence in the event of convictions. At the very least the judge's direction to ignore inadmissible evidence should be given to the jury in writing for them to take with them when they retire.

He concludes that:

While it must be recognised that the interest of the prejudiced defendant in the context of a joint trial will always be only one of several competing interests, the time may have come for greater flexibility in favour of that defendant and a less restrictive approach.

Where the defence would prefer separate trials of the defendants (for example, where the confession of one defendant implicates the other), it is worth making an application for separate trials to the trial judge but, if the judge refuses, the Court of Appeal is unlikely to interfere with his decision unless it is manifestly unreasonable (*R v Josephs* (1977) 65 Cr App R 253 and *R v Myers* [1996] 2 Cr App R 335).

9.10   BREACH OF r 9: MISJOINDER

If an indictment contains counts which should not be joined together in the same indictment, two questions arise. First, how can the defect be cured before the trial proceeds? Secondly, what happens if no remedial steps are taken and the defendant is convicted on the basis of the defective indictment?

9.10.1   Curing the defect

What should the Crown Court do if faced with an indictment which breaches r 9?

In *R v Newland* [1988] QB 402, the defendant was charged with a drugs offence and three counts alleging assault which were wholly unconnected with the drugs charge. The trial judge simply ordered separate trials (purporting to 'sever' the indictment under s 5(3) of the Indictments Act 1915), so that the drugs offence and the assault charges were tried separately. The Court of Appeal held that the judge had no power to 'sever' the indictment under s 5(3), since this power applies only to a valid indictment, and the indictment in the present case was invalid because it failed to comply with r 9 of the Indictment Rules. The court went on to say that the trial judge should have deleted from the indictment either the drugs charge or the assault charges, and proceeded with the trial on that indictment. The allegations deleted from the indictment could only be proceeded with if the prosecution brought fresh committal proceedings in respect of them or else sought a voluntary bill of indictment.

In *R v Follett* [1989] QB 338, a differently constituted Court of Appeal accepted a rather simpler solution. In this case, the indictment was invalid because it contained counts which were not sufficiently linked. The Court of Appeal upheld the decision of the trial judge to stay proceedings on the indictment as drafted and to give the prosecution leave to prefer fresh indictments (each complying with r 9) out of time. The effect of this is that the invalid indictment remains in existence but becomes irrelevant. Two or more trials then follow, based on the new indictments, without the need for fresh committal proceedings or a voluntary bill of indictment.

In the light of the case law set out below, it seems that *Newland* and *Follett* are not correct in labelling an indictment 'invalid' because of misjoinder. However, there is no reason to suppose that the methods for curing the defect of misjoinder which these two cases suggest should not still be followed where the misjoinder becomes apparent at the Crown Court trial. Thus, the 'cure' is either (a) to delete sufficient counts to leave an indictment which complies with r 9, or (b) with the leave of the court, to prefer fresh indictments, each of which must comply with r 9.

9.10.2 Validity of the indictment

There has been a plethora of case law on the exact status of proceedings on an indictment which contains counts that are improperly joined. The question which the Court of Appeal has had to consider on several occasions is this: if a person is convicted on the basis of an indictment which does not comply with r 9 of the Indictment Rules, should all the convictions on that indictment be quashed, or just the convictions on counts which were improperly joined?

In *R v Bell* (1984) 78 Cr App R 305, Lord Lane CJ said that it cannot be the law that an indictment could be made a complete nullity by the addition of a count or counts contrary to r 9.

In *Newland*, however, Watkins LJ said that although the indictment itself could not, in the light of *Bell*, properly be described as a nullity, 'the proceedings flowing from the arraignment of the appellant upon that indictment must surely be a nullity'. This was followed in *R v O'Reilly* (1990) 90 Cr App R 40.

In *R v Callaghan* (1992) 94 Cr App R 226, the Court of Appeal had to consider a case where a summary offence was added to an indictment pursuant to s 40 of the Criminal Justice Act 1988 but where the required link (which is in the same terms as r 9 of the Indictment Rules) between the summary offence and the indictable offence was missing. The Court of Appeal held cases such as *Newland* and *Follett* do not decide that an indictment becomes a nullity by the addition of a count which involves a breach of r 9. The result of this was that the misjoinder did not nullify all the proceedings on the indictment. It followed that only the conviction for the improperly joined count should be quashed.

R v Lewis (1992) 95 Cr App R 131 was another case involving the addition of a summary offence under s 40 of the Criminal Justice Act 1988. The defendant was arrested for a number of offences. While he was at the police station he spat at one of the police officers; this resulted in a charge of common assault (a summary offence to which s 40 of the Criminal Justice Act 1988 applies). The Court of Appeal held that the common assault could not be regarded as being founded on the same facts as the other offences: what occurred at the police station took place too long after the other offences to be founded on the same facts as those offences. The Court of Appeal, reaching the opposite conclusion to *R v Callaghan*, went on to hold that the indictment was invalid and so technically there had been no convictions. Thus, all the convictions on the defective indictment had to be quashed.

In *R v Simon* [1992] Crim LR 444, the appellant took one car without authority. That car ran out of petrol. He then took another car without authority and used it to get to a place where he and another defendant committed a robbery. The Court of Appeal held that the taking of the first car was properly joined, since the whole evening's criminality needed to be looked at as a continuous series of events; thus, there was no misjoinder. However, the court went on to say (*obiter*) that *Callaghan*, having been decided earlier than *Lewis*, was to be preferred.

In *R v Smith* [1997] 2 WLR 588, three summary offences were added to an indictment under s 40 of the Criminal Justice Act 1988; joinder of two of those summary offences was improper because there was no sufficient link with the indictable offence which was also on the indictment. The Court of Appeal followed *Callaghan* and the *obiter dictum* in *Simon* and held that convictions for offences which are correctly joined are valid convictions. Accordingly, the convictions on the indictable offence and the correctly joined summary offence stood; only the convictions for the two improperly joined summary offences were quashed.

In *R v Lockley and Sainsbury* [1997] Crim LR 455, the appellants were charged with conspiracy to commit burglary and dangerous driving (on the basis that the car they used in connection with the burglary was dangerously defective). Both offences are indictable offences and so only r 9 of the Indictment Rules had to be considered. The Court of Appeal held that the dangerous driving charge was improperly joined. The court confirmed that s 40 of the Criminal Justice Act 1988 and r 9 of the Indictment Rules are in all material respects in the same terms, and so the same principles regarding misjoinder and the consequences thereof must apply to both. The court went on to hold that misjoinder does not nullify the whole indictment. It followed that only the conviction on the wrongly joined count(s) should be quashed.

It is thus clear that misjoinder of counts does not render the entire indictment invalid.

9.11   DECIDING THE CONTENTS OF THE INDICTMENT

In most cases, the counts on the indictment are the same as the charges in respect of which the defendant was committed for trial (or transferred from the magistrates' court under s 51 of the Crime and Disorder Act 1998).

However, s 2(2) of the Administration of Justice (Miscellaneous Provisions) Act 1933 states that where a defendant has been committed or sent for trial at the Crown Court, the bill of indictment against the person charged may include, either in substitution for or in addition to counts charging the offence(s) for which the defendant was committed or sent for trial, any counts founded on the evidence contained in the witness statements relied on by the prosecution at the committal/transfer proceedings, provided that the various counts may 'lawfully be joined in the same indictment'.

Section 2(2) effectively confers two powers:

- the power to indict an offender for offences in addition to those for which he has been committed or sent for trial by the magistrates; and
- the power to replace the offences for which he has been committed or sent for trial with different offences.

In *R v Biddis* [1993] Crim LR 392, it was held that there need not be conclusive evidence in the papers used at the committal proceedings supporting the new count(s); it is enough if there is *prima facie* evidence in respect of them.

9.11.1 Substituting offences

An example of the power in s 2 of the Administration of Justice (Miscellaneous Provisions) Act 1933 to substitute a different offence would be a case where the magistrates send the defendant for trial on a charge of burglary (entering premises as a trespasser and then stealing). The prosecution, after the case has been sent to the Crown Court, decide that the evidence on the issue of trespass is very weak, but that they can prove that the defendant stole what he is alleged to have stolen during the course of the 'burglary'. The prosecution could indict the defendant for theft instead of burglary.

Similarly, if the magistrates send the defendant for trial on a charge of theft but the prosecution subsequently decide that there is sufficient evidence to prove that the theft was committed in the course of a burglary, the prosecution could indict the defendant for burglary instead of theft.

The power to indict for offences which differ from those in respect of which the justices committed the defendant for trial applies even if the justices expressly refused to send the defendant for trial in respect of a particular offence but sent him for trial in respect of another offence. In *R v Moloney* [1985] AC 905, for example, the justices refused to commit the defendant on a charge of murder but committed him on a charge of manslaughter instead; the prosecution charged murder in the indictment and this decision was upheld. The abolition of committal proceedings means that this principle will only be relevant in very rare cases (since the magistrates do not consider the evidence when sending a case to the Crown Court under s 51 of the Crime and Disorder Act 1998). However, there may be exceptional cases where abuse of process arguments are used in the magistrates' court in an attempt to prevent the court from sending a case for trial. In *R v C* (1995) 159 JP 205, the magistrates had stayed certain charges on the ground of abuse of process but the defendant was committed for trial on other charges. Evidence of the charges which had been stayed was contained in the witness statements which formed the bundle of evidence relied on by the prosecution at committal. The prosecution sought leave from the Crown Court to add to the indictment the charges which had been stayed by the magistrate. Leave was given and the Court of Appeal upheld this decision.

9.11.2 Adding offences

Section 2(2) of the Administration of Justice (Miscellaneous Provisions) Act 1933 also enables the prosecution to indict the defendant for charges which are additional to those in respect of which he was committed for trial. The essential restriction on this power is that the resulting indictment must satisfy the requirements of r 9 of the Indictment Rules (*R v Lombardi* [1989] 1 WLR 73).

An example of the operation of the power to add offences would be where the defendant is sent for trial on a single charge of robbery. The prosecution witness statements relied upon by the prosecution also disclose the fact that the defendant was in possession of a firearm when carrying out the robbery. The prosecution could add a firearms offence to the indictment. Even though the defendant has not been sent for trial in respect of the firearms charge, it is a charge which is sufficiently closely related to the charge in respect of which the defendant has been sent for trial to permit joinder of the two charges under r 9.

An example of where it would not be open to the prosecution to add a count to the indictment would be where the defendant is sent for trial on a charge on burglary. The prosecution witness statements also reveal evidence which would support a completely unrelated drugs charge. However, the defendant has not been sent for trial in respect of that charge. The prosecution cannot add the drugs charge to the indictment which contains the burglary charge. The two charges are wholly unrelated and so to put them on the same indictment would infringe r 9 of the Indictment Rules.

9.11.3 More than one indictment

In *Lombardi*, Lord Lane CJ said that where the magistrates have sent a defendant to the Crown Court on more than one charge, the prosecution are at liberty to prefer a number of separate indictments if they feel that it is appropriate to do so. Take, for example, the defendant who is sent for trial on a charge of burglary and a completely unrelated drugs charge. Although the two charges (being unrelated) cannot appear on the same indictment (because of r 9 of the Indictment Rules), the prosecution can prefer two separate indictments (one for the burglary and the other for the drugs offence), because the defendant has been sent for trial in respect of both offences.

However, what the prosecution *cannot* do is to prefer one indictment containing the charges in respect of which the defendant was sent for trial, and a second indictment containing only charges in respect of which the defendant has not been sent for trial. Take, for example, a case where the defendant is sent to the Crown Court for trial on a charge of burglary, but the prosecution witness statements also reveal evidence of a drugs offence. The prosecution can prefer an indictment for burglary because the defendant has been sent for trial in respect of that charge. They cannot add the unrelated drugs offence to that indictment, because that would contravene r 9 of the Indictment Rules, and they cannot prefer a separate indictment in respect of the drugs offence, because the defendant has not been sent for trial in respect of that offence and that offence is not being substituted for an offence in respect of which the defendant was sent for trial.

9.11.4 More than one defendant

If the magistrates send two or more defendants for trial at the same time, it is open to the prosecution to draft separate indictments against them if the prosecution feel that it would be appropriate to do so or if the defendants are charged with different offences and joinder of the offences in one indictment would breach r 9 of the Indictment Rules (see *R v Groom* [1977] QB 6).

If defendants are not sent for trial at the same time, it is nevertheless open to the prosecution to join those defendants in the same indictment (assuming r 9 is satisfied). This is so even if an indictment in respect of a defendant who has been sent for trial has already been signed (see para IV.34.2 of the *Practice Direction (Criminal Proceedings: Consolidation)* [2002] 1 WLR 2870; [2002] 3 All ER 904).

9.11.5 Alternative counts

In many cases, the prosecution will include alternative counts on the indictment. For instance, an allegation of wounding with intent (s 18 of the Offences Against the

Person Act 1861) may be accompanied by a separate count alleging unlawful wounding (s 20 of the same Act). This would be appropriate where the prosecution are not sure that they can prove that the accused had the requisite intent to commit the s 18 offence. There is nothing on the indictment to show that these are alternatives (the word 'or' does not appear) but counsel for the prosecution, during the opening speech, will inform the jury that the prosecution seek a conviction on one or other of the two counts but not both.

9.11.6 Overloading the indictment

In *R v Novac* (1976) 65 Cr App R 107 and *R v Thorne* (1977) 66 Cr App R 6, the Court of Appeal warned against the danger of having too many counts or too many defendants in a single trial. Splitting the case into a series of shorter trials may, in the long run, be easier.

Note also that if both conspiracy and a related substantive offence are alleged, the judge may ask the prosecution to justify charging both or else choose to proceed with one or the other. See para IV.34.3 of the Practice Direction.

9.12   AMENDING THE INDICTMENT

Section 5(1) of the Indictments Act 1915 provides:

> Where, before trial, or at any stage of a trial, it appears to the court that the indictment is defective, the court shall make such order for the amendment of the indictment as the court thinks necessary to meet the circumstances of the case, unless, having regard to the merits of the case, the required amendments cannot be made without injustice.

This provision thus allows the amendment of a defective indictment at any stage, provided the amendment can be made without causing injustice. Amendment may be necessary, for example, where the evidence at trial shows that the prosecution have charged the wrong offence.

The amendment may take the form of inserting a new count in the indictment, whether in addition to or instead of the original count (*R v Johal; R v Ram* [1972] 2 All ER 449). Where there is no injustice to the defendant, an indictment can even be amended under s 5(1) so as to add a new defendant (*R v Palmer* [2002] EWCA Crim 892; (2002) *The Times*, 18 April).

In *R v Osieh* [1996] 1 WLR 1260, prior to the start of the trial, the judge gave leave for the indictment to be amended to include a count of attempted theft. The appellant argued that the judge should not have allowed this to be done, since there was no evidence relating to the attempted theft in the committal papers (as is required by s 2(2) of the Administration of Justice (Miscellaneous Provisions) Act 1933). The Court of Appeal held that the 1933 Act and the Indictments Act 1915 are two entirely different statutory regimes. The Administration of Justice (Miscellaneous Provisions) Act 1933 governs the signing and preferment of the bill of indictment; the Indictments Act 1915 governs the indictment itself. Accordingly, the requirement in the Administration of Justice (Miscellaneous Provisions) Act 1933 that there must be evidence in the committal papers to support a count on the indictment does not apply to the power conferred by the Indictments Act 1915. The court went on to say that where the amendment relates to matters which are not foreshadowed in the committal papers, it may be appropriate for the judge to exercise his discretion against giving leave for the amendment (or else allowing the amendment but adjourning the case to enable the defence to review their case). The court went on to make the point that the 1915 Act confers a wide discretion; the Court of Appeal will not interfere lightly with the exercise of such a discretion.

Applications to amend the indictment may be made at the Plea and Directions Hearing (PDH). If an amendment is made just before the start of the trial, and the amendment changes the nature of the prosecution case, the defence must be allowed an adjournment to enable them to review their case in the light of the new allegations (see s 5(4) of the Indictments Act 1915). If a jury has already been empanelled, it may be necessary for the judge to discharge that jury and order a re-trial (see s 5(5)(a) of the Indictments Act 1915).

It is permissible (subject to the possible need for an adjournment) for the indictment to be amended in the course of the trial (although if the amendment is a fundamental one, so that defence would need a long adjournment, it may be appropriate for the judge to discharge the jury and order a re-trial).

In *R v Pople* [1951] 1 KB 53, it was held that it is not necessary that an indictment, in order to be 'defective' within the meaning of s 5(1) of the Indictments Act 1915, should be one which is bad on its face (for example, one which charges an offence unknown to the law). On the contrary, said the court, any alteration in matters of description may be made in order to meet the evidence in the case so long as the amendment causes no injustice to the accused. In that case, the appellants were charged in an indictment alleging that they had obtained sums of money by false pretences; the trial judge allowed the indictment to be amended by replacing the sums in question with the words 'a valuable security, to wit, a cheque'. The Court of Appeal upheld this amendment. They held that the defendant was not prejudiced, since the substance of the allegation was unaltered.

Such an amendment was even permitted after the jury had retired to consider their verdict in *R v Collison* (1980) 71 Cr App R 249, where the defendant was charged with one count of wounding with intent (s 18 of the Offences Against the Person Act 1861). The jury was unable to reach either a unanimous or a majority verdict on this count, but wanted to convict the defendant of the lesser offence of unlawful wounding (s 20 of the 1861 Act). Since they could not agree on an acquittal of the offence on the indictment, they could not simply return a verdict of guilty to the lesser offence under s 6(3) of the Criminal Law Act 1967, since that provision only applies where the jury first acquits of the offence on the indictment. The judge therefore allowed the prosecution to add a further count (alleging the s 20 offence) to the indictment. The Court of Appeal upheld this course of action, as no injustice was caused to the defendant by the addition of the new count. Given their power to acquit of s 18 but convict instead of s 20, the lesser offence was, effectively, already before the jury.

The important question in deciding whether or not to allow an amendment once the trial has started is whether the defence case would have been conducted differently had the amendment taken place at the outset. In *R v Harris* (1993) *The Times*, 22 March, the defendant was charged with rape but, at the close of the defence case, the prosecution applied to add an alternative count alleging attempted rape to the indictment. The judge allowed this amendment, but the Court of Appeal held that this decision was wrong, since the defence case would have been put differently (different cross-examination of prosecution witnesses and different defence evidence). Similarly, in *R v Thomas* [1983] Crim LR 619, the Court of Appeal quashed a conviction where a count of receiving stolen property was added to an indictment which hitherto alleged only theft. This amendment took place after the close of the prosecution case and the defence would have cross-examined the prosecution witnesses differently if both allegations had been made at the outset.

In *R v Piggott and Litwin* [1999] 2 Cr App R 320, the defendants were charged with a single count of conspiracy to steal motor vehicles between May 1993 and May 1996. At the close of the prosecution case, the defendants submitted that there was no case to answer. The submission made on behalf of L was that the conspiracy count was bad, as the evidence adduced did not show one overall conspiracy but a number of different conspiracies. The trial judge ruled that the count was defective, but allowed the prosecution to amend the indictment by adding a number of substantive counts against L, each alleging handling stolen goods, and a 10th count alleging a conspiracy between L and P. Due to the admission of irrelevant and highly prejudicial evidence, the judge discharged the jury and ordered a fresh trial. The appellants argued that the second trial was an abuse of process. The Court of Appeal held that the test to determine whether an amendment should be permitted is whether the trial itself can be continued without injustice. The power to amend does not affect the principle that the defendant is entitled to know the case he has to meet and the right to a fair trial. Accordingly, the prosecution are not entitled to present the case to the jury in one way and hope that leave to amend will be given if there is a successful submission of no case to answer. The amendment in the present case should not have been permitted and, therefore, the second trial was an abuse of process.

Once an indictment has been signed and preferred following the granting of a voluntary bill of indictment, the indictment is like any other indictment. It follows that the trial judge can give leave for that indictment to be amended if it is defective (for example, it does not include offences disclosed in the witness statements which were considered by the High Court judge (*R v Wells* [1995] 2 Cr App R 417)).

Where the Court of Appeal quashes a conviction but orders a re-trial under s 7 of the Criminal Appeal Act 1968, the trial judge has power under s 5(1) of the Indictments Act 1915 to allow the indictment to be amended, even if the amendment results in the defendant being tried for offences for which the Court of Appeal had no power to order a re-trial. However, this is only permissible so long as the amendment does not put the defendant in a worse position than he was in after the original trial (*R v Hemmings* [2000] 2 All ER 155).

9.13   QUASHING THE INDICTMENT

It is open to the defence to make an application to 'quash' the indictment. Such an application would normally be made at the plea and directions hearing which precedes the trial itself.

There are three grounds for quashing an indictment. Those grounds are:

(a) the indictment (or a count on the indictment) is bad on its face, as it alleges an offence which is not known to the law or a single count alleges more than one offence;

(b) the indictment (or one of its counts) has been preferred without authority, in that there have been no committal/transfer proceedings and no voluntary bill of indictment;

(c) the indictment contains a count in respect of which the defendant was not sent for trial (and there was no voluntary bill of indictment in respect of that count) and the prosecution witness statements do not disclose a case to answer on that count.

The distinction between (b) and (c) is that in the case of (b), there were no committal/transfer proceedings at all (or an acceptable alternative to them); in the case of (c), there were committal/transfer proceedings but the person drafting the indictment added a new offence in addition to the offence(s) in respect of which the defendant was originally sent for trial.

The only instance in which the trial judge is entitled to look at the prosecution witness statements to see if they disclose a case to answer is in case (c), the 'new' count (*R v Jones* (1974) 59 Cr App R 120). It follows that if the offence is one in respect of which the defendant was sent for trial (or a valid alternative to committal), the judge cannot be asked to quash the indictment on the basis that there is insufficient evidence in respect of that offence (*R v London Quarter Sessions ex p Downes* [1954] 1 QB 1).

Motions to quash are of little practical importance since these grounds are very limited and, in any event, most errors can be cured by the prosecution seeking to amend the defective indictment under s 5(1) of the Indictments Act 1915.

Furthermore, if the indictment is quashed, the defendant is not regarded as having been acquitted and so can be prosecuted again. However, if the whole indictment is quashed, the defendant can only be indicted for the same offence again if he is sent for trial a second time for that offence by the magistrates (*R v Thompson* [1975] 1 WLR 1425).

9.14 SHOULD INDICTMENTS BE MORE DETAILED?

In 1994, the Law Commission published a paper (which is no longer available) entitled *Counts in an Indictment*. It proposed that counts in an indictment should be drafted in a way that sets out the prosecution case in greater detail.

The main objectives would be to:

- assist with ensuring that the prosecution has evidence to support each of the elements of the offence charged (by setting out each element that has to be proved);
- assist the prosecutor when opening the case to the jury, by setting out (from the prosecution's perspective) the agenda for the trial;
- assist the jury's comprehension of the issues in the trial (so that they can follow more easily the evidence that they hear during the trial);
- assist in stock-taking at the end of the trial (and to assist the jury when considering their verdict).

The proposal was intended to require the prosecution to plead law or evidence, but to set out the factual nature of their case in greater detail.

Two examples given by the Law Commission illustrated what was being proposed.

One example is theft of a handbag. The 'particulars of offence' for theft would currently read: '[Defendant] on [date] stole a handbag belonging to [victim].' A more detailed indictment in that case might allege:

> [Defendant] on [date] in the White Horse Public House, Croydon, removed a handbag belonging to [victim] from the chair on which [victim] had placed it, thereby dishonestly assuming [victim's] rights as owner of the handbag and its contents. [Defendant] intended permanently to deprive [victim] of the handbag and its contents.

A second example is assault occasioning actual bodily harm. The particulars for this offence would currently read: '[Defendant] on [date] assaulted [victim], thereby occasioning him actual bodily harm.' A more detailed indictment might allege:

> [Defendant] on [date], in the Prince of Wales Public House, Croydon, at about 10.45 pm intentionally punched [victim], causing him bruising around the mouth.

One potential drawback of setting out such factual detail is that the evidence may not come out exactly as the prosecution anticipated (for example, in the theft case illustrated above, it might turn out that the handbag was under the chair, not on the chair). There would therefore probably be more cases where the indictment would have to be amended during the course of the trial.

It was also suggested by the Law Commission that the defence should also be required to set out the basis of their case. This is now done through the defence statements required by the Criminal Procedure and Investigations Act 1996 (especially given the greater level of detail required as a result of the amendments to the 1996 Act contained in Pt 5 of the Criminal Justice Act 2003).

CHAPTER 10

TRIAL ON INDICTMENT: PRELIMINARIES

10.1   INTRODUCTION

In this chapter, we examine some of the preliminary matters which are dealt with before a Crown Court trial takes place. In the next chapter, we follow the course of the trial itself.

10.2   DISCLOSURE OF EVIDENCE TO THE DEFENCE

It is a vital principle that the defence are entitled to know in advance what case they have to meet.

10.2.1   Witness to be called by the prosecution

The prosecution may only call as witnesses at the Crown Court people whose written statements have been served on the defence. Most of these witness statements will have been served on the defence in the context of committal proceedings or when the case was transferred to the Crown Court under s 51 of the Crime and Disorder Act 1998. The witness statements, or some of them, may also have been handed to the defence prior to the mode of trial hearing, under the advance information rules.

If the prosecution wish to adduce the evidence of a witness whose statement was not served on the defence when the case was sent to the Crown Court, a notice of additional evidence (including a copy of the written statement by the witness) must first be served on the defence. There is no specified time by which the notice must have been served on the defence; however, if the notice is served just before (or even during) the trial, so that there is insufficient time for the defence to consider the effect which the extra evidence has on the defence case, the judge should grant an adjournment.

10.2.2   Editing prosecution evidence

Some of the prosecution witness statements may contain matters upon which the prosecution do not wish to rely.

To ensure that editing of prosecution evidence does not result in non-disclosure to the defence, para III.24 of *Practice Direction (Criminal Proceedings: Consolidation)* [2002] 1 WLR 2870; [2002] 3 All ER 904 provides detailed rules on the editing of statements:

24   *Evidence by written statement*

24.1   Where the prosecution proposes to tender written statements in evidence either under sections 5A and 5B of the Magistrates' Courts Act 1980 or section 9 of the Criminal Justice Act 1967 it will frequently be not only proper, but also necessary for the orderly presentation of the evidence, for certain statements to be edited. This will occur either because a witness has made more than one statement whose contents should conveniently be reduced into a single, comprehensive statement or where a statement contains inadmissible, prejudicial or irrelevant material. Editing of statements should in all circumstances be done by a Crown prosecutor (or by a legal representative, if any, of the prosecutor if the case is not being conducted by the Crown Prosecution Service) and not by a police officer.

Composite statements

24.2 A composite statement giving the combined effect of two or more earlier statements or settled by a person referred to in paragraph 24.1 must be prepared in compliance with the requirements of sections 5A and 5B of the 1980 Act or section 9 of the 1967 Act as appropriate and must then be signed by the witness.

Editing single statements

24.3 There are two acceptable methods of editing single statements:

(a) By marking copies of the statement in a way which indicates the passages on which the prosecution will not rely. This merely indicates that the prosecution will not seek to adduce the evidence so marked. The original signed statement to be tendered to the court is not marked in any way. The marking on the copy statement is done by lightly striking out the passages to be edited so that what appears beneath can still be read, or by bracketing, or by a combination of both. It is not permissible to produce a photocopy with the deleted material obliterated, since this would be contrary to the requirement that the defence and the court should be served with copies of the signed original statement. Whenever the striking-out/bracketing method is used, it will assist if the following words appear at the foot of the frontispiece or index to any bundle of copy statements to be tendered: 'The prosecution does not propose to adduce evidence of those passages of the attached copy statements which have been struck out and/or bracketed (nor will it seek to do so at the trial unless a notice of further evidence is served).'

(b) By obtaining a fresh statement, signed by the witness, which omits the offending material, applying the procedure in paragraph 24.2.

24.4 In most cases where a single statement is to be edited, the striking-out/bracketing method will be the more appropriate, but the taking of a fresh statement is preferable in the following circumstances:

(a) When a police (or other investigating) officer's statement contains details of interviews with more suspects than are eventually charged, a fresh statement should be prepared and signed omitting all details of interview with those not charged except, in so far as it is relevant, for the bald fact that a certain named person was interviewed at a particular time, date and place.

(b) When a suspect is interviewed about more offences than are eventually made the subject of committal charges, a fresh statement should be prepared and signed omitting all questions and answers about the uncharged offences unless either they might appropriately be taken into consideration or evidence about those offences is admissible on the charges preferred, such as evidence of system. It may, however, be desirable to replace the omitted questions and answers with a phrase such as: 'After referring to some other matters, I then said ...', so as to make it clear that part of the interview has been omitted.

(c) A fresh statement should normally be prepared and signed if the only part of the original on which the prosecution is relying is only a small proportion of the whole, although it remains desirable to use the alternative method if there is reason to believe that the defence might itself wish to rely, in mitigation or for any other purpose, on at least some of those parts which the prosecution does not propose to adduce.

(d) When the passages contain material which the prosecution is entitled to withhold from disclosure to the defence.

24.5 Prosecutors should also be aware that, where statements are to be tendered under section 9 of the 1967 Act in the course of summary proceedings, there will be a need to prepare fresh statements excluding inadmissible or prejudicial material rather than using the striking-out or bracketing method.

24.6 None of the above principles applies, in respect of committal proceedings, to documents which are exhibited (including statements under caution and signed contemporaneous notes). Nor do they apply to oral statements of a defendant which are recorded in the witness statements of interviewing police officers, except in the circumstances referred to in paragraph 24.4(b). All this material should remain in its original state in the committal bundles, any editing being left to prosecuting counsel at the Crown Court (after discussion with defence counsel and, if appropriate, the trial judge).

24.7 Whenever a fresh statement is taken from a witness, a copy of the earlier, unedited statement(s) of that witness will be given to the defence in accordance with the Attorney General's guidelines on the disclosure of unused material (*Practice Note (Criminal Evidence: Unused Material)* [1982] 1 All ER 734) unless there are grounds under paragraph 6 of the guidelines for withholding such disclosure.

Thus, in summary, where a statement has to be edited, either:

• the maker of the original statement produces a new statement (both statements would have to be disclosed to the defence); or

• the prosecution may bracket or lightly strike out the material upon which they do not intend to rely, but in such a way that the original words remain visible.

Editing may also be necessary in the case of evidence which the jury will see. For example, the accused might make a statement to the police from which it becomes apparent that he has previous convictions or is accused of other offences. The transcript of this interview may well become an exhibit in the case which the jury will see. Such a document would have to be edited so that the inadmissible material which is deleted is no longer visible.

10.2.3 Witnesses whom the prosecution do not intend to call: unused material

The prosecution have a duty (under the Criminal Procedure and Investigations Act (CPIA) 1996) to disclose to the defence any material which has not already been disclosed but which might undermine the prosecution case against the defendant or assist the defence case. This is considered in detail in Chapter 7. In particular, it should be noted that if a prosecution witness has previous convictions, the prosecution must inform the defence that this is the case (*R v Collister* (1955) 39 Cr App R 100 and *R v Paraskeva* (1982) 76 Cr App R 162).

10.3   DISCLOSURE BY THE DEFENCE

The defence also have a duty of disclosure.

10.3.1   Disclosure of the defence case

Under the CPIA 1996, the defence have a duty to give the prosecution a written statement of the nature of the defence case and to set out the matters upon which the defence take issue with the prosecution. In particular, the defence must give full particulars of any alibi which is going to be raised at trial. Failure to comply with these requirements enables adverse inferences to be drawn by the jury. Full details of these provisions are contained in Chapter 7.

10.3.2   Expert evidence

The other specific duty of pre-trial disclosure with which the defence have to comply is under s 81 of the Police and Criminal Evidence Act 1984 (PACE) and the Crown Court (Advance Notice of Expert Evidence) Rules 1987. The Rules apply to the prosecution as well as the defence, but the prosecution have to disclose all the evidence they wish to rely on anyway (at committal/transfer or by way of notice of additional evidence).

10.4   SECURING THE ATTENDANCE OF WITNESSES

Section 2 of the Criminal Procedure (Attendance of Witnesses) Act 1965 enables the Crown Court to grant a witness summons requiring the attendance at the Crown Court of a person who is likely to be able to give material evidence but who will not attend voluntarily.

Section 2 provides that:

(1)   This section applies where the Crown Court is satisfied that—

    (a)   a person is likely to be able to give evidence likely to be material evidence, or produce any document or thing likely to be material evidence, for the purpose of any criminal proceedings before the Crown Court, and

    (b)   the person will not voluntarily attend as a witness or will not voluntarily produce the document or thing.

(2)   In such a case the Crown Court shall, subject to the following provisions of this section, issue a summons (a witness summons) directed to the person concerned and requiring him to—

    (a)   attend before the Crown Court at the time and place stated in the summons, and

    (b)   give the evidence or produce the document or thing.

Under sub-ss (4)–(6), an application for a witness summons must be made as soon as reasonably practicable after the defendant has been sent to the Crown Court for trial.

Under s 2C(1) of the Criminal Procedure (Attendance of Witnesses) Act 1965, a person against whom a witness summons was made and who was not present or represented when the order was made may apply to the Crown Court for the order to be discharged provided that he:

(b) satisfies the court that he was not served with notice of the application to issue the summons and that he was neither present nor represented at the hearing of the application, and

(c) satisfies the court that he cannot give any evidence likely to be material evidence or, as the case may be, produce any document or thing likely to be material evidence.

Furthermore, s 4(1) of the Act enables pre-emptive action if a witness summons has been obtained and there are grounds to believe that the person will not attend court. It provides that:

(1) If a judge of the Crown Court is satisfied by evidence on oath that a witness in respect of whom a witness summons is in force is unlikely to comply with the summons, the judge may issue a warrant to arrest the witness and bring him before the court before which he is required to attend:

Provided that a warrant shall not be issued under this sub-section unless the judge is satisfied by such evidence as aforesaid that the witness is likely to be able to give evidence likely to be material evidence or produce any document or thing likely to be material evidence in the proceedings.

Section 4(2) and (3) deal with the situation where the witness fails to attend court:

(2) Where a witness who is required to attend before the Crown Court by virtue of a witness summons fails to attend in compliance with the summons, that court may—

(a) in any case, cause to be served on him a notice requiring him to attend the court forthwith or at such time as may be specified in the notice;

(b) if the court is satisfied that there are reasonable grounds for believing that he has failed to attend without just excuse, or if he has failed to comply with a notice under paragraph (a) above, issue a warrant to arrest him and bring him before the court.

(3) A witness brought before the court in pursuance of a warrant under this section may be remanded by that court in custody or on bail (with or without sureties) until such time as the court may appoint for receiving his evidence or dealing with him under section 3 of this Act ...

Thus, if the person who is the subject of the summons fails to attend court, and there are reasonable grounds for believing that there is no just excuse for this non-attendance, a warrant for the arrest of the witness may be issued by the judge. Otherwise, a notice is served on the witness requiring him to attend court on a specified date (and if he fails to do so, a warrant for his arrest may be issued). Someone arrested under such a warrant will be taken before the Crown Court and may be remanded in custody or on bail until the time his evidence is required.

Failure to comply with a witness summons amounts to contempt of court under s 3(1) of the 1965 Act, which provides that:

Any person who without just excuse disobeys a witness summons requiring him to attend before any court shall be guilty of contempt of that court and may be punished summarily by that court as if his contempt had been committed in the face of the court.

Under s 3(2), the maximum penalty for contempt under s 3(1) is three months' imprisonment.

10.5　PREPARATORY AND PRE-TRIAL HEARINGS; PLEA AND DIRECTIONS HEARINGS

The CPIA 1996 makes provision for preliminary hearings to take place prior to Crown Court trials. The Act supplements the existing practice of the Crown Court, which is to hold a 'plea and directions hearing'.

10.5.1　Preparatory hearings

Section 29(1) of the CPIA 1996 empowers a Crown Court judge to order that a 'preparatory hearing' be held; such power may be exercised where 'an indictment reveals a case of such complexity, or a case whose trial is likely to be of such length, that substantial benefits are likely to accrue' from such a hearing. Section 309 of the Criminal Justice Act 2003 amends s 29(1) of the CPIA 1996, by adding 'seriousness' to the criteria justifying a preparatory hearing. The amended s 29(1) reads:

> Where it appears to a judge of the Crown Court that an indictment reveals a case of such complexity, *a case of such seriousness* or a case whose trial is likely to be of such length, that substantial benefits are likely to accrue from a hearing ...

Thus, a preparatory hearing can be held on the basis that the case appears to be:

- complex; or
- serious; or
- lengthy.

These provisions do not apply to serious fraud cases, as these have their own system of preparatory hearings (s 29(3)).

Section 45(6) of the Criminal Justice Act 2003 adds s 29(1A) to the 1996 Act, enabling a preparatory hearing to take place where there is an application for trial without a jury under s 45 of the 2003 Act.

Section 29(2) sets out the purposes of the preparatory hearing:

(a)　identifying issues which are likely to be material to the verdict of the jury [as amended by the Criminal Justice Act 2003, sub-s (a) will read, 'identifying issues which are likely to be material to the determinations and findings which are likely to be required during the trial'];

(b)　assisting their comprehension of any such issues [as amended by the Criminal Justice Act 2003, sub-s (b) will read, 'if there is to be a jury, assisting their comprehension of those issues and expediting the proceedings before them'];

(c)　expediting the proceedings before the jury [as amended by the Criminal Justice Act 2003, sub-s (c) will read, 'determining an application to which s 45 of the Criminal Justice Act 2003 applies'];

(d)　assisting the judge's management of the trial;

(e)　considering questions as to the severance or joinder of charges [(e) was added by s 310(4) of the Criminal Justice Act 2003].

Section 30 says that the arraignment will take place at the start of the preparatory hearing, unless it has taken place before then.

Section 31 sets out the powers which the judge may exercise at the preparatory hearing. This section provides that:

(3) He may make a ruling as to—

(a) any question as to the admissibility of evidence;

(b) any other question of law relating to the case;

(c) any question as to the severance or joinder of charges [(c) was added by s 310(5) of the Criminal Justice Act 2003].

(4) He may order the prosecutor—

(a) to give the court and the accused or, if there is more than one, each of them a written statement (a case statement) of the matters falling within sub-section (5);

(b) to prepare the prosecution evidence and any explanatory material in such a form as appears to the judge to be likely to aid comprehension by the jury and to give it in that form to the court and to the accused or, if there is more than one, to each of them;

(c) to give the court and the accused or, if there is more than one, each of them written notice of documents the truth of the contents of which ought in the prosecutor's view to be admitted and of any other matters which in his view ought to be agreed;

(d) to make any amendments of any case statement given in pursuance of an order under paragraph (a) that appear to the judge to be appropriate, having regard to objections made by the accused or, if there is more than one, by any of them.

(5) The matters referred to in sub-section (4)(a) are—

(a) the principal facts of the case for the prosecution;

(b) the witnesses who will speak to those facts;

(c) any exhibits relevant to those facts;

(d) any proposition of law on which the prosecutor proposes to rely;

(e) the consequences in relation to any of the counts in the indictment that appear to the prosecutor to flow from the matters falling within paragraphs (a) to (d).

(6) Where a judge has ordered the prosecutor to give a case statement and the prosecutor has complied with the order, the judge may order the accused or, if there is more than one, each of them—

(a) to give the court and the prosecutor a written statement setting out in general terms the nature of his defence and indicating the principal matters on which he takes issue with the prosecution;

(b) to give the court and the prosecutor written notice of any objections that he has to the case statement;

(c) to give the court and the prosecutor written notice of any point of law (including any point as to the admissibility of evidence) which he wishes to take, and any authority on which he intends to rely for that purpose.

(7) Where a judge has ordered the prosecutor to give notice under sub-section (4)(c) and the prosecutor has complied with the order, the judge may order the accused or, if there is more than one, each of them to give the court and the prosecutor a written notice stating—

(a) the extent to which he agrees with the prosecutor as to documents and other matters to which the notice under sub-section (4)(c) relates; and

(b) the reason for any disagreement.

(8)   A judge making an order under sub-section (6) or (7) shall warn the accused or, if there is more than one, each of them of the possible consequence under section 34 of not complying with it.

(9)   If it appears to a judge that reasons given in pursuance of sub-section (7) are inadequate, he shall so inform the person giving them and may require him to give further or better reasons.

(10) An order under this section may specify the time within which any specified requirement contained in it is to be complied with.

(11) An order or ruling made under this section shall have effect throughout the trial, unless it appears to the judge on application made to him that the interests of justice require him to vary or discharge it.

Section 34(1) provides that a party may depart from the case disclosed under s 31. However, s 34(2) provides that if a party departs from the case disclosed under s 31, or fails to comply with a requirement imposed under s 31, the judge or, with the leave of the judge, any other party may make such comment as appears to be appropriate and the jury may draw such inference as appears proper. Under s 34(3):

(3)   In deciding whether to give leave the judge shall have regard—

(a) to the extent of the departure or failure; and

(b) to whether there is any justification for it.

A Crown Court judge is entitled to hold separate preparatory hearings under s 29 in respect of defendants who are charged jointly in the same indictment (*Kanaris v Governor of Pentonville Prison* [2003] UKHL 2; [2003] 1 WLR 443).

Section 37 imposes reporting restrictions very similar to those that apply under s 52A of the Crime and Disorder Act 1998.

10.5.2   Appeals from preparatory hearings

Section 35(1) provides that:

An appeal shall lie to the Court of Appeal from any ruling of a judge under section 31(3), but only with the leave of the judge or of the Court of Appeal.

Under s 35(2):

... the judge may continue a preparatory hearing notwithstanding that leave to appeal has been granted under sub-section (1), but no jury shall be sworn until after the appeal has been determined or abandoned.

Under s 35(3):

... on the termination of the hearing of an appeal, the Court of Appeal may confirm, reverse or vary the decision appealed against.

The procedure for such an appeal is set out in the Criminal Procedure and Investigations Act 1996 (Preparatory Hearings) (Interlocutory Appeals) Rules 1997 (SI 1997/1053). Where the judge at the preparatory hearing does not give leave to appeal, an application for leave is made to a single judge of the Court of Appeal. The single judge also has the power to extend the time within which notice of application for leave to appeal must be given and the power to give leave for the defendant to be present at the hearing of the appeal if the defendant is in custody. If the single judge refuses leave to appeal, there is provision for a renewal of that application to the full Court of Appeal.

The scope of preparatory hearings, and appeals therefrom, was considered in *R v Claydon* (2004) *The Times*, 13 February. In the preparatory hearing in that case, a number of issues were raised which were formulated as abuse of process issues and issues under s 78 of the PACE. The judge rejected submissions based on abuse of process but held that some evidence should be excluded because it would be unfair to admit it on the ground of entrapment. The defendants sought leave to appeal the judge's ruling under s 35(1) of the CPIA 1996. The first issue that arose was whether the Court of Appeal had jurisdiction under the 1996 Act to grant leave and to hear the appeal. The Court of Appeal held that for there to be an interlocutory appeal, there has not only to be a ruling as to admissibility or law made at a hearing held pursuant to the judge's order that there be a preparatory hearing, but the ruling has also to be for a purpose covered by s 29(2). In the present case, it could be said that the object of the hearing was for the limited purpose of securing a fair trial by excluding or admitting evidence (usually within the context of s 78) and so was not a purpose listed in s 29(2). However, the court took the view that Parliament clearly intended, by s 31(3)(a) of the 1996 Act, to empower rulings concerning questions of admissibility of evidence to be made at preparatory hearing and for such rulings to be subject to appeal (if leave is given). Such questions pre-eminently arise under s 78, and it would largely emasculate s 31 if rulings given under s 78 were held to be outside its scope. Accordingly, the court held that the making of such rulings should be treated as being for the purpose of 'expediting the proceedings before the jury' (s 29(2)(c)). The trial judge therefore has power to determine s 78 issues within the context of the preparatory hearing (and so his rulings are, to that extent, subject to appeal); however, rulings as to abuse of process are not subject to appeal.

A hearing will only fall within s 29 if the case appears to be complex or likely to lead to a lengthy trial (or serious, taking account of the amendment made by the Criminal Justice Act 2003). In *R v Ward* [2003] EWCA Crim 814; [2003] 2 Cr App R 20, the issue as to whether the case was likely to be long or complex had never been addressed by the trial judge. It followed that the judge had erred in concluding that the case fell within s 29. The judge was entitled to make a pre-trial ruling on a point of law, but that power came from s 40 of the 1996 Act, not s 31(3). It followed that the Court of Appeal did not have jurisdiction to hold an interlocutory appeal, since there was no right of pre-trial appeal against a ruling under s 40. Similarly, in *R v van Hoogstraten* [2003] EWCA Crim 3642; (2003) *The Times*, 24 December, the defendant was to be re-tried for manslaughter (his original conviction having been quashed by the Court of Appeal). The defence made an application to the trial judge that the case should not proceed to trial because, even if the prosecution proved their factual allegations, the jury would not in law be able to convict the defendant of manslaughter. The judge acceded to the application. The prosecution sought to appeal to the Court of Appeal, arguing that the judge's ruling had been made in a preparatory hearing under s 29 of the CPIA 1996. The Court of Appeal held that where the object of the defence application before the start of the trial is to prevent the trial occurring, that application falls outside the scope of the preparatory hearing under s 29(2) of the CPIA 1996, and so there can be no appeal to the Court of Appeal.

In *Attorney General's Reference (No 1 of 2004); R v Crowley* [2004] EWCA Crim 1025; (2004) *The Times*, 30 April, it was held that, before ordering a preparatory hearing under the CPIA 1996, the judge must identify factors relevant to the criteria set out in s 29(2) of the Act. The judgment cannot be made solely on the basis of a study of the terms or length of the specific indictment. The judge is entitled to consider the evidence which is likely to be called and to make his own judgment as to whether he should order a preparatory hearing. If the judge has addressed the statutory criteria for such hearings, the Court of Appeal will be reluctant to set aside what is a matter for judicial assessment and decision by the trial judge. However, if there was no relevant material on which the judge could properly conclude that the case falls within s 29(1), there is no jurisdiction to make an order for a preparatory hearing and the Court of Appeal similarly lacks jurisdiction. It does not inevitably follow that the Court of Appeal is precluded from inviting argument and making observations about the substantive issue for the assistance of the Crown Court, if it sees fit.

10.5.3 Pre-trial hearings

The procedure that we have just looked at is concerned only with complex or lengthy (or serious) trials. Section 39 of the CPIA 1996 provides for pre-trial hearings in other cases to be tried in the Crown Court. These hearings take place before the jury is empanelled. Section 40 sets out the powers of the judge to make rulings at a pre-trial hearing:

(1)   A judge may make at a pre-trial hearing a ruling as to—

    (a) any question as to the admissibility of evidence;

    (b) any other question of law relating to the case concerned.

(2)   A ruling may be made under this section—

    (a) on an application by a party to the case, or

    (b) of the judge's own motion.

(3)   Subject to sub-section (4), a ruling made under this section has binding effect from the time it is made until the case against the accused or, if there is more than one, against each of them is disposed of; and the case against an accused is disposed of if—

    (a) he is acquitted or convicted, or

    (b) the prosecutor decides not to proceed with the case against him.

(4)   A judge may discharge or vary (or further vary) a ruling made under this section if it appears to him that it is in the interests of justice to do so; and a judge may act under this sub-section—

    (a) on an application by a party to the case, or

    (b) of the judge's own motion.

(5)   No application may be made under sub-section (4)(a) unless there has been a material change of circumstances since the ruling was made or, if a previous application has been made, since the application (or last application) was made.

(6)   The judge referred to in sub-section (4) need not be the judge who made the ruling or, if it has been varied, the judge (or any of the judges) who varied it.

At the pre-trial hearing, the judge may thus rule on any question as to the admissibility of evidence, or any other question of law relevant to the case. Any ruling is binding for the whole of the trial unless the judge (upon application by the prosecution or the defence, or of his own motion) varies or discharges that ruling. No application may be made for a ruling to be discharged or varied unless there has been a change in circumstances since the ruling was made. These provisions apply whether or not the pre-trial hearing and the trial itself are presided over by the same judge.

Again, there are similar reporting restrictions to those contained in s 52A of the Crime and Disorder Act 1998.

10.5.4 Plea and directions hearings

In 1995, the Lord Chief Justice issued Practice Rules requiring a plea and directions hearing to take place prior to all Crown Court trials. The powers conferred by s 39 of the CPIA 1996 essentially give statutory effect to the system of plea and directions hearings (PDHs). These rules are set out in para IV.41 of *Practice Direction (Criminal Proceedings: Consolidation)* [2002] 1 WLR 2870; [2002] 3 All ER 904:

41 *Plea and directions hearings*

41.1 These rules apply to all cases (other than serious fraud) in Crown Court centres which have notified the magistrates' courts that plea and directions hearings ('PDHs') have been introduced.

41.2 At the PDH pleas will be taken and, in contested cases, prosecution and defence will be expected to assist the judge in identifying the key issues and to provide any additional information required for the proper listing of the case.

41.3 The detailed operation of the rules will be a matter for the judiciary at each Crown Court centre, taking the views of other agencies and the legal profession into account.

41.4 In every case, other than serious fraud cases in relation to which a notice of transfer to the Crown Court is given under section 4 of the Criminal Justice Act 1987 and child abuse cases transferred under section 53 of the Criminal Justice Act 1991, the magistrates' court should commit the defendant to appear in the Crown Court on a specific date fixed in liaison with the Crown Court listing officer for an initial PDH. The PDH provisions will apply equally to child abuse cases, for which special arrangements will need to be made for the Crown Court to fix a PDH date on receipt of the case papers.

41.5 The purpose of the PDH will be to ensure that all necessary steps have been taken in preparation for trial and to provide sufficient information for a trial date to be arranged. It is expected that the advocate briefed in the case will appear in the PDH wherever practicable.

41.6 At least 14 days' notice of the PDH shall be given unless the parties agree to shorter notice. The PDH should be within six weeks of committal in cases where the defendant is on bail and four weeks where the defendant is in custody.

Preparation for the PDH

41.7 Where the defendant intends to plead guilty to all or part of the indictment the defence must notify the Probation Service, the prosecution and the court as soon as this is known.

41.8 The defence must supply the court and the prosecution with a full list of the prosecution witnesses they require to attend at the trial. This must be provided at least 14 days prior to the PDH or within three working days of the notice of the hearing where the PDH is fixed less than 17 days ahead.

41.9 For all class 1 offences and for lengthy and complex cases a case summary should be prepared by the prosecution for use by the judge at the PDH. All class 2 cases should be scrutinised by the prosecution to determine whether the provision of a summary is appropriate in any particular case. The summary will assist the judge by indicating the nature of the case and focusing on the issues of fact and/or law likely to be involved. The summary should also assist the judge in estimating the trial length.

Form of hearing

41.10 The PDH should normally be held, and orders made, in open court and all defendants should be present (except with the leave of the court). It shall be conducted (a) in all cases other than those in class 1 or class 2 and serious sexual offences of any class against a child, by the trial judge or such judge as the presiding judge or resident judge shall appoint; (b) in cases in class 1 or class 2 and serious sexual offences of any class against a child, by a High Court judge or by a circuit judge or recorder to whom the case has been specifically released in accordance with the directions for the allocation of business within the Crown Court (see paragraphs 33.1–33.12), or by a directions judge authorised by the presiding judges to conduct such hearings, but (i) pleas of guilty when entered before a directions judge in such cases will be adjourned for sentencing by a High Court judge, circuit judge or recorder to whom the case has been specifically released and (ii) a directions judge will deal only with those matters necessary to see that such cases are prepared conveniently for trial, including identifying any issues suitable for a preliminary hearing before the trial judge, and making such necessary directions as may facilitate the conduct of such a preliminary hearing.

Conduct of the hearing

41.11 At the PDH arraignment will normally take place.

41.12 If the defendant pleads guilty, the judge should proceed to sentencing whenever possible.

41.13 Following a not guilty plea, and where part or alternative pleas have not been accepted, the prosecution and defence will be expected to inform the court of:

(a) the issues in the case (identifying any human rights issue);

(b) issues, if any, as to the mental or medical condition of any defendant or witness;

(c) the number of witnesses whose evidence will be placed before the court either orally or in writing;

(d) the defence witnesses in (c) above whose statements have been served and whose evidence the prosecution will agree and accept in writing;

(e) any additional witnesses who may be called by the prosecution and the evidence that they are expected to give;

(f) facts which are to be admitted and which can be reduced into writing in accordance with section 10(2)(b) of the Criminal Justice Act 1967, within such time as may be directed at the hearing, and of the witnesses whose attendance will not be required at trial;

(g) exhibits and schedules which are to be admitted;

(h) the order and pagination of the papers to be used by the prosecution at the trial;

(i) any alibi which should already have been disclosed;

(j) any point of law which it is anticipated will arise at trial, any questions as to the admissibility of evidence which appear on the face of the papers, and of any authority on which the party intends to rely;

(k) any applications to be made for evidence to be given through live television links by child witnesses;

(l) any applications to submit pre-recorded interviews with a child witness as evidence-in-chief;

(m) any applications for screens, for use by witnesses seeking a visual break between themselves and any relevant parties: whether any video, tape recorder or other technical equipment will be required during a trial; where tape recorded interviews have taken place, of any dispute or agreement as to the accuracy of any transcript or summary;

(n) any other significant matter which might affect the proper and convenient trial of the case, and whether any additional work needs to be done by the parties;

(o) the estimated length of the trial, to be agreed more precisely taking account of any views expressed by the judge and the other parties;

(p) witness availability and the approximate length of witness evidence so that attendance can be staggered during lengthy trials, agreeing likely dates and times of attendance, taking into consideration real hardship and inconvenience to a witness where applicable;

(q) availability of advocates;

(r) whether there is a need for any further directions.

41.14 Subject to the provisions of sections 9 and 10 of the Criminal Justice Act 1967, admissions under paragraph 41.13(f) may be used at the trial.

41.15 The judge may make such order or orders as lie within his powers as appear to be necessary to secure the proper and efficient trial of the case. Each party shall, at least 14 days before the date of trial, confirm to the court in writing that all such orders have been fully complied with.

41.16 The questionnaire in Annex D below provides a recommended structure for use by the judiciary in conducting a PDH. A single copy of the questionnaire, completed as far as possible with the agreement of both advocates, is to be handed in to the court prior to the commencement of the PDH.

41.17 The defence shall apply to the court for the case to be listed for mention if they are unable to obtain instructions from the defendant. If the defendant fails to attend court the judge will wish to consider whether a warrant of arrest should be issued.

The Rules thus require that, at the PDH, the defendant must be asked to enter a plea to the offence(s) on the indictment (sometimes called 'arraigning' the defendant). The indictment is read out by the clerk of the court and after each count the defendant says 'guilty' or 'not guilty'. Each count must be 'put' to the defendant separately and a separate plea must be entered on each count. The plea must be entered by the defendant personally (not through his advocate), at least if the plea is one of guilty: *R v Ellis* (1973) 57 Cr App R 571; *R v Williams* [1978] QB 373.

If the defendant pleads guilty, the judge should proceed to sentencing whenever possible (although it may be necessary to adjourn in order for a pre-sentence report to be prepared).

In cases where the defendant pleads not guilty, the prosecution and defence will be expected to inform the court of the matters set out in para 41.13 of the Practice Direction.

The Practice Direction envisages that the PDH will normally be conducted by the trial judge. The PDH is normally held in open court and all defendants should be present unless the court otherwise directs. It should normally take place within six weeks of the defendant being sent for trial if he is on bail, four weeks if he is in custody. When the magistrates send the case to the Crown Court, they should (after consultation with the Crown Court listing officer) specify the date on which the PDH should take place.

The defence should inform the prosecution, the court, and the probation service as soon as it is known that the defendant intends to plead guilty to all or part of the indictment.

Paragraph 41.17 requires the defence solicitors to apply to the court for the case to be listed for mention if they are unable to obtain instructions from the defendant (sometimes called listing for 'non-co-operation'). If the defendant fails to attend this hearing, the judge is likely to issue a warrant for his arrest.

The Auld Review recommended that, in the preparation for trial in all criminal courts, there should be a move away from PDHs and other forms of pre-trial hearings to co-operation between the parties according to standard timetables (wherever necessary, seeking written directions from the court). He recommended a written 'pre-trial assessment' by the court of the parties' readiness for trial, with a pre-trial hearing only if the court or the parties are unable to resolve all matters in this way. However, the Courts Act 2003 makes no change in the Crown Court, where there will continue to be PDHs or preparatory hearings.

Active judicial management of cases is becoming increasingly important. In *R v Jisl; R v Tekin* [2004] EWCA Crim 696; (2004) *The Times*, 19 April, for example, the Court of Appeal observed that whilst the defendant is entitled to a fair trial, the prosecution are equally entitled to a reasonable opportunity to present the evidence against the defendant. The court said that it is not a concomitant of the entitlement to a fair trial that either or both sides are entitled to take as much time as they like or, for that matter, as long as counsel and solicitors or defendants themselves think appropriate. Resources are limited. Time itself is a resource. Active, hands-on case management both pre-trial and throughout the trial itself is now regarded as an essential part of a judge's duty. The profession must understand that this has become and will remain part of the normal trial process, and that cases must be prepared and conducted accordingly (see paras 114–16 of the judgment of Judge LJ).

10.6 THE TRIAL

Now, we start to examine in detail the course of a trial on indictment.

10.6.1 Presence of the defendant

In the Crown Court, the defendant must be present in order to enter a plea to the counts on the indictment. In the magistrates' court, the position is slightly different, as it is possible (where a defendant fails to attend court) for a not guilty plea to be entered on his behalf (although if the offence is triable either way, this is only possible if the accused had consented to summary trial at an earlier hearing).

If, after entering a plea, the defendant absconds (or misbehaves and disrupts the proceedings), the trial judge has a discretion to continue the trial in the defendant's absence. In practice, this would only occur if there was another defendant being tried at the same time and it would be unfair on that defendant to postpone the trial (*R v Jones (No 2)* [1972] 1 WLR 887). Further guidance was given by the House of Lords in *R v Jones* [2002] UKHL 5; [2003] 1 AC 1, where the defendants had pleaded not guilty on arraignment but absconded before the date fixed for the trial. The judge (after a number of adjournments) decided to try them in their absence. It was held by the House of

Lords that the discretion to commence a trial in the absence of the defendant should be exercised with the utmost care and caution, and that if the absence is attributable to involuntary illness or incapacity it will very rarely, if ever, be right to do so, at any rate unless the defendant is represented and has asked that the trial should begin. The judge's overriding concern must be to ensure that the trial would be as fair as circumstances permit and lead to a just outcome. These objectives are equally important whether the offence is serious or relatively minor, so the seriousness of the offence is not a matter that ought to be taken into account. It is generally desirable that a defendant be represented even if he has voluntarily absconded. That provides a valuable safeguard against the possibility of error and oversight. Trial judges should therefore ask counsel to continue to represent a defendant who has absconded and counsel should normally accede to such an invitation and defend their absent client as best they properly can in the circumstances. In the same case, the Court of Appeal ([2001] EWCA Crim 168; [2001] QB 862) had set out, in detail, the principles which should guide the English courts in relation to the trial of a defendant in his absence. They are:

(a) a defendant has, in general, a right to be present at his trial and to be legally represented;

(b) those rights could be waived, separately or together, wholly or in part, by the defendant himself. They might be waived wholly if he deliberately absents himself and/or withdraws his instructions from those representing him. They might be waived in part if the defendant, during the course of the trial, behaves in such a way as to obstruct the proper course of the proceedings and/or withdraws his instructions from those representing him;

(c) the trial judge has a discretion as to whether a trial should take place or continue in the absence of a defendant and/or his legal representatives;

(d) that discretion has to be exercised with great care and only in a rare case in favour of a trial taking place or continuing, particularly if the defendant is unrepresented;

(e) in exercising that discretion, fairness to the defence is of prime importance but fairness to the prosecution has also to be taken into account. The judge has to have regard to all the circumstances of the case, including:

(i) the nature and circumstances of the defendant's behaviour in absenting himself from the trial or disrupting it and, in particular, whether his behaviour was such as plainly waived his right to appear;

(ii) whether an adjournment might result in the defendant being caught or attending voluntarily and/or not disrupting the proceedings;

(iii) the likely length of such adjournment;

(iv) whether the defendant, although absent, was or wished to be legally represented at the trial or had, by his conduct, waived his right to representation;

(v) whether an absent defendant's legal representatives were able to receive instructions from him during the trial and the extent to which they were able to present his defence;

(vi) the extent of the disadvantage to the defendant in not being able to give his account of events, having regard to the nature of the evidence against him;

(vii) the risk of the jury reaching an improper conclusion about the absence of the defendant;

(viii) the seriousness of the offence (it should be noted that when the case went to the House of Lords, Lord Bingham CJ said (at para 14 of his speech) that the seriousness of the offence should *not* be taken into account, since fairness is important whether the offence charged is serious or relatively minor);

(ix) the general public interest and the particular interest of victims and witnesses that a trial should take place within a reasonable time of the events to which it relates;

(x) the effect of delay on the memories of witnesses;

(xi) where there is more than one defendant and not all have absconded, the undesirability of separate trials, and the prospects of a fair trial for the defendants who were present;

(f) if the judge decides that a trial should take place or continue in the absence of an unrepresented defendant, he must ensure that the trial is as fair as circumstances permit. In particular, he has to take reasonable steps, both during the giving of evidence and in the summing up, to expose weaknesses in the prosecution case and to make such points on behalf of the defendant as the evidence permits. In summing up he ought to warn the jury that absence is not an admission of guilt and adds nothing to the prosecution case.

See also paras I.13.13–19 of the *Consolidated Practice Direction* (which refers to *R v Jones*).

It follows that if a defendant is taken ill during the course of the trial and cannot attend court, the trial can continue in his absence if he consents; if he does not consent to the trial continuing in his absence, and the illness is likely to last more than a few days, the jury will be discharged and a new trial will begin when the defendant is well enough to attend court.

10.6.2 Bail

If the defendant is remanded in custody prior to his trial, he will remain in custody during the trial itself (unless the trial judge grants bail, which is very unlikely).

In *R v Central Criminal Court ex p Guney* [1996] AC 616, the House of Lords held that when a defendant who has not previously surrendered to the custody of the court is arraigned, he thereby surrenders to the custody of the court at that moment. The result is that the Crown Court judge then has to decide whether or not to grant him bail; unless the judge grants bail, the defendant will remain in custody pending and during the trial.

Guney was followed by the Divisional Court in *R v Maidstone Crown Court ex p Jodka* (1997) 161 JP 638. In that case, the court held that bail granted by magistrates ceases when the defendant surrenders to the custody of the Crown Court, whether or not the defendant is arraigned at the hearing at which he surrenders. Where the magistrates grant bail subject to a surety, the responsibility of that surety under the magistrates' court order ceases once the defendant surrenders to the custody of the Crown Court. If the Crown Court wishes to grant bail subject to the same surety, the court must consider the position of that surety before imposing such a condition.

It follows from this that the question of bail will have to be considered at the pre-trial hearing. In any event, if the defendant is on bail before the trial, his bail effectively expires at the start of the trial. It is therefore a matter for the trial judge whether or not bail is granted to the defendant for lunch-time and/or overnight adjournments. Some judges usually withhold bail at lunch-time; some grant bail on the condition that the defendant remains in the company of his solicitor; others are happy to grant unconditional bail unless there seems to be a risk of the defendant absconding. Bail might be withdrawn if, for example, the likelihood of the defendant absconding increases because the case starts to go badly for him. If a custodial sentence is likely in the event of conviction, bail is normally withheld once the judge has begun the summing up. These issues are dealt with in para III.25 of the *Practice Direction (Criminal Proceedings: Consolidation)* [2002] 1 WLR 2870; [2002] 3 All ER 904. This provides as follows:

25   *Bail during trial*

25.1 Paragraphs 25.2 to 25.5 are to be read subject to the Bail Act 1976, especially section 4.

25.2 Once a trial has begun the further grant of bail, whether during the short adjournment or overnight, is in the discretion of the trial judge. It may be a proper exercise of this discretion to refuse bail during the short adjournment if the accused cannot otherwise be segregated from witnesses and jurors.

25.3 An accused who was on bail while on remand should not be refused overnight bail during the trial unless in the opinion of the judge there are positive reasons to justify this refusal. Such reasons are likely to be:

      (a) that a point has been reached where there is a real danger that the accused will abscond, either because the case is going badly for him or for any other reason;

      (b) that there is a real danger that he may interfere with witnesses or jurors.

25.4 There is no universal rule of practice that bail shall not be renewed when the summing up has begun. Each case must be decided in the light of its own circumstances and having regard to the judge's assessment from time to time of the risks involved.

25.5 Once the jury has returned a verdict a further renewal of bail should be decided in the light of the gravity of the offence and the likely sentence to be passed in all the circumstances of the case.

Applications for bail during the course of the trial should be made in the absence of the jury (who might otherwise be prejudiced against the accused if bail is not granted, since they might take this as an indication of the judge's view that the defendant is guilty).

10.6.3 Unrepresented defendants

Where the defendant is unrepresented:

(a) the trial judge should ask such questions as he sees fit, to test the reliability of the prosecution witnesses and may ask the defendant whether there are certain matters he wishes to be put to the witnesses;

(b) the jury should be instructed (at the start of the trial and in the summing up) that the defendant is entitled to represent himself and they should also be warned of the difficulty of his doing so properly;

(c) the judge should prevent repetitious questioning of prosecution witnesses by the defendant.

Section 34 of the Youth Justice and Criminal Evidence Act 1999 provides that no person charged with a sexual offence may cross-examine the complainant, either in connection with that offence or in connection with any other offence (of whatever nature) with which that person is charged in the proceedings. Under s 35 of the Act, unrepresented defendants are not allowed to cross-examine in person a child who is either the complainant of, or a witness to the commission of, an offence of kidnapping, false imprisonment or abduction. Section 36 gives courts the power to prohibit unrepresented defendants from cross-examining witnesses in cases where a mandatory ban does not apply under ss 34 and 35, but where the court is satisfied that the circumstances of the witness and the case merit a prohibition, and that it would not be contrary to the interests of justice.

Article 6(3)(c) of the European Convention on Human Rights guarantees the right to legal representation and legal aid. However, the European Court of Human Rights has held that a court may place restrictions on the right of a defendant to appear without a lawyer (*Croissant v Germany* (1993) 16 EHRR 135). The provisions of the 1999 Act would seem to be within Art 6.

10.6.4 Adjournments

In *R v Chaaban* [2003] EWCA Crim 1012; (2003) *The Times*, 8 May, the Court of Appeal said that adjournments must be justified and, if at all possible, should be avoided. However, the court noted that the decision whether or not to adjourn is pre-eminently a matter for the trial judge, and so the Court of Appeal will not interfere with that decision unless it can be demonstrated that the decision to refuse an adjournment was wholly unreasonable and caused real (as opposed to fanciful) prejudice to the defendant, undermining the safety of the conviction.

10.7 THE JURY

In this section, we examine the composition of the jury, and how the jury to try a defendant is chosen.

One of the concerns about jury trial is that a substantial number of people are not summoned for jury service because they are not on the electoral role. In his *Review of the Criminal Courts of England and Wales*, Lord Justice Auld quotes (Chapter 5, para 22) some Home Office research showing that in 1999 some 8% of people who were eligible to register on the electoral roll had not done so. Those aged 20–24, ethnic minorities and those living in rented accommodation were most under-represented on the electoral roll. Lord Justice Auld said that jurors should be more representative than they currently are of the national and local communities from which they are drawn. To this end, Recommendation 18 in the Review is that:

> The law should be amended to substitute for the condition of registration on an electoral roll, inclusion in such a roll and/or on any one or more of a number of other specified publicly maintained lists or directories, but excluding anyone listed who, on investigation at the summons stage, is found not to be entitled to registration as an elector.

Thus, entitlement to, rather than actual, entry on an electoral role would be the basis for eligibility; this would make it possible to use other sources of information (public registers and lists) to track down people who are eligible to be on the electoral roll but are not in fact on it. The government has not so far acted upon this suggestion.

10.7.1 Who can serve on a jury?

As we have seen, jurors are drawn from the electoral register. Essentially, anyone on the register and aged between 18 and 70 can be summoned for jury service (s 1 of the Juries Act 1974). The principle underpinning the operation of the Juries Act 1974 is that the jury should be a cross-section of society, drawn at random. In practice, so many people were excluded from jury service, or were able to be excused, that juries were not really representative of society as a whole.

Prior to the amendment of the Juries Act 1974 by the Criminal Justice Act 2003, some people were ineligible to serve on a jury. This category included the judiciary (including lay magistrates), lawyers, those concerned in the administration of justice (for example, police officers, prison officers, probation officers), the clergy and the mentally disordered. Other people had the right to be excused from jury service if they so wished. This category included those aged 65 or over, those who had served on a jury within the last two years, Members of Parliament, full time serving members of the armed forces, and medical personnel (such as doctors, dentists, nurses and vets).

A major change recommended by the Auld Review was that those with criminal convictions and mental disorder should continue to be excluded from jury service, but that no one else should be ineligible for or excusable as of right from it:

> Everyone should be eligible for jury service, save for the mentally ill, and the law should be amended accordingly (Recommendation 20).

This proposal was enacted in Sched 33 to the Criminal Justice Act 2003, which was brought into force in April 2004. The effect of the reforms brought about by Sched 33 is to abolish (except in the case of mentally disordered persons) the categories of people who are ineligible for, or entitled to be excused as of right from, jury service.

Paragraph 2 of Sched 33 enacts a new version of s 1 of the Juries Act 1974 (qualification for jury service), removing the status of 'ineligibility' for jury service except in the case of mentally disordered persons. The amended version reads as follows:

(1) Subject to the provisions of this Act, every person shall be qualified to serve as a juror in the Crown Court ... and be liable accordingly to attend for jury service when summoned under this Act if—

  (a) he is for the time being registered as a parliamentary or local government elector and is not less than eighteen nor more than seventy years of age;

  (b) he has been ordinarily resident in the United Kingdom, the Channel Islands or the Isle of Man for any period of at least five years since attaining the age of thirteen;

  (c) he is not a mentally disordered person; and

  (d) he is not disqualified for jury service.

(2) In sub-section (1) above 'mentally disordered person' means any person listed in Part 1 of Schedule 1 to this Act.

(3)   The persons who are disqualified for jury service are those listed in Part 2 of that Schedule.

Paragraph 15 of Sched 33 to the 2003 Act replaces Sched 1 to the 1974 Act (ineligibility and disqualification for and excusal from jury service), so that it accords with the new s 1 of the 1974 Act by removing the judiciary, others concerned with the administration of justice, and the clergy from the list of those 'ineligible' for jury service, leaving only mentally disordered people with that status. There is a comprehensive definition of mental disorder in the new Pt 1 of Sched 1 to the Juries Act 1974.

Thus, the bar on the judiciary, those concerned with the administration of justice and the clergy is lifted; similarly, the entitlement to refuse to serve as jurors enjoyed by people over 65, Members of Parliament, medical professionals and members of certain religious bodies is also removed. This means that even lawyers and judges, and police officers, are now eligible for jury service. Such jurors will (according to guidance issued by the Central Summoning Bureau) be asked to sit in a court other than one in which they regular appear or sit as the case may be. The Auld Review specifically rejected the argument that such a person might (albeit unintentionally) unduly influence their fellow jurors (citing the fact that in some American states, where lawyers and judges are eligible for jury service, such problems do not seem to have arisen (see paras 27–32 of Chapter 5)).

Paragraph 15 of the 2003 Act also amends the categories of those who are disqualified from jury service by revising Pt 2 of Sched 1 to the Juries Act. These changes have been made necessary by changes in sentencing legislation. The following people are disqualified from jury service:

- a person who is on bail in criminal proceedings at the relevant time;
- a person who has at any time been sentenced in the UK to imprisonment or detention for life, to detention during Her Majesty's pleasure, to imprisonment or detention for public protection, to an extended sentence under s 227 or 228 of the Criminal Justice Act 2003, or to a term of imprisonment or detention of five years or more;
- a person who at any time in the last 10 years has, in the UK, served any part of a sentence of imprisonment or detention, or has had passed on him a suspended sentence of imprisonment or detention;
- a person who at any time in the last 10 years has, in England and Wales, had made in respect of him a community order under s 177 of the Criminal Justice Act 2003, a community rehabilitation order, a community punishment order, a community punishment and rehabilitation order, a drug treatment and testing order or a drug abstinence order.

Paragraph 3 of Sched 33 repeals s 9(1) of the Juries Act 1974, which provided that the groups of people listed in Pt 3 of Sched 1 to the 1974 Act (repealed by para 15 of Sched 33 of the 2003 Act) should be 'excused as of right' from jury service. The effect of these repeals is that no one is entitled to automatic excusal from jury service.

The Auld Review also noted the number of people who seek – and obtain – excusal from jury service (during a sample period in 1999, 38% of those summoned), and quotes the axiom that the scope for excusal created the impression that jury service is only for those not important or clever enough to get out of it (para 13 in Chapter 5). The effect of this (especially in the case of longer trials) was that the jury did not represent a cross-section of the community at large. To deal with this problem, the Review made three recommendations:

22 Save for those who have recently undertaken, or have been excused by a court from, jury service, no-one should be excusable from jury service as of right, only on showing good reason for excusal.

23 The Central Summoning Bureau or the court, in examining a claim for discretionary excusal, should consider its power of deferral first.

24 The Bureau should treat all subsequent applications for deferral and all applications for excusal against clear criteria identified in the jury summons.

The effect of the reforms made by the 2003 Act is that anyone who is not ineligible through mental illness, or disqualified because of a previous conviction, is required to attend for jury service if summoned. However:

- s 9(2) of the Juries Act 1974 provides that a person who has been summoned for jury service may seek excusal if they can show a 'good reason' for this; and

- s 9A(1) enables a person summoned for jury service to seek deferral of the summons (and so, if the dates specified in the summons clash with the person's holiday arrangements or business commitments, attendance can be deferred to a later date).

The discretion to excuse or defer is exercised by the Jury Central Summoning Bureau (part of the Lord Chancellor's Department) which administers the jury summoning system on behalf of the Crown Court in England and Wales. With the abolition of most of the categories of persons ineligible for jury service and the removal of excusal as of right, it is likely that there will be a large increase in the number of applications for excusal or deferral under ss 9 and 9A. Paragraph 12 of Sched 33 to the 2003 Act inserts a new s 9AA into the 1974 Act, requiring the Lord Chancellor to issue guidance as to the manner in which the functions of the 'appropriate officer' under ss 9 and 9A of this Act are to be exercised. Guidance was issued when the relevant provisions of the 2003 Act came into force, and makes it clear that deferral is preferable to excusal. The guidance states that excusal should be reserved for cases where it would be 'unreasonable to require the person to serve at any time within the following 12 months', and that a person should be excused from jury service only in 'extreme circumstances'.

Section 9B of the Juries Act 1974 enables a person to be excused from jury service because he or she is not capable of acting effectively as a juror because of a physical disability.

In *R v Guildford Crown Court ex p Siderfin* [1990] 2 QB 683, the Divisional Court said that it would be appropriate to excuse from jury service a practising member of a religious society or order the tenets or beliefs of which are incompatible with jury service. It is likely that the Central Summoning Bureau will adopt the same approach.

Paragraph IV.42 of *Practice Direction (Criminal Proceedings: Consolidation)* [2002] 1 WLR 2870; [2002] 3 All ER 904 states:

42.1 Jury service is an important public duty which individual members of the public are chosen at random to undertake. The normal presumption is that ... he or she will be required to serve when summoned to do so. There will, however, be circumstances where a juror should be excused, for instance where he is personally concerned in the facts of the particular case or is closely connected with a party or prospective witness.

42.2 He may also be excused on grounds of personal hardship or conscientious objection to jury service. Each such application should be dealt with sensitively and sympathetically.

42.3 Any person who appeals to the court against a refusal by the appropriate officer to excuse him from jury service must be given an opportunity to make representations in support of his appeal.

It is likely this part of the Practice Direction will have to be amended to reflect the changes made by the Criminal Justice Act 2003 and the change in ethos, whereby deferral is to be regarded as preferable to excusal.

Another concern that is considered in the Auld Review is the number of people who evade jury service. In para 25 of Chapter 5, Lord Justice Auld refers to Home Office research showing that some 15% of summoned jurors failed to attend court. To endeavour to counter this, the Review recommends that:

There should be rigorous and well publicised enforcement of the obligation to undertake jury service when required, and consideration should be given to doing so by way of a system of fixed penalties subject to a right of appeal to the magistrates (Recommendation 18).

This suggestion has not been taken up in the Criminal Justice Act 2003, and so it will remain incumbent on the Crown Court to deal with those who fail to answer their summons for jury service. A person who is summoned for jury service and who fails to attend without reasonable cause is guilty of an offence punishable with a fine of up to £1,000 (s 20 of the Juries Act 1974).

10.7.2 Empanelling a jury

The term 'jury panel' is used to describe the body of people who have been summoned for jury service at a particular Crown Court.

Where a defendant has pleaded not guilty to an indictment, at least 12 members of the jury panel are brought into the court room; they are then known as the 'jury in waiting'. The clerk of the court calls out the names of 12 of them, chosen at random.

Once 12 people are in the jury box, the clerk says to the defendant, 'the names that you are about to hear are the names of the jurors who are to try you. If you wish to object to them or to any of them, you must do so as they come to the book to be sworn, and before they are sworn, and your objection shall be heard'. The nature of the objection referred to is considered below when we examine challenges to jurors.

Each of the jurors (one after the other) takes the juror's oath, reading the words from a card and holding in his right hand the appropriate Holy Book (New Testament for Christians, Old Testament for Jews, Koran for Muslims). Jurors who do not wish to swear an oath are permitted to make an affirmation instead. The terms of the oath/affirmation are set out in para IV.42.4 of *Practice Direction (Criminal Proceedings: Consolidation)* [2002] 1 WLR 2870; [2002] 3 All ER 904, which stipulates that:

42.4 The wording of the oath to be taken by jurors is: 'I swear by Almighty God that I will faithfully try the defendant and give a true verdict according to the evidence.' Any person who objects to being sworn shall be permitted to make his solemn affirmation instead. The wording of the affirmation is: 'I do solemnly, sincerely and truly declare and affirm that I will faithfully try the defendant and give a true verdict according to the evidence.'

Note that Recommendation 295 of the Auld Review is that: 'The juror's oath and affirmation should be replaced with a promise in the following or similar form: "I promise to try the defendant and to decide on the evidence whether he is guilty or not."'

Once all 12 have taken the oath (or affirmed), the clerk reads out the indictment and then says, 'To this indictment the defendant has pleaded not guilty. It is your charge, having heard the evidence, to say whether he be guilty or not'. Note that if the defendant has pleaded guilty to some of the counts on the indictment, but not guilty to the others, the jury will not be told about the guilty pleas.

In some cases, there have been attempts to 'nobble' the jury. If the police fear that such an attempt is likely, an application may be made for the jurors to receive special protection. In *R v Comerford* [1998] 1 WLR 191, it was held that an application for jury protection should normally be made in the presence of the defendant, and should be supported by evidence of the need for such protection (which the defendant can cross-examine). Any departure from this approach is only possible if the trial judge is satisfied that it is necessary and would not render the trial process unfair. Furthermore, the jury must be directed not to hold it against the defendant that protective measures have been taken. In that case, the clerk in the Crown Court did not reveal the names of the jurors. The Court of Appeal held that, although the defendant is entitled under s 5(2) of the Juries Act 1974, if he wishes, to know the names of all the people on the jury panel (that is, all those summoned for jury service at that court), it is permissible, in an appropriate case, for the clerk not to follow the usual practice of calling out the names of the individual jurors as they enter the jury box.

Paragraphs 17–20 of Chapter 5 of the Auld Review discuss the (comparatively) rare cases where a trial has to be aborted because the number of jurors falls below the crucial figure of nine. This does not happen often but is a cause for concern in cases that last a very long time. Recommendation 16 of the Review is that:

A system should be introduced for enabling judges in long cases, where they consider it appropriate, to swear alternate or reserve jurors to meet the contingency of a jury otherwise being reduced in number by discharge for illness or any other reason of necessity.

This suggestion has not been adopted by the government.

10.8   CHALLENGES TO JURORS

The clerk tells the defendant that he can challenge the jury, or individual jurors. In this section, we consider the challenges which can be made to the jury as a whole and to individual jurors.

10.8.1   Challenging the whole jury

Theoretically, it is open to the defendant to challenge the way in which the jury panel was selected; this is known as 'challenging the array'. In practice, this never occurs. The only basis for objecting to the entire jury panel would be that the population of the area served by that particular Crown Court would be hostile to the defendant because of the notoriety of the case. In such a case, the appropriate course of action would be to try to secure a change in the location of the trial.

10.8.2 Challenging individual jurors

- *Challenging for cause*

Both the prosecution and the defence can challenge a potential juror on the ground that he may be biased for or against the accused. The party who alleges that a juror is biased bears the burden of proving bias.

To challenge for cause, counsel says 'challenge' just before the juror takes his oath. The reason for the challenge is then explained to the judge. In a straightforward case, the judge will ask the juror to leave the jury box, having heard submissions from counsel. Otherwise, jurors who have already been sworn in and the rest of the 'jury in waiting' will be asked to leave the court room and evidence will be called to substantiate the challenge.

Unlike the position in the United States (where jurors are questioned at length on their suitability), the challenger must provide *prima facie* evidence in support of the challenge before being allowed to question the juror (*R v Chandler (No 2)* [1964] 2 QB 322).

An example of this taking place is *R v Kray* (1969) 53 Cr App R 412. The activities of the accused had been the subject of sensational reporting in a newspaper; counsel for the accused persuaded the trial judge that anyone who had read the graphic and inaccurate material would be predisposed to convict the accused. Once the judge was satisfied of this, he allowed the defence to ask each potential juror if they had read the offending press reports.

Questioning of potential jurors can only take place in exceptional cases. In *R v Andrews* [1999] Crim LR 156, the appellant claimed that her conviction for murder was unsafe because of adverse pre-trial publicity. It was argued on her behalf that potential jurors should have been asked whether they had read or heard the reports in question. It was held that such questioning of jurors (whether done orally or by means of a questionnaire) is of doubtful efficacy and may even be counter-productive (by reminding the jurors of the adverse publicity); it should therefore only be done in the most exceptional circumstances. In *Montgomery v HM Advocate; Coulter v HM Advocate* [2001] 2 WLR 779, the Privy Council (hearing a Scottish appeal) held that, where there has been prejudicial pre-trial publicity, the court is entitled to expect the jury to follow the directions which they receive from the trial judge and to return a true verdict based only on the evidence they have heard in court. On that basis, a defendant may be regarded as having received a fair trial even if there has been adverse pre-trial publicity. The Court of Appeal took the same view in *R v Stone* [2001] EWCA Crim 297; (2001) *The Times*, 22 February, where it was held that in deciding whether to order a retrial in a case that had attracted widespread publicity, the court has to consider whether it could be satisfied, on the balance of probabilities, that if the jury empanelled at the retrial returned a verdict of guilty, the effect of the pre-trial publicity would be such as to render that conviction unsafe. In the present case, any re-trial would not start until nearly three years after the relevant publicity, and the public would have largely forgotten about that publicity. Even if they did not forget it entirely, the passage of time made it easier for them to set aside that which they would be told to disregard. It was, said the court, in the interests of justice to both the victims and the wider community that there should be a re-trial.

In any event, whilst the names of the jury panel are available to the defence before the trial, it is unlikely that the defence will have the resources to investigate each one of the potential jurors.

If the challenge is successful the juror cannot try this case but, depending on the nature of the challenge (is he or she unsuitable to be a juror or just biased in this particular case?), may be called upon to try another case.

The question is whether the fair-minded and informed observer, having considered the facts, would conclude that there was a real possibility that the tribunal was biased: see *Porter v Magill* [2002] 2 AC 357. In that case, Lord Hope of Craighead notes (in para 88) that there is a close relationship between the concept of independence and that of impartiality. He quotes from the case of *Findlay v UK* (1997) 24 EHRR 221 at 244–45 (para 73), where the European Court said:

> ... in order to establish whether a tribunal can be considered as 'independent', regard must be had *inter alia* to the manner of appointment of its members and their term of office, the existence of guarantees against outside pressures and the question whether the body presents an appearance of independence. As to the question of 'impartiality', there are two aspects to this requirement. First, the tribunal must be subjectively free from personal prejudice or bias. Secondly, it must also be impartial from an objective viewpoint, that is, it must offer sufficient guarantees to exclude any legitimate doubt in this respect. The concepts of independence and objective impartiality are closely linked ...

Lord Hope comments that, in both cases, the concept requires not only that the tribunal must be truly independent and free from actual bias (proof of which is likely to be very difficult), but also that it must not appear, in the objective sense, to lack these essential qualities.

The test for apparent bias had been set out by Lord Goff of Chieveley in *R v Gough* [1993] AC 646 at 670 in these terms:

> I think it unnecessary, in formulating the appropriate test, to require that the court should look at the matter through the eyes of a reasonable man, because the court in cases such as these personifies the reasonable man; and in any event the court has first to ascertain the relevant circumstances from the available evidence, knowledge of which would not necessarily be available to an observer in court at the relevant time ... I prefer to state the test in terms of real danger rather than real likelihood, to ensure that the court is thinking of possibility rather than probability of bias. Accordingly, having ascertained the relevant circumstances, the court should ask itself whether, having regard to those circumstances, there was a real danger of bias on the part of the relevant member of the tribunal in question, in the sense that he might unfairly regard (or have unfairly regarded) with favour, or disfavour, the case of a party to the issue under consideration by him ...

In *Porter v Magill*, Lord Hope notes that the 'reasonable likelihood' and 'real danger' tests propounded by Lord Goff in *R v Gough* had been criticised on the ground that they tend to emphasise the court's view of the facts and to place inadequate emphasis on the public perception of the irregular incident. The Scottish courts (see, for example, *Bradford v McLeod* 1986 SLT 244) had adopted a test which looked at the question of whether there was suspicion of bias through the eyes of the reasonable man who was aware of the circumstances. Lord Hope observed that this approach (sometimes described as 'the reasonable apprehension of bias' test) is in line with that adopted in most common law jurisdictions and by the European Court of Human Rights (which looks at the question of whether there was a risk of bias objectively in the light of the circumstances which the court has identified: *Piersack v Belgium* (1982) 5 EHRR 169 at 179–80 (paras 30–31); *Pullar v UK* (1996) 22 EHRR 391 at 402–03 (para 30); and *Hauschildt v Denmark* (1989) 12 EHRR 266 at 279 (para 48)).

In *R v Bow Street Metropolitan Stipendiary Magistrate ex p Pinochet Ugarte (No 2)* [2000] 1 AC 119 at 136, the House of Lords declined to review the *Gough* test. In that case, Lord Hope had expressed the view that the English and Scottish tests were described differently but their application was likely, in practice, to lead to results that were so similar as to be indistinguishable (p 142). Moreover, the Court of Appeal, having examined the question whether the 'real danger' test might lead to a different result from that which the informed observer would reach on the same facts, concluded in *Locabail (UK) Ltd v Bayfield Properties Ltd* [2000] QB 451 at 477 (para 17) that, in the overwhelming majority of cases, the application of the two tests would lead to the same outcome. However, in *Re Medicaments and Related Classes of Goods (No 2)* [2001] 1 WLR 700, the Court of Appeal reconsidered the question of bias. Lord Phillips of Worth Matravers MR, giving the judgment of the court, concluded as follows (at para 35):

> When the Strasbourg jurisprudence is taken into account, we believe that a modest adjustment of the test in *R v Gough* is called for, which makes it plain that it is, in effect, no different from the test applied in most of the Commonwealth and in Scotland. The court must first ascertain all the circumstances which have a bearing on the suggestion that the judge was biased. It must then ask whether those circumstances would lead a fair-minded and informed observer to conclude that there was a real possibility, or a real danger, the two being the same, that the tribunal was biased.

In *Porter v Magill*, Lord Hope (with whom the other Law Lords agreed) approved this 'modest adjustment' of the test in *R v Gough* subject to one modification. Lord Hope (at para 103) said the test formulated by Lord Phillips:

> ... expresses in clear and simple language a test which is in harmony with the objective test which the Strasbourg court applies when it is considering whether the circumstances give rise to a reasonable apprehension of bias. It removes any possible conflict with the test which is now applied in most Commonwealth countries and in Scotland. I would however delete from it the reference to 'a real danger'. Those words no longer serve a useful purpose here, and they are not used in the jurisprudence of the Strasbourg court. The question is whether the fair-minded and informed observer, having considered the facts, would conclude that there was a real possibility that the tribunal was biased.

It is likely that much of the earlier case law on bias would be decided applying the *Porter v Magill* formulation of the test for bias: for example, *R v Brown* [1992] Crim LR 586, where one of the jurors was distantly related to one of the police officers in the case, and *R v Wilson* (1979) 69 Cr App R 83, where convictions were quashed (and retrials ordered) because one of the jurors was the wife of a prison officer serving at the prison where the appellants had been held on remand. The Court of Appeal said that it was not necessary to inquire into the juror's actual state of mind, since there was a real danger that, consciously or not, she may have been biased against the appellants.

- *The prosecution stand by*

It used to be the case that each defendant could challenge up to three potential jurors peremptorily (that is, without giving a reason). This right was abolished in 1988, and the only challenge the defence can now make is the challenge for cause described above.

The prosecution, however, have retained their right to challenge a juror without giving reasons; this is known as the prosecution right to stand a juror by. To exercise this right, prosecuting counsel says 'stand by' just before the juror takes his oath. It is then explained to the juror that he cannot sit on this jury, but will go back to the jury panel and may be called on to try another case.

As it may be seen as unfair that the prosecution should be able to challenge a juror without giving any reason but the defence do not have such a right, the Attorney General issued guidelines which make it clear that the right of stand by should only be used in exceptional cases. In cases involving national security or terrorism, the jury panel will be 'vetted' extensively to ensure that they are suitable to try such a sensitive case. In other cases, the only check that will be carried out is to see which members of the jury panel have previous convictions. Some may have convictions which disqualify them from jury service (and this would be the subject of a challenge for cause); others may not be disqualified from service but may be unsuitable to try a particular case (for example, someone who has just been fined for theft may not be the best person to try a theft case).

Finally, the prosecution may stand a juror by, if the defence agree to this, if the juror is manifestly unsuitable to try the case (for example, clearly has difficulty in reading the words on the card when trying to take the oath and is therefore unsuited to try a case where a number of documents have to be read).

- *The judge's right of stand by*

The judge has an inherent power to stand a juror by. This power is hardly ever exercised and would only be appropriate where a juror is manifestly unsuitable to try a particular case.

In *R v Ford* [1989] QB 89, the Court of Appeal held that a judge must not use his power to stand jurors by in order to try to ensure a racially balanced jury. The statutory procedure for selecting jurors is intended to ensure random selection and the judge should not interfere with this randomness. *Ford* was followed in *R v Tarrant* [1998] Crim LR 342, where the Court of Appeal repeated that a judge cannot use his discretion to discharge individual jurors in order to interfere with the composition of the jury panel (in the present case, to select jurors from outside the court's catchment area in order to minimise the risk of intimidation). In *R v Smith* [2003] EWCA Crim 283; [2003] 1 WLR 2229, a black defendant was tried by an all-white jury with causing serious injury to a white victim. It was held that the jury summoning procedure in the Juries Act 1974 is not inconsistent with Art 6 of the European Convention on Human Rights: it is (said the court) neither unfair that a black defendant is tried by a randomly selected all-white jury, nor would a fair-minded and informed observer consider it unfair. To consider the evidence in the present case did not require knowledge of the traditions or social circumstances of a particular racial group (even though there was a racial element to the offence); rather it was a common situation of violence outside a club. The reasoning of the court appears to leave open the possibility that the judge might be allowed take steps to include ethnic minority representation on the jury if the case were one that required such knowledge.

In light of the rule that a judge cannot use the power of stand by to try to achieve a racially balanced jury, it has been a source of concern that juries do not necessarily represent the ethnic diversity of our society. It is not uncommon, for example, for a defendant to be tried by 12 people none of whom shares his ethnicity. The Auld Review said that provision should be made to enable ethnic minority representation on juries where race is likely to be relevant to an important issue in the case (not on the basis that people have a right to have represented on the jury someone from their background but on the basis of studies suggesting that white juries are, or are perceived to be, less fair to black than to white people). Recommendation 25 of the Review suggests that:

> A scheme should be devised ... for cases in which the court considers that race is likely to be relevant to an issue of importance in the case, for the selection of a jury consisting of, say, up to three people from any ethnic minority group.

The detail of this proposal is set out in paras 60 and 61 of Chapter 5 of the Review:

> The parties could be required to indicate early in their preparation for the pre-trial assessment whether race is likely to be a relevant issue and, if so, whether steps should be taken to attempt to secure some ethnic minority representation on the jury. This could be done by the empanelment of a larger number of jurors than normal from which the jury for the case is to be selected, some of whom would be identified by their juror cards as from ethnic minorities ... The first nine selected would be called to serve and, if they did not include a minimum of – say three – ethnic minority jurors, the remainder would be stood down until the minimum was reached ...
>
> 61 ... the judge's ruling would be for a racially diverse jury in the form that I have suggested, not that it should contain representatives of the particular ethnic background on either side.

This proposal was not acted upon in the Criminal Justice Act 2003.

10.8.3 Discharge of individual jurors during the trial

A jury always starts off with 12 jurors. However, under s 16 of the Juries Act 1974, up to three jurors may be discharged during the course of the trial in case of illness or other necessity (for example, bereavement).

What constitutes necessity is a matter for the trial judge. In *R v Hambery* [1977] 1 QB 924, a juror was discharged because the trial went on longer than expected and she would otherwise have had to cancel a holiday.

If more than three jurors can no longer serve, the trial has to be abandoned; a fresh trial will take place later.

10.8.4 Discharge of the entire jury

The entire jury may be discharged if, for example:

- the jury hears evidence which is inadmissible and prejudicial to the defendant and the judge decides that a direction to ignore this evidence would not be sufficient. Where something prejudicial to the defendant has inadvertently been admitted in evidence, it is not necessarily the case that the jury should be discharged; whether or not the jury should be discharged is a matter for the discretion of the trial judge (*R v Weaver and Weaver* (1967) 51 Cr App R 77); the test to be applied is the usual test for bias, namely whether there is real possibility or real danger of injustice occurring because the jury, having heard the prejudicial matter, would be biased against the accused (*R v Docherty* [1999] 1 Cr App R 274);

- the jury cannot agree on a verdict (see below);
- an individual juror has to be discharged and there is a risk that he may have contaminated the rest of the jury (for example, he happens to know that the defendant has previous convictions or is facing further trials for other offences) (*R v Hutton* [1990] Crim LR 875).

If members of the jury misbehave during the course of the trial, the jury should be discharged if there is a 'real danger of prejudice' to the accused (*R v Spencer* [1987] AC 128). In *R v Sawyer* (1980) 71 Cr App R 283, for example, some jurors were seen in conversation with prosecution witnesses during an adjournment. The trial judge questioned them and it transpired that the conversation had been on subjects unconnected with the trial. The decision of the judge not to discharge the jury was upheld by the Court of Appeal.

Where a juror has specialised knowledge of something relevant to the case against the defendant, and has communicated that knowledge to the rest of the jury, the judge is obliged to discharge the jury if this comes to light at a stage of the trial such that the defendant has had no opportunity to challenge what amounts to new evidence or to put forward his own explanation (*R v Fricker* (1999) 96(30) LSG 29).

In *R v Blackwell* [1995] 2 Cr App R 625, the Court of Appeal gave guidance on the approach to be taken by a judge where there is a suspicion that a member of the public has tried to influence members of the jury. The member of the public should be questioned by the judge (or by court officials or police at the direction of the judge) and, if it appears that there has been an attempt to influence the jurors, the jurors should be questioned to establish if their independence has been compromised. Only after a full investigation has been completed does the judge have sufficient information to decide whether any or all of the jurors should be discharged.

Where the jury is discharged from giving a verdict, the defendant can be retried, as he is not regarded as having been acquitted.

10.8.5 Composition of the jury as a ground of appeal

Composition of the jury as a ground of appeal is dealt with in Chapter 12.

10.9 SPECIAL MEASURES DIRECTIONS AND LIVE LINKS

In this section, we look at the measures which can be adopted to help witnesses who might otherwise find it difficult to testify and the use of live links to enable a witness to testify from outside the courtroom.

10.9.1 Special measures directions

Sections 16–33 of the Youth Justice and Criminal Evidence Act 1999 contain provision for various 'special measures' which the court can direct in respect of certain witnesses, including:

- screening the witness from the accused (s 23);
- giving evidence by live link (s 24) (this provision will become less relevant, as s 51 of the Criminal Justice Act 2003 enables a court to authorise witnesses, other than the defendant, to give evidence through a live link in criminal proceedings);
- ordering the removal of wigs and gowns while the witness gives evidence (s 25);
- giving evidence in private, in a sexual case or where there is a fear that the witness may be intimidated (s 26);
- video recording of evidence-in-chief (s 27) (again, this provision is made less relevant, as s 137 of the Criminal Justice Act 2003 extends the circumstances in which evidence-in-chief can take the form of a video recorded statement);
- video recording of cross-examination and re-examination where the evidence-in-chief of the witness has been video recorded (s 28);
- examination through an intermediary in the case of a young or incapacitated witness (s 29);
- provision of aids to communication for a young or incapacitated witness (s 30).

The procedure for making an application for special measures is contained in the Crown Court (Special Measures Directions and Directions Prohibiting Cross-examination) Rules 2002 (SI 2002/1688). Applications in the magistrates' court are dealt with by the Magistrates' Courts (Special Measures Directions) Rules 2002 (SI 2002/1687).

Such application has to be made in the prescribed form (set out in the Schedule to the Rules). The other parties to the proceedings may then serve notice of opposition to the application. There will then be a hearing to determine the application. The rules also contain provision for applications to vary or discharge a special measures direction (see s 20 of the 1999 Act); such applications must be based on a material change of circumstances since the direction was made. Also, where an application for a special measures direction has been refused by the court, the application may be renewed if there is a material change of circumstances since the court refused the application.

In *R (S) v Waltham Forest Youth Court* [2004] EWHC 715 (Admin); (2004) 168 JP 293, the Divisional Court held that there is no power to make a special measures direction in relation to the evidence of the accused. It was, said the court, Parliament's clear intention to exclude defendants from those provisions. The court observed that this view was not incompatible with Art 6 of the European Convention on Human Rights, since it does not in any way derogate from the powers and safeguards already in place under the provisions of domestic law (see s 19 of the 1999 Act). Special measures do not restrict the rights of defendants but augment the protection available for other witnesses. In any event, there remains the obligation to ensure a fair trial and, in particular, to see that a defendant does not suffer injustice through inequality of arms. The court added that no power exists to make an order enabling the accused to testify via a video link under any inherent or common law power.

In *R v Brown* [2004] EWCA Crim 1401, the appeal concerned a special measures direction whereby two witnesses were permitted to give evidence from behind screens but a third witness did not wish to do so; also, the applications for special measures were not made within the 28 day time limit envisaged in r 2(4) of the Rules. The Court of Appeal held that, provided that the jury are correctly instructed as to the implications of the use of screens, the fact that one witness gives evidence without screens does not require the rest to so as well; it is a matter for the judge to determine whether the justice of the case, fairness to the defendants and fairness to the witnesses require or permit him to allow them to give evidence in different ways. It was also held that the time limits provided for by the Rules are not mandatory, but are directory; any significant handicap to the defence by a late application is for the judge to take very carefully into account; the Rules apply to all special measures, including the giving of evidence by video recording; in such cases, there are obvious reasons why applications for special measures should be made well in advance, but the 28 day lead-in is much less necessary where screens are to be used. The court added that where a special measures direction has been given to the jury before a witness gave evidence, the judge is not required to repeat the direction in the summing up. The question is whether the judge had got across to the jury effectively the essential matter of the use of screens and the conclusions that should and should not be drawn therefrom. Doing so is much more likely to impress itself on the jury if it is given at the time of the witness' evidence than if it is repeated on a later date in the summing up. Further, any reversion to the matter might, in some cases, give it more emphasis (derogatory to the defendant) than it deserves.

Rule 7 in each set of Rules deals with applications for special measures directions for witnesses to give evidence by means of a live television link. A party who seeks to oppose an application for a child witness to give evidence by means of a live link must state why, in his view, the giving of a special measures direction would not be likely to maximise the quality of the witness's evidence (unless the application relates to a child witness in need of special protection within the meaning of s 21(1)(b) of the 1999 Act, in which case this provision does not apply). Rule 7 goes on to state that where a special measures direction is made enabling a witness to give evidence by means of a live link, the witness must be accompanied at the live link only by persons acceptable to the court.

Rule 8 in each set of rules deals with video recording of testimony from witnesses. Where an application is made for a special measures direction enabling a video recording of an interview of a witness to be admitted as evidence-in-chief of the witness, the application must be accompanied by the video recording which it is proposed to tender in evidence and must include (under r 8(2)):

(a)   the name of the defendant and the offence to be charged;

(b)   the name and date of birth of the witness in respect of whom the application is made;

(c)   the date on which the video recording was made;

(d)   a statement as to whether, and if so at what point in the video recording, an oath was administered to, or a solemn declaration made by, the witness;

(e)   a statement that, in the opinion of the applicant, either—

   (i)   the witness is available for cross-examination; or

   (ii) the witness is not available for cross-examination and the parties have agreed that there is no need for the witness to be so available;

(f)   a statement of the circumstances in which the video recording was made which complies with [r 8(4)]; and

(g)   the date on which the video recording was disclosed to the other party or parties.

Under r 8(4):

> The statement of the circumstances in which the video recording was made referred to in paragraphs (2)(f) and (3) above shall include the following information, except in so far as it is contained in the recording itself—
>
> (a) the times at which the recording commenced and finished, including details of interruptions;
>
> (b) the location at which the recording was made and the usual function of the premises;
>
> (c) in relation to each person present at any point during, or immediately before, the recording—
>
>   (i)   their name, age and occupation;
>
>   (ii) the time for which each person was present; and
>
>   (iii) the relationship, if any, of each person to the witness and to the defendant;
>
> (d) in relation to the equipment used for the recording—
>
>   (i)   a description of the equipment;
>
>   (ii) the number of cameras used;
>
>   (iii) whether the cameras were fixed or mobile;
>
>   (iv) the number and location of the microphones;
>
>   (v)   the video format used; and
>
>   (vi) whether it offered single or multiple recording facilities and, if so, which were used; and
>
> (e) the location of the mastertape if the video recording is a copy and details of when and by whom the copy was made.

Where a party opposes the use of the video recording, he must lodge a notice giving reasons why it would not be in the interests of justice for the recording (or part of it) to be admitted.

Rule 8(6) stipulates that any video recording which the defendant proposes to tender in evidence need not be sent to the prosecution until the close of the prosecution case at the trial.

Under r 9 of both sets of Rules, a party who proposes to adduce expert evidence (whether of fact or opinion) in connection with an application or renewal application for, or for varying or discharging, a special measures direction must furnish the other party or parties to the proceedings with a statement in writing of any finding or opinion which he proposes to adduce by way of such evidence and (if the other party so requests) provide a reasonable opportunity to examine the record of any observation, test, calculation or other procedure on which the finding or opinion is based.

Section 29 of the Youth Justice and Criminal Evidence Act 1999 allows, as part of the special measures provision, for the use of intermediaries to facilitate communication with witnesses with special communication difficulties. Section 29, which was brought into force in February 2004, specifies that:

> ... the function of an intermediary is to communicate:
>
> (a) to the witness, questions put to the witness;
>
> (b) to any persons asking such questions, the answers given by the witness in reply to them,

and to explain such questions and answers so far as necessary to enable them to be understood by the witness or person in question.

Such intermediaries have to be professionally experienced in their own specialist area of communication, and are subject to a Code of Practice and a Code of Ethics (see www.homeoffice.gov.uk/docs2/intermediaryrole.pdf).

The Crown Court (Special Measures Directions and Directions Prohibiting Cross-examination) (Amendment) Rules 2004 (SI 2004/185) and the Magistrates' Courts (Special Measures Directions) (Amendment) Rules 2004 (SI 2004/184) contain detailed procedural rules for governing use of intermediaries.

10.9.2   Evidence through television link/pre-recorded video

Part 8 of the Criminal Justice Act 2003 extends the circumstances where live links can be used. A 'live link' (defined in s 56(2)) will usually mean a closed circuit television link, but could apply to any technology with the same effect, such as video-conferencing facilities or the internet. Section 51 provides as follows:

(1)   A witness (other than the defendant) may, if the court so directs, give evidence through a live link in the following criminal proceedings.

(2)   They are—

   (a) a summary trial,

   (b) an appeal to the Crown Court arising out of such a trial,

   (c) a trial on indictment,

   (d) an appeal to the criminal division of the Court of Appeal,

   (e) the hearing of a reference under section 9 or 11 of the Criminal Appeal Act 1995,

   (f) a hearing before a magistrates' court or the Crown Court which is held after the defendant has entered a plea of guilty, and

   (g) a hearing before the Court of Appeal under section 80 of this Act.

(3)   A direction may be given under this section—

   (a) on an application by a party to the proceedings, or

   (b) of the court's own motion.

(4)   But a direction may not be given under this section unless—

   (a) the court is satisfied that it is in the interests of the efficient or effective administration of justice for the person concerned to give evidence in the proceedings through a live link,

...

(6)   In deciding whether to give a direction under this section the court must consider all the circumstances of the case.

(7)   Those circumstances include in particular—

   (a) the availability of the witness,

   (b) the need for the witness to attend in person,

   (c) the importance of the witness's evidence to the proceedings,

   (d) the views of the witness,

     (e) the suitability of the facilities at the place where the witness would give evidence through a live link,

     (f) whether a direction might tend to inhibit any party to the proceedings from effectively testing the witness's evidence.

(8)   The court must state in open court its reasons for refusing an application for a direction under this section and, if it is a magistrates' court, must cause them to be entered in the register of its proceedings.

Thus, for example, a witness may be able to give evidence from his place of work in a different part of the UK rather than have to travel to court.

Under s 52(2), where the court has given a direction under s 51 for a person to give evidence through a live link in particular proceedings, the person concerned may not give evidence in those proceedings after the direction is given otherwise than through a live link unless (under s 52(3)) the court rescinds the direction (which it can do, on the application of a party or of its own motion, if it appears to the court to be in the interests of justice to do so).

Section 54 empowers a judge in the Crown Court to give the jury 'such direction as he thinks necessary to ensure that the jury gives the same weight to the evidence as if it had been given by the witness in the courtroom or other place where the proceedings are held'.

Section 137(1) of the Criminal Justice Act 2003 also extends the cases where evidence can be given by means of a video recording. It empowers the court to allow a video recording of an interview with a witness (other than the defendant), or a part of such a recording, to be admitted as evidence-in-chief of the witness (that is, to replace live evidence-in-chief of that witness) provided that the person is called as a witness in proceedings for an offence which is triable only on indictment, or for an either way offence prescribed in regulations made under the section, and:

     (b) the person claims to have witnessed (whether visually or in any other way)—

         (i) events alleged by the prosecution to include conduct constituting the offence or part of the offence; or

         (ii) events closely connected with such events;

     (c) he has previously given an account of the events in question (whether in response to questions asked or otherwise);

     (d) the account was given at a time when those events were fresh in the person's memory (or would have been, assuming the truth of the claim mentioned in paragraph (b));

     (e) a video recording was made of the account;

     (f) the court has made a direction that the recording should be admitted as evidence in chief of the witness, and the direction has not been rescinded; and

     (g) the recording is played in the proceedings in accordance with the direction.

    ...

(3)   A direction under sub-section (1)(f)—

     (a) may not be made in relation to a recorded account given by the defendant;

     (b) may be made only if it appears to the court that—

         (i) the witness's recollection of the events in question is likely to have been significantly better when he gave the recorded account than it will be when he gives oral evidence in the proceedings; and

         (ii) it is in the interests of justice for the recording to be admitted, having regard in particular to the matters mentioned in sub-section (4).

(4) Those matters are—

    (a) the interval between the time of the events in question and the time when the recorded account was made;

    (b) any other factors that might affect the reliability of what the witness said in that account;

    (c) the quality of the recording;

    (d) any views of the witness as to whether his evidence in chief should be given orally or by means of the recording.

(5) For the purposes of sub-section (2) it does not matter if the statements in the recorded account were not made on oath.

Section 138 stipulates that where a video recording has been admitted into evidence under s 137, the witness cannot give examination-in-chief in any other way.

CHAPTER 11

CROWN COURT TRIAL –
THE COURSE OF THE TRIAL

11.1   THE START OF THE TRIAL

Once the jury has been empanelled, the prosecution present their case. Counsel for the prosecution begins by making an opening speech.

11.1.1   Content of the prosecution opening speech

In the opening speech, the prosecution remind the jury of the offences to which the defendant has pleaded not guilty. If those offences are complicated, the prosecution will summarise the relevant legal principles (making it clear that the judge is the final arbiter of the law). It should also be made clear at this stage that the prosecution bear the burden of proof and that the jury must be satisfied so that they are sure in order to convict. Prosecutors normally indicate who they will be calling as witnesses and how these witnesses fit into the overall story. The purpose of the opening speech is to enable the jury to make sense of the evidence that they will now be hearing.

In most cases, any questions of admissibility of evidence should be dealt with at the plea and directions hearing (PDH). However, if this has not happened, and counsel for the defence has indicated to the prosecution before the start of the trial that the defence will be challenging the admissibility of some of the prosecution evidence, the opening speech by the prosecution should make no mention of that evidence. If, however, the evidence in dispute is so crucial to the prosecution case that an opening speech cannot be made without referring to it, the jury will be sent out of the court room and the admissibility of this evidence will be determined before the trial begins. Usually, where such crucial evidence is ruled inadmissible at the outset, the prosecution would have little choice but to abandon the case.

11.2   THE PROSECUTION CASE

If the defendant pleads not guilty, the prosecution are put to proof of their entire case, and so must adduce evidence on all the elements of the alleged offence(s).

The only exception to this rule is where the defence make a formal admission so that something which would otherwise be in issue is no longer an issue.

11.2.1   Formal admissions

Under s 10 of the Criminal Justice Act 1967, the prosecution or the defence (in practice, usually the defence) may admit any fact which would otherwise be in issue; this admission is conclusive evidence of the fact admitted. If, for example, the defendant is charged with causing death by dangerous driving, he might admit that he was driving the car at the time of the accident.

In the Crown Court, the admission may be made in writing (in which case, it will be signed by the person making it) or orally in court by counsel. In the magistrates' court, a formal admission must be made in writing.

Formal admissions are not made very frequently. It is usually apparent from questions asked in cross-examination if some of what the witness says is accepted by the defence. If all of the evidence of a particular witness is accepted by the defence, the defence will consent to that witness's statement being read to the court.

11.2.2 Prosecution witnesses

The prosecution witnesses whose written statements the defence do not allow to be read to the court each give evidence. Evidence is usually given under oath, the witness saying 'I swear by almighty God that the evidence I shall give shall be the truth, the whole truth, and nothing but the truth'. A witness who does not wish to take the oath may affirm instead, promising to tell the truth.

Each witness is examined-in-chief by the prosecution (who are not allowed to ask leading questions, that is, questions which contain or suggest their own answer), then cross-examined by the defence, and (if necessary) re-examined by the prosecution (the rule against leading questions applying to re-examination as well).

Where a witness made a contemporaneous note of the matters on which he is about to give evidence, it is open to the party calling that witness to apply to the judge for the witness to be given permission to refresh his memory by referring to those notes (*R v Da Silva* [1990] 1 WLR 31). This is invariably done to enable police officers to refer to their notebooks while giving evidence. In *R v South Ribble Stipendiary Magistrate ex p Cochrane* [1996] 2 Cr App R 544, the Divisional Court held that the court also has a discretion to permit a witness to refresh his memory from a non-contemporaneous document; judges (and magistrates) must consider the requirements of fairness and justice in exercising that discretion. Section 139 of the Criminal Justice Act 2003 (in force since April 2004) puts this on a statutory footing. Section 139(1) provides that:

> A person giving oral evidence in criminal proceedings about any matter may, at any stage in the course of doing so, refresh his memory of it from a document made or verified by him at an earlier time if—
>
> (a) he states in his oral evidence that the document records his recollection of the matter at that earlier time, and
>
> (b) his recollection of the matter is likely to have been significantly better at that time than it is as the time of his oral evidence.

Section 139(2) allows a witness to refresh his memory from the transcript of a sound recording in the same circumstances.

11.2.3 Reading witness statements

Section 9 of the Criminal Justice Act 1967 provides as follows:

> (1) In any criminal proceedings, a written statement by any person shall, if such of the conditions mentioned in the next following sub-section as are applicable are satisfied, be admissible as evidence to the like extent as oral evidence to the like effect by that person.

(2)   The said conditions are—

    (a) the statement purports to be signed by the person who made it;

    (b) the statement contains a declaration by that person to the effect that it is true to the best of his knowledge and belief and that he made the statement knowing that, if it were tendered in evidence, he would be liable to prosecution if he wilfully stated in it anything which he knew to be false or did not believe to be true;

    (c) before the hearing at which the statement is tendered in evidence, a copy of the statement is served, by or on behalf of the party proposing to tender it, on each of the other parties to the proceedings; and

    (d) none of the other parties or their solicitors, within seven days from the service of the copy of the statement, serves a notice on the party so proposing objecting to the statement being tendered in evidence under this section:

Provided that the conditions mentioned in paragraphs (c) and (d) of this sub-section shall not apply if the parties agree before or during the hearing that the statement shall be so tendered.

This provision will be used, for example, where the defence in a theft case is not that the property was not stolen but that the defendant was not the thief: the evidence of the loser of the property, saying that the property is his and that he gave no-one permission to take it, will not therefore be disputed by the defence and so the written statement of the loser will be read out to the court. The judge should direct the jury that a statement read out under this provision has the same evidential value as 'live' testimony.

11.2.4   Section 23 of the Criminal Justice Act 1988

Section 23 of the Criminal Justice Act 1988 allows a written statement to be used in place of oral evidence without the consent of the defence in any of the following instances:

- the person who made the statement is dead or by reason of his bodily or mental condition unfit to attend as a witness (s 23(2)(a)); or

- the person who made the statement is outside the UK and it is not reasonably practicable to secure his attendance (s 23(2)(b)); or

- all reasonable steps have been taken to find the person who made the statement, but he cannot be found (s 23(2)(c)); or

- the statement was made to a police officer or some other person charged with the duty of investigating offences or charging offenders, and the person who made it does not give oral evidence through fear or because he is kept out of the way (s 23(3)).

It should be noted that, where fear is relied on, that fear must be proved by admissible evidence. Thus, in *Neill v North Antrim Magistrates' Court* [1992] 1 WLR 1221, the House of Lords held that this provision could not be relied upon to admit the written statements of two boys where a police officer gave evidence that the mother of the boys had told him that they were in fear; it would have been different if the officer had been able to give evidence that the boys themselves had told him that they were in fear. Similarly, in *R v Belmarsh Magistrates' Court ex p Gilligan* [1998] 1 Cr App R 14, the

Divisional Court held that, in order to satisfy the requirements of s 23, the court must hear oral evidence (for example, from a police officer) as to the fear of the witness: the fear cannot be proved by a written statement made by the witness who claims to be in fear.

In *R v Ricketts* [1991] Crim LR 915, it was said that the jury must not be told that a statement is being read to them on the ground that the maker of the statement is absent because of fear for his personal safety resulting from threats by the accused. Obviously this would be extremely prejudicial to the defendant.

In *R v Waters* (1997) 161 JP 249, the victim of an assault made a statement to the police in which he identified the appellant as one of his assailants. At the appellant's trial, the witness started to give evidence but then ceased to give evidence through fear, saying that he could not now remember what had happened and could not identify his assailants. The Court of Appeal (following *R v Ashford Justices ex p Hilden* [1993] QB 555) upheld the decision of the trial judge to allow the witness's earlier statement to be read to the jury under s 23. The court said that what mattered was whether or not there was, at the time when s 23 was invoked, any relevant oral evidence which the witness was still expected to give. If there is such evidence, and it was proved beyond reasonable doubt that he did not give that evidence through fear, s 23 is satisfied.

Section 25 of the Criminal Justice Act 1988 gives the court a discretion to exclude evidence which would otherwise be admissible under s 23 of that Act. Section 25(2) provides that:

> ... it shall be the duty of the court to have regard—
>
> (a)   to the nature and source of the document containing the statement and to whether or not, having regard to its nature and source and to any other circumstances that appear to the court to be relevant, it is likely that the document is authentic;
>
> (b)   to the extent to which the statement appears to supply evidence which would otherwise not be readily available;
>
> (c)   to the relevance of the evidence that it appears to supply to any issue which is likely to have to be determined in the proceedings; and
>
> (d)   to any risk, having regard in particular to whether it is likely to be possible to controvert the statement if the person making it does not attend to give oral evidence in the proceedings, that its admission or exclusion will result in unfairness to the accused or, if there is more than one, to any of them.

Section 26 of the same Act provides as follows:

> Where a statement which is admissible in criminal proceedings by virtue of section 23 or 24 above appears to the court to have been prepared ... for the purposes—
>
> (a)   of pending or contemplated criminal proceedings; or
>
> (b)   of a criminal investigation,
>
> the statement shall not be given in evidence in any criminal proceedings without the leave of the court, and the court shall not give leave unless it is of the opinion that the statement ought to be admitted in the interests of justice; and in considering whether its admission would be in the interests of justice, it shall be the duty of the court to have regard—

(i)   to the contents of the statement;

(ii)   to any risk, having regard in particular to whether it is likely to be possible to controvert the statement if the person making it does not attend to give oral evidence in the proceedings, that its admission or exclusion will result in unfairness to the accused or, if there is more than one, to any of them; and

(iii)   to any other circumstances that appear to the court to be relevant.

In *R v Arnold* [2004] EWCA Crim 1293, Leveson J (at para 30), referring to applications under s 23, said:

> Very great care must be taken in each and every case to ensure that attention is paid to the letter and spirit of the Convention and judges should not easily be persuaded that it is in the interests of justice to permit evidence to be read. Where that witness provides the sole or determinative evidence against the accused, permitting it to be read may well, depending on the circumstances, jeopardise infringing the defendant's Article 6(3)(d) rights; even if it is not the only evidence, care must be taken to ensure that the ultimate aim of each and every trial, namely, a fair hearing, is achieved.

The prosecution will not be allowed to invoke s 23 in respect of crucial evidence or where there would be another way of getting the evidence before the court. In *R v Radak* [1999] 1 Cr App R 187, the trial judge allowed a witness statement to be read to the jury under s 23 on the basis that the maker of the statement was in the United States and would not come to court to give evidence through fear. The Court of Appeal held that this decision was wrong. The witness's evidence was an essential link in the prosecution case and the defence had little or no evidence to controvert the contents of the statement; it would therefore be unfair to admit that evidence without the defence being able to cross-examine the witness. Furthermore, the prosecution had known from the outset that the witness might not attend voluntarily, and so should have taken steps to have his evidence taken in the United States. The witness statement should therefore not have been admitted.

Where the prosecution seek to adduce the written statement of a witness on the ground that the witness is unfit through illness to attend, the defence should ordinarily be given the opportunity to cross-examine the doctor who provides support for the application. If the defence dispute the unfitness of the witness, the prosecution cannot rely on a written statement setting out the doctor's view that the witness is unfit (*R v Elliott* [2003] EWCA Crim 1695; (2003) *The Times*, 15 May).

Where a statement is read to the jury without the consent of the defence, the jury should be warned that the evidence needs to be viewed in light of the fact that the defence have not had the opportunity to cross-examine the witness. It is not sufficient simply to draw the jury's attention to the fact that evidence has been given by way of a witness statement. The jury should be warned to use particular care when considering the witness statement, since the maker of the statement was not in court to be cross-examined as to its contents. Where the witness statement is vital to the prosecution case, failure to give such a direction will render any subsequent conviction unsafe (*R v Curry* (1998) *The Times*, 23 March).

Article 6(3)(d) of the European Convention on Human Rights guarantees the right to examine and call witnesses. The admission of hearsay evidence without an opportunity for the defence to cross-examine may render the trial unfair if the conviction is based wholly or mainly on such evidence (*Unterpertinger v Austria* (1991) 13 EHRR 175). This may cause problems where s 23 is relied on, though the judge's discretion to exclude the evidence may be held to be a sufficient safeguard.

The provisions of the Criminal Justice Act 1988 will be replaced by Chapter 2 of Pt 11 of the Criminal Justice Act 2003 when those provisions are brought into force. In particular, s 116(2)(e) will make an out-of-court statement admissible if 'through fear the relevant person does not give (or does not continue to give) oral evidence in the proceedings, either at all or in connection with the subject-matter of the statement, and the court gives leave for the statement to be given in evidence'. Section 116(4) provides that in deciding whether to give leave under s 116(2)(e), the court must have regard to the risk that the admission or exclusion of the statement 'will result in unfairness to any party to the proceedings (and in particular to how difficult it will be to challenge the statement if the relevant person does not give oral evidence)' and to the fact that, in appropriate cases, a special measures direction under the Youth Justice and Criminal Evidence Act 1999 could be made (thus removing the need for s 116(2)(e) to be invoked).

11.2.5 Real evidence

Real evidence means tangible evidence such as the murder weapon or the stolen goods. An item of real evidence has to be produced (that is, identified and its relevance established) by a witness. Once this has been done, counsel says to the judge 'may this be exhibit [number]?' and (assuming the judge agrees) the item then becomes an exhibit in the case. Exhibits are numbered sequentially.

11.3 CHALLENGING THE ADMISSIBILITY OF PROSECUTION EVIDENCE

If the defence object to some of the prosecution evidence, arguing that it is inadmissible, this matter may be dealt with at the pre-trial hearing (at which the judge is empowered to give binding rulings on the admissibility of evidence). Otherwise, the objection is made (in the absence of the jury) during the course of the trial. If the objection is made during the course of the trial, the prosecution evidence is called in the usual way until the part of the evidence to which there is objection is reached. At that point the jury is invited to retire to the jury room.

Although s 82 of the Police and Criminal Evidence Act 1984 (PACE) expressly preserved the common law rules on the admissibility of evidence, objections to prosecution evidence are usually made under s 76 or 78 of PACE.

11.3.1 Section 76 of the Police and Criminal Evidence Act 1984

Section 76 of PACE provides as follows:

(1) In any proceedings a confession made by an accused person may be given in evidence against him in so far as it is relevant to any matter in issue in the proceedings and is not excluded by the court in pursuance of this section.

(2) If, in any proceedings where the prosecution proposes to give in evidence a confession made by an accused person, it is represented to the court that the confession was or may have been obtained—

    (a) by oppression of the person who made it; or

    (b) in consequence of anything said or done which was likely, in the circumstances existing at the time, to render unreliable any confession which might be made by him in consequence thereof,

the court shall not allow the confession to be given in evidence against him except in so far as the prosecution proves to the court beyond reasonable doubt that the confession (notwithstanding that it may be true) was not obtained as aforesaid.

(3) In any proceedings where the prosecution proposes to give in evidence a confession made by an accused person, the court may of its own motion require the prosecution, as a condition of allowing it to do so, to prove that the confession was not obtained as mentioned in sub-section (2) above.

...

(8) In this section 'oppression' includes torture, inhuman or degrading treatment, and the use or threat of violence (whether or not amounting to torture).

Thus, where the defence allege that a confession has been obtained by oppression or in circumstances likely to render it unreliable, the prosecution must prove beyond reasonable doubt that the confession was not so obtained. The requirement for the prosecution to prove this means that they must call evidence on the point and so a *voir dire* ('trial within a trial') takes place.

Unless the witness is in the middle of giving (or has already given) evidence in the course of the trial, a witness giving evidence on a *voir dire* takes a special form of oath: 'I swear by almighty God that I will answer truthfully all such questions as the court may ask.'

Each prosecution witness called in the *voir dire* may be cross-examined by the defence. When the relevant prosecution witnesses have given evidence, the defence may call evidence (including the evidence of the defendant himself); each defence witness may be cross-examined by the prosecution.

After the evidence has been called, both counsels may address the judge and the judge then rules on the admissibility of the confession.

The only question to be determined under s 76 is *how* the confession was obtained. It is wholly irrelevant whether the confession was true or not.

If the defence case is simply that the police have fabricated the confession, that is a matter for the jury to decide and not a question of admissibility. However, there are cases where the defence allege that the confession has been fabricated but also argue that, even if that was not so, the confession is inadmissible anyway. In *Thongjai v The Queen* [1998] AC 54, the Privy Council (following *Ajodha v The State* [1982] AC 204) said that if the defendant denies confessing and also alleges that he was ill treated by the police before or at the time of the alleged confession, the two issues are not mutually exclusive. The judge has to assume that the admission was made and decide whether it is admissible; if (and only if) the judge decides that the evidence is admissible, it is for the jury to decide whether the admission was in fact made.

Where a judge conducts a *voir dire* and holds that a confession is admissible, the judge should not tell the jury of the ruling (the trial should simply continue with the prosecution leading evidence of the confession); if the judge indicates that he has ruled against the accused, this might lead the jury to think that the judge does not believe the accused (*Mitchell v The Queen* [1998] AC 695).

11.3.2 Section 78 of the Police and Criminal Evidence Act 1984

Section 78(1) of PACE provides as follows:

> In any proceedings the court may refuse to allow evidence on which the prosecution proposes to rely to be given if it appears to the court that, having regard to all the circumstances, including the circumstances in which the evidence was obtained, the admission of the evidence would have such an adverse effect on the fairness of the proceedings that the court ought not to admit it.

Where the defence object to prosecution evidence on the ground that its admission would be unfairly prejudicial, this objection is made in the absence of the jury but need not involve the judge hearing evidence. In other words, a *voir dire* need not take place if the judge is able to decide the question of admissibility under s 78 just by hearing legal argument from counsel and without hearing evidence. This will be the case, for example, where the breach of provisions of the Codes of Practice made under PACE are apparent from the custody record and/or the witness statements of the prosecution witnesses and the judge merely has to decide the effect of those breaches (*R v Keenan* [1990] 2 QB 54).

11.3.3 The European Convention on Human Rights

Under the European Convention on Human Rights, there is no absolute requirement that illegally obtained evidence should be excluded, but use of such evidence may give rise to unfairness in a particular case (*Schenck v Switzerland* (1991) 13 EHRR 242). Section 78 of PACE appears to accord with this principle.

Admission of a confession which was obtained through maltreatment will inevitably violate Art 6. Section 76 of the 1984 Act accords with this principle.

11.4 WITNESSES WHOM THE PROSECUTION MUST CALL

The prosecution must call all the witnesses whose statements were served on the defence when the case was transferred to the Crown Court (*R v Balmforth* [1992] Crim LR 825). The exceptions to this rule are as follows:

- the defence consent to the written statement of the witness being read to the court (under s 9 of the Criminal Justice Act 1967); or
- the prosecution take the view that the witness is no longer credible (*R v Oliva* [1965] 1 WLR 1028); or
- the witness would so fundamentally contradict the prosecution case that it would be better for that witness to be called by the defence (*R v Nugent* [1977] 1 WLR 789).

These principles were restated in *R v Armstrong* [1995] Crim LR 831 and *R v Russell-Jones* [1995] 3 All ER 239.

In *R v Cairns* [2002] EWCA Crim 2838; [2003] 1 WLR 796, the appeal was based partly on the fact that the prosecution had called a witness, part of whose evidence the prosecutor conceded to be unreliable. The Court of Appeal rejected this ground of appeal, holding that the overriding consideration in the exercise of the prosecution's discretion as to whether to call a witness is the interests of justice. As there is no reason

why a jury should not accept the evidence of a witness in part only, there is no principle of law which requires the prosecution to regard the whole of a witness's evidence as reliable before calling that person to testify. If the prosecution consider that part of the evidence of a witness is capable of belief, then, even though they might not rely upon other parts of his evidence, it is a proper exercise of their discretion to call the witness. The court said that, since part of the evidence of the witness might be of assistance to the jury in performing its task, it would be contrary to the interests of justice to deprive them of that assistance.

11.4.1   Tendering witnesses for cross-examination

If a witness simply duplicates the evidence of another witness, the prosecution may simply 'tender' that witness, that is, call him, establish his identity and relevance to the case, and then invite the defence to cross-examine. This is often done with police witnesses, where the evidence of one officer largely repeats that of another.

11.5   SUBMISSION OF NO CASE TO ANSWER

After the close of the prosecution case, the defence may make a submission that there is no case to answer. This submission is made in the absence of the jury, who might otherwise be prejudiced against the defendant if the submission fails (*R v Smith* (1986) 85 Cr App R 197; *Crosdale v R* [1995] 2 All ER 500).

11.5.1   Principles applied to submission of no case to answer

The principles governing this submission are to be found in *R v Galbraith* [1981] 1 WLR 1039 (*per* Lord Lane CJ) at p 1042:

How then should the judge approach a submission of 'no case'?

(1)   If there is no evidence that the crime alleged has been committed by the defendant, there is no difficulty. The judge will of course stop the case.

(2)   The difficulty arises where there is some evidence but it is of a tenuous character, for example because of inherent weakness or vagueness or because it is inconsistent with other evidence:

(a)   Where the judge comes to the conclusion that the prosecution evidence, taken at its highest, is such that a jury properly directed could not properly convict upon it, it is his duty, upon a submission being made, to stop the case.

(b)   Where however the prosecution evidence is such that its strength or weakness depends on the view to be taken of a witness's reliability, or other matters which are generally speaking within the province of the jury and where on one possible view of the facts there is evidence upon which a jury could properly come to the conclusion that the defendant is guilty, then the judge should allow the matter to be tried by the jury. It follows that we think the second of the two schools of thought is to be preferred.

There will of course, as always in this branch of the law, be borderline cases. They can safely be left to the discretion of the judge.

Two key principles flow from this:

(a) if the judge comes to the conclusion that the prosecution evidence, taken at its highest, is such that a jury properly directed could not properly convict upon it, it is his duty to hold that there is no case to answer; and

(b) if the strength or weakness of the prosecution evidence depends on the view to be taken of a witness's reliability, and on one possible view there is evidence on which a jury could properly convict, the judge should allow the matter to be tried by the jury.

Thus, a judge should only accept a submission of no case to answer in a clear case; otherwise he is trespassing on the function of the jury.

However, a judge may take account of the credibility of the prosecution evidence if no reasonable jury could believe that evidence. In *R v Shippey* [1988] Crim LR 767, for example, Turner J found no case to answer in a rape trial because of 'really significant inherent inconsistencies' in the complainant's uncorroborated evidence, which his Lordship found 'frankly incredible'. It follows that the judge can have regard to:

- the sheer improbability of what a witness says;
- internal inconsistencies in the testimony of a particular witness; and
- inconsistencies between one prosecution witness and another.

It should be noted that where identification is in issue, special rules apply. In *R v Turnbull* [1977] QB 224, the Court of Appeal said that a judge should withdraw an identification case from the jury if the quality of the identification is poor (taking into account the circumstances of the identification – length of view, distance, lighting, etc) and there is no other evidence supporting the correctness of the identification. This case is so widely used in the courts that it is worth quoting at length from the judgment of Lord Widgery CJ (at pp 228–31):

> First, whenever the case against an accused depends wholly or substantially on the correctness of one or more identifications of the accused which the defence alleges to be mistaken, the judge should warn the jury of the special need for caution before convicting the accused in reliance on the correctness of the identification or identifications. In addition he should instruct them as to the reason for the need for such a warning and should make some reference to the possibility that a mistaken witness can be a convincing one and that a number of such witnesses can all be mistaken. Provided this is done in clear terms the judge need not use any particular form of words.
>
> Secondly, the judge should direct the jury to examine closely the circumstances in which the identification by each witness came to be made. How long did the witness have the accused under observation? At what distance? In what light? Was the observation impeded in any way, as for example by passing traffic or a press of people? Had the witness ever seen the accused before? How often? If only occasionally, had he any special reason for remembering the accused? How long elapsed between the original observation and the subsequent identification to the police? Was there any material discrepancy between the description of the accused given to the police by the witness when first seen by them and his actual appearance? If in any case, whether it is being dealt with summarily or on indictment, the prosecution have reason to believe that there is such a material discrepancy they should supply the accused or his legal advisers with particulars of the description the police were first given. In all cases if the accused asks to be given particulars of such

descriptions, the prosecution should supply them. Finally, he should remind the jury of any specific weaknesses which had appeared in the identification evidence.

Recognition may be more reliable than identification of a stranger; but even when the witness is purporting to recognise someone whom he knows, the jury should be reminded that mistakes in recognition of close relatives and friends are sometimes made.

All these matters go to the quality of the identification evidence. If the quality is good and remains good at the close of the accused's case, the danger of a mistaken identification is lessened, but the poorer the quality, the greater the danger.

In our judgment when the quality is good, as for example when the identification is made after a long period of observation, or in satisfactory conditions by a relative, a neighbour, a close friend, a workmate and the like, the jury can safely be left to assess the value of the identifying evidence even though there is no other evidence to support it: provided always, however, that an adequate warning has been given about the special need for caution.

...

When, in the judgment of the trial judge, the quality of the identifying evidence is poor, as for example when it depends solely on a fleeting glance or on a longer observation made in difficult conditions, the situation is very different. The judge should then withdraw the case from the jury and direct an acquittal unless there is other evidence which goes to support the correctness of the identification.

...

The trial judge should identify to the jury the evidence which he adjudges is capable of supporting the evidence of identification. If there is any evidence or circumstances which the jury might think was supporting when it did not have this quality, the judge should say so.

...

Care should be taken by the judge when directing the jury about the support for an identification which may be derived from the fact that they have rejected an alibi. False alibis may be put forward for many reasons: an accused, for example, who has only his own truthful evidence to rely on may stupidly fabricate an alibi and get lying witnesses to support it out of fear that his own evidence will not be enough. Further, alibi witnesses can make genuine mistakes about dates and occasions like any other witnesses can. It is only when the jury is satisfied that the sole reason for the fabrication was to deceive them and there is no other explanation for its being put forward can fabrication provide any support for identification evidence. The jury should be reminded that proving the accused has told lies about where he was at the material time does not by itself prove that he was where the identifying witness says he was.

...

A failure to follow these guidelines is likely to result in a conviction being quashed and will do so if in the judgment of this court on all the evidence the verdict is either unsatisfactory or unsafe.

If the submission of no case to answer succeeds in respect of all the counts being tried, the judge directs the jury to acquit the defendant on all those counts. If the submission fails on all counts, the trial proceeds and the jury know nothing about the submission. If the submission succeeds on some, but not all, of the counts in the indictment, the

trial continues in respect of those counts in respect of which the judge has found there to be a case to answer; the jury are told that they are to consider only the counts that are left, and a formal acquittal on those counts where the submission succeeded will be directed when the jury give their verdict on the remaining counts (*R v Plain* [1976] 1 WLR 565).

If defence counsel notices a procedural error on the part of the prosecution, he should take the point at the outset, and not wait until the close of the prosecution case. For example, in *R v Gleeson* [2003] EWCA Crim 3357; [2004] 1 Cr App R 29, the defendant was charged with common law conspiracy. The charge was inappropriate and the trial judge accepted a submission of no case to answer. However, the judge also gave the prosecution leave to amend the indictment to allege statutory conspiracy. The Court of Appeal held that just as a defendant should not be penalised or unfairly prejudiced by faults or errors on the part of his legal representatives in the conduct of his defence, so also the prosecution should not be frustrated by errors on the part of the prosecutor, unless such errors have irremediably rendered a fair trial for the defendant impossible. It is, said the court, contrary to defence counsel's professional duty, and not in the legitimate interests of the defendant, to take advantage of procedural errors by the prosecution by delaying in identifying those errors as issues in the case until the last possible moment. Auld LJ, at para 36, says:

> ... we take the opportunity to repeat and adopt the extra-judicial sentiments of one of us in the Report of the Criminal Courts Review (October 2001), in paragraph 154 of Chapter 10: 'To the extent that the prosecution may legitimately wish to fill possible holes in its case once issues have been identified by the defence statement, it is understandable why as a matter of tactics a defendant might prefer to keep his case close to his chest. But that is not a valid reason for preventing a full and fair hearing on the issues canvassed at the trial. A criminal trial is not a game under which a guilty defendant should be provided with a sporting chance. It is a search for truth in accordance with the twin principles that the prosecution must prove its case and that a defendant is not obliged to inculpate himself, the object being to convict the guilty and acquit the innocent. Requiring a defendant to indicate in advance what he disputes about the prosecution case offends neither of those principles.'

If the judge wrongly holds that there is a case to answer, evidence called after the submission will not be considered by the Court of Appeal, as no further evidence would have been called had the submission been upheld. Thus, an appeal against conviction would succeed even if the defendant was clearly incriminated by evidence given on behalf of the defence (see *R v Abbott* [1955] 2 QB 497; *R v Juett* [1981] Crim LR 113; *R v Smith* [1999] 2 Cr App R 238).

In *R v S; R v C* [1996] Crim LR 346, the Court of Appeal said that it assists the Court of Appeal if a trial judge gives reasons for rejecting a submission of no case to answer. Those reasons can either be given when the submission is rejected or, if the judge prefers, after the jury has retired or after the verdict. If the judge does not give reasons, defence counsel may ask him to do so.

Section 34(2)(c) of the Criminal Justice and Public Order Act 1994 provides that adverse inferences can be drawn from failure to answer police questions when the court is considering a submission of no case to answer. However, s 34(2)(c) can only be relied upon to take the case past half time if a fact has been relied on by the defence which brings s 34 into play. This would be the case where, for example, the defence cross-examine prosecution witnesses on the basis of facts that were not mentioned by

the defendant when he was questioned by the police. In *R v Bowers* (1999) 163 JP 33, the Court of Appeal confirmed that adverse inferences can be drawn under s 34 even if the defendant does not give evidence at trial. The court said that, for s 34 to operate, the defendant must rely on a particular fact at trial, and he must have failed to mention that fact when questioned by the police. However, the defendant may rely on a fact even if he does not himself give evidence of that fact: for example, a witness called on his behalf may testify to that fact, or a prosecution witness may be cross-examined on the basis of that fact. The same conclusion was reached by the House of Lords in *R v Webber* [2004] UKHL 1; [2004] 1 WLR 404. In that case, the question of law certified by the Court of Appeal was 'Can a suggestion put to a witness by or on behalf of a defendant amount to a fact relied upon in his defence for the purpose of s 34 of the Criminal Justice and Public Order Act 1994, if that suggestion is not adopted by the witness?' The House of Lords ruled that s 34 might apply if a defendant fails to mention when questioned by the police a significant matter on which he seeks to rely in his defence at trial (a) by giving evidence of it, (b) by adducing evidence of it from another witness, or (c) by putting it to a prosecution witness. The House of Lords justified this conclusion on the basis that the word 'fact' in s 34 should be given a broad meaning. It covers any alleged fact that is put forward as part of the defence case. A defendant relies on a fact or matter in his defence not only when he gives or adduces evidence of it but also when counsel, acting on his instructions, puts a specific and positive case to prosecution witnesses, as opposed to asking questions intended to probe or test the prosecution case; this is so whether or not the witness accepts the suggestion put.

11.5.2 Acquittal by judge of his own motion

The judge can order an acquittal of his own motion (in other words, without the need for a submission of no case to answer). However, in *Attorney General's Reference (No 2 of 2000)* [2001] 1 Cr App R 36, the Court of Appeal held that where a prosecution has been properly brought (that is, it is not an abuse of process), a trial judge has no power to prevent the prosecution from calling evidence, or to direct the jury to acquit, simply on the basis that he thinks a conviction unlikely. In the case which gave rise to that Reference, when the defendant was brought before the court, the judge encouraged the prosecution to offer no evidence because he considered that it was unlikely that the defendant would be convicted. The prosecution declined to do so. A jury was empanelled and the judge informed them that he had formed a view about the quality of the evidence and that once the prosecution had begun he intended to order a verdict of not guilty. Prosecuting counsel opened the case to the jury and the judge then directed the jury to return a verdict of not guilty before the prosecution had called any of its witnesses. The Court of Appeal noted that the judge had not decided that the case was oppressive, vexatious or an abuse of process, but rather that the accused had a defence and that to proceed with the case would be a waste of time. The decision of the judge to stop the case, which had otherwise been properly brought, trespassed upon the right of the Crown Prosecution Service (CPS) to present its case in court, and the right of the jury to form their own view of the evidence and to express it by their verdict. In the circumstances of the case, it was unlikely that a submission of no case to answer, at the end of the prosecution case, would have been successful. Had the case proceeded and had the judge considered it appropriate, he could have reminded the jury of their right to stop the case (see below), but it would have been inappropriate to

issue an invitation to acquit. Accordingly, the decision of the trial judge to direct an acquittal after the prosecution had opened its case had been wrong in law.

In *R v Brown* [2001] EWCA Crim 961; [2002] 1 Cr App R 5, the Court of Appeal held that a Crown Court judge is entitled, even at the end of the defence case, to rule that there is no case to go before the jury if there is no evidence on a count or if no reasonable jury could convict on the evidence available. A judge is under a duty to keep under review the question of whether a properly directed jury could convict at the close of evidence before leaving the matter to the jury. However, the judge's power to rule that there is no case to go before the jury should be exercised very sparingly and only if the judge is satisfied that no properly directed reasonable jury could safely convict on the evidence.

11.5.3   Power of the jury to acquit at any time after the close of the prosecution case

Not to be confused with the right of the defence to seek a ruling from the judge that there is no case to answer, the jury themselves have the power to stop the case and acquit the defendant at any time after the close of the prosecution case. Jurors are, of course, generally unaware that they have this power and it is only in exceptional cases that they will be told of this power. In *R v Kemp* [1995] 1 Cr App R 151, the Court of Appeal said that where the judge does remind the jury that they may acquit the defendant without hearing further evidence, he should be cautious not to do anything other than merely inform them of their right to stop the case. Thus, the judge should not in effect invite the jury to acquit the defendant. If the judge considers that the case against the defendant is too weak to be left to the jury, then the judge should stop the case himself.

11.5.4   Judge-ordered and judge-directed acquittals – a critical evaluation

'Ordered' acquittals are those in which the judge orders an acquittal before the trial starts (usually because the prosecution has decided to offer no evidence); 'directed' acquittals occur where the judge directs the jury to acquit after the trial has started.

Figures from the case results for the year 2003–04 contained in the 2004 Annual Report of the CPS show that of those who were acquitted in the Crown Court, there was a judge-directed acquittal in 19% of cases (put another way, 7% of contested cases resulted in judge-directed acquittal). Figures in previous years were:

- 1998–99: 21% of acquittals were judge-directed (9% of contested cases resulted in judge-directed acquittal);
- 1999–00: 20.5% of acquittals were judge-directed (9% of contested cases resulted in judge-directed acquittal);
- 2000–01: 20% of acquittals were judge-directed (9% of contested cases resulted in judge-directed acquittal);
- 2001–02: 18.5% of acquittals were judge-directed (8% of contested cases resulted in judge-directed acquittal).
- 2002–03: 18.6% of acquittals were judge-directed (7% of contested cases resulted in judge-directed acquittal).

According to the official Judicial Statistics for 2003 (which cover all prosecutions, not just those brought by the CPS), during 2003, 67% of defendants who pleaded not guilty were acquitted. Of those defendants who were acquitted, 58% were discharged by the judge, 11% were acquitted on the direction of the judge, and 31% were acquitted by the jury.

Whichever set of figures is used, the rate of non-jury acquittals is very high.

John Baldwin conducted a study of judge-ordered and judge-directed acquittals (see 'Understanding judge ordered and directed acquittals in the Crown Court' [1997] Crim LR 536). He was concerned to find out the principal reasons why cases ended as such acquittals and whether those acquittals were foreseeable and (if so) preventable.

In his detailed study of 173 prosecution files, he found that early warning signs about the likelihood of the prosecution ending in acquittal were noted in no fewer than 87.3% of judge-ordered acquittals, 73.1% of judge-directed acquittals and 58.8% of jury acquittals.

It is tempting to use figures such as these to suggest that the CPS is simply allowing too many weak cases to proceed. There may be some substance to this, in that some of the CPS lawyers interviewed by Baldwin suggested that case reviews had to be carried out too quickly for the evidential sufficiency test to be applied rigorously; that some reviewing lawyers may lack the necessary experience to help them spot evidential weaknesses; that some reviewing lawyers:

> ... far from conducting a dispassionate examination of a case, uncritically accepted the initial police view ... It was sometimes clear that reviewing lawyers had been blinkered in the approach they had adopted, merely following the line that the police had already taken and not subjecting the evidence supplied by the police to a rigorous or critical examination ... Put bluntly, weak cases continue to be committed to the Crown Court because of a reluctance, even a disinclination, on the part of certain reviewing lawyers to make the tough decisions in serious cases required of them under the Code for Crown Prosecutors.

It also transpired that several CPS lawyers were considering the strength of the case as it stood, rather than considering whether the prosecution case could be improved. Baldwin also noticed a tendency to adopt 'in effect a weaker test of evidential sufficiency where allegations or injuries are serious'. Baldwin said that:

> ... the interviews also showed that some CPS lawyers share a common value system with the police, a core element of which is that serious cases ought to be prosecuted, almost irrespective of considerations as to evidential strength. Cases have developed a considerable momentum by the time of committal, and expectations build up that cases will proceed to the Crown Court. In such circumstances, it is easy to understand why some prosecutors, particularly when lacking experience or self-confidence, hesitate in making hard decisions in complex or serious cases.

He noted that:

> ... requests to the police, in so far as they were made at all, were overwhelmingly for clarification of the detail or for the taking of statements which had for some reason been overlooked by police. There were only isolated instances in the files where suggestions had been made by reviewing lawyers about the need to pursue further or fresh lines of inquiry. In practice, it seems, case review is much more concerned with tinkering with points of detail in what has already been done by police than with tackling the fundamentals in the approach adopted.

(Indeed some prosecutors complain, though Baldwin does not note this as an issue, that requests for further evidence rarely result in action by the police.) It also became apparent during Baldwin's research that some prosecuting counsel were not carrying out a review of the evidence at all (or at least not until very close to the trial date, making it too late to take remedial action). Some barristers felt that it was not appropriate for them to advise on evidence unless specifically instructed to do so; some barristers felt reluctant to point out weaknesses in case doing so jeopardised their relationship with the CPS.

A major reason for the failure of the prosecution to obtain convictions was the fact that witnesses either failed to attend court or else did not 'come up to proof' (in other words, gave evidence that was inconsistent with their original statements to the police). In some cases, there were clear warning signs that there were, or might be, problems with particular witnesses, but little or no action was taken.

11.6   THE DEFENCE CASE

If there is no submission of no case to answer, or a submission is made and the judge finds a case to answer in respect of some or all of the counts, evidence may then be adduced on behalf of the defendant.

Counsel for the defence may begin the defence case by making an opening speech if he proposes to call one or more witnesses (other than the defendant) as to the facts. If the only witness as to the facts is the defendant (that is, only the defendant gives evidence or there is evidence only from the defendant and character witnesses) there will be no defence opening speech.

Where there is more than one defence witness including the defendant, the defendant must give evidence first unless the court otherwise directs, under s 79 of PACE, which states:

If at the trial of any person for an offence—

(a)   the defence intends to call two or more witnesses to the facts of the case; and

(b)   those witnesses include the accused,

the accused shall be called before the other witness or witnesses unless the court in its discretion otherwise directs.

11.6.1   Adverse inferences

There is no obligation on the defence to call any evidence: counsel for the defence could simply address the jury and ask them to find that the prosecution have failed to prove the guilt of the accused beyond reasonable doubt. However, s 35 of the Criminal Justice and Public Order Act 1994, whilst not rendering the accused compellable to give evidence on his own behalf, does enable the court to draw such inferences as appear proper from the failure of the accused to give evidence or from his refusal, without good cause, to answer any question.

Where the accused has taken the oath but then refuses to answer a question, he will only be regarded as having good cause not to answer the question if either he is entitled to refuse to answer by virtue of an Act of Parliament or on the ground of

privilege, or the court, in the exercise of its general discretion, excuses him from answering it.

Section 35 requires the defendant to be warned that adverse inferences may be drawn from his silence unless he (or his barrister) has informed the court that he will give evidence. The details of what the judge should say are set out in para IV.44 of *Practice Direction (Criminal Proceedings: Consolidation)* [2002] 1 WLR 2870; [2002] 3 All ER 904 and are as follows:

IV.44 *Defendant's right to give or not to give evidence*

44.1 At the conclusion of the evidence for the prosecution, section 35(2) of the Criminal Justice and Public Order Act 1994 requires the court to satisfy itself that the accused is aware that the stage has been reached at which evidence can be given for the defence and that he can, if he wishes, give evidence and that, if he chooses not to give evidence, or having been sworn, without good cause refuses to answer any question, it will be permissible for the jury to draw such inferences as appear proper from his failure to give evidence or his refusal, without good cause, to answer any question.

If the accused is legally represented

44.2 Section 35(1) provides that section 35(2) does not apply if at the conclusion of the evidence for the prosecution the accused's legal representative informs the court that the accused will give evidence. This should be done in the presence of the jury. If the representative indicates that the accused will give evidence the case should proceed in the usual way.

44.3 If the court is not so informed, or if the court is informed that the accused does not intend to give evidence, the judge should in the presence of the jury inquire of the representative in these terms:

> Have you advised your client that the stage has now been reached at which he may give evidence and, if he chooses not to do so or, having been sworn, without good cause refuses to answer any question, the jury may draw such inferences as appear proper from his failure to do so?

44.4 If the representative replies to the judge that the accused has been so advised, then the case shall proceed. If counsel replies that the accused has not been so advised, then the judge shall direct the representative to advise his client of the consequences set out in paragraph 44.3 and should adjourn briefly for this purpose before proceeding further.

If the accused is not legally represented

44.5 If the accused is not represented, the judge shall at the conclusion of the evidence for the prosecution and in the presence of the jury say to the accused:

> You have heard the evidence against you. Now is the time for you to make your defence. You may give evidence on oath, and be cross-examined like any other witness. If you do not give evidence or, having been sworn, without good cause refuse to answer any question the jury may draw such inferences as appear proper. That means they may hold it against you. You may also call any witness or witnesses whom you have arranged to attend court. Afterwards you may also, if you wish, address the jury by arguing your case from the dock. But you cannot at that stage give evidence. Do you now intend to give evidence?

In *R v Bevan* (1993) 98 Cr App R 354, the Court of Appeal said that if the defendant chooses not to give evidence in his own defence, counsel should make sure that this decision is recorded (usually, this will be done by an endorsement on the brief); the

record should be signed by the defendant and should indicate that he has made the decision of his own free will, bearing in mind the advice of counsel regarding the possible consequences of not testifying.

11.6.2 Defence evidence

Each defence witness (including the defendant himself, if he chooses to give evidence) is liable to be cross-examined by the prosecution and may then be re-examined by defence counsel, if necessary.

Where the defendant gives evidence, it must be borne in mind that he may be cross-examined as to any previous convictions he has if the nature or conduct of the defence case has involved the casting of 'imputations' on the character of one or more prosecution witnesses (s 1(3)(ii) of the Criminal Evidence Act 1898). This will be the case if the defence cross-examine prosecution witnesses on the basis that they are lying, rather than mistaken, or if the defendant (or one of his witnesses) makes such an allegation. The judge has a discretion to refuse to allow such cross-examination to take place, and so the prosecutor should seek permission from the judge before embarking on such cross-examination. Leave may well be refused if there is a real risk that, because the previous convictions are for offences which are very similar to the present charges (but falling short of the similarity required for them to be admissible as similar fact evidence), the jury might use them as evidence of propensity despite a direction from the judge that they should not do so.

In *R v Taylor and Goodman* [1999] 2 Cr App R 163, the appellant was cross-examined on his previous convictions (he had cast imputations on the character of prosecution witnesses). On appeal, he argued that the judge had erred in allowing the prosecution to cross-examine him thus, as he had a very serious criminal record. The Court of Appeal held that to accept the argument that defendants with very bad criminal records should be protected against disclosure of those records would allow such defendants too much freedom to cast imputations against prosecution witnesses. However, the court said that where a defendant's criminal record was very serious, a judge was only likely to allow its admission where the allegations made by the defendant against the prosecution witnesses were equally serious.

A defendant who attacks the character of a prosecution witness is immune from questioning as to his own character under s 1(3)(ii) of the Criminal Evidence Act 1898 if he chooses not to give evidence, since that section is only concerned with cross-examination (*R v Butterwasser* [1948] 1 KB 4). However, where he elects to give evidence and has embarked on doing so, he cannot avoid evidence of his own character going before the jury simply by refusing to return to the witness box so that he cannot be cross-examined. In such circumstances, the Crown is entitled to adduce evidence as to his bad character (*R v Forbes* [1999] 2 Cr App R 501).

The provisions of the Criminal Evidence Act 1898 will be replaced by those contained in Chapter 1 of Pt 11 of the Criminal Justice Act 2003. Section 101(1) provides that:

(1)   In criminal proceedings evidence of the defendant's bad character is admissible if, but only if—

   (a) all parties to the proceedings agree to the evidence being admissible,

   (b) the evidence is adduced by the defendant himself or is given in answer to a question asked by him in cross-examination and intended to elicit it,

(c) it is important explanatory evidence,

(d) it is relevant to an important matter in issue between the defendant and the prosecution,

(e) it has substantial probative value in relation to an important matter in issue between the defendant and a co-defendant,

(f) it is evidence to correct a false impression given by the defendant, or

(g) the defendant has made an attack on another person's character.

Under s 101(3), the court must not admit evidence under sub-s (1)(d) or (g) if, on an application by the defendant to exclude it, it appears to the court that the admission of the evidence 'would have such an adverse effect on the fairness of the proceedings that the court ought not to admit it'. Section 101(4) goes on to provide that the court, when considering an application to exclude evidence under sub-s (3), must 'have regard, in particular, to the length of time between the matters to which that evidence relates and the matters which form the subject of the offence charged'.

11.7 CLOSING SPEECHES

If the accused is unrepresented and either calls no evidence at all or else was himself the only witness as to the facts, then the prosecution have no right to make a closing speech.

Otherwise, once all the defence evidence has been called, both counsel may make a closing speech. The prosecution make the first speech (although prosecuting counsel may decide not to make a speech if the trial has been a very short one). Thus, the defence have the last word before the judge sums the case up to the jury.

11.8 VARIATION IN PROCEDURE WHERE THERE IS MORE THAN ONE DEFENDANT

The procedure for putting the defence case before the jury varies slightly if there is more than one defendant.

11.8.1 Defendants separately represented

Where two or more defendants are charged in the same indictment and are separately represented, their cases are presented in the order in which their names appear on the indictment. So:

R v D1
    D2

Prosecution witnesses are cross-examined first on behalf of D1, then on behalf of D2.

The defence case is then presented as follows:

• opening speech on behalf of D1;

• D1 called as a witness (if he chooses to give evidence):

(a) examination-in-chief by his own counsel;

(b) cross-examination on behalf of D2;

    (c)   cross-examination by prosecution;

    (d)   re-examination by his own counsel (if necessary);

- any witnesses called on behalf of D1 give evidence; the order of questioning is the same as above;
- opening speech on behalf of D2;
- D2 called as a witness (if he chooses to give evidence):

    (a)   examination-in-chief by his own counsel;

    (b)   cross-examination on behalf of D1;

    (c)   cross-examination by prosecution;

    (d)   re-examination by his own counsel (if necessary);

- any witnesses called on behalf of D2 give evidence; the order of questioning is the same as the point above;
- prosecution closing speech;
- closing speech on behalf of D1;
- closing speech on behalf of D2.

It must be remembered that if one defendant (D1) gives evidence against a co-defendant (D2), D2 can cross-examine D1 as to any previous convictions recorded against him (s 1(3)(iii) of the Criminal Evidence Act 1898). The term 'evidence against' means evidence which supports the prosecution case against D2 in a material respect or which undermines D's defence (see *Murdoch v Taylor* [1965] AC 574 and *R v Crawford* [1997] 1 WLR 1329).

11.8.2   Defendants jointly represented

If the defendants are jointly represented, they are regarded as presenting a joint defence. Consequently, the defence case will be presented as follows:

- there will be a single opening speech on behalf of all the defendants;
- D1 gives evidence if he wishes to do so;
- D2 gives evidence if he wishes to do so;
- any other defence witnesses give evidence;
- prosecution closing speech;
- closing speech on behalf of all defendants.

11.9   RE-OPENING THE PROSECUTION CASE

In exceptional cases, the judge has a discretion to allow the prosecution to call additional evidence after the close of the prosecution case.

In *R v Munnery* (1991) 94 Cr App R 164, for example, the defendants were charged with shoplifting. When they were stopped by security staff, they were each carrying a carton of glassware. After the close of the prosecution case, the defence indicated that they wished to submit that there was no case to answer. The next morning, when the judge was to consider this submission, the prosecution stated that they wished to call a new witness, a shop assistant who would testify that two cartons of glassware were found to be missing from the shop. The Court of Appeal upheld the decision of the

judge to allow this witness to be called. No injustice was done to the defendant as the defence case had not yet started.

In *R v Patel* [1992] Crim LR 739, further evidence against the defendant unexpectedly came to light in the context of an unrelated investigation. The prosecution were allowed to adduce this additional evidence even though closing speeches had already been made. The Court of Appeal said that judges should generally be reluctant to grant such late applications. However, the judge had invited the defence to seek an adjournment and to call fresh evidence if they wished and so no harm had been done.

If the judge takes the view that it would be unduly prejudicial to the defence to allow the prosecution to re-open their case, it is open to him to discharge the jury (with the effect that a new trial will take place later).

11.10 THE JUDGE'S SUMMING UP

After the prosecution and defence counsel have made their closing speeches, the judge sums the case up to the jury. The judge must do this in all cases, however simple the case may seem. Although traditionally the judge produces the summing up without reference to counsel, in *R v Taylor* [2003] EWCA Crim 2447; (2003) *The Times*, 8 October, the Court of Appeal said that where complex directions are to be given to the jury, counsel in the case should be permitted to consider and comment upon the draft directions before the judge addresses the jury.

A very useful resource is the Criminal Bench Book published by the Judicial Studies Board. It contains a set of specimen directions which cover all the major matters which have to be covered in a summing up. These specimen directions are freely available on the web: www.jsboard.co.uk/criminal_law/index.htm.

11.10.1 The respective functions of the judge and the jury

Matters of law are for the judge whereas matters of fact are for the jury. This means that the jury must accept what the judge says about the law, whether they agree or not. The judge should be careful not to express an opinion on the facts and should make it clear to the jury that if he does express an opinion on the facts, the jury are free to come to a different conclusion. The direction approved in *R v Jackson* [1992] Crim LR 214 was:

> It is my job to tell you what the law is and how to apply it to the issues of fact that you have to decide and to remind you of the important evidence on these issues. As to the law, you must accept what I tell you. As to the facts, you alone are the judges. It is for you to decide what evidence you accept and what evidence you reject or of which you are unsure. If I appear to have a view of the evidence or of the facts with which you do not agree, reject my view. If I mention or emphasise evidence that you regard as unimportant, disregard that evidence. If I do not mention what you regard as important, follow your own view and take that evidence into account.

11.10.2 Burden and standard of proof

- *Burden of proof*

  It is for the prosecution to prove the defendant's guilt; it is not for the defendant to prove his innocence.

- *Standard of proof*

  In describing the standard of proof, the judge should tell the jury that they have to be satisfied so that they are sure of the defendant's guilt (sometimes expressed as the prosecution having to prove the defendant's guilt beyond reasonable doubt: *Ferguson v The Queen* [1979] 1 WLR 94; *R v McVey* [1988] Crim LR 127). In *R v Stephens* [2002] EWCA Crim 1529; (2002) *The Times*, 27 June, the jury retired and sent a note asking the judge (a) what constituted reasonable doubt and (b) how certain was it necessary for them to be. The appeal concerned the answer which should be given in such a case. The court said that the Judicial Studies Board guideline to direct a jury to be satisfied so that they were sure of guilt is a well-established direction. It is not helpful for a judge to direct a jury to distinguish between being sure and being certain and a judge should avoid doing so. If necessary, a judge should direct a jury that his telling them to be sure was the limit of the help that he could give them.

Exceptionally, the defendant may bear a burden of proof. For example, if the defendant is charged with possession of an offensive weapon (s 1 of the Prevention of Crime Act 1953), it is open to him to show that he had lawful authority or reasonable excuse. In such a case, it must be made clear to the jury that the defendant can satisfy this burden of proof on the balance of probabilities (that is, showing that it is more likely than not that he had lawful authority or reasonable excuse).

There is only a burden of proof on the defendant if statute clearly so provides; otherwise it is for the prosecution to disprove a defence. Thus, if the defendant raises the defence of self-defence, it is for the prosecution to prove beyond reasonable doubt that he was not so acting.

11.10.3 Explanation of the law involved and how it relates to the facts

Even in a straightforward case, directions on the ingredients of the offence are an essential part of the summing up (*R v McVey* [1988] Crim LR 127). Thus, the judge must explain what the prosecution have to prove and must remind the jury of the evidence they have heard (*R v O'Meara* (1989) *The Times*, 15 December). The judge should remind the jury of the main features of the prosecution and defence evidence, even if the case is a straightforward one (*R v Gregory* [1993] Crim LR 623).

The jury should thus be able to relate the evidence which they have heard to the legal principles which they have to apply.

In *R v Bowerman* [2000] 2 Cr App R 189, the grounds of appeal concerned the judge's decision not to sum up the facts of the case to the jury. After giving legal directions the judge told the jury that they had the advantage of two speeches, from the defence and prosecution, who were very experienced and had covered every salient point in the case. He told them that any repetition by him of the evidence would be otiose. It was submitted in particular that the jury were not reminded of the evidence which supported the defence case. The Court of Appeal said that counsels'

closing speeches are no substitute for an impartial review of the facts from the trial judge, who is responsible for ensuring that an accused has a fair trial. The first step to a fair trial is for the trial judge to focus the jury's attention on the issues he identifies; that responsibility should not be delegated or abandoned to counsel. The fact that members of the jury were taking notes did not relieve a judge of his responsibility; evidence needs to be marshalled and arranged issue by issue by the judge and that task could not be passed to the jurors. The instant case was not such a short and simple case that no review of the facts was required by the trial judge. Therefore, the principle set out in *R v Farr* (1999) 163 JP 193 applied: 'in a trial lasting several days or more, it is generally of assistance to the jury if the judge summarises those factual issues which are not disputed, and, where there is a significant dispute as to material facts, identifies succinctly those pieces of evidence which are in conflict.'

11.10.4 Such warnings as are appropriate

(a)   Co-defendants or more than one count

Where there is more than one count and/or more than one defendant, the judge must direct the jury to consider each count and each defendant separately.

Where there are co-defendants and each defendant says that he is not responsible for the alleged crime, the jury should be directed that:

(a) the case for and against each defendant should be considered separately;

(b) the case should be decided on all of the evidence, including the evidence of the co-defendant(s) and the defendant whose case they are considering;

(c) when considering a co-defendant's evidence against the particular defendant whose case they are considering, they should bear in mind that he may have an interest to serve;

(d) they should assess the evidence of a co-defendant in the same way as any other witness in the case (*R v Jones and Jenkins* [2003] EWCA Crim 1966; [2004] 1 Cr App R 5).

If one defendant implicated another in a police interview, the judge should instruct the jury to disregard the out-of-court statement of one defendant in so far as it relates to the other defendant (*R v Rhodes* (1959) 44 Cr App R 23). Note that if a defendant implicated a co-defendant in the witness box when giving evidence on his own behalf, that evidence is admissible against the co-defendant (*R v Rudd* (1948) 32 Cr App R 138).

(b)   Identification evidence

If the case rests on identification evidence, the judge must warn the jury that such evidence is notoriously unreliable and that they should examine very closely the circumstances in which the identification took place when assessing the weight of that evidence (*R v Turnbull* [1977] QB 224). The judge should give a detailed direction on the factors which strengthen or weaken the identification evidence.

(c)   Adverse inferences

Given the fact that a jury may draw adverse inferences from the failure of a defendant to answer police questions (s 34 of the Criminal Justice and Public Order Act 1994) or to testify in court (s 35), they will have to be given some guidance on how to approach this aspect of the case.

In *R v Cowan* [1996] QB 373, the Court of Appeal considered what should be said in the summing up if the case is one where adverse inferences might be drawn under s 35 from the defendant's failure to testify. The essential elements of the direction are as follows:

(a) the judge must remind the jury that the burden of proof remains on the prosecution throughout;

(b) (as provided by s 38(3) of the Criminal Justice and Public Order Act 1994) an inference from silence cannot on its own prove guilt;

(c) the jury has to be satisfied (on the basis of the evidence called by the prosecution) that the prosecution have established a case to answer before inferences can be drawn from the accused's silence; and

(d) they can only draw an adverse inference from the accused's silence if they conclude that the silence could only sensibly be attributed to the accused having no answer to the charge, or none that would stand up to cross-examination; where the defendant offers an explanation for his silence, the jury must reject that explanation before drawing adverse inferences from the silence.

In other words, the defendant's failure to answer police questions or testify cannot be the sole basis for his conviction and so the jury must be directed not to convict just because the defendant has not testified. Nevertheless, if the evidence adduced by the prosecution calls for an explanation which the defendant should be in a position to give, the jury may be rightly suspicious of a defendant who declines to give an explanation unless they accept any explanation for the silence.

Where the silence was failure to answer police questions, it may be that the defendant will explain this silence when he gives evidence. If the silence is a failure to testify, any explanation could come from the questions asked during the cross-examination of the prosecution witnesses.

The same approach was followed in *R v Birchall* [1999] Crim LR 311. In that case, the Court of Appeal held that where the defendant fails to testify, the judge must tell the jury that they should not start to consider whether to draw adverse inferences from the defendant's failure to testify until they have concluded that there is a case to answer (that is, that the prosecution case against him is sufficiently compelling to call for an answer by him). This is so even if there is plainly sufficient evidence to amount to a *prima facie* case against the defendant.

Thus, there are two key steps before adverse inferences can be drawn under s 35:

(a) is the jury satisfied that the prosecution have established a case to answer against the defendant?; and

(b) has the jury rejected any explanation put forward by the defendant for his refusal to give evidence?

If the answer to these questions is 'yes', the jury may draw adverse inferences from the defendant's silence.

In *R v Argent* [1997] 2 Cr App R 27, the Court of Appeal set out the conditions which have to be satisfied before adverse inferences can be drawn, under s 34 of the Criminal Justice and Public Order Act 1994, from a person's failure to answer police questions. The conditions include:

(a) the alleged failure to mention a relevant fact must take place before the person has been charged;

(b) the alleged failure must occur during questioning under caution;

(c) the questioning must be directed at trying to discover whether and by whom the alleged offence has been committed;

(d) the alleged failure must be a failure to mention a fact relied on by the defendant in his defence;

(e) the fact must be one which this particular defendant (not some hypothetical reasonable accused) could reasonably be expected to have mentioned when being questioned, taking account of all the circumstances existing at that time (for example, the time of day, the defendant's age, experience, mental capacity, state of health, sobriety, personality and access to legal advice).

In *R v Roble* [1997] Crim LR 346 and *R v Daniel* [1998] 2 Cr App R 373, it was said that legal advice to remain silent at a police interview is unlikely of itself to be an adequate explanation for refusal to answer questions. So, the fact that a defendant was following his solicitor's advice not to answer police questions does not prevent the judge from directing the jury that they could draw an adverse inference from the defendant's failure to answer questions. An important issue is whether the defendant waives legal professional privilege by saying that his solicitor has advised him not to answer questions. In *R v Condron* [1997] 1 WLR 827, the Court of Appeal held that where legal advice is given as the reason for not answering police questions, this will not amount to waiver of privilege. However, where the defendant goes a step further and asks for adverse inferences not to be drawn because his silence was based on legal advice, this might amount to a waiver of privilege. Much more detailed guidance on this point was given by the Court of Appeal in *R v Bowden* [1999] 1 WLR 823. In that case, it was held that where a defendant says (at his interview in the police station or at trial) that he refused to answer police questions because he was advised to remain silent by his solicitor, he does not thereby waive legal professional privilege. However, if the defendant or his solicitor (at the time of the interview or at trial) explains the basis for that advice, the defendant has waived privilege and it is open to the prosecution to cross-examine the defendant about the information he gave to his solicitor (that is, he can be cross-examined on the nature of that advice and the factual premises on which it had been based). Article 6 of the European Convention on Human Rights requires that the confidentiality of communications between the accused and his solicitor must be respected (*S v Switzerland* (1992) 14 EHRR 670); the decision in *R v Bowden* seems to be inconsistent with this principle.

In *R v Gowland-Wynn* [2001] EWCA Crim 2715; [2002] 1 Cr App R 41, the court said that a judge can draw the jury's attention to the fact that, when interviewed by the police, the defendant did not comment when he could be expected to comment about something which went to the heart of his defence. The court commended the specimen direction prepared in July 2001 by the Judicial Studies Board. In giving the direction, the judge must bear in mind that the burden of proof remains throughout on the prosecution.

In *R v McGarry* [1998] 3 All ER 805, the prosecution had accepted that the defendant had not relied on anything in his defence that he had not mentioned when interviewed, and so no inferences could be drawn from his failure to answer questions in those interviews. It was held that the trial judge should have given the jury a specific direction that no adverse inference should be drawn from the defendant's silence; otherwise, the jury might have been left in doubt as to whether or not it was proper to hold the defendant's silence against him.

In *R v Brizzalari* [2004] EWCA Crim 310; (2004) *The Times*, 3 March, the Court of Appeal noted that the mischief to which s 34 of the 1994 Act is primarily directed is the positive defence put forward despite a no-comment interview, and/or the ambush defence. The court said that it would counsel against the further complicating of trials and summings up by invoking s 34 unless the merits of the individual case require that it should be involved. If the section is not relied on in a particular case, it may well be sensible, said the court, for the judge to raise with counsel whether a specific direction not to draw any adverse inferences is desirable or necessary.

The right to a fair trial guaranteed by Art 6 of the European Convention on Human Rights includes 'the right of anyone charged with a criminal offence to remain silent and not to contribute to incriminating himself' (*Funke v France* (1993) 16 EHRR 297). The case of *Condron* went to the European Court of Human Rights (*Condron v UK* (2001) 31 EHRR 1). On the basis that the defendant had testified at trial and had offered an explanation for remaining silent during the police interview, the Court held that the jury should have been directed that if they were satisfied that the defendant's silence at the police interview could not sensibly be attributed to his having no answer (or none that would stand up to cross-examination), it should not draw an adverse inference.

In *R v Betts & Hall* [2001] EWCA Crim 224; [2001] 2 Cr App R 257, the defendants had elected to remain silent in interviews with the police following legal advice. The judge directed the jury that they were entitled to draw adverse inference from the defendants' silence. The Court of Appeal held that any direction that left the jury at liberty to draw an adverse inference from a defendant's failure to answer questions in the police interview, notwithstanding that they might have been satisfied as to the plausibility of the explanation for not so doing, amounts to a breach of the right to a fair trial under Art 6(1) of the European Convention on Human Rights. The court said that the genuineness of the decision to decline to answer questions, not its quality, is conclusive. If it was a plausible explanation that the reason for not mentioning facts when interviewed was that the particular defendant had acted on the advice of his solicitor and not because he had had no answer, or no satisfactory answer, to give, then no inference could be drawn. In the present case, the jury might have failed to appreciate that they could only draw inferences against a particular defendant if they were sure that he had no explanation to offer, or none that he believed would stand up to questioning or investigating. The approach taken by the Court of Appeal in this case was approved by the European Court of Human Rights in *Beckles v UK* (2003) 36 EHRR 13.

In *R v Hoare; R v Pierce* [2004] EWCA Crim 784, the court commented on the rationale behind s 34, saying (at paras 53–55, *per* Auld LJ):

> The whole basis of s 34, in its qualification of the otherwise general right of an accused to remain silent and to require the prosecution to prove its case, is an assumption that an innocent defendant – as distinct from one who is entitled to require the prosecution

to prove its case – would give an early explanation to demonstrate his innocence. If such a defendant is advised by a solicitor to remain silent, why on earth should he do so, unless ... he might wrongly inculpate himself? It is not the purpose of s 34 to exclude a jury from drawing an adverse inference against a defendant because he genuinely or reasonably believes that, regardless of his guilt or innocence, he is entitled to take advantage of that advice to impede the prosecution case against him. In such a case the advice is not truly the reason for not mentioning the facts. The s 34 inference is concerned with flushing out innocence at an early stage or supporting other evidence of guilt at a later stage, not simply with whether a guilty defendant is entitled, or genuinely or reasonably believes that he is entitled, to rely on legal rights of which his solicitor has advised him. Legal entitlement is one thing. An accused's reason for exercising it is another. His belief in his entitlement may be genuine, but it does not follow that his reason for exercising it is ... The question in the end, which is for the jury, is whether regardless of advice, genuinely given and genuinely accepted, an accused has remained silent not because of that advice but because had no or no satisfactory explanation to give.

In *R v Chenia* [2002] EWCA Crim 2345; [2003] 2 Cr App R 6, the Court of Appeal gave further detailed guidance on the drawing of adverse inferences under s 34 of the Criminal Justice and Public Order Act 1994. In that case, evidence was adduced of interviews under caution in which the appellant made no comment. He did not give evidence, but his case was put through counsel in cross-examination. The Court of Appeal ruled as follows:

(a) whilst merely putting the prosecution to proof of its case would not amount to reliance upon a fact for the purposes of s 34, an adverse inference might be drawn even though the defendant did not give evidence or call witnesses. A fact might be relied upon whether it was adduced in evidence in the course of either the prosecution or defence case. The mere putting of a fact to a witness in cross-examination might, in certain circumstances, be sufficient to amount to reliance upon it for the purposes of s 34 (see *R v Bowers* (1999) 163 JP 33 and *R v Webber* [2004] UKHL 1; [2004] 1 WLR 404);

(b) discussion between the advocates and the judge before the commencement of speeches, aimed at determining whether a s 34 direction is appropriate and, if so, how that direction should be tailored to meet the facts of the particular case, is a sensible and necessary precaution;

(c) under s 34, the jury should, in respect of any fact relied on by a defendant in his defence but not mentioned in interview, first resolve whether he could, in the circumstances existing at the time, have been expected to mention it and, if so, go on to draw such inferences as might appear proper. The facts relied upon by way of defence, but not mentioned in interview, should be identified by the trial judge to the jury. The direction must not give the impression that the jury might draw an adverse inference because the appellant was sheltering behind his solicitor's advice not to answer questions: such an inference can only be drawn if the jury are sure that the defendant had, at that stage, no explanation to offer or none that would have withstood questioning or investigation;

(d) the fact that the s 34 direction given by the trial judge was inadequate does not necessarily render either the trial unfair or the conviction unsafe. Whether there was a breach of Art 6 as the result of a failure to direct a jury in a particular way depends upon all the circumstances of the individual case.

In *R v Petkar* [2003] EWCA Crim 2668; [2004] 1 Cr App R 22, the Court of Appeal said that a well crafted and careful jury direction on s 34 should include: identification of the facts the accused failed to mention but which were relied on in his defence and the inferences or conclusions which it was suggested might be drawn from the failure, to the extent that they might go beyond the standard inference of late fabrication; that if an inference was drawn, the jury should not convict wholly or mainly on the strength of it; that an inference should only be drawn if the jury thought it a fair and proper conclusion and the only sensible explanation for the failure was that the defendant had no answer to the accusation or none that would have stood up to scrutiny; that no inference should be drawn unless the prosecution case was so strong that it clearly called for an answer. The jury should further be reminded of any evidence on the basis of which the jury were invited not to draw any inference from a defendant's silence and a special direction should be given where the explanation for silence was reliance on legal advice.

Sometimes, defendants try to avoid the effects of s 34 and yet also avoid answering police questions; this is achieved through the use of pre-prepared statement rather than submitting to police questioning. This stratagem has been considered in two cases. The first is *R v Knight* [2003] EWCA Crim 1977; [2004] 1 WLR 340. At the beginning of his interview with police, the defendant's solicitor read out a prepared statement giving an account which was wholly consistent with the testimony that he gave later at trial. On his solicitor's advice, he declined to answer any questions in interview, stating at trial that he did so because he was worried about getting confused and answering police questions incorrectly. The judge directed the jury that they might draw the adverse inference from the defendant's silence that he wished to prevent his account being scrutinised by police questioning because he believed that it would not stand up to it. The Court of Appeal said that the purpose of s 34 of the Criminal Justice and Public Order Act 1994 is to procure the early disclosure of a suspect's account, not the scrutiny and testing of it by the police in interview. That, said the court, would be a significantly greater intrusion into a suspect's general right to silence than the requirement to disclose his factual defence. There can be no adverse inference where the defendant gives his full account in the statement given to the police, mentioning all the facts he later relies on and from which he does not depart in the witness box. The fact that he does not mention the facts specifically in response to police questions is immaterial. The judge's direction therefore rendered the conviction unsafe. The court noted that a prepared statement does not of itself give automatic immunity against adverse inferences under s 34. It might be incomplete in comparison with the account given at trial or in some respects inconsistent with it. The fact that a solicitor has provided no reasons, or bad reasons, as to why the accused should stay silent does not necessarily mean that an adverse inference should be drawn, as the defendant might be weak or vulnerable, so that it would not be reasonable to expect him to give an account to the police. It was, said the court, a matter for the jury.

The second case is *R v Turner* [2003] EWCA Crim 3108; [2004] 1 All ER 1025. The defendant again relied on a pre-prepared statement in his interview with the police. The Court of Appeal ruled that where a defendant produces a pre-prepared statement in a police interview, directions to the jury in relation to potential adverse inferences should include a comparison of the defendant's evidence at trial with the pre-prepared statement to see whether there was any fact relied on at trial which the defendant did not mention in the pre-prepared statement. It is only on the basis of such unmentioned

facts that the jury is entitled to draw an adverse inference and the judge should give a specific direction in that regard. The court pointed out that the growing practice of submitting a pre-prepared statement and declining to answer any questions in interview may prove a dangerous course for an innocent person who subsequently discovers at the trial that something significant was omitted; no such problems would arise following an interview where the suspect gave appropriate answers to the questions asked. The court added that where the prosecution propose to invite the jury to draw an adverse inference under s 34, the alleged discrepancy should ordinarily be ventilated in cross-examination so that the defendant has an opportunity to deal with it, and that where there are discrepancies between the prepared statement and the defendant's evidence at trial, it may be more appropriate to deal with this through a direction on previous lies rather than a direction under s 34.

Given the importance of ss 34 and 35, it is appropriate to set them out in full here:

34(1) Where, in any proceedings against a person for an offence, evidence is given that the accused—

(a) at any time before he was charged with the offence, on being questioned under caution by a constable trying to discover whether or by whom the offence had been committed, failed to mention any fact relied on in his defence in those proceedings; or

(b) on being charged with the offence or officially informed that he might be prosecuted for it, failed to mention any such fact,

being a fact which in the circumstances existing at the time the accused could reasonably have been expected to mention when so questioned, charged or informed, as the case may be, sub-section (2) below applies.

(2) Where this sub-section applies—

(a) a magistrates' court inquiring into the offence as examining justices;

(b) a judge, in deciding whether to grant an application made by the accused under—

(i) section 6 of the Criminal Justice Act 1987 (application for dismissal of charge of serious fraud in respect of which notice of transfer has been given under section 4 of that Act); or

(ii) paragraph 5 of schedule 6 to the Criminal Justice Act 1991 (application for dismissal of charge of violent or sexual offence involving child in respect of which notice of transfer has been given under section 53 of that Act);

(c) the court, in determining whether there is a case to answer; and

(d) the court or jury, in determining whether the accused is guilty of the offence charged,

may draw such inferences from the failure as appear proper.

(2A) Where the accused was at an authorised place of detention at the time of the failure, sub-sections (1) and (2) above do not apply if he had not been allowed an opportunity to consult a solicitor prior to being questioned, charged or informed as mentioned in sub-section (1) above.

(3) Subject to any directions by the court, evidence tending to establish the failure may be given before or after evidence tending to establish the fact which the accused is alleged to have failed to mention.

(4) This section applies in relation to questioning by persons (other than constables) charged with the duty of investigating offences or charging offenders as it

applies in relation to questioning by constables; and in sub-section (1) above 'officially informed' means informed by a constable or any such person.

(5)   This section does not—

   (a) prejudice the admissibility in evidence of the silence or other reaction of the accused in the face of anything said in his presence relating to the conduct in respect of which he is charged, in so far as evidence thereof would be admissible apart from this section; or

   (b) preclude the drawing of any inference from any such silence or other reaction of the accused which could properly be drawn apart from this section.

(6)   This section does not apply in relation to a failure to mention a fact if the failure occurred before the commencement of this section.

35(1) At the trial of any person for an offence, sub-sections (2) and (3) below apply unless—

   (a) the accused's guilt is not in issue; or

   (b) it appears to the court that the physical or mental condition of the accused makes it undesirable for him to give evidence;

   but sub-section (2) below does not apply if, at the conclusion of the evidence for the prosecution, his legal representative informs the court that the accused will give evidence or, where he is unrepresented, the court ascertains from him that he will give evidence.

(2)   Where this sub-section applies, the court shall, at the conclusion of the evidence for the prosecution, satisfy itself (in the case of proceedings on indictment, in the presence of the jury) that the accused is aware that the stage has been reached at which evidence can be given for the defence and that he can, if he wishes, give evidence and that, if he chooses not to give evidence, or having been sworn, without good cause refuses to answer any question, it will be permissible for the court or jury to draw such inferences as appear proper from his failure to give evidence or his refusal, without good cause, to answer any question.

(3)   Where this sub-section applies, the court or jury, in determining whether the accused is guilty of the offence charged, may draw such inferences as appear proper from the failure of the accused to give evidence or his refusal, without good cause, to answer any question.

(4)   This section does not render the accused compellable to give evidence on his own behalf, and he shall accordingly not be guilty of contempt of court by reason of a failure to do so.

(5)   For the purposes of this section a person who, having been sworn, refuses to answer any question shall be taken to do so without good cause unless—

   (a) he is entitled to refuse to answer the question by virtue of any enactment, whenever passed or made, or on the ground of privilege; or

   (b) the court in the exercise of its general discretion excuses him from answering it.

(7)   This section applies—

   (a) in relation to proceedings on indictment for an offence, only if the person charged with the offence is arraigned on or after the commencement of this section;

(b) in relation to proceedings in a magistrates' court, only if the time when the court begins to receive evidence in the proceedings falls after the commencement of this section.

(d) Alibi evidence

Where the defendant puts forward an alibi, the judge must direct the jury that the burden of proof rests on the prosecution to disprove it (not on the defendant to prove it) beyond reasonable doubt. Where the defendant relies on an alibi at trial but either failed to give particulars of that alibi to the prosecution or gave particulars which are inconsistent with the story told in court, the judge may direct the jury that they are entitled to draw adverse inferences against the defendant (see s 11(3) of the Criminal Procedure and Investigations Act (CPIA) 1996). A conviction cannot, however, be based solely on such an adverse inference (s 11(5)). Where the evidence in court is different from the particulars of alibi given to the prosecution, regard must be had to the degree of divergence in the stories and to any justification which the defence put forward for the divergence (s 11(4)).

Where the defendant has relied on an alibi and the prosecution have sought to prove that the alibi was false, the judge should direct the jury to the effect that 'even if you conclude that the alibi was false, that does not entitle you to convict the defendant. The Crown must still make you sure of his guilt. An alibi is sometimes invented to bolster a genuine defence'. A failure to give such a direction does not automatically render a conviction unsafe; the Court of Appeal will consider whether the jury might have come to a different conclusion had the direction been given (*R v Harron* [1996] 2 Cr App R 457; *R v Lesley* [1996] 1 Cr App R 39).

(e) Lies by the defendant

Where there is evidence before the jury that the defendant has lied about something, and there is a risk of the jury thinking that, because the defendant has lied, he must therefore be guilty of the offence with which he is charged, they should be directed that proof of lying is not proof of guilt (in that an innocent defendant might lie): *R v Lucas* [1981] 1 QB 720.

(f) The defendant's previous convictions

If the prosecution have been given leave to cross-examine the defendant on his previous convictions (under s 1(f) of the Criminal Evidence Act 1898), the jury must be warned that these previous convictions are relevant only to the defendant's credibility as a witness and are not evidence of his guilt (*R v Vickers* [1972] Crim LR 101; *R v France* [1978] Crim LR 48). In *R v McLeod* [1994] 1 WLR 1500, the Court of Appeal reiterated that where a defendant is cross-examined on his previous convictions, it must be made clear that the previous convictions are relevant only to his credibility as a witness and not to show a propensity to commit offences of the type of which he is now accused.

(g)   The defendant's good character

Where the defendant has no previous convictions, the jury should be directed that this is relevant both to his credibility as a witness and to the likelihood of his having committed the offence. If the defendant does not testify, then his previous good character goes to the credibility of any denial that he made to the police when interviewed as well as being relevant to the likelihood of his having committed the offence alleged (*R v Vye* [1993] 1 WLR 471; *R v Teasdale* [1993] 4 All ER 290; *R v Aziz* [1996] 1 AC 41). In *Barrow v The Queen* [1998] AC 846, the Privy Council considered *R v Aziz* and held that the judge ought only to direct the jury on the relevance of the good character of the accused if the matter is raised by the defence (calling evidence or questioning prosecution witnesses with a view to establishing the defendant's good character).

Where a defendant has previously been cautioned by the police, it is proper for the trial judge to direct the jury as to the relevance of the defendant's lack of previous convictions in relation to his credibility as a witness but not to give the second limb of the *Vye* direction in relation to the defendant's lack of propensity to commit the offence charged (*R v Martin* (2000) 164 JP 174).

(h)   Corroboration

Where an accomplice testifies as a prosecution witness against a defendant, there is no duty to warn the jury about the dangers of convicting on the basis of that evidence (s 32 of the Criminal Justice and Public Order Act 1994 removed the mandatory corroboration warning). However, the trial judge nevertheless has a discretion to give such a warning: *R v Makanjuola; R v Easton* [1995] 1 WLR 1348. The Court of Appeal will only rarely interfere with the exercise of this discretion. Under the European Convention on Human Rights, admitting evidence of an accomplice may not violate Art 6 provided that the jury are made fully aware of the circumstances. It is open to question whether the removal of the mandatory corroboration warning by s 32 of the 1994 Act accords with this principle.

(i)   Expert evidence

In a case involving expert evidence, it is important for the judge to direct the jury that they are not bound by the opinion of an expert witness: *R v Fitzpatrick* [1999] Crim LR 832; *R v Stockwell* (1993) 97 Cr App R 260.

(j)   Separation of the jury

In *R v Oliver* [1995] 2 Cr App R 514, the Court of Appeal gave guidance on the directions which should be given to a jury which was allowed to separate before delivering its verdict. The jury must be warned that:

(a) they may only decide the case on the basis of the evidence and arguments they have seen and heard in court;

(b) they must not seek further information about the case (for example, by going and having a look at the scene of the crime);

(c) they must not talk to anyone about the case except other jurors and even discussions with other jurors may only take place while they are deliberating together in the retiring room.

11.10.5 Alternative counts

If the indictment contains alternative counts where one is more serious than the other (for example, ss 18 and 20 of the Offences Against the Person Act 1861), the judge will tell the jury to consider the more serious count first. If they convict on that count, they should not consider the other count; if they acquit on the more serious count, they should go on to consider the less serious charge.

If the alternative counts are of more or less equal gravity (for example, theft and handling), the jury will simply be told to consider both but to acquit on both or convict on only one.

11.10.6 Unanimous verdict

The jury must be directed to return a unanimous verdict; a majority verdict is only possible after an appropriate direction given later. The judge will normally say something like this to the jury: 'You may well have heard of the majority verdicts. Well, until I give you a direction to the contrary, I can only accept a verdict upon which you are all agreed. If a time comes when I can accept a verdict which is not the verdict of all of you, I will give you further directions. Until that time, you should put thoughts of majority verdicts from your minds and try to reach a verdict upon which you are all agreed.'

In *R v Guthrie* (1994) *The Times*, 23 February, the judge was asked by the jury, after they had been deliberating for a little over an hour, how long it would be before the judge could accept a majority verdict. The Court of Appeal said that the judge acted correctly in telling them how long in response to their direct question. However, it is only where there is such a direct question that the jury should be given this information before the judge actually gives a majority verdict direction.

Finally, the jury will also be advised to elect a foreman to chair their discussions and announce their verdict.

11.10.7 Summing up fairly

The judge must take care to sum up fairly. He must, for example, ensure that the defence case is put fully and fairly (*R v Gaughan* [1990] Crim LR 880). The judge should deal with the case impartially. Sarcastic and extravagant language disparaging the defence must be avoided. In the event of an appeal against conviction, the Court of Appeal will look at 'the impact of the summing up as a whole' when considering its fairness (*R v Berrada* (1990) 91 Cr App R 131).

In *R v Spencer* [1995] Crim LR 235, the defendant's conviction was held to be unsafe as a result of excessive and largely one-sided comment made by the judge when directing the jury. It was said by Henry LJ that some comment is permissible, but not to the extent that the rehearsal of the evidence is interrupted and the jury's task made more difficult. In *R v Reid* (1999) *The Times*, 17 August, the Court of Appeal made the

point that where the case against the defendant is strong, and his defence correspondingly weak, the judge has to be scrupulous to ensure that the defendant's defence is presented to the jury in an even-handed and impartial manner.

In *R v Farr* (1999) 163 JP 193, the Court of Appeal said that a judge summing up a case is under no obligation to recite all the evidence or arguments (see also *McGreevy v DPP* [1973] 1 WLR 276 and *R v Wilson* [1991] Crim LR 838). In general, the longer the trial, the greater would be the jury's need for the judge's help with the evidence. Where a trial lasts for a few days or more, it would usually assist the jury if the judge were to summarise the factual issues and identify any evidence in dispute, thereby focusing the jury's attention on the issues to be resolved. However, the Court of Appeal will not look favourably on appeals based simply on a judge's failure to refer to particular arguments or specific pieces of evidence. The summing up in the present case was defective, in that it failed to refer to a number of the key features of the defence case, and (instead of being fair and balanced) resembled a speech for the prosecution. The convictions were quashed and a re-trial was ordered.

It should be noted that it is generally inappropriate for the judge to comment on the failure of the defence to call a particular witness, as such comment can easily detract from what is said about the burden of proof (see *R v Wheeler* [1967] 1 WLR 1531, 1535; *R v Wright* [2000] Crim LR 510).

Finally, it should be borne in mind that where the judge fails to direct the jury adequately on a particular point, and that failure appears to provide a ground of appeal, defence counsel should not remain silent but should draw the matter to the attention of the judge; indeed, the duty to assist the judge rests upon both the prosecution and the defence (*R v Langford* (2001) *The Times*, 12 January).

In *R v Weller* [2003] EWCA Crim 815; [2004] 1 Cr App R 1, a murder trial where the defence of provocation was raised, the court observed that there may be considerable advantages in giving the direction on provocation to the jury in writing at the appropriate moment in the summing up before taking them through it. It is, said the court, asking a lot for a jury to absorb the direction as they listen to it and carry it in their minds into the jury room. This approach may, of course, be appropriate in the case of any directions that are at all complicated.

11.11 RETIREMENT OF THE JURY

After the summing up, the jury are delivered into the custody of the jury bailiff, who takes an oath to take them to a private place to consider their verdict and to prevent anyone from communicating with them. The jury then go to the jury room to consider their verdict.

In a serious case (especially where there are several counts and/or several defendants), the judge should not send the jury out after 3 pm save in exceptional cases. It would be better for them to start their deliberations the following day (*R v Birch* (1992) *The Times*, 27 March).

Practice Direction (Crown Court: Guidance to Jurors) (2004) *The Times*, 27 February makes an amendment to *Practice Direction (Criminal Proceedings: Consolidation)* [2002] 1 WLR 2870:

IV.42 *Jurors*

Guidance to jurors

42.5 The following directions take effect immediately.

42.6 Trial judges should ensure that the jury is alerted to the need to bring any concerns about fellow jurors to the attention of the judge at the time, and not to wait until the case is concluded. At the same time, it is undesirable to encourage inappropriate criticism of fellow jurors, or to threaten jurors with contempt of court.

42.7 Judges should therefore take the opportunity, when warning the jury of the importance of not discussing the case with anyone outside the jury, to add a further warning. It is for the trial judge to tailor the further warning to the case, and to the phraseology used in the usual warning. The effect of the further warning should be that it is the duty of jurors to bring to the judge's attention, promptly, any behaviour among the jurors or by others affecting the jurors, that causes concern. The point should be made that, unless that is done while the case is continuing, it may be impossible to put matters right.

42.8 The judge should consider, particularly in a longer trial, whether a reminder on the lines of the further warning is appropriate prior to the retirement of the jury.

42.9 In the event that such an incident does occur, trial judges should have regard to the remarks of Lord Hope of Craighead in *R v Mirza* [2004] 2 WLR 201, 241–42, paras 127–28 and consider the desirability of preparing a statement that could be used in connection with any appeal arising from the incident to the Court of Appeal (Criminal Division). Members of the Court of Appeal (Criminal Division) should also remind themselves of the power to request the judge to furnish them with any information or assistance under r 22 of the Criminal Appeal Rules 1968 (SI 1968/1262) and s 87(4) of the Supreme Court Act 1981.

11.11.1 Separation of the jury

During lunch-time and overnight adjournments during the trial, the jury are allowed to go their separate ways. Formerly, the jury were not allowed to separate after the judge had finished the summing up. Section 13 of the Juries Act 1974 now enables the court to allow the jury to separate after (as well as before) they have been sent out to consider their verdict.

Before being allowed to separate, the jurors should be warned not to discuss the case with anyone who is not on the jury *(R v Prime* (1973) 57 Cr App R 632). The jury should also be told not to continue their deliberations except when they are together in the jury room, otherwise there is a risk that discussions might take place without all jurors being present *(R v Tharakan* [1995] 2 Cr App R 368). In *R v Hastings* [2003] EWCA Crim 3730; (2003) *The Times*, 12 December, the Court of Appeal reiterated that it is extremely important that the judge warns the jury not to deliberate on their verdict until all jury members are present and after the jury bailiffs have been sworn.

11.11.2 No further evidence

Once the jury has retired, no further evidence can be called *(R v Owen* [1952] 2 QB 362). In that case, the jury came out of retirement to ask whether the premises where an indecent assault was alleged to have taken place would have been occupied or not at

the relevant time. The Court of Appeal held that no further evidence can be called after the jury has retired to consider its verdict.

The jury is, however, entitled to have with them in the jury room evidence which has been exhibited during the trial (*R v Wright* [1993] Crim LR 607). In *R v Tonge* (1993) 157 JP 1137, following *R v Emmerson* (1991) 92 Cr App R 284 and *R v Aitken* (1992) 94 Cr App R 85, the Court of Appeal considered what should be done if the jury (after they have retired) ask to hear the tape-recording of the defendant's interview at the police station. It was said that if the tape-recording had not been played in open court during the trial and the jury ask to hear the tape, it should usually be played in open court. However, if the tape has already been played in court, the jury may be allowed to hear it again in the jury room.

11.11.3 Questions from the jury after retirement

If the jury wish to communicate with the judge (for example, they need further directions on the law or to be reminded of some of the evidence), they do so by means of a note sent to the judge via the jury bailiff. If the judge receives such a note, he should show it to both counsel in open court and should invite submissions from them before sending for the jury (*R v Gorman* [1987] 1 WLR 545 and *R v Sipson Coachworks Ltd* [1992] Crim LR 666).

In *Ramstead v The Queen* [1999] AC 92, the Privy Council said that any communication between the judge and jury has to take place in open court in the presence of the entire jury, both counsel and the defendant (see also *R v McCluskey* (1993) 98 Cr App R 216). The Privy Council reiterated that where the judge receives a note from the jury, he should follow the procedure laid down in *R v Gorman*.

In *R v McQuiston* [1998] 1 Cr App R 139, it was held that where the judge reads substantial parts of the complainant's evidence to the jury after the jury have retired to consider their verdict (as may be the case if the jury ask for their memory of certain evidence to be refreshed), the judge must warn the jury not to give disproportionate weight to that evidence simply because it was repeated well after the other evidence had been heard; the judge must also remind the jury of the cross-examination of the complainant and of any relevant part of the defendant's evidence.

11.12 RETURNING A VERDICT

When the jury come back into court, the clerk asks them: 'Have you reached a verdict upon which you are all agreed?' If the answer is 'yes', the foreman will be asked to announce the verdict on each count of the indictment.

If the answer is 'yes', and the defendant is acquitted on all counts, he is told that he is free to go.

Where the defendant is charged with a number of offences and the jury indicate that they have agreed verdicts on some, but not all, of the offences, it is good practice to take the verdicts on those counts upon which the jury are agreed before they carry on considering the other counts (*R v F* [1994] Crim LR 377).

The Auld Review (paras 99–108) considers the ability of the jury to announce a verdict that does not accord with the evidence they have heard or the law as

expounded to them by the judge. Where the decision is to convict, the accused can of course appeal against that conviction. However, there is no remedy for the prosecution against a perverse acquittal. Some see this as one of the great strengths of the system of jury trial: if the jury feel that the law is wrong or is being applied oppressively, they can acquit the defendant. Others argue that a defendant has no right to be acquitted just because 12 people think that they know better than the government. Lord Justice Auld recommends (Recommendation 30) that:

> The law should be declared, by statute, if need be, that juries have no right to acquit defendants in defiance of the law or in disregard of the evidence, and that judges and advocates should conduct criminal cases accordingly.

This comparatively limited recommendation needs to be seen in the context of Recommendation 310 of the Review, which states that:

> 310 Where any special verdict [ie, a verdict where the judge has required the jury to answer publicly a series of questioned fashioned by the judge to the issues in the case] of a jury reveals on its terms that it is perverse:

> 310.1 if the verdict is guilty, the defence should have a right of appeal to the Court of Appeal, subject to the usual leave procedure, on the ground that the perversity renders the conviction unsafe; and

> 310.2 if the verdict is not guilty, the prosecution should have a right of appeal to the Court of Appeal, also subject to leave, on the ground that the perversity indicates that the verdict is probably untrue or unfair and such as to merit a re-trial.

This proposal is a very controversial one, since it would enable an appeal against an acquittal by the jury. However, as Lord Justice Auld points out in para 67 of Chapter 12, perverse decisions of magistrates have always been open to scrutiny on appeal, by the defence or the prosecution, through appeal by way of case stated to the Divisional Court. In the event, this suggestion was not taken up in the Criminal Justice Act 2003.

11.12.1 Guilty verdict

If the answer is 'yes', and the defendant is convicted on some or all of the counts, the prosecution will tell the judge if the defendant has any previous convictions and will say what else is known about him (education, family situation, employment, etc). The judge may hear a plea in mitigation or the case may be adjourned for a pre-sentence report. If there is an adjournment, the plea in mitigation will be delivered when the report has been prepared. The usual period of an adjournment for a report is three weeks if the defendant is remanded in custody, four weeks if he is on bail. Where the case is adjourned for a pre-sentence report to be prepared, the prosecution may ask to be excused from attending court on the next occasion since the judge will be aware of the facts of the case (and so there will be no need for the prosecution to summarise those facts) and the prosecution have no other part to play in the sentencing process.

11.12.2 Alternative counts

If the indictment contains counts which are in the alternative, the usual practice is for the clerk to ask for a verdict on the more serious allegation first. If the verdict on that count is 'not guilty', the clerk will go on to ask for the verdict on the other count. If, on

the other hand, the verdict on the more serious count is 'guilty', the jury should be discharged from giving a verdict on the less serious charge (*R v Harris* [1969] 1 WLR 745).

This should not be confused with the power of the jury to return an alternative verdict, acquitting the defendant of the count on the indictment but convicting him of an offence which is not on the indictment, a power dealt with below.

11.13 THE JURY IS UNABLE TO REACH A VERDICT

The answer to the question 'Have you reached a verdict upon which you are all agreed?' will be 'no' if the jury have returned to court to ask the judge for further assistance or if they have been out for some time and cannot reach a verdict. In the latter case, a majority verdict direction may be appropriate.

11.14 MAJORITY VERDICTS

According to the official Judicial Statistics for 2003, 22% of convictions that year were by way of majority verdict.

The law relating to majority verdicts is to be found in s 17 of the Juries Act 1974 and para IV.46 of *Practice Direction (Criminal Proceedings: Consolidation)* [2002] 1 WLR 2870; [2002] 3 All ER 904.

Section 17 of the 1974 Act provides as follows:

(1)   Subject to sub-sections (3) and (4) below, the verdict of a jury in proceedings in the Crown Court or the High Court need not be unanimous if—

   (a)   in a case where there are not less than eleven jurors, ten of them agree on the verdict; and

   (b)   in a case where there are ten jurors, nine of them agree on the verdict.

(2)   Subject to sub-section (4) below, the verdict of a jury (that is to say a complete jury of eight) in proceedings in a county court need not be unanimous if seven of them agree on the verdict.

(3)   The Crown Court shall not accept a verdict of guilty by virtue of sub-section (1) above unless the foreman of the jury has stated in open court the number of jurors who respectively agreed to and dissented from the verdict.

(4)   No court shall accept a verdict by virtue of sub-section (1) or (2) above unless it appears to the court that the jury have had such period of time for deliberation as the court thinks reasonable having regard to the nature and complexity of the case; and the Crown Court shall in any event not accept such a verdict unless it appears to the court that the jury have had at least two hours for deliberation.

(5)   This section is without prejudice to any practice in civil proceedings by which a court may accept a majority verdict with the consent of the parties, or by which the parties may agree to proceed in any case with an incomplete jury.

Paragraph IV.46 of the Practice Direction states:

IV.46 *Majority verdicts*

46.1 It is important that all those trying indictable offences should so far as possible adopt a uniform practice when complying with section 17 of the Juries Act 1974, both

in directing the jury in summing up and also in receiving the verdict or giving further directions after retirement. So far as the summing up is concerned, it is inadvisable for the judge, and indeed for advocates, to attempt an explanation of the section for fear that the jury will be confused. Before the jury retire, however, the judge should direct the jury in some such words as the following:

> 'As you may know, the law permits me, in certain circumstances, to accept a verdict which is not the verdict of you all. Those circumstances have not as yet arisen, so that when you retire I must ask you to reach a verdict upon which each one of you is agreed. Should, however, the time come when it is possible for me to accept a majority verdict, I will give you a further direction.'

46.2 Thereafter the practice should be as follows. Should the jury return before two hours and ten minutes since the last member of the jury left the jury box to go to the jury room (or such longer time as the judge thinks reasonable) has elapsed (see section 17(4)), they should be asked:

(a)　'Have you reached a verdict upon which you are all agreed? Please answer Yes or No';

(b)　(i)　if unanimous, 'What is your verdict?';

　　　(ii)　if not unanimous, the jury should be sent out again for further deliberation with a further direction to arrive if possible at an unanimous verdict.

46.3 Should the jury return (whether for the first time or subsequently) or be sent for after the two hours and ten minutes (or the longer period) has elapsed, questions (a) and (b)(i) in paragraph 46.2 should be put to them and, if it appears that they are not unanimous, they should be asked to retire once more and told that they should continue to endeavour to reach an unanimous verdict but that, if they cannot, the judge will accept a majority verdict as in section 17(1).

46.4 When the jury finally return they should be asked:

(a)　'Have at least ten (or nine as the case may be) of you agreed on your verdict?';

(b)　if 'Yes', 'What is your verdict? Please only answer Guilty or Not Guilty';

(c)　(i)　if 'Not Guilty', accept the verdict without more ado;

　　　(ii)　if 'Guilty', 'Is that the verdict of you all or by a majority?';

(d)　if 'Guilty' by a majority, 'How many of you agreed to the verdict and how many dissented?'

46.5 At whatever stage the jury return, before question (a) is asked, the senior officer of the court present shall state in open court, for each period when the jury was out of court for the purpose of considering their verdict(s), the time at which the last member of the jury left the jury box to go to the jury room and the time of their return to the jury box and will additionally state in open court the total of such periods.

46.6 The reason why section 17(3) is confined to a majority verdict of guilty and for the somewhat complicated procedure set out in paragraph 46.3 and paragraph 46.4 is to prevent it being known that a verdict of 'Not Guilty' is a majority verdict. If the final direction in paragraph 46.3 continues to require the jury to arrive, if possible, at an unanimous verdict and the verdict is received as in paragraph 46.4, it will not be known for certain that the acquittal is not unanimous.

46.7 Where there are several counts (or alternative verdicts) left to the jury the above practice will, of course, need to be adapted to the circumstances. The procedure will have to be repeated in respect of each count (or alternative verdict), the verdict being accepted in those cases where the jury are unanimous and the further direction in paragraph 46.3 being given in cases in which they are not unanimous. Should the jury

in the end be unable to agree on a verdict by the required majority (ie if the answer to the question in paragraph 46.4(a) be in the negative) the judge in his discretion will either ask them to deliberate further or discharge them.

46.8 Section 17 will, of course, apply also to verdicts other than 'Guilty' or 'Not Guilty', eg to special verdicts under the Criminal Procedure (Insanity) Act 1964, verdicts under that Act as to fitness to be tried, and special verdicts on findings of fact. Accordingly in such cases the questions to jurors will have to be suitably adjusted.

There is no minimum length of deliberation required before a *unanimous* verdict can be delivered. However, under s 17 of the Juries Act 1974, a *majority* verdict cannot be accepted until at least two hours, or such longer period as the judge considers necessary having regard to the nature and complexity of the case, have elapsed since the jury first retired to consider their verdict. The Practice Direction adds a further 10 minutes, to allow the jury to settle down in the jury room and elect a foreman.

If a majority verdict were to be accepted before two hours have elapsed from the time the jury left the court room to begin its deliberations, that verdict would be a nullity.

The only permissible majorities are:

- for 12 jurors: 11–1 or 10–2;
- where one juror has been discharged, leaving 11 jurors: 10–1;
- where two jurors have been discharged, leaving 10: 9–1.

A nine person jury (where three jurors have been discharged) can only deliver a unanimous verdict. As we have already seen, if more than three jurors have to be discharged, the trial has to be aborted and a re-trial takes place later.

If the judge considers that the jury have had long enough to come to a verdict (subject to the two hour minimum set out in s 17), the judge can send for the jury and give a majority verdict direction. Sometimes, the jury will take the initiative and send a note to the judge saying that they are deadlocked; if at least two hours have elapsed, the judge may, if he thinks it appropriate, give a majority verdict direction.

11.14.1 Content of majority verdict direction

A majority verdict direction will be along these lines:

> Members of the jury, it is desirable for you to reach a verdict upon which you are all agreed if that is possible. However, the time has now come when I can accept a verdict which is the verdict of at least 10 of you. Please go back into the jury room and try once again to reach a unanimous verdict or, if you are unable to do that, a verdict upon which at least 10 of you are agreed.

11.14.2 Procedure after direction is given

When the jury return to the courtroom after a majority verdict direction has been given, the clerk asks the foreman, 'Have you reached a verdict on which at least 10 of you are agreed?' (assuming there remain 12 people on the jury).

If the answer is 'yes', the clerk asks the foreman whether the verdict is guilty or not guilty. If it is not guilty, no further question will be asked of the jury; if it is guilty the clerk will ask how many jurors find the defendant guilty (s 17(3) of the Juries Act). If the size of the majority in favour of conviction is not stated, the verdict is a nullity (*R v*

Barry [1975] 1 WLR 1190 and *R v Pigg* [1983] 1 WLR 6). However, if the error is realised after the jury has been discharged, it is possible to reconvene the jury for this purpose (*R v Maloney* [1996] 2 Cr App R 303).

In *R v Austin* [2002] EWCA Crim 1796; [2003] Crim LR 426, the defendant was convicted by majority verdict but the court failed to comply with s 17(3) of the Juries Act 1974, in that the number of dissenting jurors was not stated by the foreman in open court; the defendant argued that the verdict was therefore invalid. The Court of Appeal held that whilst compliance with the requirement of s 17(3) of the Juries Act that the foreman state in open court the number of jurors who respectively agreed to and dissented from the verdict is mandatory before a judge can accept a majority verdict of guilty, all that is necessary is that the words used by the clerk of the court and the foreman are such that it would be clear to an ordinary person how the jury was divided. In the present case, the words used were such that the division of the jury could not be ascertained, and so the requirements of s 17(3) had not been complied with (thereby rendering the conviction unsafe).

The essential point is that it will not be known whether an acquittal is unanimous or by majority. However, in the case of a conviction, it is important to know whether it was unanimous or by majority, and if the latter the size of the majority (not least to ensure that the majority was a lawful one).

If the answer to the clerk's first question is 'no', the foreman will be asked by the judge if there is any prospect of the jury reaching a verdict. If there is a possibility, the judge will almost certainly give the jury more time. If there is no such possibility, the jury will be discharged and a fresh trial will probably take place later.

11.15 THE *WATSON* DIRECTION

The judge must not exert undue pressure on the jury to reach a verdict. In *R v McKenna* [1960] 1 QB 411, for example, the judge told the jury that they would be 'kept all night' if they could not reach a verdict; it was felt that this could have been interpreted by some of them that they would have to stay in the jury room and the resulting conviction was therefore quashed.

However, the judge can inquire if there is a reasonable prospect of a verdict being reached; the judge may tell the jury that if there is no reasonable prospect of them reaching a verdict they will be discharged and if there is then they can have as much time as they need (*R v Modeste* [1983] Crim LR 746).

In *R v Watson* [1988] QB 690, the Court of Appeal said that a judge must not point out to the jury that if they do not reach a verdict there will have to be a re-trial which will cause inconvenience and expense. However, Lord Lane CJ said (at p 700) that:

In the judgment of this court there is no reason why a jury should not be directed as follows:

'Each of you has taken an oath to return a true verdict according to the evidence. No one must be false to that oath, but you have a duty not only as individuals but collectively. That is the strength of the jury system. Each of you takes into the jury box with you your individual experience and wisdom. Your task is to pool that experience and wisdom. You do that by giving your views and listening to the views of the others. There must necessarily be discussion, argument and give and take within the

scope of your oath. That is the way in which agreement is reached. If, unhappily, [10 of] you cannot reach agreement you must say so.'

In *R v Buono* (1992) 95 Cr App R 338, the Court of Appeal said that a *Watson* direction should not be given at the same time as a majority verdict direction. Thus, the judge should give the majority verdict direction and then wait to see if the jury can reach a majority verdict; if the jury is still unable to reach a verdict, a *Watson* direction may then be given.

In *Buono*, and again in *R v Morgan* (1997) *The Times*, 18 April, the Court of Appeal said that where it is necessary to direct a jury on the need to reach a verdict, the judge should follow the precise terms laid down in *R v Watson*, because a conviction will be rendered unsafe if the judge says anything which might be construed as putting improper pressure on the jury.

No other pressure must be brought to bear on the jury. In *R v Duggan* [1992] Crim LR 513, for example, the jury informed the judge that they would rather deliberate into the night than have to return the following day. The trial judge indicated that they might have to go into an hotel if they could not reach a verdict by 5 pm. A verdict of guilty was returned at 4.55 pm. As some jurors had already indicated that they did not wish to spend the night in an hotel, the judge's words were held to amount to undue pressure and the convictions were quashed.

11.16 THE VERDICT OF GUILTY TO AN ALTERNATIVE OFFENCE

Under s 6(3) of the Criminal Law Act 1967, where the allegations in the indictment amount to or include (whether expressly or by implication) an allegation of another offence which may be tried on indictment, the jury may acquit on the offence charged and convict on the included offence. Section 6(3) provides as follows:

> Where, on a person's trial on indictment for any offence except treason or murder, the jury find him not guilty of the offence specifically charged in the indictment, but the allegations in the indictment amount to or include (expressly or by implication) an allegation of another offence falling within the jurisdiction of the court of trial, the jury may find him guilty of that other offence or of an offence of which he could be found guilty on an indictment specifically charging that other offence.

11.16.1 Express inclusion

An offence is expressly included in the indictment if words can be deleted from the existing count so as to leave words alleging another offence. This is sometimes called the 'blue pencil' test (*R v Lillis* [1972] 2 QB 236).

Suppose that it is alleged that the defendant 'entered 4 Gray's Inn Place as a trespasser and stole therein a typewriter'. If the words 'entered 4 Gray's Inn Place as a trespasser and' and 'therein' are deleted, that leaves an allegation that the defendant 'stole a typewriter'. Therefore, theft (s 1 of the Theft Act 1968) is expressly included in an allegation of burglary (s 9(1)(b) of the Theft Act 1968).

Thus, if a jury decides that they are not satisfied so that they are sure that the defendant entered as a trespasser but are sure that he stole the goods alleged in the indictment, they can acquit of burglary but convict of theft.

11.16.2 Implied inclusion

The meaning of implied inclusion was considered by the House of Lords in *Metropolitan Police Commissioner v Wilson* [1984] AC 242. Where the commission of the offence alleged in the indictment will, in the normal course of events (that is, in the great majority of cases) involve the commission of another offence, that other offence is impliedly included in the offence charged in the indictment.

In *Wilson*, for example, it was held that inflicting grievous bodily harm (s 20 of the Offences Against the Person Act 1861) usually involves assault occasioning actual bodily harm (s 47 of the Offences Against the Person Act 1861), and so the jury can acquit of grievous bodily harm but convict of actual bodily harm. It may well be possible to inflict grievous bodily harm without assaulting the victim (for example, by deliberately creating a panic in a crowded building intending that people are seriously hurt in the rush to escape), but, in the normal course of events, grievous bodily harm will involve assault occasioning actual bodily harm.

The same would apply to an allegation of wounding under s 20 of the Offences Against the Person Act 1861, so s 47 is an alternative offence to that charge too (*R v Savage* [1992] 1 AC 699).

A charge of causing grievous bodily harm with intent (s 18 of the Offences Against the Person Act 1861) includes a charge of inflicting grievous bodily harm (s 20 of the Offences Against the Person Act 1861) (*R v Mandair* [1994] 2 WLR 700).

Likewise, indecent assault is an alternative to rape (*R v Hodgson* [1973] QB 565) and theft is an alternative to robbery.

Where a defendant is charged with attempted murder, an alternative verdict of attempting to cause grievous bodily harm with intent can be left to the jury, since a defendant who intends to murder someone clearly intends to cause them grievous bodily harm as well (*R v Morrison* [2003] EWCA Crim 1722; [2003] 1 WLR 1859).

11.16.3 Other statutory provisions

There are also statutory provisions which set out alternative offences:

- *Section 6(2) of the Criminal Law Act 1967*

  The jury may acquit of murder but convict of (*inter alia*) manslaughter or causing grievous bodily harm with intent.

- *Section 6(4) of the Criminal Law Act 1967*

  The jury may acquit of the offence charged but convict of attempt to commit that offence or attempt to commit an offence which is expressly or implied included in the offence charged. Thus, if the indictment alleges robbery, the jury could acquit of robbery but convict of attempted robbery or attempted theft.

- *Section 12(4) of the Theft Act 1968*

  On a count of theft, the jury could acquit of theft but convict the defendant of taking a conveyance without the owner's consent (even though the latter is a summary offence).

- *Section 24 of the Road Traffic Offenders Act 1988*

  On a count alleging dangerous driving or causing death by dangerous driving, the jury may convict the defendant instead of careless driving (again, even though the latter is a summary offence).

11.16.4 Summary offences

Section 6(3) of the Criminal Law Act 1967 makes it clear that the included offence must be one which can be tried in the Crown Court, hence the need for s 12(4) of the Theft Act 1968 and s 24 of the Road Traffic Offenders Act 1988. The two included offences are both summary offences and, but for statutory provision to the contrary, the jury would not be able to convict of those summary offences.

So, in *R v Mearns* [1991] 1 QB 82, followed in *Bird v DPP* [1992] COD 351, it was held that the jury cannot convict a defendant of common assault as that is a summary offence. Note that common assault is one of the four offences to which s 40 of the Criminal Justice Act 1988 applies, and so if the jury indicated that they could not convict of, say, assault occasioning actual bodily harm (because they are not satisfied that injury occurred) but nonetheless find that an assault (which includes the threat of violence) took place, a count alleging common assault could be added to the indictment. Only then could the jury convict of common assault. *Mearns* was followed in *R v Clifford* (2003) *The Times*, 5 December, where the Court of Appeal confirmed that a defendant being tried on indictment cannot be found guilty, by way of an alternative verdict under s 6(3), of a summary offence to which s 40 of the Criminal Justice Act 1988 applies. The accused can only be convicted of the summary offence if a count specifically charging him with that offence is included in the indictment. Therefore, if (as in *Clifford*) the indictment alleges racially aggravated assault occasioning actual bodily harm, the accused cannot be convicted of common assault (a summary offence within the ambit of s 40) unless the indictment is amended to include that offence.

The position as regards criminal damage is a little more complicated. Where the value involved in a criminal damage charge is less than £5,000, a magistrates' court has to treat the offence as if it were a summary offence. In *R v Fennell* [2000] 1 WLR 2011, the defendant was charged with racially aggravated criminal damage. The judge allowed the jury to acquit him of that offence but convict him instead (under s 6(3) of the Criminal Law Act 1967) of ordinary criminal damage. The value involved was less than £5,000. The court held that it is open to a judge to leave an alternative verdict of criminal damage for the jury's consideration even if the value involved is less than £5,000 and without invoking s 40 of the Criminal Justice Act 1988 to add that offence of criminal damage to the indictment. The court held that *R v Burt* (1996) 161 JP 77, where the contrary view was expressed, was wrongly decided. *Fennell* was followed in *R v Alden* [2002] EWCA Crim 421; [2002] 2 Cr App R(S) 74, where it was held that if an offender is to be sentenced by the Crown Court for an offence of criminal damage, otherwise than under a particular provision specifically restricting the sentencing powers of the Crown Court (such as s 40 of the Criminal Justice Act 1988), then the maximum sentence available is 10 years. The basis of these decisions is that criminal damage is an offence triable either way, subject only to the fact that magistrates have to treat it as if it were triable only summarily for mode of trial purposes if the value is less than £5,000.

11.16.5 Scope of s 6(3) of the Criminal Law Act 1967

Convicting of an alternative offence is only possible if the jury first agree to acquit on the offence on the indictment. If the jury cannot agree on an acquittal of the offence charged, the only way they can convict of another offence is if that offence is added to

the indictment as a new count. See, for example, *R v Collison* (1980) 71 Cr App R 249, where a count was added to the indictment after the jury had been considering their verdict for some while for this very reason.

11.16.6 Directing the jury on alternative offences

The jury will only know about the possibility of convicting of an offence other than the offence on the indictment if they are told about this power. So, when should the judge direct the jury about the possibility of convicting on an alternative offence?

In *R v Fairbanks* [1986] 1 WLR 1202, it was said that the judge should direct the jury that it is possible for them to acquit of the offence charged but convict of an alternative offence if:

- the possibility that the defendant is guilty only of a lesser offence has fairly arisen on the evidence; and

- directing the jury about the possibility of convicting the defendant of an alternative offence will not unnecessarily complicate the case.

In *R v Wilson* [1984] Crim LR 173, CA, it was held that there must be no risk of injustice to the defendant; he must have had the opportunity of fully meeting the alternative in the course of his defence. In other words, if the possibility of an alternative offence is only canvassed at the end of the trial, would the defence have cross-examined prosecution witnesses differently or adduced different defence evidence had the alternative offence been mentioned at the start of the trial? In *R v Hammett* [1993] RTR 275, for example, the possibility of convicting of an alternative offence was first mentioned in the judge's summing up. Even though the judge then gave counsel the opportunity of addressing the jury further, it was held by the Court of Appeal to be unfair to raise the issue of an alternative offence so late in the proceedings.

The question was looked at again by the House of Lords in *R v Maxwell* [1990] 1 WLR 401. The defendant was charged with robbery. He indicated that he would have been willing to plead guilty to burglary. However, the prosecution did not wish to add a count alleging burglary to the indictment. Burglary is not an alternative to robbery, but theft (a constituent of one type of burglary) is an alternative to robbery (which comprises theft together with the use or threat of violence). The judge refused to allow the jury to consider convicting of theft instead of robbery. This refusal was upheld by the House of Lords. The essential issue, as defined by the prosecution, was whether the defendant had used violence; theft was trivial by comparison and would merely have distracted the jury from the main issue of the case.

The implication of *Maxwell* is that it is for the prosecution to define the main issue(s) in the case and the judge should not subvert their decision by directing the jury to consider an alternative offence. It should be noted that even if defence counsel takes the initiative and tells the jury that they can convict of an alternative offence, the judge could direct the jury that they are not to consider this possibility.

The arguments in favour of letting the jury consider an alternative offence were considered in *Fairbanks*. From the prosecution point of view, where the evidence is such that it is clear that the defendant ought to be convicted of the lesser offence, it would be wrong for the jury to have to acquit him altogether merely because they cannot be sure that he is guilty of the more serious offence. From the defence point of view, if the judge does not allow the jury to consider the lesser offence, it is possible

that the jury will convict the defendant of the more serious offence, not because they are sure that he is guilty of it, but so as to convict him of something rather than allow him to escape without any penalty at all.

It would of course be inappropriate for the judge to leave a lesser offence to the jury if it is inappropriate given the way the defence has been conducted (for example, where the defence is one of alibi).

Where a judge refuses to leave an alternative offence to the jury, the Court of Appeal will only quash a conviction for the offence charged on the indictment if satisfied that the jury convicted the defendant only because it was reluctant to allow him to get away completely with his misconduct (*R v O'Hadhmaill* [1996] Crim LR 509). This approach was followed in *R v Bergman and Collins* [1996] 2 Cr App R 399, where the trial judge should have directed the jury about the possibility of convicting the defendants of a lesser offence but the convictions for the offence charged on the indictment were upheld since there was no evidence which tended to show that the jury's verdict would have been different if they had been directed on the possibility of convicting of a lesser offence. Similarly, in *R v Hussain* [2004] EWCA Crim 325; (2004) *The Daily Telegraph*, 5 February, where the defendant was charged with causing death by dangerous driving, the trial judge rejected an application to leave the alternative offence of careless driving to the jury. The Court of Appeal confirmed that the test to be applied when considering whether to leave an alternative offence to the jury is:

(a) whether there is any sensible basis on which the jury might convict of the more serious offence;

(b) whether leaving an alternative charge might compromise the jury's consideration and lead to an element of confusion; and

(c) in circumstances where the criminality is graver than the alternative offence, whether it is undesirable to leave an alternative to the jury, even if that renders the situation of the defendant overly favourable on the basis that the options are only an acquittal or a conviction.

Where an alternative offence is not left to the jury, a conviction might be rendered unsafe, said the court, if the jury convicted the defendant out of reluctance to see an acquittal where they had found some misconduct. In those circumstances, it is incumbent on the judge properly to direct the jury exactly as to what they have to find in order to convict. On the facts of the present case, it was open to the judge not to leave the alternative to the jury, and the direction to the jury was clearly designed to ensure that the jury only convicted the defendant if the offence on the indictment was made out. The conviction was therefore safe.

In *R v Mandair* [1994] 2 WLR 700, Lord Mackay LC said that the simpler (and better) course of action is to add a count to the indictment alleging the lesser offence, rather than relying on s 6(3) of the Criminal Law Act 1967.

11.16.7 Summary

For the judge to leave the alternative offence to the jury:

- it must be appropriate (for example, it would not be appropriate where the defence is one of alibi, since it would distract the jury from the main issue in the case, namely the whereabouts of the defendant at the time of the alleged offence);

- it must have been at least implicit in the defence questioning of prosecution witnesses and the defence evidence (otherwise, it will be unfair to the defence);
- if the alternative is trivial in comparison with the offence charged, it must not be an unnecessary and undesirable complication.

11.17 DISCHARGE OF THE JURY

If the jury cannot reach a verdict within what the judge regards as a reasonable time, the jury will be discharged. This does not count as an acquittal and so the accused can be retried. There is no need for the case to be go back to the magistrates' court to be re-sent to the Crown Court. If the second jury is 'hung' (unable to reach a verdict) too, the prosecution are unlikely to insist on a third trial.

11.18 GUILTY PLEAS

If the defendant pleads guilty to all the counts on the indictment (or pleads guilty to some of the counts and the prosecution do not proceed with the others), no trial takes place.

11.18.1 Procedure where the defendant pleads guilty

If the defendant pleads guilty to all the counts, the prosecution summarise the facts of the case. Details of the defendant's previous convictions (if any) are handed to the judge and he will indicate which (if any) he wishes prosecuting counsel to read aloud. Usually, it is only the most recent previous convictions that are read out. The prosecution will also tell the judge what is known about the defendant's personal circumstances (employment, housing, etc); this is based on what the defendant has told the police and will be very brief.

The defence then make a plea in mitigation. If a pre-sentence report is not available, the judge may adjourn the case until one is prepared. In that case there is a presumption in favour of bail as s 4 of the Bail Act 1976 still applies. When the case is resumed, the prosecution will again summarise the facts and the defence will make a plea in mitigation. The usual period for the adjournment is three weeks if the defendant is in custody, four weeks if he is on bail.

11.19 THE *NEWTON* HEARING

If the defendant pleads guilty but challenges the version of events put forward by the prosecution, and the difference is one which will affect the sentence that is passed, the court can only reject the defence version of events after hearing evidence as to what happened. Such a hearing is known as a *Newton* hearing (from *R v Newton* (1983) 77 Cr App R 13).

11.20 MIXED PLEAS

If the defendant pleads guilty to some counts but not guilty to others, sentence will be postponed until the trial on the counts to which the defendant has pleaded not guilty has been completed, assuming that the prosecution wish to proceed with the trial of the offences to which the defendant pleaded not guilty.

This raises the question of plea bargaining between the prosecution and the defence.

11.21 PLEA BARGAINING

The usual basis of a plea bargain is either:

- that if the defendant will plead guilty to some counts on the indictment, the prosecution will not proceed with the remainder; or
- that if the defendant will plead guilty to a lesser offence, the prosecution will not proceed with the more serious offence.

This form of plea bargaining is widely accepted as a way of saving time and money. From the prosecution point of view, it may well be better to have a conviction for something rather than risk a jury acquitting on all counts.

11.22 PLEADING GUILTY TO A LESSER OFFENCE

Pleading guilty to a lesser offence is possible in the following two circumstances.

11.22.1 Pleading guilty to an offence which is not on the indictment

Under s 6(1)(b) of the Criminal Law Act 1967, the defendant 'may plead not guilty of the offence specifically charged in the indictment but guilty of another offence of which he might be found guilty on that indictment'. In other words, the defendant may plead not guilty to the count on the indictment but guilty to a lesser offence of which the jury would be able to convict him under s 6(3) of the Criminal Law Act 1967. If this plea is accepted, the defendant stands acquitted of the offence charged but convicted of the lesser offence, for which he will then be sentenced.

If the plea of guilty to the lesser offence is not accepted by the prosecution (or the judge refuses to accept it), the trial will proceed on the basis of a not guilty plea to the offence on the indictment. The defendant's plea of guilty to the lesser offence is impliedly withdrawn (so, if the jury acquit the defendant of the offence on the indictment, and do not convict of the lesser offence under s 6(3), the defendant cannot then be sentenced for the lesser offence (*R v Hazeltine* [1967] 2 QB 857)). *Hazeltine* was followed in *R v Yeardley* [2000] 1 QB 374, where the defendant was arraigned on an indictment charging possession of a Class A drug with intent to supply contrary to the Misuse of Drugs Act 1971. He pleaded not guilty to the charge but guilty to simple possession of the drug. However, his guilty plea was not accepted by the prosecution, and the trial proceeded on the charge of possession with intent to supply. The prosecution did not seek a conviction for, nor were the jury directed that they could

find the defendant guilty of, simple possession. The jury returned a verdict of not guilty of possession with intent to supply. The judge then sentenced the defendant for simple possession. The Court of Appeal held that the defendant's plea of guilty, having been rejected by the prosecution, was a nullity; there was therefore no conviction and no basis on which he could lawfully have been sentenced. The Court of Appeal went on to say that (because the conviction was a nullity) it had no jurisdiction to hear an appeal against sentence and so it had to reconstitute itself as a Divisional Court and quash the sentence. The court noted that it would be sensible in cases where a defendant is charged with supplying drugs, or being in possession of drugs with intent to supply, to include a separate count for simple possession if the quantity of drugs involved is not such that simple possession is out of the question. Such a count could be drafted on a separate sheet so that where the defendant pleads guilty to simple possession but that plea is unacceptable to either the court or the prosecution, the trial can proceed on the more serious charge and the jury can be supplied with a copy of that charge on its own.

Note that if the prosecution do not add a count alleging the lesser offence to the indictment and there is a trial on the original offence, the prosecution can adduce evidence of the defendant's earlier plea of guilty to the lesser offence if they so wish. So (using the facts of *Yeardley*) if the accused had, during his trial for possession with intent to supply, denied being in possession of the drugs, the prosecution could have adduced evidence of his plea of guilty to the possession charge.

The acceptance of a plea of guilty to a lesser offence is subject to the agreement of the judge, but it would be very rare for the judge to insist on a trial of the more serious offence if the prosecution do not wish that to happen. However, there may be cases where the judge expresses misgivings about the decision of the prosecutor to accept a plea to a lesser charge. In *R v Mulla* [2003] EWCA Crim 1881; [2004] 1 Cr App R 6, the defendant was charged with causing death by dangerous driving; he offered to plead guilty to the lesser offence of causing death by careless driving. The prosecutor initially agreed to that course of action, but the trial judge invited the prosecutor to reconsider this decision. The prosecutor subsequently decided to proceed on the original charge. The defendant argued that this amounted to an abuse of process. The Court of Appeal said that five issues are to take into account in such a case:

(a) whether the prosecution had indicated a view not to proceed;

(b) whether the judge had expressed a view;

(c) whether there had been a significant time between the offered plea and the prosecutor's change of view;

(d) whether the defendant's hopes had been inappropriately raised and then dashed; and

(e) whether there had been prejudice caused to the defendant.

In the present case, the defendant had not been prejudiced, since he had known from the beginning that the judge had not approved of the course of action the prosecutor had agreed to and he had not received any private assurance from his counsel that a lesser plea would be accepted.

11.22.2 Pleading guilty to an alternative count on the indictment

The indictment may contain alternative counts. The word 'or' does not appear, and so there is nothing on the face of the indictment to indicate that the counts are in the alternative. For example, there might be one count alleging s 18 offences under the Offences Against the Person Act 1861 and another alleging s 20.

If the defendant pleads not guilty to both counts, the trial will proceed on both counts and the prosecution will tell the jury in the opening speech that they do not seek a conviction on both counts.

If the defendant pleads not guilty to the more serious offence but guilty to the lesser offence, it is up to the prosecution to decide whether to proceed with a trial of the count to which the defendant pleads not guilty. If a trial does follow and the defendant is acquitted of the more serious offence, he will then be sentenced for the lesser offence to which he pleaded guilty. If he is convicted of the more serious offence, the lesser offence will be ignored for sentencing purposes.

Normally, the prosecution will indicate to the defence beforehand whether a plea of guilty to the lesser offence will be acceptable. Where the plea to the lesser offence is acceptable, the lesser offence is put to the defendant first and (assuming he pleads guilty to it as anticipated) the second offence will either not be put to the defendant or it will be put and the prosecution will either offer no evidence or ask it to be left on the file.

11.23   ADVISING THE DEFENDANT ON PLEA

Care must be taken that a plea of guilty is entered voluntarily. If it is not entered voluntarily, the Court of Appeal will quash the conviction and will usually order a re-trial.

In the next section, we look at safeguards to prevent pressure from the judge. However, pressure can also be exerted by the defendant's own lawyers. It would be wholly improper to advise a client to plead guilty if the defendant reveals facts amounting to a defence. If, however, the facts revealed by the defendant show that he is effectively admitting the offence, then this should be made clear to him.

The decision as to plea must be that of the accused. The defendant's legal adviser may express advice in strong terms but must make it clear that the defendant has complete freedom of choice.

It should be added that if the defendant confesses to the crime to his advocate, he can only continue to represent the defendant if he pleads guilty (otherwise the advocate would effectively be misleading the court).

If the defendant insists on pleading guilty but maintains to the advocate that he is in fact innocent, the advocate may continue to represent the defendant but cannot say anything in mitigation which is inconsistent with the plea of guilty. This should be made clear to the defendant. Where the client is represented by counsel, the client should be asked to write a signed note on counsel's brief saying that he wishes to plead guilty against the advice of counsel.

11.23.1 Seeing the judge in his chambers

When a solicitor or barrister is advising a defendant as to plea, the client will inevitably want to know the likely sentence in the event of a conviction. Experienced lawyers are usually able to predict sentences with a reasonable degree of accuracy. Sometimes, however, the question arises whether the judge can give a preliminary indication of the sentence he is minded to impose (based on a view of the offence founded on the witness statements sent from the magistrates' court and a pre-sentence report if one is already available).

The leading case on this topic is *R v Turner* [1970] 2 QB 321, where the judge told defence counsel that if the defendant pleaded guilty, he would not be sent to prison but if he was convicted by the jury, a prison sentence was a very real possibility. The Court of Appeal said that a judge must not say (or imply) that the sentence is likely to take one form if the defendant pleads guilty and a different form if the defendant is convicted following a not guilty plea. This could be construed as putting pressure on the defendant to plead guilty. All the judge is allowed to say is that, whether the defendant pleads guilty or is found guilty, the sentence will, or will not, take a particular form. So, for example, in *R v Ryan* (1977) 67 Cr App R 177, the judge said that if the defendant pleaded guilty, he would get a non-custodial sentence but, if he was found guilty by the jury, he would get a custodial sentence. Not surprisingly, the defendant pleaded guilty. Equally unsurprisingly, the Court of Appeal quashed the conviction and ordered a re-trial.

It should be remembered that if the judge does give an indication of the likely sentence, he cannot then change his mind. In *R v Atkinson* [1978] 1 WLR 425, the judge indicated that he could see no reason why the defendant should go to prison. The defendant was convicted (following trial) and sentenced to six months' imprisonment. The Court of Appeal varied the sentence to enable the defendant's immediate release from custody. Similarly, in *R v Cullen* (1984) 81 Cr App R 17, the judge indicated that, whether the defendant pleaded guilty or was found guilty, he would receive a non-custodial sentence. The judge subsequently imposed a suspended sentence of imprisonment (which is regarded as a custodial sentence); this sentence was quashed by the Court of Appeal. Again, in *R v Johnson and Lorraine* (1990) 12 Cr App R(S) 219, the judge indicated that he would impose either a community order or a suspended sentence but, when he came to pass sentence, imposed immediate custody. The Court of Appeal said that even though the sentences were proper in themselves, a sense of injustice resulted from the earlier comments of the judge and so those sentences had to be quashed.

In *R v Smith* [1990] 1 WLR 1311, the Court of Appeal said that a shorthand writer should be present if counsel see the judge in his chambers. This will prevent an 'unseemly dispute' arising later as to exactly what was said. In *R v Harper-Taylor* [1991] RTR 76, the Court of Appeal emphasised that the judge should only see counsel in private if there is a very good reason, otherwise all proceedings should be conducted in open court.

These principles were re-affirmed in *R v Ryan* (1999) 163 JP 849. Counsel for the defendant went to see the trial judge in chambers to seek an indication as to sentence if the defendant were to change her plea to guilty. The judge gave an indication, and the defendant changed her plea to guilty. The same judge was unavailable when the case

was listed for sentencing; the sentencing judge passed a more severe sentence than that indicated by the first judge. The Court of Appeal ruled that:

(a) approaches to a judge seeking an indication of the length of sentence which might be imposed in the event of a plea of guilty are to be deprecated;

(b) where such an indication is given and conveyed to a defendant, it will normally be binding, not only on the judge who gave the indication but also on any other judge before whom a defendant might appear to be sentenced; and

(c) where a defendant changes plea in the light of such an indication from the judge but subsequently receives a more severe sentence than that indicated, the Court of Appeal would often (though not invariably) feel constrained to reduce the sentence to that indicated, even if the indicated sentence was lower than the offence merited in all the circumstances.

In *R v Dossetter* [1999] 2 Cr App R(S) 248, the Court of Appeal reiterated: (a) that the judge cannot give an indication of sentence which implies a different form of sentence if the defendant is found guilty rather than pleading guilty; (b) that there should be no visits to the judge save in exceptional circumstances; and (c) that there should be a record of what was said in such visits.

These principles have been summarised in para IV.45 of *Practice Direction (Criminal Proceedings: Consolidation)* [2002] 1 WLR 2870; [2002] 3 All ER 904:

IV.45 *Discussions about sentence*

45.1 An advocate must be free to do what is his duty, namely to give the accused the best advice he can and, if need be, in strong terms. It will often include advice that a guilty plea, showing an element of remorse, is a mitigating factor which may well enable the court to give a lesser sentence than would otherwise be the case. The advocate will, of course, emphasise that the accused must not plead guilty unless he has committed the acts constituting the offence(s) charged.

45.2 The accused, having considered the advocate's advice, must have complete freedom of choice whether to plead guilty or not guilty.

45.3 There must be freedom of access between advocate and judge. Any discussion must, however, be between the judge and the advocates on both sides. If counsel is instructed by a solicitor who is in court, he too should be allowed to attend the discussion. This freedom of access is important because there may be matters calling for communication or discussion of such a nature that the advocate cannot, in his client's interest, mention them in open court, eg the advocate, by way of mitigation, may wish to tell the judge that the accused has not long to live because he is suffering maybe from cancer of which he is and should remain ignorant. Again, the advocates on both sides may wish to discuss with the judge whether it would be proper, in a particular case, for the prosecution to accept a plea to a lesser offence. It is imperative that, so far as possible, justice must be administered in open court. Advocates should, therefore, only ask to see the judge when it is felt to be really necessary. The judge must be careful only to treat such communications as private where, in fairness to the accused, this is necessary.

45.4 The judge should, subject to one exception, never indicate the sentence he is minded to impose. The exception is that it should be permissible for a judge to say, if it be the case, that, whatever happens, whether the accused pleads guilty or not guilty, the sentence will or will not take a particular form. Where any such discussion on sentence has taken place, the advocate for the defence should disclose it to the accused and, subject to the exception of those matters of which he should remain ignorant, such as cancer, of which he is unaware, inform him of what took place.

45.5 Where any such discussion takes place it should be recorded either by a tape recorder or a shorthand writer.

The same issues arose yet again in *R v Nazham* [2004] EWCA Crim 491. The appeal in that case related to a conversation which took place between counsel and the judge in the judge's chambers before the defendants changed their pleas to guilty. The defendants argued that their convictions were unsafe because, when the conversation was relayed to them by their respective counsel, it fettered their freedom of choice as to their plea. The judge had said to counsel that, 'this has got plea written all over it and bags of credit'; that even though the case was listed for trial, a plea would still attract credit; that a plea would make for a shorter term of imprisonment, that is, a term of less than four years; he added that: 'At the end of the day they know whether they are guilty or not you know and they have got an eye for a deal, I would have thought.' The Court of Appeal held that the judge should not have said what he did in his room, but the indication which he gave as to the sentence he was minded to impose in the event of a plea of guilty (which was all that was conveyed to the appellants by their counsel) did not improperly inhibit their freedom of choice, or give rise to any injustice, apparent or real. The court added that nothing in the judgment was intended to detract from the advice given in *R v Turner* and in para IV.45.4 of the Practice Direction. However, proof of such an irregularity on the part of the trial judge is not necessarily sufficient for the conviction to be quashed on appeal. The Court of Appeal seemed to be taking a very strict line in this case. It should perhaps be borne in mind that the most important things for the trial judge to avoid are (a) giving an indication that the sentence will take a different form depending on whether the defendant pleads guilty or is found guilty (for example, a custodial sentence if found guilty, a community sentence if a plea of guilty), or (b) indicating that the defendants are likely to be found guilty by a jury. Merely saying that the sentence will be shorter is simply confirming what counsel will already know (and will doubtless have told the client), that a guilty plea attracts a discount (usually of about one-third).

Lord Justice Auld, in Chapter 10 of his *Review of the Criminal Courts of England and Wales* (paras 91–114), considers whether there should be greater freedom for courts to give advance indications of likely sentence. He considers the rule set out in *Turner* restricting what the judge can say about likely sentence, and notes that:

98   The Bar Council and many others have urged a relaxation of the *Turner* rules. They propose a system of advance indication of sentence in the event of a possible plea of guilty, but without commitment as to the likely sentence in the event of a trial. They suggest that that such a system should have the following features:

(a) a publicly well defined and consistently applied scale of minimum discounts according to the stage in the proceedings that the plea is offered;

(b) the discounts should be such as to secure for the defendant a significant reduction in sentence;

(c) the level of discount above the appropriate minimum would remain a matter for the judge's discretion, but in exercising it, he should disregard the strength of the prosecution case since otherwise that could undermine the incentive to a defendant to enter an early plea;

(d) the judge should indicate the sentence he would give in the event of a plea of guilty and what his sentence might be if the matter went to trial;

(e) the present disincentive to early pleas of guilty of loss of bail or change of status for remand prisoners should be removed; and

(f) the procedure should be subject to review by the Court of Appeal on a reference by the Attorney General, but without power to the Court of Appeal to increase individual sentences.

99   The Bar Council suggests the following procedure. It would be for the defendant, through his advocate, to initiate it by requesting an advance indication of sentence from the judge. Before doing so, his advocate should advise him firmly that he should not plead guilty unless he is guilty. The application would be made formally in court, though sitting in private, in the presence of the defendant and his legal advisers and of the prosecution advocate. The proceedings would be recorded. The judge should satisfy himself through canvassing the matter with both advocates as to the mental competence and emotional state of the defendant and as to whether he might be under any pressure falsely to admit guilt. He should firmly warn the defendant that he should not plead guilty unless he is guilty. If satisfied as to those matters and as to the sufficiency of the information before him of the circumstances of the offence, the judge should indicate the maximum sentence he would give in the event of a plea of guilty.

However, Lord Justice Auld goes on to note that these proposals are far from uncontroversial. He says:

100 Arrayed against that seemingly just and pragmatic solution to the long-standing problems of 'cracked' and unnecessary trials and the advantage to defendants in knowing where they stand, there are powerful arguments of principle voiced in the main by leading academics. They are directed, not so much against a clearer articulation of the system of sentence discounting for a plea of guilty or the relaxation of the *Turner* rule, but at the very existence of pleas of guilty as part of our criminal justice process and, in any event, against the practice of discounting sentence for a plea of guilty.

101 As to the former, Professor Ashworth and others have referred to the general absence in European jurisdictions of a procedure for pleading guilty and have urged consideration of abolition of the guilty plea itself, say, in indictable cases. They suggest replacing it with some form of judicial scrutiny of the acknowledgement of guilt. However, Professor Ashworth rightly acknowledges that 'there would be tremendous difficulties in such a great cultural change'. I have to confess to timidity about such a radical approach given the state of development of our sentencing law and practice. There would be obvious problems in devising a new criminal justice system equipped to subject every serious criminal case to judicial scrutiny of some sort to test an acknowledgement of guilt against all the other evidence, in order to evaluate the fact of guilt and the extent of it. I cannot see in what practical way it would improve the quality or administration of justice or what significant, if any, advantage the public or defendants would gain from it. The comparison, often made in this context, with bench trials in Philadelphia, is unhelpful. There, they have earned the description of 'slow pleas of guilty' to meet those cases in which, under that State's plea bargaining system, the prosecutor and defendant have been unable to make a bargain as to the disposal of the case, and the defendant opts instead for trial by judge alone in the hope of persuading him of the level of culpability for which he contends.

Having considered each of these arguments, Lord Justice Auld concludes as follows:

186 There should be introduced, by way of a judicial sentencing guideline for later incorporation in a Sentencing Code, a system of sentencing discounts graduated so that the earlier the tender of plea of guilty the higher the discount for it,

coupled with a system of advance indication of sentence for a defendant considering pleading guilty.

187 On the request of a defendant, through his advocate, the judge should be entitled formally to indicate the maximum sentence in the event of a plea of guilty at that stage and the possible sentence on conviction following a trial.

188 The request to the judge and all related subsequent proceedings should be in court, in the presence of the prosecution, the defendant and his advisers and a court reporter, but otherwise in private, and should be fully recorded.

189 The judge should enquire, by canvassing the matter with both advocates, as to the mental competence and emotional state of the defendant and as to whether he might be under any pressure falsely to admit guilt.

190 The prosecution and defence should be equipped to put before the judge all relevant information about the offence(s) and the defendant, including any pre-sentence or other reports and any victim impact statement, to enable the judge to give an indication.

191 The judge should only give an indication if and when he is satisfied that he has sufficient information and if he considers it appropriate to do so.

192 Where, as a result of such an indication, a defendant's advocate indicates to the judge that he wishes to plead guilty, the judge should, by questioning the defendant direct, satisfy himself that the defendant understands the effect of his proposed plea, that it would be true and that it would be voluntary.

193 The judge should be bound by his indication, as should any other judge before whom the defendant may appear for sentence, on the consequent plea of guilty.

The Criminal Justice Act 2003 retains the duty to take account of guilty pleas but does not make provision for a graduated system; it may be that the new Sentencing Guidelines Council will take this proposal forward. However, the Criminal Justice Act 2003 (in Sched 3) does make provision for a defendant in the magistrates' court to seek a broad indication of sentence at the allocation (mode of trial) stage.

11.24 CHANGE OF PLEA

The defendant may change his plea from not guilty to guilty at any stage before the verdict is given. Counsel for the defendant simply asks for the indictment to be put again, the defendant pleads guilty and the jury is asked by the judge to return a formal verdict of guilty (*R v Heyes* [1951] 1 KB 29). However, in *R v Poole* [2001] EWCA Crim 2664; [2002] 1 WLR 1528, the Court of Appeal held that, where a defendant pleads not guilty but then changes the plea to guilty during the course of the trial, there is no requirement that the judge should ask the jury for a formal verdict of guilty; it is permissible for the judge simply to discharge the jury and proceed to sentencing.

The judge has a discretion to allow the defendant to change his plea of guilty to one of not guilty at any stage before sentence has been passed (*R v Dodd* (1981) 74 Cr App R 50). The defendant will obviously have to give a reason for his change of mind. Permission to withdraw the guilty plea is unlikely to be given unless the defendant did not realise that he had a defence when he pleaded guilty (*R v McNally* [1954] 1 WLR 933). In *R v Sheikh* [2004] EWCA Crim 492, the defendants applied to withdraw their pleas of guilty. The basis of their application was that they had not been informed that they could be made the subject of confiscation proceedings in the event of conviction.

The trial judge refused to allow a change of plea, and the Court of Appeal upheld the refusal. The court said that it is well accepted that, quite apart from cases where the plea of guilty is equivocal or ambiguous, the court retains a residual discretion to allow the withdrawal of a guilty plea where not to do so might work an injustice. Examples might be where a defendant has been misinformed about the nature of the charge or the availability of a defence or where he has been put under pressure to plead guilty in circumstances where he is not truly admitting guilt. Commonly, however, it is reserved for cases where there is doubt that the plea represents a genuine acknowledgment of guilt. The possibility of confiscation proceedings taking place could not, of itself, have any bearing upon their acceptance of guilt.

11.25   ALTERNATIVES TO TRIAL: OFFERING NO EVIDENCE; LEAVING COUNTS ON FILE

We have already seen that there may be circumstances where the prosecution do not wish to proceed with the trial. It is too late to serve a notice of discontinuance under s 23 of the Prosecution of Offences Act 1985 (since that power only applies during the preliminary stages of the case) but there are two other ways of achieving the same objective.

11.25.1 Offering no evidence

Section 17 of the Criminal Justice Act 1967 provides that:

> Where a defendant arraigned on an indictment or inquisition pleads not guilty and the prosecutor proposes to offer no evidence against him, the court before which the defendant is arraigned may, if it thinks fit, order that a verdict of not guilty shall be recorded without the defendant being given in charge to a jury, and the verdict shall have the same effect as if the defendant had been tried and acquitted on the verdict of a jury.

This section thus allows the prosecution to offer no evidence in respect of one or more counts on an indictment. This may be appropriate where a key prosecution witness refuses to testify, or where evidence exonerating the defendant comes to light, or where the defendant pleads guilty to one offence and the prosecution do not wish to proceed with another.

Section 17 says that the court *may* enter a finding of not guilty where the prosecution offer no evidence. The use of the word 'may' suggests that the court can refuse and can empanel a jury. In practice, however, the judge would not force the prosecution to present its case. Indeed, in *R v Grafton* [1992] QB 101, the Court of Appeal said that before the completion of the prosecution case, the decision whether or not to continue had to be that of the prosecution and that a trial judge therefore has no power to refuse to permit discontinuance of the prosecution. It is suggested that the same principles must necessarily apply where the prosecution do not even wish to open their case. It would seem to be wrong in principle to require a prosecutor to continue with a case that he does not wish to proceed with, and it would be wholly wrong for the judge to call and question prosecution witnesses himself. It is submitted that if a judge is unhappy with a decision to offer no evidence, he should contact the Director of Public Prosecutions (DPP) (as head of the CPS) and ask for the case to be reviewed.

11.25.2 Leaving counts on file

The prosecution may ask for one or more counts to be 'left on the file marked not to be proceeded with without leave of the Crown Court or the Court of Appeal'. This may be appropriate where the defendant pleads guilty to some counts but not guilty to others, since leaving a count on the file does not amount to an acquittal. Thus, if the conviction is for some reason overturned on appeal, the prosecution can proceed with the other counts if the Crown Court or Court of Appeal gives permission. This could happen if the trial judge gives a preliminary ruling on the law adverse to the accused, so the accused then pleads guilty but then challenges the judge's ruling by means of an appeal against conviction; the prosecution could then seek leave to proceed with the other counts.

11.25.3 Difference between offering no evidence and leaving counts on file

The main difference between offering no evidence and leaving counts on the file is that in the former case an acquittal is entered (so the defendant cannot – subject to the reforms made by Pt 10 of the Criminal Justice Act 2003 – be prosecuted again for the same offence) whereas, in the latter case, it is possible (with the leave of the court) for the case against the defendant to be revived.

11.26   DIFFERENT PLEAS FROM DIFFERENT DEFENDANTS

If more than one defendant is charged in the same indictment, it may well be that one defendant will plead guilty and another will plead not guilty.

11.26.1 What to tell the jury

Where one defendant pleads guilty but another not guilty, counsel for the prosecution should only tell the jury which tries the defendant who pleads not guilty that '[name of defendant who pleads guilty], of whom you may hear mention in the course of this case, is not before you and is none of your concern'.

Reference to the guilty plea of a co-defendant is only possible with leave of the judge, which can only be given where the evidence of the plea of the former co-defendant is admissible in evidence (in the circumstances set out in s 74 of PACE) (*R v Kempster* [1989] 1 WLR 1125). For example, in *R v Manzur and Mahmood* [1997] 1 Cr App R 414, three people had been charged with rape. One defendant pleaded guilty; the other two pleaded not guilty, saying that the victim had consented to sexual intercourse. The judge allowed the jury to be told of the third defendant's plea of guilty. The Court of Appeal accepted the argument that the jury might have taken the view, on the basis of the third defendant's guilty plea, that the two appellants must have known that the victim was not consenting and so may not have given sufficient consideration to the evidence of the two appellants that they believed the woman to be consenting to intercourse. The admission of the evidence of the plea of the third defendant was therefore unduly prejudicial to the appellants and so a re-trial was ordered.

Admission of evidence that a co-defendant pleaded guilty (under s 74 of PACE) does not violate Art 6 of the European Convention on Human Rights (*MH v UK* [1997] EHRLR 279).

11.26.2 When should sentence be passed on the defendant who pleads guilty?

Where one defendant pleads guilty and the other not guilty, the usual procedure is to adjourn sentence of the defendant who pleads guilty until after the trial of the defendant who pleads not guilty. There is less risk of disparity between the sentences if the judge sentences them together, and the judge is in a better position to sentence as he will have heard the evidence about the gravity of the offence and the respective roles played by the defendants during the course of the trial (*R v Payne* [1950] 1 All ER 102).

However, where it is accepted by the prosecution that the defendant who pleads guilty played a very minor role in the offence, or where the other defendant absconds, the defendant who pleads guilty will generally be sentenced as soon as the plea is entered.

11.26.3 'Turning Queen's evidence'

If the defendant who pleads guilty also indicates that he is willing to give evidence for the prosecution, the arguments are slightly different. This is because 'turning Queen's evidence' attracts a discount in sentence well beyond the one-third discount that a plea of guilty normally receives. Such a person becomes a competent witness for the prosecution once he has pleaded guilty.

If the defendant who pleads guilty is sentenced after he has given evidence against the other accused, it could be thought that the sentence is determined by the quality of his evidence for the Crown rather than by the level of criminality revealed in his involvement in the offence. If, on the other hand, he is sentenced before he gives his evidence, he will receive a substantial discount for his promise to give evidence for the Crown and if (having achieved a more lenient sentence) he then refuses to testify, he cannot be re-sentenced (see *R v Stone* [1970] 1 WLR 1112).

Ultimately, it is a matter for the trial judge whether he sentences the defendant who is expected to testify for the Crown immediately after his plea of guilty or after the trial of the other defendant (*R v Sheffield Crown Court ex p Brownlow* [1980] QB 530). However, in most cases, sentence will be postponed; see, for example, *R v Potter* [1977] Crim LR 112. In *R v Weekes* (1980) 74 Cr App R 161, the Court of Appeal confirmed that in such a case sentence should normally be postponed until after the trial of the defendant who pleads not guilty. Nevertheless, in *R v Clement* (1991) *The Times*, 12 December, it was held that the decision whether or not to postpone sentence on a defendant who pleads guilty and indicates that he is willing to give evidence against a co-defendant until the end of the trial is a matter for the discretion of the trial judge, and would not in itself give rise to a ground of appeal.

11.27   VARIATION OF SENTENCE

Section 155 of the Powers of Criminal Courts (Sentencing) Act 2000 states:

(1)   Subject to the following provisions of this section, a sentence imposed, or other order made, by the Crown Court when dealing with an offender may be varied or rescinded by the Crown Court within the period of 28 days beginning with the day on which the sentence or other order was imposed or made or, where sub-section (2) below applies, within the time allowed by that sub-section.

(2)   Where two or more persons are jointly tried on an indictment, then, subject to the following provisions of this section, a sentence imposed, or other order made, by the Crown Court on conviction of any of those persons on the indictment may be varied or rescinded by the Crown Court not later than the expiry of whichever is the shorter of the following periods, that is—

(a) the period of 28 days beginning with the date of conclusion of the joint trial;

(b) the period of 56 days beginning with the day on which the sentence or other order was imposed or made.

(3)   For the purposes of sub-section (2) above, the joint trial is concluded on the latest of the following dates, that is any date on which any of the persons jointly tried is sentenced or is acquitted or on which a special verdict is brought in.

(4)   A sentence or other order shall not be varied or rescinded under this section except by the court constituted as it was when the sentence or other order was imposed or made, or, where that court comprised one or more justices of the peace, a court so constituted except for the omission of any one or more of those justices.

Section 155(1) thus enables the judge who imposed a sentence to vary or rescind that sentence within 28 days of the sentence being passed. This power is rarely invoked. It would be appropriate where, for example, an unlawful sentence has inadvertently been passed (*R v Newsome* [1970] 2 QB 711). However, it can also be used to increase sentence in exceptional cases where the original sentence was imposed on an erroneous factual basis. In *R v Hart* (1983) 5 Cr App R(S) 25, for example, a defendant boasted to the press that he had invented a false story to trick the judge into passing a lenient sentence. The judge re-listed the case and replaced a suspended sentence of imprisonment with immediate custody. The Court of Appeal upheld this use of s 155.

The power to vary a sentence (which can only be exercised by the judge who imposed the original sentence (s 155(4)) can be used to substitute one form of sentence for another. In *R v Sodhi* (1978) 66 Cr App R 260, for example, a prison sentence was replaced with a hospital order under the Mental Health Act 1983. In *R v Hadley* (1994) 16 Cr App R(S) 358, the judge thought that the maximum sentence for the offence of which the defendant had been convicted was lower than in fact it was. When the judge discovered his error, he increased the defendant's sentence. The Court of Appeal upheld the use of the power to vary the sentence, saying that where a judge decides that the original sentence is too low, in the sense that it is outside the bracket of sentences which could reasonably be imposed for a particular offence, the judge will be justified in increasing the sentence.

Before a sentence is varied (especially if the variation amounts to an increase), the offender and his legal representative should be given the chance to make representations (*R v May* (1981) Cr App R(S) 165; *R v Shacklady* (1987) 9 Cr App R(S) 258). Sentence should only be varied in open court (*R v Dowling* (1988) 88 Cr App R 88).

Subject to the provision about joint trials, the power to vary a sentence under s 155(1) can only be exercised within the period of 28 days from the passing of the sentence (*R v Menocal* [1980] AC 598). This means that not only must the original sentence be rescinded but a new sentence must be imposed within the 28 day period (*R v Stillwell* (1991) 94 Cr App R 65).

11.28   OTHER PLEAS

In this section, we consider the case where the plea of the defendant is unclear and we look at the special situations where the accused may not be fit to plead or where he claims the benefit of the doctrine of *autrefois convict* or *autrefois acquit* (otherwise known as 'double jeopardy').

11.28.1 The ambiguous plea

If the defendant pleads guilty but, either then or when addressing the court in mitigation, says something which shows that he may have a defence, the judge will explain to the defendant that he is putting forward a defence and the defendant will be asked to plead again. If the defendant confirms his plea of guilty but still tries to put forward a defence, a not guilty plea will be entered by the court.

11.28.2 If the defendant refuses to plead

If the defendant refuses to enter a plea of guilty or not guilty when the indictment is put to him, a not guilty plea will be entered on his behalf.

11.28.3 Fitness to plead

Either the prosecution or the defence may raise the issue of whether the accused is fit to plead.

A defendant is unfit to plead if he suffers from a disability which prevents him from being able to understand the course of the proceedings and the evidence which is given. Such a defendant would not be able to give proper instructions to his lawyer. It is not enough for the accused to be mentally disturbed or to be suffering from amnesia so that he cannot remember the events in question (see *R v Podola* [1960] 1 QB 325).

The procedure to be followed in such a case is contained in the Criminal Procedure (Insanity) Act 1964 (as amended by the Criminal Procedure (Insanity and Unfitness to Plead) Act 1991).

The court may postpone consideration of the question of the defendant's fitness to be tried until any time up to the opening of the defence case if this is in the defendant's interests (s 4(2) of the Criminal Procedure (Insanity) Act 1964). This means that there is an opportunity for a submission of no case to answer to be made before the question of fitness is considered. If the submission of no case to answer is successful, an acquittal is entered and the issue of fitness is not determined.

The issue of fitness to plead is determined by a jury and the evidence of at least two doctors (at least one of whom must specialise in mental disorder) is required.

If the issue of fitness is determined at the start of the trial and the defendant is found fit to plead, a fresh jury must be empanelled to try the case. If the issue of fitness is considered later, it can be considered either by the jury which is trying the defendant or by a separate jury (s 4(5) of the Criminal Procedure (Insanity) Act 1964).

If the accused is found fit to plead, the trial will take its usual course. Where the defendant is found unfit to plead, a jury has to consider whether the defendant committed the *actus reus* of the offence. If the issue of fitness was determined before arraignment, a fresh jury must be empanelled to decide whether the defendant committed the *actus reus* of the offence. If determination of the question of fitness to plead was postponed, the issue of fitness may be considered either by the jury trying the case or by a separate jury; however, if the defendant is found unfit to plead, the jury which was trying the case should determine whether the accused did the *actus reus*: s 4A(5) of the Criminal Procedure (Insanity) Act 1964. If the jury finds that he did not do the act alleged, then he must be acquitted (s 4A(4) of the Criminal Procedure (Insanity) Act 1964).

If the defendant is found unfit to plead and it is also found that he committed the *actus reus* of the offence, the court may order that the defendant be detained in a mental hospital, or make other orders appropriate to a mentally ill defendant, or order an absolute discharge (that is, impose no penalty): s 5 of the Criminal Procedure (Insanity) Act 1964.

The procedure laid down by s 4A of the Criminal Procedure (Insanity) Act 1964 for determining whether the accused has done the act charged against him does not involve the determination of a criminal charge but is, in any event, compatible with the rights of the accused under Art 6 of the European Convention on Human Rights (*R v H* [2003] UKHL 1; [2003] 1 WLR 411).

Paragraphs 212–13 of the Auld Review consider how the question of fitness to plead should be determined. Lord Justice Auld notes that in the majority of cases the question of unfitness is little more than a formality, since there is no dispute between the prosecution and the defence that the defendant is unfit to plead. However, the procedure remains 'cumbrous' because of the need to empanel a jury. Lord Justice Auld took the view that it is difficult to see what a jury can bring to the determination of the issue that a judge cannot. Accordingly, Recommendation 51 is that: 'Legislation should be introduced to require a judge, not a jury, to determine the issue of fitness to plead.' The government has not chosen to act on this recommendation.

11.28.4 *Autrefois convict* and *autrefois acquit* (double jeopardy)

The basic principle of *autrefois convict* and *autrefois acquit* is that a person should not be tried twice for the same offence. In other words, a person should not be tried for a crime in respect of which he has already been acquitted or convicted (*Connelly v DPP* [1964] AC 1254). In *Connelly*, the House of Lords identified three other principles:

- the defendant cannot be tried for a crime in respect of which he could have been convicted on an earlier occasion (that is, he cannot be convicted of an offence which was an alternative offence of which the jury could have convicted him under s 6(3) of the Criminal Law Act 1967). Thus, if the defendant was earlier tried for robbery, he cannot now be tried for the theft which comprised that robbery;

- the defendant cannot be tried for a crime, proof of which would necessarily entail proof of another crime of which he has already been acquitted (that is, the offence of which he has been acquitted is a necessary step towards establishing the second offence). Thus, if the defendant is acquitted of theft, he cannot later be charged with robbery alleging that same theft; and
- the defendant cannot be tried for a crime which is, in effect, the same (or substantially the same) as one of which he has previously been acquitted or convicted, or of which he could have been convicted by way of a verdict of guilty to an alternative offence.

In *R v Beedie* [1998] QB 356, a tenant died from carbon monoxide poisoning due to a defective gas fire. Her landlord was convicted of offences under health and safety legislation. He was subsequently charged with manslaughter, arising from the same facts. The Court of Appeal pointed out that in *Connelly*, the majority of the House of Lords had confined the strict operation of the *autrefois convict* doctrine to cases where the second indictment charged the same offence as the first; in such a case, the later prosecution must be struck out as an abuse of process. In the other three situations identified in *Connelly*, the court has a discretion whether or not to strike out the later prosecution. In the present case, the court decided that a stay should have been ordered, because the manslaughter charge was based on substantially the same facts as the earlier prosecution and gave rise to a prosecution for an offence of greater gravity, no new facts having occurred.

In *R v Dabhade* [1993] QB 329, the Court of Appeal confirmed the general principle that where a charge or count is dismissed without a hearing, the prosecution may not thereafter institute fresh proceedings on the same or an essentially similar charge or count. However, the court held that if the summary dismissal of the charge or count is because it is defective or because the prosecution wished to reorganise their case (because the charge was inappropriate given the evidence they had), it cannot properly be said that the defendant was ever in jeopardy of conviction. In *Dabhade*, the defendant was originally charged with obtaining property by deception, but the prosecution offered no evidence on that charge (which was then dismissed). The prosecution then brought proceedings on a charge of theft arising out of the same incident, as this was felt to be more appropriate given the facts. The Court of Appeal rejected the argument that the defendant could plead *autrefois acquit*. The court held that the original charge was so fundamentally incorrectly framed that the prosecution had decided before a trial could take place that a different charge would have to be brought; the defendant was therefore never, in any real sense, in jeopardy of being convicted on that original charge.

Dabhade applies only where the original charge is fundamentally flawed. In *R v G* [2001] EWCA Crim 1215; [2001] 1 WLR 1727, the appellant was charged with common assault and pleaded not guilty. Counsel for the prosecution then applied to amend the indictment by adding a count of assault occasioning actual bodily harm. The prosecution offered no evidence on the common assault charge and a verdict of not guilty was entered under s 17 of the Criminal Justice Act 1967. The question to be decided was whether the defendant was entitled to rely on *autrefois acquit* to avoid prosecution on the ABH charge. It was held that where the prosecution offer no evidence against a defendant and a verdict of not guilty is entered, the prosecution cannot then proceed against the defendant on a charge alleging a more serious offence

based on the same facts, as the defendant is entitled to rely on the defence of *autrefois acquit*.

Section 122 of the Criminal Justice Act 1988 provides that where the issue of *autrefois* is raised, it must be determined by a judge alone (that is, sitting without a jury).

11.28.5 Scope of the *autrefois* doctrine

The following situations do *not* amount to acquittal and so the defendant can be re-prosecuted:

- the quashing of an indictment (for example, because it is defective) (*R v Newland* [1988] QB 402);
- the withdrawal of a summons in the magistrates' court at any time prior to the defendant entering a plea (*R v Grays Justices ex p Low* [1990] 1 QB 54);
- the dismissal of an information by the magistrates where the prosecution failed to attend court or where the information is defective in a way that cannot be cured by amendment (*R v Dabhade* [1993] QB 329);
- the prosecution serve a notice of discontinuance under s 23(9) of the Prosecution of Offences Act 1985 providing that, where the prosecution serve a notice of discontinuance, proceedings in respect of that offence may be instituted at a later date;
- the jury is discharged from giving a verdict.

In all of these cases, the defendant cannot be said to have been in jeopardy of a conviction. For the *autrefois* doctrine to be applicable, the defendant must have been in jeopardy of a conviction (*R v Old Street Magistrates' Court ex p Davies* [1995] Crim LR 629).

Where a defendant asks for offences to be taken into consideration (TICs), the defendant is not in fact convicted of these offences and so could, theoretically, be prosecuted for them even though they were taken into account when he was sentenced for offences for which he had been convicted. However, in practice, offences which have been taken into consideration are never prosecuted.

11.28.6 Tainted acquittals

A further exception to the *autrefois convict* doctrine was introduced by ss 54–57 of the Criminal Procedure and Investigations Act 1996. Section 54 provides that where:

(a) a person has been acquitted of an offence; and

(b) a person has been convicted of an administration of justice offence involving interference with, or intimidation of, a juror or witness (or potential witness) in any part of the proceedings which led to that acquittal,

the court before which the latter person was convicted may certify that:

(i) there is a real possibility that, but for the interference or intimidation, the acquitted person would not have been acquitted; and

(ii) it is not contrary to the interests of justice (because of lapse of time or for any other reason) for the acquitted person to be re-prosecuted.

An application may then be made to the High Court for an order quashing the acquittal. The acquitted person may then be re-prosecuted for the offence of which he was acquitted.

Section 55 requires that four conditions must be satisfied before the High Court will quash the acquittal. They are:

(a) the High Court must agree that it is likely that, but for the interference or intimidation, the acquitted person would not have been acquitted;

(b) the High Court must agree that it is not contrary to the interests of justice for the acquitted person to be re-prosecuted;

(c) the acquitted person must be given a reasonable opportunity to make written representations to the High Court; and

(d) it must appear to the High Court that the conviction for the administration of justice offence will stand (and so there must not be an appeal against that conviction pending and the time limit for lodging such an appeal must have expired).

Under the Crown Court (Criminal Procedure and Investigations Act 1996) (Tainted Acquittals) Rules 1997 (SI 1997/1054) and the Magistrates' Court (Criminal Procedure and Investigations Act 1996) (Tainted Acquittals) Rules 1997 (SI 1997/1055), certification by the court under s 54 must made no later than immediately after the court has sentenced or otherwise dealt with the person convicted of the administration of justice offence.

11.28.7 Re-trial for serious offences under the Criminal Justice Act 2003

One of the most controversial changes contained in the Criminal Justice Act 2003 is the provision (in Pt 10 of that Act) for re-trials in certain cases, by way of exception to the normal rule against 'double jeopardy'.

Section 75 of the 2003 Act sets out the types of case which may be retried. The main restriction is that these new provisions apply only to 'qualifying offences' (defined in s 75(8) as offences listed in Pt 1 of Sched 5); the offences in the list are all very serious ones (most of them carry a maximum sentence of life imprisonment). As the Explanatory Notes issued along with the Act suggest, these offences were chosen because they are 'considered to have a particularly serious impact either on the victim or on society more generally'.

For s 75 to apply, the defendant must have been:

- acquitted of the qualifying offence at the Crown Court; or

- acquitted of the qualifying offence through the quashing of his conviction on appeal (but note that in the latter case the Court of Appeal would have the power to order a re-trial under s 7 of the Criminal Appeal Act 1968, which empowers the Court of Appeal to order a re-trial when it considers that it is in the interests of justice to do so); or

- (under s 75(2)) impliedly acquitted of a lesser qualifying offence of which he could have been convicted at the time.

The Explanatory Notes explain the latter provision thus:

> This takes into account cases of 'implied acquittals', in which, under the current law, an acquittal would have prevented a further prosecution being brought for a lower

level offence on the same facts. For example, an acquittal for murder may also imply an acquittal for the lower level offence of manslaughter, but new evidence may then come to light which would support a charge of manslaughter.

Where s 75 applies, s 76 allows a prosecutor to apply to the Court of Appeal for an order quashing the defendant's acquittal and ordering him to be retried for the qualifying offence. Section 95 defines a 'prosecutor' as 'an individual or body charged with duties to conduct criminal prosecutions' (in other words, persons or bodies responsible for bringing public prosecutions, such as the CPS or HM Customs and Excise).

Under s 76(3), a prosecutor may only make an application under s 76 with the written consent of the DPP. Under s 76(4), the DPP may give his consent:

... only if satisfied that—

(a)   there is evidence as respects which the requirements of section 78 [see below] appear to be met,

(b)   it is in the public interest for the application to proceed, and

(c)   any trial pursuant to an order on the application would not be inconsistent with obligations of the United Kingdom under Article 31 or 34 of the Treaty on European Union relating to the principle of *ne bis in idem*.

Furthermore, to protect against possible abuse of process, s 76(5) provides that 'not more than one application may be made' under s 76 in relation to an acquittal. Thus, only one application for an acquittal to be quashed may be made in respect of any acquittal, giving the prosecution only one further 'bite at the cherry'.

The powers of the Court of Appeal are set out in s 77. On an application under s 76(1), the Court of Appeal:

(a)   if satisfied that the requirements of sections 78 and 79 are met, must make the order applied for;

(b)   otherwise, must dismiss the application.

Where the application is under s 76(2) – implied acquittal – the court declares that the acquittal is not a bar to the person being tried for the offence of which he was impliedly acquitted (s 77(3)).

The key criteria, which are relevant both to the decision of the DPP to permit an appeal and to the Court of Appeal in deciding whether to order a re-trial, are set out in ss 78 and 79 of the 2003 Act. Those sections provide as follows:

78   *New and compelling evidence*

(1)   The requirements of this section are met if there is new and compelling evidence against the acquitted person in relation to the qualifying offence.

(2)   Evidence is new if it was not adduced in the proceedings in which the person was acquitted (nor, if those were appeal proceedings, in earlier proceedings to which the appeal related).

(3)   Evidence is compelling if—

(a)   it is reliable,

(b)   it is substantial, and

(c)   in the context of the outstanding issues, it appears highly probative of the case against the acquitted person.

(4) The outstanding issues are the issues in dispute in the proceedings in which the person was acquitted and, if those were appeal proceedings, any other issues remaining in dispute from earlier proceedings to which the appeal related.

(5) For the purposes of this section, it is irrelevant whether any evidence would have been admissible in earlier proceedings against the acquitted person.

79 *Interests of justice*

(1) The requirements of this section are met if in all the circumstances it is in the interests of justice for the court to make the order under section 77.

(2) That question is to be determined having regard in particular to—

(a) whether existing circumstances make a fair trial unlikely;

(b) for the purposes of that question and otherwise, the length of time since the qualifying offence was allegedly committed;

(c) whether it is likely that the new evidence would have been adduced in the earlier proceedings against the acquitted person but for a failure by an officer or by a prosecutor to act with due diligence or expedition;

(d) whether, since those proceedings or, if later, since the commencement of this Part, any officer or prosecutor has failed to act with due diligence or expedition.

Thus, s 78 requires the court to make a decision on the strength of the new evidence and the impact it would have had if it had been adduced at the original trial. In considering the interests of justice, the court will have regard to factors such as whether a fair trial would be made more difficult because of, for example, adverse publicity about the case or the length of time that has elapsed since the original trial. The court is specifically required to consider whether the police and prosecution acted with due diligence and expedition in relation to both the original trial and the new evidence that has come to light.

Under s 80(5), the acquitted person is entitled to attend the hearing and to be represented at the hearing.

Under s 81(2), there is a right to appeal on a point of law to the House of Lords from decisions made by the Court of Appeal under s 77.

Section 82 empowers the Court of Appeal to impose reporting restrictions to ensure that any potential jury is not influenced by these developments:

Where it appears to the Court of Appeal that the inclusion of any matter in a publication would give rise to a substantial risk of prejudice to the administration of justice in a re-trial, the court may order that the matter is not to be included in any publication while the order has effect (s 82(1)).

Under s 84, the acquitted person must be arraigned for the re-trial within the two months (or such longer time as the Court of Appeal may allow); if this does not occur, he can apply to the Court of Appeal to set aside the order for re-trial and restore the previous acquittal.

Section 85 requires the police to obtain the consent of the DPP before re-investigating cases where new evidence has come to light, or where there are reasonable grounds to believe that new evidence is likely to be obtained as a result of re-investigation. If the previous acquittal would ordinarily constitute a bar to prosecution (on the basis of the *autrefois* doctrine), the DPP's consent is required before the police can take any of the steps set out in s 85(3), namely arresting or questioning the defendant; searching him, or premises owned or occupied by him; searching a

vehicle owned by him, or anything in or on such a vehicle; seizing anything in his possession; or taking his fingerprints or a sample from him. The DPP is only allowed to give his consent if:

(a)   there is, or there is likely as a result of the investigation to be, sufficient new evidence to warrant the conduct of the investigation, and

(b)   it is in the public interest for the investigation to proceed (s 85(6)).

These restrictions are intended to provide a safeguard against any potential harassment of acquitted persons. As is pointed out in the Explanatory Notes that accompany the Act, there must therefore be some 'trigger' for the application to the DPP; it is not intended that the re-investigation of an acquitted person can take place without any element of new evidence. It should be noted, however, that the DPP's consent is not required in order to enable the police to make enquiries that do not directly affect the acquitted person (for example, interviewing new or previous witnesses, or comparing fingerprint or DNA samples with records which they already hold).

Section 86 provides for the situation where investigative steps have to be taken urgently and there is insufficient time to seek consent from the DPP. In such a case, a police officer of at least the rank of Superintendent can authorise the action. In such a case, s 87 empowers a magistrate to issue an arrest warrant in respect of the arrested person. After his arrest under the warrant, he can be charged with the offence for which he has been arrested if there is sufficient evidence to do so but only with the agreement of an officer of the rank of Superintendence or above.

11.29   THE EFFECT OF THE EUROPEAN CONVENTION ON HUMAN RIGHTS

Several references have already been made in this chapter to the European Convention on Human Rights. In particular, Art 6 of the Convention guarantees the right to a fair trial.

However, it has been held by the European Court of Human Rights that Art 6 does not apply to preliminary hearings concerning trial arrangements: *X v UK* (1983) 5 EHRR 273.

An important aspect of the operation of Art 6 is the principle of 'equality of arms'. This requires that the defendant should have a reasonable opportunity of presenting his case to the court under conditions which do not place him at a substantial disadvantage vis à vis his opponent (*Foucher v France* (1997) 25 EHRR 234). For example, handcuffing the accused during the trial may violate Art 6: *Kaj Raninen v Finland* [1998] EHRLR 344.

The trial must take place before an unbiased tribunal. In the case of trial on indictment, that requirement applies to both the judge and the jury. There is a presumption that the court has acted impartially (*Hauschildt v Denmark* (1989) 12 EHRR 266; compare the UK case of *Locabail (UK) Ltd v Bayfield* [2000] 1 All ER 65). The test applied by the European Court is whether a legitimate doubt as to the impartiality of the tribunal can be objectively justified (*Hauschildt v Denmark*). This seems very similar to the test applied by UK courts ('a real danger or possibility of bias': *R v Gough* [1993] AC 646; *Porter v Magill* [2002] 2 AC 357).

11.30 TRIALS ON INDICTMENT WITHOUT A JURY

The Auld Review makes the controversial suggestion that some trials on indictment should take place without a jury. He says that:

(a) defendants in the Crown Court should be entitled, with the court's consent, to opt for trial by judge alone;

(b) in serious and complex frauds, the trial judge should have the power to direct trial by himself and two lay members drawn from a panel established by the Lord Chancellor for the purpose or, if the defendant so requests, by himself alone.

In paras 110–18 of Chapter 5 of the Review, Lord Justice Auld considers the arguments for and against the defendant having the option to choose trial by judge alone ('bench trial' or 'jury waiver'). This mode of trial (which is available in some other jurisdictions) might be attractive to defendants in a number of circumstances, for instance in cases where the defendant is concerned about whether a jury would understand the defence case (perhaps where the defence is a technical one), or where the defendant is charged with an offence which might evoke strong emotional reactions or where there has been adverse pre-trial publicity, or where the evidence against the accused rests on evidence, such as identification evidence, which needs very careful and thorough scrutiny. Lord Justice Auld concluded that there may be cases where this form of trial would not be appropriate (and so the court needs to be able to insist that the ordinary trial process should take place) but that little harm can be done by giving the accused the option to choose trial by judge alone. Accordingly, Recommendation 31 of the Review was to the effect that defendants, with the consent of the court (given after hearing representations from both sides), should be able to opt for trial by judge alone in all cases tried on indictment.

This recommendation was accepted by the government and appeared in the Criminal Justice Bill; however, it was removed at the last minute as part of a deal with the Opposition to enable the Bill to receive Royal Assent.

It is perhaps odd that judge-only trial without the agreement of the defence – surely the more controversial measure – remained in the Bill. In paras 173–206 of Chapter 5, the Auld Review considers whether there should continue to be trial by jury in fraud and other complex cases. This topic has been considered on several previous occasions; for example, by the Fraud Trials Committee chaired by Lord Roskill, which reported in 1986 (the 'Roskill Committee'). Lord Justice Auld helpfully sets out the arguments for and against:

181   The arguments for and against the present form of jury trial in cases of serious and complex fraud have been canvassed many times. Arguments for include:

- jury trial is a hallowed democratic institution and a citizen's right in all serious cases which necessarily include serious and complex frauds;

- the random nature of selection of juries ensures their fairness and independence;

- mostly the question is one of dishonesty, which is essentially a matter for a jury who, by reason of their number and mix, are as well as, or better equipped than, a smaller tribunal, however professional, to assess the reliability and credibility of witnesses;

- there is no evidence, for example in the form of jury research, that juries cannot cope with long and complex cases or that their decisions in them are contrary to the evidence; on the contrary, most judges and legal practitioners'

assessment, based on their trial experience, is that their verdicts are in the main 'correct'; and

- there is an openness and public intelligibility in the parties having to accommodate the jury's newness to the subject matter by presenting their respective cases in a simple and easily digestible form, and that there is scope for improvements in such presentation.

Arguments against include:

- if jurors are truly to be regarded as the defendant's peers, they should be experienced in the professional or commercial discipline in which the alleged offence occurred;
- although the issue of dishonesty is essentially a matter for a jury, the volume and complexities of the issues and the evidence, especially in specialist market frauds, may be too difficult for them to understand or analyse so as to enable them to determine whether there has been dishonesty;
- the length of such trials, sometimes of several months, is an unreasonable intrusion on jurors' personal and, where they are in employment, working lives, going way beyond the conventional requirement for such duty of about two weeks' service;
- that has the effect of making juries even less representative of the community than they are already, since the court excuses many who would otherwise be able and willing to make short-term arrangements to do their civic duty;
- such long trials are also a great personal strain and burden on everyone else involved, not least the defendant, the victim and witnesses;
- judges, with their legal and forensic experience, and/or specialist assessors would be better equipped to deal justly and more expeditiously with such cases;
- that would also have the benefit of greater openness, since there would then be a publicly reasoned and appealable decision instead of the present inscrutable and largely unappealable verdict of the jury; and
- the length of jury trials in fraud cases is very costly to the public and also, because of limited judicial and court resources, unduly delays the efficient disposal of other cases waiting for trial.

In para 182, Lord Justice Auld writes:

I have considered these conflicting arguments with care. Like the Roskill Committee, I have concluded that those for replacing trial by judge and jury with some other form of tribunal in serious and complex fraud cases are the more persuasive.

On this basis, the Auld Review makes the following Recommendations:

37 As an alternative to trial by judge and jury in serious and complex fraud cases, the nominated trial judge should be empowered to direct trial by himself sitting with lay members or, where the defendant has opted for trial by judge alone, by himself alone.

38 The category of cases to which such a direction might apply should, in the first instance, be frauds of seriousness or complexity within sections 4 and 7 of the Criminal Justice Act 1987.

39 The overriding criterion for directing trial without jury should be the interests of justice.

40 Either party should have a right of appeal against such decision to the Court of Appeal (Criminal Division).

41 Judges trying such cases, by whatever form of procedure, should be specially nominated for the purpose as now, and provided with a thorough, structured and continuing training for it.

42 There should be a panel of experts, established and maintained by the Lord Chancellor in consultation with professional and other bodies, from which lay members may be selected for trials.

43 The nominated trial judge should select the lay members after affording the parties an opportunity to make written representations as to their suitability.

44 Lay members should be paid appropriately for their service.

45 In a court consisting of a judge and lay members, the judge should be the sole judge of law, procedure, admissibility of evidence and as to sentence; as to conviction, all three should be the judges of fact.

46 The decision of a court so constituted should wherever possible be unanimous, but a majority of any two could suffice for a conviction.

47 The judge should give the court's decision by a public and fully reasoned judgment.

Part 7 of the Criminal Justice Act 2003 makes provision for trial by judge alone in complex fraud cases, but makes no provision for the judge to sit with lay members; Pt 7 also enables trial by judge alone to take place in cases where there is a danger of jury tampering.

Section 43 of the 2003 Act enables an application to be made by the prosecution for certain fraud trials to be conducted without a jury. Such an order can only be made with the approval of the Lord Chief Justice or a judge nominated for this purpose by the Lord Chief Justice (s 43(4)). It only applies where notice has been given under s 51B of the Crime and Disorder Act 1998 (notices in serious or complex fraud cases) in respect of the offence(s) (s 43(1)(b)) and the judge can only accede to the request if:

> ... the complexity of the trial or the length of the trial (or both) is likely to make the trial so burdensome to the members of a jury hearing the trial that the interests of justice require that serious consideration should be given to the question of whether the trial should be conducted without a jury [s 43(5)].

In deciding whether or not he is satisfied that this condition is fulfilled, the judge must have regard to any steps which might reasonably be taken to reduce the complexity or length of the trial (s 43(6)); in other words, a trial without a jury is very much a last resort. However, under s 43(7), 'a step is not to be regarded as reasonable if it would significantly disadvantage the prosecution'.

Section 44 of the Act enables an application to be made by the prosecution for a trial to be conducted without a jury where there is a danger of jury tampering. The judge may only make such an order if two conditions are satisfied: the first condition is that 'there is evidence of a real and present danger that jury tampering would take place' (s 44(4)) and the second condition is that 'notwithstanding any steps (including the provision of police protection) which might reasonably be taken to prevent jury tampering, the likelihood that it would take place would be so substantial as to make it necessary in the interests of justice for the trial to be conducted without a jury' (s 44(5)). Section 44(6) gives some examples of cases where there may be evidence of a real and present danger that jury tampering would take place:

(a)   a case where the trial is a re-trial and the jury in the previous trial was discharged because jury tampering had taken place,

(b)   a case where jury tampering has taken place in previous criminal proceedings involving the defendant or any of the defendants,

(c)   a case where there has been intimidation, or attempted intimidation, of any person who is likely to be a witness in the trial.

The word 'examples' indicates that this is not intended to be an exhaustive list of the cases where s 44 may apply.

Under s 45 of the Criminal Justice Act 2003, an application for an order under s 43 or s 44 must be made at a preparatory hearing; all parties must be given an opportunity to make representations about the application. Section 45(6) adds a s 29(1A) to the CPIA 1996, providing that:

(1A) A judge of the Crown Court may also order that a preparatory hearing shall be held if an application to which section 45 of the Criminal Justice Act 2003 applies (application for trial without jury) is made.

Section 45(7) amends s 29(2) of the 1996 Act (which sets out the purposes of preparatory hearings), so that paras (a) to (c) provide that a preparatory hearing may be used for:

(a)   identifying issues which are likely to be material to the determinations and findings which are likely to be required during the trial,

(b)   if there is to be a jury, assisting their comprehension of those issues and expediting the proceedings before them,

(c)   determining an application to which section 45 of the Criminal Justice Act 2003 applies.

Section 45(9) amends s 35(1) of the 1996 Act to enable an appeal to the Court of Appeal against the refusal by a judge to make an order under s 43 or 44 or the decision to make an order under those sections.

Section 46 of the Criminal Justice Act 2003 makes provision for the discharge of a jury because of jury tampering. That section provides as follows:

(1)   This section applies where—

(a) a judge is minded during a trial on indictment to discharge the jury, and

(b) he is so minded because jury tampering appears to have taken place.

(2)   Before taking any steps to discharge the jury, the judge must—

(a) inform the parties that he is minded to discharge the jury,

(b) inform the parties of the grounds on which he is so minded, and

(c) allow the parties an opportunity to make representations.

(3)   Where the judge, after considering any such representations, discharges the jury, he may make an order that the trial is to continue without a jury if, but only if, he is satisfied—

(a) that jury tampering has taken place, and

(b) that to continue the trial without a jury would be fair to the defendant or defendants;

but this is subject to sub-section (4).

(4)   If the judge considers that it is necessary in the interests of justice for the trial to be terminated, he must terminate the trial.

(5)   Where the judge terminates the trial under sub-section (4), he may make an order that any new trial which is to take place must be conducted without a jury if he is satisfied in respect of the new trial that both of the conditions set out in section 44 are likely to be fulfilled.

(6)   Sub-section (5) is without prejudice to any other power that the judge may have on terminating the trial.

(7)   Subject to sub-section (5), nothing in this section affects the application of section 43 or 44 in relation to any new trial which takes place following the termination of the trial.

Section 47 of the 2003 Act makes provision for an appeal to the Court of Appeal against an order under s 46(3) or (5). However, under s 47(2), such an appeal may be brought only with the leave of the trial judge or the Court of Appeal. To enable an appeal to be commenced, s 47(3) provides that:

An order from which an appeal under this section lies is not to take effect—

(a)   before the expiration of the period for bringing an appeal under this section, or

(b)   if such an appeal is brought, before the appeal is finally disposed of or abandoned.

Under 47(4), the Court of Appeal may either confirm or revoke the order.

In an attempt to allay fears about potential unfairness in a trial by judge alone, s 48(5) requires the judge to give reasons for convicting the defendant. It provides that:

Where a trial is conducted or continued without a jury and the court convicts a defendant—

(a)   the court must give a judgment which states the reasons for the conviction at, or as soon as reasonably practicable after, the time of the conviction, and

(b)   the reference in section 18(2) of the Criminal Appeal Act 1968 (notice of appeal or of application for leave to appeal to be given within 28 days from date of conviction etc) to the date of the conviction is to be read as a reference to the date of the judgment mentioned in paragraph (a).

Section 48(6) makes it clear that these new powers do not affect the requirement under s 4 of the Criminal Procedure (Insanity) Act 1964 that any question of fitness to be tried must be determined by a jury, or the requirement under s 4A of that Act that any question, finding or verdict mentioned in that section must be made by a jury.

The basis of the recommendation by Lord Justice Auld, in the *Review of the Criminal Courts of England and Wales* (and that of the Fraud Trials Committee Report (1986)), was essentially that jurors are ill-equipped to understand the evidence in such cases, and it is very difficult to find jurors who cannot validly seek excusal from sitting on a trial lasting several months (in para 183 of Chapter 5, Lord Justice Auld quotes the Director of the Serious Fraud Office as saying that in fraud trials lasting upwards of six months, the jury consists largely of 'the unemployed and the unemployable').

Some would argue that rather than removing the right to trial by jury in complex cases, efforts should be made to find ways of presenting complex cases to jurors in a way that they will be able to comprehend. This may be something of a counsel of perfection. However, jury comprehension is not the only issue: given the length of the trial that is necessary to deal with a very complex case, many of those who are summoned for jury service will have valid reasons to seek excusal from trying such a case (because of family and/or work commitments). This means that juries in such cases tend to be drawn exclusively from those people with time on their hands, thus subverting the randomness which is supposed to be a feature of the system of trial by jury.

In 'Trying fraud cases without juries' [2002] Crim LR 282, David Corker argues that the safeguards suggested by Auld were inadequate. He argues that the 'interests of justice' and 'complexity' tests are too vague (leaving what he calls 'undue and excessive scope for subjective and relativist judicial decision-making'); and that the right of appeal to the Court of Appeal will be 'emasculated' by the fact that the Court of Appeal will probably be reluctant to interfere with the exercise of the trial judge's discretion. He goes on to argue that:

> The absence of the jury combined with the new role of trier of fact will inevitably cause the judge to play a far greater role. His/her position of judge both of law and fact, likely long experience of trials and ability to explore issues of fact with witnesses must place the judge in a position of near-dominance in the courtroom ... The enhanced role of the judge is ... likely to have implications upon adversarial protections for the defence. If for example the judge will be free to open up new lines of inquiry not known in advance to the defence, to cross-examine witnesses and generally act more like a coroner than a judge this must surely entail that there must be far greater interaction, if not challenge, between judge and counsel than at present ... It is submitted that whatever the consequences of a non-jury trial, the character of the trial will be significantly changed. The vacuum left behind by the jury will be filled somehow by an active and dominant judge.

He also considers the requirement that the judge must produce a judgment explaining why the defendant has been convicted. He writes:

> This requirement ... has perhaps been commonly regarded as the most important safeguard ensuring a fair conviction. The assumption is that whatever prejudicial evidence the tribunal has heard, the eventual judgment will be untainted because of the need to justify it on the basis of the admissible evidence with detailed reasoning. Thus if error or prejudice has crept in, this will be exposed upon scrutiny of the judgment leading to a successful appeal ... Two issues arise in consequence. First the workload of the Crown Court judiciary ... will be substantially increased. The intellectual feat of writing an inevitably lengthy and detailed judgment should not be underestimated and trial judges may need a considerable period of time away from the courtroom to accomplish this. Secondly it is also inevitable that there will be an increased number of appeals by those convicted. In a complex case it would be rare for them not to find some inaccuracy or infelicity in the written judgment about which to appeal. The Court of Appeal, already overworked, will be awarded a burdensome new source of business.

11.30.1 Research in how juries reach their verdicts

In 'Summing up to juries in criminal cases: what jury research says about current rules and practice' [2003] Crim LR 665, William Young notes some of the research that has been done about how juries reach their verdicts. He suggests that reluctance to countenance research into real juries (as opposed to research using mock juries or shadow juries) might be explicable on the basis of concern about what such research might reveal. However, his verdict on the system suggests that these fears are unfounded. He says that:

> Overall, the research ... suggests that the strength of the jury system lies in the collective understanding, recall and diligence of the jury as a whole and that in most (but not all) cases, inadequacy, misunderstanding, predisposition, or prejudice on the part of individual jurors do not adversely impact on the ultimate determination.

However, he does not suggest that the system is perfect. He says:

> Plainly there are imperfections in the system. A significant proportion of acquittals and a much smaller proportion of convictions are highly suspect. A perverse verdict may result from a jury consciously setting out to decide the case outside the legal framework identified by the judge. Sometimes the random nature of jury selection produces a jury without sufficient unprejudiced and competent jurors to ensure that a rational approach is taken. Occasionally, the complexity of a case is beyond the collective competence of the jury. These risks are inherent in the jury system. But a wayward verdict is perhaps more likely to result from the jury misunderstanding either the law or the evidence. It follows that if such misunderstandings can be avoided, the likelihood of perverse verdicts is much reduced.

In 'What can we learn from published jury research? Findings for the criminal courts review' [2001] Crim LR 969, Penny Darbyshire considers the question whether s 8 of the Contempt of Court Act 1981 should be repealed, so as to enable research to be carried out amongst jurors. She begins by considering the composition of juries. She found that:

> The new central summoning system for jurors has not solved the problem of a high avoidance and excusal rate. In London in 2000, the [Jury Summoning Central] Bureau found they had to summon six times as many jurors as needed and four times as many elsewhere in England and Wales. We found if jurors ignore their summons and reminder letter, many Crown Court centres will take no steps to pursue a non-respondent.

She notes that:

> Research in England and Wales, California and New Zealand found that the causes for high excusal and avoidance rates are problems with childcare, family commitments, employment problems and potential lost income.

She also notes that some people escape from the pool of potential jurors. She comments that:

> ... selection from the electoral roll is a flawed system. Research as long ago as the 1960s, in the USA, showed electoral lists are not representative of communities and this has since been confirmed in Australia and New Zealand. This is caused by factors such as population mobility and residential status, which are linked to class and income levels. Census data in England and Wales show non-registration to be high among ethnic minorities, the 20–24 age group and renters. Also, it is well known that non-registration may be an attempt to evade council tax. As long ago as 1968, Federal US legislation required supplementary source lists, such as drivers' licence and public utility lists to be used to correct this unrepresentativeness. Most research shows that merging electoral rolls with other lists increases the proportion of young people and non-whites in jury pools.

On the decision-making process, Darbyshire notes that:

> ... there is much sophisticated research on jury instruction in the United States. Virtually every involved researcher agrees that juries have a great deal of difficulty in understanding instructions, even though research shows that most juries conscientiously try to follow them ... Improvements in comprehension have been achieved experimentally in the United States, by reorganising instructions, reducing sentence length and complexity, avoiding jargon and uncommon words and using concrete rather than abstract concepts ... It is well known that audible information is lost soon after receipt. Written instructions do not reduce deliberation time but they

result in better comprehension, retention and application. They make jurors more satisfied and efficient and they participate in higher quality deliberations. American researchers have suggested a juror notebook with witness photos, key documentation and a written instruction. Similar conclusions have been reached in recent New Zealand research on real jurors, who found a written summary of the law useful. We encountered English circuit judges who have given word- processed instructions to juries for some years. The pros and cons of pre-instruction have been analysed. Most writers appear to conclude in favour of pre-instruction, which confirms accounts of real jurors in England and Wales that it is illogical and confusing to receive a mass of verbal information (the trial evidence) and then be verbally instructed on the decisions the group has to reach on that information. Judges were less surprised by and more satisfied with the verdicts of pre-instructed juries (in American experiments with real juries) and tend to favour their use, finding no difficulty and no extra burden in preparing them.

Accordingly, she recommends that:

> Juries should be given written as well as verbal instructions on the law after the trial. These should be drafted by the judge and agreed by counsel and explained verbally by the judge. Where possible, juries should be given a pre-trial summary of the issues. Certain basic instructions, such as on burden and quantum of proof could be written into the juror's introductory pamphlet and pinned, as reminders, onto the walls of the jury room.

In a similar vein, Young (in the article mentioned at the beginning of this section) concludes that:

> If some of the rules which have developed around the way judges sum up are under-pinned by unnecessarily gloomy views of juror competence, many practical aspects of the criminal trial process rest on unrealistically high assessments of juries' powers of analysis, comprehension and recall. Jurors are unlikely to have had experience in breaking down complex factual controversies into issues of manageable size. If there are a number of such issues, they will struggle to match these issues to the relevant evidence. Limits to their collective powers of comprehension and recall will be most apparent in lengthy or complex cases. All of this requires inputs from the judge. This should be in language that is appropriate to the occasion – simple concrete language firmly tied to the facts of the case at hand. At the start of the trial, jurors should be told what is truly in issue. In the summing up, if not before, the judge should marshal the evidence around those questions. In cases of any length, the oral process of the criminal trial process requires some written supplementation if jurors are to recall enough of the evidence and the summing up to be able to deliberate efficiently and to reach verdicts on the evidence and in accordance with the law.

It is sometimes suggested that jurors should be encouraged to take notes. Darbyshire suggests that, in fact, this would be disadvantageous, as it is more difficult to concentrate on observing witnesses if one is taking notes.

An important issue is whether the jurors understand the direction that they receive from the judge on the standard of proof. Darbyshire noted that:

> Recent English research found that subjects thought the quantum of proof varied with the gravity of the offence. Most subjects instructed with the English instruction, including the word 'sure' equated BRD ['beyond reasonable doubt'] with an impossible 100 per cent proof and this was confirmed by very recent English research. A survey of American studies showed that the percentage proof at which jurors were

prepared to convict varied from 51 to 92 per cent, very close to their interpretation of the balance of probabilities.

She concludes that:

Juries have immense difficulty in understanding 'beyond reasonable doubt'. Depending on how it is interpreted by the judge, they may equate it with 51–100 per cent proof. Modern lay persons are used to evaluating probability in terms of percentages. English research findings confirm real jurors' accounts that when judges use the word 'sure', some or even the majority of jurors will equate BRD with absolute proof. On the other hand, with different instructions, jurors may equate BRD with the balance of probabilities. It may be thought desirable to describe BRD in percentage proof terms. In any event, the word 'sure' should be eliminated from the BRD direction.

Young raises the same issue. He notes that:

In Professor JW Montgomery's study (*The Criminal Standard of Proof* (1998) 148 NLJ 582), 73.5 per cent of those surveyed took the 'satisfied so that you are sure' formula to require 100 per cent confidence of guilt.

Professor Michael Zander carried out a broadly similar study ('The criminal standard of proof' (2000) 150 NLJ 1517). In that study, the formula used was 'Only convict if the prosecution have made you sure of the defendant's guilt [which is the same as proving the case beyond reasonable doubt]'. Half of those surveyed received the words included in square brackets and the other half did not. Just over half the respondents regarded the direction (in both forms) as requiring 100 per cent certainty. Young suggests that:

The difference between that figure and the corresponding figure of 73.5 per cent in Professor Montgomery's survey may suggest that the formula that Professor Zander used (in both its iterations) is less stringent than the 'satisfied so that you are sure' formula used by Professor Montgomery.

This is a rather worrying conclusion, since a number of judges seem to use 'sure' and 'satisfied so you are sure' interchangeably.

In his *Review of the Criminal Courts in England and Wales*, Lord Justice Auld made several recommendations aimed at making the task of the juror more manageable. He recommends that jurors should receive more assistance to help them understand what is going on. Recommendation 235 is as follows:

In all cases tried by judge and jury:

1   each juror should be provided at the start of the trial with a copy of the charge or charges;

2   the judge at the start of the trial should address the jury, introducing them generally to their task as jurors and giving them an objective outline of the case and the questions they are there to decide;

3   the judge should supplement his opening address with, and provide a copy to each juror of, a written case and issues summary prepared by the parties' advocates and approved by him;

4   the judge, in the course of his introductory address, and the case and issues summary, should identify:

(a) the nature of the charges;

(b) as part of a brief narrative, the evidence agreed, reflecting the admissions of either side at the appropriate point in the story;

(c) also as part of the narrative, the matters of fact in issue; and

(d) with no, or minimal, reference to the law, a list of likely questions for their decision.

Thus, the judge, by reference to a case and issues summary produced by the parties, would give the jury a fuller introduction to the case than is now conventional.

Given the fact that the issues can change during the course of a trial, Recommendation 236 is that:

If and to the extent that the issues narrow or widen in the course of the trial, the case and issues summary should be amended and fresh copies provided to the judge and jury.

Recommendation 238 concerns the role of defence counsel is setting the scene for the jury. It states that:

I endorse the Runciman Royal Commission's recommendation that a defence advocate should be entitled to make a short opening speech to the jury immediately after that of the prosecution advocate, but normally of no more than a few minutes.

Recommendation 240 makes it clear that:

... a defence advocate who makes a short opening speech after the prosecution opening should not, thereby, forfeit his right to make an opening speech at the beginning of the defence case.

In his Review, Lord Justice Auld took the view (Recommendation 241) that defence counsel should always have the right to make an opening speech:

A defence advocate's entitlement to make an opening speech at the start of the defence case should no longer depend on whether he intends to call a witness as to fact other than the defendant.

To give further assistance to the jury, the Auld Review recommends as follows:

242 At the close of evidence and before speeches, the judge and advocates, in the absence of the jury, should finally review the case and issues summary and, if necessary, amend it for the jury.

...

244 If, and to the extent that, the law and professional codes of conduct do not require a defending, as well as a prosecuting, advocate to seek to correct a judge's error of law or of material fact of which he becomes aware, both the law and the codes should be changed to require it.

The Auld Review also looks at the role of the summing up in helping the jury with their task. The Recommendations are:

245 Consideration should be given to ... a requirement that a judge should use a case and issues summary and any other written or visual aid provided to a jury, as an integral part of his summing-up, referring to the points in them, one by one, as he deals with them orally.

246 Courts should equip judges with, and in cases meriting it they should consider using, other visual aids to their summings-up, such as PowerPoint and evolving forms of presentational soft-ware.

247 So far as possible, the judge should not direct the jury on the law, save by implication in the questions of fact that he puts to them for decision.

248 The judge should continue to remind the jury of the issues and, save in the most simple cases, the evidence relevant to them, and should always give the jury an adequate account of the defence; but he should do it in more summary form than is now common.

249 The judge should devise and put to the jury a series of written factual questions, the answers to which could logically lead only to a verdict of guilty or not guilty; the questions should correspond with those in the updated case and issues summary, supplemented as necessary in a separate written list prepared for the purpose; and each question should be tailored to the law as the judge knows it to be and to the issues and evidence in the case.

250 The judge, where he considers it appropriate, should be permitted to require a jury to answer publicly each of his questions and to declare a verdict in accordance with those answers.

Thus, Lord Justice Auld suggests that in the summing up the judge should make use of the written case and issues summary, and should try, so far as possible, to 'filter out' the law and fashion factual questions to the issues and the law as he knows it to be. Where he considers it appropriate, the judge should require the jury publicly to answer each of the questions and to declare a verdict in accordance with those answers. These proposals would perhaps have made the task of the jury a little easier (and the requirement to answer a series of questions, as well as delivering a verdict on guilt or innocence, might answer the point made by some that the right to a fair trial should require juries to give reasons for their verdict). However, the Criminal Justice Act 2003 does not enact these suggestions.

CHAPTER 12

APPEALS FROM THE CROWN COURT

12.1 INTRODUCTION

Appeal against conviction and/or sentence lies from the Crown Court to the Court of Appeal (Criminal Division). In this chapter, we look at the procedure for appealing against conviction and/or sentence following trial on indictment and at the criteria applied by the Court of Appeal when disposing of such appeals.

Criminal appeals are governed by the Criminal Appeal Act 1968 and the Criminal Appeal Rules 1968 (SI 1968/1262). There is also very helpful information in 'A guide to the proceedings of the Court of Appeal Criminal Division' (1997), available online at www.courtservice.gov.uk/cms/media/proc_guide.pdf.

Practice Direction (Court of Appeal, Criminal Division: Listing) (2004) *The Times*, 10 March, amongst other things, sets out targets for hearing dates in the Court of Appeal: for sentencing appeals, 28 days from receipt by the listing officer; for conviction appeals, 63 days from receipt by the listing officer; for conviction appeals where witnesses are to attend, 80 days from receipt by the listing officer.

12.2 THE COURT OF APPEAL

The constitution of the Court of Appeal (Criminal Division) is governed by the Supreme Court Act 1981. The court is presided over by the Lord Chief Justice of England (although, of course, he will not hear every appeal). It comprises Lords Justices of Appeal, together with High Court judges whom the Lord Chief Justice has asked to assist with the work of the Court of Appeal (ss 2, 3 and 9 of the Supreme Court Act 1981).

The number of judges required for a sitting of the Court of Appeal is governed by s 55 of the Supreme Court Act 1981:

- when determining an appeal against conviction, the Court of Appeal must comprise at least three judges; one or more of the judges must be a Lord Justice of Appeal. The decision is by majority (the presiding judge does not have a casting vote). Usually, only one judgment will be delivered;
- when determining an appeal against sentence, the Court of Appeal may consist of only two judges, but again one of them should be a Lord Justice of Appeal. Should an appeal be heard by a two-judge court (again, one would have to be a Lord Justice of Appeal) and the two judges disagree, the appeal will be re-heard by a three-judge court.

We shall see later that some of the powers of the Court of Appeal may be exercised by a single judge (for example, the granting of leave to appeal). The single judge may be a Lord Justice of Appeal or else a High Court judge whom the Lord Chief Justice has asked to assist with the work of the Court of Appeal.

Certain Circuit judges may be approved by the Lord Chancellor to sit in the Court of Appeal (Criminal Division). A sitting of the court must not include more than one

Circuit judge, and a Circuit judge is not permitted to exercise the powers of the single judge. Under s 67 of the Courts Act 2003 (in force since January 2004), the selected Circuit judges who sit in the Court of Appeal are permitted to hear or determine any appeal against conviction and/or sentence, even if the judge who presided at the trial, or passed the sentence, was a High Court judge.

The administrative work of the court is carried out by the Registrar of Criminal Appeals.

Recommendation 314 of the Auld Review considers the composition of the Court of Appeal and would require amendment of s 55 of the 1981 Act. It includes the following:

> 314.2 in straightforward appeals against conviction, or in respect of short sentences where the law and procedures are clear and the only issue is whether the trial judge has correctly followed them, or where the issue turns on his treatment of the facts, the Court should consist of two High Court Judges or one High Court Judge and one Circuit Judge; and

> 314.3 consideration should be given to introducing a system under which, in cases of exceptional legal importance and complexity, a distinguished academic could either be appointed ad hoc to act as a judge of the Court or be invited to submit a written brief to the Court on the point(s) in issue.

12.3 PROCEDURE

12.3.1 The need for leave to appeal

Under s 1(2) of the Criminal Appeal Act 1968 (as amended by the Criminal Appeal Act 1995), an appeal against conviction may only be made if either:

(a) the Court of Appeal gives leave to appeal (s 1(2)(a)); or

(b) the trial judge certifies that the case is 'fit for appeal' (s 1(2)(b)).

Certificates from the trial judge are very rare and are only granted if the case has raised a point of law where there is no authority giving an answer or where there are conflicting decisions of the Court of Appeal. In *R v Williams* [1992] 1 WLR 380, it was emphasised that a certificate should only be given by the trial judge if exceptional circumstances are present; it is not enough that the trial judge simply disagrees with the verdict. In *R v Bansal* [1999] Crim LR 484, the Court of Appeal confirmed that a trial judge should only certify that a case is fit for appeal if there are exceptional features to the case; otherwise, the granting of leave to appeal is a matter for the Court of Appeal. It follows that leave to appeal is required in almost every case.

It should be noted that although Art 6 of the European Convention on Human Rights does not necessarily require there to be a possibility of appeal against conviction or sentence, where there is a mechanism for appeal, any appellate proceedings will be treated as an extension of the trial process and so will be subject to the requirements of Art 6 of the Convention, which guarantees the right to a fair trial (*Monnell and Morris v UK* (1988) 10 EHRR 205). It should also be borne in mind that, for the purposes of the European Convention on Human Rights, unfairness at first instance can be remedied by an effective appellate process: *Adolf v Austria* (1982) 4 EHRR 313.

12.3.2 Appeal against conviction where the defendant has pleaded guilty

A defendant who pleads guilty in the magistrates' court cannot appeal against conviction to the Crown Court if he pleaded guilty (s 108 of the Magistrates' Courts Act 1980). There is no such rule in s 1 of the Criminal Appeal Act 1968. However, the Court of Appeal is very unwilling to give leave to appeal against conviction to a defendant who pleaded guilty in the Crown Court. In *R v Forde* [1923] 2 KB 400, Avory J said that leave should only be given in such a case if either the appellant did not appreciate the nature of the charge or did not intend to admit he was guilty of it, or else that upon the admitted facts he could not in law have been convicted of the offence charged. In *R v Eriemo* [1995] 2 Cr App R 206, the Court of Appeal reaffirmed its reluctance to entertain appeals where the defendant pleaded guilty. In that case, the applicant (who had changed his plea to guilty following the trial judge's refusal to sever the indictment on the basis that the applicant was going to allege that he committed the offence under the duress of the co-defendant) was refused leave to appeal. It was said by Glidewell LJ that where a defendant pleads guilty, he is making an admission of the facts which form the basis of the offence with which he is charged and therefore loses his right to appeal against conviction.

There have, however, been a considerable number of cases where a defendant who has pleaded guilty was allowed to appeal against conviction. For example, if a defendant is pressurised (for example, by comments from the judge) into pleading guilty, he will be allowed to appeal (*R v Turner* [1970] 2 QB 321). Similarly, in *R v Bane* [1994] Crim LR 134, the judge told counsel that he was not willing to leave the defence of self-defence to the jury. The defendant changed his plea to guilty. The conviction was quashed because of the pressure to plead guilty which was caused by the judge's refusal to allow the jury to consider Bane's defence. Similarly, in *R v Boal* [1992] QB 591, the defendant pleaded guilty because of erroneous legal advice by his counsel and so the Court of Appeal entertained his appeal against conviction. Another situation where the defendant might be able to appeal against conviction even though he pleaded guilty is where the plea of guilty was entered after the judge made an incorrect ruling on the law. In *R v Kenny* [1994] Crim LR 284, for example, the defendant changed his plea to guilty following a decision by the trial judge that a confession (the only evidence against him) was admissible.

However, in *R v Greene* [1997] Crim LR 659, the Court of Appeal took a tougher line. The defendant had changed his plea to guilty following the rejection by the trial judge of a submission that the confession should be excluded under s 78 of the Police and Criminal Evidence Act 1984. The Court of Appeal said that his plea of guilty was an acknowledgment of the truth of the confession and the commission of the offence. The court said that had the defendant maintained his plea of not guilty and been convicted, he could then have complained on appeal about the judge's ruling under s 78.

In *R v Chalkley* [1998] QB 848, the Court of Appeal returned to the vexed question of whether a defendant who pleads guilty in the Crown Court can appeal against conviction to the Court of Appeal. The defendants had originally pleaded not guilty, but the judge ruled that certain evidence against them (covertly obtained tape-recordings of conversations) was admissible; the defendants then changed their pleas to guilty. The court held that s 2(1) of the Criminal Appeal Act 1968 entitles the Court of Appeal to quash as unsafe a conviction based on a guilty plea if that plea was

mistaken or uninformed or without intention to admit the truth of the offence charged. Furthermore, said Auld LJ, a conviction would be unsafe where the effect of an incorrect ruling of law on admitted facts was to leave the defendant with no legal escape from a verdict of guilty on those facts. In other words, on the basis of the ruling, an acquittal would be legally impossible (for example, where the judge rejects the defendant's submission that admitted facts do not in law amount to the offence charged, and so there is no issue of fact for the jury to try). However, a conviction will not normally be unsafe where the defendant is influenced to change his plea to guilty because he recognises that, as a result of the judge's ruling that compelling evidence is admissible against him, his case on the facts is hopeless. Pleading guilty would, in such a case, amount to acknowledgment of the truth of the facts constituting the offence charged (unless, of course, the plea was mistaken or made without intention to admit guilt of the offence charged).

It is therefore important to distinguish between two situations:

(a) where, in the light of an erroneous ruling, the defendant is left with no legal basis for a verdict of not guilty (and so an appeal will be entertained despite the guilty plea); and

(b) where the guilty plea is influenced by an erroneous ruling of law, for example, to admit strong evidence against the defendant (where, because of the guilty plea, no appeal would be entertained).

In *R v Sales* [2000] 2 Cr App R 431, the Court of Appeal confirmed that because a plea of guilty is normally to be regarded as an acknowledgment of the truth of the facts constituting the offence charged, it is only in rare cases that the Court of Appeal could consider a conviction to be unsafe because an appellant who had pleaded guilty is now claiming that he did not do the act relied upon. However, such rare cases do occur. In *R v Early* [2002] EWCA Crim 1904; [2003] 1 Cr App R 288, it was held that where the prosecution have failed to make proper pre-trial disclosure and prosecution witnesses have lied to the court on a *voir dire*, and the defendant enters a plea of guilty on the assumption that full disclosure has been made, the Court of Appeal will set aside that guilty plea however strong the prosecution case might appear to be. Furthermore, in *R v Togher* [2001] 1 Cr App R 33, it was held that the strict approach taken in *Chalkley* could not be applied to a situation where the appeal is based on alleged abuse of process and the defendants were unaware, when they pleaded guilty, of the matters relied upon in the appeal as amounting to the abuse of process. Lord Woolf CJ said (at para 33) that if the appellants can establish an abuse, the Court of Appeal will give very serious consideration to whether justice requires the conviction to be set aside; however, it has to be a situation where it would be inconsistent with the due administration of justice to allow the pleas of guilty to stand.

An example of an exceptional case, where an appeal was permitted despite a guilty plea, may be found in *R v Montague-Darlington* [2003] EWCA Crim 1542. The defendant had pleaded guilty to illegal importation of a Class A drug. Almost a year after the conviction, it came to light that the prosecution were in possession of certain information that would have been disclosable under the Criminal Procedure and Investigations Act 1996 but which was highly sensitive and therefore likely to attract public interest immunity. The court held that the prosecution would indeed have been obliged to disclose the material (in other words, the right of the defendant to a fair trial would have overridden the public interest immunity in withholding the material from the defence). The result would have been that the prosecution would have been

dropped. The Court of Appeal reaffirmed that it will only consider an appeal against conviction following a guilty plea in rare cases. The court's task was to determine whether the appellant had had a fair trial. It was said to be difficult to see how she could have had a fair trial when she should not have been tried at all had the sensitive material been available at that stage. The conviction was therefore set aside.

12.3.3 Procedure for obtaining leave to appeal

A barrister (usually, but not necessarily, the one who conducted the case in the Crown Court) will be asked to write an advice on the merits of an appeal. If the barrister advises that an appeal is appropriate, draft grounds of appeal will be attached to the advice.

As a matter of professional conduct, counsel should only advise in favour of an appeal if there are proper grounds for doing so (*R v Morson* (1976) 62 Cr App R 236). Paragraph 2.4 of the Guide to the Proceedings of the Court of Appeal (Criminal Division) states that 'Counsel should not settle or sign grounds unless they are reasonable, have some real prospect of success and are such that he is prepared to argue them before the Court'.

In a similar vein, para II.15 of *Practice Direction (Criminal Proceedings: Consolidation)* [2002] 1 WLR 2870; [2002] 3 All ER 904 states:

II.15 *Grounds of appeal*

15.1 Advocates should not settle grounds or support them with written advice unless they consider that they are properly arguable. Grounds should be carefully drafted and properly particularised. Advocates should not assume that the court will entertain any ground of appeal not set out and properly particularised. Should leave to amend the grounds be granted it is most unlikely that further grounds will be entertained.

15.2 A copy of the advocate's positive advice about the merits should be attached as part of the grounds.

A notice of application for leave to appeal is then lodged at the Crown Court where the defendant was convicted (see para II.14.1 of the Practice Direction). This must be done within 28 days of conviction (s 18(2) of the Criminal Appeal Act 1968). The notice must be accompanied by grounds of appeal (r 2 of the Criminal Appeal Rules). These grounds should be particularised so that the matters relied upon are clearly identified and set out in some detail.

The text of s 18(2) is as follows:

(2) Notice of appeal, or of application for leave to appeal, shall be given within twenty-eight days from the date of the conviction, verdict or finding appealed against, or in the case of appeal against sentence, from the date on which sentence was passed or, in the case of an order made or treated as made on conviction, from the date of the making of the order.

In *R v Long* [1998] 2 Cr App R 326, the Court of Appeal pointed out that, under s 18(2) of the Criminal Appeal Act 1968, a notice of application for leave to appeal against conviction must be lodged within 28 days of conviction even if there is lapse of time between conviction and sentence. In other words, for an appeal against conviction, time begins to run from the date of conviction (and not from the date of sentence).

The Crown Court then passes the papers to the Registrar of Criminal Appeals.

12.3.4   Transcript of evidence and summing up

The Registrar (when he receives the grounds of appeal) decides whether a transcript is necessary and, if so, how extensive it should be. Normally, the transcript is limited to the summing up and to any judgment given by the judge during the course of the trial. If counsel for the would-be appellant wants a more extensive transcript, reasons for this request must be given. A transcript of the evidence should only be sought if genuinely essential, as it is an expensive and time consuming procedure (*R v Flemming* (1987) 86 Cr App R 32).

12.3.5   'Perfecting' the grounds of appeal

The original advice and grounds of appeal will be based on counsel's notes taken at the time of the trial. It may be that these notes are not entirely accurate (for example, some of the judge's comments may have been omitted or mis-recorded). The transcript is sent to counsel for the would-be appellant (free of charge if the appellant is publicly funded), who then has the chance to 'perfect' the grounds of appeal. Paragraph 4.2 of the Guide says that:

> The purpose of perfection is (a) to give counsel the opportunity to reconsider his original grounds in the light of the transcript and (b) to save valuable judicial time by enabling the judge or Court to identify at once the relevant parts of the transcript.

Paragraph 4.4. of the Guide goes on to say:

> 4.4   Perfected grounds should consist of a fresh document which supersedes the original grounds of appeal and contains *inter alia* references by page number and letter to all relevant passages in the transcript. Authorities on which counsel relies should be cited, where possible in the Criminal Appeal Reports.

Thus, counsel should amend the original grounds of appeal so that they refer to specific passages of the transcript – for example, 'the learned trial judge erred in that at [specific page number] he ...'. The grounds of appeal, or the advice on appeal written by counsel which accompanies the grounds, should also cite any authorities upon which counsel for the appellant proposes to rely.

Once the grounds of appeal have perfected, the papers are referred to a single judge to decide the question of leave to appeal.

12.3.6   Granting of leave to appeal: the single judge

The single judge considers the papers (without a hearing) and decides whether the appeal has a sufficient prospect of success to justify the granting of leave of appeal (s 31(2)(a) of the Criminal Appeal Act 1968).

In most cases, a single judge granting leave to appeal will give leave to appeal generally. However, the single judge has the power to grant leave on some grounds and refuse leave on others. Where leave to appeal has been refused on particular grounds, those grounds can only be argued before the court with its leave (*R v Cox* [1999] 2 Cr App R 6; *R v Jackson* [1999] 1 All ER 572).

The determination of the application for leave to appeal without the applicant being present or represented is not incompatible with Art 6 of the European Convention on Human Rights (*Monnell and Morris v UK* (1988) 10 EHRR 205).

12.3.7 Challenging the decision of the single judge

If the single judge refuses leave to appeal, the appellant has 14 days (which can only be extended if there is very good reason (*R v Doherty* [1971] 1 WLR 1454)) in which to renew the application for leave (r 12). If the appellant does renew the application, it will be heard by two or three Court of Appeal judges sitting in open court (s 31(3) of the Criminal Appeal Act 1968). If the applicant is serving a custodial sentence, there is a risk in renewing the application for leave – namely that a 'direction for loss of time' could be made if the Court of Appeal confirms the refusal of leave to appeal.

12.3.8 The 'direction for loss of time'

This is governed by s 29 of the Criminal Appeal Act 1968 and para II.16 of *Practice Direction (Criminal Proceedings: Consolidation)* [2002] 1 WLR 2870; [2002] 3 All ER 904.

Section 29 of the 1968 Act says:

(1) The time during which an appellant is in custody pending the determination of his appeal shall, subject to any direction which the Court of Appeal may give to the contrary, be reckoned as part of the term of any sentence to which he is for the time being subject.

(2) Where the Court of Appeal give a contrary direction under sub-section (1) above, they shall state their reasons for doing so; and they shall not give any such direction where—

   (a) leave to appeal has been granted; or

   (b) a certificate has been given by the judge of the court of trial [that the case is fit for appeal]; or

   (c) the case has been referred to them under section 9 of the Criminal Appeal Act 1995 [Criminal Cases Review Commission].

Paragraph II.16 of the Practice Direction says:

II.16 *Loss of time*

16.1 Both the court and the single judge have power in their discretion to direct that part of the time during which an applicant is in custody after putting in his notice of application for leave to appeal should not count towards sentence. Those who contemplate putting in such a notice and their legal advisers should bear this in mind. It is important that those contemplating an appeal should seek advice and should remember that it is useless to appeal without grounds and that grounds should be substantial and particularised and not a mere formula. Where an application devoid of merit has been refused by the single judge and a direction for loss of time has been made, the full court, on renewal of the application, may direct that additional time shall be lost if it, once again, thinks it right so to exercise its discretion in all the circumstances of the case.

A 'direction for loss of time' is only relevant if the appellant is serving a custodial sentence. The direction is that some or all of the sentence served by the appellant between the date of the commencement of the appeal proceedings and the date when the application for leave or (as the case may be) the renewed application for leave to appeal is dismissed does not count towards the service of the appellant's sentence.

Where the single judge gives leave to appeal (or the application is successfully renewed) but the Court of Appeal ultimately dismisses the appeal, a direction for loss

of time cannot be made even though the appeal is ultimately unsuccessful (s 29(2)(a) of the Criminal Appeal Act 1968).

A direction for loss of time under s 29 does not amount to arbitrary detention and so is compatible with the right to liberty under Art 5 of the European Convention on Human Rights (*Monnell and Morris v UK* (1988) 10 EHRR 205).

12.3.9 Procedure where leave is not required

In the very few cases where leave to appeal is not required because the trial judge certified that the case is fit for appeal, the barrister who conducted the case still has to draft grounds of appeal. The only difference in procedure is that the Registrar will not refer the papers to a single judge; instead, the case will be listed for a full hearing by the Court of Appeal.

12.3.10 Frivolous appeals

Section 20 of the Criminal Appeal Act 1968 provides as follows:

> If it appears to the registrar that a notice of appeal or application for leave to appeal does not show any substantial ground of appeal, he may refer the appeal or application for leave to the Court for summary determination; and where the case is so referred the Court may, if they consider that the appeal or application for leave is frivolous or vexatious, and can be determined without adjourning it for a full hearing, dismiss the appeal or application for leave summarily, without calling on anyone to attend the hearing or to appear for the Crown thereon.

Thus, if the Registrar of Criminal Appeals takes the view that a notice of appeal or an application for leave to appeal is frivolous or vexatious, he can refer it to a sitting of the Court of Appeal for summary determination without a full hearing. If the Court of Appeal dismisses the application summarily, this decision cannot be challenged. The Court of Appeal may thus dispose summarily of appeals which are obviously without merit and have no reasonable prospect of success (*R v Taylor* [1979] Crim LR 649).

12.3.11 By-passing the single judge

If the Registrar takes the view that an application for leave to appeal discloses grounds which make an appeal likely to succeed, he may refer the case to the Court of Appeal so that the court itself can give leave and then go on to hear the appeal itself. This would be appropriate, for example, where a number of other cases are awaiting trial and the present appeal will be a test case to clarify the law and needs to be dealt with urgently.

12.3.12 Other powers of the Registrar of Criminal Appeals

Under s 31A(2) of the Criminal Appeal Act 1968 (as amended by the Criminal Appeal Act 1995), the Registrar of Criminal Appeals is empowered to:

(a) extend the time within which notice of appeal or of application for leave to appeal may be given: the 28 day time limit may be extended under s 18(3) of the Criminal Appeal Act 1968. The test to be applied in deciding whether to grant an extension of time is whether the case is an exceptional one (*R v Hawkins* [1996] 1 Cr App R

234) and so the applicant has to show a very good reason for missing the time limit (see *R v Ramsden* [1972] Crim LR 547; *R v Burley* (1994) *The Times*, 9 November);

(b) order a witness to attend for examination; and

(c) vary the conditions of bail granted to an appellant by the Court of Appeal or the Crown Court (provided that the respondent does not object: s 31A(3)).

If the Registrar refuses an application on behalf of an appellant to exercise any of these powers, the appellant is 'entitled to have the application determined by a single judge' (s 31A(4)).

12.4 OTHER POWERS OF THE SINGLE JUDGE

As well as granting leave to appeal, the single judge also has jurisdiction (under s 31 of the Criminal Appeal Act 1968) to deal with the following matters.

12.4.1 Presence of the appellant

Section 22 of the Criminal Appeal Act 1968 provides as follows:

(1) Except as provided by this section, an appellant shall be entitled to be present, if he wishes it, on the hearing of his appeal, although he may be in custody.

(2) A person in custody shall not be entitled to be present—

(a) where his appeal is on some ground involving a question of law alone; or

(b) on an application by him for leave to appeal; or

(c) on any proceedings preliminary or incidental to an appeal; or

(d) where he is in custody in consequence of a verdict of not guilty by reason of insanity or of a finding of disability,

unless the Court of Appeal give him leave to be present.

(3) The power of the Court of Appeal to pass sentence on a person may be exercised although he is for any reason not present.

Where the appellant is not in custody, he may be present on any occasion when his appeal is being heard or where interlocutory applications in respect of his appeal are being made in open court.

However, an appellant who is in custody has no right to attend interlocutory applications in respect of his appeal or, if the appeal is on a ground of law alone, the hearing of the appeal itself. The single judge may make an order permitting the appellant to be present at the hearing of the appeal if the appellant does not have a right to attend (s 31(2)(c)). No order is needed, as the appellant has the right to attend, if the appeal involves questions of fact (s 22 of the Criminal Appeal Act 1968).

Where an appellant absconds before his appeal has been heard, the normal practice is to adjourn the appeal or, if the justice of the case permits, to dismiss the appeal. However, in exceptional cases, the court might allow the appeal to be heard in the absence of the appellant (*R v Gooch* [1998] 1 WLR 110). In *R v Charles* [2001] EWCA Crim 129; [2001] 2 Cr App R 15, the defendant had absconded during his trial. After his capture, he sought leave to appeal against his conviction. The Court of Appeal held that, notwithstanding policy issues regarding absconders, the defendant should not be denied the right to apply for leave to appeal simply because of the delay caused by his

being at large (since that might be a breach of his right to a fair trial under Art 6(1) of the Convention). The court went on to hold that it is open to the Court of Appeal to consider such applications by assuming that the legal representatives of an absconder had instructions to act.

12.4.2 Bail

Bail may be granted to the appellant under s 19 of the Criminal Appeal Act 1968. Section 19 provides that:

(1) The Court of Appeal may ... if they think fit—

    (a) grant an appellant bail pending the determination of his appeal; or

    (b) revoke bail granted to an appellant by the Crown Court under paragraph (f) of section 81(1) of the Supreme Court Act 1981 or paragraph (a) above; or

    (c) vary the conditions of bail granted to an appellant in the exercise of the power conferred by either of those paragraphs.

(2) The powers conferred by sub-section (1) above may be exercised—

    (a) on the application of an appellant; or

    (b) if it appears to the registrar of criminal appeals of the Court of Appeal ... that any of them ought to be exercised, on a reference to the court by him.

The application for bail is considered by the single judge (under s 31(2)(e)) without a hearing. If the single judge refuses bail, the appellant can renew his bail application in open court if he gives notice that he wishes to do so within 14 days of the single judge's decision.

Bail pending appeal will only be granted if there are exceptional circumstances which drive the court to the conclusion that justice can only be done by the granting of bail (*R v Watton* (1978) 68 Cr App R 293). The case where the grant of bail is most likely is where it is likely that the appellant will have served his sentence before the appeal is disposed of (especially if he appears to have very strong grounds of appeal):

- *Restrictions on Crown Court granting bail pending appeal*

  It should be noted that the Crown Court only has jurisdiction to grant bail to someone who is appealing against conviction and/or sentence if the trial judge has certified that the case is fit for appeal (s 81 of the Supreme Court Act 1981). Such certificates are, as we have seen, very rare, and so in most cases it will only be the single judge of the Court of Appeal who can grant bail to an appellant.

- *Expedited appeals*

  If the single judge refuses to grant bail but the appellant may have served his sentence before the appeal is disposed of, the single judge may order an expedited appeal so that the appellant does not have to wait as long as usual for the appeal to be heard.

12.4.3 Public funding

Under s 26 of the Access to Justice Act 1999, representation under the trial representation order includes advice on the question of whether there appear to be reasonable grounds of appeal and, if such grounds appear to exist, assistance in the preparation of an application for leave to appeal or in the giving of a notice of appeal.

Publicly funded representation is also available for the appeal itself. Regulation 10 of the Criminal Defence Service (General) (No 2) Regulations 2001 (SI 2001/1437) provides as follows:

(1) An application for a representation order in respect of proceedings in the Court of Appeal or the House of Lords may be made:

   (a) orally to the Court of Appeal, or a judge of the court; or

   (b) in writing to the Court of Appeal, a judge of the court, or the appropriate officer of the court.

(2) Where an application is made to the court, it may refer it to a judge or the appropriate officer for determination.

(3) Where an application is made to a judge, he may refer it to the appropriate officer for determination.

(4) The appropriate officer may:

   (a) grant the application; or

   (b) refer it to the court or a judge of the court.

(5) A representation order shall not be granted until notice of leave to appeal has been given in respect of the proceedings which are the subject of the application.

(6) Where a representation order is granted in respect of proceedings in the Court of Appeal, a judge or the appropriate officer may specify the stage of the proceedings at which the representation order shall take effect.

Thus, the Registrar is empowered to make a representation order or to refer the application to the single judge (in other words, the Registrar cannot refuse an order).

12.4.4 Direction for loss of time

As we have already seen, where the appellant received a custodial sentence, the single judge may make a direction for loss of time (s 31(2)(h)), ordering that the time spent in custody since conviction shall not count towards the service of the appellant's sentence. Such an order should only be made where the application is devoid of merit.

12.4.5 The Courts Act 2003: procedural directions

The Auld Review recommended that a judge of the Court of Appeal should be empowered, when considering applications for leave to appeal, to give procedural directions for the hearing of the application for leave, or of the appeal itself, that need not trouble the full court (subject to a right on the part of the applicant or the prosecution to renew the application to the full court). To achieve this, s 87 of the Courts Act 2003 will enable either a single judge or the Registrar to give such procedural directions, thus reducing delay.

Section 87(1) of the Courts Act 2003 amends s 31(2) of the Criminal Appeal Act 1968 (powers of the Court of Appeal exercisable by a single judge), by adding a new sub-s (2)(i) empowering a single judge to make orders under s 23(1)(a) (ordering the production of any document, exhibit or other thing connected with the appeal proceedings, the production of which appears necessary for the determination of the case). Section 87(2) of the 2003 Act amends s 31A of the 1968 Act (powers of Court of Appeal exercisable by Registrar), by adding a new sub-s (2)(d) conferring the same power on the Registrar.

Section 87(3) of the Courts Act 2003 also adds two new sections, ss 31B and 31C, to the Criminal Appeal Act 1968. Section 31B provides as follows:

31B   *Procedural directions: powers of single judge and registrar*

(1)   The power of the Court of Appeal to determine an application for procedural directions may be exercised by—

     (a)   a single judge; or

     (b)   the registrar.

(2)   'Procedural directions' means directions for the efficient and effective preparation of—

     (a)   an application for leave to appeal; or

     (b)   an appeal,

     to which this section applies.

(3)   A single judge may give such procedural directions as he thinks fit—

     (a)   when acting under sub-section (1);

     (b)   on a reference from the registrar;

     (c)   of his own motion, when he is exercising, or considering whether to exercise, any power of his in relation to the application or appeal.

(4)   The registrar may give such procedural directions as he thinks fit—

     (a)   when acting under sub-section (1);

     (b)   of his own motion.

Section 31C deals with appeals against procedural directions, providing that:

(1)   Sub-section (2) applies if a single judge gives, or refuses to give, procedural directions.

(2)   The Court of Appeal may, on an application to it under sub-section (5)—

     (a)   confirm, set aside or vary any procedural directions given by the single judge; and

     (b)   give such procedural directions as it thinks fit.

(3)   Sub-section (4) applies if the registrar gives, or refuses to give, procedural directions.

(4)   A single judge may, on an application to him under sub-section (5)—

     (a)   confirm, set aside or vary any procedural directions given by the registrar; and

     (b)   give such procedural directions as he thinks fit.

(5)   An application under this sub-section may be made by—

     (a)   an appellant;

     (b)   a respondent, if the directions—

         (i)   relate to an application for leave to appeal and appear to need the respondent's assistance to give effect to them,

         (ii)   relate to an application for leave to appeal which is to be determined by the Court of Appeal, or

         (iii) relate to an appeal.

12.5 THE HEARING OF THE APPEAL

Prior to the hearing, the judges and all counsel will have received a summary of the case from the Registrar. These case summaries are prepared by the Registrar's staff.

Paragraph II.17 of the *Practice Direction* [2002] 1 WLR 2870 lays down the requirements for skeleton arguments in appeals against conviction. The advocate for the appellant must lodge a skeleton argument with the Registrar, and serve it on the prosecuting authority, within 14 days of receipt by the advocate of leave to appeal against conviction (unless a longer period is directed). The prosecutor should lodge a skeleton argument within 14 days of receipt of the appellant's skeleton argument (unless directed otherwise).

The appeal takes the form of argument based on the grounds of appeal, the transcript of the summing up and any other documentary evidence.

Counsel for the appellant presents his case first and counsel for the respondent (the prosecution) then replies. Unless it is a case where the conviction is said to be unsafe because of fresh evidence, no oral evidence will be heard by the court.

12.6 GROUNDS OF APPEAL AGAINST CONVICTION

Section 2 of the Criminal Appeal Act (as amended by the Criminal Appeal Act 1995) provides as follows:

(1) Subject to the provisions of this Act, the Court of Appeal—

    (a) shall allow an appeal against conviction if they think that the conviction is unsafe; and

    (b) shall dismiss such an appeal in any other case.

(2) In the case of an appeal against conviction the Court shall, if they allow the appeal, quash the conviction.

(3) An order of the Court of Appeal quashing a conviction shall, except when under section 7 below the appellant is ordered to be retried, operate as a direction to the court of trial to enter, instead of the record of conviction, a judgment and verdict of acquittal.

Thus, the Court of Appeal must allow an appeal against conviction if they think that the conviction is unsafe; otherwise, they must dismiss the appeal.

Prior to its amendment by the Criminal Appeal Act 1995, s 2(1) of the 1968 Act required the Court of Appeal to allow an appeal against conviction if it thought that the conviction was 'unsafe or unsatisfactory', or there had been a 'wrong decision on any question of law', or a 'material irregularity in the course of the trial'. This was subject to the proviso that the Court of Appeal could dismiss an appeal if they considered 'that no miscarriage of justice has actually occurred'. This proviso does not appear in the amended version of s 2(1) as it is unnecessary: a conviction could not be 'safe' if a miscarriage of justice has occurred.

According to the Home Secretary, who had consulted with the Lord Chief Justice, the revised version of s 2(1), 'in substance ... restates the existing practice of the Court of Appeal' (*Hansard*, HC (6 March 1995) cols 53–55 and *Hansard*, HL (15 May 1995) cols 310–12).

There is no statutory definition of the word 'unsafe'. However, under the original version of s 2(1), a conviction would be held to be 'unsafe' if the members of the Court of Appeal feel that there is 'some lurking doubt in our minds which makes us wonder whether an injustice has been done' (*R v Cooper* [1969] 1 QB 267 at p 271, *per* Lord Widgery CJ; *Stafford v DPP* [1974] AC 878 at p 912, *per* Lord Kilbrandon).

In *R v Graham* [1997] 1 Cr App R 302 at p 308, Lord Bingham CJ said of the amended s 2(1):

> This new provision ... is plainly intended to concentrate attention on one question: whether in the light of any arguments raised or evidence adduced on appeal the Court of Appeal considers a conviction unsafe. If the Court is satisfied despite any misdirection of law or any irregularity in the conduct of the trial or any fresh evidence, that the conviction is safe, the Court will dismiss the appeal. But if, for whatever reason, the Court concludes that the appellant was wrongly convicted of the offence charged or is left in doubt whether the appellant was rightly convicted of that offence or not, then it must of necessity consider the conviction unsafe. The Court is then subject to a binding duty to allow the appeal.

It follows from this that the Court of Appeal is not concerned with the guilt or innocence of appellants, but only with the safety of their convictions.

In *R v Farrow* [1999] Crim LR 306, the Court of Appeal deprecated the use of the 'lurking doubt' test for appeals against conviction and said that the court should focus on the wording of the statutory test of whether the conviction is unsafe, rather than applying a gloss to that test. However, in *R v Criminal Cases Review Commission ex p Pearson* [2000] 1 Cr App R 141, Lord Bingham CJ (at pp 146–47) said:

> The expression 'unsafe' in section 2(1)(a) Criminal Appeal Act 1968 does not lend itself to precise definition. In some cases unsafety will be obvious, as (for example) where it appears that someone other than the appellant committed the crime and the appellant did not, or where the appellant has been convicted of an act that was not in law a crime, or where a conviction is shown to be vitiated by serious unfairness in the conduct of the trial or significant legal misdirection ... Cases however arise in which unsafety is much less obvious: cases in which the Court, although by no means persuaded of an appellant's innocence, is subject to some lurking doubt or uneasiness whether an injustice has been done ... If, on consideration of all the facts and circumstances of the case before it, the Court entertains real doubts whether the appellant was guilty of the offence of which he has been convicted, the Court will consider the conviction unsafe. In these less obvious cases the ultimate decision of the Court of Appeal will very much depend on its assessment of all the facts and circumstances.

12.6.1 Errors in the course of the trial

Matters which are capable of rendering a conviction unsafe include the following:

(a) A decision by the judge that certain evidence against the defendant was admissible. If the Court of Appeal decides that the evidence in question ought to have been excluded, the judges will go on to consider what impact this mistake had on the trial: for example, how strong was the other (admissible) evidence against the accused.

(b) The wrongful rejection by the judge of a submission that there is no case to answer. Where a defendant appeals against conviction on the ground that the trial judge

wrongly rejected a submission of no case to answer at the end of the prosecution case, the Court of Appeal should ignore any evidence admitted after the submission of no case. Therefore, if the defendant admits his guilt during cross-examination, the conviction should still be set aside if the submission of no case was rejected wrongly (*R v Abbott* [1955] 2 QB 497; *R v Cockley* (1984) 79 Cr App R 181; *R v Smith* [1999] 2 Cr App R 238).

(c) Irregularities occurring during the course of the trial, for example, misconduct on the part of a juror (as where a juror is seen in conversation with a prosecution witness during an adjournment). An example of something going wrong in the course of the trial is provided by *R v Maguire* [1997] 1 Cr App R 61. A witness called by the defendant repeatedly refused to answer certain questions regarding his own whereabouts at the time of the alleged offence. The judge, in the presence of the jury, ordered the witness to be arrested and taken down to the cells. The Court of Appeal accepted the argument that the jury might have been affected by seeing an important defence witness being arrested. The judge should have invited the jury to retire before ordering the arrest of the witness. The appeal was therefore allowed and a re-trial was ordered.

(d) Errors in the summing up: details of what the summing up must contain and how the various components should be dealt with are set out later in this chapter.

(e) The judge's conduct of the trial: in *R v Whybrow* (1994) 144 NLJ 124, the Court of Appeal expressed support for the recommendation of the 1993 Royal Commission on Criminal Justice that judges should be more interventionist in order to prevent trials becoming protracted. However, such intervention must not go beyond legitimate bounds. If, for example, a witness gives an ambiguous answer, the judge should have it clarified. If a witness gives a long answer, the judge may ask the witness to confirm the gist of that answer so that there is no misunderstanding. What the judge must not do is to become an advocate. The court approved a *dictum* of Cumming-Bruce LJ in *R v Gunning* (1994) 98 Cr App R 303, comparing the function of the judge with that of an umpire in a cricket match:

> He is certainly not the bowler, whose business is to get the batsman out. If a judge ... descends into the forum and asks great numbers of pointed questions of the accused when he is giving his evidence-in-chief, the jury may well get the impression that the judge does not believe a word that the witness is saying and by putting these pointed questions, to which there is sometimes only a lame answer, he blows the evidence out of the water during the stage that counsel ought to be having the opportunity to bring the evidence of the accused to the attention of the jury in its most impressive pattern and shape.

In both cases, it was stressed that the opportunity to examine-in-chief without interruption is particularly important 'if the evidence emerging in chief is a story that takes a bit of swallowing'. In *R v Wiggan* (1999) *The Times*, 22 March, after the defendant had been re-examined by her counsel, the judge asked some 64 questions of a testing nature, suggesting scepticism of the defendant's evidence. The Court of Appeal held that after a witness has been re-examined, it is open to the judge to ask questions to clear up uncertainties, to fill gaps, or to answer queries which might be lurking in the jury's mind. However, it is not appropriate for the judge to cross-examine the witness. Similarly, in *R v Tuegel* [2000] 2 All ER 872, the Court of Appeal held that although a judge should avoid asking a witness questions which appear to suggest that the judge is taking sides, he has a duty to ask questions which clarify ambiguities in answers previously given or which

identify the nature of the defence, if that is unclear. Such questions should usually be asked at, or close to, the time when the ambiguity first becomes apparent. The court went on to say that although it might exceptionally be necessary for a judge, in the presence of the jury, to interrupt a speech by counsel, it is generally preferable for him not to do so. Ideally, interventions for the purpose of clarifying or correcting something said, either by judge or counsel, should be made in the first instance in the absence of the jury and at a break in the proceedings, so that, if necessary, the point can be dealt with before the jury in an appropriate fashion.

(f) Errors by defence counsel: in *R v Ullah* [2000] 1 Cr App R 351, defence counsel was aware of the existence of evidence that cast doubt on the veracity of the complainant's evidence; this evidence was not put before the court (possibly because its admissibility was rather doubtful). Had the jury known about this evidence, it would have seriously damaged the prosecution case. The Court of Appeal held (following *R v Clinton* (1993) 97 Cr App R 320) that a conviction will not be unsafe merely because defence counsel took a decision that another counsel might not have taken; the Court of Appeal will only have regard to 'significant' fault by trial counsel or solicitor. The court said that it may well be appropriate to apply the *Wednesbury Corp* ([1948] 1 KB 223) test of unreasonableness: was the decision one that no reasonable advocate could have reached? In *Boodram v State of Trinidad & Tobago* [2001] UK PC 20; [2002] 1 Cr App R 12, the Privy Council said that when the conduct of a case forms the ground of appeal against conviction, the court ought normally to focus on the impact which the faulty conduct of the case had on the trial and the verdict. However, where counsel's conduct was so extreme as to result in a denial of due process to his client, the question of the impact of counsel's conduct on the result of the case is no longer of any relevance: whenever a person is convicted without having enjoyed the benefit of due process, there is a miscarriage of justice, regardless of his guilt or innocence. In such circumstances, the conviction has to be quashed, since a conviction following a fundamental flaw in the conduct of a trial cannot be allowed to stand. In *R v Thakrar* [2001] EWCA Crim 1096, the appeal was brought on the grounds that the appellant had not had a fair trial because his solicitors did not properly prepare or advise on his case prior to trial. It was held that the appellant's solicitors had fallen below the level of reasonably competent solicitors in the way in which they had prepared the trial on behalf of the appellant. However, the mere fact that an appellant's solicitors may have failed to carry out their duties to an appellant in a proper manner does not of itself mean that a conviction is automatically unsafe. Nor could a conviction be quashed as a means of expressing the court's disapproval of a solicitor's failure. The issue, said the court, was whether the failures had prevented the appellant from having a fair trial within the meaning of Art 6 of the European Convention on Human Rights. Some errors on the part of counsel are tactical decisions which turn out to be wrong. In *Popat v Barnes* [2004] EWCA Civ 820, the Court of Appeal said that where counsel made a tactical decision not to raise a particular point at the trial, this should not necessarily inhibit counsel from raising the matter on appeal, although it should be borne in mind that the Court of Appeal may well look with disfavour on arguments based on deliberate decisions made at the trial by counsel.

(g) Events before the trial: a conviction may be rendered unsafe by events which occurred before the trial started. In *R v Mullen* [2000] QB 520, for example, the

appellant's deportation to this country had been procured by unlawful means. There was no complaint about the conduct of the trial, but it was argued that the trial should never have taken place, since there had been abuse of process by the prosecution prior to the trial. The Court of Appeal confirmed that a conviction can be 'unsafe' under s 2 of the Criminal Appeal Act 1968 as a result of matters occurring prior to the trial itself.

A key question is the relationship between the safety of the conviction (the test applicable under the Criminal Appeal Act) and the fairness of the trial (the test applicable under Art 6 of the European Convention on Human Rights). Put simply, the question is whether a conviction can be regarded as 'safe' if the trial process was 'unfair'.

In *R v Chalkley* [1998] QB 848 (where the defendants pleaded guilty following an erroneous ruling by the trial judge on a question of admissibility), Auld LJ said, 'The Court has no power under ... s 2(1) [of the Criminal Appeal Act 1968] to allow an appeal if it does not think the conviction unsafe but is dissatisfied in some way with what went on at trial'. However, his Lordship went on to say that this is subject to the jurisprudence of the European Court of Human Rights. The view of the European Court was given in *Condron v UK* (2001) 31 EHRR 1, where the Court said (at para 65): 'The question whether or not the rights of the defence guaranteed to an accused under Article 6 of the Convention were secured in any given case cannot be assimilated to a finding that his conviction was safe in the absence of any enquiry into the issue of fairness.' This is significant, as it suggests that the European Court was concerned that the two tests – the safety of the conviction and the fairness of the trial – might not necessarily lead to the same result.

In *R v Francom* [2001] 1 Cr App R 237, the Court of Appeal agreed that the tests are different but said that this does not mean that the results of applying the two tests should be different. Lord Woolf CJ said (at para 43) that the test of whether a conviction is unsafe applied by the Court of Appeal is not identical to the issue of unfairness before the European Court of Human Rights. However, his Lordship said (at para 47) that the Court of Appeal should approach the issue of lack of safety in the same way that the European Court of Human Rights approaches lack of fairness. The appeal is this case arose (as in *Condron v UK*) from the failure of the trial judge to direct the jury correctly on adverse inferences under s 34 of the Criminal Justice and Public Order Act 1994. Lord Woolf CJ said that the issue was whether the omission of the required direction had in fact resulted in unfairness or had impaired the safety of the conviction. No distinction should be drawn between the two tests (para 48). In the present case, no reasonable jury, properly directed, could have reached a different conclusion, and so the conviction was not unsafe and there had been no unfairness to the defendants.

Similarly, in *R v Togher* [2001] 1 Cr App R 33, the Court of Appeal said that since the coming into force of the Human Rights Act 1998, it would be extremely rare for there to be room for a different result before the Court of Appeal and before the European Court of Human Rights. Lord Woolf CJ said that if the defendant has been denied a fair trial, it is almost inevitable that his conviction will be regarded as unsafe. It followed that, if it would have been right to stop a prosecution on the basis that it was an abuse of process, the Court of Appeal would be most unlikely to conclude that the conviction should not be set aside.

In *R v Davies, Rowe and Johnson* [2001] 1 Cr App R 115, the Court of Appeal had to decide how to deal with the fact that the European Court of Human Rights had held that there had been a breach of Art 6(1) of the Convention during the trial of these defendants, and that this had not been cured by the appeal process. In other words, the Court had to consider the effect of this ruling on the application of s 2 of the Criminal Appeal Act 1968 to the defendants' convictions. It held that the Court of Appeal is concerned only with the safety of a conviction, whereas the jurisdiction of the European Court of Human Rights is to examine the fairness of the trial, not to express an opinion on the safety of the conviction under domestic law. Even if there has been a finding by the European Court of Human Rights that Art 6(1) of the Convention has been violated, that would not necessarily lead to the quashing of a conviction, since it is for the domestic court to examine the safety of the conviction in accordance with s 2 of the Criminal Appeal Act 1968. Mantell LJ said that a conviction can never be safe if there is doubt about the appellant's guilt. However, his Lordship said that the converse is not true: a conviction might be unsafe even where there is no doubt about guilt, but the trial process was vitiated by serious unfairness or significant legal misdirection. It follows that if a trial is found to be unfair, that could have an impact on the safety of the conviction even in the face of overwhelming evidence against the defendant (see, for example, *R v Smith* [1999] 2 Cr App R 238). His Lordship went on to hold that, usually, the court should apply the test in *Stirland v DPP* [1944] AC 315 and ask itself: 'Assuming the wrong decision on law or the misdirection had not occurred and the trial had been free from legal error, would the only reasonable and proper verdict have been one of guilty?' The European Court of Human Rights is charged with inquiring into whether there has been a breach of a Convention right; the Court of Appeal is concerned with the safety of the conviction. Obviously, the first question might intrude upon the second, but the extent to which it does so would depend upon the circumstances of the particular case. A finding of a breach of Art 6(1) of the Convention would not lead 'inexorably' to the quashing of a conviction. The effect of any unfairness upon the safety of a conviction would vary according to its nature and degree. The Court went on to hold that, in the present case, the unfairness did cast doubt of the safety of the convictions, which were accordingly quashed.

In *R v Williams* [2001] EWCA Crim 932; (2001) *The Times*, 30 March, the court reiterated the point made in *R v Davis, Rowe and Johnson* that a conviction following a trial which involved a breach of Art 6 of the European Convention on Human Rights is not *necessarily* unsafe. In the case of a misdirection or failure to give a direction, the court should ask itself whether, if an appropriate direction had been given, the jury might have acquitted the defendant. If the answer is no, then the conviction should be regarded as safe.

On the other hand, in *R v A (No 2)* [2001] 2 Cr App R 21, Lord Steyn said at para 38 that: 'It is well established that the guarantee of a fair trial under Article 6 is absolute: a conviction obtained in breach of it cannot stand ... The only balancing permitted is in respect of what the concept of a fair trial entails: here account may be taken of the familiar triangulation of interests of the accused, the victim and society.' It is submitted that this approach may offer one way of resolving the uncertainty in the case law: a breach of the right to a fair trial should result in the conviction being held unsafe, but not every error in the course of a trial is of sufficient gravity to result in unfairness. In *R v Lambert* [2002] 2 AC 545, Lord Clyde (at para 159) (with whom Lords Steyn (at para 43) and Hutton (paras 199–200) agreed) said that:

... an unfairness is not always fatal to a conviction ... If there is doubt about guilt then the conviction must be held to be unsafe. But if there is no doubt about guilt it is not every case where an unfairness can be identified that will necessarily and inevitably lead to a quashing of the conviction.

In *R v Hanratty* [2002] 2 Cr App R 30, Lord Woolf (at para 95) reiterated the point that a conviction can be unsafe even if the defendant is in fact guilty of the offence:

Here it is important to have in mind that a conviction may be unsafe for two distinct reasons that may, but do not necessarily, overlap. The first reason being that there is a doubt as to the safety of the conviction and the second being that the trial was materially flawed. The second reason can be independent of guilt because of the fundamental constitutional requirement that even a guilty defendant is entitled, before being found guilty, to have a trial which conforms with at least the minimum standards of what is regarded in this jurisdiction as being an acceptable criminal trial.

In *R v Dundon* [2004] EWCA Crim 621; (2004) *The Times*, 28 April, the Court of Appeal said (at para 16): 'We are unable to envisage any circumstance in which, an Article 6 breach having arisen from want of independence and impartiality in the tribunal, it would be possible to conclude that the conviction is safe.' Presumably this would encompass cases where the defendant was clearly guilty.

In 'Mind the gaps: safety, fairness and moral legitimacy' [2004] Crim LR 266, Nick Taylor and David Ormerod write:

... we suggest that the appropriate benchmark for the degree of unfairness sufficient to constitute unsafety is not a question of 'grossness' but a matter of when the procedure is flawed to the extent that it jeopardises the moral integrity of the process. In such cases, the conviction cannot be upheld even if the defendant is factually guilty, and conversely can be upheld in the face of minor infractions of 'fairness' ... We cannot offer a definitive answer to the question of the boundaries of unfairness and unsafety. We would, however, submit that failings in fairness that would not fall within the scope of unsafety should be restricted to technical breaches that do not prejudice the accused. There ought to be only a small gap between unsafety and unfairness. Viewed from a different angle, it is easier to identify what should be treated as being so unfair as to constitute unsafety. Breaches of Convention rights should presumptively be viewed as generating such unfairness as to render a conviction unsafe.

Given the uncertainty created by conflicting *dicta* in the case law, it is perhaps unsurprising that Lord Justice Auld, in his *Review of the Criminal Courts of England and Wales*, notes the potential tension between safety of conviction and fairness of trial. Recommendation 301 is that:

Consideration should be given to amendment of the statutory test of unsafety as the ground for quashing a conviction so as to clarify whether and to what extent it is to apply to convictions that would be regarded as safe in the ordinary sense, but that follow want of due process before or during trial.

12.6.2 Appeals relating to the jury

Apart from instances of misconduct by jurors, there are special rules which deal with appeals which are based on complaints about the jury. Those rules are contained in s 18 of the Juries Act 1974. This provides that a conviction may not be quashed on any of the following grounds:

(a) that the provisions of the Act regarding the selection of the jury have not been complied with;

(b) that a juror was not qualified to serve;

(c) that a juror was unfit to serve. In *R v Chapman and Lauday* (1976) 63 Cr App R 75, this was held to include an allegation that one of the jurors was partially deaf and so missed most of the evidence. The Court of Appeal did say in that case that although such unfitness could not amount to a material irregularity, it could be used as one factor amongst others rendering the conviction unsafe.

In addition to the statutory restriction contained in s 18, it is a strict rule that the Court of Appeal will not investigate what went on in the jury room while the jury were considering their verdict: see *R v Bean* [1991] Crim LR 843, where the defence wanted to adduce evidence from the jury bailiff that he had overheard an exchange which could be regarded as one juror being pressurised into voting in favour of conviction but the Court of Appeal refused to entertain this evidence. This is a long-standing rule. In *R v Thompson* [1962] 1 All ER 65, the Court of Appeal refused to hear evidence that most of the jury had been in favour of an acquittal until the foreman of the jury had read out a list of the defendant's previous convictions (which had not been referred to in court). Likewise, in *R v Roads* [1967] 2 QB 108, the Court of Appeal would not hear evidence that one of the jurors had in fact disagreed with the verdict announced by the foreman. In *R v Less* (1993) *The Times*, 30 March, the Court of Appeal disregarded letters from jurors saying that they disagreed with the verdict. Similarly, in *R v Scholfield* [1993] Crim LR 217, the Court of Appeal refused to entertain evidence of a conversation between a juror and the jury bailiff in which it became apparent that the jury did not understand the legal definition of the charge. In *R v Miah; R v Akhbar* [1997] 2 Cr App R 12, the Court of Appeal reaffirmed once again the rule that it will not receive evidence of discussions which take place in the jury room. In any event, it was pointed out in *R v Mickleburgh* [1995] 1 Cr App R 297 that taking a statement from a juror about the deliberations which took place in the jury room could well amount to contempt under s 8 of the Contempt of Court Act 1981; following *R v McCluskey* (1993) 98 Cr App R 216, it was held that such inquiries should only take place with the consent of the Court of Appeal.

In *R v Millward* [1999] 1 Cr App R 61, after a majority verdict direction had been given, the jury later returned to court. They were asked if they had reached a verdict on which at least 10 of them were agreed. The foreman said that they had. The verdict was guilty. The clerk asked whether it was a verdict of all the jury or by a majority. The foreman replied 'all'. A juror subsequently wrote to the court saying that in fact it was a 10:2 majority verdict in favour of conviction. The Court of Appeal said that there had been a clear statement from the foreman that the verdict was unanimous, and so the court did not have to make the further inquiries required by s 17(3) of the Juries Act 1974. Furthermore, the Court of Appeal was not entitled to inquire into what went on in the jury room.

Allegations of dissent amongst a jury remain immune from investigation notwithstanding the coming into force of the Human Rights Act 1998: *R v Lewis* [2001] EWCA Crim 749; (2001) *The Times*, 26 April; *R v Qureshi* [2001] EWCA Crim 1807; [2002] 1 WLR 518. In *R v Austin* [2002] EWCA Crim 1796; [2003] Crim LR 426, the jury verdict was announced as unanimous but the following day one of the jurors stated that he and possibly other jurors had in fact disagreed with the verdict. The judge refused to make any inquiries of jurors in relation to the verdict. The Court of Appeal

held that where a verdict is given in the sight and hearing of the entire jury without any dissent by any member of it, there is a presumption that they all assent to it. There was nothing in the present case to rebut that presumption.

In *R v Young* [1995] QB 324, it was said by the Court of Appeal that this rule of secrecy applies only to deliberations which take place in the jury room. Thus, it did not prevent the court from inquiring into what took place if the jury were not allowed to go home after they had retired to consider their verdict but had been sent to stay in an hotel overnight instead. In that case (a murder trial), a re-trial was ordered because, during the overnight adjournment, some members of the jury had used an Ouija board to try to get in touch with the murder victim to ask him who had committed the murder.

In *Gregory v UK* (1997) 25 EHRR 577, the European Court of Human Rights observed (p 594, para 44):

> The court acknowledges that the rule governing the secrecy of jury deliberations is a crucial and legitimate feature of English trial law which serves to reinforce the jury's role as the ultimate arbiter of fact and to guarantee open and frank deliberations among jurors on the evidence which they have heard.

The rationale of the secrecy rule was explained by Arbour J, in giving the judgment of the Canadian Supreme Court in *Sawyer* [2001] 2 SCC 344 at pp 373–75:

> The first reason supporting the need for secrecy is that confidentiality promotes candour and the kind of full and frank debate that is essential to this type of collegial decision making. While searching for unanimity, jurors should be free to explore out loud all avenues of reasoning without fear of exposure to public ridicule, contempt or hatred. This rationale is of vital importance to the potential acquittal of an unpopular accused, or one charged with a particularly repulsive crime. In my view, this rationale is sound, and does not require empirical confirmation.
>
> The Court of Appeal also placed considerable weight on the second rationale for the secrecy rule: the need to ensure finality of the verdict. Describing the verdict as the product of a dynamic process, the court emphasized the need to protect the solemnity of the verdict, as the product of the unanimous consensus which, when formally announced, carries the finality and authority of a legal pronouncement. That rationale is more abstract, and inevitably invites the question of why the finality of the verdict should prevail over its integrity in cases where that integrity is seriously put in issue. In a legal environment such as ours, which provides for generous review of judicial decisions on appeal, and which does not perceive the voicing of dissenting opinions on appeal as a threat to the authority of the law, I do not consider that finality, standing alone, is a convincing rationale for requiring secrecy.
>
> [T]he third main rationale for the jury secrecy rule [is] the need to protect jurors from harassment, censure and reprisals. Our system of jury selection is sensitive to the privacy interests of prospective jurors … and the proper functioning of the jury system, a constitutionally protected right in serious criminal charges, depends upon the willingness of jurors to discharge their functions honestly and honourably. This in turn is dependent, at the very minimum, on a system that ensures the safety of jurors, their sense of security, as well as their privacy.

In *R v Connor; R v Mirza* [2004] UKHL 2; [2004] 1 AC 1118, the House of Lords was called upon to review the rule that the court will not investigate, or receive evidence about, anything said in the course of the jury's deliberations while they are considering

their verdict in their retiring room. The questions certified by the Court of Appeal were:

> Should the common law prohibition on the admission of evidence of the jury's deliberations prevail even if the Court of Appeal is presented with a statement from the juror, which, if admitted, would provide *prima facie* evidence of jury partiality in breach of Article 6?

> Does section 8 of the Contempt of Court Act 1981, when interpreted in the light of section 3 of the Human Rights Act 1998 and Article 6 of the European Convention, prohibit the admission into evidence of a statement from a juror which if admitted, would provide prima facie evidence of partiality in breach of Article 6? If so, is section 8 incompatible with Article 6 to the extent that it prohibits the admission into evidence of such a statement?

Section 8 of the Contempt of Court Act 1981 provides:

> (1)   Subject to sub-section (2) below, it is a contempt of court to obtain, disclose or solicit any particulars of statements made, opinions expressed, arguments advanced or votes cast by members of a jury in the course of their deliberations in any legal proceedings.

> (2)   This section does not apply to any disclosure of any particulars—

>> (a) in the proceedings in question for the purpose of enabling the jury to arrive at their verdict, or in connection with the delivery of that verdict; or

>> (b) in evidence in any subsequent proceedings for an offence alleged to have been committed in relation to the jury in the first mentioned proceedings,

> or to the publication of any particulars so disclosed.

There have been many calls for s 8 of the Contempt of Court Act 1981 to be amended to enable research to take place into how juries reach their verdicts. The Auld Review concluded that the law should not be amended to permit more intrusive research than is already possible into the workings of juries. However, Lord Justice Auld did add that, in appropriate cases, trial judges and/or the Court of Appeal should be entitled to examine alleged improprieties in the jury room. On the issue of research into jury verdicts, the Recommendations steer a very cautious path. They are:

> 26 There should be no amendment of section 8 of the Contempt of Court Act 1981 to enable research into individual juries' deliberations.

> 27 Careful consideration should be given to existing research material throughout the common law world on jury trial in criminal cases, with a view to identifying and responding appropriately to all available information about how juries arrive at their verdicts.

> 28 If and to the extent that such research material is insufficient, consideration should be given to jury research of a general nature that does not violate the 1981 Act.

> 29 Section 8 of the Contempt of Court Act 1981 should be amended to permit, where appropriate, enquiry by the trial judge and/or the Court of Appeal (Criminal Division) into alleged impropriety by a jury, whether in the course of its deliberations or otherwise.

It is submitted that this final recommendation is unnecessary in so far as the trial judge is concerned, in that the trial judge is already fully entitled to enquire into irregularities that occur during the course of the trial (that is, prior to the verdict).

In *Mirza*, it becomes clear that the rules preventing the Court of Appeal from enquiring into what takes place in the jury room result from the common law, not from the effect of s 8. *Mirza* involved two separate appeals. In one of them, it was suggested that some of the jurors may have been motivated by racism; in the other, it was contended that the jury had decided to convict both of them because it would have taken too long to consider the case against each of them separately and, in any event, this would 'teach them a lesson'. In both appeals the allegations were based on a letter sent by a member of the jury after the trial was over. The House of Lords had to consider both the common law rules relating to the secrecy of the jury room and the effect of s 8 of the Contempt of Court Act 1981.

Lord Slynn of Hadley says (at para 55) that:

> The admission of evidence as to what happened in the jury room cannot be allowed without seriously detracting from the advantages which flow from the present system and which in my view need to be protected. If a case arose when all the jurors agreed that something occurred which in effect meant that the jury abrogated its functions and eg decided on the toss of a coin the case might be, and in my opinion would be, different.

His Lordship then refers to In *R v Young* [1995] QB 324 (where it was alleged that four jurors, during their accommodation overnight in an hotel, had conducted a session with a Ouija board and that a discussion had taken place about this with the other jurors afterwards). In that case, Lord Taylor of Gosforth CJ had said at p 330F–H:

> ... As a matter of principle, the object of [s 8] is clearly to maintain the secrecy of the jury's deliberations in their retiring room. To give the court power, after verdict, to inquire into those deliberations, would force the door of the jury room wide open. If one dissentient juror or sharp-eared bailiff alleged irregularities in the jury room, the court would be pressed to inquire into the jury's deliberations. We are in no doubt that section 8(1) applies to the court as to everyone else.

Lord Slynn, holding that *Young* was wrongly decided on this point, says:

> ... in enacting s 8 of the Contempt of Court Act 1981 ... Parliament did not intend to fetter the power of a court to make investigation as to the conduct of a trial. Properly construed, section 8(1) does not apply to the court of trial or to the Court of Appeal hearing an appeal in that case. It cannot properly be read as categorising what the court does in the course of its investigation as a contempt of the court itself. What was said in *R v Young* [1995] QB 324, at p 330 should not be followed. The court is restricted in its inquiry into what happened in the jury's deliberations, not by section 8 of the Act but by the longstanding rule of the common law.

Lord Hope said (at para 90):

> ... a court cannot be in contempt of itself. In my opinion section 8(1) is addressed to third parties who can be punished for contempt, and not to the court which has the responsibility of ensuring that the defendant receives a fair trial. The observations to the contrary in *R v Young* at p 330 F–H should now be disapproved.

It follows, said his Lordship (para 92), that:

> Where allegations are made which suggest that a defendant is not receiving, or did not receive, the fair trial to which he was entitled under article 6(1) of the Convention, they must be considered and investigated. Any investigation must, of course, be within the limits that are set by the common law. Evidence which is struck at by the common law rule will be inadmissible, and the court should not ask for or receive such evidence.

But there is nothing in the statute that expressly inhibits or restricts the court in its performance of this task ...

Lord Hope went on (para 93) to say:

> ... it is going too far to suggest, as the Court of Appeal appears to have done in Young's case, that the trial court will be in contempt of itself if during the trial, having received allegations such as those made by the jurors in these cases, it investigates them and discloses the result of these investigations to counsel so that they may have an opportunity of making submissions about them to the court; or that the Court of Appeal in its turn, or persons acting under its direction, will be in contempt if the Court of Appeal decides that in the interests of justice the allegations must be investigated. The court must look to the common law for guidance as to the extent to which any such investigation is permissible.

Having established that the only restriction on the court is to be found in the common law, his Lordship went on to consider the common law rules (and whether those rules are compatible with Art 6(1) of the European Convention on Human Rights). He takes as his starting point three propositions (para 61): that confidentiality is essential to the proper functioning of the jury process; that there is merit in finality; and that jurors must be protected from harassment. At para 107, Lord Hope summarises the exceptions to the common law rules as disclosed by case law:

- matters which were extrinsic to the deliberations in the jury room;
- events that took place outside the jury room;
- irregularities which may have led to the jury being provided with information which they should not have had;
- the possession by a juror of knowledge or characteristics which made it inappropriate for that person to serve on the jury.

The present appeals concerned allegations that were directed to what took place during the jury's deliberations in the jury room and so fell squarely within the common law rule.

Lord Hope refers to the *dictum* of the Canadian judge, Arbour J (cited above) and comments (at para 115) that:

> These observations take us to the heart of the matter. The appeals raise questions about a rule which makes it impossible, after a guilty verdict has been returned, to investigate allegations that the jurors were biased or that they ignored directions by the trial judge. But the rigour of the secrecy rule operates, and is designed to operate, in exactly the same way if the verdict is one of not guilty. A defendant does not need to invoke his article 6(1) right where he has been acquitted. But the rule protects jurors who acquit the unpopular, such as members of minority groups, or who acquit those accused of crimes that the public regards as repulsive, such as the abuse of children who were in their care. It protects them too against pressure that might otherwise be brought to bear, in less enlightened times, by the executive.

He goes on (para 116):

> This is an important safeguard against biased verdicts. One cannot have a rule that operates in one way where the jury acquits but operates differently where they convict. Full and frank discussion, in the course of which prejudices may indeed be aired but then rejected when it comes to the moment of decision-taking, would be inhibited if everything that might give rise to allegations of prejudice after the verdict is delivered were to be opened up to scrutiny. Attempts to soften the rule to serve the

interests of those who claim that they were unfairly convicted should be resisted in the general public interest, if jurors are to continue to perform their vital function of safeguarding the liberty of every individual.

Lord Hope concludes (at para 123) that he would be:

> ... inclined to make only one modification to the rule that distinguishes, after the verdict has been delivered, between things which are intrinsic to the deliberation process and those which are extrinsic to it ... it is arguable that an allegation that the jury as a whole declined to deliberate at all, but decided the case by other means such as drawing lots or by the toss of a coin, can be placed into a different category. Conduct of that kind, were it ever to occur, would amount to a complete repudiation by the jury of their only function which, as the juror's oath puts it, is to give a true verdict according to the evidence. A trial which results in a verdict by lot or the toss of a coin, or was reached by consulting an ouija board in the jury room, is not a trial at all. If that is what happened, the jurors have no need to be protected as the verdict was not reached by deliberation – that is, by discussing and debating the issues in the case and arriving at a decision collectively in the light of that discussion. The law would be unduly hampered if the court were to be unable to intervene in such a case and order a new trial.

Having held that the common law should continue to require that the deliberations of the jury must remain confidential, Lord Hope suggested two 'refinements to current practice with a view to strengthening the system of jury trial and retaining public confidence': first, that jurors should be informed that they are under a duty to inform the court at once of any irregularity which occurs during their deliberations (if that step is taken before the verdict is delivered, the trial can – indeed must – investigate and deal with the matter); second, that where an irregularity involving the jury is a ground of appeal, the Court of Appeal should call for a report from the trial judge, so that the Court of Appeal has a complete and accurate account of the events of the trial.

Lord Hobhouse of Woodborough, at para 131, makes the point that 'it is fundamentally wrong to use the phrase "miscarriage of justice" selectively as if it only related to perverse convictions ... a perverse verdict of not guilty, whatever the reason for it, is also a miscarriage of justice'. His Lordship points out (at para 135) that approximately 20% of all convictions after a trial on indictment result from majority verdicts and suggests that:

> This is inevitably a fertile scenario for a dissident juror, maybe honestly, maybe not, to claim that the majority disregarded or misunderstood the judge's direction, did not understand the facts, were not prepared to listen to argument or were prejudiced in some way.

At para 142, Lord Hobhouse reiterates the arguments in favour of the confidentiality of jury deliberations:

> It underpins the independence and impartiality of the jury as a whole. It enables them to be true to their oath to return a true verdict according to the evidence without fearing the consequences of the reporting of things individual jurors have said or the arguments they have advanced. They can play their part in the collective deliberations of the jury without fear of quotation, embarrassment or victimisation.

Lord Rodger of Earlsferry recalls (at para 156) that:

> Allegations of misconduct by jurors may surface at any stage of a trial before the jury has returned a verdict. In such cases there is no reason why the allegations should not be investigated. Judges must accordingly take appropriate steps to investigate and deal with any such matter that arises then ... If it turns out on investigation of an allegation that the jury as a whole is fatally compromised, the judge will discharge them. Where only one particular juror is fatally compromised, the judge will discharge that juror and the trial will proceed with the remaining jurors. In less serious cases the judge will deal with the matter by giving the jury appropriate directions.

His Lordship quotes from the judgment of the European Court of Human Rights in *Gregory v UK* (1997) 25 EHRR 577, and comments (at para 161):

> In other words, faced with a situation where the rule that jurors' deliberations had to be kept secret made it impossible for the trial judge to find out what had given rise to the note, the European Court acknowledged that that rule was not only a legitimate, but a 'crucial', feature of English trial law which served worthwhile objectives. Thus the incorporation of Article 6 of the Convention into our domestic law can be regarded as reinforcing, rather than as calling into question, the rule that jury deliberations should be kept secret.

At para 165, his Lordship says that:

> Once returned ... the verdict becomes the verdict of the jury as a whole and, as such, it cannot be impugned by any of the individual jurors who have publicly assented to it. To hold otherwise would not only call into question the entire status and authority of the jury's verdict but would also expose jurors to pressure, especially from convicted defendants and their associates, to make such allegations.

It should be noted that the government has stated that consideration is to be given to the question of whether the section should be repealed or amended to permit research into how the jury system operates (*Hansard*, HL (11 September 2003) col WA 135). At para 173, Lord Rodgers points out that the Auld Review (Chapter 5, para 98) recommended that the Court of Appeal should be able to inquire into alleged impropriety by a jury, whether in the course of their deliberations or otherwise. His Lordship continues:

> This would involve a substantial, if not complete, departure from the present law and from its underlying policies. There is, as yet, no sign that the Government intend to bring forward legislation to implement the recommendation. Any such far-reaching reform of the law on this topic must, however, be a matter for Parliament rather than for this House in its judicial capacity. Only Parliament is in a position to weigh the competing policy arguments and, if so advised, to produce a new and suitably sophisticated solution. Unless and until that happens, the existing law must be applied.

It seems likely that this factor will have weighed heavily on the other three Law Lords who agreed that the House of Lords should affirm the common law rules on the secrecy of the jury room. It could be argued that if Parliament is examining an area of law, the courts should not pre-empt that examination by making their own modifications to that area of law.

Nonetheless, in a powerful dissenting speech, Lord Steyn disagreed vehemently with the view expressed by the other four Law Lords:

If the law requires individual cases to be subordinated to systemic considerations affecting the jury system, one may question whether the law has not lost its moral underpinning (para 5).

Lord Steyn emphasises the importance of the jury to public confidence in our criminal justice system. At para 7, his Lordship says:

> Lord Devlin observed 'that trial by jury is more than an instrument of justice and more than one wheel of the constitution: it is the lamp that shows that freedom lives': Trial by Jury, (1956), p 164 ... The jury is an integral and indispensable part of the criminal justice system. The system of trial by judge and jury is of constitutional significance. The jury is also, through its collective decision-making, an excellent fact finder. Not surprisingly, the public trust juries. What public opinion would not tolerate are jury verdicts arrived at by perverse processes.

To ensure the integrity of the jury system, Lord Steyn said (para 8) that:

> ... it is necessary to accept that the Court of Appeal has the power in exceptional cases to examine material regarding jury deliberations tending to show that the jury or some of them were false to their oath.

His Lordship accepted that 'there must be a general rule that the deliberations of the jury must remain secret' (para 9). However, he took the view that there should be exceptions to this rule where the justice of the case so requires. At para 12, he quotes from the commentary to the Court of Appeal decision in *R v Qureshi* [2002] Crim LR 62 by Professor Sir John Smith QC:

> If the allegations in the present case were true and if the court had been able to inquire into them, it seems likely that the conviction would have been held to be unsafe. As it is, we shall never know. Not a happy situation ...

Lord Steyn goes on to quote from Professor JR Spencer [2002] 61 CLJ 291 at p 293:

> The nub of the decision in *Qureshi*, one suspects, is the remark that if the appeal were allowed it might lead 'to many such complaints, some perhaps owing their origin to friends or relatives of the defendant'. But this simply will not do. The fact that many allegations of this sort are false cannot justify ignoring all of them because, as *Young* [the ouija board case] so painfully reminds us, some of them regrettably are true.

Turning to the interpretation of the decided cases, Lord Steyn said (at para 14):

> In none of the judgments is there any clear indication that the courts would have been prepared to uphold an absolute rule excluding evidence about jury deliberations in cases where there is credible evidence, disclosed after verdict, showing that the jury was not impartial. In none of the decided cases has it been held that the court may in the interests of the efficient functioning of the jury system tolerate real identifiable risks of miscarriages of justice.

At para 16, Lord Steyn says:

> In cases where there is cogent evidence demonstrating a real risk that the jury was not impartial and that the general confidence in jury verdicts was in the particular case ill reposed, what possible public interest can there be in maintaining a dubious conviction?

At para 19, Lord Steyn says:

> In my view it would be an astonishing thing for the ECHR to hold, when the point directly arises before it, that a miscarriage of justice may be ignored in the interests of the general efficiency of the jury system ... such a view would be utterly indefensible.

At para 22, Lord Steyn says that the consequence of the ruling of the majority is that the jury is immune from scrutiny:

> ... on the basis that such immunity is a price worth paying. This restrictive view will gnaw at public confidence in juries. It is likely in the long run to increase pressure for reducing the scope of trial by jury. A system which forfeits its moral authority is not likely to survive intact. The question will be whether such a system provides a better quality of justice than trial by professionals.

12.7   FRESH EVIDENCE IN THE COURT OF APPEAL

One reason for a conviction being unsafe is that new evidence has come to light which casts doubt on the safety of the conviction. Another reason is that the trial judge wrongly declared certain evidence to be inadmissible. In either case, the Court of Appeal has a discretion to receive evidence which was not adduced at the trial.

Section 23 of the Criminal Appeal Act 1968 empowers the Court of Appeal to receive fresh evidence. It provides as follows:

(1)   For the purposes of an appeal under this Part of this Act the Court of Appeal may, if they think it necessary or expedient in the interests of justice—

    (a) order the production of any document, exhibit or other thing connected with the proceedings, the production of which appears to them necessary for the determination of the case;

    (b) order any witness who would have been a compellable witness in the proceedings from which the appeal lies to attend for examination and be examined before the Court, whether or not he was called in those proceedings; and

    (c) receive any evidence which was not adduced in the proceedings from which the appeal lies.

(2)   The Court of Appeal shall, in considering whether to receive any evidence, have regard in particular to—

    (a) whether the evidence appears to the Court to be capable of belief;

    (b) whether it appears to the Court that the evidence may afford any ground for allowing the appeal;

    (c) whether the evidence would have been admissible in the proceedings from which the appeal lies on an issue which is the subject of the appeal; and

    (d) whether there is a reasonable explanation for the failure to adduce the evidence in those proceedings.

(3)   Sub-section (1)(c) above applies to any evidence of a witness (including the appellant) who is competent but not compellable.

(4)   For the purposes of an appeal under this Part of this Act, the Court of Appeal may, if they think it necessary or expedient in the interests of justice, order the examination of any witness whose attendance might be required under sub-section (1)(b) above to be conducted, in manner provided by rules of court, before any judge or officer of the Court or other person appointed by the Court for the purpose, and allow the admission of any depositions so taken as evidence before the Court.

Thus, the criteria to which the court must have regard when deciding whether or not to receive fresh evidence are:

- the *credibility* of the new evidence (s 23(2)(a));
- the *relevance* of the new evidence – would it have made a difference had it been adduced at trial? (s 23(2)(b));
- the *admissibility* of the evidence, applying the usual rules of evidence (s 23(2)(c)); and
- the *reason for that evidence not being adduced at trial* (s 23(2)(d)).

To assess the credibility of the witness for the purpose of s 23(2)(a), the court should either be provided with an affidavit or a written witness statement or else the Registrar must have been asked to arrange for an out-of-court deposition to be taken by an examiner appointed by the court. In *R v Gogana* (1999) *The Times*, 12 July, the Court of Appeal emphasised the importance of this requirement, particularly where it is suggested that a witness who has previously made a statement is now prepared to give different evidence. In such a case, the court must be supplied with affidavit evidence from all those involved in the taking of the new statement (since the circumstances in which that new statement came into existence are highly relevant to its potential credibility). In assessing credibility, the court will consider whether the evidence is intrinsically credible and whether it fits in with at least some of the evidence adduced at trial (*R v Parks* [1961] 1 WLR 1484).

As far as s 23(2)(b) is concerned, in *R v Gilfoyle* [1996] 3 All ER 883, Beldam LJ said 'We are satisfied that the interests of justice are not simply confined to receiving evidence which would result in an appeal being allowed, particularly when the court is being asked to review as unsafe ... the verdict of a jury after an impeccable summing up on the ground that it has a lurking doubt' (*per* Beldam LJ at p 898). The court is therefore empowered to receive admissible evidence which reinforces or dispels a lurking doubt.

Section 23(2)(c) simply requires that the evidence be admissible (for example, not hearsay). Where the trial judge ruled that certain evidence was inadmissible, it is open to the Court of Appeal, if it rules that the evidence was in fact admissible, to receive that evidence itself.

The fact that counsel for the defence took a tactical decision not to call a particular witness is not a reasonable explanation for the failure to adduce the evidence at trial for the purpose of s 23(2)(d), and so the Court of Appeal is unlikely to hear the evidence of that witness. In *R v Sharp* [2003] EWCA Crim 3870, the Court of Appeal was asked to entertain evidence relating to diminishing responsibility even though that defence had not been raised at the trial. The court noted that there are two conflicting principles. The first principle is that facts 'establishing innocence should not be excluded because of a previous mistaken decision by the appellant or by his advisers'. The second (and conflicting) principle is that it is not open to appellants to choose not to run a defence at trial and then to go back on that decision at the appeal. The Court of Appeal cited with approval the words of Lord Bingham CJ in *R v Campbell* [1997] 1 Cr App R 492:

> This Court has repeatedly underlined the necessity for defendants in criminal trials to advance their full defence before the jury and call any necessary evidence at that stage. It is not permissible to advance one defence before the jury and when that has failed, to devise a new defence, perhaps many years later, and then to seek to raise the defence on appeal.

This *dictum* was itself based closely on earlier guidance given by Lord Taylor CJ in *R v Ahluwalia* (1992) 96 Cr App R 133 at p 142:

Ordinarily, of course, any available defences should be advanced at trial. Accordingly, if medical evidence is available to support a plea of diminished responsibility, it should be adduced at the trial. It cannot be too strongly emphasised that this court would require much persuasion to allow such a defence to be raised for the first time here if the option had been exercised at the trial not to pursue it. Otherwise, as must be clear, defendants might be encouraged to run one defence at trial in the belief that if it fails, this court would allow a different defence to be raised and give the defendant, in effect, two opportunities to run different defences.

In *Sharp*, the Court of Appeal concluded that the inhibition on running a different defence on appeal is not limited to cases where the original decision was in some way dishonest or manipulative, or one purely of tactics. It will only be in very exceptional cases that a different defence can be adduced.

Where evidence could not have been obtained with 'reasonable diligence' in time for the trial (for example, a relevant witness has only just come forward), there is of course a reasonable explanation for not adducing that evidence at the trial: see *R v Beresford* (1971) 56 Cr App R 143, where the appellant wished to rely on the evidence of alibi witnesses who had not been called at the trial. The defence solicitors had not been given the names and addresses of the potential witnesses. However, as the appellant could have supplied this information to his solicitors before the trial, the Court of Appeal held that there was no reasonable explanation for the failure to adduce the evidence at trial.

Even if there is no reasonable explanation for the failure to adduce particular evidence at trial, it might nevertheless be expedient in the interests of justice to receive that fresh evidence (provided that it would have been admissible at the trial, is capable of belief, and might afford a ground for allowing the appeal): see *R v Cairns* [2000] Crim LR 473, where the Court of Appeal noted that it is possible for the court to receive fresh evidence under s 23 of the Criminal Appeal Act 1968 even if all of the four criteria in sub-ss 2(a)–(d) are not satisfied. In *R v Sales* [2000] 2 Cr App R 431, the Court of Appeal said that it is only in rare cases that the Court of Appeal will receive fresh evidence in respect of a defence that was not only not advanced at trial but was completely different to the defence given at trial, and that it is also rare for the Court of Appeal to receive evidence from an appellant who chose not to give evidence before the jury. However, the court confirmed that it is possible for the Court of Appeal to receive fresh evidence even if all four of the considerations under s 23(2) of the Criminal Appeal Act 1968 are not satisfied, providing that the Court of Appeal has had regard to those matters. Where an appellant wishes the Court of Appeal to receive fresh evidence under s 23 of the Criminal Appeal Act 1968 and the circumstances give rise to the need for a lengthy or complex explanation of why the evidence was not adduced at the original trial, an affidavit or signed statement from the appellant or his solicitor, setting out the grounds relied on, should be usually be supplied to the court.

In *R v Jones* [1997] 1 Cr App R 86, the Court of Appeal considered the position of expert witnesses. The court noted that, as far as s 23(2)(d) is concerned (the requirement of a reasonable explanation for the failure to adduce the evidence at trial), this applies more aptly to factual evidence of which a party was unaware or could not adduce at the trial. Expert witnesses, unlike factual witnesses, even though they may vary in standing, are interchangeable. A defendant who is unable to call a particular expert at the trial should either apply for a postponement of the trial or else should try to find a different expert witness. Having said that, the Court of Appeal decided that it

was in the interests of justice in the present case to receive the evidence of the three expert witnesses upon whom the appellant wishes to rely.

In *R v Garner* [1997] *Archbold News*, 13 March, the Court of Appeal drew a distinction between (on one hand) cases involving the new discovery of an earlier suppression or mistake, or evidence dealing with an area hitherto unknown, or unappreciated, scientific or technical advance, or a confession of error or change of opinion by an expert who was called at the trial, and (on the other hand) cases where the relevant facts were known at the trial, and opinion within the relevant profession – as represented by the experts called at (or consulted before) the trial – was broadly agreed, but the defence have since found an expert who is in significant disagreement with such opinion. In the latter case, the court said that it would think long and hard before permitting the new evidence to be adduced on appeal.

As we have seen, the Court of Appeal decides whether or not to receive fresh evidence on the basis of written witness statements. If the Court of Appeal decides to receive the evidence, the witnesses have to attend court to give their evidence unless the court regards the written statement it has already seen as sufficient. Each witness is usually examined-in-chief on behalf of the appellant and cross-examined on behalf of the Crown.

In *R v Pendleton* [2001] UKHL 66; [2002] 1 WLR 72, the House of Lords considered the test to be applied in deciding whether or not to allow an appeal against conviction where fresh evidence has been received under s 23 of the Criminal Appeal Act 1968. It was held (following *Stafford v DPP* [1973] 3 All ER 762) that the correct test to be applied by the Court of Appeal when considering whether or not to allow an appeal against conviction, where fresh evidence had been received, is the effect of the fresh evidence on the minds of the members of the court, and not the effect that it would have had on the minds of the jury, so long as the court bears very clearly in mind that the question for its consideration is whether the conviction is safe and not whether the accused was guilty. Such a test reminds the Court of Appeal that it is not and should never become the primary decision-maker, and that it has an imperfect and incomplete understanding of the full processes which had led the jury to convict. The court can make its assessment of the fresh evidence it has heard but, save in a clear case, it is at a disadvantage in seeking to relate that evidence to the rest of the evidence which the jury heard. It would therefore usually be wise for the Court of Appeal, in a case of any difficulty, to test its own provisional view by asking whether the evidence, if given at the trial, might reasonably have affected the decision of the trial jury to convict. If it might, the conviction must be held unsafe.

In *R v Jamil* [2001] EWCA Crim 1687; (2001) *The Times*, 25 October, the appeal was based on the existence of a police report which had not been disclosed to the defence. It was held that in cases in which fresh evidence is uncovered following a trial, this evidence should be considered within the actual context of the case, bearing in mind the material available to the defence at the time, the instructions given by the defendant and the manner in which the defence conducted the trial. The test as to whether or not the fresh evidence is such as to render the conviction unsafe is whether, having regard to all these matters, the fresh evidence is likely to have been used by the defence. If the answer to this question is in the negative, then it is very unlikely that the discovery of the fresh evidence will render the conviction unsafe.

Most applications to receive fresh evidence are made by the appellant. However, there is no reason why the prosecution cannot invite the court to receive fresh evidence. In *R v Hanratty* [2002] EWCA Crim 1141; [2002] 3 All ER 534, the Court of Appeal said that the overriding consideration, when deciding whether to admit fresh evidence at the request of the prosecution, is whether that evidence could assist the court to achieve justice, bearing in mind that the conviction could be unsafe either because there was a doubt as to the guilt of the defendant or because the trial was materially flawed. The court rejected the submission that the prosecution could only place evidence before the court if it was used to evaluate or rebut fresh evidence adduced by the appellant.

12.8 RESULT OF APPEAL AGAINST CONVICTION

The Court of Appeal has a number of options open to it when disposing of an appeal against conviction.

12.8.1 Appeal dismissed

If the Court of Appeal decides that the appellant's conviction was safe, it will dismiss the appeal and the appellant's conviction will stand.

12.8.2 Successful appeal

If the Court of Appeal decides that one or more of the statutory grounds of appeal is made out, the Court of Appeal has up to four options:

- *To quash the conviction*

  The appellant is regarded for all purposes as if he had been acquitted by the jury. The doctrine of *autrefois acquit* applies, so the appellant cannot be re-prosecuted for the same offence (save in the limited circumstances set out in the Criminal Justice Act 2003).

  If the Court of Appeal allows the appellant's appeal on some counts of an indictment but not others, the Court of Appeal may also review the sentence. However, if the sentence is altered, it must not be more severe than that imposed by the Crown Court.

- *To order a re-trial*

  Section 7 of the Criminal Appeal Act 1968 provides that the Court of Appeal may order a re-trial if the interests of justice so require. Section 7 states that:

  (1) Where the Court of Appeal allow an appeal against conviction and it appears to the Court that the interests of justice so require, they may order the appellant to be retried.

  (2) A person shall not under this section be ordered to be retried for any offence other than—

      (a) the offence of which he was convicted at the original trial and in respect of which his appeal is allowed as mentioned in sub-section (1) above;

      (b) an offence of which he could have been convicted at the original trial on an indictment for the first-mentioned offence; or

(c) an offence charged in an alternative count of the indictment in respect of which the jury were discharged from giving a verdict in consequence of convicting him of the first-mentioned offence.

If the appeal is allowed after the Court of Appeal has heard fresh evidence, a re-trial will usually be ordered so that a jury can hear all the evidence. If, on the other hand, the fresh evidence clearly establishes that the appellant is innocent of the charge, the Court of Appeal will simply quash the conviction.

No re-trial will be ordered if the original trial took place so long ago that the memories of the witnesses would have faded, making a fair trial impossible (*R v Saunders* (1973) 58 Cr App R 248). Furthermore, if the appellant has already spent time in custody so that he has, in effect, already served whatever sentence would be appropriate were he to be found guilty on a re-trial, no re-trial will be ordered (*R v Newland* [1988] QB 402).

In *Nicholls v The State* (2001) *The Times*, 30 January, it was held by the Privy Council that where an appeal against conviction is allowed because the trial judge failed to mention to the jury that there were inadequacies in the prosecution case, and those inadequacies could have been remedied by the prosecution calling further evidence (in the present case, expert evidence), the proper course is simply to quash the conviction, and not to order a re-trial. It would be wrong in principle to allow the prosecution another chance to make good the deficiencies in its case by calling further evidence.

Section 8 of the Criminal Appeal Act 1968 says that where a re-trial has been ordered, a fresh indictment must be preferred within two months of the order; if it is not preferred within that time, the defendant may apply to the Court of Appeal for the order to be set aside. Such an application will succeed unless the prosecution can show that they have acted with all due expedition (that is, all reasonable promptness) and there is good and sufficient cause for a re-trial despite the delay.

It is permissible to introduce a new count to the indictment where there is a re-trial, provided that this can be done without injustice to the defendant (*R v Swaine* (2000) *The Times*, 1 November).

- *To order a venire de novo*

There will be some (very rare) cases where the statutory power to order a re-trial is not available. This will be the case where the proceedings at the trial were a nullity. Examples of this are where some irregularity of procedure has occurred so that no trial was validly commenced (an extreme instance of this would be if a defendant were to be tried in the Crown Court without having been sent for trial by a valid method) or where the trial comes to an end without a properly constituted jury ever having returned a valid verdict (an instance of this would be where the number of jurors remaining falls below the statutory minimum of nine but the judge nevertheless allows the trial to continue and accepts a 'verdict' from the remaining jurors). In such a case, if the Court of Appeal wishes to order a re-trial, it does so by means of a writ of *venire de novo* (see *R v Rose* [1982] 2 All ER 731).

In *R v O'Donnell* [1996] 1 Cr App R 286, for example, the question arose as to the defendant's fitness to plead. The judge decided to postpone consideration of this issue until the completion of the prosecution case. At the end of the prosecution case, the judge empanelled a different jury to determine whether the defendant

was fit to plead. That jury decided that the defendant was not fit to plead. In breach of s 4A(2) of the Criminal Procedure (Insanity) Act 1964, the judge then recalled the first jury and carried on with the trial. That jury subsequently found the defendant guilty of the offence. Because the trial should not have continued after the finding that the defendant was unfit to plead, the conviction was a nullity; thus, there was no conviction for the defendant to appeal against for the purposes of s 2 of the Criminal Appeal Act 1968. Nonetheless, the Court of Appeal used its inherent jurisdiction to set aside and annul the 'conviction' and then exercised its discretion to order a *venire de novo*.

Where the Court of Appeal allows an appeal on the ground that there has been an irregularity which vitiates the whole trial but decides not to grant an order for re-trial (*venire de novo*), the proper form of order is that the conviction 'be set aside and annulled and that there be no new trial'. There is no conviction to quash (since the purported conviction is a nullity) and so there is no power to grant a statutory acquittal under the Criminal Appeal Act 1968 (*R v Booth* [1999] 1 Cr App R 457).

- *To substitute a conviction for an alternative offence*

Section 3 of the Criminal Appeal Act 1968 provides that:

(1) This section applies on an appeal against conviction, where the appellant has been convicted of an offence *to which he did not plead guilty* and the jury could on the indictment have found him guilty of some other offence, and on the finding of the jury it appears to the Court of Appeal that the jury must have been satisfied of facts which proved him guilty of the other offence. [NB: words in italics were added by s 316(2) of the Criminal Justice Act 2003.]

(2) The Court may, instead of allowing or dismissing the appeal, substitute for the verdict found by the jury a verdict of guilty of the other offence, and pass such sentence in substitution for the sentence passed at the trial as may be authorised by law for the other offence, not being a sentence of greater severity.

Therefore, if:

(a) the jury could, on the indictment, have found the appellant guilty of some other offence; and

(b) the jury must have been satisfied of facts which proved him guilty of the other offence,

the Court of Appeal may quash the conviction appealed against but replace it with a conviction for that other offence.

For example, in *R v Spratt* [1980] 1 WLR 554, a conviction for manslaughter was substituted for the conviction of murder and, in *R v Blackford* (1989) 89 Cr App R 239, a conviction for possession of cannabis with intent to supply was replaced by a conviction for possession of cannabis.

The first requirement in s 3 of the Criminal Appeal Act 1968 means that the Court of Appeal must consider whether the jury could, on the indictment they were trying, have found the appellant guilty of some other offence (under s 6 of the Criminal Law Act 1967 or other statutory provisions dealing with specific offences).

The second requirement in s 3 means that the Court of Appeal has to consider the evidence which was put before the jury. In *R v Graham* [1997] 1 Cr App R 302, the Court of Appeal said that, in considering this requirement, the court would have regard to whether or not the jury had been given a proper direction on the other

offence and to the question whether there were reasonable grounds for concluding that the conduct of the defence would have been materially affected if the appellant had been charged with that other offence.

If the Court of Appeal does quash the conviction appealed against but substitutes a conviction for a different offence, it must then go on to review the sentence imposed by the Crown Court. If the Court of Appeal alters the sentence, it must not impose a sentence which is more severe than the original sentence.

In *R v Horsman* [1997] 3 All ER 385, the Court of Appeal held that where the defendant pleads guilty in the Crown Court to an offence and then appeals against that conviction, and the Court of Appeal quashes the conviction, the Court of Appeal has no power under s 3 of the Criminal Appeal Act 1968 to substitute a conviction for an alternative offence. The effect of this case is reversed by s 316 of the Criminal Justice Act 2003, which adds a new section, s 3A, to the Criminal Appeal Act 1968. This new provision empowers the Court of Appeal (instead of allowing or dismissing the appeal) to substitute a conviction of an alternative offence, where the facts admitted by the appellant by virtue of a guilty plea justify a conviction of that other offence (so that power to substitute a conviction no longer applies only where the defendant was found guilty by a jury and then appealed against his conviction).

Section 3A provides as follows:

Power to substitute conviction of alternative offence after guilty plea

(1) This section applies on an appeal against conviction where—

   (a) an appellant has been convicted of an offence to which he pleaded guilty,

   (b) if he had not so pleaded, he could on the indictment have pleaded, or been found, guilty of some other offence, and

   (c) it appears to the Court of Appeal that the plea of guilty indicates an admission by the appellant of facts which prove him guilty of the other offence.

(2) The Court of Appeal may, instead of allowing or dismissing the appeal, substitute for the appellant's plea of guilty a plea of guilty of the other offence and pass such sentence in substitution for the sentence passed at the trial as may be authorised by law for the other offence, not being a sentence of greater severity.

12.9 APPEAL AGAINST SENTENCE

Section 9 of the Criminal Appeal Act 1968 provides as follows:

(1) A person who has been convicted of an offence on indictment may appeal to the Court of Appeal against any sentence (not being a sentence fixed by law) passed on him for the offence, whether passed on his conviction or in subsequent proceedings.

(2) A person who on conviction on indictment has also been convicted of a summary offence under section 41 of the Criminal Justice Act 1988 (power of Crown Court to deal with summary offence where person committed for either way offence) or paragraph 6 of Schedule 3 to the Crime and Disorder Act 1998 (power of Crown Court to deal with summary offence where person sent for trial

for indictable-only offence) may appeal to the Court of Appeal against any sentence passed on him for the summary offence (whether on his conviction or in subsequent proceedings) under sub-section (7) of that section or sub-paragraph (4) of that paragraph.

'Sentence' includes an order to pay prosecution costs (*R v Hayden* [1975] 1 WLR 852) and a compensation order (*R v Vivian* [1979] 1 WLR 291).

Section 10 of the Criminal Appeal Act 1968 currently states that a person who was convicted by a magistrates' court but was sentenced by the Crown Court following committal for sentence may appeal to the Court of Appeal if:

- the Crown Court imposed a sentence in excess of the sentence which the magistrates could have imposed (that is, more than six months' imprisonment for a single offence or the sentence is otherwise in excess of the power of the magistrates (in the rare cases where a maximum of less than six months is applicable)); or
- the Crown Court disqualifies the defendant from driving; or
- the Crown Court activates a suspended sentence because the offence for which he was committed for sentence was in breach of that suspended sentence.

Section 319(2) of the Criminal Justice Act 2003 amends s 10(3) of the 1968 Act by removing the limitation that appeal is not available if the defendant received less than six months' imprisonment. The effect of this reform is that a defendant who is sentenced by the Crown Court even though he was not tried there will have the right to seek leave to appeal to the Court of Appeal against the Crown Court's sentence. The simplified version of s 10(3) reads as follows:

> An offender dealt with for an offence before the Crown Court in a proceeding to which sub-section (2) of this section applies may appeal to the Court of Appeal against any sentence passed on him for the offence by the Crown Court.

12.9.1   Leave to appeal

Section 11(1) and (1A) of the Criminal Appeal Act 1968 provide that leave is always required in order to appeal against sentence unless the trial judge certifies the sentence fit for appeal. Certificates are hardly ever given and are discouraged by the Court of Appeal. In *R v Grant* (1990) 12 Cr App R(S) 441, for example, it was said that if the judge has second thoughts about a sentence he has imposed, he should use his power under s 155 of the Powers of Criminal Courts (Sentencing) Act 2000 to vary the sentence (provided that no more than 28 days have elapsed since the sentence was imposed) or else allow the case to proceed through the ordinary process of appeal; he should not grant a certificate that the sentence is fit for appeal.

It should be emphasised that leave to appeal is needed even if the sentence is wrong in law.

12.9.2   Procedure

The procedure for obtaining leave to appeal is virtually identical to that for obtaining leave to appeal against conviction. Within 28 days of sentence, the appellant has to lodge a notice of application for leave to appeal against sentence at the Crown Court which passed the sentence. Grounds of appeal (usually drafted by counsel), based on

the remarks made by the judge when passing sentence, are drafted. The papers are sent to the Registrar of Criminal Appeals, who refers them to a single judge to decide whether leave to appeal should be given. Again, the test is whether the appeal has a reasonable prospect of success. The appellant has 14 days to renew the application for leave to appeal if the single judge refuses leave.

12.9.3   The hearing

At the hearing of the appeal (assuming leave is granted), the appellant will usually be represented by counsel (and the single judge will grant public funding for this purpose if the appellant's means are insufficient).

The Crown will not usually be represented, however, as it is not part of the role of the prosecution to advocate for a higher sentence. It should be noted, however, that Recommendation 321 of the Auld Review says that:

> The Crown Prosecution Service should consider on a case by case basis whether to appear on the hearing of an appeal against sentence so as to be able to assist the Court, if required, on matters of fact, including the effect on any victim, or of law.

Paragraph II.1.1 of the *Consolidated Practice Direction* provides that the prosecution should be notified if a defendant has been granted leave to appeal against sentence (or, if the application for leave has been referred, by the Registrar or the single judge, to the full court) so that they may be represented at the hearing if they so wish. The ever-increasing complexity of sentencing legislation means that it is more often desirable for the Court of Appeal to hear adversarial argument rather than simply hearing argument from the appellant.

A cautionary note on the use of authorities in sentencing appeals was sounded in *Attorney General's Reference (No 17 of 2002)* [2002] EWCA Crim 1292, at para 21, where Judge LJ said:

> Before leaving this case, we would like to highlight the authorities cited in the reference. Some of the authorities appear in well-known, respected reports. But two of the authorities include sentencing decisions of this Court, which appear in the neutral citation system only. Ignoring guideline decisions, sentencing decisions by this Court almost always reflect the specific and individual facts of the offence and the circumstances of the offender. Accordingly, generally speaking, citation of sentencing decisions should, to put it no higher, be circumspect. If a sentencing decision is not regarded as worthy of the attention of the Criminal Appeal (Sentencing) Reports, or the Criminal Law Review, or *The Times* or any other recognised authoritative series of reports, we believe that it can only be in the most exceptional circumstances that unreported decisions will be of any value to the Court. The wonder of modern technology means that all the decisions of this Court are preserved and published and available through the neutral citation system. That, however, does not normally justify citation of them on sentencing appeals, whether those appeals are brought by an appellant or take form of a reference by the Attorney-General.

12.10   GROUNDS OF APPEAL AGAINST SENTENCE

Unlike appeals against conviction, the Criminal Appeal Act 1968 does not specify grounds for appeal against sentence. However, the following grounds may be derived from a reading of the case law.

12.10.1 Sentence is wrong in law

If the judge imposes a sentence which he has no jurisdiction to impose, that sentence can be set aside by the Court of Appeal. This would apply, for example, if the judge imposed a sentence of three years' imprisonment for an offence which carries a maximum of two years' imprisonment. In *R v Corcoran* (1986) 8 Cr App R(S) 118, a Crown Court judge imposed a sentence of long-term detention on a juvenile, purportedly under what is now s 91 of the Powers of Criminal Courts (Sentencing) Act 2000, even though that power was not available in the circumstances of the case being dealt with; that sentence was therefore unlawful.

Such cases are, of course, very rare as most judges know the extent of their sentencing power. Furthermore, it is the duty of both prosecuting and defence counsel to make themselves aware of the sentencing options that are available and to draw the judge's attention to any mistake he makes (*R v Clarke* (1974) 59 Cr App R 298; *R v Kennedy* [1976] Crim LR 508; *R v Komsta* (1990) 12 Cr App R(S) 63; *R v Hartrey* (1993) 14 Cr App R(S) 507).

12.10.2 Sentence is wrong in principle

A sentence which is wrong in principle occurs where the Crown Court judge imposes the wrong form of sentence. For example, an appellant who receives a custodial sentence argues that the offence was not so serious that only a custodial sentence was appropriate and so the custody threshold had not been crossed.

In *R v Nuttall* (1908) 1 Cr App R 180, it was said that the appellant must show that he was dealt with in a way which was outside the broad range of penalties appropriate to the case.

12.10.3 Sentence is manifestly excessive

This is where the Crown Court judge imposed the correct form of sentence but nevertheless imposed too severe a sentence. For example, the judge imposes a sentence of three years' imprisonment in a case where 18 months would be more appropriate.

In *R v Gumbs* (1926) 19 Cr App R 74, Lord Hewart CJ said:

This court never interferes with the discretion of the court below merely on the ground that this court might have passed a somewhat different sentence; for this court to revise a sentence there must be some error in principle.

For example, in *R v Gleeson* [2001] EWCA Crim 2023; [2002] 1 Cr App R(S) 112, the Court of Appeal found that the case was one where some judges might have passed a slightly shorter sentence. However, the court repeated that it does not interfere with sentences passed in the Crown Court save in wholly exceptional cases, where the sentence passed was wrong in principle or manifestly excessive.

12.10.4 Wrong approach to sentencing

The Court of Appeal will interfere with a sentence if the judge adopted the wrong approach to the sentencing process. This occurs where the judge ignores relevant factors or takes account of irrelevant factors. In *R v Skone* (1965) 51 Cr App R 165, for example, the judge incorrectly penalised the defendant for casting imputations on the veracity of the prosecution witnesses. Similarly, in *R v Doab* [1983] Crim LR 569, the judge wrongly increased the sentence because the defendant had chosen Crown Court trial for an offence which could have been tried in the magistrates' court.

12.10.5 Procedural errors

The Court of Appeal will also interfere if there has been a procedural error. An example of a procedural error is where the judge failed to hold a *Newton* hearing where defence and prosecution versions of events differ significantly where the defendant has pleaded guilty.

12.10.6 Legitimate sense of grievance

If a judge gives an indication that a custodial sentence will not be imposed, the Court of Appeal will interfere if a custodial sentence is subsequently imposed for that offence (*R v Moss* (1984) 5 Cr App R(S) 209).

If a court adjourns for pre-sentence reports, it should therefore be made clear to the defendant that the court is nevertheless keeping all its sentencing options open (*R v Gillam* (1980) 2 Cr App R(S) 267; *R v Horton* (1985) 7 Cr App R(S) 299).

12.10.7 Disparity

In *Attorney General's Reference (Nos 62, 63 and 64 of 1995)* [1996] 2 Cr App R(S) 223, the Court of Appeal pointed out that it is wrong to pass the same sentence on two defendants when one has strong personal mitigation and the other does not; in such a case, disparity is to be encouraged.

Where two offenders are sentenced for an offence for which they have committed jointly, any difference in sentence should only result from differing degrees of involvement in the offence or from personal mitigating circumstances. Even if a difference cannot be so justified, an appeal on the basis of disparity will only succeed in rare cases.

If the heavier of the two sentences is the correct one, the Court of Appeal will not generally reduce it to bring it into line with the more lenient sentence: this would convert one right sentence and one wrong sentence into two wrong sentences. The main question is whether the appellant's sentence is excessive in itself (*R v Stroud* (1977) 65 Cr App R 150; *R v Nooy* (1982) 4 Cr App R(S) 308).

An appeal will only succeed on the ground of disparity if the appellant would otherwise be left with a justifiable and burning sense of grievance (*R v Potter* [1977] Crim LR 112 and *R v Dickinson* [1977] Crim LR 303). As Lawton LJ put it in *R v Fawcett* (1983) 5 Cr App R(S) 158: 'would right thinking members of the public, with full knowledge of the facts and circumstances, hearing of this sentence consider that something has gone wrong with the administration of justice?'

12.11   EFFECT OF APPEAL AGAINST A SENTENCE

If the appeal is dismissed, the original sentence stands.

If the Court of Appeal allows the appeal, it may quash the sentence and replace it with the appropriate sentence.

Section 11(3) of the Criminal Appeal Act 1968 provides that:

> On an appeal against sentence the Court of Appeal, if they consider that the appellant should be sentenced differently for an offence for which he was dealt with by the court below may—
>
> (a)   quash any sentence or order which is the subject of the appeal; and
>
> (b)   in place of it pass such sentence or make such order as they think appropriate for the case and as the court below had power to pass or make when dealing with him for the offence;
>
> but the Court shall so exercise their powers under this sub-section that, taking the case as a whole, the appellant is not more severely dealt with on appeal than he was dealt with by the court below.

Thus, taking the case as a whole, the appellant should not be dealt with more severely by the Court of Appeal than he was dealt with by the Crown Court.

Section 319(3) of the 2003 Act adds a new sub-section, s 11(7), to the 1968 Act, which provides as follows:

> For the purposes of this section, any two or more sentences are to be treated as passed in the same proceeding if—
>
> (a)   they are passed on the same day; or
>
> (b)   they are passed on different days but the court in passing any one of them states that it is treating that one together with the other or others as substantially one sentence.

Two examples may assist in interpreting the restrictions imposed by s 11(3):

- An appellant is sentenced to two years' imprisonment on count 1 and 12 months' imprisonment on count 2 and the judge ordered the terms to run consecutively, making a total of three years. The Court of Appeal could substitute sentences of 12 months on count 1 (a reduction) and two years on count 2 (an increase), to run consecutively: the original total of three years is not exceeded.

- An appellant is sentenced to two years on count 1 and three years on count 2, these terms to run consecutively (making a total of five years). The Court of Appeal could theoretically substitute sentences of five years on each count to run concurrently, as the total of five years is not exceeded.

Note that the Court of Appeal cannot replace a suspended sentence of imprisonment with a sentence of immediate custody, even if the term is the same as or less than the original term that was suspended (*R v Peppard* (1990) 12 Cr App R(S) 88). However, where a term of imprisonment is reduced, the Court of Appeal may impose a fine as well (*R v Walton* (1989) unreported, 29 August).

12.12   APPEALS BY THE PROSECUTION

If a person is acquitted by the jury at the Crown Court, that acquittal cannot be challenged. Unlike cases which were tried by a magistrates' court, the prosecution cannot appeal against an acquittal even if the acquittal was based on a mistaken understanding of the law. However, the prosecution can ask the Court of Appeal to clarify the law. The prosecution can also, in certain cases, challenge an excessively lenient sentence imposed by the Crown Court.

It should also be noted that Pt 9 of the Criminal Justice Act 2003 confers a right to appeal against terminating and evidentiary rulings (see below).

12.12.1 Attorney General's reference

Where a defendant has been acquitted following trial on indictment and the Attorney General thinks that the trial judge misdirected the jury on a point of law, he may refer the case to the Court of Appeal. This power is contained in s 36 of the Criminal Justice Act 1972.

The acquittal is not in jeopardy as the Court of Appeal cannot reverse that acquittal, but the reference does enable the Court of Appeal to clarify the law. Thus, judges in subsequent trials will not make the same mistake (*Attorney General's Reference (No 1 of 1975)* [1975] QB 773).

The acquitted defendant cannot be named unless he gives his permission.

This power is only relevant to acquittal following trial on indictment. Where the defendant was acquitted following summary trial and there was an error of law, the prosecution can challenge the acquittal by asking the magistrates to state a case for the opinion of the High Court (s 111 of the Magistrates' Courts Act 1980) and the High Court has power to quash the acquittal.

12.12.2 Attorney General's reference: excessively lenient sentences

Sections 35 and 36 of the Criminal Justice Act 1988 enable the Attorney General to appeal against excessively lenient sentences imposed by the Crown Court. Three restrictions apply:

- this power only applies in respect of offences which are triable only on indictment or which are triable either way and have been prescribed by statutory instrument (currently the latter category comprises a comparatively small number of either way offences);
- the Attorney General requires leave from a single judge of the Court of Appeal in order to bring such an appeal;
- the Court of Appeal may increase the sentence (but not beyond the maximum which the Crown Court could have imposed) only if it holds that the original sentence was excessively lenient.

Section 36(3) of the Criminal Justice Act 1988 and s 10(4) of the Criminal Appeal Act 1968, taken together, provide that if the Crown Court sentences the defendant for two offences, one triable only on indictment and the other triable either way and not in the list of offences to which s 36 applies, the Attorney General may refer both sentences to the Court of Appeal provided that either:

- the sentences were imposed on the same day by the Crown Court; or
- the Crown Court, in passing sentence, said that it was treating the two sentences as a single sentence. The Court of Appeal can then increase the sentence on both offences, if it thinks it appropriate to do so.

In *Attorney General's Reference (No 4 of 1989)* [1990] 1 WLR 41, the Court of Appeal gave guidance on the use of s 36 references:

- a sentence is unduly lenient if it falls outside the range of sentences which the judge could reasonably consider appropriate;
- even if the Court of Appeal does consider the original sentence to be unduly lenient, it does not have to increase that sentence. It may be that the sentence can be justified in the light of events since the trial or that increasing the sentence would be unfair to the offender or detrimental to others for whose well-being the court should be concerned;
- if the Attorney General is given leave to refer a sentence to the Court of Appeal on the ground that it is unduly lenient, the court's powers are not confined to increasing the sentence. In theory, the sentence could be reduced.

In *Attorney General's Reference (No 31 of 2004); R v McInerney* (2004) *The Times*, 20 July, the Court of Appeal reiterated that it will only interfere with a sentence under s 36 if it is shown that there was some error of principle in the sentence, so that public confidence would be damaged if the sentence were not altered. Where the sentence under appeal is a community order, the court should be provided with up-to-date information on the progress made by the offender since the sentence was passed: even if such a sentence were not appropriate at the time it was passed, the fact that the offender is responding to the community order could affect the outcome of the reference.

Where a sentence is referred to the Court of Appeal by the Attorney General (under s 36 of the Criminal Justice Act 1988), the Court of Appeal will not inquire into the facts of the offence but will base its decision on the findings made by the Crown Court (*Attorney General's Reference (No 95 of 1998); R v Highfield* (1999) *The Times*, 21 April).

In *Attorney General's Reference (No 17 of 1998); R v Stokes* [1999] 1 Cr App R(S) 407, a judge gave an indication that he was not minded to impose a sentence of immediate custody. The defendant pleaded guilty (and received a suspended sentence). The prosecution sought to appeal against the sentence as unduly lenient (s 36 of the Criminal Justice Act 1988). The Court of Appeal rejected the argument that it should not increase the sentence because the defendant had pleaded guilty on the basis of the judge's indication as to likely sentence. In *Attorney General's References (Nos 87 & 86 of 1999); R v Webb & Simpson* [2001] 1 Cr App R(S) 141, the Court of Appeal said that the fact that a trial judge gives an indication that he feels a custodial sentence to be inappropriate does not fetter the discretion of the Court of Appeal on an appeal by the Attorney General under s 36, although it is a relevant factor (especially where the defendant acted to his detriment, for example, by pleading guilty in light of that indication). The dangers of plea bargaining were highlighted in *Attorney General's Reference (No 44 of 2000); R v Peverett* [2001] 1 Cr App R 27. In that case it was said that if the Crown (whether acting through the Crown Prosecution Service, Customs & Excise or the Inland Revenue) makes representations to a defendant on which he is entitled to rely, and on which he acts to his detriment (for example, by pleading guilty

in circumstances in which he would not otherwise have pleaded guilty), that can properly be regarded as giving rise to a legitimate expectation on the part of the defendant that the Crown would not subsequently seek to resile from those representations, for example, by the Attorney General appealing against the sentence under s 36 of the 1988 Act.

An order deferring sentence (s 1 of the Powers of Criminal Courts (Sentencing) Act 2000) is a sentence within the meaning of s 36 of the Criminal Justice Act 1988 and so the Attorney General can seek leave to refer that order to the Court of Appeal as unduly lenient (*R v L*; *R v Jones* (1999) 163 JP 97).

In *R v Lea*; *R v Shatwell* [2002] EWCA Crim 215; [2002] 2 Cr App R 24, the Court of Appeal said that where the defendant is convicted following a re-trial ordered by the Court of Appeal, the Attorney General has no power to appeal against the sentence imposed following the re-trial if he feels it is unduly lenient, as the judge is precluded (by para 2 of Sched 2 to the Criminal Appeal Act 1968) from passing a greater sentence than that passed at the original trial. In appropriate cases, the Attorney General would therefore have to appeal against the sentence passed at the original trial.

12.13   APPEALS TO THE HOUSE OF LORDS

Under ss 33 and 34 of the Criminal Appeal Act 1968, either the prosecution or the defence can appeal to the House of Lords against a decision of the Court of Appeal. This is subject to two conditions:

- the Court of Appeal must certify that a point of law of general public importance is involved; and
- leave to appeal is given by the Court of Appeal or by the Appeals Committee of the House of Lords.

Given the ability of the prosecution to appeal, it should be noted that even if a conviction is quashed by the Court of Appeal, that conviction could be reinstated by the House of Lords.

Section 88 of the Courts Act 2003 amends s 2 of the Administration of Justice Act 1960 and s 34 of the Criminal Appeal Act 1968 in order to extend the time, from 14 to 28 days, in which an application by either the defence or the prosecution for leave to appeal from a decision of the Court of Appeal can be made and to make it clear that time begins to run against either the prosecution or the defendant from the date of the Court of Appeal's reasoned judgment, rather than from the date of the court's decision. It will remain the case that although the House of Lords or the Court of Appeal have power to extend a defendant's time for application for leave, neither has power to do so if the prosecutor wishes to seek leave to appeal but fails to apply within time. The Explanatory Notes to the 2003 Act explain that if the prosecution were to be allowed to apply for an extension of time, this would leave a defendant with the indefinite possibility of the original conviction being restored by the House of Lords.

12.14   THE ROLE OF THE DIVISIONAL COURT

Section 29(3) of the Supreme Court Act 1981 provides that the High Court may judicially review a decision of the Crown Court provided the decision is not in respect of a matter relating to trial of indictment. In *DPP v Manchester Crown Court and Huckfield* [1993] 1 WLR 1524, the House of Lords held that any decision which arises in the issue between the Crown and the defendant formulated in the indictment is likely to be outside the scope of judicial review. In that case, the decision of a Crown Court judge to quash an indictment was held to be incapable of judicial review. This followed the earlier decision of the House of Lords in *DPP v Manchester Crown Court and Ashton* [1993] 2 All WLR 846, where it was held by the House of Lords that an order to stay proceedings because they amounted to an abuse of process could not be the subject of judicial review. Similarly, a decision as to the date the trial of an indictment would commence (in the present case, the decision at issue was the order in which indictments against the same defendant were to be tried) is not susceptible to judicial review (*R v Southwark Crown Court ex p Ward* [1996] Crim LR 123).

In *R v Leeds Crown Court ex p Hussain* [1995] 1 WLR 1329, the Divisional Court declined to follow *R v Maidstone Crown Court ex p Clark* [1995] 1 WLR 831 and *R v Maidstone Crown Court ex p Hollstein* [1995] 3 All ER 503, holding that the decision when to arraign a defendant (and indeed the conduct of the plea and directions hearing generally) is sufficiently closely related to the trial on indictment that s 29(3) of the Supreme Court Act 1981 operates to exclude judicial review of the decision.

The Divisional Court has jurisdiction to entertain an application for judicial review of an order made by the Crown Court lifting reporting restrictions imposed under s 39 of the Children and Young Persons Act 1933: *R v Manchester Crown Court ex p H* [2000] 1 WLR 760 (*R v Harrow Crown Court ex p Perkins* (1998) 162 JP 527 followed; *R v Winchester Crown Court ex p B* [1999] 1 WLR 788 not followed).

12.15   FREE PARDONS

It is open to the Home Secretary to advise the Queen to pardon someone who has been convicted of an offence. This may be the only remedy if the Court of Appeal (usually after a reference by the Home Secretary under s 36 of the Criminal Justice Act 1972) has failed to secure the quashing of the conviction.

This exercise of the royal prerogative of mercy does not, however, have the effect of quashing the conviction (*R v Foster* [1985] QB 115); only a successful appeal to the Court of Appeal (or House of Lords, on further appeal) can achieve that.

12.16   THE CRIMINAL CASES REVIEW COMMISSION

Section 8(1) of the Criminal Appeal Act 1995 creates a new body called the Criminal Cases Review Commission ('the Commission'). Its function is to investigate possible miscarriages of justice.

12.16.1 Membership

The Commission is to consist of at least 11 members (s 8(3)). The members are appointed by the Queen on the recommendation of the Prime Minister (s 8(4)). At least one-third of the members should be legally qualified and at least two-thirds of the members should have 'knowledge or experience of any aspect of the criminal justice system' (s 8(5), (6)).

12.16.2 References

Section 9(1) of the Criminal Appeal Act 1995 says that where a person has been convicted by the Crown Court, the Commission may at any time refer the conviction and/or the sentence to the Court of Appeal.

Section 11(1) of the Criminal Appeal Act 1995 says that where a person has been convicted by a magistrates' court, the Commission may at any time refer the conviction and/or the sentence to the Crown Court. The power to refer a conviction to the Crown Court applies whether or not the defendant pleaded guilty (s 11(2)). Section 11(6) says that on a reference under s 11, the Crown Court may not impose a more severe punishment than that inflicted by the magistrates' court. Section 11(7) empowers the Crown Court to grant bail to someone whose conviction or sentence has been referred to the Crown Court under s 11.

Section 13(1)(a)–(c) sets out the three conditions which have to be satisfied before a reference can be made:

(a) the Commission consider that there is a 'real possibility' that the conviction or sentence 'would not be upheld were the reference to be made';

(b) the Commission so consider:

    (i)   in the case of a conviction, 'because of an argument, or evidence, not raised in the proceedings which led to it or on any appeal or application for leave to appeal against it';

    (ii) in the case of a sentence, 'because of an argument on a point of law, or information, not so raised';

(c) an appeal against the conviction or sentence has been dismissed or leave to appeal has been refused.

Section 13(2) says that 'nothing in sub-s 1(b)(i) or (c) shall prevent the making of a reference if it appears to the Commission that there are exceptional circumstances which justify making it'.

Section 14(1) says that a reference may be made whether or not the person to whom it relates has applied for a reference to be made.

In *R v Mills and Poole* [2003] EWCA Crim 1753; [2003] 1 WLR 2931, the Court of Appeal noted that the Criminal Cases Review Commission may only refer a conviction to the Court of Appeal if it considers that there is a real possibility that the court would not uphold the conviction because of new argument or evidence, or because there are exceptional circumstances for making it (s 13 of the Criminal Appeal Act 1995). However, the court went on to hold that once the matter is referred, the appeal is not confined to the Commission's reasons for the referral; rather, it may be on any ground (s 14(5) of the 1995 Act). That may consist of, or include, a ground that has already been aired in a previous appellate hearing in the matter. However, the proper exercise

of the court's discretion under s 14(5) involving departure from its previous reasoning should normally be confined to exceptional circumstances: *R v Thomas* [2002] EWCA Crim 941; [2003] 1 Cr App R 11 and *R v Smith* [2002] EWCA Crim 2907; [2003] 1 Cr App R 37. Exceptional circumstances may exist where, for example, there was some cogent argument advanced (but not properly developed) at the previous appellate hearing, but which (as now developed) could persuade the court that the conviction was unsafe; or where there has been a development of the law requiring the adoption of a different approach by the court to the issue before it. The exceptional circumstances must be such as would convince the court that if the matter had been arguable and argued in that way before the previous court, it would (not might) have quashed the conviction. The court should in any such cases be very slow to differ from its previous judgment. The court must also keep in mind that it needs to be sure of the safety of the conviction, as distinct from sureness of the appellant's guilt. However, this requirement of exceptional circumstances does not govern the court's consideration of grounds rejected by the Commission. Whilst the court will treat the Commission's reasoning on making a reference with considerable respect, its discretion to consider a ground not included in the Commission's reasons for the reference, or to reject the Commission's reasoning on any matter considered by it, is unfettered. The court added that the *Pendleton* 'jury impact' test ([2001] UKHL 66; [2002] 1 WLR 72), looked at as a range of permissible intrusion into the jury's thought processes for confirmatory purposes, is equally applicable where the new matter is one of argument, either of law or of interpretation of, or of inference from, the evidence at trial. The court may also have to ask itself similar questions as to the effect on the jury of evidence improperly given or of other irregularities at trial.

12.16.3 References by the Home Secretary

Section 3 of the Criminal Appeal Act 1995 repeals s 17 of the Criminal Appeal Act 1968, which empowered the Secretary of State to refer cases tried on indictment to the Court of Appeal. This power is effectively replaced by the Criminal Cases Review Commission.

12.16.4 Power to order investigations

Section 5(1) of the Criminal Appeal Act 1995 inserts s 23A into the Criminal Appeal Act 1968. Section 23A(1) states that, on an appeal against conviction, the Court of Appeal may direct the Criminal Cases Review Commission to investigate and report to the court on any matter if it appears to the court that:

(a) the matter is relevant to the determination of the case and ought, if possible, to be resolved before the case is determined;

(b) an investigation of the matter by the Commission is likely to result in the court being able to resolve it; and

(c) the matter cannot be resolved by the court without an investigation by the Commission.

The court may make the Commission's report available to the appellant and the respondent (s 23A(4)).

Section 313 of the Criminal Justice Act 2003 amends s 23A of the 1968 Act to empower the Court of Appeal to direct the Criminal Cases Review Commission to investigate and report to it on any matter relevant to the determination of the case, and which is likely to assist in resolving it, where the defendant is still applying for leave to appeal against conviction (and not just after the defendant has been given leave to appeal). This amendment reverses the effect of *R v Shillibier* [2004] 1 Cr App R 31, where it was held that the power of the Court of Appeal to direct the Criminal Cases Review Commission to investigate and report can only be used on the hearing of an appeal; the court had no such power on the hearing of an application for leave to appeal.

Section 313 also adds a new sub-section, s 23A(1A), to s 23A of the 1968 Act. This new sub-section stipulates that a direction to the Criminal Cases Review Commission to investigate may not be given by a single judge of the Court of Appeal. The purpose of this stipulation is to require the full court to consider such directions before they are made, and thus ensure that they are used sparingly.

Section 15(1) of the 1995 Act says that where such a direction is given by the Court of Appeal, the Commission must investigate the matter in such manner as the Commission thinks fit. Section 15(2) provides that where, in investigating a matter pursuant to a direction from the Court of Appeal, it appears to the Commission that another matter 'which is relevant to the determination of the case by the Court of Appeal ought, if possible, to be resolved before the case is determined by that court' and an investigation of that other matter 'is likely to result in the court's being able to resolve it', the Commission may investigate the related matter.

Section 315 of the Criminal Justice Act 2003 adds two new sub-sections, s 14(4A) and (4B), to the Criminal Appeal Act 1995. Under s 14(5) of the 1995 Act, the appellant is not confined to the grounds of appeal identified by the Commission. However, s 14(4A) and (4B) of the 1995 Act introduce a requirement that the appellant must obtain leave in order to add grounds of appeal that are unrelated to the reasons upon which the Commission based its reference to the Court of Appeal.

12.16.5 Investigative powers of the Commission

Section 17 of the Criminal Appeal Act 1995 empowers the Commission to order 'a person serving in a public body' to produce documents or other material which may assist the Commission. A 'public body' is defined in s 22 as meaning a police force, any government department, or local authority, or any other body whose members are appointed by the Queen or whose revenue comes from the government.

Section 19 of the Criminal Appeal Act 1995 enables the Commission to require the appointment of an 'investigating officer' to carry out inquiries which the Commission believe are necessary. This may be an appropriate official of a public body or a police officer.

12.17 PROSECUTION APPEALS UNDER THE CRIMINAL JUSTICE ACT 2003

Prior to the enactment of Pt 9 of the Criminal Justice Act 2003, there was statutory provision only for appeals to the Court of Appeal by the defendant. Whereas the defendant has a right of appeal at the end of the trial against conviction and/or sentence, there was no corresponding right for the prosecution to appeal against an acquittal. In some ways this was anomalous, since the prosecution enjoy a right of appeal to the High Court (through an appeal by way of case stated or through judicial review) if an acquittal in the magistrates' court is based on an error of law.

The possibility of a right of appeal against certain acquittals was considered in the Law Commission's Paper *Double Jeopardy and Prosecution Appeals* (Law Com 267). In that Paper, the Commission endeavoured to identify 'the main principles and aims which have a bearing on the question whether it would be fair to extend the prosecution's existing rights of appeal'. They identified two such aims: (a) 'accuracy of outcome' – to ensure, as far as possible, that those who are guilty are convicted and that those who are not guilty are acquitted; and (b) a 'process aim' – ensuring that the system shows respect for the fundamental rights and freedoms of the individual. They noted that accuracy of outcome may benefit either the prosecution or the defendant, depending on whether the defendant is guilty or innocent. Process aims, however, by their nature work only in favour of the defendant (see para 7.12). When this approach was first mooted in a Law Commission Consultation Paper (Law Com 158), it was criticised by some on the basis that the prosecution and defendant are not the only interested parties in a criminal trial. The victim of the alleged offence, for example, clearly has an interest in the case.

The Law Commission argued that, in general, the existence of prosecution rights of appeal may be expected to militate in favour of accurate outcomes, because an accurate outcome is more likely to be achieved if the law is correctly applied than if it is not; on the other hand, they noted that the existence of such rights might detract from the process aims of the system. They decided that the correct approach to the question whether to grant the prosecution a particular right of appeal was:

(1)   to identify the extent (if any) to which that right of appeal would enhance or detract from the aim of ensuring accuracy of outcome;

(2)   to identify the extent (if any) to which it would detract from process aims; and,

(3)   by balancing these factors, to come to a conclusion whether the trial process would thus be rendered unfair (paragraph 7.13).

On this basis, the Commission recommended (in para 7.49) that:

> ... the prosecution should have a right of appeal against an acquittal arising from a terminating ruling made during the trial up to the conclusion of the prosecution evidence (Recommendation 26).

The Law Commission gave separate consideration to rulings that there is no case to answer.

In its Consultation Paper (Law Com 158), the Commission had argued that the existence of a prosecution right of appeal against a successful submission of no case would put the defence in an invidious position: if a submission of no case is made, and is successful, there is a danger that the prosecution will appeal and there will be a re-

trial (and so it might be better for the defence not to make a submission of no case, simply hoping the jury will acquit at the end of the trial). In that Consultation Paper, the Law Commission concluded that it would be wrong for the defence to face this disincentive to the making of a submission of no case, and they concluded that there should be no right of appeal by the prosecution against a ruling of no case to answer made at the conclusion of the prosecution case. On the other hand, the possibility of a prosecution appeal in such a case already exists in the context of magistrates' courts. If the magistrates uphold a submission of no case to answer, it is open to the prosecution to ask the magistrates to state a case for the opinion of the High Court if it appears that the ruling may be based on an error of law; the High Court may then quash the acquittal. This possibility does not seem to have dissuaded defendants in the magistrates' court from making submissions of no case to answer.

At para 7.56 of the Paper, the Commission summarises some of the arguments in favour of allowing a challenge to erroneous acquittals following submissions of no case in this way:

> A successful submission of no case, erroneously acceded to, deprives the jury of a proper opportunity to judge the case, diminishes the legitimacy of the resulting acquittal, may appear to interested persons and the public to be the product of bizarre technicality, and damages public confidence in the system.

In the next paragraph, they put forward a further argument:

> The possibility of an appeal against an acquittal arising from an erroneous ruling of no case would help to 'keep the judges honest'. A senior trial judge with Court of Appeal experience argued that 'It is a temptation for a weak judge with a difficult case to rule against there being a case to answer...'

The Law Commission's conclusions were as follows:

> 7.61 ... we agree that there is no logical distinction between a terminating ruling of law made during the prosecution case and one made at its conclusion.

> 7.62 We also accept that there may be a temptation for trial judges too readily to accept defence submissions where they know that their reasoning will not be susceptible to scrutiny by the Court of Appeal. In any event the discipline of possible appeal to the Court of Appeal would serve to concentrate minds and improve both the quality of decision taken and its expression.

> 7.63 If a case is to fail on a legal argument it is better for public confidence in the system of criminal justice that it be susceptible to the second opinion of a higher court than that it be unappealable.

> 7.64 We also agree that the case stated procedure in the magistrates' court is a template, at least for a prosecution appeal on a point of law, and that there is no evidence that defendants labour under a disadvantage in pursuing a submission of no case at that level because of it.

> 7.65 On the other hand we do not accept the arguments which seek to diminish the dilemma for the defence which we described ... Arguments were presented which suggested that there is no particular disadvantage to a defendant in being required either (i) to make a submission and to face a re-trial after an appeal; or (ii) to forgo a submission and give evidence for fear that an appealed ruling of no case would deprive the defendant of the chance of an acquittal by a jury in a trial which is going well ... It is a truism, recognised by most experienced practitioners, that the high point of the defence case is invariably at the close of the prosecution case. This is quite apart

from the obvious fact that at a re-trial witnesses will have had a dry run, tactics will have been revealed and weaknesses in the prosecution case will have been spotted and possibly plugged.

7.66 In our view, it is possible to reconcile these different arguments in a principled way.

7.67 There is no doubt that the two limbs identified in *Galbraith* are distinct. The first limb [that there is no evidence that the alleged offence was committed by the defendant] concerns a question of law, and there is no logical reason why the prosecution should not have a right of appeal against an acquittal arising from such a terminating decision if it is to have a right of appeal against acquittals arising from other terminating rulings made in the course of its case.

7.68 On the other hand, the second limb of *Galbraith* [that the prosecution evidence, taken at its highest, is such that a jury properly directed could not properly convict on it] does not involve a point of law at all. Rather, the judge is required to perform a quasi-jury role. Without usurping the role of the jury, the judge has to assess the strength of the prosecution case. If the judge is of the view that, taking that case at its highest, no jury properly directed could properly convict, the judge's duty is to protect the defendant from any further risk by removing the case from the jury.

7.69 There is no more reason to give the prosecution a right of appeal against such a decision than there is to give it a right of appeal against an acquittal by a jury ...

7.70 In CP 158 we expressed the opinion that it would be difficult in practice to distinguish the two limbs of *Galbraith* ... On reflection we believe that we were over-pessimistic on this score. The limbs are distinct. Whilst submissions are often made under both limbs and the arguments may merge, the tests are sufficiently distinct so that we are confident that trial judges will be able sufficiently to separate them in their own minds, and in their reasons for their decisions, to enable the parties and the Court of Appeal to see whether the ruling is one of law under limb one, susceptible to appeal, or one of no case on the basis of limb two, not susceptible to appeal. Where the ruling is on both bases, in practice there would, of course, be no appeal.

...

7.72 ... If the defence has decided to try to persuade the judge to dismiss the case on a legal basis which turns out to be wrong, it can have no cause to complain if on appeal it is denied the benefit of an error of law which it by its own arguments has induced.

7.73 It follows from the above analysis that we do not recommend any prosecution right of appeal where the case is one of identification and it is withdrawn from the jury because the quality of the identifying evidence is poor, such as where it depends solely on a 'fleeting glance'. The judge in such a case is as much exercising a quasi-jury function as in applying *Galbraith* limb two ...

7.74 We recommend that the prosecution should have a right of appeal against an acquittal arising from a ruling of no case to answer made at the conclusion of the prosecution evidence, but only where that ruling is made on a point of law under the first limb of *Galbraith* (Recommendation 27).

The Law Commission's proposals (as contained in the original Consultation Paper No 158) were considered by Rosemary Pattenden in 'Prosecution appeals against judges' rulings' [2000] Crim LR 971. She says that, 'The question is whether an innovation that promotes accuracy, and is therefore presumptively desirable, detracts so seriously from process values that lend the criminal justice system moral authority that it must be rejected', and concludes that 'Judges are at present unaccountable to the Court of

Appeal as to a crucial aspect of their responsibilities: directed acquittals and other rulings that abort the proceedings' and that this should be remedied in order to 'protect public confidence in the criminal process'.

In Recommendation 309 of the *Review of the Criminal Courts of England and Wales*, Lord Justice Auld says:

> I ... support the general thrust of the Law Commission's recommendations for:
>
> 309.1 extending the present preparatory hearing regime to include appealable rulings on potentially terminating matters such as severance, joinder, quashing the indictment or staying the prosecution as an abuse of process;
>
> 309.2 giving the prosecution a right of appeal against an acquittal in certain cases arising from a terminating ruling during the trial up to the close of the prosecution case; and
>
> 309.3 giving the prosecution a right of appeal against an acquittal arising from a ruling of no case to answer under the first limb of the rule in *R v Galbraith*.

Part 9 of the 2003 Act introduces an interlocutory prosecution right of appeal against two categories of ruling by a Crown Court judge: (a) rulings, made either at a pre-trial hearing or at any time during the trial before the start of the summing up, that have the effect of terminating the trial (which includes both rulings that are terminating in themselves and those that are so fatal to the prosecution case that the prosecution proposes to treat them as terminating and, in the absence of the right of appeal, would offer no, or no further, evidence); and (b) evidentiary rulings made in certain trials for qualifying offences listed in Sched 4, where the rulings significantly weaken the prosecution case.

Thus, the Criminal Justice Act 2003 does not entirely accord with the recommendations of the Law Commission and the Auld Review, in that it does not exclude any submissions of no case to answer from the prosecution right of appeal against terminating rulings (in s 58), and it goes further than the Law Commission recommendation by including rulings that are, in effect, terminating rulings where key prosecution evidence is excluded (s 62).

Leave to appeal must be obtained either from the trial judge or the Court of Appeal. Depending upon the circumstances of the case, the judge will decide whether the appeal follows either an expedited route (where the trial is adjourned pending the conclusion of the appeal) or a non-expedited route (where any jury that has been empanelled may be discharged). In both cases, any judicial ruling effectively acquitting the defendant or otherwise terminating the trial will not take effect while the prosecution is considering whether to appeal and, if an appeal is pursued, until the conclusion of the appeal (or its abandonment). When appealing a terminating or effectively terminating ruling, the prosecution must agree to the acquittal of the defendant(s) for the offence(s) to which the ruling applies, if leave to appeal is not granted or the appeal is abandoned. This does not apply to appeals against significantly weakening evidentiary rulings where the trial will usually continue or a fresh trial will take place, whatever the outcome of the appeal.

12.17.1 Right of appeal against terminating rulings

Section 58 sets out the procedure to be followed when the prosecution wish to appeal against a terminating ruling. Under s 58(4), following the ruling, the prosecution must either inform the court that they intend to appeal or request an adjournment to consider whether to appeal (s 58(4)(a)). If such an adjournment is requested, the judge has the discretion to grant it (s 58(5)). Following such an adjournment, the prosecution must advise the court whether or not they in fact intend to appeal (s 58(4)(b)). By virtue of s 58(3), (10) and (11), the judge's ruling has no effect while the prosecution are considering whether to appeal or are pursuing an appeal. However, if the prosecution inform the court under s 58(4) that they intend to appeal, proceedings may be continued in respect of any offence which is not the subject of the appeal (s 60).

Under s 58(8) and (9), where the prosecution either fail to obtain leave to appeal or abandons the appeal, the prosecution must agree that the defendant should be acquitted.

Section 59 provides two different appeal routes (an 'expedited' appeal and a 'non-expedited' appeal). The judge must decide whether or not the appeal should be expedited (s 59(1)). If the judge decides that the appeal should be expedited, the trial may be adjourned (s 59(2)). If the judge decides that the appeal should not be expedited, he may either adjourn the trial or discharge the jury, if one has been sworn in (s 59(3)).

Under s 61, the Court of Appeal may confirm, reverse or vary a ruling appealed against under s 58. Under s 61(3) and (7), where the Court of Appeal confirms the ruling, it must order the acquittal of the defendant(s) for the offence(s) which are the subject of the appeal. If the Court of Appeal reverses or varies a ruling, under s 61(4), it must make one of the following orders:

- that the proceedings be resumed in the Crown Court; or
- that a fresh trial should take place; or
- that the defendant(s) should be acquitted of the offence(s) that are subject to the appeal.

The Court of Appeal will only order the resumption of the Crown Court proceedings or the start of a fresh trial where it considers it 'necessary in the interests of justice to do so' (s 61(5)).

12.17.2 Evidentiary rulings

Section 62 confers on the prosecution a right of appeal in respect of 'qualifying' evidentiary rulings. Section 62(9) defines an evidentiary ruling as 'a ruling which relates to the admissibility or exclusion of any prosecution evidence'. Under s 68(2), a 'qualifying' evidentiary ruling is one made by a judge in relation to a trial on indictment at any time before the opening of the case of the defence (as defined in s 62(8)). Under s 62(3) and (4), the prosecution may only appeal against qualifying evidentiary rulings that relate to 'qualifying' offences (whether or not the ruling also relates to other, non-qualifying, offences); s 62(9) defines a qualifying offence as 'an offence described in Part 1 of Schedule 4'.

To appeal under s 62, the prosecution must (before the opening of the defence case) inform the court that they intend to appeal and identify the ruling(s) and the qualifying offence(s) to which the appeal relates.

Section 63 places a further limitation on the right of the prosecution to appeal under s 62. It provides that leave to appeal should not be given (whether by the trial judge or by the Court of Appeal itself) unless the effect of the ruling(s) is to significantly weaken the prosecution case in relation to the offence(s) subject to appeal.

As is the case with the general right of appeal against terminating rulings, appeals under s 62 can be either expedited or non-expedited (and it is a matter for the trial judge to decide which).

Section 65 mirrors s 60 in providing that where the trial involves one or more offences which are not subject to appeal, the proceedings in respect of those offences may be continued.

Section 66 empowers the Court of Appeal to confirm, reverse or vary any ruling to which the appeal under s 62 relates. Under s 66(2), the Court of Appeal must also do one of the following:

- order that proceedings for the offence(s) be resumed in the Crown Court proceedings; or
- order that a fresh trial be started in respect of the offence(s); or
- order the acquittal of the defendant(s) for the offence(s) subject to appeal.

The Court of Appeal may only order an acquittal if the prosecution have indicated that they do not intend to continue with the prosecution of that offence (which might be the case where the prosecution take the view that the effect of the ruling is so damaging that they do not wish to proceed with the prosecution).

12.17.3 Reversal of rulings

Section 67 applies to both appeals against terminating rulings and appeals against evidentiary rulings. It states that:

> The Court of Appeal may not reverse a ruling on an appeal under this Part unless it is satisfied—
>
> (a)   that the ruling was wrong in law,
>
> (b)   that the ruling involved an error of law or principle, or
>
> (c)   that the ruling was a ruling that it was not reasonable for the judge to have made.

It remains to be seen how the Court of Appeal will interpret s 67(c). It seems probable that it will be interpreted as enabling the Court of Appeal to interfere only if the trial judge reached a decision that no reasonable judge, properly directing himself on the law, could have reached (in other words, the *Wednesbury* standard of unreasonableness familiar within the field of judicial review). This would seem appropriate, since the Court of Appeal is carrying out a task similar to the judicial review task carried out by the High Court in relation to errors of law in the magistrates' court. Furthermore, it seems likely to be Parliament's intention that the new right to appeal should be exercised sparingly, and certainly not routinely.

It should also be noted that s 74(5) provides that:

> Where two or more defendants are charged jointly with the same offence, the provisions of this Part are to apply as if the offence, so far as relating to each defendant, were a separate offence (so that, for example, any reference in this Part to a ruling which relates to one or more offences includes a ruling which relates to one or more of those separate offences).

Thus, where a ruling affects several defendants, the prosecution may (if they so wish) appeal against that ruling in so far as it relates to just one of the defendants.

12.17.4 Further appeal

Section 68 of the Criminal Justice Act 2003 amends s 33(1) of the Criminal Appeal Act 1968 so as to give both the prosecution and defence a right of appeal to the House of Lords from a decision by the Court of Appeal on a prosecution appeal against a ruling made under Pt 9 of the Act.

12.17.5 Custody time limits

Section 70 inserts a new section, s 22(6B), into the Prosecution of Offences Act 1985. The new section provides that:

> Any period during which proceedings for an offence are adjourned pending the determination of an appeal under Part 9 of the Criminal Justice Act 2003 shall be disregarded, so far as the offence is concerned, for the purposes of the overall time limit and the custody time limit which applies to the stage which the proceedings have reached when they are adjourned.

This provision thus disapplies the overall time limit and the custody time limit for the period during which proceedings are adjourned pending a prosecution appeal under Pt 9 of the 2003 Act.

12.17.6 Reporting restrictions

Section 71 of the Criminal Justice Act 2003 prevents reporting of appeal proceedings under Pt 9, except the reporting of basic factual details (set out in s 71(8)), for example, details of the court, the defendants, witnesses, legal representatives and the offences charged. Section 71(2), (3) and (4) gives the trial judge, the Court of Appeal and the House of Lords respectively power to lift the reporting restrictions either completely or to a specified extent. Where there are two or more defendants and one or more of them objects to the lifting of the restrictions, the restrictions may only be lifted if the court is satisfied, after hearing the representations of each of the defendants, that it is in the interests of justice to do so (s 71(6)).

Under s 72, breach of the reporting restrictions is a summary offence punishable with a fine up to level 5 (£5,000) (s 72(9)); proceedings for such an offence can only be instituted by or with the consent of the Attorney General (s 72(10)).

12.18   COMPENSATION FOR MISCARRIAGES OF JUSTICE

If a defendant successfully appeals against conviction so that his conviction is quashed, and this occurs within the ordinary time limits for appeals, there is no right to compensation. However, where a conviction is quashed after the defendant has been allowed to appeal out of time, there may be a right to compensation. Section 133 of the Criminal Justice Act 1988 provides as follows:

(1)   Subject to sub-section (2) below, when a person has been convicted of a criminal offence and when subsequently his conviction has been reversed or he has been pardoned on the ground that a new or newly discovered fact shows beyond reasonable doubt that there has been a miscarriage of justice, the Secretary of State shall pay compensation for the miscarriage of justice to the person who has suffered punishment as a result of such conviction or, if he is dead, to his personal representatives, unless the non-disclosure of the unknown fact was wholly or partly attributable to the person convicted.

(2)   No payment of compensation under this section shall be made unless an application for such compensation has been made to the Secretary of State.

(3)   The question whether there is a right to compensation under this section shall be determined by the Secretary of State.

(4)   If the Secretary of State determines that there is a right to such compensation, the amount of the compensation shall be assessed by an assessor appointed by the Secretary of State.

(4A) In assessing so much of any compensation payable under this section to or in respect of a person as is attributable to suffering, harm to reputation or similar damage, the assessor shall have regard in particular to—

   (a)   the seriousness of the offence of which the person was convicted and the severity of the punishment resulting from the conviction;

   (b)   the conduct of the investigation and prosecution of the offence; and

   (c)   any other convictions of the person and any punishment resulting from them.

(5)   In this section 'reversed' shall be construed as referring to a conviction having been quashed—

   (a)   on an appeal out of time; or

   (b)   …

As well as the statutory scheme, there is also an *ex gratia* scheme whereby the Home Secretary can award compensation to claimants who fall outside s 133 but whose claim is nonetheless meritorious.

In *R v Secretary of State for the Home Department ex p Mullen* [2004] UKHL 18; [2004] 2 WLR 1140, the House of Lords had to grapple with the meaning of the phrase 'miscarriage of justice'. Lord Bingham of Cornhill said:

The expression 'wrongful convictions' is not a legal term of art and it has no settled meaning. Plainly the expression includes the conviction of those who are innocent of the crime of which they have been convicted. But in ordinary parlance the expression would, I think, be extended to those who, whether guilty or not, should clearly not have been convicted at their trials. It is impossible and unnecessary to identify the manifold reasons why a defendant may be convicted when he should not have been. It may be because the evidence against him was fabricated or perjured. It may be because flawed expert evidence was relied on to secure conviction. It may be because evidence helpful to the defence was concealed or withheld. It may be because the jury

was the subject of malicious interference. It may be because of judicial unfairness or misdirection. In cases of this kind, it may, or more often may not, be possible to say that a defendant is innocent, but it is possible to say that he has been wrongly convicted. The common factor in such cases is that something has gone seriously wrong in the investigation of the offence or the conduct of the trial, resulting in the conviction of someone who should not have been convicted (para 4).

'[M]iscarriage of justice' is an expression which, although very familiar, is not a legal term of art and has no settled meaning. Like 'wrongful conviction' it can be used to describe the conviction of the demonstrably innocent ... But, again like 'wrongful conviction', it can be and has been used to describe cases in which defendants, guilty or not, certainly should not have been convicted ... courts of appeal, although well used to deciding whether convictions are safe, or whether reasonable doubts exist about the safety of a conviction, are not called upon to decide whether a defendant is innocent and in practice very rarely do so (para 9).

Lord Steyn concluded that the term 'a miscarriage of justice' extends only to 'clear cases of miscarriage of justice, in the sense that there would be acknowledgment that the person concerned was clearly innocent' (para 56). Lords Rodgers and Walker adopted the narrower interpretation put forward by Lord Steyn. Lord Scott noted that, as a result of the existence of the *ex gratia* scheme to supplement the statutory scheme, in most, if not all, of the miscarriage of justice cases in which Lord Steyn would refuse but Lord Bingham would allow a s 133 claim, the facts would be likely to be such as to attract a discretionary payment of compensation by the Home Secretary. On that basis he expressed doubt whether there would be much practical difference in result between the two rival views.

CHAPTER 13

REPRESENTATION ORDERS AND COSTS

13.1 INTRODUCTION

In this chapter, we see how State funds can be made available to pay for the defence of people who are charged with criminal offences. We then go on to look at the various orders for costs which can be made when a case has been disposed of.

The main legislative source for public funding in criminal matters is the Access to Justice Act 1999 (which replaced the Legal Aid Act 1988). It created the Criminal Defence Service (the civil counterpart of the Community Legal Service). The 1999 Act is supplemented by various regulations, including the:

- Criminal Defence Service (General) (No 2) Regulations 2001 (SI 2001/1437).
- Criminal Defence Service (Representation Order Appeals) Regulations 2001 (SI 2001/1168).
- Criminal Defence Service (Recovery of Defence Costs Orders) Regulations 2001 (SI 2001/856).
- Criminal Defence Service (Funding) Order 2001 (SI 2001/855).

The Criminal Defence Service (General) (No 2) Regulations 2001 (SI 2001/1437) govern the provision of advice and assistance and representation by the Criminal Defence Service (CDS) under Pt 1 of the Access to Justice Act 1999. They:

(a) define the ambit of 'criminal proceedings';

(b) define the assistance which can be provided through the CDS and, where applicable, how financial eligibility is to be determined;

(c) set out the procedure for seeking a representation order (and, in Sched 2, give the standard forms for use when making written applications);

(d) specify what representatives may provide services; and

(e) make provision for withdrawal of representation.

The CDS is run by the Legal Services Commission (the successor to the Legal Aid Board). Its purpose is set out in s 12(1) of the 1999 Act:

> ... securing that individuals involved in criminal investigations or criminal proceedings have access to such advice, assistance and representation as the interests of justice require.

The CDS relies heavily on a system of contracting, based on the 'General Criminal Contract'. Solicitors in private practice are authorised to carry out publicly funded criminal defence work only if they have such a contract. Once it has been awarded, the firm is subject to a periodic audit to ensure that it meets the standards set out in the contract.

Traditionally, defendants in criminal cases have been represented by lawyers who are in private practice and whose fee is paid either by the client or by the State. However, in 2001, the government published its conclusions following a consultation exercise on the establishment of a system of salaried criminal defence services lawyers (along the lines of the public defender system that is a feature of American criminal

justice). The Paper is entitled *Criminal Defence Service: Establishing a Salaried Defence Service – The Government's Conclusions*, and is available on www.dca.gov.uk/consult/saldef/saldefresp.htm.

The government announced that a pilot scheme would start in 2001 and last for four years, during which the effectiveness of the scheme would be evaluated. The final results of the research will be published in 2005.

The Paper announces the intention to employ as public defenders lawyers with higher rights of audience (whether barristers or solicitors who have completed the Rights of Audience in the Higher Courts training), as well as those who would be limited to appearing in the magistrates' court. The salaried defenders are also entitled to instruct specialist advocates (whether solicitors or barristers). The public service is governed by the same quality standards and system of auditing that applies to contracted firms.

The aim of the research is to compare the salaried CDS service to services being provided through private practice and to test it against what the paper describes as 'the most commonly voiced criticisms – independence, choice of representative, under-funding, case overload and restriction of access'.

It is noteworthy that the Paper points out a particular clause (cl 2.2) in the Code of Conduct for Salaried Defenders, designed to ensure that public defenders are not 'too ready to plea bargain':

> A professional employee shall not put a client under pressure to plead guilty, and in particular, shall not advise a client that it is in his or her interests to plead guilty unless satisfied that the prosecution is able to discharge the burden of proof.

Despite some negative responses from practitioners and interest groups in the consultation exercise, the government maintained its view that the independence of the Public Defenders could be assured 'by the appointment of a professional head of service and the effective implementation of the Code of Conduct'. Nonetheless, the government agreed that 'public perception of independence will remain a concern until experience proves otherwise'.

The long-term objective is to achieve a CDS which uses both lawyers in private practice and salaried defenders (employed directly by the Commission or by non-profit making organisations established for the purpose). This will necessarily mean that suspects and defendants seeking publicly funded representation will be limited in their choice of representative: the choice will be limited to contracted or salaried defenders. However, it is apparently the government's intention to offer a choice between contracted or salaried defenders in all but exceptional cases.

13.1.1 Grant of right to representation

Section 14(1) of the Access to Justice Act 1999 provides that the Legal Services Commission 'shall fund representation to which an individual has been granted a right in accordance with Schedule 3 to the Act'.

Paragraph 1 of Sched 3 provides that a right to representation may be granted to an individual in relation to any kind of criminal proceedings mentioned in s 12(2), and to enable him to resist an appeal to the Crown Court. Any court before which proceedings take place has the power to grant the right of representation. Where the

right is granted, it includes representation for any related bail or other preliminary or incidental proceedings: see para 2 of Sched 3, which provides as follows:

(1) A court before which any criminal proceedings take place, or are to take place, has power to grant a right to representation in respect of those proceedings except in such circumstances as may be prescribed.

(2) Where a right to representation is granted for the purposes of criminal proceedings it includes the right to representation for the purposes of any related bail proceedings and any preliminary or incidental proceedings; and regulations may make provision specifying whether any proceedings are or are not to be regarded as preliminary or incidental.

(3) A court also has power to grant a right to representation for the purposes of criminal proceedings before another court in such circumstances as may be prescribed.

(4) The form of the application for a grant of a right to representation under this paragraph, and the form of the grant of such a right, shall be such as may be prescribed.

(5) A right to representation in respect of proceedings may be withdrawn by any court before which the proceedings take place; and a court must consider whether to withdraw a right to representation in such circumstances as may be prescribed.

(6) The powers of a magistrates' court for any area under this paragraph may be exercised by a single justice of the peace for the area.

(7) Any rules under section 144 of the Magistrates' Courts Act 1980 which provide for the functions of a single justice under sub-paragraph (6) to be exercised by a justices' clerk may make different provision for different areas.

The decision whether or not to grant representation by the Criminal Defence Service is to be determined 'according to the interests of justice' (para 5). The specific factors which must be taken into account mirror the factors that were relevant under s 22 of the Legal Aid Act 1988 (and so case law decided under s 22 is relevant to the criteria contained in para 5 of the 1999 Act).

Those criteria, as set out in para 5, are:

(1) Any question as to whether a right to representation should be granted shall be determined according to the interests of justice.

(2) In deciding what the interests of justice consist of in relation to any individual, the following factors must be taken into account—

(a) whether the individual would, if any matter arising in the proceedings is decided against him, be likely to lose his liberty or livelihood or suffer serious damage to his reputation,

(b) whether the determination of any matter arising in the proceedings may involve consideration of a substantial question of law,

(c) whether the individual may be unable to understand the proceedings or to state his own case,

(d) whether the proceedings may involve the tracing, interviewing or expert cross-examination of witnesses on behalf of the individual, and

(e) whether it is in the interests of another person that the individual be represented.

In assessing whether the accused is likely to lose his liberty, regard must be had to the facts alleged by the prosecution, rather than the maximum penalty that could

theoretically be imposed (*R v Highgate Justices ex p Lewis* [1977] Crim LR 611). So it is not enough that the offence carries a custodial sentence: the court must consider whether a custodial sentence might be imposed in this particular case. In *R v Liverpool City Magistrates ex p McGhee* (1994) 158 JP 275, the Divisional Court rejected the contention that what is now called a community punishment order (a community order which imposes an unpaid work requirement) could be regarded as a sentence which deprives the accused of liberty. However, Rose LJ did add that the list of criteria in s 22 (now para 5) is not exhaustive, and so the possibility that such an order may be made may be a factor in deciding whether or not to make a representation order.

The factor which includes expert cross-examination of witnesses means expert cross-examination of witnesses, not cross-examination of expert witnesses (*R v Liverpool City Magistrates ex p McGhee*). In *R v Scunthorpe Justices ex p S* (1998) *The Times*, 5 March, the Divisional Court considered that refusal of legal aid to an accused aged 16 who sought to challenge whether a police officer had acted in the execution of his duty was irrational. The expertise needed to cross-examine police witnesses, and to find, select and proof defence witnesses was beyond an accused aged 16.

In *R v Oates* [2002] EWCA Crim 1071; [2002] 1 WLR 2833, the applicant sought permission to appeal to the Court of Appeal against her conviction; the application was refused by the single judge and she wished to renew the application orally. She sought public funding for representations to be made on her behalf. It was held that legal assistance by way of a representation order will not, save in exceptional circumstances, be granted on a renewed application for permission to appeal against conviction following refusal by the single judge. The court added that this restriction is not contrary to the right of an accused to defend himself through legal assistance of his own choosing under Art 6(3)(c) of the European Convention on Human Rights.

13.1.2 Recovery of costs

Section 17 of the Access to Justice Act 1999 provides as follows:

(1) An individual for whom services are funded by the Commission as part of the Criminal Defence Service shall not be required to make any payment in respect of the services except where sub-section (2) applies.

(2) Where representation for an individual in respect of criminal proceedings in any court other than a magistrates' court is funded by the Commission as part of the Criminal Defence Service, the court may, subject to regulations under sub-section (3), make an order requiring him to pay some or all of the cost of any representation so funded for him (in proceedings in that or any other court).

Paragraph 3 of the Criminal Defence Service (Recovery of Defence Costs Orders) Regulations 2001 (SI 2001/856) provides:

(1) Where an individual receives representation in respect of criminal proceedings which is funded by the Commission or the Lord Chancellor as part of the Criminal Defence Service, the court before which the proceedings are heard, other than a magistrates' court, shall make an order requiring him to pay some or all of the cost of any representation so funded for him in the circumstances set out in these Regulations.

(2) An order of the type mentioned in paragraph (1) shall be known as a Recovery of Defence Costs Order (an 'RDCO').

It follows from the exclusion of magistrates' courts from para 3 that a person convicted by a magistrates' court cannot be required to contribute to the costs incurred on their behalf by the CDS.

Under para 4 of the Regulations:

(1)   The judge hearing the case shall make an RDCO against a funded defendant except as provided in paragraph (2).

(2)   An RDCO may not be made against a funded defendant who:

(a) has appeared in the magistrates' court only;

(b) is committed for sentence to the Crown Court;

(c) is appealing against sentence to the Crown Court; or

(d) has been acquitted, other than in exceptional circumstances.

Under para 5:

(1)   An RDCO may be made up to a maximum amount of the full cost of the representation incurred in any court under the representation order.

(2)   An RDCO may provide for payment to be made forthwith, or in specified instalments.

Thus, where the defence is paid for by the Legal Services Commission, there is no means test, no contribution order, and no payment is required from the person granted representation. However, a court other than a magistrates' court may make an order that an individual repay some or all of the cost of any such representation. Such an order is known as a Recovery of Defence Costs Order (RDCO). The procedure relating to the RDCO is set out in the Criminal Defence Service (Recovery of Defence Costs Orders) Regulations 2001. The Crown Court may not make an RDCO against an accused who has appeared in the magistrates' court but who is committed for sentence to the Crown Court or appeals sentence to the Crown Court. Nor may the Crown Court make an RDCO against an accused who has been acquitted, other than in exceptional circumstances (which phrase is not further defined). It is implicit in para 4 that RDCOs will most commonly be made where a publicly funded defendant is convicted on indictment, or unsuccessfully appeals from the magistrates' court to the Crown Court (para 4(2)(c) excludes only appeals against sentence), or unsuccessfully appeals against conviction and/or sentence to the Court of Appeal (Criminal Division).

As originally drafted, paras 3 and 4 conferred a power on courts other than magistrates' courts to make an RDCO. This paragraph was amended by the Criminal Defence Service (Recovery of Defence Costs Orders) (Amendment) Regulations 2004 (SI 2004/1195) to change the power into a duty.

Paragraph XI.1.6 of the *Practice Direction (Costs: Criminal Proceedings)* [2004] 2 All ER 1070 says that 'Where a person of modest means properly brings an appeal against conviction, it should be borne in mind that it will not usually be desirable or appropriate for the court to make an RDCO for a significant amount, if to do so would inhibit an appellant from bringing an appeal'. This would appear to conflict with the mandatory obligation to make an RDCO but the spirit of this paragraph may perhaps be reflected in the amount of the RDCO.

13.1.3 Applying for a representation order

Under para 4 of the Criminal Defence Service (General) (No 2) Regulations 2001 (SI 2001/1437):

> The Commission shall fund such advice and assistance, including advocacy assistance, as it considers appropriate in relation to any individual who:
>
> (a) is the subject of an investigation which may lead to criminal proceedings;
>
> (b) is the subject of criminal proceedings;
>
> (c) requires advice and assistance regarding his appeal or potential appeal against the outcome of any criminal proceedings or an application to vary a sentence;
>
> (d) requires advice and assistance regarding his sentence;
>
> (e) requires advice and assistance regarding his application or potential application to the Criminal Cases Review Commission;
>
> (f) requires advice and assistance regarding his treatment or discipline in prison (other than in respect of actual or contemplated proceedings regarding personal injury, death or damage to property);
>
> (g) is the subject of proceedings before the Parole Board;
>
> (h) requires advice and assistance regarding representations to the Home Office in relation to a mandatory life sentence or other parole review;
>
> (i) is a witness in criminal proceedings and requires advice regarding self-incrimination; or
>
> (j) is a volunteer [NB: this means a person attending a police station voluntarily, 'helping the police with their enquiries']; or
>
> (k) is detained under Schedule 7 to the Terrorism Act 2000.

Under para 5:

> (1) The following advice and assistance may be granted without reference to the financial resources of the individual:
>
> (a) all advice and assistance provided to an individual who is arrested and held in custody at a police station or other premises;
>
> (b) all advocacy assistance before a magistrates' court or the Crown Court;
>
> (c) all advice and assistance provided by a court duty solicitor in accordance with his contract with the Commission;
>
> (d) all advice and assistance provided to a volunteer during his period of voluntary attendance;
>
> (e) all advice and assistance provided to an individual being interviewed in connection with a serious service offence; and
>
> (f) all advice and assistance provided in respect of an individual who is the subject of an identification procedure carried out by means of video recordings in connection with that procedure, notwithstanding the individual's non-attendance at a police station at the time the procedure is carried out.
>
> ...
>
> (4) Except where paragraph (1) applies, the Commission, or a person acting on behalf of the Commission where such function has been delegated in accordance with section 3(4) of the Act, shall determine the financial eligibility of the individual ...

(5) Except where paragraph (1) ... applies, an individual is eligible for advice and assistance if his weekly disposable income does not exceed [figure specified in regulations, varied annually] and his disposable capital does not exceed £1,000.

...

(7) Where the Commission is satisfied that any person whose disposable income is to be assessed ... is directly or indirectly in receipt of any qualifying benefit, it shall take that person's disposable income as not exceeding the [eligibility limit].

(8) The following are qualifying benefits for the purposes of paragraph (7):

    (a) income support;

    (b) income-based jobseeker's allowance;

    (c) working tax credit claimed together with child tax credit where the gross annual income is not more than [figure specified in regulations, varied annually] ...

    (d) working tax credit with a disability element or severe disability element (or both) where the gross annual income is not more than [figure specified in regulations, varied annually]; and

    (e) guarantee state pension credit under section 1(3)(a) of the State Pension Credit Act 2002.

(9) Where the Commission is satisfied that any person whose disposable capital is to be assessed ... is directly or indirectly in receipt of income support, income-based jobseeker's allowance or guarantee state pension credit, it shall take that person's disposable capital as not exceeding the [eligibility limit].

Paragraph 6 requires the application for a representation order to be made on a standard form and stipulates that public funding is effective from the date of the receipt of a properly completed application form.

Under para 7:

The court, a judge of the court, the head of the Civil Appeals Office, or the registrar of criminal appeals may grant a representation order at any stage of the proceedings in the circumstances set out in these Regulations whether or not an application has been made for such an order.

Regulations 8, 9 and 10 of the Criminal Defence Service (General) (No 2) Regulations 2001 go on to set out the procedure governing an application for a representation order. In respect of proceedings in the magistrates' court, application may be made orally to the court, or in writing to the court or the justices' clerk. For proceedings in the Crown Court, the application may be made orally or in writing to the Crown Court, or in writing to the court manager. Applications in respect of Crown Court proceedings may also be made to the magistrates' court, in the manner specified in reg 9(1)(c)–(g). Where a re-trial is ordered as a result of an appeal, application is to the court ordering the re-trial.

In all the above cases, where an application is refused, the applicant must be provided with written reasons for the refusal and details of the appeal process.

The text of these paragraphs is as follows:

8   *Proceedings in a magistrates' court*

(1) Other than where regulation 6(3) applies, an application for a representation order in respect of proceedings in a magistrates' court may be made:

    (a) orally or in writing to the court; or

    (b) in writing to the appropriate officer.

(2)   Where an application is made to the court, it may refer it to the appropriate officer for determination.

(3)   Where an application is refused, the appropriate officer shall provide to the applicant:

(a) written reasons for the refusal; and

(b) details of the appeal process.

9   *Proceedings in the Crown Court*

(1)   Other than where regulation 6(3) applies, an application for a representation order in respect of proceedings in the Crown Court may be made:

(a) orally or in writing to the Crown Court;

(b) in writing to the appropriate officer of that court;

(c) orally or in writing to a magistrates' court at the conclusion of any proceedings in that magistrates' court;

(d) orally or in writing to a magistrates' court inquiring into the offence as examining justices or sending for trial under section 51 of the Crime and Disorder Act 1998;

(e) where a magistrates' court has been given a notice of transfer under section 4 of the Criminal Justice Act 1987 (serious fraud cases), in writing to the appropriate officer of that magistrates' court [to be replaced by s 51B of the Crime and Disorder Act 1998, when the amendments made by the Criminal Justice Act 2003 come into effect];

(f) in the case of an appeal to the Crown Court from a magistrates' court, in writing to the appropriate officer of that magistrates' court;

(g) where the applicant was granted a representation order for proceedings in a magistrates' court and was committed for trial in the Crown Court under section 6(2) of the Magistrates' Courts Act 1980, in writing to the appropriate officer of the magistrates' court ordering the committal [this will cease to be relevant when the abolition of committal proceedings by the Criminal Justice Act 2003 takes effect]; and

(h) in the case of a retrial ordered under section 7 of the Criminal Appeal Act 1968, orally or in writing to the court ordering the retrial.

(2)   An application for a representation order in respect of representations to the High Court against a voluntary bill of indictment may be made:

(a) in writing to the appropriate officer of the Crown Court; or

(b) orally to the judge considering the voluntary bill

and where any such order is granted it shall also apply to any proceedings to which the applicant is indicted.

(3)   Where an application is made to the court, it may refer it to the appropriate officer for determination.

(4)   Where an application is refused, the appropriate officer shall provide to the applicant:

(a) written reasons for the refusal; and

(b) details of the appeal process.

10   *Appeals to the Court of Appeal and the House of Lords*

(1)   An application for a representation order in respect of proceedings in the Court of Appeal or the House of Lords may be made:

(a) orally to the Court of Appeal, or a judge of the court; or

(b) in writing to the Court of Appeal, a judge of the court, or the [appropriate officer] of the court.

(2) Where an application is made to the court, it may refer it to a judge or the appropriate officer for determination.

(3) Where an application is made to a judge, he may refer it to the appropriate officer for determination.

(4) The appropriate officer may:

(a) grant the application; or

(b) refer it to the court or a judge of the court.

(5) A representation order shall not be granted until notice of leave to appeal has been given in respect of the proceedings which are the subject of the application.

(6) Where a representation order is granted in respect of proceedings in the Court of Appeal, a judge or the appropriate officer may specify the stage of the proceedings at which the representation order shall take effect.

(7) The House of Lords may not grant a representation order in respect of any proceedings.

13.1.4 Nature of representation

Section 15(1) of the Access to Justice Act 1999 says that:

> An individual who has been granted a right to representation in accordance with Schedule 3 may select any representative or representatives willing to act for him; and, where he does so, the Commission is to comply with the duty imposed by section 14(1) by funding representation by the selected representative or representatives.

The form taken by the representation is dealt with in regs 11–17 and 19–24 of the Criminal Defence Service (General) (No 2) Regulations 2001. These regulations deal with the circumstances in which orders for representation by an advocate or advocates (including Queen's Counsel) may be granted. They also lay down the procedure for a change of representative, for withdrawal of representation, and for the authorisation and restriction of expenditure incurred.

In *Attorney General's Reference (No 82a of 2000) (R v Lea; R v Shatwell)* [2002] 2 Cr App R 342, the Court of Appeal held that the principle of equality of arms does not require that where the Crown instructs leading counsel and the defence is being funded at public expense, the accused is entitled to be represented by leading counsel as well.

Paragraph 11 of the 2001 Regulations deals with representation in magistrates' courts and some Crown Court proceedings:

(1) The right conferred by section 15(1) of the Act, as regards representation in respect of any proceedings to which this regulation applies, shall be exercisable only in relation to those representatives who are:

(a) employed by the Commission to provide such representation; or

(b) authorised to provide such representation under a crime franchise contract with the Commission which commences on or after 2nd April 2001 and specifies the rate of remuneration for such representation.

(2) This regulation applies to:

(a) any criminal proceedings in a magistrates' court;

(b) any proceedings in the Crown Court mentioned in regulation 3(2);

(c) any appeal by way of case stated from a magistrates' court; and

(d) any proceedings which are preliminary or incidental to proceedings mentioned in sub-paragraphs (a) to (c).

(3) This regulation does not apply to proceedings referred to in section 12(2)(f) of the Act (proceedings for contempt in the face of a court).

Paragraph 12 deals with advocates in magistrates' courts:

(1) A representation order for the purposes of proceedings before a magistrates' court may only include representation by an advocate in the case of:

(a) any indictable offence, including an offence which is triable either way;

...

where the court is of the opinion that, because of circumstances which make the proceedings unusually grave or difficult, representation by both a solicitor and an advocate would be desirable.

(2) A representation order for the purposes of proceedings before a magistrates' court may not include representation by an advocate other than as provided in paragraph (1).

Paragraph 13 makes provision for advocates in the Crown Court, the Court of Appeal and the House of Lords.

Paragraph 14 deals with the appointment of Queen's Counsel or more than one advocate. This is permissible where, in the opinion of the court, the case for the assisted person involves substantial novel or complex issues of law or fact which could not be adequately presented without the appointment of a QC or second advocate, and the prosecution will be represented by a QC or by two or more advocates.

Paragraph 16 enables one representative to be replaced by another (for example, where the representative considers himself to be under a duty to withdraw from the case in accordance with his professional rules of conduct, or where there has been a breakdown in the relationship between the assisted person and the representative (such that effective representation can no longer be provided)).

Paragraph 17 deals with the withdrawal of representation:

(1) The court before which the proceedings are heard, or, in respect of any proceedings mentioned in regulation 3(2)(a) to (g), the Commission, must consider whether to withdraw the representation order in any of the following circumstances:

(a) where any charge or proceedings against the assisted person are varied, the court or the Commission, as appropriate, must consider whether the interests of justice continue to require that he be represented in respect of the varied charge or proceedings;

(b) where the assisted person declines to accept a representation order in the terms which are offered;

(c) at the request of the assisted person; or

(d) where the representative named on the representation order declines to continue to represent the assisted person.

(2) Where representation is withdrawn, the appropriate officer or the Commission, as appropriate, shall provide written notification to the assisted person and to the solicitor (or, where there was no solicitor assigned, to the advocate), who shall inform any assigned advocate (or, where notification is given to the advocate, any other assigned advocate).

(3) On any subsequent application by the assisted person for a representation order in respect of the same proceedings, he shall declare the previous withdrawal of representation and the reason for it.

Paragraph 19 covers the need for authorisation of expenditure:

(1) Where it appears to the solicitor necessary for the proper conduct of proceedings in the Crown Court for costs to be incurred under the representation order by taking any of the following steps:

    (a) obtaining a written report or opinion of one or more experts;

    (b) employing a person to provide a written report or opinion (otherwise than as an expert);

    (c) obtaining any transcripts or recordings; or

    (d) performing an act which is either unusual in its nature or involves unusually large expenditure

he may apply to the Costs Committee for prior authority to do so.

(2) The Commission may authorise a person acting on behalf of the Costs Committee to grant prior authority in respect of any application made under paragraph (1).

(3) Where the Costs Committee or a person acting on its behalf authorises the taking of any step specified in paragraph (1), it shall also authorise the maximum to be paid in respect of that step.

13.1.5 Appeals against refusal of representation

Where an applicant for the grant of a representation order is refused, he may appeal by way of a renewed application to the body which refused the application. The procedure is set out in the Criminal Defence Service (Representation Order Appeals) Regulations 2001 (SI 2001/1168).

Paragraph 3 deals with appeals against refusals of representation orders:

(1) A person whose application for the grant of a representation order has been refused may appeal against such refusal by way of a renewed application to the body which refused the application.

(2) Any appeal in writing shall be made on such form as is from time to time specified by the Lord Chancellor.

(3) Subject to the provisions of the Criminal Defence Service (General) (No 2) Regulations 2001, the date of any representation order shall be the date upon which the original application was received in accordance with those Regulations.

Paragraph 4 deals with Crown Court and magistrates' court, and provides that:

(1) A person whose application for the grant of a representation order has been refused by the Crown Court or a magistrates' court may make a renewed application, either orally or in writing to the same court, or in writing to the appropriate officer of that court.

(2) Where a renewed application is made to the appropriate officer, he may:

    (a) grant the order; or

    (b) refer the renewed application:

        (i) in the Crown Court, to a judge of the court; or

        (ii) in a magistrates' court, to the court, a District Judge (Magistrates' Court) or a single justice who may grant the order or refuse the application.

(3) The judge hearing the application shall give reasons for the refusal of any application.

(4) Where the application was made in writing, the reasons for any refusal shall be given in writing.

Paragraph 5 deals with the Court of Appeal, and provides that:

(1) A person whose application for the grant of a representation order has been refused by the Court of Appeal or the registrar of criminal appeals [or the head of the Civil Appeals Office] may make a renewed application, either orally or in writing to the court, or in writing to the registrar or the head of the Civil Appeals Office.

(2) Where a renewed application is made to the registrar or the head of the Civil Appeals Office, he may:

    (a) grant the order; or

    (b) refer the renewed application to:

        (i) a judge of the court, who may grant the order; or

        (ii) the court, which may grant the order or refuse the application.

(3) The court shall give reasons for the refusal of any application.

(4) Where the application was made in writing, the reasons for any refusal shall be given in writing.

Paragraph 6 deals with refusals of representation by the Legal Services Commission. It provides that:

(1) A person whose application for the grant of a representation order has been refused by the Commission may make a renewed application in writing to the Funding Review Committee, which may grant the order or refuse the application.

(2) The Commission shall give written reasons for the refusal of any application.

Paragraph 7 provides for appeals against withdrawals of representation orders:

(1) A person whose representation order has been withdrawn may appeal against such withdrawal on one occasion to the body which withdrew the order.

(2) Equivalent provisions to those set out in regulations 4 to 6 shall apply in respect of such appeals.

(3) Any appeal in writing shall be made on such form as is from time to time specified by the Lord Chancellor.

13.1.6 Forthcoming changes to the funding scheme

In *Delivering Value for Money in the Criminal Defence Service – A Consultation on Proposed Changes to the Criminal Defence Service* (www.dca.gov.uk/consult/leg-aid/cdserv.htm), published in June 2003, the government expressed concern at the escalating cost of providing representation for defendants in criminal cases, making the point that:

> Legal aid has to compete with other calls on taxpayers' money, such as schools and hospitals. Any efficient publicly funded system of legal aid must be clearly focused on eliminating duplication and waste where they exist and delivering efficient, effective and sustainable services within budget.

The Paper expressed the desire to ensure that the legal aid scheme is focused firmly on what it describes as the 'core functions' of a Criminal Defence Service, namely 'to

ensure that people have the right to a fair trial and that people accused of a crime have their rights protected and are treated fairly'. This requires, according to the paper, that resources should be focused primarily in two areas:

- advice in the police station where such advice is necessary to protect and advance the client's interests;
- representation in court where the interests of justice require such representation.

In May 2004, the government published a Criminal Defence Service Bill. The Bill was discussed in a Consultation Paper (Cmnd 6194) and seeks to achieve two main objectives: the transfer of the responsibility for the grant of criminal legal aid from the courts to the Legal Services Commission; and the re-introduction of a means test for legal aid in criminal cases. Under these proposals, the 'interests of justice' test would be administered not by the courts but by solicitors acting on the basis of binding instructions in the General Criminal Contract. Solicitors would be responsible for ensuring that the individual qualifies for help and for the recovery of contributions.

The government also proposes the abolition of advocacy assistance for early hearings in the magistrates' court (to enable help to be focused on more serious cases where representation is necessary according to the interests of justice test) and to restrict the scope of the duty solicitor scheme to those who are in custody or who are charged with an imprisonable offence (encouraging solicitors to apply for representation at the earliest possible stage in the proceedings). If an individual meets the means criteria, and the case satisfies the interests of justice test, the solicitor will automatically be able to grant representation and proceed to case preparation immediately.

The government also plans to abolish post-charge advice and assistance and to limit the provision of legal advice in the police station to telephone advice in those cases where a solicitor would not be able to advance the client's case by attending the police station (for example, drink-driving cases).

It is perhaps important to remember the words of Lord Justice Auld in his *Review of the Criminal Courts of England and Wales*. He was critical of the funding arrangements for defence lawyers (see paras 13–27 of Chapter 10) and recommends that:

> Urgent consideration should be given to changing the structure of public funding of defence fees in the criminal courts so as properly to reward and encourage adequate and timely preparation of cases for disposal on pleas of guilty or by trial, rather than discourage such preparation as it perversely does at present (Recommendation 153).

13.2   COSTS

The powers of the criminal courts to award costs are contained in ss 16–21 of the Prosecution of Offences Act 1985 and the Costs in Criminal Cases (General) Regulations 1986 (SI 1986/1335).

Reference should also be made to *Practice Direction (Costs: Criminal Proceedings)* [2004] 2 All ER 1070, which gives detailed guidance on costs in criminal cases.

Three types of order have to be considered:

- an order that the defendant's costs be paid out of central funds (s 16 of the 1985 Act);
- an order that the prosecution costs be paid out of central funds (s 17); and
- an order that the defendant pay the prosecution costs (s 18).

13.3   DEFENDANT'S COSTS ORDER

Section 16 makes provision for the award of defence costs out of central funds (that is, government funds pay some or all of the defendant's legal bill). Such an order may be made in any of the following circumstances:

- the prosecution decide not to proceed with an information;
- the defendant is discharged when the magistrates find no case to answer in committal proceedings (this will cease to be relevant when committal proceedings are abolished for either way offences in the same way they have been for indictable-only offences, save for the exceptional cases where the magistrates refuse to send a case for trial to the Crown Court on the basis that it would be an abuse of process);
- the defendant is acquitted following summary trial;
- the prosecution at the Crown Court offer no evidence or ask that all counts remain on the file marked not to be proceeded with without leave;
- the defendant is acquitted following trial on indictment;
- the defendant successfully appeals against conviction and/or sentence.

Paragraphs II.1.1 and II.2.1 of the Practice Direction stipulate that where s 16 of the Act applies, 'an order should normally be made unless there are positive reasons for not doing so. For example, where the defendant's own conduct has brought suspicion on himself and has misled the prosecution into thinking that the case against him was stronger than it was, the defendant can be left to pay his own costs'. However, para II.1.2 (dealing with magistrates' courts) makes it clear that the decision 'whether to make such an award is a matter in the discretion of the court in the light of the circumstances of each particular case', effectively reducing the scope for challenging a refusal to make an order under s 16. This paragraph makes it clear that magistrates' courts should adopt the same approach as the Crown Court to the making of orders under s 16. Paragraph II.2.1, dealing with the Crown Court, says that if the court declines to make an order under s 16, it should be explained, in open court, 'that the reason for not making an order does not involve any suggestion that the defendant is guilty of any criminal conduct but the order is refused because of the positive reason that should be identified'.

Paragraph II.2.2 goes on to provide that 'Where a person is convicted of some count(s) in the indictment and acquitted on other(s) the court may exercise its discretion to make a defendants costs order but may order that only part of the costs incurred be paid. The court should make whatever order seems just having regard to the relative importance of the two charges and the conduct of the parties generally. Where the court considers that it would be inappropriate that the defendant should recover all of the costs properly incurred, the amount must be specified in the order'. The same approach applies in the magistrates' court: see para II.1.1.

Paragraph II.4.3 provides that where the Court of Appeal has jurisdiction to make an order under s 16, 'In considering whether to make such an order the court will have in mind the principles applied by the Crown Court in relation to acquitted defendants'.

It follows that (unless the defence is publicly funded) there is a strong presumption that a costs order should be made in favour of a defendant who has been acquitted. Where the prosecution resist the application on the basis that the defendant brought

suspicion on himself, the court is entitled to rely on a statement of facts from the prosecution – the court does not have to hear oral evidence on this matter (*Mooney v Cardiff Justices* (2000) 164 JP 220).

The court should not refuse to make an order that the defence recover their costs from central funds merely because the prosecution acted properly in bringing the case or that the accused was acquitted on a meritless technicality (*R v Birmingham Juvenile Court ex p H* (1992) 156 JP 445).

A defendant's costs order under s 16 does not have to be made by the bench which acquits the defendant, and so a differently constituted court (for example, the bench which sentences the defendant for other offences) can make such an order regarding an earlier acquittal (*R v Clerk to Liverpool Justices ex p Abiaka* (1999) 163 JP 497).

R (McCormick) v Liverpool City Magistrates' Court [2001] 2 All ER 705 concerned costs incurred by a defendant before he was granted publicly funded representation. The defendant did not have the means to pay those costs. It was held that costs are incurred by a defendant for the purpose of s 16(6) of the Act if he is contractually obliged to pay for them. There is no requirement for the defendant to prove that he has in fact paid, or is likely to pay, those costs.

In *R (Cunningham) v Exeter Crown Court* [2003] EWHC 184; (2003) 167 JP 93, it was held that, where the Crown Court allows an appeal from the magistrates' court, the successful defendant should be awarded his costs under s 16 unless there are positive reasons for not doing so. Where the court takes the view that there are such reasons for not awarding costs, it should set out (albeit briefly) its reasons for coming to that view. In *R (Barrington) v Preston Crown Court* [2001] EWHC 599 (Admin); [2001] All ER (D) 199, the defendant was convicted in the magistrates' court of failing to provide a breath specimen. She appealed to the Crown Court. At the Crown Court, the prosecution offered no evidence after a crucial witness failed to attend and the defendant's conviction was quashed. However, the judge refused an application for a defendant's costs order under s 16. Having regard to the fact that the case against the defendant collapsed not because of anything she had said or done, or any misleading behaviour on her part, but simply because a prosecution witness had failed to attend court, it was held that an application for a defendant's costs order should have been successful.

The amount of the costs order is governed by s 16(6) which provides:

> A defendant's costs order shall ... be for the payment out of central funds, to the person in whose favour the order is made, of such amount as the court considers reasonably sufficient to compensate him for any expenses properly incurred by him in the proceedings.

The order can only cover expenses properly incurred in the proceedings; it cannot include expenses that do not relate directly to the proceedings themselves, such as loss of earnings. See also para I.3.1 of the Practice Direction.

In *R v Dudley Magistrates' Court ex p Power City Stores Ltd* (1990) 154 JP 654, where the defendant wanted to recover the cost of employing leading counsel (that is, a QC), the Divisional Court held that in calculating the amount of costs to be paid under s 16, the officer doing the assessment has to carry out a two-stage test. First, he has to consider whether the expenses claimed were properly incurred by the defendant. If so, the second step is to ask what amount would be reasonably sufficient to compensate the defendant for those costs. The test is whether the defendant acted reasonably in

instructing the counsel he did. There are cases in which junior counsel or a solicitor could conduct the case, but in which it is reasonable to instruct leading counsel. In *R (Hale) v North Sefton Justices* [2002] EWHC 257; (2002) *The Times*, 29 January, it was held that the question to be decided under s 16(6) is whether the defendant had acted reasonably in the circumstances by instructing a solicitor at a particular hourly rate, not whether he could have instructed a more junior solicitor. In the instant case, the justices' clerk had applied the statutory criterion of reasonable sufficiency in s 16(6) to the wrong issue, namely the quality of representation, rather than the costs incurred.

In *Henry A Coff Ltd v Environment Agency* [2003] EWHC 1305; [2003] All ER (D) 145 (May), a District judge declined to make a defendant's costs order under s 16 on the ground that the amount sought was unreasonable on its face and the court should not allow costs that reflect extravagance. The Divisional Court said that the District judge was wrong to refuse to make a defendant's costs order on this basis. What had been asked for was an order for costs to be assessed. It would therefore be for the person subsequently assessing the costs to determine whether the costs claimed were excessive.

Under s 16(7):

> Where a court makes a defendant's costs order but is of the opinion that there are circumstances which make it inappropriate that the person in whose favour the order is made should recover the full amount mentioned in sub-section (6) above, the court shall—
>
> (a) assess what amount would, in its opinion, be just and reasonable; and
>
> (b) specify that amount in the order.

This allows the court to make a defendant's costs order in respect of only part of the costs incurred. If, for example, the defendant is convicted of some offences but acquitted of others, it may be appropriate to award him some costs, or none at all.

13.4   PROSECUTION COSTS FROM CENTRAL FUNDS

An order that the prosecutor's costs be paid out of central funds may be made under s 17 of the Prosecution of Offences Act 1985. Section 17 applies only to private prosecutors, and so excludes the Crown Prosecution Service and any other public authority (for example, Customs & Excise, local authorities, etc). Furthermore, this section applies only to the prosecution of indictable offences (whether triable only on indictment or triable either way). According to para III.1.1 of the Practice Direction, an order should be made, save where there is good reason for not doing so, for example, where 'proceedings have been instituted or continued without good cause'. Such an order can be made even though the defendant was acquitted.

The order under s 17(1) is an order for:

> ... the payment out of central funds of such amount as the court considers reasonably sufficient to compensate the prosecutor for any expenses properly incurred by him in the proceedings.

Under s 17(3):

> Where a court makes an order under this section but is of the opinion that there are circumstances which make it inappropriate that the prosecution should recover the full amount mentioned in sub-section (1) above, the court shall—
>
> (a) assess what amount would in its opinion, be just and reasonable; and
>
> (b) specify that amount in the order.

13.5 DEFENDANT TO PAY PROSECUTION COSTS

Section 18 of the Prosecution of Offences Act 1985 provides as follows:

> (1) Where—
>
> > (a) any person is convicted of an offence before a magistrates' court;
> >
> > (b) the Crown Court dismisses an appeal against such a conviction or against the sentence imposed on that conviction; or
> >
> > (c) any person is convicted of an offence before the Crown Court;
> >
> > the court may make such order as to the costs to be paid by the accused to the prosecutor as it considers just and reasonable.
>
> (2) Where the Court of Appeal dismisses—
>
> > (a) an appeal or application for leave to appeal under Part I of the Criminal Appeal Act 1968; or
> >
> > (b) an application by the accused for leave to appeal to the House of Lords under Part II of that Act; or
> >
> > (c) an appeal or application for leave to appeal under section 9(11) of the Criminal Justice Act 1987 or an appeal or application for leave to appeal under section 35(1) of the Criminal Procedure and Investigations Act 1996 [NB: the latter was added by s 312(3) of the Criminal Justice Act 2003];
> >
> > it may make such order as to the costs to be paid by the accused, to such person as may be named in the order, as it considers just and reasonable.
>
> ...
>
> (5) Where any person under the age of eighteen is convicted of an offence before a magistrates' court, the amount of any costs ordered to be paid by the accused under this section shall not exceed the amount of any fine imposed on him.

Thus, s 18 allows the court to order a defendant who has been convicted (or whose appeal against conviction and/or sentence has been dismissed) to pay the prosecution costs. Section 18(3) provides that the amount of the order is whatever sum the court considers just and reasonable.

Paragraph VI.1.4 of the Practice Direction says that an order for costs under s 18 against a person convicted of an offence or an unsuccessful appellant 'should be made where the court is satisfied that the offender or appellant has the means and the ability to pay', thus establishing a clear presumption (subject to means) that an order will be made. Such an order will only be made if the defendant has sufficient means to enable him to pay some or all of the prosecution costs. In *R v Newham Justices ex p Samuels* [1991] COD 412, the Divisional Court quashed a costs order which had been made without proper account being taken of the defendant's means. In *R v Northallerton Magistrates' Court ex p Dove* [2000] 1 Cr App R(S) 136, the Divisional Court held that a costs order against a defendant under s 18 should never exceed the sum which, having

regard to his means and any other financial order imposed on him, he is able to pay. Where a fine is imposed as well, a costs order should not be grossly disproportionate to the fine. The court should begin by deciding on the appropriate fine (taking account of the seriousness of the offence and the offender's means) and should then consider what costs he should be ordered to pay. If the offender cannot afford to pay both, the fine has priority. It is for the defendant to disclose such information as is necessary for the court to decide what he can reasonably afford to pay; in the absence of such disclosure, the court can draw reasonable inferences as to his means from evidence they have heard and from all the circumstances of the case. In *R v Ghadami* [1998] Cr App R(S) 42, it was held that mortgage debts must be taken into account in deciding whether it is appropriate to make a costs order against a defendant.

Where costs are awarded against several defendants and one of them lacks the means to pay costs, the court should divide the total amount payable between the number of defendants (not just those who are able to pay) so that each defendant pays only his own share of the costs and does not subsidise the defendant who cannot pay (*R v Ronson* (1992) 13 Cr App R(S) 153). In *R v Ronson*, there were four defendants of whom one could not afford to pay costs. It was held by the Court of Appeal that the defendants who could afford to pay costs should each pay one-quarter of the total, not one-third. In *R v Harrison* (1993) 14 Cr App R(S) 419, however, the Court of Appeal upheld an order made against only one of the defendants: he was the principal offender (the other defendants had played relatively minor roles in the offences) and he had the means to pay the amount ordered.

When seeking an order for costs against a defendant, the prosecution must give notice to the defendant of its intention to apply for such an order (*R v Emmett* (1999) *The Times*, 15 October).

In *R v Associated Octel Co Ltd* [1996] 1 WLR 1543, the Court of Appeal held that where a defendant is ordered to pay costs under s 18 of the Prosecution of Offences Act 1985, the amount can include the cost of investigating the offence (as well as the costs of preparing and presenting the prosecution). In *R v Bow Street Stipendiary Magistrate ex p Multimedia Screen Ltd* (1998) *The Times*, 28 January, the defendant sought judicial review of a costs order requiring him to pay £15,000 although he had made only a tiny profit from the offence of which he was convicted. The Divisional Court held that the prosecution had had to do a lot of research and so the order was appropriate.

A judge in the Crown Court should not use a costs order as a means of penalising a defendant for electing Crown Court trial of an offence which could have been dealt with in the magistrates' court (*R v Hayden* [1975] 1 WLR 852). Nevertheless, it has been recognised by the Court of Appeal that trial on indictment is necessarily more expensive than summary trial and this will inevitably be reflected in the costs order (*R v Bushell* (1980) 2 Cr App R(S) 77; *R v Boyle* (1995) 16 Cr App R(S) 927).

A costs order is more likely to be made against a defendant where the prosecution case is manifestly strong and the defendant must have known all along that he was guilty (*R v Singh* (1982) 4 Cr App R(S) 38, following *R v Mountain* (1978) 68 Cr App R 4).

If the prosecution in the Crown Court accept a plea of guilty to an offence to which the defendant would have pleaded guilty in the magistrates' court if the prosecution had not at that stage wanted to proceed with a more serious offence, the defendant will only be ordered to pay the costs appropriate to a guilty plea in the magistrates'

court (*R v Hall* (1988) 10 Cr App R(S) 456). In that case, the defendant was willing to plead guilty to careless driving but the prosecution insisted on proceeding with a charge of reckless (now known as dangerous) driving. At the Crown Court, the prosecution offered no evidence on the reckless driving and the defendant pleaded guilty to careless driving (made possible even though careless driving is a summary offence by what is now s 24 of the Road Traffic Offenders Act 1988). On appeal, the costs order was reduced to the figure he would have had to pay had his plea been accepted in the magistrates' court.

A costs order may (and, subject to means, usually will) be made where the defendant pleads guilty. However, the order will be for less than would be the case upon conviction following a not guilty plea, not least because less expense will probably have been incurred, especially if a plea of guilty is intimated at the earliest opportunity (see *R v Maher* [1983] QB 784).

13.5.1 Appeals on costs

Neither party has a right of appeal to the Crown Court in respect of a costs order made by a magistrates' court: the prosecution have no right of appeal to the Crown Court, and s 108(3)(b) of the Magistrates' Courts Act 1980 precludes a defence appeal to the Crown Court against a costs order. However, it was held in *Johnson v RSPCA* (2000) 164 JP 345 that the Crown Court does have jurisdiction to make an order as to costs incurred before the conclusion of the magistrates' court proceedings (either under s 18(1) of the Prosecution of Offences Act 1985 or s 48(2) of the Supreme Court Act 1981). Usually, following an unsuccessful appeal against conviction, the Crown Court should hesitate to modify the magistrates' costs order. If the prosecutor wishes to seek an increase in the costs the defendant has to pay, he should give written notice to this effect to the defendant, so that the defendant is aware of the possible consequences of pursuing an appeal against conviction.

In *R (Commissioners of Customs & Excise) v Crown Court at Leicester* [2001] EWHC 33 (Admin); (2001) *The Times*, 23 February, the prosecution had refused to disclose some documents and there was an application to stay the trial as an abuse of process. The prosecution offered no evidence and the judge ordered verdicts of not guilty to be recorded. The judge ordered the prosecution to pay defence costs incurred. The question to be decided was whether the costs order was a matter relating to trial on indictment and so excluded from judicial review by s 29 of the Supreme Court Act 1981. The Divisional Court held that under reg 3 of the Costs in Criminal Cases Regulations 1986 (which enables the court to order the payment of any costs incurred as a result of any act or omission by or on behalf of a party to the proceedings (see para VII.1 of the Practice Direction)), the judge had to consider first whether there had been an unnecessary or improper act or omission by, or on behalf, of the prosecution. Secondly, he had to determine whether the costs that were incurred by the defendants were as a result of that unnecessary or improper act or omission. Thirdly, he had to decide whether he would, as a matter of discretion, order all or part of the costs to be paid by the party in default. It is implicit in the last stage that, before an order can be made, the judge is required to identify the costs incurred as a result of the unnecessary or improper act or omission. Having performed those exercises, the judge had to specify the amount to be paid. In the present case, the judge had not complied with reg 3. However, that was not a decision made without jurisdiction, since the judge was

entitled to make a costs order once he was seised of the issue of whether the relevant documents had been disclosed. In those circumstances, the High Court had no jurisdiction to reconsider the judge's decision on an application for judicial review.

13.6   PUBLICLY FUNDED DEFENDANTS

Section 21(4A)(a) of the Prosecution of Offences Act 1985 provides that:

Where one party to any proceedings is a legally assisted person then—

(a)   for the purposes of sections 16 and 17 of this Act, his costs shall be taken not to include the cost of representation funded for him by the Legal Services Commission as part of the Criminal Defence Service; and

(b)   for the purposes of sections 18 ... of this Act, his costs shall be taken to include the cost of representation funded for him by the Legal Services Commission as part of the Criminal Defence Service.

Thus, a defendant's costs order will not be made in respect of costs covered by a representation order, as these costs are being paid out of the public purse anyway.

13.7   WASTED COSTS ORDERS

Section 19A of the Prosecution of Offences Act 1985 empowers the court to make a 'wasted costs order' against a lawyer acting for a party to criminal proceedings. It was held in *Re A Barrister (Wasted Costs Order) (No 9 of 1999)* (2000) *The Times*, 18 April (following the civil case of *Ridehalgh v Horsefield* [1994] Ch 205) that such an order is only appropriate where the lawyer has made an error that no reasonably well-informed and competent lawyer could have made. A wasted costs order against a solicitor is not appropriate where the solicitor relied on the advice of experienced counsel; such a solicitor cannot be said to have acted in a way that no reasonably competent solicitor could have acted (*Re Hickman and Rose (Wasted Costs Order) (No 10 of 1999)* (2000) *The Times*, 3 May).

Paragraph VIII.1.1 of the Practice Direction makes it clear that the power under s 19A of the Act to disallow or order the legal or other representative to meet the whole or any part of the wasted costs is applicable against 'any person exercising a right of audience or a right to conduct litigation (in the sense of acting for a party to the proceedings)'. The paragraph says that 'wasted costs' are 'costs incurred by a party (which includes an LSC funded party) as a result of any improper, unreasonable or negligent act or omission on the part of any representative or his employee, or which, in the light of any such act or omission occurring after they were incurred, the court considers it unreasonable to expect that party to pay'. Paragraph VIII.1.2 stipulates that 'the Judge has a much greater and more direct responsibility for costs in criminal proceedings than in civil and should keep the question of costs in the forefront of his mind at every stage of the case and ought to be prepared to take the initiative himself without any prompting from the parties'.

Paragraph VIII.1.4 says that judges contemplating making a wasted costs order should bear in mind the guidance given by the Court of Appeal in *Re A Barrister (Wasted Costs Order) (No 1 of 1991)* [1993] QB 293:

(i) There is a clear need for any Judge or court intending to exercise the wasted costs jurisdiction to formulate carefully and concisely the complaint and grounds upon which such an order may be sought. These measures are draconian and, as in contempt proceedings, the grounds must be clear and particular.

(ii) Where necessary a transcript of the relevant part of the proceedings under discussion should be available and in accordance with the rules a transcript of any wasted cost hearing must be made.

(iii) A defendant involved in a case where such proceedings are contemplated should be present if, after discussion with counsel, it is thought that his interest may be affected and he should certainly be present and represented if the matter might affect the course of his trial. Regulation 3B(2) of the Costs in Criminal Cases (General) (Amendment) Regulations 1991 furthermore requires that before a wasted costs order is made 'the court shall allow the legal or other representative and any party to the proceedings to make representations'. There may be cases where it may be appropriate for counsel for the Crown to be present.

(iv) A three-stage test or approach is recommended when a wasted costs order is contemplated: (a) Has there been an improper, unreasonable or negligent act or omission? (b) As a result have any costs been incurred by a party? (c) If the answers to (a) and (b) are 'yes', should the court exercise its discretion to disallow or order the representative to meet the whole or any part of the relevant costs, and if so what specific sum is involved?

(v) It is inappropriate to propose any settlement that the representative might forego fees. The complaint should be formally stated by the Judge and the representative invited to make his own comments. After any other party has been heard the Judge should give his formal ruling. Discursive conservations may be unfair and should certainly not take place.

(vi) The Judge must specify the sum to be allowed or ordered. Alternatively the relevant available procedure should be substituted should it be impossible to fix the sum.

Paragraph VIII.1.5 goes on to refer to the additional guidance given by the Court of Appeal in *Re P* [2001] EWCA Crim 1728; [2002] 1 Cr App R 207:

(i) The primary object is not to punish but to compensate, albeit as the order is sought against a non party, it can from that perspective be regarded as penal.

(ii) The jurisdiction is a summary jurisdiction to be exercised by the court which has 'tried the case in the course of which the misconduct was committed'.

(iii) Fairness is assured if the lawyer alleged to be at fault has sufficient notice of the complaint made against him and a proper opportunity to respond to it.

(iv) Because of the penal element a mere mistake is not sufficient to justify an order: there must be a more serious error.

(v) Although the trial Judge can decline to consider an application in respect of costs, for example on the ground that he or she is personally embarrassed by an appearance of bias, it will only be in exceptional circumstances that it will be appropriate to pass the matter to another Judge, and the fact that, in the proper exercise of his judicial function, a Judge has expressed views in relation to the conduct of a lawyer against whom an order is sought, does not of itself normally constitute bias or the appearance of bias so as to necessitate a transfer.

(vi) If the allegation is one of serious misconduct or crime the standard of proof will be higher but otherwise it will be the normal civil standard of proof.

It follows that the standard of proof to be applied is on the balance of probabilities. However, in applying that standard of proof, the court should bear in mind that the more serious the allegation, the less likely it is that the event had occurred and, hence, the stronger the evidence should be before the court concludes that the allegation has been established to the required standard.

Paragraph VIII.1.7 of the Practice Direction notes that the court may postpone the making of a wasted costs order to the end of the case if it appears more appropriate to do so. This might be the case if, for example, there is a possibility of conflict between the legal representatives as to the apportionment of blame, or the legal representative concerned is unable to make full representations because of a possible conflict with the duty to the client.

13.8   AWARD OF COSTS AGAINST THIRD PARTIES

Section 93 of the Courts Act 2003 adds a new section, s 19B, to the Prosecution of Offences Act 1985. This section (which will be supplemented by regulations) enables costs to be awarded against third parties where there has been serious misconduct by the third party and the court considers it appropriate, having regard to that misconduct, to make a third party costs order against him.

CHAPTER 14

SENTENCING PROCEDURE AND PRINCIPLES

In this chapter, we examine the procedure which takes place between conviction and the passing of sentence and at some of the factors which affect the sentence passed by the court.

For the first time, the objectives of sentencing have been enshrined in statute: s 142(1) of the Criminal Justice Act 2003 describes the purposes of sentencing, to which 'any court dealing with an offender in respect of his offence must have regard' as:

(a)   the punishment of offenders,

(b)   the reduction of crime (including its reduction by deterrence),

(c)   the reform and rehabilitation of offenders,

(d)   the protection of the public, and

(e)   the making of reparation by offenders to persons affected by their offences.

Section 142(2) states that sub-s (1) does not apply in a number of cases:

- offenders who are aged under 18 at the time of conviction;
- where the sentence is fixed by law (that is, murder);
- where the sentence is a mandatory one (for example, under s 110 or 111 of the Powers of Criminal Courts (Sentencing) Act 2000 (repeat offending – Class A drug trafficking or domestic burglary) or s 51A of the Firearms Act 1968 (possession of illegal weapons));
- in relation to the making of hospital orders under the Mental Health Act 1983.

The exclusion of young offenders reflects the different ethos of the youth court system, where the court has to take account of the interests of the young offender in a way that does not apply in the case of older defendants.

Section 142(3) defines 'sentence' as including any order made by a court when dealing with the offender in respect of his offence.

14.1   THE HALLIDAY REPORT AND THE PRINCIPLES OF SENTENCING

In July 2001, the Report of the *Review of the Sentencing Framework for England and Wales: Making Punishments Work* by John Halliday was published. Halliday's brief was to examine whether the sentencing framework for England and Wales could be changed to improve results, especially by reducing crime, at justifiable expense.

To this end, the Review looked at a broad range of matters, including:

- the types of sentence that should be available to the courts (with the aim of designing more flexible sentences that work effectively whether the offender is in prison or in the community);
- the ways in which sentences are enforced;
- the systems that govern release from prison;

- the role of the courts in decision-making while the sentence is in force;
- judicial discretion in sentencing and the guidelines governing its use.

The Halliday Report begins by identifying the perceived deficiencies in the present sentencing framework. These shortcomings include the following:

- the present system is too narrowly focused on 'just deserts' and does not encourage sentencers to consider crime reduction and reparation (paras 1.8–1.10);
- the present system adopts a 'muddled approach' towards persistent offenders (paras 1.11–1.15) and fails to deal satisfactorily with the relevance of previous convictions (para 1.34);
- short-term prison sentences (that is, those under 12 months) are inadequate because they 'literally mean half what they say' and 'to all intents and purposes [the second half] is meaningless and ineffective' (paras 1.16–1.19 and 3.13);
- although longer prison terms 'are closer to meaning what they say', the last quartile of the sentence 'lacks any obvious purpose' and has a questionable impact on offenders' behaviour (paras 1.20–1.23);
- community sentences do not inspire confidence because their purpose and 'punitive weight' lack clarity and transparency (paras 1.24–1.27);
- the existing arrangements for sentence enforcement 'are inconsistent and unclear' and lack continuity (paras 1.28–1.30);
- the statutory sentencing framework is unnecessarily rigid; in particular, the division that the 'community sentence threshold' creates between financial and non-financial community penalties is irrational (paras 1.31–1.33);
- the 'just deserts' approach has 'failed to take root because deterrence was soon reinstated [by the courts] as an aim of sentencing' (paras 1.34–1.36);
- the present sentencing framework is inaccessible and lacking in transparency (paras 1.37–1.41) (put another way, the present system is overly complicated); and
- significant disparities exist in sentencing patterns, particularly as between magistrates' courts (paras 1.42–1.44).

In considering the case for change, the Report highlights two particular shortcomings in the existing system of sentencing:

- the unclear and unpredictable approach to persistent offenders; and
- the fact that prison sentences of less than 12 months have little meaningful impact on criminal behaviour.

The Report points out that the purpose of sentencing is not confined to punishment; rather, the aims of sentencing include both crime reduction and reparation. The Report therefore concludes that the sentencing framework should do more to reduce re-offending through working with offenders under sentence, and that more should be done to build on the contributions that reparation and 'restorative justice' schemes can make.

The Report expresses the view that the principles that severity of sentence should be 'proportionate' to the seriousness of criminal conduct, and that imprisonment should be reserved for cases in which no other sentence will do, both remain valid. Thus, the Report says that the principle of 'just deserts' should be retained (so that the sentence ought to be commensurate with the seriousness of the offence) but that in assessing the seriousness of the offence, greater account should be taken of any

previous convictions recorded against the offender. Thus, persistent criminality would result in more severe sentencing than would otherwise have been the case (para 2.7). The reasoning goes along the lines that the existence of previous convictions is a strong indicator of the risk that the offender will re-offend and therefore, if a key aim of sentencing is crime reduction, previous convictions must be an essential part of the information that is taken into account in deciding how to deal with the offender.

The Report thus suggests that the law relating to previous convictions requires reform. It calls for a new presumption that the severity of the sentence will be increased by the existence of recent and relevant convictions showing a continuing course of criminal conduct. To prevent sentencing practice becoming unpredictable and to prevent disproportionately severe sentences being passed, the Report recommends that guidelines be created to help sentencers match the severity of sentence with the seriousness of the offence and to show the ranges within which previous convictions may impact on sentence severity.

The Report also suggests that sentencing decisions should be structured so that sentencers would consider whether a non-custodial sentence would meet the needs of crime reduction, punishment and reparation rather than imposing a short custodial sentence.

The Report called for the general principles of sentencing to be set out in statute. It identified the key principles as being that:

- the severity of the sentence should reflect the seriousness of the offence(s), and the offender's criminal history;
- the seriousness of the offence should reflect the harm caused, threatened or risked, and the offender's degree of blame in committing the offence;
- the severity of the sentence should increase as a consequence of sufficiently recent and relevant previous convictions;
- a prison sentence should be imposed only when no other sentence would be adequate to reflect the need for punishment;
- non-custodial sentences (including financial penalties) should be used, when they are adequately punitive, in ways designed to reduce the risk of re-offending and to protect the public.

A critique of the Halliday Report can be found in Baker, E and Clarkson, C, 'Making punishments work? An evaluation of the Halliday Report on sentencing in England and Wales' [2002] Crim LR 81. Their first criticism is that the Report's approach seems to give undue weight to previous convictions:

> ... the Report proposes that, in future, sentencing should be based on 'limited retributivism'. This means that the limits of punishment (the punitive envelope) would be shaped by desert while the content of the envelope would be determined according to utilitarian objectives. In principle, the pursuit of such a strategy is intellectually defensible. However, there are good reasons for questioning the manner in which the Report's proposals would put it into effect.
>
> The first difficulty lies with the way in which, in seeking to ensure that persistence is punished more effectively, the Report's modified just deserts philosophy has the potential to attach a disproportionate weight to an offender's criminal history in defining the punitive envelope. Although it is asserted that 'sentence severity should be commensurate with the seriousness of criminal conduct', later in the same paragraph [para 2.7] the Report proceeds to propose 'a clear presumption that

sentence severity should increase as a consequence of sufficiently recent and relevant previous convictions'. Allowing previous convictions to lead to an increase in sentence severity can be reconciled with desert-based sentencing through the principle of 'progressive loss of mitigation' [see Wasik, M and von Hirsch, A, 'Section 29 revisited: previous convictions in sentencing' [1994] Crim LR 409]. At the outset of a criminal career an offender can argue that a first offence was 'out of character' and that this should be reflected in mitigated punishment. However, with each successive conviction the argument loses plausibility as the offender's failure to respond to the State's censure and to learn lessons from previous convictions and punishments becomes increasingly patent. Consequently, the degree of mitigation of subsequent sentences progressively diminishes. Importantly though, the reasoning that supports this principle suggests that there ought to be a ceiling on the extent to which previous convictions can justifiably increase sentencing severity.

This leads onto another key criticism made by Baker and Clarkson, that the Halliday approach, as well as being based on predictive sentencing (itself controversial), will lead to an unacceptable level of disparity in the sentencing process:

Having established the parameters of the [punitive] envelope according to the Report's modified desert principles, the next stage in the proposed sentencing process is all-important. The actual sentence to be imposed will be determined by utilitarian considerations. Within the range the sentencer will select the punishment that would most closely serve the purpose of crime reduction (and reparation) in the individual case [see para 2.30]. This will involve an assessment of the likelihood of re-offending and the measures most likely to reduce that risk [see para 2.31]. It is, of course, appropriate that crime reduction should be a consideration in sentencing, particularly with regard to the type of sentence imposed, as opposed to the severity of sentence. However, the difficulty with the Report's proposals is that they invite inconsistent results. Because the 'desert'-based sentencing range is defined according to previous convictions and aggravating and mitigating circumstances, two offenders who commit substantially similar crimes with similar records could end up receiving very different sentences on the grounds that their predicted risk and assessed suitability for programmes aimed at reducing re-offending were significantly divergent ... The important point to note is this. While predictive sentencing is already practised in relation to 'dangerous' offenders (and would continue in the guise of the new 'special' and discretionary life sentences), the effect of the Report's proposals would be to extend a risk assessment approach to all cases. The only possible outcome is sentencing disparity, the avoidance of which is one of the Report's stated goals [in paras 1.42–1.44].

14.2 PROCEDURE FOLLOWING A PLEA OF GUILTY

Where the defendant pleads guilty, the first step is for the court to ascertain the facts of the case. The prosecution therefore summarise the facts of the offence so that the court is able to form a view of how serious the offence was. The prosecutor will also draw the court's attention to the defendant's antecedents, including previous convictions.

The prosecution adopt a neutral stance when it comes to sentencing. It is considered wrong for a prosecutor to try to persuade the court to impose a heavy sentence or to argue for a particular sentence. The prosecutor should therefore summarise the facts fairly.

All the allegations which are made by the prosecution should be based on admissible evidence and should be apparent from the written witness statements which have been disclosed to the defence. In *R v Hobstaff* (1993) 14 Cr App R(S) 605, for example, the Court of Appeal criticised prosecuting counsel for making allegations about the effect of the offence on the victim because he used emotive language and made allegations which were not contained in the witness statements which had been supplied to the defence.

14.2.1 The *Newton* hearing

In cases where the defendant pleads guilty but does so on a factual basis which is different from the prosecution version of what took place, the conflict must be resolved in accordance with the rules laid down by the Court of Appeal in *R v Newton* (1983) 77 Cr App R 13.

In *R v Newton*, the defendant was charged with buggery of his wife. He claimed that she consented to this (at that time not a defence, but relevant to sentence) but the prosecution alleged that she had not consented. The judge wrongly accepted the prosecution version without hearing evidence on the issue of consent. The Court of Appeal held that if, on a plea of guilty, there is a substantial conflict between the prosecution and the defence (that is, there is sharp divergence between the prosecution version of the facts and the defence version of the facts), the judge or magistrates must either:

- accept the defence version and sentence accordingly; or
- hear evidence on what happened and then make a finding of fact as to what happened, and sentence accordingly.

In other words, where there is a substantial divergence between the two stories (that is, a divergence which will have a material effect on the sentence imposed), the judge or magistrates can only reject the defence version after hearing evidence on what happened.

In the Crown Court, if the judge hears evidence, then he sits alone (that is, a jury is not empanelled for the *Newton* hearing). The parties are given the opportunity to call such evidence as they wish and to cross-examine witnesses called by the other side.

An example of a situation where a *Newton* hearing was appropriate is to be found in *R v McFarlane* (1995) 16 Cr App R(S) 315. The defendant was charged with assault occasioning actual bodily harm. The prosecution case was that he had jabbed his wife in the face with a fork and repeatedly punched her about the face. The defendant pleaded guilty but claimed that he had not jabbed her in the face with a fork and that he had slapped her (and had not punched her).

The judge cannot compel the prosecution or the defence to call evidence or cross-examine witnesses. However, if a party refuses to co-operate, the judge is entitled to draw the appropriate adverse inferences. In *R v Mirza* (1993) 14 Cr App R(S) 64, for example, the trial judge directed that a *Newton* hearing should take place. The defendant refused to give evidence, however. The judge accepted the prosecution version of events, and the defendant appealed on the ground that a *Newton* hearing had not taken place. Not surprisingly, the Court of Appeal dismissed the appeal.

If the defendant wants to plead guilty on the basis that he committed the offence but not in the way alleged by the prosecution (for example, he might admit the offence

but deny the presence of aggravating features alleged by prosecution witnesses), the defence should warn the prosecution that this is so, to enable the prosecution to ensure that the relevant witnesses attend court on the relevant date (see *R v Mohun* (1993) 14 Cr App R(S) 5). That way, a *Newton* hearing can take place without the need for an adjournment.

As we have seen, a *Newton* hearing in the Crown Court takes the form of the judge himself hearing evidence and deciding issues of the fact. However, in *R v Newton*, it was suggested that there may be cases where the difference between the versions put forward by the prosecution and the defence ought to be resolved by use of a jury. This can only be done where the difference in stories amounts to an allegation that the defendant committed an additional offence. For example, in a robbery case, if the offender admits threatening the use of violence but denies brandishing a weapon, this dispute should be resolved by adding a count alleging possession of an offensive weapon (s 1 of the Prevention of Crime Act 1953). Indeed, the *Newton* hearing should not be used in a way that effectively defeats the defendant's right to be tried by a jury for an allegation which amounts to an additional offence. For example, in *R v Eubank* [2001] EWCA Crim 891; [2002] 1 Cr App R(S) 4, the defendant was charged with robbery. The prosecution alleged that he was carrying a firearm in the course of the robbery. The defendant pleaded guilty to robbery but denied carrying a firearm. The judge held a *Newton* hearing and decided that the defendant was carrying a firearm. The Court of Appeal said that the judge had been wrong to resolve the question through a *Newton* hearing. The allegation that the defendant had a firearm amounted to a separate and additional offence, on which the defendant was entitled to the verdict of a jury, and so should have been reflected by a separate count on the indictment.

Another example of where it might have been appropriate to empanel a jury comes from the case of *R v Gandy* (1989) 11 Cr App R(S) 564. The defendant pleaded guilty to a charge of violent disorder. The prosecution alleged that the defendant threw a glass which caused serious injury to the victim. The defendant denied that this was the case. The judge held a *Newton* hearing, but the Court of Appeal said that it would have been more appropriate to add a count alleging wounding with intent (s 18 of the Offences Against the Person Act 1861) or alternatively a count alleging unlawful wounding (s 20 of the Offences Against the Person Act 1861); this would have enabled a jury to determine whether the defendant threw the glass.

In fact, cases where this method of resolving the difference between the two versions of events will be quite rare. A jury should not be empanelled needlessly. In *R v Dowdall* (1992) 13 Cr App R(S) 441, for example, the defendant was charged with stealing a pension book from a bag carried by a woman in a supermarket. He offered to plead guilty to theft on the basis that he had found the book and subsequently dishonestly appropriated it, but he denied that he had taken the book from the victim's bag (which would have been a more serious offence, given the closer proximity to the victim). The judge allowed the prosecution to amend the indictment so that it contained a count alleging theft by finding and an alternative count alleging theft from the woman's bag. The Court of Appeal said that the judge erred in allowing the prosecution to amend the indictment in this way. He should have accepted the defendant's plea of guilty and then held a *Newton* hearing (without empanelling a jury) to determine the circumstances in which the defendant stole the pension book. It is only appropriate to empanel a jury where the prosecution allege one offence and the

defendant admits a different offence; in the present case, the only offence alleged was theft.

It should be borne in mind that if there is a *Newton* hearing and the judge rules against the accused (in other words, having heard evidence, accepts the prosecution version), the accused will lose some (though not all) of the credit that he would otherwise have received for pleading guilty (see, for example, *R v Webster* [2004] EWCA Crim 417).

14.2.2 Exceptions to the rule

The only exception where a *Newton* hearing need not be held is the case where the defendant's story is manifestly false or implausible (see *R v Hawkins* (1985) 7 Cr App R(S) 351; *R v Walton* (1987) 9 Cr App R(S) 279; and *Attorney General's References (Nos 3 and 4 of 1996)* [1997] 1 Cr App R(S) 29).

14.2.3 Standard of proof

The judge, in making findings of fact on a *Newton* hearing, should apply the criminal standard of proof; in other words, he must be satisfied so that he is sure that the prosecution version is correct before sentencing on that basis (*R v Kerrigan* (1993) 14 Cr App R(S) 179).

In *R v Gandy* (1989) 11 Cr App R(S) 564, it was stressed by the Court of Appeal that where the judge holds a *Newton* hearing, the rules of evidence must be followed strictly and the judge must direct himself in the same terms as he would direct a jury. In that case, for example, the Court of Appeal rejected the finding of the fact made by the judge that it was the defendant that had caused injury to the victim because the judge had not taken proper account of the weaknesses in the identification evidence against the accused (cf *R v Turnbull* [1977] QB 224).

14.2.4 Appeals

In *R v Wood* [1991] Crim LR 926, the Court of Appeal said that it would not interfere with the judge's findings of fact in a *Newton* hearing unless no reasonable jury could have reached the conclusion reached by the judge.

If the judge wrongly fails to conduct a *Newton* hearing, the Court of Appeal will allow an appeal against sentence and will impose the sentence which would be appropriate on the basis that the defendant's version of events is the correct one (*R v Mohun* (1993) 14 Cr App R(S) 5), effectively giving the benefit of the doubt to the defendant.

14.2.5 Responsibility of the sentencer and of counsel

In *Attorney General's Reference (Nos 3 and 4 of 1996)* [1997] 1 Cr App R(S) 29, the defendants pleaded guilty to robbery but, when speaking to the probation officer, denied some of the allegations made by the victim. These denials were set out in the pre-sentence reports. Counsel for the defendants, when addressing the court in mitigation, referred to the pre-sentence reports but did not make specific reference to

the fact that the defendants denied some of the allegations made by the prosecution. The Court of Appeal said that it was the duty of defence counsel to make it known to the prosecution, and to the court, that there was a dispute (so that a *Newton* hearing could be held). The Court of Appeal went on to consider the dispute (since it had not been considered in the Crown Court) but upheld the sentence on the basis that a *Newton* hearing need not be held if the defendant's story is manifestly false or implausible.

However, in *R v Oakley* [1998] 1 Cr App R(S) 100, it was said that the court must itself be alert to differences between the prosecution case and the defence case. In that case, sentence was passed on a factual basis which was inconsistent with the defence version of what had happened as set out in the pre-sentence report. Defence counsel did not invite the judge to hold a *Newton* hearing. The Court of Appeal held that the judge should have been alert to the conflict and should have resolved the conflict with the *Newton* hearing whether or not the defence or prosecution asked for such a hearing.

In *R v Tolera* [1999] 1 Cr App R 29, the Court of Appeal gave further guidance on this issue. The Court preferred the approach taken in *Attorney General's Reference (Nos 3 and 4 of 1996)* and re-emphasised that it is not enough for the defence version to be set out in the pre-sentence report. It was said that while the judge will normally read that part of the report, he will not ordinarily pay attention, for the purposes of sentence, to any account of the crime given by the offender to the probation officer where it conflicts with the prosecution case. If the defendant wants to rely on such an account, the defence must expressly draw those paragraphs to the court's attention and ask that sentence be passed on that basis.

Tolera also gives guidance on what should be done where the defendant puts forward a version of events which is inconsistent with the prosecution case but which the prosecutor is unable to challenge by adducing evidence to contradict what the defendant is saying. This might be the case if, for example, the defendant alleges the existence of mitigating circumstances relating to the commission of the offence. If the court is unwilling to accept the defence version, the court should make its views known so that a *Newton* hearing can take place before sentence is passed. That will normally involve the defendant giving evidence; the prosecutor should ask appropriate questions to test the defendant's evidence rather than simply leaving it to the court to question the defendant.

14.3 PROCEDURE FOLLOWING CONVICTION AFTER A NOT GUILTY PLEA

Where the defendant was convicted following a plea of not guilty, the facts of the offence will have emerged during the evidence. However, the prosecution may have to summarise the facts of the case where there has been an adjournment after conviction, as will usually be the case where a pre-sentence report has to be prepared. In the Crown Court, it is usually the judge who presided over the trial who passes sentence and it is likely that he will use his note of the evidence to refresh his memory, and so will not need the prosecution to remind him of the facts. In magistrates' courts, however, it is very common for a bench other than the bench which convicted the

defendant to pass sentence, and so the bench which passes sentence will need a summary of the facts from the prosecution.

14.4 PROCEDURE AFTER THE PROSECUTION SUMMARY OF FACTS (IF GIVEN)

After the prosecution have summarised the facts of the case (if the defendant pleaded guilty), or after the defendant has been found guilty, the prosecution supply the court with details of the defendant's character and antecedents. In *R v Egan* [2004] EWCA Crim 630; (2004) *The Times*, 9 March, the Court of Appeal pointed out that sentencers should have available to them, as part of a defendant's antecedent history, details of any previous sentences imposed, the dates of release from such sentences and the relevant sentence expiry dates.

The way in which the court is made aware of the defendant's previous convictions is dealt with in para III.27 of the *Practice Direction (Criminal Proceedings: Consolidation)* [2002] 1 WLR 2870. This makes provision for information relating to a defendant's previous convictions to be provided by the police directly from the Police National Computer (PNC). Paragraph III.27 provides as follows:

III.27 *Antecedents*

Standard for the provision of information of antecedents in the Crown Court and magistrates' courts

27.1 In the Crown Court the police will provide brief details of the circumstances of the last three similar convictions and/or of convictions likely to be of interest to the court, the latter being judged on a case-by-case basis. This information should be provided separately and attached to the antecedents as set out below.

27.2 Where the current alleged offence could constitute a breach of an existing community order, eg community rehabilitation order, and it is known that that order is still in force then, to enable the court to consider the possibility of revoking that order, details of the circumstances of the offence leading to the community order should be included in the antecedents as set out below.

Preparation of antecedents and standard formats to be used

27.3 In magistrates' courts and the Crown Court: personal details and summary of convictions and cautions—Police National Computer ('PNC') court/ defence/probation summary sheet; previous convictions—PNC court/defence/ probation printout, supplemented by Form MG16 if the police force holds convictions not shown on PNC; recorded cautions—PNC court/defence/probation printout, supplemented by Form MG17 if the police force holds cautions not shown on PNC. In addition, in the Crown Court: circumstances of the last three similar convictions; circumstances of offence leading to a community order still in force; Form MG(c). The detail should be brief and include the date of the offence.

Provision of antecedents to the court and parties

Crown Court

27.4 The Crown Court antecedents will be prepared by the police immediately following committal proceedings, including committals for sentence, transfers under

section 4 of the Criminal Justice Act 1987 or section 53 of the Criminal Justice Act 1991 or upon receipt of a notice of appeal, excluding non-imprisonable motoring offences.

27.5 Seven copies of the antecedents will be prepared in respect of each defendant. Two copies are to be provided to the Crown Prosecution Service ('CPS') direct, the remaining five to be sent to the Crown Court. The court will send one copy to the defence and one to the Probation Service. The remaining copies are for the court's use. Where following conviction a custodial order is made one copy is to be attached to the order sent to the prison.

27.6 The antecedents must be provided, as above, within 21 days of committal or transfer in each case. Any points arising from them are to be raised with the police by the defence solicitor as soon as possible and, where there is time, at least seven days before the hearing date so that the matter can be resolved prior to that hearing.

27.7 Seven days before the hearing date the police will check the record of convictions. Details of any additional convictions will be provided using the standard format above. These will be provided as above and attached to the documents already supplied. Details of any additional outstanding cases will also be provided at this stage.

Magistrates' courts

27.8 The magistrates' court antecedents will be prepared by the police and submitted to the CPS with the case file.

27.9 Five copies of the antecedents will be prepared in respect of each defendant and provided to the CPS, who will be responsible for distributing them to others at the sentencing hearing. Normally two copies will be provided to the court, one to the defence and one to the Probation Service when appropriate. Where following conviction a custodial order is made, one of the court's copies is to be attached to the order sent to the prison.

27.10 In instances where antecedents have been provided to the court some time before the hearing the police will, if requested to do so by the CPS, check the record of convictions. Details of any additional convictions will be provided using the standard format above. These will be provided as above and attached to the documents already supplied. Details of any additional outstanding cases will also be provided at this stage.

27.11 The above arrangements whereby the police provide the antecedents to the CPS for passing on to others will apply unless there is a local agreement between the CPS and the court that alters that arrangement.

In cases being dealt with by either the magistrates' court or the Crown Court, the antecedents form will contain:

(a) personal details (domestic circumstances, financial commitments, employment, etc; this is based on information provided by the defendant to the police following arrest and no action will be taken by the police to verify this information);

(b) a list of previous convictions (showing, for each conviction, the date of the conviction, the court, the offence, and the sentence imposed);

(c) details of any cautions recorded against the offender.

In cases being dealt with by the Crown Court, the antecedents form should also:

(a) show the circumstances of the last three similar convictions; and

(b) set out the circumstances of the offence leading to any community order which is still in force.

In the Crown Court, the police will provide brief details of the circumstances of the last three similar convictions, and/or of convictions likely to be of interest to the court. Where the current alleged offence was committed during the term of an existing community order which is still in force, brief details of the circumstances (including the date) of the offence leading to the community order must be included in the antecedents form (in case the Crown Court decides to revoke the community order and re-sentence for the earlier offence). Where the defendant disputes the accuracy of the information provided by the police, this matter should (where possible) be raised at least seven days before the date of the hearing.

In the magistrates' court, unless there is a local agreement between the CPS and the court, the CPS is responsible for distributing the copies: two to the court, one to the defence and one to the Probation Service (when appropriate). Where the antecedents were provided some time before the hearing, the police should, if requested to do so by the CPS, check the record of convictions. Details of any additional convictions, and of any additional outstanding cases, should be provided at this stage.

It used to be the practice, at least in the Crown Court, for a police officer to give sworn evidence about the defendant's antecedents. However, this information is now given by the prosecutor, who simply reads details from the standard forms.

Where the offender has a large number of previous convictions, the court will indicate which of those convictions should be referred to by the prosecutor; it is only the convictions referred to by the prosecutor that the court will take into account in passing sentence for the present offence.

If the offender disputes the accuracy of the list of previous convictions, the convictions which he disputes have to be proved. Section 73 of the Police and Criminal Evidence Act 1984 enables proof of previous convictions to be by way of a certificate of conviction from the convicting court. Alternatively, s 39 of the Criminal Justice Act 1948 enables a previous conviction to be proved by showing that the fingerprints of the defendant are the same as those of the person previously convicted. A further option is for someone (for example, a police officer) to give evidence that he was present in court when the defendant was convicted of the offence on the earlier occasion and that that person is the defendant in the present proceedings. However, a previous conviction can be proved by any admissible evidence; for example, if the defendant admits the previous conviction to the police (*R v Derwentside Magistrates' Court ex p Swift* (1996) 160 JP 468).

If the present conviction means that the offender is in breach of a previous order (for example, suspended sentence or conditional discharge), it is necessary to ask the defendant whether he admits that he is in breach of the earlier order. If the defendant denies the breach, the breach has to be proved by means of admissible evidence that the earlier order was made.

14.5   REPORTS ON THE OFFENDER

As well as considering the prosecution summary of the facts (if given) and the defendant's antecedents, the court will usually have to consider a pre-sentence report.

14.5.1 Pre-sentence report

Section 81(1) of the Powers of Criminal Courts (Sentencing) Act 2000 requires the court to obtain and consider a pre-sentence report before imposing a custodial sentence, unless the court takes the view that a report is unnecessary. Section 36(4) of the Act requires the court to obtain and consider a pre-sentence report before imposing a community rehabilitation order, a community punishment order, a community punishment and rehabilitation order, or a supervision order with additional requirements (again, unless the court takes the view that a report is unnecessary).

In the case of offenders who have attained the age of 18, pre-sentence reports are compiled by probation officers. For offenders who are under 13, reports are prepared by local authority social workers. In the case of young offenders who have attained the age of 13, reports are prepared either by social workers or probation officers. Such reports are usually prepared by a social worker, but the report would be prepared by a probation officer if, for example, the probation service was already having dealings with a member of the offender's family.

The court is not bound to accept the conclusions in a pre-sentence report. So, for example, if the report says that the offender is suitable for a community rehabilitation order, the court does not have to accept that view. In *R v Smith* [1998] 1 Cr App R(S) 138, for instance, the defendant was convicted, following trial, of causing actual bodily harm by stalking his victim. A psychiatric report said that the defendant did not represent a continuing threat to the victim. The judge rejected that view. The Court of Appeal held that the judge was entitled to take the view that he did and to sentence accordingly.

The Criminal Justice Act 2003 re-enacts the procedural requirements (in ss 36 and 81 of the Powers of Criminal Courts (Sentencing) Act 2000) which have to be met before the imposition of a community sentence or a custodial sentence. Section 156 of the Act provides that before forming an opinion about the appropriateness of a community sentence or the appropriateness of a custodial sentence, the court 'must take into account all such information as is available to it about the circumstances of the offence or (as the case may be) of the offence and the offence or offences associated with it, including any aggravating or mitigating factors'; also, in forming an opinion about the suitability of imposition of specific requirements as part of a community sentence, the court may take into account any information about the offender which is before it. Section 156(3) provides that a court must obtain and consider a pre-sentence report before:

(a) in the case of a custodial sentence, deciding that the case is so serious that neither a fine nor a community sentence could be justified (s 152(2)), that the term imposed is commensurate with the seriousness of the offence (s 153(2)), that life imprisonment is necessary for the protection of the public because of the risk of serious harm posed by the offender (s 225(1)(b); s 226(1)(b) for young offenders), that an extended sentence is necessary to protect the public where the offender is convicted of certain violent or sexual offences and poses a significant risk to the public (s 227(1)(b); s 228(1)(b)(i) for young offenders); or

(b) in the case of a community sentence, deciding that the offence is sufficiently serious to warrant a community sentence (s 148(1)), that the restrictions on the offender's liberty are commensurate with the seriousness of the offence (s 148(2)(b); s 148(3)(b) for young offenders), or forming any opinion as to the

suitability for the offender of the particular requirement(s) to be imposed by the community order.

Under s 156(4), the court need not obtain and consider a pre-sentence report if, in the circumstances of the case, the court is of the opinion that it is unnecessary to obtain a pre-sentence report. However, where the offender is under the age of 18, the court cannot dispense with a pre-sentence report unless (a) there exists a previous pre-sentence report obtained in respect of the offender, and (b) the court has had regard to the information contained in that report or, if there is more than one such report, the most recent report (s 156(5)).

Section 156(6) provides that no custodial sentence or community sentence is invalidated by the failure of a court to obtain and consider a pre-sentence report as required by s 156. However, if the sentence court did not obtain a pre-sentencing report in a case where it was required to do so under s 156, the court hearing the appeal should obtain a pre-sentence report (if one is required under s 156) unless that court is of the opinion (a) that the sentencing court was justified in forming an opinion that it was unnecessary to obtain a pre-sentence report, or (b) that although the court below was not justified in forming that opinion, in the circumstances of the case at the time it is before the appeal court, it is unnecessary to obtain a pre-sentence report (s 156(7)). If the offender is under 18, the appeal court can only dispense with a pre-sentence report if (a) there exists a previous pre-sentence report obtained in respect of the offender, and (b) the court has had regard to the information contained in that report, or, if there is more than one such report, the most recent report (s 156(8)).

14.5.2 Disclosure of the pre-sentence report

Disclosure of the pre-sentence report is governed by s 156 of the Powers of Criminal Courts (Sentencing) Act 2000. This provision is re-enacted, with some modifications, in s 159 of the Criminal Justice Act 2003.

The defence advocate invariably has sight of a copy of the pre-sentence report if one has been prepared. It is good practice to ask the defendant if he has seen a copy of the report. If he has not, then he should be asked to read through it and check its accuracy (or the advocate should summarise its contents). The report is normally based on a single interview between the defendant and a probation officer and there is the potential for errors to creep in. In any event, s 156 of the Powers of Criminal Courts (Sentencing) Act 2000 (s 159(2) of the 2003 Act) requires the pre-sentence report to be disclosed to the offender and to his counsel or solicitor.

Under s 159(2)(b) of the 2003 Act, if the offender is under 18, a copy of the report must also be given to a parent or guardian (if present in court); this is subject to the proviso in s 159(3) that:

> If the offender is aged under 18 and it appears to the court that the disclosure to the offender or to any parent or guardian of his of any information contained in the report would be likely to create a risk of significant harm to the offender, a complete copy of the report need not be given to the offender or, as the case may be, to that parent or guardian.

Where the offender is under 18 and is in local authority care, a copy of the report goes to the local authority (s 159(6)).

Section 156 of the 2000 Act (s 159(2)(c) of the 2003 Act) also requires the report to be disclosed to the prosecutor. This may seem unnecessary, since the prosecutor generally has little further part to play once a conviction has been recorded (apart from ensuring that the court does not exceed its sentencing powers and drawing the courts attention to any relevant sentencing guidelines). Section 156(5) of the 2000 Act (s 159(5) of the 2003 Act) stipulates that the prosecutor can only use information gleaned from the report for the purpose of deciding whether to make representations to the court about the content of the report and for making any such representations. The disclosure of the report to the prosecutor under this provision means that prosecutors will have a chance to check that any factual information contained in the report agrees with information contained in the prosecution file. Any representations made by the prosecutor are likely to be confined to drawing the attention of the court to any factual inaccuracies in the report.

14.5.3 Juveniles

Before passing sentence on a juvenile, the court must give the juvenile and a parent or guardian a chance to make representations about the appropriate sentence. The court must also consider all available information about the offender's general conduct, home environment, school record and medical history. In addition to the report from a local authority social worker (or a probation officer), there will also be a report from the juvenile's school (and, if appropriate, the GP) (see rr 10 and 11 of the Magistrates' Courts (Children and Young Persons) Rules 1992 and s 9 of the Children and Young Persons Act 1969).

14.5.4 Adjournments prior to sentence

Section 10(3) of the Magistrates' Courts Act 1980 empowers a magistrates' court to adjourn before passing sentence in order to enable inquiries to be made as to the most suitable method of dealing with the offender.

Section 10(3) stipulates that adjournments between conviction and sentence should be for no more than four weeks at a time if the offender is on bail (note that the presumption in favour of bail created by s 4 of the Bail Act 1976 applies to such an offender) and for no more than three weeks at a time if the offender is in custody.

The Crown Court has inherent jurisdiction to adjourn and there is no statutory limit on the length of the adjournment. However, the Crown Court will usually adopt the same periods as magistrates' courts.

14.5.5 Other reports

Before the court can make a hospital order or a community rehabilitation order with a requirement for medical treatment, a psychiatric report is required (see s 37 of the Mental Health Act 1983; para 5 of Sched 2 to the Powers of Criminal Courts (Sentencing) Act 2000; s 157 of the Criminal Justice Act 2003).

Section 157 of the 2003 Act re-enacts s 82 of the Powers of Criminal Courts (Sentencing) Act 2000 and sets out additional requirements to be satisfied in the case of mentally disordered offenders:

(1) Subject to sub-section (2), in any case where the offender is or appears to be mentally disordered, the court must obtain and consider a medical report before passing a custodial sentence other than one fixed by law.

(2) Sub-section (1) does not apply if, in the circumstances of the case, the court is of the opinion that it is unnecessary to obtain a medical report.

(3) Before passing a custodial sentence other than one fixed by law on an offender who is or appears to be mentally disordered, a court must consider—

   (a) any information before it which relates to his mental condition (whether given in a medical report, a pre-sentence report or otherwise), and

   (b) the likely effect of such a sentence on that condition and on any treatment which may be available for it.

(4) No custodial sentence which is passed in a case to which sub-section (1) applies is invalidated by the failure of a court to comply with that sub-section, but any court on an appeal against such a sentence—

   (a) must obtain a medical report if none was obtained by the court below, and

   (b) must consider any such report obtained by it or by that court.

(5) In this section 'mentally disordered', in relation to any person, means suffering from a mental disorder within the meaning of the Mental Health Act 1983.

Section 161 of the Criminal Justice Act 2003 re-enacts, with some modifications, s 36A of the Powers of Criminal Courts (Sentencing) Act 2000, and provides for pre-sentence drug testing:

(1) Where a person aged 14 or over is convicted of an offence and the court is considering passing a community sentence or a suspended sentence, it may make an order under sub-section (2) for the purpose of ascertaining whether the offender has any specified Class A drug in his body.

(2) The order requires the offender to provide, in accordance with the order, samples of any description specified in the order.

(3) Where the offender has not attained the age of 17, the order must provide for the samples to be provided in the presence of an appropriate adult.

(4) If it is proved to the satisfaction of the court that the offender has, without reasonable excuse, failed to comply with the order it may impose on him a fine of an amount not exceeding level 4.

14.5.6 Keeping sentencing options open

When the court adjourns the case so that a report can be prepared, great care must be exercised when the court explains to the defendant what is happening.

In *R v Gillam* (1980) 2 Cr App R(S) 267, the judge adjourned the case so that a report could be prepared to assess whether the defendant was suitable for what was then known as community service (community punishment/unpaid work under a community order). The circumstances were such that the defendant was led to believe that if the report was favourable, he would receive community service rather than a custodial sentence. In the event, the report was favourable but a custodial sentence was passed nonetheless. The Court of Appeal said that the judge should have imposed a non-custodial sentence, otherwise a feeling of injustice would be aroused. Similarly, in *R v Howard* (1989) 11 Cr App R(S) 583, the court adjourned for a pre-sentence report and the defendant was told that the court was minded to deal with the case by means

of a community service order. A custodial sentence was subsequently imposed and this sentence was quashed by the Court of Appeal.

In *R v Keily* (1989) 11 Cr App R(S) 273, a judge at a pre-trial review said that if the defendant were to plead guilty, a custodial sentence would not be imposed. The case was later tried by a different judge; the defendant pleaded not guilty but was convicted and was sent to prison. The Court of Appeal quashed the custodial sentence on the grounds that the first judge had erred in giving an indication which put pressure on the defendant to plead guilty (infringing the rule set out in *R v Turner* [1970] 2 QB 321) and that the second judge was bound by the indication given by the first judge that an immediate custodial sentence would not be imposed (following *R v Wilkinson* (1988) 9 Cr App R(S) 468).

This principle only applies if there was something 'in the nature of a promise, express or implied, that, if a particular proposal is recommended, it will be adopted' (*R v Moss* (1984) 5 Cr App R(S) 209, *per* Croom-Johnson LJ).

Thus, if the court makes it clear that it is not committing itself to a non-custodial sentence if the pre-sentence report recommends a non-custodial sentence, no legitimate sense of injustice is created if a custodial sentence is passed, even if the court rejects a recommendation for a non-custodial sentence contained in the report (*R v Horton* (1985) 7 Cr App R(S) 299).

Thus, in *R v Renan* (1994) 15 Cr App R(S) 722, the judge granted the defendant bail pending the preparation of a pre-sentence report, but said nothing about sentencing options. It was held that this did not, in the circumstances of the particular case, create an expectation that a custodial sentence would not be passed. A custodial sentence was, accordingly, upheld.

In *R v Jones* [2003] EWCA Crim 1631; [2004] Cr App R(S) 23, the judge adjourned sentence with a view to hearing an application for a confiscation order, but made no mention of the possibility of making a compensation order; at the adjourned hearing, the judge imposed a compensation order. It was held (quashing the compensation order) that if a judge postpones his decision on all or part of a sentence, it is essential that he states fully his reasons for doing so and makes it clear what sentence will be considered at the adjourned hearing.

14.6   THE PLEA IN MITIGATION

A plea in mitigation usually comprises a speech by the barrister or solicitor appearing for the defence. If the defendant is unrepresented, he will be asked if there is anything he wishes to say before sentence is passed.

Occasionally, witnesses will be called to show the good character of the offender or to explain why he acted out of character by committing an offence.

The matters which the prosecution will draw to the court's attention will be matters which relate to the seriousness of the offence; the plea in mitigation by the defence may address the seriousness of the offence, together with mitigating factors relating to the offender. In the next section, we consider factors which make an offence more or less serious.

14.7 AGGRAVATING AND MITIGATING FACTORS

The decision as to what sentence to pass involves a two-stage process:

- the court first has to decide what sentence is appropriate given the seriousness of the offence committed by the defendant;

- the court then goes on to consider whether that sentence should be reduced in the light of any mitigating circumstances which relate to the defendant.

Thus, the court looks first at the offence and then at the offender.

Section 143(1) of the Criminal Justice Act 2003 states that:

> In considering the seriousness of any offence, the court must consider the offender's culpability in committing the offence and any harm which the offence caused, was intended to cause or might foreseeably have caused.

In other words, the starting point is to consider the harm that was actually caused and the harm that the offender intended to cause.

14.8 THE OFFENCE ITSELF

Some factors are matters of statute; others are derived from case law. Relevant factors relating to the offence include the following:

- Section 151(2) of the Powers of Criminal Courts (Sentencing) Act 2000 (re-enacted in s 143(3) of the Criminal Justice Act 2003) provides that if an offence is committed whilst the offender is on bail in respect of another offence, that is an aggravating factor as far as the later offence is concerned. This is so even if the two offences are different in nature or relative seriousness, and even if the accused is in fact acquitted of the first offence. In *R v Thackwray* [2003] EWCA Crim 3362; (2003) *The Times*, 25 November, the defendant was sentenced for an offence committed while he was on bail for another offence; the judge treated that fact as an aggravating feature even though the defendant had been acquitted of the original offence. The Court of Appeal confirmed that this was the correct approach, saying that the fact that defendant had been on bail at the time of the present offence is to be regarded as an aggravating feature, whether or not the defendant was subsequently convicted of that other offence.

- The fact that an offence was 'racially aggravated' must be treated as an aggravating factor which increases the seriousness of the offence (s 153 of the Powers of Criminal Courts (Sentencing) Act 2000; s 145 of the Criminal Justice Act 2003). In *R v Saunders* [2000] 1 Cr App R 458, the Court of Appeal said that where an offence involves racial aggravation, a term of up to two years' custody may be added to the sentence. Also, the presence of racial aggravation may make a custodial sentence appropriate for an offence which would otherwise have merited a non-custodial sentence.

- Section 146(3) of the Criminal Justice Act 2003 provides for an increase in sentences because of aggravation related to disability (in the sense of physical or mental impairment) or sexual orientation. Section 146(2) provides that s 146 applies where:

... at the time of committing the offence, or immediately before or after doing so, the offender demonstrated towards the victim of the offence hostility based on (i) the sexual orientation (or presumed sexual orientation) of the victim, or (ii) a disability (or presumed disability) of the victim,

or where the offence was:

... motivated (wholly or partly) (i) by hostility towards persons who are of a particular sexual orientation, or (ii) by hostility towards persons who have a disability or a particular disability.

Under sub-s (4), it is immaterial whether or not the offender's hostility was also based, to any extent, on any other factors apart from disability or sexual orientation.

- In a case involving money, the amount involved is an important factor in determining the seriousness of the offence. The greater the sum stolen or the greater the value of the property damaged, the more serious the offence.

- Using or threatening the use of violence makes the offence more serious, and the use or threatened use of a weapon makes it more serious still.

- The offence is more serious if the victim is vulnerable. The term vulnerable includes not only the aged and infirm (as in *Attorney General's Reference (No 13 of 1992)* (1993) 14 Cr App R(S) 756), but also those whose work brings them into contact with the public, and so places them at greater risk (for example, police officers, taxi drivers, bus drivers, milkmen and, as in *R v Rigg* (1997) *The Times*, 4 July, a publican).

- Where an offence is committed in breach of trust, the offence is made more serious by that breach (see *R v Barrick* (1985) 81 Cr App R 78 and *R v Clark* [1998] 2 Cr App R 137). This includes the employee who steals from his employer and the postman who steals or destroys the mail. In a case involving breach of trust, a custodial sentence may be appropriate even if the sum involved is small (*R v McCormick* (1995) 16 Cr App R(S) 134).

- If the offence was committed on impulse, that is a mitigating factor. On the other hand, an offence is made more serious if it is premeditated. The greater the degree of planning and sophistication, the more serious the offence. See, for example, *Attorney General's Reference (No 13 of 1992)* (1993) 14 Cr App R(S) 756.

- Where more than one person is involved in the commission of an offence, this fact may make the offence more serious. A mugging by a gang is worse than a mugging carried out by one person.

- Where more than one person is involved, the level of a particular person's involvement affects the seriousness of the offence as regards that offender. For example, the lookout and the getaway driver will be dealt with more leniently than those who actually carry out the burglary or the robbery as the case may be.

- If the offender is able to show that the offence was committed out of something approaching necessity (but the necessity falls short of being a defence), that offence may be regarded as less serious than one committed for purely personal gain.

- Provocation is only a defence to murder but may be used as a mitigating circumstance for any offence. Usually, of course, the question of provocation arises only in offences of violence. See, for example, *R v Brookin* (1995) 16 Cr App R(S) 78.

- The effect of the offence on the victim. The use of statements from victims of crime about the impact of the offence is governed by para III.28 of *Practice Direction (Criminal Proceedings: Consolidation)* [2002] 1 WLR 2870:

III.28 *Personal statements of victims*

28.1 This section draws attention to a scheme, which started on 1 October 2001, to give victims a more formal opportunity to say how a crime has affected them. It may help to identify whether they have a particular need for information, support and protection. It will also enable the court to take the statement into account when determining sentence.

28.2 When a police officer takes a statement from a victim the victim will be told about the scheme and given the chance to make a victim personal statement. A victim personal statement may be made or updated at any time prior to the disposal of the case. The decision about whether or not to make a victim personal statement is entirely for the victim. If the court is presented with a victim personal statement the following approach should be adopted:

(a) The victim personal statement and any evidence in support should be considered and taken into account by the court prior to passing sentence.

(b) Evidence of the effects of an offence on the victim contained in the victim personal statement or other statement must be in proper form, that is a witness statement made under section 9 of the Criminal Justice Act 1967 or an expert's report, and served upon the defendant's solicitor or the defendant, if he is not represented, prior to sentence. Except where inferences can properly be drawn from the nature of or circumstances surrounding the offence, a sentencer must not make assumptions unsupported by evidence about the effects of an offence on the victim.

(c) The court must pass what it judges to be the appropriate sentence having regard to the circumstances of the offence and of the offender, taking into account, so far as the court considers it appropriate, the consequences to the victim. The opinions of the victim or the victim's close relatives as to what the sentence should be are therefore not relevant, unlike the consequence of the offence on them. Victims should be advised of this. If, despite the advice, opinions as to sentence are included in the statement, the court should pay no attention to them.

(d) The court should consider whether it is desirable in its sentencing remarks to refer to the evidence provided on behalf of the victim.

14.9 MITIGATION RELATING TO THE OFFENDER

After consideration of the seriousness of the offence itself, the court goes on to examine any mitigation which relates to the offender.

14.9.1 A plea of guilty

Section 152 of the Powers of Criminal Courts (Sentencing) Act 2000 (which is re-enacted in s 144 of the Criminal Justice Act 2003) gives statutory effect to the already well established principle that credit should be given for pleading guilty. The court is required to take account of the stage in the proceedings at which the offender indicated his intention to plead guilty and the circumstances in which this indication was given. It is difficult to see what this statutory provision added to the existing law. There is still

no statutory guidance on the amount of the discount, and so the case law on that issue remains important.

The reasons for this credit are:

- it shows contrition on the part of the accused;
- it saves court time, in that no trial takes place;
- if the defendant admitted the offence when first questioned by the police (or, better still, surrendered himself to police custody), police time is saved, in that unnecessary enquiries do not have to be made;
- in cases where the experience of giving evidence would be traumatic to a witness (for example, a victim of a sexual assault), the plea of guilty spares the witness this trauma.

The usual credit for pleading guilty in a case where a custodial sentence is imposed is a one-third reduction in that sentence (*R v Buffery* (1993) 14 Cr App R(S) 511). This credit may be withheld if, for example, it is clear that the offender is only pleading guilty because the prosecution case against him is overwhelming.

The court is specifically required to have regard to when the defendant pleads guilty. In *R v Barber* [2001] EWCA Crim 2267; [2002] 1 Cr App R(S) 130, the Court of Appeal said that it is of the greatest importance that those who enter pleas of guilty before venue is decided receive the maximum possible discount for so doing. The court said that pleas entered before venue has been decided attract a greater discount than pleas which are delayed and entered to an indictment in the Crown Court. The appropriate discount for a prompt guilty plea entered at the Crown Court to an offence triable only on indictment is one-third; however, a greater discount than one-third is often appropriate for a plea entered before venue is decided in relation to an offence triable either way. The court did not specify how much greater than one-third the discount should be.

In the case of an offence which is triable either way, the earliest stage at which the defendant can effectively enter a plea of guilty is at the 'plea before venue' hearing. If the defendant indicates an intention to plead not guilty (or gives no indication of likely plea) at the 'plea before venue' hearing, but then (at the trial) enters a plea of guilty, he may forfeit some of the credit which he would otherwise have earned for pleading guilty. In the case of an offence which is triable only on indictment, the earliest point at which the defendant can plead guilty is when he is arraigned in the Crown Court; however, the defendant can nevertheless give an informal indication that he intends to plead guilty at an earlier stage.

Section 152 of the 2000 Act (and s 174(2)(d) of the Criminal Justice Act 2003) makes it mandatory for a sentencing judge to state in express terms that account was taken of any guilty plea before imposing sentence; however, it was held in *R v Wharton* [2001] EWCA Crim 622; (2001) *The Times*, 27 March, that this requirement is purely procedural and so the court, on an appeal, is not required to interfere with what is otherwise an appropriate sentence, notwithstanding the fact that the sentencer failed to state expressly that the guilty plea had been taken into account.

In *R v Marsh* [2002] EWCA Crim 551; [2002] 2 Cr App R(S) 98, the judge had refused to give any discount for the defendant's guilty plea on the basis that he felt that the Crown had wrongly decided to accept pleas to lesser offences. It was held that he had erred in not giving some discount for the guilty plea. A judge cannot pass a

sentence which reflects charges which the Crown has chosen not to pursue. In *R v Wilson* [2004] EWCA Crim 281; (2004) *The Times*, 12 February, the appellant argued that his sentence was manifestly excessive because insufficient account had been taken of his offer of early guilty pleas. At the plea and directions hearing, offers of pleas of guilty were made to the offences to which the appellant ultimately pleaded guilty, but prosecuting counsel took the view that he was not in a position to decide what to do about two lesser pleas on the indictment. The matter was adjourned. No further steps were taken either by counsel for the defence or by counsel for the prosecution, and so the case came on for trial. The appellant, who pleaded guilty at the start of trial, argued that this should not redound to his disadvantage, since he had been prepared to plead guilty at an earlier stage. The Court of Appeal held that if a defendant, advised properly on the nature of his pleas, wishes to gain full credit for those pleas, those pleas must be entered at the first available opportunity. If there is a practice of delaying the entering of a guilty plea until after plea and directions, in order to maintain a negotiating advantage, then it should stop. Full credit will not be given for a plea that could have been entered earlier. It is always unacceptable that the discussion as to the nature of the pleas to be tendered should be left from the plea and directions hearing to the morning of the trial. The court said that it behoves all members of the Bar conducting such litigation to ensure that trials take place only when all avenues for discussion have been explored and exhausted.

Credit should also be given if the offender has assisted the police, perhaps by helping them to trace stolen property or to arrest other offenders. Where an accomplice pleads guilty and gives evidence for the prosecution against his erstwhile co-defendants, substantial credit should be given. In *R v Wood* [1997] 1 Cr App R(S) 347, the Court of Appeal said that the discount for someone who 'turns Queen's evidence' (that is, gives evidence against an accomplice) should reflect the seriousness of the offence, the importance of the evidence, and the effect which giving the evidence will have on the future circumstances of the witness (for example, placing him in danger of retribution).

In *R v A (Informer: Reduction of Sentence)* [1999] 1 Cr App R(S) 52, the Court of Appeal reiterated that where an offender gives information which is accurate, detailed, useful and hitherto unknown to the authorities, enabling serious criminal activity to be stopped and serious criminals brought to book, a substantial discount in sentence may be appropriate. Where, by supplying such valuable information, the offender exposes himself or his family to personal jeopardy, this should be taken into account. However, where the offender gives information to the authorities after he has been sentenced, the Court of Appeal will not normally take account of that information. On the other hand, if the offender expresses willingness to help prior to sentence but the value of the help is not fully appreciated at that stage, or the help thereafter given greatly exceeds the help anticipated by the sentencer, the Court of Appeal can adjust the sentence to reflect the value of the help given after sentence. In *R v R (Informer: Reduction in Sentence)* (2002) *The Times*, 18 February, the Court of Appeal said that where the defendant pleads guilty and, within a reasonable time of sentence being passed, gives information to the authorities (albeit in relation to a different case), he is entitled to rely on that subsequent information. Information given in those circumstances, however, will not carry the same discount potential as would have been the case had the same information been provided prior to sentence.

It is also very good mitigation, because it is a sign of remorse, if the offender has tried to compensate the victim of the crime.

The other side of the coin is that the defendant should not be penalised for pleading not guilty. In *R v Blaize* (1997) *The Times*, 12 June, for example, the Court of Appeal said that a defendant ought to be sentenced for the offence of which he has been convicted, not for the manner in which the defence was conducted. By contesting the charge, the defendant loses the benefit of the discount which a plea of guilty usually earns but, by pleading not guilty, the defendant does not run the risk of the sentence being increased. It followed, said the Court of Appeal, that false accusations of racial prejudice made in the course of the defence case should not serve to increase the sentence imposed on conviction.

The system of giving a discount for a guilty plea has been heavily criticised. See, for example, Henham, R, 'Bargain justice and justice on demand? Sentence discounts and the criminal process' (1999) 62 MLR 515 and Darbyshire, P, 'The mischief of plea bargaining and sentencing rewards' [2000] Crim LR 895.

In para 102 of Chapter 10 his *Review of the Criminal Courts of England and Wales*, Lord Justice Auld considers the arguments that have been put forward against having a system of discounting sentence for pleas of guilty (for example, by Andrew Ashworth in *The Criminal Process: An Evaluative Study* (OUP, 1998, pp 276–97) and Penny Darbyshire in 'The mischief of plea bargaining and sentencing rewards' [2000] Crim LR 895). He summarises the arguments against discounts for guilty pleas as follows:

- defendants who plead guilty, and by that means secure a lower sentence than would have been imposed on conviction, receive a benefit that they do not deserve, since a plea of guilty does not reduce their culpability or need for punishment and/or containment;
- it is contrary to the presumption of innocence and, by implication, the defendant's entitlement to require the prosecution to prove his guilt that, as a result of requiring it to do so, he should receive a more severe sentence than if he had admitted guilt;
- although a defendant can waive that entitlement, a system of discounting sentences is an incentive and is therefore capable of amounting to an improper pressure on him to do so;
- in other jurisdictions, for example, Scotland, no discount is given for a plea and to do so would be regarded as an improper inducement; and in many European countries, at least formally, admission of guilt is not a mitigating factor for the purpose of determining sentence;
- victims, though relieved of the ordeal of having to give evidence, may be unhappy about the lower sentence secured by the plea and untested mitigation; and
- discounting sentence for pleas of guilty indirectly discriminates against defendants from ethnic minorities who, regardless of their guilt or innocence, tend to maintain a plea of not guilty and, in consequence on conviction, face a greater risk of custody and longer sentences than white offenders.

Having considered and rejected each of these arguments, Lord Justice Auld concludes (Recommendation 186) that there should be a 'system of sentencing discounts graduated so that the earlier the tender of plea of guilty the higher the discount for it'.

14.9.2 Previous convictions

Section 151(1) of the Powers of Criminal Courts (Sentencing) Act 2000 states that:

> In considering the seriousness of any offence, the court may take into account any previous convictions of the offender or any failure of his to respond to previous sentences.

The statute is, however, silent on what effect previous convictions should have. The best view appears to be that expressed in *R v Carlton* (1994) 15 Cr App R(S) 335, namely that s 151(1) preserves the common law principle that in fixing the sentence to be imposed, the starting point is to assess the seriousness of the offence. A more lenient sentence can be imposed than that justified by the seriousness of the offence if the defendant is of previous good character. The effect of previous convictions is that the offender is deprived of what would otherwise be the very strong mitigation that he has no previous convictions. Thus, a defendant who has previous convictions will not receive the discount in sentence which a person who does not have previous convictions will receive. It would, however, be wrong in principle to impose a sentence greater than that appropriate to the seriousness of the offence merely because the offender has previous convictions.

Thus, the more previous convictions recorded against an offender, the greater the loss of 'good character' mitigation. This effect is sometimes called 'progressive loss of mitigation'. What the court must not do is to impose a sentence greater than that justified by the seriousness of the offence merely because the offender has previous convictions. To do so is, in effect, to sentence the defendant again for his previous misdemeanours (see *R v Queen* (1981) 3 Cr App R(S) 245). So, to take a case where the custody threshold has been met, if the appropriate sentence is between six and nine months, an offender with previous convictions might receive a sentence closer to nine months than six. However, it would be wrong in such a case to impose 12 months.

If the offender has previous convictions, but those convictions were some time ago, this conviction-free period should be taken into account when sentence is passed.

It has frequently been recognised (for example, in *R v Bowles* [1996] 2 Cr App R(S) 248) that there are occasions when, in the case of persistent offenders, it is appropriate to impose a community order, rather than a custodial sentence, provided that there is sufficient reason to think that it might be possible to break the defendant's cycle of offending once and for all. To take such a course of action, the court should be satisfied that the offender is highly motivated to change his ways.

It is also very strong mitigation to have good character that goes beyond merely the absence of previous convictions. For example, in *R v Clark (Joan)* (1999) *The Times*, 27 January, the defendant had defrauded the public of a total of £18,000 over a period of six years (a very serious offence, almost certain to carry a lengthy prison sentence). However, there was a moving tribute from the nephews and nieces whom she had brought up following the death of their mother, and her parish priest gave evidence of a number of local community and charitable activities with which she had been involved. The Court of Appeal held (maybe a little surprisingly) that the judge should have placed greater weight on her positive good character (that is, good character going beyond the legal sense of an absence of convictions); the sentence of six months' imprisonment was reduced to seven days.

Section 143(2) of the Criminal Justice Act 2003, which replaces s 151 of the 2000 Act, appears to place greater emphasis on previous convictions. It says that:

In considering the seriousness of an offence ('the current offence') committed by an offender who has one or more previous convictions, the court must treat each previous conviction as an aggravating factor if (in the case of that conviction) the court considers that it can reasonably be so treated having regard, in particular, to—

(a) the nature of the offence to which the conviction relates and its relevance to the current offence, and

(b) the time that has elapsed since the conviction.

In essence, however, this guidance reflects the existing practice of the courts, namely that the existence of previous convictions results in a progressive loss of mitigation.

14.9.3 Failures to respond

The provision in s 151(1) of the Powers of Criminal Courts (Sentencing) Act 2000 which entitles the court to take account of failure to respond to previous sentences operates in this way: if the sentence appropriate to the seriousness of the offence is a custodial sentence but it is argued on behalf of the defendant that a non-custodial sentence should be imposed, that argument can be rejected if the offender has previously been given a community sentence but has nonetheless re-offended. Re-offending may be taken as showing that non-custodial sentences do not prevent this offender from re-offending (see *R v Oliver and Little* [1993] 1 WLR 177).

This argument is strongest where the offender has committed offences whilst being subject to a community order.

If some time has elapsed since the offender's last conviction, some credit may be given for the conviction-free period in determining the effectiveness of non-custodial sentences in preventing the offender from re-offending.

In *R v Southwark Crown Court ex p Ager* (1990) 91 Cr App R 322, it was held (interpreting earlier legislation) that a failure to respond can only be established by the existence of at least two previous sentences.

Under the Criminal Justice Act 1991, conditional discharges, fines and community orders are all regarded as sentences for these purposes.

The provision about failures to respond does not feature in the Criminal Justice Act 2003 (which repeals s 151 of the 2000 Act). However, the fact that the offender has previously received non-custodial sentences, and yet has re-offended, may well be relevant under s 143(2) of the Act (quoted above).

14.9.4 Other factors

Mitigation may be derived from the personal circumstances of the offender. The courts tend to look more favourably on people who have stable homes and secure jobs, partly by giving credit for a past contribution to society and partly because such people have more to lose as a result of acquiring a criminal record (effectively a punishment in addition to the sentence imposed by the court).

In appropriate cases, a plea in mitigation should try to explain why the offender has turned to crime. For example, it may well be that a person with no previous

convictions suddenly starts committing offences at a time when suffering stress at work or as a result of a family break-up. A related argument is that, if the source of the stress has been removed, the risk of re-offending is negligible. See, for example, *R v Khan* (1994) *The Times*, 24 February and *R v Edney* (1994) 15 Cr App R(S) 889.

The age of the offender may be relevant. Account is taken particularly of the youth of an offender, perhaps because the young are more easily led astray. However, in *R v Dodds* (1997) *The Times*, 28 January, the Court of Appeal said that, in a serious case, such as aggravated burglary involving the use of violence, a substantial reduction in sentence should no longer be given because of the offender's youth. It should also be added that where an offence is committed predominantly by young offenders (such as taking cars without the owner's consent), the fact that the offender is young will not amount to mitigation.

Account is also taken of any mental disorder from which the offender is suffering.

The fact that the offender was acting under the influence of drink or drugs is regarded by some as a mitigating factor on the basis that the offender did not know what he was doing. Others, however, regard it as an aggravating factor that the offender deprived himself of self-control.

In some cases, it will be appropriate to consider the likely effect of a particular sentence on people other than the offender. For example, if a single parent is sent to prison, the children may well have to go into the care of the local authority.

14.9.5 Associated offences

In assessing seriousness where there is more than one offence, the court looks at the seriousness of the combination of associated offences.

Section 161(1) of the Powers of Criminal Courts (Sentencing) Act 2000 (which is not affected by the Criminal Justice Act 2003) provides that an offence is associated with another offence (which we may call the main offence) if:

- it is an offence of which the defendant has been convicted, or for which he is to be sentenced, in the same proceedings as the main offence; or
- it is an offence which the offender has asked the court to take into consideration when passing sentence for the main offence.

In *R v Godfrey* (1993) 14 Cr App R(S) 804, it was held that if the defendant is being re-sentenced for an offence in respect of which a conditional discharge was imposed at the same time as he is being sentenced for the offence which put him in breach of the conditional discharge, the earlier offence is associated with the later one. The same would apply where the offender is re-sentenced following the revocation of a community sentence.

In *R v Crawford* (1993) 14 Cr App R(S) 782 and *R v McQuillan* (1994) 15 Cr App R(S) 159, it was held that where an offence is committed in breach of a suspended sentence, the present offence and the offence for which the suspended sentence was imposed are not associated offences. This is because the court is not imposing a sentence for the earlier offence, but merely activating a sentence imposed on an earlier occasion.

14.10 RULE THAT THE DEFENDANT SHOULD BE SENTENCED ONLY FOR OFFENCES OF WHICH HE HAS BEEN CONVICTED AND EXCEPTIONS TO THAT RULE

It is an important principle of sentencing that the offender should only be sentenced for offences to which he has pleaded guilty or been found guilty. For example, if the offender is charged with an indictment containing a count alleging wounding with intent (s 18 of the Offences Against the Person Act 1861) and an alternative count alleging unlawful wounding (s 20), and the jury acquits the offender of the s 18 offence but convicts him of the s 20 offence, the judge must ensure that the sentence reflects the fact that the offender is guilty only of the lesser offence. This is so even if the judge disagrees with the verdict of the jury. The same applies where the prosecution agree to accept a plea of guilty to a lesser offence and the more serious offence is left on the file or the prosecution offer no evidence in respect of it (see *R v Booker* (1982) 4 Cr App R(S) 53; *R v Stubbs* (1988) 88 Cr App R 53).

A good example of the operation of this principle is to be found in *R v Lawrence* (1981) 3 Cr App R(S) 49. The defendant was charged with two offences under the Misuse of Drugs Act 1971; he pleaded guilty to cultivating cannabis and the prosecution did not proceed with a count alleging possession of cannabis with intent to supply. The Court of Appeal reduced his sentence because it was apparent that the judge had sentenced him on the basis that he was growing cannabis in order to sell it.

Moreover, the judge must not sentence the offender on the basis that he has committed similar offences on other occasions, even if the circumstances of the offence of which the defendant has been convicted (or even admissions made by the defendant to the police) suggest that the offence of which the defendant has been convicted is just part of a course of criminal conduct (*R v Ayensu* (1982) 4 Cr App R(S) 248; *R v Reeves* (1983) 5 Cr App R(S) 292).

In *R v Perkins* (1994) 15 Cr App R(S) 402, the defendant was accused of breaching a notice under planning legislation preventing him from tipping waste onto certain land. The summons alleged a breach of the notice on one particular day. However, the judge imposed a fine on the basis not of one incident, but on the basis that breaches of the notice had been taking place over an extensive period of several months. The Court of Appeal said that since the basis of the appellant's conviction was a single breach of the notice, that should be the basis of the sentence. The appellant had not admitted other breaches of the notice and so should only have been sentenced for the offence of which he had actually been convicted.

The same principle applies to compensation orders. In *R v Crutchley and Tonks* (1994) 15 Cr App R(S) 627, the offenders pleaded guilty to specimen offences arising out of a social security fraud; the appellants accepted that the charges to which they had pleaded guilty were sample counts representing a substantial number of other offences. However, no other offences were taken into consideration. The compensation order made by the Crown Court reflected the whole amount lost as a result of the fraud, not just the offences to which the appellants had pleaded guilty. The Court of Appeal held that there was no power to make such an order since it was not open to the court to make a compensation order in respect of loss or damage arising from offences which, even though admitted by the defendant, have not been subject to a conviction and have not been taken into consideration.

14.10.1 Offences taken into consideration ('TICs')

It is very common for an offender to ask for offences with which he is not charged to be taken into consideration when he is sentenced for offences with which he is charged and to which he pleads guilty. These other offences are colloquially known as 'TICs'.

Suppose that a person is arrested for an offence and when he is interviewed by the police admits that he has committed a large number of similar offences. In such a case, the defendant is usually charged with a number of the offences which he has admitted. The prosecution also draw up a list of the other offences which the offender has admitted to the police. The offender is asked to sign the list to confirm that he wishes those offences to be taken into consideration. Any offences which he subsequently denies should be deleted from the list.

When the prosecution summarise the facts of the case, they will refer to the list of TICs and the court will ask the offender to confirm that he wishes the offences to be taken into consideration.

The offender does not stand convicted of offences which are taken into consideration. This means that the maximum sentence which the court may impose is fixed by the offences to which the offender has pleaded guilty or of which he has been found guilty.

It follows from this that no separate penalty can be imposed in respect of an offence which has been taken into consideration. However, TICs are regarded as associated offences under s 161 of the Powers of Criminal Courts (Sentencing) Act 2000 and so the presence of TICs may result in an increase in the sentence imposed for the offences of which the defendant actually stands convicted.

Because the offender does not stand convicted of offences which have been taken into consideration, the doctrine of *autrefois convict* does not apply to those offences (*R v Nicholson* [1947] 2 All ER 535). Thus, in theory, the offender could subsequently be prosecuted for offences which have been taken into consideration. However, such action would only be taken in exceptional circumstances.

There is no statutory basis for the practice of taking offences into consideration. However, it enables the police to close their files on the offences which have been dealt with in this way (which has a good effect on that force's 'clear up rate'). As far as the offender is concerned, although the existence of TICs may result in a slightly increased sentence, the defendant is able to 'wipe the slate clean' (which is a good indicator of remorse) at a minimal cost in terms of increased sentence. The amount of the increase will almost certainly be considerably less than the sentence would have been had the offences been prosecuted separately.

The court has a discretion whether or not to comply with the defendant's request to take offences into consideration. There is very little authority on the subject, but it is regarded as inappropriate for offences to be taken into consideration if they are of a different type to the offence(s) of which the defendant actually stands convicted. In *R v Simons* [1953] 1 WLR 1014, it was held that magistrates should not take into consideration offences which are triable only on indictment. In *R v Collins* [1947] KB 560, it was held that a court should not take into consideration offences which carry endorsement or disqualification from driving unless the offences of which the offender stands convicted also carry such penalty.

14.10.2 Specimen or sample counts

A 'specimen' (or 'sample') count is where the defendant is charged with one or more offences occurring on specific occasions, but the prosecution allege that such conduct was representative of other criminal conduct of the same kind on other occasions which are not the subject of specific charges. Take, for example, the case of a defendant who dishonestly receives a stolen cheque book and then dishonestly obtains property using each of the 20 cheques: if the indictment contains one count of receiving (the cheque book itself) and, say, three counts of obtaining property by deception (the use of three of the 20 cheques), those three counts would be sample counts.

In a number of cases, such as *R v Huchison* [1972] 1 WLR 398, *R v McKenzie* (1984) 6 Cr App R(S) 99 and *R v Burfoot* (1990) 12 Cr App R(S) 252, the Court of Appeal made it clear that the offender could only be sentenced on the basis that the counts of which he stood convicted were sample counts, illustrative of an overall course of conduct (rather than being sentenced on the basis that he had only committed the offences of which he stood convicted), if the offender accepted that the convictions represented an overall course of conduct. For example, in *R v Clark* [1996] 2 Cr App R(S) 351, the appellant was convicted of a single count of indecent assault. This single count was said by the prosecution to reflect a series of offences committed over a two year period. However, the appellant did not admit committing any offence. The judge passed sentence on the basis that the defendant had committed a series of offences. The Court of Appeal said that, having been convicted on a single count particularising a single act and not having admitted any offence beyond that, the appellant could only be sentenced on the basis of that single act.

However, in *R v Kidd* [1998] 1 WLR 604, the Court of Appeal went further and effectively put a stop to the practice of using counts as 'specimen counts'. The court held that the defendant can only be sentenced for an offence which has been proved against him (that is, where he pleads guilty to it or is found guilty of it) or which he has asked the court to take into consideration when passing sentence. Therefore, when passing sentence, the court must not take account of the fact that the charges are said by the prosecution to be 'specimen' or 'sample' charges. If the prosecution want other incidents to be taken account of, those other incidents must be the subject of individual charges (or offences 'taken into consideration' under the procedure set out in the previous section). In *R v Rosenburg* [1999] 1 Cr App R(S) 365 and *R v T (Michael Patrick)* [1999] 1 Cr App R(S) 419, the Court of Appeal repeated that a defendant should not be sentenced for offences of which he has not been convicted (whether by pleading guilty or being found guilty) and which he has not asked the court to take into consideration under the TIC procedure.

It should be noted, however, that if the prosecution do use specimen counts, despite the prohibition in *R v Kidd*, but the offender pleads guilty to an indictment on an agreed factual basis that it charges a course of conduct involving multiple offences, he is admitting to having committed those multiple offences and may therefore be lawfully sentenced accordingly (*Attorney General's Reference (No 82 of 2002)* [2003] EWCA Crim 1078; [2003] 2 Cr App R(S) 115).

14.11 SENTENCING GUIDELINES

There are currently two sources of guidelines: sentencing guidelines issued by the Magistrates' Association (for offences triable in the magistrates' court) and guideline judgments of the Court of Appeal (for some offences triable in the Crown Court). The former contain guidance on 'entry points' (that is, the type of sentence likely to be imposed for a particular offence); the latter give guidance on likely length of prison sentence. Both sources are useful for identifying aggravating and mitigation factors associated with particular offences.

Prior to the passing of the Criminal Justice Act 2003, the Court of Appeal was assisted in its task of handing down sentencing guidelines for particular offences by the Sentencing Advisory Panel. The Panel would identify those offences where it felt that guidelines (or revised guidelines) were required, and would suggest specific guidelines to the Court of Appeal. It was a matter for the Court of Appeal whether it acceded to the suggestion that it lay down guidelines for a particular offence, and it was open to the Court of Appeal to accept or reject (wholly or in part) the suggestions made by the Panel.

Dealing with the Sentencing Advisory Panel, the *Review of the Criminal Courts of England and Wales* by Lord Justice Auld recommended as follows:

324 The law should be amended to widen the remit of the Sentencing Advisory Panel to include general principles of sentencing, in particular as to the courts' use of the various sentencing options available to them regardless of the category of offence.

325 The law should be amended, to enable the Court of Appeal to work more closely with and respond more speedily to the Panel's advice, by empowering it to issue guidelines without having to tie them to a specific appeal before it.

To ensure consistency in applying these principles (especially as regards the sentencing of persistent offenders), the Halliday Report called for new guidelines to be provided for sentencers. The Report said that these guidelines should apply to all criminal courts (rather than having separate guidelines for magistrates' courts and the Crown Court). The guidelines should:

- specify graded levels of seriousness of offence;
- provide 'entry points' of sentence severity in relation to each level of seriousness;
- set out how severity of sentence should increase in relation to numbers and types of previous convictions;
- explain other possible grounds for mitigation and aggravation.

The Report argued that responsibility for producing, monitoring, revising and accounting for the guidelines should be placed on an independent judicial body. The Report sets out various options for the composition of this body:

- the Court of Appeal (Criminal Division) sitting in a new capacity, with the Sentencing Advisory Panel in an expanded remit providing a resource to the court;
- a new judicial body set up for the purpose, which would be independent of the Court of Appeal, but under strong judicial leadership complemented by professionals and academics. The Sentencing Advisory Panel could be subsumed within this body; or
- an independent body with a more mixed membership, not necessarily judicially dominated, and into which the Sentencing Advisory Panel would be subsumed.

Rather than widening the remit of the Sentencing Advisory Panel, the Criminal Justice Act 2003 creates a new body, the 'Sentencing Guidelines Council', which (working alongside the Panel) takes over responsibility for issuing guidelines on sentencing matters. These provisions came into effect in February 2004. Section 167 of the 2003 Act establishes the Sentencing Guidelines Council. The Council is to be chaired by the Lord Chief Justice and is to comprise seven other 'judicial members' (appointed by the Lord Chancellor after consultation with the Secretary of State and the Lord Chief Justice) and four 'non-judicial members' (appointed by the Secretary of State after consultation with the Lord Chancellor and the Lord Chief Justice). To be eligible to act as one of the judicial members, a person must be a Lord Justice of Appeal, a High Court judge, a Circuit judge, a District judge (magistrates' courts) or a lay justice; the judicial members must include a Circuit judge, a District judge (magistrates' courts) and a lay justice. To be eligible for appointment as a non-judicial member, a person must have experience in policing, criminal prosecution, criminal defence, or the promotion of the welfare of victims of crime; the non-judicial members must include at least one person with experience in each of these areas. Section 167(9) empowers the Secretary of State to appoint a person with experience of sentencing policy and the administration of sentences to attend and speak at any meeting of the Council.

The function of the Sentencing Guidelines Council is to promulgate guidelines to enable all courts dealing with criminal cases to approach the sentencing of offenders from a common starting point. The new Council will work alongside, not supplant or replace, the Sentencing Advisory Panel. To make this clear, s 169(1) provides that 'There shall continue to be a Sentencing Advisory Panel ... constituted by the Lord Chancellor after consultation with the Secretary of State and the Lord Chief Justice'.

The functions of the Council are set out in s 170 of the 2003 Act. This section provides as follows:

Guidelines relating to sentencing and allocation

(1) In this Chapter—

    (a) 'sentencing guidelines' means guidelines relating to the sentencing of offenders, which may be general in nature or limited to a particular category of offence or offender, and

    (b) 'allocation guidelines' means guidelines relating to decisions by a magistrates' court under section 19 of the Magistrates' Courts Act 1980 as to whether an offence is more suitable for summary trial or trial on indictment.

(2) The Secretary of State may at any time propose to the Council—

    (a) that sentencing guidelines be framed or revised by the Council—

        (i) in respect of offences or offenders of a particular category, or

        (ii) in respect of a particular matter affecting sentencing, or

    (b) that allocation guidelines be framed or revised by the Council.

(3) The Council may from time to time consider whether to frame sentencing guidelines or allocation guidelines and, if it receives—

    (a) a proposal under section 171(2) from the Panel, or

    (b) a proposal under sub-section (2) from the Secretary of State,

    must consider whether to do so.

(4) Where sentencing guidelines or allocation guidelines have been issued by the Council as definitive guidelines, the Council must from time to time (and, in

particular, if it receives a proposal under section 171(2) from the Panel or under sub-section (2) from the Secretary of State) consider whether to revise them.

(5) Where the Council decides to frame or revise sentencing guidelines, the matters to which the Council must have regard include—

(a) the need to promote consistency in sentencing,

(b) the sentences imposed by courts in England and Wales for offences to which the guidelines relate,

(c) the cost of different sentences and their relative effectiveness in preventing re-offending,

(d) the need to promote public confidence in the criminal justice system, and

(e) the views communicated to the Council, in accordance with section 171(3)(b), by the Panel.

(6) Where the Council decides to frame or revise allocation guidelines, the matters to which the Council must have regard include—

(a) the need to promote consistency in decisions under section 19 of the Magistrates' Courts Act 1980, and

(b) the views communicated to the Council, in accordance with section 171(3)(b), by the Panel.

(7) Sentencing guidelines in respect of an offence or category of offences must include criteria for determining the seriousness of the offence or offences, including (where appropriate) criteria for determining the weight to be given to any previous convictions of offenders.

(8) Where the Council has prepared or revised any sentencing guidelines or allocation guidelines, it must—

(a) publish them as draft guidelines, and

(b) consult about the draft guidelines—

(i)   the Secretary of State,

(ii) such persons as the Lord Chancellor, after consultation with the Secretary of State, may direct, and

(iii) such other persons as the Council considers appropriate.

(9) The Council may, after making any amendment of the draft guidelines which it considers appropriate, issue the guidelines as definitive guidelines.

The role of the Sentencing Advisory Panel is set out in s 171 of the Act. This provides as follows:

Functions of Sentencing Advisory Panel in relation to guidelines

(1) Where the Council decides to frame or revise any sentencing guidelines or allocation guidelines, otherwise than in response to a proposal from the Panel under sub-section (2), the Council must notify the Panel.

(2) The Panel may at any time propose to the Council—

(a) that sentencing guidelines be framed or revised by the Council—

(i)   in respect of offences or offenders of a particular category, or

(ii) in respect of a particular matter affecting sentencing, or

(b) that allocation guidelines be framed or revised by the Council.

(3) Where the Panel receives a notification under sub-section (1) or makes a proposal under sub-section (2), the Panel must—

    (a) obtain and consider the views on the matters in issue of such persons or bodies as may be determined, after consultation with the Secretary of State and the Lord Chancellor, by the Council, and

    (b) formulate its own views on those matters and communicate them to the Council.

(4)   Paragraph (a) of sub-section (3) does not apply where the Council notifies the Panel of the Council's view that the urgency of the case makes it impracticable for the Panel to comply with that paragraph.

The two main consequences that flow from these provisions are as follows:

(a) responsibility for handing down guidance on sentencing passes from the Court of Appeal (or, in the case of offences triable summarily, the Magistrates' Association) to the Council, as does responsibility for amending the allocation/mode of trial guidelines currently contained in the 2002 consolidating Practice Direction;

(b) the Panel will make proposals for guidelines to the Council, not direct to the Court of Appeal.

The force of the sentencing guidelines issued by the Council is spelled out by s 172(1) of the 2003 Act, which states that:

(1)   Every court must—

    (a) in sentencing an offender, have regard to any guidelines which are relevant to the offender's case, and

    (b) in exercising any other function relating to the sentencing of offenders, have regard to any guidelines which are relevant to the exercise of the function.

14.12   REASONS FOR SENTENCING DECISIONS

Section 174 of the Criminal Justice Act 2003 imposes a general statutory duty on courts to give reasons for, and to explain the effect of, the sentence passed. The Explanatory Notes that accompany the Act point out that, in doing so, s 174 is seeking to bring together in a single provision many of the obligations on a court to give reasons when passing sentence which are currently scattered across sentencing legislation.

To achieve this objective, s 174(1) provides that:

… any court passing sentence on an offender—

    (a) must state in open court, in ordinary language and in general terms, its reasons for deciding on the sentence passed, and

    (b) must explain to the offender in ordinary language—

        (i) the effect of the sentence,

        (ii) where the offender is required to comply with any order of the court forming part of the sentence, the effects of non-compliance with the order,

        (iii) any power of the court, on the application of the offender or any other person, to vary or review any order of the court forming part of the sentence, and

        (iv) where the sentence consists of or includes a fine, the effects of failure to pay the fine.

This requires the court to explain its reasons for passing a particular sentence in non-technical terms. The aim of this is to ensure that the offender and other interested

parties (such as the victim of the offence or the family and friends of the victim) understand why this particular sentence was chosen by the court. The court is also required to explain to the offender what the sentence requires him to do, what will happen if he fails to comply, and any power that exists to vary or review the sentence.

Section 174(2) requires the court to deal with certain specific matters (as well as those set out in sub-s (1)). Under s 174(2)(a):

> ... where guidelines indicate that a sentence of a particular kind, or within a particular range, would normally be appropriate for the offence and the sentence is of a different kind, or is outside that range, state the court's reasons for deciding on a sentence of a different kind or outside that range.

Thus, where the Sentencing Guidelines Council has issued definitive guidelines relevant to the sentence, and the court departs from those guidelines, it must give reasons for doing so.

In the case of a custodial sentence or a community sentence, the court must explain why it regards the offence as being sufficiently serious to warrant such a sentence (s 174(2)(b) and (c)).

By virtue of s 174(2)(d), where, as a result of taking account of a plea of guilty:

> ... the court imposes a punishment on the offender which is less severe than the punishment it would otherwise have imposed, [it must] state that fact.

Under s 174(2)(e), the court must:

> ... mention any aggravating or mitigating factors which the court has regarded as being of particular importance.

Section 174(3) excludes from the obligations created by s 174 those cases where the sentence is fixed by law (although a separate duty to give reasons in such cases is created by s 270 of the Act) or where there is a mandatory minimum sentence under ss 110 and 111 of the Powers of Criminal Courts (Sentencing) Act 2000 (minimum sentences for repeat offenders convicted of drug trafficking or domestic burglary) and s 51A of the Firearms Act 1968 (minimum sentences for certain firearms offences).

Section 175 of the Criminal Justice Act 2003 amends s 95 of the Criminal Justice Act 1991 so as to require the Secretary of State to publish information each year on the effectiveness of sentencing in (a) preventing re-offending, and (b) in promoting public confidence in the criminal justice system (in addition to the existing obligation to publish information on race, gender and costs in the criminal justice system).

14.13 SENTENCING POWERS OF MAGISTRATES' COURTS

The sentence which may be imposed by a magistrates' court often depends on whether the offence is summary or triable either way.

14.13.1 Summary offences

The statute creating a summary offence indicates whether or not the offence is punishable with imprisonment. Prior to the changes made by the Criminal Justice Act 2003, if the summary offence is an imprisonable offence, the maximum sentence is six

months or that prescribed by the statute which creates the offence, whichever is less (s 78(1) of the Powers of Criminal Courts (Sentencing) Act 2000). If the statute creating the offence expressly overrides the limit of six months, then the statute creating the offence prevails (s 78(2)).

These powers are altered by the Criminal Justice Act 2003. Section 280 gives effect to Scheds 25 and 26. Schedule 25 lists a number of summary offences that are no longer punishable with imprisonment. Schedule 26 lists a number of summary offences where the maximum term of imprisonment is increased to 51 weeks (to fit in with the new framework of custodial sentences created by the Act). Section 281(1)–(3) empowers the Secretary of State to amend the penalty for other summary offences (that is, those not listed in Sched 25 or 26), so as to remove the possibility of imprisonment or to increase the maximum sentence to 51 weeks. Section 281(4) and (5) provides for all summary offences contained in Acts passed before or in the same Session as the 2003 Act with a maximum penalty of six months' imprisonment to have this maximum penalty raised automatically to 51 weeks.

14.13.2 Offences which are triable either way

The maximum sentence for an offence which is triable either way because it is listed in Sched 1 to the Magistrates' Courts Act 1980 is currently six months' imprisonment or a fine not exceeding £5,000 (s 32(1)).

Where the offence is triable either way because the statute creating it gives alternative penalties for summary conviction and conviction on indictment, the maximum penalty is six months' imprisonment or the term specified in the statute creating the offence, whichever is the less (s 78(1) of the Powers of Criminal Courts (Sentencing) Act 2000). If the statute creating the offence expressly overrides the six month limit, the statute creating the offence prevails (s 78(2)). The maximum fine which may be imposed is a fine not exceeding £5,000 or the amount prescribed by the statute, whichever is greater (s 32(2) of the 1980 Act).

Section 282 of the Criminal Justice Act 2003 increases the maximum custodial term that may be imposed following summary conviction of an either way offence from six months to 12 months. Furthermore, under s 154(1) of the Criminal Justice Act 2003, the powers of magistrates are extended, so that they can pass a sentence of up to 12 months' custody for a single either way offence.

14.13.3 Consecutive terms of imprisonment

Prior to amendment by the Criminal Justice Act 2003, s 133(1) of the Magistrates' Courts Act 1980 empowered a magistrates' court to order that custodial sentences (imprisonment or detention in a young offender institution) which it imposes may run concurrently or consecutively. However, the maximum aggregate sentence which may be imposed is six months (s 133(1)) unless the court is dealing with the offender for two or more offences which are triable either way; in that case, the maximum aggregate sentence is 12 months (s 133(2)). Thus, if an offender is convicted of three summary offences each of which is punishable with three months' imprisonment, the maximum aggregate term is six months; the magistrates could, for example, impose a sentence of three months on each offence but one of the terms would have to be concurrent, so that the maximum does not exceed six months; alternatively, they could

impose a sentence of two months on each to run consecutively. If the offender is being dealt with for one either way offence and a number of summary offences, the maximum aggregate sentence is six months. It is only where the court is dealing with an offender for at least two either way offences that a total of up to 12 months' imprisonment may be imposed. It should be noted that where a magistrates' court activates a suspended sentence (which it can only do if that sentence was imposed by a magistrates' court), the provisions of s 133 do not apply; the effect of this is that whilst the sentence(s) for the present offence(s) must not exceed the limit set by s 133, the suspended sentence may be activated even if doing so has the effect of imposing a total term in excess of the limit set by s 133 (*R v Chamberlain* (1992) 13 Cr App R(S) 525).

Section 155(1) amends s 133 of the Magistrates' Court Act 1980 to empower magistrates to impose consecutive sentences such that the aggregate term is up to 65 weeks (which equates roughly to 15 months). The effect of s 155 is to give magistrates the power to impose an aggregate custodial term of 65 weeks in respect of two or more offences where the terms are to be served consecutively.

14.13.4 Fines

The maximum fine for a summary offence is that prescribed by the statute which creates the offence. Most enactments refer to a level on the standard scale of fines, rather than to a specific sum of money.

The maximum fine for an either way offence is £5,000 (unless the statute creating the offence specifies a different amount).

Although there is a limit to the amount of a fine for an individual offence, there is no limit on the aggregate fine which may be imposed. Thus, if the court is dealing with an offender for 10 offences which are triable either way, it could impose a fine of £5,000 on each, making a total of £50,000.

14.13.5 Compensation orders

The maximum compensation order which can be made by a magistrates' court is £5,000 per offence, and this applies whether the offence is summary or triable either way (s 131(1) of the Powers of Criminal Courts (Sentencing) Act 2000).

Apart from the limit of £5,000 per offence, there is no limit on the aggregate amount of compensation which may be awarded.

Where the offender asks for offences to be taken into consideration, compensation may be ordered in respect of offences taken into consideration but the total amount of the order must not exceed the maximum which could be ordered for the offence(s) of which the offender has actually been convicted (s 131(2)). Thus, if the offender is convicted of three offences and asks for six others to be taken into consideration, the maximum compensation order is £15,000.

14.13.6 Other sentences

In respect of other sentences (for example, community sentences), the powers of the magistrates' courts are identical to those of the Crown Court.

14.13.7 Offenders aged 18 to 20

Where a magistrates' court is dealing with an offender aged between 18 and 20, all of the principles set out above apply, save that references to imprisonment should read detention in a young offender institution.

14.13.8 Sentencing juveniles in the magistrates' court

There are some circumstances in which a person under the age of 18 may be tried in an adult magistrates' court.

If an adult magistrates' court convicts an offender who is under 18, the following options are available to the court under s 8(8) of the Powers of Criminal Courts (Sentencing) Act 2000:

- discharge the offender absolutely or conditionally;
- impose a fine not exceeding £1,000 (£250 if the offender is under 14);
- order a parent or guardian to enter into a recognisance to take proper care of, and exercise proper control over, the offender.

In addition, the court may disqualify the offender from driving and make ancillary orders such as orders to pay compensation and costs.

If none of these powers is appropriate, the adult magistrates' court will remit the offender to the youth court to be dealt with under s 8(2) of the 2000 Act.

Note that an adult magistrates' court dealing with a juvenile cannot impose a custodial sentence or a community sentence, nor can it commit the juvenile to the Crown Court for sentence.

14.13.9 Sentencing the defendant in his absence

Section 11 of the Magistrates' Courts Act 1980 empowers a magistrates' court to try a defendant in his absence in certain circumstances. This power extends to sentencing a defendant who has been convicted in his absence. The power to sentence a defendant in his absence is subject to two restrictions:

- a person may not be sentenced to a custodial sentence in his absence (s 11(3)); and
- a person may not have any disqualification imposed on him in his absence (s 11(4)). Section 11(4) applies to any disqualification and so would include, for example, the most common disqualification, namely, disqualification from driving under the Road Traffic Offenders Act 1988, but would also include, for example, disqualification from keeping an animal under the Protection of Animals (Amendment) Act 1954.

If a custodial sentence or a disqualification is imposed in the absence of the defendant, the order is a nullity and would be quashed by the Divisional Court on an application for judicial review (*R v Llandrindod Wells Justices ex p Gibson* [1968] 1 WLR 598; [1968] 2 All ER 20).

Where the defendant has pleaded guilty by post under s 12 of the Magistrates' Courts Act 1980, the court will have to adjourn the case if it is minded to impose a custodial sentence or to make an order involving disqualification. There is no power to

issue an arrest warrant against the defendant unless the court has adjourned once and the defendant fails to appear on the occasion of the adjourned hearing.

Where the defendant was tried in his absence under s 11, the court has the power to issue a warrant for the defendant's arrest under s 13(1), provided that the offence is an imprisonable one (s 13(3)(a)). This power also applies if the defendant has been convicted of a non-imprisonable offence provided that the court is minded to impose a disqualification on the defendant (s 13(3)(b)).

14.14 SENTENCING POWERS OF YOUTH COURTS

Under ss 100 and 101 of the Powers of Criminal Courts (Sentencing) Act 2000, where the offender has attained the age of 12 at the date of conviction (which is the relevant date for determining the offender's age for sentencing purposes (*R v Danga* [1992] QB 476)), the youth court may impose a detention and training order for up to 24 months.

Note that the youth court cannot make an order for long-term detention under s 91 of the Powers of Criminal Courts (Sentencing) Act 2000, as this power can only be exercised by the Crown Court.

The maximum fine which the youth court can impose is £1,000 per offence (£250 if the offender is under 14).

As regards other sentences, the powers of the youth court are identical to the Crown Court.

14.15 DUTIES OF COUNSEL

In *R v Hartrey* (1993) 14 Cr App R(S) 507 and in *R v Street* (1997) 161 JP 281, the Court of Appeal reiterated that it is the duty of both prosecution and defence counsel to acquaint themselves with the sentencing powers of the court in the particular case, so that they know what options are available to the judge, and to correct the judge if he passes a sentence which is unlawful. This principle applies equally in the magistrates' court. In *Attorney General's Reference (No 52 of 2003)* [2003] EWCA Crim 3731; (2003) *The Times*, 12 December, the Court of Appeal (doubtless mindful of the ever-increasing complexity of the law of sentencing) stated that it is the duty of prosecuting counsel to draw to a sentencing judge's attention any relevant guideline cases before sentence is passed, and to have copies of those cases available so that the judge can look at them if he wishes to do so.

14.16 DEFERRING SENTENCE

Section 1 of the Powers of Criminal Courts (Sentencing) Act 2000 empowers a court to defer passing sentence on an offender for up to six months. The court may only defer sentence if the offender consents and if the court considers that it is in the interests of justice to do so, having regard to the nature of the offence and the character and circumstances of the offender. The purpose of deferring sentence is to enable the court to have regard to the offender's conduct after conviction (including, where appropriate, the making by him of reparation for the offence) or to any change in the

offender's circumstances. When sentence is deferred, this does not count as a remand and so bail does not have to be granted in order that the offender remain at liberty. However, if the defendant fails to appear on the date to which sentence is deferred, a bench warrant for his arrest may be issued. When the court eventually deals with the offender, it may deal with him in any way in which he could have been dealt with by the court which deferred sentence. Where sentence is deferred by a magistrates' court, the magistrates retain their power to commit the defendant for sentence to the Crown Court at the end of the period of deferment.

Section 278 of the Criminal Justice Act 2003 gives effect to Sched 23, which amends s 1 of the 2000 Act and inserts new provisions about deferment of sentence into the Act. The court retains the power to defer sentence for up to six months in order to have regard to the conduct of the offender and any change in his circumstances. However, the court is also empowered to require the offender to undertake reparative activities during the period of deferment; in assessing the offender's conduct during the deferment period, the court will assess how well the offender has complied with such requirements.

The amended provisions are as follows:

1   *Deferment of sentence*

(1)   The Crown Court or a magistrates' court may defer passing sentence on an offender for the purpose of enabling the court, or any other court to which it falls to deal with him, to have regard in dealing with him to—

(a)   his conduct after conviction (including, where appropriate, the making by him of reparation for his offence); or

(b)   any change in his circumstances;

but this is subject to sub-sections (3) and (4) below.

(2)   Without prejudice to the generality of sub-section (1) above, the matters to which the court to which it falls to deal with the offender may have regard by virtue of paragraph (a) of that sub-section include the extent to which the offender has complied with any requirements imposed under sub-section (3)(b) below.

(3)   The power conferred by sub-section (1) above shall be exercisable only if—

(a)   the offender consents;

(b)   the offender undertakes to comply with any requirements as to his conduct during the period of the deferment that the court considers it appropriate to impose; and

(c)   the court is satisfied, having regard to the nature of the offence and the character and circumstances of the offender, that it would be in the interests of justice to exercise the power.

(4)   Any deferment under this section shall be until such date as may be specified by the court, not being more than six months after the date on which the deferment is announced by the court; and, subject to section 1D(3) below, where the passing of sentence has been deferred under this section it shall not be further so deferred.

...

(7)   Where—

(a)   a court which under this section has deferred passing sentence on an offender proposes to deal with him on the date originally specified by the court; or

(b)   the offender does not appear on the day so specified,

the court may issue a summons requiring him to appear before the court at a time and place specified in the summons, or may issue a warrant to arrest him and bring him before the court at a time and place specified in the warrant.

...

1A   *Further provision about undertakings*

(1)   Without prejudice to the generality of paragraph (b) of section 1(3) above, the requirements that may be imposed by virtue of that paragraph include requirements as to the residence of the offender during the whole or any part of the period of deferment.

(2)   Where an offender has undertaken to comply with any requirements imposed under section 1(3)(b) above the court may appoint—

(a) an officer of a local probation board; or

(b) any other person whom the court thinks appropriate,

to act as a supervisor in relation to him.

...

(4)   It shall be the duty of a supervisor appointed under sub-section (2) above—

(a) to monitor the offender's compliance with the requirements; and

(b) to provide the court to which it falls to deal with the offender in respect of the offence in question with such information as the court may require relating to the offender's compliance with the requirements.

1B   *Breach of undertakings*

(1)   A court which under section 1 above has deferred passing sentence on an offender may deal with him before the end of the period of deferment if—

(a) he appears or is brought before the court under sub-section (3) below; and

(b) the court is satisfied that he has failed to comply with one or more requirements imposed under section 1(3)(b) above in connection with the deferment.

(2)   Sub-section (3) below applies where—

(a) a court has under section 1 above deferred passing sentence on an offender;

(b) the offender undertook to comply with one or more requirements imposed under section 1(3)(b) above in connection with the deferment; and

(c) a person appointed under section 1A(2) above to act as a supervisor in relation to the offender has reported to the court that the offender has failed to comply with one or more of those requirements.

(3)   Where this sub-section applies, the court may issue—

(a) a summons requiring the offender to appear before the court at a time and place specified in the summons; or

(b) a warrant to arrest him and bring him before the court at a time and place specified in the warrant.

1C   *Conviction of offence during period of deferment*

(1)   A court which under section 1 above has deferred passing sentence on an offender may deal with him before the end of the period of deferment if during that period he is convicted in Great Britain of any offence.

(2)   Sub-section (3) below applies where a court has under section 1 above deferred passing sentence on an offender in respect of one or more offences and during

the period of deferment the offender is convicted in England and Wales of any offence ('the later offence').

(3) Where this sub-section applies, then (without prejudice to sub-section (1) above and whether or not the offender is sentenced for the later offence during the period of deferment), the court which passes sentence on him for the later offence may also, if this has not already been done, deal with him for the offence or offences for which passing of sentence has been deferred, except that—

(a) the power conferred by this sub-section shall not be exercised by a magistrates' court if the court which deferred passing sentence was the Crown Court; and

(b) the Crown Court, in exercising that power in a case in which the court which deferred passing sentence was a magistrates' court, shall not pass any sentence which could not have been passed by a magistrates' court in exercising that power.

(4) Where a court which under section 1 above has deferred passing sentence on an offender proposes to deal with him by virtue of sub-section (1) above before the end of the period of deferment, the court may issue—

(a) a summons requiring him to appear before the court at a time and place specified in the summons; or

(b) a warrant to arrest him and bring him before the court at a time and place specified in the warrant.

Under s 1D, deferment of sentence is to be regarded as an adjournment, and if the offender does not appear before the court when required to, he is to be dealt with accordingly. When the court deals with an offender at the end of the period of deferment (or earlier if he does not comply with the requirements or commits another offence), it has the same powers as if the offence had just been committed (including committal to the Crown Court for sentence where appropriate).

In *R v George* [1984] 1 WLR 1082, it was said that:

- deferring sentence is especially appropriate where there are improvements in the offender's conduct, or steps which the court wants him to take, which are not sufficiently specific to be requirements under a probation order. Sentence should not be deferred if the court's objective could be achieved by means of a community order;

- the court should make it clear to the offender why sentence is being deferred and what conduct is expected of him during the period of deferment;

- a careful note should be made by the court of what the offender is told and, ideally, the offender should have a copy of that note;

- at the end of the period of deferment, the court which passes sentence should consider whether the offender has substantially conformed with what was required of him; if the defendant has conformed with what was required of him, a non-custodial sentence should be imposed. If the defendant has not conformed, a custodial sentence may be passed but the offender should be told in what respects he has failed to conform. A fresh pre-sentence report should be available to the sentencing court.

It will always be a requirement that the offender does not commit any further offences, but merely refraining from committing further offences will not be enough. In *R v Smith* (1976) 64 Cr App R 116, for example, sentence was deferred to see if the offender could find regular work and reduce his consumption of alcohol. He did not commit

any further offences but failed to achieve either of the objectives set by the court and so a custodial sentence was upheld by the Court of Appeal.

In *Attorney General's Reference (No 22 of 1992)* [1994] 1 All ER 105, it was held that a deferred sentence is a sentence for the purposes of appeal and so the Attorney General may use his powers under s 36 of the Criminal Justice Act 1988 to appeal to the Court of Appeal on the ground that it is too lenient.

Where the offender is convicted of a further offence which was committed during the period of the deferment, the court passing sentence on him for the later offence may also pass sentence on him in respect of the offence for which sentence was deferred. The only exception to this is that if sentence on the original offence was deferred by the Crown Court, a magistrates' court cannot deal with the original offence. If sentence on the original offence was deferred by a magistrates' court and the offender is being dealt with for the later offence by the Crown Court, the Crown Court may only impose a sentence which the magistrates could have imposed when it is dealing with the original offence.

If the offender does re-offend during the period of the deferment, it is of course highly likely that a custodial sentence will be imposed for the original offence.

However, it may well be that the defendant is charged with a further offence allegedly committed during the period of the deferment but the offender has not been convicted of that offence before the date when the court passes sentence in respect of the original offence. In such a case, the allegation of a later offence should be ignored by the court dealing with the offence for which sentence was deferred. It is only where the offender is convicted of an offence committed during the period of deferment that account can be taken of the later offence when sentence is passed for the offence in respect for which sentence was deferred. An unproved allegation of a further offence should be disregarded (*R v Aquilina* (1989) 11 Cr App R(S) 431).

14.17 REHABILITATION OF OFFENDERS: SPENT CONVICTIONS

The Rehabilitation of Offenders Act 1974 allows a person who has been convicted of an offence to regard himself as rehabilitated after a period of time has elapsed and the conviction is deemed to be 'spent'. However, s 7(2) of the Rehabilitation of Offenders Act 1974 says that the provisions of the Act do not apply to criminal proceedings. Nonetheless, para I.6 of the *Practice Direction (Criminal Proceedings: Consolidation)* [2002] 1 WLR 2870 requires that:

- spent convictions which appear on an offender's record should be marked as such;
- no reference should be made in open court to any spent convictions without leave of the court, which should only be given where the interests of justice so require; and
- when passing sentence, the sentencer should make no reference to spent convictions unless it is necessary to do so to explain the sentence being passed.

In some instances, a conviction can never become spent. Sentences which are outside the scope of the Rehabilitation of Offenders Act 1974 (and so never become spent) are:

- life imprisonment (custody for life or detention during Her Majesty's pleasure in the case of young offenders);

- imprisonment (detention in a young offender institution or detention under s 91 of the Powers of Criminal Courts (Sentencing) Act 2000 in the case of young offenders) for a period exceeding 30 months.

The Rehabilitation of Offenders Act 1974 applies to all other convictions. The rehabilitation period (that is, the time which must elapse before the conviction is regarded as spent) depends on the sentence imposed for the original offence. In some cases, the rehabilitation period is shortened if the offender was under 18 at the date of conviction.

The rehabilitation periods are as follows:

- A sentence of imprisonment, detention in a young offender institution, or youth custody, for more than six months but not more than 30 months: 10 years for an adult, five years for a juvenile.
- A sentence of imprisonment, detention in a young offender institution, or youth custody, of six months or less: seven years for an adult, three and a half years for a juvenile.
- Detention and training order where person aged at least 15 at date of conviction: five years if the order exceeded six months, three and a half years if six months or less.
- Detention and training order where person aged under 15 at date of conviction: one year after the order expires.
- A fine: five years for an adult, two and a half years for a juvenile.
- A community punishment order or community punishment and rehabilitation order: five years for an adult, two and a half years for a juvenile.
- Community rehabilitation order: five years for an adult, two and a half years for a juvenile.
- Supervision order: the date the order ceases or one year, whichever is the longer.
- Attendance centre order: one year after the order expires.
- Referral order: when the contract ceases to have effect.
- Disqualification: the date the order ceases to have effect.
- Absolute discharge: six months.

The rehabilitation period for a sentence of imprisonment is the same whether the imprisonment is immediate or suspended.

In *Power v Provincial Insurance plc* (1997) 161 JP 556, it was held that, under the Rehabilitation of Offenders Act 1974, an endorsement on a driving licence is not a 'penalty' for the purposes of the 1974 Act and so the driver does not have to wait until he can apply for a 'clean' licence for the conviction to be spent. It follows that once the rehabilitation period for the fine/disqualification has expired, the driver can lawfully say to an insurer that he has not been disqualified from driving.

These rehabilitation periods only apply if the offender is not convicted of a further offence during the rehabilitation period.

If the offender is convicted of a further offence during the rehabilitation period, the rehabilitation period for the first offence continues to run until the expiry of the rehabilitation period for the subsequent offence.

14.18 REMISSION OF CASES BETWEEN MAGISTRATES' COURTS

Section 10 of the Powers of Criminal Courts (Sentencing) Act 2000 provides that:

(1) Where a person aged 18 or over ('the offender') has been convicted by a magistrates' court ('the convicting court') of an offence to which this section applies ('the instant offence') and:

   (a) it appears to the convicting court that some other magistrates' court ('the other court') has convicted him of another such offence in respect of which the other court has neither passed sentence on him nor committed him to the Crown Court for sentence nor dealt with him in any other way; and

   (b) the other court consents to his being remitted under this section to the other court, the convicting court may remit him to the other court to be dealt with in respect of the instant offence by the other court instead of by the convicting court.

(2) This section applies to:

   (a) any offence punishable with imprisonment; and

   (b) any offence in respect of which the convicting court has a power or duty to order the offender to be disqualified under section 34, 35 or 36 the Road Traffic Offenders Act 1988 (disqualification for certain motoring offences).

(3) … the other court may deal with the case in any way in which it would have power to deal with it if all proceedings relating to the instant offence which took place before the convicting court had taken place before the other court.

14.19 RESPONSIBILITY FOR ENFORCEMENT OF ORDERS

For many of the orders that can be imposed, there is a 'responsible officer'. Section 198(1) of the Criminal Justice Act 2003 sets out the duties of the responsible officer:

(a) to make any arrangements that are necessary in connection with the requirements imposed by the order,

(b) to promote the offender's compliance with those requirements, and

(c) where appropriate, to take steps to enforce those requirements.

Supervision of an offender is generally a matter for his local magistrates' court. Section 216 of the Criminal Justice Act 2003 identifies the petty sessions area to be specified in relevant orders. Under sub-s (1), a community order or suspended sentence order must specify the petty sessions area in which the offender resides or will reside; under sub-s (2), a custody plus order or an intermittent custody order must specify the petty sessions area in which the offender will reside during the licence periods.

CHAPTER 15

OFFENDERS OVER 21: CUSTODIAL SENTENCES

In this chapter, we examine the sentences of imprisonment (immediate and suspended) which may be imposed on an offender who has attained the age of 21. We look at the regime of custodial sentencing contained in the Powers of Criminal Courts (Sentencing) Act 2000 and the new regime established by the Criminal Justice Act 2003.

However, we begin by considering the statutory criteria which govern the imposition of custodial sentences; these statutory criteria apply to all custodial sentences and so are equally applicable to custodial sentences for offenders under the age of 21.

15.1 STATUTORY CRITERIA FOR IMPOSING CUSTODIAL SENTENCES

First, we consider the criteria for imposing custodial sentences under the Powers of Criminal Courts (Sentencing) Act 2000. Section 79(2) of the Powers of Criminal Courts (Sentencing) Act 2000 provides that a court shall not pass a custodial sentence on an offender unless it is of the opinion:

    (a) that the offence, or the combination of the offence and one or more offences associated with it, was so serious that only such a sentence can be justified for the offence; or

    (b) where the offence is a violent or sexual offence, that only such a sentence would be adequate to protect the public from serious harm from him.

Section 79(3) of the Act sets out a third ground for imposing a custodial sentence, namely where the offender fails to express his willingness to comply with a requirement which is proposed by the court to be included in a community rehabilitation order or supervision order and which requires an expression of such willingness.

These pre-conditions apply to sentences of imprisonment (both immediate custody and suspended sentences) and to sentences of detention in a young offender institution (offenders aged 18–20), detention and training orders (offenders under 18) and detention under s 91 of the 2000 Act (offenders under 18).

15.1.1 Seriousness of offence: s 79(2)(a) of the Powers of Criminal Courts (Sentencing) Act 2000

A very important case on the 'custody threshold' in s 79(2)(a) of the Powers of Criminal Courts (Sentencing) Act 2000 is *R v Howells* [1999] 1 WLR 307. In it, Lord Bingham CJ gave detailed guidance on the application of the test of whether an offence is so serious that only a custodial sentence can be justified. Lord Bingham described the problem of dealing with cases which are on the borderline of the custody threshold as 'one of the most elusive problems of criminal sentencing'.

Corresponding provisions in earlier legislation had been interpreted by Lawton LJ in *R v Bradbourn* (1985) 7 Cr App R(S) 180, 182 thus:

> The phrase 'so serious that a non-custodial sentence cannot be justified' comes to this: the kind of offence which when committed by a young person would make right-thinking members of the public, knowing all the facts, feel that justice had not been done by the passing of any sentence other than a custodial one.

In *R v Cox* [1993] 1 WLR 188, this 'right-thinking members of the public' test was held to apply to the slightly different criterion for custody set out in s 1(2)(a) of the Criminal Justice Act 1991 (now s 79(2)(a) of the Powers of Criminal Courts (Sentencing) Act 2000). However, in *Howells*, Lord Bingham said that this test is unhelpful, since the court has no means of ascertaining the views of right-thinking members of the public. The essential problem with the test is its circularity: the court can only regard itself as epitomising the thinking of 'right-thinking members of the public', and so the test is saying little more than 'a custodial sentence is justified if the court thinks it is justified'.

In deciding which side of the custodial/non-custodial line a case falls, Lord Bingham said that the starting point should be a consideration of the 'nature and extent to the defendant's criminal intention and the nature and extent of any injury or damage caused to the victim'. As regards the defendant's criminal intention, his Lordship re-stated the well established principle that a deliberate and premeditated offence will usually be regarded as more serious than a 'spur of the moment', unpremeditated offence. His Lordship went on to say that an offence which causes 'personal injury or mental trauma, particular if permanent, will usually be more serious than an offence which inflicts financial loss only'. Lord Bingham also pointed out that under what is now s 151 of the Powers of Criminal Courts (Sentencing) Act 2000, the court may take into account any previous convictions of the offender or any failure of his to respond to previous sentences and must, where an offence is committed while the offender was on bail, treat that fact as an aggravating factor.

Lord Bingham then went on to list a number of matters which the court should normally take into account when deciding whether or not to impose a custodial sentence in a borderline case. Those factors are as follows:

(a) An admission of responsibility for the offence. Section 152 of the Powers of Criminal Courts (Sentencing) Act 2000 requires the court to take account of the fact of a guilty plea, and also of the stage at which that plea is entered. The best mitigation obviously comes from an early admission of responsibility when the offender is first questioned by the police, together with a guilty plea tendered at the earliest opportunity (in the case of an offence which is triable either way, the guilty plea should be entered at the 'plea before venue' hearing if the offender is to receive the maximum credit for that guilty plea: *R v Rafferty* (1998) 162 JP 353). Lord Bingham added that the court should also look for 'hard evidence of genuine remorse' (for example, an expression of regret to the victim of the offence and an offer to pay compensation).

(b) Where the offence is connected with addiction to drink or drugs, the court should look favourably on an offender who has already started to take practical steps which demonstrate a genuine and self-motivated determination to rid himself of the addiction.

(c) Youth and immaturity would often justify a less rigorous penalty than that appropriate to an adult offender. (This may be contrasted with *R v Dodds* (1997) *The Times*, 28 January, where the Court of Appeal said that in a serious case, such

as aggravated burglary involving the use of violence, a substantial reduction in sentence should no longer be given because of the offender's youth.)

(d) Some measure of leniency should be extended to an offender who is of previous good character. More credit should be given to a person who can demonstrate 'positive good character' rather than just an absence of previous convictions. Lord Bingham gave examples of a 'solid employment record or faithful discharge of family duties'. The list could also include actions which have benefited the community, or charitable deeds.

(e) There should be even greater than usual reluctance to impose a custodial sentence on someone who has never before served such a sentence. The reasoning behind this is that the most traumatic part of a custodial sentence is the first part of the offender's first custodial sentence (the effect of the so-called 'clang of the prison gates'), and so the court should be reluctant to put someone through this.

Lord Bingham added that it was right for the court to bear in mind that the purpose of sentencing is to protect the public (by punishing the offender, by reforming him, or by deterring him and others from offending). In *Attorney General's References (Nos 62 and 63 of 1997); R v McMaster* [1998] 2 Cr App R(S) 300, for example, the Court of Appeal referred to the need for sentences to have a proper deterrent effect on those who embark on brutal attacks. In *R v Cunningham* [1993] 1 WLR 183, it was held that the prevalence of a particular type of offence (and public concern about it) could be regarded as an aggravating factor.

In assessing the seriousness of the offence, the court should consider the facts of the case and not just the label which is attached to the offence. Thus, although most cases involving the burglary of a dwelling house will result in a custodial sentence, domestic burglary should not be regarded as automatically so serious that a custodial sentence is justified.

Where the offender is convicted of two or more offences, the court should consider the offences together and should decide whether the combination of offences is such that a custodial sentence is justified. In *R v Oliver and Little* [1993] 1 WLR 177, the Court of Appeal considered what should be done where an offender is convicted of a number of offences, some of which merit a custodial sentence and some of which do not. It was held to be permissible to impose custodial sentences for the lesser offences but those sentences should be concurrent with the sentences for the offences which do merit custody.

In *R v Oliver and Little*, the Court of Appeal also considered the approach to be taken where a court which is sentencing an offender for one offence is also re-sentencing him for an earlier offence. For example, the earlier offence may well have been dealt with by means of a community rehabilitation order, and the court may now take the view that such an order is ineffective to prevent this offender from re-offending. The Court of Appeal said that the fact that the earlier court dealt with the offence by means of a community order does not necessarily mean that the offence was not so serious that only a custodial sentence could be justified; it may well be that the earlier court found that the custody threshold had been passed but there was sufficient personal mitigation to allow the court to pass a more lenient sentence. If the offender commits a subsequent offence and is re-sentenced to the earlier offence, he will have deprived himself of much of the mitigation which led the earlier court to pass a non-

custodial sentence for the original offence; the later court would therefore be entitled to impose a custodial sentence for that original offence.

This mirrors the approach taken in *R v Cox* [1993] 1 WLR 188. In that case, following *R v Baverstock* [1993] 1 WLR 202, the Court of Appeal pointed out that even if the court decides that an offence is sufficiently serious to justify the imposition of a custodial sentence, the court is not prevented from imposing a non-custodial sentence in the light of mitigating circumstances. Indeed, this is expressly permitted by s 158 of the Powers of Criminal Courts (Sentencing) Act 2000 .

There has been some pressure from the senior judiciary to reduce the number of defendants being sent to prison: see *R v Kefford* [2002] EWCA Crim 519; [2002] 2 Cr App R(S) 106 and *R v Baldwin* [2002] EWCA Crim 2647; (2002) *The Times*, 22 November, where the Court of Appeal encourages greater use of fines rather than imprisonment. This has to be handled quite carefully in a plea in mitigation, as it would be wrong to give the impression that the offender is trying to 'buy his way out of prison' by offering to pay a substantial fine. The essential point is that a fine can have a substantial punitive effect.

15.1.2 The custody threshold under the Criminal Justice Act 2003

The Criminal Justice Act 2003 repeals s 79 of the 2000 Act (see Pt 7 of Sched 37). However, the 2003 Act maintains the position that a custodial sentence may only be passed where no other sentence would be appropriate; in other words, the 'custody threshold' must have been crossed.

This test is set out in s 152(2), which provides:

> The court must not pass a custodial sentence unless it is of the opinion that the offence, or the combination of the offence and one or more offences associated with it, was so serious that neither a fine alone nor a community sentence can be justified for the offence.

This is subject to the rider contained in s 152(3), that:

> Nothing in sub-section (2) prevents the court from passing a custodial sentence on the offender if—
>
> (a) he fails to express his willingness to comply with a requirement which is proposed by the court to be included in a community order and which requires an expression of such willingness, or
>
> (b) he fails to comply with an order under section 161(2) (pre-sentence drug testing).

The similarity between the tests in s 79 of the 2000 Act and s 152 of the 2003 Act means that the case law decided under the former provision is likely to remain valid when the courts consider how to apply the new provision.

15.1.3 Procedural requirements before imposing a custodial sentence

Section 81(1) of the Powers of Criminal Courts (Sentencing) Act 2000 requires that the court, in order to determine whether the criteria set out in s 79(2) of the Act are satisfied, 'shall obtain and consider a pre-sentence report', unless the court considers a report to be unnecessary (s 81(2)). Such a report is prepared by a probation officer (or, in the case of a young offender, by a probation officer or a local authority social

worker). In determining the length of the sentence, s 81(4)(a) of the Powers of Criminal Courts (Sentencing) Act 2000 requires the court to take into account all available information about the circumstances of the offence(s), including aggravating and mitigating factors, and s 158(1) enables the court to take into account any mitigation put forward on behalf of the offender.

In *R v Gillette* (1999) *The Times*, 3 December, the Court of Appeal said that in all cases where a court is contemplating sentencing a defendant to prison for the first time, other than for a very short period, it should be the invariable practice that a pre-sentence report should be obtained before such a sentence is passed. However, the Court of Appeal subsequently re-considered this point in *R v Armsaramah* (2000) 164 JP 709, holding that there may be cases where it is permissible for the court to pass a first custodial sentence without first obtaining a pre-sentence report. In the instant case, it was held that the judge had been entitled to decide that a pre-sentence report would have added nothing.

Under s 79(4) of the 2000 Act (re-enacted in s 174(2)(b) of the Criminal Justice Act 2003), the court must explain to the offender in open court and in ordinary language why it is passing a custodial sentence on him.

Section 83(1) of the 2000 Act (a provision that is not repealed by the Criminal Justice Act 2003) provides that a sentence of imprisonment (whether immediate or suspended) cannot be imposed on someone who has not previously served a sentence of imprisonment (that is, was sentenced on an earlier occasion to immediate custody or received a suspended sentence which was subsequently activated) unless he is legally represented, or has refused to apply for representation funded by the Criminal Defence Service.

The provisions contained in s 81 of the 2000 Act are replaced by s 156 of the Criminal Justice Act 2003, which effectively repeats the requirements set out in that section. Section 156 requires the court to obtain and consider a pre-sentence report before deciding that a case is sufficiently serious to justify the imposition of a custodial sentence and, if so, the length of sentence that would be commensurate with the seriousness of the offence (s 156(3)). Where the offender has attained the age of 18, the court may refrain from seeking a pre-sentence report if it considers that it is unnecessary to obtain one (s 156(4)).

15.1.4 Determining length of sentence: s 80(2)(a) of the Powers of Criminal Courts (Sentencing) Act 2000

If the case is sufficiently serious to justify the imposition of a custodial sentence, the next question is how long that sentence should be. Section 80(2)(a) of the 2000 Act states that the length of the sentence, which must not exceed the maximum sentence prescribed for the offence(s) being dealt with, should be 'commensurate with the seriousness of the offence, or the combination of the offence and one or more offences associated with it'.

In *R v Cunningham* [1993] 1 WLR 183, the Court of Appeal considered the question of deterrence. Lord Taylor of Gosforth CJ said that the phrase 'commensurate with the seriousness of the offence' must mean 'commensurate with the punishment and deterrence which the seriousness of the offence requires'. However, his Lordship added the rider that s 80(2)(a) prohibits the court from adding any extra length to the

sentence which is commensurate with the seriousness of the offence, simply to make a special example of the defendant. However, Lord Taylor then went on to hold that the prevalence of the kind of offence of which the offender has been convicted is a legitimate factor in determining the length of the custodial sentence to be passed (presumably with the implication that a stiff sentence on the present occasion might make it less prevalent in the future!).

In *R v Howells* [1999] 1 WLR 307, Lord Bingham CJ endorsed the observations of Rose LJ in *R v Ollerenshaw* [1999] 1 Cr App R(S) 65. In that case, it was said that where a court is considering a comparatively short custodial sentence (that is, a sentence of about 12 months or less), it should generally ask itself (especially if the offender has not served a custodial sentence before) whether custody for an even shorter period might be equally effective in protecting the public and in punishing and deterring criminal behaviour. For example, said Rose LJ, six months might be just as effective as nine months, and two months just as effective as four months. This echoes observations made by Lord Lane CJ in *R v Bibi* [1980] 1 WLR 1193, where he said that a sentence should be 'as short as possible, consistent only with the duty to protect the interests of the public and to punish and deter the criminal'. This point will be of particular relevance where the offender has been remanded in custody prior to conviction and/or sentence: it may well be possible to mitigate on the basis that the period already spent behind bars on remand is sufficient punishment.

The Court of Appeal has laid down guidelines as to the approach to be taken to particular offences (for example, *R v Barrick* (1985) 81 Cr App R 78 and *R v Clark* [1998] 2 Cr App R 137, for theft involving breach of trust). In *R v Johnson* (1994) 15 Cr App R(S) 827, it was said that such decisions of the Court of Appeal are no more than guidelines and within those guidelines there is a great deal of flexibility. The Court of Appeal recognised that a judge has to take into account many factors when passing sentence (for example, it may be that a particular crime is too prevalent in that area, or the offence may have had a particularly distressing effect on the victim, or the offender may have behaved in an especially vicious manner). Nevertheless, judges must pay attention to the guidance given by the Court of Appeal and sentences should be broadly in line with guideline cases unless the particular case presents factors which allow the judge to depart from the tariff set by the Court of Appeal. What a judge must not do is to state that he is applying some personal tariff of his own because he feels that the range of sentences set by the Court of Appeal is wrong.

When considering earlier guideline cases on the level of sentence to be imposed for a particular offence where the statutory maximum for that offence has subsequently been increased, the court must take account of the increase in statutory maximum since the guideline case was decided and must adjust the guidelines accordingly (*R v L (Indecent Assault: Sentencing)* [1999] 1 Cr App R 117).

15.1.5 Length of sentence under the Criminal Justice Act 2003

Section 80 of the 2000 Act is repealed by the Criminal Justice Act 2003 (see Pt 7 of Sched 37). However, the provisions in the 2003 Act on length of custodial sentence are very similar. Section 153 of the 2003 Act provides as follows:

Length of discretionary custodial sentences: general provision

(1)   This section applies where a court passes a custodial sentence other than one fixed by law or falling to be imposed under section 225 or 226 [imprisonment for protection of public].

(2)   Subject to section 51A(2) of the Firearms Act 1968, sections 110(2) and 111(2) of the Sentencing Act [mandatory minimum sentences] and sections 227(2) and 228(2) of this Act [extended sentences for certain violent or sexual offences], the custodial sentence must be for the shortest term (not exceeding the permitted maximum) that in the opinion of the court is commensurate with the seriousness of the offence, or the combination of the offence and one or more offences associated with it.

The principle underpinning the restriction is that of 'just deserts', in other words that there should be a direct correlation between the sentence imposed and the seriousness of the offence that is being dealt with.

15.1.6   Public protection: s 79(2)(b) of the Powers of Criminal Courts (Sentencing) Act 2000

Protecting the public from serious harm is the second ground for imposing a custodial sentence. It is only a relevant factor where the offender has been convicted of a 'violent or sexual offence' (as defined in s 161 of the 2000 Act).

A violent offence is one 'which leads, or is intended or likely to lead, to a person's death or to physical injury to a person'. In *R v Robinson* [1993] 1 WLR 168, the Court of Appeal held that whether a particular offence is a violent offence depends on the individual facts of each case. The court also held that the phrase 'physical injury' does not require serious physical harm to be caused.

The term 'sexual offence' connotes specific sexual offences listed in s 161.

Although there is nothing to stop a magistrates' court from invoking s 79(2)(b) of the 2000 Act, it will be rare for a magistrates' court to do so. Offences where the considerations set out in s 79(2)(b) are applicable will normally be regarded by the magistrates as too serious for summary trial and so the justices are likely to refuse jurisdiction at the mode of trial hearing.

Length of sentence in such a case is governed by s 80(2)(b) of the Powers of Criminal Courts (Sentencing) Act 2000. The sentence must still not exceed the maximum term prescribed for the offence(s) being dealt with, but may be 'for such longer term ... as in the opinion of the court is necessary to protect the public from serious harm from the offender' (s 80(2)(b)). Where the court invokes s 80(2)(b) to pass a sentence longer than that commensurate with the seriousness of the offence, it must state why it is of that opinion and must explain this to the offender in ordinary language (s 80(3)).

An example of the use of s 80(2)(b) is to be found in *R v Bowler* (1994) 15 Cr App R(S) 78. The defendant pleaded guilty to indecent assault on a six year old girl: he had put his hand up her skirt and touched her genitals through her knickers. The defendant had eight previous convictions for similar offences committed on adult women. The defendant had received drug treatment to curb his offending but was unwilling to undergo any further treatment. The Court of Appeal upheld a sentence of six years' imprisonment. Even though no physical harm had been caused to any of his

previous victims, the court felt that if the offender were to re-offend by assaulting another young girl, serious psychological harm could be caused to her. Similarly, in *R v Carpenter* [1997] 1 Cr App R(S) 4, the Court of Appeal accepted that a longer than normal sentence may be appropriate even if the offence itself is towards the lower end of the scale of seriousness, but only if other factors (in this case, which involved indecent assault, breach of trust, use of alcohol to achieve seduction, lack of remorse and past offences) show that the offender is a danger to the public.

Detailed guidance on the use of sentences under s 80(2)(b) was given by the Court of Appeal in *R v Fawcett* (1983) 5 Cr App R(S) 158. For a sentence under s 80(2)(b) to be appropriate, the offender must pose a danger to the public which is more than merely minimal. A medical report should be sought first, to ensure that a medical disposal would not be more appropriate. There must be a repetition of similar offending. A longer than normal sentence might be appropriate where there is a mixture of minor offending and a severe personality disorder or other mental abnormalities. The court should hear evidence of the facts of the previous convictions. Relevant considerations would include the irrationality of the behaviour, the selection of vulnerable people or particular classes of people, unexplained severe violence, unusual obsessions or delusions, any inability on the part of the offender to understand the consequences of his actions, or lack of remorse on his part, or unwillingness on the part of the offender to accept medication. The court must be satisfied beyond reasonable doubt that such a sentence is appropriate. In *R v Auger* [1996] 1 Cr App R(S) 431 and *R v Etchells* (1991) 1 Cr App R(S) 163, the Court of Appeal emphasised that there must be evidence that the risk of further offending on the part of the defendant is of such a nature that the applicant is likely to cause serious harm – whether physical or psychological – to members of the public.

The danger of serious psychological injury to a potential future victim can trigger the power to impose a longer than normal sentence (*R v Kaye* [1996] 2 Cr App R(S) 17). However, there must be some basis in fact for the belief that future victims are likely to suffer serious psychological injury (*R v Fishwick* [1996] 1 Cr App R(S) 359).

In *R v Cameron* [2003] EWCA Crim 328; (2003) *The Times*, 12 February, the Court of Appeal said that where the judge is minded to impose a sentence which is longer than that which would be commensurate with the seriousness of the offence, he should inform counsel, so that counsel can make submissions on whether the conditions for such a sentence have been met. A longer than commensurate sentence should only be imposed where there is a need to protect the public from serious harm from the offender. Before imposing such a sentence, the judge therefore has to consider both the likelihood that the offender will re-offend and the extent of injury or damage which he would be likely to cause if he did re-offend.

Some of the sentencing guidelines handed down by the Court of Appeal for particular offences already include an element for the protection of the public (for example, rape). It follows that where a court wishes to impose a longer than normal sentence in such a case, the correct starting point is to consider what the appropriate sentence would be without taking into account any increase for the protection of the public already included in the sentencing guidelines for that offence. Thus, where public protection is already included in the guidelines, the starting point should be lower than in a case where a longer than normal sentence is not being imposed. The second stage is then to increase the sentence in accordance with s 80(2)(b): see *R v Campbell* [1997] 1 Cr App R(S) 119.

In *R v Henshaw* [1996] 2 Cr App R(S) 310 and *R v Palmer* [1996] 2 Cr App R(S) 68, the Court of Appeal held that where the trial judge incorrectly passes a sentence under s 80(2)(b) (for example, where there is no evidence that the appellant is likely to commit violent offences in the future), the Court of Appeal is not obliged to interfere with the sentence if that court takes the view that the length of the sentence is proper (in that it is commensurate with the seriousness of the offence).

In *R v Smith (Wayne Anthony)* (1999) *The Times*, 22 June, the Court of Appeal pointed out that the court may pass a 'longer than normal sentence' under s 80(2)(b) of the Powers of Criminal Courts (Sentencing) Act 2000 even if the defendant has no previous convictions.

In *R v Everleigh* [2001] EWCA Crim 1276; [2001] 1 Cr App R(S) 32, it was held (following *R v Johnson* [1998] 1 Cr App R(S) 126) that a longer than normal sentence should not be imposed to run consecutively to another sentence imposed on the same occasion, because a longer than normal sentence is intended in itself to protect the public from serious harm, without the need for any additional penalty in relation to other conduct punishable at the same time. However, there is nothing objectionable in passing a longer than normal sentence to run consecutively to a sentence passed on an earlier occasion.

In *R (Giles) v Parole Board* [2003] UKHL 42; [2004] 1 AC 1, it was held that extended sentences under s 80(2)(b) fall squarely within Art 5(1)(a) of the European Convention on Human Rights, permitting lawful detention after conviction by a competent court. On review of the sentence by the Parole Board, the prisoner is entitled to the same rights as any other long-term prisoner serving a determinate sentence but has no other or greater rights. It follows that there is no right to an oral hearing before the Parole Board after the punitive period of the sentence has expired.

15.1.7 Dangerous offenders under the Criminal Justice Act 2003

The provisions in s 80 of the 2000 Act are replaced by Chapter 5 of Pt 12 of the Criminal Justice Act 2003 (ss 224–36). These provisions apply only to certain offences. Section 224 defines the key terms used in Chapter 5 of the Act. A 'specified offence' means a violent offence specified in Pt 1 of Sched 15 to the Act or a sexual offence specified in Pt 2 of that Schedule. A 'serious offence' means a violent or sexual offence specified in Sched 15 and punishable (ignoring the effect of s 225, below) with life imprisonment or a determinate sentence of at least 10 years' imprisonment. The phrase 'serious harm' means death or serious personal injury (whether physical or psychological).

15.1.7.1 *Life sentence or imprisonment for public protection*

Section 225 enables the court to impose imprisonment for public protection where an offender aged 18 or over is convicted of a 'serious offence' and the court is of the opinion that there is a significant risk to members of the public of serious harm occasioned by the commission by him of further specified offences (that is, offences specified in Sched 15).

Under s 225(2), if the offence is punishable with life imprisonment and the court considers that the seriousness of the offence (or of the offence and one or more offences associated with it) is such as to justify the imposition of a sentence of imprisonment for

life, then the court *must* impose a life sentence. In all other cases which fall within s 225 but not within s 225(2), the court must impose a sentence of imprisonment for public protection (s 225(3)); this sentence is for an indeterminate period (s 225(4)).

Section 226 deals with cases where the offender is under 18. It provides that where an offender under the age of 18 is convicted of an offence that falls within s 225, the same consequences result, save that the sentence is detention for life (or for an indeterminate period, as the case may be) under s 91 of the Powers of Criminal Courts (Sentencing) Act 2000.

15.1.7.2 Extended sentences for violent or sexual offences

We have already seen that the usual principle of sentencing is based on the principle of 'just deserts', so that the length of any custodial sentence should be commensurate with the seriousness of the offence. Section 227, however, requires the court to impose an 'extended sentence' where the offender has attained the age of 18 and is convicted of a specified violent or sexual offence and the court considers that there is a significant risk to members of the public of serious harm occasioned by the commission by the offender of further specified offences (that is, offences specified in Sched 15). Section 227(2) defines an 'extended sentence of imprisonment' as:

> ... a sentence of imprisonment the term of which is equal to the aggregate of—
>
> (a)   the appropriate custodial term, and
>
> (b)   a further period ('the extension period') for which the offender is to be subject to a licence and which is of such length as the court considers necessary for the purpose of protecting members of the public from serious harm occasioned by the commission by him of further specified offences.

Sub-section (3) defines 'the appropriate custodial term' as:

> ... a term of imprisonment (not exceeding the maximum term permitted for the offence) which—
>
> (a)   is the term that would (apart from this section) be imposed in compliance with section 153(2) [commensurate with seriousness of offence], or
>
> (b)   where the term that would be so imposed is a term of less than 12 months, is a term of 12 months.

Under sub-section (4), the extension period must not exceed:

> (a)   five years in the case of a specified violent offence, and
>
> (b)   eight years in the case of a specified sexual offence.

In any event, the term of an extended sentence of imprisonment must not exceed the maximum term permitted for the offence.

Section 228 applies the same provisions to offenders under the age of 18.

15.1.7.3 Assessing dangerousness

Section 229 sets out the criteria for assessing dangerousness in cases to which any of ss 225–28 apply. Section 229(2) provides that:

> If at the time when that offence was committed the offender had not been convicted in any part of the United Kingdom of any relevant offence or was aged under 18, the court in making the assessment ...

(a) must take into account all such information as is available to it about the nature and circumstances of the offence,

(b) may take into account any information which is before it about any pattern of behaviour of which the offence forms part, and

(c) may take into account any information about the offender which is before it.

Section 229(3) provides that:

If at the time when that offence was committed the offender was aged 18 or over and had been convicted in any part of the United Kingdom of one or more relevant offences, the court must assume that there is [a significant risk to members of the public of serious harm from the offender] unless, after taking into account—

(a) all such information as is available to it about the nature and circumstances of each of the offences,

(b) where appropriate, any information which is before it about any pattern of behaviour of which any of the offences forms part, and

(c) any information about the offender which is before it,

the court considers that it would be unreasonable to conclude that there is such a risk.

This creates a strong presumption that the court will find that the offender is dangerous, since the court 'must' do so unless it would be 'unreasonable'. This would seem to place a burden on the offender to show a lack of danger; it is questionable whether the imposition of this burden is consistent with the Human Rights Act.

Section 230 gives effect to Sched 18 to the 2003 Act, which deals with the release of prisoners serving sentences of imprisonment or detention for public protection.

15.1.8 Discount where the offender pleads guilty

Where the offender pleads guilty, the length of the custodial sentence is usually reduced. In *R v Buffery* (1993) 14 Cr App R(S) 511, a serious fraud case, Lord Taylor CJ said that where a defendant pleads guilty, a discount of approximately one-third from the sentence which would have been imposed on conviction following a not guilty plea is usually appropriate.

In *R v Marsh* [2002] EWCA Crim 551; [2002] 2 Cr App R(S) 98, the judge had refused to give any discount for the defendant's guilty plea on the basis that he felt that the Crown had wrongly decided to accept pleas to lesser offences. It was held that he had erred in not giving some discount for the guilty plea. A judge cannot pass a sentence which reflects charges which the Crown has chosen not to pursue.

However, it was held in *R v Costen* (1989) 11 Cr App R(S) 182 that any discount may be lost or reduced in any of the following circumstances:

- where the offender has been caught red-handed, and a plea of guilty was virtually inevitable (for example, *R v Landy* (1995) 16 Cr App R(S) 908);

- where the protection of the public makes a long sentence necessary (thus, the discount may not be applicable where s 80(2)(b) is invoked);

- where the offender does not plead guilty at the earliest opportunity.

The credit may also be increased. *R v Claydon* (1994) 15 Cr App R(S) 526, for example, concerned a defendant who voluntarily approached the police and admitted the offences to which he later pleaded guilty. Had he not done so, it was highly unlikely

that he would have been caught. Where an offender who would otherwise have escaped detection gives himself up and confesses, a discount of 50% may be appropriate.

If the defendant pleads guilty but there is a significant difference between the defence version and prosecution version of events, and a *Newton* hearing takes place, the defendant may lose some of the credit which he would otherwise have received for pleading guilty if the judge, having heard evidence, rejects the defence version of events (*R v Stevens* (1986) 8 Cr App R(S) 291; *R v Jauncey* (1986) 8 Cr App R(S) 401). However, the defendant remains entitled to some credit for pleading guilty; even if the victim has not been spared the trauma of giving evidence, some court time has been saved (*R v Williams* [1992] 1 WLR 380).

15.1.9   Concurrent and consecutive sentences

Where an offender is convicted of more than one offence, a separate sentence will usually be imposed for each offence. In the case of custodial sentences, prison terms may be concurrent or consecutive. Sentences are concurrent if they are to be served simultaneously. In other words, a sentence of nine months on count 1 and three months concurrent on count 2 means that the offender receives a total sentence of nine months. Sentences are consecutive if they have to be served one after the other. In other words, a sentence of nine months on count 1 and three months consecutive on count 2 means that the offender receives a total sentence of 12 months.

It is possible to have a mixture of consecutive and concurrent sentences. For example, an offender could be sentenced to six months on count 1, nine months consecutive on count 2 and three months concurrent on count 3. The total sentence would be 15 months.

If the court fails to specify whether sentences are concurrent or consecutive, they are deemed to be concurrent.

It would be wrong in principle to impose consecutive sentences if the two offences in question essentially amount to a single crime. For example, in *R v Coker* [1984] Crim LR 184, the defendant was convicted of indecent assault and assault occasioning actual bodily harm. He had struck a young woman repeatedly about the face, removed most of her clothes and then indecently assaulted her. The judge imposed consecutive terms of imprisonment but the Court of Appeal held that the two offences were so inextricably linked that the sentences should have been concurrent.

Generally, concurrent sentences will be imposed where the offences arise out of the same transaction; for example, dangerous driving and driving while disqualified on the same occasion (*R v Skinner* (1986) 8 Cr App R(S) 166), driving with excess alcohol and driving while disqualified on the same occasion (*R v Jones* (1980) 2 Cr App R(S) 152). However, this is not an invariable rule. In *R v Wheatley* (1983) 5 Cr App R(S) 417, consecutive sentences were imposed for driving while disqualified and driving with excess alcohol on the same occasion on the ground that it would be wrong to lead the offender to believe that he could drive with excess alcohol and incur no extra penalty for driving while disqualified: though the offences were committed on the same occasion, they were in fact completely separate offences.

In *R v Ling* (1993) 157 JP 931, the defendant was convicted of burglary, affray, dangerous driving, driving while disqualified, refusing to provide a specimen, and

making off without payment. It was said that his offending, which took place over a single (and rather eventful!) evening, was due to the effects of diabetes. The Court of Appeal held that these events should have been regarded as a single ongoing offence. Likewise, in *R v Tutu Sikwabi* (1993) 157 JP 1182, the defendant was convicted of dangerous driving, driving while disqualified, taking a vehicle without the owner's consent and making off without payment. The offences had been committed over a period of three days (beginning with the taking of the car and ending with a police car chase). It was held that the offences arose out of a single series of incidents and that the sentences for the various parts of the series should be made concurrent.

Consecutive sentences are usually imposed where the offences are committed on different occasions, even if there is a link between the offences. For example, in *Attorney General's Reference (No 1 of 1990)* (1990) 12 Cr App R(S) 245, consecutive sentences were imposed for indecent assault and attempting to pervert the course of justice, the latter offence arising out of an attempt to dissuade the victim of the assault from giving evidence. See also *Attorney General's Reference (No 4 of 1994)* (1995) 16 Cr App R(S) 81, where consecutive sentences were imposed for robbery and wounding with intent committed on separate occasions.

Consecutive sentences are also appropriate where, though the offences were committed on the same occasion, they are not part of the same transaction. Thus, a sentence for using violence to resist arrest or in an attempt to escape from the scene of the crime will normally lead to a consecutive sentence being imposed (*R v Fitter* (1983) 5 Cr App R(S) 168). Similarly, a sentence for a firearms offence will usually be consecutive to the sentence for the main offence where that offence involves the use or possession of a firearm (*R v French* (1982) 4 Cr App R(S) 57). For example, in *R v Greaves* [2003] EWCA Crim 3229; [2004] 2 Cr App R(S) 10, it was held that if a defendant uses a weapon in the course of committing a robbery, the proper course as regards sentencing is to impose a separate and consecutive sentence in respect of possession of the weapon. Likewise, in *R v McNaughten* [2003] EWCA Crim 3479; (2004) *The Times*, 15 January, which concerned a woman who had been the subject of systematic and very brutal domestic violence, the court observed that if there had been a separate victim for each count, consecutive sentences would have been justified. The court could see no reason why consecutive sentences would be inappropriate simply because the victim of each assault was the same, not a different person.

In *R v Gorman* (1993) 14 Cr App R(S) 120, the Court of Appeal said that where a custodial sentence of 12 months is passed and the court is also dealing with the offender for another offence for which a very short custodial sentence is appropriate, the sentences should normally be concurrent rather than consecutive.

Terms of imprisonment may be ordered to run consecutively even if the total sentence is greater than the maximum which could have been imposed for one of the offences (*R v Prime* (1983) 5 Cr App R(S) 127). In other words, where the defendant is convicted of more than one offence, the total period of custody can exceed the statutory maximum sentence for a single offence. For example, in *R v Backwell* [2003] EWCA Crim 3213; (2003) *The Times*, 15 December, the defendant pleaded guilty to seven offences of indecent assault on a female, for which the statutory maximum (for a single offence) was 10 years' imprisonment. The judge passed six sentences of six years to run concurrently for six of the offences, and a further six years to run consecutively for the seventh offence (making a total of 12 years). The Court of Appeal upheld this

sentence, holding that it was not wrong in principle even though it exceeded the statutory maximum for a single offence. There is, said the court, no legal principle which states that, irrespective of the circumstances, consecutive sentences which exceed the statutory maximum for a single offence cannot be imposed for a series of offences.

15.1.10 The principle of 'totality'

Sentencers must, however, have regard to the total length of sentence passed, particularly where consecutive sentences have been imposed, to ensure that the sentence properly reflects the overall seriousness of the behaviour (*R v Jones* [1996] 1 Cr App R(S) 153). Thus, where an offender is being sentenced for a number of offences, and terms of imprisonment are ordered to run consecutively rather than concurrently, the court should ensure that the total sentence is commensurate with the overall seriousness of the offender's crimes. This is known as the principle of 'totality', a principle expressly preserved by s 158(2)(b) of the Powers of Criminal Courts (Sentencing) Act 2000 (re-enacted in s 166(3)(b) of the Criminal Justice Act 2003).

15.1.11 Effect of time spent on remand

Section 87 of the Powers of Criminal Courts (Sentencing) Act 2000 (re-enacted in s 240 of the Criminal Justice Act 2003) provides that, if an offender has spent time in custody awaiting trial and/or sentence, the length of time spent in custody counts towards the service of a custodial sentence passed in respect of that offence. This means that, where an offender has been remanded in custody before conviction and/or sentence, the period for which he has already been detained is deducted from the sentence he has to serve. Section 87 applies to sentences of imprisonment and to detention in a young offender institution or a sentence of long-term detention under s 91 of the 2000 Act.

In *R v Governor of Haverill Prison ex p McMahon* (1997) *The Times,* 24 September, the Divisional Court held that, where the defendant is remanded in custody at the same time for related offences but those offences are subsequently tried and dealt with separately, any time spent on remand for the first offence which exceeds the time the defendant has to serve for that offence is to be credited as service of the second sentence.

15.2   EARLY RELEASE

15.2.1   Relative to length of sentence

The length of time which a prisoner actually has to serve before early release can take place depends on the length of sentence imposed by the court:

- Where the offender was sentenced to a term of less than 12 months, he will automatically be released after he has served half of the sentence. The release is unconditional.

- Where the offender was sentenced to a term of 12 months or more but less than four years (a 'short-term prisoner'), he will automatically be released after he has

served half of the sentence. However, from the date of release until the three-quarter point of the sentence is reached, the offender will be on licence and will be under the supervision of a probation officer. If the offender fails to comply with the conditions of his licence, he may be punished (on summary conviction) with a fine.

- Where the offender was sentenced to a term of four years or more (a 'long-term prisoner'), there is no automatic release. However, there is discretionary release (subject to the recommendation of the Parole Board) after half the sentence has been served. The release is on licence, again under the supervision of a probation officer. Once two-thirds of the sentence has been served, a long term prisoner must be released on licence. If the offender fails to comply with the terms of the licence, there is no provision for a fine but the Home Secretary may revoke the licence, requiring the offender to return to prison.

In *R v Secretary of State for the Home Department ex p Probyn* [1998] 1 WLR 809, it was held that in determining whether a prisoner is a short-term or long-term prisoner, the relevant sentence is the sentence pronounced by the court (not the sentence as reduced by any time spent in custody while on remand). In *R v Secretary of State for the Home Department ex p Francois* [1998] 1 All ER 929, the House of Lords held that where a person is sentenced to a term of imprisonment on one occasion and is subsequently sentenced to a further term of imprisonment for another offence, the two terms are to be treated as if they are one term for the purpose of calculating the prisoner's release date, even if this has the effect of converting a prisoner from a short-term prisoner to a long-term prisoner.

15.2.2 Home detention curfew

Section 246 of the Criminal Justice Act 2003 (which replaces s 34A of the Criminal Justice Act 1991) revises the arrangements for 'home detention curfew'. Under s 246(1), the Secretary of State may release a prisoner on licence at any time during the period of 135 days ending with the day on which the prisoner will have served the requisite custodial period under the sentence. Section 246 thus maintains the maximum period available for home detention curfew at 135 days. Under s 246(4), prisoners serving one of the sentences applicable to dangerous offenders are not eligible for the scheme; prisoners who have less than 14 days to serve of their required custodial period following sentence (for example, due to remand time being deducted from the required custodial period) are not eligible either. Under s 246(2) and (3), the periods spent on home detention curfew are tapered according to the length of sentence: where the length of the requisite custodial period is at least six weeks, the offender must have served at least four weeks of his sentence and at least one-half of the requisite custodial period; where the length of the requisite custodial period is at least 42 days, the offender must have served at least 28 days and at least one-half of the total number of days.

Section 246(1)(b) enables prisoners serving a sentence of intermittent custody to benefit from the scheme. On intermittent custody, the offender will spend a number of days on home detention curfew equal to the days he would have spent in custody had he not been granted home detention curfew.

The curfew element is governed by s 253. The curfew condition specifies periods during which the offender must remain in a specified place, and includes a

requirement that the curfew is electronically monitored. Under sub-s (2) the curfew condition can specify more than one place and/or more than one period. The curfew cannot last for less than 9 hours in any one day. Under sub-s (3), the curfew condition lasts until the date the offender would have been released on licence from prison if he had not been granted early release through home detention curfew. Sub-section (4) provides for the curfew condition in sentences of intermittent custody.

In *R v Alkazraji* [2004] EWCA Crim 204; (2004) *The Times*, 2 March, the Court of Appeal said that when fixing a sentence, a judge should ignore the possibility that an offender might be granted early release on 'home detention curfew'. Since such release is discretionary, it would introduce undesirable uncertainty into the sentencing process.

Figures produced by the Home Office showed that of some 80,000 offenders, 90% complied with the curfew. However, in his commentary on *R v Al-Buhairi* [2003] EWCA Crim 2922; [2004] 1 Cr App R(S) 83, Dr David Thomas roundly criticised the home detention curfew scheme. He says that:

> First, it reduces or eliminates the differential between sentences imposed by the courts, particularly at the lower end of the scale. Three months' imprisonment requires the defendant to serve six weeks before release; six months' imprisonment also requires him to serve six weeks, followed by six weeks subject to curfew. Secondly, the scheme effectively transfers to the prison governors a sentencing function performed in secret, without appropriate procedural safeguards of any kind and any publicly declared criteria ... [I]t is difficult to imagine that individual governors of different institutions are able to act consistently in this situation. Thirdly, the scheme operates arbitrarily with regard to different categories of offenders ... Fourthly, the scheme operates in a manner that is wholly lacking in transparency. It is an elementary requirement that sentencing should take place in public view. Little or nothing can be easily discovered about the working of the scheme in practice ...

15.2.3 Commission of further offences

Section 116 of the Powers of Criminal Courts (Sentencing) Act 2000 (to be repealed by the Criminal Justice Act 2003 when the revisions to custodial sentencing made by that Act come into force) provides that where a short-term or long-term prisoner is released and, before the date on which he would have served his sentence in full, he commits a further offence punishable with imprisonment, the court dealing with him for the new offence may, whether or not it passes any other sentence on him, order him to be returned to prison. The maximum period of the return to prison is equal to the length of time between the date of the offence and the date when he would have served his sentence in full (s 116(2)).

However, a magistrates' court cannot order a person's return to prison for more than six months but may commit the offender (in custody or on bail) to the Crown Court, which may make an order for any period up to the maximum set out in s 116(2) of the Criminal Justice Act 1991 (s 116(3)).

The order for return counts as a sentence of imprisonment and may be ordered to be served consecutively with, or concurrently to, any custodial sentence imposed for the new offence. However, in *R v Worthing Justices ex p Varley* (1998) 1 Cr App R(S) 223, it was held that where the justices impose the maximum custodial sentence they can for the offences committed while the offender was on licence (six months or, if two or

more either way offences, 12 months), the court can nonetheless order that the sentence(s) for the new offence(s) be served consecutively with the period of return order under s 116.

It was held by the Divisional Court in *R v Burton-on-Trent Justices ex p Smith* [1997] Crim LR 685 (following *R v Harrow Justices ex p Jordan* [1997] 1 WLR 84) that where the defendant commits a new offence during his release from prison on licence, the magistrates must either (a) deal with both the question of the defendant's return to prison and the sentence for the new offence, or (b) commit the defendant to the Crown Court for that court to determine both questions. This is so even if the new offence is a purely summary offence. Thus, it is not open to the magistrates to impose a sentence for the new offence and then to commit the offender to the Crown Court so that the Crown Court can decide whether to make an order for return to prison.

Thus, the options open to a magistrates' court in such a case are:

- to sentence for the new offence, but make no order for return to prison;
- to sentence for the new offence and make an order for return to prison for up to six months; or
- to commit the offender to the Crown Court to be sentenced for the new offence (even if the new offence is a summary offence), thus leaving it to the Crown Court to decide whether or not to make an order for return to prison.

In *R v Taylor* [1998] 1 All ER 357, the Court of Appeal held that where an offender commits an offence while on licence from prison, the sentencing court must first decide what it is the appropriate sentence for the new offence (disregarding, at this stage, the possibility of an order for the offender's return to prison). Then, in considering whether an order for return should be made, the court should have regard to:

(a) the nature and extent of any progress made by the offender since his release on licence;

(b) whether the new offence calls for a custodial sentence;

(c) the question of 'totality' (that is, whether the overall punishment reflects the seriousness of what the offender has done).

The court may also have regard to the length of time between the offender's release on licence and the commission of the new offence.

In *R v Secretary of State for the Home Department ex p Probyn* [1998] 1 WLR 809, it was held by the Divisional Court that where an offender commits an offence while on licence and the court orders his return to prison and also imposes a sentence of imprisonment for the later offence, the two terms are to be regarded as a single term for the purpose of deciding whether the offender is a short-term prisoner or a long-term prisoner (which affects whether he has to serve half or two-thirds of his sentence before release).

The rules relating to release on licence under the new custodial sentencing regime established by the Criminal Justice Act 2003 are set out later in this chapter.

15.2.4 Murder

A person convicted of murder must be sentenced to life imprisonment (s 1(1) of the Murder (Abolition of Death Penalty) Act 1965). In the case of an offender who is under 18, the appropriate sentence is one of detention during Her Majesty's pleasure under s 90 of the Powers of Criminal Courts (Sentencing) Act 2000.

Prior to the coming into force of Chapter 7 of Pt 12 of the Criminal Justice Act 2003, the trial judge made a recommendation as to the minimum period which should elapse before the offender is released on licence; this recommendation was communicated to the Home Secretary, along with the view of the Lord Chief Justice. The recommendation was not binding on the Home Secretary, who could shorten or lengthen the period. The prisoner's case would, in due course, be reviewed by the Parole Board, which could recommend that the prisoner be released on licence. The Home Secretary was not bound by that recommendation. However, in *R (Anderson) v Secretary of State for the Home Department* [2002] UKHL 46; [2003] 1 AC 837, the House of Lords held that the Home Secretary's power to fix sentencing tariffs was incompatible with the right to a fair trial guaranteed by Art 6 of the European Convention. This was because the European Court had made it clear that the fixing of a tariff is to be regarded as a sentencing exercise rather than the administrative implementation of a life sentence that has already been passed (see *Stafford v UK* (2002) 35 EHRR 32). It followed that the fixing of the tariff forms part of the trial and therefore has to be conducted by an independent court or tribunal; the Secretary of State, as a member of the executive, should not perform functions of the judiciary. Section 275 of the Criminal Justice Act 2003 deals with the release of mandatory life prisoners in order to give effect to the ruling of the European Court of Human Rights in *Stafford v UK* and brings the arrangements for the release of mandatory life prisoners into line with those for discretionary life prisoners (s 28 of the Crime (Sentences) Act 1997). Thus, a mandatory lifer is able to require the Secretary of State to refer his case to the Parole Board once he has served the 'minimum term' (specified under s 269(2) of the 2003 Act). Once a case has been referred to it, the Parole Board decides whether the prisoner is to be released; it may only direct his release if satisfied that the continued detention of the lifer is no longer necessary for the protection of the public. If the Parole Board decides that this is the case, the Secretary of State must release the offender on a lifelong licence. Guidance on the fixing of the minimum term is contained in para IV.49 of the *Consolidated Practice Direction*.

15.2.5 Discretionary life sentences

Several offences carry a maximum sentence of life imprisonment (for example, rape, robbery, inflicting grievous bodily harm with intent).

In *R v Whittaker* [1997] 1 Cr App R(S) 261 (following *Attorney General's Reference (No 34 of 1992)* (1994) 15 Cr App R(S) 167), the Court of Appeal set out the conditions which must be satisfied before a discretionary life sentence can be imposed. First, the offender must have been convicted of a very serious offence. Secondly, it must be established that there are good grounds for believing that the offender might remain a serious danger to the public for a period that could not be estimated reliably at the time when the sentence was passed.

Further guidance on discretionary life sentences was given in *R v Chapman* [2000] 1 Cr App R 77, where the offender was given a discretionary life sentence after pleading guilty to arson. The offender, aged 19, had started a fire in the room he shared in an adult residential unit where it could be, and was, quickly discovered and extinguished. The property had not been extensively damaged; no personal injuries had been sustained, nor were they likely or intended to have been. The Court of Appeal held as follows:

(a) a discretionary life sentence imposed for purposes of public protection and not for pure retribution or deterrence can only be passed under s 80(2)(b) of the Powers of Criminal Courts (Sentencing) Act 2000. The pre-conditions for imposing an indeterminate life sentence for purposes of public protection are that:

   (i) the offender has committed an offence grave enough to merit an extremely long sentence; and

   (ii) there are good grounds for believing that the offender might remain a serious danger to the public for a period which could not be reliably estimated at the date of sentence;

(b) a longer than commensurate sentence under s 80(2)(b) should not be longer than judged necessary to achieve the object of protecting the public, but there is no necessary ratio between the part of the sentence intended to punish and that intended to protect. Thus, there was no objection in principle if the court regarded, for example, a term of two years as that necessary to punish and additionally, say, six to eight years as that necessary for protection purposes, making a total of eight to 10 years. A sentence so constructed, if justified by the grounds relied on in its support, is to be preferred to an indefinite life sentence which leaves a defendant uncertain when, if ever, he might hope for release and exposes him to the risk of extremely protracted incarceration;

(c) the more likely it is that the offender will re-offend and the more grave such offending is likely to be if it does occur, the less emphasis the court might place on the gravity of the original offence (this is because of the fact that such sentences are essentially intended to protect the public and so involve a prediction of future behaviour on the part of the offender). However, a life sentence should never be imposed unless the circumstances are such as to call for a serious sentence based on the offence committed. In the present case, the offence was not sufficiently grave to justify imposition of a life sentence. Despite the prospect of continuing risk, a life sentence was inappropriate and a determinate sentence under s 80(2)(b) was appropriate; the life sentence was therefore replaced with a determinate sentence of three years to which seven years was added for purposes of public protection under s 80(2)(b), giving a total sentence of 10 years.

When imposing a discretionary life sentence, the trial judge is empowered to specify a minimum length of time which the offender should serve before release on licence (s 82A of the Powers of Criminal Courts (Sentencing) Act 2000). A minimum recommendation should be made unless the case is an exceptional one, where the judge considers the offence to be so serious that detention for life is justified by the seriousness of the offence alone, irrespective of the risk to the public. Guidance is given in para IV.47 of the *Consolidated Practice Direction*.

Release on licence is considered by the Parole Board. The prisoner has the right to attend the hearing and to be legally represented. The Parole Board should only recommend release if satisfied that it is no longer necessary for the protection of the public that the prisoner be detained (s 28(6) of the Crime (Sentences) Act 1997). If the Board decides that the prisoner should be released, that decision is final and binds the Home Secretary (s 28(5) of the 1997 Act). If the Board does not decide to release the prisoner, he can require his case to be considered every two years (s 28(7)(b)).

Where a life prisoner is released on licence, he is liable to be recalled to prison at any time during the rest of his life (s 31(1) of the Criminal Justice Act 1991).

Section 31 stipulates that where a life prisoner is released on licence, the licence (unless revoked) remains in force until his death. Section 32 enables the Secretary of State (subject to the approval of the Parole Board) to revoke the licence of a life prisoner who has been released on licence, thus recalling the offender to prison.

15.3   SUSPENDED SENTENCES OF IMPRISONMENT

Section 118(1) and (2) of the Powers of Criminal Courts (Sentencing) Act 2000 provides that where a court imposes a prison sentence of two years or less, it may order that the sentence is not to take effect unless, during a specified period of between one and two years from the date the sentence is imposed, the offender commits a further imprisonable offence and the court dealing with the later offence orders that the original sentence of imprisonment take effect. The length of the original sentence imprisonment is known as the 'term' and the period during which it is to remain suspended is known as the 'operational period'. Section 118(7) of the 2000 Act requires the court to warn the offender that he will be liable to serve the suspended sentence if he commits a further imprisonable offence during the operational period.

Only a sentence of imprisonment can be suspended. The power does not, therefore, apply to detention in a young offender institution or to long-term detention under s 91 of the Act. It follows that a suspended sentence can only be imposed on an offender who has attained the age of 21.

Where an offender is being dealt with for more than one offence and consecutive sentences of imprisonment are imposed, those sentences can only be suspended if the aggregate total is two years or less (s 125(1) of the Act).

Where two suspended sentences are imposed on the same occasion, the court should indicate whether they are to run concurrently or consecutively if they are activated (*R v Wilkinson* [1970] 1 WLR 1319). In *R v Gall* (1970) 54 Cr App R 292, it was held that if the sentences run consecutively, they constitute a single suspended sentence for the purpose of activation in the event of the commission of a later offence.

Section 118(2) of the 2000 Act stipulates that a suspended sentence may only be imposed if:

- '... a sentence of imprisonment would have been appropriate even without the power to suspend the sentence'; and
- the exercise of the power to suspend the sentence 'can be justified by the exceptional circumstances of the case'.

The fact that a suspended sentence may only be imposed if the court is satisfied that immediate custody would have been appropriate in the absence of the power to

suspend the sentence serves to emphasise that s 79 of the Act applies equally to suspended sentences. In other words, the offence must be sufficiently serious to justify a custodial sentence (*R v Fletcher* (1991) 12 Cr App R(S) 671).

By requiring the presence of exceptional circumstances before a suspended sentence can be imposed, it is clearly the intention of Parliament that the suspended sentence 'should be used far more sparingly than it has been in the past' (*R v Lowery* (1993) 14 Cr App R(S) 485). There is no statutory definition of exceptional circumstances: in *R v Okinikan* [1993] 1 WLR 173, Lord Taylor CJ declined to provide a judicial definition of the phrase, saying that it will depend on the facts of each individual case whether it can be said that exceptional circumstances are present. However, it was held in that case that good character (that is, lack of previous convictions), youth and an early plea of guilty cannot amount to exceptional circumstances. The rationale is that such factors are present in a large number of cases and so can hardly be described as exceptional.

The term 'exceptional circumstances' can include the poor health of the defendant (*R v Weston* [1995] Crim LR 900). In *R v French* [1993] Crim LR 893, the defendant had experienced severe financial and emotional difficulties and was receiving psychiatric care for depression; there was evidence that a custodial sentence would impede her recovery. These factors were said to amount to exceptional circumstances justifying the suspension of the custodial sentence. In *R v Brookin* (1995) 16 Cr App R(S) 78, provocation resulting in violence was said to be capable of amounting to exceptional circumstances.

The decision in *R v Lowery* (1993) 14 Cr App R(S) 485 appears rather more harsh. The defendant was a police officer whose duties included collecting fines. He stole a total of just over £1,500. It was argued in the Court of Appeal that a suspended sentence was appropriate because the defendant's wife had become disabled and the money had been stolen to pay for adaptations to the family home for her benefit; as a result of the offence, the defendant was unemployed and had lost most of his pension rights; the defendant was very depressed and had attempted suicide twice. The Court of Appeal held that these circumstances were not exceptional because theft in breach of trust will usually involve far-reaching adverse consequences to the offender which go far beyond the immediate impact of any sentence which might be imposed on him. Accordingly, a suspended sentence was not appropriate. However, as an act of mercy, the Court of Appeal substituted a sentence of immediate custody of such length as would mean the offender's immediate release. Likewise, in *R v Murti* [1996] 2 Cr App R(S) 152, the defendant was convicted of social security fraud. She was a postal worker and she allowed two women to cash DSS benefit vouchers which she knew were stolen. In mitigation, reliance was placed on her initial reluctance to become involved in the offence, the fact that she was suffering from post-natal depression, the fact that her husband had threatened to leave her, so that she would be the sole carer for two small children, the fact that her employer had re-engaged her and that she had pleaded guilty and testified against a co-defendant. The Court of Appeal rejected the argument that any of these factors amounted to exceptional circumstances. However, since the sentence was passed, she had attempted suicide in prison and her husband had left her, taking the children with him. The Court of Appeal, as an act of mercy, substituted a probation (community rehabilitation) order for the prison sentence.

15.3.1 Combining a suspended sentence with other orders

Section 118(5) of the Powers of Criminal Courts (Sentencing) Act 2000 requires the court to consider imposing a fine and/or making a compensation order in addition to imposing a suspended sentence.

In *R v Sapiano* (1968) 52 Cr App R 674, it was held to be wrong in principle to impose an immediate sentence of imprisonment and a suspended sentence of imprisonment on the same occasion: the two are incompatible.

Section 118(6) of the Powers of Criminal Courts (Sentencing) Act 2000 provides that if the court imposes a suspended sentence, it may not impose a community sentence in respect of the same offence or for any other offence being dealt with by the court.

15.3.2 Suspended sentence supervision order

There is an indirect method of combining a form of probation/community rehabilitation with some suspended sentences. Section 122 of the Powers of Criminal Courts (Sentencing) Act 2000 states that where a sentence of more than six months is suspended, the court may make a suspended sentence supervision order. The effect of such an order is to place the offender under the supervision of a probation officer for a specified period not exceeding the operational period of the suspended sentence.

This power only applies if there is a sentence of six months or more for one offence. It does not apply if sentences which are each shorter than six months are imposed but made to run consecutively so that the aggregate term exceeds six months (*R v Baker* (1988) 10 Cr App R(S) 409). This restriction has the effect that a magistrates' court (which cannot impose a sentence of more than six months' imprisonment for a single offence (s 78 of the 2000 Act)) cannot make a suspended sentence supervision order.

If a supervision order is made, the offender is required to keep in touch with the probation officer in accordance with the probation officer's instructions and must notify the probation officer of any change of address. No other conditions may be added to the supervision order. Failure without reasonable cause to comply with the requirements of the order is punishable with a fine of up to £1,000 (s 123(3)).

The supervision order ceases to have effect if either the suspended sentence is activated because of the commission of a later offence or else the supervision order is discharged (which is possible on the application of the offender or the probation officer) (s 124).

15.3.3 Length of a suspended sentence

In *R v Mah-Wing* (1983) 5 Cr App R(S) 347, it was held that the court, when determining the length of a suspended sentence, must first consider what would be the appropriate sentence of immediate custody and then go on to consider whether there are grounds for suspending it. 'What the court must not do is pass a longer custodial sentence than it would otherwise do, because it is suspended' (*per* Griffiths LJ). In determining the length of the sentence, the court must impose a term which is commensurate with the seriousness of the offence (cf s 80(2)(a) of the 2000 Act).

When fixing the duration of the term of a suspended sentence, the sentencer should take account of any period spent in custody by the offender in respect of that offence (see, by analogy, para I.9.1 of the *Practice Direction (Criminal Proceedings: Consolidation)* [2002] 1 WLR 2870). Accordingly, where a suspended sentence is activated, account should not be taken of the period spent in custody by ordering the suspended sentence to take effect with a reduced term (*R v Williams* (1989) 11 Cr App R(S) 152). A second consequence is that where the offender has been in custody on remand for a period equivalent to the appropriate term of immediate imprisonment for the offence, so that the offender has effectively served his sentence on remand, the sentence should be such as to secure his immediate release; it would therefore be wrong to pass a suspended sentence in such a case (*R v Peppard* (1990) 12 Cr App R(S) 88).

15.4 ACTIVATION OF A SUSPENDED SENTENCE

Section 119(2) of the Powers of Criminal Courts (Sentencing) Act 2000 creates a presumption that where an offender is convicted of an imprisonable offence committed during the operation period of a suspended sentence, the court dealing with him for the later offence should activate the suspended sentence.

Section 119(2) stipulates that the whole of the suspended sentence should be brought into effect unless the court takes the view that it would be unjust to do so. If the court does not activate the whole of the suspended sentence, it must give its reasons for not doing so.

Section 119(1) sets out the options available to the court if it decides not to activate the whole of the suspended sentence. Those options are:

- To activate part of the suspended sentence. The effect of this is best illustrated by an example. Suppose that an offender is sentenced to nine months' imprisonment, suspended for two years, and during that two year period he commits a further offence. Suppose that, for the second offence, the defendant is sentenced to three months' imprisonment. It would be open to the court to take the view that it would be excessive to activate the whole of the nine months' suspended sentence consecutive to the three months for the later offence (which would make a total sentence of 12 months); the court could, for example, activate the suspended sentence but reduce its term to six months. Where part of a suspended sentence is activated, the rest lapses and the defendant can never be required to serve it.

- To vary the operational period of the original suspended sentence by replacing it with a new operational period of up to two years from the date of the variation. For example, if the court wishes to make a community punishment (unpaid work) order in respect of the later offence, it would be inappropriate to activate any part of the suspended sentence (the offender could not do community work if he were in prison!) but if the court does not wish to ignore the breach of the suspended sentence, increasing the operational period may well be the appropriate solution.

Where the court varies the operational period, it may also make a suspended sentence supervision order (see above) provided that at least six months' imprisonment is suspended (s 122(8) of the 2000 Act).

- To take no action at all in respect of the breach of the suspended sentence.

Where the court activates all or part of a suspended sentence, it should be ordered to run consecutively to a prison sentence for the later offence unless there are exceptional circumstances (*R v Ithell* [1969] 1 WLR 272). In *R v Bocskei* (1970) 54 Cr App R 519, it was pointed out that the 'totality' principle applies to the activation of suspended sentences. Therefore, if the activation of a suspended sentence to run consecutively with a custodial sentence for the present offence would result in a total sentence which is too harsh, the court may activate part of the suspended sentence and/or order that the two sentences be served concurrently.

It must be emphasised that a defendant is only in breach of a suspended sentence if he commits an imprisonable offence during the operational period of the suspended sentence. It follows from this that the defendant will be in breach of the suspended sentence even if he is convicted of the later offence after the expiry of the operational period, provided that the offence was committed during the operational period. It is the date of the commission of the later offence, not the date when the defendant is convicted of that offence, which determines whether there is a breach of a suspended sentence.

Where an offender commits an offence during the operational period of a suspended sentence but is conditionally discharged for the later offence, it does not count as a conviction for the purpose of activating the suspended sentence and so the suspended sentence cannot be activated (*R v Moore* [1995] 2 WLR 728).

15.4.1 Determining action to be taken for breach of a suspended sentence

As we have seen, s 119(2) of the Powers of Criminal Courts (Sentencing) Act 2000 creates a presumption that the court will activate the suspended sentence in full in the event of a breach. In *R v Craine* (1981) 3 Cr App R(S) 198, it was emphasised that it is only in exceptional circumstances that a suspended sentence will not be activated if a further imprisonable offence is committed.

The mere fact that the later offence is of a different type to the offence for which the suspended sentence was imposed does not justify refraining from activating the suspended sentence (*R v Saunders* (1970) 54 Cr App R 247; *R v Craine* (1981) 3 Cr App R(S) 198; *R v Clitheroe* (1987) 9 Cr App R(S) 159).

However, in most cases (though not all), it will be inappropriate to activate a suspended sentence where the later offence is dealt with by means of a non-custodial sentence (*R v McElhorne* (1983) 5 Cr App R(S) 53; *R v Jagodzinski* (1986) 8 Cr App R(S) 150). This is so even if the later offence is of the same nature as the offence for which the suspended sentence was imposed (*R v Dobson* (1989) 11 Cr App R(S) 332).

Thus, in *R v Brooks* (1990) 12 Cr App R(S) 756, the defendant was convicted of possessing a small quantity of cannabis for his own use. This conviction placed him in breach of a suspended sentence for possession of cannabis with intent to supply. It was held by the Court of Appeal that the later offence was not sufficiently serious to justify a custodial sentence. The comparative triviality of the second offence, making a custodial sentence for that offence inappropriate, meant that it would be wrong to activate the suspended sentence for the earlier offence.

Another argument in favour of leniency is that the later offence was committed when the operational period of the suspended sentence had almost expired (*R v Carr* (1979) 1 Cr App R(S) 53); *R v Fitton* (1989) 11 Cr App R(S) 350). In that case, the later offence was committed when the offender had completed 22 months of a two year suspended sentence. He was sentenced to two years' imprisonment for the later offence, but the Court of Appeal ordered that the suspended sentence run concurrently with the sentence for the later offence. An alternative in such a case may well be to activate only part of the suspended sentence.

In *R v Stacey* (1994) 15 Cr App R(S) 585, a non-custodial sentence was imposed for an offence committed in breach of a suspended sentence, but the suspended sentence was activated in full. The Court of Appeal affirmed the general principle that where a non-custodial sentence is imposed for the later offence, it is inappropriate to activate the suspended sentence unless there are exceptional circumstances. In the present case, however, the appellant had breached the suspended sentence shortly after its imposition (and had committed another offence while on bail for the present offence) and so the decision to activate the suspended sentence was justified (although, in fact, the Court of Appeal decided that, because of personal mitigation, only half the period of the suspended sentence should be activated).

The law relating to suspended sentences is amended by the Criminal Justice Act 2003 (see below).

15.5 MANDATORY SENTENCES

15.5.1 Life sentence for second serious offence

Section 109 of the Powers of Criminal Courts (Sentencing) Act 2000 provides for the imposition of a mandatory life sentence for an offender who commits a second serious offence. The section states that where:

(a) a person is convicted of a serious offence; and

(b) at the time when that offence was committed, the offender had attained the age of 18 years and had also been convicted in any part of the United Kingdom of another serious offence,

then the court must impose a sentence of imprisonment for life (custody for life in the case of an offender who is under 21) unless the court is of the opinion that there are exceptional circumstances (relating to either of the offences or of the offender) which justify it passing a lesser sentence.

Sub-section (5) lists the offences that are encompassed by the definition 'serious offence'. The list includes attempted murder, manslaughter, wounding or causing grievous bodily harm with intent, rape and attempted rape.

In the joined cases of *R v Kelly* and *Attorney General's Reference (No 53 of 1998)* [2000] 1 QB 198, the Court of Appeal held that, to be exceptional, a circumstance need not be unique, or unprecedented or very rare, but it could not be one that was regularly or routinely or normally encountered. The court added that it is not enough that the circumstances are exceptional: they must also be such as to justify the court in not imposing the mandatory sentence. The court went on to hold that it is not enough that the offender does not present a serious threat to the safety of the public (this part of the

decision can no longer stand, in light of subsequent authority). Also, the court said that the offender's age when convicted of the first offence, the interval of time between the two offences, and the difference in nature between the two offences do not give rise to exceptional circumstances.

In *R v Buckland* [2000] 1 All ER 907, the Court of Appeal gave further guidance on the mandatory life sentence provisions, saying acute mental illness at the time of committing a 'serious offence' is not of itself an exceptional circumstance which justifies the court in not passing a life sentence. The court went to hold that the judgment whether exceptional circumstances exist is qualitative as well as quantitative: if the court finds that exceptional circumstances exist, it must go on to consider whether those exceptional circumstances justify not imposing a life sentence. The court added that in any case where it appears that the defendant presents a serious and continuing danger to public safety, it is hard to see how the court could consider itself justified in not imposing a life sentence even if exceptional circumstances are found to exist. However, if there are exceptional circumstances and the offender does not represent a serious and continuing danger to the safety of the public, the court may be justified in imposing a lesser penalty.

In *R v Stephens* [2000] 2 Cr App R(S) 320, defence counsel had failed to inform the defendant that, if he were to be convicted of causing grievous bodily harm with intent (s 18 of the Offences Against the Person Act 1861), he faced a mandatory life sentence under s 109 of the 2000 Act. If the defendant had been aware of this fact, he might have pleaded guilty to the alternative charge of inflicting grievous bodily harm (s 20 of the 1861 Act), a plea that would have been acceptable to the prosecution, and which would not have attracted a mandatory life sentence. The Court of Appeal held that the lack of appropriate advice gave rise to exceptional circumstances justifying the court in not imposing a life sentence.

In *R v Offen* [2001] 1 WLR 253, the Court of Appeal said that the intention of Parliament in enacting the provision was to protect the public. It follows that if an offender does not constitute a significant risk to the public, that will constitute an exceptional circumstance which would justify the court in not imposing an automatic life sentence. If the two offences are of a different kind, or if a long period has elapsed between the offences (during which he has not committed other offences), that could be a very relevant indicator as to the degree of risk to the public which the offender poses. If an offender is a significant risk to the public, the court can impose a life sentence under s 109 without contravening the European Convention on Human Rights. Likewise, in *R v Kelly (No 2)* [2001] EWCA Crim 1751; [2002] 1 Cr App R(S) 85, the court confirmed that s 109 establishes a norm, namely that those who have committed two serious offences constitute a danger or risk to the public. If, taking into account all the circumstances relating to a particular offender, he does not create an unacceptable risk to the public, he is an exception to that norm. If the offences are of a different kind, or if a long period of time has elapsed between the offences during which the offender has not committed other offences, that might be a very relevant indicator as to the degree of risk to the public that he constitutes. Under s 109, it is the responsibility of judges to assess the risk to the public that offenders constitute, whether by reference to criminal records, or assessments made in reports which were available to the court. In the present case, in the light of the conclusions of the defendant's psychiatric report, it was apparent that the defendant did not constitute a significant risk to the public from which it required protection, and so a life sentence

should not have been imposed under s 109. Similarly, in *R v Stark* [2002] EWCA Crim 542; [2002] 2 Cr App R (S) 104, it was held that it is necessary to begin with the assumption that the defendant presents a significant risk to the public; however, this assumption is capable of rebuttal by evidence. Where the court is satisfied that the defendant is not a significant risk to the public in terms of either violent or sexual offences, exceptional circumstances exist under s 109. In such a case, a determinate sentence of imprisonment (not an automatic life sentence) is appropriate.

In *R v Drew* [2003] UKHL 25; [2003] 1 WLR 1213, the House of Lords held that a sentence of life imprisonment passed under s 109 on a mentally ill defendant is not an infringement of the European Convention on Human Rights. The House also confirmed that s 109 does not contravene the European Convention on Human Rights if the courts apply it so that it does not result in offenders being sentenced to life imprisonment when they do not constitute a significant risk to the public.

15.5.2 Minimum sentences for a third Class A drug trafficking offence

Section 110 of the Powers of Criminal Courts (Sentencing) Act 2000 provides for the imposition of a minimum sentence of seven years for conviction of a third Class A drug trafficking offence. The section states that where:

(a) a person is convicted of a Class A drug trafficking offence (as defined by the Drug Trafficking Act 1994); and

(b) at the time when that offence was committed the offender was 18 or over and had been convicted in any part of the United Kingdom of two other Class A drug trafficking offences; and

(c) one of those other offences was committed after he had been convicted of the other (so where the offender is convicted of more than one offence on a single occasion that only counts as one conviction for these purposes),

then the court must impose a custodial sentence of at least seven years unless the court takes the view that there are particular circumstances which relate to any of the offences or to the offender and which would make it unjust in all the circumstances to impose the minimum sentence.

In *R v Stenhouse* [2000] 2 Cr App R(S) 386, the Court of Appeal decided that there were 'particular circumstances' making it unjust to impose the seven year minimum: the last of the offender's previous convictions had led to a community rehabilitation order; that fact, together with other mitigating features, made the minimum sentence unjust in all the circumstances.

15.5.3 Minimum sentence for a third domestic burglary

Section 111 of the Powers of Criminal Courts (Sentencing) Act 2000 prescribes a minimum sentence of three years for conviction of a third domestic burglary. It states that where:

(a) a person is convicted of a domestic burglary (that is, a burglary committed in respect of a building or part of a building which is a dwelling); and

(b) at the time when that offence was committed the offender had attained the age of 18 and had been convicted in England or Wales of two other domestic burglaries; and

(c) one of those other burglaries was committed after he had been convicted of the other, and both were committed after 30 November 1999,

then the court must impose a custodial sentence of at least 3 years unless the court takes the view that there are particular circumstances which relate to any of the offences or to the offender and which would make it unjust in all the circumstances to impose the minimum sentence.

Section 111(3) provides that where a person is charged with a domestic burglary which could otherwise be triable either way but the case is one to which s 4 applies, the burglary is to be regarded as triable only on indictment.

15.5.4 Minimum sentence for certain firearms offences

Section 287 of the Criminal Justice Act 2003 (enacted in response to the rapid growth of gun-crime) prescribes minimum sentences for certain firearms offences under s 5 of the Firearms Act 1968 (possession, etc, of prohibited weapons). The section (in force since January 2004) inserts a new section, s 51A, into the 1968 Act. Under s 51A(5), the minimum sentence for a person aged 18 or over at the time of the offence is five years (three years where the offender was under 18 at the time of the offence). Section 51A(2) provides that:

The court shall impose an appropriate custodial sentence ... for a term of at least the required minimum unless the court is of the opinion that there are exceptional circumstances relating to the offence or to the offender which justify its not doing so.

15.5.5 Discount for guilty plea

Where s 110 or 111 of the 2000 Act is applicable, the court can still give credit for a guilty plea under s 152 of the 2000 Act (re-enacted in s 144 of the Criminal Justice Act 2003). However, the amount of discount is limited by s 152(3) of the 2000 Act (s 144(2) of the 2003 Act), which provides that in a case under s 110 or 111, the court can take account of a guilty plea by passing a sentence which is not less than 80% of what would otherwise be the minimum sentence prescribed by the 2000 Act. The 2003 Act does not contain similar provision for mandatory sentences under s 51A of the Firearms Act (possibly this was an oversight).

15.6   CUSTODIAL SENTENCES UNDER THE CRIMINAL JUSTICE ACT 2003

The Halliday Report says that one of the most serious failures in the present system is seen in prison sentences of under 12 months. Only half of this time is served in custody (or less with a Home Detention Curfew), and the remainder is not subject to any conditions. The Prison Service has little opportunity to tackle criminal behaviour as the time served in custody is so limited.

The Report calls for a structured framework to deal with the large number of offenders who persist in the type of criminality that does not require longer prison sentences. To this end, the Report calls for a new sentence of 'custody plus', under which those who serve short prison sentences would be required to undertake

supervised programmes after release (under conditions, which – if breached – could result in swift return to custody). The Report suggests an initial period in custody of between two weeks and three months, and a period of supervision between six months and whatever would take the sentence as a whole to less than 12 months. The Report notes that such a sentence would, potentially, be more punitive in its effect on offenders who breach their conditions than an existing prison sentence of under 12 months. The Report suggested that for the comparatively few offenders for whom post-custody supervision is not needed, a sentence of ordinary custody of up to three months should be available.

One particular advantage identified by the Report is that all short-term prison sentences would then mean what they say in terms of time served.

The Halliday Report called for more supervision of short-term and long-term prisoners following their release. It proposed that the supervisory period should run until the end of the total sentence, making (as the Report suggests) these sentences more 'real' and increasing opportunities for crime reduction through work with offenders after release. To achieve this enhanced degree of supervision, the Report suggests that all sentences of 12 months or more should, effectively, be served in full: half in custody and half under supervision in the community, with the second half being subject to conditions whose breach could result in recall to prison. It is perhaps noteworthy that this is the model already adopted for juvenile offenders (the detention and training order, which is a period of custody, followed by the same period being supervised in the community).

The Report recommends that before the offender is released, the Prison and Probation Services (which have since been combined into a single offender management service) should design a package of measures to be complied with by the offender after release. These conditions should, according to the Report, be geared to public protection, rehabilitation and resettlement, and would run until the end of the sentence. Emphasising the need for the courts to be involved after sentence has been passed, the Report says that the package of measures should be subject to review in a criminal court before the offender is released.

The Report also said that it should be possible to include curfews and electronic monitoring in post-release conditions for all custodial sentences.

The Halliday report recommended a new sentence of 'intermittent custody', to allow the offender to spend part of a custodial sentence out of prison.

The Report also recommended the creation of a new sentence of 'suspended sentence plus', which would combine a community sentence with a suspended sentence of imprisonment (which could be activated if the offender fails to comply with the conditions of the non-custodial part of the sentence). The Report said that there were no grounds for removing the current restrictions on the use of suspended sentences, and concluded that when a prison sentence has to be passed, suspending it entirely should continue to be possible only in exceptional circumstances. The Report recommends that when a non-custodial sentence is passed for an imprisonable offence, it would be beneficial to make clear to offenders the 'conditional' nature of the sentence (in the sense that, if the offender does not comply with the agreed conditions, a custodial sentence may be passed instead).

The sentencing provisions contained in Pt 12 of the Criminal Justice Act 2003 are, in large measure, a response to the Halliday Report and enact many of the suggestions that are set out in that Report.

15.7   PRISON SENTENCES OF LESS THAN 12 MONTHS

Section 181 of the Criminal Justice Act 2003 provides that, in general, all prison sentences of less than 12 months should consist of a short period of custody (the 'custodial period') followed by a longer period on licence (the 'licence period'), during which the offender has to comply with requirements fixed by the courts as part of the 'custody plus order'. Under s 181(5), the custodial period must be between two and 13 weeks; under s 181(6), the licence period must be at least 26 weeks. Section 181(7) provides for consecutive sentences and limits the total term of imprisonment for two or more offences to 65 weeks (15 months), with a maximum of 26 weeks (six months) in custody.

Section 181 provides as follows:

(1)   Any power of a court to impose a sentence of imprisonment for a term of less than 12 months on an offender may be exercised only in accordance with the following provisions of this section unless the court makes an intermittent custody order (as defined by section 183).

(2)   The term of the sentence—

(a) must be expressed in weeks,

(b) must be at least 28 weeks,

(c) must not be more than 51 weeks in respect of any one offence, and

(d) must not exceed the maximum term permitted for the offence.

(3)   The court, when passing sentence, must—

(a) specify a period (in this Chapter referred to as 'the custodial period') at the end of which the offender is to be released on a licence, and

(b) by order require the licence to be granted subject to conditions requiring the offender's compliance during the remainder of the term (in this Chapter referred to as 'the licence period') or any part of it with one or more requirements falling within section 182(1) and specified in the order.

...

(5)   The custodial period—

(a)   must be at least 2 weeks, and

(b) in respect of any one offence, must not be more than 13 weeks.

(6)   In determining the term of the sentence and the length of the custodial period, the court must ensure that the licence period is at least 26 weeks in length.

(7)   Where a court imposes two or more terms of imprisonment in accordance with this section to be served consecutively—

(a) the aggregate length of the terms of imprisonment must not be more than 65 weeks, and

(b) the aggregate length of the custodial periods must not be more than 26 weeks.

(8)   A custody plus order which specifies two or more requirements may, in relation to any requirement, refer to compliance within such part of the licence period as is specified in the order.

(9)   Sub-section (3)(b) does not apply where the sentence is a suspended sentence.

Section 182 of the 2003 Act lists the requirements which the court may attach to the licence period under the 'custody plus order' provided for by s 181. Under s 182(1), the following conditions may be attached:

(a) an unpaid work requirement (as defined by s 199);

(b) an activity requirement (as defined by s 201);

(c) a programme requirement (as defined by s 202);

(d) a prohibited activity requirement (as defined by s 203);

(e) a curfew requirement (as defined by s 204);

(f) an exclusion requirement (as defined by s 205);

(g) a supervision requirement (as defined by s 213); and

(h) where the offender is aged under 25, an attendance centre requirement (as defined by s 214).

Section 182(3) stipulates that where the court makes a custody plus order requiring a licence to contain a curfew requirement or an exclusion requirement, it must also require the licence to contain an electronic monitoring requirement (as defined by s 215) unless, in the particular circumstances of the case, it considers it inappropriate to do so. Under s 182(4), where the court makes a custody plus order requiring a licence to contain any of the other requirements listed above, the court may also require the licence to contain an electronic monitoring requirement.

Section 182(5) adds the stipulation that where the licence contains two or more different requirements, the court must consider whether, in the circumstances of the case, the requirements are compatible with each other.

15.8   INTERMITTENT CUSTODY

Section 183 of the Criminal Justice Act 2003 provides for 'intermittent custody' (in force since February 2004). Under s 183(1), a court passing a sentence of imprisonment of under 12 months may specify the number of days the offender must serve in prison, and at the same time provide for his release on licence, subject to specified conditions, at set intervals throughout his sentence. Under s 183(4), the sentence must, like a 'custody plus' sentence under s 165, be at least 28 weeks but no more than 51 weeks in respect of any one offence. Section 183(5) specifies the minimum and maximum amount of time the offender must spend in prison: the number of custodial days must be at least 14 and (in respect of any one offence) must not be more than 90. Such a sentence cannot be passed without the consent of the offender (s 183(6)). Section 183(7) makes provision for consecutive sentences, but limits the total term to 65 weeks, with a maximum of 180 days in custody. Section 183(8) enables the Secretary of State, by order, to make provision about licence periods that the court may specify: he may make provision about the length of licence periods, so as to enable the custodial days to be served during the week or at the weekend; he may specify particular days of the week on which licence periods may begin or end (to restrict custodial periods to

weekends, for example), and periods including or not including specified parts of the week (for example 'not Fridays').

Section 183 provides as follows:

(1) A court may, when passing a sentence of imprisonment for a term complying with sub-section (4)—

    (a) specify the number of days that the offender must serve in prison under the sentence before being released on licence for the remainder of the term, and

    (b) by order—

        (i) specify periods during which the offender is to be released temporarily on licence before he has served that number of days in prison, and

        (ii) require any licence to be granted subject to conditions requiring the offender's compliance during the licence periods with one or more requirements falling within section 182(1) and specified in the order.

...

(4) The term of the sentence—

    (a) must be expressed in weeks,

    (b) must be at least 28 weeks,

    (c) must not be more than 51 weeks in respect of any one offence, and

    (d) must not exceed the maximum term permitted for the offence.

(5) The number of custodial days—

    (a) must be at least 14, and

    (b) in respect of any one offence, must not be more than 90.

(6) A court may not exercise its powers under sub-section (1) unless the offender has expressed his willingness to serve the custodial part of the proposed sentence intermittently, during the parts of the sentence that are not to be licence periods.

(7) Where a court exercises its powers under sub-section (1) in respect of two or more terms of imprisonment that are to be served consecutively—

    (a) the aggregate length of the terms of imprisonment must not be more than 65 weeks, and

    (b) the aggregate of the numbers of custodial days must not be more than 180.

Section 184 of the 2003 Act places restrictions on the power of the court to make an intermittent custody order. It provides that an intermittent custody order may only be made where suitable prison accommodation is available for the offender during the custodial periods, and he will have suitable accommodation available to him during the licence periods.

Section 185(1) limits requirements which can be added to the licence conditions for intermittent custody:

(a) unpaid work requirement (see s 199);

(b) activity requirement (see s 201);

(c) programme requirement (see s 202);

(d) prohibited activity requirement (see s 203).

Section 185(2) provides that s 182(3) to (5) (electronic monitoring of licence conditions and compatibility of licence conditions in the context of custody plus orders) apply equally to intermittent custody orders.

Section 187 of the 2003 Act gives effect to Sched 10 to the Act, which contains provisions relating to the revocation or amendment of custody plus orders and the amendment of intermittent custody orders.

Paragraph 3 of Sched 10 provides that:

(1)   Where at any time while a custody plus order or intermittent custody order is in force, it appears to the appropriate court on the application of the offender or the responsible officer that, having regard to circumstances which have arisen since the order was made, it would be in the interests of justice to do so, the court may—

(a) in the case of a custody plus order, revoke the order, and

(b) in the case of an intermittent custody order, amend the order so that it contains only provision specifying periods for the purposes of section 183(1)(b)(i) [quoted above].

(2)   The revocation under this paragraph of a custody plus order does not affect the sentence of imprisonment to which the order relates, except in relation to the conditions of the licence.

Paragraph 4 enables the court to amend the order to refer to another petty sessions area if the offender changes his residence.

Paragraph 5 provides that:

(1)   At any time during the term of imprisonment to which a custody plus order or intermittent custody order relates, the appropriate court may, on the application of the offender, the Secretary of State or the responsible officer, by order amend any requirement of the custody plus order or intermittent custody order—

(a) by cancelling the requirement, or

(b) by replacing it with a requirement of the same kind imposing different obligations, which the court could include if it were then making the order.

Paragraph 6(1) provides that:

At any time during the term of imprisonment to which an intermittent custody order relates, the appropriate court may, on the application of the offender, the Secretary of State or the responsible officer, amend the order—

(a)   so as to specify different periods for the purposes of section 183(1)(b)(i), or

(b)   so as to provide that he is to remain in prison until the number of days served by him in prison is equal to the number of custodial days.

The Explanatory Notes that accompany the Act comment that this provision could be used if (for example) the offender loses his job, which had provided the reason for intermittence. In such a case, the offender might wish to serve his sentence in the normal manner in order to get the custodial days over with as soon as possible. Another example given in the Notes is where the offender turns out to be unsuitable for intermittent custody, in which case the responsible officer could apply to have the intermittence removed from the sentence (so that the custodial periods are served consecutively, followed by a single licence period).

Where a court is amending an order other than following an application by the offender, the court must summon the offender to appear before the court (and may issue a warrant if he does not appear) unless the court is cancelling a requirement (para 8).

15.9   SUSPENDED SENTENCES OF IMPRISONMENT

The Criminal Justice Act 2003 (which repeals the provisions relating to suspended sentences in the Powers of Criminal Courts (Sentencing) Act 2000) makes radical changes to the law relating to suspended sentences. The key changes are:

(a) the removal of the requirement that there must be 'exceptional circumstances' before the court can impose a suspended sentence; and

(b) the inclusion of a supervisory element into the suspended sentence to increase the rehabilitative effect of the sentence.

The new law on suspended sentences is contained in s 189 of the 2003 Act. It provides as follows:

Suspended sentences of imprisonment

(1)   A court which passes a sentence of imprisonment for a term of at least 28 weeks but not more than 51 weeks in accordance with section 181 may—

    (a) order the offender to comply during a period specified for the purposes of this paragraph in the order (in this Chapter referred to as 'the supervision period') with one or more requirements falling within section 190(1) and specified in the order, and

    (b) order that the sentence of imprisonment is not to take effect unless either—

        (i) during the supervision period the offender fails to comply with a requirement imposed under paragraph (a), or

        (ii) during a period specified in the order for the purposes of this sub-paragraph (in this Chapter referred to as 'the operational period') the offender commits in the United Kingdom another offence (whether or not punishable with imprisonment),

    and (in either case) a court having power to do so subsequently orders under paragraph 8 of Schedule 12 that the original sentence is to take effect.

(2)   Where two or more sentences imposed on the same occasion are to be served consecutively, the power conferred by sub-section (1) is not exercisable in relation to any of them unless the aggregate of the terms of the sentences does not exceed 65 weeks.

(3)   The supervision period and the operational period must each be a period of not less than six months and not more than two years beginning with the date of the order.

(4)   The supervision period must not end later than the operational period.

(5)   A court which passes a suspended sentence on any person for an offence may not impose a community sentence in his case in respect of that offence or any other offence of which he is convicted by or before the court or for which he is dealt with by the court.

In summary, s 189(1) enables a court which passes a prison sentence of between 28 and 51 weeks (or between 28 and 65 weeks in the case of consecutive sentences for two or more offences (s 189(2)) to suspend that sentence for a period of between six months and two years and to order the offender to undertake certain requirements in the community. The custodial part of the sentence only takes effect if the offender either fails to comply with those requirements or commits another offence within the period of suspension.

The period during which the offender undertakes the requirements is called 'the supervision period' and the entire length of period of suspension is (as in the case of suspended sentences prior to the implementation of these provisions) called 'the operational period'.

Under s 189(3), the supervision period and the operational period must each be between six months and two years. Section 189(4) provides that the supervision period must not end later than the operational period. However, the supervision period may be less than the operational period.

Section 189(5) prohibits the court from imposing a community sentence at the same time as a suspended sentence (although it is open to the court to impose a fine or compensation order at the same time).

Section 189(6) provides that a suspended sentence is to be treated as a sentence of imprisonment.

15.9.1 Requirements added to a suspended sentence

Section 190 of the 2003 Act deals with the imposition of requirements in a suspended sentence order. This section provides as follows:

Imposition of requirements by suspended sentence order

(1)   The requirements falling within this sub-section are—

    (a)   an unpaid work requirement (as defined by section 199),

    (b)   an activity requirement (as defined by section 201),

    (c)   a programme requirement (as defined by section 202),

    (d)   a prohibited activity requirement (as defined by section 203),

    (e)   a curfew requirement (as defined by section 204),

    (f)   an exclusion requirement (as defined by section 205),

    (g)   a residence requirement (as defined by section 206),

    (h)   a mental health treatment requirement (as defined by section 207),

    (i)   a drug rehabilitation requirement (as defined by section 209),

    (j)   an alcohol treatment requirement (as defined by section 212),

    (k)   a supervision requirement (as defined by section 213), and

    (l)   in a case where the offender is aged under 25, an attendance centre requirement (as defined by section 214).

Section 190(3) requires that where the court makes a suspended sentence order imposing a curfew requirement or an exclusion requirement, it must also impose an electronic monitoring requirement (as defined by s 215) unless, in the particular circumstances of the case, it would be inappropriate to do so. Under s 190(4), where the court makes a suspended sentence order imposing any of the other requirements listed above, it may also impose an electronic monitoring requirement. Where two or more different requirements are imposed, the court must consider whether, in the circumstances of the case, the requirements are compatible with each other (sub-s (5)).

Section 191(1) confers a discretion on the court to provide that a suspended sentence order passed under s 189(1) should be subject to periodic review at review hearings (which the offender is required to attend). Sub-section (2) excludes cases where the offender is subject to an order that imposes a drug rehabilitation requirement that is subject to court review, since reviews will be taking place anyway

(under s 210). A review hearing is conducted by the court responsible for the order (as defined in s 191(3) to (5)).

Section 192 sets out what is to take place at a review hearing. Section 192(1) provides that the court may amend the community requirements of the suspended sentence order, following consideration of the responsible officer's report. However, under s 192(2)(a), the court cannot impose a requirement of a different kind unless the offender consents, although (under s 192(3)) it can impose a requirement of the same kind. The offender's consent is required before a mental health treatment, drug rehabilitation or alcohol treatment requirement can be amended (s 192(2)(b)). The court may extend the supervision period, but not so that it lasts longer than two years or ends later than the operational period (s 192(2)(c)); however, the court has no power to amend the operational period (s 192(2)(d)).

Where, based on a report from the responsible officer, the court is of the opinion that 'the offender's progress in complying with the community requirements of the order is satisfactory', it can dispense with a review hearing, or may amend the order to provide that subsequent reviews can be held without a hearing (s 192(4)). Under s 192(5), if a review is held without a hearing and the court takes the view that the offender's progress is no longer satisfactory, the offender may be required to attend a review hearing. Section 192(6) empowers the court to adjourn a review hearing where it wishes to deal with the offender in respect of a breach of a requirement under formal breach proceedings (under para 8 of Sched 12).

15.9.2 Breach of suspended sentence orders

Section 193 of the 2003 Act gives effect to Sched 12 to the Act, which provides for the revocation or amendment of suspended sentence orders, and sets out the effect of further convictions.

Paragraph 4 of Sched 12 provides that:

(1) If the responsible officer is of the opinion that the offender has failed without reasonable excuse to comply with any of the community requirements of a suspended sentence order, the officer must give him a warning under this paragraph unless—

(a) the offender has within the previous twelve months been given a warning under this paragraph in relation to a failure to comply with any of the community requirements of the order, or

(b) the officer causes an information to be laid before a justice of the peace [or, if the suspended sentence order was made by the Crown Court and does not include a direction that any failure to comply with the community requirements of the order is to be dealt with by a magistrates' court, the Crown Court] in respect of the failure.

(2) A warning under this paragraph must—

(a) describe the circumstances of the failure,

(b) state that the failure is unacceptable, and

(c) inform the offender that if within the next twelve months he again fails to comply with any requirement of the order, he will be liable to be brought before a court.

Paragraph 5 sets out the consequences of a breach of the order after a warning has been administered:

(1) If—

  (a) the responsible officer has given a warning under paragraph 4 to the offender in respect of a suspended sentence order, and

  (b) at any time within the twelve months beginning with the date on which the warning was given, the responsible officer is of the opinion that the offender has since that date failed without reasonable excuse to comply with any of the community requirements of the order,

  the officer must cause an information to be laid before a justice of the peace [or, if the suspended sentence order was made by the Crown Court and does not include a direction that any failure to comply with the community requirements of the order is to be dealt with by a magistrates' court, the Crown Court] in respect of the failure in question.

Under para 6, where a suspended sentence order made by a magistrates' court, or a suspended sentence order which was made by the Crown Court, includes a direction that any failure to comply with the community requirements of the order is to be dealt with by a magistrates' court, and it appears to a justice of the peace that the offender has failed to comply with any of the community requirements of the order, the justice may issue a summons requiring the offender to appear at the court or (if the information is in writing and on oath) issue a warrant for his arrest.

Paragraph 7 confers the same power on the Crown Court where the suspended sentence order was made by the Crown Court and does not include a direction that any failure to comply with the community requirements of the order is to be dealt with by a magistrates' court.

Paragraph 8 sets out the powers of the court following the breach of a community requirement or where the offender is convicted of a further offence. Under this paragraph, where:

(a) it is proved to the satisfaction of the court that the offender has failed, without reasonable excuse, to comply with any of the community requirements of the suspended sentence order; or

(b) the offender is convicted of an offence committed during the operational period of a suspended sentence,

the court must deal with him in one of the following ways (set out in para 8(2)):

(a) make an order that the suspended sentence is to take effect with its original term and custodial period unaltered; or

(b) make an order that the sentence is to take effect with either or both of the following modifications—

  (i) the substitution for the original term of a lesser term (under s 181(2)); and

  (ii) the substitution for the original custodial period of a lesser custodial period (under s 181(5) and (6)), or

(c) amend the order by doing any one or more of the following—

  (i) imposing more onerous community requirements which the court could include if it were then making the order;

  (ii) extending the supervision period; or

  (iii) extending the operational period.

Paragraph 8(3) stipulates that the court must make an order under para (2)(a) or (b) unless it is of the opinion that it would be unjust to do so in view of all the circumstances, including the matters mentioned in sub-para (4). The factors set out in para 8(4) are:

(a) the extent to which the offender has complied with the community requirements of the suspended sentence order; and

(b) where the offender has been convicted of a subsequent offence, the facts of that subsequent offence.

Where the court does not order that the suspended sentence take effect, it must state its reasons.

The new provisions thus maintain the presumption that a suspended sentence will be activated following a breach, unless the court finds that it would be unjust to do so. If it does activate the suspended sentence, the court can set a shorter custodial term for the offender to serve if it wishes. If the court finds that it would be unjust to activate the suspended sentence, it can maintain the sentence suspended but amend the order to make the community requirements more onerous or to extend either the supervision or operational periods.

Under para 8(6), where the suspended sentence order was made by the Crown Court and the offender is appearing before a magistrates' court, the magistrates may commit him (in custody or on bail) to the Crown Court to be dealt with.

Under para 8(8), if the Crown Court has to decide whether the offender has failed to comply with the community requirements of a suspended sentence order, this question is dealt with by a judge sitting alone.

Paragraph 9(1) requires that where a court orders (under para 8(2)(a) or (b)) that a suspended sentence is to take effect (with or without any variation of the original term and custodial period), the court:

(a) must also make a custody plus order, and

(b) may order that the sentence is to take effect immediately or that the term of that sentence is to commence on the expiry of another term of imprisonment passed on the offender by that or another court.

Thus, where a suspended sentence is activated, the court must make a custody plus order, setting out the licence conditions that will apply on the offender's release from custody at the end of the custodial period of his sentence. The court has a discretion over whether the new sentence is to take effect immediately or after any other sentence that the offender is serving.

Paragraph 10(1) makes it clear that an offender who is subject to a suspended sentence order that contains a mental health treatment, drug rehabilitation or alcohol treatment requirement, and who refuses to undergo any surgical, electrical or other treatment, is not to be regarded as being in breach of the order if the court takes the view that his refusal was, in all the circumstances, reasonable having regard to all the circumstances. Under para 10(2), the court cannot amend a mental health treatment, drug rehabilitation or alcohol treatment requirement unless the offender agrees to comply with the requirement as amended.

Paragraph 11 sets out which court may deal with a breach of a suspended sentence order. Paragraph 11(1) provides that the Crown Court may deal with breach of any suspended sentence (whether imposed by the Crown Court or a magistrates' court),

and that any magistrates' court dealing with the offender can deal with breach of a suspended sentence order made by that or any other magistrates' court.

Under para 11(2), where an offender is convicted by a magistrates' court of an offence committed during the operational period of a suspended sentence passed by the Crown Court, the magistrates may commit him (in custody or on bail) to the Crown Court, otherwise they must give written notice of the conviction to the appropriate officer of the Crown Court. In the latter case, para 12 enables the Crown Court to issue a summons requiring the offender to appear before the court, or to issue a warrant for his arrest.

15.9.3 Amendment of suspended sentence orders

Part 3 of Sched 12 to the Criminal Justice Act 2003 deals with the amendment of suspended sentence orders.

Paragraph 13(1) empowers the court to cancel community requirements that form part of a suspended sentence order. It provides that:

> Where at any time while a suspended sentence order is in force, it appears to the appropriate court on the application of the offender or the responsible officer that, having regard to the circumstances which have arisen since the order was made, it would be in the interests of justice to do so, the court may cancel the community requirements of the suspended sentence order.

Paragraph 13(2) states that these circumstances include 'the offender's making good progress or his responding satisfactorily to supervision'. Another reason might be illness or disability making it impossible for the offender to comply with the original requirements.

Paragraph 14 enables the order to be amended if the offender moves to a different area.

Paragraph 15(1) empowers the court (at any time during the supervision period), upon application by the offender or the responsible officer, to amend any community requirement of a suspended sentence order either by cancelling the requirement, or by replacing it with a requirement of the same kind, which the court could include if it were then making the order. Under para 15(3), the court cannot amend a mental health treatment, drug rehabilitation or alcohol treatment requirement without the consent of the offender; however, where the offender withholds consent, the court may (under para 15(4)) revoke the suspended sentence order and the suspended sentence to which it relates, and deal with the offender, for the offence in respect of which the suspended sentence was imposed in any way in which it could deal with him if he had just been convicted by the court of that offence. If the court does re-sentence the offender, it must take into account the extent to which the offender has complied with the requirements of the order (para 15(5)).

Paragraph 16 provides that where a community order includes a drug rehabilitation, alcohol treatment or mental health treatment requirement and the medical practitioner responsible for the treatment is of the opinion that:

- the treatment should be extended beyond the period specified in the order;
- the offender should receive different treatment;

- the offender is not susceptible to treatment; or
- the offender does not require further treatment,

he must make a report to the responsible officer.

Similarly, if for any reason the medical practitioner is unwilling to continue to treat the offender, he must report this fact to the responsible officer. Where this has occurred, the responsible officer will apply to the court to have the requirement amended or cancelled.

Paragraph 17 provides that where a suspended sentence order contains a drug rehabilitation requirement, the responsible officer may apply to the court to change a review without a hearing to a review with a hearing, or vice versa.

Under para 18, where the suspended sentence order includes an unpaid work requirement, the offender or the responsible officer may apply to the court to extend the 12 months limit on unpaid work if it is in the interests of justice to do so. This might be necessary if, for example, the offender became ill during the 12 months and was unable to complete all the hours of unpaid work during the first 12 months.

15.10   RELEASE ON LICENCE

Chapter 6 of the Criminal Justice Act 2003 deals with release on licence.

Section 240 of the 2003 Act (which is based on s 87 of the Powers of Criminal Courts (Sentencing) Act 2000) sets out the effect of remand in custody prior to the passing of a custodial sentence. Section 240(3) provides that:

> ... the court must direct that the number of days for which the offender was remanded in custody in connection with the offence or a related offence is to count as time served by him as part of the sentence.

Under s 240(4)(b), this does not apply if it is, in the opinion of the court, just in all the circumstances not to give a direction under sub-s(3). Where the court does not give a direction under sub-s (3), it must give its reasons (sub-s (6)).

Section 240(5) requires that where the court gives a direction under sub-s (3), it must state in open court:

(a)   the number of days for which the offender was remanded in custody; and

(b)   the number of days in relation to which the direction is given.

Under s 240(2):

> ... it is immaterial ... whether the offender—

(a)   has also been remanded in custody in connection with other offences; or

(b)   has also been detained in connection with other matters.

For these purposes, a suspended sentence is treated as a sentence of imprisonment when it takes effect (sub-s (7)). Where the offender is sentenced to consecutive terms, those terms are to be treated as a single term if they were passed on the same occasion or, although they were passed on different occasions, the offender has not been released between the two terms (sub-s (8)).

Section 244 sets out when prisoners (except those subject to a life sentence or one of the new sentences for dangerous offenders under Chapter 5 of the Act) must be released. Prisoners must spend the 'requisite custodial period' in custody before the Secretary of State is required to release them on licence. This period varies according to the length of the sentence:

- prisoners serving a sentence of 12 months or more (apart from dangerous offenders and life sentence prisoners) must be released on licence after serving one-half of their sentence;

- prisoners serving a sentence of less than 12 months must be released at the end of the 'custodial period' defined by s 181;

- prisoners serving a sentence of intermittent custody must be released at the end of each custodial period defined by s 183.

Section 247 deals with the release on licence of prisoners who are serving extended sentences under s 227 or 228. Under s 247(2), once the offender has served one-half of the 'appropriate custodial term', he must be released on licence if the Parole Board so directs. The Parole Board 'may not give a direction under sub-section (2) unless the Board is satisfied that it is no longer necessary for the protection of the public that the prisoner should be confined' (s 247(3)). Under s 247(4), once the offender has served the full 'appropriate custodial term' (that is, the period determined by the court as the appropriate custodial term under s 227 or 228), he must be released on licence. Where a fixed term prisoner is released on licence, the licence remains in force (unless he is recalled to prison) for the remainder of his sentence: s 249(1).

15.10.1 Conditions of release on licence

Section 250 of the Criminal Justice Act 2003 sets out the licence conditions that may be imposed. Under s 250(2), where the prisoner is serving a sentence of less than 12 months, the conditions *must* include:

(a) the conditions required by the relevant court order;

(b) the 'standard conditions' in so far as they are not inconsistent with (a).

The conditions in such a case *may* include:

(i) conditions authorised by s 62 or 64 of the Criminal Justice and Court Services Act 2000 (electronic monitoring or drug testing requirements);

(ii) conditions prescribed by the Secretary of State (by statutory instrument).

Section 238 (which does not apply to sentences of detention under s 91 of the Powers of Criminal Courts (Sentencing) Act 2000) empowers the court to recommend licence conditions when sentencing an offender to imprisonment for 12 months or more. It provides that:

(1) A court which sentences an offender to a term of imprisonment of twelve months or more in respect of any offence may, when passing sentence, recommend to the Secretary of State particular conditions which in its view should be included in any licence granted to the offender under this Chapter on his release from prison.

Under s 250(4), where the prisoner is serving a sentence of 12 months or more, the conditions *must* include the standard conditions and *may* include:

(a) conditions authorised by s 62 or 64 of the Criminal Justice and Court Services Act 2000 (electronic monitoring or drug testing requirements);

(b) conditions prescribed by the Secretary of State (by statutory instrument).

The 'standard' and 'prescribed' conditions are set out in the Criminal Justice (Sentencing) (Licence Conditions) Order 2003 (SI 2003/3337), which came into force on 26 January 2004.

The 'standard' conditions required by para 2(2) are that the prisoner must:

(a)   keep in touch with the responsible officer in accordance with instructions;

(b)   receive visits from the responsible officer in accordance with instructions;

(c)   permanently reside at an address approved by the responsible officer, and obtain the prior permission of the responsible officer for any stay of one or more nights at a different address;

(d)   undertake work (including voluntary work) only with the approval of the responsible officer, and obtain his prior approval in relation to any change in the nature of that work;

(e)   not travel outside the United Kingdom without the prior permission of the responsible officer;

(f)   be of good behaviour, and not behave in a way which undermines the purposes of the release on licence, which are to protect the public, prevent re-offending and promote successful re-integration into the community;

(g)   not commit any offence.

Paragraph 3 sets out other conditions of licence for prisoners serving a sentence of imprisonment of less than 12 months. The prisoner must:

(a)   attend appointments arranged with a named psychiatrist, psychologist or medical practitioner, and co-operate fully with any recommended care or treatment;

(b)   not take work (including voluntary work) or participate in any organised activity which will involve a person below an age specified by the responsible officer;

(c)   not spend one or more nights in the same household as any person below an age specified by the responsible officer;

(d)   not seek to approach or communicate with any person specified by the responsible officer without the prior permission of—
      (i)   the responsible officer; and
      (ii) where the specified person is under the age of 18, a social services authority specified by the responsible officer;

(e)   not enter a place (including an area) specified by the responsible office except with the prior permission of the responsible officer;

(f)   remain at a specified place for periods specified by the responsible officer.

Paragraph 4 sets out other conditions of licence for prisoners serving a sentence of imprisonment of 12 months or more. The prisoner:

... must comply with any instructions given by the responsible officer in relation to participation by the offender in an activity or set of activities designed to promote the prevention of re-offending and the successful re-integration of the prisoner into the community.

Section 254 of the Criminal Justice Act 2003 empowers the Secretary of State to revoke a prisoner's licence and thereby to recall the prisoner to prison. Section 254(2) provides that:

(2) A person recalled to prison under sub-section (1)—

    (a) may make representations in writing with respect to his recall, and

    (b) on his return to prison, must be informed of the reasons for his recall and of his right to make representations.

Section 255 governs the recall of prisoners who have been released under s 246 (home detention curfew). Such recall may be ordered where the offender fails to comply with any licence condition or if his whereabouts can no longer be electronically monitored.

Finally, s 257 of the Criminal Justice Act 2002 re-enacts s 42 of the Criminal Justice Act 1991, enabling additional days to be added to a prisoner's sentence if he is found guilty of disciplinary offences whilst in custody.

15.11 LIFE SENTENCES

Chapter 7 of the Criminal Justice Act 2003 sets out the effect of a life sentence. It was enacted partly as a result of concern that life prisoners were being released on licence too early.

Section 269 governs the determination of the minimum term in relation to mandatory life sentences imposed for murder. Under s 269(2), a court passing a mandatory life sentence must make an order specifying a period of time the prisoner must serve before the Parole Board can consider release on licence under the provisions of s 28 of the Crime (Sentences) Act 1997 (often called the 'minimum term'). Under sub-s (3), the minimum term:

... is to be such as the court considers appropriate taking into account ... the seriousness of the offence, or of the combination of the offence and any one or more offences associated with it.

However, under s 269(4), where the offender was aged 21 or over at the time of the offence, and the court takes the view that the murder is so serious that the offender ought to spend the rest of his life in prison, the court must order that the early release provisions are not to apply. Under s 269(5)(a), the court must have regard to the principles set out in Sched 21 to the Act.

Schedule 21 provides that where the offender was aged 21 or over when he committed the offence, the appropriate starting point is a 'whole life order' if the court considers the seriousness of the offences is 'exceptionally high'. Under para 4(2), this will normally be the case where:

(a) in the case of the murder of two or more persons, each murder involves any of the following—

    (i) a substantial degree of premeditation or planning,

    (ii) the abduction of the victim, or

    (iii) sexual or sadistic conduct,

(b) the murder of a child, if involving the abduction of the child or sexual or sadistic motivation,

(c)   a murder done for the purpose of advancing a political, religious or ideological cause, or

(d)   a murder by an offender previously convicted of murder.

Where the offender was aged 18 or over when he committed the offence, the appropriate starting point is a minimum term of 30 years if the court considers that the seriousness of the offence is 'particularly high'. Under para 5(2), this will normally be the case where the murder:

- was of a police officer or prison officer in the course of his duty,
- involved the use of a firearm or explosive,
- was done for gain (such as a murder done in the course or furtherance of robbery or burglary, done for payment or done in the expectation of gain as a result of the death),
- was intended to obstruct or interfere with the course of justice,
- involved sexual or sadistic conduct,
- was of two or more persons,
- was racially or religiously aggravated or aggravated by sexual orientation, or
- falls within paragraph 4(2) [quoted above] but was committed by an offender who was aged under 21 when he committed the offence.

In other cases where the offender was aged 18 or over when he committed the offence, the appropriate starting point, in determining the minimum term, is 15 years (para 6). If the offender was aged under 18 when he committed the offence, the appropriate starting point, in determining the minimum term, is 12 years (para 7).

Paragraph 8 goes on to provide that:

Having chosen a starting point, the court should take into account any aggravating or mitigating factors, to the extent that it has not allowed for them in its choice of starting point.

These aggravating or mitigating factors may result in a minimum term of any length (whatever the starting point), or in the making of a whole life order (para 9).

Paragraph 10 lists some aggravating factors (additional to those mentioned in paras 4(2) and 5(2)):

(a)   a significant degree of planning or premeditation,

(b)   the fact that the victim was particularly vulnerable because of age or disability,

(c)   mental or physical suffering inflicted on the victim before death,

(d)   the abuse of a position of trust,

(e)   the use of duress or threats against another person to facilitate the commission of the offence,

(f)   the fact that the victim was providing a public service or performing a public duty, and

(g)   concealment, destruction or dismemberment of the body.

Paragraph 11 lists some mitigating factors that may be relevant to the offence of murder:

(a)   an intention to cause serious bodily harm rather than to kill,

(b)   lack of premeditation,

(c)   the fact that the offender suffered from any mental disorder or mental disability which (although not falling within section 2(1) of the Homicide Act 1957, lowered his degree of culpability,

(d)   the fact that the offender was provoked (for example, by prolonged stress) in a way not amounting to a defence of provocation,

(e)   the fact that the offender acted to any extent in self-defence,

(f)   a belief by the offender that the murder was an act of mercy, and

(g)   the age of the offender.

Under s 270 of the Act, the court has to give reasons for making an order under s 269(2) or (4). Under s 270(2):

> ... in stating its reasons the court must ... (a) state which of the starting points in Schedule 21 it has chosen and its reasons for doing so, and (b) state its reasons for any departure from that starting point.

(a)   that ... that the offender suffered from any mental disorder or mental disability within subsection 2(b) or the formula in Chapter 8:2; and the degree of culpability.

(b)   the fact that the offender was proved or not proved, by prolonged stress or was an admission to the offence of provocation;

(c)   ... whether the offender acted under any external self-defence;

(d)   ... acted by fire of under that the offence was an act of necessity; and

(e)   the age of the offender.

Under ... 270 of the Act the court has to give reasons for making an order under section 26, Chapter 8:2(2).

In passing its sentence the court must ... (2) state which of the starting points in Schedule 21 it has chosen, an 2 set out its reasons for doing so and (b) state its reasons for any departure from that starting point.

CHAPTER 16

OFFENDERS OVER 16: COMMUNITY SENTENCES

In this chapter, we look at the community sentences which may be imposed on adult offenders, namely the community rehabilitation order, the community punishment order, and the community punishment and rehabilitation order. The statutory criteria which have to be met before any of these orders can be made also have to be met for supervision orders and attendance centre orders (which may be made in respect of young offenders). We look at community orders under the Powers of Criminal Courts (Sentencing) Act 2000 and at the new regime for such orders established by the Criminal Justice Act 2003.

16.1 STATUTORY CRITERIA FOR IMPOSING COMMUNITY ORDERS

Under the Powers of Criminal Courts (Sentencing) Act 2000, a community order means:

- a community punishment order (formerly known as a 'community service order');
- a community rehabilitation order (formerly known as a 'probation order');
- a community punishment and rehabilitation order (formerly known as a 'combination order'), which combines community punishment and community rehabilitation;
- a supervision order;
- an attendance centre order;
- a curfew order;
- a drug treatment and testing order;
- an action plan order;
- a drug abstinence order;
- an exclusion order.

Before imposing a community sentence (that is, a sentence which consists of or includes one or more community orders), the court must be satisfied that 'the offence, or the combination of the offence and one or more offences associated with it, was serious enough to warrant such a sentence' (s 35(1) of the 2000 Act). As with custodial sentences, associated offences include offences which are taken into consideration (s 161(1) of the 2000 Act).

Furthermore, s 35(3) of the Act provides that:

- the community order(s) must be 'the most suitable for the offender'; and
- the restrictions on the offenders liberty imposed by the community order(s) must be commensurate with the seriousness of the offence(s).

Section 36(1) of the Act states that in deciding whether a community sentence is appropriate, the court must take into account:

- information about the circumstances of the offence (including any aggravating or mitigating factors); and
- information about the offender.

Section 36(3) provides that a pre-sentence report must be obtained before any of the following community orders is imposed:

- a community punishment order;
- a community rehabilitation order where additional requirements are imposed;
- a community punishment and rehabilitation order;
- a supervision order where additional requirements are imposed;
- a drug treatment and testing order.

It follows that the obtaining of a pre-sentence report is not mandatory (although one will often be obtained) before any of the following sentences is imposed:

- a community rehabilitation order which does not contain any additional requirements;
- a supervision order which does not contain any additional requirements;
- an attendance centre order;
- a curfew order.

Section 36A of the Powers of Criminal Courts (Sentencing) Act 2000 provides that where a person aged 18 or over is convicted of an offence and the court is considering passing a community sentence, it may make a 'pre-sentence drug testing order' for the purpose of ascertaining whether the offender has any specified Class A drug in his body. The order requires the offender to provide samples for analysis. Failure without reasonable excuse to comply with the order will be an offence punishable with a fine of up to level 4 (£2,500).

16.2   COMMUNITY PUNISHMENT ORDERS

Section 46 of the Powers of Criminal Courts (Sentencing) Act 2000 provides that where a person who has attained the age of 16 is convicted of an offence which is punishable with imprisonment, the court may make a community punishment order. The effect of the order is to require the offender to perform unpaid work under the direction of a probation officer or, where the offender is under 18, a social worker or a member of a youth offending team.

The obligations imposed by a community punishment order are contained in s 47(1) of the Act, namely:

- to keep in touch with the probation officer and to notify the probation officer of any change of address; and
- to perform the number of hours of work specified in the order at such times as he may be instructed by the probation officer.

Section 47(2) says that the instructions given by the probation officer should, so far as practicable, be such as to avoid any conflict with the offender's religious beliefs and to avoid any interference with the times (if any) at which the offender normally works or attends a school or other educational establishment.

16.2.1   Requirements to be met before an order is made

Section 46 of the 2000 Act states that a community punishment order cannot be made unless the following requirements are satisfied:

- there must be a pre-sentence report (s 36(3)(b));
- there must be evidence before the court from a probation officer (usually part of the pre-sentence report procedure) that the offender is a suitable person to perform community service (s 46(4));
- the court must be satisfied that provision can be made for the offender to perform community service in the area in which he resides (s 46(6)).

Where the court adjourns the case so that a report can be prepared to assess the offender's suitability for community service, the court will usually warn the offender that the court may nonetheless impose a custodial sentence. The reason for this is that if the court does not warn the defendant in this way and the report shows that the offender is suitable for community service, the offender will be left with a legitimate sense of grievance if the court later imposes a custodial sentence. In such a case, the custodial sentence would almost certainly be overturned on appeal (see *R v Gillam* (1980) 2 Cr App R(S) 267; *R v Millwood* (1982) 4 Cr App R(S) 281; *R v Stokes* [1983] RTR 59).

Section 46(10) of the Act provides that before a court makes a community punishment order, it must explain to the offender:

- the purpose and effect of the order;
- the consequences of failing to comply with the order;
- that the court may review the order on the application of the offender or the probation officer.

16.2.2   Number of hours

Section 46(3) of the 2000 Act provides that the aggregate number of hours of community service imposed under a community punishment order must be between 40 and 240. Section 46(8) says that where a court makes community punishment orders in respect of two of more offences, the hours of work specified in the orders may be concurrent or cumulative, provided that the total does not exceed 240 hours.

Section 46(8) only applies where a court is imposing two or more community punishment orders on the same occasion. However, in *R v Siha* (1992) 13 Cr App R(S) 588, the defendant was sentenced in April 1990 to 180 hours' community service and in October 1990 to 90 hours for a separate offence. The Court of Appeal held that even though the legislation does not prevent a court from making a community punishment order where the offender is already subject to a community punishment order imposed on an earlier occasion, with the effect that orders imposing more than a total of 240 hours are in force against that offender, a court should not impose a consecutive community punishment order on an offender who is already subject to a community punishment order if the effect of the two orders is to impose a total of more than 240 hours.

The community service should normally be completed within one year of the making of the order. However, the order remains in force (unless revoked by the court)

until the total number of hours specified in the order have been completed (see s 47(3) of the 2000 Act).

Note that in *R v Porter* (1992) 13 Cr App R(S) 258, it was pointed out by the Court of Appeal that there is no hard and fast rule that where the offence is not sufficiently serious to justify the imposition of a custodial sentence, the number of hours of community service which the offender is ordered to perform should be small. The court should make sure that the number of hours ordered reflects the gravity of the offence.

16.2.3   Mixing community punishment with other orders

A community punishment order cannot be imposed with a community rehabilitation order imposed for the same offence, although a community punishment and rehabilitation order achieves the same effect. Furthermore, where an offender is convicted of more than one offence and is being sentenced for those offences at the same hearing, there is no power to impose a community rehabilitation order for one offence and a community punishment order in respect of another offence (*Gilding v DPP* (1998) 162 JPN 523).

It would be wrong in principle to impose a community punishment order and a sentence of immediate imprisonment (even where the court is sentencing for two offences) as the two are clearly incompatible (*R v Starie* (1979) 69 Cr App R 239). By virtue of s 118(6) of the Powers of Criminal Courts (Sentencing) Act 2000, it is not permissible to impose a suspended sentence and make a community punishment order on the same occasion.

16.3   COMMUNITY REHABILITATION ORDERS

Section 41(1) of the Powers of Criminal Courts (Sentencing) Act 2000 provides that a court which is dealing with an offender who has attained the age of 16 may make a community rehabilitation order if the court is of the opinion that supervision of the offender by a probation officer (or member of a youth offending team if the offender is under 18) is desirable in the interests of:

- securing the rehabilitation of the offender; or
- protecting the public from harm from him or preventing the commission by him of further offences.

The minimum period of a community rehabilitation order is six months; the maximum period is three years.

16.3.1   Effect of a community rehabilitation order

The offender's principal duty under a community rehabilitation order is to keep in touch with the probation officer in accordance with instructions given by the probation officer and to notify the probation officer of any change of address (s 41(11)).

16.3.2   Imposing additional requirements under a community rehabilitation order

The court is empowered by s 42 of the Powers of Criminal Courts (Sentencing) Act 2000 to impose additional requirements in the community rehabilitation order where it takes the view that these are necessary to secure the rehabilitation of the offender or to protect the public from harm from him or to prevent him from committing further offences.

Before imposing any additional requirements, the court must first obtain a pre-sentence report on the offender (s 36(3)(a) of the 2000 Act). In practice, courts are generally reluctant to make a community rehabilitation order at all unless a pre-sentence report has been prepared.

The additional requirements which may be imposed are set out in Sched 2 to the 2000 Act. They are:

- *Requirements as to residence (para 1)*

Before imposing such a requirement, the court must consider the home surroundings of the offender.

Where the residence requirement is that the offender must reside in an approved hostel, the period for which this requirement applies must be stated in the order.

- *Requirements as to activities (para 2)*

The court may require the offender:

(a) to present himself to a specified person at a specified place for up to a total of 60 days;

(b) to participate (for up to 60 days) or to refrain from participating in specified activities.

The offender may be required to comply with instructions given by the person in charge of the place or activities in question.

Such requirements should avoid, so far as possible, interference with the times (if any) during which the offender is normally at work or attends a school or other educational establishment.

- *Requirements as to attendance at a probation centre (para 3)*

A probation centre is a place at which non-residential facilities are provided for use in connection with the rehabilitation of offenders (para 3(8)). A community rehabilitation order may require the offender to attend a probation centre for up to a total of 60 days. If the offender was convicted of a sexual offence, then the 60 hours maximum does not apply (para 4).

Again, the requirement should avoid, so far as possible, interference with the times (if any) during which the offender is normally at work or attends a school or other education establishment.

The offender must comply with instructions given by staff at the probation centre.

- *Requirements as to treatment for mental condition (para 5)*

Where the court is satisfied, on the evidence of a duly qualified medical practitioner, that the mental condition of the offender is such that he requires (and may be susceptible to) treatment but is not such as to warrant the making of a

hospital order or a guardianship order (under the Mental Health Act 1983), the court may impose a requirement that the offender submit to treatment with a view to improving his mental condition. This requirement can be imposed for the duration of the community rehabilitation order or for such lesser period as may be specified in the order.

The treatment which may be required by a community rehabilitation order must be one of the following:

(a) treatment as a resident patient in a mental hospital;

(b) treatment as a non-resident patient at a place specified in the order;

(c) treatment by a qualified medical practitioner.

However, the nature of the treatment to be administered cannot be specified in the order.

- *Requirements as to treatment for alcohol or drug dependency (para 6)*

  If the court is satisfied that:

  (a) the offender is dependent on drugs or alcohol or has a propensity towards the misuse of drugs or alcohol; and

  (b) this dependency or propensity caused or contributed to the offence in respect of which the community rehabilitation order is to be made; and

  (c) the offender's dependency or propensity is such that it requires and may be susceptible to treatment,

  the court can impose a requirement that the offender attend a specified place for such treatment. This requirement may be imposed for the duration of the community rehabilitation order or some shorter period specified in the order.

Schedule 2 of the Powers of Criminal Courts (Sentencing) Act 2000 was amended by the Criminal Justice and Court Services Act 2000 to enable a community rehabilitation order to include further additional requirements.

The first of the new additional requirements is the 'curfew requirement' (para 7 of Sched 2). This is a requirement that the offender remain, for periods specified in the order, at a place specified in the order. The maximum duration of the requirement is six months, and the curfew period must be for between two and 12 hours per day. The order may specify different curfew addresses or different periods of curfew on different days.

Before imposing a curfew requirement, the court must obtain and consider information about the curfew address and, in particular, must take account of the attitude of anyone likely to be affected by the enforced presence of the offender in the place to be specified in the order.

The second of the new additional requirements is the 'exclusion requirement' (para 8 of Sched 2). This is a requirement that prohibits the offender from entering a place specified in the order for a specified period of up to two years. The order may provide for the prohibition to operate continuously or only during the periods specified in the order, and may specify different places for different periods or days.

16.3.3   Procedure for making a community rehabilitation order

Section 41(7) of the Powers of Criminal Courts (Sentencing) Act 2000 states that before making a community rehabilitation order, the court must explain the effect of the order (including the consequences of failing to comply with any additional requirements that have been imposed under the order) and must inform the offender that the court has power to review the order on the application of the offender or of the probation officer. The court may only include a requirement in a community rehabilitation order that the offender undergo treatment for a mental condition, or for drug or alcohol dependency, if the offender expresses willingness to comply with such requirements.

16.3.4   Combining a community rehabilitation order with other sentences

A community rehabilitation order cannot be made if the offender receives an immediate custodial sentence on the same occasion (whether in respect of the same offence or separate offences) as the two forms of sentence are clearly incompatible (*R v Mullervy* (1986) 8 Cr App R(S) 41).

Furthermore, a community rehabilitation order cannot be combined with a suspended sentence of imprisonment (s 118(6) of the 2000 Act). However, the 'suspended sentence supervision order' provides a means of achieving the same end.

A community rehabilitation order cannot be combined with a community punishment order where the two sentences are imposed for a single offence (s 35(2) of the 2000 Act), although a community punishment and rehabilitation order will achieve the same effect. If the offender is to be sentenced for two offences, there is power to impose a community rehabilitation order for one and community punishment order for another (*Gilding v DPP* (1998) 162 JPN 523). The court can, of course, make a community punishment and rehabilitation order instead.

Section 42(3) of the 2000 Act specifically prohibits the court from imposing a requirement in a community rehabilitation order that the offender pay compensation to the victim of the offence. The court may, however, make a compensation order under s 130 of the Act even if it imposes a community rehabilitation order for the offence itself.

16.4   COMMUNITY PUNISHMENT AND REHABILITATION ORDERS

Although s 35(2) of the 2000 Act prevents the court imposing a community rehabilitation order and a community punishment order for the same offence, the same effect can be achieved by means of a community punishment and rehabilitation order.

Section 51(1) of the 2000 Act states that where the court is dealing with an offender who has attained the age of 16 who has been convicted of an imprisonable offence, the court may make a community punishment and rehabilitation order.

The effect of the order is that:

• the offender is under the supervision of a probation officer (or member of a youth offending team if the offender is under 18) for the period specified in the order, which must be between 12 months and three years; and

- the offender is required to perform unpaid work for the number of hours specified in the order, which must be between 40 and 100 hours.

A community punishment and rehabilitation order can only be made if the court is of the opinion that it is desirable to do so in the interests of securing the rehabilitation of the offender or of protecting the public from harm by preventing him from committing further offences (s 51(3)).

Before making a community punishment and rehabilitation order, the court must obtain a pre-sentence report (s 36(3)(c)).

Under s 51(4), the court may impose any additional requirements into the probation part of the order which it could impose if the order were merely a community rehabilitation order.

16.5   CURFEW ORDERS

The power to make curfew orders is contained in s 37 of the Powers of Criminal Courts (Sentencing) Act 2000. The effect of a curfew order is to require the offender to remain, for periods specified in the order, at a place or places specified in the order.

A curfew order can be made in respect of an offender of any age. However, where the offender has not attained the age of 16, the maximum duration of the curfew order is three months. Where the offender has attained the age of 16, the maximum duration of the order is six months. In either case, the curfew order can only apply for between two and 12 hours per day.

Where the offender is under 16, the court must, before making a curfew order, obtain and consider information about his family circumstances and the likely effect of making such an order on those circumstances.

Whatever the age of the offender, the order should avoid conflict with the offender's religious beliefs and interference with the times he normally works or attends a school or other education establishment.

Before making a curfew order, the court must also seek information about the attitude of anyone likely to be affected by the enforced presence of the offender at the place specified in the order.

The effect of the order and the consequences of failing to comply with it must be explained to the offender by the court.

Section 38 of the 2000 Act provides for the imposition of a requirement for the electronic monitoring of the offender's whereabouts to assist in the enforcement of the curfew order.

16.6   DRUG TREATMENT AND TESTING ORDERS

Section 52 of the Powers of Criminal Courts (Sentencing) Act 2000 empowers the court to make a drug treatment and testing order where it convicts someone aged 16 or over of an offence, provided that the court is satisfied that he is dependent on (or has a propensity to misuse) drugs and that his dependency (or propensity) requires, and

may be susceptible to, treatment (s 52(3)). An order cannot be made unless the offender expresses his willingness to comply with its requirements (s 52(7)).

The order is for a specified period of between six months and three years (s 52(1)). It includes a requirement that the offender must submit, during the period covered by the order, to treatment by a qualified person with a view to reducing or eliminating his dependency or propensity to misuse drugs (s 53(2)). The treatment may include a period of residential or non-residential treatment at a place specified in the order (s 53(2)). During this period, the offender can also be required to provide samples for the purpose of ascertaining whether he has any drugs in his body (s 53(4)).

Before making a drug treatment and testing order, the court must explain its effect to the offender and the consequences which may follow if he fails to comply with the order (s 52(6)).

During the period covered by the order, the offender is also under the supervision of a probation officer (s 54(2)).

Section 55 provides for periodic reviews by the court of the offender's progress. The court may amend the order, but only with the consent of the offender. If the offender withholds consent, the court may revoke the order and sentence the offender for the original offence as if the court had just convicted him of that offence (s 55(3)). In such a case, the court must take into account the extent to which the offender has complied with the order; a custodial sentence may be imposed notwithstanding the restrictions in s 79(2) of the 2000 Act (s 55(4)).

Schedule 3 of the 2000 Act deals with breach of drug treatment and testing orders.

The Court of Appeal gave detailed guidelines on the factors to be considered before imposing a drug treatment and testing order in *Attorney General's Reference (No 64 of 2003)* [2003] EWCA Crim 3514; [2004] 2 Cr App R(S) 22:

(a) the court should consider whether it is a realistic possibility that the order will reduce the defendant's addiction to drugs;

(b) the fact that the defendant has been influenced by drugs to commit the offence is not in itself a reason to impose an order; an order is therefore not necessarily appropriate merely because an offender has committed offences under the influence of drugs;

(c) it is a necessary prerequisite that the defendant has made a clear and determined effort to become free from drugs;

(d) a drug treatment and testing order will generally have a greater prospect of success with defendants who are caught early in their criminal career, although in exceptional circumstances it might be suitable to impose an order at a later stage of a criminal career;

(e) an order will rarely be suitable in cases of serious violence;

(f) an order will generally be appropriate for offences involving acquisition where the motive was to get money for drugs to feed an addiction;

(g) an order might be suitable even where the defendant has committed a substantial number of offences;

(h) an order would be unlikely to be suitable where there are substantial cases of minor violence which have had a damaging effect on the victims (because there has to be proportionality between offences and sentences, rather than excessive emphasis on rehabilitation);

(i) particular significance has to be given to all the material in the case including pre-sentence reports.

In *R (Inner London Probation Service) v Tower Bridge Magistrates' Court* [2001] EWHC 401 (Admin); [2002] 1 Cr App R(S) 43, it was held by the Divisional Court that where a court is considering the imposition of a drug treatment and testing order and the Probation Service says that the defendant is not suitable for such an order, the court should be slow to act against the conclusions of a reasoned probation service assessment unless it has cogent reasons for doing so. In such a case, the court should ask the person who made the assessment to attend court, so that the court can discuss the matter. Where the court disagrees with the assessment of the probation service, it should set out the reasons for its decision. Lord Bingham CJ added that the Crown Prosecution Service should make sure that the appropriate steps have been taken by the court before a particular sentence is passed, especially where the defendant is unrepresented.

In *R v Chute* [2003] EWCA Crim 177; [2003] 2 Cr App R(S) 74, the defendant was made the subject of a drug treatment and testing order for a period of 12 months following his commission of two offences of burglary. He failed to comply with the terms of that order and failed to attend a review after a request to do so. The order was revoked and he was committed to the Crown Court for sentence, pursuant to s 4 of the Powers of Criminal Courts (Sentencing) Act 2000. It was held that the magistrates did not have the power to commit the defendant to the Crown Court for sentence where there has been a breach of a drug treatment and testing order.

16.7 ORDERS FOR PERSISTENT PETTY OFFENDERS

Section 59 of the Powers of Criminal Courts (Sentencing) Act 2000 applies where someone aged 16 or over is convicted of an offence in respect of which the court would be minded to impose a fine, but the offender has one or more unpaid fines imposed for previous convictions and, if a fine commensurate with the seriousness of the offence were to be imposed for the present offence, the offender would not have sufficient means to pay it. In such a case, the court may make a curfew order or community punishment order instead of imposing a fine.

Section 151 of the Criminal Justice Act 2003 replaces s 59 of the 2000 Act. It provides that where an offender aged 16 or over has been sentenced only to a fine on at least three previous occasions, the court may impose a community sentence even if the current offence does not cross the community sentence threshold. It does not matter whether the offender has, on previous sentencing occasions, received community or custodial sentences.

Section 151 applies where:

(a) a person aged 16 or over is convicted of an offence ('the current offence'),

(b) on three or more previous occasions he has, on conviction by a court in the United Kingdom of any offence committed by him after attaining the age of 16, had passed on him a sentence consisting only of a fine, and

(c) despite the effect of section 143(2) [assessing the seriousness of the offence], the court would not (apart from this section) regard the current offence, or the

combination of the current offence and one or more offences associated with it, as being serious enough to warrant a community sentence (s 151(1)).

Under s 151(2):

> The court may make a community order in respect of the current offence instead of imposing a fine if it considers that, having regard to all the circumstances including the matters mentioned in sub-section (3), it would be in the interests of justice to make such an order.

> (3)   The matters referred to in sub-section (2) are—
>
>> (a) the nature of the offences to which the previous convictions mentioned in sub-section (1)(b) relate and their relevance to the current offence, and
>>
>> (b) the time that has elapsed since the offender's conviction of each of those offences.

Under s 151(5), for the purposes of sub-s (1)(b), a compensation order does not form part of an offender's sentence. Section 151(6) goes on to provide that it is immaterial if the offender has received a sentence other than a fine for offences other than the three or more offences taken into account under sub-s (1)(b).

Section 151(7) makes it clear that s 151 is not intended to 'limit the extent to which a court may, in accordance with section 143(2), treat any previous convictions of the offender as increasing the seriousness of an offence'.

16.8   THE CRIMINAL JUSTICE AND COURT SERVICES ACT 2000

The Criminal Justice and Court Services Act 2000 introduced some additional community orders, detailed below.

16.8.1   Exclusion orders

Section 40A of the Powers of Criminal Courts (Sentencing) Act 2000 enables the court to make an order prohibiting the offender from entering a place specified in the order for a specified period of up to one year (three months where the offender is under 16). The order may provide for the prohibition to operate only during the periods specified in the order, and may specify different places for different periods or days. The order may contain an additional requirement that the offender submit to electronic monitoring of his whereabouts to ensure compliance with the order.

The requirements of the order should avoid conflict with the offender's religious beliefs or with the requirements of any other community order to which he is subject, and should avoid interference with the times at which he attends work or school or any other educational establishment.

Where the offender is under 16, the court must first obtain and consider information about his family circumstances and the likely effect of the order on those circumstances. Before making an exclusion order, the court must always explain the effect of the order and the consequences of failing to comply with it.

Breach of an exclusion order is dealt with under the procedure set out in Sched 3 to the Powers of Criminal Courts (Sentencing) Act 2000.

16.8.2 Drug abstinence orders

Section 58A of the Powers of Criminal Courts (Sentencing) Act 2000 enables the court to make a drug abstinence order against an offender aged 18 or over. The order requires the offender to abstain from misusing specified Class A drugs and to provide samples for the purpose of ascertaining whether he has any specified Class A drug in his body. The court cannot make a drug abstinence order unless satisfied that the offender is dependent on (or has a propensity to misuse) specified Class A drugs and either the offence in question is a 'trigger offence' (as defined in Sched 6 to the Criminal Justice and Court Services Act 2000) or else the misuse by the offender of any specified Class A drug caused or contributed to the offence of which he has been convicted. The trigger offences include various offences under the Theft Act 1968 and the Misuse of Drugs Act 1971.

The order can last for a specified period between six months and three years. Before making the order, the court must explain its effect and the consequences of non-compliance. Breach of a drug abstinence order is dealt with under the procedure set out in Sched 3 to the Powers of Criminal Courts (Sentencing) Act 2000.

Section 42(2A) of the Powers of Criminal Courts (Sentencing) Act 2000 (added by the Criminal Justice and Court Services Act 2000) enables the court to add a 'drug abstinence requirement' to a community rehabilitation order. This is a requirement that the offender abstain from misusing specified Class A drugs and that he must provide samples for analysis to determine whether he has any specified Class A drug in his body. Such a requirement may be imposed if the offender was aged 18 or over on the date of his conviction for the offence and, in the opinion of the court, is dependent on or has a propensity to misuse specified Class A drugs, and either the offence of which he has been convicted is a trigger offence or, in the opinion of the court, the offender is dependent on or has a propensity to misuse specified Class A drugs and the misuse by the offender of any specified Class A drug caused or contributed to the offence of which he has been convicted.

A community rehabilitation order cannot include a drug abstinence requirement if it includes a requirement of treatment for drug dependency (under para 2 of Sched 6 to the 2000 Act); also, a community sentence cannot include a drug abstinence requirement if it includes a drug treatment and testing order or a drug abstinence order.

16.8.3 Electronic monitoring of community orders

Section 36B of the Powers of Criminal Courts (Sentencing) Act 2000 enables a community order to include requirements for securing the electronic monitoring of the offender's compliance with any requirement imposed by the community order. Where the co-operation of someone other than the offender is required in order for electronic monitoring of the offender to be practicable, an electronic monitoring requirement cannot be imposed without that person's consent.

16.9 ENFORCING COMMUNITY SENTENCES

Enforcement of community sentences is primarily a matter for the Probation Service and the offender's local magistrates' court.

16.9.1 Dealing with breaches of community orders

In this section, we examine what happens if a community order is not complied with. This will be the case, for example, if a person subject to a community rehabilitation order fails to keep appointments with the probation officer or fails to comply with an additional requirement imposed by the court, or if a person subject to a community punishment order fails to perform the requisite number of hours.

The enforcement of community punishment orders, community rehabilitation orders, community punishment and rehabilitation orders, curfew orders and drug treatment and testing orders is dealt with by Sched 3 to the Powers of Criminal Courts (Sentencing) Act 2000.

No matter which court imposes a community order, enforcement proceedings are taken in the magistrates' court which serves the place where the offender resides. If a court in Newcastle-upon-Tyne imposes a community order on an offender who lives in Croydon, the offender will perform his obligations under the order in Croydon and if he fails to do so will have to appear before the Croydon magistrates' court.

If a person who is subject to a community order fails to comply with the terms of the order, a probation officer will lay an information at the local magistrates' court. A summons will then be issued requiring the offender to appear before the magistrates' court (Sched 3, para 2).

When the offender attends the court, he will be asked whether he admits or denies failing to comply with the order. If the offender denies the allegation, the court can only deal with him for breaching the order if that breach is proved by evidence (*R v Devine* (1956) 40 Cr App R 45).

Schedule 3, para 4 provides that if it is proved to the satisfaction of the magistrates that the offender has failed without reasonable excuse to comply with any of the requirements of the relevant order, the court may either:

- impose a fine of up to £1,000; or
- impose a community punishment order for up to 60 hours' community service.

If the court takes the latter option, and the order breached was a community punishment order, the total number of hours of community service imposed under the two orders must not exceed 240 hours (para 7(3)(b)).

Paragraph 4 also provides that if the order breached is a community rehabilitation order, or a community punishment and rehabilitation order and the offender is under 21, or if the order is a curfew order and the offender is under 16, the court may make an attendance centre order instead of imposing a fine or community punishment order.

These powers apply whether the original order was made by a magistrates' court or a Crown Court. If the breach is dealt with by the imposition of a fine, a community punishment order or an attendance centre order, the original community order remains in force.

If the original order was made by a magistrates' court, the magistrates' court dealing with the breach may (instead of imposing a fine or community punishment order or, if appropriate, an attendance centre order) revoke the original order and impose a new sentence for the original offence (Sched 3, para 4(1)(d)).

If the original order was made by a Crown Court, the magistrates' court dealing with the breach may (instead of imposing a fine, a community punishment order or an attendance centre order) commit the offender (in custody or on bail) to the Crown Court (para 4(4)). The Crown Court may impose any of the punishments for non-compliance which the magistrates could have imposed or it may impose a new sentence for the original offence (see para 5).

The important point to note is that a magistrates' court dealing with an offender for the breach of a community order imposed by the Crown Court can never revoke the community order and re-sentence the offender for the original offence.

If the original community order is revoked and the offender is re-sentenced for the original offence, para 4(2) (magistrates' court) or 5(2) (Crown Court) applies. This states that:

- the court must take into account the extent to which the offender has complied with the requirements of the original order; and
- where the offender has 'wilfully and persistently' failed to comply with the requirements of the community order, the court may impose a custodial sentence notwithstanding the restrictions contained in s 79(2) of the 2000 Act.

The requirement for wilful and persistent non-compliance means that a custodial sentence could not be substituted for the community order merely on the basis of a single allegation of non-compliance.

In *Caton v Community Service Officer* (1995) 159 JP 444, the offender had twice threatened to hit a community service officer. It was held by the Divisional Court (dismissing an appeal against a finding that the offender was in breach of the order) that it was implicit in the concept of 'performing' community service that the offender was under an obligation to behave in a reasonable manner during the required performance; it followed that unacceptable (in this case, violent) behaviour could amount to a failure to comply with the requirements of the community punishment order.

Also, under the Criminal Justice and Court Services Act 2000, Sched 3 to the Powers of Criminal Courts (Sentencing) Act 2000 is amended to create a warning scheme (para 2A). There is a duty on the probation service to issue a warning to an offender who has unacceptably failed to comply with the requirements of the order if the offender has not already been referred back to court for the failure. The warning must describe the circumstances of the failure, state that the failure is unacceptable, and inform the offender of the consequence of a further failure: namely, that if there is a second unacceptable failure to comply within 12 months, or six months in the case of a curfew order, the offender must be referred back to court to be dealt with for breach of the order. If two or more orders were imposed at the same time, they will be considered as one order to which the warning scheme applies, so only one warning in total can be given in any 12 month period.

Where the offender has attained the age of 18 and the matter is referred back to the court (whether a magistrates' court or the Crown Court), the court must impose a custodial sentence for the offence in respect of which the community order was

imposed (if he is found to be in breach of the order) unless it is of the opinion either that the offender is likely to comply with the requirements of the order during the period for which it remains in force, or that there are exceptional circumstances that justify not imposing a sentence of imprisonment. Where the offence is punishable with imprisonment, the sentence imposed should be what the court would have imposed had it not imposed a community order; otherwise, the maximum term is three months. The court must take account of the extent to which he has complied with the requirements of the order.

These warning and punishment measures do not apply to any failure to abstain from misusing specified Class A drugs.

16.9.2   Revocation of community orders on grounds other than breach

Paragraph 10 of Sched 3 to the Powers of Criminal Courts (Sentencing) Act 2000 enables a person subject to a community order made by a magistrates' court, or the probation officer concerned, to apply to the magistrates' court which serves the area where the offender resides, on the ground that – having regard to circumstances which have arisen since the order was made – it is in the interests of justice that:

- the original community order should be revoked; or
- the offender should be dealt with in some other manner for the original offence.

The magistrates' court to which the application is made may:

- revoke the order; or
- revoke the order and impose a different sentence for the original offence.

If the original order was made by the Crown Court, the application to revoke it is made to the Crown Court, which is similarly empowered to revoke the order or revoke the order and re-sentence the offender (para 11).

It should be noted that if an order is revoked by a magistrates' court, the offender cannot afterwards be committed to the Crown Court to be dealt with for breach of the order (*R v Brent Justices ex p Ward* (1993) 157 JP 192).

Revocation under para 10 or 11 is on the basis that the circumstances have changed since the original order was made. For example, a community rehabilitation order may be revoked if the offender has made such good progress that the order is no longer necessary; a community punishment order may be revoked if the offender is no longer physically capable of doing community service.

In *R v Fielding* (1993) 14 Cr App R(S) 494, for example, it was held inappropriate to impose a custodial sentence (even a suspended sentence) where the community punishment order is revoked because the offender is unable, through no fault of his own (for example, illness or injury), to carry out the work.

16.9.3   Commission of a subsequent offence

The commission of a subsequent offence does not amount to a breach of a community sentence. It follows that if a magistrates' court convicts an offender of an offence committed during the currency of a community rehabilitation order, they cannot revoke the community rehabilitation order (even if it was made by a magistrates' court) and they cannot commit the offender to the Crown Court to be dealt with for

breaching the community rehabilitation order (see *R v Adams* (1994) 15 Cr App R(S) 417). The order can only be revoked (by a magistrates' court if the original order was made by a magistrates' court, by the Crown Court if the original order was made in the Crown Court) if there is an application by the Probation Service for its revocation (on the ground that it is not working).

However, para 11(1)(b) of Sched 3 to the Powers of Criminal Courts (Sentencing) Act 2000 says that where an offender is convicted by the Crown Court, or convicted by a magistrates' court but committed for sentence to the Crown Court, and the offence was committed during the currency of a community sentence, the Crown Court may revoke the community order and, if the Crown Court thinks it appropriate, re-sentence the offender. This power only applies if the community order is in force at the date when the Crown Court is sentencing the offender. If the community order has expired by the time the Crown Court is dealing with the offender, there is no power to revoke the order and re-sentence the offender for the original offence (*R v Bennett* (1994) 15 Cr App R(S) 213; *R v Cousin* (1994) 15 Cr App R(S) 516).

In *R v Kenny* [1996] 1 Cr App R(S) 397, the appellant was charged with burglary. While on bail for that offence, he committed a further burglary. For the first burglary, he was given a community punishment order. Having performed a few hours' community service, he was tried in respect of the other burglary. Upon his conviction for that second burglary, the Crown Court judge revoked the community punishment order and substituted a short prison sentence (to be served consecutively to a custodial sentence for the burglary of which the appellant had just been convicted). The Court of Appeal said that the power conferred by para 11(1)(b) of Sched 3 to revoke a community order and re-sentence an offender is not confined to cases where the offender has committed an offence during the currency of the community order. The judge was entitled to come to the view that it was in the interests of justice to revoke the community punishment order and re-sentence the appellant.

Where the Crown Court re-sentences an offender in a case where the original community order was imposed by a magistrates' court, the powers of the Crown Court are limited to those of the magistrates' court (see *R v Ogden* [1996] 2 Cr App R(S) 386 and *R v Kosser* [1996] 16 Cr App R(S) 737).

Even though the commission of a further offence during the currency of a community rehabilitation order does not constitute a breach of the order, the fact that a further offence has been committed may be regarded by the court as evidence that the community sentence is ineffective as regards this offender. This can be regarded as a 'failure to respond' to a previous sentence (under s 151(1) of the 2000 Act), something which affects the seriousness of the subsequent offence. However, in *R v Rowsell* (1988) 10 Cr App R(S) 411, the offender committed an offence within weeks of being put on probation. The court accepted the argument that the community rehabilitation order had not had time to have any effect on the offender. It was thus premature to say that probation would not work for this offender and so the order should be left in place.

Also of relevance in such a situation is para 13 of Sched 3 to the Powers of Criminal Courts (Sentencing) Act 2000. This provides that where a magistrates' court convicts someone of an offence and decides to impose a custodial sentence for that offence, and that person is currently subject to a community order imposed because of an earlier offence, the magistrates can revoke that community order (if it was imposed by a magistrates' court) or commit the offender to the Crown Court (if the order was made by the Crown Court).

16.9.4 Re-sentencing for the original offence

In *R v Hewitt* [1996] 2 Cr App R(S) 14, the Court of Appeal made the point that, in deciding what custodial sentence to pass in place of a community order, the offender must be given credit if he pleaded guilty to the offence for which community service was imposed and, where the original sentence was a community punishment order, he must also be given credit for the hours of community service which he has performed.

Furthermore, where the community order is replaced with a custodial sentence, the offender should be given credit for any time spent in custody on remand for the offence in respect of which the community order was made (see *R v Wiltshire* (1992) 13 Cr App R(S) 642 and *R v Henderson* [1997] 2 Cr App R(S) 266).

16.9.5 Age of the offender

Where the offender is under 21 when the community order is made but is over 21 when the order is revoked and he is re-sentenced for the offence for which the community order was imposed, the replacement sentence must be one which is appropriate to the age of the offender at the date when the original order was made. So, if such an offender is given a custodial sentence in place of the community order, it would have to be a sentence of detention in a young offender institution, not imprisonment (*R v Pesapane* (1992) 13 Cr App R(S) 438).

16.10 COMMUNITY SENTENCES UNDER THE CRIMINAL JUSTICE ACT 2003

The Halliday Report says that in order to ensure that non-custodial sentences reduce the likelihood of re-offending, courts should have the power to impose a single, non-custodial penalty made up of specific elements. This new sentence would replace all existing community sentences. These elements which could be included in the new community sentence would include:

- treatment for substance abuse or mental illness;
- curfew and exclusion orders;
- electronic monitoring;
- reparation to victims and communities;
- compulsory work;
- attendance at offending behaviour programmes.

The Report says that supervision in all cases would be geared towards managing and enforcing the sentence, and supporting resettlement.

In deciding which particular elements to include in the sentence passed on an offender, the court should, said the Report, consider the aims of punishment, including reparation and prevention of re-offending. The 'punitive weight' of the sentence should reflect the seriousness of offence(s), subject to any increase in the severity of the offence resulting from the existence of previous convictions.

Under this new framework, financial penalties would be available at all levels of seriousness, both on their own and in combination with other non-custodial penalties.

The Report also argued that there should be a new 'interim review order', strengthening the existing power to defer sentences. This power would be available where a court decided that it would be appropriate to allow time for an offender to meet commitments (such as reparation, voluntary attendance at drug/alcohol treatment programmes, or participation in restorative justice schemes) voluntarily, before being sentenced.

The Report noted that the procedures for enforcing sentences, and the penalties for breach of conditions of sentences, are very complex and vary greatly as between different sentences. The Report also noted a 'sharp division of roles' between the courts (where the only concern is what sentence should be passed) and the Prison and Probation Services (who implement the sentences passed by the courts). The result of this dichotomy is that sentencers rarely receive feedback on the progress of the offenders they have sentenced. The Report expresses the view that 'visible involvement' of the court for the duration of the sentence would exert additional leverage over the offender during periods in the community (whether after release from prison, or under a community sentence). Offenders would realise that when they were under sentence in the community, whether they stay there or face return to prison will depend on their own good behaviour and compliance. This would, said the Report, be more transparent to the public (and, it might be added, could increase the level of public confidence in community sentences as an effective form of punishment rather than some sort of 'let-off' or 'soft option').

Under the new framework proposed by the Halliday Report:

- all non-custodial sentences would be enforced by the court, which would be empowered, if the terms of the sentence are breached, to replace the community sentence with a custodial one;

- in cases where there is a high risk of re-offending and swift action is required, the probation service should make more use of their power to apply for an arrest warrant (which could lead to remand in custody, pending a full court hearing);

- all custodial sentences would be enforced administratively on breach of requirements, subject to a right of appeal to the court.

The Report recommended that the court should deal with breaches of community sentences, hear appeals against recall to prison, authorise pre-release plans and review progress during community sentences or the community part of custodial sentences.

The broad thrust of these proposals was accepted by the government. The Criminal Justice Act 2003 therefore aims to simplify the regime of community sentences. Essentially it gives the court a 'pick and mix' menu to enable it to construct a community order that is appropriate to the particular offender.

The starting point is the definition of 'community order' in s 177 of the Act. This provides as follows:

(1)   Where a person aged 16 or over is convicted of an offence, the court by or before which he is convicted may make an order (in this Part referred to as a 'community order') imposing on him any one or more of the following requirements—

     (a) an unpaid work requirement (as defined by section 199),

     (b) an activity requirement (as defined by section 201),

     (c) a programme requirement (as defined by section 202),

     (d) a prohibited activity requirement (as defined by section 203),

(e) a curfew requirement (as defined by section 204),

(f) an exclusion requirement (as defined by section 205),

(g) a residence requirement (as defined by section 206),

(h) a mental health treatment requirement (as defined by section 207),

(i) a drug rehabilitation requirement (as defined by section 209),

(j) an alcohol treatment requirement (as defined by section 212),

(k) a supervision requirement (as defined by section 213), and

(l) in a case where the offender is aged under 25, an attendance centre requirement (as defined by section 214).

...

(5) A community order must specify a date, not more than three years after the date of the order, by which all the requirements in it must have been complied with; and a community order which imposes two or more different requirements falling within sub-section (1) may also specify an earlier date or dates in relation to compliance with any one or more of them.

(6) Before making a community order imposing two or more different requirements falling within sub-section (1), the court must consider whether, in the circumstances of the case, the requirements are compatible with each other.

Two general points worth underlining from this section are:

• a community order can last for up to three years; and

• the components of the order must be compatible with each other.

It is also worth noting that s 178 of the Act empowers the Secretary of State to introduce delegated legislation which enables or requires a court making a community order to provide for that order 'to be reviewed periodically by that or another court'. In other words, the court should continue to have involvement with the case after it has passed sentence.

As was the case prior to the passing of the Criminal Justice Act 2003, a community sentence can only be imposed if the seriousness of the case merits such a sentence; in other words, the community sentence 'threshold' has to be met. Section 148 of the 2003 Act provides that:

(1) A court must not pass a community sentence on an offender unless it is of the opinion that the offence, or the combination of the offence and one or more offences associated with it, was serious enough to warrant such a sentence.

(2) Where a court passes a community sentence which consists of or includes a community order—

(a) the particular requirement or requirements forming part of the community order must be such as, in the opinion of the court, is, or taken together are, the most suitable for the offender, and

(b) the restrictions on liberty imposed by the order must be such as in the opinion of the court are commensurate with the seriousness of the offence, or the combination of the offence and one or more offences associated with it.

It may well be that an offender who ultimately receives a community sentence was remanded in custody prior to conviction and/or sentence. Section 149 of the 2003 Act provides that in such a case:

(1) In determining the restrictions on liberty to be imposed by a community order or youth community order in respect of an offence, the court may have regard to

any period for which the offender has been remanded in custody in connection with the offence or any other offence the charge for which was founded on the same facts or evidence.

In other words, the offender may receive a more lenient community sentence to reflect the fact that he has already spent some time in custody in connection with the offence for which sentence is now being passed. This enshrines in statute the effect of case law.

The next stage in understanding the new regime introduced by the Criminal Justice Act 2003 is to examine each of the requirements that may be imposed as part of a community order (listed in s 177(1), quoted above).

16.10.1 Unpaid work requirement (s 199)

Section 199 sets out details concerning the 'unpaid work requirement':

(1)   ... 'unpaid work requirement' ... means a requirement that the offender must perform unpaid work in accordance with section 200.

(2)   The number of hours which a person may be required to work under an unpaid work requirement must be specified in the relevant order and must be in the aggregate—

(a) not less than 40, and

(b) not more than 300.

(3)   A court may not impose an unpaid work requirement in respect of an offender unless after hearing (if the courts thinks necessary) an appropriate officer, the court is satisfied that the offender is a suitable person to perform work under such a requirement.

(4)   In sub-section (3) 'an appropriate officer' means—

(a) in the case of an offender aged 18 or over, an officer of a local probation board, and

(b) in the case of an offender aged under 18, an officer of a local probation board, a social worker of a local authority social services department or a member of a youth offending team.

(5)   Where the court makes relevant orders in respect of two or more offences of which the offender has been convicted on the same occasion and includes unpaid work requirements in each of them, the court may direct that the hours of work specified in any of those requirements is to be concurrent with or additional to those specified in any other of those orders, but so that the total number of hours which are not concurrent does not exceed the maximum specified in sub-section (2)(b).

It will be apparent from this description that the unpaid work requirement is the same as community punishment, save that the maximum order is increased from 240 to 300 hours.

Under s 200(1), the offender 'must perform for the number of hours specified in the order such work at such times as he may be instructed by the responsible officer'. Sub-section (2) states that the work should normally be performed during a period of 12 months. However, under sub-s (3), unless it is revoked, a community order imposing an unpaid work requirement remains in force until the offender has worked under it for the number of hours specified in it.

Section 200(4) states that where an unpaid work requirement is imposed by a suspended sentence order, the supervision period of the suspended sentence continues until the offender has worked under the order for the number of hours specified in the order, but does not continue beyond the end of the operational period.

16.10.2 Activity requirements (s 201)

Section 201 of the Act gives details about the 'activity requirement':

(1)   ... 'activity requirement' ... means a requirement that the offender must do either or both of the following—

(a) present himself to a person or persons specified in the relevant order at a place or places so specified on such number of days as may be so specified;

(b) participate in activities specified in the order on such number of days as may be so specified.

(2)   The specified activities may consist of or include activities whose purpose is that of reparation, such as activities involving contact between offenders and persons affected by their offences.

(3)   A court may not include an activity requirement in a relevant order unless—

(a) it has consulted—

(i)   in the case of an offender aged 18 or over, an officer of a local probation board,

(ii) in the case of an offender aged under 18, either an officer of a local probation board or a member of a youth offending team, and

(b) it is satisfied that it is feasible to secure compliance with the requirement.

(4)   A court may not include an activity requirement in a relevant order if compliance with that requirement would involve the co-operation of a person other than the offender and the offender's responsible officer, unless that other person consents to its inclusion.

(5)   The aggregate of the number of days specified under sub-section (1)(a) and (b) must not exceed 60.

(6)   A requirement such as is mentioned in sub-section (1)(a) operates to require the offender—

(a) in accordance with instructions given by his responsible officer, to present himself at a place or places on the number of days specified in the order, and

(b) while at any place, to comply with instructions given by, or under the authority of, the person in charge of that place.

(7)   A place specified under sub-section (1)(a) must be—

(a) a community rehabilitation centre, or

(b) a place that has been approved by the local probation board for the area in which the premises are situated as providing facilities suitable for persons subject to activity requirements.

(8)   Where the place specified under sub-section (1)(a) is a community rehabilitation centre, the reference in sub-section (6)(a) to the offender presenting himself at the specified place includes a reference to him presenting himself elsewhere than at the centre for the purpose of participating in activities in accordance with instructions given by, or under the authority of, the person in charge of the centre.

(9) A requirement to participate in activities operates to require the offender—

    (a) in accordance with instructions given by his responsible officer, to participate in activities on the number of days specified in the order, and

    (b) while participating, to comply with instructions given by, or under the authority of, the person in charge of the activities.

Under sub-s (10), a 'community rehabilitation centre' is defined as premises, approved by the Secretary of State, 'at which non-residential facilities are provided for use in connection with the rehabilitation of offenders'.

16.10.3 Programme requirements (s 202)

Section 202 of the Act deals with 'programme requirements':

(1) ... 'programme requirement' ... means a requirement that the offender must participate in an accredited programme specified in the order at a place so specified on such number of days as may be so specified.

    ...

(3) In this section—

    (a) 'programme' means a systematic set of activities,

    ...

(4) A court may not include a programme requirement in a relevant order unless—

    (a) the accredited programme which the court proposes to specify in the order has been recommended to the court as being suitable for the offender—

        (i) in the case of an offender aged 18 or over, by an officer of a local probation board, or

        (ii) in the case of an offender aged under 18, either by an officer of a local probation board or by a member of a youth offending team, and

    (b) the court is satisfied that the programme is (or, where the relevant order is a custody plus order or an intermittent custody order, will be) available at the place proposed to be specified.

(5) A court may not include a programme requirement in a relevant order if compliance with that requirement would involve the co-operation of a person other than the offender and the offender's responsible officer, unless that other person consents to its inclusion.

(6) A requirement to attend an accredited programme operates to require the offender—

    (a) in accordance with instructions given by the responsible officer, to participate in the accredited programme at the place specified in the order on the number of days specified in the order, and

    (b) while at that place, to comply with instructions given by, or under the authority of, the person in charge of the programme.

(7) A place specified in an order must be a place that has been approved by the local probation board for the area in which the premises are situated as providing facilities suitable for persons subject to programme requirements.

16.10.4 Prohibited activity requirements (s 203)

Section 203 of the Act deals with 'prohibited activity requirements':

(1)   ... 'prohibited activity requirement' ... means a requirement that the offender must refrain from participating in activities specified in the order—

    (a) on a day or days so specified, or

    (b) during a period so specified.

(2)   A court may not include a prohibited activity requirement in a relevant order unless it has consulted—

    (a) in the case of an offender aged 18 or over, an officer of a local probation board;

    (b) in the case of an offender aged under 18, either an officer of a local probation board or a member of a youth offending team.

(3)   The requirements that may by virtue of this section be included in a relevant order include a requirement that the offender does not possess, use or carry a firearm within the meaning of the Firearms Act 1968.

16.10.5 Curfew requirements (s 204)

Section 204 of the 2003 Act covers 'curfew requirements':

(1)   ... 'curfew requirement' ... means a requirement that the offender must remain, for periods specified in the relevant order, at a place so specified.

(2)   A relevant order imposing a curfew requirement may specify different places or different periods for different days, but may not specify periods which amount to less than two hours or more than twelve hours in any day.

(3)   A community order or suspended sentence order which imposes a curfew requirement may not specify periods which fall outside the period of six months beginning with the day on which it is made.

(4)   A custody plus order which imposes a curfew requirement may not specify a period which falls outside the period of six months beginning with the first day of the licence period as defined by section 181(3)(b).

(5)   An intermittent custody order which imposes a curfew requirement must not specify a period if to do so would cause the aggregate number of days on which the offender is subject to the requirement for any part of the day to exceed 182.

(6)   Before making a relevant order imposing a curfew requirement, the court must obtain and consider information about the place proposed to be specified in the order (including information as to the attitude of persons likely to be affected by the enforced presence there of the offender).

16.10.6 Exclusion requirements (s 205)

Section 205 of the Act deals with 'exclusion requirements':

(1)   ... 'exclusion requirement' ... means a provision prohibiting the offender from entering a place specified in the order for a period so specified.

(2)   Where the relevant order is a community order, the period specified must not be more than two years.

(3) An exclusion requirement—

    (a) may provide for the prohibition to operate only during the periods specified in the order, and

    (b) may specify different places for different periods or days.

(4) In this section 'place' includes an area.

16.10.7 Residence requirements (s 206)

Section 206 covers 'residence requirements':

(1)   ... 'residence requirement', in relation to a community order or a suspended sentence order, means a requirement that, during a period specified in the relevant order, the offender must reside at a place specified in the order.

(2)   If the order so provides, a residence requirement does not prohibit the offender from residing, with the prior approval of the responsible officer, at a place other than that specified in the order.

(3)   Before making a community order or suspended sentence order containing a residence requirement, the court must consider the home surroundings of the offender.

(4)   A court may not specify a hostel or other institution as the place where an offender must reside, except on the recommendation of an officer of a local probation board.

16.10.8 Mental health treatment requirements (s 207)

Section 207 of the Act sets out the mental health treatment requirement:

(1)   ... 'mental health treatment requirement', in relation to a community order or suspended sentence order, means a requirement that the offender must submit, during a period or periods specified in the order, to treatment by or under the direction of a registered medical practitioner or a chartered psychologist (or both, for different periods) with a view to the improvement of the offender's mental condition.

(2)   The treatment required must be such one of the following kinds of treatment as may be specified in the relevant order—

    (a) treatment as a resident patient ...;

    (b) treatment as a non-resident patient ...;

    (c) treatment by or under the direction of such registered medical practitioner or chartered psychologist (or both) as may be so specified;

but the nature of the treatment is not to be specified in the order except as mentioned in paragraph (a), (b) or (c).

(3)   A court may not by virtue of this section include a mental health treatment requirement in a relevant order unless—

    (a) the court is satisfied, on the evidence of a registered medical practitioner approved for the purposes of section 12 of the Mental Health Act 1983, that the mental condition of the offender—

       (i) is such as requires and may be susceptible to treatment; but

       (ii) is not such as to warrant the making of a hospital order or guardianship order within the meaning of that Act;

(b) the court is also satisfied that arrangements have been or can be made for the treatment intended to be specified in the order (including arrangements for the reception of the offender where he is to be required to submit to treatment as a resident patient); and

(c) the offender has expressed his willingness to comply with such a requirement.

Section 208 permits mental health treatment at a place other than that specified in the order:

(1) Where the medical practitioner or chartered psychologist by whom or under whose direction an offender is being treated for his mental condition in pursuance of a mental health treatment requirement is of the opinion that part of the treatment can be better or more conveniently given in or at an institution or place which—

(a) is not specified in the relevant order, and

(b) is one in or at which the treatment of the offender will be given by or under the direction of a registered medical practitioner or chartered psychologist,

he may, with the consent of the offender, make arrangements for him to be treated accordingly.

(2) Such arrangements as are mentioned in sub-section (1) may provide for the offender to receive part of his treatment as a resident patient in an institution or place notwithstanding that the institution or place is not one which could have been specified for that purpose in the relevant order.

16.10.9 Drug rehabilitation requirements (s 209)

Section 209 covers 'drug rehabilitation requirements':

(1) ... 'drug rehabilitation requirement', in relation to a community order or suspended sentence order, means a requirement that during a period specified in the order ('the treatment and testing period') the offender—

(a) must submit to treatment by or under the direction of a specified person having the necessary qualifications or experience with a view to the reduction or elimination of the offender's dependency on or propensity to misuse drugs, and

(b) for the purpose of ascertaining whether he has any drug in his body during that period, must provide samples of such description as may be so determined, at such times or in such circumstances as may (subject to the provisions of the order) be determined by the responsible officer or by the person specified as the person by or under whose direction the treatment is to be provided.

(2) A court may not impose a drug rehabilitation requirement unless—

(a) it is satisfied—

(i) that the offender is dependent on, or has a propensity to misuse, drugs, and

(ii) that his dependency or propensity is such as requires and may be susceptible to treatment,

(b) it is also satisfied that arrangements have been or can be made for the treatment intended to be specified in the order (including arrangements for the reception of the offender where he is to be required to submit to treatment as a resident),

(c) the requirement has been recommended to the court as being suitable for the offender—

    (i) in the case of an offender aged 18 or over, by an officer of a local probation board, or

    (ii) in the case of an offender aged under 18, either by an officer of a local probation board or by a member of a youth offending team, and

(d) the offender expresses his willingness to comply with the requirement.

(3) The treatment and testing period must be at least six months.

(4) The required treatment for any particular period must be—

    (a) treatment as a resident in such institution or place as may be specified in the order, or

    (b) treatment as a non-resident in or at such institution or place, and at such intervals, as may be so specified,

but the nature of the treatment is not to be specified in the order except as mentioned in paragraph (a) or (b) above.

Sections 210 and 211 provide for review by the court where a drug rehabilitation requirement has been imposed:

210(1)A community order or suspended sentence order imposing a drug rehabilitation requirement may (and must if the treatment and testing period is more than 12 months)—

    (a) provide for the requirement to be reviewed periodically at intervals of not less than one month,

    (b) provide for each review of the requirement to be made, subject to section 211(6), at a hearing held for the purpose by the court responsible for the order (a 'review hearing'),

    (c) require the offender to attend each review hearing,

    (d) provide for the responsible officer to make to the court responsible for the order, before each review, a report in writing on the offender's progress under the requirement, and

    (e) provide for each such report to include the test results communicated to the responsible officer ... and the views of the treatment provider as to the treatment and testing of the offender.

  ...

211(1)At a review hearing ... the court may, after considering the responsible officer's report ... amend the community order or suspended sentence order, so far as it relates to the drug rehabilitation requirement.

(2) The court—

    (a) may not amend the drug rehabilitation requirement unless the offender expresses his willingness to comply with the requirement as amended,

    (b) may not amend any provision of the order so as to reduce the period for which the drug rehabilitation requirement has effect below the minimum specified in section 209(3), and

    (c) except with the consent of the offender, may not amend any requirement or provision of the order while an appeal against the order is pending.

(3) If the offender fails to express his willingness to comply with the drug rehabilitation requirement as proposed to be amended by the court, the court may—

(a) revoke the community order, or the suspended sentence order and the suspended sentence to which it relates, and

(b) deal with him, for the offence in respect of which the order was made, in any way in which he could have been dealt with for that offence by the court which made the order if the order had not been made.

(4) In dealing with the offender under sub-section (3)(b), the court—

(a) shall take into account the extent to which the offender has complied with the requirements of the order, and

(b) may impose a custodial sentence (where the order was made in respect of an offence punishable with such a sentence) notwithstanding anything in section 152(2).

(5) Where the order is a community order made by a magistrates' court in the case of an offender under 18 years of age in respect of an offence triable only on indictment in the case of an adult, any powers exercisable under sub-section (3)(b) in respect of the offender after he attains the age of 18 are powers to do either or both of the following—

(a) to impose a fine not exceeding £5,000 for the offence in respect of which the order was made;

(b) to deal with the offender for that offence in any way in which the court could deal with him if it had just convicted him of an offence punishable with imprisonment for a term not exceeding twelve months.

(6) If at a review hearing ... the court, after considering the responsible officer's report, is of the opinion that the offender's progress under the requirement is satisfactory, the court may so amend the order as to provide for each subsequent review to be made by the court without a hearing.

(7) If at a review without a hearing the court, after considering the responsible officer's report, is of the opinion that the offender's progress under the requirement is no longer satisfactory, the court may require the offender to attend a hearing of the court at a specified time and place.

(8) At that hearing the court, after considering that report, may—

(a) exercise the powers conferred by this section as if the hearing were a review hearing, and

(b) so amend the order as to provide for each subsequent review to be made at a review hearing.

(9) In this section any reference to the court, in relation to a review without a hearing, is to be read—

(a) in the case of the Crown Court, as a reference to a judge of the court;

(b) in the case of a magistrates' court, as a reference to a justice of the peace ...

16.10.10 Alcohol treatment requirements (s 212)

Section 212 deals with 'alcohol treatment requirements':

(1) ... 'alcohol treatment requirement', in relation to a community order or suspended sentence order, means a requirement that the offender must submit during a period specified in the order to treatment by or under the direction of a specified person having the necessary qualifications or experience with a view to the reduction or elimination of the offender's dependency on alcohol.

(2) A court may not impose an alcohol treatment requirement in respect of an offender unless it is satisfied—

(a) that he is dependent on alcohol,

(b) that his dependency is such as requires and may be susceptible to treatment, and

(c) that arrangements have been or can be made for the treatment intended to be specified in the order (including arrangements for the reception of the offender where he is to be required to submit to treatment as a resident).

(3) A court may not impose an alcohol treatment requirement unless the offender expresses his willingness to comply with its requirements.

(4) The period for which the alcohol treatment requirement has effect must be not less than six months.

(5) The treatment required by an alcohol treatment requirement for any particular period must be—

(a) treatment as a resident in such institution or place as may be specified in the order,

(b) treatment as a non-resident in or at such institution or place, and at such intervals, as may be so specified, or

(c) treatment by or under the direction of such person having the necessary qualification or experience as may be so specified;

but the nature of the treatment shall not be specified in the order except as mentioned in paragraph (a), (b) or (c) above.

16.10.11   Supervision requirements (s 213)

Section 213 covers 'supervision requirements':

(1) ... 'supervision requirement' ... means a requirement that, during the relevant period, the offender must attend appointments with the responsible officer or another person determined by the responsible officer, at such time and place as may be determined by the officer.

(2) The purpose for which a supervision requirement may be imposed is that of promoting the offender's rehabilitation.

(3) In sub-section (1) 'the relevant period' means—

(a) in relation to a community order, the period for which the community order remains in force,

(b) in relation to a custody plus order, the licence period as defined by section 181(3)(b),

(c) in relation to an intermittent custody order, the licence periods as defined by section 183(3), and

(d) in relation to a suspended sentence order, the supervision period as defined by section 189(1)(a).

16.10.12   Attendance centre requirements (s 214)

Section 221(2) defines an 'attendance centre' as 'a place at which offenders aged under 25 may be required to attend and be given under supervision appropriate occupation or instruction ...'. Thus, the definition of the attendance centre is unchanged.

Attendance centre requirements are governed by s 214, which provides that:

(1)   In this Part 'attendance centre requirement' ... means a requirement that the offender must attend at an attendance centre specified in the relevant order for such number of hours as may be so specified.

(2)   The aggregate number of hours for which the offender may be required to attend at an attendance centre must not be less than 12 or more than 36.

(3)   The court may not impose an attendance centre requirement unless the court is satisfied that the attendance centre to be specified in it is reasonably accessible to the offender concerned, having regard to the means of access available to him and any other circumstances.

...

(6)   An offender may not be required under this section to attend at an attendance centre on more than one occasion on any day, or for more than three hours on any occasion.

16.10.13   Electronic monitoring requirements

These are dealt with by s 215:

(1)   ... 'electronic monitoring requirement' ... means a requirement for securing the electronic monitoring of the offender's compliance with other requirements imposed by the order during a period specified in the order, or determined by the responsible officer in accordance with the relevant order.

(2)   Where—

(a)   it is proposed to include in a relevant order a requirement for securing electronic monitoring in accordance with this section, but

(b)   there is a person (other than the offender) without whose co-operation it will not be practicable to secure the monitoring,

the requirement may not be included in the order without that person's consent.

16.10.14   Restrictions on community orders

Section 217 requires that:

(1)   The court must ensure, as far as practicable, that any requirement imposed by a relevant order is such as to avoid—

(a)   any conflict with the offender's religious beliefs or with the requirements of any other relevant order to which he may be subject; and

(b)   any interference with the times, if any, at which he normally works or attends school or any other educational establishment.

(2)   The responsible officer in relation to an offender to whom a relevant order relates must ensure, as far as practicable, that any instruction given or requirement imposed by him in pursuance of the order is such as to avoid the conflict or interference mentioned in sub-section (1).

16.10.15   Other duties of offenders subject to community orders

Section 220 imposes a duty on the offender to keep in touch with the responsible officer:

(1)   An offender in respect of whom a community order or a suspended sentence order is in force—

(a) must keep in touch with the responsible officer in accordance with such instructions as he may from time to time be given by that officer, and

(b) must notify him of any change of address.

Under s 220(2), these obligations are enforceable as if they were requirements imposed by the order itself.

16.11 REVOCATION AND AMENDMENT OF COMMUNITY ORDERS UNDER THE CRIMINAL JUSTICE ACT 2003

Section 179 of the Criminal Justice Act 2003 gives effect to Sched 8, which deals with breach, revocation and amendment of community orders.

16.11.1 Breach of community orders

This Schedule largely reproduces (with some amendments) the provisions of Sched 3 to the Powers of Criminal Courts (Sentencing) Act 2000 (which will continue to apply to certain orders for young offenders).

Under para 5(1):

If the responsible officer is of the opinion that the offender has failed without reasonable excuse to comply with any of the requirements of a community order, the officer must give him a warning under this paragraph unless—

(a) the offender has within the previous twelve months been given a warning under this paragraph in relation to a failure to comply with any of the requirements of the order, or

(b) the officer causes an information to be laid before a justice of the peace [or, if the order was made by the Crown Court and did not include a direction that any failure to comply was to be dealt with by a magistrates' court, the Crown Court] in respect of the failure.

Paragraph 5(2) requires that such a warning must:

(a) describe the circumstances of the failure,

(b) state that the failure is unacceptable, and

(c) inform the offender that, if within the next twelve months he again fails to comply with any requirement of the order, he will be liable to be brought before a court.

There has been some concern that the Probation Service has been insufficiently robust in bringing offenders before the court when they fail to comply with community orders. It should be noted that para 6(1), which deals with further non-compliance after a warning, is cast in mandatory terms. It provides that:

If—

(a) the responsible officer has given a warning under paragraph 5 to the offender in respect of a community order, and

(b) at any time within the twelve months beginning with the date on which the warning was given, the responsible officer is of the opinion that the offender has since that date failed without reasonable excuse to comply with any of the requirements of the order,

the officer must cause an information to be laid before a justice of the peace [or, if the order was made by the Crown Court and did not include a direction that any failure to comply was to be dealt with by a magistrates' court, the Crown Court] in respect of the failure in question.

Under para 7, a justice of the peace may issue a summons requiring the attendance of the offender, or (if the information is in writing and on oath) a warrant for his arrest, if it appears that he has failed to comply with any of the requirements of:

- a community order made by a magistrates' court; or

- a community order made by the Crown Court which includes a direction that any failure to comply with the requirements of the order is to be dealt with by a magistrates' court.

However, this power only applies if the community order is still in force (thus preventing enforcement proceedings being commenced after the order has expired).

Under para 7(4), if the offender fails to appear in answer to the summons, the magistrates' court may issue a warrant for his arrest.

Paragraph 8 confers the same powers on the Crown Court where it has made a community order which does not include a direction that a failure to comply with the requirements be dealt with by the magistrates' court.

Paragraph 9(1) provides that:

If it is proved to the satisfaction of a magistrates' court before which an offender appears or is brought under paragraph 7 that he has failed without reasonable excuse to comply with any of the requirements of the community order, the court must deal with him in respect of the failure in any one of the following ways—

(a) by amending the terms of the community order so as to impose more onerous requirements which the court could include if it were then making the order;

(b) where the community order was made by a magistrates' court, by dealing with him, for the offence in respect of which the order was made, in any way in which the court could deal with him if he had just been convicted by it of the offence;

(c) where—

(i) the community order was made by a magistrates' court,

(ii) the offence in respect of which the order was made was not an offence punishable by imprisonment,

(iii) the offender is aged 18 or over, and

(iv) the offender has wilfully and persistently failed to comply with the requirements of the order,

by dealing with him, in respect of that offence, by imposing a sentence of imprisonment for a term not exceeding 51 weeks.

Option (a) would, for example, empower the court to extend the duration of a particular requirement, but not beyond the maximum duration applicable to that requirement and not beyond the three year limit applicable to the duration of a community order (para 9(3)).

Option (b) involves revocation of the order (if it is still in force at the date of the hearing) and then re-sentencing (subject to the limitation on the court's sentencing powers when it was first dealing with the offender). Paragraph 9(4) empowers the court to impose a custodial sentence even if the offence did not cross the custody

threshold where the offender has wilfully and persistently failed to comply with the requirements of the community order .

Option (c) enables the court to punish wilful and persistent non-compliance with a custodial sentence even though the offence for which the order was made was non-imprisonable. As with (b), the community order is revoked if this option is chosen.

When dealing with the non-compliance, the court must take into account the extent to which the offender has complied with the order (para 9(2)).

If the offender is re-sentenced, he can appeal to the Crown Court against the new sentence (para 9(8)).

Where the order was made by the Crown Court (and that court directed that failures to comply should be dealt with by the magistrates' court), the magistrates' court dealing with the breach can commit him, in custody or on bail, to be dealt with by the Crown Court (para 9(6)).

Paragraph 10 sets out how the Crown Court must deal with failure to comply with a community order (whether the Crown Court is dealing with the case under para 8 or para 9). The options open to the Crown Court are the same as those available to the magistrates' court (making the order more onerous; revoking the order and re-sentencing the offender; imposing a custodial sentence for up to 51 weeks even though offence for which order made is non-imprisonable). The determination of whether or not the defendant is in breach of the order (if the breach is not admitted by the defendant) is made by a Crown Court judge sitting alone.

Paragraph 11(1) provides that:

(a) if an offender has refused to comply with a mental health treatment requirement, a drug rehabilitation requirement or an alcohol treatment requirement; and

(b) the refusal was a refusal to undergo 'any surgical, electrical or other treatment'; and

(c) the court decides that the refusal was reasonable in all the circumstances,

then the refusal is not to be treated as a breach of the order.

Under para 11(2), the court may not amend a mental health treatment requirement, a drug rehabilitation requirement or an alcohol treatment requirement 'unless the offender expresses his willingness to comply with the requirement as amended'.

Paragraph 12 deals with cases where a community order was made by a magistrates' court in respect of an offender who was being dealt with for an indictable-only offence and who was under 18 years of age when the order was made but has attained the age of 18 by the time of the enforcement proceedings. Where the court revokes the community order and re-sentences the offender, its powers are limited to:

(a) imposing a fine not exceeding £5,000 for the offence in respect of which the order was made; or

(b) dealing with the offender for that offence in any way in which a magistrates' court could deal with him if it had just convicted him of an offence punishable with imprisonment for a term not exceeding 51 weeks.

16.11.2 Revocation of community orders other than for breach

Part 3 of Sched 8 deals with the revocation of community orders other than in the case of a breach of the requirement of the order.

Paragraph 13 states that (provided the order is still in force) either the offender or the responsible officer may apply to the magistrates' court for the revocation of the order, or for the offender to be dealt with in some other way for the offence in respect of which the order was made, if – having regard to circumstances which have arisen since the order was made – it would be in the interests of justice to do so.

Under para 13(3), the circumstances in which a community order may be revoked include the fact that the offender is making good progress or is responding satisfactorily to supervision or treatment under the order. The revocation of the order may also be appropriate if, for example, the offender is taken ill or becomes disabled, and so becomes unable to complete the requirements of the order.

If the court re-sentences the offender, it must take into account the extent to which the offender complied with the original order (para 13(4)).

If a new sentence is passed, the offender can appeal against that sentence (para 13(5)).

Unless it is the offender who is applying for the revocation of the order, the court must summon him to appear in order to revoke or revoke and re-sentence; if he does not appear in answer to the summons, the courts may issue a warrant for his arrest (para 13(6)).

Paragraph 14 confers the same powers to the Crown Court in the case of orders it has made which do not contain a direction that failure to comply with the requirements is to be dealt with by the magistrates' court.

Under para 15, if the offender was convicted of an indictable-only offence and was under the age of 18 when the community order was made, but attained the age of 18 by the time the court is considering revocation, the court can impose a fine of up to £5,000 or else re-sentence him as if he had just been convicted of an offence punishable with imprisonment for up to 51 weeks.

16.11.3 Amendment of community orders

Part 4 of Sched 8 deals with the amendment of community orders.

Paragraph 16 deals with amendments made necessary because the offender has changed residence and is living in a different area.

Under para 17(1), the court may, on the application of the offender or the responsible officer, amend a community order by cancelling any of the requirements of the order, or by replacing any of those requirements with a requirement of the same kind, which the court could include if it were then making the order.

Under para 17(2), the court may not amend a mental health treatment requirement, a drug rehabilitation requirement or an alcohol treatment requirement unless the offender expresses his willingness to comply with the requirement as amended. If the offender fails to express his willingness to comply with a mental health treatment requirement, drug rehabilitation requirement or alcohol treatment requirement as proposed to be amended by the court, the court may revoke the community order and

deal with him, for the offence in respect of which the order was made, in any way in which he could have been dealt with for that offence by the court which made the order (para 17(3)). If re-sentencing under para 17(3), the court must take account of the extent to which the offender has complied with the requirements of the order, and may impose a custodial sentence if the original offence was punishable with imprisonment (para 17(4)).

The court cannot add a wholly new requirement or substitute a different requirement for one that was originally specified in the order. However, the court can cancel a requirement or adjust it (for example, changing the hours of a curfew or substituting one specified activity for another). The court is also empowered to add electronic monitoring to any of the original requirements under the order.

Paragraph 18 provides that, where a community order includes a drug rehabilitation, alcohol treatment or mental health treatment requirement, and the medical practitioner (or other person responsible for the treatment) is:

(a) of the opinion that:

   (i) the treatment of the offender should be continued beyond the period specified in the order;

   (ii) the offender needs different treatment;

   (iii) the offender is not susceptible to treatment; or

   (iv) the offender does not require further treatment; or

(b) is for any reason unwilling to continue to treat or direct the treatment of the offender,

he must make a written report to that effect to the responsible officer; the responsible officer must then apply (under para 17) to the court for the variation or cancellation of the requirement.

Paragraph 19 provides that where a community order includes a drug rehabilitation requirement with provision for review, the responsible officer may apply to the court (under para 17) to amend the order to provide for each subsequent periodic review (see s 211) to be made without a hearing instead of at a review hearing, or vice versa.

Paragraph 20 provides that on the application of the offender or the responsible officer, the court may extend an unpaid work requirement beyond the 12 month limit (specified in s 200(2)) if it believes it to be in the interests of justice to do so having regard to circumstances which have arisen since the order was made.

16.11.4 Commission of further offences

Part 5 of Sched 8 deals with the powers of the court in relation to a community order where the offender is subsequently convicted of another offence.

Paragraph 21 provides that where an offender in respect of whom a community order made by a magistrates' court is in force is convicted of an offence by a magistrates' court, and it appears to the court that it would be in the interests of justice to do so, having regard to circumstances which have arisen since the community order was made, the magistrates' court may either (a) revoke the order, or (b) revoke the

order and deal with the offender, for the offence in respect of which the order was made, in any way which he could have been dealt with for that offence by the court which made the order.

If it re-sentences him, the court must take into account the extent to which he complied with the order (para 21(3)), and the offender has a right of appeal to the Crown Court (para 21(4)).

If the magistrates' court is dealing with the later offence but the community order was made in the Crown Court, the magistrates may commit the offender (in custody or on bail) to appear at the Crown Court (para 22(1)).

Paragraph 23 confers the same powers to revoke and/or re-sentence on the Crown Court where the offender is convicted by the Crown Court of a subsequent offence.

CHAPTER 17

FINES, DISCHARGES AND BINDING
OVER TO KEEP THE PEACE

In this chapter, we consider fines, conditional and absolute discharges and the power to bind a person over. These powers apply irrespective of the age of the offender, although special limits exist on the amount of a fine that may be imposed on a juvenile.

17.1   FINES

A fine may be imposed for any offence except one which carries mandatory life imprisonment. There has been some encouragement for the courts to make greater use of the fine as a penalty. In *R v Kefford* [2002] EWCA Crim 519; [2002] 2 Cr App R(S) 106, the Court of Appeal said that only those who need to be sent to prison ought to be sent to prison and those who are sent to prison would not be sent there for longer than necessary. This, said the court, is not intended to deter courts from sending to prison those who commit offences involving violence or intimidation, or other grave crimes. However, there are other categories of offences where community punishment or a fine would be a more appropriate sentence (for example, where a person with no previous convictions commits an economic crime, such as obtaining credit by fraud). In appropriate cases, it could be better that an offender repay his debt to society by performing some useful task for the public rather than spending a short time in prison. Again, in *R v Baldwin* [2002] EWCA Crim 2647; (2002) *The Times*, 22 November, Lord Woolf CJ, at para 9, observed:

> It is not today the practice to use the penalty of a fine as frequently as it has been used in the past. Bearing in mind the stress in our prisons today from overcrowding, if there are good prospects that an offender is not going to prey upon the public again, there are advantages in using the penalty of a fine rather than sentencing someone to a further period of imprisonment. This is especially true in the case of an offender in the situation of the appellant, who is able to gain steady employment and is able to earn a substantial salary.

17.1.1   Crown Court fines

Section 127 of the Powers of Criminal Courts (Sentencing) Act 2000 (which is re-enacted in s 163 of the Criminal Justice Act 2003) empowers the Crown Court to impose a fine on an offender instead of, or in addition to, dealing with the offender in any other way. This power applies both where the offender has been convicted on indictment and where the offender has been convicted summarily but is then committed to the Crown Court for sentence under s 3 of the Powers of Criminal Courts (Sentencing) Act 2000.

There is no statutory limit on the amount of a fine imposed by the Crown Court following conviction on indictment or following a s 3 committal for sentence. Note, however, that where a Crown Court is dealing with an offence following committal under s 6 of the 2000 Act, the Crown Court cannot exceed the amount of the fine

which the magistrates could have imposed (since the object of that committal is not to increase the sentencing powers available to the court).

Section 139(2) of the 2000 Act provides that where the Crown Court imposes a fine, it must fix a term of imprisonment (if the offender is 21 or over) or detention in a young offender institution (if the offender is aged between 18 and 20) in default.

Section 139(2) of the 2000 Act sets out the maximum term of imprisonment or detention which may be imposed under s 139. This depends on the amount of the fine:

Fine (£)	Term
1–200	7 days
201–500	14 days
501–1,000	28 days
1,001–2,500	45 days
2,501–5,000	3 months
5,001–10,000	6 months
10,001–20,000	12 months
20,001–50,000	18 months
50,001–100,000	2 years
100,001–250,000	3 years
250,001–1,000,000	5 years
over 1,000,000	10 years

17.1.2 Magistrates' courts fines for either way offences

Where a magistrates' court convicts a person of an offence which is triable either way because it is listed in Sched 1 to the Magistrates' Courts Act 1980, the court may impose a fine not exceeding the 'prescribed sum' (s 32(1) of the Magistrates' Courts Act 1980, currently £5,000).

Where a magistrates' court convicts a person of an offence which is triable either way because the statute creating the offence specifies penalties both for summary conviction and conviction on indictment, the court may impose a fine not exceeding the amount fixed in the statute creating the offence or the prescribed sum (that is, £5,000), whichever is greater (s 32(2)). Where the statute creating the offence states that the fine may not exceed 'the statutory maximum', the maximum referred to is the prescribed sum (that is, £5,000).

If the statute creating the offence refers only to imprisonment as a punishment, a fine on level 3 (£1,000) is deemed to be included (s 34(3)).

17.1.3 Magistrates' courts fines for summary offences

Fines for summary offences are expressed in terms of a standard scale (s 37(2) of the Criminal Justice Act 1982). The standard scale has five levels:

Level	Current maximum fine (£)
1	200
2	500
3	1,000
4	2,500
5	5,000

17.1.4   Imprisonment in default (magistrates' court fines)

Section 82(1) of the Magistrates' Courts Act 1980 provides that a magistrates' court which imposes a fine may only fix a term of imprisonment (or detention in a young offender institution) if:

- the offence is punishable with imprisonment and it appears to the court that the offender has sufficient means to pay the fine immediately; or

- it appears to the court that the offender is unlikely to remain long enough at an address where he can be found so that enforcement of the fine by other methods is possible; or

- the court also imposes a custodial sentence on the offender or the offender is already serving a custodial sentence.

Where a magistrates' court does fix a term of imprisonment in default of payment of a fine, the same periods apply as in the Crown Court (save that a magistrates' court cannot fix more than 12 months' imprisonment in default) (Sched 4 to the Magistrates' Courts Act 1980).

17.1.5   Fixing the amount of the fine

Section 128 of the Powers of Criminal Courts (Sentencing) Act 2000 sets out the procedure for fixing the amount of a fine. Section 128 is re-enacted (with some minor modifications) by s 164 of the Criminal Justice Act 2003. The process is as follows:

(1)   Before fixing the amount of any fine to be imposed on an offender who is an individual, a court must inquire into his financial circumstances.

(2)   The amount of any fine fixed by a court must be such as, in the opinion of the court, reflects the seriousness of the offence.

(3)   In fixing the amount of any fine to be imposed on an offender (whether an individual or other person), a court must take into account the circumstances of the case including, among other things, the financial circumstances of the offender so far as they are known, or appear, to the court.

(4)   Sub-section (3) applies whether taking into account the financial circumstances of the offender has the effect of increasing or reducing the amount of the fine.

Sub-section (1) says that before fixing the amount of the fine, the court must inquire into the financial circumstances of the offender, and sub-s (3) requires the court to take into account the financial circumstances of the offender so far as they are known to the court. It should be noted that sub-s (1) applies only where the offender is an individual (that is, not a company); sub-s (3) applies both to individuals and to companies. Sub-

section (4) states that the financial circumstances of the offender must be taken into account whether this has the effect of increasing or reducing the amount of the fine. The purpose of sub-s (4) is to ensure that no-one is ordered to pay a fine that is beyond their financial means (and to try to ensure that the effect of the fine on this particular offender would be the same as the effect of an equivalent fine on someone who is noticeably richer or poorer than this offender).

Thus, the court first fixes an amount related to the seriousness of the offence (taking account of any aggravating features, and any relevant mitigating circumstances) and then considers whether that amount should be increased or reduced as a result of the offender's means. See, for example, *R v Cowley* (1995) *The Times*, 2 February, where a fine was reduced because proper account had not been taken of the offender's means.

In *R v Chelmsford Crown Court ex p Birchall* (1989) 11 Cr App R(S) 510, the Divisional Court emphasised that where the offender is fined for a number of offences, the court must also ensure that the total amount to be paid is proportionate to the totality of the offending.

In 'The use of financial penalties and the amounts imposed: the need for a new approach' [2003] Crim LR 13, Robin Moore notes that use of the fine has declined recently, and that there are growing concerns regarding its credibility as a means of punishment; these concerns arise from the fact that a large proportion of those ordered to pay fines are in arrears, and significant amounts of money are simply being written-off. He says that:

> ... it is important to clarify the underlying principles behind any proposals for change. One such principle is that the fine should have a detrimental impact upon offenders' means, short of actual financial hardship. It should also be capable of payment within 12 months, enabling offenders to make a fresh start once a year has passed.

He advocates a return to a version of the short-lived 'unit fines' system, which was related much more closely to ability to pay. Under that system, the fine was essentially based on weekly disposable income: s 18(2) of the Criminal Justice Act 1991 provided that the amount of the fine should be the product of a number of units, 'commensurate with the seriousness of the offence', and the value given to each unit, representing 'the offender's disposable [weekly] income'. However, after being in force for only a very short time, the unit fine system was abolished by s 65 of the Criminal Justice Act 1993. The system attracted criticism from magistrates and from the media, with magistrates saying that the scheme was too rigid and the press protesting at the fact that people who had committed similar offences were receiving very different fines (which was, of course, the whole point of the scheme!). The unit fines scheme was replaced with the more general requirement that the court should take account of the offender's means when fixing a fine (whether doing so served to decrease or increase the amount of the fine). The widespread problems over fine enforcement suggest that this more flexible approach is not working.

Moore's suggestion is as follows:

> First, a financial penalty could be imposed for a specified number of weeks according to the gravity of the offence. The offence would rightly remain paramount, and fines, like other sentencing disposals, would be imposed for a period of time. Second, the amount to be paid in each week throughout the specified period could be set according to the offender's spare income, subject to a fixed minimum and maximum

so as to maintain a level of proportionality with the offence. To maintain correspondence with both offence and offender, subsequent financial penalties would need to be set consecutively, unless the offender was judged able to afford concurrent maximum rates of payment. The time periods appropriate for the various offences, along with the maximum and minimum rates of payment, would have to be calculated carefully and set out in the magistrates' guidelines.

Moore also comments on the dilemma faced by courts where a fine is the appropriate sentence but the offender lacks the means to pay. Often the only alternative is a conditional discharge (which is regarded by many as a complete let-off). Moore concludes that 'the full range of community sentences should be available as options so that the sentence can be tailored to both offence and offender'.

If the offender does not have the means to pay a fine which adequately reflects the seriousness of the offence but the offence is not sufficiently serious to justify a custodial sentence, it is wrong in principle to impose a custodial sentence (*R v Reeves* (1972) 56 Cr App R 366). The same applies even if the sentence of imprisonment is to be suspended. On the other hand, if the seriousness of the offence does justify a custodial sentence, the offender should not escape custody merely because he has the means to pay a large fine (*R v Markwick* (1953) 37 Cr App R 125).

In *R v Warden* (1996) 160 JP 363, it was held that in determining a non-custodial sentence, the offender should normally be given credit for any time spent in custody on remand. In that case, a fine of £2,000 was reduced to £1,000 on that basis.

In *R v F Howe & Son Ltd* [1999] 2 All ER 249, the Court of Appeal gave some guidance on fines where the defendant is a company. The starting point should be the company's annual accounts; these need to be scrutinised with some care to avoid reaching a superficial or erroneous conclusion. Where accounts or other financial information are deliberately not supplied, the court is entitled to conclude that the company can afford to pay any fine the court is minded to impose. The fine needs to be large enough to bring home the seriousness of the offending to the managers and to the shareholders. Where the defendant is a small company, with limited resources, it must be borne in mind that the fine (and costs) are not tax deductible and so the full burden will fall on the company. In *R v Rollco Screw and Rivet Co Ltd* [1999] 2 Cr App R(S) 436, the Court of Appeal pointed out that, in a small company, the directors might also be the shareholders and so the court must be alert to this if a fine is imposed on both the directors and on the company; however, the penalties imposed should make it clear that there is personal responsibility on the part of the directors which cannot be shuffled off to the company. When deciding the period for payment of the fine, it is proper for the court to fix a longer period in the case of a company than would be appropriate in the case of an individual.

17.1.6   Obtaining information about the offenders' means

Section 126 of the Powers of Criminal Courts (Sentencing) Act 2000 is re-enacted in s 162 of the Criminal Justice Act 2003. It empowers a court to make a 'financial circumstances order' against any person convicted by that court. The order requires the offender to provide a statement of his financial circumstances within the period specified in the order.

Under sub-s (4), failure to comply without reasonable excuse is a summary offence punishable with a fine not exceeding level 3 (£1,000). Where a financial circumstances

order has been made, it is an offence under sub-s (5) to make a statement which is known to be false, or recklessly to furnish a statement which is false, or knowingly to fail to disclose a material fact. These offences are punishable with a fine not exceeding level 4 (£2,500).

Furthermore, under s 164(5) of the 2003 Act, where the offender has been convicted in his absence (either under s 11 or 12 of the Magistrates' Courts Act 1980), or fails to comply with a financial circumstances order, or otherwise fails to co-operate with the court's inquiry into his means, 'and the court considers that it has insufficient information to make a proper determination of the financial circumstances of the offender, it may make such determination as it thinks fit'.

Section 165 of the Criminal Justice Act 2003 re-enacts s 129 of the Powers of Criminal Courts (Sentencing) Act. It applies 'where a court has, in fixing the amount of a fine, determined the offender's financial circumstances under section 164(5)'. The section goes on:

(2) If, on subsequently inquiring into the offender's financial circumstances, the court is satisfied that had it had the results of that inquiry when sentencing the offender it would—
   (a) have fixed a smaller amount, or
   (b) not have fined him,
   it may remit the whole or part of the fine.
(3) Where under this section the court remits the whole or part of a fine after a term of imprisonment has been fixed under section 139 of the Sentencing Act (powers of Crown Court in relation to fines) or section 82(5) of the Magistrates' Courts Act 1980 (magistrates' powers in relation to default) it must reduce the term by the corresponding proportion.

17.1.7 Summary

The fixing of a fine is essentially a three-stage process:

* deciding what amount would appropriately reflect the seriousness of the offence;
* considering whether that amount should be reduced in light of personal mitigation relating to the offender; and
* considering whether the amount reached after the second stage should be increased or decreased in light of the offender's means.

17.1.8 Enforcement of fines

Whether the fine was imposed by the Crown Court or a magistrates' court, enforcement is the responsibility of a magistrates' court. If the fine was imposed by a magistrates' court, enforcement is the responsibility of that court. If the fine was imposed by the Crown Court, responsibility for enforcement rests with the magistrates' court which committed the offender for trial or sentence (as the case may be). If the offender resides outside the area served by the enforcing magistrates' court, the order will usually be transferred to the offender's local magistrates' court.

Under s 75 of the Magistrates' Courts Act 1980, the court may allow time (or extend the time already allowed) for payment or may order payment by instalments.

Where a fine is to be paid by instalments, the instalments should usually be calculated so that the fine is paid off within 12 months. However, there is no rule of law to this effect and there may be cases where a period longer than a year may be appropriate (*R v Olliver* (1989) 11 Cr App R(S) 10).

Where the court allows time (or further time), it may also set a date when the offender must attend court for an inquiry into his means if any part of the fine remains unpaid (s 86).

We have already seen that the offender's means are taken into account when the decision is taken to impose a fine. However, if the offender fails to pay some or all of the fine and an inquiry into his means shows that the default results from inability (rather than refusal) to pay, then the magistrates' court may remit the whole or part of the fine (s 129 of the 2000 Act).

Otherwise, the sanctions for non-payment of a fine are:

- to issue a 'distress warrant' (this authorises the seizure and sale of goods belonging to the offender; the proceeds of sale go to meet the outstanding fine);

- where the offender is in employment, to make an attachment of earnings order (this requires the offender's employer to deduct a regular sum from the offender's wages and to pay that sum direct to the court (the Attachment of Earnings Act 1971));

- where the offender is in receipt of income support or income-based jobseekers allowance, to make an order for the deduction of regular sums from the offender's income support (under the Fines (Deduction from Income Support) Regulations 1992);

- where the offender is under 25, to make an attendance centre order;

- to commit the offender to prison. This is possible if either:

  (a) the offence for which the fine was imposed was imprisonable and it appears to the court that the offender has the means to pay the outstanding amount forthwith; or

  (b) the court is satisfied that the offender's failure to pay the fine is due to wilful refusal or culpable neglect, and no other method of enforcement would be effective.

Where a term of imprisonment is ordered, it must be for the term originally specified as the term in default (see above); if no term in default was specified when the fine was imposed, the court dealing with the default fixes a term which must not exceed the term which could have been fixed in the first place (see Sched 4 to the Magistrates' Courts Act 1980).

Prior to the issue of a distress warrant (authorising seizure of goods) where a fine remains unpaid, there is no need (indeed, there is no power) to hold a means inquiry. It is only where the court is considering issuing a warrant of committal (sending the defaulter to prison) that such an inquiry is required (*R v Hereford Magistrates' Court ex p MacRae* (1999) 163 JP 433).

Before an offender can be committed to prison for non-payment of a fine, all other methods of enforcing payment must have been considered or tried; where other methods have been considered inappropriate, reasons for that determination must be given (*R v St Helen's Justices ex p Jones* [1999] 2 All ER 73).

Where magistrates are considering a warrant of commitment to prison and the defendant is not present, the hearing should be adjourned if the justices are aware that the defendant has not received notice of the proceedings (*R v Doncaster Justices ex p Hannan* (1999) 163 JP 182).

17.1.9 Enforcement of fines under the Crime (Sentences) Act 1997

The Crime (Sentences) Act 1997 adds a number of additional ways of enforcing the fines.

Under s 35 of the Crime (Sentences) Act 1997, where the offender has attained the age of 16, the court may impose a community punishment order or a curfew order as a penalty for default in paying a fine. Section 300 of the Criminal Justice Act 2003 modifies the fine default provisions in s 35 of the Crime Sentences Act 1997. Section 300 provides that where the court has the power to commit an offender to custody in default of payment of a fine, it may order the offender to comply with an unpaid work requirement or a curfew requirement (with electronic monitoring) instead. Such an order is to be known as a 'default order'. If the offender subsequently pays part of the sum due, the number of hours of unpaid work or days of curfew will be reduced by a proportion corresponding to the amount repaid; if the fine is paid in full, the default order will cease to have effect.

Section 301 of the 2003 Act re-enacts the provisions of s 40 of the Crime (Sentences) Act 1997. This provides that instead of committing an offender to custody for non-payment of a fine, the court may disqualify an offender from driving for a period of up to 12 months. If part of the fine is repaid, the length of disqualification is reduced *pro rata*; the disqualification ceases to have effect if the fine is paid in full.

17.1.10 Enforcement of fines under the Courts Act 2003

Schedule 5 to the Courts Act 2003 puts in place an additional set of powers to aid the enforcement of fines. It complements (rather than replacing) the existing mechanisms for enforcement.

Schedule 5 applies where the offender is over 18 and is liable to pay a sum which consists of or includes a fine; 'fine', in this context, does not include compensation. If the offender is not liable to pay a fine, no collection order can be made. However, if he is liable to pay a fine, then any other sums that he is liable to pay (such as compensation) can be collected under the same collection order as the fine (para 1). Paragraph 2 accordingly defines 'the sum due' so as to include compensation and costs.

Under para 3, the offender is to be regarded as an 'existing defaulter' if he is currently in default on any fine or similar sum ordered to be paid by the court (whether or not a collection order has been made under Sched 5), unless he can show an adequate reason for the default.

Part 2 (paras 4–6) of Sched 5 deals with fines which are paid immediately. The offender is eligible for a discount if the sum due (less the amount of the discount) is paid immediately. The amount of the discount (which cannot exceed 50%) is fixed by statutory instrument. The discount does not apply to any compensation or costs forming part of the sum due.

This discount is not available if the offender is an 'existing defaulter' (unless the court has accepted that there is a good reason for the default and is prepared to allow the discount).

Part 3 of the Schedule covers attachment of earnings orders and applications for deduction from benefits (income support or jobseekers allowance). Under para 7, Pt 3 applies if the sum due is not paid immediately. This will be the case if the court decides that the offender should be allowed time to pay, or if the offender was required to pay immediately but failed to do so. Under para 8, if the court finds that the offender is an 'existing defaulter' who can show no good reason for being in default, the court must (unless it is impracticable or inappropriate to do so) either make an attachment of earnings order if the offender is employed, or apply to the Secretary of State for Work and Pensions for deduction from benefits. Where the offender is not an existing defaulter, para 9 enables the court to make an attachment of earnings order or seek deduction from benefits if he consents.

Part 4 governs the making of 'collection orders'. Under para 11, these provisions apply if the court decides that the offender should be allowed time to pay, or if the offender was required to pay immediately and failed to do so. Paragraph 11 makes it clear that these provisions apply whether or not the court has made an attachment of earnings order or sought deduction from benefits. Paragraph 12 provides that the court must, unless it appears impracticable or inappropriate to do so, make a collection order to enable enforcement of payment of the sum due.

Under para 14, if the court has not made an attachment of earnings order or sought deduction from benefits, the collection order must either require the offender to pay the sum due within a specified period or by instalments. If the court has made an attachment of earnings order or sought deduction from benefits, the collection order must give directions for payment of the fine if, as the case may be, the attachment of earnings order fails (that is, the employer fails to comply with the order or the order is discharged before the entire sum due is paid) or the application for deduction from benefits fails (for example, if the Secretary of State refuses to make deductions, or ceases to make deductions, because of other deductions being made from the offender's benefits).

Part 5 provides for a discount for prompt payment where a collection order has been made (provided that the offender is not an 'existing defaulter'). Under para 19, the offender is entitled to a discount on the fine (but not costs or compensation) if the sum due (that is, all monies owing, including any compensation and costs) is paid without the offender at any time having been in default on the order. If the offender defaults, the discount is lost. The amount of the discount is fixed by statutory instrument but cannot exceed 50%.

Part 6 enables the 'fines officer' (the person responsible for collecting the fine) to vary the payment terms in the collection order. Under para 22, the offender can apply for such a variation (provided that he is not in default) if there has been a material change in his circumstances since the collection order was made (or since the fines officer last varied the collection order), or if the offender has since provided more information about his circumstances. The offender might seek, for example, to be allowed to pay the sum due by instalments rather than within a fixed period, or (if the order requires payment by instalments) to vary the number or amount of the instalments.

Part 7 of the Schedule sets out the effect of the first default on a collection order containing payment terms. Under para 26, provided it is not impracticable or inappropriate to do so, the fines officer must either make an attachment of earnings order (if the offender is employed) or apply to the Secretary of State for Work and Pensions for deductions to be made from benefit. Paragraph 27 provides for the fine (but not compensation or costs) to be increased if this attachment of earnings or deduction from benefits fails or if the fines officer does not make an attachment of earnings order or seek deduction from benefits. The amount of the increase is fixed by statutory instrument, but cannot exceed 50%. If the sum due is paid in full, without further default, the offender's liability to pay the increase is waived.

Part 8 of the Schedule deals with what happens if an attachment of earnings order or deduction from benefits (under Pt 3 or Pt 6) fails. The attachment of earnings order or application for deduction from benefits will contain 'reserve terms', and these terms come into operation if the order or application fails.

Under para 31, the offender can apply to the fines officer for these reserve terms to be varied provided that the offender is not in default on the collection order, and either there has been a material change in his circumstances since the reserve terms were set (or last varied) or the offender has since provided more information about his circumstances. Under para 32, the offender can appeal to the magistrates' court against the fines officer's decision. Paragraph 33 provides for an increase to be imposed on the fine (the increase being waived if the offender pays the sum due without further default).

Part 9 deals with the operation of collection orders after an increase in the fine has been imposed as a result of default on the part of the offender. Under para 35, the fines officer may vary the payment terms. If he does so, there is a right of appeal to the magistrates' court.

Paragraph 37 sets out what happens if the offender fails to contact the fines officer when he receives notice that the fine has been increased as a result of the first default, or if the offender does contact the fines officer but the latter decides not to vary terms of payment, or if, after the increase has been imposed and payment terms have been varied to accommodate this, the offender again defaults. In such a case, the fines officer must either refer the case to the magistrates' court, or issue a notice (a 'further steps notice') stating that he intends to take one or more of the enforcement measures set out in para 38 of the Schedule, namely to:

- issue a distress warrant;
- register the sum in the register of judgments set up under the Act (which may adversely affect the offender's credit rating);
- make an attachment of earnings order or apply for deduction from benefits;
- make a clamping order (that a vehicle registered in the offender's name be immobilised);
- take any other step that may be permitted under regulations governing the collection of fines.

The magistrates' court will become involved if the offender appeals against the fines officer's decision about variation of the collection order following an increase because of default or against a 'further steps notice', or if the fines officer refers the case to the court. Where this occurs, the magistrates' court may (under para 39) make an order

waiving the increase, provided that the court is satisfied that there are exceptional circumstances and the sum due is paid without further default. The court may also:

- vary or quash any decision made by the fines officer;
- take any of the 'further steps' set out in para 38 (see above); or
- discharge the collection order and deal with the case itself using any of its standard powers (that is, the powers it would have had if no collection order had been made).

Paragraph 41 empowers the court to order the sale of a vehicle that has been clamped pursuant to a clamping order under para 38 (and the court should consider whether the sale of the vehicle is proportionate to the amount of the fine outstanding).

Paragraph 42 enables the fines officer to refer a case to the magistrates' court (and, if necessary, issue a summons requiring the offender to attend court) at any time before the fine is paid in full. This would be appropriate if circumstances arise which require action but the fines officer lacks the necessary powers. This would be the case if, for example, the offender fails to co-operate with the fines officer or circumstances arise under which the offender ceases to have the means to pay any fine.

Paragraph 48 allows a fines officer to request information about the offender's means. It is an offence (punishable with a level 4 fine, that is, up to £2,500) to give false information to a fines officer or to fail to disclose relevant information. It is also an offence (punishable with a level 2 fine, that is, up to £500) to fail to provide a statement of financial circumstances to the fines officer upon request.

The Fines Collection Regulations 2004 (SI 2004/176) implement Sched 5 to the Courts Act 2003 ('Sched 5'), which has been brought into force in some areas by way of a pilot scheme.

Part II of the Regulations amends Pt 1 of Sched 3 to the Attachment of Earnings Act 1971 and sets out tables for the calculation of the amounts to be deducted under attachments of earnings orders. Part III of the Regulations contains provisions setting out the detailed implementation of Sched 5. For example, reg 7 specifies the amount of the increase imposed on a fine under para 27 or 33 of Sched 5. Section 87 of the Magistrates' Courts Act 1980, which enables a fine to be enforced as if it were imposed by a judgment or order of the High Court or the county court, is specified as another step which may be taken under Sched 5 as listed in para 38(1) of that Schedule (reg 9). A fines officer may issue a summons requiring the offender to attend the magistrates' court to which he has referred the offender's case under Sched 5 (reg 11).

Part IV of the Regulations provides detailed rules on the clamping of vehicles under Sched 5 for default in the payment of fines, and for the storage and sale of clamped vehicles. Provision for the payment of the fine and any charges due and the release of the vehicle is made in reg 21. Provision is made for the ultimate sale of clamped vehicles if, after the expiry of the period of three months from the date the vehicle was clamped, a magistrates' court so orders under para 41 of Sched 5 (reg 24).

Schedule 6 to the Courts Act 2003 is even more innovative. It enables the court to allow an offender to discharge a fine by means of unpaid work (under a 'work order'). This power only applies to offenders who are over the age of 18. Under para 2, a 'work order' may be made if it appears to the court, from the information before it of the offender's financial circumstances, that the normal methods of fine collection are likely to be impracticable or inappropriate. The court must be satisfied that the offender

appears suitable to carry out the work; also, the order can only be made with the consent of the offender.

Under para 3, the offender's performance of the work order will be carried out under supervision. The number of hours to be worked will be calculated by dividing the sum owed by the prescribed hourly sum (fixed by regulations). The order must specify a date by which the number of hours is to be performed. Under para 6, if the work is completed before the specified date, the liability to pay the amount due is discharged. Paragraph 7 allows the offender to discharge his liability by paying the sum in respect of which the work was set. He can also reduce the number of hours he has to work by paying part of the sum.

Under para 8, the work order may be revoked or varied on application to the fines officer. If the offender fails to carry out the work but has a reasonable excuse (or if a change in circumstances means that he is unlikely to be able to comply), the court may revoke the order or allow more time to do the work. Where a work order is revoked and the offender has carried out some work under it, the sum due is reduced *pro rata* (para 9).

17.1.11 Combining fines with other orders

A fine may be combined with any other sentence.

However, it will usually be wrong in principle to impose a fine and an immediate custodial sentence unless the object of the fine is to deprive the offender of the profit which he has made from committing the offence (*R v Savundranayagan* [1968] 1 WLR 1761), although it should be noted that this object may be achieved through a confiscation order made under the Proceeds of Crime Act 2002 in cases where that Act applies.

A fine may be imposed at the same time as a compensation order. However, s 130(12) of the Powers of Criminal Courts Act 2000 provides that if an offender has insufficient means to pay both a fine and a compensation order, the compensation order takes priority; thus, in such a case, the fine will be reduced or a different sentence altogether imposed.

A fine may be imposed in addition to an order to pay the costs incurred by the prosecution, but the court should ensure that the total sum is within the offender's means.

17.2   ABSOLUTE AND CONDITIONAL DISCHARGES

Section 12(1) of the Powers of Criminal Courts (Sentencing) Act 2000 provides that where a court has convicted a person of an offence but is of the opinion, having regard to the nature of the offence and the character of the offender, that it is inexpedient to inflict punishment, the court may either:

- discharge the offender absolutely; or
- discharge the offender subject to a condition that he does not commit a further offence during the period (of up to three years) specified in the order.

17.2.1 Absolute discharge

The effect of an absolute discharge is that, apart from the fact that a conviction is recorded against the offender, no penalty is imposed.

An absolute discharge is appropriate where the court decides that it would be wrong to take any action against the accused. For example, an absolute discharge may be ordered if the defendant is convicted of a very trivial offence or if the circumstances of the commission of the offence show little or no blame on the part of the defendant. In *R v O'Toole* (1971) 55 Cr App R 206, for example, an ambulance driver who collided with another vehicle while answering a 999 call received an absolute discharge.

17.2.2 Conditional discharge

The only condition of a conditional discharge is that the offender does not commit another offence during the period of the conditional discharge. No other condition can be imposed.

Before ordering a conditional discharge, the court must explain to the offender that, if he commits another offence during the period of the conditional discharge, he is liable to be sentenced for the original offence (as well as the subsequent offence) (s 12(4) of the Powers of Criminal Courts (Sentencing) Act 2000).

A conditional discharge may be appropriate instead of a fine where the offence is not sufficiently serious to justify a community sentence or there is sufficient personal mitigation to render a community sentence too harsh.

17.2.3 Breach of conditional discharge

If the offender commits an offence during the period of a conditional discharge, the court dealing with the breach may deal with the offender in any way in which the offender could have been dealt with when the conditional discharge was ordered (s 13(6) of the Powers of Criminal Courts (Sentencing) Act 2000).

A magistrates' court can only deal with the breach of a conditional discharge imposed by a magistrates' court; the Crown Court can deal with the breach of a conditional discharge imposed by a Crown Court or a magistrates' court (s 13(2) of the Powers of Criminal Courts (Sentencing) Act 2000).

In practice, little is usually done in respect of a breach of a conditional discharge. A custodial sentence can only be imposed in respect of the original offence if that offence was sufficiently serious to justify a custodial sentence; this will rarely be the case. Similarly, a community sentence can only be imposed if the original offence merited such a sentence but there was sufficient personal mitigation in respect of the offender for a conditional discharge to be imposed instead.

Thus, the breach of a conditional discharge is often ignored, or else a fine is imposed for the original offence.

17.2.4 Combining discharges with other orders

As a discharge is only to be imposed where it is inexpedient to inflict punishment (s 12(1) of the 2000 Act), it would be wrong in principle to combine a discharge with

any other sentence for the same offence (*R v Savage* (1983) 5 Cr App R(S) 216). So, for example, a conditional discharge cannot be combined with a fine (*R v Sanck* (1990) 12 Cr App R(S) 155).

Section 12(7) of the 2000 Act, however, enables the court to make an order for costs and/or compensation even if it discharges the offender.

17.2.5   Effect of conditional or absolute discharge

Section 14(1) of the Powers of Criminal Courts (Sentencing) Act 2000 provides that a conditional or absolute discharge only counts as a conviction for certain purposes.

It follows that where an offence is dealt with by way of a discharge, conviction for that offence cannot amount to a breach of an earlier order. So, for example, if the offender commits an offence during the currency of a conditional discharge or during the operational period of a suspended sentence, but the later offence is dealt with by way of a discharge, the court cannot re-sentence the offender for the earlier offence or activate the suspended sentence.

However, an offence which is dealt with by way of conditional discharge does amount to a conviction where an offence is committed during the currency of that conditional discharge and the offender is re-sentenced for the offence for which the conditional discharge was imposed (s 14(2) of the Powers of Criminal Courts (Sentencing) Act 2000).

Furthermore, an offence dealt with by way of discharge appears on the offender's criminal record.

17.3   BINDING OVER TO KEEP THE PEACE

Section 1 of the Justices of the Peace Act 1968 declares that any 'court of record' with criminal jurisdiction (that is, a magistrates' court, the Crown Court or the Court of Appeal) has the power to bind a person over to be of good behaviour. This may be done by requiring the person to enter into his own recognisance or to find sureties, or both, and he may be committed to prison if he does not comply.

A similar power arises under s 115 of the Magistrates' Courts Act 1980 where the court has finished hearing a 'complaint' (a method of bringing proceedings of a civil or quasi-civil nature before magistrates).

The effect of the order is that the offender promises to pay a specified sum of money (or sureties promise to pay money on his behalf) if he misbehaves during a period specified by the court.

When exercising its power to bind over, the court must fix the period during which the bind over is to last (that is, the period during which misbehaviour will result in forfeiture of the recognisance) and must also fix the amount to be forfeited if the person breaches the order.

There is no statutory maximum for the amount of the recognisance. A person could, therefore, be convicted of an offence and bound over in a sum which exceeds the maximum fine that could be imposed for that offence (*R v Sandbach Justices ex p Williams* [1935] 2 KB 192).

Similarly, there is no statutory maximum for the length of time for which the order is to run.

The only conditions which may be imposed are that the person bound over must keep the peace and be of good behaviour. No other conditions may be imposed (*R v Randall* (1986) 8 Cr App R(S) 433).

A person may be bound over at any stage of criminal proceedings. It may be done, for example, where the prosecution discontinue the case, or offer no evidence.

The power to bind over arises 'not by reason of any offence having been committed, but as a measure of preventive justice' to prevent a future breach of the peace (*Veater v Glennon* [1981] 1 WLR 567). It follows that:

- the power to bind over does not apply only to defendants. It also applies to a witness appearing before the court (see *Sheldon v Bromfield Justices* [1964] 2 QB 573) and to the alleged victim of the defendant's wrongdoing (see *R v Wilkins* [1907] 2 KB 380);

- it does not depend on a conviction being recorded against the person to be bound over. So, a defendant who has been acquitted can be bound over (*R v Inner London Crown Court ex p Benjamin* (1986) 85 Cr App R 267). However, in *R v Middlesex Crown Court ex p Khan* (1997) 161 JP 240, the Divisional Court held that where a defendant is acquitted, he may only be bound over if the judge is satisfied beyond reasonable doubt that he is a potential threat to other people and a person of violence.

In *R v Lincoln Crown Court ex p Jude* [1997] 3 All ER 737, the Divisional Court held that where a court intends to bind a person over, there is no requirement that the person must consent to the order.

17.3.1 Procedure

Where the court is minded to bind over a person who has not been charged with an offence or a defendant who has been acquitted, that person should be given the opportunity to make representations (*R v Hendon Justices ex p Gorchein* [1973] 1 WLR 1502; *R v Woking Justices ex p Gossage* [1973] QB 448).

Where the court proposes to bind over a defendant who has been convicted (in other words, using the power to bind over as a form of sentence), the defendant must be given the opportunity to make representations and the amount of the recognisance must take account of the defendant's means (*R v Central Criminal Court ex p Boulding* [1984] 1 QB 813).

17.3.2 Refusal to enter into recognisance

If the person refuses to be bound over, the court can impose a custodial sentence.

Where the bind over is ordered under s 115 of the Magistrates' Courts Act 1980, the maximum period of the custodial sentence is six months. There is no statutory limit to the custodial sentence where the defendant refuses to be bound over under s 1 of the Justices of the Peace Act 1968, although it would seem to be wrong in principle for a magistrates' court to exceed the usual limit on its sentencing powers.

Although the penalty for failing to enter into the recognisance is expressed to be committal to prison, this is deemed to include detention in a young offender institution (and so the power to impose a custodial sentence applies to the offender who is aged 18 to 20) (*Howley v Oxford* (1985) 81 Cr App R 246).

There is no power in these circumstances to order the detention of a person who is under the age of 18, but a magistrates' court may order such a person to attend at an attendance centre (see s 60(1)(b) of the Powers of Criminal Courts (Sentencing) Act 2000).

17.3.3 Failure to comply with conditions of bind over

If the person who has been bound over fails to keep the peace and to be of good behaviour, the court may order the payment of some or all of the amount of the recognisance.

The Crown Court, when forfeiting a recognisance, must fix a term of imprisonment or detention to be served in default (s 139(2) of the Powers of Criminal Courts (Sentencing) Act 2000).

Forfeiture proceedings in respect of a bind over ordered by a magistrates' court are commenced by means of a complaint to the court which made the original order (s 120 of the Magistrates' Courts Act 1980). Such forfeiture proceedings are regarded as civil, not criminal, and so the civil standard of proof (the balance of probabilities) applies (*R v Marlow Justices ex p O'Sullivan* [1984] QB 381). Nevertheless, the person should be given an opportunity to present evidence (including calling witnesses) and to make representations as to why the recognisance should not be forfeited (*R v McGregor* [1945] 2 All ER 180).

CHAPTER 18

YOUNG OFFENDERS: CUSTODIAL SENTENCES

There are currently three types of custodial sentence which apply to offenders who have not attained the age of 21:

- 'detention in a young offender institution' under s 96 of the Powers of Criminal Courts (Sentencing) Act 2000 (18–20 year olds);
- a 'detention and training order' under s 100 of the Act (offenders under 18); and
- long-term detention under s 91 of the Act.

The two main differences between custodial sentences for those under 21 as against those over 21 are:

- young offenders and adults do not serve their sentences together: young offenders are detained separately from adult offenders;
- unlike a sentence of imprisonment, a sentence of detention in a young offender institution or a detention and training order cannot be suspended. A custodial sentence on an offender who has not attained the age of 21 must therefore be immediate.

18.1 DETENTION AND TRAINING ORDERS

Section 100 of the Powers of Criminal Courts (Sentencing) Act 2000 provides for the making of a detention and training order where an offender between the ages of 12 and 17 is convicted of an offence which (in the case of an adult offender) is punishable with imprisonment.

A detention and training order is a custodial sentence and so the requirements set out in ss 79–81 of the Powers of Criminal Courts (Sentencing) Act 2000 apply. In particular, the court must be satisfied that the seriousness of the offence requires such a sentence or, in the case of a violent or sexual offence, such a sentence is needed to protect the public from serious harm from the offender. Section 83 restricts the power of the court to impose a detention and training order on someone who is not legally represented.

Where the offender has not attained the age of 15 at the date of conviction, a detention and training order can only be imposed if he is a 'persistent offender' (s 100(2)(a)). The term 'persistent offender' is (rather surprisingly) not defined in the legislation. In *R v Charlton* (2000) 164 JP 685, the court noted Home Office guidance which suggested that the phrase meant that the offender had been convicted on three or more separate occasions in the past. In the present case, however, the offender had been held by the Crown Court to be a persistent offender solely on the basis of the offences currently before the court (of which there were several!). The Divisional Court held that it would not be appropriate to adopt the Home Office guidance as the definition of the term 'persistent offender'; the court went on to say that the sentencing court in the present case was entitled to regard the offender as a persistent offender on the basis of the offences currently before the court. Similarly, in *R v B (D) (A Juvenile)* [2001] 1 Cr App R(S) 113 (where the offender was aged 12 and was

sentenced to a detention and training order following his conviction for burglary), the Court of Appeal held that it is not necessary to establish a pattern of offences of the same or similar character in order to categorise a person as a persistent offender.

Where the offender is aged 10 or 11 at the date of conviction, a detention and training order cannot be imposed unless the Secretary of State extends such orders to offenders of this age group (and there are apparently no immediate plans to do so) and if such a sentence is the only way of protecting the public from further offending by that offender (s 100(2)(b)).

18.1.1   Duration of a detention and training order

The total length of a detention and training order can be four, six, eight, 10, 12, 18 or 24 months (s 101(1)). However, the term of a detention and training order cannot exceed the maximum term of imprisonment that the Crown Court could impose on an adult offender for that offence (s 101(2)).

Where the offender is convicted of more than one offence for which a detention and training order could be imposed, the court can impose consecutive detention and training orders, but the total term imposed must not exceed 24 months (s 101(3) and (4)).

Section 102(2) provides that the period of detention under a detention and training order is to be one-half of the total term of the order.

Section 101 empowers both the Crown Court and a youth court to impose a detention and training order for up to 24 months. As half of the period of the detention and training order is spent in custody, this means that the youth court is empowered to impose 12 months' custody (plus 12 months' supervision) for a single offence. The youth court's powers in this regard are therefore greater than those currently enjoyed by the adult magistrates' court (although the powers of that court are increased by the Criminal Justice Act 2003). In *R v Medway Youth Court ex p A* [2000] 1 Cr App R(S) 191, a youth court sentenced a young offender to a 12 month secure training order under the Criminal Justice and Public Order Act 1994 (the secure training order was effectively the precursor to the detention and training order). It was argued that this sentence was unlawful, given the general restriction on the sentencing powers of magistrates to six months' custody for a single offence (or 12 months for two or more either way offences). The Divisional Court held that Parliament had clearly intended to permit magistrates in the youth court to exceed the usual six months' limit in the case of secure training centre orders. The court went on to refer to the new detention and training orders and noted that, so far as these orders are concerned, magistrates are to 'have the power to make the sentences of any length the Crown Court could impose' up to the limit of 24 months and that the old restrictions on the justices' powers were 'not to be presumed to apply to new sentencing powers'. It follows that the aggregate sentence is not restricted to the maximum aggregate that a magistrates' court could impose on an adult offender. So, for example, an aggregate sentence of 10 months' detention and training is permissible even though a magistrates' court dealing with an adult offender would be limited to a total of six months' imprisonment (see, for example, *C (A Child) v DPP* [2001] EWHC 453 (Admin); [2002] 1 Cr App R(S) 45, where the Divisional Court upheld a total sentence of a 10-month detention and training order imposed on a 16 year old defendant in respect of a series of summary-only offences in respect of which an adult could not have received more than a total of six months' custody).

Section 298 of the Criminal Justice Act 2003 adds a new sub-section, sub-s (2A), to s 101 of the Powers of Criminal Courts (Sentencing) Act 2000. This provides that the maximum sentence for a summary offence in the case of offenders under the age of 18 will remain as a six month detention and training order despite the increase, in the case of adults, in the maximum sentence for some summary-only offences from six months to 51 weeks.

18.1.2 Supervision under a detention and training order

Section 103(1) provides that the period of supervision under a detention and training order begins with the offender's release from custody (whether that is at the half-way point or not) and lasts until the expiry of the total term of the detention and training order. During the period of supervision, the offender is under the supervision of a probation officer, a social worker or a member of a youth offending team (s 103(3)).

The offender receives a notice setting out any requirements with which he must comply during the period of supervision (s 103(6)(b)). Section 104 provides that failure to comply with such requirements will lead to the issue of a summons requiring the offender to appear before the youth court which made the order or the youth court for the area where the offender lives. If breach of the requirement(s) is proved, the court may order detention of the offender for a period of up to three months, or the remainder of the term of the detention and training order (whichever is shorter) or it may impose a fine of up to £1,000 (s 104(3)).

Failure to comply with the terms of supervision under a detention and training order was considered in *Stewart v Doncaster Youth Offending Team* [2003] EWHC 1128 (Admin); (2003) 167 JP 381. The offender had been sentenced to detention and training orders of 18 months for one offence, and four months for each of three other offences, all to run concurrently. After his release from detention, he failed on four occasions to report as instructed to the youth offending team and he also failed to reside where directed by that team. He was charged with four offences of failing to comply with the terms of each of the four orders. The justices heard evidence of the offender's breaches and were shown the log which indicated that he had not attended as required by the conditions of his supervision. The justices found the case proved and the offender was recalled to serve 13 weeks' detention. The offender appealed by way of case stated. The questions to be resolved were:

(a) whether the information, which alleged four breaches, was bad for duplicity;

(b) whether the memorandum of conviction, which recorded four offences, was wrong; and

(c) whether direct evidence of proof of service of the notice of the requirements under the order was required.

The Divisional Court held as follows:

(a) the memorandum of conviction was wrong because it suggested a conviction for four different offences reflecting four detention and training orders, whereas in each case the conduct constituting the offence was the same;

(b) the information related to a single detention and training order, in that the four orders should be treated as a single term;

(c) the charges of failing to report and failing to live at the address approved by the supervising officer represented two separate offences and so they should not have been tried on the same information. However, that error had not caused any prejudice to the offender;

(d) although it is desirable that when an offender is given a notice of the requirements of the order, he should be asked to sign a copy so that there can be no dispute that he was given it, and that where it is alleged that there has been a failure to comply with a specific direction (such as to live at a specified address or attend on a specific occasion), the person who gave that direction should, if the breach is disputed, be at court to give evidence about it, proof by inference (as occurred in the present case) is sufficient.

18.1.3   Commission of further offences during the supervision period

Section 105 applies where a person is convicted of an imprisonable offence committed after release from detention but before the expiry of the term of a detention and training order (that is, during the period of supervision). The court which convicts him of the later offence may (as well as dealing with him for the later offence) order his detention for a period equal in the length to the period between the date of the commission of the later offence and the date when the original detention and training order would have expired.

18.1.4   Early release from a detention and training order

Section 102(4) provides for discretionary early release: in the case of an order for a term of eight months or more but less than 18 months, one month before the half-way point of the total term of the order; in the case of an order for a term of 18 months or more, one or two months before that half-way point. If the youth court (on an application by the Secretary of State) so orders, release can be postponed until one month after the half-way point (for detention and training orders of eight months or more but less than 18 months) or one or two months after the half-way point (for detention and training orders of 18 months or more): s 102(5).

Time spent in custody on remand prior to the imposition of a detention and training order is not automatically deducted, so s 101(8) requires the court, when determining the duration of a detention and training order, to take account of any period for which the offender was remanded in custody in connection with that or a closely related offence. In *R v Ganley* [2001] 2 Cr App R(S) 17, the Court of Appeal highlighted the fact that time spent in custody on remand is not automatically deducted from the period to be served under a detention and training order but has to be taken into account by the court when passing sentence.

18.2   DETENTION IN A YOUNG OFFENDER INSTITUTION

Section 96 of the Powers of Criminal Courts (Sentencing) Act 2000 provides that where an offender who has attained the age of 18 but is under 21 is convicted of an offence which is punishable with imprisonment in the case of an offender who has attained the age of 21, the court may impose a sentence of detention in a young offender institution.

The criteria for imposing a sentence of detention in a young offender institution (being a custodial sentence) are the same as for the imposition of a sentence of imprisonment on an adult offender. In summary, a sentence of detention in a young offender institution may be imposed if:

- the offence, or the combination of the offence and one or more offences associated with it, was so serious that only a custodial sentence can be justified for the offence; or

- the offence is a violent or sexual one and only a custodial sentence would be adequate to protect the public from serious harm from the offender; or

- the offender refuses to consent to the imposition of an additional requirement in a probation order where consent is necessary for that requirement.

It should be noted that s 61 of the Criminal Justice and Court Services Act 2000 abolishes the sentence of the detention in a young offender institution. However, this provision has not been brought into force. If and when this sentence is abolished, a court imposing a custodial sentence on a defendant aged 18 or over at the time of sentence will impose a sentence of imprisonment (as it would in the case of an offender who has attained the age of 21).

18.2.1 Procedural requirements

The same provisions regarding the procedure to be followed before imposing a sentence of imprisonment on someone who has attained the age of 21 apply to the imposition of detention in a young offender institution. In particular, the court must first obtain a pre-sentence report (and can only refrain from doing so if the offence in question is triable only on indictment) and must explain why it is imposing a custodial sentence (see ss 79–81 of the Powers of Criminal Courts (Sentencing) Act 2000). Furthermore, s 83 of the 2000 Act prevents the court from imposing a sentence of detention in a young offender institution on an offender who is not legally represented unless either the offender was granted a right to representation funded by the Criminal Defence Service but that right was withdrawn because of his conduct, or he has been informed of his right to apply for such representation but he has refused or failed to apply.

18.2.2 Relevant date for determining the age of the offender

Section 96 of the 2000 Act applies where 'a person aged at least 18 but under 21 is convicted of an offence'. In R v Danga [1992] QB 476, it was confirmed that the sentence to be imposed is determined according to the offender's age at the date of conviction, not at the date when sentence is passed. Thus, an offender who is 20 when convicted, but 21 at the date of sentence, is sentenced to detention in a young offender institution not to imprisonment. Thus, in R v Cassidy (2000) The Times, 13 October, the offender was aged 17 when convicted but was 18 at the date of sentence. The question at issue was whether the appropriate sentence was one of detention in a young offender institution (the custodial sentence for 18–20 year olds) or a detention and training order (the custodial sentence for offenders under the age of 18). The Court of Appeal held (following Danga) that the appellant fell to be sentenced as a 17 year old because the determining factor is the date of conviction.

In *R v Ghafoor* [2002] EWCA Crim 1857; [2003] 1 Cr App R(S) 84, the offender was 17 at the date of the offence but, by the time he pleaded guilty, he had reached the age of 18. The court confirmed that the relevant date for determining a defendant's age when the court is about to exercise its powers of sentence is the date of conviction, since the form of sentence is dictated by the defendant's age at that date. In the present case, since the offender had passed his 18th birthday before he pleaded guilty, the sentencing powers available to the court permitted the judge to pass a sentence of up to a maximum of 10 years' detention in a young offender institution. If he had pleaded guilty when he was still only 17, the maximum available custodial sentence would have been a term of 24 months' detention and training order. Dyson LJ said that the approach to be adopted where a defendant crosses a relevant age threshold between the date of the commission of the offence and the date of conviction is as follows. The starting point is the sentence that the defendant would have been likely to receive if he had been sentenced at the date of the commission of the offence. His Lordship emphasised that the 'starting point' is not the maximum sentence that could lawfully have been imposed, but the sentence that the offender would have been likely to receive. Thus, the sentence that would have been passed at the date of the commission of the offence is what his Lordship described as a 'powerful factor'. However, it is only the starting point, and other factors may have to be considered. Nonetheless, there have to be good reasons for departing from the starting point, since justice requires there to be good reason to pass a sentence higher than would have been passed at the date of the commission of the offence. His Lordship noted that departure from the starting point may well be appropriate if there has been a long interval between the date of commission of the offence and the date of conviction. By the date of conviction, circumstances may have changed significantly. For example, by the date of conviction, the tariff for the offence in question may have increased, and this is a factor that may be taken into account and could, in an appropriate case, properly lead to the passing of a sentence somewhat higher than the sentence that would have been passed at the date of the commission of the offence. His Lordship added, however, that it would rarely be necessary for a court even to consider passing a sentence that is more severe than the maximum that it would have had jurisdiction to pass at the date of commission of the offence. In a case where the date of conviction is only a few months after the date of the offence, it will rarely be appropriate to pass a longer sentence than that which would have been passed at the date of the offence.

In *Aldis v DPP* [2002] EWHC 403 (Admin); [2002] 2 Cr App R(S) 88, the defendant, who was aged 17 at the time of the offence, was charged with wounding with intent. The youth court decided that it would not be appropriate to commit him to the Crown Court for trial (to enable a sentence of detention under s 91 of the Powers of Criminal Courts (Sentencing) Act 2000 to be imposed in the event of conviction). The defendant pleaded not guilty. Before the trial started, the defendant had had his 18th birthday. The questions posed for the Divisional Court were '(a) Can the Court impose a detention and training order on a youth who has attained the age of 18 prior to conviction and sentence? (b) Does s 29 Children and Young Persons Act 1963 (which provides that where proceedings in respect of a young person in respect of a offence have begun, but he attains the age of 18 before the conclusion of those proceedings, the court can deal with the case and make any order which it could have made if he had not attained that age) apply in such situations?'. The Divisional Court decided that both questions would be answered in the affirmative. Section 100 of the 2000 Act plainly contemplates the possibility of a detention and training order being made in

respect of someone over 18, for the crucial date was the date of conviction. There is no basis, said the court, to suggest that s 29 of the 1963 Act was impliedly repealed. Parliament's intention must be that s 100 should be interpreted as subject to the provisions of s 29. The justices were entitled to sentence a defendant to a detention and training order even though the defendant had attained the age of 18 prior to the sentencing hearing provided the defendant was under 18 at the date when the court decided whether they were obliged to try him summarily.

18.2.3 Length of detention

The minimum period of detention in a young offender institution is 21 days (s 97(2) of the 2000 Act).

The maximum period of detention is the same as the maximum sentence of imprisonment in the case of an offender who has attained the age of 21. It follows that where a young offender aged between 18 and 21 is convicted of a single offence which is triable either way, the magistrates may impose up to six months' detention; where such an offender is convicted of two or more offences which are triable either way, the magistrates may impose up to 12 months' detention. The Crown Court may impose detention of any length up to the maximum sentence applicable to the offence in question (that is, the maximum prison sentence for an adult offender). It should be borne in mind that the Criminal Justice Act 2003 increases the powers of the magistrates when dealing with adult offenders (generally speaking, 51 weeks' custody for a single offence and 65 weeks for two or more offences).

Section 97(4) of the 2000 Act allows the court to impose consecutive sentences of detention in a young offender institution in the same way that consecutive sentences of imprisonment can be imposed on an offender who has attained the age of 21.

18.3   CUSTODY FOR LIFE/DURING HER MAJESTY'S PLEASURE

Section 93 of the Powers of Criminal Courts (Sentencing) Act 2000 provides that where an offender under 21 is convicted of murder, the Crown Court must sentence the offender to custody for life. An offender aged 10–17 who is convicted of murder is sentenced to be detained during Her Majesty's pleasure under s 90 of the 2000 Act.

Section 94 provides that where an offender aged 18–20 is convicted of an offence which carries discretionary life imprisonment in the case of an adult offender, the Crown Court may impose custody for life. Usually, custody for life is only appropriate in a case other than murder if the offender is dangerous and is suffering from mental instability (R v Powell (1989) 11 Cr App R(S) 113). The mental instability does not have to be sufficiently severe to amount to mental illness (R v Silson (1987) 9 Cr App R(S) 282).

When the repeal of this section by the Criminal Justice and Court Services Act 2000 comes into effect, offenders aged 18–20 who would have been sentenced to custody for life will be sentenced to life imprisonment instead.

18.4   DETENTION UNDER s 91 OF THE POWERS OF CRIMINAL COURTS (SENTENCING) ACT 2000

As we have seen, once an offender has attained the age of 18, the courts can impose the same length of custody (by way of detention in a young offender institution) that they could in the case of an adult (by way of imprisonment). However, in the case of an offender who is under 18 at the date of conviction, the usual custodial sentence (the detention and training order) is limited to a total of 24 months (of which only half is served in custody). Plainly, this would not be adequate punishment where an offender under the age of 18 committed a really serious offence. Section 91 of the Powers of Criminal Courts (Sentencing) Act 2000 provides for long-term detention in the following cases:

- an offence punishable (in the case of an adult offender) with 14 years' imprisonment or more; or
- an offence under s 3 of the Sexual Offences Act 2003 (sexual assault); or
- an offence under s 13 of the 2003 Act (child sex offences committed by children or young persons); or
- an offence under s 25 of the 2003 Act (sexual activity with a child family member); or
- an offence under s 26 of the 2003 Act (inciting a child family member to engage in sexual activity).

The original version of s 91 included the offences of causing death by dangerous driving, and causing death by careless driving while under the influence of drink or drugs. However, the Criminal Justice Act 2003 increased the maximum penalty for these offences to 14 years, and so they fall within s 91 by virtue of that fact.

Section 91 currently only applies to an offender who has been convicted in the Crown Court. Thus, a youth court cannot impose a sentence under this section. When the plea before venue procedure is extended to the youth court in cases where the juvenile is charged with an offence that falls within the ambit of s 91, the youth court will be empowered to commit the juvenile to the Crown Court for sentence if the juvenile indicates a guilty plea and the magistrates take the view that a sentence of detention under s 91 may well be appropriate given the seriousness of the offence (see s 24A of the Magistrates' Courts Act 1980, inserted by para 10 of Sched 3 to the Criminal Justice Act 2003).

18.4.1   Length of detention

The maximum sentence which can be imposed under s 91 is the same as the maximum sentence of imprisonment which can be imposed on an adult offender for that offence (s 91(3)). If the offence carries life imprisonment in the case of an adult, detention for life can be ordered under s 91.

Usually, a sentence under s 91 of the Powers of Criminal Courts (Sentencing) Act 2000 will be for more than two years (see also the 24 month detention and training order). However, unless the Secretary of State exercises his power under s 100(2) of the Act to extend the scope of detention and training orders to 11–12 year olds, there is no custodial sentence for offenders in that age group apart from detention for life for

murder (s 90) or detention under s 91. In the case of offenders in that age group, a relatively short sentence under s 91 may be appropriate in some cases. In *R v LH* [1997] 2 Cr App R(S) 319, for example, the Court of Appeal upheld a sentence of 12 months' detention under s 91 for indecent assault where the offender was too young for any other custodial sentence; see also *R v Nicholls and Warden* [1998] 1 Cr App R(S) 66, where the Court of Appeal reduced a sentence on such a youngster of two years' detention to 12 months' detention.

18.4.2   Procedure to be followed before imposing a sentence under s 91

A sentence of detention under s 91 cannot be imposed on an offender who is not legally represented unless either the offender has refused to apply for legal representation funded by the Criminal Defence Service or representation has been withdrawn because of misconduct on the part of the offender (s 83 of the 2000 Act).

18.4.3   Effect of time spent on remand

Where a young offender has spent time in custody (or in local authority secure accommodation) because bail was withheld before conviction and/or sentence, the time spent in custody or in secure accommodation counts towards the service of any custodial sentence (whether detention in a young offender institution or long-term detention under s 91 of the 2000 Act) subsequently imposed for the offence for which bail was withheld, and so that period will be deducted from the sentence which is imposed by the court in order to calculate how long the offender will actually have to serve in custody (s 67 of the Criminal Justice Act 1967, as amended by para 2 of Sched 11 to the Criminal Justice Act 1991).

18.4.4   Early release

The provisions relating to early release from sentences of imprisonment apply equally to sentences of detention in a young offender institution and to sentences of long-term detention under s 91 of the 2000 Act.

CHAPTER 19

YOUNG OFFENDERS: NON-CUSTODIAL SENTENCES

In this chapter we look at the various non-custodial sentences that are applicable to young offenders.

19.1 POWERS OF AN ADULT MAGISTRATES' COURT

There are some circumstances in which a juvenile may be tried and sentenced by an adult magistrates' court. However, the range of sentences available to the adult court is very limited. An adult magistrates' court may:

- order an absolute or conditional discharge;
- impose a fine (see below);
- order the parents of the juvenile to enter into a recognisance to take proper care of, and to exercise proper control over, a juvenile who has not attained the age of 16 (see below);
- make ancillary orders such as compensation and disqualification from driving.

19.2 POWERS OF THE YOUTH COURT AND CROWN COURT

As regards non-custodial sentences, the powers of the youth court and the Crown Court are identical.

19.3 FINES

A fine may be imposed on a juvenile (that is, someone under the age of 18) by a youth court, an adult magistrates' court and by the Crown Court.

19.3.1 Maximum fine

Under s 135 of the Powers of Criminal Courts (Sentencing) Act 2000, the maximum fine which may be imposed by a youth court or an adult magistrates' court on an offender who has not attained the age of 18 is £1,000. Where the offender has not attained the age of 14, s 36 limits the fine to a maximum of £250. There is, however, no limit on the fine which may be imposed by the Crown Court.

19.3.2 Payment of fine

Under s 137(1) of the Powers of Criminal Courts (Sentencing) Act 2000, where the offender is under 16, the court must order that the fine be paid by the parent or guardian of the offender unless either:

- the parent or guardian cannot be found; or
- it would be unreasonable to order the parent or guardian to pay the fine.

Under s 137(3) of the 2000 Act, where the offender has attained the age of 16, the court has a discretion (not a duty) to order the parent or guardian to pay the fine.

Where a parent or guardian is ordered to pay the fine, s 136 of the 2000 Act provides that it is the means of the parent or guardian (not those of the young offender) which are taken into account in fixing the amount of the fine. Accordingly, s 136 empowers the court to make a 'financial circumstances order' requiring the parent or guardian to provide a statement of means.

19.4   PARENTAL RECOGNISANCE

In the case of offenders under 16, there is a special form of bind over. Section 150(1) of the Powers of Criminal Courts (Sentencing) Act 2000 empowers the Crown Court, a youth court or a magistrates' court to order the parent or guardian of an offender who has not attained the age of 18 to enter into a recognisance to take proper care of the offender and to exercise proper control over him. The effect of such an order is that the parent or guardian promises to pay a sum specified by the court, which must not exceed £1,000, if they fail to comply with the terms of the order. Such an order can only be made if the court is satisfied that it is desirable to do so in the interests of preventing the offender from committing further offences. Where the offender has not attained the age of 16 (that is, is under school-leaving age), the court must state in open court why it has not exercised the power under s 150 if it decides not to bind the parents over.

A parent or guardian can only be ordered to enter into a recognisance with their consent. However, a parent or guardian who unreasonably refuses to consent may be fined up to £1,000 (that is, a fine on level 3) (s 150(2)).

In fixing the amount of the recognisance, the court must take account of the means of the parent or guardian, whether this has the effect of increasing or reducing the amount of the recognisance (subject always to the maximum of £1,000): s 150(7).

Under s 150(2), when a court imposes a community sentence on a young offender, the order may include a requirement that the offender's parent or guardian enter into a recognisance to ensure that the young offender complies with the terms of the order.

19.5   SUPERVISION ORDERS

Section 63 of the Powers of Criminal Courts (Sentencing) Act 2000 enables a youth court or the Crown Court (but not an adult magistrates' court) to make a supervision order against an offender who has attained the age of 10 but who is under 18.

The effect of a supervision order is to place the juvenile under the supervision of a social worker, a member of a youth offending team or a probation officer. The supervisor will usually be a social worker unless the probation service is already in contact with other members of the offender's family. The role of the supervisor, according to s 64(4) of the Act, is to 'advise, assist and befriend' the offender.

A supervision order is a community order and so has to be justified by the seriousness of the offence(s) being dealt with by the court (s 35(1) of the 2000 Act).

Before a supervision order can be made, the court must obtain a pre-sentence report if the supervision order is to contain any of the additional requirements set out below (s 36(3)(e) of the Act).

19.5.1 Duration of an order

A supervision order may last for up to three years (s 63(7) of the 2000 Act).

19.5.2 Additional requirements

The following additional requirements (set out in Sched 6 to the 2000 Act) may be added to a supervision order.

19.5.2.1 Residence

Paragraph 1 of Sched 6 allows the court to require the offender to reside with an individual named in the order. Before such a requirement may be imposed, the person named in the order must agree to the offender residing with him.

19.5.2.2 Complying with directions of supervisor

Paragraph 2(1) of Sched 6 enables the court to require a person who is subject to a supervision order to comply with any directions given by the supervisor to:

- live at a specified place for a specified period;
- present himself to a specified person at a specified place on a specified day;
- participate in activities specified by the supervisor.

Paragraph 2(5) stipulates that the maximum number of days in respect of which the supervisor may give directions is 180 (increased from 90 days by Sched 2 to the Anti-Social Behaviour Act 2003). These days need not be consecutive.

The directions are at the discretion of the supervisor, in that it is for the supervisor to decide whether to exercise any of the powers conferred by the order. These directions are intended to help the offender to develop his abilities and to become involved in worthwhile activities. The object is to show the offender that spare time can be used constructively. Directions may involve, for example, learning a new skill or going on an outward-bound adventure holiday.

19.5.2.3 Court-nominated activities

Under para 3(2)(a)–(c) of Sched 6, the court may itself specify requirements that the offender live at a particular place, or attend at a specified place, or take part in specified activities. In other words, the court removes the discretionary element from the directions under para 2(1) of Sched 6 by deciding itself what the offender is to do.

The maximum number of days in respect of which the court may impose such requirements is 180 (increased from 90 days by Sched 2 to the Anti-Social Behaviour Act 2003): para 3(3).

19.5.2.4 Reparation

Paragraph 3(2)(d) of Sched 6 enables the court to add a requirement to a supervision order that the offender make the reparation (otherwise than by payment of compensation) to the victim(s) of the offence or to the community at large.

19.5.2.5 Night restrictions

Paragraph 3(2)(e) of Sched 6 enables the court to make an order that the offender remain in a specified place (or one of a number of places) for specified periods between 6 pm and 6 am.

The supervised person may not be required to remain at a place for longer than 10 hours on any one night (para 4(2)).

Night restrictions cannot be imposed in respect of more than a total of 30 days (para 4(4)) and cannot continue in operation for more than three months from the date of the making of the supervision order (para 4(3)).

19.5.2.6 Negative requirements

Under para 3(2)(f) of Sched 6, the court may order the supervised person to refrain from participating in specified activities on specified days or for a specified period. The restrictions may apply for the entire duration of the supervision order:

* *Procedural requirements*

    Before making an order under any of the provisions of para 3(2), the court must be satisfied:

    (a) that compliance with the requirement(s) is feasible (para 3(4)(a));

    (b) that the requirements are necessary for securing the good conduct of the supervised person or for preventing him from committing further offences (para 3(4)(b));

    Where the offender is under 16, the court has to consider the likely effects of the requirements it wishes to impose upon the offender's family circumstances (para 3(4)(c)).

    Where compliance with the requirement requires the co-operation of a third party, the requirement can only be imposed with that person's consent (para 5(6)).

19.5.2.7 Requirement of residence in local authority accommodation

Under para 5 of Sched 6, the court may add a requirement that the supervised person live in local authority accommodation for a specified period. The maximum period which may be specified in a residence requirement is six months (para 5(6)).

The residence requirement may also stipulate that the supervised person must not live with a person named in the order (para 5(2)).

A residence requirement may only be added to a supervision order if each of the conditions laid down in para 5(2) are met. Those conditions are as follows:

- a supervision order has previously been made in respect of the offender;
- that the supervision order contained a requirement of residence, or compliance with supervisor's directions, or court-nominated directions or night restrictions, or negative requirements, or contained a local authority residence requirement;
- the offender has failed to comply with the requirement, or has been found guilty of an offence which was committed while the original supervision order was in force;
- the court is satisfied that the failure to comply with the requirement, or the behaviour which constituted the offence was due, to a significant extent, to the circumstances in which the offender was living.

A requirement may only be imposed under para 5 if the offender is legally represented or has refused to apply for representation funded by the Criminal Defence Service (para 5(9)).

The other requirements which may be added to a supervision order may be imposed in addition to a residence requirement (para 5(9)).

19.5.2.8 Treatment for a mental condition

Paragraph 7 of Sched 6 enables the court to insert a requirement that the offender receive treatment for a mental condition. The court must have evidence from a duly qualified medical practitioner that the mental condition of the offender is such as requires, and may be susceptible to, treatment but is not sufficiently serious to require a hospital order under the Mental Health Act 1983. Such a requirement may specify treatment by a qualified medical practitioner, treatment (as a resident or non-resident patient) at a place specified in the order or treatment in a mental hospital. The consent of the offender is required if he has attained the age of 14. A condition requiring mental treatment lapses when the offender attains the age of 18 (para 6(3)).

19.5.2.9 Educational requirements

Paragraph 7 of Sched 6 enables the court to add a requirement to a supervision order that the offender, so long as he is of compulsory school age (that is, under 16), must comply with arrangements made by his parents and approved by the local education authority for his education.

Under para 7(5), such a requirement may only be imposed if it is necessary to secure the good conduct of the offender or to prevent the commission of further offences by him.

19.5.2.10 Residence with foster parents

Schedule 2 of the Anti-Social Behaviour Act 2003 adds a para 5A to Sched 6 to the 2000 Act; this enables the court to include in a supervision order a requirement that the offender live with local authority foster parents for a specified period of up to 12 months (although this period may be extended up to a total of 18 months). This requirement is available only where the court is satisfied that the case would otherwise meet the criteria for a custodial sentence, that the youngster's offending was due, to a great extent, to the circumstances in which he was living, and that the imposition of a foster parent residence requirement will assist in his rehabilitation. Such a requirement must not be imposed on an offender who is not legally represented unless either he

was represented through the Criminal Defence Service but the representation was withdrawn because of his conduct, or else he has declined to apply for such representation.

19.5.2.11 Drug treatment and testing requirements

Section 279 of the Criminal Justice Act 2003 gives effect to Sched 24 to the Act, which deals with drug treatment and testing requirements in supervision orders (and action plan orders). The Schedule amends Sched 6 to the Powers of Criminal Courts (Sentencing) Act 2000 (adding a para 6A) to allow drug treatment (including testing) to be imposed as a requirement in a supervision order.

These powers may be exercised where the court is satisfied that:

(a) the offender is dependent on, or has a propensity to misuse, drugs; and

(b) his dependency or propensity is such as requires and may be susceptible to treatment.

The object of the treatment (which may be in-patient or out-patient treatment) is to reduce or eliminate the offender's dependency on, or propensity to misuse, drugs. The testing element may only be included if the offender has attained the age of 14 and consents to the inclusion of that requirement.

The intention of the government, faced with the problem of drug-related offending by young people, is to enable their drug misuse and their offending behaviour to be addressed at the same time.

19.5.3   Breach of a supervision order

Schedule 7 to the Powers of Criminal Courts (Sentencing) Act 2000 deals with the enforcement of supervision orders. A person who fails to comply with a supervision order and who is under the age of 18 will be summoned to appear before the youth court; if the offender has attained the age of 18, he will be summoned to attend before the adult magistrates' court. Paragraph 2 of Sched 7 enables the supervisor to take action in respect of a breach of a supervision order. Where it is proved to the satisfaction of the court that the offender has failed to comply with any of the requirements of the supervision order, the court may impose a fine of up to £1,000, or may make a curfew order or an attendance centre order (para 2(2)(a) of Sched 7). The fine or curfew order or attendance centre order may be imposed in addition to, or instead of, the discharge of the order.

Under para 2(2)(b), where the supervision order was made by a magistrates' court, the court dealing with the breach can revoke the order and re-sentence the offender for the original offence. The court can impose any sentence which it could have imposed if it had had jurisdiction to try the offender for that original offence.

If the supervision order was made by the Crown Court, the magistrates dealing with the breach may simply commit the offender (in custody or on bail) to the Crown Court (para 2(2)(c)). The Crown Court may revoke the supervision order and re-sentence the offender for the original offence (para 2(4)).

When an offender is re-sentenced following breach of a supervision order, the court must take into account the extent to which the offender has complied with the requirements of the order (and make any necessary reduction) (para 4(7)).

19.5.4   Revocation or amendment of an order

We have already seen that a supervision order can be discharged under para 2 of Sched 7 if the offender fails to comply with any of its requirements.

Paragraph 5 of Sched 7 enables the supervisor or the supervised person to make an application for the order to be discharged or varied. The application is made to the youth court if the offender is under 18 and to the adult magistrates' court if he has attained the age of 18.

If the court decides to vary the order, it may do so by cancelling any of the additional requirements imposed in the original order or by adding new requirements; any of the requirements (except night restrictions) which could have been imposed originally may be added when the order is varied.

19.6   ATTENDANCE CENTRE ORDERS

An attendance centre is 'a place at which offenders aged under 21 may be required to attend and be given, under supervision, appropriate occupation or instruction' (s 62(2) of the Powers of Criminal Courts (Sentencing) Act 2000).

Attendance centres are generally run by off-duty police officers or teachers on Saturday mornings or afternoons. Premises such as schools, youth clubs and church/community halls are often used.

The power to make an attendance centre order is conferred by s 60 of the 2000 Act:

- where the court is dealing with an offender who is under 21 for an imprisonable offence, it may make an attendance centre order;

- an attendance centre order may be made as an alternative to the imposition of a custodial term for non-payment of a fine; and

- an attendance centre order may be used as a method of punishing a failure to comply with the requirements of a supervision order or a probation order.

An attendance centre order may only be made if an appropriate centre is reasonably accessible to the offender (s 60(6)).

19.6.1   Number of hours

The aggregate number of hours must be specified in the order:

- *Minimum*

  The total number of hours must not be less than 12, unless the offender is under 14 and the court takes the view that 12 hours would be excessive (s 60(3)).

- *Maximum*

  Section 60(4) provides that the aggregate number of hours should not exceed 12 unless the court takes the view that, in all the circumstances, 12 hours would be inadequate. In that case, the total number of hours must not exceed 24 in the case of an offender who is under 16 and must not exceed 36 hours if the offender is aged between 16 and 20.

This maximum aggregate number of hours applies only to attendance centre orders made on the same occasion. If an attendance centre order is made against someone who has not yet completed the number of hours under an earlier attendance centre order, the earlier order is disregarded in fixing the number of hours under the later order (s 60(6)).

Under s 60(10), an offender may not be required to attend a centre on more than one occasion on any day and cannot be ordered to attend for more than three hours on any one occasion.

19.6.2   Use of an attendance centre order

The object of an attendance centre order is partly punitive, in that the offender is deprived of free time on a Saturday morning or afternoon, and partly preventative (Home Office Circular 69/1990 points out that such an order can be effective in keeping football hooligans away from matches).

There is also a substantial element of rehabilitation. The Home Office Circular says that such an order should benefit the offender by 'bringing him under the influence of representatives of the authority of the State' and by 'teaching him something of the constructive use of leisure'. Thus, there should be firm discipline at an attendance centre, but the emphasis will be on physical exercise (for example, sports) and skills (for example, car maintenance).

19.6.3   Breach of an attendance centre order

Paragraph 1 of Sched 5 to the Powers of Criminal Courts (Sentencing) Act 2000 empowers a magistrates' court to issue a summons where an information has been laid by the person in charge of the attendance centre alleging that the offender has failed to attend the attendance centre or has broken the rules of the centre.

Where the original order was made by a magistrates' court, the magistrates' court dealing with the breach may either impose a fine of up to £1,000 (para 2(1)(a)) or revoke the order and re-sentence the offender for the original offence. Any sentence which could have been imposed by the original court may be imposed by the court dealing with the breach (para 2(1)(b)).

If the original order was made by the Crown Court, the magistrates' court may impose a fine of up to £1,000 for the breach but it cannot re-sentence the offender for the original offence. It can, however, commit the offender (in custody or on bail) to the Crown Court to be dealt with for the breach. The Crown Court can re-sentence the offender for the original offence (para 3(1)).

Where the offender is re-sentenced for the original offence, account must be taken of the extent to which he has complied with the original order (paras 2(5)(a) and 3(3)(a)).

It should also be noted that if the offender has 'wilfully and persistently failed to comply' with an attendance centre order, the court may impose a custodial sentence notwithstanding anything in s 79(2) of the 2000 Act (paras 2(5)(b) and 3(3)(b)).

19.6.4 Discharge or variation of an attendance centre order

As well as the power to deal with a breach of an attendance centre order under paras 2 and 3 of Sched 5, the court may discharge or vary an order, on the application of the person in charge of the attendance centre or of the offender, under para 4 of Sched 5. If the order is revoked, the court has the power to re-sentence for the original offence under para 4(3) of Sched 5.

19.7 CURFEW ORDERS

These orders are also available in the case of adult offenders. Schedule 2 to the Anti-Social Behaviour Act 2003 amends s 37 of the Powers of Criminal Courts (Sentencing) Act 2000 by repealing s 37(4); this has the effect of increasing the maximum length of a curfew order for an offender who has attained the age of 10 but is under 16 from three months to six months. The Schedule also adds a new section, s 64A, to the 2000 Act; this makes it clear that a curfew order and a supervision order may be imposed at the same time.

19.8 ACTION PLAN ORDERS

Section 69 of the Powers of Criminal Courts (Sentencing) Act 2000 provides for 'action plan orders'. Under s 69(1), where a person aged under 18 is convicted of an offence, the court may, if it considers it desirable in the interests of securing his rehabilitation or preventing him from re-offending (s 69(3)), make an action plan order.

This is an order which (under s 69(2)):

(a) requires the offender, for a period of three months from the date of the order, to comply with a series of requirements with respect to his actions and whereabouts during that period (the 'action plan');

(b) places the offender, for that three month period, under the supervision of a probation officer, a social worker or a member of a youth offending team; and

(c) requires the offender to comply with any directions given by his supervisor with a view to the implementation of the action plan.

An action plan order cannot be made if the offender is already the subject of such an order (s 69(5)(a)). Furthermore, an action plan order cannot be combined with a custodial sentence or a community rehabilitation order, a community punishment order, a community punishment and rehabilitation order, an attendance centre order, a supervision order or a referral order (s 69(5)(b)).

Under s 70 of the 2000 Act, the requirements under the action plan order itself and the directions given by the supervisor, can require the offender to:

• participate in specified activities;

• attend at a particular place at a particular time;

• attend an attendance centre;

• keep away from a particular place or places;

• comply with arrangements for his education; and

- make reparation (otherwise than by payment of compensation) to the victim of the offence (or to someone affected by it), provided that this person consents, or to the community at large.

The requirements specified in the order should avoid any conflict with the offender's religious beliefs, with the requirements of any community order to which he is subject as a result of a previous conviction, and with the times (if any) when he attends school or any other educational establishment (s 70(4)).

Section 279 of the Criminal Justice Act 2003 gives effect to Sched 24 of that Act. It amends s 70 of the Powers of Criminal Courts (Sentencing) Act 2000 (adding sub-ss (4A)–(4H)) to enable drug treatment (including testing) to be a requirement that may be included in an action plan order where the court is satisfied that the offender is dependent on, or has a propensity to misuse, drugs, and that his dependency or propensity is such as requires and may be susceptible to treatment. The testing element may only be included if the offender has attained the age of 14 and consents to the inclusion of that requirement.

An action plan order is a community sentence and so can only be made if justified by the seriousness of the offence (s 35(1) of the 2000 Act). Before an action plan order is made, the court must have a written report from the proposed supervisor setting out the requirements he thinks ought to be included in the order, the benefits to the offender that these requirements are designed to achieve, the attitude of the parent or guardian of the offender to those proposed requirements, and (where the offender is under the age of 16) information about the likely effect of the order on the offender's family circumstances (s 69(6)).

Before making the order, the court has to explain its effect, and the consequences which may follow from failure to comply with it, to the offender (s 69(11)).

19.9   REPARATION ORDERS

Section 73 of the Powers of Criminal Courts (Sentencing) Act 2000 provides for 'reparation orders'. These orders can only be made where a person aged under 18 has been convicted of an offence.

The order requires the offender to make the form of reparation specified in the order (but not payment of compensation) either to the victim of the offence or someone otherwise affected by it (in either case, the person must be named in the order) or to the community at large (s 73(1)).

A reparation order cannot require the offender to work for more than a total of 24 hours or to make reparation to any person without the consent of that person (s 74(1)(a)). The form of reparation ordered must be commensurate with the seriousness of the offence(s) for which the offender is being dealt with (s 74(2)). The reparation has to be made under the supervision of a probation officer, a social worker or a member of a youth offending team specified in the order and has to be made within three months of the making of the order (s 74(8)).

The requirements specified in the order should avoid any conflict with the offender's religious beliefs, with the requirements of any community order to which he is subject as a result of a previous conviction, and with the times (if any) when he attends school or any other educational establishment (s 74(3)).

Before making a reparation order, the court must obtain and consider a report written by a probation officer, a social worker, or a member of a youth offending team, indicating the type of work that is suitable for the offender and the attitude of the victim(s) to the requirements proposed to be included in the order (s 73(5)). Also, before making a reparation order, the court must explain to the offender the effect of the order and the consequences of failing to comply with it (s 73(7)).

Section 73(8)) requires the court to give reasons if it does not make a reparation order in any case where it has power to make such an order.

A reparation order cannot be made at the same time as a custodial sentence, or a community punishment order, a community punishment and rehabilitation order, a supervision order which includes requirements authorised by Sched 6 to the Act, an action plan order or a referral order (s 73(4)).

19.9.1 Breach of an action plan order and a reparation order

Schedule 8 to the Powers of Criminal Courts (Sentencing) Act 2000 deals with the enforcement of action plan orders and reparation orders.

If the magistrates' court, on the application of the supervisor, finds that the offender has failed to comply with the requirements of the order, it may impose a fine of up to £1,000, or make a curfew order, or make an attendance centre order (para 2(2)(a) of Sched 8).

Where the original order was made by a magistrates' court, the magistrates may revoke the order and re-sentence the offender (para 2(2)(b)). If the order was made by a Crown Court, the magistrates may commit the offender (in custody or on bail) to be dealt with by the Crown Court, which may re-sentence the offender for the original offence (para 2(2)(c); para 2(4)).

Where the offender is re-sentenced, account must be taken of the extent to which he complied with the requirements of the order (para 2(7)).

Paragraph 5 of Sched 8 contains a general power to revoke or amend the order on the application of the supervisor or of the offender.

19.10 REFERRAL ORDERS FOR YOUNG OFFENDERS: YOUTH OFFENDER PANELS

These orders are contained in ss 16–28 of the Powers of Criminal Courts (Sentencing) Act 2000.

A referral order may be either compulsory or discretionary. The provisions apply where a youth court or adult magistrates' court is dealing with an offender aged under 18 and the court is not minded to impose a custodial sentence, or to make a hospital order under the Mental Health Act 1983, or to grant an absolute discharge (s 16(1)).

The court *must* make a referral order if the offender pleads guilty to an imprisonable offence and to any connected offence (whether or not imprisonable) and has not previously been convicted of any offence (s 17(1)). The court *may* make a referral order if the offender is being dealt with for at least two connected offences, he pleads guilty to at least one of them but also pleaded not guilty to at least one of them,

and has not previously been convicted of any offence (s 17(2)). The Referral Orders (Amendment of Conditions) Regulations 2003 increase the court's discretionary power to make a referral order, in that the court is given the power to make a referral order in respect of an offence which is not imprisonable when the conditions for a compulsory referral order would otherwise have been met.

A referral order requires the offender to attend meetings of a youth offender panel. The court may also specify the period for which any youth offender contract is to have effect; that period must be between three and 12 months. Where the court is dealing with the offender for more than one offence, separate periods may be specified; those periods may be concurrent or consecutive (but, if they are consecutive, the total period may not exceed 12 months): s 18(6).

Where the court makes a referral order in respect of an offence, the court is prohibited from imposing a community sentence, or a fine, or a reparation order, or granting a conditional discharge (s 19(4)). Where the court is dealing with the offender for two or more connected offences, and makes a referral order in respect of one of them, the court must either make a referral order or grant an absolute discharge in respect of the other offence(s): s 19(3)(a).

Unless the child is in the care of the local authority, a parent or guardian is required to attend meetings of the youth offender panel established for their child, unless (and to the extent that) it would be unreasonable so to require (s 20). Membership of the youth offender panel for an offender is governed by s 21 and will include a member of the youth offending team and two other appropriately qualified people. If the offender fails to attend a panel meeting, the matter may be referred back to the court (s 22(2)).

At the first meeting of the youth offender panel established for the offender, the panel seeks to reach agreement with the offender on 'a programme of behaviour the aim (or principal aim) of which is the prevention of re-offending by the offender' (s 23(1)).

Under s 23(2), the programme may include provision for:

(a)   the offender to make financial or other reparation to any person who appears to the panel to be a victim of, or otherwise affected by, the offence, or any of the offences, for which the offender was referred to the panel;

(b)   the offender to attend mediation sessions with any such victim or other person;

(c)   the offender to carry out unpaid work or service in or for the community;

(d)   the offender to be at home at times specified in or determined under the programme;

(e)   attendance by the offender at a school or other educational establishment or at a place of work;

(f)   the offender to participate in specified activities (such as those designed to address offending behaviour, those offering education or training or those assisting with the rehabilitation of persons dependent on, or having a propensity to misuse, alcohol or drugs);

(g)   the offender to present himself to specified persons at times and places specified in or determined under the programme;

(h)   the offender to stay away from specified places or persons (or both);

(i)   enabling the offender's compliance with the programme to be supervised and recorded.

The programme cannot provide for electronic monitoring of the offender's whereabouts, or for any physical restriction to be placed on his movements (s 23(3)). Where anyone else will be affected by a requirement in the programme, that person's consent must first be obtained (s 23(4)).

The programme is reduced into writing and is signed by the offender and a member of the panel.

If the first meeting with the panel does not produce a contract with the offender, there may be a further meeting (s 25(1)). If it appears that there is no prospect of an agreement being reached within a reasonable period, the matter is referred back to the court (s 25(2)).

Section 26 provides for progress meetings to review the offender's progress in implementing the programme. Progress meetings are also convened if the offender wishes the terms of the contract to be varied or if he wishes the order to be revoked because of a significant change in his circumstances (such that compliance with the contract is no longer practicable). A progress meeting is also appropriate if it appears to the panel that the offender is in breach of any of the terms of the contract.

Section 27 deals with the final meeting held when the compliance period of the contract is due to expire. At the final meeting, the panel reviews the offender's compliance with the contract and decides whether he has satisfactorily completed the contract (s 27(2)). If the panel decides that the offender has complied with the contract, this has the effect of discharging the referral order (s 27(3)). Otherwise, the panel refers the offender back to the court (s 27(4)).

Schedule 1 to the 2000 Act makes detailed provision for what happens where a youth offender panel refers the offender back to the court or where the offender is convicted of further offences during the currency of the order.

Under para 5 of Sched 1, if the court is satisfied that the offender has failed to comply with the requirements of the referral order, the court may revoke the referral order and sentence the offender for the original offence as if the case were one where a referral order was not appropriate.

Under para 12 of Sched 1, where the offender re-offends during the period of a referral order, the court may extend his compliance period, but only if there is evidence of exceptional circumstances indicating that an extension of the compliance period is likely to help prevent further re-offending by him. Otherwise, unless the court grants an absolute discharge for the subsequent offence, the court revokes the referral order and sentences the offender for the original offence as if the case were one where a referral order was not appropriate.

In the 1997 Consultation Paper issued by the Home Office, *No More Excuses – A New Approach to Tackling Youth Crime in England and Wales* (Cmnd 3809), the government emphasises the underlying foundation of restorative justice on which the referral order is based (requiring as it does that the offender should make some sort of reparation, either to the victim – for example, through a letter of apology or a direct meeting with the victim; by putting right the damage caused by the offence; or through financial compensation – or, where the victim does not want direct reparation, making amends to the community as a whole). The Consultation Paper also emphasises the need for continued engagement with the offender:

Although the formal referral would be for a fixed period of time, the youth panel would be encouraged to identify ways of supporting the young person at the end of the referral through community based schemes such as mentoring, to help prevent further offending (para 9.31).

19.11 CRIME PREVENTION PROVISIONS

The Crime and Disorder Act 1998 introduced a number of crime prevention measures to reduce the amount of crime committed by young people.

19.11.1 Parenting orders

Section 8 of the Crime and Disorder Act 1998 creates 'parenting orders'. Such an order can be made in respect of the parent or guardian of a child or young person if:

(a) a child safety order (see below) has been made in respect of the child;

(b) an anti-social behaviour order has been made in respect of the child or young person;

(c) the child or young person has been convicted of an offence; or

(d) there has been a conviction for an offence involving truancy.

A parenting order can only be made if the court considers that a parenting order would be desirable in the interests of preventing:

(a) the repetition of the behaviour which led to the making of the child safety order or the anti-social behaviour order; or

(b) the child or young person from re-offending; or

(c) the child or young person from truanting.

The order requires the parent to comply, for a period of up to 12 months, with such requirements as are specified in the order, and (during that period) to attend, for a period of up to three months (but not more than once in any week), counselling or guidance sessions specified by the probation officer, the social worker or the member of the youth offending team specified in the order. Section 18 of the Anti-Social Behaviour Act 2003 amends s 8 of the 1998 Act to allow a programme of guidance and counselling sessions to consist of, or to include, a residential course, provided that the court is satisfied that this is likely to be more effective than a non-residential course and that any interference with family life is proportionate.

The requirements which may be imposed are anything that the court considers desirable in the interests of preventing repetition of the anti-social behaviour, preventing further truanting or preventing the youngster from re-offending.

Section 9 of the 1998 Act provides that where a person under the age of 16 is convicted of an offence, and the court is satisfied that any of the pre-conditions for the making of a parenting order are satisfied, a parenting order must be made.

Before making a parenting order, the court must explain to the parent the effect of the order and the consequences of non-compliance with it.

An application to vary or discharge the parenting order can be made by the probation officer or social worker specified in the order or by the parent. Where an

application for discharge of the order is dismissed, a further application for its discharge can only be made with the consent of the court which made the order.

Failure by the parent without reasonable excuse to comply with the requirements of the order is a summary offence punishable with a fine up to level 3 (£1,000).

Section 10 provides that where a parenting order was made because a child safety order had been made, appeal lies to the High Court. Where the order was made because an anti-social behaviour order had been made, appeal lies to the Crown Court. Where the order is made following the commission of an offence (or as a result of truanting offences), the order can be the subject of an appeal as if that order were a sentence passed by the court (and so the appeal takes the form of an ordinary appeal against sentence).

Section 25 of the Anti-Social Behaviour Act 2003 makes provision for 'parenting contracts' to be entered into when a child or young person has been referred to a youth offending team and a member of that team has reason to believe that he has engaged, or is likely to engage, in criminal conduct or anti-social behaviour. The 'contract' is defined in sub-s (3) as a document containing a statement by the parent that he or she will comply with the requirements specified in the contract and a statement on behalf of the youth offending team that it agrees to provide support to the parent to help with compliance with the requirements of the contract. Under sub-s (4), the contract may include a requirement that the parent attend a counselling or guidance programme. The purpose of such a parenting contract is set out in sub-s (5): to prevent the child or young person from engaging in criminal conduct or anti-social behaviour. There is no direct sanction if the parent breaches the terms of the agreement, but it would be open to the youth offending team to seek a parenting order under s 26.

Sections 26–29 of the Anti-Social Behaviour Act 2003 extend the circumstances in which parenting orders in respect of criminal conduct or anti-social behaviour can be made. Section 26(1) and (2) provides that where a child or young person has been referred to a youth offending team, a member of the team may apply to the magistrates' court for a parenting order in respect of the youngster. Under sub-s (3), the court can make a parenting order if it is satisfied that the youngster has engaged in criminal conduct or anti-social behaviour and the making of the order would be desirable in the interests of preventing this from continuing. Under s 26(4), the order requires the parent, for a period of up to 12 months, to comply with the requirements specified in the order, and to attend a counselling or guidance programme specified by the person who is acting as the 'responsible officer' under the order. This may consist of, or include, a residential course, provided that the court is satisfied that this is likely to be more effective than a non-residential course and that any interference with family life is proportionate (sub-s (6)).

Under s 27(1), in deciding whether to make a parenting order, the court must consider any refusal by the parent to enter into a parenting contract under s 25 or any failure to comply with the requirements of such a contract. Under s 27(3), parents convicted of failing to comply with requirements in, or directions given under, a parenting order are liable to a fine.

Under s 29, 'anti-social behaviour' is defined as meaning behaviour by a person which causes, or is likely to cause, harassment, alarm or distress to one or more other persons not of the same household as himself; 'criminal conduct', in this context, includes behaviour by children below the age of criminal responsibility (that is, age 10) that would be criminal were they above that age.

Section 324 of the Criminal Justice Act 2003 gives effect to Sched 34 to the Act (in force since February 2004). This amends the parenting order provisions in the Crime and Disorder Act 1998 and the referral order provisions in the Powers of Criminal Courts (Sentencing) Act 2000 to enable courts to make a parenting order when a referral order is being made. Section 9(2A) of the Crime and Disorder Act 1998, as amended by the 2003 Act, provides that where a court proposes to make both a referral order and a parenting order, the court must, before making the parenting order, obtain and consider a report by a probation officer, a local authority social worker or a member of a youth offending team. The report should indicate what requirements should be included in the parenting order and why those requirements would be desirable in the interests of preventing the commission of any further offences by the child/young person.

A new sub-section, s 22(2A), is inserted into the Powers of Criminal Courts (Sentencing) Act 2000. This provides that a court making a referral order may require a parent or guardian to attend the meetings of the youth offender panel under s 20 of the 2000 Act. Where the parent or guardian fails to comply with such an order, the panel may to refer the case back to the youth court. Part 1A of Sched 1 to the Powers of Criminal Courts (Sentencing) Act 2000 sets out the arrangements when a youth offender panel refers a parent or guardian to the youth court under s 22(2A). The panel must make a report to the court explaining why the parent is being referred to it and the court can require the parent to appear before it (by issuing a summons or an arrest warrant). When the parent then appears before the youth court, the court may make a parenting order if the court is satisfied that the parent has failed without reasonable excuse to comply with an order made by the court under s 20 to attend the youth referral panel, and that it is desirable in the interests of preventing the commission of further offences by the offender. The parenting order requires the parent, for 12 months, to comply with the requirements specified in the order (which are aimed at preventing the youngster from re-offending) and to attend (during a period of up to three months) a counselling or guidance programme (which can include attendance at a residential course (provided the court is satisfied that this is likely to be more effective than a non-residential course and that any interference with family life is proportionate). There is a right of appeal to the Crown Court against the making of the parenting order.

19.11.2 Child safety orders

Section 11 of the Crime and Disorder Act 1998 creates 'child safety orders'. A magistrates' court, on the application of a local authority, is empowered to make a child safety order if the court is satisfied that one of more of the following conditions has been fulfilled with respect to a child under the age of 10:

(a) the child has committed an act which, if committed by someone over 10, would have constituted a criminal offence;

(b) a child safety order is necessary for the purpose of preventing the child from doing so again;

(c) the child has contravened a ban imposed by a curfew notice; or

(d) the child has acted in a manner that caused, or was likely to cause, harassment, alarm or distress to one or more persons not in the same household as himself.

The effect of the order is:

(a) to place the child under the supervision of a social worker or a member of a youth offending team for up to three months (or 12 months if the court regards the circumstances of the case as exceptional); and

(b) to require the child to comply with requirements specified in the order. The court may impose any requirements which it considers desirable in the interests of:

   (i) securing that the child receives appropriate care, protection and support and is subject to proper control; or

   (ii) preventing any repetition of the kind of behaviour which led to the child safety order being made.

This order is made in the context of family proceedings (not the criminal jurisdiction of the magistrates); the standard of proof is therefore that applicable to civil proceedings (that is, the balance of probabilities): s 11(6).

Before making a child safety order, the court must explain to the parent the effect of the order and the consequences of non-compliance with it.

An application to vary or discharge the order can be made by the social worker or the member of the youth offending team specified in the order or by the parent/guardian. Where an application for discharge of the order is dismissed, a further application for its discharge can only be made with the consent of the court which made the order.

Where the child fails to comply with any requirement included in the order, the magistrates may, on the application of the social worker or the member of the youth offending team specified in the order, replace the order with a care order (under s 31(1)(a) of the Children Act 1989) or vary the child safety order.

Under s 13 of the 1998 Act, appeal against the making of a child safety order lies to the High Court.

19.11.3 Local child curfew schemes

Section 14 of the Crime and Disorder Act 1998 empowers a local authority to ban children of specified ages under 10 from being in a public place within a specified area, during specified hours (between 9 pm and 6 am), otherwise than under the effective control of a parent or responsible person aged 18 or over. The order can last for a maximum of 90 days and only comes into operation if confirmed by the Secretary of State. The scheme is publicised by means of curfew notices.

Where the police have reasonable cause to believe that a child is in contravention of a ban imposed by a curfew notice, they must inform the local authority and may remove the child to the child's place of residence (unless there is reasonable cause to believe that the child would suffer significant harm there).

19.12   THE CRIMINAL JUSTICE ACT 2003

The Criminal Justice Act 2003 has comparatively little effect on sentencing young offenders. However, it should be noted that s 147(1) of the Act defines 'community sentence' as including 'a sentence which consists of or includes ... (b) one or more youth community orders'.

Section 147(2) defines 'youth community order' as:

(a)   a curfew order as defined by section 163 of the [2000] Sentencing Act,

(b)   an exclusion order under section 40A(1) of that Act,

(c)   an attendance centre order as defined by section 163 of that Act,

(d)   a supervision order under section 63(1) of that Act, or

(e)   an action plan order under section 69(1) of that Act.

Section 148(3) of the Criminal Justice Act 2003 provides that:

Where a court passes a community sentence which consists of or includes one or more youth community orders—

(a)   the particular order or orders forming part of the sentence must be such as, in the opinion of the court, is, or taken together are, the most suitable for the offender, and

(b)   the restrictions on liberty imposed by the order or orders must be such as in the opinion of the court are commensurate with the seriousness of the offence, or the combination of the offence and one or more offences associated with it.

It is likely that the sentencing of young offenders will eventually be reformed to bring it into line with the approach taken (under the Criminal Justice Act 2003), creating a single community order for young offenders and giving the court a variety of options as regards the impositions contained in that order: see the government's 2004 Consultation Paper *Youth Justice — The Next Steps*.

CHAPTER 20

ANCILLARY ORDERS

In this chapter, we consider the powers of the court to order an offender to pay compensation to the victim, to order forfeiture of articles used to commit crime and to confiscate the proceeds of crime. We also consider the special orders which can be made in respect of offenders who are mentally disordered and examine the power of the court to recommend that a person be deported. Finally, we look at various orders involving exclusion and disqualification.

20.1 COMPENSATION ORDERS

Section 130 of the Powers of Criminal Courts (Sentencing) Act 2000 empowers a court which has convicted someone of an offence to require that person to pay:

(a) compensation for any personal injury, loss or damage resulting from that offence or any other offence which is taken into consideration by the court in determining sentence; or

(b) to make payments for funeral expenses or bereavement in respect of a death resulting from any such offence, other than a death due to an accident arising out of the presence of a motor vehicle on a road.

The 'personal injury' does not have to be physical injury. It can include distress and anxiety (*Bond v Chief Constable of Kent* [1983] 1 WLR 40). The Magistrates' Association Sentencing Guidelines point out that 'compensation for personal injury may include compensation for terror, shock or distress caused by the offence'.

In *R v Donovan* (1981) 3 Cr App R(S) 192, Eveleigh LJ said that:

> ... a compensation order is designed for the simple, straightforward case where the amount of the compensation can be readily and easily ascertained.

Similarly, in *R v Watson* [1991] Crim LR 307, it was held that a compensation order should only be made if there is evidence of the amount of the victim's loss or else the prosecution and the defence agree on the amount of the order. The same approach was followed in *R v White* [1996] 2 Cr App R(S) 58, where the Court of Appeal said that where a case raises difficult or complex issues as to liability, a compensation order is not appropriate. However, in *R v James* [2003] EWCA Crim 811; [2003] 2 Cr App R (S) 97, it was said that where a court is of the opinion that a complete reconciliation between the parties as to the proper amount of a compensation order would present a complex and difficult task, but that the calculation of the minimum loss arising is a comparatively simple task, and it would be in the interest of justice to make a compensation order in a sum representing the minimum loss arising, it should make such an order rather than decline on the ground of complexity.

In *Holt v DPP* [1996] 2 Cr App R(S) 314, two youths stole £1,900 from an elderly lady. She died before sentence was passed on the youths. The Divisional Court held that the case was a simple and straightforward one, and so a compensation order was appropriate. The amount of the loss (£1,900) was not in issue, nor was the defendants' responsibility for that loss. The youths had the means to pay and there were no factors

which made it more appropriate to leave the matter of compensation to the civil courts. Furthermore, there was no reason why a compensation order could not be made in favour of the victim's estate if the victim had died by the time the compensation order was made.

Section 130(3) requires the court to give reasons if it does not make a compensation order where it has power to make one (which effectively creates a presumption that a compensation order ought to be made where the loss is readily quantifiable and the offender has the means to pay). A compensation order should be considered whether or not there is an application for compensation by or on behalf of the victim, although in practice the prosecution will normally indicate that there is a claim for compensation.

20.1.1 Causation

In *R v Horsham Justices ex p Richards* [1985] 1 WLR 986, it was held that the prosecution must show that the loss or damage suffered by the victim occurred as a result of the offence of which the offender has been convicted. However, in *R v Corbett* (1993) 14 Cr App R(S) 101, it was held that for a compensation order to be made, whilst there must be some causal link or connection between the offence and the injury sustained by the victim, the offence need not be the *sole* cause of the injury. The question is simply whether the injury could fairly be said to have resulted from the offence.

For example, in *R v Derby* (1990) 12 Cr App R(S) 502, the defendant pleaded guilty to a charge of affray. It was accepted by the prosecution that the offender was not the person who used violence against the victim. Although the defendant was part of the disturbance, he did not inflict any actual violence. It was therefore held that he could not be ordered to pay compensation to the victim of the violence, since the injury had been inflicted by someone else, albeit in the same incident. See also *R v Deary* (1994) 14 Cr App R(S) 502, where the Court of Appeal quashed a compensation order because there was no proven causal link between the offender's part in an affray and the injury sustained by the victim.

However, other cases have placed less importance on the need to prove causation. In *R v Taylor* (1993) 14 Cr App R(S) 276, the defendant was convicted of affray following an incident in which a person had been kicked while on the ground. The offender was ordered to pay compensation to the person who was kicked. He appealed on the basis that it had not been proved that it was he who had kicked the victim. It was held that a compensation order may be made against someone who is involved in a fight in which someone is injured even if the injuries were not caused by that offender. In *Taylor*, it was seen as important that the defendant's behaviour was a factor leading to the start of the fighting in which the injury to the victim was inflicted. A similar approach was taken in *R v Denness* [1996] 1 Cr App R(S) 159. In that case, there were three appellants. One of them was being arrested. There was a struggle as the other two appellants tried to pull the first away from the police officer. Another officer intervened and a struggle ensued. One of the officers was injured. The appellants pleaded guilty to affray but were found not guilty of assault occasioning actual bodily harm. The Court of Appeal upheld the making of compensation orders against each of the appellants, on the basis that they were all involved in the incident in which the officer was injured.

Section 130(5) of the 2000 Act provides that in the case of an offence under the Theft Act 1968, where the property is recovered but has been damaged while out of the owner's possession, the damage is deemed to result from the offence. In *R v Ahmad* (1992) 13 Cr App R(S) 212, for example, the defendant pleaded guilty to taking a conveyance. What is now s 130(5) was held to apply to damage which had been caused to the car but not to the loss of property which had been in the vehicle (as the defendant had not been convicted of the theft of that property).

A compensation order for injury, loss or damage (apart from loss suffered by dependents where the victim dies) cannot be made where the loss is due to an accident arising out of the presence of a motor vehicle on a road unless either s 130(5) applies or else it is loss which is not covered by any insurance held by the offender or by the Motor Insurers' Bureau scheme (s 130(6)). Where an order is made in a road accident case, its amount can include compensation for loss of a no claims bonus.

20.1.2 Amount of compensation

In calculating the amount of compensation, the court must have regard to any evidence as to the amount of the loss and to any representations made by the defendant or the prosecution (s 130(4)). In other words, the amount of the damage should be proved if it is not agreed between the parties.

Section 131(1) of the 2000 Act sets a limit of £5,000 compensation for an offence where the order is made by a magistrates' court. There is, however, no limit on the total amount of compensation ordered provided that no more than £5,000 is ordered in respect of any one offence. Thus, if there are five offences, the maximum compensation is £25,000.

There is no limit on the amount of compensation which can be awarded in respect of an offence by the Crown Court.

However, it should be noted that where a compensation order includes an award in respect of bereavement, such an award can only be made in favour of the person entitled to damages for bereavement under s 1A of the Fatal Accidents Act 1976 (the spouse of the deceased or, if the deceased was a minor, the parents) and the amount of the award must not exceed the sum prescribed in the 1976 Act (currently £7,500) (s 130(10) of the 2000 Act).

The Magistrates' Association Sentencing Guidelines include guidance to be used as a starting point in deciding how much compensation to order. The guidelines include the following suggestions:

Type of injury	Description	Starting point
Graze	Depending on size	Up to £75
Bruise	Depending on size	Up to £100
Black eye		£125
Cut: no permanent scar	Depending on size and whether stitched	£100–£500
Sprain	Depending on loss of mobility	£100–£1,000
Finger	Fractured little finger, recovery within month	£1,000

Type of injury	Description	Starting point
Loss of non-front tooth	Depending on cosmetic effect	£500–£1,000
Loss of front tooth		£1,500
Eye	Blurred or double vision	£1,000
Nose	Undisplaced fracture of nasal bone	£1,000
Nose	Displaced fracture of bone requiring manipulation	£1,500
Nose	Not causing fracture but displaced septum requiring sub-mucous resection	£2,000
Facial scar	However small, resulting in permanent disfigurement	£1,500
Wrist	Closed fracture, recovery within month	£3,000
Wrist	Displaced fracture, limb in plaster, recovery in six months	£3,500
Leg or arm	Closed fracture of tibia, fibula, ulna or radius, recovery within month	£3,500

20.1.3 Means of the offender

Section 130(11) of the Powers of Criminal Courts (Sentencing) Act 2000 requires the court to take account of the offender's means in deciding whether to make a compensation order and, if so, the amount of the order. So, in *R v Ellis* (1994) 158 JP 386, a compensation order was quashed because the judge made it without there being any evidence that the defendant, who was unemployed, would be able to pay it. Such an order can only be made against an unemployed defendant if there is evidence that he will be able to find employment. Similarly, in *R v Love and Tomkins* [1999] 1 Cr App R(S) 484, the Court of Appeal said that it is wrong to make a compensation order where the defendant has no assets and his means of earning income are being suspended or brought to an end by the imposition of a sentence of imprisonment. The court should also be very careful before making an order based on the defendant's capacity to earn money after release from prison. However, the court said that it is not necessarily wrong to combine a compensation order with a sentence of imprisonment. A compensation order may be appropriate in those cases where there is evidence that the defendant has sufficient assets or will have sufficient earning capacity after release from prison. The same approach was adopted in *R v Aitkens* [2003] EWCA Crim 2587, where the Court of Appeal said that if an offender is sentenced to immediate imprisonment, a compensation order should not be made where it would subject the defendant, on release from prison, to a financial burden that could not be met. In the present case, the sentence of imprisonment necessarily led to the defendant's loss of employment; since he had no assets, the compensation order was wrong in principle.

In *R v Harrison* (1980) 2 Cr App R(S) 313, it was said that a compensation order should not generally be made if its effect would be to require the offender to sell his home. However, in *R v McGuire* (1992) 13 Cr App R(S) 454, it was held that a compensation order could properly be made, even though it would have the effect of forcing the offender to sell his home, at least if it appears that he will have sufficient money left over to buy a cheaper house. Indeed, in *R v Griffiths* [2001] EWCA Crim 2093; (2001) *The Times*, 17 October, whilst the court re-affirmed the general principle

that a compensation order is not generally appropriate if the defendant's principal asset is the matrimonial home and the innocent spouse and children might suffer if a sale were to be forced, it went on to point out that a compensation order would be permissible in such a case if the husband and wife were both involved in the offending or where the sale of the home was almost inevitable anyway to satisfy a confiscation order made against the defendant.

Similarly, there is usually no objection to making an order which will require the offender to sell other assets (*R v Workman* (1979) 1 Cr App R(S) 335).

In *R v Barney* (1989) 11 Cr App R(S) 448, it was pointed out that the court should avoid giving the impression that the offender will receive a more lenient sentence if he has sufficient funds to pay compensation; in other words, the impression should not be given that a person can buy their way out of prison. However, there is some tension between this laudable principle and the fact that willingness of the offender to pay compensation is relevant in mitigation to the extent that it indicates remorse.

It should be noted that if the offender misleads the court into thinking he can pay more compensation than he is in fact able to pay, the court will not subsequently vary the compensation order on the ground that he lacks the means to pay (*R v Hayes* (1992) 13 Cr App R(S) 454).

A compensation order should only be made if it is likely that the offender will be able to pay it (if necessary by instalments under s 75(1) of the Magistrates' Courts Act 1980) within a reasonable time. Ideally, compensation should be paid within a year; however, in *R v Olliver* (1989) 11 Cr App R(S) 10, it was said that a fine may be imposed if it can be paid within two or three years and presumably the same principle applies to a compensation order.

It follows from this that co-defendants may – and indeed should – be required to pay different sums under compensation orders if their capacity to pay is different (*R v Beddow* (1987) 9 Cr App R(S) 235).

20.1.4 Juveniles

Where an offender under the age of 18 is convicted of an offence, a compensation order may be made. However, where the offender is under 16, the court must order the parent or guardian to pay the compensation unless either the parent or guardian cannot be found or it would be unreasonable to require the parent or guardian to pay the compensation (s 137(1) of the Powers of Criminal Courts (Sentencing) Act 2000). Where the offender is aged 16 or 17, the court has a discretion to order the parent or guardian to pay the compensation (s 137(3) of the 2000 Act). Where the compensation is to be paid by a parent or guardian, it is their means (not the means of the offender) which are taken into account (s 136 of the 2000 Act).

In *R v JJB* [2004] EWCA Crim 14, the Crown Court had made an order that a compensation order be paid by the parents of a young offender (under s 137 of the Powers of Criminal Courts (Sentencing) Act 2000). The Court of Appeal noted that the court must first give the parent an opportunity to be heard (see s 137(4)) and went on to hold that it is unreasonable to make an order against a parent who has done what they can to keep the youngster from criminal ways (see *R v Sheffield Crown Court ex p Clarkson* (1986) 8 Cr App R(S) 454) and that a court should normally find some causative link between any fault proved on the part of the parent and the offence(s) committed by the youngster before making an order under s 137. If no such causative

fault is shown to the satisfaction of the court, it is unreasonable to order the parent to pay compensation (see *Bedfordshire County Council v DPP* [1996] 1 Cr App R(S) 322, 323).

20.1.5 Combining compensation orders and other orders

Section 130(1) of the Powers of Criminal Courts (Sentencing) Act 2000 allows the court to make a compensation order as well as, or instead of, imposing a punishment on the offender.

It should be noted that s 130(12) of the Act gives priority to compensation over fines. If the offender cannot afford to pay both compensation and a fine, the amount of the fine should be reduced or no fine should be imposed.

It must be borne in mind (as we have already seen) that a sentence of immediate custody may well have the effect that the offender will not be able to pay compensation (as it will have the effect of preventing him from earning the money with which to comply with the order) and, in such a case, the custodial sentence would preclude a compensation order (*R v Webb* (1979) 1 Cr App R(S) 16; *R v Gill* (1992) 13 Cr App R(S) 36). This would not be the case if the offender had substantial savings or other realisable assets and so would be able to meet the order from his existing resources (*R v Panayioutou* (1989) 11 Cr App R(S) 535), or if he had good prospects of finding employment on release from custody (*R v Townsend* (1980) 2 Cr App R(S) 328), or if the custodial sentence is relatively short and there is evidence that the offender's previous job will be open to him when he is released from custody (*R v Clark* (1992) 13 Cr App R(S) 124).

20.1.6 Enforcement of compensation orders

Essentially, compensation orders are enforced in the same way as fines. Enforcement is carried out by a magistrates' court, with a term of custody in default of payment. The maximum term of custody for non-payment of compensation is the same as the term for a fine of the same amount. Note, however, that the Crown Court does not have power to fix a term in default when making a compensation order (although it does when imposing a fine): *R v Komsta* (1990) 12 Cr App R(S) 63.

As with a fine, if the offender has paid part of the compensation due under the order, the custodial term will be reduced proportionately.

Where the offender is in receipt of income support or income-based jobseekers allowance, the Fines (Deduction from Income Support) Regulations 1992 enable the court to order deduction of compensation from the offender's benefits in the same way that fines may be deducted at source.

20.1.7 Other methods of obtaining compensation

Compensation orders should not be confused with the Criminal Injuries Compensation Authority nor with the Motor Insurers' Bureau scheme (which provides compensation from a fund set up by insurance companies to compensate victims of road accidents where the driver at fault cannot be traced or is uninsured). The Criminal Injuries Compensation Act 1995 put the criminal injuries compensation

scheme on a statutory footing, with s 2 of the Act setting out the basis on which compensation is payable under the scheme. A standard amount of compensation is payable depending on the nature of the injury suffered by the victim, the amount being calculated according to a tariff published by the Home Secretary. Loss of earnings may also be recovered.

It is always open to a victim of crime to bring civil proceedings against the perpetrator. If the victim receives money under a compensation order from a magistrates' court or the Crown Court, that money will be deducted from any damages awarded by the county court or the High Court, and vice versa.

20.2 RESTITUTION ORDERS

Section 148 of the Powers of Criminal Courts (Sentencing) Act 2000 applies where goods have been stolen and a person is convicted of theft (or asks for theft to be taken into consideration) in respect of those goods. For these purposes, 'theft' includes robbery, burglary, blackmail, obtaining property by deception and handling stolen goods (see s 24(4) of the Theft Act 1968).

Three orders are possible:

- The court may order anyone who has possession or control of the goods to restore them to the person who is entitled to have those goods (s 148(2)(a)).

  Where the person who has possession or control of the goods is not the offender but an innocent purchaser who bought them in good faith, the court may order the offender to pay compensation to the purchaser under s 148(2)(c) below (s 148(4)).

- Where the stolen goods have been sold and the proceeds used to purchase other goods which are in the possession of the offender, the court may order the offender to hand over those goods to the person who was entitled to the stolen goods (s 148(2)(b)).

- The court may order the offender to pay a sum not exceeding the value of the stolen goods to the person who was entitled to those goods provided that this sum can be paid out of money which was in the offender's possession when he was arrested (s 148(2)(c)). In *R v Ferguson* [1970] 1 WLR 1246, it was held that this provision also applies to money seized from the offender after his arrest (in that case, £2,000 seized from a safe deposit box some 11 days after the offender's arrest was held susceptible to an order under s 148).

An order should only be made under s 148 where it is clear that the person benefiting under the order owned the goods; if there is any doubt, the matter is best left to the civil courts (*R v Calcutt* (1985) 7 Cr App R(S) 385).

20.3 FORFEITURE ORDERS

Section 143 of the Powers of Criminal Courts (Sentencing) Act 2000 empowers a Crown Court or magistrates' court to make a forfeiture order in two situations:

- Under s 143(1), the court may make an order in respect of property which has lawfully been seized from the offender or which was in his possession or under his

control at the time he was arrested for the offence (or when the summons was issued if proceedings were commenced by the laying of an information).

This power only applies if the property was used for the purpose of committing, or facilitating the commission of, an offence committed by the offender or if it was intended by him to be used for that purpose.

Section 143(6) of the 2000 Act provides that:

(a) if the offence in question is either manslaughter or an offence under the Road Traffic Act 1988 which is punishable with imprisonment; and

(b) if the offence involved the use of a vehicle and the offender was driving or in charge of the vehicle,

the vehicle is automatically regarded as having been used for the purpose of committing the offence.

• Under s 143(2) of the 2000 Act, the court may make a forfeiture order where the offence consists of unlawful possession of property which has lawfully been seized from the offender or which was in his possession or under his control at the time he was arrested for the offence (or when the summons was issued if proceedings were commenced by the laying of an information).

In deciding whether or not to make a forfeiture order, the court must have regard to the value of the property and to the likely effect of the order on the offender (s 143(5)). An order is inappropriate if it would have a disproportionately severe impact on the offender (*R v Highbury Corner Magistrates ex p Di Matteo* [1991] 1 WLR 1374).

20.3.1 Effect of a forfeiture order

Property which is subject to a forfeiture order is taken into the possession of the police and is held by them under the Police (Property) Act 1897. If the property is owned by someone other than by the offender, that person has six months in which to claim the property (in which case the claimant must show that he did not consent to the offender having the property and did not know it was being used for the commission of an offence). Property which has not been claimed within six months is sold.

Section 145 of the 2000 Act provides that if the offender has been convicted of an offence resulting in loss in respect of which a compensation order could be made, or such an offence is taken into consideration by the court, but the offender does not have the means to pay compensation, the court may order that when property subject to a forfeiture order is sold, the proceeds should be paid to the victim.

20.3.2 Other powers of forfeiture

Other specific statutory powers to make forfeiture orders are contained in the following legislation:

• Section 27 of the Misuse of Drugs Act 1971 enables the court to order forfeiture (and destruction where appropriate) of property related to drugs offences or drug trafficking offences.

For s 27 to apply, it must be shown that the property is related to the offence of which the offender has been convicted (*R v Morgan* [1977] Crim LR 488).

In *R v Cuthbertson* [1981] AC 470; [1980] 2 All ER 401, it was held by the House of Lords that forfeiture orders apply to 'tangible' property such as the drugs, the equipment for making them, vehicles used for transporting them and cash handed over (or ready to be handed over) for them.

The object of a forfeiture order is not to strip drug traffickers of the profits of their crime. This object is achieved by means of confiscation orders, which are dealt with below.

- Section 52 of the Firearms Act 1968 provides that where a person is convicted of a firearms offence, or is convicted of a crime for which a custodial sentence is imposed, the court may order the forfeiture or disposal of any firearm or ammunition in his possession.

- Section 1 of the Prevention of Crime Act 1953 provides that where the offender is convicted of being in possession of an offensive weapon, the court may order the forfeiture or disposal of the weapon.

- Section 1 of the Obscene Publications Act 1964 states that where the offender is convicted of having obscene articles in his possession for gain (s 2 of that Act), the court may order the forfeiture of those articles.

- Section 24 of the Forgery and Counterfeiting Act 1981 empowers the court to order the forfeiture (including the destruction) of counterfeit currency.

20.4 CONFISCATION ORDERS UNDER THE PROCEEDS OF CRIME ACT 2002

The Proceeds of Crime Act (PCA) 2002 replaces the pre-existing dual scheme for the confiscation of the proceeds of crime, previously contained in the Drug Trafficking Act 1994 and the Criminal Justice Act 1988.

A magistrates' court has no power to make a confiscation order under the PCA 2002. It may, however, commit an offender to the Crown Court where the prosecutor asks the court to commit for sentence with a view to a confiscation order being made (s 70). If the offence is triable either way, the magistrates' court should indicate whether, apart from s 70, it would have committed the offender for sentence anyway. If it would have so committed, the Crown Court may sentence the offender in any way in which it could have dealt with him if he had just been convicted before it. If the magistrates' court would not have committed the offender but for the provisions of s 70, the Crown Court is limited to the sentencing powers of the magistrates' court (s 71).

20.4.1 Making of a confiscation order

The basic procedure for making a confiscation order under the PCA 2002 is set out in s 6 of the Act. The power to make a confiscation order only arises if the defendant is:

(a) convicted of one or more offences in the Crown Court; or

(b) committed to the Crown Court for sentence in respect of one or more offences under s 3, 4 or 6 of the Powers of Criminal Courts (Sentencing) Act 2002; or

(c) committed to the Crown Court in respect of one or more offences under s 70 of the PCA 2002 (which, as we have seen, empowers the magistrates' court to commit a

defendant to the Crown Court with a view to a confiscation order being considered).

A confiscation order can only be made if either:

(a) the prosecutor (or the Director of the Assets Recovery Agency) asks the court to proceed under s 6; or

(b) the court believes that it is appropriate for it to proceed under s 6.

Where s 6 is invoked, the court has to proceed as follows:

(a) the court must first decide whether the defendant has 'a criminal lifestyle';

(b) if it decides that the defendant has a criminal lifestyle, it must then decide whether he has benefited from 'general criminal conduct';

(c) if the court decides that the defendant does not have a criminal lifestyle and has not benefited from 'general criminal conduct', it must then decide whether the defendant has benefited from 'particular criminal conduct' (that is, the offence(s) of which he has been convicted in the present proceedings);

(d) if the court decides that the defendant has benefited from general criminal conduct or particular criminal conduct, the court must go on to:

(i) decide the recoverable amount; and

(ii) make a confiscation order requiring the defendant to pay that amount.

If any victim of the defendant's criminal conduct has started (or intends to start) civil proceedings against the defendant in respect of loss, injury or damage sustained in connection with the conduct, then the court is no longer obliged to decide the recoverable amount and to make a confiscation order; nonetheless, the court retains the power to do so in such a case.

In deciding whether the defendant has a criminal lifestyle, whether he has benefited from particular or general criminal conduct, and in determining the recoverable amount, the court must decide any question which arises on a balance of probabilities (s 6(7)).

The phrase 'criminal lifestyle' is comprehensively defined in s 75. Under s 75(2), a defendant has a criminal lifestyle if (and only if) the offence (or any of the offences):

(a) is specified in Sched 2 to the Act (s 75(2)(a));

(b) constitutes conduct forming part of a course of criminal activity and the offender has obtained benefit from this conduct of at least £5,000 (s 75(2)(b)); or

(c) is an offence committed over a period of at least six months, and the defendant has obtained benefit of at least £5,000 from the conduct which constitutes the offence (s 75(2)(c)).

The offences specified in Sched 2 include:

(a) drug trafficking;

(b) money laundering;

(c) directing terrorism;

(d) people trafficking;

(e) arms trafficking;

(f) counterfeiting;

(g) intellectual property offences;

(h) offences related to pimps and brothels;

(i) blackmail;

(j) inchoate offences of attempt, conspiracy or incitement of an offence specified above or aiding, abetting, counselling or procuring the commission of such an offence.

Under s 75(3), conduct forms part of a course of criminal activity for the purposes of s 75(2)(b) where the offender has benefited from the conduct, and:

(a) in the proceedings in which he was convicted, he was convicted of three or more other offences, each of three or more of them constituting conduct from which he has benefited (s 75(3)(a)); or

(b) in the period of six years ending with the day when those proceedings were started (or, if there is more than one such day, the earliest day), he was convicted on at least two separate occasions of an offence constituting conduct from which he has benefited (s 75(3)(b)).

Under s 75(5), relevant 'benefit', for the purposes of s 75(2)(b), is benefit from conduct which constitutes the offence, or benefit from any other conduct which forms part of the course of criminal activity and which constitutes an offence of which the offender has been convicted, or benefit from conduct which constitutes an offence which has been (or will be) taken into consideration in sentencing; relevant 'benefit' for the purposes of s 75(2)(c) is benefit from conduct which constitutes the offence, or benefit from conduct which constitutes an offence which has been (or will be) taken into consideration in sentencing.

The terms 'criminal conduct', 'general criminal conduct' and 'particular criminal conduct' are each defined in s 76:

- 'Criminal conduct' is conduct which constitutes an offence in England and Wales.
- 'General criminal conduct' is all the offender's criminal conduct, it being irrelevant whether the conduct occurred before or after the passing of the PCA 2002, or whether property constituting a benefit from conduct was obtained before or after the passing of the Act.
- 'Particular criminal conduct' is all the offender's criminal conduct which constitutes:
  (a) the offence or offences concerned;
  (b) offences of which he was convicted in the same proceedings; or
  (c) offences which the court will be taking into consideration in sentencing.

20.4.2 Recoverable amount

Section 7(1) of the PCA 2002 defines the 'recoverable amount' for the purposes of s 6 as being 'an amount equal to the defendant's benefit from the conduct concerned'. However, under s 7(2), if the defendant shows that the available amount is less than that benefit, the recoverable amount is 'the available amount' or, if the available amount is nil, a nominal amount. Section 7(5) states that the court must include in the confiscation order a statement of its findings as to the matters relevant for deciding the available amount.

Section 8 of the PCA 2002 provides that in deciding whether the defendant has benefited from conduct, and in deciding his benefit from the conduct, the court must take account of conduct occurring up to the time it makes its decision and must take account of property obtained up to that time.

Section 9 provides that for the purposes of deciding the recoverable amount, the 'available amount' is the aggregate of:

(a) the total of the values (at the time the confiscation order is made) of all the free property (that is, property that is not subject to a forfeiture order: see s 82) then held by the defendant, minus the total amount payable in pursuance of obligations which then have priority, that is, a fine in respect of an earlier conviction or a preferential debt as defined by s 386 of the Insolvency Act 1986); and

(b) the total of the values (at that time) of all tainted gifts – if the court has decided that the defendant has a criminal lifestyle, a gift is to be regarded as tainted if either:

(i) it was made by the defendant at any time during the period of six years before the start of the proceedings for the present offence; or

(ii) it was made by the defendant at any time and was of property obtained by the defendant as a result of, or in connection with, general criminal conduct; if the court has decided that the offender does not have a criminal lifestyle, a gift is to be regarded as tainted if it was made by the defendant at any time after the date on which the present offence was committed: see s 77.

Under s 76(4) and (7), a person 'benefits' from conduct if he obtains property as a result of, or in connection with, that conduct. The 'benefit' is the value of the property so obtained. If a person obtains a pecuniary advantage as a result of or in connection with the conduct, he is to be regarded as having obtained a sum of money equal to the value of the pecuniary advantage (s 76(5)).

Valuation of property obtained by a defendant from criminal conduct is dealt with by s 80 of the PCA 2002. Under s 80(2), the value of the property at the material time (that is, the time when the court makes its decision) is the greater of the following:

(a) the value of the property (at the time the person obtained it), adjusted to take account of later changes in the value of money;

(b) the value (at the material time) of the property found under s 80(3).

The property found under s 80(3) is as follows:

(a) if the person holds the property obtained, the property found under s 80(3) is that property;

(b) if he holds no part of the property obtained, the property found under s 80(3) is any property which directly or indirectly represents it in his hands;

(c) if he holds part of the property obtained, the property found under s 80(3) is that part and any property which directly or indirectly represents the other part in his hands.

20.4.3 Criminal lifestyle: assumptions

Section 10 of the PCA 2002 states that if the court decides that the defendant has a criminal lifestyle, it must make four assumptions for the purpose of deciding whether the defendant has benefited from general criminal conduct, and deciding the value of the benefit from that conduct. Those assumptions are as follows:

(a) that any property transferred to the defendant at any time after the relevant day was obtained as a result of the general criminal conduct, and at the earliest time the defendant appears to have held it;

(b) that any property held by the defendant at any time after the date of conviction was obtained as a result of the general criminal conduct, and at the earliest time the defendant appears to have held it;

(c) that any expenditure incurred by the defendant at any time after the relevant day was met from property obtained by the defendant as a result of his general criminal conduct; and

(d) that, for the purpose of valuing any property obtained (or assumed to have been obtained) by the defendant, he obtained it free of any other interests in it.

Under s 10(8), the 'relevant day' is the first day of the period of six years ending with the day when proceedings for the present offence were started against the defendant or, if there are two or more offences and proceedings for them were started on different days, the earliest of those days.

By virtue of s 10(6), the court must not make a required assumption in relation to particular property or expenditure if either:

(a) the assumption is shown to be incorrect; or

(b) there would be a serious risk of injustice if the assumption were made.

If the court does not make one or more of the required assumptions, it must state its reasons (s 10(7)).

In *R v Rezvi; R v Benjafield* [2002] UKHL 1; [2003] 1 AC 1099, the House of Lords held that similar assumptions to be made in confiscation proceedings under the Criminal Justice Act 1988 and the Drug Trafficking Act 1994 were not incompatible with the rights of a defendant under the European Convention on Human Rights. In *Phillips v UK* [2001] 11 BHRC 280, the European Court of Human Rights held that the statutory assumptions contained in the Drug Trafficking Act 1994 did not contravene Art 6 of the Convention. It seems likely, therefore, that the provisions of the PCA 2002, although draconian, are consistent with the Convention.

20.4.4 Statements of information

Under s 16 of the PCA 2002, where the prosecutor or the Director of the Assets Recovery Agency has asked the court to proceed under s 6, the prosecutor or the Director (as the case may be) must give the court a statement of information within the period specified by the court. If the court is proceeding under s 6 of its own motion, it may order the prosecutor to give it a statement of information within a specified period.

If the prosecutor or the Director (as the case may be) believes that the defendant has a criminal lifestyle, the statement of information must take the form of a statement of matters that the prosecutor or the Director believes are relevant in connection with deciding whether the defendant has a criminal lifestyle, whether he has benefited from general criminal conduct and what his benefit from the conduct has been. It must also include information the prosecutor or Director believes to be relevant in connection with the making by the court of a required assumption under s 10 and for the purpose

of enabling the court to decide if the circumstances are such that it must not make such an assumption (s 16(3), (4)).

If the prosecutor or the Director (as the case may be) does not believe the defendant has a criminal lifestyle, the statement of information should take the form of a statement of matters which the prosecutor or the Director believes to be relevant in connection with deciding whether the defendant has benefited from particular criminal conduct and the benefit from that conduct (s 16(5)).

Under s 17(1), if the prosecutor or the Director gives the court a statement of information and a copy is served on the defendant, the court may order the defendant to indicate (within the period it orders) the extent to which he accepts each allegation in the statement and, in so far as he does not accept such an allegation, to give particulars of any matters he proposes to rely on.

If the defendant accepts an allegation in a statement of information, the court may treat his acceptance as conclusive of the matters to which it relates for the purpose of deciding the issues referred to in s 16(3) or (5): s 17(2).

If the defendant fails to comply with an order under s 17(1), he may be treated as accepting every allegation in the statement of information apart from any allegation in respect of which he has complied with the requirement, and any allegation that he has benefited from general or particular criminal conduct.

Section 18 empowers the court, for the purpose of obtaining information to help it in carrying out its functions, to order the defendant to give it information specified in the order.

If the defendant fails without reasonable excuse to comply with an order under s 18, the court may draw such inference as it believes is appropriate (s 18(4)). It should also be borne in mind that the failure to comply with the order could amount to contempt of court.

If the prosecutor or the Director (as the case may be) accepts an allegation made by the defendant in giving information required by an order under s 18, or in any other statement given to the court in relation to any matter relevant to deciding the available amount under s 9, the court may treat that acceptance as conclusive of the matters to which it relates.

20.4.5 Time for payment

Section 11 of the PCA 2002 provides that the amount ordered to be paid under a confiscation order must normally be paid when the order is made. However, where the offender is unable to pay immediately, the court may make an order allowing payment to be made within a specified period; this time must not exceed six months from the date on which the confiscation order is made. The offender may, in exceptional circumstances, apply to the court for an extension of that period (up to a total of 12 months from the date of the confiscation order).

20.4.6 Effect of a confiscation order on the sentencing powers of the court

Under s 13 of the PCA 2002, the court must take account of the confiscation order before imposing a fine on the defendant, or (for example) a forfeiture order under s 27

of the Misuse of Drugs Act 1971. Apart from that, the court must leave the confiscation order out of account in deciding the appropriate sentence for the defendant (s 13(4)).

If the court makes both a confiscation order and a compensation order (under s 130 of the Powers of Criminal Courts (Sentencing) Act 2000) against the same person in the same proceedings, and the court believes that the offender does not have sufficient means to satisfy both orders in full, the court must direct that so much of the compensation as it specifies is to be paid out of any sums recovered under the confiscation order. The amount it specifies must be the amount it believes will not be recoverable because of the insufficiency of the offender's means.

20.4.7 Enforcement

Detailed provisions on the enforcement of confiscation orders are contained in ss 34–69 of the PCA 2002. Sections 34–37 enable the appointment by the court of the Director of the Assets Recovery Agency as enforcement authority for the order. Sections 38 and 39 provide for the setting of a term of imprisonment in default of payment of the amount ordered to be paid under a confiscation order. The maximum terms to be served in default are the same as in relation to fines.

Where the defendant is ordered to serve a term of imprisonment in default of payment of a confiscation order, this term does not start to run until the defendant has served any prison sentence imposed for the offence(s) which led to the confiscation order being made. If the defendant does serve a sentence in default of payment, that does not prevent the order from continuing to apply for the purposes of enforcement by other means (see s 38(5)).

Sections 40–69 deal with restraint orders and receivership.

In *R (Lloyd) v Bow Street Magistrates' Court* [2003] EWHC 2294 (Admin); [2004] 1 Cr App R 11, the claimant was made the subject of a confiscation order (under the Criminal Justice Act 1988). The order provided that if payment was not made within 12 months, 18 months' imprisonment was to be served in default. In December 1999, the prosecution invited the court to consider enforcement action. A summons was issued in January 2001, but the hearing of the summons did not take place until October 2002. The claimant argued that the proceedings should be stayed on the ground that the delay involved a violation of his rights under Art 6(1) of the European Convention on Human Rights. It was held that the reasonable time guarantee afforded by Art 6(1) applies to enforcement proceedings in respect of a confiscation order. In deciding what is a reasonable time, the court has to have regard to the efforts made to extract money by other methods, such as the appointment of a receiver. Dyson LJ said:

> If a receiver has been appointed within a reasonable time and has proceeded with reasonable expedition, then the fact that all of this may have taken some time will not prevent the court from concluding that there has been no violation of the defendant's Article 6.1 rights if the unsuccessful attempts to recover the money have led to delay in the institution of proceedings to commit. Likewise, if the defendant has been evasive and has avoided diligent attempts to extract the money from him, he will be unable to rely on the resultant delay in support of an argument that his right to a determination within a reasonable time has been violated.

In the present case, a delay of two years and nine months was unacceptable and therefore breached Art 6(1). It is likely that the same principles would be applicable to confiscation orders made under the PCA 2002.

20.4.8 Postponement

The court should normally proceed under s 6 of the PCA 2002 before it sentences the offender for the offence(s) of which he has been convicted. However, s 14 enables the court to postpone proceedings under s 6 for a specified period. Such a period of postponement may be extended, but it should not (unless there are exceptional circumstances) extend for more than two years from the date of conviction (s 14(3)).

If the offender appeals against sentence, proceedings under s 6 may be postponed for a period of up to three months after the appeal is determined or disposed of (s 14(6)). A postponement or extension may be made on application by the offender, the prosecutor or the Director of the Assets Recovery Agency, or may be made by the court of its own motion.

Section 15 provides that if proceedings under s 6 are postponed, the court may proceed to sentence the offender for the offence(s), but must not impose a fine or make a compensation order. When the postponement period comes to an end, the court may vary the sentence by imposing one or more of the financial orders, but it must do so within 28 days of the end of the postponement period (s 15(4)).

20.4.9 Reconsideration

Sections 19–22 of the PCA 2002 enable questions relating to confiscation orders to be re-opened. Section 19 provides that where the court did not proceed against the offender under s 6, and there is now evidence available to the prosecutor which was not then available, the Director may apply to the Crown Court for consideration of the evidence at any time prior to the end of the period of six years from the date of conviction.

Section 20 provides that where the court proceeded against the offender under s 6 but found that he had not benefited from general criminal conduct, or particular criminal conduct, and there is now evidence available to the prosecutor which was not then available, the Director may apply to the Crown Court for consideration of the evidence at any time prior to the end of the period of six years from the date of conviction.

Section 21 provides that where the court has made a confiscation order, and there is now evidence available to the prosecutor which was not then available, the Director may apply to the Crown Court to make a new calculation of the offender's benefit from the conduct concerned.

Sections 22–25 allow for applications to be made to the court for reconsideration of the available amount, and for variation or discharge of the confiscation order in light of the inadequacy of the available amount.

20.4.10 Appeals by the prosecution

Section 31 of the PCA 2002 enables the prosecutor or the Director to appeal to the Court of Appeal against a decision of the court not to make a confiscation order, or in respect of the amount of a confiscation order which has been made.

20.4.11 Effect of the Proceeds of Crime Act 2002 on lawyers

In *P v P* [2003] EWHC 2260 (Fam); [2004] Fam 1, Butler-Sloss P considered the effect of the PCA 2002 on family law practitioners, but her comments will be highly relevant to other areas of practice, including crime:

(a) If, having taken instructions from the client, the solicitor or barrister knows or suspects that he or his client will become involved in an arrangement that might involve the acquisition, retention, use or control of criminal property, then an authorised disclosure should be made (usually to the National Criminal Intelligence Service (NCIS)) and the appropriate consent sought under s 335. If it seems to the solicitor or barrister that there are grounds for suspicion that any arrangement being sought from the court or negotiated between the parties is contrary to the requirements of s 328(1), then authorisation should be sought. It is important for the legal profession to take into account that the Act makes no distinction between degrees of criminal property: an illegally obtained sum of £10 is no less susceptible to the definition of 'criminal property' than a sum of £1 million.

(b) In general terms, the professional duties in family proceedings appear to attract the protection of ss 333(3) and 342(4) in order to permit a legal adviser to inform, for instance, the other side that a disclosure either will be, or has been, made to the NCIS. Sections 333 and 342 specifically recognise a legal adviser's duty in ordinary circumstances to make the relevant disclosures, even where the result would be to tip off their client, where to do so would fall within the ambit of being in connection with the giving of legal advice or with legal proceedings actual or contemplated. The exemption is lost if a disclosure to a client is made 'with the intention of furthering a criminal purpose'. There may well be instances where a solicitor's disclosure to a client is in breach of s 333(4) or 342(5), because the solicitor makes the disclosure with an improper purpose; in such a case, the legal professional exemption would be lost. However, unless the requisite improper intention is there, the solicitor should be free to communicate such information to his client or opponent as is necessary and appropriate in connection with the giving of legal advice or acting in connection with actual or contemplated legal proceedings. As a matter of good practice (as opposed to statutory obligation), the investigation authorities should be permitted time to do their job without frustration. In most cases, a delay of, at most, seven working days before informing a client would not generally cause particular difficulty to the solicitor's obligations to his client or his opponent. Where appropriate consent is refused by the NCIS and a 31 day moratorium is imposed, best practice would suggest that the legal adviser and the NCIS try to agree on the degree of information which can be disclosed during the moratorium period without harming the investigation. In the absence of agreement, or in other urgent circumstances where even a short delay in disclosure would be unacceptable (such as where a hearing is imminent, or orders for discovery require immediate compliance), the guidance of the court may be sought. It would be appropriate for the legal advisers to make the application without notice to the other side, making the NCIS the respondent to the application.

In light of this judgment, the NCIS revised its guidance to legal advisers (see the NCIS website: www.ncis.co.uk). In particular, the NCIS now states that where a solicitor has

already made disclosure and obtained consent, there is no need for a barrister instructed subsequently to do so (where there is no change of circumstances).

Under s 328(1), a person commits an offence if he enters into, or becomes concerned in, an arrangement which he knows or suspects facilitates (by whatever means) the acquisition, retention, use or control of criminal property by or on behalf of another person. Section 340(3) states that property is criminal property if (a) it constitutes a person's benefit from criminal conduct or it represents such benefit (in whole or part and whether directly or indirectly), and (b) the alleged offender knows or suspects that it constitutes or represents such a benefit. For example, property representing the benefit of the non-payment of tax constitutes criminal property for the purposes of the Act.

If, for example, a lawyer advises a client on how to enforce his rights in respect of certain property, the lawyer may well be 'concerned in an arrangement which ... facilitates the acquisition etc of criminal property' (if the property is criminal within the meaning of the Act).

If the parties to litigation agree a settlement where the subject matter of the litigation is (at least in part) criminal property within the meaning of the Act, this too would amount to an arrangement under the Act.

Section 328(2) provides defences. Under s 328(2)(a), a person does not commit an offence if he makes an authorised disclosure under s 338 and (if the disclosure is made before he does the act mentioned in s 328(1)) he has the appropriate consent. Under s 335, disclosure is made to the NCIS.

Guidance from the Bar Council says that:

14 Where the barrister considers that, in order to continue to act without committing a criminal offence, he should make disclosure (and the solicitor has not already done so), subject to his assessment of the impact of Sections 333 and 342 as to which see below, he should inform his client that in order to continue to act without committing a criminal offence the barrister must make a disclosure to NCIS and seek NCIS consent before continuing to act. He should also inform his client that in order for the client to proceed without committing a criminal offence the client should seek NCIS consent. Thereafter events will take one of three courses:

(i)   The client objects to this course of action in which case he will no doubt withdraw instructions. If he does so there is no difficulty and there is no need for the barrister to make a disclosure.

(ii)   If the client objects to the report and does not withdraw instructions the barrister should withdraw from the case to avoid committing the offence. There is no duty upon the barrister to make a disclosure in those circumstances.

(iii) If the client agrees to the proposed course of action the barrister makes disclosure to NCIS and seeks consent. The barrister should consider (and advise his client in this regard) whether he should make the disclosure jointly with his client. If the client makes a report, he also has the protection of the defence. In practical terms it may well be the case that the disclosure is made jointly by barrister, solicitor and client.

Disclosure must be made to the NCIS in writing. The NCIS then has seven working days (the notice period) within which to notify the person making the disclosure of its consent/refusal, starting with the first working day after the person makes disclosure. If no notice is received from NCIS during the notice period, a person is deemed to have appropriate consent. If a notice of refusal is served on the person making the

disclosure, there is then a moratorium period (31 days starting with the day on which the person receives notice of refusal). At the expiry of that period, the person is deemed to have consent.

Where a solicitor has already made a disclosure to the NCIS, there is no need for the barrister instructed by that solicitor to make a disclosure and seek consent before continuing to act.

Section 333(1) creates the offence of tipping off: a person commits this offence if (a) he knows or suspects that a disclosure falling within s 337 or 338 has been made and (b) he makes a disclosure which is likely to prejudice any investigation which might be conducted following that disclosure. Under s 333(2)(c), there is a defence if a person is a professional legal adviser and the disclosure is a disclosure to a client in connection with the giving by the adviser of legal advice to the client. Thus, a lawyer is entitled to tell his client of the disclosure if he does so in connection with the giving of legal advice. However, such a disclosure would amount to an offence (by virtue of s 333(4)) if it was made with the intention of furthering a criminal purpose. It is plain from the decision in *P v P* that the intention must be that of the legal adviser, not the client.

Under s 342, if a person knows or suspects that a confiscation investigation, a civil recovery investigation or a money laundering investigation is being or is about to be conducted, he commits an offence if he makes a disclosure which is likely to prejudice the investigation.

Once again, there is a defence where the disclosure is made by a professional legal adviser in connection with the giving of legal advice to the client, etc (see s 342(3)(c)) unless the disclosure is made with the intention of furthering a criminal purpose (s 342(5)).

20.5   MENTALLY DISORDERED OFFENDERS

In an attempt to ensure that custodial sentences are not imposed unnecessarily on mentally disordered offenders, s 82 of the Powers of Criminal Courts (Sentencing) Act 2000 requires the court to obtain a medical report before imposing a custodial sentence on someone 'who is or appears to be mentally disordered'. Under s 82(3), the court must consider the likely effect of a custodial sentence on the person's mental condition and on any treatment which may be available for it.

There are a number of different orders which may be made in respect of a mentally disordered offender.

A community rehabilitation order may contain a requirement that the offender undergo treatment for his mental condition (para 3 of Sched 2 to the 2000 Act); a supervision order may also contain such a requirement (para 6 of Sched 6 to the 2000 Act).

Where the offender's condition is more serious, it may be necessary for the court to make an order under the Mental Health Act 1983. There are two main orders under this Act: the hospital order and the guardianship order.

20.5.1 Hospital orders

Section 37 of the Mental Health Act 1983 provides that, where a mentally disordered person is convicted of an offence which is punishable with imprisonment, the court may make an order for his admission to, and detention in, a mental hospital.

Under s 37(2) of the Mental Health Act 1983, a number of conditions have to be satisfied before a hospital order can be made. Those conditions are as follows:

- The court must be satisfied on the evidence of two duly qualified medical practitioners that the offender is suffering from 'mental illness, psychopathic disorder, severe mental impairment or mental impairment' and either:

  (a) the mental disorder is of a nature or degree which makes it appropriate for the offender to be detained in a hospital for medical treatment and, in the case of psychopathic disorder or mental impairment, such treatment is likely to alleviate or prevent a deterioration in his condition; or

  (b) the offender has attained the age of 16 and his mental disorder is of a nature or degree which warrants a guardianship order (see below).

- The court must be of the opinion that such an order is the most suitable method of disposing of the case.

A hospital order may be made even if there is no causal link between the offender's mental disorder and the offence of which he has been convicted (*R v McBride* [1972] Crim LR 322).

As with compulsory civil committal under Pt II of the Mental Health Act 1983, the order lapses after six months, but may be renewed for a further six months and may thereafter be renewed for periods of one year at a time, where the doctors dealing with the offender consider further detention to be necessary for the protection of the public or in the interests of the health or safety of the patient (s 20 and Sched 1 to the Mental Health Act 1983). There is no limit to the total length of detention in the hospital, but an application for the patient's release may be made to the Mental Health Review Tribunal.

20.5.2 Interim hospital orders

Section 38 of the Mental Health Act 1983 enables the court to make an interim hospital order before finally disposing of the case. The conditions which have to be met are the same as for a hospital order (so it is likely that a hospital order will be made when the case is finally disposed of). An interim order may last for up to 12 weeks; it may then be renewed for further periods of up to 28 days at a time; an interim order cannot last for a total of more than six months.

20.5.3 Restriction orders

Section 41 of the Mental Health Act 1983 empowers the Crown Court to make a 'restriction order' as well as a hospital order. The court may do so if it considers:

> ... having regard to the nature of the offence, the antecedents of the offender and the risk of his committing further offences if set at large, that it is necessary for the protection of the public from serious harm to do so.

The effect of the restriction order is that the offender cannot be discharged from the mental hospital without the permission of the Secretary of State or the Mental Health Review Tribunal.

A restriction order may be for a fixed period (in which case it lasts for that period, with no need for it to be renewed when the hospital order is renewed) or it may be for an indefinite period.

Such an order can only be made where it is necessary to protect the public from serious harm: it cannot be made simply to reflect the gravity of the offence committed by the offender (see *R v Birch* (1990) 90 Cr App R 78).

20.5.4 Hospital orders and limitation directions

Sections 45A and 45B of the Mental Health Act 1983 provide for the making of a hospital order coupled with a limitation direction. Before making such an order, the court must be satisfied, on the basis of evidence from two medical practitioners (one of whom must give oral evidence), that the offender is suffering from a psychopathic disorder, that the disorder is of a nature or degree which makes it appropriate for him to be detained in a hospital for medical treatment, and that such treatment is likely to alleviate (or prevent a deterioration of) his condition. Such an order is made in addition to a sentence of imprisonment. When an order is made, the offender is conveyed to the hospital named in the direction. If the offender ceases to need treatment, he is returned to prison; if he is still in hospital when the sentence expires, he will cease to be subject to restriction and will remain in hospital as if detained under an ordinary hospital order made under s 37 of the 1983 Act. The offender is eligible for release on the decision of the responsible medical officer.

20.5.5 Guardianship orders

Under s 40(2) of the Mental Health Act 1983, a guardianship order may be made to confer certain powers in respect of the offender on an authority or person. These powers are the same as those conferred by a guardianship order made in the civil context (see Pt II of the Mental Health Act 1983). The powers include determining where the offender will reside and the power to require him to attend for treatment, occupational therapy, education or training. The pre-conditions for the making of a guardianship order are the same as those for making a hospital order, except that there is no requirement that the offender's mental disorder be treatable. A guardianship order lasts for 12 months, but can be renewed.

20.5.6 Juveniles

An adult magistrates' court may not make a hospital order or guardianship order on a juvenile (s 7(8) of the Children and Young Persons Act 1969). Otherwise, the same principles apply as to adult offenders.

20.6   ANTI-SOCIAL BEHAVIOUR ORDERS; INDIVIDUAL SUPPORT ORDERS

Section 1 of the Crime and Disorder Act 1998 (as amended by s 85 of the Anti-Social Behaviour Act 2003) provides for 'anti-social behaviour orders' (ASBOs). The police, a local authority or certain other bodies may apply to the local magistrates' court for such an order if:

(a) any person aged 10 or over has acted in an anti-social manner (defined as acting in a manner that caused or was likely to cause harassment, alarm or distress to one or more persons not in the same household as himself); and

(b) such an order is necessary to protect people in the area from further anti-social acts by that person.

The ASBO is an order which prevents the person from doing anything described in the order; the prohibitions imposed under the order can be anything the magistrates consider necessary to protect people in the locality from further anti-social acts by the defendant.

The minimum period of such an order is two years (no maximum period is specified by the Act).

Section 1(10) provides that if, without reasonable excuse, a person does anything which he is prohibited from doing by an ASBO, he commits an offence (carrying up to six months' imprisonment and/or a fine of up to £5,000 following summary conviction or up to five years' imprisonment and an unlimited fine following conviction in the Crown Court).

Section 4 of the Act provides for an appeal to the Crown Court against the making of an ASBO.

The same power to make an ASBO is available to the county court and the Crown Court under ss 1B and 1C respectively of the 1998 Act.

Section 85(8) of the 2003 Act inserts a new sub-section (1B) into s 9 of the 1998 Act. This provides that where a court makes an ASBO against a person under the age of 16, it must also make a parenting order (see Chapter 19) against the parents of that child if it is satisfied that the parenting order would be desirable in the interests of preventing repetition of the behaviour which led to the ASBO.

Section 86(1) of the 2003 Act amends s 1C of the 1998 Act to make clear that, following conviction, a court may make an ASBO either at the request of the prosecutor or of its own volition; s 86(2) inserts new sub-sections, (3A) and (3B), allowing for evidence that was not admissible in the criminal proceedings to be presented for the purpose of deciding whether to make an ASBO. Section 86(3) inserts a new sub-section, (9A), into s 1C to allow a local authority, where a person subject to an ASBO resides in its area, to prosecute for breach of the ASBO. This sub-section also inserts new sub-sections, (9B) and (9C), to remove automatic reporting restrictions (under s 49 of the Children and Young Persons Act 1933) where an ASBO is made following conviction in the youth court, although the court will retain a discretion (under s 39 of the 1933 Act) to apply reporting restrictions.

Sections 322 and 323 of the Criminal Justice Act 2003 (in force since May 2004) provide for an 'individual support order', aimed at preventing further anti-social behaviour where an ASBO has already been made against a person under the age of

18. The individual support order may require the young person to undertake activities aimed at tackling the underlying causes of their anti-social behaviour.

Section 322 of the 2003 Act inserts two new sections, ss 1AA and 1AB, after s 1A of the Crime and Disorder Act 1998. Section 1AA stipulates that the court must consider making an individual support order after it has made an ASBO against a child or young person (that is, a person aged 10–17). Under s 1AA(2), the court must (unless the juvenile is already subject to an individual support order) make an individual support order if it is satisfied that an individual support order would be desirable in the interests of preventing any repetition of the kind of behaviour which led to the making of the ASBO.

The maximum duration of an individual support order is six months. Under s 1AA(5), the court may impose requirements under the order which the court considers desirable in the interests of preventing a repetition of the anti-social behaviour which led to the ASBO. Under sub-s (6), the offender may be required to participate in specified activities, to attend a specified place (or places), or to comply with specified arrangements for his education. The offender cannot be required to attend a place (or different places) on more than two days per week. Sub-section (8) obliges the court, when imposing requirements, to (so far as practicable) avoid conflict with religious beliefs and avoid interference with school or with work commitments. Under s 1AA(9), the court is required to obtain information from a social worker of a local authority social services department or a member of a youth offending team in order to determine what requirements should be included in an order.

Section 1AB(1) requires the court to explain to the defendant in open court the effect of the order, the consequences of failure to comply with its requirements and the court's power to review the order. Under s 1AB(3), failure without reasonable excuse to comply with the requirements under the individual support order is a summary offence, punishable with a fine of up to £1,000 for an offender aged 14–17, and £250 for an offender aged 10–14.

Under s 1AB(5), an individual support order ceases to have effect (if it has not already expired) when the ASBO to which it is linked ceases to have effect. Section 1AB(6) allows the offender or the responsible officer to apply to the court for the order to be varied or discharged; sub-s (7) allows a court to vary or discharge an individual support order if it is varying the ASBO to which it is linked.

Section 323 of the 2003 Act amends s 4(2) of the Crime and Disorder Act 1998 to enable an appeal to the Crown Court against the making of an individual support order.

Section 1D of the Crime and Disorder Act 1998 (as amended by the Police Reform Act 2002) enables an interim ASBO to be made if the court considers that it is just to do so pending the determination of the main application. Such orders can, where necessary, be made for a limited period without notice, but there is a right to seek review of the interim order once it has been served and this power is not inconsistent with Art 6 of the European Convention on Human Rights (see *R (M) v Secretary of State for Constitutional Affairs* [2004] EWCA Civ 312; [2004] 2 All ER 531).

20.7 OTHER ANCILLARY ORDERS

Finally, we consider various orders which can be made at the time the offender is being sentenced.

20.7.1 Recommendation for deportation

Under s 6(3) of the Immigration Act 1971, a court which is dealing with someone who is not a British citizen and who has been convicted of an imprisonable offence may make a recommendation to the Home Secretary that the person be deported. In *R v Nazari* [1980] 1 WLR 1366, Lawton LJ said that the seriousness of the offence and the extent of the offender's criminal record should be taken into account in deciding whether or not to make a recommendation for deportation. Such a recommendation may be combined with any sentence, but is most common where the offender has received a custodial sentence; in such a case, the Home Secretary can order the offender's deportation once he is released from prison.

20.8 EXCLUSION ORDERS

The courts have various statutory powers to exclude offenders from particular places.

20.8.1 Licensed premises

Section 1 of the Licensed Premises (Exclusion of Certain Persons) Act 1980 empowers a court which is dealing with a person who has been convicted of an offence of violence to prohibit the offender from entering licensed premises without the express consent of the licensee for a specified period of between three months and two years.

20.8.2 Football matches

Section 14A of the Football Spectators Act 1989 (as amended by the Football (Disorder) Act 2000) requires the court to make a banning order where the offender is convicted of certain offences and the court is satisfied that there are reasonable grounds to believe that making a banning order would help to prevent violence or disorder at or in connection with regulated football matches. Unless there are exceptional circumstances, the offender is required to surrender his passport. If the order is made in addition to a sentence of immediate custody, the banning order must last for a specified period between six and 10 years; otherwise it must last for three to five years.

20.9 DISQUALIFICATIONS

The courts also have a number of disqualification orders at their disposal.

20.9.1 Company directors

Sections 1 and 2 of the Company Directors Disqualification Act 1986 apply where a court is dealing with a person who has been convicted of an indictable (including triable either way) offence which is connected with the formation, management, liquidation, receivership or management of a company. The effect of the order is to prevent the offender from being a company director or being involved in the setting up or running of a company. The usual maximum period of disqualification is five years (magistrates' court) and 15 years (Crown Court). Disqualification is usually appropriate where the offender has been guilty of dishonesty or gross incompetence, so that he would be a danger to the public if he were to be allowed to continue to be involved in the management of companies (*per* Hoffmann J in *Re Dawson Print Group Ltd* [1987] BCLC 601).

20.9.2 Animals

Section 1 of the Protection of Animals (Amendment) Act 1954 enables a court to disqualify the offender from keeping any animal where the offender has been convicted of causing unnecessary suffering to an animal.

20.9.3 Road traffic offenders

Under s 34 of the Road Traffic Offenders Act 1988, where a person has been convicted of a road traffic offence involving obligatory disqualification, the court must order that he be disqualified from driving for at least 12 months unless the court finds that there are special reasons for not disqualifying him or for disqualifying him for less than 12 months. A special reason must be connected with the commission of the offence itself; mitigation which is personal to the offender is not a special reason (*R v Wickins* (1958) 42 Cr App R 236).

Other road traffic offences carry discretionary disqualification (see Sched 1 to the Road Traffic Offenders Act 1988). In such cases, disqualification is only imposed in the more serious examples of those offences (*per* Morland J in *R v Callister* [1993] RTR 70).

Many road traffic offences carry a number of penalty points which have to be endorsed on the offender's driving licence in the event of conviction. The number of points to be endorsed is set out in Sched 1 to the Road Traffic Offenders Act 1988; sometimes, the number is fixed; sometimes, there is a range, with a minimum and a maximum number specified. If the offender is convicted of more than one offence, the points to be endorsed are those which relate to the offence which carries the highest number of points (s 28); thus, if the offender is convicted on one occasion of careless driving (which carries three to nine points) and failing to comply with a traffic sign (three points), the maximum number of points which can be endorsed is nine.

Under s 35 of the Road Traffic Offenders Act 1988, where a person is convicted of an offence which carries discretionary disqualification and mandatory endorsement and the number of penalty points on the offender's driving licence (including those imposed for the present offence) number 12 or more, the court must disqualify the offender from driving for at least six months (if it is his first disqualification) or 12 months (if it is his second) or two years (if he has already been disqualified twice) unless the court takes the view that there are grounds for not doing so or for disqualifying for a shorter period. Penalty points are taken into account if they were imposed within the last three years (s 29(2)). This is known as a 'totting up' disqualification.

In deciding whether there is mitigation to justify not disqualifying the offender (or for shortening the disqualification), the court cannot take account of:

- circumstances alleged to make the present offence less serious;
- hardship (unless it is exceptional hardship); or
- circumstances which the offender has relied on to escape a 'totting up' disqualification within the last three years (s 35(4)).

In *R v Thames Magistrates' Court ex p Levy* (1997) *The Times*, 17 July, the defendant had been disqualified from driving after being convicted of various driving offences. He appealed against these convictions but did not apply to have the disqualification suspended pending the appeal. The convictions were subsequently quashed following a successful appeal. Prior to the quashing of the convictions, he drove a motor vehicle. He was charged with driving while disqualified. The Divisional Court held, unsurprisingly, that he was guilty of driving while disqualified because he drove a motor vehicle while an order for disqualification was lawfully in force.

20.9.4 Disqualification under the Powers of Criminal Courts (Sentencing) Act 2000

Section 146 of the Powers of Criminal Courts (Sentencing) Act 2000 provides that, in addition to, or instead of, dealing with an offender in any other way, a court may disqualify him from driving for such period as it thinks fit. Thus, the penalty of disqualification from driving can be imposed for any offence, not just driving offences. This power became available on 1 January 2004. When this Act was passing through Parliament, it was said that (HC Official Report, SCA, 10 December 1996):

> ... it is important that the courts regard disqualification from driving as a heavy penalty, especially if someone is employed. There will therefore be occasions when they will not apply this penalty if it might result in a person losing his job, because that may seem disproportionate ... The important point ... is the idea that the use of the sentence should be appropriate to the nature of the offence, and that in most if not all cases there should be some relevance to the use of a vehicle.

20.9.5 Disqualification from working with children

Sections 26–34 of the Criminal Justice and Court Services Act 2000 empower the Crown Court to impose a disqualification order on a person who has committed an offence against a child and who has received a custodial sentence of 12 months or more. The effect of the order is to disqualify that person from working with children in the future.

20.10 RESTRAINING ORDERS

The court also enjoys a range of restraining orders (in addition to the anti-social behaviour orders considered earlier).

20.10.1 Sex offenders

Sections 80–92 of the Sexual Offices Act 2003 re-enact (with amendments) Pt 1 of the Sex Offenders Act 1997, which established a requirement that those convicted of specified sexual offences must notify certain personal details to the police. This process is popularly known as registering on the 'sex offenders' register'.

Section 104 of the Sexual Offences Act 2003 creates 'sexual offences prevention orders'. Where the court is dealing with an offender for a specified sexual offence and that offender has previously been dealt with for a specified offence, the court may make a sexual offences prevention order if it is satisfied that the person's behaviour, since the date on which he was first dealt with in this way, means it is necessary to make the order 'for the purpose of protecting the public or any particular members of the public from serious sexual harm from the offender'. Alternatively, where an offender has been dealt with for a specified sexual offence, the police may apply to a magistrates' court for a sexual offences prevention order if that person's behaviour gives rise to reasonable cause to believe that it is necessary for such an order to be made. Section 107 of the Act sets out the effect of the order: the order may prohibit the offender from doing anything specified in it; the only restriction on the prohibitions that may be contained in the order is that they must be necessary 'for the purpose of protecting the public or any particular members of the public from serious sexual harm from the defendant'. The order must last for a specified period of no less than five years. Section 108 enables applications to vary or discharge the order. Under s 113, failure to comply with the order is an offence punishable with up to five years' imprisonment.

Section 114 of the Sexual Offences Act 2003 creates a new preventative order, the 'foreign travel order'. The order prohibits offenders convicted of specified sexual offences (essentially, certain sexual offences against children under the age of 16) from travelling abroad where and insofar as it is necessary to do so to protect a child or children from serious sexual harm outside the UK. The order can prohibit travel either to a named country or countries, to anywhere in the world other than a named country, or to anywhere in the world. Breach of the order is an offence under s 122 of the Act (again punishable with up to five years' imprisonment).

20.10.2 Protection from harassment

A court which is dealing with a person convicted of an offence under s 2 or 4 of the Protection from Harassment Act 1997 may make a restraining order under s 5 of the Act. For the purpose of protecting the victim of the offence (or any other person mentioned in the order) from further conduct which amounts to harassment, or which will cause a fear of violence, the order may prohibit the offender from doing anything described in the order. The order has effect for a specified period or until further order. The prosecutor, the defendant or any other person mentioned in the order may apply to the court which made the order for it to be varied or discharged. If, without reasonable excuse, the offender does anything which he is prohibited from doing under the order, he is guilty of an offence punishable with up to five years' imprisonment.

20.10.3 Travel restrictions on drug traffickers

Under ss 33–37 of the Criminal Justice and Police Act 2001, the court may impose a travel restriction order on an offender who is convicted of a drug trafficking offence and who has been sentenced by that court to a term of imprisonment for four years or more. The effect of the order is to restrict the offender's freedom to leave the UK for a period specified by the court, and it may require him to surrender his passport. The minimum duration of a travel restriction order is two years, starting from the date of the offender's release from custody. No maximum period is prescribed in the Act. The court must always consider whether such an order should be made and must give reasons in any case where it does not consider such an order to be appropriate.

In *R v Mee* [2004] EWCA Crim 629; (2004) *The Times*, 1 April, the court gave guidance on travel restriction orders made under s 33 of the Criminal Justice and Police Act 2001. The power to make the order has to be exercised proportionately, and for the purpose for which it was granted, namely the prevention or reduction of the risk of re-offending after release from prison. It is not intended to be a substitute for the appropriate period of imprisonment. The mere fact that a defendant has imported drugs does not necessarily give rise to the risk that, on release from prison, he will abuse his freedom to travel by engaging in that activity again. A distinction should be drawn between a one-off importation by a holidaymaker in a non-commercial quantity, and an established pattern of travel between one or more foreign drug sources, with the likelihood that a network of contracts in the trade had been established. Where such a risk has been identified, the principles of proportionality and fairness require a balanced approach to the determination of the length of the order. The length of an order should be that which is required to protect the public in the light of the degree of risk. Factors such as age, previous convictions, risk of re-offending, family contacts and employment prospects might be taken into account in that determination.

CHAPTER 21

SOURCES AND THEORETICAL PERSPECTIVE

In this chapter, we look at further reading (both practitioner textbooks and texts that are written from a more theoretical perspective) and at some websites that are of use to those interested in criminal justice. There is also a brief examination of some of the theoretical perspectives that underpin our criminal justice system.

21.1 PRACTITIONER TEXTS

The main sources used by criminal practitioners are:

Blackstone's Criminal Practice: a one-volume book re-published annually (also available on the internet through subscription to the LexisNexis Butterworths' Crime Online service at http://grenville.butterworths.co.uk). It contains substantive criminal law as well as procedure, evidence and sentencing, and covers both the Crown Court and magistrates' courts. There is a companion website at www.oup.com/uk/booksites/content/0199263612.

Archbold: Criminal Pleading Evidence and Practice: a one-volume book re-published annually, with supplements issued during the course of the year (also available on the internet through subscription to Westlaw at www.westlaw.co.uk). It contains substantive criminal law as well as procedure, evidence and sentencing, but it only covers the Crown Court. In 2004, *Archbold Magistrates' Courts Criminal Practice*, a new one-volume work covering magistrates' courts, was published for the first time.

Stone's Justices Manual: a three-volume annual publication (also available on the internet through subscription to the LexisNexis at www.lexisnexis.co.uk). It contains substantive law (both criminal and civil) as well as procedure, evidence and sentencing, but it covers only the magistrates' courts.

The *Criminal Law Review* is a good source of articles and commentaries on case law on both substantive criminal law and evidence, procedure and sentencing.

21.2 ACADEMIC TEXTBOOKS

Academic textbooks which offer critical analysis of some of the issues raised by the English criminal justice system include:

Ashworth, Andrew: *The Criminal Process: An Evaluative Study*, 1998, Oxford: OUP

McConville, Mike and Wilson, Geoffrey: *Handbook of the Criminal Justice Process*, 2002, Oxford: OUP

Sanders, Andrew and Young, Richard: *Criminal Justice*, 2000, London: Butterworths

Uglow, Steve: *Criminal Justice*, 2002, London: Sweet & Maxwell

21.3 WEBLINKS

The following websites are of particular interest to anyone with an interest in the criminal justice system.

The 'official' government website for matters relating to criminal justice is: www.cjsonline.gov.uk/home.html.

Criminal justice has, in recent years, been at the forefront of party politics. The most recent, and most substantial, changes are made in the Criminal Justice Act 2003, which is available at www.hmso.gov.uk/acts/acts2003/20030044.htm.

The Criminal Justice Act 2003 arose, in part, out of two major reviews that were published in 2001:

- *The Review of the Criminal Courts of England and Wales* by the Right Honourable Lord Justice Auld (September 2001) is available at www.criminal-courts-review.org.uk.

- The Halliday Report (*Making Punishments Work: Review of the Sentencing Framework for England and Wales*, July 2001) is available at www.homeoffice.gov.uk/docs/halliday.html.

For information on sentencing guidelines, see www.sentencing-guidelines.gov.uk.

Useful government department websites include:

- The Home Office: www.homeoffice.gov.uk.

- The Department for Constitutional Affairs (formerly the Lord Chancellor's Department): www.dca.gov.uk.

- The Crown Prosecution Service: www.cps.gov.uk (the CPS Annual Reports contain useful statistics on the work carried out by the CPS: www.cps.gov.uk/home/CPSPublications/Scheme/reports.htm.)

Some useful statistics can be found in the official Judicial Statistics, published annually: www.dca.gov.uk/jsarlist.htm.

There are some particularly useful 'portal' sites containing links related to crime and criminal justice:

- Delia Venables: www.venables.co.uk/sitesc.htm#crime.

- The Institute of Advanced Legal Studies: http://ials.sas.ac.uk/links/eicrime.htm.

- The University of Kent: http://library.kent.ac.uk/library/lawlinks/special.htm#crim.

21.4 THEORETICAL PERSPECTIVES – A BRIEF INTRODUCTION

What should our criminal justice system be trying to achieve? In para 7 of Chapter 1 of his *Review of the Criminal Courts in England and Wales*, Lord Justice Auld refers to the two key 'aims' identified in the government's Paper, *Criminal Justice System: Strategic Plan 1999–2002*. Those aims are:

(a) reducing crime and the fear of crime and their social and economic costs; and

(b) dispensing justice fairly and efficiently to promote confidence in the law.

The second of those aims was said to give rise to a series of objectives:

- to ensure just processes and just and effective outcomes;
- to deal with cases throughout the criminal justice process with appropriate speed;
- to meet the needs of victims, witnesses and jurors within the system;
- to respect the rights of defendants and to treat them fairly;
- to promote confidence in the criminal justice system.

Herbert L Packer, an American jurist, in 'Two models of the criminal process' ((1964) 113 U PA L Rev 1) and *The Limits of the Criminal Sanction* (Stanford University Press, 1968) proposed two models of criminal justice:

- the 'crime control' model: this has as its primary objective the repression of crime (in other words, the lowering of crime rates), achieved by the efficient apprehension and punishment of criminals; and
- the 'due process' model: this has as its primary objective procedural fairness (in other words, the protection of the rights of the accused), achieved by presenting formidable impediments to carrying them past each step in the legal process.

These two models are considered in much greater detail in the academic textbooks listed earlier in this chapter.

Packer makes it clear that neither model is presented as corresponding to reality or as representing the ideal criminal justice system. Rather, the two models offer a basis for examining how a criminal justice system might take account of the competing demands of differing value systems which have differing (and inconsistent) priorities. In other words, these models offer a framework for examining the tensions between competing claims within a criminal justice system. Packer suggests that it may be worthwhile examining where, on the spectrum between the extremes represented by the two models, our present practices seem to fall and what appears to be the direction and thrust of current trends within our system. Moreover, we can compare our own values with the values which underlie the two models.

21.4.1 'Crime control'

Turning to the crime control model, Packer says that the:

> ... value system that underlies the Crime Control model is based on the proposition that the repression of criminal conduct is by far the most important function to be performed by the criminal process. The failure of law enforcement to bring criminal conduct under tight control is viewed as leading to the breakdown of public order and thence to the disappearance of an important condition of human freedom. If the laws go unenforced – which is to say, if it is perceived that there is a high percentage of failure to apprehend and convict in the criminal process – a general disregard for legal controls tends to develop ... the crime control model requires that primary attention be paid to the efficiency with which the criminal process operates to screen suspects, determine guilt, and secure appropriate dispositions of persons convicted of crime.

The two risks inherent in the failure to repress crime are (a) the risk that people will take the law into their own hands (in other words, becoming vigilantes), leading to public disorder, and (b) the risk that crime rates will increase further because people believe they will be able to get away with offending. This model seeks a system that is efficient, in the sense of being able to apprehend, try, convict and sentence a high proportion of offenders whose offences become known. The system will thus be operating successfully (according to the values underpinning crime control) if there is a high rate of apprehension and conviction of offenders. This places a premium on speed (which requires that the hands of the investigators and prosecutors are not tied) and finality (in the sense of minimising the occasions for challenge).

Packer writes that the criminal process according to this model is seen as a 'screening process', in which each successive stage (investigation, arrest, subsequent investigation, preparation for trial, trial or plea, conviction, sentence) involves 'a series of routinised operations whose success is gauged primarily by their tendency to pass the case along to a successful conclusion'. For these purposes, Packer defines a successful conclusion as one that 'throws off at an early stage those cases in which it appears unlikely that the person apprehended is an offender and then secures, as expeditiously as possible, the conviction of the rest, with a minimum of occasions for challenge'.

This requires that, at the stage of the police investigation (and maybe charge review and evidence review by the prosecuting authority), those who are probably innocent are 'screened out' and those who are probably guilty are 'passed quickly through the remaining stages of the process'. Packer notes that this approach requires what he terms 'a presumption of guilt'. This is because 'the screening processes operated by police and prosecutors are reliable indicators of probable guilt'. Once the police (and the prosecution) have determined to their own satisfaction that there is enough evidence of guilt to justify taking the case forward, 'all subsequent activity directed toward him is based on the view that he is probably guilty'. The instinct of the police officer or prosecutor may well be to look for further evidence that the suspect is guilty, rather than evidence that would exonerate the suspect. This is one of the tensions in the law relating to the disclosure of unused prosecution material (where the law requires the prosecution to retain, and then disclose to the defence, material which weakens the prosecution case or strengthens the defence case).

This 'presumption of guilt' stems from confidence in the reliability of the fact-finding that takes place at the investigative stage (and the subsequent evidential review stage). According to the crime control model, if we can be confident in the accuracy of those initial stages, the remaining stages of the process can be relatively perfunctory. Indeed, the crime control model would suggest that the trial process is likely to be less capable of producing reliable fact-finding as the earlier investigative stages. On this basis, the criminal process must put special weight on the quality of that earlier fact-finding. This, in turn, makes it important to place as few restrictions as possible on the investigative process. If the early fact-finding stages are the most important, the corollary is that the subsequent stages are relatively unimportant and should therefore be truncated as much as possible.

Packer contrasts this *de facto* presumption of guilt with the (legal) presumption of innocence, which he defines as a direction to those involved in the process to 'ignore the presumption of guilt in their treatment of the suspect. It tells them, in effect, to close their eyes to what will frequently seem to be factual probabilities' or, put another way, to close their eyes to 'the probability that, in the run of cases, the preliminary screening process operated by the police and the prosecuting officials contains adequate guarantees of reliable fact-finding'.

In an ideal 'crime control world', the initial investigative stages would result in either the exoneration of the suspect, or else the entering of a plea of guilty.

21.4.2 'Due process'

In contrast to the value of crime control, Packer says that according to due process values, each successive stage of the criminal process 'is designed to present formidable impediments to carrying the accused any further along in the process'. He makes it clear, however, that those who subscribe to due process values will not necessarily reject some of the foundations of crime control. Proponents of due process do not, for example, have to argue that it is not desirable to repress crime.

The due process approach places much less faith in the reliability of the initial investigative stages of the process. It points out that witnesses can make mistakes, that confessions may be induced by various forms of coercion (whether intentional or not), and that the police are looking for evidence of guilt not innocence. The due process model would argue additionally that the trial process itself may not lead to reliable fact-finding, and so there must be the possibility of further scrutiny (by ways of appeals) open to the accused (with the result that finality has a low priority in the due process model).

This takes us to questions of efficiency and resourcing. As Packer puts it: 'How much reliability is compatible with efficiency?' In other words: 'how much weight is to be given to the competing demands of reliability (a high degree of probability in each case that factual guilt has been accurately determined) and efficiency (expeditious handling of the large numbers of cases that the process ingests)?'

The crime control model is not only more optimistic about the improbability of error in a significant number of cases, but is also, at least to an extent, more tolerant about the number of errors that it will put up with. The due process model insists on the prevention and elimination of mistakes to the greatest extent possible, whereas the crime control model accepts the probability of mistakes up to the level at which they interfere with the goal of repressing crime (either because too many guilty people are escaping justice or because a general lack of confidence in the process leads to a decrease in the deterrent efficacy of the criminal law). Under the due process model, the aim of the process is at least as much to protect the factually innocent as it is to convict the factually guilty.

The combination of stigma and loss of liberty that can result from conviction of a criminal offence is viewed by the due process model as very serious. For this reason, the due process model is prepared to accept a substantial diminution in the efficiency with which the criminal process operates in the interest of preventing oppression of the individual by the State. Packer highlights the importance of the concept of 'legal guilt'. He writes that:

> According to this doctrine, a person is not to be held guilty of a crime merely on a showing that in all probability, based upon reliable evidence, he did factually what he is said to have done. Instead, he is to be held guilty if and only if these factual determinations are made in procedurally regular fashion and by authorities acting within competences duly allocated to them. Furthermore, he is not to be held guilty, even though the factual determination is or might be adverse to him, if various rules designed to protect him and to safeguard the integrity of the process are not given effect.

This requires, for example, that there must not be unacceptable delay (a concept that is given full expression in the European Convention on Human Rights: *Attorney General's*

Reference (No 2 of 2001) [2003] UKHL 68; [2004] 2 WLR 1); moreover, only an impartial tribunal can be trusted to make determinations of legal as opposed to factual guilt.

Packer goes on to note that by 'forcing the state to prove its case against the accused in an adjudicative context, the presumption of innocence serves to force into play all the qualifying and disabling doctrines that limit the use of the criminal sanction against the individual, thereby enhancing his opportunity to secure a favourable outcome'. The key point is the proposition that 'the factually guilty may nonetheless be legally innocent and should therefore be given a chance to qualify for that kind of treatment'. This is exemplified by the fact that a conviction may be unsafe even if there is clear evidence showing the guilt of the accused (see the discussion in Chapter 12). Similarly, a crime control model would admit evidence even if it was obtained illegally, whereas the due process model would exclude such evidence (this example perhaps also shows that the reality lies between the two extremes – in the UK, evidence that was obtained illegally may be admissible if its probative value exceeds its prejudicial effect).

Packer notes that one of the hallmarks of due process is the notion that 'there can be no equal justice where the kind of trial a man gets depends on the amount of money he has'. This concept is what the European Court of Human Rights refers to as 'equality of arms', and is seen as a fundamental characteristic of a fair trial under Art 6 of the European Convention. It follows that the State must institute a system of legal aid, and that a defendant whose defence is publicly funded should be in no worse a position than a defendant who is paying for his own defence.

One of the challenges faced by the European Court is that the provisions of the Convention have to be applied both to accusatorial systems such as ours and to inquisitorial systems adopted elsewhere. In the inquisitorial system, the court takes an active role in fact-finding (and may, to a greater or lesser extent, even direct the conduct of the investigation); in the accusatorial system, the court essentially acts as a neutral umpire as the prosecutor presents the case against the accused and the defence advocate tries to highlight reasonable doubt in that case. It could be said that the accusatorial approach is not actually a quest for the truth: the court is not concerned with what actually happened, but whether it is satisfied so that it is sure that the case against the accused is proven. So far as the due process model is concerned, the defence advocate plays a role of central importance in protecting the interests of the accused; similarly, the court plays a vital role in excluding evidence that has been obtained improperly.

The two models essentially represent extremes but are marked by a very important difference. The due process model requires individual liberties to be protected even at the cost of guilty people sometimes going free, whereas the crime control model can tolerate innocent people occasionally being mistakenly convicted. Of course, the crime control model could not accept a large number of mistaken convictions (since that would reduce confidence in the system, thereby diminishing its effectiveness).

21.4.3 Competing interests in the criminal justice system

Packer's two models are in some ways best regarded as descriptive rather than evaluative. In order to evaluate the efficacy of a criminal justice system, it is necessary to examine the interests of all those with a stake in that system. Those stakeholders include:

- the State itself, acting on behalf of society as a whole: a key purpose of the criminal law is to ensure that retribution for criminal conduct is meted out by the State, making it less likely that individuals, or their friends and family, will seek their own revenge against the perpetrator (in other words, reducing the risk of vigilantism);

- the victim (whose interests are now formally recognised through victim impact statements and who may want to see the perpetrator punished and may want to receive some sort of compensation for the harm suffered);

- the accused (whether an individual or a corporate body): the accused enjoys the right not to be wrongly convicted. This in turn encompasses three key rights:

  (a) the right not to be convicted if he is, in fact, innocent;

  (b) the right not to be convicted (irrespective of whether or not he is, in fact, guilty) if the prosecution cannot prove their case against the accused beyond reasonable doubt; and

  (c) the right not to be convicted through an unfair process (one aspect of which is the concept in the jurisprudence of the European Court of Human Rights that there should be 'equality of arms' between the accused and the prosecution);

- the family and friends of the victim (who want to 'see justice done');

- the family and friends of the accused (who will suffer wrongly if the accused is wrongly convicted);

- the police and prosecuting authorities (whose task could be made impossible by too many rules and regulations limiting what they can do in the investigation and prosecution of crime);

- the courts (who cannot administer the law if cases are not disposed of efficiently and so take an excessive time to be resolved, leading to intolerable backlogs);

- the prosecuting lawyers (who, in the UK, are meant to be independent from the police but who have to have a very close working relationship with the police if they are to perform their role effectively, and who are supposed to be 'ministers of justice', putting the facts fairly before the court rather than striving for a conviction at all costs);

- the defence lawyers (who have to represent clients whom they may well believe to be guilty); and

- the taxpayer, who ultimately pays for the criminal justice system (the police, the courts, the prosecuting authorities and publicly funded defence work).

These tensions become even more apparent in the case of serious offences. The more serious the offence, the more important it is that the perpetrator is caught and punished (to deter that person – and others – from committing such offences and to give the public confidence that they are being protected by the law). However, the consequences of a wrongful conviction in such a case are particularly dire for the person suspected of the offence if he is innocent (given the likely sentence for a really serious offence and the effect on the reputation of the accused).

In *R v Ward* (1993) 96 Cr App R 1 at 52, Glidewell LJ, giving the judgment of the court, said that the trial process should be:

> ... developed so as to reduce the risk of conviction of the innocent to an absolute minimum. At the same time we are very much alive to the fact that, although the avoidance of the conviction of the innocent must unquestionably be the primary consideration, the public interest would not be served by a multiplicity of rules which merely impede effective law enforcement.

It follows, as was said by Lord Bingham in *Brown v Stott* [2003] 1 AC 681 at 704, that 'a fair balance [has to be struck] between the general interest of the community and the personal rights of the individual'.

One of the leading concepts in the jurisprudence of the Strasbourg Court is that of proportionality: it is a legitimate aim to prevent crime, but measures to achieve this objective must be proportionate (in other words, no more than necessary to achieve the legitimate objective).

There are tensions or competing interests within the criminal justice system. On the one hand, the system should ensure that the guilty are convicted and the innocent are protected from wrongful conviction. However, if there are too many protections in place to make the conviction of the accused more difficult, it becomes more difficult to convict those who are guilty. These tensions are equally present when the concept of human rights is applied: the accused (whether in fact innocent or guilty) should enjoy protection from arbitrary or oppressive treatment; on the other hand, the victim has rights too. This ambivalence also appears when one looks at the interests of the State: on one hand, it is not in the interests of society to have a criminal justice system that allows improper treatment of those suspected of crime; on the other hand, if there are so many barriers to convicting defendants, more people who are in fact guilty will go free (reducing public confidence in the effectiveness of the criminal justice system to protect its members, leading to people being less willing to co-operate with the police and the prosecuting authorities and increasing the risk of people taking the law into their own hands).

It also has to be borne in mind that criminal justice comes at a price. On one reading of the crime control model, the investigation by the police would be so effective that there would be little need for trials, since all of those (or virtually all of those) brought before the courts would be guilty. However, such thorough investigation would place an intolerable demand on the resources of the police. If one were to go to the extreme version of the due process model, trials would take an inordinate length of time (because of the procedural protections which could be invoked) and could result in the cost of investigations being wasted because so many cases are thrown out on the basis of technicalities. Inevitably, there has to be compromise, since the goals of the criminal justice system have to be achieved without disproportionate cost. There is essentially a finite amount of money for public services: the more that is spent on the justice system, the less there is available for other important public services (education, health, etc). It is for this reason that there has been a major drive for efficiency and cost effectiveness (for example, Martin Narey's *Review of Delay in the Criminal Justice System* (Home Office, 1997) and the moves to curb the ever-growing cost of the criminal defence service set out in the draft Criminal

Defence Service Bill contained in the Consultation Paper (Cmnd 6194) published in May 2004 by the Department for Constitutional Affairs).

21.4.4 Trying to achieve the balance: the Criminal Procedure Rules

Section 69 of the Courts Act 2003 makes provision for the creation of Criminal Procedure Rules (mirroring the Civil Procedure Rules). These rules will govern the practice and procedure to be followed in the criminal courts. The Rules will be made by a committee known as the Criminal Procedure Rules Committee.

The membership of the Criminal Procedure Rules Committee is governed by s 70 of the 2003 Act. It comprises the Lord Chief Justice and a number of members appointed by the Lord Chancellor. Under s 70(2), the Lord Chancellor must appoint:

(a) a person nominated by the Secretary of State,

(b) three persons each of whom is either a *puisne* judge of the High Court or an ordinary judge of the Court of Appeal,

(c) two Circuit judges with particular experience of sitting in criminal courts,

(d) one District Judge (Magistrates' Courts),

(e) one lay justice,

(f) one justices' clerk,

(g) the Director of Public Prosecutions or a person nominated by the Director,

(h) two persons who have a Supreme Court qualification and who have particular experience of practice in criminal courts,

(i) two persons who—

    (i) have been granted by an authorised body, under Part 2 of the 1990 Act, the right to conduct litigation in relation to all proceedings in the Supreme Court, and

    (ii) have particular experience of practice in criminal courts,

(j) one person who appears to represent the Association of Chief Police Officers, and

(k) two persons who appear to represent voluntary organisations with a direct interest in the work of criminal courts.

The intention is to produce a common set of rules of criminal procedure in order to promote greater integration of the courts and more consistency of practice. Under s 69(4) of the Courts Act 2003, the power to make or alter Criminal Procedure Rules:

... is to be exercised with a view to securing that—

(a) the criminal justice system is accessible, fair and efficient, and

(b) the rules are both simple and simply expressed.

A draft of the first part of the Rules – setting out the objectives of the Rules – was published by the Lord Chief Justice in the summer of 2004 (and was discussed briefly in [2004] Crim LR 397).

The draft begins (like the Civil Procedure Rules) with an 'overriding objective':

1.1(1) The overriding objective of this new code is that criminal cases be dealt with justly.

(2)　Dealing with a criminal case justly includes:

    (a)　acquitting the innocent and convicting the guilty;

    (b)　dealing with the prosecution and the defence fairly;

    (c)　recognising the rights of a defendant, particularly those under Article 6 of the ECHR;

    (d)　respecting the interests of witnesses, victims and jurors;

    (e)　dealing with the case efficiently and expeditiously;

    (f)　ensuring that appropriate information is available to the court when bail and sentence are considered;

    (g)　dealing with the case in ways that take into account—

        (i)　the gravity of the offence alleged,

        (ii)　the complexity of what is in issue,

        (iii)　the severity of the consequences for the defendant and others affected, and

        (iv)　the needs of other cases.

The Rules go on to set out the duty of the participants in a criminal case:

1.2　Each participant, in the conduct of each case, shall:

    (a)　prepare and conduct the case in accordance with the overriding objective, with or without specific orders by the court;

    (b)　comply with these Rules, practice directions and orders made by the court;

    (c)　at once inform the court and all parties of any failure (whether or not that participant is responsible for that failure) to take any procedural step required by these Rules, any practice direction or any direction of the court.

Next, the Rules set out the duty of the court:

1.3　The court must further the overriding objective when:

    (a)　exercising any power given to it by legislation (including these Rules);

    (b)　applying any practice direction;

    (c)　interpreting any Rule or practice direction.

1.4(1) The court must further the overriding objective by actively managing cases.

(2)　Active case management includes:

    (a)　the early identification of the real issues;

    (b)　the early setting of a timetable for the preparation and trial of the case;

    (c)　monitoring the preparation of the case and compliance with orders;

    (d)　ensuring that evidence, whether disputed or not, is presented in the shortest and clearest way;

    (e)　dealing with as many aspects of the case as possible on the same occasion and avoiding unnecessary hearings;

    (f)　encouraging the participants to co-operate in the conduct of the proceedings;

    (g)　making use of technology.

(3)　The court may make any order and take any step actively to manage a criminal case in pursuit of the overriding objective, unless legislation, including these Rules, prohibits it.

Rule 1.1(2) emphasises two things as aspects of dealing with cases justly: accuracy of outcome and respecting the rights of all the participants in the criminal process.

The duty to inform the court of any failure to comply with the Rules (r 1.2(c)) may be drawn a little widely, as it seems to run the risk of large numbers of applications being made to the court to complain about the conduct of the other side. It remains to be seen what sanctions will be available to the court in the event of such failures to comply with the Rules.

Rule 1.3 comes as no surprise given the encouragement in the Auld Review that there should be more active case management by the courts (similar to the position in the civil courts).

It is anticipated that the first Criminal Procedure Rules will be made in the autumn of 2004, probably coming into force in April 2005. It is intended that these Rules will apply to all criminal cases (magistrates' courts, youth courts, the Crown Court and the Court of Appeal (Criminal Division)).

INDEX